Fox
SER*
IXD331912

Activation Key
PMZVBRKV

S0-AFH-766

WT51
Lic# ACEWPCNR145538

Computers and Information Processing: The Complete Course

with BASIC

Fifth Edition

Computers and Information Processing: The Complete Course

with BASIC

Fifth Edition

Steven L. Mandell

BOWLING GREEN STATE UNIVERSITY

Includes educational versions of the following software:
dBase III® PLUS ™, VP-Planner Plus™,
WordPerfect® 4.2, and VP*Expert 2.0

WEST PUBLISHING COMPANY

St. Paul ■ New York ■ Los Angeles ■ San Francisco

Copy Editor: Benjamin Shriver
Illustrations: John and Jean Foster, Carlisle Graphics, and Rolin Graphics
Composition: Parkwood Composition Service, Inc.

Credits appear following the Index.

A STUDENT STUDY GUIDE

A study guide has been developed to assist students in mastering the concepts presented in this text. It reinforces chapter material presenting it in a concise format with review questions. An examination copy is available to instructors by contacting West Publishing Company. Students can purchase the study guide from the local bookstore under the title *Study Guide to Accompany Computers and Information Processing: A Complete Course, Fifth Edition* prepared by Steven L. Mandell.

COPYRIGHT © 1979, 1982, 1985, 1987   By WEST PUBLISHING COMPANY
COPYRIGHT © 1989   By WEST PUBLISHING COMPANY
                                      50 W. Kellogg Boulevard
                                      P.O. Box 64526
                                      St. Paul, MN 55164-1003

All rights reserved

Printed in the United States of America

96 95 94 93 92 91 90   8 7 6 5 4 3 2

Library of Congress Cataloging-in-Publication Data

Mandell, Steven L.
    Computers and information processing: a complete course with
  dBASE III PLUS, VP-Planner Plus, WordPerfect 4.2, and VP-Expert /
  Steven L. Mandell.—5th ed.
        p.   cm.
    Includes index.
    ISBN 0-314-47016-6
    1. Electronic data processing.   2. Electronic digital computers.
  3. dBase III Plus (Computer program) 4. WordPerfect (Computer
  program) 5. VP-expert (Computer program)   I. Title.
  QA76.M27472   1989b
  004—dc19   88-39051
                                                                      CIP

Contents

Introduction to Information Processing   1

■ ARTICLE: Dreaming the Impossible at M.I.T.   2
Introduction   4
Computers Today   4
  Computers in Business   4
  Computers in Other Areas   7
  ■ HIGHLIGHT: Saginaw Vanguard   7
Overview of Information Processing   8
  Data Organization   9
  The Data Flow   11
  ■ HIGHLIGHT: Computers Are Part of the Pros   12
Concept Summary 1–1: Overview of Information Processing   14
Operation of Computers   14
  Analog and Digital Computers   14
  The Computer Advantage   15
Concept Summary 1–2: Computer Functions   17
Computer Classifications   17
  Supercomputers   17
  Mainframes   19
  Minicomputers   20
  Microcomputers   20
Concept Summary 1–3: Factors to Consider in Buying a Computer System   22
Summary Points   22
Review Questions   22
  ■ APPLICATION: Wall Street Journal   24

CHAPTER

1

The Evolution of Computers   27

■ ARTICLE: The Next Major Battleground   28
Introduction   29
The Technology Race   29
  Early Developments   30
  ■ HIGHLIGHT: Who Was First?   34
  First Generation: 1951–1958   34
  Second Generation: 1959–1964   37
  Third Generation: 1965–1970   38

CHAPTER

2

Fourth Generation: 1971–Today   40
Concept Summary 2–1: The Technology Race: Generations of Computer
  Development   42
The Computer Industry   42
  The Hardware Industry   43
  The Software Industry   44
Careers In Computers   45
  Data-Processing Operations Personnel   45
  System Development Personnel   46
  HIGHLIGHT: New Careers in Computers   47
  Data-Base Specialists   48
  Information System Managers   49
Professional Associations   50
  AFIPS   50
  ACM   50
  DPMA   51
  ASM   51
  ICCP   51
  SIM   52
Concept Summary 2–2: Professional Associations   52
Summary Points   52
Review Questions   54
  APPLICATION: National Semiconductor Corporation   55

CHAPTER

3

Introduction to Information Systems   57

  ARTICLE: Real Strategic Successes   58
Introduction   59
Qualities of Information   59
  HIGHLIGHT: You Are Here   61
Concept Summary 3–1: Qualities of Information   61
Fundamental Principles of Information Systems   62
  A System's Interaction with Other Systems   63
  The Organization as a System   63
Components of an Information System   64
  Hardware as Part of an Information System   65
  Software as Part of an Information System   65
  Data as Part of an Information System   66
  People as Part of an Information System   66
  HIGHLIGHT: Portrait of a Programmer   67
The Value of Information Systems   67
How Businesses Use Information Systems   68
  Accounting/Payroll   68
  Finance/Budgeting   69
  Marketing/Sales Order Processing   69
  Human Resources Management/Personnel   69
  HIGHLIGHT: Customized Grocery Stores   70
  Production Management/Materials Requirement Planning (MRP)   70
  Engineering/Computer-Aided Engineering   71

Summary Points   72
Review Questions   73
▨ APPLICATION: PRUPAC   74

Hardware   78

▨ ARTICLE: Supercomputers Offer Keys to Cures   78
Introduction   80
Central Processing Unit   80
Instruction   81
Concept Summary: 4–1: Components of the Central Processing Unit   82
Stored-Program Concept   83
▨ HIGHLIGHT: Where Do Old Computers Go?   84
Storage   84
Storage Location   84
Primary Storage   85
Read-Only Memory (ROM)   87
Concept Summary 4–2: RAM and ROM   89
Registers   90
Cache Memory   90
Data Representation   90
Binary Representation   90
Octal Number System   92
Hexadecimal Number System   93
Easy-to-Do-Conversion   95
Computer Codes   95
▨ HIGHLIGHT: Fault Tolerance   97
Code Checking   98
Summary Points   99
Review Questions   100
▨ APPLICATION: IBM   101

Input and Output   105

▨ ARTICLE: Shopping Club Finds a Bargain   106
Introduction   107
Data Input   107
▨ HIGHLIGHT: Before Magnetized Media   108
Key-to-Magnetic Media   108
Source-Data Automation   109
▨ HIGHLIGHT: When Security Counts   116
Concept Summary 5–1: Types of Data Input   116
Information Output   116
Printers   116
Concept Summary 5–2: Impact and Nonimpact Printers   122
Plotters   122
Visual Display Terminals   122
Summary Points   123
Review Questions   124
▨ APPLICATION: Wendy's International, Inc.   125

CHAPTER

6

Storage Devices   127

■   ARTICLE: The World on a Silver Platter   128
Introduction   129
Classification of Storage Media   129
Sequential-Access Media   129
  Magnetic-Tape   129
  Cassette Tape   134
Concept Summary 6–1: Characteristics of Magnetic Tape   136
Direct-Access Media   136
  Magnetic Disk   136
  Floppy Disk   141
Concept Summary 6–2: Characteristics of Magnetic Disks   142
Mass Storage   143
■   HIGHLIGHT: Move Over, Magnetic Media   144
Trends in Data Storage   144
  Charged-Couple Devices   144
  Laser Technology   144
■   HIGHLIGHT: What's All the Hype?   146
  RAM Disks   146
  Compact Disks   147
  Josephson Junction   147
  Superconductors   147
Summary Points   148
Review Questions   149
■   APPLICATION: American Airlines   150

CHAPTER

File Organization and Data Base Design   154

■   ARTICLE: It's Grab-Your-Partner Time for Software Makers   154
Introduction   155
File Processing   156
■   HIGHLIGHT: Laying Down the Law   157
Methods of File Access   158
  Batch File Access   158
  Online File Access   158
File Designs   158
  Sequential File Design   158
  Direct-Access File Design   163
  Indexed-Sequential File Design   166
■   HIGHLIGHT: SQL to the Rescue   169
Concept Summary 7–1: Comparison of File Designs   169
Data Bases   169
  Structuring Data   170
  Data-Base Management Systems   175
  Assessment of the Data-Base Approach   176
Summary Points   176
Review Questions   177
■   APPLICATION: SupeRx   178

CONTENTS

Microcomputers 181

■ ARTICLE: Put Enough PCs Together and You get a Supercomputer   182
Introduction   183
Microcomputers: An Overview   183
　The New Technology   184
Concept Summary 8–1: Early Microcomputers and Their Microprocessors   187
　The Machines Themselves   187
■ HIGHLIGHT: Executives and Micros   192
Concept Summary 8–2: Microcomputer Sizes   194
Understanding the Microchips   194
　The Microprocessor's Speed   194
■ HIGHLIGHT: Amazing Microcomputers   195
　Primary Memory   195
　The Instruction Set   196
　Operating Systems   196
　Compatibility   197
Using Microcomputers   198
　Peripherals   198
　Software Packages   202
　Users Groups   204
Purchasing Microcomputers   204
　The Big Picture   205
　Evaluating Software   206
　Choosing the Hardware   209
　Buyer's Checklist   212
Summary Points   213
Review Questions   214
■ APPLICATION: Compaq Computer Corporation   216

Telecommunications and Distributed Computing 219

■ ARTICLE: Security Problems Greater Than Ever   220
Introduction   221
Data Communications   221
　Message Transmission   222
　Input/Output Operations   223
Communication Channels   225
　Types of Channels   225
■ HIGHLIGHT: When Computers Speak   226
　Grades of Channels   227
　Modes of Channels   228
Concept Summary 9–1: Communication Channels   229
Communication Hardware   229
　Multiplexers and Concentrators   229
　Programmable Communications Processors   231
Data Communication Applications   231
　Local Area Networks (LANs)   231
■ HIGHLIGHT: The End of the Minis?   233
　Electronic Banking   233
　Telecommuting   235

Distributed Computing   236
Distributed Computing Networks   237
  Single CPU Networks   237
  Multiple CPU Networks   238
  ■ HIGHLIGHT: EDI   239
Concept Summary 9–2: Network Configurations   239
Telecommunication Standards   241
A Guide to Networks   241
  Information Services   241
  Bulletin Boards   244
  Proprietary and Nonproprietary Networks   245
Summary Points   246
Review Questions   247
  ■ APPLICATION: Texas Instruments   248

CHAPTER

10

System Software   251

  ■ ARTICLE: Unix: The Soul of a Lot of New Machines   252
Introduction   254
Categories of Programs   254
  System Programs   254
  Application Programs   255
Operating Systems   255
  Development of Operating Systems   255
  Functions of Operating Systems   255
*Concept Summary 10–1: Relationships Among User, Operating System, and
    Computer Hardware*   256
  Types of Processing Handled by Operating Systems   256
  ■ HIGHLIGHT: What It Means to Be Open   257
  Components of Operating Systems   257
Concept Summary 10–2: Types of Operating System Programs   260
Multiprogramming   261
Virtual Storage   263
  ■ HIGHLIGHT: SAA, Systems Application Architecture   266
Multiprocessing   266
Concept Summary 10–3: Developments that Improved Computer Efficiency   268
Summary Points   270
Review Questions   271
  ■ APPLICATION: Microsoft Corporation   272

CHAPTER

11

Software Development   275

  ■ ARTICLE: Trying Times: Lawsuits Threaten Developers   276
Introduction   277
Defining and Documenting the Problem   277
Concept Summary 11–1: The Steps in the Software Development Process   270
  ■ HIGHLIGHT: Groupware Can Make Groups Work   279
Designing and Documenting a Solution   281
  The Four Basic Logic Patterns   281
  Structured Programming Techniques   283
  Top-Down Design   286
  Pseudocode   290

Flowcharts   291
Action Diagrams   293
Using Structured Design Techniques in Industry   293
Writing and Documenting the Program   297
Structured Coding   297
Concept Summary 11–2: Structured Programming Techniques   298
Types of Statements   299
Debugging and Testing the Program   299
Summary Points   301
Review Questions   303
APPLICATION: Eli Lilly   304

Programming Languages   309

ARTICLE: C Edging Out Pascal as Developers' Language of Choice   310
Introduction   311
Standardization of Languages   312
Categorizing Languages   312
Concept Summary 12–1: Special-Purpose Languages   313
Translating Languages   313
HIGHLIGHT: That Really Bugs Me!   314
Low-Level Languages   314
Machine Language   314
Assembly Language   315
Concept Summary 12–2: Levels of Programming Languages   317
High-Level Languages   317
FORTRAN   317
BASIC   318
Pascal   320
COBOL   322
Logo   324
APL   326
Ada   327
HIGHLIGHT: Ada   328
RPG   328
C   331
Modula-2   334
FORTH   335
LISP   336
Very-High-Level Languages   337
Natural Languages   337
Programming Languages—A Comparison   338
Summary Points   339
Review Questions   341

Application Software   345

ARTICLE: Financial Software: Brokers Power Up   346
Introduction   347
Advantages and Disadvantages of Commercial Application Software   347
General Categories of Application Software Packages   348
Productivity Tools   349

CHAPTER 12

CHAPTER 13

Word Processors   349
Graphics Packages   349
Spreadsheets   350
File Managers   350
Other Productivity Tools   351
Functional Tools   352
Desktop Publishing Packages   352
Accounting Packages   352
Manufacturing Packages   353
CASE Packages   355
Sales and Marketing Packages   355
Turnkey Systems   355
End-User Development Tools   356
Simulation Software   356
Concept Summary 13–1: Illustration of Relationship between Reality and Simulation   357
Expert Systems   359
Statistical Packages   360
Data-base Management Systems   361
■ HIGHLIGHT: Expert Systems   362
Concept Summary 13–2: Categories of Application Software Packages   362
Choosing an Application Software Package   363
Summary Points   363
Review Questions   365
■ APPLICATION: Chase Manhattan   366

CHAPTER 14

System Analysis and Design   369

■ ARTICLE: Expert System Cuts Diagnosis Time   370
Introduction   371
System Analysis   371
Reasons for Conducting System Analysis   372
Data Gathering   374
Concept Summary 14–1: Types of Data Gathering   377
Data Analysis   377
Systems Analysis Report   383
System Design   383
Reviewing Goals and Objectives   384
Developing a System Model   384
Evaluating Organizational Constraints   384
Developing Alternative Designs   386
Performing Feasibility Analysis   389
Performing Cost/Benefit Analysis   390
Preparing the Design Report   391
System Programming   392
Programming   392
Testing   392
Documentation   393
Special Considerations   393
System Implementation   394
Personnel Training   394
Conversion   394
■ HIGHLIGHT: The Design Team   395

Systems Audit and Review 396
   Evaluating System Performance 396
   Making Modifications and Improvements 396
   Responding to Change 396
Prototyping 397
Concept Summary 14–2: The Purposes and Steps of System Development
   Stages 398
Summary Points 398
Review Questions 408
   ▨ APPLICATION: General Dynamics 401

Management Information Systems and Decision Support Systems 405

   ▨ ARTICLE: DSS/EIS Aids in Corporate Downsizing 406
Introduction 407
Definition of a Management Information System (MIS) 407
   ▨ HIGHLIGHT: Chief Information Officer 408
Concept Summary 15–1: Data Processing vs. Management Information
   Systems 408
Levels of Management 408
   Top-Level Management 408
   Middle-Level Management 408
   Lower-Level Management 409
   Problems and Differences 409
Concept Summary 15–2: Differences among Decision-Making Levels 411
Types of Reports 411
   Scheduled Listings 411
   Exception Reports 411
   Predictive Reports 412
   Demand Reports 412
Management and MIS 412
   ▨ HIGHLIGHT: Information Center 413
Design Methodology 413
   Top-Down Design 413
   Design Alternatives 413
Decision Support Systems 415
   The Purpose and Scope of a DSS 418
   A Model: The Heart of a DSS 418
   The Future of DSS 419
Summary Points 421
Review Questions 422
   ▨ APPLICATION: Pepsi-Cola Company 423

CHAPTER

15

The Impact of Computers on People and Organizations 427

   ▨ ARTICLE: The Goal is Working Smarter, Not Longer 428
Introduction 429
Behavioral Aspects of Computer Use 429

CHAPTER

16

Computer Anxiety   429
Computer Literacy   430
Job Displacement and Retraining   431
Changes in the Workplace   432
■ HIGHLIGHT: Health Problems and VDTs   433
Office Automation   434
Word Processing   435
Communications   437
■ HIGHLIGHT: Lending a Helping Hand   438
Computers in Business and Industry   440
Computers in Business   441
Concept Summary 16–1: Forms of Electronic Communication   441
Computers in Industry   444
Concept Summary 16–2: Computers in Industry   447
Summary Points   448
Review Questions   449
■ APPLICATION: EDS   450

CHAPTER

17

Computer Security, Crime, Ethics, and the Law   453

■ ARTICLE: A Bold Raid on Computer Security   454
Introduction   455
Computer Crime and Security   455
Computer Crime Defined   456
Types of Computer Crime   456
Concept Summary 17–1: Types of Computer Crime   459
Crime Prevention and Detection   459
Computer Security   461
Concept Summary 17–2: Computer Security   464
■ HIGHLIGHT: Who Goes There?   465
Computer Ethics   465
■ HIGHLIGHT: Hackers—No Longer Harmless   466
Privacy   467
Issues   467
Legislation   468
■ HIGHLIGHT: Do Computers and Medicine Really Mix?   471
Warranties, Copyright Law, Public-Domain Software, and Shareware   472
Warranties   472
Copyright Law   473
Public-Domain Software and Shareware   474
Summary Points   475
Review Questions   476
■ APPLICATION: ALCOA   477

CHAPTER

18

Computers in Our Lives: Today and Tomorrow   479

■ ARTICLE: Computer "Virus" Plague Is Feared   480
Introduction   482
Trends in Hardware Technology   482
Chip Technology   483

CONTENTS

Laser Technology   483
Parallel Processing   484
Artificial Intelligence   485
▨   HIGHLIGHT: Neurocomputing   486
Voice Recognition   487
Robotics   488
Concept Summary 18–1: Improvements in Technology   489
Computers in Medicine   489
Computer-Assisted Diagnosis   491
Computer-Assisted Treatment   493
Computers in Science   494
Computers for All of Us   496
Concept Summary 18–2: Computers in Medicine and Science   497
Microcomputers at Home   497
▨   HIGHLIGHT: I'd Rather Stay Home   499
Interactive Video   500
The Card: Who's Watching Whom?   501
Education: The Newly Disadvantaged   502
Summary Points   504
Review Questions   505
▨   APPLICATION: Marshall & Melhorn   507

Basic Supplement   509

Preface   510

SECTION I: Introduction to BASIC   511

Introduction   511
What is Programming?   511
The Programming Process   511
Defining and Documenting the Problem   512
Designing and Documenting a Solution   512
Writing and Documenting the Program   515
Debugging and Testing the Program   516
Interacting with the Computer   516
The VAX   518
The IBM Personal Computer   520
The Macintosh   521
The Apple IIe and IIGS   523
The TRS-80 Model 4   523
Summary Points   524
Review Questions   525

SECTION II: BASIC Fundamentals   526

Introduction   526
Components of the BASIC Language   526
Line Numbers   526
Constants   528
Variables   529
Reserved Words   530
Elementary BASIC Statements   530

The REM Statement   530
The LET Statement   531
The PRINT Statement   534
The END Statement   535
Comprehensive Programming Problem   536
Problem Definition   536
Solution Design   536
The Program   537
Summary Points   539
Review Questions   539

SECTION III: Input and Ouput   542

Introduction   542
The INPUT Statement   542
The READ and DATA Statements   544
A Comparison of Two Methods of Data Entry   547
Printing Results   548
Print Zones and Commas   548
Using Semicolons   550
Comprehensive Programming Problem   551
Problem Definition   551
Solution Design   552
The Program   553
Summary Points   555
Review Questions   555
Debugging Exercises   556
Programming Problems   556

SECTION IV: The Decision Statement and Functions   558

Introduction   558
The GOTO Statement: Unconditional Transfer   558
The IF Statement: Conditional Transfer   558
The Single-Alternative IF Statement   559
The Double-Alternative IF Statement   560
Library Functions   562
Numeric Functions   562
For Apple Users: Simulating The IF/THEN/ELSE Statement   563
String Functions   565
User-Defined Functions   567
Comprehensive Programming Problem   567
The Problem   567
Solution Design   569
The Program   570
Summary Points   571
Review Questions   571
Debugging Exercises   572
Programming Problems   572

SECTION V: Looping   574

Introduction   574
The FOR/NEXT Loop   574
Processing Steps for the FOR/NEXT Loop   576

Rules for Using the FOR/NEXT Loop   577
Nested FOR/NEXT Loops   578
Advantages and Disadvantages of Using the FOR/NEXT Loop   578
The WHILE Loop   580
For Apple Users: Simulating the WHILE Loop   581
Comprehensive Programming Problems   582
Problem Definition   582
Solution Design   583
The Program   583
Summary Points   587
Review Questions   588
Debugging Exercises   589
Programming Problems   589

SECTION VI: Modularizing Programs   591

Introduction   591
The Importance of Modularizing Programs   591
Writing Subroutines   591
The GOSUB Statement   591
The RETURN Statement   592
A Program Containing Multiple Calls to the Same Subroutine   592
The ON/GOSUB Statement   594
Using the Structure Chart to Modularize a Program   596
Single Entry, Single Exit Subroutines   599
Comprehensive Programming Problem   600
Defining the Problem   600
Solution Design   601
The Program   604
Summary Points   607
Review Questions   608
Debugging Exercises   608
Programming Problems   609

BASIC Glossary   611

West Student Pro Pack™ (IBM®/ MS-DOS®) Supplement   A-1

Section A: Introduction to Word Processing and WordPerfect   A-2
Section B: Advanced WordPerfect   A-33
Section C: Introduction to Spreadsheets and VP-Planner PLUS   A-60
Section D: Advanced VP-Planner PLUS   A-98
Section E: Introduction to Data Managers and dBase III PLUS   A-128
Section F: Advanced dBase III PLUS   A-189
Section G: Introduction to Expert Systems and VP-Expert   A-220
Section H: Advanced VP-Expert   A-254

West Student Pro Pack™ (IBM®/MS-DOS®) Supplement Index   A-281

Glossary   G-1

Index   I-1

Preface

Computers and Information Processing, Fifth Edition, marks an exciting departure from its earlier versions. Today, because of the different emphasis on programming, microcomputers and hands-on application software coverage, the Fifth Edition is available in two versions:

■ The Complete Course with BASIC educational software versions of WordPerfect 4.2, dBASE III PLUS, VP-Planner Plus, and VP-Expert 2.0, and applications documentation
■ Alternate version with BASIC and a generic application software supplement.

The revision work associated with the Fifth Edition has been more challenging than the efforts involved with the four earlier editions. Major developments and advances in information systems have occurred so rapidly that providing current examples is more difficult than ever before. Feedback from instructors using the text continued to provide an excellent source of ideas for making improvements. When it comes to improving content, nothing can replace the actual classroom testing of material. While prior editions of this text have been highly successful, a great deal of care went into updating and refining the latest edition. The final result is a Fifth Edition textbook vastly improved in structure and substance.

It is appropriate at this point to thank the following people who reviewed the book and provided invaluable comments based on their experience using the Fourth Edition of *Computers and Information Processing:*

Thomas M. Krueger
Waukesha County Technical Institute, Wisconsin

Frances Grodzinsky
Sacred Heart University, Connecticut

Richard G. Stearns
Parkland College, Illinois

Paul Tymann
SUNY College at Oswego, NY

Virginia B. Bender
William Rainey Harper College, Illinois

Robert Froese
Red River College, Canada

Earl Chrysler
California State University, Chico

New Features

Readers familiar with the fourth edition of the text will notice several changes incorporated into the Fifth Edition:

- As mentioned previously, two versions of the book are available reflecting the different views instructors have concerning laboratory-based microcomputer activities. The Complete Course version includes an application software supplement and educational software for WordPerfect 4.2, dBASE III PLUS, VP-Planner Plus, and VP-Expert 2.0. The alternate version contains a generic application software supplement for classroom support.
- New *articles* and *highlights*.
- New and updated corporate *applications*.
- Redesigned *Concept Summaries* with more concise reviews of key topics.
- Improved coverage of business systems.
- Increased coverage of the computer industry and professional associations.
- Increased coverage of decision support systems.
- Updated chapter on microcomputers.
- Improved chapter on programming with emphasis on top-down design.
- Rewritten and condensed BASIC supplement with emphasis on structured programing.
- Extended coverage of the impact of computers on our society.

The most inspiring lectures on computers that I have had the good fortune to attend were presented by Rear Admiral Grace Hopper (Ret.), a leader in the development of early computers. In analyzing her material, which always seemed so interesting, it became apparent to me that no new concept was permitted to remain abstract. Rather, actual examples were described, encouraging the listener to visualize their applications. Following Admiral Hopper's example, each chapter in this book is followed by an application that shows how a corporation implements the concepts presented.

Several other important features are included within each chapter. The introductory section serves a dual purpose: as a transition between chapters and a preview of material. An *article* with high interest appeal draws the student into the chapter. *Highlights* containing interesting computer applications or controversial topics are interspersed throughout the chapter to maintain reader interest. *Concept summaries* enable students to review quickly the important key topics covered in the chapter. Chapter summary points and review questions are also provided. A comprehensive glossary and index are placed at the end of the text.

Throughout the development of this book the emphasis has been on orienting material to students. All incorporated approaches are designed to assist students in the learning process. Important concepts are never avoided regardless of their complexity. Many books on information processing emphasize one or two aspects of the subject—either informational relationships or computer capabilities. This book attempts to balance and blend both subjects.

Supplementary Educational Materials

Coupons inside the Complete Course version offer students the chance to upgrade to fully functioning commercial versions of WordPerfect 4.2 and VP-Planner Plus at a discounted price. (The coupons are available only with the Complete Course version.)

West's User's Guides by Steven L. Mandell are available for purchase to accompany the text. They are:

■ West Soft Pack 2.5 Version (IBM/MS-DOS); includes WestWord 2.5, WestCalc 2.5, WestGraph 2.5, WestData 2.5, WestSoft 1.0 and a student file disk.

■ Educate-Ability 1.1 Version (IBM/MS-DOS); includes Educate-Ability 1.1, an integrated application software program consisting of word processing, spreadsheets, graphics, and data manager programs.

■ Popular Commercial Software Version (IBM/MS-DOS); for WordStar 2000, WordPerfect, Lotus 1-2-3 and dBASE III (a student file disk is included along with WestSoft 1.0; students must have access to the commercial software).

■ West Soft Pack 2.2 Version (Apple II-e, II-c, II-cs); includes WestWord 2.2, WestCalc 2.2, WestGraph 2.2, WestData 2.2, WestSoft 1.0, and student file disk.

These user's guides offer maximum flexibility by providing Professors with the choice of using popular commercial software, which may be installed at their college or university, West's 2.2 Apple or 2.5 IBM/MS-DOS software.

The instructor's manual with test bank, by Steven L. Mandell, includes answers to the exercises and problems in the Pro Pack and generic application software sections, a classroom administration section, enrichment lectures, complete test bank, and additional Applications.

The Student Study Guide, also by the author, includes a summary, review of Key Terms and definitions, and various self-testing formats for review of each chapter.

Masters are available; transparency acetates (many in color) are available to qualified adopters.

WESTEST, a computerized testing service with more than 1800 questions, is available from West Publishing Company.

Acknowledgments

I would like to give special recognition to Professor Donald J. Weinshank and the staff of Computer Science 115 at Michigan State University for their suggestions with respect to Action Diagrams.

Many individuals and companies have been involved in the development of the material for this book. The corporations whose applications appear in this book have provided invaluable assistance. Many professionals provided the assistance required for completion of a text of this magnitude: Russ Thompson and Lynnette Radigan on chapter development; Meredith Flynn on the Application Software Supplement and the West Student Pro Pack (IBM/MS-DOS) Supplement; Sue Baumann on the BASIC Supplement and instructor material; Shannan Christy, Linda Cupp, and Sally Oates on manuscript preparation.

The design of the book is a tribute to the many talents of Kristen Weber. One final acknowledgment goes to my publisher and valued friend, Clyde Perlee, Jr., for his encouragement and ideas.

Steven L. Mandell

Computers and Information Processing: The Complete Course

with BASIC

Fifth Edition

CHAPTER

1

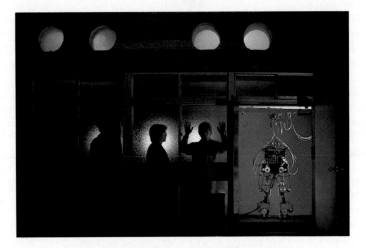

Introduction to Information Processing

O U T L I N E

Introduction
Computers Today
  Computers in Business
  Computers in Other Areas
Overview of Information Processing
  Data Organization
  The Data Flow

Operation of Computers
  Analog and Digital Computers
  The Computer Advantage
Computer Classifications
  Supercomputers
  Mainframes
  Minicomputers
  Microcomputers

Summary Points
Review Questions

Dreaming the Impossible at M.I.T.

By Philip Elmer DeWitt. Reported
by Robert Buderi
TIME

What if television sets were equipped with knobs that let viewers customize the shows they watch? If they could adjust the sex content, for example, or regulate the violence, or shift the political orientation to the left or right? What if motion pictures were able to monitor the attention level of audiences and modify their content accordingly, lengthening some scenes while cutting others short if they evoke yawns. What if the newspapers that reach subscribers' homes every morning could be edited with each particular reader in mind—filled with stories selected because they affected his neighborhood, or had an impact on his personal business interests, or mentioned his friends and associates?

There are a lot of "what ifs," but none of these is mere futuristic fantasy. All of them, in fact, are the goals of research projects now under way at the Media Laboratory, a dazzling new academic facility at the Massachusetts Institute of Technology. The lab's unique mission is to transform today's passive mass media, particularly TV, into flexible technologies that can respond to individual tastes. Because of advances in computers, says Nicholas Negroponte, 43, the co-founder and director, "all media are poised for redefinition. Our purpose is to enhance the quality of life in an electronic age."

Two years ago, when the lab first opened its doors in Cambridge, Mass., the announced intention of "inventing the future" seemed like an impossibly vague undertaking. But Negroponte has made believers of much of the corporate and academic estab-

lishment. Bankrolled by more than 100 business and government sponsors, he has filled his $45 million facility with a group of 120 gifted researchers that includes some of the brightest and quirkiest minds in computer science: Marvin Minsky, dean of artificial-intelligence research; Seymour Papert, disciple of Child Psychologist Jean Piaget and a leading advocate of computerized education; Alan Kay, one of the most influential designers of personal computers.

Some of the projects are still in the visionary stage, but several investigative teams have come up with working products and prototypes. In many cases, research relating to electronic media has led to spin-offs that could have wide applications for both individuals and businesses. Consider the following:

■ The lab's Conversational Desktop is a voice-controlled computer system that acts like an automatic receptionist, personal secretary and travel agent—screening calls, taking messages, making airline reservations. "Get me two seats to the Bahamas," says Research Scientist Chris Schmandt to his com-

puter. "When do you want to go?" replies the machine.

■ NewsPeek is a selective electronic newspaper made of material culled daily from news services and television broadcasts. By sliding their fingers across the screen of a computer terminal, viewers can ask to see lengthier versions of particular stories, roll selected videotapes or call up related articles. The computer remembers what it has been asked to show and the next day tailors its news gathering to search for similar stories. Says Associate Director Andrew Lippman: "It's a newspaper that grows to know you."

■ The lab has developed the world's first computer-generated freestanding hologram—a three-dimensional image of a green Camaro sedan suspended in midair. Unlike most holographic images, which are put onto flat photographic plates, the Camaro is recorded on a concave plate and projected into the air by laser beams. The hologram was designed with funding from General Motors, which still painstakingly builds scale models of new car designs out of clay. In the future, GM and other automakers may be able to use holograms to see what a car will look like before it is actually manufactured. Eventually, such images may be made by laserage copying machines for a few dollars apiece.

■ In the field of fine arts, the world-class music research center in the lab has already produced the Synthetic Performer, a computerized piano-playing accompanist. The system not only plays along with soloists but also adapts to changes in their tempo and cadence without losing a beat. The project is part of an ongoing effort to explore the mysteries of harmony and composition by teaching music appreciation to computers.

Negroponte began raising funds for the Media Lab in 1980 with the help of Jerome Wiesner, former M.I.T. president. The two men sought out publishers, broadcasters and electronics manufacturers whose businesses were being transformed by the advent of VCRs, cable television and personal computers. Then they hinted broadly that the faculty at M.I.T. knew precisely where all this was headed. Money came in from such leading sponsors as IBM, CBS, Warner Communications, 20th Century Fox, Mitsubishi, Time Inc. and the Washington *Post*. Sponsors can send scientists and other observers to the Media Lab and make commercial use of any of the facility's research. Though many of the projects may never yield commercial or educational applications, only one company, Toshiba, has failed to renew its funding.

Visitors to the lab, a sleek four-story maze of gadget-filled work areas, are assaulted by strange sights. In a 64-ft.-high atrium. 7-ft.-long computer-controlled blimps may be flying overhead—part of a project to develop stimulating science activities for elementary and high schools. In another area visitors encounter computers that can read lips. After spending three months at M.I.T. last year, Stewart Brand, the counterculture guru who originated the *Whole Earth Catalog*, was impressed enough to write a flattering book titled *The Media Lab*, which will

be published next month by Viking Press.

But the lab's high-tech razzle-dazzle masks plenty of serious business. Investigators are experimenting with new forms of teleconferencing. One idea involved projecting video images of individuals onto plaster casts of their faces. The resulting "talking heads" were so lifelike that people using the system felt they were "meeting" with colleagues who were actually in another city. A major effort is also being made to enhance computer animation. Assistant Professor David Zeltzer, building on research he started at Ohio State, is developing new ways of simulating human figures and movement. One application would allow playwrights to see just how scenes would look without having to hire live actors to try them out.

Within the Media Lab there is a lurking fear that the research might prove too successful. Some of the scientists, who point to TV's mesmerizing impact, worry about creating new media so powerfully seductive that they might keep many viewers from venturing into the real world. Minsky, for one, has given that a lot of thought. "Imagine what it would be like if TV actually were good," he told Brand. "It would be the end of everything we know." Yet he and his groundbreaking colleagues seem more than willing to take that risk.

In many ways we have already grown accustomed to computers in our lives—consider the automatic teller machines at banks or the computer scanners at the checkout counters of grocery stores. Yet scientists are constantly designing new uses for computers in business and leisure-time activities. How will computers affect us in the future? Will they select the articles for our personal newspaper or monitor our television shows? It's possible!

■ INTRODUCTION

Hard copy, modem, data base, peripherals: all these words refer to a relatively new and rapidly changing technology—that of the computer. Computers are changing our language, and they are also changing us. No longer are computer experts the only people who interact with computers. Today, the lives of most of us are affected by computers every day.

■ Your morning newspaper was written, edited, and typeset on computers.

■ Your late-model car contains a computer chip that governs its fuel mixture and controls emissions from its exhaust.

■ Your pharmacist consults a data base and warns you that your new medication will not be as effective if you take it with milk.

■ At the supermarket, the clerk slides your groceries over a counter-mounted scanner that reads coded data into a computer about each item you bought.

■ At home, you slip a potato into the microwave oven. Once you punch in the length of time and degree of heat, a computer takes over the baking process.

■ The evening newscast on TV receives information from an elaborate computer-controlled communications network.

■ You can get cash at the bank even after it is closed by using the automatic teller machine.

This chapter examines many current uses of computers, explains the basic terminology of computers, and shows the differences between the four classifications of computers.

■ COMPUTERS TODAY

Yesterday's **computers** were tools for scientists, mathematicians, and engineers. When computers became commercially available, only the largest businesses acquired them, often simply for the prestige of owning one. Today, many businesses and organizations own computers although they may have different types of computers and use them for different purposes.

Computer equipment is generally divided into two categories, hardware and software. **Hardware,** the tangible parts of a computer, ranges from equipment that fills a large room to computers that fit on your lap. Hardware also includes **peripheral devices** that can be attached to the computer, such as a printer. **Software** consists of the instructions to the computer that enable it to do things, such as finding the best spot to drill for oil, or playing a competitive game of bridge. These computer instructions are also called **programs.**

Computers in Business

Hardly a day goes by when we do not make a computer-controlled business transaction. Each time we visit the bank, use a credit card, pay a bill, or buy groceries, a computer lurks behind the scene, recording each transaction. Computers can process data in a fraction of the time it would take to perform the same jobs manually. They reduce the paperwork involved in these transaction and also reduce costs.

Until recently, computer capabilities were limited primarily to large corporations due to the expenses associated with purchasing a computer. As the cost of computer hardware decreased, more small businesses were able to use computers. Today a host of programs for small computers are available for handling typical business activities such as accounting.

Computers in business provide many services. Airlines, travel agencies, and hotels use extensive networks of computer equipment for scheduling reservations. The computers in branches of a business across the country from one another can be connected by communication lines. Businesses use computers for sharing data, preparing documents, sending messages, and performing clerical duties. Since computers can work very fast, handle large amounts of data, and provide results exactly when needed, they are almost indispensable in banking, manufacturing, management, and general office functions.

BANKING. A bank processes huge amounts of paper and figures daily, as in checks, loan records, deposits, savings clubs, and investment plans. The balances of all accounts must be kept up to date. Funds and data must be exchanged among banks. Banks also use computers for the typical clerical and communications procedures found in businesses.

Many banks now offer automated services, such as direct deposit of paychecks into customers' accounts and automatic payment of their bills. Customers can also request that a regular amount be transferred periodically from checking accounts to savings accounts. Cash does not actually change hands in any of these transactions; only data changes. In addition, many banks also offer 24-hour banking services through their customers' use of a computer-controlled machine, the automatic teller machine (see Figure 1–1).

MANUFACTURING. Computers have greatly increased productivity in industry. Manufacturing involves designing and building products, all of which takes extensive planning and scheduling. Computers help manufacturers handle the routine scheduling of inventory, machinery, and labor.

Engineers use computers in drawing plans for products and in designing machines for building the products and machines for building *those* machines. During the manufacturing process, computers are used in controlling the operation of machinery (see Figure 1–2). Computers are also helpful in testing prototypes of products, whether car seats, lenses in sunglasses, sport shoes, or practically any product you can name. Major computer manufacturers even use computers to design better computers.

MANAGEMENT. Managers oversee the daily operations of a company. In addition, they make decisions about short-term goals and long-range plans. In order to effectively carry out their responsibilities, managers need information. Often it is processed and stored by a computer. Managers in companies with large computers may obtain the information in the form of reports. Recently more managers also have smaller computers in their offices. They use the small computer to prepare documents and analyze financial data.

FIGURE 1–1

Automatic Teller Machine
Automatic teller machines offer customers 24-hour self-service banking.

FIGURE 1–2

Computer-Aided Manufacturing
Entire rolling operation for the 13-inch bar mill at Bethlehem's Lackawanna, N.Y., facility is supervised from mill pulpit, the main monitor and control center of the mill.

Because computers make it so easy to generate and **retrieve** information, many managers find they suffer from information overload. In some cases, computers are used to graphically represent information so that relationships, trends, and comparisons can be highlighted. Software can be used to put information in the form of pie charts, bar graphs, and line graphs (see Figure 1–3).

Recently managers have begun using computers to project the probable outcome of a decision. If a manager dislikes the outcome the computer predicts, the variables in the problem can be changed to see if that improves the situation.

FIGURE 1–3

Bar Graph
This image was created using Lumena software by Time Arts Inc. They combine video digitizing, hand drawing, image manipulation, enhanced resolution and color mapping effects. Images were output to a 35 m.m Samurai file recorder.

OFFICE AUTOMATION. If we believe the advertisements on television and in business magazines, the office as we now know it is doomed. In the future the typewriters, bulky desks, and cumbersome filing cabinets will all be gone. Recent developments in communications, in information storage and retrieval, and in software have permanently changed the office environment. Organizations are realizing that computer technology is efficient, cost effective, and—in fact—*necessary* for handling their exploding amounts of data. The increasing amount of reporting required by federal government agencies particularly lends itself to computer technology in the office.

Almost every office function—typing, filing, communications, all of it—can be automated. The term applied to the integration of computer and communication technology with traditional office procedures is **office automation.** Among the specific applications in office automation are word processing, information retrieval, electronic mail including facsimiles and voice mail, teleconferencing, and telecommuting (see Chapter 16). **Word processing** is using computer equipment to prepare text; it can involve writing, editing, formatting, and printing. Word processing is much faster and more efficient than traditional typing. At least 75 percent of U.S. companies use some form of word processing.

Computers in Other Areas

No area of enterprise seems without computers nowadays. Scientists build computer models of airplane crashes in order to determine the "crash behavior" of airplanes, which in turn helps aircraft designers plan safer seats, windows, and fabrics to decrease fire hazards during a crash. Ecologists use computers to monitor environmental problems like acid rain and suggest solutions. Engineers use computers to design replacements for damaged bones. Educators use computers in the classroom to perform chemistry experiments that might otherwise be dangerous. There seems to be no limit to computer applications.

The federal government is the largest user of computers in the United States. This fact is not surprising considering the many government agencies that collect, process, and store information about the population. Typical examples are taking the U.S. census every ten years, processing the millions of income tax returns received each year, maintaining the large data bases in the Library of Congress and Federal Bureau of Investigation, and managing the welfare and social security systems (see Figure 1–4).

Computers are used in the areas of science and medicine not just for routine clerical functions. More importantly, in only seconds they can make calculations and test designs that human beings unaided could not complete in months. Data analyzed by computers can be collected by satellites for military intelligence and environmental planning, by seismographs for earthquake prediction, by CAT scans for medical diagnosis, and by sensors for determination of toxicity levels. For example, a crisis such as the horribly fatal gas leak at the Union Carbide plant in Bhopal, India, might have been prevented with computerized warning systems.

Educators are becoming more involved in computer use, too. Although computers cannot replace teachers, they are an effective learning tool. Computers are private tutors for students who need extra help or additional challenges. They not only help students learn foreign languages and programming languages such as Pascal or BASIC. Videodisks combined with

H I G H L I G H T

Saginaw Vanguard

A viewer watching the workings of one new auto manufacturing plant will see very few human workers. The majority of the assembling is performed by computer-controlled robots. These assemblers are unlike robots of the past because they have a vision system enabling them to "see" the parts. They then retrieve from their memory the image of how the parts should be connected. Furthermore, the robots work in the same way humans do—by actually holding up pieces in the air and attaching parts. The parts the robots use to assemble the automobile are delivered by automated vehicles that are also controlled by computers.

Are there any humans around? The whole system is overseen by human engineers who are in an elevated glass control room.

This plant sounds like a scene from a science fiction movie, but it is actually a research and development plant developed by General Motors. The plant is located in Saginaw, Michigan; it is called Saginaw Vanguard. The purpose of the plant is to develop new ways of automating manufacturing. The successful new technologies developed at Saginaw Vanguard will eventually be used in other GM plants. Although additional automation may eliminate human positions, when U.S. manufacturers compare themselves to Japanese competitors, they realize they must either automate or be left behind.

FIGURE 1-4

FBI Data Base
Huge data bases such as the ones
maintained by the government lead
many people to fear abuse of their
privacy.

computers offer a learning aid that, unlike books, includes motion and
sound. Using videodisk lessons, students can see reproductions of the early
colonists preparing for the Revolutionary War or the Wright brothers trying
out their first airplane. They can interact with lessons about current events
and watch news footage from old newscasts.

Computer use does not end at school or work. Increasingly, American
families are buying computers for use at home. At first they may only use
the computer to play games, but later they realize the tremendous potential
of home computers. They use word processing to prepare documents. Many
users store such information as addresses and recipes. Others use financial
planning software to help manage their budget and record their finances
(see Figure 1–5).

We have seen how computers can be powerful tools both in large-scale
applications and in the everyday functions of our lives. By knowing how
computers work, what they do, and what their benefits and problems are,
we can use computers to our best advantage.

OVERVIEW OF INFORMATION PROCESSING

Many people use the terms **data processing** and **information processing**
interchangeably, yet the two have a subtle difference in meaning. Data
processing refers to the steps involved in collecting, manipulating, and distributing data to achieve certain goals. Data processing can be performed
manually or electronically. Using computers for data processing is called
electronic data processing (EDP). The term *data processing* historically has
been used to mean EDP.

The objective of all data processing, whether manual or electronic, is the
conversion of data into information that can be used in making decisions.
The term *information processing*, then, includes all the steps involved in

FIGURE 1—5

Computers at Home
This computer is being used for controlling the home environment, including heating, lighting, and security.

converting data into information. Thus it includes data processing as well as the process of changing data to information.

What is the difference between data and information? **Data** refers to raw facts collected from various sources, but not organized or defined in a meaningful way. Data cannot be used to make meaningful decisions. For example, a bank manager may have very little use for a daily list of the amounts of all checks and deposit slips from the branch offices. But once data is organized, it can provide useful information—perhaps in the form of a summary report giving the dollar value and total number of deposits and withdrawals at each branch. **Information,** then, is processed data that increases understanding and helps people make intelligent decisions (see Figure 1–6). To be useful, information must be accurate, timely, complete, concise, relevant, and in a form easily understood by the user. It must be delivered to the right person at the right time. If information fails to meet these requirements, it fails to meet the needs of those who must use it and is of little value.

Data Organization

Data must be organized before it can be processed effectively. For that reason, data items are placed in the following groups:

1. *Bit.* Data is represented by on and off states of the computer's electronic circuitry (see the section on Analog and Digital Computers that follows.) The symbols that represent on and off are the binary digits 0 and 1. Each 0 or 1 is called a **bit,** short for **bi**nary digi**t.** The bit is the smallest unit of data a computer can handle.

2. *Character.* There are obviously more letters and numbers than two, but the computer only recognizes the two. Therefore, combinations of bits (0s and 1s) are used to represent **characters**—letters, digits, and special symbols such as %, #, or $. In the employee name E. J. Barnes, the characters are

FIGURE 1—6

The Data Processing Flow

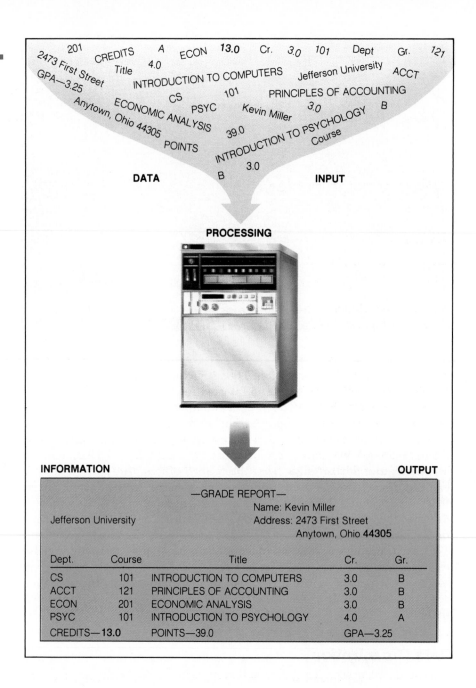

the letters, E, J, B, a, r, n, e, and s, the two periods, and the two spaces. A fixed combination of adjacent bits that represents a character is called a **byte.** Since eight bits are sufficient to represent any character, many computers are designed to accept eight-bit bytes.

3. *Field.* A business firm maintains specific data about its employees, such as home address, social security number, hourly wage, withholding tax, gross income, and so on. Each of these categories is called a **field.** A field is a collection of related characters that conveys a unit of information. Note that the size of a field depends upon the information placed in the field. For

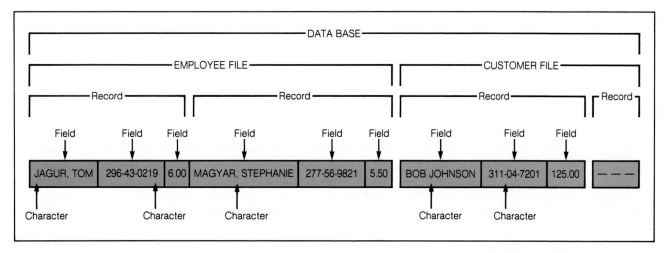

FIGURE 1—7

Organization of a Data Base

example, the field for names would need to be larger than the field for hourly wages (see Figure 1–7).

4. *Record.* A collection of fields that relate to a single unit is a **record.** An inventory record might consist of fields for item number, item name, description, price, supplier, quantity on hand, and location.

5. *File.* A grouping of related records is a **file.** All the client records for a construction firm would constitute the firm's client file. Many times different departments of a company will have their own separate files stored on the computer. For example, marketing may have sets of files and billing may have sets of files.

6. *Data base.* If each department in a company has its own set of files, the same information may be stored more than once. For example, both marketing and billing will need a customer's name, address, and telephone number. In order to eliminate this redundancy, a data base system can be used. A **data base** consolidates various independent files into one integrated unit. All users who need the information can access this one main file. In the above example both marketing and billing would access the same customer file to obtain a customer's address and telephone number.

The Data Flow

In order to change data into information, data must be manipulated, or processed. All processing follows the same basic flow: input, processing, and output. Each step is described in detail below.

INPUT. Input is the process of capturing data and putting it in a form that the computer can "understand." Input includes both the data that is to be manipulated and the software to do that.

Data can be input into a computer by typing on a keyboard, using a scanning device such as the counter-mounted scanners found in grocery stores, speaking into a microphone connected to the computer, or running a magnetic tape or disk. Such devices are described in greater detail in Chapters 4 and 5.

H I G H L I G H T

Computers Are Part of the Pros

Pro football enthusiasts all have their opinions on who their teams should select in the college draft. Yet player selection is not based solely on coaches' appraisals of a player. Many pro teams use a computerized information system called Scouting Information Systems (SIS). A scouting information system is used to compare college players and to project how well players will do in pro football. Players are evaluated on factors such as speed, intelligence, and durability. They are also evaluated on their height and weight in relation to the position they play. These factors are then assigned a weight when calculating a player's potential. Players are also evaluated on skills specific to their position. For example, a quarterback is judged on areas such as arm strength, touch, and the ability to lead the team. In comparison, an offensive lineman is judged on factors such as leg strength and ability to stay on his feet. The system also assigns a weight to the school the player attended.

These weighted factors are fed into the computer. The computer processes the data and then ranks the players for the college draft. Pro football is not only one of America's favorite games, it is also a business that bases decisions on computer-processed information

Input involves three steps:

■ Collecting the raw data and assembling it at one location.
■ Verifying, or checking, the accuracy and completeness of data (facts), and the programs. This step is very important since most computer errors are caused by human error.
■ Coding the data into a machine-readable form for processing.

PROCESSING. Once the data has been input, it is processed. **Processing** occurs in the part of the computer called the **central processing unit (CPU)**, examined in Chapter 4. The CPU includes the circuitry needed for performing arithmetic and logical operations and **primary memory.** Primary memory (also called **primary storage**) is the internal storage that holds programs and data used in immediate processing.

Once an instruction or data element is stored at a particular location in primary memory, it stays there until new data or instructions are written over the old material. This means the same data can be **accessed** repeatedly during processing, or the same instructions can be used repeatedly to process many different pieces of data.

Processing entails several types of manipulations (see Figure 1–8):

■ Classifying, or categorizing, the data according to certain characteristics so that it is meaningful to the user. For example, sales data could be grouped according to salesperson, product type, or customer.
■ Sorting, or arranging, the data alphabetically or numerically. An employee file may be sorted by social security number or by last name.
■ Calculating the data arithmetically or logically. Examples include computation of students' grade-point averages, customers' bank balances, and employees' paychecks.
■ Summarizing data; that is, reducing it to concise, usable forms. All grades for all students in all classes can be summarized by grade point averages, naming those students who earn a place on the dean's list. Sales figures can be summarized by salesperson in order to provide a list of those who exceeded their quota.
■ Storing, or retaining, data on storage media such as magnetic disks, tapes, or microfilm for later retrieval and processing.

OUTPUT. After data has been processed according to some or all of the steps above, information can be distributed to users. There are two types of **output:** soft copy and hard copy. **Soft copy** is information that is seen on a televisionlike screen or monitor attached to most computers. It is temporary; as soon as the monitor is turned off or new information is required, the old information vanishes. **Hard copy** is output printed in a tangible form such as on paper or microfilm. It can be read without using the computer and can be conveniently carried around, written on, or passed to other readers. Hardware that produces hard copy includes printers, discussed in Chapter 5.

The output phase of data flow consists of three steps:

■ Retrieving, or pulling, data from storage for use by the decision maker.
■ Converting data into a form that humans can understand and use (words or pictures displayed on a computer screen or printed on paper).

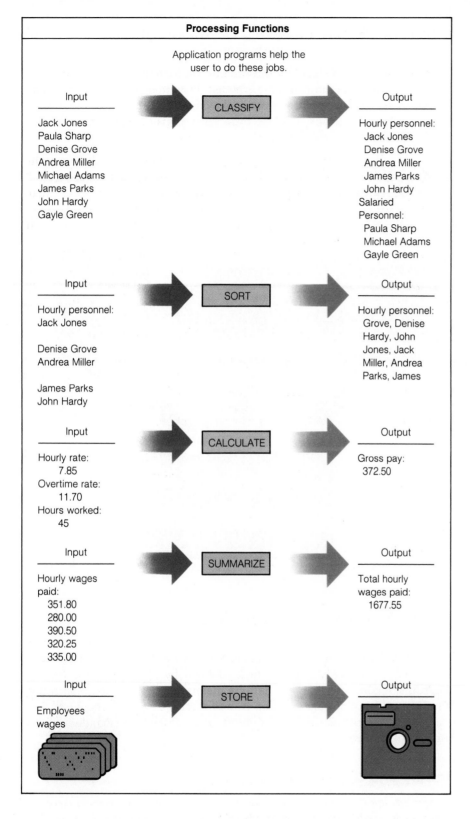

Processing Functions

Application programs help the user to do these jobs.

Input

Jack Jones
Paula Sharp
Denise Grove
Andrea Miller
Michael Adams
James Parks
John Hardy
Gayle Green

CLASSIFY

Output

Hourly personnel:
Jack Jones
Denise Grove
Andrea Miller
James Parks
John Hardy
Salaried
Personnel:
Paula Sharp
Michael Adams
Gayle Green

Input

Hourly personnel:
Jack Jones

Denise Grove
Andrea Miller

James Parks
John Hardy

SORT

Output

Hourly personnel:
Grove, Denise
Hardy, John
Jones, Jack
Miller, Andrea
Parks, James

Input

Hourly rate:
7.85
Overtime rate:
11.70
Hours worked:
45

CALCULATE

Output

Gross pay:
372.50

Input

Hourly wages
paid:
351.80
280.00
390.50
320.25
335.00

SUMMARIZE

Output

Total hourly
wages paid:
1677.55

Input

Employees
wages

STORE

Output

FIGURE 1–8

Processing Functions

■ Communicating, that is, providing information to the proper users at the proper time and in an appropriate form.

Information processing is monitored and evaluated in a step called **feedback.** Over time, the information provided through processing may lose its effectiveness. Feedback is the process of evaluating the output and making adjustments to the input or to the processing steps to ensure that the processing continues to result in good information.

CONCEPT SUMMARY 1—1

Overview of Information Processing

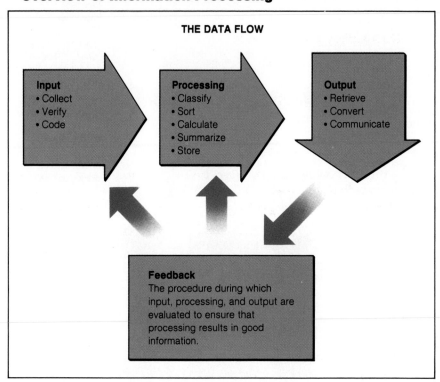

THE DATA FLOW

Input
• Collect
• Verify
• Code

Processing
• Classify
• Sort
• Calculate
• Summarize
• Store

Output
• Retrieve
• Convert
• Communicate

Feedback
The procedure during which input, processing, and output are evaluated to ensure that processing results in good information.

■ OPERATION OF COMPUTERS

When some people hear the word "computer" they envision an electronic marvel with superhuman intelligence. Yet a computer has no intelligence of its own. It can only perform tasks defined by humans in the form of programs. A computer handles data by means of simple yes/no operations. It pulls data from storage, acts on it, and stores it again, directed by programs that determine the yes/no, on/off, or conducting/nonconducting operations of its circuits.

Analog and Digital Computers

Computers are divided into two main types, analog computers and digital computers. **Analog computers** measure change in continuous physical or electrical states, such as pressure, temperature, voltage, length, volume, or shaft rotations. A speedometer is an example of an analog device. The computer measures the rotations of the driveshaft and then uses a pointer to indicate the speed of the car.

Unlike analog computers, **digital computers** count. In a digital computer, data is represented by discrete "on" and "off" (conducting/nonconducting or yes/no) states of the computer's electronic circuitry. Numbers, letters, and symbols are represented by a code based on the binary number system, a number system consisting of two digits, 1 and 0. This number system is well suited to represent the on/off states of electric current. The digital computer must convert all data to binary form. The computers discussed in this book are digital computers.

The Computer Advantage

Within the limits of its circuits, a computer can perform three basic functions:

1. Arithmetic operations (addition, subtraction, multiplication, division).
2. Logical comparisons of relationships among values (greater than, less than, equal to).
3. Storage and retrieval operations.

If the three functions named above are all computers can do, then why have these machines become so widely used? Computers are useful because they are very fast, their circuits are reliable, and they can store vast amounts of data. In other words, computers are used because of their speed, accuracy, and storage capabilities.

SPEED. The speed of a computer is controlled by a number of physical factors. First, the switching speed of its electronic components, such as switching the state from on to off or switching the direction the current travels, affects the speed of the computer. A second factor is the distances that electric currents must travel within the circuits. By packing circuits closer together and increasing the switching speed, engineers have been able to increase the speed of computers vastly. Other factors that affect computer speeds are the **programming language** (that is, type of code) used in writing programs (see Chapter 12), the amount of data a computer can handle at one time, and the amount of data and instructions readily available in the computer's primary memory.

Modern computers can perform millions of calculations in one second. Their speed is fast reaching the physical limitation of the speed of light, 186,000 miles per second. Generally, computer speed describes the time required to perform one operation and is measured in terms of nanoseconds and other small units (see Figure 1–9). In the past, the time required for performing one addition ranged from 4 microseconds to 200 nanoseconds. In the future, it may be 200 to 1,000 times faster.

ACCURACY. The accuracy of a computer refers to the inherent reliability of its electronic components. The same type of current passed through the same circuits yields the same results each time. We take advantage of this aspect of circuitry every time we switch on an electric device. When we

FIGURE 1—9

Divisions of a Second

Unit	Symbol	Fractions of a Second	
Millisecond	ms	one-thousandth	(1/1,000)
Microsecond	μs	one-millionth	(1/1,000,000)
Nanosecond	ns	one-billionth	(1/1,000,000,000)
Picosecond	ps	one-trillionth	(1/1,000,000,000,000)

turn on a light switch a light comes on, not a radio or a fan. The computer is reliable for the same reason—its circuitry is reliable. A computer can run for hours, days, and weeks at a time, giving accurate results for millions of activities. Of course, if the data or programs submitted to the computer are faulty, the computer will not produce correct results. The output will be useless and meaningless, illustrating the human error involved. This concept is called garbage in—garbage out (GIGO) and is fundamental in understanding computer "mistakes."

STORAGE. Besides being very fast and reliable, computers can store large amounts of data. Some data is held in primary memory for use during immediate operations. The amount of data held in primary memory varies among computers. Some small computers hold as few as 16,000 characters, whereas large computers can hold billions of characters. Data can also be recorded on magnetic disks and tapes (see Figure 1–10); this **secondary storage** makes a computer's "memory" almost limitless. Secondary storage (also called **secondary memory**) holds data that is not immediately needed by the computer.

The ability of the computer to store, retrieve, and process data—all without human intervention—separates it from a simple calculator and gives

FIGURE 1—10

Tape Storage

COMPUTERS AND INFORMATION PROCESSING

it its power and appeal to humans. So while humans can perform the same functions as the computer, the difference is that the computer can reliably execute millions of instructions in a second and store the results in an almost unlimited memory.

CONCEPT SUMMARY 1–2

Computer Functions

- The computer performs three functions: arithmetic operations, comparison operations, and storage and retrieval operations.

- A computer's appeal is based on its speed, accuracy, and memory.

- A computer's internal memory is called **primary storage,** and media used to hold data outside the computer constitute **secondary storage.** Secondary storage makes the computer's memory almost limitless.

COMPUTER CLASSIFICATIONS

Computers are categorized by size, capability, price range, and speed of operation. It is becoming increasingly difficult to distinguish among the different classifications of computers, however, because smaller computers have increasingly larger primary memories and are able to handle an increasing number of peripheral devices such as printers and secondary storage devices. The four major categories of computer systems are supercomputers, mainframes, minicomputers, and microcomputers.

Supercomputers

Supercomputers are the largest, fastest, and most expensive computers made (see Figure 1–11). Some supercomputers have as many as eight central processing units. Manufacturers of supercomputers claim they will soon produce supercomputers that can execute more than one billion instructions per second. The computers are so fast that their chips must be surrounded by a liquid coolant to prevent melting. As for price, the newest supercomputers cost as much as $20 million.

Supercomputers are used for figuring lengthy and complex calculations. Scientists use them in weather forecasting, oil exploration, energy conservation, seismology, nuclear reactor safety analysis, and cryptography. In addition, supercomputers are used for simulations in nuclear energy research and for stress tests in automotive and aircraft design.

Most organizations have no need for supercomputers, nor can they justify the large cost of the hardware and software. Software development for supercomputers is much more complex and expensive because the design of the machines is so different from the design of less powerful computers. Still, the demand for supercomputers is increasing. In 1980, there were only 21 supercomputers in the world. Today, about 300 supercomputers are busy crunching numbers, and the appetite for them seems insatiable. Even universities are beginning to install supercomputers for their extensive research projects.

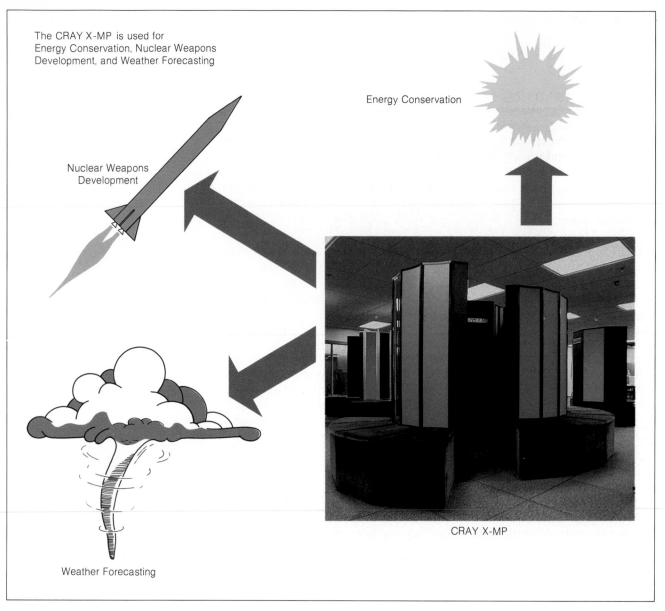

The CRAY X-MP is used for
Energy Conservation, Nuclear Weapons
Development, and Weather Forecasting

Energy Conservation

Nuclear Weapons
Development

Weather Forecasting

CRAY X-MP

FIGURE 1—11

**The Cray X-MP Supercomputer
System**

Research in supercomputer development has become a heated race between the United States and Japan. Whoever develops and commercializes the technology that improves supercomputers will have the competitive edge in all computer-related industries—an important consideration for both economics and national defense. Companies developing supercomputers include Cray Research, Fujitsu, ETA Systems, Inc., and Evans and Sutherland. Scientific Computer Systems Corporation and Supertek Computers, Inc., are producing what they call mini supercomputers. These manufacturers hope to capture the market for products between regular supercomputers and mainframes.

Mainframes

During the 1960s, the term *mainframe* was synonymous with CPU. Today the word refers simply to a category of computers between the supercomputer and the minicomputer.

Mainframes operate at very high speeds and support main input and output devices that also operate at very high speeds. They can be subdivided into small, medium, and large systems. Most mainframes are manufactured as "families" of computers. A family consists of several mainframe models varying in size and power. An organization can purchase or lease a small system and, if processing needs expand, upgrade to a medium or large system. Purchase prices range from $200,000 to several million dollars for a large mainframe with peripherals. Mainframes are used chiefly by large businesses, hospitals, universities, and banks with large data processing needs (see Figure 1–12).

A mainframe requires special installation and maintenance procedures. It creates a fair amount of heat, so it requires a cooling system. A mainframe cannot be plugged into a standard electrical outlet; it needs special electrical wiring. It may rest on special platforms so that wires and cables can be housed beneath it. Furthermore, a mainframe runs day and night and provides access to a large amount of data. Because this access needs to be controlled, users must implement some type of security system. All these factors add to the cost of using a mainframe.

Mainframe computers are sold or leased with a great deal of support from the vendor. The vendor may invest considerable time and money in helping a customer select and install a mainframe. Once the system is installed, the vendor spends additional effort training the customer's employees from top executives to clerical workers to use the system, servicing and repairing the mainframe, and solving questions and problems that arise periodically.

FIGURE 1–12

IBM System 4381 Mainframe

Major mainframe manufacturers are International Business Machines (IBM), Unisys, Honeywell, and National Cash Register (NCR).

Minicomputers

Minicomputers were developed in the 1960s for doing specialized tasks. They were smaller, less powerful, and less expensive than the large computers available at the time. As they became increasingly sophisticated, their capabilities, memory size, and overall performance have overlapped those of mainframes. The more powerful minicomputers are called *superminis.*

Minicomputers are easier to install and operate than mainframe computers. They take up less floor space than mainframes; they may fit on a desk, or they may be as large as a file cabinet (see Figure 1–13). They require few special environmental conditions. Minicomputers can be plugged into standard electrical outlets and often do not require facilities such as air conditioning and special platforms. Prices for minicomputers range from a few thousand dollars to two or three hundred thousand dollars.

Minicomputers are used for multiuser applications, numerical control of machine tools, industrial automation, and word processing. They are also used in conjunction with communication facilities for sharing data and peripherals or serving a geographically dispersed organization. They can use **packaged software,** that is, standardized commercial software developed for solving general problems such as preparing a general ledger or payroll.

A minicomputer system can easily be enlarged to meet the needs of a growing organization since it can be implemented in a modular fashion. For example, a hospital may install one minicomputer in its out-patient department for record keeping and another in the pharmacy or laboratory. As additional minicomputers are installed, they can be connected to existing ones to share common data.

In the late 1970s and early 1980s, the minicomputer industry grew at a rate of 35 to 40 percent annually. Today, the market for minicomputers is weakening. The increased capabilities and improved software of microcomputers has led to the increased use of micros in traditional minicomputer markets. Many companies now link microcomputers with mainframes or existing minicomputers to hold down equipment investment costs and still meet processing needs. This practice, however, creates new security problems for many corporations.

Manufacturers of minicomputers include Digital Equipment Corporation (DEC), Hewlett-Packard, Data General, Honeywell, General Automation, Unisys, Texas Instruments, Wang Laboratories, Prime Computer Inc., and IBM.

Microcomputers

Once technology had advanced to the point where many circuits could be etched onto a single silicon chip, the **microprocessor** was developed. A microprocessor is a chip that contains the portions of the CPU that control the computer and perform arithmetic and logic operations. It may contain

FIGURE 1–13

Minicomputer System with Peripherals

COMPUTERS AND INFORMATION PROCESSING

some primary storage also. The microprocessor became the foundation for the **microcomputer,** also called the personal computer.

Microcomputers are the most popular type of computer today. The demand for microcomputers continues to increase. Even the stock market crash of October 1987, did not have an adverse effect on the sales of microcomputers. In addition, the sale of microcomputer software is greatly increasing.

The prefix *micro* applies more to size and cost than to capability. They may fit on a desktop or in a briefcase (see Figure 1–14). Some microcomputers designed for home use cost as little as $100, while microcomputers for professional use may cost over $10,000. Yet current microcomputers are very powerful for their size. Microcomputers cannot perform as many complex functions as today's large computers, and they have much smaller primary memories; however, technology continues to give them more speed and memory at decreasing costs.

Most microcomputers are single-user systems. As such they must be easy to operate. One important aspect of microcomputer design involves the development of user-friendly hardware and software; that is, equipment that is easy to learn and easy to use. The concern for user friendliness has overflowed into the development of other computers, too.

Microcomputers are available in computer stores, office supply stores, and department stores. In some cases, they are sold much as an appliance, like a television or a videocassette recorder. Software for microcomputers is often packaged, but many users like the challenge of developing their own and many businesses need custom-developed software. Chapter 8 provides a detailed discussion of microcomputers.

FIGURE 1—14

IBM PS/2 Model 25

Factors to Consider in Buying a Computer System

	Super-Computer	Mainframe	Mini-Computer	Micro-Computer
Cost	Several million dollars	$200,000 to several million dollars	A few thousand to two or three hundred thousand dollars	$100 to $10,000
Other facts	Largest, fastest computer. Good for complex, lengthy calculations. Hard to justify costs. Software development complex.	Additional costs: platforms, security, wiring, air conditioning. Vendor support. Easily upgraded to next size in family.	Fits in small space. Uses standard electrical outlets. Often needs no air conditioning. Expandable in modular fashion. Micros rapidly approaching minicomputer capabilities.	Can fit on desk or lap. Many applications. Can be linked to mainframes or minicomputers. Newer computers and software are user-friendly.

■ SUMMARY POINTS

■ Computers are powerful tools in many areas such as business, manufacturing, banking, government, education, and personal use. Most of today's transactions and procedures involve computer equipment, office automation, and data bases.

■ Electronic data processing, often simply called data processing, involves the use of computers in collecting, manipulating, and distributing data to achieve goals. The terms *hardware* and *software* describe the physical components of a computer and the instructions or programs used in electronic data processing.

■ Data refers to unorganized, raw facts, whereas information is data that has been organized and processed so that it can be used in making intelligent decisions.

■ For effective data processing, data is organized in meaningful units. The units, from smallest to largest, are bit, character, field, record, file, and data base.

■ Converting data into information follows this pattern: input, processing, output.

■ Input involves collecting, verifying, and coding data.

■ Processing involves classifying, sorting, calculating, summarizing, and storing data.

■ Information retrieved and converted so that it can be communicated to the user in an intelligible form is output.

■ Analog computers measure the change in continuous physical and electric states, while digital computers count data in the form of yes/no, on/off, conducting/nonconducting states of electronic circuitry. The digital computer must convert all data to binary form, which is based on the binary number system of two digits, 0 and 1.

■ The computer performs three functions: arithmetic operations, logic comparisons, and storage and retrieval operations.

■ The computer's appeal is based on its speed, accuracy, and memory.

■ A computer's internal memory is called primary storage. Media used to hold data outside the computer constitute secondary storage. Secondary storage makes the computer's memory almost limitless.

■ Computers are categorized by size, capability, price range, and speed of operation. The four classifications are supercomputer, mainframe, minicomputer, and microcomputer.

■ Advances in technology have blurred the distinctions between the classifications of computers, to the point where some minicomputers have capabilities as great as mainframes and some microcomputers have capabilities as great as minicomputers.

■ Many companies are linking microcomputers to existing systems so as to increase capabilities yet hold down costs.

▨ REVIEW QUESTIONS

1. In your job or school today, name some ways that computers affect you. Relate these ways to applications discussed in the first sections of this chapter.

2. Distinguish between data and information in the context of data processing. Give some examples.

3. Define data processing. Why is it often referred to as EDP?

4. Describe the relationship that exists among data within a data base, mentioning the bit, character, field, record, file, and data base.

5. Using data that a store might collect when you purchase groceries, describe the five types of manipulations that may occur in the processing stage of the data flow.

6. Name the three basic functions that a computer can perform.

7. Although computer processing is essentially error free, mistakes can and do occur. What is meant by the phrase *garbage in—garbage out?* Name two procedures mentioned in the discussion of the data flow that could prevent GIGO.

8. Describe two types of storage involved in data processing. Why is the computer's "memory" almost limitless?

9. For what purposes are supercomputers used? Have you heard of any uses other than the ones mentioned in the text? What are they?

10. What market trends are currently causing the downturn in sales of mainframes and minicomputers?

Wall Street Journal

COMPANY HISTORY

The largest newspaper in the country, with a circulation of approximately two million, *The Wall Street Journal* began more than a hundred years ago as a two-page publication known as the *Customers' Afternoon Letter*. The *Letter* was the brainchild of Charles H. Dow and Edward D. Jones, two financial news reporters who worked for a New York news agency. The two men formed Dow Jones & Company and were soon joined in their publishing efforts by Charles M. Bergstresser.

The *Letter*, which was delivered to subscribers in the Wall Street area, appeared each afternoon and summarized the financial bulletins that were issued during the day. Charles Dow added a daily feature called the Dow Jones Average, a stock price index based on a formula he devised. The publication prospered and, soon after Clarence W. Barron of the Boston News Bureau became associated with Dow Jones & Company, the *Letter* became a full-fledged newspaper called *The Wall Street Journal*. The first issue of *The Wall Street Journal* was printed on July 8, 1889, cost two cents, and was four pages long. Although the *Journal's* stories emphasized business and finance, general news stories appeared in the first issue and continue to this day.

The *Journal's* reputation and circulation grew. Clarence Barron bought a controlling interest in the company following the death of Charles Dow in 1902. Barron increased circulation, expanded news coverage, and introduced modern printing equipment during the years in which he controlled the paper. A Pacific Coast edition of the *Journal* was first published eight days before the stock market crash of 1929.

With the collapse of the stock market, the *Journal* fell upon hard times. Circulation dropped as the financial community struggled to survive. Help came from Barney Kilgore, who was named managing editor in 1941. The changes in the paper that Kilgore implemented exist today. He insisted the paper acquire a broader scope, including all aspects of business, economics, and consumer affairs. Kilgore also made the Pacific Coast edition of the paper a duplicate of the Eastern edition.

Serving readers promptly was another of Kilgore's goals. This goal provided the impetus for a Southwest edition of the *Journal* in 1948 complete with a printing plant in Dallas. Although three editions of the paper ensured that readers all over the country would have access to up-to-the minute news, the diverse locations created technical problems of a new magnitude. How could the same newspaper with the same staff of writers and editors be published in different locations around the country? The answer involved the use of a new technology. Once stories were typed, they were coded on perforated tape and passed through a reader that converted the stories into electrical pulses. The pulses were sent via telephone lines to linecasters and then were automatically set into type.

Continued circulation growth and expansion in news coverage brought the *Journal* worldwide fame. A number of the paper's writers have received Pulitzer Prizes. Old printing plants were replaced, and early in the sixties, a breakthrough came on the production front. Microwave transmissions were used to send full-page images from one plant to another. By the mid-seventies, all *Journal* printing plants were using a sophisticated internal communications system. A central computer directed typesetting in multiple printing plants.

Computer Usage Today

Computers play an essential role in getting news stories into print. A sophisticated electronic network brings *Wall Street Journal* stories from their points of origin to the homes and offices of subscribers. Computer terminals are used to write and edit stories. Once a story has been edited, it is transmitted electronically from New York City to Chicopee, Massachusetts, and Dallas, Texas. There it is entered into a production computer system that electronically transmits the story to computers at five "mother" plants (Chicopee, Massachusetts; Dallas, Texas; Orlando, Florida; Naperville, Illinois; Palo Alto, California) where type is set. Typeset stories are printed out as paper galleys that are then pasted onto pages. From this point, the pages may take one of two routes. They may be photographed, with printing plates made from the film and subsequently mounted onto high-speed presses. Or they may be made into paper proofs, which in turn are scanned by a laser device, and transmitted via satellite to other printing plants, at the same time as the pages are printed at the "mother" plant itself. Computer-controlled printing systems can print fifteen copies per second. Once printed, the papers are automatically labeled with a computer-produced label, bundled and loaded on trucks that carry the papers to distribution points.

Computers are used in a number of other ways at *The Wall Street Journal*. Financial systems are run on IBM mainframes using MVS/XA and VM operating systems. A computerized advertising system provides page makeup information and produces invoices. Circulation records are kept current on a Unisys computer that contains a master file of all subscribers. Each printing plant is sent a list of subscribers daily.

When Charles Dow and Edward Jones began their two-page *Afternoon Letter* in a tiny basement office in 1882, they could hardly have imagined how large their news organization would become.

DISCUSSION POINTS

1. Describe how computers are directly involved in bringing stories to print.
2. Other than bringing stories to print, how are computers used at *The Wall Street Journal?*

CHAPTER

2

The Evolution of Computers

OUTLINE

The Technology Race
Early Developments
First Generation: 1951–1958
Second Generation: 1959–1964
Third Generation: 1965–1970
Fourth Generation: 1971–today
The Computer Industry
The Hardware Industry
The Software Industry

Careers in Computers
Data-Processing Operations
Personnel
System Development Personnel
Data-Base Specialists
Information System Managers
Professional Associations
AFIPS
ACM
DPMA
ASM
ICCP
SIM

Summary Points
Review Questions

The Next Major Battleground

By Philip Elmer-DeWitt. Reported
by Thomas McCarroll
and Edwin M. Reingold
TIME

Silicon Valley has not seen such a bumper crop since it stopped growing peaches and prunes and began producing computer chips. Hardly a week has gone by this spring without a ballyhooed announcement of a new semiconductor or a line of high-speed computers. At the center of the excitement is a new breed of microprocessors that promises to give computer manufacturers their biggest performance boost in a decade. Lightning fast, the chips make it possible to put the power of ten to 20 refrigerator-size minicomputers into a single desktop-size machine.

Of all the announcements, none has generated as much anticipation as the one to be made this week by Motorola, the largest U.S. supplier of semiconductors (1987 sales: $6.7 billion). The electronics giant has etched 1.7 million transistors into a three-chip microprocessor called the 88000 that it hopes will become a standard component of the next generation of high-performance computers. Motorola may be right. Even before the new product was formally unveiled, more than 30 prospective customers, including Data General, Convergent and Tektronix, had formed a users group to set guidelines for designing hardware and software to take advantage of the new chips. Says Motorola Vice President Murray Goldman: "This is the next major battleground in the computer world."

How do the new chips achieve their performance breakthroughs? In a word: RISC, for reduced instruction set computer. RISC is not a new technology, but a fresh approach to computing that challenges 25 years of semiconductor design. It focuses on a computer's most basic commands: the instructions that are embedded, or hard-wired, into the silicon circuitry of the machine's central processing unit. The first computers made do with a handful of primitive commands, such as LOAD, ADD and STORE, which programmers combined to perform complex tasks. Lacking a command to multiply 6 times 5, for example, they had to instruct their computers to add five 6s together.

Over the years, the basic instruction sets grew in length, as miniaturization allowed computer designers to etch more circuits into silicon chips. The most advanced microprocessors began to resemble state-of-the-art calculators that could compute everything from square roots to compound interest at the touch of a button. By the time Digital Equipment introduced its best-selling VAX 11/780 computer in 1977, the machine's instruction set had swelled to 304 commands.

But the increased complexity had its cost. Studies showed that 20% of the instructions were doing 80% of the work. The rest were like expensive extras on a limousine: rarely used luxuries that took up space and slowed performance. The advocates of RISC, declaring that it was time to go back to basics, stripped away the nonessentials and optimized the performance of the 50 or so most frequently used commands. Says Ben Anixter, vice president at Advanced Micro Devices, a Sunnyvale, Calif., firm that is introducing its first RISC chip in two weeks: "It is like going from the complicated old piston airplane engine to the turbojet."

At first, the industry was reluctant to switch to RISC. But the new crop of chips has made believers out of almost everybody. Sun, a company best known for its engineering computers, got into the chip business last summer when it began licensing a RISC processor to AT&T, Unisys and Xerox. MIPS, which introduced its second generation of the chips last month, supplies microprocessors to Tandem, Prime, and Silicon Graphics. Hewlett-Packard has built an entire line of computers around RISC technology.

Most important, IBM is making a major commitment to RISC. IBM Vice President Andrew Heller suggests that RISC technology could produce startling advances in electronic speech recognition, machine vision and artificial intelligence—

ARTICLE

all of which require superfast microprocessors. Says Heller: "Computers that can listen and talk back, and recognize objects on sight, are not so farfetched. RISC will help make all that a reality, and it's going to happen this century."

Today's computers differ significantly from the early computers of forty years ago which filled a room with vacuum tubes and other components. New computers have decreased in size, yet new methods of processing such

as RISC are increasing computer speeds. If scientists continue to develop technological advances at their present rate, the future capabilities of computers seem almost limitless.

INTRODUCTION

Although the computer is a relatively recent innovation, its development rests on centuries of research, thought, and discovery. Advances in information-processing technology are responses to the growing need to find better, faster, cheaper, and more reliable methods of handling data. The search for better ways to store and process data is not recent. Data-processing equipment has gone through generations of change and improvement. An understanding of the evolution of data processing is especially helpful in understanding the capabilities and limitations of modern computers.

This chapter presents a discussion of significant people and events that led to the development of the modern computer. Each of the four computer generations is described. Additionally, an overview of the computer industry, including both the hardware and software industries, is presented. The chapter concludes with brief descriptions of computer careers and of several professional associations.

CHAPTER

THE TECHNOLOGY RACE

True electronic computers entered the technological revolution less than fifty years ago. They can be traced through a long line of calculating and recording methods that began with tying knots in pieces of rope to keep track of livestock and carving marks on clay or stone tablets to record transactions.

Later, the **abacus,** a device made of beads strung on wires, was used for adding and subtracting (see Figure 2–1). The abacus, along with hand calculations, was adequate for computation until the early 1600s when John Napier designed a portable multiplication tool called **Napier's Bones,** or Napier's Rods. The user slid the ivory rods up to figure multiplication and division problems. Napier's idea led to the invention of the slide rule in the mid-1600s.

These tools were anything but automatic. As business became more complicated and tax systems expanded, people needed faster, more accurate aids for computation and record-keeping. The idea for the first mechanical

FIGURE 2–1

The Abacus

The abacus is still used by some Chinese as the primary calculating device. It is also a popular disk accessory and educational toy.

calculating machine grew out of the many tedious hours a father and his son spent preparing tax reports. Once this machine was introduced, the way opened for more complex machines as inventors built upon each succeeding development. The race for automation was on.

Early Developments

In the mid-1600s, Blaise Pascal, a mathematician and philosopher, and his father, a tax official were compiling tax reports for the French government in Paris. As they agonized over the columns of figures, Pascal decided to build a machine that would do the job much faster and more accurately. His machine, the **Pascaline,** could add and subtract (see Figure 2–2). The

FIGURE 2–2

Blaise Pascal and the Pascaline

The Pascaline worked very well for addition, but subtraction was performed by a roundabout adding method.

Pascaline functioned by a series of eight rotating gears, much as an odometer keeps track of a car's mileage. But the market for the Pascaline never grew. Clerks and accountants would not use it. The were afraid it might replace them on their jobs and thought it could be rigged, like a scale or a roulette wheel.

About fifty years later, in 1694, the German mathematician Gottfried Wilhelm von Leibniz designed the **Stepped Reckoner** that could add, subtract, multiply, divide, and figure square roots. Although the machine did not become widely used, almost every mechanical calculator built during the next 150 years was based on its design.

The first signs of automation benefited France's weaving industry when Joseph-Marie Jacquard built a loom controlled by punched cards. Heavy paper cards linked in a series passed over a set of rods on the loom. The pattern of holes in the cards determined which rods were engaged, thereby adjusting the color and pattern of the product (see Figure 2–3). Prior to Jacquard's invention, a loom operator adjusted the loom settings by hand before each glide of the shuttle, a tedious and time-consuming job.

Jacquard's loom emphasized three concepts important in computer theory. One was that information could be coded on **punched cards.** A second key concept was that cards could be linked to provide a series of instructions—essentially a program—allowing a machine to do its work without human intervention. Finally, the loom illustrated that programs could automate jobs.

The first person to use these concepts in a computing machine was Charles Babbage, a professor at Cambridge University in England. As a mathematician, Babbage needed an accurate method for computing and printing tables of the properties of numbers (squares, square roots, logarithms, and so on). A model of his first machine worked well, but the technology of the day was too primitive for manufacturing parts precise enough to build a full-sized version (see Figure 2–4).

FIGURE 2–3

The Jacquard Loom
Although other weavers had already designed looms that used punched cards, Jacquard refined the idea and he receives credit for the invention.

FIGURE 2–4

Charles Babbage and the Difference Engine
Even very slight flaws in the brass and pewter rods and gears designed for a larger version of the difference engine threw the machine out of whack and invalidated results.

Later, Babbage envisioned a new machine, the **analytical engine,** for performing any calculation according to instructions coded on cards. The idea for this steam-powered machine was amazingly similar to the design of computers. It had four parts: a "mill" for calculating, a "store" for holding instructions and intermediate and final results, an "operator" or system for carrying out instructions, and a device for "reading" and "writing" data on punched cards. Although Babbage died before he could construct the machine, his son built a workable model based on Babbage's notes and drawings. Because of the ideas he introduced, Babbage is known as the "father of computers."

Punched cards played an important role in the next advance toward automatic machines. Dr. Herman Hollerith, a statistician, was commissioned by the U.S. Census Bureau to develop a faster method of tabulating census data. His machine read and compiled data from punched cards. These cards were the forerunners of today's standard computer card. Thanks to Hollerith's invention, the time needed to process the census data was reduced from seven and a half years in 1880 to two and a half years in 1890, despite an increase of thirteen million people in the intervening decade (see Figure 2–5).

Encouraged by his success, Hollerith formed the Tabulating Machine Company in 1896 to supply equipment to census takers in western Europe and Canada. In 1911, Hollerith sold his company, which later combined with twelve others to form the Computing-Tabulating-Recording Company (CTR).

In 1924, Thomas J. Watson, Sr. became president of CTR and changed the name to International Business Machines Corporation (IBM). The IBM machines made extensive use of punched cards. After Congress set up the social security system in 1935, Watson won for IBM the contract to provide

FIGURE 2–5

Herman Hollerith and the Tabulating Machine
Hollerith's code fit the grid of twelve rows and eighty columns on his cards. Once data was punched onto the cards, a tabulator read the cards as they passed over tiny brushes. Each time a brush found a hole, it completed an electrical circuit and caused special counting dials to increment the data. The cards were then sorted into 24 compartments by the sorting component of the machine.

machines needed for this massive accounting and payment distribution system. The U.S. Census Bureau also bought IBM equipment.

During the late 1920s and early 1930s, **accounting machines** evolved that could perform many record-keeping and accounting functions. Although they handled the U.S. business data-processing load well into the 1950s, they did little more than manipulate vast quantities of punched cards. These machines were limited in speed, size, and versatility.

World War II also had an impact on the development of computers. Cryptologists on the Allied side were determined to build a computer that would decipher the codes developed by the German machine, Enigma. The Allies smuggled Richard Lewinski, a Jewish factory worker, out of Poland because he had made parts for the Enigma. He designed a mockup of the German machine for the Allies. Two Englishmen, Dilwyn Knox and Alan Turing, used this model to build the **Bletchley Park** computer, which successfully deciphered the German codes.

A major advance toward modern computing came in 1944 when Howard Aiken's team at Harvard University designed a machine called the **Mark I.** This machine, the first automatic calculator, consisted of seventy-eight accounting machines controlled by punched paper tapes. The U.S. Navy used the Mark I for designing weapons and calculating trajectories until the end of World War II.

Regardless of its role in computer history, the Mark I was outdated before it was finished. Only two years after work on it was begun, John Mauchly and J. Presper Eckert, Jr. introduced the first electronic computer for large-scale, general use at the University of Pennsylvania Moore School of Engineering. This machine was called the **ENIAC**, short for **Electronic Numerical Integrator and Calculator** (see Figure 2–6). It represented the shift from mechanical/electromechanical devices that used wheels, gears, and relays for computing to devices that depended upon electronic parts such as vacuum tubes and circuitry for operations.

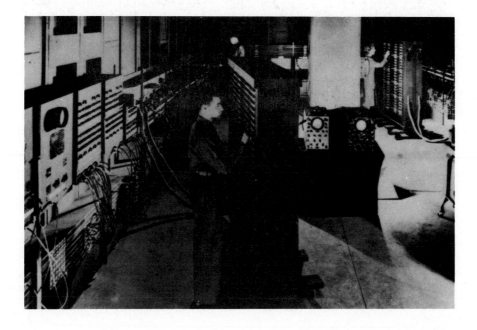

FIGURE 2–6

The ENIAC
The ENIAC's first job was calculating the feasibility of a proposed design for the hydrogen bomb. The computer was also used for studying weather and cosmic rays.

HIGHLIGHT

Who Was First?

Who invented the first electronic computer? The first electronic computer built in the United States was thought to be the ENIAC, built by John W. Mauchly and J. Presper Eckert, Jr. Recently a lawsuit on the patent of the concepts of the ENIAC brought to light the name John V. Atanasoff.

Atanasoff was a graduate student at the University of Wisconsin in the late 1920s when he became fascinated with the possibility of an electronic digital computer. Later, while a professor of physics at Iowa State College, he and a graduate student started to build the ABC, Atanasoff-Berry Computer. The two men were unable to complete their work because of their involvement in World War II.

Many of Atanasoff's concepts are evident in early computers such as the ENIAC. The concepts include data being represented in digital form; switches being electronic, not mechanical; memory separated from processing; and the use of rules of logic and binary numbers.

Although historians are late in recognizing Atanasoff's contributions to the computer field, they now credit him with having a major impact on the development of computer technology.

The ENIAC was a huge machine; its 18,000 vacuum tubes took up a space eight feet high and eighty feet long. It weighed thirty tons and gobbled 174,000 watts of power. It could multiply two ten-digit numbers in three-thousandths of a second, compared with the three seconds required by the Mark I. At the time, the ENIAC seemed so fast the scientists predicted that seven computers like it could handle all the calculations the world would ever need.

The ENIAC had two major problems, however. First, the failure rate of the **vacuum tubes** was very high. Research showed that it was often the new tubes that failed, so Richard Clippinger developed a method for curing the tubes. New tubes were burned for about six hours, after which weak tubes would be isolated and discarded.

A second problem with ENIAC was that operating instructions had to be fed into it manually by setting switches and connecting wires on control panels called plugboards. This was a tedious, time-consuming, and error-prone task. In the mid-1940s, the mathematician John von Neumann proposed a way to overcome the difficulty. The solution involved the **stored-program concept,** the idea of storing both instructions and data in the computer's primary memory. Although Eckert and Mauchly actually conceived of the stored-program concept long before von Neumann, they had not outlined a plan for its use.

Von Neumann's principles spurred the development of the first stored-program computer in the United States, the **EDVAC (Electronic Discrete Variable Automatic Computer).** The EDVAC's stored instructions decreased the number of manual operations needed in computer processing. This development marked the beginning of the modern computer era and the information society (see Figure 2–7). Subsequent refinements of the computer concept have focused on speed, size, and cost.

First Generation: 1951–1958

Improvements in computer capabilities are grouped in generations based upon the electronic technology available at the time. The first generation of computers—based upon the designs of the ENIAC and EDVAC—began with the sale of the first commercial electronic computer. This machine, called the **UNIVAC I,** was developed by Mauchly and Eckert, who had approached Remington Rand for financing (see Figure 2–8). Remington Rand (later Sperry Corporation) bought Mauchly and Eckert's company and propelled itself into the computer age with a product that was years ahead of the machines produced by competitors. In 1951, the first UNIVAC I replaced IBM equipment at the U.S. Census Bureau. Another UNIVAC was installed at General Electric's Appliance Park in Louisville, Kentucky. For the first time, business firms saw the possibilities of computer data processing.

The UNIVAC I and other **first-generation computers** were huge, costly to buy, expensive to power, and often unreliable. They were slow compared to today's computers, and their internal storage capacity was limited. They depended upon the first-generation technology of vacuum tubes for internal operations. The masses of vacuum tubes took up a lot of space and generated considerable heat, requiring an air-conditioned environment. Vacuum tubes could switch on and off thousands of times per second, but one tube would

FIGURE 2—7

John von Neumann and the EDVAC
As it turned out, two groups of people were working simultaneously on a stored-program computer. Scientists at Cambridge University in England were building the EDSAC (Electronic Delay Storage Automatic Computer). The EDSAC received the title of first stored-program computer, although it was completed only a few months before the EDVAC.

fail about every fifteen minutes. Too much time was wasted hunting for the burned-out tubes (see Figure 2–9).

Punched cards were used to enter data into the machines. Internal storage consisted of **magnetic drums,** cylinders coated with magnetizable material. A drum rotated at high speeds while a device was poised just above it either to write on the drum by magnetizing small spots or to read from it by detecting spots already magnetized. Then results of processing were punched on blank cards.

Early first-generation computers were given instructions coded in **machine language,** that is, a code that designates the electrical states in the

FIGURE 2—8

The UNIVAC I
The most popular business uses for the UNIVACs were payroll and billing.

FIGURE 2-9

Racks of Vacuum Tubes
Vacuum tubes were used in the architecture of first-generation computers.

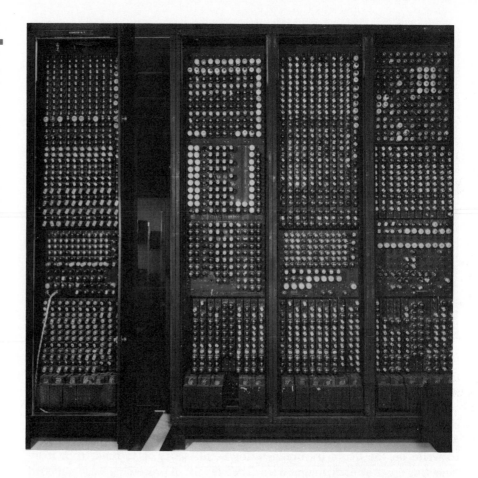

computer as combinations of 0s and 1s. Preparing the program or instructions was extremely tedious and errors were common. In order to overcome the difficulty, symbolic languages were developed. **Symbolic languages** use mnemonic symbols to represent instructions. For example, ADD would stand for addition. These symbols were easier for people to use than the strings of 0s and 1s of binary code, but the computer had to translate each symbol into machine language. A special set of language-translator programs was developed for this job. Rear Admiral Grace Murray Hopper of the U.S. Navy worked with a team that developed the first of these programs.

In the early 1950s, the public was not yet aware of the amazing computing machines. This changed with the 1952 presidential election. After analyzing only 5 percent of the tallied vote, a UNIVAC I computer predicted that Dwight David Eisenhower would defeat Adlai E. Stevenson. CBS doubted the accuracy of the prediction and did not release the information to the public until the election results were confirmed by actually counting the votes. The electronic prediction became the first in a burgeoning trend that has culminated in today's controversy about predicting election results from East Coast tallies before polls are closed on the West Coast.

Business acceptance of computers grew quickly. In 1953, Remington Rand and IBM led the infant industry, having placed a grand total of nine installations. But by the late 1950s, IBM alone had leased one thousand of its first-generation computers.

Second Generation: 1959–1964

Four hardware advances led to the **second-generation computers** of the early 1960s: the transistor, magnetic core storage, magnetic tapes, and magnetic disks. **Transistors** replaced the vacuum tubes of first-generation machines. A transistor is a small component made of solid material that acts like a vacuum tube in controlling the flow of electric current (see Figure 2–10). Using transistors in computers resulted in smaller, faster, and more reliable machines that used less electricity and generated much less heat than the first-generation computers.

Just as transistors replaced vacuum tubes as primary electronic components, **magnetic cores** replaced magnetic drums as internal storage units. Magnetic cores consisted of tiny rings of magnetic material strung on fine wires. Each magnetic core was placed at the intersection of a vertical and horizontal wire. To turn on a core, half the electricity needed was run through each wire. Thus, only at the intersection of specific wires would a core become charged. In this way, groups of cores stored instructions and data (see Figure 2–11). The development of magnetic cores resulted from the U.S. Navy's need for a more advanced, reliable high-speed flight trainer. Known as Whirlwind I, the navy project was one of the most innovative and influential projects in the history of the computer. Because of the high speed with which instructions and data could be located and retrieved using magnetic cores (a few millionths of a second), the Whirlwind allowed the real-time processing necessary in flight simulation. (Real time describes the ability of the computer to provide output fast enough to control the outcome

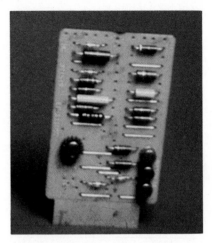

FIGURE 2–10

Transistors
Transistors were mounted close together and connected with tiny, flat wires on small cards called circuit boards.

FIGURE 2–11

A Frame of Magnetic Cores
An assembled core unit looked much like a window screen.

of an activity.) The development led to other real-time functions such as air traffic control, factory management, and battle simulations.

This new type of internal storage was supplemented by external storage on magnetic tapes and disks. During World War II, the Germans used huge, heavy steel tapes for sound recording. Plastic magnetic tapes eventually replaced the metal tapes, and later were tried for recording computer output. Output was recorded in the form of magnetized spots on the tape's surface. Another by-product of sound recording, the platter, led to the introduction of the magnetic disk. Much as a record is "accessed" on a jukebox, magnetic disks allowed direct access to data, contributing to the development of real-time activities such as making airline reservations. Disks and tapes greatly increased the speed of processing and enlarged storage capacities, and they soon replaced punched cards (see Figure 2–12).

During this period, more sophisticated, English-like computer languages such as COBOL and FORTRAN were commonly used.

Third Generation: 1965–1970

At the same time that transistors were replacing vacuum tubes, Jack S. Kilby of Texas Instruments and Robert Noyce at Fairchild Semiconductor were separately developing the **integrated circuit (IC).** Using separate methods, they discovered that the components of electronic circuits could be placed together—or integrated—onto small chips. Soon a single silicon chip less than one-eighth inch square could hold sixty-four complete circuits. This seems crude to us since today's chips may contain as many circuits as five hundred thousand transistors.

The chips marked the beginning of **third-generation computers,** computers that used less power, cost less, and were smaller and much more reliable than previous machines. Although computers became smaller, their internal memories increased due to the placement of memory on chips (see Figure 2–13).

FIGURE 2–12

A Second-Generation Computer System
This IBM 7070 system relied heavily on magnetic tape secondary storage and required many tape drives to read from and write to the tapes.

COMPUTERS AND INFORMATION PROCESSING

FIGURE 2–13

A Third-Generation Minicomputer
The development of minicomputers allowed many small businesses to acquire computer power since the costs were much less than the costs of mainframes.

A major third-generation innovation resulted when IBM realized that its company was turning out too many incompatible products. The company responded to the problem by designing the System/360 computers, which offered both scientific and business applications and introduced the family concept of computers. The first series consisted of six computers designed to run the same programs and use the same input, output, and storage equipment. Each computer offered a different memory capacity. For the first time, a company could buy a computer and feel that its investment in programs and peripheral equipment would not be wasted when the time came to move to a machine with a larger memory. Other manufacturers followed IBM's lead, and before long, more than 25,000 similar computer systems were installed in the United States.

Other developments in this period included minicomputers. Although these machines had many of the same capabilities as large computers, they were much smaller, had less storage space, and cost less. Use of remote terminals also became common. **Remote terminals** are computer terminals that are located some distance away from a main computer and linked to it through cables such as telephone lines.

The software industry also began to emerge in the 1960s. Programs to perform payroll, billings, and other business tasks became available at fairly low costs. Yet software was rarely free of "bugs," or errors. The computer industry experienced growing pains as the software industry lagged behind advances in hardware technology. The rapid advancements in hardware meant that old programs had to be rewritten to suit the circuitry of the new machines, and programmers skilled enough to do this were scarce. Software problems led to a glut of computer-error horror stories: a $200,000 water bill or $80,000 worth of duplicate welfare checks.

Fourth Generation: 1971—Today

Although the dividing lines between the first three generations of computers are clearly marked by major technological advances, historians are not so clear about when the fourth generation began. They do agree that in **fourth-generation computers** the use of magnetic cores had been discontinued, replaced by memory on silicon chips.

Engineers continued to cram more circuits onto a single chip. The technique by which this was accomplished was called **large-scale integration (LSI),** which characterized fourth-generation computers. LSI put thousands of electronic components on a single silicon chip for faster processing (the shorter the route electricity has to travel, the sooner it gets there). At this time, the functions that could be performed on a chip were permanently fixed during the production process.

Ted Hoff, an engineer at Intel Corporation, introduced an idea that resulted in a single, programmable unit—the microprocessor, or "computer on a chip." He packed the arithmetic and logic circuitry needed for computations onto one microprocessor chip that could be made to act like any kind of calculator or computer desired. Other functions, such as input, output, and memory, were placed on separate chips. The development of the microprocessor led to a boom in computer manufacturing that gave computing power to homes and schools in the form of microcomputers.

As microcomputers became more popular, many companies began producing software that could be run on the smaller machines. Most early programs were games. Later, instructional programs began to appear. One important software development was the first electronic spreadsheet for microcomputers, VisiCalc, introduced in 1979. VisiCalc vastly increased the possibilities for using microcomputers in the business world. Today, a wide variety of software exists for microcomputer applications in business, school, and personal use.

Currently, **very-large-scale integration (VLSI)** is replacing large-scale integration. In VLSI, thousands of electronic components can be placed on a single silicon chip. This further miniaturization of integrated circuits offers even greater improvements in price, performance, and size of computers (see Figure 2–14). A single microprocessor based on VLSI is more powerful than a room full of 1950s computer circuitry.

Trends in miniaturization led, ironically, to the development of the largest and most powerful computers, the supercomputers. By reducing the size of circuitry and changing the design of the chips, companies that manufacture supercomputers were able to create computers powerful enough and with memories large enough for computing the complex calculations required in aircraft design, weather forecasting, nuclear research, and energy conservation (see Figure 2–15). In fact, the main processing unit of some supercomputers is so densely packed with miniaturized electronic components that, like the early mainframe computers, it needs to be cooled and so is submerged in a special liquid coolant bath that disperses the tremendous heat generated during processing.

When will the fifth-generation begin? Many experts believe that the fifth-generation will begin in the 1990s, when the Japanese perfect the technology of parallel processing to perform artificial intelligence operations. **Parallel processing** is linking processors so that they work together to solve problems. Parallel processing is faster than processing with a single processor

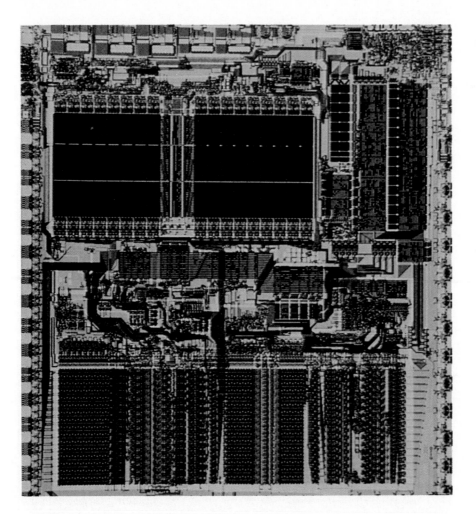

FIGURE 2-14

A 16-Bit Microprocessor
This microprocessor was designed on the principles of very-large-scale integration.

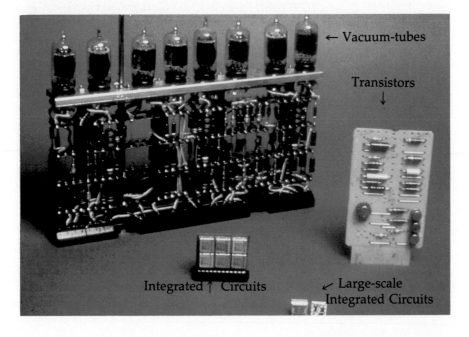

← Vacuum-tubes

Transistors
↓

Integrated ↑ Circuits

↙ Large-scale
Integrated Circuits

FIGURE 2-15

First-, Second-, and Third-Generation Components
Vacuum tubes gave way to transistors and transistors gave way to chips in the effort to reduce the size of computer components.

because it can search many data bases simultaneously. Unlike most computer processing today that mainly performs arithmetic operations, the next generation of computers will imitate human thinking and perform logically (i.e., will display **artificial intelligence**). In addition, experts predict that users will be able to easily communicate with these computers simply by using English or Japanese. Computer capabilities have improved drastically in the past forty-five years; fifth-generation computers that will actually "think" are just around the corner.

CONCEPT SUMMARY 2–1

The Technology Race: Generations of Computer Development

Period	Characteristics
First Generation 1951–1958	Vacuum tubes for internal operations. Magnetic drums for internal storage. Limited internal storage. Heat and maintenance problems. Punched cards for input and output. Slow input, processing, and output. Low-level symbolic languages for programming.
Second Generation 1959–1964	Transistors for internal operations. Magnetic cores for internal storage. Increased internal storage capacity. Magnetic tapes and disks for external storage. Reductions in size and heat generation. Increase in processing speed and reliability. Increased use of high-level languages.
Third Generation 1965–1970	Integrated circuits on silicon chips for internal operations. Increased internal storage capacity. Compatible systems. Introduction of minicomputers. Emergence of software industry. Reduction in size and cost. Increase in speed and reliability. Operating systems on external storage media.
Fourth Generation 1971–Today	Large-scale integration for internal operations. Development of the microprocessor. Introduction of microcomputers and supercomputers. Greater versatility in software. Introduction of very-large-scale integration. Increase in speed, power, and storage capacity.

▨ THE COMPUTER INDUSTRY

Computers have become powerful machines that have played a significant role in our country's growth and economic development in the last forty years. In the process, computer manufacturing and marketing have become big business. In this section we will examine briefly the hardware and software industries and vendor maintenance and support.

The Hardware Industry

The hardware industry encompasses manufacturers of computer equipment, including makers of the different sizes of computer systems and makers of peripheral devices such as monitors, disk drives, communications equipment, and printers.

There are many hardware manufacturers in existence today, but the number of manufacturers of large computer systems is fairly limited, primarily due to the huge capital investment required to produce large systems. The leading manufacturer of large computer systems is IBM. Unisys, NCR, Control Data, and Honeywell are all major competitors in the large-system market (see Figure 2–16). Some of these companies, such as IBM and Honeywell, also compete in the production of minicomputer systems against Digital Equipment Corporation, Hewlett-Packard, Data General, and Wang Laboratories, among others. In the last few years some Japanese companies have began to manufacture large computers, creating more competition in the international market. The leading Japanese manufacturers are Toshiba, Fujitsu, and Hitachi.

There are far fewer supercomputers built than any other type of computer. Cray Research and Control Data are the leading manufacturers of these powerful systems. For information on manufacturers of microcomputers, see Chapter 8.

Large computer vendors do more than just sell their systems. A computer is useless to an organization that lacks the knowledge needed to operate it. Most vendors provide support services along with the initial purchase. These services normally include education and training for all levels of users from top executives to data-entry personnel. Training can involve classes and seminars of self-study in which users pace their own learning while studying

FIGURE 2—16

IBM 4341 Mainframe

manuals and practicing hands-on exercises. Other services such as maintenance and repair may be included in the purchase or lease price of a computer system. Recent technological advances have contributed to a yearly decline in hardware costs. In contrast, service costs have increased significantly each year, making good vendor support after the initial purchase even more important to users.

Since a large percentage of the money spent on hardware goes toward the purchase of peripherals such as printers, monitors, and disk drives, many of the major companies mentioned earlier also produce peripheral equipment to support their computers. For example, IBM and Hewlett-Packard manufacture printers, monitors, and disk drives (see Figure 2–17). Leading exclusive manufacturers of peripherals include NEC (monitors), Epson (printers), and Kodak (disk drives).

Because of rapidly changing technology in the computer industry, many new product announcements are made over the course of a year. New technology leads to new companies. Often, a new company will introduce a product that incorporates the latest technology, creating a highly successful business year for them. That successful year may be followed by a lean one after a competitor introduces an even more sophisticated product a short time later. Many times in the past, situations such as this have led to the failure of peripheral companies, so the market is in a constant state of flux.

The Software Industry

Early computer systems came complete with software that was specially designed to operate on a specific system. Most of the software consisted of **operating systems** and **utility programs** designed by the manufacturer. Users were responsible for designing programs to meet their own specific needs, and companies hired programming staffs to write the programs in-house. Companies found this practice very expensive and looked for other ways to

FIGURE 2–17

Laser Printer
The HP LaserJet PLUS printer from Hewlett-Packard Company has an assortment of font cartridges.

solve their programming needs. During this period, a court decision in 1969 forced IBM, the industry leader, to "unbundle" its software, or offer hardware and software for sale separately. This action, more than any other, led to the development of independent software companies and the emergence of a new industry.

Early software companies often consisted of one person working at home, developing a clever idea. Today there are thousands of software companies in existence, creating programs capable of running on all sizes and brands of computers. Many companies specialize in producing a particular type of program to satisfy a particular industry or need; other companies create "generic" software for a variety of applications. A few software companies work under contract, custom-designing programs to meet the needs of specific customers. Some hardware companies still offer their own company-designed software to hardware buyers. Of all the options presently available to users, off-the-shelf software is generally the most cost-effective; programming your own is expensive because it is labor-intensive and requires a high degree of skill.

CAREERS IN COMPUTERS

Today a great many organizations, including businesses, hospitals, schools, government agencies, banks, and libraries, are using computers to help organize and store information. This has created the demand for a large class of professionals who can design and operate effective computer systems. This section describes various career opportunities in the computer field.

Data-Processing Operations Personnel

Data-processing operations personnel are responsible for entering data and instructions into the computer, operating the computer and attached devices, retrieving output, and ensuring the smooth operation of the computing center and its associated libraries. An efficient operations staff is crucial to the effective use of an organization's resources.

The **librarian** is responsible for classifying, cataloging, and maintaining the files and programs stored on cards, tapes, disks, and diskettes, and all other storage media in a computer library. The librarian's tasks include transferring backup files to alternate storage sites, purging old files, and supervising the periodic cleaning of magnetic tapes and disks. As for job qualifications, the librarian should have a high-school diploma, clerical record-keeping skills, and a knowledge of basic data-processing concepts.

A **computer operator's** duties include setting up equipment; mounting and removing tapes, disks, and diskettes; and monitoring the operation of the computer. A computer operator should be able to identify operational problems and take appropriate corrective actions. Most computers run under sophisticated operating systems that direct the operator through messages generated during processing. However, the operator is responsible for reviewing errors that occur during operation, determining their causes, and maintaining operating records.

An operator should be able to read and understand technical literature. Although few operators have a four-year college degree, some have degrees from technical schools and junior colleges. Many operators receive apprentice and on-the-job training.

A **data-entry operator's** job involves transcribing data into a form suitable for computer processing. A **keypunch operator** uses a keypunch machine to transfer data from source documents to punched cards. Operators of other key-entry devices transfer data to magnetic tape and magnetic disk for subsequent processing.

A **remote terminal operator** is involved with the preparation of input data. The operator is located at a site that is probably some distance from the computer itself. The data is entered into the computer directly from the remote location at which it is generated.

Data-entry jobs usually require manual dexterity, typing or keying skills, and alertness. They do not require more than a high school education. Usually data-entry personnel receive several weeks of on-the-job training so they can become familiar with the documents they will be reading. This training minimizes errors.

Occupations in computer operations are affected by changes in data-processing technology. For example, the demand for keypunch operators has declined as new methods of data preparation have developed. Yet the expanding use of computers, especially in small businesses, will require additional computer operating personnel.

System Development Personnel

PROGRAMMERS. Generally, three types of programming are done in an organization:

1. *Application programming*, that is, developing programs for specific functions such as accounting.
2. *Maintenance programming*, which is keeping already developed programs current and error free.
3. *System programming*, which is developing and maintaining the programs that operate the computer.

Persons working in any of these areas should possess the following basic skills:

■ Good command of the programming language(s) in which programs are written.
■ A knowledge of general programming methodology and the relationships between programs and hardware.
■ Analytical reasoning ability and attention to detail.
■ Creativity and discipline for developing new problem-solving methods.
■ Patience and persistence.

Application programmers convert a design for a system into instructions for the computer. They are responsible for testing, debugging, documenting, and implementing programs. Applications programmers in business generally have at least a two-year degree. They should know the objectives of an organization and have a basic understanding of accounting and management science in addition to the skills outlined earlier.

Scientific application programmers work on scientific or engineering problems, which usually require complex mathematical solutions. Thus,

New Careers in Computers

As computer technology continues to advance, the number of people in computer-related careers has grown tremendously. Programmers will continue to be in demand. The outlook for systems analysts has never been brighter. The U.S. Labor Department predicts the number of systems analyst positions will increase over 60 percent in the next ten years.

In addition to these traditional computer positions, a number of new jobs are being created to oversee the expanding technology. For example, some companies have created Information Centers (ICs),

which support users of departmental microcomputers. Personnel in ICs must not only have technical skills, they must be able to work well with people. Within an IC a company may employ a manager, trainers, analysts, and programmers.

Another growing area of professionals in information systems is that of the security expert. Security experts are responsible for protecting data from natural disasters such as

floods and fires. They must also secure systems against "hackers," people who try to gain unauthorized access to data. Part of a security expert's job may also include developing backup systems in the event data is damaged or destroyed.

Telecommunications is another area where computer-related positions such as the Local Area Network (LAN) manager, are now being created. Changes occur rapidly in the computer field, and new positions will continue to be created to keep abreast of technological advances.

scientific application programming usually requires a degree in computer science, information science, mathematics, engineering, or a physical science. Some jobs require graduate degrees. Few scientific organizations are interested in applicants with no college training.

Program maintenance is an important but often neglected activity. Many large programs are never completely **debugged**; furthermore, there is a continuing need to change and improve major programs. In some organizations, maintenance programming is done by application programmers. To be effective, a **maintenance programmer** needs extensive programming experience and a high level of analytical ability. Occasionally personnel in computer operations are promoted to maintenance programming positions, but they often are required to take additional data-processing courses.

System programmers are responsible for creating and maintaining system software. System programmers do not write programs that solve day-to-day organizational problems. Instead, they develop utility programs; maintain operating systems, data-base packages, compilers, and assemblers; and are involved in decisions concerning additions and deletions of hardware and software. Because of their knowledge of operating systems, system programmers typically offer technical help to application programmers. A system programmer should have at least one year of assembly language programming experience or a college degree in computer science. He or she should have (a) a background in the theory of computer language structure and syntax, and (b) extensive and detailed knowledge of the hardware being used and the software that controls it. Some employers may look for specialized skills in system programmers. For example, the advanced technology of today's communication networks offers excellent opportunities for programmers skilled in designing, coding, testing, debugging, documenting, and implementing data communication software. Application and system programmers will continue to be in high demand.

SYSTEM ANALYSTS. The **system analyst** plays a significant role in the analysis, design, and implementation of a formal system. The analyst has the following responsibilities:

■ Helping the user determine information needs.
■ Gathering facts about existing systems and analyzing them to determine the effectiveness of current processing methods and procedures.
■ Designing new systems, recommending changes to existing systems, and being involved in implementing these changes.

The analyst's role is critical to the success of any information system. He or she acts as an interface between users of the system and technical personnel such as programmers, machine operators, and data-base specialists. This role becomes more important as the cost of designing, implementing, and maintaining information systems rises.

An effective system analyst should have:

■ A general knowledge of the firm, including its goals, objectives, products, and services.
■ Familiarity with the organizational structure of the company and management's rationale for selecting that structure.
■ Comprehensive knowledge of data-processing methods and current hardware; familiarity with available programming languages.
■ The ability to plan and organize work and to cooperate and interact effectively with both technical and nontechnical personnel.
■ A high degree of creativity.

Minimum requirements for a job as a system analyst generally include work experience in system design and programming and specialized industry experience. System analysts seeking jobs in a business environment should be college graduates with backgrounds in business management, accounting, economics, computer science, information systems, or data processing. For work in a scientifically oriented organization, a college background in physical sciences, mathematics, or engineering is preferred. Many universities offer majors in management information systems; their curricula are designed to train people to be system analysts.

The need for system analysts is growing. There is a continuing high demand for system professionals by computer manufacturers, and the increasing use of minicomputers and microcomputers will create even greater need for analysts to design systems for small computers.

Data-Base Specialists

Data-base specialists are responsible for designing and controlling the use of data resources. A **data-base analyst**—the key person in the analysis, design, and implementation of data structures—must plan and coordinate data use within a system. A data-base analyst has the following responsibilities:

■ Helping the system analyst or user analyze the interrelationships of data.

■ Defining the physical data structures and logical views of data.

■ Designing new data-base systems, recommending changes to existing ones, and being involved in the implementation of these changes.

■ Eliminating data redundancy.

A data-base analyst needs technical knowledge of programming and system methodologies. A background in system software is valuable for persons planning physical data-base structures. The job requires a college education and courses in computer science, business data processing, and data-base management system design. Many colleges offer courses in data-base management to train people to be data analysts.

The person who controls all the data resources of an organization is called the **data-base administrator (DBA).** The primary responsibilities of this position include:

■ Developing a dictionary of standard data definitions so that all records are consistent.

■ Designing data bases.

■ Maintaining the accuracy, completeness, and timeliness of data bases.

■ Designing procedures to ensure data security and data-base backup and recovery.

■ Facilitating communications between analysts and users.

■ Advising analysts, programmers, and system users about the best ways to use data bases.

A data-base administrator must have a high level of technical expertise, as well as the ability to communicate effectively with diverse groups of people. He or she also needs supervisory and leadership skills. The demand for data-base specialists is high. With the increasing trend toward data-base management, the need for people with the technical knowledge to design data-base application systems is increasing.

Information System Managers

Historically, data processing managers have been programmers or system analysts who worked their way up to management positions with little formal management training. But the increasing emphasis on information systems and information management has brought a change; professional managers with demonstrable leadership qualities and communication skills are being hired to management information system departments.

The **management information system (MIS) manager** is responsible for planning and tying together all the information resources of a firm. The manager is responsible for organizing the physical and human resources of a department. He or she must devise effective control mechanisms to monitor progress toward company goals. The following knowledge and skills are useful assets for an MIS manager:

■ A thorough understanding of an organization, its goals, and its business activities.

■ Leadership qualities to motivate and control highly skilled people.

■ Knowledge of data-processing methods and familiarity with available hardware and software.

A person seeking a career in information system management should have a college degree. A degree in business administration with a concentration in the area of management information systems is desirable for managing business data-processing centers. Some employers prefer an individual with an MBA degree. To handle high-level management responsibilities, a candidate should have at least two years of extensive management experience, advanced knowledge of the industry in which the individual hopes to work, and competence in all technical, professional, and business skills.

PROFESSIONAL ASSOCIATIONS

Societies have been formed that increase communication among professional people in computer fields. The purposes of these organizations vary, but most attempt to share current knowledge through the publication of professional journals and encourage the ongoing professional education of members.

AFIPS

The American Federation of Information Processing Societies (AFIPS), organized in 1961, is a national federation of professional societies established to represent member societies on an international basis and to advance and disseminate knowledge of these societies. These are two categories of AFIPS participation: (a) member societies that have a principal interest in computers and information processing; and (b) affiliated societies that, although not primarily concerned with computers and information processing, have a major interest in this area. Some of the prominent constituent societies of AFIPS are the Association for Computing Machinery (ACM), the Data Processing Management Association (DPMA), the Institute of Electrical and Electronic Engineers (IEEE), and the American Society for Information Science (ASIS). Affiliated societies of AFIPS include the American Institute of Certified Public Accountants (AICPA) and the American Statistical Association (ASA).

ACM

The Association for Computing Machinery (ACM) is the largest scientific, educational, and technical society of the computing community. Founded in 1947, this association is dedicated to the development of information processing as a discipline and to the responsible use of computers in increasingly complex and diverse applications. The objectives of the association are:

■ To advance the science and art of information processing, including the study, design, development, construction, and application of modern machinery, computing techniques, and programming software.
■ To promote the free exchange of ideas in the field of information processing in a professional manner, among both specialists and the public.
■ To develop and maintain the integrity and competence of individuals engaged in the field of information processing.

DPMA

Founded in Chicago as the National Machine Accountants Association, the Data Processing Management Association (DPMA) was chartered in December 1961. At that time the first electronic computer had yet to come into commercial use. The name "machine accountants" was chosen to identify persons associated with the operation and supervision of punched-card equipment. The society took its present name in 1962.

DPMA is one of the largest worldwide organizations serving the information-processing and management communities. It comprises all levels of management personnel. Through its educational and publishing activities, DPMA seeks to encourage high standards in the field of data processing and to promote a professional attitude among its members.

One of DPMA's specific purposes is to promote and develop educational and scientific inquiry in the field of data processing and data-processing management. It sponsors college student organizations interested in data processing and encourages members to serve as counselors for the Boy Scout computer merit badge. The organization also presents DPMA's Distinguished Information Sciences Award for outstanding contributions to computer use in information management.

ASM

The Association of Systems Management (ASM), founded in 1947, is headquartered in Cleveland, Ohio. The ASM is an international organization engaged in keeping its members abreast of the rapid growth and change occurring in the field of systems management and information processing. It provides for the professional growth and development of its members and of the systems profession through:

■ Extended programs in local and regional areas in the fields of education and research.
■ Annual conferences and committee functions in research, education, and public relations.
■ Promotion of high standards of work performance by members of the ASM and members of the systems profession.
■ Publication of the *Journal of Systems Management*, technical reports, and other works on subjects of current interest to systems practitioners.

ICCP

The Institute of Certification of Computer Professionals is a nonprofit organization established in 1973 for the purpose of testing and certifying the knowledge and skills of computing personnel. A primary objective of the ICCP is to pool the resources of constituent societies so that the full attention of the information-processing industry can be focused on the vital tasks of development and recognition of qualified personnel.

The establishment of the ICCP was an outgrowth of studies made by committees of the DPMA and the ACM, which developed the concept of a "computer foundation" to foster testing and certification programs of DPMA. The ICCP has four certificates: Associate Systems Professional (ASP), Certified Systems Professional (CSP), Certificate in Computer Programming

(CCP), and Certificate in Data Processing (CDP). Candidates for certificates must pass examinations on material related to their area. For example, a candidate for the CDP certificate must pass exams covering data processing equipment, computer programming and software, principles of management, quantitative methods, and system analysis and design. In addition, certification requirements require varying degrees of work experience.

Because the computer field changes so rapidly, certificate holders must be recertified every three years. Candidates for recertification can either take a new exam or they can earn recertification credit by participating in educational activities such as attending seminars or writing for publication.

SIM

The Society for Information Management (SIM) was founded in 1968 to serve persons concerned with all aspects of management information systems in the electronic data-processing industry, including business system designers, managers, and educators. The organizational aims include providing an exchange or marketplace for technical information about management information systems and enhancing communications between MIS directors and executives responsible for the management of business enterprises. SIM also offers educational and research programs, sponsors competitions, bestows awards, and maintains placement programs.

CONCEPT SUMMARY 2—2

Professional Associations	
Association	**Purpose**
AFIPS	To represent member societies on an international basis and to advance and disseminate knowledge of the member societies
ACM	To develop information processing as a discipline and promote responsible use of computers in diverse applications
DPMA	To encourage high standards in the field of data processing and to promote a professional attitude among members
ASM	To keep members abreast of rapid change and growth in the field of systems management and information processing
ICCP	To test and certify knowledge and skills of computing personnel
SIM	To provide an exchange or marketplace for technical information about MIS and to enhance communication between MIS directors and executives

■ SUMMARY POINTS

■ Humans have been searching for ways to calculate answers to problems and keep track of the results for thousands of years. Early attempts to succeed at this goal include the abacus, Napier's Bones, Pacal's and von Leibniz's machines, and Jacquard's punched cards.

■ Charles Babbage, the father of computers, designed the analytical engine, a machine that was similar in design to a computer, but it was doomed to failure because it was too advanced to be produced by the technology of its time.

■ Punched cards played an important role in the advance toward automatic machines when Dr. Herman Hollerith designed a tabulating machine that could read census data from the 1890 census punched onto cards.

■ Hollerith's tabulating machine became the basis for a company that Thomas Watson joined and later led. Today that company is known as IBM. During the 1920s accounting machines evolved that could perform many record-keeping and accounting functions.

■ Howard H. Aiken invented the first large-scale electromechanical automatic calculator, the Mark I. The first general-purpose electronic digital computer, ENIAC, was built by John W. Mauchly and J. Presper Eckert. It was huge and required tremendous amounts of electricity, but it was much faster than the Mark I.

■ To solve the problem of manually feeding operating instructions into ENIAC and setting switches, John von Neumann proposed the idea of storing both instructions and data in the computer's primary memory. This is the stored-program concept. The first computer of this type in the United States was called EDVAC.

■ First-generation computers relied on vacuum tubes for power and used magnetic drums for storage. Instructions were coded in machine language until symbolic languages (mnemonic symbols representing instructions) were invented.

■ Second-generation computers were characterized by magnetic core memory and transistors for power. Internal storage was supplemented by external storage on magnetic tapes and disks. More sophisticated, English-like languages such as COBOL were commonly used.

■ The integrated circuit developed by Jack S. Kilby of Texas Instruments and Robert Noyce at Fairchild Semiconductor led to the third computer generation. These machines were even smaller, faster, and more powerful than computers in earlier generations. They were also less costly, more reliable, and used less electricity.

■ A major third-generation innovation resulted when IBM developed the System/360 computers, the first series designed to run the same programs and use the same input, output, and storage equipment. Other developments in this period included minicomputers and the emergence of the software industry.

■ Fourth-generation computers rely on large-scale integration and very-large-scale integration to cram more circuits onto a chip. Ted Hoff, an engineer at Intel Corporation, introduced the microprocessor, or "computer on a chip."

■ Trends in miniaturization led to the development of the largest and most powerful of computers, the supercomputers. These machines perform complex calculations required in aircraft design, weather forecasting, nuclear weapons research, and energy conservation.

■ Fifth-generation computers will use parallel processing to perform artificial intelligence operations. Parallel processing is linking processors so they can work together to solve problems.

■ The hardware industry encompasses manufacturers of computer equipment, including makers of different sizes of computer systems and makers of peripheral devices such as monitors, disk drives, communications equipment, and printers.

■ Large computer vendors generally offer support services to users. While hardware costs are declining, costs associated with training, maintenance, and repair are increasing, making good vendor support an important consideration for potential buyers.

■ A large percentage of the money spent on hardware goes toward the purchase of peripherals such as printers, monitors, and disk drives. Rapidly changing technology leads to the rise and fall of many makers of peripheral equipment.

■ Early computer systems came complete with software that was specially designed to operate on that specific system. A court decision in 1969 forced IBM, the industry leader, to "unbundle" its software, or offer hardware and software for sale separately. This action, more than any other, led to the development of independent software companies.

■ Today software companies offer users many options to meet their computing needs, from custom-designed programs to off-the-shelf software. Off-the-shelf software is generally the most cost-effective way of meeting needs because programming is labor-intensive and requires a high degree of skill.

■ Computer-related personnel such as programmers, analysts, data-base specialists and information systems managers are increasingly in demand.

■ Programmers perform three types of programming: application programming, maintenance programming, and system programming.

■ As more and more people have chosen careers in computer-related fields, societies have been formed that increase communication among professionals. Most of these societies attempt to share current knowledge through the publication of professional journals and to encourage the ongoing professional education of members. Some of these societies are AFIPS, ACM, DPMA, ASM, ICCP, and SIM.

▦ REVIEW QUESTIONS

1. What contributions did Pascal and von Leibniz make to the development of computers?

2. How is Babbage's analytical engine similar in design to modern computers?

3. What was the first automatic calculator? What machine made the Mark I outdated before it was finished? How did this machine differ from the Mark I and other earlier computing devices?

4. Explain the stored-program concept.

5. What are some of the drawbacks of the first-generation computers?

6. What replaced vacuum tubes and magnetic drums in second-generation computers? What advances were noteworthy in storage?

7. What significance did the IBM System/360 computers have in the third computer generation?

8. What is a microprocessor? What effect did its development have on the computer industry?

9. Explain how a court decision that forced IBM to unbundle its software led to the growth of the software industry.

10. Explain the three types of programming often performed by programmers in organizations using large computer systems. Explain the difference between a systems analyst and a programmer.

National Semiconductor Corporation

As transistors replaced vacuum tubes in second-generation computers, the demand for this special circuitry grew. National Semiconductor Corporation was founded in 1959 in Danbury, Connecticut, to help meet the growing demand for the new technology. Despite this demand, the business of manufacturing transistors was filled with problems, which National Semiconductor worked hard to overcome. In 1964, Peter Sprague secured a major interest in the struggling company, and in 1966, he acquired Molectro, a small integrated circuit company based in Santa Clara, California. When Charles Sporck was named president and chief executive officer of National a year later, company headquarters were moved from Danbury to Santa Clara, an area known today as the "Silicon Valley."

Today, the Silicon Valley is known throughout the world as the center of new computer technology, and National is known as a leader in the high-tech industry. The company has evolved from a small transistor manufacturer into one of the foremost developers of advanced semiconductor and system products. National manufactures more than 5,000 types of integrated circuits and has introduced hundreds of products.

Although the company now manufactures a wide variety of products, in 1959 National began modestly with just three product lines. Transistors, the first of many National product lines, are still produced in large numbers at the Danbury, Connecticut, plant. Linear integrated circuits (ICs), a second product line, are used in computers, communications equipment, instrumentation and a variety of consumer products, including stereos, radios and TVs. Today, National

boasts the world's broadest linear line. The third product line combines transistors or ICs and other components in the same package, called a hybrid. Today, National is the world's largest standard hybrid manufacturer.

By the middle of the third computer generation in 1968, sales increases and newer technology prompted National to add two more product lines. Logic devices, which are used to perform mathematical and logical operations in computers, became a standard product. Also added to the product line were MOS memory integrated circuits. The tiny, high-density ICs were put to use in computers and instrumentation systems.

As the product lines expanded and National's reputation for manufacturing quality products grew, sales increased. The demand for National's products spread throughout the world. In 1969, to meet world-wide demand and to ensure effective participation in European and Pacific Rim markets, the company expanded its operations to Germany, Scotland, and Singapore. Today, in addition to these countries, National has facilities in Hong Kong, Malaysia, Thailand, the Philippines, and Israel.

During the early 1970s, as the construction of new facilities around the world neared completion, National became the world's fourth largest semiconductor supplier. Despite an industry slowdown in 1971, National quadrupled its investments in new facilities and equipment and introduced microprocessor, CMOS, and bipolar products.

Also during the 1970s National formed a new division and entered the systems business. One of the systems division's (now called Information Systems Group) first successes was in the retail industry. National introduced a line of point-of-sale systems designed especially for supermarkets by National's subsidiary, Datachecker Systems Inc. In a period of only five years, DATACHECKER® systems were installed in 1400 locations nationwide. Encouraged by Datachecker's growth, National's management expanded the systems division by creating the computer Products Group, the predecessor of National Advanced Systems.

During the late 1970s and early 1980s, National Semiconductor and the industry experienced unprecedented growth. In addition to becoming the first Silicon Valley semiconductor company to achieve a billion dollars in sales, National broke new ground in the area of integrated circuit design. It established the Customer Specific Products Group in 1983, enabling

customers to create custom products, tailored specifically to their own needs. Two years later, National had introduced more than 100 custom products. The Customer Specific Products Group later became National's ASIC (application-specific integrated circuits) division.

In autumn 1987, National acquired Fairchild Semiconductor, the company that pioneered the Silicon Valley. With the acquisition, National became one of America's best technologically balanced semiconductor suppliers, combining its expertise in CMOS with Fairchild's leading position in bipolar and BiCMOS technologies.

National Today

Today National Semiconductor has two business segments: semiconductor and systems. On the semiconductor side, National's focus is on proprietary LSI (Large Scale Integration) and VSLI (Very Large Scale Integration) products in four key, high-growth areas: high-end microprocessors, computer peripherals, application-specific integrated circuits (ASICs) and memory products.

On the systems side, National's Information Systems Group, which accounted for nearly half of the corporation's total sales in 1987, is composed of National Advanced Systems, a leader in the IBM-compatible mainframes and peripherals market; and Datachecker Systems, a leader in the manufacture, marketing and service of point-of-sale systems and applications software to the supermarket, general merchandise, and hospitality industries worldwide.

National Semiconductor's strategies for the 1990s include: becoming increasingly customer-driven; continuing to develop long-term strategic partnerships; showing excellence in technology and productivity; and focusing on high-growth markets.

Also, National will continue to be an active participant in SEMATECH, a consortium of U.S. semiconductor manufacturers dedicated to restoring America's leadership in semiconductor manufacturing technology.

National Semiconductor, headquartered in Santa Clara, California, employs some 36,000 people in 29 countries worldwide.

DISCUSSION POINTS

1. What are the first three products that National manufactured?
2. How did National counter the industry slowdown in 1971 and continue the company's pattern of growth and expansion?

CHAPTER

3

Introduction to Information Systems

O U T L I N E

Introduction
Qualities of Information
**Fundamental Principles of
    Information Systems**
  What Is a System?
  A System's Interaction with Other
    Systems
  The Organization as a System
**Components of an Information
  System**
  Hardware as Part of an
    Information System

Software as Part of an Information
    System
Data as Part of an Information
    System
People as Part of an Information
    System
The Value of Information Systems
**How Businesses Use Information
  Systems**
  Accounting/Payroll
  Finance/Budgeting
  Marketing/Sales Order Processing
  Human Resources Management/
    Personnel

Production Management/Materials
    Requirement Planning (MRP)
Engineering/Computer-Aided
    Engineering
Summary Points
Review Questions

Real Strategic Successes

By Paul Berger
Computer Decisions

With all the attention given to the strategic use of information technology, it's easy to miss the real gains corporations are making by using information systems for strategic advantage. Strategic systems are more than hype; three recent developments provide solid evidence that information systems are making direct contributions to corporate success.

Item: The domestic apparel industry fights back, with computers. U.S.-based apparel manufacturers have turned to technology in the effort to stop the inroads made by foreign apparel manufacturers. The stakes for American clothing makers are high: Foreign manufacturers now control over 50 percent of the domestic clothing market.

Information technologies are being employed to link retailers, apparel manufacturers, and fabric producers in a single network. The objectives are to shorten the time between order and delivery, reduce inventory levels, and slash waste by more closely matching consumer demands and production.

Among the leading implementations of information technology in the apparel business is the network tying Levi Strauss & Co. to other suppliers. The companies involved agreed on standards that allow them to share information on availability of products, prices, and delivery schedules.

Item: A major retailing chain hires as its president an executive noted for his uses of information technology. Robert Morosky moved to Allied Stores from The Limited, where he was responsible for building a computerized

distribution system that helped fuel high growth. Allied stands to gain the benefit of Morosky's aggressive use of information technology. In a recent presentation, Morosky specifically identified state-of-the-art computerized information systems as the most critical innovation for retailers.

If Allied's parent, Campeau Corp., is successful in acquiring rival retail conglomerate Federated Stores, Morosky's emphasis on innovative uses of information technology is likely to spread to most of the large U.S. retail chains. Clearly, information technologies have become a big factor in the retail trade.

Item: Texas Instruments looks to forge closer ties with customers through the use of computers, communications, and software. Texas Instruments' business is changing. More of its revenue will come from services, systems, and software than from hardware sales. The vendor is striving to perpetuate its position as a major player in the electronics business by locking in its customers through its network and local design centers. Semiconductors will be delivered to customers with customized soft-

ware. In addition, Texas Instruments is setting up custom design centers around the world to offer integration and customization services. The result is customer lock-in—an extremely close, and hard to end, relationship between supplier and customer.

The fact that these success stories have appeared in the general business press signals that a significant change is taking place. Strategic systems once were the domain of academicians and researchers. Now, newspapers report on the strategic use of information technology as part of their regular business coverage.

It takes a while for awareness to be converted to action. In a presentation on information systems planning last summer, one IS executive advised his colleagues that the phrase "strategic and competitive uses of information technologies" was in vogue for IS planning and was important to include in IS plans presented to management. However, he did not advise his listeners to become leaders in carrying out this aspect of the plan. By treating strategic uses of IS as merely a catchphrase, the executive performed a disservice to his colleagues.

Use of information technology has become part of business practice. Operations and line managers see its value as necessary to growth and profitability and, in some cases, to business survival. Real measurements can be made of technology's impact in business performance. The IS organizations that recognize this and take a leadership role will guarantee their place in the future. IS organizations that only

ARTICLE

provide operational and support functions will always be treated as an overhead cost, not as a bottom-line contributor.

Paul Berger, a consultant on the strategic use of information systems, is president of the Society for Information Management.

Most large companies have computer systems for processing transactions such as payroll. Now, however, business leaders are realizing that computers can be used for more than number crunching. Computer systems

can link departments of businesses together and link businesses to customers. Companies who want to stay competitive must be able to see and apply the potential of new technologies.

INTRODUCTION

CHAPTER

3

In the eighteenth century the United States changed from an agricultural country to an industrial society. Most of the country's workers no longer worked on farms, but were employed in jobs related to manufacturing. The United States has now evolved from an industrial society into an information society. Information is increasing at an astounding rate. Of the total amount of information known today, 75 percent became available in the last twenty years. U.S. workers must process over 35 billion pieces of paper each year. In order to meet this demand for information, more people in this country are now employed in information-related jobs than in manufacturing.

This chapter discusses how technology developed to meet information needs as the United States evolved from an industrial to an information society. The chapter includes discussions of qualities and value of information. The term *system*, so frequently associated with computers, is defined, and the relationships among systems, subsystems, and information systems is explored. The chapter also examines the ways businesses use information systems.

QUALITIES OF INFORMATION

As explained in Chapter 1, information is processed data that increases understanding and helps people make intelligent decisions. Yet not all information is equally valuable. The value of information varies depending upon when and how the data was gathered and processed.

A business manager does not need outdated information, or information that is not complete. Furthermore, managers only want accurate, relevant information. The most valued information is accurate, verifiable, timely, relevant, complete, and clear.

Information should be *accurate* (error-free). It is difficult to provide error-free information; inaccuracies can occur when data is put into the system, or it can be inappropriately processed. Erroneous data entered into the computer system brings about a situation known as **"GIGO"** or **"garbage in–garbage out."** The degree of accuracy acceptable to most decision makers depends on the circumstances. When decisions must be made quickly, there are trade-offs between speed and accuracy. Information produced quickly may not be error free.

Accurate information is *verifiable*. In other words, it can be confirmed. Verification can be accomplished in different ways. One approach compares the new information with other information that is accurate. Another approach involves reentering new data and comparing the processed information with the original. A third approach, an **audit trail,** traces the information back to its original source. An audit trail describes the path that leads to the data on which information is based. A decision maker evaluates the audit trail description to verify the accuracy of information. Any well-designed information system should include a plan for an audit trail. Information that cannot be verified cannot be depended upon for decision making.

The *timeliness* of information is important because information frequently loses its value as it ages. Information necessary for routine business operations must be current. For example, a warehouse manager needs up-to-the-minute reports on inventory levels to fill orders promptly. A report generated last year would be useless in determining inventory levels for the current week. The type of information needed for long-term planning, however, may require more than current information. A future sales campaign may be based on sales figures that span a five-year period, revealing past sales trends. Therefore *timely* does not always mean *current;* timely information is appropriate information that is available when needed.

Even the most timely information is useless if it does not actually contribute to making a good decision. Extraneous information can complicate decision making, whereas relevant information makes it easier. *Relevant* information is information that a manager or a staff specialist "needs to know" in order to make a particular decision. A company comptroller performing an audit does not need the plant maintenance schedule for the past year, he needs financial records. Relevant information is new knowledge that actually assists in decision making getting to the appropriate person.

Before making decisions, managers must determine if the information is *complete* or if more is needed. Accurate, verifiable, timely, relevant information is meaningless if it is incomplete. The completeness of information refers not to the quantity of information, but rather its content. Large volumes of information may be present, but one crucial detail may have been overlooked. Circumstances influence whether or not the missing information hampers decision making. At one time incomplete information may have little effect, whereas at another the missing information could have serious consequences. For example, a fire department will respond immediately to a report of a fire in a chemical plant. Once at the scene, however, firefighters may need more complete information to fight the fire effectively. The chemicals inside the building affect decisions about techniques used to combat the blaze. Without this information, firefighters could use the wrong containment techniques and actually spread the fire instead of putting it out.

Finally, information should be *clear*. It should contain no ambiguous terms and should be stated in a way that leaves no doubts concerning the meaning of facts. A report that contains vague generalities and ambiguous terms quickly loses its value to an organization.

You Are Here

Many of us have had the experience of stopping our car and asking a gas station attendant or a pedestrian for directions. Sometimes the vague instructions we received were helpful—but other times they just didn't get us where we wanted to go. A new solution to this problem is to have a computer screen on your car's dashboard that shows on a map where you are and how to get to where you want to go. In one type of computer system, the Driver-Guide, the driver tells the computer where she is and where she is going. In a few minutes a map displays the best route to her destination. Another system, The

Navigator, shows you where you are on the map and gives you directions on getting to your destination. As you drive, the map on the screen moves up and down and right to left so the map can continue to show your location.

Cab companies were among the first businesses to use the electronic maps. The screens in their cars show where all the company's cabs are located and which cabs are empty. This allows the drivers to provide service to areas

with few empty cabs and to avoid areas with a large number of available cabs.

Car rental company owners also see the potential of these electronic maps. Renters—especially clients who use the offices near airports—are likely to be people from out of town. Many of them prefer to rent a car that displays a map and provides directions to their destinations.

Will the average car owner soon have an electronic map on the dashboard? Right now prices range from $1000 to $1395. Developers predict we will all be using them in the next ten years.

All these attributes are equally important if the receiver of the information is to have complete confidence in using the information for decision making. Unfortunately, limitations in time and money may necessitate compromises in any of these areas.

CONCEPT SUMMARY 3—1

Qualities of Information

Quality	Explanation
Timely	Information frequently loses value as it ages. Different management levels have different information needs.
Accurate	Information should be without errors. The degree of accuracy depends on different circumstances.
Verifiable	The accuracy of information can be confirmed by comparing, rekeying, or performing an audit trail.
Relevant	Information should contribute to making decisions more easily or more successfully. Extraneous information can complicate decision making.
Complete	Information may be meaningless if it is not complete. Circumstances help determine if more information is needed.

◼ FUNDAMENTAL PRINCIPLES OF INFORMATION SYSTEMS

What Is a System?

A **system** is a group of related elements that work together toward a common goal. The term *system* is often associated with computers, but it actually refers to a wider concept, used in many areas such as science and the social sciences. For example, physiologists see the human body as a system made up of smaller systems such as the respiratory system and the circulation system. In our study, an information system is made up of input, processes, and output. **Input** enters the system from the surrounding environment and is transformed by some **process** into output. Information can flow within the system or between it and its larger environment. Most **output** leaves the system and flows into the external environment. Some may remain in the internal environment.

A system requires **feedback,** which can come from either internal or external sources. Feedback keeps the system functioning smoothly. In system theory, a system's primary goal is survival. Feedback helps the system survive by pinpointing the system's strengths and weaknesses (Figure 3–1).

A newspaper is an example of a system with input, processes, output, and feedback. Input consists of the news items that are collected by reporters. The writing, editing, typesetting, and printing of the stories is the process that turns the news items into output (the printed paper). Feedback to this

FIGURE 3–1

The Environment of a System

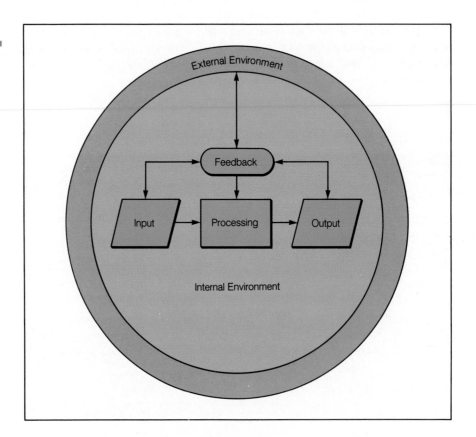

system may come from internal or external sources. The opinions of the publisher are a source of internal feedback. Letters to the editor from readers and people dropping their subscriptions are sources of external feedback.

A System's Interaction with Other Systems

Every system can be viewed in terms of inputs, processes, outputs, and feedback mechanisms, but the boundaries between systems are not always clear. Which elements of a system are actually subsystems? The boundaries and elements of a system depend upon the level from which one views the system. In medicine, for instance, a general practitioner views the human body as the system, whereas an opthalmologist views just the eye as the system. In a business, payroll, accounts receivable, and accounts payable can all be subsystems of the accounting system. An important concept in system theory is that subsystems (such as payroll in accounting) interact with the system. Accounting is, of course, a subsystem of the business and interacts with other departments such as marketing.

The Organization as a System

System theory is also applicable to organizations. Organizations have groups of related elements (departments and employees) working toward common goals (survival, growth, or profit). Figure 3–2 shows a state university as a subsystem of a larger system, the community. The university uses inputs from the surrounding environment and transforms them into useful outputs.

As shown in Figure 3–2, the university is affected by external factors beyond its control. Examples of external factors are the economy; federal, state, and local legislation; and competition from other universities. Internal factors affecting the university include the quality of its faculty and

FIGURE 3–2

The University as an Interacting System

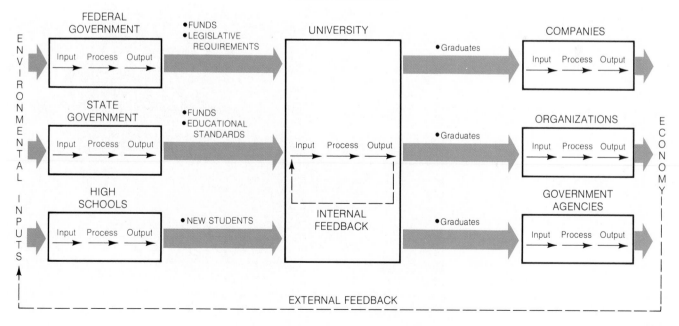

students, relationships among administrators, departmental relations, and internal communication channels. An analysis of its information needs must consider both internal and external factors.

Each department in a university is a subsystem within the university. The goal of each department is to educate students according to predetermined standards. But each department must interact with other departments. The history department must obtain enrollment and eligibility information from the registrar. The registrar finds out from the bursar's office which students have not paid their tuition.

External information, such as the number of high school graduates, SAT scores, and new tax laws affecting education, comes from state agencies among other sources. Information about present and future economic conditions that will affect university enrollments is supplied by external sources such as federal agencies. Some of the many interactions are shown in Figure 3–3.

COMPONENTS OF AN INFORMATION SYSTEM

Information is data that has been processed and made useful for decision making. Decision makers use information to increase knowledge and reduce uncertainty. Organizations cannot function without information. An information system, therefore, is designed to transform data into information and make it available to decision makers in timely fashion. An information system consists of many components. The four major components—hardware, software, data, and people—are discussed in the following sections.

FIGURE 3–3

**The Internal and External
Interactions of a University**

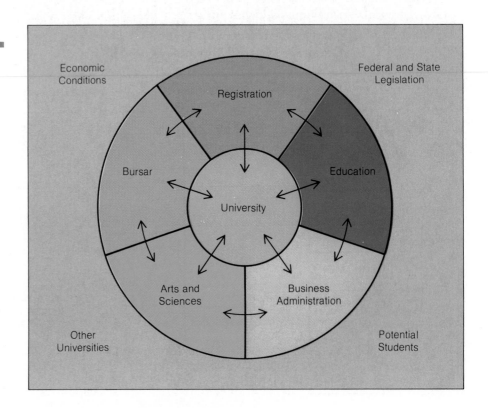

Hardware as Part of an Information System

In a computer-based information system, hardware consists of equipment, or the parts of the computer that can be seen. Hardware is used to input the data into the computer system (see Figure 3–4). Once inside the computer the data is processed by the hardware into information. Output equipment is then used either to place the information on storage devices or to present the information in human-readable form such as on a display screen.

Software as Part of an Information System

Software programs are specific sequences of instructions needed to run computers. Without specific instructions provided by software, a computer-based system could not function. Software not only processes the information needed by users but also provides the instructions needed just to get the computer running.

FIGURE 3–4

Input Equipment (Bottom Left)

Data as Part of an Information System

Before it can flow through an information system, data must be collected and changed into a form on which the computer can operate. Although collection methods vary widely, the most common data-input method is using a keyboard to "type" the data. Data can also be input directly from sources by scanning devices such as the ones used at the check-out counters of grocery stores. Remember that data refers to raw facts collected from various sources, facts not yet organized or defined in a meaningful way. Information is processed data that helps people make intelligent decisions. Processing data through an information system involves manipulating data by hardware and software.

People as Part of an Information System

People are an essential part of an information system. They put together and coordinate all activities within the system (Figure 3–5). People in an information system can be categorized by their roles, such as providers, users, and clients.

Providers are the people who design and operate the computer information system. They include many of the information system personnel

FIGURE 3–5

People are an important component of an information system.

discussed in Chapter 2, such as system analysts, programmers, and operators. Users interact directly with the information system. They provide input or use the output in their jobs. Users often are clerks or data-entry personnel, although more and more managers are becoming "hands-on" users. Clients, on the other hand, may not interact directly with the system, although they do benefit from it in other ways. A customer purchasing a product through a computer-based information system benefits when the product is received even though the customer does not enjoy direct use of the computer.

▇ THE VALUE OF INFORMATION SYSTEMS

The number of businesses and organizations with computer-based information systems is growing. Companies find that combining hardware, software, data, and people to create information systems is so successful that the term **synergism** is frequently used to describe the relationship. A synergistic relationship is one in which the combined effort of all the parts is greater than the sum of the efforts of each part operating independently.

Science has many synergistic relationships. In chemistry, an area in which synergism abounds, tensile strength is one example. Chrome-nickel steel has a tensile strength of approximately 350,000 pounds per square inch. That figure exceeds, by 100,000 pounds per square inch, the sum of the tensile strength of each of the several elements that, when combined, form chrome-nickel steel. In other words, the whole is greater than the sum of its parts.

We can also observe synergistic relationships in a political campaign. Suppose a candidate's staff must decide the most effective way to use personal appearances, television ads, and direct-mail flyers in a campaign. The staff knows that when used one at a time, a direct-mail flyer will generate 5,000 votes, personal appearances will generate 7,000 votes, and television ads will generate 10,000 votes. If each of the tactics is used in succession over the course of three separate months, the candidate can depend on receiving 22,000 votes. However, voter surveys show that if all three tactics are used in combination the month before an election, the joint effect will generate 30,000 votes. With this information, a knowledgeable staff would combine the techniques.

Regardless of the situation, political campaign or information system, combining resources for maximum effectiveness demonstrates good management practice. A person working alone to input data in an information system is slower than a computer and more prone to errors. A computer can input data faster and more accurately than humans, but it can only input data that people have found a way to put in computer-readable form. Thus, humans and computers working together can input huge amounts of data with a high degree of accuracy.

After the input phase, recall that data is processed to be turned into useful information. The question that businesses face is, since a computer-based information system is a major expense, what is the value of that processed information to the organization?

Decisions are made with the hope that they will produce the best outcome either by maximizing or minimizing a result. A major consideration in determining the value of information is whether it reduces the uncertainty

HIGHLIGHT

Portrait of a Programmer

People are an integral part of a computerized information system. And programmers are the people who write the code that puts human concepts into computer-readable form. Who are these programmers? A recent survey by the computer journal *Datamation* found that more women are becoming programmers—18 percent of the respondents to their survey were women. Furthermore, the respondents were well educated; 81 percent had college degrees, while 27 percent held advanced degrees.

What type of people choose computer programming as a career? Experts in career decision making sometimes categorize a position based on the extent to which the person in the position works with three items: people, things (objects), or ideas. Although many positions require the person to work in all three areas, people who choose programming as a career often say they enjoy working with ideas and things. Programmers enjoy the challenge of creating new, more effective ways of using the computer. They must be patient, meticulous, and persistent in order to work with the computer to solve problems and create new systems. Is there anything programmers dislike about their positions? Many say they dislike the lack of appreciation and support coming their way from management. Yet many programmers find their positions exciting most of the time. For them, becoming a programmer proved to be a good decision.

that surrounds the outcome of a decision. A decision is generally chosen from among a number of options, or choices, each with a different degree of uncertainty. The degree to which information reduces uncertainty determines its value to the organization or firm.

Businesses quantify the value of information by determining the cost of obtaining the information and comparing that with the cost of making a decision without the information. If the cost of obtaining information exceeds the ill effects of making a decision without that information, then the information loses its value to the firm.

◼ HOW BUSINESSES USE INFORMATION SYSTEMS

Businesses use computer-based information systems in a variety of ways. When computers were first introduced to businesses, the machines were used to solve specific processing problems. Little emphasis was placed on centralized planning or on using computers in the most effective way to benefit the entire organization. The primary applications for computers were clerical and record-keeping tasks. Today, computer-based information systems have expanded and developed into information systems that include all types of applications from record keeping to operational functions to strategic planning. The following sections show how businesses are using computers to improve their effectiveness.

Accounting/Payroll

Payroll, essentially a record-keeping function, is a common application of information systems in the accounting department of most businesses (see Figure 3–6). Accounting machines were among the first forms of automated machines. Accountants, therefore, made some of the first applications of electronic computers. Since a major purpose of accounting is to maintain

FIGURE 3–6

Rockwell International's Graphics Systems Division in Reading, PA, which manufactures newspaper printing presses, monitors factory time, attendance, and labor productivity with a Honeywell factory data collection system. Terminals on the factory floor and in the managers' offices supply the factory's 1200 employees with timely information on job status, job cost, and payroll.

COMPUTERS AND INFORMATION PROCESSING

and represent financial data accurately, the speed, accuracy, and memory advantages offered by computers make them ideal for such applications.

A payroll system designed to compute wages for hourly employees has informational requirements above mere hours and rate of pay. A typical payroll system also computes taxes and appropriate deductions for each employee. Vacation time and sick leave must be reflected in the paychecks. Checks and W-2 forms must be printed. A payroll system must also accommodate changes in employee information, such as change of address or number of deductions. Although these information requirements are complex, most systems break them into phases so as to perform without error.

Finance/Budgeting

Budgeting, a subsystem of finance, is an indispensable function in all businesses. An information system designed for budgeting can process data and generate reports that are used to manage financial resources. Reports in cost accounting are used to determine how and where money is spent. It is essential for managers to have this information whether they are planning their payroll or the purchase of new materials or equipment.

A budgeting system receives input from several sources, including marketing, production, accounts payable, and accounts receivable. After processing all the data, the system produces a projected budget. Management can use the projected budget to keep track of actual spending and identify discrepancies in spending before expenditures get out of control. Because information systems are capable of processing huge amounts of data, some firms use their budget systems to process hypothetical data for planning purposes.

Marketing/Sales Order Processing

In the area of marketing, sales order processing is a frequent application of an information system. Order processing must provide for a fast and accurate fulfillment of customer orders. A computerized inventory system is often used in conjunction with order processing. By combining the two in the same information system, orders can be filled more quickly, accurately, and efficiently.

Most businesses receive orders placed alternately in person, by phone, by mailed orders, or by online computer systems. Items are also returned for credit. The firm's information system must be designed to handle all of these situations.

An inventory control system can help process orders. Inventory control systems facilitate sales by preventing delays in filling orders that are caused by running out of stock. For example, a computerized inventory system may indicate reorder points when inventory levels are low. Inventory control systems also help keep costs down by making sure that warehouses do not become overstocked with items that tie up operating capital.

Human Resources Management/Personnel

Human resources management departments are involved in many functional areas of businesses. Employee assistance programs, such as relocation

Customized Grocery Stores

Grocery shoppers have grown accustomed to computer scanners at the checkout counter. They understand that the computer "sees" the Universal Product Code (UPC) and then assigns the appropriate price to the item. This enables stores to change the prices of products without remarking all the items—they simply enter new prices into the computer.

Yet the scanners are also used for functions such as inventory control. The manager can specify that the inventory of a product must remain at a certain level. The computer records the number of items sold and monitors the stock of the item. At the appropriate time it automatically reorders the item.

Data collected by the scanners is used to customize the stores to the population they serve. For example, the records may show that certain ethnic foods are in high demand. The manager may decide to increase the stock for those items or to add additional items to the ethnic foods department. The manager can use the record of products sold to learn other demographics. If many of the customers are older, the store may stock items that are packaged in small quantities. If the neighborhood serviced by the store has a lot of young families, the manager may expand the number of items for young children.

Computer scanners not only enable checkout personnel to ring up a customer's groceries faster, they also supply the managers with valuable information about how to increase sales.

and benefits, fall under human resources management, as do training and development, policies and procedures, and personnel record keeping.

Personnel record keeping is a functional area ideally suited to computerization because the volume of processed information is large and records must be updated frequently. Most organizations keep employee records in a centralized data base to which additions, deletions, and other changes can be made. Each record may include information such as the employee's name, address, phone number, social security number, date of hiring, job assignment, salary, and performance ratings. Human resource management seeks to bring about efficient planning and control for career path planning and skills development. By computerizing the personnel record-keeping functions, organizations can reach this goal.

Production Management/Materials Requirement Planning (MRP)

Manufacturers transform raw materials into finished products. This transformation usually involves many complex activities: Products are designed and engineered; raw materials are purchased; components are assembled; and facilities and equipment must be scheduled. **Materials requirement planning (MRP)** assists in the planning, purchasing, and control of raw materials used in the manufacture of goods (see Figure 3–7).

A well-designed MRP system has many interacting subsystems. Inventory control regulates the quantity of raw materials available. The scheduling of facilities helps eliminate wasted machine time and scheduling conflicts.

Engineering systems assist in designing and testing new products. Sophisticated engineering systems speed up the design process and hold down costs by reducing the need for building and testing prototypes (see Figure 3–8).

Engineering/Computer-Aided Engineering

Engineering departments are responsible for product design. In the early 1970s, computer-aided design (CAD) systems were first introduced to help engineers draw and analyze physical structures. CAD systems were and still are used to convert designs into production drawings, and are therefore considered "tail end" systems. While CAD systems have greatly reduced product development time and costs, computer-aided engineering (CAE) systems go one step beyond CAD.

Computer-aided engineering systems, which are used in the design of electronic products, are tools for the "front end" of product design. Engineers use CAE systems for everything from the initial design concept to production drawings. A CAE works a little like a word processing system. Word processors allow users to make changes to text at any point during the creation of a document. Users can correct mistakes as soon as they are identified. Similarly, CAE systems allow engineers to interact with the computer during simulation runs as errors are identified. Most CAD systems, on the other hand, run through an entire simulation before mistakes are identified, and a simulation for a complex chip design can take several days. Because CAE allows engineers to make design changes as they are identified, product prototypes frequently work on the first try. Using a CAE system, Hewlett-Packard designed a chip in seven months that normally would have taken two years to design. By cutting design time, CAE systems can significantly affect company profits.

FIGURE 3–7

MRP is being used increasingly by manufacturers.

FIGURE 3–8

Using computers to assist in product design and engineering can speed up the design process and reduce manufacturing costs.

Businesses are continually looking for ways to use computers to improve efficiency and increase profits. In many instances those companies that have developed creative ways of using computers have gained a competitive edge over their competition. For example, Ford Motor Company introduced an information storage system to improve customer relations and create dealer loyalty. Ford recognized that dealers who needed parts for repairs often had difficulty locating them. While dealers were trying to locate the necessary parts, customers waited impatiently for repairs. Together with AT&T Information Systems, Ford developed a greatly improved parts inventory system for dealers. A digital network, Net/1000, helps dealers search the inventories of other dealers for needed parts. Now customers are enjoying faster service; Ford is enjoying improved customer relations; and dealers are experiencing customer loyalty. In order to compete, other companies must also develop sophisticated information systems like the one used at Ford.

■ SUMMARY POINTS

■ As information needs increase, information systems are in great demand for processing information and presenting it in meaningful ways to decision makers.

■ In order to be meaningful and appropriate for decision making, information must be timely, relevant, accurate, verifiable, complete, and clear. Information that meets these criteria is suitable for decision making.

■ A system is a group of related elements that work together toward a common goal. A system includes inputs, processes, outputs, and feedback. Many systems are subsystems of larger systems.

■ The boundaries between systems are seldom easy to define. It is also difficult to identify the elements of a system that might stand alone as systems in themselves. The determination of boundaries and elements depends on the level or scope at which we view the system.

■ System theory can be applied to an organization: It has a group of related elements (departments and employees) working together toward a common goal (survival, growth, or profit).

■ The four main components of an information system include hardware, software, data, and people.

■ Hardware consists of equipment, or the parts of the computer that can be seen. An information system has several kinds of hardware. Input equipment is used to place data in the computer. Processing equipment performs operations on data placed in the computer. Output equipment transfers data or information from one location to another. Storage devices hold data before and after processing.

■ Software consists of the specific sequences of instructions required to run a computer.

■ People are a necessary part of an information system, for they bring together the other parts and coordinate all activities within the system. People in an information system are categorized by the roles they perform: providers, users, and clients.

■ Synergistic relationships are those in which the combined effort of all the parts is greater than the sum of each part operating independently.

■ One consideration in determining the value of information to a firm is whether it reduces the uncertainty that surrounds the outcome of a decision. The degree to which information reduces uncertainty determines its value to the organization.

■ Businesses quantify the value of information by determining the cost of obtaining the information and then comparing that with the cost of making a decision without the information.

■ Businesses use computer-based information systems in different ways to meet the needs of management, employees, and customers. Information systems are commonly used in accounting, finance, marketing, human resources, product management, and engineering.

■ Businesses that develop creative ways of using computers to improve efficiency and increase profits gain an edge over their competition.

■ REVIEW QUESTIONS

1. How can managers determine if information is meaningful and appropriate for decision making?

2. What do the information traits of accuracy and verifiability mean?

3. What is the purpose of feedback? Give an example of how feedback works.

4. Think of an example of a system. Describe its inputs, processes, and outputs. Then describe a larger system of which it is part.

5. What are the four components of a computerized information system? What role do people play in the system? Which component is the most important?

6. Explain how synergism affects the performance of an information system. Describe a synergistic effect not explained in the chapter.

7. How can a business manager determine the value of information to the firm?

8. Explain how businesses quantify the value of information. At what point does information begin to lose its value to a firm?

9. What is the difference between computer-aided design (CAD) and computer-aided engineering (CAE)?

10. What is materials requirement planning (MRP)?

PRUPAC

COMPANY HISTORY

Prudential Property and Casualty Insurance Company (PRUPAC) is a wholly owned subsidiary of the Prudential Insurance Company of America, the largest life insurance company in the United States. The company markets four types of insurance—private passenger auto, homeowners, personal catastrophe liability, and dwelling fire insurance—through Prudential agents. A relatively young organization, PRUPAC was created in 1971, after studies indicated an interest on the part of the public in dealing with one agent for all their personal insurance needs: life, health, auto, and homeowner. At the same time, Prudential recognized a need to keep its agents competitive with those of several large property and casualty insurers (who had begun marketing life and health insurance through subsidiary companies) by adding auto and homeowners insurance to their portfolios.

PRUPAC began its operations in June 1971, in a one-room office in Chicago, with 18 employees. By the end of that year, it had 112 employees and insured 14,200 cars and homes in Illinois alone. Within five years, the company had expanded nationwide, insuring nearly 1.5 million risks; its staff numbered more than 3,000. Today, with the same size staff, PRUPAC insures about two million cars and homes, making it one of the twenty largest personal-line property and casualty insurers in the country.

GENERAL COMPUTER USE

Such rapid expansion would not have been possible without computers. Prudential bought its original computers in the early 1950s, when the first commercially available vacuum tube models appeared. As the computer evolved during the following decade, so did Prudential's applications. By the time PRUPAC was founded in 1971, it could build on the software and hardware expertise of its parent company and start its corporate life as a fully computerized operation. Unlike many of its competitors, PRUPAC never had to undergo the expense, both in time and personnel dislocation, of converting a massive, manual record-keeping system to a computerized information system. This heavy reliance on computers right from the start enabled the company to handle more business with fewer people in less time, making explosive growth financially and operationally feasible.

The basic product sold by insurance companies is an intangible: the promise to pay should a loss occur. The concrete embodiment of that promise is the insurance contract and all the records and paperwork that go with it. Computerized information systems have made it possible to handle the millions of transactions involved both efficiently and economically.

Besides the computer systems that handle the records dealing with policyholders, their bills, and their claims, other systems help manage the finances of the company. These are the common general ledger, accounts payable, accounts receivable, tax, and payroll systems used by most companies, although they are specifically tailored for PRUPAC's needs.

Although the basic product of insurance is simple—a promise to pay for a loss—the trick is in knowing how much to charge so that all losses can be paid off and the company can make a profit without charging rates so high that customers go elsewhere. This is the realm of the actuaries, trained specialists in the mathematical discipline of probability theory. In addition to past experience with losses, the kinds of people who have had losses, and the circumstances under which those losses occurred, actuaries must take into consideration economic projections regarding inflation, return on investment, and so forth. Capturing and analyzing this mass of statistical data would be an awesome task without computer assistance. The computer has enabled insurance companies to analyze and adjust their rates on a more timely basis than previously possible.

All of these systems are part of the information system that helps senior management understand what is happening with the company's business and finan-

cial picture before a crisis occurs. These include systems for projecting and planning for the future, analyzing current results against set objectives, and facilitating corrective action.

TELECOMMUNICATIONS AND MICROCOMPUTERS

Although PRUPAC was born a child of the computer age, since its founding in 1971 there have been two major technological advances, telecommunications and microcomputers, that have affected both the company's organization and its people. The growth of telecommunications and on-line storage capacity has changed the structure of the organization and the way it operates. Telecommunications and on-line storage allow access to millions of records in a central location from anywhere in the company. Once accessed, the records can be updated quickly. The advent of the microcomputer, on the other hand, brought the power of the computer out of the data-processing center and placed it in the hands of the layperson.

Perhaps the most outstanding example of microcomputer use at PRUPAC is at the point of sale. Rating insurance policies is a complex process. For example, variables in quoting an auto insurance premium in most states include, but are not limited to, the age, sex, and marital status of the driver, the kind of car,

how far the car is driven each year, what use is made of the car, where the car is garaged, whether the driver has any points or convictions for motor vehicle violations, which of a dozen or more possible coverages the driver wants and in what amounts, and so forth. Add to these factors the number and ages of the drivers and the number of cars owned, and the calculations in figuring a rate are formidable.

To facilitate the rate process, PRUPAC furnished agents with a loose-leaf binder containing numerous rate tables, rating rules, and worksheets to guide the agent through the necessary calculations. Even with this aid, though, calculating rates often took fifteen or more minutes during which prospective clients waited and fidgeted. Recalculating the premium with different coverages or different amounts to try to tailor a package to meet the client's needs meant going through the whole process again.

Portable Sharp 1500A computers came to the rescue of beleaguered agents. These machines can fit easily into a briefcase or jacket pocket, yet they provide more than 32K of storage. To use the small computers, agents key in a policy and the client's answers to a series of questions. Most of the answers can be entered in the computer with a single keystroke (Y for "Yes"; N for "No"). When all necessary data has been input, the computer calculates all the rates and displays a final figure. The entire process, including keying in data, takes no more than five minutes. When rates change,

APPLICATION

the portable machines are reprogrammed in agency offices via modems and telephone lines.

At PRUPAC, computers, from large information systems to tiny portables, play an important role in the day-to-day operations of the company.

DISCUSSION POINTS

1. Explain how starting corporate life as a fully computerized operation helped PRUPAC gain an edge over the competition?

2. Discuss the benefits that hand-held computers have created in PRUPAC, its agents, and its customers.

CHAPTER

4

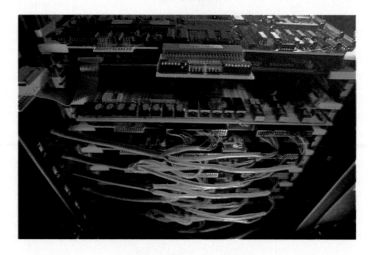

Hardware

OUTLINE

Introduction
Central Processing Unit
Instructions
Stored-Program Concept
Storage
  Storage Location
  Primary Storage
  Read-Only Memory (ROM)
  Registers
  Cache Memory

Data Representation
  Binary Representation
  Octal Number System
  Hexadecimal Number System
  Easy-to-Do Conversion
  Computer Codes
  Code Checking

Summary Points
Review Questions

Super-computers Offer Keys to Cures

By Dave Peters
St. Paul Pioneer Press Dispatch.

No matter how tangled in chicken wire you've gotten trying to fence rabbits out of your garden, what Terry Lybrand had on the computer screen in his University of Minnesota office looked a thousand times worse.

In patterns of blue, orange and green, a three-dimensional web of hundreds of hexagons and other shapes rotated and folded back and forth on itself in a seemingly random pattern.

The strange image was a good look at where the next lucrative market for supercomputers might be—the drug industry.

Since the supercomputer industry was spawned in the Twin Cities in the 1970s, the giant number-crunchers have changed the way automakers design cars and the way petroleum companies look for oil. Now they are beginning to help pharmaceutical companies streamline the way they design new drugs.

The picture on Lybrand's screen represented one-sixtieth of the surface of a virus that causes the common cold. Each line in the web represented the bond between two of the 12,000 to 15,000 atoms that make up that protein complex.

Lybrand's goal in the supercomputer work he did for a pharmaceutical company was to determine ways the clump of protein might react to certain potential drugs.

So far, no drug maker has purchased a supercomputer from Cray Research in Minneapolis, ETA Systems in St. Paul or any of the big three Japanese manufacturers.

But, intent on avoiding expensive lab work, they are buying time on supercomputers at universities and other research institutions, and they are counting on university researchers such as Lybrand to lay the groundwork for drug design methods.

"Within the next six to 10 months we will see several major drug companies making the move, purchasing a supercomputer," predicted Erich Wimmer, manager of the computational chemistry group in the industry, sciences and technology department at Cray's Mendota Heights facility.

"That will really trigger an avalanche because the pharmaceutical market is very competitive," Wimmer said.

Some analysts predict that the first supercomputer sale to a drug company will come by the end of the year. Jeff Canin of Hambrecht & Quist in San Francisco predicts that the value of the supercomputers and their smaller cousins, mini-supercomputers, used for molecular modeling could hit $1 billion within five years.

In fact, biology could be as big a market for supercomputer makers as the aerospace and petroleum industries, Canin said.

Barry Willman of Sanford C. Bernstein & Co. in New York, agreed that drugs "represent one of the larger opportunities" for supercomputer use.

Supercomputers are the most powerful computers built, able to conduct millions of calculations far faster than mainframe computers and thus able to produce mathematical models of complex natural phenomena. Many of their applications are for the military, but the commercial world has become increasingly interested.

About 300 supercomputers, most of them Crays, have been installed around the world. About 40 percent of the machines, which can cost more than $20 million, have been bought or leased by businesses.

Car makers create models of new cars and "test crash" them before ever building one. Oil companies make models of geological formations to determine the best places to find oil. Airplane builders simulate the aerodynamic characteristics of new designs without having to build and test them in wind tunnels.

Biologists are making mathematical models not simply of the chemical compounds that might become drugs, but of the huge, complex proteins that make up such disease agents as viruses and enzymes. They can examine these models—both visually on the screen and via other computer-driven analyses—for likely places a drug molecule would fit, or bind, like a key in a lock.

The closer the fit between a binding site and the drug molecule, the more likely the drug would attach itself to the virus in a patient's body. That would increase the drug's chances of changing the virus so it could not cause disease.

Whether the drug, once attached, has the desired effect might be a much larger question than today's supercomputing can answer. But using a computer simply to identify and screen out the chemical compounds that won't fit can save millions of dollars.

"The goal is to cut out 50 percent of the false leads," said David Dixon, a research scientist for E.I. DuPont de Nemours & Co. DuPont is generally thought of as a chemical company but spends about half the time available on its Cray X-MP 24 on life science work, Dixon said.

Typically, a drug company tests 30,000 compounds in the laboratory to come up with a single drug, he said. "If you can cut that to 15,000, you could save between $50 million and $100 million per drug."

The university's Lybrand did his work on the cold virus in connection with Sterling Drug, a New York pharmaceutical company recently bought by Eastman Kodak. He doesn't know whether the screening of some of Sterling's potential drugs will speed the creation of an anti-cold drug.

But screening compounds wasn't the only goal. The work "helps you generate ideas that weren't obvious," he explained. For example, he recognized a way the cold virus might be made ineffective, essentially by causing its surface to tighten around the RNA inside and not release it to replicate the virus elsewhere in the sick person's body.

"The simulation of biological molecules is only now moving out of its infancy," Lybrand said.

"The molecules are no longer some abstract entity in someone's head."

Similar kinds of modeling are being done on the structure of genes in the hope that genetic disorders might be tackled.

Computer modeling of biological molecules can be done on smaller computers, but as the tasks become more complex, the power of a supercomputer is needed.

"To search all these patterns involves a lot of adding two and two together," said Mike Pique, a scientific associate at Scripps Clinic and Research Foundation in La Jolla, Calif.

Industry observers are guessing which drug company will take the plunge first.

"What we'll see here in a phenomenon we've seen before," said Hambrecht & Quist's Canin. "It seems to take forever to get the first order and then there's a rush of orders."

The pharmaceutical companies themselves won't say much about their plans, but some already have waded into the water.

Eli Lilly & Co. and Kodak have invested $3 million each in a supercomputing consortium at the University of Illinois, for example.

Lilly won't talk much about what it's doing there, but Kodak has a variety of interests, including learning more about life science applications for supercomputers, said John McKelvey, senior staff member of Kodak's computational science laboratory.

A significant milestone in the use of supercomputers for biological work came in 1986 when the National Cancer Institute bought a Cray to study molecular structure.

"Understanding the basic molecular biology of diseases leads to a better understanding of those diseases," said Robert Jernigan, deputy chief of the cancer institute's laboratory of mathematical biology. For cancer research, too, "the intent is to model those processes and circumvent some of the experiments," Jernigan said.

Last year, the Scripps Clinic bought a Cray to look at models of enzymes, DNA molecules and other large proteins. One use is comparing the proteins of humans and animals to gain clues about how they work, Pique said.

Among the companies working with Scripps is drug and medical products maker Johnson & Johnson.

Restraining the market is the limited availability of software, Canin said. Programs need to be written to help biologists calculate the energy with which potential drugs bind to proteins, for example, and complicated graphics need to improve to let scientists see their work on the screen, he said.

Cray's Wimmer said there are perhaps 20 big drug makers in the world which are likely prospects to buy supercomputers in the near future. But he predicted that success with molecule modeling by those companies will lead several hundred more potential customers to become interested in supercomputer work on chemicals and agricultural products.

Most of the discussion about supercomputer drug design involves Cray, the world's dominant supercomputer maker. Wimmer's group works closely with the people developing software at universities and other research institutions.

Rival ETA Systems, smaller and later to the game, says it isn't neglecting the potential drug company market. But it is trying to look beyond it as well.

"That's the hot topic, but there's so much more in life sciences," said Matthew Witten, who came to ETA in June from the University of Kentucky.

Witten outlined a variety of potential uses of supercomputers in hospitals, for example. Different treatments for hearts, livers and other organs might someday be simulated before the actual treatment of a patient, he said. Voluminous patient records, including scanning images, can be stored in a supercomputer for fast reference, he said.

ETA is hoping to sell two of its small air-cooled supercomputers to research hospitals within the next six months for such uses, Witten said.

One quest of biologists is to map the entire DNA sequence of all human genes. The ability to store such a large database and search through it quickly will be another job for a supercomputer, Witten said.

"We've got enough problems to keep ourselves busy for 50 years," he said. "But the window for pharmaceutical companies is now. If you don't do it in the next six months to a year, forget it."

Scientists have been using supercomputers to research aerodynamic designs and to forecast the weather for some time. They are now beginning to use supercomputers to study viruses and to develop drugs to treat the viruses. In the future a supercomputer may help develop what has eluded scientists for ages—the cure for the common cold.

CHAPTER

4

■ INTRODUCTION

It is possible to obtain a general understanding of electronic data processing without undertaking a detailed study of computer technology, just as it is possible to generally comprehend how a car operates without undertaking a detailed study of the internal combustion engine. Moreover, with cars as well as computers, a general understanding of the machines' capabilities and limitations can be useful.

This chapter focuses on the parts of a computer system. The central processing unit, or CPU, and its key components are identified and their functions explained. The chapter also examines various forms of primary storage and briefly discusses read-only memory (ROM) and programmable read-only memory (PROM). Data representation in relation to computer processing is discussed. Binary, octal, and hexadecimal number systems are covered, along with computer codes. The chapter concludes with a brief discussion of code checking.

■ CENTRAL PROCESSING UNIT

The **central processing unit (CPU)** is the heart of the computer system. It is composed of three parts that function together as a unit. These components are the control unit, the arithmetic/logic unit, and primary storage. Each part of the CPU performs its own unique functions (see Figure 4–1).

While the CPU incorporates all three components, the control unit and the arithmetic/logic unit are often referred to collectively as the **processor.** A processor may incorporate one or more circuit elements, or "chips." In a large computer, the processor may be built on several circuit boards in boxlike structures or frames, hence the term *mainframe.* Processors in microcomputers have been reduced in size to fit onto a single plug-in chip and are referred to as microprocessors.

When data and programs enter the CPU, they are held in primary storage. Generally the primary storage that holds the data and programs is a form of semiconductor memory called **random-access memory (RAM).** RAM is the working area of the computer. Since RAM is volatile, or nonpermanent, data or programs will be erased when the electric power to the computer is turned off or disrupted in any other way. When any changes or results are to be preserved, they must be saved on an external form of storage, for example, on disks or magnetic tapes.

To begin work, data and programs to be manipulated are written into RAM. What happens to the contents of RAM depends on the processor. The processor, as stated earlier, consists of two processing units: the control unit and the arithmetic/logic unit. The **control unit** maintains order and controls activity in the CPU. It does not process or store data; it directs the sequence of operations. The control unit interprets the instructions of a program in storage and produces signals that "command" circuits to execute the instructions. Other functions of the control unit include communicating with an input device in order to begin the transfer of instructions and data into storage and, similarly, communicating with an output device to initiate the transfer of results from storage.

The manipulation of the data occurs in the **arithmetic/logic unit (ALU)** of the CPU. The ALU performs arithmetic computations and logical operations. Arithmetic computations include addition, subtraction, multiplication, and division. Logical comparisons include six combinations of equality: equal to, not equal to, greater than, less than, equal to or greater than, and equal to or less than. Since the bulk of internal processing involves calculations or comparisons, computer capabilities often depend upon the design and capabilities of the ALU.

Primary storage (also known as **primary memory, internal storage/memory,** or **main storage/memory**) holds instructions, data, and intermediate and final results of processing. At the start of processing, data is transferred from some form of input media by an input device to primary storage, where it is kept until needed for processing. Data being processed and intermediate results of ALU calculations are also stored here. After all computations and manipulations are completed, the final results remain in memory until the control unit causes them to be transferred to an output device. See Concept Summary 4–1 for a review of the central processing unit.

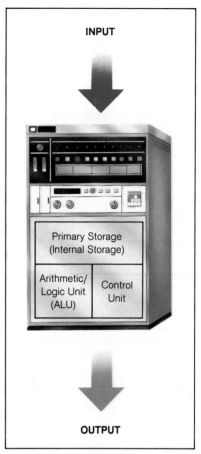

F I G U R E 4—1

Computer System Components

▨ INSTRUCTIONS

A computer functions by processing a series of instructions. Each computer instruction has two basic parts: the operation code and the operand. The **operation code (op code)** indicates to the control unit what function is to be performed (such as ADD, MOVE, DATA, or COMPARE). The **operand**

Components of the Central Processing Unit	
Component	**Function**
Control Unit	Maintains order
	Controls CPU activity
	Directs sequence of operations
Arithmetic/Logic Unit (ALU)	Manipulates data
	Performs arithmetic computations
	Performs logical operations
Primary Storage	Holds instructions, data, and intermediate and final results of processing

FIGURE 4–2

Memory Segmentation

INPUT

Instructions

| 1 | 2 | 3 | 4 |

Input Area   Output Area

OUTPUT

indicates the primary storage location of the data on which to operate. (Op codes and operands will be discussed in more detail in Chapter 12.)

The computer performs instructions sequentially, in the order they are given, unless instructed to do otherwise. This **next-sequential-instruction** feature requires that instructions be placed in consecutive locations in memory. Otherwise, the computer would be unable to differentiate between instructions and data. Since input must be brought into the computer for processing, a separate area must be designated for the input. The output generated by processing also requires an area isolated from the instructions (see Figure 4–2).

Input to a computer can take many forms. In one form, data and instructions can be entered into the computer from magnetic tape by pressing keys on a terminal keyboard. Another method relies on data that is stored on magnetic disks. No matter what method is used to enter data into a computer, once the process begins, the control unit directs the input device to transfer instructions and data to primary storage. Then the control unit takes one instruction from storage, examines it, and sends electronic signals to the ALU and storage, which causes the instruction to be carried out. The signals sent to storage may tell it to transfer data to the ALU, where it is manipulated. The result may then be transferred back to storage.

After an instruction has been executed, the control unit takes the next instruction from the primary storage unit. Data may be transferred from storage to the ALU and back several times before all instructions are executed. When all manipulations are complete, the control unit directs the storage unit to transfer the processed data (information) to the output device.

The most widely used output devices are printers, which provide results on paper; visual-display units, which project results on a television-like screen; and tape and disk drives, which produce machine-readable magnetic information. (These devices will be discussed in Chapters 5 and 6.)

If more than one input record is to be processed, the steps that have been described will be repeated for each record. These steps can be summarized as shown in Figure 4–3. Notice that, like humans, computers can only execute one instruction at a time. The power of computers comes from the fact that they can work at incredibly high speeds.

STORED-PROGRAM CONCEPT

In Chapter 1 a program was defined as a series of instructions that direct the computer to perform a given task. In early computers, instructions had to be either wired on control panels and plugged into the computer at the beginning of a job or read into the computer from punched cards in distinct steps as the job progressed. This approach slowed down processing because the computer had to wait for instructions by a human operator. To speed up processing, the memory of the computer began to be used to store the

FIGURE 4-3

CPU Operations

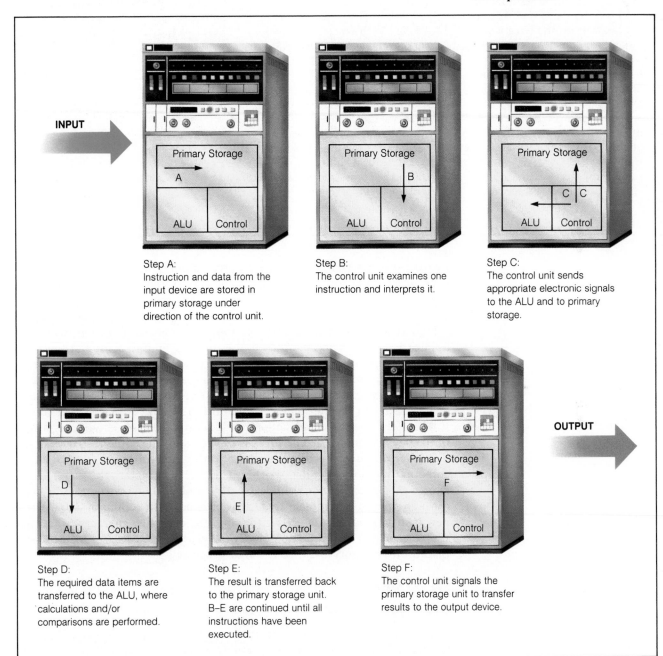

Step A:
Instruction and data from the input device are stored in primary storage under direction of the control unit.

Step B:
The control unit examines one instruction and interprets it.

Step C:
The control unit sends appropriate electronic signals to the ALU and to primary storage.

Step D:
The required data items are transferred to the ALU, where calculations and/or comparisons are performed.

Step E:
The result is transferred back to the primary storage unit. B–E are continued until all instructions have been executed.

Step F:
The control unit signals the primary storage unit to transfer results to the output device.

Where Do Old Computers Go?

Although the thrust of the computer industry is for businesses to upgrade their computer systems by buying the latest equipment, some companies are buying used computers instead. Buyers of older computers have decided they do not need the speed and the multiple capabilities the latest computers provide. After considering the cost/benefit ratio, these businesspeople say they are further ahead by purchasing used equipment.

The obvious advantage of buying a used computer is the lower price. For example, a mainframe IBM 4381 costs $550,000 new, the same computer—used for four years—can be bought for about $70,000. In the microcomputer market, a new Macintosh SE costs about $2,450; a used SE can be purchased for about $1,900.

What are the disadvantages of buying used hardware? First, the buyer needs to consider whether or not maintenance services are available for the used product. A good deal for a computer isn't so good if the computer breaks down right away and cannot be fixed.

Many major manufacturers provide maintenance unless the model has been discontinued. Secondly, the buyer must make sure parts are available for the used computer. Finally, the buyer must be sure maintenance service companies have qualified technicians. Some technicians are not familiar with older computers.

Buying a used computer can be risky; but if the purchaser determines that maintenance service, parts, and technicians are available, buying a used computer can be a good business decision.

---

instructions as well as the data. This development, the **stored-program concept,** was significant; since instructions were stored in computer memory in electronic form, no human intervention was required during processing. The computer could proceed at its own speed—close to the speed of light!

Modern computers can store programs. Once instructions required for an application have been determined, they are placed into computer memory so the appropriate operations will be performed. The storage unit operates much as a tape recorder. Once instructions are stored, they remain in storage until new ones are stored over them. This same process holds true for data as well. Data in the computer is held until new data is placed over top of it. Therefore, the same instructions or data can be used over and over again until they are changed. The process of accessing the same instructions or data over and over is called **reading.** Storing new instructions or data in computer memory is called **writing.** The basic characteristic, therefore, is known as **nondestructive read/destructive write.** When instructions or data are read, they do not replace or destroy previous instructions or data. When new instructions or data are written into the computer memory, whatever was formerly in that area of memory is destroyed. A series of instructions placed into memory is called a **stored program.**

STORAGE

Storage Location

In order to direct processing operations, the control unit of the CPU must be able to locate each instruction and data item in storage. Therefore, each location in storage is assigned an **address.** One way to understand this concept is to picture computer storage as a large collection of mailboxes. Each mailbox is a specific location with its own number or address (see Figure 4–4). Each can hold one item of information. Since each location in storage has a unique address, items can be located by use of stored-program instructions that provide their addresses. Sometimes data at a location must be changed added to, or deleted during execution of the program. The programmer assigns a **variable,** or symbolic name for the kind of data to be changed, to that storage location.

To understand variables, consider this example. Suppose the computer is directed to subtract TAX from GROSS PAY to determine an employee's salary. Suppose further that TAX is stored at location 104 and has a value of 55.60 and that GROSS PAY is stored at location 111 and has a value of 263.00. To determine an employee's salary, the programmer instructs the computer to subtract TAX from GROSS PAY. The computer interprets this to mean that it should subtract the contents of location 104 from the contents of location 111.

Programmers must keep track of what is stored at each location, and variables help in this task. It is easier for the programmer to use names such as TAX and GROSS PAY and let the computer translate them into addresses assigned to storage locations. The term *variable* means that while the variable name (storage address) does not change, data stored at the location may. The values of TAX and GROSS PAY are likely to change with each employee. The addresses of TAX and GROSS PAY will not.

Primary Storage

Primary storage is the section of the CPU that holds instructions, data, and intermediate results during processing. It may, in some cases, be supplemented by **secondary storage** (also called **auxiliary,** or **external storage**), which is separate from the CPU. Information is transferred between primary and secondary storage through electrical lines. The most common secondary storage media are discussed more fully in Chapter 6.

Second- and third-generation computers contained primary storage units composed of magnetic cores. Each core could store one bit (short for *binary*

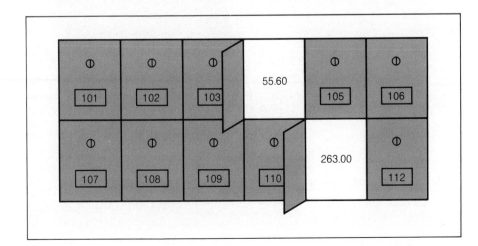

FIGURE 4—4

Each Mailbox Represents a Storage Location with a Unique Address

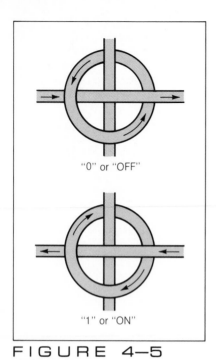

FIGURE 4—5

Magnetizing a Core

digi*t*). When electricity flowed through the wires making up the cores, a magnetic field was created. The direction of the magnetic field determined which binary state a core represented. A magnetic field in one direction indicated an "on" (1) condition; a magnetic field in the other direction indicated an "off" (0) condition (see Figure 4–5).

Technological developments have led to the use of semiconductors in primary storage units. **Semiconductor memory** is composed of circuitry on **silicon chips.** Each chip, only slightly bigger than a single core, can hold as much data as thousands of cores, and operate at significantly faster speeds. Storage for most computers in use today consists mostly of semiconductors (see Figure 4–6).

Semiconductors are designed to store data in locations called **bit cells,** which are capable of being either "on" or "off." An "on" state is represented by a 1, an "off" state by a 0. The bit cells are arranged in matrices; often these matrices are eight rows by eight columns. Unlike core memory, semiconductor memory does not store data magnetically. With semiconductor memory, electrical current is sent along the wires leading to the bit cells. At the points where the electrically charged wires intersect, the bit cells are in "on" states. The remaining cells are in "off" states (see Figure 4–7).

There are many different kinds of semiconductor memory, but most require a constant power source. Since they rely on currents to represent data, all stored data is lost if the power source fails and no emergency (backup) system exists. Core memory retains its contents even if the power source fails because it relies on magnetic charges rather than on currents. Despite this disadvantage of semiconductor memory, its speed makes it a more popular form of memory than core.

A form of memory called **bubble memory** has been introduced as a replacement medium for both primary and secondary storage. This memory consists of magnetized spots, or **magnetic domains,** resting on a thin film of semiconductor material. The magnetic domains (called bubbles) have a

FIGURE 4—6

IBM 3090 1-Megabit Memory Chip
This 1-megabit memory chip can hold as much data as thousands of cores.

COMPUTERS AND INFORMATION PROCESSING

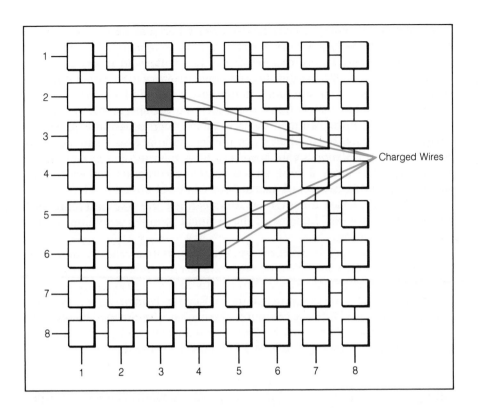

FIGURE 4—7

The shaded areas represent electrically charged bit cells. At the point where electrically charged wires intersect, the bit cells are "on."

Charged Wires

polarity opposite that of the semiconductor material on which they rest. Data is stored by shifting the bubbles into place on the surface of the material (see Figure 4–8). When data is read, the presence of a bubble indicates a 0 bit. Bubbles are similar to magnetic cores in that they retain their magnetism indefinitely. They are much smaller than magnetic cores and store more data in a smaller area. A bubble memory module only slightly larger than a quarter can store 20,000 characters of data. While some manufacturers are using bubble memory in computers, high costs, and production problems have led to the limited use of it.

Read-Only Memory (ROM)

Computers are capable of performing complex functions such as taking square roots and evaluating exponents. Such functions can be built into the hardware or software of a computer. When the functions are built into the hardware, they provide the advantage of speed and reliability since the operations are part of the actual computer circuitry. Building functions into software allows more flexibility, but carrying out functions built into software is slower and more prone to error.

When functions are built into the hardware of a computer, they are placed in **read-only memory (ROM).** Read-only memory instructions are **hard-wired** and cannot be changed or deleted by other stored-program instructions. Since ROM is permanent, it cannot be occupied by common stored-program instructions or data and can only be changed by altering the physical construction of the circuits. Sometimes ROM chips are called *firmware*. Building

FIGURE 4—8

Bubble Memory

instructions into ROM makes the distinction between hardware and software less clear-cut (see Figure 4–9).

Microprograms are a direct result of hard wiring. Microprograms are sequences of instructions built into read-only memory to carry out functions (such as calculating square roots) that otherwise would have to be directed by stored-program instructions at a much slower speed. Although some machines can be programmed by users at the microprogram level, microprograms are usually supplied by computer manufacturers and cannot be altered by users. Vendors can, however, tailor microprograms to meet the specific needs of users. If all instructions that a computer can execute are located in ROM, a new set of instructions can be obtained by changing the ROM. When selecting a computer, users can get the standard features of the machine plus their choice of the optional features available through microprogramming.

Read-only memory is different from nondestructive read. With nondestructive read, items stored in memory can be read repeatedly without loss of information. New items can then be stored over old ones if the stored program instructs the computer to do so. Read-only memory, on the other hand, is hard-wired into the computer and can only be changed by rewiring.

A version of ROM that can be programmed by the end user is **programmable read-only memory (PROM)**. PROM can be programmed by the man-

FIGURE 4–9

ROM Chip

ufacturer, or it can be shipped "blank" to the end user for programming. Once programmed, its contents are unalterable. With PROM the end user has the advantages of ROM along with the flexibility to meet unique needs. A problem with it, though, is that mistakes programmed into the unit cannot be corrected. To overcome this drawback, **erasable programmable read-only memory (EPROM)** has been developed (see Figure 4–10). EPROM can be erased but only when it is submitted to a special process, such as being bathed in ultraviolet light. Concept Summary 4–2 presents a review of RAM and ROM.

CONCEPT SUMMARY 4–2

RAM and ROM	
RAM	**ROM**
Stands for random-access memory	Stands for read-only memory
Form of primary storage for holding temporary data and instructions	Form of primary storage for holding permanent data and instructions
Volatile: Programs and data are erased when the power is disrupted	Permanent: Programs and data remain intact even when power is off
	Other forms of ROM: PROM—Programmable ROM EPROM—Erasable PROM

FIGURE 4–10

EPROM Chip

Registers

Registers are temporary holding areas in the CPU for instructions and data, but they are not considered part of primary storage. Registers can receive information, hold it, and transfer it very quickly as directed by the control unit of the CPU.

The CPU has a number of different types of registers, but essentially they all operate in the same way. A register functions much as a standard pocket calculator does. The person using the calculator acts as the control unit by transferring numbers from a sheet of paper to the calculator. This paper is analogous to the primary storage unit of the CPU. When the calculation is complete, the calculator (register) displays the result. The person (control unit) then transfers the result displayed on the calculator back to the sheet of paper (primary storage). This process is very similar to the way most modern computers work. Intermediate calculations are performed in registers, and the final results are transferred back to primary storage.

Cache Memory

Cache memory, also called a **high-speed buffer,** is a portion of primary storage used to speed the processing operations of the computer. Cache memory serves as a working buffer or temporary area to store both instructions and data. The program looks ahead and tries to anticipate what instructions and data must be accessed often and places these in cache memory. By storing the data or instructions in a temporary area of primary storage, the computer does not need to access secondary storage. Accessing secondary storage slows down the processing considerably. Although more expensive than secondary storage, cache memory increases processing speeds, which sometimes warrants its use.

▪ DATA REPRESENTATION

Humans communicate information by using symbols that have specific meanings. Symbols such as letters or numbers are combined in meaningful ways to represent information. For example, the twenty-six letters of the English alphabet can be combined to form words, sentences, paragraphs, and so on. By combining individual words in various ways, we construct various messages. This enables us to communicate with one another.

The human mind is much more complex than the computer. A computer is only a machine; it is not capable of understanding the inherent meanings of symbols used by humans to communicate. To use a computer, therefore, humans must convert their symbols to a form the computer is capable of "understanding." This is accomplished through binary representation and the "on" and "off" states discussed earlier.

Binary Representation

Data is represented in the computer by the electrical state of the machine's circuitry: magnetic states for core storage, current for semiconductor storage, and the position of magnetic bubbles for bubble memory. In all cases, only two states are possible, "on" and "off." This two-state system is known as the **binary system,** and its use to represent data is known as **binary representation.**

The **binary (base 2) number system** operates in a manner similar to the way the familiar **decimal number system** works. For example, the decimal number 4,672 can be analyzed as follows:

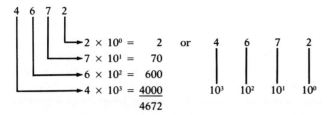

Each position represents a specific power of 10. The progression of powers is from right to left; that is, digits further to the left in a decimal number represent larger powers of 10 than digits to the right of them (see Figure 4–11).

The same principle holds for binary representation. The difference is that in binary representation each position in the number represents a power of 2 (see Figure 4–12). For example, consider the decimal number 14. In binary, the value equivalent to 14 is written as follows:

$$
\begin{array}{ll}
1 \quad 1 \quad 1 \quad 0 & \\
0 \times 2^0 = 0 & \\
1 \times 2^1 = 2 & \\
1 \times 2^2 = 4 & \text{or} \\
1 \times 2^3 = \underline{8} & \\
\qquad\qquad 14 &
\end{array}
$$

$$
\begin{array}{cccc}
1 & 1 & 1 & 0 \\
2^3 & 2^2 & 2^1 & 2^0
\end{array}
$$

As a further example, the value represented by the decimal number 300 is represented in binary form below:

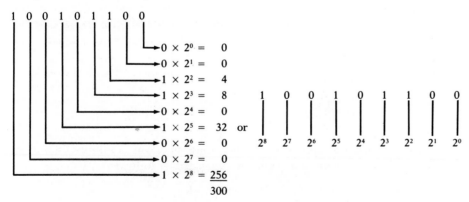

10^5	10^4	10^3	10^2	10^1	10^0
100,000	10,000	1,000	100	10	1

FIGURE 4—11

Decimal Place Value

HARDWARE   91

FIGURE 4–12

Binary Place Value

2^6	2^5	2^4	2^3	2^2	2^1	2^0
64	32	16	8	4	2	1

As indicated by the examples above, the binary number system uses 1s and 0s in various combinations to represent various values. Recall that each digit position in a binary number is called a bit. A 1 in a bit position indicates the presence of a specific power of 2; a 0 indicates the absence of a specific power. As in the decimal number system, the progression of powers is from right to left.

Octal Number System

Although all digital computers must store data as 0s and 1s, the sizes of the storage locations vary. Storage locations within primary memory are referred to as **words,** and one word is equal to one "mailbox" (see discussion on storage locations and addresses earlier in this chapter). Word sizes are measured in bits and are typically 8, 16, 24, 32, 48, and 64 bits in length.

The **octal (base 8) number system,** which uses digits 0 to 7, can be employed as a shorthand method of representing the data contained within one word, or addressable memory location. In the case of 24- and 48-bit word size computers, the octal number system provides a shorthand method of representing what is contained in memory. This is true because three binary digits, or bits, can be represented by one octal digit and both 24 and 48 are divisible by three.

As noted above, three binary digits can be represented by one octal digit. This is done by considering the first three binary place values from right to left that sum to seven, the highest digit value in the octal number system.

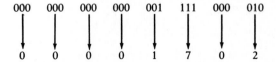

$$
\begin{array}{l}
1 \times 2^0 = 1 \\
1 \times 2^1 = 2 \\
1 \times 2^2 = \underline{4} \\
7
\end{array}
$$

If we wanted to represent a binary value that was contained in a 24-bit word as an octal value, it could be converted as follows:

000	000	000	000	001	111	000	010
0	0	0	0	1	7	0	2

The octal value can be converted to its decimal equivalent. The octal number 1,702 is equivalent to the decimal number 962. Consider the conversion below, keeping in mind that each digit of the octal number represents a power of 8.

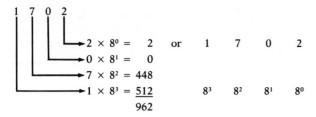

$$2 \times 8^0 = 2 \quad \text{or} \quad 1 \quad 7 \quad 0 \quad 2$$
$$0 \times 8^1 = 0$$
$$7 \times 8^2 = 448$$
$$1 \times 8^3 = \underline{512} \qquad 8^3 \quad 8^2 \quad 8^1 \quad 8^0$$
$$962$$

For another example, the value represented by the decimal number 10,000 is displayed in octal form below.

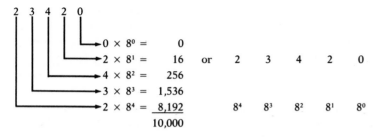

$$0 \times 8^0 = 0$$
$$2 \times 8^1 = 16 \quad \text{or} \quad 2 \quad 3 \quad 4 \quad 2 \quad 0$$
$$4 \times 8^2 = 256$$
$$3 \times 8^3 = 1,536$$
$$2 \times 8^4 = \underline{8,192} \qquad 8^4 \quad 8^3 \quad 8^2 \quad 8^1 \quad 8^0$$
$$10,000$$

Hexadecimal Number System

When a program fails to execute correctly, it is sometimes necessary to examine the contents of certain memory locations to discover what is wrong. This can be done by obtaining a printout, or **dump,** of the contents of the memory locations (see Figure 4–13). If everything were printed in binary representation, the programmer would see page after page of 1s and 0s. Error detection would be difficult.

To alleviate this problem, the contents or storage locations in computers can be represented by the octal number system or the **hexadecimal (base 16) number system.** In the hexadecimal number system, sixteen symbols

9000D203	9000C11E	41330004	4650C05A
0010E020	C1220064	E020C186	006407FE
40F0F740	40F0F840	4040F540	40F2F340
40404040	40404040	40F2F340	40F2F340
40F4F640	40F2F540	40F1F240	40F2F440
4040F640	40F6F640	40F8F540	40404040
40F0F840	40F2F540	40F3F140	4040F540
F2F5F640	F7F8F940	F1F2F540	F6F2F440
00000005	00000005	00000006	00000007
0000000F	00000010	00000015	00000017
00000018	00000018	00000019	00000019
00000035	00000035	00000037	00000038
00000055	00000055	00000060	0000007D
0000022B	0000022B	0000022B	0000022B
0000022B	00000315	F0E3C8C5	40E4D5E2
E2D6D9E3	C5C440C1	D9D9C1E8	F1F5F5F5
F5F5F5F5	F5F5F5F5	F5F5F5F5	F5F5F5F5
F5F5F5F5	F5F5F5F5	F5F5F5F5	F5F5F5F5

FIGURE 4—13

Core Dump

are used to represent the digits 0 through 15 (see Figure 4–14). Note that the letters A through F designate the numbers 10 through 15. The fact that each position in a hexadecimal number represents a power of 16 allows for easy conversion from binary to hexadecimal since 16 is equal to 2^4. A single hexadecimal digit can be used to represent four binary digits.

As noted above, four binary digits can be represented by one hexadecimal digit. This is done by considering the first four binary place values (from right to left) that sum 15, the highest single digit value in the hexadecimal number system.

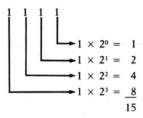

A binary value contained in a 32-bit word as a hexadecimal value could be converted as follows:

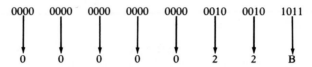

The hexadecimal value can be converted to its decimal equivalent. Keep in mind that each digit of the hexadecimal number represents a power of 16.

FIGURE 4–14

Binary, Hexadecimal, and Decimal Equivalent Values

BINARY SYSTEM (PLACE VALUES)				HEXADECIMAL EQUIVALENT	DECIMAL EQUIVALENT
8	4	2	1		
0	0	0	0	0	0
0	0	0	1	1	1
0	0	1	0	2	2
0	0	1	1	3	3
0	1	0	0	4	4
0	1	0	1	5	5
0	1	1	0	6	6
0	1	1	1	7	7
1	0	0	0	8	8
1	0	0	1	9	9
1	0	1	0	A	10
1	0	1	1	B	11
1	1	0	0	C	12
1	1	0	1	D	13
1	1	1	0	E	14
1	1	1	1	F	15

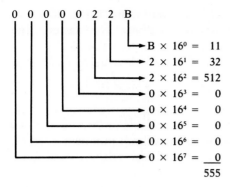

$$0 \quad 0 \quad 0 \quad 0 \quad 0 \quad 2 \quad 2 \quad B$$

$$B \times 16^0 = 11$$
$$2 \times 16^1 = 32$$
$$2 \times 16^2 = 512$$
$$0 \times 16^3 = 0$$
$$0 \times 16^4 = 0$$
$$0 \times 16^5 = 0$$
$$0 \times 16^6 = 0$$
$$0 \times 16^7 = \underline{0}$$
$$555$$

Easy-to-Do-Conversion

The division multiplication method is a simpler way to convert any decimal number to its equivalent in any other base system. Following this method first, divide the number by the value of the base you have chosen until nothing is left to divide. The remainders of each division, written in each place starting with the ones place, form the new equivalent number. Here's how it works in base 2:

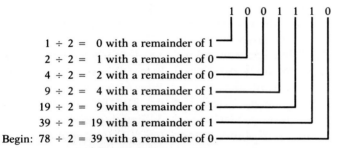

$$1 \quad 0 \quad 0 \quad 1 \quad 1 \quad 1 \quad 0$$

$$1 \div 2 = 0 \text{ with a remainder of } 1$$
$$2 \div 2 = 1 \text{ with a remainder of } 0$$
$$4 \div 2 = 2 \text{ with a remainder of } 0$$
$$9 \div 2 = 4 \text{ with a remainder of } 1$$
$$19 \div 2 = 9 \text{ with a remainder of } 1$$
$$39 \div 2 = 19 \text{ with a remainder of } 1$$
$$\text{Begin: } 78 \div 2 = 39 \text{ with a remainder of } 0$$

Now convert the decimal number 325 to a base 2 number. Did you get 101000101? Very good! So try something more difficult: Change 325 to a base 8 number. Was your answer 505? Good! That means 5 in the 64s place, 0 in the 8s place, and 5 in the 1s place. Try some more problems you make up.

Computer Codes

Many computers use coding schemes other than simple binary notation to represent numbers. One of the most basic coding schemes is called **four-bit binary coded decimal (BCD).** Rather than represent a decimal number as a string of 0s and 1s (which gets increasingly complicated for large numbers), BCD represents each decimal digit in a number by using four bits. For instance, the decimal number 23 is represented by two groups of four bits, one group for the "2," the other for the "3." Representations of the number 23 in four bit BCD and in binary are compared below:

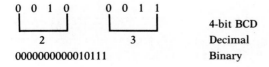

0 0 1 0	0 0 1 1	4-bit BCD
2	3	Decimal
0000000000010111		Binary

The representation of a three-digit decimal number in four-bit BCD consists of three sets of four bits, or twelve binary digits. For example, the decimal number 637 is coded as follows:

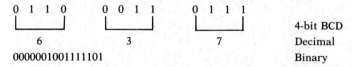

Use of four-bit BCD saves space when large decimal numbers must be represented. Furthermore, it is easier to convert a four-bit BCD to its decimal equivalent than to convert a binary representation to decimal.

The four-bit code allows sixteen (2^4) possible unique bit combinations. We have already seen that ten of them are used to represent the decimal digits 0 through 9. Since that leaves only six remaining combinations, this code in practice is used only to represent numbers.

To represent letters and special characters as well as numbers, more than four bit positions are needed. Another coding scheme, called **six-bit BCD,** allows for sixty-four (2^6) unique combinations. Thus, six-bit BCD can be used to represent the decimal digits 0 through 9, the letters A through Z, and twenty-eight characters, such as the period and the comma.

The four rightmost bit positions in six-bit BCD are called **numeric bits.** The two leftmost bit positions are called **zone bits** (see Figure 4–15). The zone bits are used in various combinations with the numeric bits to represent numbers, letters, and special characters.

Another approach to data representation is an eight-bit code known as **Extended Binary Coded Decimal Interchange Code (EBCDIC).** An eight-bit code allows 256 (2^8) possible bit combinations. Whereas six-bit BCD can be used to represent only uppercase letters, eight-bit EBCDIC can be used to represent uppercase and lowercase letters and additional special characters, such as the cent sign and the quotation mark. The EBCDIC bit combinations for uppercase letters and numbers are given in Figure 4–16.

In EBCDIC, the four leftmost bit positions are zone bits, and the four rightmost bit positions are numeric bits. As with six-bit BCD, the zone bits are used in various combinations with the numeric bits to represent numbers, letters, and special characters.

The **American Standard Code for Information Interchange (ASCII)** is a seven-bit code developed cooperatively by several computer manufacturers who wanted to develop a standard code for all computers. Because certain machines are designed to accept eight-bit rather than seven-bit code patterns, an eight-bit version of ASCII, called **ASCII-8,** was created. ASCII-8 and EBCDIC are similar, the key difference between them being in the bit patterns used to represent certain characters.

As described earlier, a fixed number of adjacent bits operated on as a unit is called a byte. Usually, one alphabetic character or two numeric characters are represented in one byte. Since eight bits are usually sufficient to represent a character, eight-bit groupings are basic units of memory. In com-

FIGURE 4—15

Bit Position in 6-Bit BCD Representation

ZONE BITS		NUMERIC BITS			
B	A	8	4	2	1

COMPUTERS AND INFORMATION PROCESSING

Fault Tolerance

Although computer systems are capable of processing data quickly and accurately, users must remember that computers are machines—and machines can break. A computer system that is down even for a few minutes can cause major havoc in businesses such as banks that require up-to-the-minute information. In order to avoid this problem, many businesses have established a fault tolerance system. A fault tolerance system is essentially a hardware backup system; that is, the company has duplicates of processors and peripherals. When the system is functioning correctly, the hardware devices work in parallel. If

the software senses a problem in one system, then all the data is switched to the other hardware system.

Sometimes other security measures are also considered part of fault tolerance, such as an alternative power supply called a UPS (uninterrupted power source) that provides power in a blackout. Often the definition of fault tolerance depends upon the company supplying the system.

Hardware backup systems are very expensive; therefore they are

only used by companies where minute-by-minute information is critical. Companies in locations that are subject to earthquake tremors or other disruptions are also more concerned with fault tolerance. Some experts project that the need for fault tolerance systems will double in the next few years. But so far most office environments have not found that the need of the backup system justifies the cost of duplicating hardware. Still, fault tolerance is crucial for some. Would you want your bank to lose its record of your deposit because the power went off?

puters that accept eight-bit characters, then, a byte is a group of eight adjacent bits. When large amounts of storage are described, the symbol **K** (for kilobyte) is often used. Generally, one K equals 1,024 (2^{10}) units. Thus, a computer that has a 256K bytes of storage can store $256 \times 1,024$, or 262,144 characters.

FIGURE 4—16

EBCDIC Representation: 0–9, A–Z

Character	EBCDIC Bit Configuration	Character	EBCDIC Bit Configuration
A	1100 0001	S	1110 0010
B	1100 0010	T	1110 0011
C	1100 0011	U	1110 0100
D	1100 0100	V	1110 0101
E	1100 0101	W	1110 0110
F	1100 0110	X	1110 0111
G	1100 0111	Y	1110 1000
H	1100 1000	Z	1110 1001
I	1100 1001	0	1111 0000
J	1101 0001	1	1111 0001
K	1101 0010	2	1111 0010
L	1101 0011	3	1111 0011
M	1101 0100	4	1111 0100
N	1101 0101	5	1111 0101
O	1101 0110	6	1111 0110
P	1101 0111	7	1111 0111
Q	1101 1000	8	1111 1000
R	1101 1001	9	1111 1001

Code Checking

Computers do not always function perfectly; errors can and do occur. For example, a bit may be lost while data is being transferred from the ALU to the primary storage unit or over telephone lines from one location to another. This loss can be caused by varied factors such as dust, moisture, magnetic fields, or equipment failure. Thus, it is necessary to have a method to detect the occurrence of an error and to isolate the location of the error.

Most computers accomplish this by having an additional bit, called a **parity bit,** or **check bit,** at each storage location. Computers that use parity bits are specifically designed always to have either an even or an odd number of 1 (or "on") bits in each storage location. If an odd number of 1 bits is used to represent each character, the characters are said to be written in **odd parity.** If an even number of 1 bits is used to represent each character, the characters are written in **even parity.** Internal circuitry in the computer constantly monitors its operation by checking to ensure that the required number of bits is present in each location.

For example, if the six-bit BCD code is used, a seventh bit is added as a check bit (see Figure 4–17). Suppose the number 6 is to be represented in six-bit BCD using odd parity (see Figure 4–18.) In this case, the check bit must be set to 1, or "on," to make the number of 1 bits odd. If a parity error is detected, the system may retry the read or write operation occurring when the error was detected. If retries are unsuccessful, the system informs the computer operator that an error has occurred.

Notice that the checking circuitry of the computer can only detect the miscoding of characters. It cannot detect the use of incorrect data. In the previous example, for instance, the computer circuitry could determine whether a bit had been dropped, making the representation of the number 6 invalid. However, if the number 5 had been mistakenly entered into the computer instead of 6 (perhaps because of incorrect keying), no error would be detected.

FIGURE 4—17

Bit Positions of 6-Bit BCD with Check Bit

CHECK BIT	ZONE BITS		NUMERIC BITS			
C	B	A	8	4	2	1

FIGURE 4—18

Detection of Error with Parity Check (Odd Parity)

	C	B	A	8	4	2	1
Valid — →	1	0	0	0	1	1	0
Invalid— ←	1	0	0	0	0	1	0

COMPUTERS AND INFORMATION PROCESSING

■ SUMMARY POINTS

■ The central processing unit, the heart of the computer, is composed of three parts: the control unit, the arithmetic/logic unit (ALU), and primary storage. The control unit maintains order and controls what is happening in the CPU; the ALU performs arithmetic and logical operations; and the primary storage unit holds all data and instructions necessary for processing.

■ Instructions are placed in consecutive locations in memory so that they can be accessed consecutively. This is called the next-sequential-instruction feature.

■ The stored-program concept involves storing both data and instructions in the computer's memory, eliminating the need for human intervention during processing.

■ The nondestructive read/destructive write characteristic of memory allows a program to be re-executed, since the program remains intact in memory until another is stored over it.

■ Each location in storage has a unique address, which allows stored-program instructions and data items to be located by the control unit of the CPU as it directs processing operations. Variables (names for storage addresses) are often used by programmers to facilitate data location.

■ One method of storing data in primary storage uses electrical currents to set magnetic cores to "on" and "off" states. Another form of storage is semiconductor memory, which uses circuitry on silicon chips. Semiconductor units are smaller and faster than cores, but they usually demand a constant power source. Bubble memory consists of magnetized spots that rest on a thin film of semiconductor material. These bubbles retain their magnetism indefinitely and have the ability to store much more data in a smaller space than core memory.

■ Read-only memory (ROM), part of the hardware of a computer, stores items in a form that can be deleted or changed only by rewiring. Microprograms are sequences of instructions built into read-only memory to carry out functions that otherwise would be directed by stored-program instructions at a much slower speed.

■ Programmable read-only memory (PROM) can be programmed either by the manufacturer or by users to meet unique needs. Thus, it provides greater flexibility and versatility than ROM.

■ Registers are devices that facilitate the execution of instructions. They act as temporary holding areas and are capable of receiving information, holding it, and transferring it very quickly as directed by the control unit of the CPU.

■ Cache memory is a portion of primary storage designed to speed the CPU's processing of instructions or data by anticipating what instructions or data a program will need and placing these in this high-speed buffer area.

■ Data representation in the computer is based on a two-state, or binary system. A 1 in a given position indicates the presence of a power of 2; a 0 indicates its absence. The four-bit binary coded decimal (BCD) system uses groups of four binary digits to represent the decimal digits 0 through 9.

■ The six-bit BCD system allows for sixty-four unique bit combinations; alphabetic, numeric, and twenty-eight special characters can be represented. Both EBCDIC and ASCII-8 are eight-bit coding systems and are capable of representing up to 256 different characters.

■ Octal (base 8) and hexadecimal (base 16) notation can be used to represent binary data in a more concise form. For this reason, the contents of computer memory are sometimes viewed or printed in one of these notations. Programmers use these number systems to help in locating errors.

■ Parity bits, or check bits, are additional bits in a coding scheme used to detect errors in the transmission of data. They can only detect the miscoding of characters and cannot detect the use of incorrect data.

■ REVIEW QUESTIONS

1. Name the three major components of the central processing unit (CPU) and discuss the function of each.

2. What is the difference between the operation code and the operand?

3. What is meant by the next-sequential-instruction feature?

4. How does the nondestructive read/destructive write feature of a computer work?

5. What technological developments have occurred in primary storage media and what impact have these developments had on modern computers?

6. How does the concept of read-only memory (ROM) relate to microprogramming?

7. Why are computer codes necessary? What advantages does EBCDIC offer over six-bit BCD?

8. Why are concepts of the binary number system important to an understanding of digital computers?

9. What relationship does the first four binary place values (from right to left) have in the hexadecimal number system?

10. What is the purpose of code checking? By using a parity bit, or check bit, can incorrect data be detected?

11. Convert the following binary value to an octal value. Then convert the octal value to a decimal value.

101100101

IBM

GENERAL CORPORATE INFORMATION

In the 1880s, Herman Hollerith developed a mechanical method of processing census data for the United States Bureau of Census. His method included two devices: one that coded population data as punched holes in cards and another that sensed the data. The success of his method led Hollerith to form his own company in 1896 to manufacture and sell these devices. In 1911, the company became part of the Computing-Tabulating-Recording (CTR) Company, which manufactured recording equipment. In 1924, CTR became the International Business Machines (IBM) Corporation.

Today, IBM is a leader of the worldwide data-processing community and is the leading vendor of mainframe computers. IBM's Entry Systems Division is the second largest producer of small computers. IBM's products include data-processing machines and systems, information processors, electric typewriters, copiers, dictation equipment, educational and testing materials, and related supplies and services. Most products can be either leased or purchased through IBM's worldwide marketing organizations.

IBM'S FAMILY SERIES

IBM's major business is information handling. IBM computers range from small, powerful microcomputers to ultra-high-performance computers for high-speed, large-scale scientific and commercial applications. The wide range of computer applications in scientific, industrial, and commercial areas today requires machines of different sizes and capabilities. For example, a computer used to forecast the weather has capabilities different from those of a computer used mainly for payroll processing. Consequently, computers with similar characteristics are usually grouped together into a family, series, or system. The family members differ from each other in range of available memory, number of input-output channels, execution speed, and types of devices with which interface can be established.

In the spring of 1987, IBM introduced the Personal System/2, a new family of microcomputers to replace the existing IBM PC. The market was broadened as the number of available models was expanded significantly. New proprietary technology was implemented to differentiate this product from existing personal computers and make it difficult for other companies to imitate (clone) the PS/2. In addition, IBM launched a massive advertising campaign to assure consumer awareness of the advantages of these new personal computers.

The smaller models (Model 25 and Model 30) both incorporate a faster version of the older processor chip found in the IBM PC, an Intel 8086. Moreover, the graphics and sound capabilities of these PC/2 models are significantly more sophisticated than comparable PCs. These computers are totally compatible with existing IBM PC software, including the operating system (DOS). Therefore, the transition for an existing user has been made painless; the vast library of existing PC programs (most of them) will run without modification on these machines. These models have been advertised as the choice for education.

The middle of the line models in this family (Model 50 and Model 60) use a more advanced processor chip, the Intel 80286. In addition to providing faster operating speeds, the computer has the ability to address a significantly larger block of internal memory, up to 15 million bytes. Associated with many of the advanced applications for this computer is a newly designed operating system, IBM Operating System 2 (OS/2). The combination of the newer hardware and software will open the next generation of applications that can take advantage of the memory and graphics features.

At the top of the PS/2 line, IBM is offering the Model 80. It is differentiated from the rest of the family by its implementation of a much more sophisticated processor chip, the Intel 80386. Although this hardware technology will permit much greater internal processing speeds, the application software available will be fundamentally identical to the 80286 machines. With the high end of the family exhibiting such processing power, the distinction formerly afforded microcomputers is blurring. Desktop publishing and other users of graphics along with large-scale data manipulators will benefit from these advances.

The newest series, the IBM Application System/400, is a family of high-function, easy-to-use processors designed to provide solutions in multi-user medium sized business environments. There are currently six processor models in the family, ranging from the Compact B10 to the rack-mounted B60. This family of computers has been designed to replace the existing System 36 and System 38 computers. Many industry observers believe that the AS400 will become the standard for the 1990s for the medium sized business.

Certain design and marketing features of the AS400 series help assure success. The system can be sold as a Total System Package (TSP). This concept includes a prepackaged, preconfigured system shipped to your location "ready to go," including preloaded software. Online educational and support software is also available with the system. In addition the computer has been designed so that transferring (migrating) data and programs from existing computers is extremely simple.

The AS400 series incorporates the latest hardware and software technology. The system processor uses Very Large Scale Integration (VLSI) logic and has the ability to provide direct access to 281 trillion bytes of storage. This architecture accommodates the needs of advanced applications such as voice, image, and artificial intelligence. The Operating System 400 integrates a powerful relational data-base system with a simple menu-driven interface for users to provide ease of connectivity and flexibility with other computer systems.

For the large system user, IBM has taken a slightly different product approach. The System 370 family of computers was introduced in the 1970s designed for large-scale, high-speed scientific and commercial applications. As new technology was implemented, more advanced computer models were added to the series. This allowed the user to expect total compatibility for software developed for an older machine in the 370 line. In 1985, IBM introduced the 3090 E Processor family based upon the System 370 architecture. Thus there was created a specialized family of powerful computers within the System 370 family of large-scale general-purpose systems.

The marketing of the 3090 E Processor family is based upon its evolutionary advances over the traditional System 370 architecture. The new design has been named the ESA/370, for Enterprise Systems Architecture/370, to further identify its position within the existing family. The processing power of the 3090 E is based upon high-speed buffers, large data paths, multiprocessing, and advanced chip packaging. This new processor family has been identified by IBM as "the base for growth into the 90s."

Table 4–1 summarizes the major IBM series and their various models. As data-processing requirements have expanded, hardware capabilities such as those provided by IBM have been developed to give the necessary support.

DISCUSSION POINTS

1. What characteristics do computers within a family have in common?
2. Why is it important for new computer systems to maintain compatibility with existing computers?

TABLE 4–1

Major IBM Computers

Series	Date Introduced	Comments	Series	Date Introduced	Comments
700	1953	Vacuum tubes	System/38	1973	Powerful, general-purpose, supporting extensive data bases
Type 650	1954	Magnetic-drum machine			
1400	1960	Oriented to business	5100	1975	Portable computer
7000	1960	Transistors, business-oriented and scientific-oriented	5110	1978	Small business computer
			5120	1980	Small business system
1620	1960	Scientific-oriented, decimal minicomputer	Datamaster	1981	Small system with data, word processing
1130	1962	Integrated circuits, small, special-purpose	Personal Computer	1981	Microcomputer for home and office
1800	1963	Integrated circuits, small, special-purpose	S/36	1983	Small business system
			9370	1986	Mid-range departmental system
360	1965	Systems designed for all purposes—business and scientific	PS/2	1987	New generation of personal computers
System/3	1969	Midi-small computer	AS400	1988	Replaced S/36 and S/38; relational data base system; middle-range family of computers based upon a relational data-base system
System/7	1970	Replacement for 1800			
370	1973	IBM's most popular system—extends capabilities of System/360			
3031	1977				
3033	1980				
3090	1985	IBM's most powerful processors			
System/32	1975	Small system for business			
System/34	1977	Small system for business			
Series/1	1976	Versatile small computer for experienced users			

Input and Output

OUTLINE

Introduction
DATA INPUT
  Key-to-Magnetic Media
  Source-Data Automation

Information Output
  Printers
  Plotters
  Visual Display Terminals

Summary Points
Review Questions

Shopping Club Finds a Bargain

By Alan J. Ryan,
Computer World

"Hi! This is Tootie. We are now taking orders for the four-piece necklace, earrings and key ring set."

For television junkies and mail-order aficionados, the voice of Tootie might be akin to heaven on earth. Shoppers can order merchandise ranging from personal computers to faux diamonds, 24 hours a day, 364 days a year from home while watching the Home Shopping Club.

Tootie answers each incoming call to the Home Shopping Club—a number that can climb to hundreds or even thousands per minute. She either handles the order herself or passes the call on to another operator. It is no secret that she is considered an extremely efficient worker: She works day and night, takes no coffee breaks or vacations and voices no complaints about being left off the company's payroll. She is not programmed to complain.

The voice response system nicknamed Tootie handles some one million calls monthly for the shopping club, more than one-third of the club's total monthly calls, according to Woody Boyd, president of Precision Software, Inc., the developer of Tootie and similar systems.

The Home Shopping Club learned of Precision Software's technology through its Unisys Corp. marketing representative, Boyd explains. In November 1986, Precision Software presented an analysis to the club and was quickly awarded a contract for the voice response system. Less than a year later, the mammoth Home Shopping Net-

work, parent of the club, acquired the software firm.

The Home Shopping Network recorded sales of $582.1 million and earnings of $29.5 million in the year ended last August, reflecting increases of 363% in sales and 174% in earnings over the prior year.

The television-based shopping program is available to 43 million homes across the U.S. on cable and broadcast TV stations and through satellite dish broadcasts. During fiscal 1987, the program shipped 17 million packages, compared with 4.9 million in fiscal 1986.

Tootie steals the show

The network employs more than 4,400 people, but its shining star is the voice response system.

For approximately $3,000 per phone line, network users of Precision Software's voice response technology receive one or more IBM Personal Computer ATs or compatibles, depending on the size of the installation. The computer acts as a series of telephones would to a phone system. "You could unplug the phone on your desk and plug in the unit," Boyd says.

The maximum number of phone lines per micro is 64,

Boyd says. The system also comes with applications to address user needs like home banking and trucking dispatching.

At the Home Shopping Club, each microcomputer in use has the equivalent of 24 voice positions on it, according to Jerry Troupe, executive assistant to the chairman of the board for special projects.

Troupe explains that in the main location, there is a network of 28 PCs offering the equivalent of 670 agent positions. In a remote facility in Clearwater, Fla., there are two more computers that create another 40 agent positions.

The club works like this: An item is brought out to the podium and displayed for the home audience; then the order taking begins. Order taking occurs only while the item is on display.

Limited time only

Because the items being sold are all in-stock inventoried items at the Home Shopping Network warehouse, orders are taken until the inventory has been depleted. The show host can view a window indicating the number of calls being taken by Tootie at any time. That information cues the host as to when items should be rotated. A typical item remains on display for approximately six minutes, Troupe says.

With the operators and Tootie combined, 2,000 or more calls can be handled per minute during peak periods with heavy-volume items.

Callers to the voice response system become computer users, and their Touch-Tone telephones act as the computer, Boyd says.

ARTICLE

"The difference is that the user communicates with the sense of sound rather than the sense of sight," as he would on a computer terminal screen, he adds.

"Every phone call that comes into the building on an 800 line is routed to a voice response line before it has the opportunity to go to a human operator," Troupe explains. The caller can either place an order with the voice system, punching in a membership number from previous orders, or punch in 0 to contact the human operator.

All information about a customer is kept on a data base on the Home Shopping Club's Unisys A 15J mainframe, so repeat callers can make purchases without having to repeat credit card numbers and address information each time.

Operators on duty

During peak periods, the company employs up to 1,200 operators in each of its two locations. The locations are connected via a fiber-optic link.

Advantages the voice response system offers the Home Shopping Club include the ability to move more merchandise in addition to labor, space, time and phone-line savings, Troupe says.

According to Boyd, the voice system is fast. "The average length of call for a human operator is between 50% and 100% longer," he says. "Tootie has reduced significantly the call length," he adds, allowing more products to be sold faster.

In the past a person had to be familiar with computers in order to put data into the computer. New developments in voice recognition systems enable anyone who can speak to interact with the computer. Voice recognition systems are used on jobs such as assembly lines; the user can work with his hands and at the same time record progress, note errors, or request parts simply by speaking into the system. The ease of voice recognition will almost surely increase the number of people who use computers.

◼ INTRODUCTION

CHAPTER

5

A computer system is much more than a central processing unit with different kinds of storage. Auxiliary devices enter data into and receive output from the CPU. **Input** is data submitted to the computer for processing. **Output** is the information produced by the computer as a result of computer processing. The processes of input and output are often referred to as **I/O.** I/O methods are important activities in any computer-based system because they are the communication links between people and the machine. If these interfaces are weak, the overall performance of the computer system suffers. This chapter describes the primary media used for computer input: key-to-magnetic tape and key-to-magnetic disks. The growing field of source-data automation is also examined. A discussion of printers and other forms of output concludes the chapter.

◼ DATA INPUT

Until recently most data was entered into a computer by punched cards, which are about the size of a business envelope. Some companies still use them for user-oriented documents such as time cards and invoices. Punched cards are not widely used today, however, because more efficient methods such as key-to-magnetic media have been developed.

H I G H L I G H T

Before Magnetized Media

Presently nearly all businesses use magnetic media or keyboards to enter data into a computer. Yet when computers were first being used by companies most of the data was entered on punched cards. These cards were about 7½ inches wide and 3½ inches high. The standard punched card had eighty vertical columns and twelve horizontal rows. Each column contained either a letter, number, or special character. Holes were punched in the columns by a keypunch machine to represent the characters.

The cards were called Hollerith cards, after their developer Herman Hollerith. The pattern of holes used to represent characters is known as the Hollerith code.

A few businesses still use punched cards. For example, some utility companies use punched cards for customer billing. Yet many businesses moved from punched cards to magnetic media because punched cards have a number of disadvantages: data does not always fit on a single card; if data is short, the remainder of the card is left blank and is wasted; cards can be easily mutilated; keypunching data on the cards is slow and costly; and cards require large amounts of storage space. Punched cards, once a major part of computer input, are now mainly part of computer history.

Key-to-Magnetic Media

Key-to-magnetic media comprise the most widely used method of input today. Data is entered by using a keyboard similar to a typewriter. Most keyboards have the standard typewriter arrangement for keying letters, numbers, and some special characters. Many keyboards have additional keys for issuing commands to the computer. The data keyboarded onto **magnetic tapes** or **magnetic disks** is stored in the form of magnetized spots on the surface of a tape or disk. Magnetic media have several advantages over the punched card method of entering data. First, data can be stored indefinitely because the spots retain their magnetism. Secondly, magnetic tapes and disks can store large quantities in a small space. Finally, the tapes and disks can be erased and reused.

There are two types of key-to-tape configurations available to users, and with both types data is recorded on magnetic tape in reels, cartridges, or cassettes. The first type, a **stand-alone key-to-tape device,** is a self-contained unit. An operator keys the data onto magnetic tapes, cartridges, or cassettes, which are then collected from all the stand-alone devices. Next, data from the various media is combined onto a single magnetic tape that is used for computer processing. The second type of key-to-tape configuration, a **clustered key-to-tape device,** uses several keyboards linked to one or two magnetic-tape units, which accept data from the operators and combine it as keying takes place. This configuration eliminates the extra step needed for the stand-alone devices. Clustered key-to-tape devices tend to be less expensive than stand-alone devices because the hardware for recording data onto the tape is centralized. Clustered devices are used in applications where large quantities of similar data are keyed. One advantage of both configurations is that data on the tape can be checked for accuracy and corrected prior to being forwarded to the computer for processing.

A typical key-to-disk configuration consists of several keying devices connected to a minicomputer (see Figure 5–1). Data is keyed onto magnetic disks. Before that, however, the data is usually stored and checked for accuracy by the minicomputer using stored-program instructions. If an error is detected, the system interrupts the operator and waits until a correction has been entered.

An increasingly popular data-entry system is the key-to-diskette system. A **flexible** (or **floppy**) **diskette** is used instead of the conventional (hard) disk. The data is entered on a keyboard, displayed on a screen for error detection, and recorded on diskette. A key-to-diskette system can operate as a stand-alone device or in a cluster configuration. Data recorded on the diskettes is collected and pooled onto a magnetic tape for computer processing.

The key-to-magnetic media are efficient for several reasons:

■ Magnetic tapes, disks, and diskettes are reusable.
■ Errors can be corrected by backspacing and rekeying correct data over the incorrect data.
■ The devices work electronically rather than mechanically.
■ Record lengths are not limited; however, most key-to-magnetic media can accommodate data in the eighty-column format used for punched cards.
■ Storage on tape, disk, or diskette is much more compact, which reduces handling and saves storage space.

FIGURE 5—1

Key-to-disk configurations are often connected to minicomputers such as this one.

Perhaps the biggest disadvantage to key-to-magnetic systems is that they cost more than punched card systems. Generally, magnetic systems are cost-effective where large amounts of data are prepared for processing on medium-sized or large computers.

Source-Data Automation

Data entry has traditionally been the weakest link in the chain of data-processing operations. Although it can be processed electronically at extremely high speeds, significantly more time is required to prepare the data, enter it, and then check its accuracy before it can actually be processed. Another method of data entry, **source-data automation,** collects data about an event, in computer-readable form, when and where the event takes place. This eliminates the possibility of keying incorrect information into the computer. Source-data automation improves the speed, accuracy, and efficiency of data-processing operations.

Source-data automation is implemented by several methods. Each requires special machines for reading data and converting it into machine language. The most common implementations of source-data automation are discussed in the following paragraphs.

Magnetic-ink was introduced in the late 1950s to speed check processing in the banking industry. Because magnetic-ink characters can be read by both humans and machines, no special data-conversion step is needed. Magnetic-ink characters are formed with magnetized particles of iron oxide. Each character is composed of certain sections of a seventy-section matrix (see Figure 5–2). The characters can be read and interpreted by a **magnetic-ink character reader.** This process is called **magnetic-ink character recognition (MICR).**

With MICR each character area is examined to determine the shape of the character represented. The presence of a magnetic field in a section of the area represents a 1 bit; the absence of a magnetic field represents a 0 bit. Each magnetic-ink character is composed of a unique combination of 0 bits and 1 bits. When all sections in a character area are combined and translated into binary notation in this manner, the character represented can be determined. MICR devices automatically check each character read to ensure accuracy.

Processing bank checks is a major application of magnetic-ink character recognition. The magnetic ink characters are printed along the bottom of the check (see Figure 5–3). The **transit field** is preprinted on the check. It includes the bank number, which is an aid in routing the check through the Federal Reserve System. The customer's account number appears in an **"on-us" field.** A clerk manually inserts the amount of the check in the **amount field** after the check has been used and received at a bank.

All magnetic-ink characters on checks are formed with the standard fourteen-character set shown in Figure 5–4. Other character sets may be used in other applications. As the checks are fed into the MICR device, it reads them and sorts them by bank number at a Federal Reserve Bank and by account number at the issuing bank. In this manner, checks are routed back to each issuing bank and then back to its customers. A MICR device can read and sort hundreds of checks per minute.

In another form of source-data automation, optical recognition devices read marks or symbols coded on paper documents and convert them into electrical pulses. The pulses can then be transmitted directly to the CPU or stored on magnetic tape for input at a later time. The simplest approach to optical recognition is known as **optical-mark recognition (OMR),** or **mark-sensing.** This approach is often used for machine scoring of multiple-choice examinations (see Figure 5–5). A heavy lead pencil is used to mark the location of each desired answer. The marks on an OMR document are sensed by an **optical-mark page reader** as the document passes under a light source.

FIGURE 5–2

Matrix Patterns for Magnetic-Ink Characters

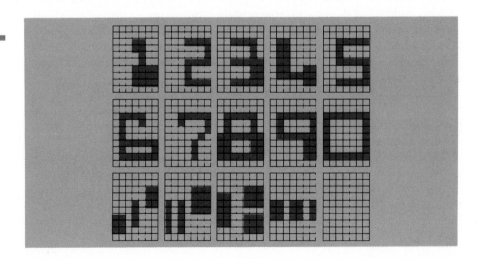

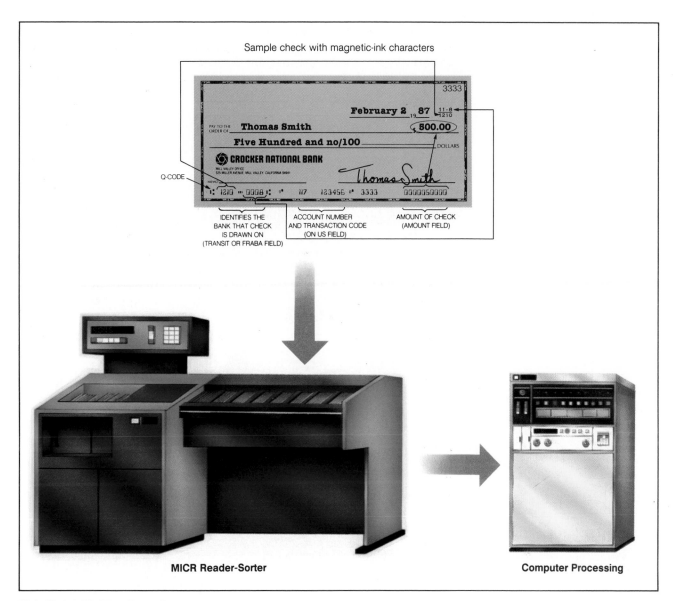

Sample check with magnetic-ink characters

FIGURE 5—3

Magnetic-Ink Character Recognition

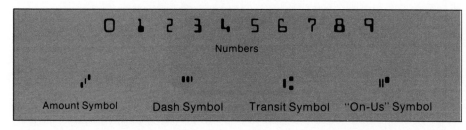

FIGURE 5—4

Magnetic-Ink Character Set

Numbers

Amount Symbol   Dash Symbol   Transit Symbol   "On-Us" Symbol

The presence of marks in specific locations is indicated by light reflected at those locations. As the document is read, the optical-mark data is automatically translated into machine language. When the optical-mark page

FIGURE 5—5

**Optical-Mark Recognition for a
Multiple-Choice Test**

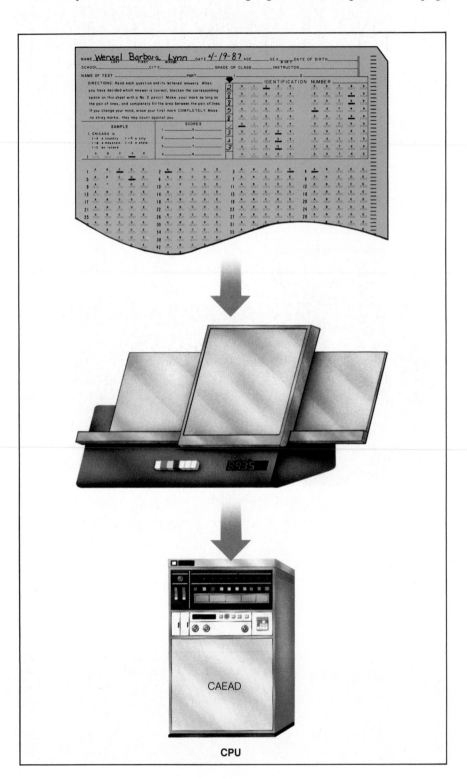

COMPUTERS AND INFORMATION PROCESSING

reader is directly connected to the computer, thousands of forms of the same type can be read and processed in an hour.

Optical-mark recognition is also used in order writing, inventory control, surveys and questionnaires, and payroll applications. Since optical-mark data is initially recorded by people, forms that are easy for them to understand and complete must be devised. Instructions, with examples, are generally provided to aid those who must use the forms. Good design helps prevent errors and lessens the amount of time required to complete forms.

Another type of optical reader, the **bar-code reader,** can read special line or bar codes. Bar codes are patterns of optical marks that represent information about the object on which the code appears. Some bar codes in use today are shown in Figure 5–6. They are suitable for many applications, including **point-of-sale (POS) systems,** credit card verification, and freight identification to facilitate warehouse operations.

Data is represented in bar code by the widths of the bars and the distances between them. Probably the most familiar bar code is the **Universal Product Code (UPC)** found on most grocery items. This code consists of pairs of vertical bars, which identify both the manufacturer and the item, but not

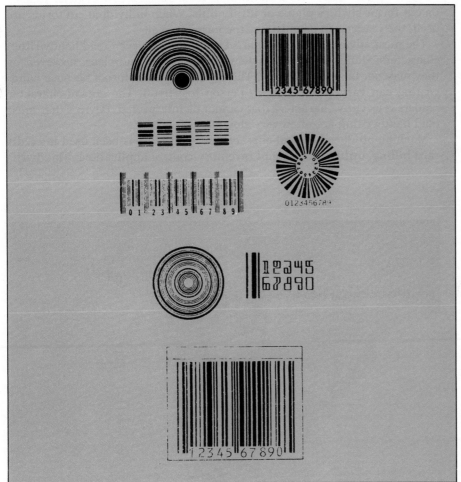

FIGURE 5–6

Bar Codes

the item's price. The code for each product is a unique combination of these vertical bars. The UPC symbol is read by a hand-held **wand reader** (see Figure 5–7) or by a fixed scanner linked to a cash register–like device (see Figure 5–8). The computer system identifies the product, its brand name, and other pertinent information and uses this data to find the item's price. It then prints out both name and price. The computer keeps track of each item sold and thus helps the store manager to maintain current inventory status.

Optical-character readers can read special types of characters known as **optical characters.** Some **optical-character recognition (OCR)** devices can read the characters of several type fonts, including both uppercase and lowercase letters. The most common font used in OCR is shown in Figure 5–9.

A major difference between optical-character recognition and optical-mark recognition is that optical-character data is represented by the shapes of characters rather than by the positions of marks. However, both OCR and OMR devices rely on reflected light to translate written data into machine-readable form.

Acceptable OCR input can be produced by computer printers, adding machines, cash registers, accounting machines, and typewriters. Data can be fed into the reader via a **continuous form** such as cash register tape or on **cut forms** such as phone or utility bills. When individual cut forms are used, the reader can usually sort the forms as well.

The most advanced optical-character readers can even read handwritten characters. Handwritten characters must be neat and clear, however, or they may not be read correctly. The system is not foolproof because handwriting can vary so much from person to person. The optical-character readers reject any characters that cannot be interpreted. Devices that must read handwriting are often very slow.

Machine-produced optical-character recognition has been used in credit card billing, utility billing, and inventory-control applications. Handwrit-

FIGURE 5–7

UPC Wand Reader

FIGURE 5-8

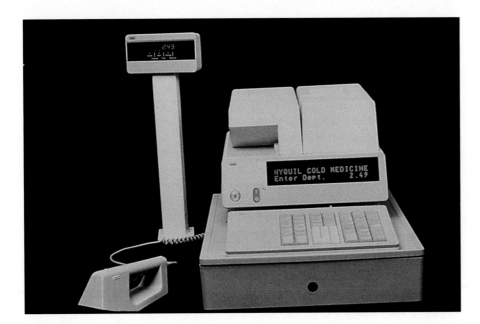

Point-of-Sale Terminal
This NCR 7000/Department Store
System is one of a new generation of
advanced point-of-sale systems. It
consists of a programmable terminal 7050 and the 7830 hand-held
scanner.

ten optical-character recognition has been used widely in mail sorting. The
reliability of optical-character recognition systems is generally very good.

In addition to recognizing small symbols such as letters, numbers, and
UPCs, full pages of hardcopy can also be interpreted by scanners. The scanner converts images to a pattern of dots and then displays the image on the
computer screen. Full page scanners are often used in conjunction with
desktop publishing.

Remote terminals collect data at its source and transmit the data to a
central computer for processing. Generally, data is transmitted over telecommunications equipment. The many types of remote terminals available
can increase the versatility and expand the applications of the computer.

Remote terminals that perform the functions of a cash register and also
capture sales data are referred to as **point-of-sale (POS) terminals.** Such
terminals have a keyboard for data entry, a panel to display the price, a
cash drawer, and a printer that provides a cash receipt. A POS terminal
typical of those found in many supermarkets is pictured in Figure 5-10.

FIGURE 5-9

OCR Characters

ABCDEFGHIJKLMN
OPQRSTUVWXYZ,.
$/*-1234567890

HIGHLIGHT

When Security Counts

The security guard at the office building may no longer be wearing a uniform or carrying a walkie-talkie. The new guard may be a computer. Persons wishing to enter the security area would be identified by placing their finger or hand on a scanner. This process, called biometrics, is the science of assigning computer codes to physical characteristics. Often a finger or a hand is used as the identifying body part, but in some cases individuals are identified by the retina in their eye. A low-intensity infrared light scans the vascular pattern in each user's eyes, then digitizes and stores the image for comparison. Because the retinal vascular pattern of each person is unique, it can be used for identification in much the same way fingerprints are used.

Biometrics is used by organizations which require high security, such as government offices. The methods eliminate the possibility of unauthorized individuals gaining access to a building by learning someone else's security number or by stealing a security card.

Presently biometric systems are expensive, and often companies cannot justify their cost. But if the prices decrease, banks and even retail stores may begin using the method for customer identification. Customers would no longer need to worry about their credit cards being stolen or someone making a phony card from stolen carbons. Soon fingerprints may be used to identify more than criminals—they may be used for everyday transactions.

Some POS terminals have wand readers that can read either the Universal Product Code (UPC) or the OCR characters stamped on or attached to an item. The sale is registered automatically as the checkout person passes the wand reader over the code; there is no need to enter the price via a keyboard unless the wand malfunctions. Thus, POS terminals enable sales data to be collected at its source. If the terminals are directly connected to a large central computer, useful inventory and sales information can be provided to the retailer almost instantaneously.

Touch-tone devices are remote terminals used together with ordinary telephone lines to transfer data from remote locations to a central computer. The data is entered via a special keyboard on the terminal. Generally, slight modifications need to be made to the telephone connection to allow data to be transferred over the line (see Figure 5–11).

There are several types of touch-tone devices. One that reads a magnetic strip on the back of plastic cards is often used to verify credit card transactions. Another stores large amounts of data on a magnetic belt similar to a magnetic tape before transmitting it. This type of terminal is best suited for large-volume processing. Concept Summary 5–1 reviews the various types of data input.

CONCEPT SUMMARY 5—1

Types of Data Input	
Type of Input	**Method of Implementation**
Punched Card	Keypunch
Key to Magnetic Media	Key-to-Tape System Key-to-Disk System Key-to-Diskette System
Source-Data Automation	Magnetic-Ink Character Recognition (MICR) Optical-Mark Recognition (OMR) Bar-Code Reader Optical-Character Recognition (OCR)

■ INFORMATION OUTPUT

Output is data that has been processed into information by the computer. Output must be in a form that is convenient for the users. Output can be produced by printers, plotters, and visual display terminals. Printers and plotters produce hard copies of output; visual display terminals (VDT) produce soft copy.

Printers

Printers print processed data in a form humans can read. To produce hard copy, the printer first receives electronic signals from the central processing unit. In an **impact printer,** these signals activate print elements, which are pressed against paper. Newer, **nonimpact printers** use heat, laser technology, or photographic techniques to print output.

COMPUTERS AND INFORMATION PROCESSING

IMPACT PRINTERS. Impact printers come in a variety of shapes and sizes. Some print one character at a time, while others print a line at a time. Printer-keyboards, dot- or wire-matrix printers, and daisy-wheel printers are the three principal character-at-a-time devices.

The **printer-keyboard** is similar to an office typewriter (see Figure 5–12). All instructions, including spacing, carriage returns, and printing of characters, are sent from the CPU to the printer. The keyboard allows an operator to communicate with the system, for example, to enter data or instructions. Printer-keyboards produce output at a relatively slow rate.

Dot-matrix (also called **wire-matrix**) **printers** are based on a design principle similar to that of a football or basketball scoreboard. The matrix is a rectangle composed of pins, usually seven pins high and five pins wide. Certain combinations of pins are activated to represent characters. For example, the number 4 and the letter L are formed by a combination of pins being pressed against paper (see Figure 5–13). The dot combinations used to represent various numbers, letters, and special characters are shown in Figure 5–14. Letter- or typewriter-quality characters produced by dot-matrix printers contain more dots placed closer together. Dot-matrix printers can typically print up to fifteen characters per second or 900 characters per minute.

FIGURE 5—10

Point-of-Sale Terminal with Fixed Scanner

FIGURE 5—11

Touch-Tone Device

FIGURE 5—12

Printer Keyboard

Daisy-wheel printers use a daisy wheel, which is a flat disk with petal-like projections (see Figure 5–15). Daisy wheels come in several type fonts that can be interchanged quickly to suit application needs. The daisy-wheel printer offers high-quality type and is often used in word-processing systems to give output a typewriter quality appearance. Daisy-wheel printers can produce up to 3,000 characters per minute.

Types of line-at-a-time printers include print-wheel, chain, and drum printers. A **print-wheel printer** typically contains 120 print wheels, one for each of 120 print positions on a line (see Figure 5–16). Each print wheel contains forty-eight alphabetic, numeric, and special characters. The wheel rotates until the desired characters move into the corresponding print position on the current print line. When all wheels are in their correct positions, a hammer drives the paper against the wheels and an entire line of output is printed. Print-wheel printers can produce about 150 lines per minute, which makes them rather slow as compared to other line-at-a-time printers.

FIGURE 5—13

Character Patterns for Dot-Matrix Printers

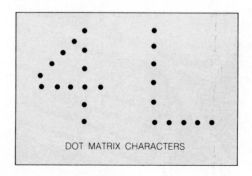

DOT MATRIX CHARACTERS

COMPUTERS AND INFORMATION PROCESSING

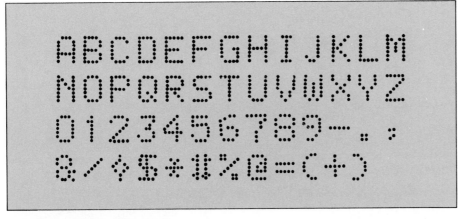

FIGURE 5-14

Dot-Matrix Character Set

FIGURE 5-15

Daisy Print Wheel

A **chain printer** has a character set assembled in a chain that revolves horizontally past all print positions (see Figure 5–17). The printer has one print hammer for each column on the paper. Characters are printed when hammers press the paper against an inked ribbon, which in turn presses

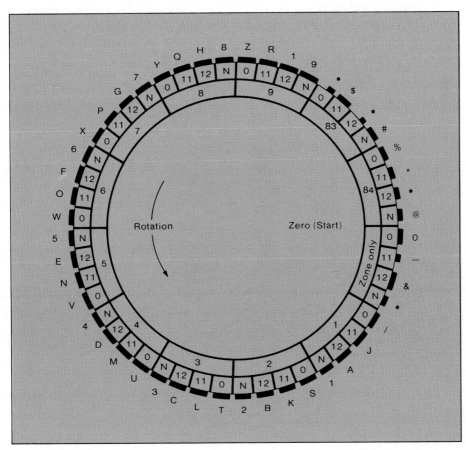

FIGURE 5-16

Print Wheel

FIGURE 5—17

Chain Printer Print Element

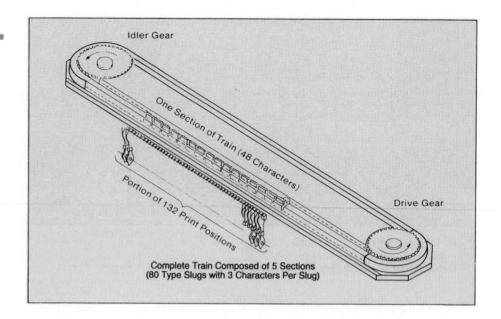

Idler Gear

One Section of Train (48 Characters)

Drive Gear

Portion of 132 Print Positions

Complete Train Composed of 5 Sections
(80 Type Slugs with 3 Characters Per Slug)

against appropriate characters on the print chain. The fonts can be changed easily on chain printers, allowing a variety of fonts, such as italic or boldface, to be used. Some chain printers can produce up to 2,000 lines per minute.

A **drum printer** uses a metal cylinder with rows of characters engraved across its surface (see Figure 5–18). Each column on the drum contains a complete character set and corresponds to one print position on the line. As the drum rotates, all characters are rotated past the print position. A hammer presses the paper against the ink ribbon and drum when the appropriate character is in place. One line is printed for each revolution of the drum, since all characters eventually reach the print position during one revolution. Some drum printers can produce 2,000 lines per minute.

FIGURE 5—18

Print Drum

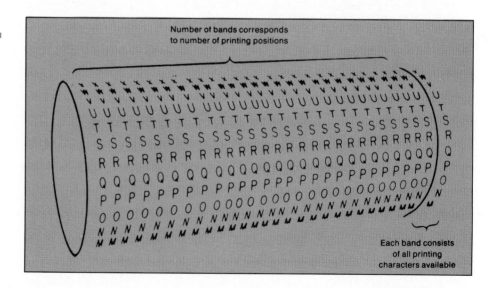

Number of bands corresponds
to number of printing positions

Each band consists
of all printing
characters available

COMPUTERS AND INFORMATION PROCESSING

NONIMPACT PRINTERS. Nonimpact printers do not print characters by means of a mechanical printing element that strikes paper. Instead, a variety of other methods are used. Electrostatic, electrothermal, ink-jet, laser, and xerographic printers are some of these types.

An **electrostatic printer** forms an image of a character on special paper using a dot matrix of charged wires or pins. The paper is moved through a solution containing ink particles that have a charge opposite that of the pattern. The ink particles adhere to each charged pattern of the paper, forming a visible image of each character.

Electrothermal printers generate characters by using heat and heat-sensitive paper. Rods are heated in a matrix. As the ends of the selected rods touch the heat-sensitive paper, an image is created. Both electrothermal and electrostatic printers operate quietly. They are often used in applications where noise may be a problem. Some of these printers are capable of producing 5,000 lines per minute.

In an **ink-jet printer,** a nozzle is used to shoot a stream of charged ink toward the paper. Before reaching it, the ink passes through an electrical field that arranges the charged particles into characters. These printers can produce up to 12,000 characters per minute.

Laser printers combine laser beams and electrophotographic technology to create output images (see Figure 5–19). A beam of light is focused through a rotating disk containing a full font of characters. The character image is projected onto a piece of film or photographic paper, and the print or negative is developed and fixed in a manner similar to that used for ordinary photographs. The output consists of high-quality, letter-perfect images. The process is often used to print books. Laser printers, which can operate at speeds of up to 21,000 lines per minute, are often replacing the slower printers that have been used with word-processing systems in the past.

Xerographic printers use printing methods much like those used in common xerographic copying machines. For example, Xerox, the pioneer of this type of printing, has one model that prints on single 8½-by-11-inch sheets of plain paper rather than on the continuous-form paper normally used. Xerographic printers operate at speeds of up to 4,000 lines per minute.

Nonimpact printers are generally faster than impact printers because they involve less physical movement. They offer a wider choice of type faces and better speed-to-price ratios than impact printers, and their technology implies a higher degree of reliability because they use fewer movable parts in printing. The disadvantages of nonimpact printers include the special paper requirements and the poor type-image quality of some printers. Also, nonimpact printers cannot make carbon copies. Yet nonimpact printers can produce several copies of a page in less time than it takes an impact printer to produce one page with several carbon copies.

New print systems now on the market combine many features of the printing process into one machine. For example, collating, routing, hole punching, blanking out of proprietary information, and perforating may be performed. Some printers produce both text and form designs on plain paper, reducing or eliminating the need for preprinted forms. Furthermore, some laserwriters and ink jet printers can also print in color. For a summary of the types and speeds of impact and nonimpact printers, see Concept Summary 5–2.

FIGURE 5—19

Laser Printer—Xerox 4045

Impact and Nonimpact Printers	
Impact Printers	**Speed**
Printer-Keyboard	Very slow
Dot Matrix	Up to 900 characters per minute
Daisy Wheel	Up to 3,000 characters per minute
Chain Printer	Up to 2,000 lines per minute
Drum Printer	Up to 2,000 lines per minute
Nonimpact Printers	**Speed**
Electrostatic	Up to 5,000 lines per minute
Electrothermal	Up to 5,000 lines per minute
Laser	Up to 21,000 lines per minute
Xerographic	Up to 4,000 lines per minute
Ink-jet	Up to 12,000 characters per minute

Plotters

Sometimes the best way for a computer to present information to a user is not in the form of text, but in graphic form. **A plotter** is an output device that prepares graphic, hard copy of information. It can produce lines, curves, and complex shapes. Plotters are often used to produce line and bar charts, graphs, organizational charts, engineering drawings, maps, trend lines, and supply and demand curves, among other things.

A typical plotter has a pen, a movable carriage, a drum, and a chart-paper holder (see Figure 5–20). Shapes are produced as the pen moves back and forth across the paper along the y-axis while the drum moves the paper up and down along the x-axis. Both the paper movement and the pen movement are bi-directional. The pen is raised from and lowered to the paper surface automatically. Many plotters use more than one pen at a time. The colors of graphics can be changed by changing the colors of the pens.

Visual Display Terminals

Visual display terminals are output devices that display data on cathode-ray tubes (CRTs) similar to television screens (see Figure 5–21). A typical screen can hold twenty-four lines, each containing eighty characters. These terminals supply soft copy output, which means the screen image is not a permanent record of what is shown. CRTs are well suited for applications involving inquiry and response, where no permanent (printed) records are required, and can be used for capturing data transmitted to the screen for verification as it is keyed.

Visual display terminals have some advantages over printers. First, they can display output much faster than printers—some CRT terminals can

FIGURE 5—20

Plotter

FIGURE 5—21

Visual Display Terminal

display up to 10,000 characters in a second. Also, they are much quieter in operation than impact printers. It is usually possible to connect a printer or a copier to a CRT terminal, making it possible to obtain hard copy output of the screen contents.

Another type of CRT, known as a **graphic display device,** is used to display drawings as well as characters on a screen. Graphic display devices are generally used to show graphs and charts, but they can also display complex curves and shapes. Graphic display devices are being used in highly technical fields such as the aerospace industry to aid in the design of new wing structures. They are also being used heavily in computer-assisted design/computer-assisted manufacturing (CAD/CAM) areas, where objects can be designed and tested and the manufacturing process specified on the computer system in an interactive fashion.

■ SUMMARY POINTS

■ Key-to-magnetic media are increasingly used for computer input because they overcome the disadvantages of punched cards, such as mutilation during handling and slow-processing time. Tapes, disks, and diskettes allow easy correction of errors, are reusable, and can store more data in less space than cards.

■ Source-data automation refers to collection of data at the point where a transaction occurs. Common approaches to source-data automation employ optical-recognition devices and other types of remote terminals.

■ Magnetic-ink characters can be read by humans and also by machines, since they are magnetically inscribed. Magnetic-ink character recognition (MICR) devices can convert the magnetic characters into machine code for computer processing. MICR devices are used extensively by the banking industry for processing checks.

■ Optical-mark recognition devices can sense marks made with a heavy lead pencil and convert them into machine code. Other optical-character recognition devices are capable of reading bar codes, documents printed in various type fonts, and even handwritten characters. The main advantage of optical-character recognition is that it eliminates the intermediate process of transcribing data from source documents to an input medium.

■ Remote terminals can collect data at its source and transmit it over communication lines for processing by a central computer. Each device satisfies distinct needs for input and output. Which device is most appropriate for a certain application depends on the particular input/output requirements.

■ Printers provide output in a permanent (hard copy) form, which people can read. Impact printers can be classified as either character-at-a-time (such as printer-keyboards, dot-matrix printers, and daisy-wheel printers) or line-at-a-time (such as print-wheel printers, drum printers, and chain printers).

■ Nonimpact printers use more recent technological developments such as photographic, thermal, or laser techniques to print output. They are faster than impact printers, offer a wider choice of type faces, better speed-to-price ratios, and are very reliable.

■ Plotters produce hard copy in graphic form. They are used to present information in the form of charts and graphs.

■ Visual display terminals display data on cathode-ray tubes (CRTs). Typically a CRT screen can hold twenty-four lines, each containing eighty columns of soft copy output. A graphic display device can display drawings as well as characters.

■ REVIEW QUESTIONS

1. What is the difference between input and output? What methods are often used for gathering input? What are common methods for producing output?

2. What are the advantages and disadvantages of using key-to-magnetic media for data input?

3. Explain the difference between a stand-alone key-to-tape device and a clustered key-to-tape device.

4. Explain source-data automation.

5. Discuss three types of optical-recognition devices. Identify applications in which each type can be used.

6. What is the Universal Product Code (UPC)?

7. Discuss the two major divisions of printers. Name at least two types of printers in each group.

8. Distinguish between character-at-a-time and line-at-a-time printers, giving examples of each.

9. What is a POS system? What types of retailers might be using POS systems?

10. What is a plotter? For what purposes might it be used?

Wendy's International Inc.

COMPANY HISTORY

Wendy's International Inc., the fourth largest restaurant chain in the world, began with the dream of R. David Thomas, Wendy's founder and senior chairman. That dream became a reality in Columbus, Ohio, in 1969 when Thomas named his first restaurant after his daughter Melinda Lou, nicknamed "Wendy" by her brother and sisters.

Today, Wendy's has over 3,800 restaurants in all fifty states and twenty countries overseas. Systemwide sales have grown from less than $300,000 in 1970 to $2.9 billion in 1987. Wendy's was the first chain to exceed $1 billion in sales in its first ten years and reached the one-thousandth and two-thousandth restaurant opening marks faster than any competitor.

More than three million meals are served each day in Wendy's Old Fashioned Hamburgers restaurants.

To operate an organization as large and as successful as Wendy's requires extensive use of computers. About twelve years ago, computer technology was introduced to automate the accounting and financial functions. As these applications proved successful, Wendy's invested more money in equipment to computerize other areas of operation.

Between 1977 and 1979, Wendy's developed and implemented data processing through a local service bureau computing facility (CompuServ). By 1979, the company created an information systems organization to transfer and develop basic applications for in-house processing. Payroll, general ledgers, accounts payable, and sales audit systems were developed on a centralized basis. Inputs for these systems were manually derived from field locations and processed at headquarters. Pertinent reports for field management and site locations were mailed through a courier service organization. These procedures were workable until Wendy's business grew and the number of stores and locations also grew at a significant rate.

Computer-based technologies were needed at the store level to accommodate the growth in (1) the number of product offerings, (2) the number of different types of raw materials, (3) the management control functions needed to adequately run a larger sales-based store, and (4) the amount of information needed to manage the business competitively. The years 1982–1985 brought significant investments in minicomputers at the area locations.

CURRENT COMPUTER USE

Currently, Wendy's network consists of 1,200 stores with POS systems (IBM 3683-84), and a Corporate Data Center with IBM/3081K and IBM 3033 computers. Approximately 400 personal computers are in use with field locations using 200 of these. Applications for PCs include word processing, electronic mail, data-base access, spreadsheet analysis, crew scheduling, product analysis, sales projections, and so on. The network is a means of obtaining data/information through daily polling of the stores. This creates a data base for (1) daily sales, (2) product mix reporting, (3) audit applications, (4) financial accounting, and (5) price elasticity analysis and other marketing applications.

Wendy's use of point-of-sale (POS) systems is extensive. The 1,200 stores equipped with POS systems use the systems predominantly for cash register operations and management control. Specific applications include customer receipts, cash control, inventory control, labor scheduling, sales analysis, slogans on receipts, and point-of-purchase displays. Application software for the POS systems is developed internally by programmers using assembler language. Changes in the software (such as price changes or on-site messages) are downloaded from headquarters. A Field Operations Support Center is maintained twenty-four hours a day seven days a week to support problem resolution at the store level. When operation reports

are requested by management in corporate head-quarters the mainframe polls the POS systems located in retail outlets and collects the data required for the reports. On occasion, the process is reversed when reports such as financial statements and marketing reports are sent back to remote area office locations from corporate headquarters.

Each area office at Wendy's is equipped with an IBM PC/XT and peripherals. The major uses of these machines are for restaurant operation systems and electronic mail. The restaurant operation systems are used to project certain operating requirements, such as raw products and personnel, on a weekly basis.

The trend in the restaurant industry is to have a communication network within the corporation that can serve the stores, field locations, and corporate offices with a data/information flow that is fast and cost efficient. At Wendy's, computers are helping make fast and efficient operations a reality.

DISCUSSION POINTS

1. How are personal computers used at Wendy's?
2. Describe how point-of-sale systems are used to prepare operation reports for management at Wendy's.

CHAPTER

6

Storage Devices

OUTLINE

Introduction
Classification of Storage Media
Sequential-Access Media
  Magnetic Tape
  Cassette Tape
Direct-Access Media
  Magnetic Disk
  Floppy Disk

Mass Storage
Trends in Data Storage
  Charge-Coupled Devices
  Laser Technology
  RAM Disks
  Compact Disks
  Josephson Junction
  Superconductors

Summary Points
Review Questions

The World on a Silver Platter

Philip Elmer-DeWitt.
Reported by Charles Pelton
Time

At first glance, the union of the personal computer and the compact disc would seem to be a perfect match. The same CD that holds an hour of Mendelssohn or Madonna can be used to store more information than a thousand floppy disks. But the coupling of the two technologies has been stalled by a kind of Catch-22. Computer owners will not buy the special disk drives required to play CDs on their desktop machines until they know there is something worth playing. And software publishers are reluctant to develop new CD programs until there are enough disk drives in place to justify the investment.

Now there are encouraging signs on both fronts. In the past year, the library of commercially available CD computer programs has doubled, from 150 to more than 300, and the number is expected to double again by the end of the year. Meanwhile, the market for CD players has received a boost from two of the computer industry's leading manufacturers. Last month Tandy announced that it would begin selling a $995 computer CD player at many of its 7,000 Radio Shack stores. Apple has introduced a $1,195 CD drive that not only plugs into its Macintosh and Apple II computers but also can be hooked up to a stereo to play music CDs.

A computer CD, known in the industry as a CD ROM (for "read only memory"), is just 4.72 in. in diameter but can store as much information as a stack of typewritten pages nine stories high. Dozens of reference books, from Grolier's *Academic American Encyclopedia* to Roget's *Thesaurus*, have appeared in CD form, and many more are on the way.

The newest discs take advantage of the medium's vast capacity for storing pictures and sounds as well as words. Laser Scan Systems of Miami sells a CD that displays maps showing the location of 520,000 real estate properties in Broward County, Fla. British Airways has put the entire maintenance manual for a Boeing 757 on CD, so its repair people can find the illustration of a missing part with a few taps on a keyboard. Soon, travel agents who use American Airlines' SABRE reservation system will be able to show customers photographs of vacation spots and hotel rooms on the same screens that display flight information and fares.

Still more variations of CD technology are on the way. Two giants of consumer electronics, Sony and Philips, are getting ready to unveil a CD device that comes with a built-in computer and can be hooked up to a TV set. A hand-held controller allows users to interact with the images on the screen. Sony and Philips, which call their new system CD-Interactive, hope it will be as big a hit as the music CD player. Philips conducted the first public demonstration of CD-I last month, and industry sources say the system could be ready for delivery as early as next year.

The trend in computer hardware is to increase capabilities while at the same time decreasing the size of the computer. In data storage the methods have moved from cumbersome punched cards and tapes to magnetic media. Now the vast storage capabilities of compact disks may make them the storage medium of the future.

▇ INTRODUCTION

Organizations store large amounts of data for a variety of purposes. Many businesses commonly store data regarding their employees, customers, suppliers, inventory levels, sales figures, and expenses, in addition to the specific types of data required to perform their particular business functions. Organizations that use electronic methods of processing data must store it in computer-accessible form. The arrangement of computer-based files and, ultimately, the type of media used for data storage depend on the needs and constraints of the organization. Each type of storage media has certain characteristics that must be considered.

This chapter examines the two most popular types of data storage media, magnetic tape and magnetic disk, and begins the discussion of two of the most common types of file arrangement using these media, sequential and direct-access. (These topics are elaborated in the next chapter.) Emphasis is placed on the storage media used with mainframe computer systems. Storage devices commonly used with microcomputers will be covered in more detail in Chapter 8. Mass storage devices and future trends in data storage are also covered.

▇ CLASSIFICATION OF STORAGE MEDIA

A computer system generally includes two types of storage: **primary storage** and **secondary** (or **auxiliary storage**). Primary storage, discussed in Chapter 4, is part of the CPU and is used to store instructions and data needed for processing. Semiconductor memory, the circuitry on silicon chips capable of extremely fast processing, is the most widely used form of primary storage. Bubble memory is also in limited use.

In most cases, the amount of data required by a program exceeds the capacity of primary storage. To compensate for limited primary storage, data can be stored on secondary storage devices. Secondary storage is not part of the CPU. The most common types of secondary storage are magnetic tapes and magnetic disks. Mass storage devices are useful in some situations. Media such as punched cards and magnetic drums can also be used, but they have become outdated. Secondary storage media costs much less than primary storage. Therefore, they make the storage of large amounts of data economically feasible for most organizations.

Secondary storage media are connected to the CPU. Once data has been stored on a secondary storage device, it can be retrieved for processing as needed. However, the retrieval of items from secondary storage is significantly slower than retrieval of items from primary storage. After processing has been completed, the data or results can be written back onto the secondary storage media (see Figure 6–1).

▇ SEQUENTIAL-ACCESS MEDIA

Magnetic Tape

A **magnetic tape** is a continuous plastic strip wound onto a reel, quite similar to the tape used in reel-to-reel audio recorders. The magnetic tape's plastic base is treated with an iron oxide coating that can be magnetized. Typically, the tape is one-half inch in width. It is wound in lengths from 400 to 3,200 feet. Some magnetic tapes are also packaged in plastic cartridges and cassettes for use with personal computers.

Data is stored on magnetic tape by magnetizing small spots of the iron oxide coating on the tape. Although these spots can be read (detected) by

FIGURE 6–1

**Computer System Utilizing
Secondary Storage Media**

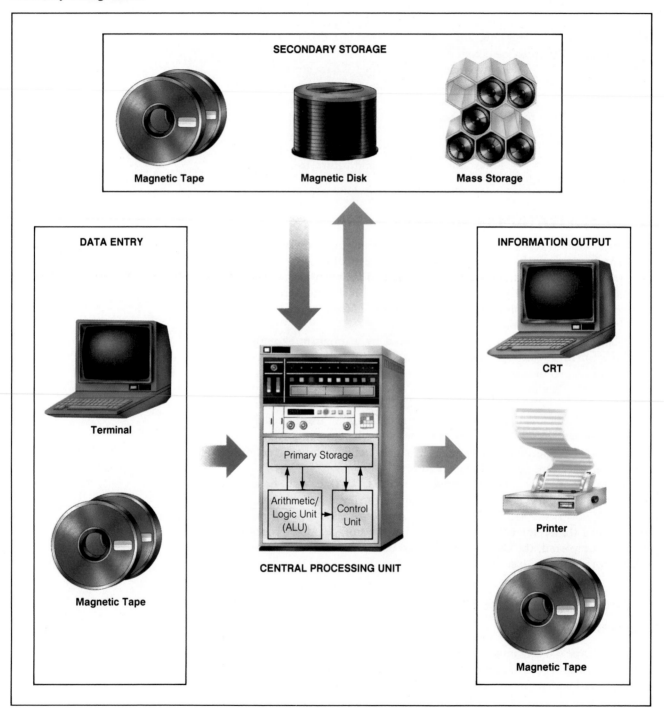

the computer, they are invisible to the human eye. Large volumes of information can be stored on a single tape; densities of 1,600 characters per inch are common, and some tapes can store up to 6,250 characters per inch. A typical tape reel 2,400 feet long can store as much data as 24,000 pages of doubled-spaced text, while costing only $20 to $30.

The most common method of representing data on magnetic tape uses a nine-track coding scheme, although other coding schemes are also used. When the nine-track method is used, the tape is divided into nine horizontal rows called **tracks** (see Figure 6–2). Data is represented vertically in columns, one character per column. This method of coding is identical to the Extended Binary Coded Decimal Interchange Code (EBCDIC) used to represent data in primary storage. In this way, eight bits and eight of the nine tracks are used to represent each character. The ninth bit and ninth track function as a parity bit.

A magnetic tape is mounted on a **tape drive** when a program needs the data it contains (see Figure 6–3). The tape drive has a **read/write head** (which is actually an electromagnet) that creates or detects the magnetized bits as the tape moves past it (see Figure 6–4). When the read/write head is reading data, it detects the magnetized spots and converts them into electrical pulses

FIGURE 6–2

Nine-Track Tape with Even Parity

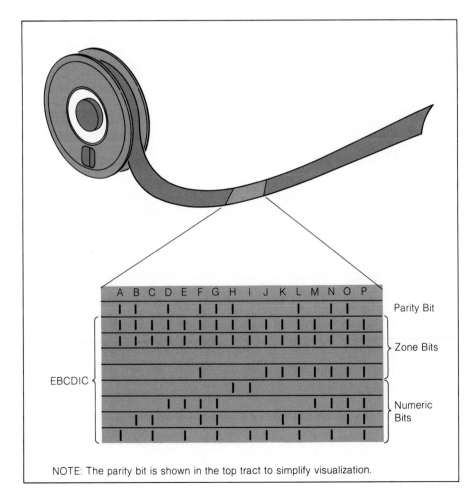

NOTE: The parity bit is shown in the top tract to simplify visualization.

FIGURE 6–3

Magnetic Tape Drive

FIGURE 6–4

Recording on Magnetic Tape

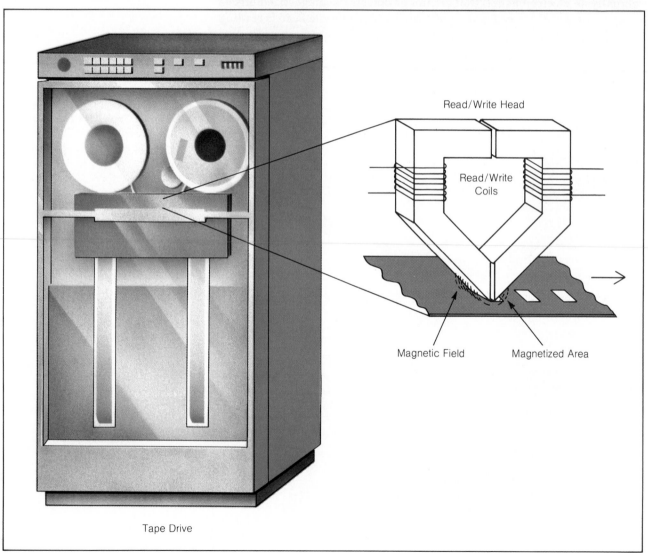

Read/Write Head

Read/Write Coils

Magnetic Field

Magnetized Area

Tape Drive

COMPUTERS AND INFORMATION PROCESSING

to send to the CPU. When writing data, the head magnetizes the appropriate spots on the tape, while erasing any data stored there previously.

Individual records on magnetic tape are separated by **interrecord gaps (IRGs),** as shown in Figure 6–5. These gaps do not contain data but they perform a specific function. When a tape is being read, its entire contents are rarely read all at once. Rather, it is stopped when the end of a record is reached. The tape must then be accelerated to the proper speed before the next record can be read accurately. If this were not the case, the result would be similar to what happens when a phonograph record is played at the wrong speed. The IRG gives the tape time to regain the proper speed before the next record is read. The length of the IRG depends on the speed of the tape drive. If the tape drive is very fast, longer gaps are needed. A slower tape drive requires shorter gaps.

If the records stored on a tape are very short and the IRGs are long, it would be possible for the tape to be more than 50 percent blank, causing the tape drive to stop and accelerate constantly. To avoid this situation, records may be grouped, or blocked, together. These **blocked records,** or **blocks,** are separated by **interblock gaps (IBGs)** as shown in Figure 6–6. Instead of reading a short record and stopping, then reading another short record and stopping, the read/write head reads a block of records at one time and stops, then reads another block and stops, and so forth. Using the interblock gap method of reading data has two advantages over the interrecord gap method:

1. The amount of storage available on the tape is used more efficiently.
2. The number of read/write operations required is significantly reduced, which makes the use of computer time more efficient.

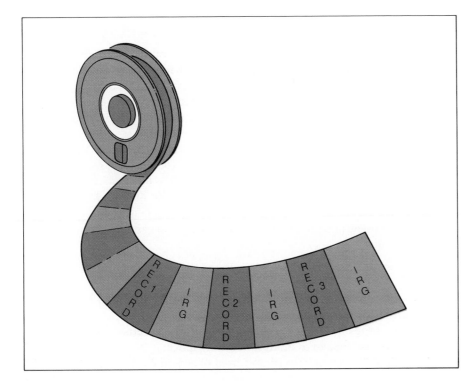

FIGURE 6–5

Magnetic Tape with Interrecord Gaps

FIGURE 6–6

Magnetic Tape with Interblock Gaps

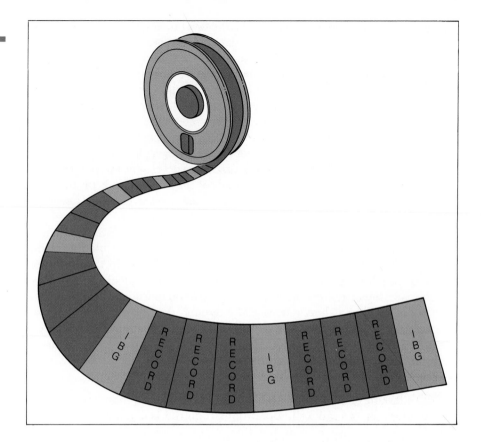

Cassette Tape

Small computer systems may not need a large amount of secondary storage. For these systems, **tape cassettes** and tape cartridges have been developed. Tape cassettes look like those used in audio recording; some can even be used with a typical cassette player. The major difference between the two types of cassettes is the tape itself: cassettes used for storing data have a high-quality digital recording tape (see Figure 6–7).

The recording densities for tape cassettes range between 125 and 200 characters per inch. They are usually between 150 and 200 feet long. Tape cartridges, on the other hand, can store from 200 to 800 characters per inch and they are available in standard lengths of 300, 450, and 555 feet (see Figure 6–8).

The advantages of using magnetic tape as a means of data storage include the following:

■ Data can be transferred between magnetic tape and the CPU at high speeds.

■ Magnetic tape records can be any length (unlike punched cards, which are usually limited to eighty characters).

■ Magnetic tapes have high recording densities; therefore they can store a large amount of data in a small amount of space.

■ Magnetic tape can be erased and used over and over again.

FIGURE 6—7

Tape Cassette Used for Data Storage

■ Magnetic tape provides high-capacity storage and backup storage at a relatively low cost.

■ Magnetic tape is perfectly suited for sequential processing (explained in Chapter 7). It is the most common storage medium for systems utilizing sequential processing.

Use of magnetic tape has the following disadvantages:

■ Magnetic tape is a sequential medium, which means the entire tape must be read from beginning to end when changes are made in the data. The

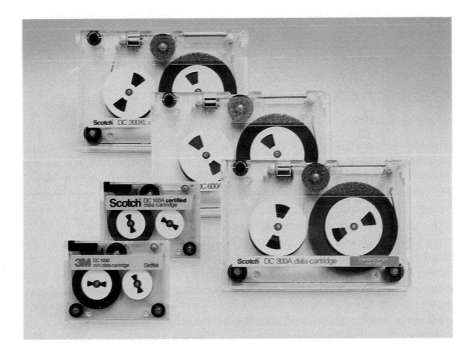

FIGURE 6—8

Tape Cartridge Used for Data Storage

amount of time required to retrieve data precludes its use when instantaneous retrieval is required.

■ All tape and reel containers must be properly labeled to identify the contents.

■ The data on the tape must be printed in order for humans to read the data.

■ Environmental factors can distort data stored on magnetic tape. Dust, moisture, extreme heat or cold, and static electricity can alter the data. **Backup copies,** that is, second copies of original tapes, must be made to prevent data loss.

CONCEPT SUMMARY 6—1

Characteristics of Magnetic Tape		
Features	**Advantages**	**Disadvantages**
A continuous strip of plastic tape wound onto a reel	Transfers data between tape and the CPU rapidly	Data must be read sequentially
Tape is treated with a magnetizable iron oxide coating	Records can be any length	Tapes require proper labels for content identification
Data are represented as magnetized spots on the surface of the tape	Stores large amounts of data in a small space	Environmental factors can distort data stored on tape
Data are accessed sequentially	Erasable and reusable	Humans cannot read the data stored on tape
	Low-cost backup media	
	Well suited for sequential processing	

DIRECT-ACCESS MEDIA

Magnetic Disk

The conventional **magnetic disk** is a metal platter fourteen inches in diameter, coated on both sides with a magnetizable material such as iron oxide. In many respects, a magnetic disk resembles a phonograph record. However, it does not have grooves etched onto its surface like a phonograph record; the surface of a magnetic disk is smooth.

A magnetic disk does store and retrieve data in much the same fashion as a phonograph record is played. The disk is rotated while a read/write head is positioned above its magnetic surface. Instead of spiraling into the center of the disk as the needle does on a phonograph record, the read/write head stores and retrieves data in concentric circles. Each circle is referred to as a **track.** One track never touches another (see Figure 6–9). A typical disk has between 200 and 500 tracks per side.

In most disk storage devices, several disks are assembled to form a **disk pack** (see Figure 6–10). The disks are mounted on a central shaft. The in-

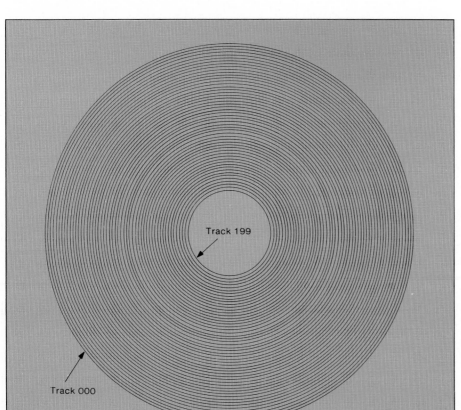

FIGURE 6—9

Top View of Disk Surface Showing
200 Concentric Tracks

Track 199

Track 000

dividual disks are spaced on the shaft to allow room for a read/write mechanism to move between them (see Figure 6–11). The disk pack in Figure
6–11 has eleven disks and provides twenty usable recording surfaces. The

FIGURE 6—10

Disk Pack

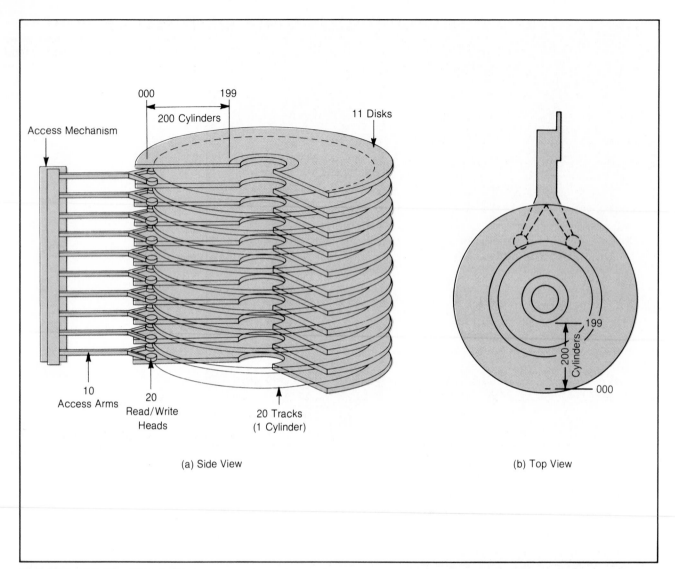

000   199

200 Cylinders

11 Disks

Access Mechanism

10
Access Arms

20
Read/Write
Heads

20 Tracks
(1 Cylinder)

199

200 Cylinders

000

(a) Side View

(b) Top View

FIGURE 6—11

**Side View (a) and Top View (b) of a
Disk Pack**

top and bottom surfaces are not used for storing data because they are likely to become scratched or nicked. A disk pack may contain anywhere from five to one hundred disks.

A disk pack is positioned in a disk drive when the data on the pack is to be processed. The **disk drive** rotates all disks in unison at speeds up to 3,600 revolutions per minute. In some models, the disk packs are removable; in others, the disks are permanently mounted on the disk drive. Removable disk packs allow disks to be removed when the data they contain is not needed (see Figure 6–12). Users of removable disk packs typically have many more disk packs than disk drives.

The data on a disk is read or written by the read/write heads located between the disks. Most disk units have one read/write head for each disk recording surface. All the heads are permanently connected to an **access mechanism.** When reading or writing occurs, the heads are positioned over

COMPUTERS AND INFORMATION PROCESSING

FIGURE 6–12

Disk Storage Units with Removable Disk Packs

the appropriate track by the in-and-out movements of the access mechanism.

When data stored on the surface of one disk in the disk pack is required, all heads move to the corresponding tracks on the surfaces of the other disks

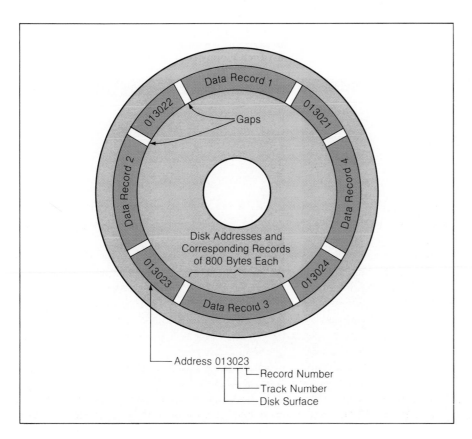

FIGURE 6–13

Disk Address

Gaps

013022

Data Record 1

013021

Data Record 2

Data Record 4

Disk Addresses and Corresponding Records of 800 Bytes Each

013023

013024

Data Record 3

Address 013023
Record Number
Track Number
Disk Surface

because they are connected to the same access mechanism. Since all the read/write heads move together, they are positioned over the same tracks on all disk surfaces at the same time. All the number-1 tracks on the disk surfaces form a **cylinder;** the number-2 tracks on all surfaces form another cylinder enclosed within the first; and so on (see Figure 6–11 again). The number of cylinders per disk pack equals the number of tracks per surface.

Some disk units have one read/write head for each track. The access time is much faster with this type of disk unit since the access mechanism does not move from track to track. Units such as this are rarely used because they are very expensive. The placement of data on the disk pack, therefore, can be an important factor if the amount of access time is critical. When access time is an important factor, it is best to store data that is accessed most frequently on the same or adjacent tracks of the disk surfaces. This will reduce the motion of the read/write heads and thus reduce the access time.

Each track on a disk can store the same amount of data even though the tracks get smaller toward the center of the disk. Consider a disk pack with 4,000 usable tracks (20 surfaces × 200 tracks per surface) on which 7,294 characters can be stored on each track. The disk pack could conceivably store 29,176,000 characters of data (4,000 tracks × 7,294 characters per track).

The computer locates data stored on a magnetic disk by its disk surface number, track number, and record number. The numbers make up the data's

FIGURE 6–14

Floppy Disks of 8 Inches and 5¼ Inches

FIGURE 6–15

3½ Inch Floppy Disk

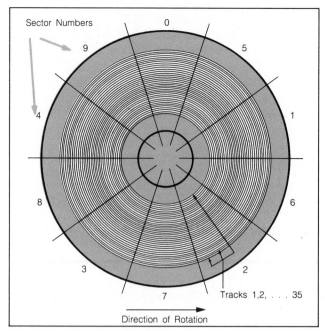

FIGURE 6-16

Sectors and Tracks on a Floppy Disk

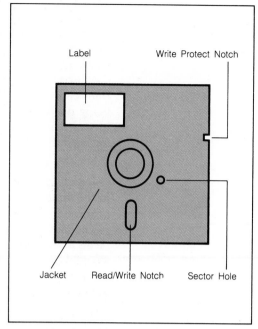

FIGURE 6-17

Parts of a Floppy Disk

disk address. The disk address of a record is stored immediately before the record (see Figure 6–13). Disk records are separated by gaps similar to the interrecord gaps on magnetic tape. Also similarly, the presence of gaps in each track reduces the amount of data that can be stored on a disk. Therefore, the usable storage capacity in the disk pack described in the previous paragraph would be slightly less than the potential 29,176,000 characters.

Since disks provide direct access, they are typically used to store data that is accessed frequently (direct-access systems are discussed in Chapter 7). Depending on the disk drive, it is possible for up to 850,000 characters to be read per second.

Floppy Disk

The **floppy disk, flexible disk,** or **diskette,** was introduced in 1973 to replace punched cards as a medium for data entry, but it can also store programs and data files. They come in varying sizes, including 8 inches, 5¼ inches, and 3½ inches, with the 5¼ being the most popular (see Figure 6–14). Micro floppy disks are about 3¼ inches square and are quickly becoming popular with microcomputer users (see Figure 6–15). Floppy disks are made of plastic and coated with a magnetizable oxide substance. In most respects, they are miniature magnetic disks. Since the diskettes are relatively inexpensive (some sell for less than $1.00), they are popular for use with microcomputer systems and point-of-sale terminals. They are reusable, easy to store, and weigh less than two ounces. Floppy disks can even be mailed. In addition, they can add security to a computer system because they can be removed and stored in a safe place.

Data is stored on a floppy disk as magnetized spots in tracks, as on conventional magnetic disks, and elements are addressed by track number and sector number (see Figure 6–16). The read/write head accesses the disk through the oblong or rectangular opening in the jacket, called the **read/write notch** (see Figure 6–17). The head moves back and forth to read the data or write data to the disk. Unlike the one used in hard disk systems, this read/write head actually rides on the surface of the disk rather than being positioned slightly above it. The disk rotates at a speed of 360 revolutions per minute (as compared to as many as 3,600 revolutions per minute for hard disk drives).

Magnetic disks have several advantages over magnetic tapes:

■ Disk files on magnetic disks can be organized sequentially and processed in the same way as magnetic tape, or they can be organized for direct-access processing.

■ The fast access time offered by magnetic disk storage allows data files to be accessed or changed immediately.

■ Quick response can be made to inquiries (normally, response is made in seconds).

■ With the appropriate software, a single transaction can simultaneously update or change several files stored on disks.

The major disadvantages of magnetic disk storage include the following:

■ Magnetic hard disks are a relatively expensive storage medium; their cost may be ten times that of magnetic tape in terms of cost per character stored. However, reductions in disk cost and the introduction of floppy disks are making these storage devices more affordable.

■ When data stored on a disk is changed, the original data is erased and the new data is stored in its place. Therefore, magnetic disks do not provide backup files. Data can be lost if there are inadequate provisions for error checking and backup files.

CONCEPT SUMMARY 6–2

Characteristics of Magnetic Disks

Features	Advantages	Disadvantages
A metal platter coated on both sides with a magnetizable material	Files can be organized for sequential or direct-access storage	More expensive than magnetic tape
Data are represented as magnetized spots on the surface of the disk	Data can be accessed immediately	Requires backup files so data is not lost when changes are made
Disks come in varying sizes	Files can be altered simultaneously	Requires complex programming to gain access to files
		Easy access to data may pose security problems

■ Disk storage requires more complicated programming to gain access to records and to update files. The technicians who maintain the highly complicated hardware must be highly skilled.

■ The ease of gaining access to data stored on disk files can create security problems.

MASS STORAGE

As stated earlier, accessing data and instructions from primary storage is very fast because it requires no physical movement of hardware devices. The speed of electricity is, in effect, the only limiting factor. However, the capacity of primary storage is limited and also very expensive. Disk storage is less expensive and provides direct-access capabilities, but even disk storage tends to be expensive when very large amounts of data must be stored for direct-access processing.

To meet the need for a low-cost method of storing vast amounts of data, mass storage devices have been developed. They allow rapid access to data. Large files, backup files, and infrequently used files can be placed in mass storage at a relatively low cost.

One type of mass storage uses a cartridge tape as the storage medium (see Figure 6–18). The cartridges are similar to cassette tapes and permit sequential access of data. The high-density tape used requires 90 percent less storage space than common magnetic tapes. A mass storage system such as this can hold the equivalent of up to 1,000 tape reels. Tape mounting is controlled by the system, rather than by a human operator, and tends to be much faster than the traditional operator-controlled mounting of magnetic tapes.

Mass storage is not limited to high-density magnetic tape. A mass storage system for minicomputers using small floppy disks as the storage medium

FIGURE 6—18

A Mass Storage Device Using Cartridge Tape

HIGHLIGHT

Move Over, Magnetic Media

Until recently, organizations have been reluctant to use optical disk storage. Although optical disks can store much more data in a smaller space than magnetic media, companies are leery of the new medium. New developments may now increase the use of optical disks.

Initially, optical disks were slower than magnetic media for accessing information. Now information is placed on recording film called "digital paper" (a phrase coined by ICI Electronics). The medium can retrieve data as quickly as magnetic media, and ICI says it is cheaper than even regular paper for storing data. Another advantage of optical disks is that they accurately store data for fifteen to twenty years. The data on magnetic media may not last even ten years.

Although optical disks are still not erasable, the new advances make this data-storage method attractive to organizations that need to store historical data; it is a low-cost method of large-volume storage. Organizations such as government offices may soon be transferring their archival data to optical disks.

has been introduced. However, unlike the cartridge system described above, most mass storage systems such as this require extensive physical movement because the needed files must first be found and then mounted (or loaded) mechanically before data can be read or written. Although direct access is possible, the retrieval time is relatively slow (although still measured in seconds) compared to systems utilizing magnetic tapes and disks.

TRENDS IN DATA STORAGE

Charge-Coupled Devices

As technology continues to advance, smaller, faster, and less-expensive storage devices will become commonplace. Advances are rapidly being made in semiconductor and laser technology. An innovation in semiconductor technology is the development of **charge-coupled devices (CCDs)** for use in data storage. CCDs are made of silicon similar to semiconductor memory. They are nearly 100 times faster than magnetic bubble memory but are somewhat slower than semiconductor RAM. As in semiconductor memories, data in CCDs can be lost if a power failure occurs. CCDs are used primarily with large computer systems such as minicomputers and mainframes.

Laser Technology

Laser technology provides an opportunity to store mass quantities of data at greatly reduced costs. A **laser storage system** can store nearly 128 billion characters of data at about one-tenth the cost of standard magnetic media. In a laser storage system, data is recorded when a laser beam forms patterns on the surface of a polyester sheet coated with a thin layer of rhodium metal. To read data from this sheet, the laser reflects light off the surface, reconstructing the data into a digital bit stream. Data stored by laser resists alterations and any attempt to change it can easily be detected. Therefore, it provides a very secure storage system. In addition, unlike magnetic media, laser storage does not deteriorate over time and it is immune to electromagnetic radiation. Another advantage is that there is no danger of losing data as a result of power failures.

A more recent development is a laser system used as a mass storage device for minicomputers. This system uses a helium-neon laser, delivering about ten milliwatts of optical power to a disk coated with a film of a nonmetallic substance called tellurium. Data is recorded when the laser creates a hole approximately one micrometer in diameter in the film. The disk used in this system is thirty centimeters in diameter and can store ten billion bits on its 40,000 tracks. The data cannot be erased once it is written, so this system is best suited for archival storage purposes.

Another development in laser technology is the optical, or laser, disk (see Figure 6–19). **Optical disks** are much faster than hard disks but are still fairly slow compared to semiconductor RAM. One big advantage, though, is their large capacity. A single optical disk can hold more than 600 megabytes of data. That is over 225,000 pages of manuscript, or the entire contents of the *Encyclopedia Britannica* with space left over. Bits of data are stored on an optical disk as the presence or absence of a tiny pit burned into the disk by a pinpoint laser beam. A single line one inch long contains about 5,000 pits, or bits of data.

FIGURE 6—19

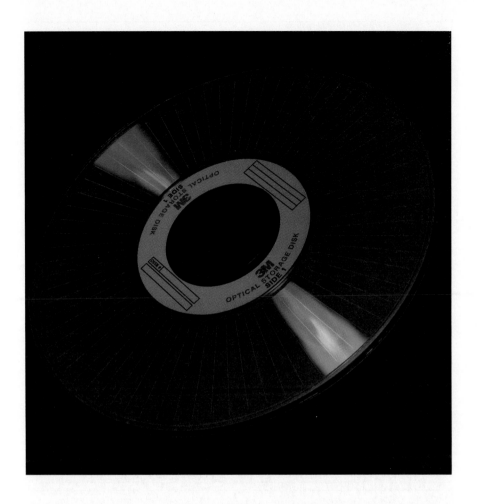

Optical Disk

FIGURE 6—20

RAM Disk Chip

What's All the Hype?

Computers themselves are very powerful tools. But combine computers with interactive videos, slides, stereo music, and a vast amount of data storage and you have—hypermedia. Hypermedia uses optical disks to store not only large amounts of text, but the other data, such as videos, as well. Most hypermedia systems require two video monitors, a computer keyboard, and a mouse. The user employs the keyboard and mouse to access the stored data in any order desired. So far universities are the main users of hypermedia.

For example, Apple Computer's HyperCard, used on a Macintosh, has a system called Slice of Life. It is used at the University of Utah to teach brain anatomy. The student can read text about the brain while at the same time viewing any of the 22,000 images on file.

In addition, medical students can review the actual case studies of patients. Another medical system, used at Cornell University Medical College, allows the student to view an organ such as a liver on one screen and then view a diseased organ for comparison on the second screen. If surgery is required, the student can watch a video of surgeons performing the necessary operation.

Hypermedia is used in many areas other than medicine. In history classes the system not only provides text about the era, it also plays music and talk shows, displays still photography, and presents TV news programs, all from the era the student is studying.

Many businesses have not yet explored the possibilities of hypermedia but it can be used there as well. Imagine a travel video that allows the user to hear the waves on the beach and actually see the different hotel options.

The hardware for a hypermedia system, sometimes called compact disc interactive (CD-I) or interactive multimedia, costs about $3,000. Some manufacturers such as Sony and Philips hope to develop a system that will connect to a regular TV, so that only one monitor would be needed. This could lower the cost to less than $1,000. Hypermedia may soon be as common as TV.

RAM Disks

Accessing data on disks is relatively slow compared to the speed at which a microprocessor can manipulate data. **Random-access memory (RAM) disks** are currently the only type of storage device that can approximate the speed of a microprocessor. A new peripheral device using RAM chips is now available (see Figure 6–20). A RAM card that contains RAM chips plugs into the computer in the same slot as the disk drive card. The computer treats the RAM card just as it does a disk drive. Even though RAM disks are not separate physical disks, they function like regular diskettes. A RAM disk instructs the computer to set aside storage space in RAM to function like a disk. A typical RAM disk used with a microcomputer stores up to 265K of data and has a retrieval rate fifty times faster than a floppy disk.

The advantage of using RAM disks is speed. Data stored in RAM can be transferred from one part of RAM to another faster than it can be transferred from a disk to RAM. The disadvantage of RAM disks is that they require a continuous power supply. As with any internal memory, when the power supply is discontinued, data is erased from memory. However, some manufacturers provide battery backup units for use with RAM disks in case of power failure.

Compact Disks

Compact disks (CDs), the type used for high quality audio recordings, are now being used as a storage medium for microcomputers. These 4¾ inch disks can store about 1,000 times more bytes than a single-sided floppy disk. Although the retrieval time of compact disks is slower than magnetic media, CDs are effective in searching data bases to locate data. Because they can store large amounts of data, they are often used in customer service areas. Travel agencies can now store mass amounts of data about hotels and resorts on CDs instead of in travel books. Furthermore, the disks store pictures as well.

Considering the advantages of CDs, why aren't more companies using them? One reason is that a compact disk system requires a large investment of time and money. Correctly structuring the data base is critical and time consuming. Some professionals say it can take nearly two years to get a CD system operative. Because CDs are not erasable, companies must develop a prototype of a disk and test it before it can be used. This process is very costly; a company must plan to spend at least $100,000 to get a CD system running.

Another disadvantage of CDs is the fact that they are not erasable. Presently CDs come in two forms: ROM (Read Only Memory) and WORM (Write Once Read Many). The information on CD-ROM is placed on the CD when it is manufactured. A company buying a CD-ROM uses it to access information, but cannot place information on the disk. In the case of CD-WORM, a company can place information on the CD, but it is a permanent copy. Therefore, CDs are used for information that does not change often. For example, some companies are using CDs for new employee orientations. In the near future erasable CDs may be developed; they will have a greater impact on how data is stored.

Josephson Junction

The **Josephson junction** is a form of primary storage named for Brian Josephson, a British Nobel Prize winner. Josephson junctions are in an early stage of development. When the technology for these devices is perfected, the speed at which primary storage operates is estimated to increase tenfold. Current semiconductor memory is slower than that proposed with Josephson junctions because of the environment in which a semiconductor is housed. By surrounding its circuits in liquid helium, the Josephson junction will eliminate the resistance to the flow of electricity that exists in semiconductor memory. The use of the Josephson junction, along with other technological advances, is expected to lead to further reduction in the size of computer hardware.

Superconductors

Superconductors are metals that are capable of transmitting high levels of current. Until recently superconductors have been impractical for most applications because they have a very limiting quality; they can only be used in extremely cold environments. In 1911, when superconductors were first discovered, they had to be cooled to almost absolute zero, which is

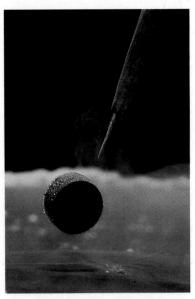

FIGURE 6—21

Superconductivity
Some scientists feel supercomputers may be reduced to the size of microcomputers once superconductors are perfected.

−459°F. Since 1986, however, scientists have made great progress in developing superconductors. A superconductor compound that contains bismuth can function at −243°F. Scientists feel they will continue to discover superconductors that can function at even warmer temperatures.

Why all the excitement about superconductors? Scientists and businesses feel superconductors will have a major impact on technology. For example, once superconductors are perfected some scientists feel supercomputers will no longer be so large they fill a room; instead, they may be reduced to about the size of a minicomputer! (see Figure 6–21).

Technology advances so rapidly that accurate predictions of what future storage media will be like is nearly impossible. Even though the state of the art changes from day to day, the objectives of making storage less expensive, faster, and more compact will continue to be pursued.

▨ SUMMARY POINTS

■ Secondary storage, which is not part of the CPU, can store large amounts of data and instructions at a lower cost than primary storage. The most common secondary storage media are magnetic tapes and magnetic disks.

■ Magnetic tape consists of a plastic base coated with iron oxide. Data is stored as small magnetized areas on the surface of the tape.

■ Records are separated on magnetic tape by interrecord gaps (IRGs). When the tape is stopped while reading records, these gaps allow the tape to regain the proper speed before the next record is read.

■ Data is often recorded on magnetic tape in groups of records called blocks. Blocks are separated from each other by interblock gaps (IBGs). Blocking reduces overall input/output time and also makes more efficient use of available storage.

■ Tape cassettes are similar to audio cassettes. They can store up to 200 characters per inch and are used when small amounts of storage are required.

■ Magnetic disks provide direct access to data. Any record can be located by referring to its address—disk surface number, track number, and record number.

■ A disk pack is positioned on a disk drive, which rotates all disks in the pack in unison. Some disk packs are removable; others are permanently mounted on disk drives.

■ Floppy, or flexible, disks provide low-cost, direct-access storage. Floppy disks are easy to store and are frequently used with minicomputers and microcomputers.

■ Mass storage devices are appropriate when large amounts of data must be stored at low costs. Commonly used mass storage media are cassette and cartridge tapes and floppy disks. Floppy disk mass storage devices provide direct access, but the retrieval time is much slower than with standard disk storage.

■ Compact disks are an excellent form of storage for data base retrieval, but the medium is used by few companies because the initial investment of a CD system is expensive and it is difficult to develop an appropriate data base.

■ Optical disks allow faster access to data than hard disks, but they provide fairly slow data retrieval compared to RAM. The advantage of optical disks as a storage medium is their storage capacity.

■ A RAM disk is an area of RAM that temporarily functions like a storage diskette.

■ Josephson junction technology allows primary memory to be housed in liquid helium to eliminate the resistance to the flow of electricity in semi-conductor memory.

■ REVIEW QUESTIONS

1. Distinguish between primary and secondary storage. Name three common secondary storage devices.

2. What is the function of interrecord gaps (IRGs) in magnetic tape storage?

3. Explain the purpose of blocking records with an interblock gap (IBG).

4. What is a disk pack?

5. Name the three components of a record's disk address.

6. Discuss the advantages and disadvantages of magnetic tape storage.

7. Discuss the advantages and disadvantages of magnetic disk storage.

8. Describe two types of mass storage devices.

9. Explain how a laser storage system stores data. What is the main advantage of a laser storage system?

10. What are the advantages and disadvantages of using compact disks for data storage?

American Airlines

The first regularly scheduled flight of what was to become American Airlines was made on April 15, 1926, when Charles Lindbergh flew the mail in a biplane from St. Louis to Chicago as chief pilot for the Robertson Company. Between 1929 and 1930, 85 small airline companies, including Robertson, were consolidated into an airline called American Airways, forerunner of today's American Airlines. In 1933, American introduced the first U.S. sleeper plane, the 18-passenger Curtice Condor, marking the debut of flight attendants on board. In 1934, the company formally reorganized with the current American Airlines and rapidly expanded air travel throughout the United States.

In the forties, American entered the airline catering business through a subsidiary called Sky Chefs and became the first airline to modernize with an all postwar fleet. In the fifties, American pioneered nonstop transcontinental service and built the world's first special facility for flight attendants in Dallas-Fort Worth. In the sixties, teaming with IBM, American introduced SABRE, the largest electronic data processing system designed for business use. Throughout the seventies and eighties, American has introduced revolutionary marketing programs and thoroughly upgraded its fleet with major acquisitions of new model Boeing 757 and 767 aircraft.

Today American Airlines is an international air carrier. With over 50,000 employees, American has been rapidly expanding its base of operations through merger agreements domestically and increased route service overseas. With yearly passenger revenue in excess of $5 billion, American has established itself as a major factor in the future of airline transportation.

American's first step at automating the reservation process came in 1952 with a device known as The Magnetronic Reservisor . . . in essence a computerized blackboard. By 1962, American and IBM had linked the electronic blackboard to the telephone with a computer system called "Semi-Automated Business Research Environment"—SABRE. In 1976 American introduced a version of SABRE tailored specifically for travel agents. In the late 1970s, SABRE was used to develop American's sophisticated yield management system which predicts booking trends on specific flights and maximizes airline passenger revenue. SABRE also handles the reservations functions of many other airlines as well as other operational functions for American.

SABRE is the world's largest privately owned real time computer network. It is driven by five large IBM mainframe computers running at the same time (TANDEM) at American's central processing site near Tulsa, Oklahoma. Today, nearly half of all U.S. air travel is booked through SABRE and more than 95 percent of U.S. travel agencies are automated.

Professional SABRE, used by the travel agent, is the most comprehensive system. It can be linked electronically to Agency Data Systems (ADS), which is a powerful accounting and office management system. Another software service available is CAPTURE, which gives a company positive control of its travel and entertainment expenses and greatly simplifies its expense accounting.

Companies that want to manage their own travel arrangements but do not need all of SABRE's features can use a subset, manual Commercial SABRE. With this program, a company can use an ordinary personal computer or terminal to make arrangements for air

travel, hotels, and rental cars. Finally, a smaller subset yet is available for individuals called EAASY SABRE and may be accessed through several different services.

SABRE FACTS

Subscribers: More than 15,000 locations with more than 80,000 terminals.

Peak Hour Usage: 1,651 messages per second

Peak Day Usage: 57.8 million messages

Fares in Data Base: 32.5 million

Fare Changes Entered Daily: Up to 1,550,000

Airlines with Schedules in Data Base: 650

Hotel Properties: More than 16,000

Rental Car Companies: 39

SABRE also plays a major role in American Airlines operations. The system tracks more than 8,500 items on each airplane and maintains inventory control on more than 250 million spare parts. The computer calculates flight plans, weight and balance, fuel requirements, and takeoff power settings for more than 2,000 flights per day. The system also handles all aircraft and crew scheduling, while tracking baggage and freight.

The data bases required to support such wide-scale operations are extremely large. SABRE has divided its data structures into five physical environments. The Passenger Service System (PSS) is the heart of the operation and provides the booking services. It utilizes 224 IBM 3380s [each capable of storing 2.5 billion bytes or gigabytes (GB)]. This data is stored in a com-

plete backup mode, thereby allocating half the drive for duplicate data. This current storage capacity of 550 GB will be increased by over 50 percent during the next year.

The Flight Operating System FOS maintains flight plan generation and scheduled maintenance. This subsystem uses 40 IBM 3380 F-series (each capable of storing 5 GB) providing over 200 gigabytes of online storage. The Commercial System providing airline accounting, payroll, and parts tracking utilizes a continuation of storage devices permitting 650 gigabytes. The remaining two environments are for software development and communication and require around 300 gigabytes.

The responsibility of maintaining such a large online data base requires extensive hardware and operational support. American Airlines has designed and implemented one of the largest communication networks in the world. Massive data storage with redundant backup is essential to maintain the performance expected and required by the users.

DISCUSSION POINTS

1. Explain how SABRE operates as a management information system rather than merely a reservation system.

2. What special concerns must be addressed for SABRE to support independent travel agents and other airline bookings?

CHAPTER

7

File Organization and Data Base Design

O U T L I N E

Introduction
File Processing
Methods of File Access
  Batch File Access
  Online File Access
File Designs
  Sequential File Design
  Direct-Access File Design
  Indexed-Sequential File Design

Data Bases
  Structuring Data
  Data-Base Management Systems
  Assessment of the Data-Base
    Approach

Summary Points
Review Questions

It's Grab-Your-Partner Time for Software Makers

Richard Brandt
Business Week

It was a jolt in mid-January when two of the Big Three in personal computer software, Microsoft and Ashton-Tate, teamed up with minicomputer software maker Sybase on a key product. Each company had decided not to go it alone in pursuing one of the most important software developments of the 1990s: a way to run so-called relational data base programs using personal computers. The three expect to have a product ready late this year. And they hope their reputations as software power-houses will make it a product that dominates its market so quickly that other competitors withdraw.

It's a goal that, suddenly, everyone has. Since last November, three other alliances between microcomputer and minicomputer companies have been announced, all aimed at cornering the same market. And Lotus Development Corp., the No. 2 personal computer software maker, is expected to announce a project next month with Gupta Technologies Inc. in Menlo Park, Calif., to design a product much like the one the Microsoft group is working on. Says Paul V. Cubbage, an analyst with market research Dataquest Inc.: "It's gonna be a real dogfight."

Relational data-base programs, which have been on the market for a decade, make it much simpler for professional computer operators to find information stored in a data base that's sitting in a mainframe or minicomputer. But with the proliferation of personal computers in the office, companies want more of their employees to use the corporate data bases. The trick is to link all these personal computers to the mainframes and minis with a program that lets non-professional computer operators work with the relational data bases.

These days no major company can function without data-base systems. Increasingly, manager base major decisions on information stored in them: United Parcel Service uses a data-base program to plan its flight schedules, for instance. Indeed, U.S. sales of data-base programs should jump 19% this year, to $1.4 billion, according to Dataquest, and at least 70% of programs sold will be relational products.

NO CINCH. Only a decade ago, working with a data-base program could be an excruciating exercise. It meant going through a series of rigidly defined steps. The process became simpler in the late 1970s, when an International Business Machines Corp. researcher came up with the relational model for data bases. Essentially, it cross-references information so completely that a single computer command can generally track down a piece of information. This technology also created a market for a new kind of software company. With the rise of minicomputers in the mid-1970s as a cheap alternative to mainframes, a cluster of startups developed relational systems for the new machines. Thanks partly to slick marketing, Oracle Corp. in Belmont, Calif., emerged the leader. Its sales should double to about $270 million for the fiscal year ending May 31.

Now the cycle is occurring again—with personal computers. Just as minicomputers took over some jobs of mainframes, local area networks of personal computers are taking over some functions of minicomputers. A key step in hastening this process is writing bridges between microcomputer applications programs, such as spreadsheets or word processing packages, and the increasingly popular relational data bases that run either on a minicomputer or a specially outfitted microcomputer.

It's the effort to achieve this that's prompting the new alliances. Consider the Microsoft-Sybase-Ashton-Tate group. It's adapting Sybase's relational data base to make it easier to use through a personal computer. And it's developing so-called software tools that other microcomputer software developers can use to adapt applications programs so they communicate with Sybase's revised data-base product. Says Ashton-Tate Chief Executive Edward M. Esber: "We can create a standard."

That won't be a cinch. By yearend, IBM will have a

A R T I C L E

competing data base for its PS/2 computer to link to DB2, its relational data base for mainframes. Then there's next month's anticipated announcement from Lotus. Some experts speculate that the company will work with IBM to adapt the popular 1-2-3 spreadsheet program to work with IBM's data-base software. And last November, Informix Corp. bought its own microcomputer software company, Innovative Software Inc., to create personal computer programs that will work with its minicomputer relational data base.

TIME WILL TELL. Other alliances aim at more than IBM's personal computers. Relational Technology Inc. is working with Sun Microsystems Inc. to create a data-base standard for

workstations. And last summer, Apple Computer Inc. bought 5% of Sybase, which is developing a data-base program for the Macintosh. With so many alliances, says Sybase marketing Vice-President Stewart A. Schuster, "this is marketing warfare."

One exception to the joint-venture trend is Oracle. Leveraging off its installed base of 50,000 programs and its strong presence in the market for Digital Equipment Corp. minicomputers, Oracle is trying to set its own data-base standard for personal computers. It is selling a scaled-down version of its program for micros. Moreover, in January it announced a program that will let 1-2-3 work with Oracle's data base. Another version, due this quarter, will work with WordPerfect Corp.'s word processing program.

Most analysts expect it to be a couple of years before a market leader emerges. There may even be three competing standards: Oracle, IBM, and Microsoft/ Ashton-Tate/Sybase. Indeed, this is one market that no one's going to relinquish without a grueling battle.

Companies cannot function without data bases, so the marketing prospects for a good PC data base are excellent. Yet developing relational data bases for microcomputers is very complex. Some companies are joining forces with competitors in order to develop the best product and therefore eliminate competitors.

■■ INTRODUCTION

C H A P T E R

7

All organizations maintain a wide variety of files containing data about employees, customers, inventory levels, production, sales, and other information pertinent to the firm. An organization's method of processing this data is determined largely by its information needs. Does new data need to be processed immediately, or can data be held and grouped and processed at a later time? The structure of the organization's files is also based on its information needs; file structures can minimize overall processing time and increase processing efficiency.

This chapter examines three types of file arrangement, or data design: sequential, direct-access, and indexed-sequential. It discusses the characteristics of each method and offers representative applications of these methods to illustrate how they are used. The chapter also explains the concept of a data base and describes how it uses physical and logical data design.

■ FILE PROCESSING

File processing is the activity of updating permanent files to thoroughly reflect any changes in data. Files can be organized in several ways, with or without a computerized system. Without computers, files must be recorded on paper and updated manually. Some companies do not need their file system computerized in order to be efficient; perhaps the small amount of paperwork they have would not justify the cost of computer hardware and software. In other companies, however, a computerized system could increase efficiency and profits. For example, consider the case of American Sporting Goods, a small supplier of sports equipment. The company carries an inventory of 110 items, supplies equipment to thirty customers and maintains a staff of twenty employees. All of American Sporting Goods' records are kept on paper, and transactions are recorded manually.

Every time a customer places an order, a clerk must prepare a sales order. The customer's file is checked to obtain all necessary data about the customer, such as billing address, shipping address, and credit status. The clerk fills in the type and quantity of item ordered, and the sales order is sent to the warehouse where the inventory is stored. At the warehouse, an employee determines if the requested items are available. To do this, the employee must actually count the number of items in stock. If the items are available, they can be packaged and prepared for shipping. If the order cannot be filled, the employee must prepare a backorder. The sales order is sent on to the accounting department, where the customer's bill is prepared. In the accounting department, a clerk checks the company catalog to determine the current cost of each item on the order. The total bill is calculated, including tax and shipping charges. The total amount is recorded on the customer's record, and the order is then shipped.

Even this simplified transaction includes many time-consuming activities. In addition to handling customer orders, the company must prepare monthly payrolls, sales reports, purchase orders to replenish inventory supplies, and many other types of records. The American Sporting Goods Company could save time and money by computerizing its activities.

Several computerized files could be designed to facilitate American Sporting Goods' operations. An employee file could be set up containing records of each employee. An employee record might contain the employee's home address, social security number, company identification number, hourly wage, withholding tax bracket, and gross income. In order for this data to be used in a variety of ways by several departments, it must be stored in a file accessible by all departments that require the data. Figure 7–1 shows a portion of an employee file and reintroduces several terms useful in a discussion of data design. Recall from Chapter 1 that a field is one data item, a record is a group of data items related to a single unit, and a file is a group of related records.

The company could also use an inventory file with one record for each item carried in inventory. Each record could contain a description of the item, its cost, the quantity in stock, and information about the manufacturer of the item. Finally, a customer file containing fields such as billing and shipping addresses, current balance due, and credit status would be useful.

Each of these files would be accessed, or read, in different ways. For example, the entire employee file would be read every time the payroll was prepared. The inventory file, however, would only need to be accessed one

Laying Down the Law

After the patrolmen pulled over a speeder, they called the driver's license number in to their office where a computerized data base was used to check for outstanding warrants. They found that the woman was wanted in several states. Computers have been used for a number of years to help fight and solve crimes. The FBI has a data base that maintains the criminal histories of lawbreakers. It is called the National Crime Information Center (NCIC). States and local communities also maintain data bases not only of histories, but of current warrants.

A new data-base system developed by Microrim is used in forensic dentistry. The data base contains the dental charts of hundreds of missing people. If remains are found, the system is used to help identify the victim. This system can also be used to identify victims of disasters such as plane crashes and floods.

Although computers have greatly aided crime solving, such systems do have drawbacks. First, if incorrect data is entered into the computer, the police may arrest the wrong person. For example, a man from Los Angeles was arrested five times because of inaccurate information in a criminal data base. Other people are concerned about what type of information will be recorded in the data bases and who will have access to the information. Some people feel that maintaining files on criminals and alleged criminals is an invasion of privacy.

Computer data bases are effective tools for solving crimes. Yet they can also contain confidential information. They should only be accessed by authorized personnel and only be used for crime solving purposes.

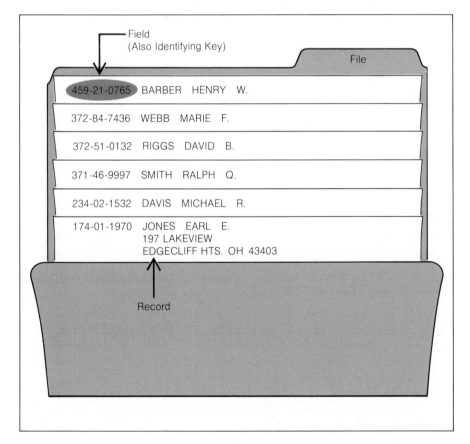

FIGURE 7–1

Employee File for the American Sporting Goods Company

record at a time; that is, only one record would be read each time an order was placed for a certain item. The customer file would be accessed in two ways. When a customer placed an order, only the record containing the data about the customer would be read. The entire file would be read each time the American Sporting Goods Company prepared customer bills or needed a report on overdue accounts.

▓ METHODS OF FILE ACCESS

Two important considerations in determining the best file design for an organization are how quickly data must be processed and the manner in which data will be retrieved. An organization must consider these factors when determining whether to use batch file access or online file access.

Batch File Access

With **batch file access,** all transactions to be processed are gathered for a certain period of time and then processed all at once. The length of time during which transactions are gathered before processing may be one work shift (eight hours), one calendar day (twenty-four hours), or any other logical time period dictated by the information needs of the user.

Batch file access is most useful when current information is needed only at set times, rather than at all times. For example, student grades can be processed at the end of a term or employee payrolls at the end of a pay period.

Online File Access

Online file access provides the ability to retrieve current information at any time. Each time a transaction occurs, the affected records are simultaneously updated. Online file access is often used for inventory control, airline reservations, and banking transactions.

▓ FILE DESIGNS

A computer file can be arranged in a number of ways. Generally, file arrangement depends upon the method used to access the file. If the information in the file is retrieved by batch file access, then the best file design may be sequential. If the file will be accessed online, a direct-access file design or indexed-sequential file design must be used.

Sequential File Design

If a particular record must be found in a file and the number of records in the file is very small, then it may not be difficult to search the file from beginning to end to find the desired record. For files containing large numbers of records, however, this method is inefficient. A special ordering technique is needed so that records can be retrieved more easily. For this reason, records may be arranged according to a **key** value. The key is one data field chosen to identify the record. Since a key is used to locate a particular record, it must be unique; that is, no two records in a file can have the same key value. In Figure 7–1, the social security number field is used as the key. Social security numbers are excellent keys for employee records because no two people in the United States have the same number. An employee record is located by searching for the appropriate value in the social security field. The key value in an inventory file could be the item number. When records are ordered according to their key values, a **sequential file** is formed.

Updating a sequential file involves two sets of files: the master file and transaction file. The **master file** is the file containing all existing records. The **transaction file** is the file containing the changes to be made to the master. During the updating process a third file, the new master file, is created.

Before updating begins, the old master file must be in sequential order according to the key field. The transaction file should then be sorted on the same key as the master file. The computer compares the key of the first master file record with the key from the first record in the transaction file. If the keys do not match, the computer writes the record to the new master file as is, and then it reads the next record on the master file. When a match between the master and transaction records occurs, the computer updates the master record. Sometimes if a transaction record has no matching master record, the computer may generate an error message.

Some transactions may add a new record, while others may delete an existing record. Since records are stored one after another on a sequential file, these types of transactions cannot be handled using the old master file alone. To allow for the insertion or deletion of records, a new master file is created whenever changes are made to the old master file. Each master record not deleted from the file must be written into a new master, whether or not it is changed during the update. The process of creating an entirely new master file each time transactions are processed is called **sequential processing.**

With sequential processing, there is no direct way to locate the matching master record for a transaction. Each time a certain master record is to be updated, the entire master file must be read and a new master file created. Since this makes updating one record in a file very time-consuming, transactions are collected over a period of time and processed in one run (see Figure 7–2). Therefore, batch file access must be used with sequential file design.

The amount of time required to update a record with sequential processing includes the time needed to process the transaction, read and rewrite the master file until the proper record is reached, update the master record, and finish rewriting the master file. To reduce the time needed, the transactions are sorted in the same order as the master file. For security, the old master file and the transaction records are kept for a period of time; then if the new master is accidentally destroyed, it can be reconstructed from the old master and the transaction files. In many instances, two generations of old masters are kept, giving rise to "father" and "grandfather" backup copies.

EXAMPLE OF SEQUENTIAL PROCESSING. The preparation of customer bills is well suited to sequential processing. Customers' bills are usually prepared only at scheduled intervals. Standard procedures apply and large numbers of records must be processed.

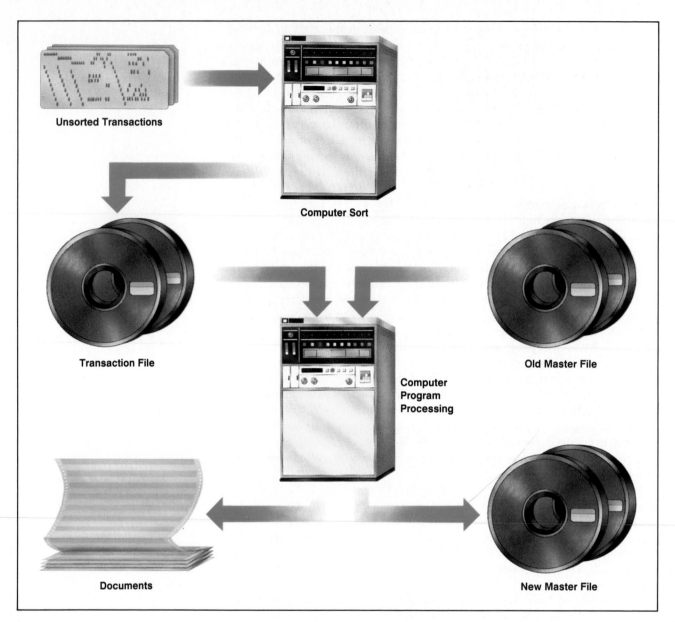

Unsorted Transactions

Computer Sort

Transaction File

Old Master File

Computer Program Processing

Documents

New Master File

FIGURE 7–2

Sequential Processing

Processing customer records results in the preparation of bills for customers and updates of the amount they owe. Magnetic tape is an appropriate medium for this application because the customer records can be arranged in order by customer number and processed in sequence accordingly.

The procedure for preparing the billing statements involves the following steps:

1. The transaction records indicating which items have been shipped to customers are keyed and verified. The key-to-tape operation also provides a report of invalid transactions so that they can be corrected (see Figure 7–3a).

2. The transaction records are sorted according to customer number be-

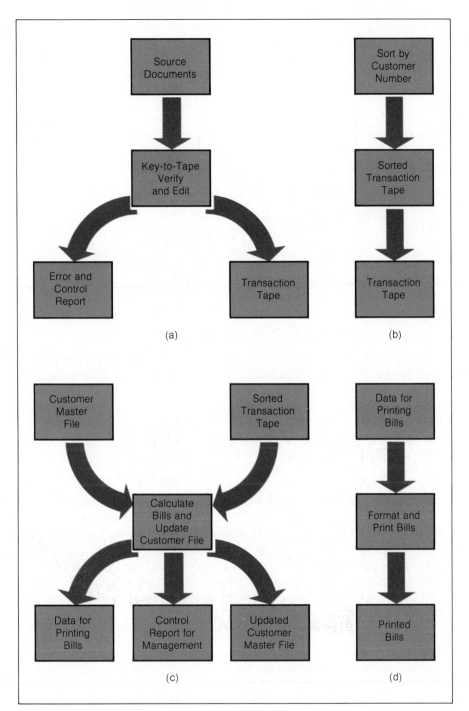

FIGURE 7-3

Billing Operations Using Sequential Processing

(a)

(b)

(c)

(d)

cause the customer master file is arranged in order by customer number (see Figure 7–3b).

3. The sorted transactions are used to update the customer master file. The process involves reading the transaction records and master records into primary storage (there may be more than one transaction record for a master record). The master record is updated to reflect the final amount owed by the customer, and a report is usually printed for management. For example, during the billing update, the computer may print a listing of customers who have exceeded their credit limits (see Figure 7–3c).

4. The customers' bills are prepared from the data generated in Step 3 (see Figure 7–3d).

MAKING INQUIRIES TO SEQUENTIAL FILES. How inquiries into a sequential file on magnetic tape are handled depends on the type of inquiry. Consider the following two inquiries into the employee file shown in Figure 7–1.

1. List the records of employees with social security numbers 234–02–1532 and 372–84–7436.

The employee file is sequenced according to social security number. In this case the file will be searched from beginning to end by checking the social security number key. As soon as the required social security numbers are located and the required records listed, the search is stopped. Of course, if the numbers are the last two records on the file, then the entire file must be searched.

2. List all employees from the area with zip code 43403.

For this inquiry the entire file will again be searched. In this case, the zip code field of each record must be checked to see if it matches 43403. This illustrates one problem with referring to a non-key field on sequential files. If an inquiry is based on a field other than the key, a great deal of time may be wasted in the search process. To alleviate this problem a second employee file, ordered by zip code, could be created; however, this approach requires multiple files with duplicate data.

ASSESSMENT OF SEQUENTIAL FILE DESIGN. Sequential processing and file design are suitable for applications with high activity and low volatility. **Activity** refers to the proportion of records processed during an updating run. **Volatility** is the frequency of changes to a file during a given time period. Examples of applications with high activity and low volatility (requiring large numbers of records to be updated at specific times) include payroll processing, updating the addresses of magazine subscribers, and preparing student grades.

Advantages of sequential processing and file design include the following:

■ It can be cost-effective when at least half the records in a master file are updated during one processing run.
■ The design of sequential files is simple.
■ Magnetic tape, a low-cost medium, can be used to maximum advantage.
■ Old master and transaction files provide automatic backup for the system.

Certain disadvantages characterize this method of processing, however:

■ The entire master file must be processed and a new master file written even when only a few master records have to be updated.
■ Transactions must be sorted in a particular sequence; this takes time and can be expensive.
■ The master file is only as up to date as the last processing run. In many

instances, using information from a master file that has not been recently updated results in the use of old, and sometimes incorrect, information.

■ The sequential nature of the file organization makes it difficult to provide information for unanticipated inquiries such as the status of a particular record, because all information is retrieved by reading the tape from beginning to end.

Direct-Access File Design

Direct-access file design also uses the key field of the records but in a different way from sequential design. The key field provides the only way of accessing data within a direct-access file design. Therefore, records are not stored in any particular order.

The data record being sought is retrieved according to its key value, so records before or after it are not read. Usually, a mathematical process called **randomizing** or **hashing** is applied to the record key, with that process yielding the storage addresses of the records. The address is usually a number from five to seven digits that is related to the physical characteristics of the storage medium. When a file is created, this address determines where the record is written. During retrieval, the address determines where to locate the record. Another way to obtain the address of a record is to place the record keys and their corresponding addresses in a **directory** (see Figure 7–4). During processing, the computer searches the directory to locate the address of a particular record.

Direct-access file design is much more efficient than searching an entire data file for a particular record. It is useful when information must be updated and retrieved quickly and when current information is crucial. A common application of direct-access file organization is for airline seat reservations. Current information about available flights and seats must be available at all times so that flights are not overbooked.

In contrast to a batch-processing system, a direct-access system does not require transaction records to be grouped or sorted before they are processed. Data is submitted to the computer in the order it occurs, usually using an online access method. **Direct-access storage devices (DASDs),** such as magnetic-disk drive units, make this type of processing possible. A particular record on a master file can be accessed directly, using its assigned keys, and updated without all preceding records on the file being read. Only the key to the record needs to be known. Thus, up-to-the-minute reports can be provided. For example, assume Ralph Smith's address in the employee master file in Figure 7–1 had to be changed. With direct-access processing, the computer can locate the record to be updated without processing all records that precede it. Figure 7–5 shows how direct-processing would be used in a business.

MAKING INQUIRIES TO DIRECT-ACCESS FILES. Consider again the two inquiries discussed in connection with sequential files. This time the inquiries will be made to direct-access files.

1. List the records of employees with social security numbers 234–02–1532 and 372–84–7436.

FIGURE 7—4

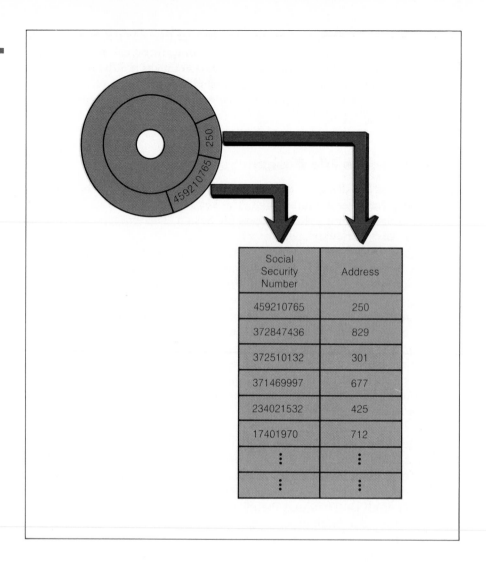

With the social security number as the key to the employee files, these two employees' records can be located directly. The computer retrieves each record from the address assigned for each social security number. It does not have to read all the records in the file.

2. List all employees from the area with zip code 43403.

The approach used for this inquiry will depend on the organization of the file. If the file is large and much processing is done based on a geographic breakdown of employees, a directory using zip codes and their record addresses can be created (as in Figure 7–6). However, if there are not many employees and processing is seldom based on the geographic breakdown of employees, a directory to locate employee records by zip code may have little value. In this case, the situation is the same as with sequential files— the entire file must be read to obtain the desired information.

FIGURE 7-5

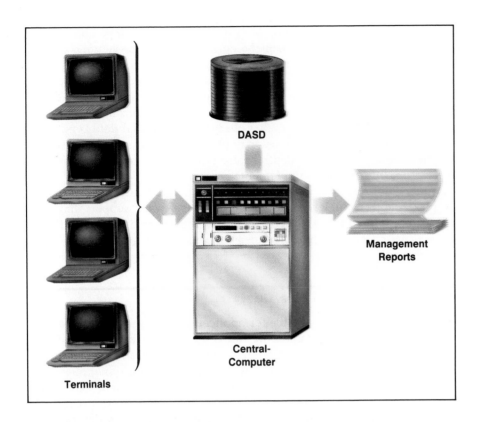

DASD

Management
Reports

Central-
Computer

Terminals

ASSESSMENT OF DIRECT-ACCESS FILE DESIGN. Direct-access processing and file design is suitable for applications with low activity and high volatility. Examples of such applications (systems requiring only a few records to be updated frequently) include banking operations and hotel and airline reservation systems.

Advantages of direct-access processing and file design are the following:

■ Transaction data can be used directly to update master records via online terminals without first being sorted. Transactions are processed as they occur.

■ The master file is not read completely each time updating occurs; only the master records to be updated are accessed. This saves time and money.

■ Gaining access to any record on a direct-access file takes only a fraction of a second.

■ Direct-access files provide flexibility in handling inquiries.

■ Several files can be updated at the same time by use of direct-access processing. For example, when a credit sale is made, the inventory file can be updated, the customer file can be changed to reflect the current accounts receivable figure, and the sales file can be updated to show which employee made the sale. Several runs would be required to accomplish all these operations if sequential processing were used.

Disadvantages of direct-access design include the following:

■ During processing, the original record is replaced by the updated record. In effect, it is destroyed. (In batch processing, a completely new master file is created, but the old master file remains intact.) Consequently, to provide

FIGURE 7-6

Directory for Zip Codes

ZIP CODE	ADDRESS
43403	12043
43403	12140
44151	12046
44153	12143
44200	12146
44201	12045

backup, an organization may have to make a magnetic-tape copy of the master file weekly and also keep the current week's transactions so that master records can be reconstructed if necessary.

■ Since many users may have access to records stored on direct-access devices in online systems, the chances of accidental destruction of data are greater than with sequential processing. Special programs are required to edit input data and to perform other checks to ensure that data is not lost.

■ Direct-access could present security problems for organizations. Users may be able to access confidential information. Therefore additional security procedures must be implemented.

■ Implementation of direct-access systems is often difficult because of their complexity and the high level of programming (software) support that such systems need. In addition, the cost of developing and maintaining a direct-access system is greater than the expense of a sequential processing system.

Indexed-Sequential File Design

Sequential processing is suitable for applications in which the proportion of records processed in an updating run is high. However, sequential files provide slow response times and cannot adequately handle file inquiries. On the other hand, direct-access processing is inappropriate for applications like payroll, where most records are processed during a single run. When a single file must be used for both batch processing and online processing, neither direct-access nor sequential file organization is appropriate. The same customer file that is used in a weekly batch run for preparing bills by the accounting department may be used daily by order-entry personnel to record orders and check credit status. To some extent, the limitations of both types of file design can be minimized by using another approach to file organization, indexed-sequential design.

In this structure, the records are stored sequentially on a direct-access storage device according to a primary key. A **primary key** is a field that will be unique for each record on the file. In addition, secondary keys can also be established. **Secondary keys** are fields that are used to gain access to records on the file but may not be unique. For instance, if zip code is chosen as a secondary key, there may be several records with the same value. Records on an indexed-sequential file can be accessed randomly by using either the primary or one of the secondary keys, or the file can be read sequentially, in order according to primary key.

The method used to gain access to a record on an indexed-sequential file is a little different from the method used for a direct-access file. Every record on an indexed-sequential file may not have its own unique address. Rather, several records may be grouped together and one address given for the entire group. An index table is created for all fields that are primary or secondary keys. The index table lists the value of the key (such as social security number) and the corresponding address on the direct-access storage device at which the group containing that record can be found. (The index table can either be stored at the beginning of the file or a separate file of indexes may be created.) A key given by the user is matched against the index table to get an approximate address for the required record. The computer then goes to that location on the direct-access storage device and checks records sequentially until the desired record is found. In the case of secondary keys, all records with that key may be retrieved.

Figure 7–7 shows the employee file from Figure 7–1 set up as an indexed-sequential file. The primary key is the social security number, while zip code is a secondary key. Notice how the records are in sequence according to the social security number on the file. To locate an employee with a zip

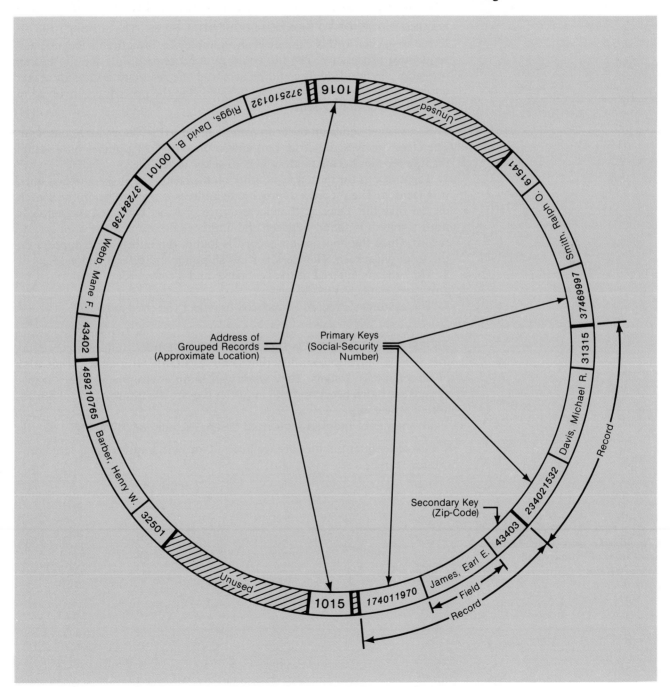

code of 43403, the computer goes to the index table for zip code (see Figure 7–8). Next to the value 43403 is the address on the direct-access storage device at which the group containing the record can be found, 1015. The computer goes to that address and reads each record in the group until the one with zip code 43403 is found. In this case, it is the first record in the group.

Thus, an indexed-sequential file provides direct-access capability. Since all the records are ordered according to a primary key, it also allows efficient sequential processing.

MAKING INQUIRIES TO INDEXED-SEQUENTIAL FILES. The customer file referred to earlier in this chapter is an example of a file suitable for indexed-sequential processing. The file could be read sequentially for the billing operation. In addition, it could be accessed one record at a time for order-entry transactions. The following steps outline the procedures involved in preparing a customer order:

1. A customer sends an order to American Sporting Goods for equipment. The clerk receives the order and enters the customer number on a visual display terminal. This number acts as a key to the file.
2. The index to the customer number on the customer file is searched until it is located. The record's approximate address is used to begin the search on the disk file. Once at that location, records are searched sequentially until a match is found between the number entered and the appropriate record. Once the appropriate record is found, the information appears on the terminal screen. The clerk verifies shipping and billing addresses.
3. The order is entered at the keyboard, and a sales order is generated by a printer connected to the system.
4. The customer's record is updated to reflect the current order.

ASSESSMENT OF INDEXED-SEQUENTIAL FILE DESIGN. Indexed-sequential files have a built-in flexibility that is not available with either sequential or direct-access designs. They work well in an environment where transactions are batch processed and inquiries require the fast response of direct-access processing.

Advantages of indexed-sequential design include the following:

■ Indexed-sequential files are well suited for both inquiries and large processing runs.

FIGURE 7–8

Index Tables of Primary and Secondary Keys

PRIMARY KEY (Social Security Number)		SECONDARY KEY (Zip Code)	
Number	*Address*	*Number*	*Address*
174–01–1970	1015	00101	1016
234–02–1532	1015	31315	1015
371–46–9997	1015	32501	1016
372–51–0132	1016	43402	1016
372–84–7436	1016	43403	1015
459–21–0765	1016	61541	1015

COMPUTERS AND INFORMATION PROCESSING

■ Access time to specific records is faster than it would be if the file were sequentially organized.

Disadvantages of indexed-sequential design include the following:

■ More direct-access storage space is required for an indexed-sequential file than for a sequential file holding the same data because of the storage space required for indexes. Therefore this type of system is more costly.
■ Processing time for specific record selection is longer than it would be in a direct-access system.

CONCEPT SUMMARY 7–1

Comparison of File Designs

	Sequential	Direct-Access	Indexed-Sequential
Types of Access	batch	online	batch or online
Data Organization	sequentially by key value	no particular order	sequentially and by index
Flexibility in Handling Inquiries	low	high	very high
Availability of Up-to-Date Data	no	yes	yes
Speed of Retrieval	slow	very fast	fast
Activity	high	low	high
Volatility	low	high	high
Examples	payroll processing billing operations	airline reservations banking transactions	customer ordering and billing

■ DATA BASES

Organizations such as hospitals, banks, retailers, and manufacturers have special information needs. Usually, data is collected and stored by many departments in these organizations, which often results in duplication of data. A hospital, for example, may keep files on patients treated in the emergency room. If a patient is then admitted, separate records may be compiled and kept for admissions, surgical procedures, X-rays, insurance, and billing purposes. The patient's name, address, personal physician, and medical history might be repeated in most or all of the records.

A data-base approach to file design treats all data from every department as one entity. A **data base** is a single collection of related data that can be used in many applications. Data is usually stored only once in a data base, which minimizes data duplication.

In a data base, data is stored in such a way that the same data can be accessed by many users for various applications. Data elements are grouped to fit the needs of all departments in the organization rather than the needs of one particular application. Eliminating duplication of data also increases

H I G H L I G H T

SQL to the Rescue

Parent Company A needs data from one of its subsidiaries, Company S. The two companies cannot exchange data, however, because they use different types of computers and different data bases. This sounds like a textbook problem, yet it is the situation faced by many businesses today. For example, Nabisco uses data-base products developed by Cincom in Cincinnati; its parent company uses Software AG products. How can these different systems communicate?

Enter SQL, Structured Query Language. SQL is a language used by many software developers for accessing relational data bases. It is becoming the standard in the software industry. SQL enables users to access information from any system that follows its standard, even when the architecture of the systems is different.

SQL is different from many programming languages because it uses English-like commands. It also provides end users with features such as help screens and prompts on the screen that help them interact with the system.

If Company A and Company S both used Structured Query Language could they pass data back and forth between each other? No problem!

efficiency. When a data element is updated, the change needs to be made only once because the data files are shared by all users. Once the update is made, current information is readily available to all departments.

Consider the case of a student at a large university. The student's name, home address, and social security number are often stored by a number of offices, such as the registrar, financial aid office, housing office, and the health center. If the student's home (permanent) address is changed, all these offices will need this information. Without a data base the student would need to notify each office individually about the change of address. If the university has a data base, the information needs to be changed only once because all the offices would share the personal data file.

The task of determining the design of data in a data base is the responsibility of the system analyst and the data-base analyst. The system analyst helps the users define their data-base needs. The data-base analyst is responsible for the analysis, design, and implementation of the data base. Together, they try to model the actual relationships that exist among data elements. The physical design of the data base is performed by the data-base administration (DBA) team. The DBA team must consider the problems of data redundancy, access time, and storage constraints in order to develop a logical design that works for the physical records and files actually stored in the data base.

The key to a successful data base is to incorporate more than one physical file into a logical file. The **physical file** is the way data is stored by the computer. The **logical file** is the combination of data needed to meet a user's needs. What one user views as a logical unit of data may include data from several physical files. For example, if a user needs an employee's identification number, address, and salary, all that information can be obtained from two files, the employee file and the payroll file (see Figure 7–9).

Data-base systems depend on direct-access storage devices (DASDs) to allow easy retrieval of data elements. The capabilities of DASDs are needed to handle the many logical relationships that exist among data elements. Combinations of data elements can be retrieved from a number of DASDs.

Structuring Data

Data elements in a computer file can be arranged in many ways according to how they are related to one another. These relationships, called **data structures,** represent the ways in which data elements can be joined together in logical ways. The user determines the way in which the elements are linked. The most common data structures are: simple, hierarchical, network, and relational structures. These structures determine the possible ways in which data contained in a data base can be organized.

SIMPLE STRUCTURE. The **simple structure** is a sequential arrangement of data records. All records are viewed as independent entities, as illustrated in Figure 7–10. Each record in this file has five characteristic fields called **attributes**—name, title, education, department, and sex. If the records are ordered—that is, arranged in a specific sequence—then the list is referred to as a **linear structure.** Simple file structure is appropriate for generating large reports but cumbersome for handling inquiries. To overcome this limitation, an **inverted structure** can be used. The inverted structure con-

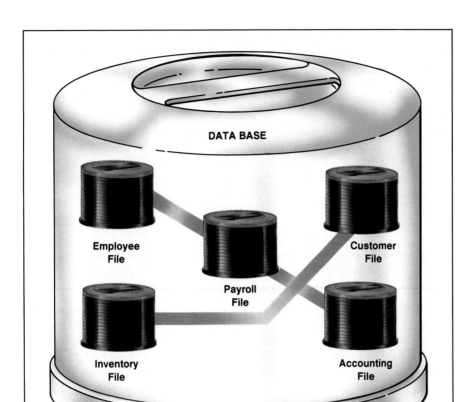

FIGURE 7—9

Example of a Data Base

tains indexes for selected attributes in a file, similar to those used in indexed-sequential files; the addresses of records having those attributes are also listed so that these records can be referenced by address. Figure 7–11 demonstrates an inverted file. Thus, the computer can handle complex inquiries because it searches the indexes rather than the actual files.

An advantage of the inverted structure is that it enables a variety of inquiries to be handled quickly and efficiently. A major disadvantage is that

FIGURE 7—10

File with Simple Structure

ADDRESS	NAME	TITLE	EDUCATION	DEPARTMENT	SEX
018021	Borgelt	Asst. Prof.	Ph.D.	Marketing	Male
018024	Henkes	Professor	D.Sc.	Management	Male
018046	Pickens	Instructor	M.S.	Accounting	Male
018020	Deluse	Asst. Prof.	Ph.D.	Marketing	Female
018016	Kozak	Assoc. Prof.	Ph.D.	Accounting	Male
018412	Gadus	Assoc. Prof.	Ph.D.	Accounting	Male
018318	Cross	Asst. Prof.	M.B.A.	Management	Female

| NAME | | TITLE | | EDUCATION | | DEPARTMENT | | SEX | |
Value	Address	Value	Address	Value	Address	Value	Address	Value	Address
Borgelt	018021	Instructor	018046	M.S.	018046	Marketing	018021	Male	018021
Henkes	018024	Asst. Prof.	018021	M.B.A.	018318		018020		018024
Pickens	018046		018020	Ph.D.	018021	Management	018024		018046
Deluse	018020		018318		018020		018318		018016
Kozak	018016	Assoc. Prof.	018016		018016	Accounting	018046		018412
Gadus	018412		018412		018412		018016	Female	018020
Cross	018318	Professor	018024	D.Sc.	018024		018412		018318

FIGURE 7—11

File with Inverted Structure

the attributes to be used in searches must be indexed. In some cases, the indexes for a particular file may be larger than the file itself.

HIERARCHICAL STRUCTURE. When a primary data element has many secondary data elements linked to it at various levels, it is called a **hierarchical** (or **tree**) **structure.** The primary data element is the parent element. Each parent may have many children (secondary elements) related to it, but each child may have only one parent. Figure 7–12 shows a hierarchical structure. A is the parent of B1 and B2; B1 is the parent of C1, C2, and C3; and so forth. The organization of corporations is typically a hierarchical structure.

A school system may use the hierarchical data structure for its student records. Figure 7–13 shows the relationship between data elements of a student's course schedule. A student's social security number is linked to the courses in which he is enrolled. Each course is linked to one teacher's meeting time and a room number. Therefore, if the principal needs to know

FIGURE 7—12

Hierarchical Data Structure

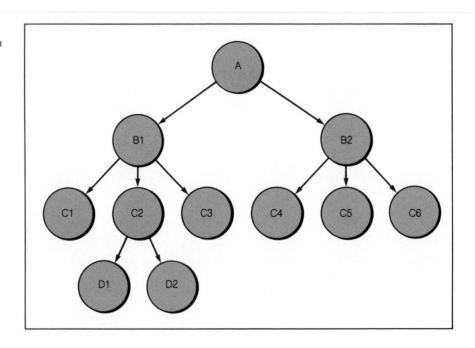

COMPUTERS AND INFORMATION PROCESSING

FIGURE 7–13

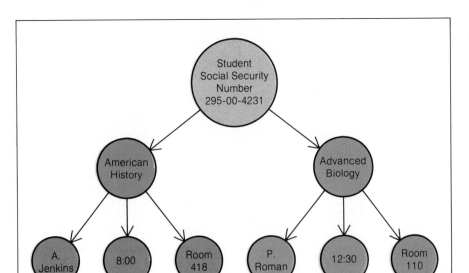

where a particular student is at 1:00, for example, she could enter the student's social security number into the computer and the student's course schedule would be displayed on the terminal screen.

NETWORK STRUCTURE. Similar to the hierarchical data structure, a **network structure** allows a parent data element to have many children. It differs from a hierarchical structure, however, because it also allows a child to have more than one parent. With network structure, any data element can be related to any other data element. There is no longer a simple hierarchy of data elements with relationships flowing only from a high level to a lower level. Data elements at a lower level can be related to several elements at a higher level, although these structures are quite complex. Figure 7–14 graphically illustrates this structure.

Figure 7–15 shows the relationship between data elements of a student course file. Each course is related to a student, a teacher, a meeting time, and a room number. Courses may have two parents, a student's social security number and a teacher's name. With this relatively simple example, the principal could locate either a student or a teacher by entering the student's social security number or the teacher's name.

RELATIONAL STRUCTURE. The newest type of data base is the **relational structure.** Relational data bases were developed to provide a more user-friendly approach to data accessing. Although relational data bases are easy for the user to access, they are the most sophisticated of the types of data bases discussed in this chapter. A relational data structure places the data elements in a table (called a relation) with columns and rows. The rows represent records, and the columns represent fields or individual data elements. With this structure, a data element can be related to other elements in the column in which it is located or to elements in the row in which it is located. With a relational data structure, the user can access either the

FIGURE 7–14

Network Data Structure

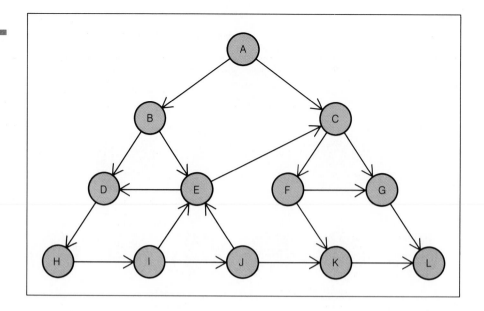

data elements that comprise a record (one row) or the data elements contained in one field (one column). It is also possible to join two or more relations to develop a third relation, or to select records within a record according to user-specified criteria.

Figure 7–16 shows a relational data structure of authors, books, publishers, and copyright dates. Each record contains one author, one title, a book publisher, and a copyright date. For example, Ernest Hemingway, *The Sun Also Rises*, Charles Scribner's Sons, and 1926 make up one record. Every record has those four fields.

Each data element has a unique location in the table identified by the column number and row number. The row and column numbers are called

FIGURE 7–15

Student Course Schedule Shown in a Network Data Structure

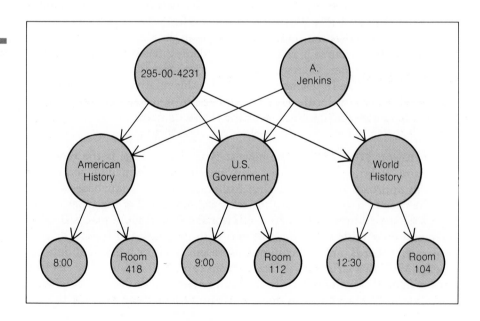

		Author (1)	Book (2)	Publisher (3)	Copyright (4)	
ROWS (RECORDS)	(1)	Ernest Hemingway	The Sun Also Rises	Charles Scribner's Sons	1926	
	(2)	F. Scott Fitzgerald	The Last Tycoon	Charles Scribner's Sons	1941	
	(3)	Richard Adams	Watership Down	Avon	1972	
	(4)	J. R. R. Tolkien	The Silmarillion	George Allen 7 Unwin	1977	
	(5)	James Joyce	Ulysses	Random House	1934	
	(6)	William Faulkner	The Sound and the Fury	Random House	1946	
	(7)	J. D. Salinger	The Cather in the Rye	Bantam Books	1945	

FIGURE 7—16

Relational Data Structure

subscripts. For example, the subscript (1,5) identifies the data element James Joyce, located in column 1, row 5.

This sample data structure in Figure 7–16 might be used at a bookstore. A clerk could then obtain all the records with J. R. R. Tolkien data, for example, or a list of all book titles carried at the store (all the data elements in that one field).

DATA-BASE STRUCTURE SUMMARY. From a logical perspective, a relational data-base structure is easier to understand than a hierarchical or network structure. This is because in hierarchical and network structures, the user establishes the logical record structure (relationships) of the datafields at the time the data base is created through logical connections (hierarchical structure) and relationships (network structure). In a relational data-base structure, however, logical record structures do not have to be established when the database is created. Therefore, when compared to either hierarchical or network data bases, users find relational data bases more flexible and useful for inquiry processing and ad hoc reports.

Data-Base Management Systems

An organization can use a **data-base management system (DBMS)** to help set up a data base. A DBMS is a set of programs that serves as the interface between the data base and the programmer, operating system, and users. With a DBMS, the programmer does not have to pay attention to the physical nature of the file; the programmer's main concern is the specific data the program needs.

A DBMS can perform the following functions:

- Organizing the data into logical structures that model the actual relationships among the data elements.
- Storing the data required to meet the needs of multiple users.
- Providing for concurrent retrieval and updating of data.
- Arranging data to eliminate data duplication.
- Providing privacy controls to prevent unauthorized access to data.

Assessment of the Data-Base Approach

Using a data base has a number of advantages:

- Data redundancy is minimized.
- Data can be stored in a manner that is useful for a wide variety of applications.
- Updating involves only one copy of the data.
- The system can handle requests that previously may have spanned several departments.

Limitations of the data-base approach include the following:

- An error in one input data record may be carried throughout the data base.
- Design and implementation of a data-base system requires highly skilled, well-trained people.
- Major attention must be given to the security of the system since all the data resources of the organization are collected in a place that is readily accessible to data-base users.
- Traditional processing jobs may run more slowly.

▨ SUMMARY POINTS

- Batch file access methods require transactions to be gathered for processing at one time.
- Online file access methods provide the ability to retrieve data and update it at any time.
- In sequential file design, all data is stored in sequential order on a master file; it may be ordered by some key field. Transactions to be processed against the master file are stored on a transaction file. Transactions are usually collected and processed against the master in one batch. During processing, transactions are matched against the master file, and updates to the master file are made by writing a new master during processing. The entire master file must be read when sequential processing is used.
- Batch access methods are generally used with sequential file design.
- In direct-access processing, records are accessed according to their key. The computer determines the location of the record on the disk by a transformation process on the key or by using a directory. Once the physical address is known, the record can be retrieved.
- Direct-access file designs are accessed using online methods.
- Indexed-sequential processing is used when the same file may be required for sequential processing and for single-record updates. A primary key is used to identify each unique record, and records are stored in sequence according to the primary key. Secondary keys are set up for those fields used to gain access to the file. The computer uses the key value to determine the approximate physical location of the record (or records), and then reads the records sequentially until the desired one is found.
- A data base is a grouping of data elements structured to fit the information needs of all departments of an organization. The data base reduces data duplication and increases efficiency and flexibility.

■ Data within a data base can be structured in many ways. Four ways are the simple structure, the hierarchical structure, the network structure, and the relational structure.

■ In a simple structure, records are arranged sequentially. Inverted structures are used to index files with simple structures according to attributes which are characteristic fields.

■ In a hierarchical structure, a given parent element may have many children, but a given child can have only one parent. In network structures, on the other hand, a parent can have many children, and each child can also have more than one parent.

■ The newest type of data-base structure, the relational structure, has data elements placed in tables called relations. The rows represent records and the columns contain fields.

■ A data-base management system is a set of programs that provides a method of arranging data to limit duplication; the ability to make changes to the data easily; and the ability to handle direct inquiries.

■ REVIEW QUESTIONS

1. Explain the two most common methods of accessing a data file.

2. Define the term *key*. Explain how a key is used in sequential processing.

3. How does the use of a key in direct-access processing differ from its use in sequential processing?

4. Distinguish between a master file and a transaction file.

5. Explain the similarities between indexed-sequential processing and sequential processing.

6. Explain the similarities between direct-access processing and indexed-sequential processing.

7. How does the computer use a directory during data retrieval?

8. What is a data base? What are the advantages of developing a data base?

9. Explain four different types of data structures that are used to organize data bases.

10. How does the inverted file structure assist in the handling of inquiries?

SupeRx

GENERAL COMPUTER USE

The success of SupeRx drugstores is due largely to one philosophy: The pharmacy is the heart of the business, and concern for the health of the customers and their families lies within the professional and quality service of that pharmacy. In 1960, when the Kroger Company decided to go into the drugstore business, they began by purchasing a chain of New Jersey drugstores. From the purchase of those stores, the SupeRx philosophy of the drugstore management evolved. Kroger sold its drug store holdings in 1986 and a new company called Hook-SupeRx Inc. was formed through a leveraged buy-out, but the continuity of management philosophy has continued.

Computers play an integral part in the operation of SupeRx Drugs. Their introduction into store operations in 1980 effected dramatic changes. Automating pharmacy procedures created additional time for more meaningful consultation between customers and pharmacists. Use of hand-held wand scanning devices in the product-ordering process improved clerk productivity and reduced errors. Electronic cash registers began to capture sales and gross profit information for evaluation of advertising effectiveness.

The SupeRx general office staff relies heavily on computers to capture, maintain, and report all information associated with daily store operations. A communications network linking all stores, offices, and data centers provides for electronic movement of data seven days a week, twenty-four hours a day. Major system applications that depend on this network include store ordering, product distribution, prescription billing, and financial reporting.

DATA RECORD STORAGE

One of the primary reasons for the success of the computerized pharmacy system is the method by which the data records are stored in the computer. SupeRx selected an IBM-supplied utility called IAM (Index Access Method). This utility allowed the retrieval of data records as well as the efficient management of data storage space on a disk.

The IAM method of data record storage has several requirements in defining a file structure. The first requirement is that all data records to be retained in the file must be the same length. IAM cannot accommodate variable length records in a single file. The second requirement is that all data fields in the data record must be the same length and position. This allows standardization of the data elements. A third requirement is the selection of the "key" field in the data record. The key is used to access each data record and therefore must be unique to each data record. When a specific data record is required, the key is used to locate the data record in the file.

The IAM method of storage provides a rapid retrieval of data records by storing the keys of each data record in index blocks. An index block contains a group of the keys and points to the location on the disk of each associated data record. The index blocks are stored in multiple levels depending on the size of the data file. They are linked in a series of levels until they point directly to the data records. The method of index block storage from a high level to lower levels to data records gives a cascading effect for data record lookups. This downward flow is the basis for a speedy retrieval of a requested data record.

At the heart of the computerized pharmacy system is a series of intricately related IAM files. The most important of these is the customer information file. The customer data record contains the personal data for each person—name, address, phone number, birthdate, and so on. To furnish a unique key to each customer, the name is processed through a hashing algorithm, which generates a unique hash value. Identical names, such as John Smith, will produce identical key values. When a duplicate hash value is found, a sequence byte is incremented and a unique key is created.

The customer data record also contains a link to another important file in the pharmacy system, the prescription history file. This file contains information about each prescription filled for each customer. As a new prescription is filled or an old one is refilled, a new entry is made in the prescription history file. To allow the pharmacist to review the customer's prescription history, each prescription is linked by the order in which it was filled. Also stored in this file for each prescription is the link to the drug item file.

The drug item file contains the data records for each drug item in the pharmacy system. The data records are made up of the information about each item, such as drug name, strength, package size, DEA class, pricing breakdown, and so forth. This file is updated weekly from a corporate data base to ensure that all information is up to date.

The files for the computerized pharmacy system are a network of interdependent data files. Each file contains pieces of information that individually mean very little, but when used in conjunction with one another, form the basis of a successful computerized application.

DISCUSSION POINTS

1. Describe the general use of computers at SupeRx.
2. How is the Index Access Method used for file storage at SupeRx? Discuss the requirements in the definition of a file structure.

CHAPTER

8

Microcomputers

O U T L I N E

Introduction
Microcomputers: An Overview
  The New Technology
  The Machines Themselves
Understanding the Microchips
  The Microprocessor's Speed
  Primary Memory
  The Instruction Set
  Operating Systems
  Compatibility

Using Microcomputers
  Peripherals
  Software Packages
  Users Groups
Purchasing Microcomputers
  The Big Picture
  Evaluating Software
  Choosing the Hardware
  Buyer's Checklist

Summary Points
Review Questions

Put Enough PCs Together, and You Get a Supercomputer

**Otis Port
Jonathan B. Levine and
Keith H. Hammonds**
Business Week

Who says those little computers-on-a-chip that power desktop PCs can't take on giant mainframes? Ganged together, those tiny Davids can match the big "brains" of Goliath computers—and for so much less money that the new technology just wipes out the old. "It will cause a revolution," declares Casey Powell, president of Sequent Computer Systems Inc. in Beaverton, Ore.

Sequent is one of the small band of pioneers in the burgeoning field known as parallel processing. Using gangs of microprocessors, they build computers that deliver the performance of a mainframe for roughly 10% of the cost. Sequent has sold 450 of its systems directly, and Siemens of West Germany has sold 1,500 others based on Sequent's technology. Co-founder C. Scott Gibson is particularly proud of a recent order from Coca-Cola Enterprises Inc., heretofore an IBM bastion. That makes Gibson more confident than ever that microprocessors will be the brains in computers of every size—"whether it takes 3 or 5 or 10 years" to generate sufficient software and overcome lingering skepticism.

The economics are telling indeed: Sequent's heftiest Symmetry system can deliver 120 mips (millions of instructions per second) and support hundreds of people sitting at terminals and running programs, all at the same time. That puts it "in the range of IBM's largest 3090 mainframe," according to an analysis by William F. Zachmann, executive vice-president of market researcher International Data Corp. But the per-mips cost with Symmetry is about $5,000 vs. roughly $120,000 for a comparable 3090.

The Symmetry system is a cluster of 30 of Intel's latest 80386 chips. Other micro-based parallel-processing machines with more chips can even surpass the blinding speed of supercomputers. For example, Intel's new Scientific Computers division puts 128 of the chips in its top-of-the-line system, and it spews out 512 mips, more than any commercial mainframe.

Running a widely used scientific program, an Intel IPSC machine with only 32 microprocessors outraces a Cray Research Inc. X-MP/12 by 40%. It turns in 100 megaflops (millions of floating-point operations per second, the customary way to measure scientific computers), against 70 megaflops for the supercomputer. Cost per megaflop: less than $10,000 for Intel, more than $100,000 for Cray. That low cost, says Leslie L. Vadasz, an Intel executive vice-president spells "the end of one era and the start of another."

COVERING THE SPECTRUM. Other newcomers—Bolt Beranek & Newman, Encore, Ncube, and Teradata—are building systems by patching together chips from Motorola, Inmos, National Semiconductor or Intel. By the end of last year, Boston's Stratus Computer Inc., which bases its system on Motorola chips, had installed 1,444 computers at places such as Gillette, Visa International, and the National Association of Securities Dealers. Stratus' sales, compounding at roughly 50% a year, hit $184 million in 1987.

Sequent is betting that its Intel based computers will score big in the market for all classes of office computers. But in engineering markets, where Motorola's chips are dug in and various so-called RISC processors may provide even more muscle, it could be a different story. There, says Sequent's Gibson, "it'll be a huge dogfight."

Microprocessors have already changed the use of computers in business. Users at all levels of the organization often process their own information on desktop personal computers. Now, groups of linked microcomputers can process more than mainframes and even supercomputers. This new way of using microcomputers may be the beginning of a new computer era.

■ INTRODUCTION

Few technological changes equal the impact that microcomputers have had on our lives in so short a period of time. In just one decade, microcomputers evolved from primitive toys for hobbyists to sophisticated machines that far surpass the early mainframe computers in both speed and capabilities. Microcomputers have become so common that they now appear in every area of our lives, from work to play.

The proliferation of microcomputers has introduced a new set of options and vocabulary to explore. This chapter examines the terms and hardware associated with microcomputers and describes some unique aspects and ramifications of using them.

■ MICROCOMPUTERS: AN OVERVIEW

Microcomputers, also called personal computers or home computers, are the smallest computers. They differ from minicomputers, mainframes, and supercomputers in capability, price, and size. The list of things they can do is rapidly expanding, however, and clear distinction no longer exists between their capabilities and those of the next class of computers, minicomputers. Some microcomputers, often referred to as supermicrocomputers, are so powerful that they are being used instead of minicomputers by some organizations. (These machines are discussed later in the chapter.)

Microcomputers can usually sit on a desk top (see Figure 8–1). They are less expensive than minicomputers and mainframes, due largely to their less complex and less expensive operating systems. Microcomputer prices range from about $100 to $15,000.

The prefix *micro* should be thought of as applying more to size and cost than to capability. Microcomputers are very powerful for their size. Today's microcomputers exceed the power of the early room-sized mainframe computers. Although they cannot perform as many complex functions as the

FIGURE 8–1

Microcomputer
Microcomputers, the least expensive category of computers, are general-purpose machines used in many applications in homes, schools, and offices.

large computers available today, technology continues to give them more speed and more memory at an ever-decreasing cost.

The New Technology

The invention of the microprocessor ushered in the fourth generation of computers in 1971. The microprocessor is a single chip containing arithmetic and logic circuitry as well as control capability for memory and input/output access (see Figure 8–2). It controls the sequence of operations and the arithmetic and logic operations. It also controls the storage of data, instructions, and intermediate and final results of processing, much as the CPU of a mainframe computer does.

Microprocessors quickly increased in power while they decreased in size. This combination of power and miniaturization paved the way for microcomputers as they exist today.

The first microprocessor was not even designed for microcomputers. Ted Hoff, an engineer at Intel, designed the first microprocessor chip for a Japanese company that wanted an integrated, programmable circuit chip for its line of calculators. At the time, calculators used several circuit chips, each chip performing only one function. Hoff's chip, the Intel 4004, could be programmed to perform numerous calculator functions.

The Intel 4004 had a very limited instruction set, could not perform many functions, and could manipulate only four bits of data at a time. By 1974, however, microprocessors could manipulate eight bits of data at a time. Popular early eight-bit chips still in use today are the Zilog Z-80, Intel 8080, and Motorola 6809. These powerful eight-bit microprocessors were used in the first microcomputers, among them the MITS Altair 8800.

Ed Roberts, the founder of a company called MITS, foresaw the start of the microcomputer revolution. He developed a computer that could be built

FIGURE 8–2

Microprocessor
This microprocessor has as much processing power as some mini-computers.

COMPUTERS AND INFORMATION PROCESSING

from a kit, the Altair 8800. In January 1975, his computer received cover billing in *Popular Electronics* magazine (now *Computers and Electronics*). The computer came unassembled for $397 or fully assembled for $498. It used the Intel 8080 microprocessor, had only 256 bytes of RAM, and offered no software. Yet the Altair 8800 created so much interest that MITS received more than 5,000 orders. This response indicated that the market for microcomputers was well worth pursuing. Other microcomputers in kit form followed: the Scelbi-8B, the Sphere I, the Jolt, and the Mike. Most featured from 1K to 4K of memory.

In 1976, not long after the introduction of the Altair, Stephen Wozniak, an employee of Hewlett-Packard, finished building a small, easy-to-use computer. His computer, the Apple I, used the MOS 6402 microprocessor chip, which cost $20. Steven Jobs, a friend of Wozniak's and a former Hewlett-Packard employee, persuaded Wozniak to leave Hewlett-Packard and start a business with him. The two men raised $1,300 and began building Apple computers. Their first commercial microcomputer, the Apple II, was a huge success (see Figure 8–3). Since then, Apple has produced a series of computers, including the Apple II Plus, Apple IIc, Apple IIe, Apple IIGS, the Macintosh, the Macintosh Plus, and the Macintosh II.

Both Wozniak and Jobs have left Apple and are working on new ideas in computer technology and applications. Apple's chairman is now John Sculley, whom Jobs brought in from Pepsi Cola Company in order to improve Apple's efficiency.

The year 1976 was a busy one in microcomputer development. Commodore Business Machines, headed by Jack Tramiel, had acquired MOS Technology, the semiconductor manufacturer that was developing the 6502 microprocessor. The chip was incorporated in the Commodore PET. Tramiel also sold the 6502 chip to Apple and Atari.

FIGURE 8–3

Steven Jobs, Stephen Wozniak, and the Apple II.

In 1977, the PET was introduced at an electronics show and received tremendous enthusiasm from those attending the show. Later, Commodore developed two popular and inexpensive computers, the VIC 20 and Commodore 64 microcomputers. Commodore's product line has expanded to include the Amiga and the Commodore 128 Personal Computer.

Today, Jack Tramiel is the chairman of the board of Atari. His philosophy—to provide more sophisticated technology for home computer users—is culminating in the introduction of the ST line of computers, the eight-bit Atari EX microcomputer, and a portable computer, the Atari XEP.

Meanwhile, the chairman of Tandy Corporation, John Roach, was busy persuading Tandy president Charles Tandy to manufacture a microcomputer and market it through Radio Shack stores. Roach's marketing sense led him to believe that the distribution potential of Radio Shack stores would help make Tandy's computer a success. He was right. Radio Shack offered the first opportunity for a consumer to walk into a retail store and purchase a low-priced personal computer. The TRS-80 Model I used the Zilog Z-80 microprocessor. The TRS-80 microcomputer Models I, II, III, and 4, the portable TRS 200, and the advanced TRS 2000 have made Radio Shack and Tandy Corporation a driving force in the microcomputer industry.

Industry giant IBM entered the microcomputer race in 1981 under the leadership of chief executive officer John Opel. The IBM Personal Computer (PC), developed under the direction of the late Philip D. Estridge, quickly became the standard in small business computers. IBM's reputation as a producer of high-quality business products quickly helped boost the sales of the PC. The original IBM PC used the Intel 8088 microprocessor, which could manipulate sixteen bits of data at a time. The success of the IBM PC prompted other microcomputer manufacturers to develop sixteen-bit computers. IBM then introduced the IBM PC jr and the more advanced IBM PC XT and IBM PC AT (see Figure 8–4).

FIGURE 8–4

IBM PC AT

In 1987 IBM introduced its next generation of personal computers, the PS/2 Models 30, 60, 70, and 80. These microcomputers incorporate micro channel architecture and are capable of running PC-DOS as well as an operating system called OS/2, which was also introduced in 1987. Since the original introduction of the PS/2 line of microcomputers IBM has also added the Model 25, Model 50, and Model 50Z.

Since 1974, more than 150 companies have introduced microcomputers. Some, such as DEC, Wang, Hewlett-Packard, and NCR, were already established manufacturers of larger computer systems. Others were new companies attempting to capture a share of the booming new industry. Not all the companies were successful. A number, among them Osborne Computer, Texas Instruments, DEC, and Timex Sinclair, were forced either to abandon their efforts or to regroup.

The shakeout of microcomputer companies is not over, and the market for microcomputers is still growing, although at a slower rate than it did in the early 1980s. Prices of microcomputers should continue to decline while more and more capabilities are added. Two factors affecting the microcomputer market are more powerful microprocessors and better manufacturing methods.

Today, sixteen-bit and thirty-two-bit microprocessors are common in microcomputers. So far, the most powerful microprocessor is the sixty-four-bit microprocessor developed by Control Data Corporation. This chip has not yet been implemented in any commercial microcomputers.

Microprocessors are being used for controlling the functions of many devices other than microcomputers. They are commonly found in microwave ovens, calculators, typewriters, sewing machines, vending machines, traffic lights, and gas pumps. Current-model cars have microprocessors that control the ignition system, the flow and mix of gasoline, and the timing of sparks.

CONCEPT SUMMARY 8—1

Early Microcomputers and Their Microprocessors			
Microcomputer	Year Introduced	Manufacturer	Microprocessor
Altair 8800	1974	MITS	Intel 8080
Apple II	1976	Apple Computer	MOS 6502
PET	1977	Commodore	MOS 6502
TRS-80 Model I	1977	Tandy Corporation	Zilog Z-80
IBM PC	1981	IBM	Intel 8086

The Machines Themselves

Most microcomputers today are desktop models (see Figure 8–5). They are small enough to place on a desk, but too large to carry around easily. A fairly versatile system includes the computer, a keyboard for input, a disk drive or two as storage devices, and a monitor and a printer for output. Other peripheral devices can be added to most systems.

FIGURE 8-5

Desktop computers fit on the surface of work spaces but are too large to be carried around comfortably.

Inside the computer itself is a main system board, often called the motherboard, that holds the microprocessor, other circuits, and memory chips (see Figure 8–6). The system board may contain slots for plugging in cards that expand the capabilities of the computer. For example, you can insert cards for adding memory, changing the number of characters per line that appear on the monitor, or using printers, modems, voice recognition units, music synthesizers, and bar code readers (see Figure 8–7). Of course, there is a limit to the number of cards that can be added at once.

FIGURE 8-6

The Main System Board
This main system board, sometimes called the motherboard, holds the microprocessor, some memory chips, slots for additional cards, and other electronic components necessary for running a microcomputer.

FIGURE 8—7

Add-on Card

Microcomputers can also have ports that can be used for plugging in peripherals (see Figure 8–8). A port may be designed for serial communication, in which the bits are transferred one at a time much as people pass through a turnstile, or parallel communication, in which the bits are transferred eight at a time much as cars drive down an eight-lane expressway.

FIGURE 8—8

Ports

Cables for telephone connections and printers require serial ports; parallel ports are used for communicating with some printers.

Although most computers are desktop models, there are three other major groups of microcomputers: portables, transportables, and supermicrocomputers.

PORTABLES AND TRANSPORTABLES. The smallest microcomputers available are **portables.** Portables are light enough to be carried and do not need an external source of power. They are powered by either rechargeable or replaceable batteries. Portables usually need some form of direct-access mass storage medium, such as floppy disks.

Portables can be divided further by size into briefcase, notebook, and hand-held. The IBM PC Convertible is a briefcase computer noted for being much faster than other portables (see Figure 8–9). Radio Shack's Model 100 and Model 200 are notebook computers used mostly for word processing (see Figure 8–10).

Portables should be distinguished from another class of small microcomputers, the **transportables.** Transportables are generally larger than portables but are still small enough to be carried. They differ from portables by requiring an external power source. The Compaq Portable III, for example, is a transportable because it does not contain its own power source (see Figure 8–11).

Some portables are capable of performance almost equal to that of small desktop microcomputers, and their prices reflect it, ranging from around $3,000 to $5,000. Other portables are dedicated to certain functions and carry a much lower price tag, between $800 and $2,000.

FIGURE 8—9

PC Convertible
This computer can fit into a briefcase, which makes carrying it on business trips easy.

COMPUTERS AND INFORMATION PROCESSING

FIGURE 8—10

Radio Shack Model 100 Portable Computer
This lower-priced portable is used mostly for special functions such as word processing.

FIGURE 8—11

Compaq Portable III
The Compaq Portable III is a transportable microcomputer that requires an external power source.

HIGHLIGHT

Executives and Micros

Microcomputers are becoming common in offices. By the year 2000 some researchers project the number of micros in the office will reach 46 million—four times the number presently being used. Many of these micros will be used in executives' offices. In the past some executives avoided PCs. They found the early micros difficult to use and the software too complex. Furthermore, many executives are uncomfortable using keyboards. Menu-driven software and devices such as a mouse are helping top management overcome their reservations about microcomputers.

Executives are now using micros to gain quick access to data they need for decision making. They like the advantage of using the computer themselves rather than waiting for someone else to make a report. This advantage is especially useful for executives who work unusual hours—such as early mornings or late at night. A growing number of executives have also gotten microcomputers for their homes.

Top management has found systems such as electronic mail ena-

ble them to communicate more effectively with personnel. Executives can send comments directly to a subordinate. The PC also provides a two-way communication system, so staffers have access to their supervisor. Top managers feel that E-mail enables them to interact more often with their staff.

In the past micros often sat unused on the desks of executives. Now many executives are finding them indispensable.

Each portable has different features, so users must evaluate their particular needs before selecting a portable. Some useful features include built-in modems and telecommunications software for transmitting and receiving data by telephone. Some portables have ports for connecting floppy disk drives or bar code readers. Most portables have built-in software such as a word processor, spreadsheet, or data-base manager (see the section on software later in this chapter). Built-in programming languages such as BASIC are also included with some portable computers.

Three technologies are responsible for the sophistication of portables:

1. Microprocessors give portables the power of some full-sized computers in a single chip.
2. Flat display panels allow portables to be slim and therefore easy to carry.
3. Finally, battery power can free portables from dependency on external power sources.

Portables have been found to be especially useful for reporters, businesspeople, and students. For example, a salesperson might use a portable to compose reports that are sent to the main office via telephone lines. Journalists use portables in similar ways. A reporter can cover a presidential news conference two thousand miles from the newspaper's headquarters, write the story using a word processor and a portable computer, and use a modem to send the finished product over telephone lines to the editor's desk. Students carry briefcase or notebook computers to classes and type notes into the computers from lectures. The typed notes are easy to decipher and hard copies can be printed out for studying at a later time.

SUPERMICROCOMPUTERS. Some microcomputers are so powerful that they can compete with low-end minicomputers. These **supermicrocomputers** are usually built around powerful thirty-two-bit microprocessors (see Figure 8–12). Because microprocessors are very inexpensive compared to the CPUs of minicomputers, supermicrocomputers offer a significant price edge over minicomputers. The low cost of microprocessors also makes it possible to build supermicrocomputers with several microprocessors, each dedicated to a particular task. For example, individual microprocessors can be dedicated to each user workstation, disk drive, or printer.

Supermicrocomputers must be able to store large amounts of data. Hard disks can store much more data than the traditional floppy disks used with microcomputers. Fortunately, the prices of hard disk drives have fallen, making them ideal storage devices for supermicrocomputers.

One problem hindering full-scale implementation of supermicrocomputers is the limited amount of available software. But as they gain in popularity, there will be more interest in developing software for these machines just as a great deal of software was developed for traditional microcomputers.

Another problem is the loyalty of minicomputer users to their machines. Many users are skeptical of the power a supermicrocomputer has and would not readily choose a supermicrocomputer over a minicomputer system. Time will remedy this problem as the power of the small supermachines increases and as more uses are found for them. In fact, the minicomputer market is already weakening as more customers upgrade their systems by linking microcomputers to existing minicomputers or mainframes. Several developments, including lower prices, networking capabilities, better software packages, and increased storage capacity, help explain the market's preference for microcomputers in the mid- to late 1980s.

FIGURE 8–12

Supermicrocomputer

CONCEPT SUMMARY 8-2

Microcomputer Sizes			
Desktop Models	**Portables**	**Transportables**	**Super-microcomputers**
Small enough to put on a desk Large and bulky to carry	Small enough to be called brief-case, notebook, and hand-held computers	Require external power source Easy to carry	Overlap power of minicomputers Store large amounts of data

▆ UNDERSTANDING THE MICROCHIPS

Earlier we stated that a computer's power is derived from its speed and memory and the accuracy of electronic circuits. This section explains two of those factors, speed and memory, as related to microprocessors. It also discusses the software that integrates the workings of a microcomputer's circuitry.

The Microprocessor's Speed

The power behind a microcomputer comes from the microprocessor, a silicon chip only fractions of an inch wide. Microprocessors can be categorized by their speed and the amount of primary storage they can directly access. The speed with which the microprocessor can execute instructions affects the speed of the microcomputer. Speed depends on two factors: word size and clock speed.

Word size is the number of bits that can be manipulated at one time. An eight-bit microprocessor, for example, can manipulate eight bits, or one byte, of data at a time. A sixteen-bit microprocessor can handle sixteen bits—two eight-bit bytes of data—at a time. Therefore, a sixteen-bit microprocessor can manipulate twice as much data as an eight-bit microprocessor in approximately the same amount of time. This does not mean, however, that there is a direct relationship between word size and speed. A sixteen-bit microprocessor is not necessarily twice as fast as an eight-bit microprocessor. It may be more than twice as fast in performing some operations but less than twice as fast in performing others. Generally, though, a sixty-four-bit microprocessor is faster than a thirty-two-bit microprocessor and the thirty-two-bit microprocessor is faster than either a sixteen-bit or an eight-bit microprocessor.

The **clock speed** of a microprocessor is the number of electronic pulses the chip can produce each second. Clock speed is built into a microprocessor and is measured in **megahertz (MHz).** *Mega* means million and *hertz* means number of cycles per second; one megahertz is one million cycles per second. The electronic pulses affect the speed with which program instructions are executed because instructions are executed at predetermined intervals, which are timed by the electronic pulses. To illustrate this concept, assume that one instruction is executed every 100 pulses. A 4 MHz microprocessor, then, could process 40,000 instructions per second (4 million pulses divided by

100 pulses). An 8 MHz microprocessor could process 80,000 instructions, or twice as many as a 4 MHz microprocessor. Thus, the more pulses produced per second, the faster instructions can be executed. Most microcomputers have clock speeds ranging between 4 MHz and 25 MHz.

The amount of data that can be directly accessed in primary storage also affects the speed with which instructions can be executed. Each microprocessor can directly access only a certain amount of data in primary storage. This means that the microprocessor can manipulate a certain number of bytes of data without switching from primary storage to a supplementary storage bank. (A supplementary storage bank is part of primary storage and should not be confused with secondary storage such as floppy disks.) Typically, an eight-bit microprocessor can directly access 64K bytes of data and a sixteen-bit microprocessor can directly access 256K.

Primary Memory

Primary memory is important in microcomputer speed because the more data directly accessible by the CPU, the faster the machine. In addition, the computer can use more complex programs. Primary memory consists of thousands of on/off devices. Each holds one bit. Common types of primary memory are RAM and ROM.

RAM. The primary storage that holds the data and programs for immediate processing is a form of semiconductor memory called random-access memory (RAM). RAM is the working area of the computer. Since RAM is volatile or nonpermanent, data or programs will be erased when the electric power to the computer is turned off or disrupted in some other way. When any changes or results are to be saved, they must be saved on an external form of storage; on magnetic disks or tapes, for example.

The size of RAM memory is stated in bytes. Today, the most common sizes in microcomputers are 256K, 512K, and 640K. Some of the new models of microcomputers are capable of RAM sizes up to 4MB (4 Million Bytes). The sizes are related to the word sizes of microprocessors in that microcomputers with smaller word sizes can access directly only a small amount of RAM. As the word size increases, so does the amount of RAM that can be accessed.

ROM. When functions are built into the hardware of a microcomputer, they are placed in read-only memory (ROM). Read-only memory instructions cannot be changed or deleted by another program's instructions. Since ROM is permanent, it cannot be occupied by instructions or data read from a disk or tape. The various versions of ROM—PROM, EPROM, and EEPROM—are available for microcomputers. See Chapter 4 for a complete discussion of these chips.

RAM DISKS. Accessing data on disks is a relatively slow process when compared to the speed at which the microprocessor itself accesses data. The transfer of data within memory is significantly faster than transferring data from a disk to memory or vice versa. Random-access memory disks, or RAM

HIGHLIGHT

Amazing Microprocessors

Microprocessors, the heart of microcomputers, were developed less than 30 years ago. The speed at which microprocessors have been processing instructions has been increasing ever since. Chip makers are now able to produce microprocessors that can process faster than some mainframes. For example, Texas Instruments' new 32-bit chip can process 100 million instructions per second (MIPS). The company says it will soon have a chip for supercomputers that processes 200 MIPS.

The Intel 80386 chip, when used in a personal computer such as the Compaq 386, provides the same processing power as a small mainframe like the VAX 8600. Soon Intel says it will release its latest chip, the 80486 (often referred to by the shorter name 486). This chip contains one million transistors. The chip is said to provide as much processing speed as a medium-size mainframe, such as the IBM 3090.

The new microprocessors may change the look of future mainframes. Some mainframe manufacturers are no longer installing traditional CPUs (Central Processing Units); instead they are using groups of super-speed microprocessors—which reduces the cost and the size of the mainframe.

Where will all this lead? Perhaps in the future the computer sitting on your desk may be a micro-mainframe.

disks, can be used to take advantage of the speed at which data can be transferred within memory. A RAM disk is a portion of the microprocessor's memory that is used to simulate a disk drive. A typical RAM disk has a retrieval rate fifty times faster than a floppy disk drive.

The Instruction Set

Instructions are designed into a microcomputer's circuitry for performing the arithmetic and logic operations and storage and retrieval functions. The set of instructions that a microprocessor can perform is called its **instruction set.** The number of instructions in a set is often quite limited, ranging from 100 to 300. By manipulating the instruction set, programmers produce software that harnesses the computer's power in order to achieve the desired results.

Instruction sets approaching 300 instructions on thirty-two-bit microprocessors occupy a lot of space on the chip, leaving less room for other components and slowing processing speeds. A new development, the Reduced Instruction Set Computer (RISC), uses a very simple instruction set that simplifies the design of the microprocessor. The implementation of RISC is still controversial, because the benefits of using RISC do not yet justify the costs. Even though RISC may not be widely used, it will encourage the more efficient use of space on microprocessors. Companies trying the RISC chips are Hewlett-Packard and IBM.

Operating Systems

Computer operating systems will be discussed in greater detail in Chapter 10; however, an operating system is a collection of programs used by the computer to manage its operation and provide an interface between the user or application program and the computer hardware. A number of operating systems have been designed for use with microcomputers.

Most operating systems are loaded into a computer's RAM from floppy disks, a process called **booting.** The word *boot* derives from the expression "to lift yourself up by your own bootstraps," which is essentially what a computer does. In order to read and write data on a disk, the disk operating system (or DOS) must be in memory. The disk operating system, however, is kept on a disk. Therefore, it seems impossible for the computer to load its operating system when it must have the operating system in memory in order to read from a disk. In actuality, the computer already has a small program built into ROM that starts the process of reading the operating system code from a disk. Some systems require you to turn on the computer before inserting the operating system diskette; others require you to insert the diskette into the disk drive first. Care should be taken that the proper procedure is followed for booting the microcomputer you are using.

The first operating system developed for use with microcomputers was Digital Research's CP/M (Control Program for Microprocessors). CP/M was stored on a floppy disk so that it could be loaded into any microcomputer, provided the computer used the Intel 8080 or 8085 or the Zilog Z-80 eight-bit microprocessor.

In 1981, Microsoft introduced its operating system, called MS-DOS, for sixteen-bit microprocessors. Microsoft licensed MS-DOS to IBM to be used in the IBM PC. MS-DOS (also called PC-DOS) quickly became the most popular sixteen-bit operating system, as IBM PC sales increased. More than 100 different computers—also referred to as compatibles—use MS-DOS, and many application programs have been written to run on it. MS-DOS is designed to run on the Intel 8088 and 8086 sixteen-bit microprocessors and subsequent updates of those, such as the 80286 and 80386.

Other microcomputer operating systems include Apple DOS and Apple ProDOS, which are used on the Apple II family of microcomputers; Unix (or Xenix), which is used on a number of microcomputers; and TRS-DOS (Tandy/Radio Shack Disk Operating System), which is used on the TRS-80 family of microcomputers. Newer, **transparent** operating systems have recently been introduced to lessen the amount of operating system knowledge required by the user of the microcomputer. The Macintosh Finder and graphical interface portion of OS/2 allow the user to point to *icons* and use pull-down menus on the screen with the help of a mouse (see Figure 8–13). An icon is a pictoral representation or graphic image that appears on the computer screen. Icons represent commands or menu choices. On the Apple Macintosh, for example, an icon of a trash can is used to signify delete a file.

Compatibility

When a microcomputer does not perform a desired task, the owner may solve the problem by adding peripheral equipment to the system, such as disk drives, color monitors, printers, and modems. Internal circuitry can even be added to expand the memory, increase the speed, or change the text windows of most computers. It is not always necessary to choose peripherals from the manufacturer of the microcomputer. Another manufacturer's equipment may have the same or better capabilities at a less expensive price. The peripherals do have to be **compatible,** however. The word

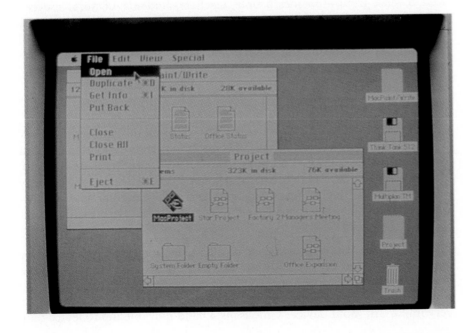

FIGURE 8–13

The icons (graphic images) on the screen are used with a mouse to enter commands on the Macintosh. Icons and pull-down menus make the Macintosh one of the most user-friendly microcomputers on the market.

compatible describes the ability to use one manufacturer's equipment or software with another manufacturer's equipment. The term *compatible* is also used to refer to entire computers that are compatible with other manufacturers' computers. A number of companies have become successful by manufacturing and or selling microcomputers that are compatible with the IBM PC line of microcomputers. Compaq, for example, has become a very successful and profitable company by manufacturing and marketing microcomputers that will run software that is identical to the software that runs on the IBM PC.

Software also must be compatible. Programs designed for one operating system cannot be used on computers with different operating systems. Compatibility in software includes the ability to read and write data on the same diskette and to use common data files.

Compatibility can be extended by adding another microprocessor to a computer. The second microprocessor makes the computer compatible with another operating system. It is a microprocessor that can be plugged into the original computer to replace or work with the original microprocessor. It allows software written for its operating system to be run on a machine that could not run the software otherwise. The second microprocessor usually comes on a plug-in board or card, along with other chips necessary for it to run. The original microprocessor and the second microprocessor share the computer's disk drives, keyboard, and other peripherals.

In addition to a second microprocessor, a coprocessor can also be added to a microcomputer to assist the microprocessor with such things as arithmetic functions. A math coprocessor can be added to IBM PC computers to speed up complicated calculations.

▊ USING MICROCOMPUTERS

Microcomputers are general-purpose machines; that is, they are designed to perform a variety of tasks. The people who buy and use microcomputers are a diverse group—businesspeople, teachers, students, doctors, lawyers, and farmers—and their computing needs are just as diverse. They may need different types of peripheral equipment. They may need various types of services, such as information services and users groups. The following section describes some of the many options available for microcomputers.

Peripherals

Certain peripheral devices work especially well in a microcomputer environment despite some limitations. The first limitation is cost; users of small systems often have limited budgets. The second limitation is ease of use. The devices must be easy to use because microcomputer users are generally not experienced programmers. Business users in particular may be discouraged from using microcomputers if the peripherals are difficult to use.

INPUT DEVICES. The increased use of microcomputers has promoted the popularity of a variety of input and output devices, many of which have become essential for easy use of microcomputers.

In addition to the microcomputer's keyboard, the mouse has become a very important input device. A mouse is a hand-movable input device that controls the position of the cursor on the computer's display screen. (The cursor is a symbol on a computer display screen that shows where the next typed character will appear.) On the bottom of the mouse is a small ball similar to a roller bearing. On the top are from one to three pushbuttons used for activating commands. When the mouse is rolled across a flat surface, the cursor on the display screen moves accordingly. Using a mouse eliminates a considerable amount of typing (see Figure 8-14).

Graphics tablets are flat, boardlike surfaces directly connected to the microcomputer screen (see Figure 8–15). The user draws on the tablet using a pencil-like device, and the image is transmitted to the screen. Graphics tablets enable the user to employ colors, textures, and patterns when creating images.

A **light pen** is a pen-shaped object with a light-sensitive cell at its end. Users can select from a list of choices displayed on the screen by touching a light pen to the proper item. Light pens may also be used in highly technical fields for altering graphs and other drawings.

Relatively new input devices are *scanners*. Scanners are input devices that read printed material so that it can be put in a computer readable form without having to retype, redraw, reprint, or rephotograph the material. Scanners have become very popular as desktop publishing software (see Chapter 12) has become more and more popular.

OUTPUT DEVICES. The most common output device is the monitor. Monitors allow users to view information before sending it to the microprocessor for processing, as well as to view information sent from the microprocessor. The information displayed on the monitor can be in either character or graphic form.

Monitors are generally divided into three categories: (a) monochrome, (b) composite color, and (c) RGB (red-green-blue). **Monochrome monitors**

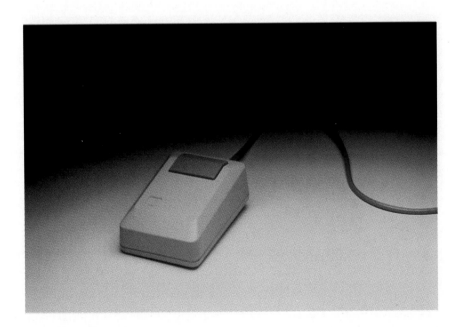

FIGURE 8—14

A Mouse
Some microcomputers allow the user to bypass the keyboard by using a mouse to enter data. The mouse is similar to a track ball: in the mouse, the roller is on the underneath surface of the device, and in the track ball the roller is on the upper surface. The user rolls the mouse around on the desk and a cursor on the screen moves according to the movements of the mouse. A click of the button on the mouse commands the computer.

FIGURE 8—15

Graphics Tablet
Macintizer allows the user to enter data by writing on a flat pad that transfers impulses of the movements of the writing to the proper positions on the screen.

display a single color, such as white, green, or amber, against a black background. They display text clearly and are inexpensive, ranging from $100 to $300. Most monochrome monitors are composite monitors, so called for their single video signal. They usually require no additional video circuitry in the computer.

Composite color monitors display a composite of colors received in a single video signal and are slightly more expensive than monochrome monitors (see Figure 8–16). They do deliver less clarity in displaying text, however, than monochrome monitors. Images on a composite color monitor are also less crisp than images on RGB monitors.

RGB monitors receive three separate color signals, one for each of three colors, red, green, and blue. Commonly used for high-quality graphics displays, they display sharper images than the composite color monitors, but produce fuzzier text than monochrome monitors. They are more expensive than composite color monitors, generally costing from $500 to $900. An add-on display card is necessary for using RGB monitors with most computers.

Color graphics adapters (CGA) were the first graphics adapters used in the IBM PC microcomputer. Enhanced graphics adapters (EGA) were later introduced for the IBM PC to provide users with sharper images on the computer's monitor. In order to produce even sharper images on the PS/2 line of microcomputers IBM introduced the multicolor graphics array (MCGA) and video graphics array (VGA) adapters.

Flat panel displays are available for portable computers. They are less bulky and require less power than the cathode ray tubes used in most monitors. They also show the image less clearly; looking at a flat panel display from an angle or in direct lighting makes the image faint or even invisible. Two common types of flat panel displays are liquid crystal display (LCD) and electroluminescence. LCDs generally show poor contrast and

FIGURE 8—16

RGB Color Monitor

visibility, although new technology is improving the LCD display. The electroluminescent panel shows a better display and a wider viewing angle, but also costs more than the LCD. In the future, it is expected that electroluminescent panels will show full color and high-contrast designs that make the displays readable even in sunlight.

Another common output device used with microcomputers is the printer, discussed in greater detail in Chapter 5. Both impact and nonimpact printers are used with microcomputers. Dot-matrix printers are usually used for rough drafts or cases when the quality of the print is not an important factor. Some dot-matrix printers produce more dots per letter and are used for good-quality textual output as well as for printing graphics such as bar graphs, varying sizes and fonts of type, and logos. Letter-quality printers, such as the daisy wheel or laser printers, are used when output must have the quality of typewritten pages.

ONLINE STORAGE. The storage media commonly used with microcomputers are floppy diskettes and hard disks. These storage devices were discussed in Chapter 6, but their features are reviewed here with respect to microcomputers. Floppy diskettes are inexpensive and small, which makes them ideal for microcomputer data storage. They are not suitable for storing large amounts of data, however. Hard disks are more expensive than floppy disks, but they can hold more than ten times more data.

Floppy disks come in three sizes and are reusable, lightweight, easy to store, and safe to mail. They are accessed by disk drives, which may be built into the computer or be separate units attached to the computer. A 5¼-inch floppy disk can hold as much as 1.2 Mb (megabytes) of data.

Hard magnetic disks hold more data than floppy disks (see Figure 8–17). Common capacities are from 10 Mb to 80 Mb, although some very expensive

FIGURE 8–17

Hard Disk Unit

hard disks for special purposes hold more than 400 Mb. Data access is also faster with hard disks than with floppy disks.

There are two varieties of hard disks: fixed and removable. A fixed disk is a sealed unit the user cannot open and is better protected from dust and other environmental factors. Often the disk drive unit comes installed in the computer. It may contain one or more polished aluminum platters covered with a high-quality magnetic coating. Fixed disks are reliable and hold a large amount of data. A removable disk allows the user to change disks. The disk is enclosed in a cartridge, which is simply inserted in the hard disk drive. This feature provides security because the disks can be removed and locked away from the computer. Removable disks are not as popular as fixed disks because most have less capacity than fixed disks. No matter what type of hard disk is used, a backup system such as floppy disks or tape is necessary.

Optical disks are changing the way microcomputers are used. With such tremendous storage capacity (550 Mb on a single 5¼-inch disk), they make possible a wide range of training and instructional capabilities for busi-nesses. The great storage capacity of the optical disk makes it possible to store video images, which take up a great deal of storage space. Combined with computer data, the video images stored on one optical disk can provide instruction similar to that given in films, yet allow the user to interact through the computer rather than watch passively. Today's optical disks cannot be erased or recorded on, but that is expected to change in the near future.

Software Packages

A **software package** is a set of standardized computer programs, procedures, and related documentation necessary for solving problems of a specific application. Many packages available for business use are discussed in the following sections and later in Chapter 13.

THE BIG FOUR. Software for business use often fills the needs of four basic tasks: doing word processing jobs, analyzing financial data, filing data, and producing pictures that summarize data.

Word processing software allows the user to handle text in four basic ways: writing, editing, formatting, and printing. What is written appears on a screen during the first three stages (the soft copy) and on paper during the printing process (the hard copy). During the writing and editing stages, text can be entered, moved, deleted, or searched. When text is formatted, it is designed for appearance on paper. Formatting may entail spacing be-tween lines, setting margins, adding page numbers, underlining or bold-facing text, merging two or more documents, or centering headings. Printing may involve producing a rough draft or a final copy of the text on paper.

Electronic spreadsheets are used in preparing financial data for sum-maries (see Figure 8–18). Many are prepared like tables with data arranged in columns and rows. Each column and row has a heading. The user looks across the desired row and down the desired column in order to find the needed data. Some parts of the spreadsheet contain formulas using data from other parts of the spreadsheet. As the data is changed, the results of the calculations in the formulas change.

COMPUTERS AND INFORMATION PROCESSING

FIGURE 8—18

Electronic Spreadsheet

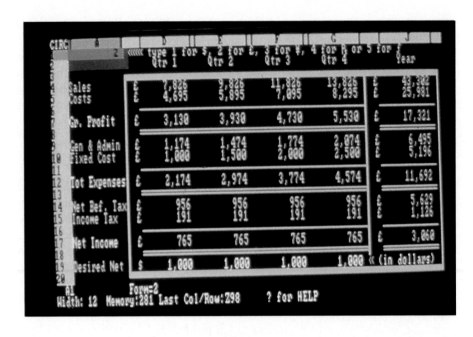

Data can be filed using data-management software. One type is the file handler, which copies traditional filing methods. Material is filed by category and data can appear in several files. The other type is the data-base manager, which allows entry of thousands of records that can be accessed in many types of ways.

Graphics software packages are designed for displaying data in chart form. Depending upon the hardware, the charts are displayed on the monitor screen or are printed using dot-matrix printers or plotters. Common charts drawn by graphics software are bar charts, line graphs, and pie charts.

INTEGRATED SOFTWARE. Integration suggests the blending of two or more parts into a whole. When the term *integration* is used in conjunction with software, it means that two or more types of software are blended into one application package. Integrated software generally conforms to three standards:

1. The software consists of what are usually separate application packages.
2. The software provides easy movement of data among the applications.
3. A common group of commands is used for all the applications in the package.

Integration may occur when several applications are combined into one, such as a data manager, spreadsheet, and graphics package, which can share data and pass data to another application. Integration can also occur when one type of software is enhanced. An example would be the addition of a spelling program, thesaurus, or grammar program to a word processing program.

UTILITIES AND OTHER FUNCTIONS. Software can be used for many other functions that a typical office employee or businessperson might encounter every day. Some software provides a calendar for entering appointments and business functions. Others set alarm clocks, dial telephone numbers, or act like calculators and notepads. Some programs provide the mechanism for writing outlines in preparation for a paper or presentation. Other programs check spelling and grammar, offer alternate word choices, and allow you to program functions into one or two keys in order to save you time while typing.

Users Groups

Where can a microcomputer owner go for help in getting the machine to operate? When a $150 software package will not run on the machine, who can identify the problem? Which word-processing package priced under $200 works best on a certain microcomputer? Questions such as these often baffle the proud new owner of a microcomputer. One answer is a **users group.** A users group is a relatively informal group of owners of a particular microcomputer model or software package who exchange information about hardware, software, service, and support. Users groups may also form around applications and related topics, such as real estate, medicine, telecommunications, education, and computer-aided publishing.

The value of users groups comes from the accumulation of knowledge and experience ready to be shared by members. The best evaluation of hardware and software comes from one who has actually purchased and tried it. As software becomes more sophisticated and more hardware becomes available for enhancing microcomputers, users groups will become even more valuable.

Users groups may be beneficial to small companies because their internal computing experience is limited. Top management may join users groups to learn about new technology and how it can be used in maintaining a competitive position in a particular business field. Individual businesspeople may be interested in improving personal productivity.

Since users groups do not normally have telephones or office space, finding a local group is not always easy. However, dealers who sell microcomputers usually know how to contact users groups, and groups often post notices and flyers in computer stores. Information on national groups is sometimes included in the microcomputer package when it is sold. Contacting the manufacturer directly may also yield the name of the person to contact about a local group.

■ PURCHASING MICROCOMPUTERS

For a number of reasons, buying a microcomputer and software can be a difficult and time-consuming task. As with stereo components and other appliances, there are many models of microcomputers. Choosing one out of 150 models can seem impossible. Add to that choice the hundreds of peripheral devices, add-ons, and worthwhile software packages from which to select and the task is indeed complex and confusing.

The purchase of a computer is a major investment for most people, so care must be taken not to make expensive mistakes. Spend time learning about the different systems on the market and analyzing what you want to do with a computer before making a decision. Otherwise, your computer purchase may end up in the closet gathering dust.

The Big Picture

Experts often recommend that you choose the software and then match the hardware needs to the software. Although this is a good policy, there may be important hardware factors involved in a final decision. Use the following list as a general guide before considering specific requirements.

1. You should have a good idea of what you want to do with your computer and software. Do you want to write papers, analyze financial data, file data, create graphs and charts, publish a newsletter, or use the same data interchangeably among several programs?

2. Know about how much data you will be using at once—ten pages or fifty pages of text, a day's figures or a month's figures of financial data. Both software needs and data needs determine how much memory and speed you need in hardware as well as required storage capacities.

3. Know the functions and names of basic hardware devices.

4. Know some basic functions of various software packages. (See Chapters 10, 11, 12, and the Applications Software Supplement for details about software, programming, and languages.)

5. Test computers and programs at the store. Test programs with data similar to what you will be entering. You may narrow your choice of software to two or three packages, then list a few machines that will run your software.

6. Find out whether the machines on your final list can be used for other purposes in the future.

7. Decide whether the hardware and software must be compatible with those used at work.

8. Be sure that all equipment and software is compatible within the system. Printers, for example, require certain types of connections. Be sure you have the proper connections.

9. Check with friends, computer magazines, and users groups for further information about the software and hardware you are considering.

10. Try different products at different stores.

11. Get firm prices. Find out how much is included in the basic package. The price may include the CPU only, or the CPU, monitor, and disk drive. You may need additional cash outlays for cards that drive a printer or produce graphics.

12. Find out about warranties, service, and exchange policies.

13. Set price limits, but don't be too price conscious. By identifying your intended uses, you already will have defined some price limits.

WHERE TO BUY. Once you have analyzed your needs and determined the appropriate software, you can purchase your computer from several sources: microcomputer vendors, retailers, and mail-order houses.

Computer vendors such as IBM, DEC, Burroughs, and NCR offer their line of microcomputers through a direct sales force. Buying through a computer manufacturer can have several benefits. Often, the salespeople are highly trained in the use of microcomputers in business and can assist you in determining which microcomputer system will meet your needs. Microcomputer vendors can also provide maintenance contracts for on-site repair and can offer replacement equipment if some part of your system should be down for a period of time.

Microcomputer manufacturers also market their products through department stores and computer specialty stores. The sales personnel at some outlets may lack the knowledge you need in making your choices. Be sure you feel comfortable with the salespeople. Computer specialty stores are often staffed with knowledgeable people and in most cases have an in-house service department.

Buying from a mail-order house can be to your advantage if you know exactly what you want to purchase. In many cases, mail-order houses offer products for less than computer specialty stores. Before you buy from a mail-order house, determine what you can expect in the way of services, and make sure you are dealing with a reputable dealer.

OTHER CONSIDERATIONS. You may wonder whether you should buy your system now or wait for newer technology. This question should always be considered before making a decision. Of course, advances will be made and prices will continue to fall. On the other hand, waiting could prevent you from realizing the benefits that technology has already provided.

If you do not have enough money for purchasing the system you want, you may be tempted to buy a cheaper system. Money spent on a cheaper system may be wasted if you do not like the software or hardware and do not use it. Under these circumstances, it may be better to wait a few months while you earn extra money or make alternative arrangements for purchasing the system you do want.

When you are considering various software and hardware for purchase, one of the most important factors should be the documentation. The importance of documentation can be overlooked by hardware and software vendors; however, you will undoubtedly refer to documentation for resolving questions you will have. Good documentation is complete, accurate, and easy to use. Documentation includes both the manuals that accompany hardware and software and on-screen help.

TRAINING. If you will require some training after purchasing your hardware and software, there are a number of options. Seminars offered by microcomputer software vendors and independent training firms are available for some of the more popular software packages. These seminars will guide you in using all the features of the packages. Local computer stores often offer similar classes and seminars (see Figure 8–19).

Colleges and high schools also offer classes in computer use and programming through the normal program or adult education programs. User groups can help resolve questions you have about equipment or programs. A final form of training is through individual home study. Many hardware and software vendors provide tutorials on the use of their products. Tutorials may also be available from independent sources and can be purchased in many bookstores.

Evaluating Software

You must know what you plan on doing with your software before you can evaluate the features of software packages. Consider the following specific factors in your final decision.

FIGURE 8—19

Computer Store Training Seminar
Local computer stores frequently offer training seminars to new computer owners. Here a businesswoman receives hands-on experience with a Macintosh in a computer store.

LEARNING. Gain knowledge about software by reading computer magazines, asking a knowledgeable friend, or joining a users group.

TESTING. Test several programs of the type you are considering. Use data similar to what you plan to use after the purchase. Have a checklist of requirements.

HARDWARE REQUIREMENTS. Check the hardware requirements for using the software. Be sure there are no problems with compatibility.

FLEXIBILITY. Be sure the software can grow as your needs expand. A good program will let you run the program using only the basic commands needed to accomplish the application, and then allow you to incorporate more sophisticated commands as you learn and need them.

ORGANIZATION. Look for a clear and logical screen appearance. A screen that is cluttered and poorly organized will take more time to learn and will not be efficient to use. Some programs are so clear that they let you learn almost by instinct. Look at how the program handles movement between the program modes.

ERROR HANDLING. Determine how the program deals with errors. Error handling capability is an area that, if overlooked in the selection of a program, can spring up as one of the most annoying and disastrous aspects of the program. You should consciously try to make the program you are testing fail, in order to see how it handles the error conditions. A good program will let you recover from common errors. For example, if you are in the middle of a save operation and you get an error message that the disk is full, the program should allow you to replace the disk and then redo the save operation without losing any data.

DATA REQUIREMENTS. Be sure the program will handle the amount of data you will be entering. For example, check the number of records a data manager can support, the number of pages of text a word processor can work with, or the number of columns and rows that a spreadsheet can support.

COMMAND STYLE. Check the type of command style used in the program. Command style refers to the approach used to command the program. Several approaches are the full menu with explanation, the menu alone, a single command with explanation, memorization of all commands with no menus available, or menus with alternative key command options. Although menus are helpful to beginners, experienced users may find that menus slow down the input and processing stages.

HELP SCREENS. Make sure the help screens are really helpful. Help screens that you can call from any point in the program and that return you to where you left off are the most efficient and helpful.

COPY PROTECTION. The question of copy protection can be important. Being able to copy a program allows a great deal of flexibility. If the software cannot be copied, you may not be able to use it with a hard disk, local area network, or electronic disk simulator because you cannot move the copy from a floppy disk. You should also be able to make backup copies of the program. Several software developers are now offering special versions of their software for use with hard disks.

VENDOR POLICIES. Find out the policy of the vendor if the software is updated or if there are programming errors in the software.

MACROS. Not essential, but very helpful, is the program's ability to use macro commands. A macro command allows you to string together several commands and define them as a single key. When that key is struck, the sequence of commands is executed automatically. For example, in a word processing program it may be necessary to search for a word or phrase, replace the word or phrase with another, and save the change. Performing operations such as this with a single keystroke increases the efficiency and ease of use of a program. Macros may be offered in a separate software package that is compatible with the one you will be using.

DEFAULTS. Examine the program for default values. A default is a value that the computer assumes when you do not tell it what value to use. For example, many word processors are set up to produce a standard business letter on 8½ by 11 inch paper without your having to specify this size.

Default values make the program more flexible. They should be easy to change, allowing you to set them so the most often used formats will automatically be used when the program is run. They should also be easy to override temporarily while you are using the program.

Choosing the Hardware

The most important consideration in buying hardware is whether it can handle the software you have chosen. Other factors include ease of use, expected output, storage, and devices that can be added to expand the capabilities of your system.

THE MICROPROCESSOR. Early microcomputers had 8-bit microprocessors. These computers are still popular today and will remain so because software for them is proven, and many users do not need the speed and primary storage available with 16-bit and 32-bit microprocessors.

The 16-bit and 32-bit microprocessors have greater primary memories and allow the computer to process instructions at a much faster rate. If you intend to use your computer for jobs like financial analysis or want to run two or three programs at once, a larger microprocessor is necessary.

MONITORS. Some computers have a built-in video display. Most, however, require the purchase of a separate video display or monitor. There are several things to consider when purchasing a monitor. First, you must decide whether you want a color monitor or a monochrome monitor.

Second, decide on screen dimensions. Microcomputer monitors come in various dimensions. If you are going to use your system for word processing or desktop publishing, a monitor that displays an entire page of text may be more desirable than one that only displays a portion of a printed page.

Third, consider the resolution of the characters displayed on the monitor. Resolution refers to the clarity of those characters. Characters are created using small dots called pixels (picture elements). The smaller the dots and the more closely packed they are, the clearer the images on the screen.

Fourth, make sure there is a way to control the brightness, contrast, and focus of the display. Controlling these factors permits you to adjust the display to suit the lighting conditions of the room in which you are working. Glare can be a stubborn nuisance, too. Most monitors now incorporate some kind of antiglare coating, either inside or outside the glass. Snap-on glare covers are available for most monitors as well. Tilt and swivel display stands, an extra for most monitors, can provide a better viewing angle for the elimination of glare and muscle tension in the neck.

Fifth, check whether the image leaves a ghostlike trail or flickers and blurs when text is scrolled or when you enter data.

KEYBOARDS. Keyboards for microcomputers can come in one of two forms. They can be attached to the computer enclosure or detached from it. Detached keyboards may be either connected to the computer by a cord or operated by batteries (see Figure 8–20).

FIGURE 8–20

Monitor, CPU, and Keyboard
Choosing the appropriate hardware is an important step in the computer buying process.

The angle of the keyboard is important. Keyboards that are part of the machine's enclosure cannot be adjusted, and typing for long periods on these can be tiresome. Detachable keyboards adjust to various angles.

Keyboard touch is another consideration. Most microcomputers have standard touch-sensitive keys that make a noise similar to typewriter keys. A few offer pressure-sensitive keyboards (membrane keyboards). These may be more suitable for use around small children or heavy industry because they protect the keyboard from dirt and spills. Pressure-sensitive keyboards are difficult for touch-typing and would not be a wise choice for word processing.

Some keyboards offer special features such as repeating keys, function keys, and numeric keypads. Numeric keypads are helpful when a considerable amount of numeric data is to be entered.

SECONDARY STORAGE. Secondary storage for microcomputers typically includes floppy disks, hard disks, and tape cartridges. When selecting which type of secondary storage to buy, consider price, amount of storage, access time, and security.

Floppy disks are fairly inexpensive and provide direct access to data, thereby making data retrieval faster than tape storage. Floppy disks commonly come in two sizes: 5¼-inch and 3½-inch. To date, the 5¼-inch size has been the most common. The 3½-inch disks are usually packaged in hard plastic for better protection when handling outside the disk drive.

Hard disks are the most expensive form of storage but allow very rapid access to data. They may be shared by more than one microcomputer, and offer more system flexibility. Some software cannot be placed on hard disks without also inserting the program disk in a regular disk drive.

Tape cartridges are typically used on microcomputers for online storage backup. A separate peripheral hardware device is required for this application. The tape cartridges' capacities are at least large enough to store an entire hard disk's contents.

PRINTERS. Printers can be one of the most expensive peripherals you purchase. There are a number of features that should be considered when shopping for a printer:

■ The speed with which printing occurs.
■ The amount of noise the printer makes. If the printer of your choice makes considerable noise, purchase a sound shield to cover the printer during operation.
■ The availability of supplies such as ribbons, cartridges, or special paper required by the printer.
■ The number of characters per inch (the pitch).
■ The size of the platen (the carriage roller). (A larger size may be needed in printing spreadsheets, for example.)
■ The type of paper feed—tractor feed, which uses tiny pins in pulling the paper through the printer, and friction feed, which is the type of paper feed used by typewriters.
■ The quality of print. Letter-quality printers produce solid characters suitable for formal communication, while dot-matrix printers produce char-

acters made of tiny dots. Some dot matrix printers produce near-letter-quality characters and can be used for most purposes.

■ The flexibility of different fonts and sizes of print. Letter-quality impact printers produce one size of print. The font can be changed by exchanging the removable print element. Dot-matrix printers allow flexibility in printing many fonts, or styles of type, and many sizes of type. These printers may be more suitable for newsletters. For a more expensive printer with high-quality output and a high degree of flexibility in fonts and sizes, consider the laser printer.

■ The number of copies to be made. Dot-matrix printers do not print through multiple copies, so an impact printer is needed if carbon copies are to be made.

ADD-ONS. Add-ons are printed circuit boards or expansion boards that can increase the capabilities of your computer. They can be used for several purposes:

■ Changing the number of characters displayed on the width of the screen.
■ Adding graphics capabilities to the computer.
■ Adding a coprocessor to the computer so that software for a different operating system can be run.
■ Adding memory.
■ Providing interfaces for input and output devices such as printers, mice, and graphics tablets.

The software you choose may require the use of one or more add-on circuit boards. Check the requirements carefully before purchasing equipment. Some computers are sold with interfaces for video displays and graphics, for example, while others need additional boards.

When buying an expansion board, test it at the dealer's, making sure all the functions work. If you are not knowledgeable about computers, it is best to have the board installed in your machine by the dealer. Power to the computer should be off and the cords removed from wall outlets before installation takes place. In addition, you should discharge static from your body before touching the components. The best way is to touch the metal chassis of any grounded appliance, such as an office copier.

Again, be sure the expansion board is compatible with all the other elements of your computer system.

OTHER HARDWARE DEVICES. Depending on your intended uses and specific needs, your microcomputer system may require other specialized hardware devices. For example, a particular graphics package may require the use of a graphics tablet or light pen for data input. Special hardware devices includes the following: joystick, Koala pad or other graphics tablet, game paddle, modem for using a telephone with your computer, track ball, light pen, mouse, digitizer, touch screen, voice recognition or voice synthesizer system, and music synthesizer. Descriptions of these items are found in this text and in popular computer literature such as magazines and paperback books.

Buyer's Checklist

When selecting a microcomputer, a checklist is often helpful. The following checklist can help you identify the items you need.

1. List the expected uses of your computer.
2. List the software requirements for handling your intended uses.
3. List the application programs that can meet your designated needs.
4. Given the software requirements listed above, check the specific hardware requirement below.

THE MICROPROCESSOR
—— 8-bit
—— 16-bit
—— 32-bit
—— K internal memory needed

THE MONITOR
—— Dimension
—— Monochrome display
     —— White
     —— Green
     —— Amber
—— Color display
     —— Composite
     —— RGB
—— Glare shield

THE KEYBOARD
—— Detachable
—— Upper- and lower-case letters
—— Repeating keys
—— Numeric keypad
—— Function keys

THE PRINTER
—— Dot-matrix
—— Letter-quality
—— Friction feed
—— Tractor feed
—— Individual sheet feed
—— Carriage width
     —— 80-column
     —— 132-column
—— Speed
—— Pitch
—— Noise shield

ADD-ON (EXPANSION) CIRCUIT BOARD
—— Graphic display
—— Printer interface
—— Interface for other devices such as joystick, graphics tablet, and so on
—— Additional memory
—— Coprocessor

OTHER HARDWARE DEVICES
—— Joystick
—— Graphics tablet
—— Track ball
—— Paddle
—— Modem
—— Light pen
—— Mouse
—— Touch screen
—— Voice recognition
—— Voice synthesis
—— Music synthesis
—— Digitizer
—— Plotter
—— Scanner

■ SUMMARY POINTS

■ Microcomputers are the smallest and least expensive computers; they differ from minicomputers, mainframes, and supercomputers in capability, price, and size. The distinctions between microcomputers and larger systems are fading as microcomputers become more powerful.

■ The increased power and miniaturization of microprocessors paved the way for the development of microcomputers.

■ The first microprocessors could manipulate four bits of data at a time. Most microcomputers today can manipulate eight, sixteen, or thirty-two bits of data.

■ Some early microcomputer pioneers include Ed Roberts of MITS, Stephen Wozniak and Steven Jobs of Apple, Jack Tramiel of Commodore Business Machines, John Roach of Tandy, and John Opel of IBM. Though their contributions vary, they all played important roles in making microcomputers available to the general public.

■ Portable computers can be classified by size as briefcase, notebook, or hand-held. They are light enough to be carried and do not need an external power source. Transportables are larger than portables but are still light enough to be carried. They require an external power source.

■ Supermicrocomputers are less expensive than minicomputers and provide users with high performance at a relatively low cost.

■ The speed of microcomputers depends on word size and clock speed. Word size refers to the number of bits that can be manipulated at one time. Clock speed is the number of electronic pulses the microprocessor can produce each second.

■ Primary memory consists of random-access memory (RAM) and read-only memory (ROM). A RAM disk is an add-on card that contains RAM chips and acts like a disk, providing speeds that approximate that of the microprocessor.

■ Instructions for basic computer functions such as arithmetic and logic operations and storage and retrieval functions constitute the instruction set of the computer.

■ An operating system is a collection of programs used by the computer to manage its operation and provide an interface between the user or application program and the computer hardware. Since there is no single standard operating system for microcomputers, microcomputers with different operating systems are not compatible.

■ Some input and output devices popular for use with microcomputers are the mouse, graphics tablets, light pens, printers, and plotters. Keyboards and monitors are among the essential peripherals for microcomputers.

■ Floppy disks and hard disks are the storage media commonly used with microcomputers. Hard disks are used in situations where large amounts of data must be stored. Optical disks are also becoming a popular storage medium for use with microcomputers, although they cannot yet be erased and reused.

■ Popular software includes programs for word processing, electronic spreadsheets, data management, and graphics. Combinations of programs—such as a data manager, spreadsheet, and graphics package, or a word processor and spelling program—are called integrated software.

■ Users groups offer owners advice and information from other microcomputer users about machines, programs, and topics of special interest such as electronic publishing or telecommunications.

■ It is recommended that when purchasing a microcomputer you first select the software you will require and then match the hardware to the needs of the software.

■ Microcomputer training is available in a number of forms, including seminars provided by manufacturers and microcomputer dealers, college and high school classes, users groups, and self study.

■ The parts of the microcomputer to be considered before purchasing include the microprocessor, monitors, keyboards, secondary storage, printers, and other add-on devices such as modems, a mouse, a light pen, and a graphics tablet.

■ REVIEW QUESTIONS

1. What differentiates microcomputers from larger computers?

2. Describe the development of the microprocessor and explain how it contributed to the development of the microcomputer.

3. Differentiate between portables, supermicrocomputers, and the desktop models of microcomputers.

5. Explain how word size and clock speed affect the speed of a microcomputer.

5. Explain what is meant by *booting* the microcomputer.

6. What is meant by microcomputer compatibility? What determines microcomputer compatibility?

7. Name some input devices that allow you to bypass the keyboard, reducing the amount of typing needed.

8. Name two disk technologies that allow greater computer capacities than floppy disks. What is special about each?

9. What is a users group?

10. What should be considered first when purchasing a microcomputer—software or hardware? Why?

11. List four factors that you feel would be important in selecting a word processor. Describe why you feel these factors are important?

12. What types of secondary storage are most common on microcomputers? How are tape cartridges typically used on microcomputers?

Compaq Computer Corporation

Compaq Computer Corporation is the world's leading manufacturer of portable business personal computers and the leading supplier of desktop personal computers based on the advanced Intel® 80386 microprocessor. Compaq employs more than 4,700 people worldwide, with U.S. and international manufacturing facilities and office facilities worldwide totaling more than 3.3 million square feet.

Compaq was founded in February 1982 by Rod Canion, Jim Harris, and Bill Murto, three senior managers who left Texas Instruments and invested $1,000 each to form their own company. Sketched on a paper placemat in a Houston pie shop, the new company's first product was a portable personal computer, able to run all of the software being developed for the original IBM PC, introduced in 1981.

The founders presented their idea to Ben Rosen, president of Sevin-Rosen Partners, the high-tech venture capital firm that would later fund Compaq and other fast-growth companies, including Lotus Development Corp. The venture capitalists were impressed with the idea of a portable product innovating within the emerging IBM PC standard and agreed to fund the new company.

In the six years following its founding in February 1982, the Houston, Texas-based company set sales and financing records, rapidly expanded its work force and facilities and built a corporate organization poised to achieve even greater long-term growth. In 1983, its first full year of operation, Compaq achieved revenues of $111.2 million, a record in U.S. business history for the most successful first year of sales. The company's 1984 sales of $329 million also set a record for the greatest second-year sales in the history of the U.S. computer industry.

In 1985, when many other computer companies reported lower revenues, Compaq Computer Corporation reported record sales of $503.9 million, making it the first company to achieve "Fortune 500" status in less than four years. In the same year the company doubled net income, while revenues rose 53 percent from 1984. In 1987, Compaq surpassed $1 billion in annual sales, just five years after shipping the first COMPAQ® Portable computer. The company reached this milestone faster than any other company in business history.

COMPAQ personal computers are compatible with personal computer industry standards, meaning they support the largest base of business software programs, peripherals, and hardware add-ons. The company, unique in its dedication to maintaining full compatibility with established industry standards, believes innovation within these standards is a key to success. It has established standards for performance, quality of design, reliability and superior features that meet real user needs.

Its first two products, the COMPAQ Portable and COMPAQ PLUS® personal computers, were introduced in 1983 and quickly set the standard for full-function portable personal computers. Within a year, they were the world's best-selling portable personal computers. In June 1984, the company introduced the COMPAQ DESKPRO® family of 8086-based desktop personal computers and within four months it became one of the top selling lines of desktop business personal computers.

In April 1985, the company introduced the COMPAQ DESKPRO 286® personal computer. This advanced business personal computer utilizes the 80286 architecture and is compatible with, yet offers features and performance superior to, the IBM PC AT®. In February 1986, Compaq introduced the COMPAQ Portable II®, which at the time set the standard as the world's smallest and lightest high-performance, portable personal computer and is now the standard for mainstream 80286-based portable personal computing.

On Sept. 9, 1986, Compaq established a new high-performance personal computing standard by introducing the COMPAQ DESKPRO 386®, the first industry standard personal computer based on the 32-bit architecture of the 80386 microprocessor. In doing so, the company achieved a major technology breakthrough and ushered in the third generation of personal computer technology.

In 1987 Compaq continued to expand the boundaries of full-function portable business personal computing with the February introduction of the COMPAQ PORTABLE III®, its lightest and smallest portable personal computer. By incorporating a 12 MHz 80286 microprocessor, the COMPAQ PORTABLE III provides the power and functionality of a high-performance desktop computer in a small and rugged self-contained unit weighing only 18 pounds. Compaq again revolutionized the personal computer industry in September 1987 with its introductions of the COMPAQ DESKPRO 386/20™, the world's most powerful high-performance personal computer, and the COMPAQ PORTABLE 386™, pound-for-pound the most powerful computer ever built.

The company sells its personal computer products exclusively through more than 3,000 Authorized COMPAQ Computer Dealers in 42 countries. Gaining valuable shelf space while developing and maintaining strong relationships with authorized COMPAQ computer dealers has been a major factor in the company's success.

International sales were almost triple those in 1986, and contributed 32 percent of the company's 1987 revenue. Compaq was the fourth leading supplier of personal computers to Europe in 1987, up from sixth the year before. Compaq has established a network of manufacturing facilities to better meet the particular needs of international users and provide enhanced support for the company's Houston-based assembly operations. These include a portable and desktop production facility in Erskine, Scotland, and a printed-circuit board assembly plant in Singapore, Compaq's first satellite manufacturing facility outside the U.S. In addition, the company markets its full line of personal computer products through wholly-owned overseas subsidiaries in Australia, Canada, France, Germany, Italy, the Netherlands, Spain, Sweden, Switzerland, and the United Kingdom.

DISCUSSION POINTS

1. What corporate design strategy has been critical to the success of Compaq?
2. Discuss the product mix of Compaq computers.

CHAPTER

9

Telecommunications and Distributed Computing

O U T L I N E

Introduction
Data Communications
  Message Transmission
  Input/Output Operations
Communication Channels
  Types of Channels
  Grades of Channels
  Modes of Channels
Communication Hardware
  Multiplexers and Concentrators
  Programmable Communications
    Processors

Data Communication Applications
  Local-Area Networks (LANs)
  Electronic Banking
  Telecommuting
Distributed Computing
Distributed Computing Networks
  Single CPU Networks
  Multiple CPU Networks
Telecommunication Standards

A Guide to Networks
  Information Services
  Bulletin Boards
  Proprietary and Nonproprietory
    Networks
Summary Points
Review Questions

ARTICLE

Security Problems Greater Than Ever

Barbara Bates
InformationWEEK

This is the information age. Technology gains have placed enormous computer power in the hands of end users and have also made it possible for them to communicate faster and more easily than ever before. Distributed processing is credited with fostering huge productivity gains, especially through the use of sophisticated decision-support systems using sensitive strategic data.

However, along with the gift of increased productivity, distributed processing brings a new challenge: network security. The network that makes possible these productivity gains also introduces distributed vulnerability in a variety of ways:

■ Competitors can copy your product, pricing, or acquisition plans as they are transmitted.
■ Thieves can alter monetary transactions.
■ Dissidents, terrorists, and hackers can introduce programmed viruses that destroy your computer's files and programs.

How, then, can you quantify the threat so you know how much to spend to protect against it? Look at the applications that use the network and start by determining what is worth protecting. The applications (funds transfer, sales forecasts, pricing systems, etc.) tell you what sort of information flows over or through the network and will enable you to determine the sensitivity of that information.

For each application, program, and file, determine the impact on your company if a competitor/thief/terrorist/hacker obtains access. If your company's style is extremely analytic, you may want to utilize risk-analysis software models and consulting services to help assign probability of occurrence and a monetary value to each vulnerability.

Next you determine what you can do to eliminate or minimize the risks identified. Generally, the technical solutions can be classified into one of three technologies: access control, privacy, or authentication.

Access control limits access to an asset. For example, passwords, personal or terminal authentication devices, and dialback systems all endeavor to limit the access to a computer to authorized individuals as long as the passwords are kept secret and secure. These methods, though, do not limit access to the network itself. Dialback or password systems don't prevent your competitor from tapping your transmission lines while authorized users are passing sensitive data over those lines.

Barbara Bates is principal product manager, data communications security, for Codex Corp. She has been an MIS director, software consultant, and systems analyst for a major bank.

Privacy controls therefore become important to the network. You may not be able to limit access to the network transmission lines, but you can ensure that data flowing across those lines is unintelligible to the unauthorized user. Encryption technologies, which enforce privacy, may be performed in software for a particular application and provide privacy for the entire path from one computer to another or to a PC. Or it may be performed in hardware/firmware that secures all data transmitted between two communications devices (like encryption).

Encryption uses a special algorithm (like a computer program) and a key (a variable number) to scramble data at one end of a line and unscramble it at the other end. The security of this approach depends on the strength of the algorithm (few people are competent to evaluate them, so pick a standard like DES), and the security of the keys (change the keys frequently and make sure your "change procedure" is secure).

Encryption also offers some assurance of data authenticity/integrity as long as no unauthorized person has a copy of the scrambler key. However, once the data is unscrambled, you have no proof that it was ever secured by encryption.

Authentication involves proof that no one has tampered with the data exchanged between authorized individuals. Authentication technology provides assurance of data integrity in software by using an encryption algorithm and key to create a special message authentication code (MAC) at the end of each trans-

ARTICLE

action—almost like a check sum. The transaction is not scrambled, but the MAC at its end provides a digital signature that, when unscrambled, proves the integrity of the transaction.

Whatever technology you choose to implement should be relatively easy to use and manage, and the need for the security should be well understood by all people involved. If this is not the case, the users will disregard or subvert the security systems. Network security measures, like so much of management, must be based on common sense to be effective.

Companies often do not report computer crimes, such as theft

of funds, to the police because the company fears they will gain a poor reputation. Yet computer crimes can and do happen. Companies must be aware of the ways data and funds can be stolen and use the methods necessary to prevent these problems.

■ INTRODUCTION

Earlier chapters have presented information on both large and small computer systems. Discussions have focused on the physical components of computers (hardware, storage, input, and output) and on file organization and data design. This chapter focuses on data communications and how computer systems of all sizes are used in data communications.

Managing today's diverse businesses is a complex task, and management information needs extend beyond routine summary reports. A manager must have current knowledge of company operations in order to control business activities and to ensure that effective customer service is provided. Decisions must be made on short notice and on the basis of data gathered and analyzed from geographically remote locations. An efficient, fast way to capture, process, and distribute large amounts of data is needed. Data communication systems developed to meet this need help to reduce delays in the collection and dissemination of data.

This chapter explains how communication systems allow users at remote locations to gain fast, easy access to computer resources. Included are discussions on the concepts and techniques involved in message transmission and the types of equipment that make data communication possible. Alternative methods of using communications technology to implement management information systems are also explored.

CHAPTER

■ DATA COMMUNICATIONS

Data communication is the electronic transmission of data from one location to another, usually over communication channels such as telephone or telegraph lines or microwaves. In a data communication system, data is transmitted between terminals and a central computer or between two or more computers. As people and equipment become geographically dispersed, the computer and input and output devices, or **terminals,** are hooked into a communication network. The communication network provides the means for the input and output devices to communicate with both themselves and the computer(s) tied into the network. The combined use of communication facilities, such as telephone systems, and data-processing equipment is called **telecommunication.**

Data communication using communication channels can take place between terminals that are in the same room or separated by an ocean. The difference between these two situations is the type of communication channel through which the data flows.

Message Transmission

Data can be transmitted over communication lines in one of two forms: analog or digital. Transmission of data in continuous wave form is referred to as **analog transmission.** An analog transmission can be compared to the waves created in a pan of still water by a stick. By sending "waves" down a wire electronically, messages are sent and received. In the past, analog transmission was the major means of relaying data over long distances. This was due largely to the type of communication lines provided by American Telephone and Telegraph (AT&T). **Digital transmission,** on the other hand, involves the transmission of data as distinct on and off pulses. Digital transmission tends to be faster and more accurate than analog transmission. Figure 9–1 illustrates the concepts of digital and analog transmission.

FIGURE 9–1

Analog and Digital Transmission

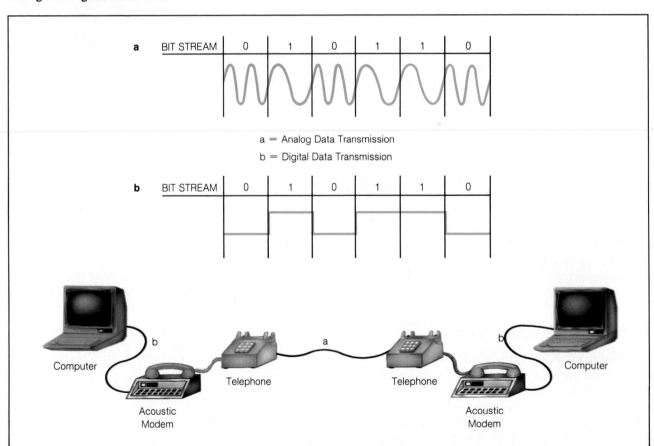

Analog transmission requires that the sender convert the data from the pulse form in which it is stored to wave form before transmitting it. This conversion process is called **modulation.** The opposite conversion—from wave to pulse form—is required at the receiving end before the data is entered into the computer. This conversion is called **demodulation.** Both modulation and demodulation are accomplished by devices called **modems** or **data sets.** The term *modem* is derived from the terms *mod*ulation and *dem*odulation.

There are three types of modems: (a) acoustic coupler, (b) direct connect, and (c) internal. An **acoustic-coupler modem** is linked to a terminal and has a special cradle that holds a standard telephone handset (see Figure 9–2a). The modem processes audible analog tones that pass through the receiver, thus the term *acoustic* coupler. A **direct-connect modem** connects a computer directly into a telephone line (see Figure 9–2b). An **internal modem** consists of a circuit board that is plugged into the internal circuitry of the computer, eliminating the need for a connection directly to a telephone (see Figure 9–2c).

Since the computer stores data in pulse form, when digital transmission is used there is no need to convert data from wave to digital form. This reduces the time required to send messages and eliminates the data errors that frequently occur in the conversion process. Users can transmit large amounts of data faster and more reliably with digital transmission.

Input/Output Operations

One of the key functions of the input/output (IO) devices of a computer system is the conversion of data into a machine-readable form. For instance, data on punched cards must be converted from Hollerith code into a machine-readable form such as ASCII or BCD (see the section on Computer Codes in Chapter 4). Code conversion must be performed when data is input from devices such as remote terminals and magnetic-ink character recognition devices and also at output when information is sent to a printer or display terminal. Code conversion is performed by the **input/output (I/O) control unit.** This unit is different from the control unit of the CPU. It is

FIGURE 9–2a

Acoustic-Coupler Modem

FIGURE 9–2b

Direct-Connect Modem

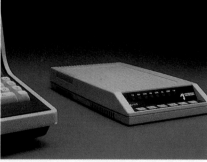

FIGURE 9–2c

Internal Modem

located between one or more I/O devices and the CPU and is used only to facilitate I/O operations.

In addition to code conversion, I/O control units perform **data buffering.** A **buffer** is a separate storage unit (normally contained in the I/O control unit) for a particular input or output device. It is used as a temporary holding area for data being transferred to or from the CPU.

When data is read by an input device, it is converted to a machine-readable form and stored in a buffer. Once a specific amount of data has been collected in the buffer, it is transferred to the CPU. The buffer allows a large quantity of data to be transferred much faster than if the data items were transferred individually. For example, a buffer is used to temporarily hold data being entered from a remote terminal; this allows an entire record to be keyed on the terminal, held, and transferred all at once to the CPU. While the record is being keyed, the CPU processes other data (see Figure 9–3). The buffer serves a similar purpose when information is transferred from the computer to a printer or terminal as output.

Although the CPU is very fast and accurate, it can execute only one instruction at a time. If it executes an instruction that requires input or output, it must wait while data is retrieved from or sent to an input/ output device. Compared with the CPU's internal processing speeds, I/O speeds are extremely slow. Even high-speed I/O devices often work only one-tenth as fast as the CPU. When the CPU slows down to wait for input/output operations to take place, it is **input/output bound.**

The flow of data shown in Table 9–1 indicates that in this system the CPU does the process step when it has the necessary data but sits idle while input and output occur. To increase use of the CPU, **channels** have been developed to take over the task of transferring data to and from the CPU (see Table 9–2). Each channel is a small, limited-capacity computer that serves as a data roadway. The channel may be within the CPU or a separate piece of equipment connected to it. During processing, when the CPU encounters an instruction requiring input or output, the CPU indicates to the channel what is needed. The channel then goes to the required input device for data or sends information to the appropriate output device. The CPU,

FIGURE 9–3

Data Buffering

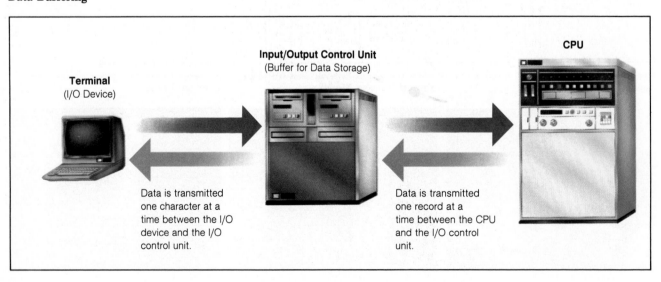

Terminal
(I/O Device)

Input/Output Control Unit
(Buffer for Data Storage)

CPU

Data is transmitted one character at a time between the I/O device and the I/O control unit.

Data is transmitted one record at a time between the CPU and the I/O control unit.

COMPUTERS AND INFORMATION PROCESSING

TABLE 9—1

Input/Output Bound

	Time 1	Time 2	Time 3
Input	Item 1		
Process		Item 1	
Output			Item 1

The CPU is input/output–bound—it can operate only one item at a time.

meanwhile, is free to execute other instructions; it is relieved of its responsibility to transfer data and can process the data more efficiently.

There are two types of channels: selector and multiplexor. A **selector channel** can accept input from only one device at a time and is used with high-speed I/O devices such as a magnetic-tape or magnetic-disk unit. A **multiplexor channel** can handle more than one I/O device at a time. A byte multiplexor channel is normally associated with multiple high-speed devices but is less frequently encountered.

▩ COMMUNICATION CHANNELS

A **communication channel** is the link that permits transmission of electrical signals between **distributed data processing (DDP)** locations. The purpose of a communication channel is to carry data from one location to another. Communication channels can be classified in a number of different ways. The following discussion classifies channels by type, grade, and mode.

Types of Channels

Several types of media are used as communication channels for data transfer, the most common of which are telephone lines, coaxial cables, fiber-optic cables, and microwaves.

Telephone lines are one of the most widely used communication channels for the transmission of both data and voices. Ordinary telephone lines are composed of strands of copper wire that are twisted into pairs. Copper is an excellent conductor of electrical signals, and data travels along the wire from one location to another.

TABLE 9—2

Processing with Channels

	Time 1	Time 2	Time 3
Input	Item 1	Item 2	Item 3
Process		Item 1	Item 2
Output			Item 1

With the aid of channels, the CPU can be active a greater percentage of the time.

HIGHLIGHT

When Computers Speak

When you place a call to a company, you may not speak to the operator. Instead you may hear the following:

Hello, this is company XYZ. If you would like to speak to someone in our sales department, press 123; if you want to talk to someone in product support, dial 345; if you need further assistance, please stay on the line."

The above statements will be spoken by one of the newest members of the automated office—the automated attendant. Many companies are now staffing their phones with this new technology because they are efficient, effective—and they don't call in sick! Two companies—Dytel, Inc. and Microvoice—are the main manufacturers of these communication systems. These companies have found processing phone calls very profitable; sales are expected to be over a billion dollars in the next few years.

What new developments are expected in the future for automated receptionists? Dytel hopes to develop a system where the caller dials the company number and then uses a touch tone telephone to spell the name of the person he is trying to reach. Again, this will eliminate the need for operator assistance.

What do callers think of the automated system? Some callers do not like listening to a computer; they would rather speak to an operator. But since companies find the systems cost effective, we all may be listening more often to computer voices.

Coaxial cable is composed of groups of both copper and aluminum wires. The wires are insulated to reduce the distortion that interferes with signal transmission (see Figure 9–4). Coaxial cables permit high-speed transmission of data and can be used to replace ordinary telephone lines.

Fiber optics is a relatively new form of technology that permits digital transmission. In fiber-optic cables, light impulses (laser beams) are sent along clear, flexible tubing approximately half the diameter of a human hair (see Figure 9–5). A fiber-optic cable is about one-tenth the diameter of a wire cable. Because fiber-optic cables permit data to be transmitted without conversion to analog form, there are few errors in data transmission. The small tubing makes the cables easy to install. One drawback of fiber-optic cables, however, is that the light impulses lose signal strength over distance. However, fiber optic cables are not susceptible to electrical interference; hence, they are ideal for data transmission because of the reduced chance of error.

Microwave communication channels transmit data in analog form. Microwaves are sent through the atmosphere at high speeds in a way that is similar to radio or television transmission. Microwaves are transmitted from one ground station to another or from earth to satellite or vice versa. Unlike other communication channels, however, microwaves cannot bend. Since they must be transmitted in a straight line between two points, microwave transmission is frequently used in conjunction with satellites. Communication satellites rotate about the earth at approximately the same speed that the earth rotates about the sun. Microwaves are sent in a straight line from an earth station to the satellite and then redirected from the receiving satellite to another satellite or earth station (see Figure 9–6).

Microwave transmission is relatively error free and offers a great deal of flexibility because there is no need for a physical link between transmission

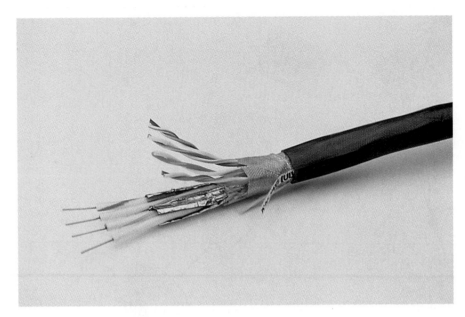

FIGURE 9—4

Coaxial Cable

points. On the negative side, microwave transmission is expensive because of the high cost of constructing ground stations and launching satellites.

Grades of Channels

Communication channels can also be classified by grade. The **grade** or **bandwidth** of a channel determines the range of frequency at which it can transmit data. The rate at which data can be transmitted across the channel is directly proportional to the width of the frequency band. **Narrow bandwidth**

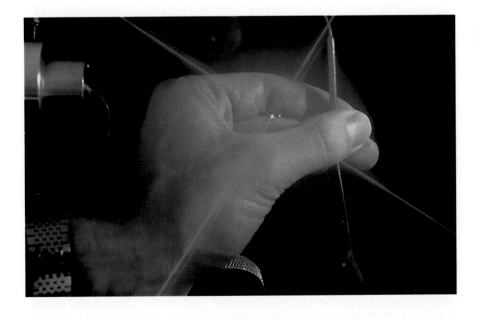

FIGURE 9—5

Fiber-Optic Cable

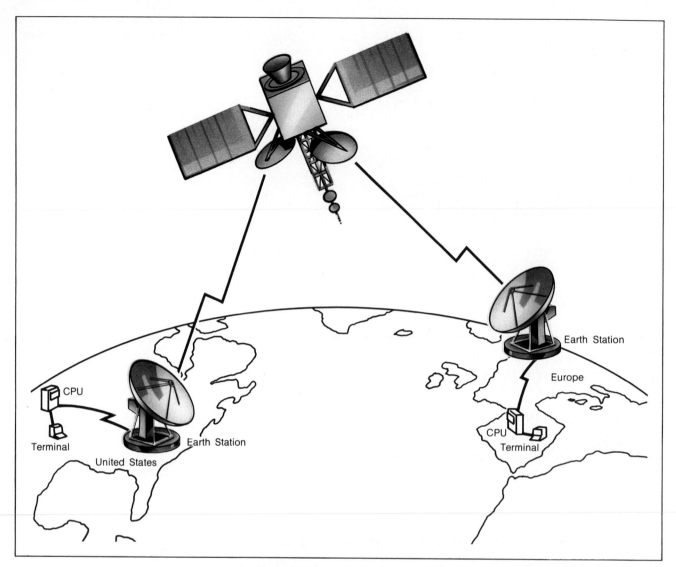

FIGURE 9—6

Satellite Communication System Using Microwaves

channels, such as telegraph lines, can transmit data at rates between forty-five and ninety bits per second.

Voice-grade channels have wider frequency ranges. They can transmit at rates between 300 and 9,600 bits per second. Voice-grade channels such as telephone lines are used by AT&T for the Wide Area Telephone Service (WATS) line.

For applications that require high-speed transmission of large volumes of data, **broad-band channels** are most suitable. Coaxial cables, microwaves, and fiber-optic cables fall into this category. Broad-band transmission services can be leased from both Western Union and AT&T. Broad-band channels can transmit data at a rate of up to 120,000 bits per second.

Modes of Channels

Communication channels operate in one of three basic transmission modes: simplex, half-duplex, or full-duplex. The mode of transmission is dependent

COMPUTERS AND INFORMATION PROCESSING

upon the application and the terminal equipment used. A simplex transmission is unidirectional, or one-way. A simplex modem can either send or receive data; it cannot do both. Half-duplex transmission permits data to flow in two directions but only one way at a time. Modems capable of half-duplex transmission are commonly used in telephone services and networks. Full-duplex transmission permits data to flow in both directions simultaneously. A modem capable of full-duplex transmission is the most versatile type available. Figure 9–7 illustrates the channel transmission modes.

CONCEPT SUMMARY 9–1

Communication Channels

Type of Channel	Characteristics of Channel	Grade of Channel
Telephone line	Twisted copper strands Excellent conductor of electricity Most widely used media Analog transmission	Voice-grade
Coaxial cable	Copper and aluminum wires insulated to reduce distortion High-speed analog transmission	Broad-band
Fiber-optic cable	Flexible, narrow tubing Light impulses are sent along clear flexible tubing Digital transmission	Broad-band

Microwave	Similar to radio or television
	    transmission
	Transmission must be in a straight
	    line
	Used with satellites
	Analog transmission
		Broad-band

▧ COMMUNICATION HARDWARE

Data communication involves the use of computer terminals or microcomputers acting as computer terminals with input/output devices. Often data communication requires the use of special hardware to speed the transfer of data.

Multiplexers and Concentrators

Multiplexers and **concentrators**, also known as **datacom handlers**, increase the number of input/output devices that can use a communication channel. They allow multiple I/O devices to share one channel. It is advantageous to increase the number of I/O devices because these devices operate at much lower speeds (100 to 150 bits per second) than communication channels (300 to 9,600 bits per second for voice-grade channels). Thus, a channel is not used to full capacity by a single I/O device.

Multiplexing can promote more economical use of a communication channel; it acts as a communication interface, combining the input streams from

FIGURE 9—7

Channel Transmission Modes

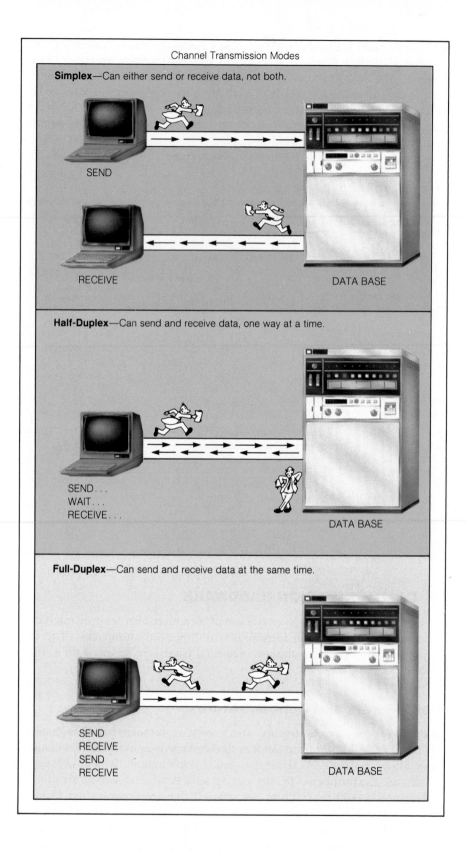

Channel Transmission Modes

Simplex—Can either send or receive data, not both.

SEND

RECEIVE

DATA BASE

Half-Duplex—Can send and receive data, one way at a time.

SEND...
WAIT...
RECEIVE...

DATA BASE

Full-Duplex—Can send and receive data at the same time.

SEND
RECEIVE
SEND
RECEIVE

DATA BASE

several devices into a single stream that can be sent over a single channel to the computer system. This allows a single communication channel (typically voice-grade) to substitute for many slower subvoice channels that might otherwise have been operating at less than full capacity. Once the computer system has completed processing, the data is sent to the multiplexer, which then routes the data to the appropriate device.

A concentrator differs from a multiplexer in that it allows data to be transmitted from only one terminal at a time over a communication channel. The concentrator **polls** the terminals one at a time to see if they have any messages to send. When a communication channel is free, the first terminal ready to send or receive data will get control of the channel and continue to control it for the length of the transaction. The use of a concentrator relies on the assumption that not all terminals will be ready to send or receive data at a given time. Figure 9–8 shows examples of communication systems with and without multiplexers and concentrators.

Programmable Communications Processors

A **programmable communications processor** is a device that relieves the CPU of many of the tasks typically required in a communication system. When the volume of data transmission surpasses a certain level, a programmable communications processor can handle these tasks more economically than the CPU. Examples of such tasks include handling messages and priorities, terminating transmission after messages have been received, requesting retransmission of incomplete messages, and verifying successfully transmitted messages.

The two most frequent uses of communications processors are message switching and front-end processing. The principal task of the processor used for **message switching** is to receive messages and route them to appropriate destinations. A **front-end processor** performs message switching as well as more sophisticated operations, such as validating transmitted data and processing data before it is transmitted to the central computer.

▩ DATA COMMUNICATION APPLICATIONS

The technology used to facilitate data communications is being used in a number of practical applications. In the following sections some of the more popular applications are described.

Local-Area Networks (LANs)

A local-area network (LAN) operates within a well-defined and generally self-enclosed area, such as a small office building. The communication stations are usually linked by cable and are generally within 1,000 feet of each other. Distance among terminals in a LAN is limited by the time required for the signal to travel from one workstation to the next and by the decrease in the strength of the signal as it travels.

In local-area networks, microcomputers can be linked together to share peripheral devices and information and also to provide the ability to communicate between members of the network. Sharing peripheral devices such as printers and mass storage devices can reduce costs on a per-computer

FIGURE 9—8

**Communication Systems with and
without Multiplexers and
Concentrators**

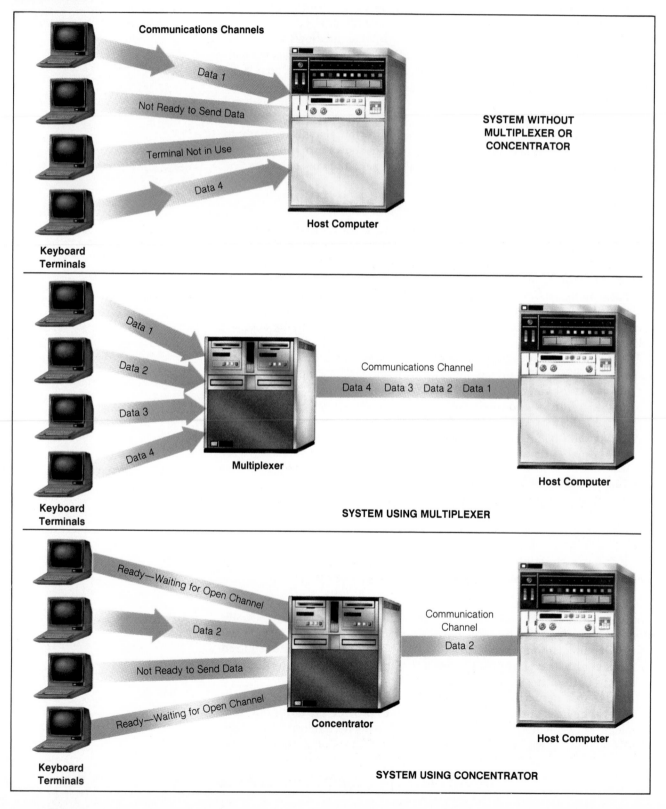

Communications Channels

Data 1

Not Ready to Send Data

Terminal Not in Use

Data 4

**SYSTEM WITHOUT
MULTIPLEXER OR
CONCENTRATOR**

Host Computer

**Keyboard
Terminals**

Data 1

Data 2

Data 3

Data 4

Multiplexer

Communications Channel

Data 4   Data 3   Data 2   Data 1

Host Computer

**Keyboard
Terminals**

SYSTEM USING MULTIPLEXER

Ready—Waiting for Open Channel

Data 2

Not Ready to Send Data

Ready—Waiting for Open Channel

Concentrator

Communication
Channel

Data 2

Host Computer

**Keyboard
Terminals**

SYSTEM USING CONCENTRATOR

HIGHLIGHT

The End of the Minis?

Many companies are finding that distributed processing is an effective way to do business. Rather than send all data to a central location for processing, they are performing many of these functions in departments. This situation is having an effect on the type of hardware that companies use. In the past departmental processing was often performed by minicomputers. But now, as the capabilities of microcomputers expand so quickly, minicomputers are being shoved aside. Businesses are finding that PCs connected by a local area network (LAN) are equally effective and in some cases more powerful than minis.

Another advantage of a PC LAN over a mini is the network flexibility. More PCs and peripherals can be added when needed. If the use in a particular department decreases, the PCs can simply be moved to another area. Furthermore, PC LANs are less expensive than minis. For these reasons companies are not upgrading their minis, but are installing PC LANS. For example many of the Hilton hotels are replacing their minicomputers with PC networks.

Some experts feel the only advantage minis have over micro networks at the moment is that there has not yet been enough application software developed for the networks. Once the software is available, will minis become computers of the past? It is hard to predict. So far there has been no decline in the sale of minicomputers, but a number of midrange manufacturers are also entering the micro and LAN market. Yet some IS professionals say they still need the capabilities of a mini. So the minis may continue to be used, but may be overshadowed by their powerful smaller relatives, the PCs.

basis. For example, four or five microcomputers may share a high-speed, letter-quality printer and a hard-disk unit. The ability to share information is also very important; information contained at a central location provides greater data integrity (accuracy and timeliness) and is accessed or updated in a timely fashion from any number of locations within the network.

The ability to communicate among members of the network is also an important consideration. **Electronic mail** is one means of network communication. It allows one member of the network to send a message to another member. If the member receiving the message is not currently connected to the network, the message will be saved until the next time he or she makes the connection. Electronic mail can eliminate many of the unnecessary calls and return calls of a telephone message process.

There are many advantages to implementing a local-area network. Among other things, a LAN permits users to share hardware, software, and data. This sharing of resources reduces costs for the users and helps provide a more direct means of communicating.

Electronic Banking

Banks process huge amounts of paper in the form of checks, loan records, deposits, savings clubs, investment information, and so forth. The account balance of every customer must be kept up to date and funds and data must be exchanged among banks. Computers are used to facilitate these activities in every banking institution across the country.

Data communication is now being used by banks in the form of **electronic funds transfer (EFT).** In an EFT system, the accounts of a party or parties involved in a transaction are adjusted by electronic communication between computers and/or computer terminals. No cash or checks actually change hands. Many banks now offer automated services such as direct deposit of checks into customers' accounts by their employers and automatic payment of bills.

One popular form of EFT is the **automatic teller machine (ATM). ATMs** are unattended remote devices that communicate with a bank's computer (see Figure 9–9). Many banks have installed the machines in the outside walls of bank buildings. The machines are also located at supermarkets, airports, college campuses, and shopping malls. Bank customers can use them twenty-four hours a day to check their account balances, transfer funds, make deposits or withdrawals, and draw out cash from a credit card account. Customers identify themselves by inserting plastic cards (often their credit cards) and entering identification codes. The cards contain account numbers and credit limits encoded on strips of magnetic tape. Once identification is approved, the customers select transactions by pushing a series of buttons.

Another application of EFT involves home banking. Using a telephone or a microcomputer and a modem, a customer can perform banking transactions by entering account numbers and transaction codes through the keypad of the telephone or the keyboard of the microcomputer. A voice synthesizer, which is programmed to give transaction instructions and information, may respond to the customer. The same tasks can be performed if a customer has a keypad device attached to a television set and two-way cable television lines.

Some institutions accept the use of the "smart" card. A customer obtains from the bank a plastic card about the size of a normal credit card. Embedded in the thin plastic is a microcomputer—a chip that has programmable functions and a memory. Rather than operating on the basis of a credit limit, the card functions on a debit basis. To use the card, the customer

FIGURE 9–9

Local Area Network (LAN)

COMPUTERS AND INFORMATION PROCESSING

transfers money from a savings account to the card account. When a purchase is made, the card is inserted into the reader at the store. The amount of a purchase is deducted from the customer's account and added to the store's account. Fraud is less likely than with an ordinary charge card since this card is personalized by a sequence of four digits, which make up the personal identity number (PIN). After three incorrect PINs are entered, part of the codes on the card self-destruct, rendering the card useless. An unauthorized user can almost never guess the correct PIN in three tries.

Banks also perform transactions with each other by computers. The Federal Reserve System, for example, operates the Fed Wire transfer network for use by member banks. Another EFT network, BankWire, serves several hundred banks in the United States. EFT facilitates international banking through a system called SWIFT (Society for Worldwide Interbank Financial Telecommunications).

Telecommuting

Perhaps one of the most interesting aspects of data communication to contemporary office workers is **telecommuting**—commuting to the office by computer rather than in person (see Figure 9–10). The system offers advantages in cities where office rent is high and mass transit systems or parking facilities are inadequate, and in businesses that do not require frequent face-to-face meetings among office workers. Telecommuting also provides greater flexibility for disabled employees and working parents.

Salespeople and journalists, who are often away from their offices, have successfully used a kind of telecommuting by taking portable computers and tiny printers with them on assignments. The portable computer is used to type memos, letters, stories, or reports. Using a modem, the person sends information over telephone lines to the office. Once the information has been received at the office, phone messages, edited copy, or other information can be sent back to the original writer.

Telecommuting does have disadvantages, however. Some employees may not have the discipline to work away from the office. They may fear that

FIGURE 9–10

Telecommuting

"out of sight is out of mind," particularly when promotions and raises are considered. In addition, managers may be uneasy about the amount of control they have over employees who work away from the office.

■ DISTRIBUTED COMPUTING

The concept of **distributed computing** involves processing that to some degree is done at a site independent of a central computer system. The amount and type of processing that takes place at a distributed site varies from company to company, depending on the structure and the management philosophy of the company. Figure 9–11 illustrates a distributed system in which three dispersed minicomputers are connected by communication links to a large central computer. The three minicomputers may be located in three different functional areas of the organization; for example, finance, marketing, and production.

This type of approach to distributed processing gives the various functional areas the ability to process data independently of the central com-

FIGURE 9—11

Distributed Computing System

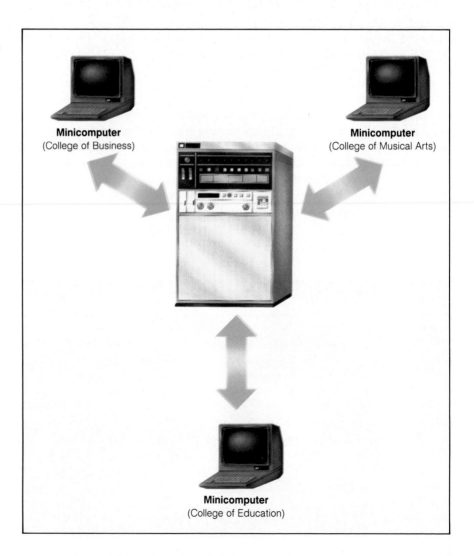

Minicomputer
(College of Business)

Minicomputer
(College of Musical Arts)

Minicomputer
(College of Education)

COMPUTERS AND INFORMATION PROCESSING

puter as well as to communicate data required by the entire organization to the central computer. Thus, some of the information generated in the functional areas can be communicated to the central computer to be used in corporate-wide planning and control.

The increase in popularity of microcomputers has led to their inclusion in distributed computing systems. Use of microcomputers by managers for planning and control in a distributed system has seen a dramatic increase.

A company's managerial philosophy normally determines the type of system and the amount of processing done at a distributed site. A company with a decentralized managerial philosophy will do a large amount of processing at distributed sites, with the central computer serving primarily as a communication link among various sites. As the technology in data communication improves and computers become more widely used at dispersed locations, the importance and use of distributed computing will undoubtedly grow.

▨ DISTRIBUTED COMPUTING NETWORKS

Distributed computing systems can encompass a number of different configurations designed to meet the varying needs of users. The development of the communication channels discussed earlier made possible the development and widespread use of computer networks. A computer **network** is the linking together of CPUs and terminals via a communication system. A network allows users at different locations to share files, devices, and programs. Many terminals may share the resources of one CPU, or multiple CPUs may be linked together. Terminals and CPUs may be geographically dispersed or situated within the physical constraints of a single office or building.

Single CPU Networks

A typical computer system consists of a single mainframe linked to a variety of peripherals. When peripherals are connected directly to the CPU, the system is called a **local system.** Advancements in computer technology have made it possible to place terminals (or other devices) in locations removed from the mainframe and connect them to the central computer by a communication channel. The resulting system is called a **remote system.**

Many businesses could benefit from a computer facility but find the costs prohibitive. For organizations that only infrequently need the power of a large computer system, **time-sharing systems** have been developed. Under time sharing, many different businesses with diverse requirements can access the same central computer and receive what seems to be simultaneous responses. Each user seems to have total control of the computer, but in reality the computer divides its time among the users. Each user is charged only for the computer resources actually used. This time-sharing system may be accessed by remote users via I/O devices and telephone lines or by local users whose I/O devices are connected directly to the system.

A system that supports time sharing must allocate computing time to users. The purpose of the time-sharing system would be defeated if one user had to wait a long time while another monopolized the CPU's processing facilities. A technique called **time slicing** can solve this problem. Each user is allocated a small portion of processing time. If the user's program is completely executed during this time, or if the programmer reaches a point at which input or output activity must occur before the allotted time is used up, the CPU begins (or resumes) execution of another user's program. If execution of the program is not completed during that allocated time, control of the CPU is transferred to another user's program and the first program is placed at the end of a waiting list. Once the program returns to the top of the list, execution is resumed at the point where it was stopped when control of the CPU was transferred to another user's program. This switching of programs occurs at such a rapid rate that users are generally unaware of it.

There are two methods of establishing time-sharing capability. One is to set up a time-sharing system **in-house** to obtain quick answers to such problems as production and cost analysis, forecasting, and accounts receivable. The other is to purchase time-sharing capability from a service company that owns and maintains one or more computer systems. Because of the intense competition in this area, many service companies have expanded to provide not only time-sharing capability but also specialized programs and technical assistance.

The major advantages of time-sharing systems include the following:

■ They provide an economical means for small users to access the resources of a large computer system.
■ They allow each user to seem to possess a private computer.
■ They offer the advantage of quick response capabilities.
■ Through resource poolings, they provide access to greater numbers of application programs at a lower unit cost than privately owned and maintained computers.
■ They relieve worry about equipment obsolescence.

Time sharing also has some inherent problems:

■ Users connected to the system by telephone lines must worry about breakdowns in the lines or increases in amount of communication; these lines are not the best medium for transmission of data. Thus, applications involving extensive I/O operations may not be suited to time sharing.
■ Because data can be accessed quickly and easily in a time-sharing system, concern for security must be increased. All programs and data must be safeguarded from unauthorized persons or use.
■ When quick response is not a necessity, time-sharing capability may be a needless expense.
■ System reliability may be lower than in non-time-sharing systems. The additional equipment and communication channels are possible areas for both mechanical and system-related problems.

Multiple CPU Networks

As with a single CPU and its terminals, a network's CPUs can be hooked together to form either local or remote systems. All networks are comprised of two basic structures: nodes and links. A **node** refers to the end points of a network. Nodes consist of CPUs, printers, terminals, and other physical devices. **Links** are the transmission channels that connect the nodes.

Nodes and links can be arranged in a number of different ways to form a network configuration or topology. Some of the more common are star, ring, hierarchical, bus, and fully distributed. Figure 9–12 illustrates these configurations.

In a **star configuration,** all transactions must go through a central computer before being routed to the appropriate network computer. This creates a central decision point, which facilitates workload distribution and resource sharing but exposes the system to single-point vulnerability. When the central computer breaks down, all the nodes in the network are disabled. An alternative approach uses a number of computers connected to a single transmission line in a **ring configuration.** This type of system can bypass a malfunctioning unit without disrupting operations throughout the network.

A more sophisticated approach is the **hierarchical configuration,** which consists of a group of small computers tied into a large central computing complex. Under this approach, an organization's needs are divided into multiple levels, which are controlled by the single computer at the top of the hierarchy. The lowest level is the user level, where only routine transaction-processing power is supplied. This level is connected to the next higher level and its associated information system. At each level, the machine size increases while the need for distribution decreases. In a **bus configuration,** each computer plugs into a single bus cable that runs from workstation to workstation. Each computer must have its own interface that connects it to the network. As messages travel along the bus cable, stations monitor the cable and retrieve their own messages. If one node in a bus configuration breaks down, the system can still function effectively.

A **fully distributed configuration** is one in which every set of nodes in the network can communicate with every other set of nodes through a single communication link. Each local system has its own processing capabilities.

CONCEPT SUMMARY 9–2

Network Configurations	
Structure	**Feature**
Star	All transactions go through a central computer; single-point vulnerability
Ring	All computers connected to a single transmission line, and malfunctioning units are bypassed
Hierarchical	Organizational needs are divided into multiple levels; a single computer controls the hierarchy
Bus	Each computer must have an interface to connect to the bus cable that links the machines
Fully Distributed	Every set of nodes can communicate directly with every other set of nodes; local systems have their own processing capabilities

HIGHLIGHT

EDI

Although electronic data interchange (EDI) was first used about ten years ago, it is only recently being implemented by most companies. EDI is a method of buying and purchasing products electronically. For example, in a manufacturing company a manager could designate a point when certain parts had to be ordered from a supplier. The inventory could be kept on computer and when the specified point was reached the computer would automatically reorder the parts. This method enables the company to eliminate the cost of storing surplus inventory, and yet have the stock always on hand.

Sellers also benefit from EDI. It reduces the cost of processing order forms. Some companies estimate the ratio of benefit to cost may be as much as twenty-to-one.

Of course, in order for both suppliers and buyers to benefit from EDI both must have the system. Buyers with the system often pressure their suppliers to obtain EDI. For example, General Motors has told suppliers they prefer suppliers with EDI.

Researchers believe the number of EDI users will triple in the next few years. Suppliers are adopting the system either because they feel it will give them a competitive advantage, or because their buyers are demanding it.

FIGURE 9—12

Network Configurations

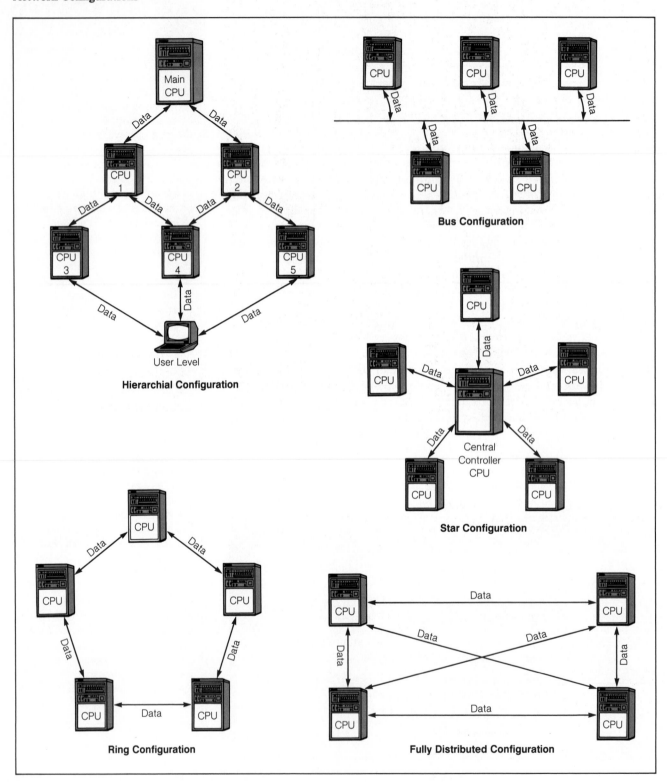

Hierarchial Configuration

Bus Configuration

Star Configuration

Ring Configuration

Fully Distributed Configuration

COMPUTERS AND INFORMATION PROCESSING

TELECOMMUNICATION STANDARDS

Telecommunication standards are a set of rules that are agreed upon by government agencies that make and enforce standards and by leading companies within the telecommunication industry. The standards are proposed and adopted so that telecommunication architectures, physical design specifications, and communication protocols can be dealt with in a consistent fashion. The fact that leading companies within the telecommunication industry participate in the process of developing standards demonstrates the companies' willingness to produce products that adhere to the standards. Organizations that are involved in the establishment of telecommunication standards include the International Organization for Standardization (ISO), American National Standards Institute (ANSI), Consultative Committee on International Telephone and Telegraph (CCITT), Institute of Electrical and Electronics Engineers (IEEE), Electronic Industries Association (EIA), National Bureau of Standards (NBS), Exchange Carrier Standards Association, and the Corporation for Open Systems (COS).

The Consultative Committee on International Telephone and Telegraph (CCITT) has proposed standards that relate to how electrical connections used in telecommunication systems should be accomplished. The X.nn series of standards describes how digital equipment should be connected to public data networks using digital data transmission. The X.25 standard in particular describes how the interface between microcomputers with modems and public data networks should be accomplished. The CCITT has also proposed a standard that deals with the transmission of voice, data, and images over worldwide networks in a digital format. The Integrated Services Digital Network (ISDN) standard would lead to a single, consistent, worldwide telecommunication network from a user's viewpoint. The X.25 and ISDN are just two of a number of telecommunication standards that are being developed by international standards making organizations.

A GUIDE TO NETWORKS

One of the benefits of buying a microcomputer is having the opportunity to access computer networks. Accessing a network through your microcomputer's modem can provide you with an opportunity to obtain resources and information and communicate with other computer users.

Information Services

Information services, also known as commercial data bases, allow the personal computer user to gain access to vast storehouses of information. Most services require payment of an initial fee. You are then issued a special user identification number and/or a password. This ensures that only paid subscribers have access to the service. All services also charge an hourly connect rate, which will vary with the time of the day you are connected and the type of information you wish to access. The information services will provide their rates to subscribers and all interested persons. The hours of availability of the services also vary; not all services can be accessed twenty-four hours a day. Another cost that may be associated with the services is telephone line charges by your local telephone company. There may be local phone numbers for you to use, but these are only available in areas where there are a lot of potential users. If local numbers exist, the services will provide them.

COMPUSERVE. CompuServe is the largest information service available to individual and family users. The initial fee includes a user's guide, a free first hour of connect-time, and a subscription to *Today* magazine (a CompuServe publication). Hourly connect rates vary depending on the day and time of day you use the service and the type of modem you have. Some of CompuServe's special services (such as stock price and dividend information) may have additional charges.

CompuServe uses a menu-choice and word-search approach. Menu-choice allows the user to access the desired information by selecting a topic and entering the numbers (see Figure 9–13). Word-search allows the user to enter a word or topic into designated areas of CompuServe while the computer looks for the related information.

Some of the topics of information provided by CompuServe include: Public and Marine Weather, which provides information on conditions throughout the country; CB, which is a simulation of Citizen's Band radio; and Family Matters Forum, which offers subscribers helpful assistance on parenting and family-related topics. CompuServe also offers many computer

FIGURE 9–13

CompuServe Menu
Users of CompuServe make menu selections from among a wide range of topics.

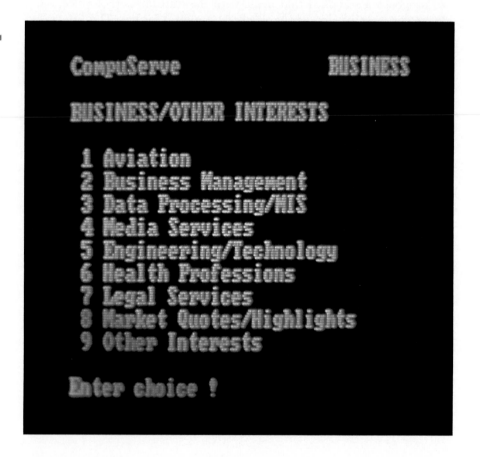

COMPUTERS AND INFORMATION PROCESSING

games and allows users to shop at home by browsing through an electronic catalog.

You can send messages to other subscribers by using CompuServe's EMAIL. In addition to the Associated Press wire service, you can also access newspapers such as the *St. Louis Post-Dispatch*, the *Middlesex Daily*, and the *Washington Post*. CompuServe also links together special-interest groups. Each group shares a common interest such as music or owning an IBM-PC. Subscribers can communicate directly with CompuServe, giving their comments and suggestions, which may be used to add new services. CompuServe is always changing and adding to its resources.

THE SOURCE. Like CompuServe, The Source is geared toward individual and family users. There is a one-time subscription fee plus a monthly minimum charge. Hourly connect rates vary. Again, some services may charge additional fees. The Source also uses a menu-choice approach.

When connected to The Source, you can consult the *Official Airline Guide, Electronic Edition*, to find the best route and fare for your next flight. If your destination is New York, Washington, or other major U.S. cities, you can even select restaurants before you go, by using the restaurant guide. The Source also offers you the convenience of shopping at home or playing computer games.

Through the EMPLOY option, you can look for job openings or potential employees in about forty different fields, ranging from accounting to utilities. The Source also allows you to send messages to other subscribers through the Mailgram service. If you want to talk with others who are connected to The Source at the same time, you can use the CHAT option. Do you need help with finances? The Source offers programs that figure depreciation schedules, balance your checkbook, and amortize a loan. As a Source subscriber, you can access the United Press International (UPI) wire service.

The Source calls its special-interest groups Private Sector. There are special-interest groups, groups for school administrators, public utilities, and radio stations. A group sponsor pays a service charge for twenty-five membership account numbers and the ability to put data bases on The Source. Like CompuServe, The Source is always updating its services and keeps its users informed through its newsletter, *SourceWorld*.

DOW JONES NEWS/RETRIEVAL. The Dow Jones News/Retrieval Service is designed with business information in mind and its primary users are business professionals and individuals interested in business. There are various user levels available with varying subscription fees. Connect rates per hour also vary. Dow Jones News/Retrieval uses a menu-choice approach to its services.

The Dow Jones News/Retrieval system provides information on every company listed on the New York and American stock exchanges, as well as some selected companies whose stock is traded over the counter. You can get historical stock market quotes and current information that is only fifteen minutes behind the action on the exchange floors. The service also gives corporate earnings estimates and price/volume data.

With a Dow Jones News/Retrieval subscription, you can get UPI summaries of local and national news, news stories from various financial newspapers and magazines, and access to the *Academic American Encyclopedia*. The service also has movie reviews and weather information, and allows you to shop at home.

Three software packages are available with which you can record and manipulate information from the News/Retrieval data bases. The Market Analyzer performs seventeen analytical functions and charts the results. The Market Microscope ranks companies and industries by sixty-eight financial indicators. The Market Manager monitors and updates investment portfolios.

DIALOG INFORMATION SERVICES. DIALOG Information Services offers two different data base collections for the serious researcher. The Information Retrieval Service data base collection has no subscription or minimum fee; however, there is a charge for a user's manual. Online hourly fees vary, depending on the data base you wish to access. The Knowledge-Index data base has variable hourly rates and limited hours of access. DIALOG uses a word-search approach for both of these services.

DIALOG Information Retrieval Service has comprehensive coverage of virtually every area of study—history, science, arts and humanities, law, medicine, and current affairs. More than 60,000 journals have been referenced as well as books, dissertations, patents, and pamphlets. You enter the word or words about which you want to gather information and DIALOG gives you a list of all references.

The Knowledge Index consists of about fifteen of the Information Retrieval data bases containing data from 10,000 journals. Some of the topics include computers, government publications, magazines, and psychology. Subscribers use a simplified word search to get the abstracts and references to the articles.

SPECIALTY SERVICES. In addition to the networks mentioned above, there are also many specialty services. BRS/After Dark, which operates evenings and weekends, is a bibliographic retrieval service. LEXIS is a service for the legal profession that includes cases, regulations, laws, and decisions in the United States, Britain, and France. AMA/NET has four different data bases that provide medical personnel with information on drugs, diagnosing, medical legislation, and public health issues. HORSE has information on the breeding and race records of more than one million racehorses in North America. The number of information services or commercial data bases is increasing daily and the variety of information available is always expanding.

Bulletin Boards

Electronic bulletin boards provide a place for users to post notices of all kinds. Although information services such as CompuServe and The Source provide bulletin board space for their subscribers, all you need to access most boards is the phone number and the proper communications link on your computer. Bulletin boards are free to the users (unless long-distance phone calls are placed). There are hundreds of bulletin boards throughout the country, and the number is constantly rising.

Bulletin board users log onto a "host" computer. Once they are connected, users can send or receive data, messages, and information, copy programs from the board, and leave programs to be copied. The "host" computer is frequently another microcomputer whose owner decided to start the bulletin board. The flexibility of the board depends upon the host.

Bulletin boards are usually good sources for hardware and software reviews, new product information, and free programs. They also offer users the opportunity to meet other computer enthusiasts. Local computer dealers and user groups can provide information on bulletin boards in the areas near you.

Proprietary and Nonproprietary Networks

As was previously discussed, local area networks (LANs) help link computers to share peripherals and information. Most LANs operate in business or academia. Since dozens of microcomputers can be linked together, LANs eliminate the need for each computer to have its own printer and floppy disks containing the same general information. The microcomputers on the LAN can access the data stored on the others.

Some microcomputer vendors have developed networks for use with their own machines. These networks are called proprietary networks. Other vendors have developed LANs that were adopted by other companies, which are called nonproprietary networks.

PROPRIETARY NETWORKS. There are a number of proprietary networks from which users can choose. Applenet was introduced by Apple Computer in 1983. It can connect 128 workstations over a distance of 8,000 feet. Digital Microsystems (not to be confused with Digital Equipment Corporation) provides HiNet, which connects up to thirty-two stations over a distance of 1,000 feet. Users can share disks and printers. Proprietary networks also provide the capability for electronic mail.

NorthNet by North Star Computers was developed for use on their Advantage microcomputers. It allows the sharing of resources over 4,000 feet. Vector Graphic developed LINC (an acronym for Local Interactive Network Communications) for use on Vector-4 products. LINC can connect up to sixteen stations over a 2,000-foot distance.

NONPROPRIETARY NETWORKS. Nonproprietary networks include Omninet, Ethernet, PLAN, and ARCnet. Omninet, developed by Corvus Systems, can connect up to sixty-four workstations over a distance of up to 1,000 meters. The users can share a central hard disk unit and printer. Omninet is compatible with Apple IIs and IIIs, IBM Personal Computers, the DEC LSI-11, and Texas Instruments' Professional. It is a CSMA/CD access method.

Xerox Corporation provides Ethernet, which can support up to 1,024 workstations over a limited distance. Different distributors sell Ethernet-compatible products. The IBM-PC Ethernet connection is known as EtherSeries. EtherLink has software to allow the transferring of files and the sharing of printers. EtherShare offers a shared hard disk and several software packages including EtherMail, which provides the ability for all workstations to send and receive electronic mail.

PLAN (Personal Local Area Network) 4000 from Nestar Systems is compatible with Apple IIs and IBM-PCs. PLAN 4000 can link up to sixty-four microcomputers over a distance of up to four miles. This LAN uses the token-passing access method. Software is available for sharing disks and printers and for electronic mail.

Datapoint Corporation introduced ARCnet in 1977. It can link up to 255 stations as far as four miles apart. ARCnet uses a token-passing access method and can connect users to a hard disk drive.

The LANs on the market combine the aspects of the technology in various ways. Each network is suited to slightly different environments. Since industry standards change with the development of LANs, it is best to find a consultant who can analyze your needs and match them to a LAN, or contact your vendor to see what is available for your equipment.

■ SUMMARY POINTS

■ Data communication is the electronic transmission of data from one location to another, usually over communication channels such as telephone, telegraph, or microwaves. The combined use of data-processing equipment and communication facilities such as telephone systems is called telecommunication.

■ Modulation is the process of converting data from the pulse form used by the computer to a wave form used for message transmission over communication lines. Demodulation is the process of converting the received message from wave form back to pulse form. These functions are performed by devices called modems, or data sets.

■ Digital transmission involves transmitting data as distinct on and off pulses rather than as waves. This mode of transmission eliminates the specialized steps of conversion from pulse to wave form and subsequent reconversion from wave to pulse form at the destination.

■ I/O control units and channels are used in an I/O subsystem to increase the efficiency of the CPU. A control unit converts input data into machine-readable form, and vice versa. It is also used in data buffering.

■ Channels control I/O operations and free the CPU to do other processing; this allows input, output, and processing to overlap.

■ A communication channel is the link permitting transmission of electrical signals from one location to another. Types of communication channels include telegraph lines, telephone lines, coaxial cables, and microwaves. Communication channels can also be classified by grade, or bandwidth, and mode of transmission (simplex, half-duplex, and full-duplex).

■ Multiplexers, concentrators, and programmable communications processors are hardware devices that reduce the costs associated with data transmission in a communication system.

■ Local-area networks involve interconnecting computers in a single building or a complex of buildings. Electronic mail is a means of network communication in which one member of the network sends a message to another member.

■ Distributed computing involves processing that, to some degree, is done at a site independent of the central computer system.

■ Communication networks may have single or multiple CPUs and may be either local or remote. A time-sharing system allows several users to access the same computer at the same time. An in-house time-sharing system can be installed, or time-sharing capability can be purchased from a service company.

■ Multiple CPU networks are characterized by several computers linked together to form either local or remote systems. Five common multiple CPU configurations are star, ring, hierarchical, bus, and fully distributed.

■ The star configuration directs all transactions through a central computer. A ring configuration uses a number of computers connected to a single transmission line. A malfunctioning unit can be bypassed without disrupting operations throughout the network. A hierarchical configuration consists of a group of small computers tied into a large central computing complex.

■ In a bus configuration, each computer plugs into a single bus cable that runs from workstation to workstation. A fully distributed network is one in which every set of nodes can communicate directly with every other set of nodes through a single communications link.

■ Information services, or commercial databases, allow personal computers equipped with a modem to access vast banks of information that are stored on a central computer system.

■ Information services such as COMPUSERVE, The Source, and Dow Jones News/Retrieval offer a variety of types of information.

■ Bulletin boards are also accessed by microcomputers through modems and provide a place for users to post notices and communicate with each other.

▦ REVIEW QUESTIONS

1. What is telecommunication?
2. Explain the difference between digital and analog transmission.
3. What are modems and what purpose do they serve in data communication systems?
4. How does a data buffer help speed up data communication?
5. Distinguish among simplex, half-duplex, and full-duplex transmission modes.
6. How does the manner in which a concentrator communicates with an I/O device differ from the way in which a multiplexer performs the same function?
7. What is a programmable communications processor?
8. Which configuration for multiple CPU networks has the disadvantage of single-point vulnerability? Why?
9. What are some advantages of a time-sharing system?
10. What is meant by distributed computing?
11. What is an information service? How do information services charge for the services they provide?
12. How do bulletin boards differ from information services?
13. What is a proprietary network? How does a nonproprietary network differ from a proprietary network?

Texas Instruments

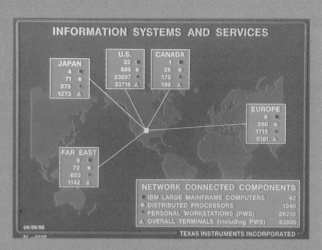

The company was founded in 1930 as Geophysical Service [later known as Geophysical Service Inc. (GSI)] to provide geophysical exploration services to the petroleum industry. During World War II, GSI manufactured electronic equipment for the U.S. Navy. In 1946 GSI formally added electronic systems manufacturing to its operations. In 1951 the company adopted its current name, Texas Instruments Incorporated (TI), and the following year entered the semiconductor business—the most significant event in its history.

TI's position as a world leader in electronics is founded on a long tradition of transforming technological ideas into useful products and services. TI "firsts" include the development of the commercial pocket radio, the commercial silicon transistor, the integrated circuit, the terrain-following airborne radar, the hand-held calculator, the single chip microcomputer, and the single-chip artificial intelligence microprocessor or LISP chip. These and other innovations give TI a technological base that spans materials, components, systems, and software.

Headquartered in Dallas, Texas, TI has manufacturing operations in more than 50 facilities in 17 countries, and sales offices and service centers throughout the world. TI has revenues in excess of $5 billion and employs more than 76,000 employees. Semiconductors are TI's principal business, as well as the technological foundation for the rest of the company.

TI's business mix is well balanced between components—principally semiconductors—and electronic systems. Defense electronics is TI's largest electronic systems business, currently representing about one-third of TI's billings. TI's materials and controls business is based on the technology of bonding two or more dissimilar metals together. The consumer products business is concentrated on calculators and electronic educational products. Each business of TI is built upon a technological base and worldwide support.

Texas Instruments has implemented one of the most sophisticated private computer networks in the world to support corporate communication and control. The integrated network includes 43,500 workstation/terminals, 1,340 minicomputers, and 42 large mainframe computers.

This multiple CPU network has been designed around a distributed computing architecture. At various functional levels of the organization a standard computer system is placed. Therefore a TI department in Europe will have computer system power with an architecture supporting access to one in the Pacific region.

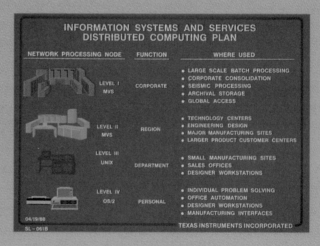

High-speed communication links permit data transfer at rates reading 768,000 bits per second. The mainframe computers alone handle about 5 million daily requests for information through regional hubs in Singapore, Bedford (U.K.), Dallas, and Miho (Japan). Each request for information overseas is beamed from a TI-owned earth station at the company's headquarters to a leased satellite which in turn beams the information to the hubs. The information is then fanned out to major TI sites. Bedford serves Europe, Miho serves Japan, and Singapore serves the rest of Southeast Asia.

One of TI's most innovative and strategic uses of the network is connecting the 15 advanced software development and semiconductor design facilities located in strategic markets. This network enables customers in Europe and Asia to design their products at technical centers a continent away. Software is distributed worldwide on more than 300 computers linked in about 35 local area networks. Therefore the same software development tools can be used in any design centers in the world.

DISCUSSION POINTS

1. How does the computer system parallel the TI corporate philosophy?

2. Why is a distributed computing approach appropriate for TI?

C H A P T E R

10

System Software

O U T L I N E

Introduction
Categories of Programs
  System Programs
  Application Programs

Operating Systems
  Development of Operating Systems
  Functions of Operating Systems
  Types of Processing Handled by
    Operating Systems
  Components of Operating Systems

Multiprogramming
Virtual Storage
Multiprocessing
Summary Points
Review Questions

Unix: The Soul of a Lot of New Machines

**Richard Brandt and
John W. Verity**
Business Week

Sporadically, over the past decade, practically every major computer maker has tried to convince Gary D. Handler that its machines were the answer to his every problem. But Handler, the executive in charge of computer systems for Shearson Lehman Brothers' trading floor, didn't believe it. He knew that committing himself to just one brand of computer might make it harder to buy the best products in the future.

So when Handler saw the chance to avoid this trap, he took it. In 1986, just after arriving at Shearson from Merrill Lynch & Co., he decided to base its trading operations on Unix. Unix is an operating system, a piece of software that controls the basic functions of a computer and has to be in place before the machine can run applications software that does useful work, such as financial analysis or text editing.

VERSATILE. Unix was obscure and a bit hard to use, but it had one huge advantage: Unlike the proprietary operating systems of IBM, DEC, or Apple, it was available on many different machines. Now Handler is confident that he can mix brands and sizes of computers to build any network he needs. "I'm prepared for the future," he says.

Suddenly, Unix is catching on everywhere. In just the past year, it has become available on scores of machines, from personal computers to supercomputers. Unisys Corp., an old-line mainframe maker, says its sales of Unix systems topped $500 million last year. The program is rumored to be the basis for an academic workstation soon to be unveiled by Next Inc., the latest venture of former Apple Computer Inc. Chairman Steven P. Jobs. International Business Machines Corp. says it now spends as much on the development of Unix-based systems as it does on PCs. And last month, Apple began shipping Unix for its Macintosh. International Data Corp. predicts that by 1991, Unix will be the main operating system for a quarter of the worldwide computer market (chart, page 96).

As the popularity of Unix grows, it will threaten the proprietary operating systems that have produced huge profits for companies such as IBm and Digital Equipment Corp. "The industry powerhouses don't want Unix," says William N. Joy, chief technologist at Sun Microsystems Inc. Indeed, nonproprietary systems such as Unix "put more bargaining power in the buyer's hands," comments Melvyn E. Bergstein, a managing partner at Arthur Andersen & Co.'s $1 billion computer consulting practice. "The marketplace is getting a lot smarter."

Unix has come a long way since Bell Laboratories developed it in the 1970s for AT&T's internal use. Prohibited as a regulated company from selling Unix, AT&T licensed it to universities, and eventually to computer makers, on the understanding that it wouldn't support the product. As its use spread, an entire generation of programmers became fans of Unix. But producers of applications software were not about to tailor their programs to it, since not many business customers used Unix.

MANY VERSIONS. This began to change in 1983. AT&T had already signed the consent decree leading to its 1984 breakup, which let the company enter the computer business through a separate subsidiary. It began promoting Unix and by 1987 had licensed it to some 225 computer makers. By then, Unix' main drawback was a multiplicity of versions. The original program essentially was a nugget that every licensee embellished. By late 1986 there were perhaps a dozen major varieties, all slightly different. The question that confronted customers and producers of applications software was which version to bet on.

AT&T started trying last year to answer that question. Aiming to create a single dominant Unix version, it decided to pluck the best features from the three most widely used varieties: Its own, called System V; Microsoft Corp.'s Xenix, for personal computers; and Berkeley 4.2, used by Sun Microsystems on its engineering workstations. Now, AT&T, Microsoft, and Sun are working together on a new version of Unix, to be released later this year.

While they applaud this effort, other Unix licensees are increasingly worried that AT&T may be making Unix more proprietary. They complain that the company has changed its license policy from a perpetual to an annual license. Moreover, AT&T has said that if other computer makers enhance Unix without getting a waiver, it may revoke their licenses. And critics say the company has been slow to grant waivers.

BEDFELLOWS. The biggest worry of rivals is AT&T's increasingly cozy relationship with Sun, currently one of the fastest-growing computer makers. Last year Sun licensed its basic computer design to AT&T, and the two are implying that Sun's design plus Unix equals superior machines, from personal computers to supercomputers. Then in January, AT&T announced plans to buy 20% of Sun. Now other Unix licenses fear that Unix will be tailored to run best with the Sun architecture, giving AT&T a lever for improving its disappointing computer sales.

"AT&T's been trying to argue lately that there's only one place standards can come from—AT&T," complains Glenn B. Johnson, engineering manager of the Ultrix Engineering Group at DEC. Jack Scanlon, AT&T's executive in charge of computer

product development, disagrees: "We will continue to deliver Unix on an evenhanded basis."

Despite the controversy, Unix' reputation continues to grow. "I've been at it for three years, and I still don't know everything about Unix," says D. Brent Chapman, a 19-year-old Unix whiz who has left college to write currency-hedging programs. "But once you learn it, you're more productive on Unix than on any other operating system." Tom Love, chairman of Stepstone Corp. in Sandy Hook, Conn., says it takes a few weeks at most to convert a major program from one Unix machine to another. That's a long changeover that AT&T and others are still working to shorten. But it compares with months or even years on systems without Unix.

Major commercial demand for Unix is being led by the U.S. government, the biggest computer customer in the world. The Air Force has specified Unix as a requirement on a $4 billion contract for which it is taking bids. Amdahl Corp. and National Advanced Systems are selling mainframes that run Unix, while Italy's Olivetti is aiming Unix systems at law firms. Unix is a key selling point for Hewlett-Packard Co.'s new Spectrum minicomputers. And Datapoint Corp. in San Antonio finds Unix demand particularly strong in Europe, says Chief Executive Robert J. Potter.

Cost is a big selling point for Unix. Because it is available on a wide range of machines, makers of those computer have had to compete on price. Indeed, Unix

systems frequently deliver two to three times as much performance as comparably priced machines using proprietary operating systems, notes Richard R. Janssen, president of Delphi Systems Inc. in Westlake Village, Calif. Delphi is a supplier of Unix systems to insurance brokers. Adding to Unix' appeal, says Janssen, are the 2,000 applications programs now available for it, a number that's growing fast.

Many customers also see Unix as the one major alternative to IBM. The No. 1 computer maker is promoting a concept called Systems Application Architecture, a set of software standards that will let a customer transport programs between different types of computers. But as currently envisioned, SAA would only work on IBM machines. So many customers view it as a sophisticated attempt to lock them in . Bergstein, who keeps up on product developments for Arthur Andersen, says "SAA is driving people to consider Unix." That may be all the endorsement Unix needs.

Other software developers realize that in order to compete with Unix they must develop their own open system or else Unix will become the market standard. Users should benefit from the struggle among software companies for control of the market, because the result should be a greater choice in deciding what operating system they can use on their hardware.

▨ INTRODUCTION

The computer is a powerful machine that can be used to solve a variety of problems. Previous chapters have covered the major hardware components of a computer system and have shown how these components are used to store and process data and generate information. However, the computer cannot solve problems without using programs. Programming is a critical step in data processing. If the computer is not correctly programmed, it cannot deliver the needed information. This chapter explains the differences between system programs and application programs and discusses the various functions performed by operating system software. The chapter also describes some of the more advanced software developments that have been made in recent years. The concepts of multiprogramming and multiprocessing are introduced, and the use of virtual storage to overcome primary storage limitations is discussed.

▨ CATEGORIES OF PROGRAMS

Despite the apparent complexity and power of the computer, it is merely a tool manipulated by an individual. It requires step-by-step instructions to reach a solution to a problem. As stated earlier, this series of instructions is known as a program, and the individual who creates the program is the programmer. There are two basic categories of programs: (1) **system programs,** which coordinate the operation of computer circuitry and assist in the development of application programs; and (2) **application programs,** which solve particular user problems.

System Programs

System programs directly affect the operation of the computer. They are designed to facilitate the efficient use of the computer's resources and aid in the development and execution of application programs. For example, one system program allocates storage for data being entered into the system; another system program instructs output to be sent to the appropriate device such as a line printer. We have already seen that computers differ in primary storage capacity, in the methods used to store and code data, and in the number of instructions they can perform. Consequently, system programs are written specifically for a particular type of computer and cannot be used (without modification) on different machines.

A system programmer maintains the system programs in good running order and tailors them, when necessary, to meet organizational requirements. Because system programmers serve as a bridge between the computer and application programmers, they must have the technical background needed to understand the complex internal operations of the computer. Because each organization uses a different set of application programs, system programs must be modified to execute the needed application programs in the most efficient manner and obtain the resulting information in an appropriate form.

System programs are normally provided by the computer manufacturer or a specialized programming firm. Thus, they are initially written in a general fashion to meet as many user requirements as possible. However, they can be modified, or tailored, to meet a particular organization's specific needs.

Application Programs

Application programs perform specific data-processing or computational tasks to solve an organization's information needs. They can be developed within the organization or purchased from software firms. Typical examples of application programs are those used in inventory control and accounting; in banks, application programs update checking and savings account balances.

The job of the application programmer is to use the capabilities of the computer to solve specific problems. A programmer need not have an in-depth knowledge of the computer to write application programs. Instead, the programmer concentrates on the particular problem to be solved. If the problem is clearly defined and understood, the task of writing a program to solve it is greatly simplified. Application software will be discussed in greater detail in Chapter 13.

▪ OPERATING SYSTEMS

In early computer systems, human operators monitored computer operations, determined the order (or priority) in which submitted programs were run and readied input and output devices. While early electronic development increased the processing speeds of CPUs, the speed of human operators remained constant. Time delays and errors caused by human operator intervention became a serious problem.

Development of Operating Systems

In the 1960s, operating systems were developed to help overcome this problem. An **operating system** consists of an integrated collection of system programs that control the functions of the CPU, input and output, and storage facilities of the system. This portion of the operating system is often referred to as the supervisor, monitor, executive, or resource manager. By performing these tasks, the operating system provides an interface between the user or the application program and the computer hardware. Concept Summary 10–1 shows the relationship among the user, operating system, and computer hardware.

Functions of Operating Systems

The functions of an operating system are geared toward attaining maximum efficiency in processing operations. As already mentioned, eliminating human intervention is one method. Allowing several programs to share computer resources is another; the operating system allocates these resources to the programs requesting them and resolves conflicts that occur when, for example, two or three programs request the use of the same tape drive or primary storage locations. In addition, the operating system performs an accounting function; it keeps track of all resource usage so that user fees can be determined and the efficiency of CPU utilization evaluated.

Relationships Among User, Operating System, and Computer Hardware

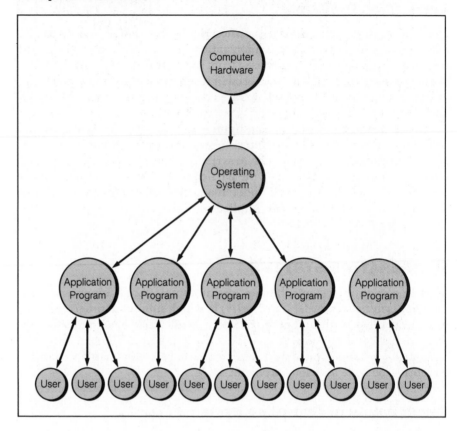

Another important function performed by the operating system is scheduling jobs on a priority basis. Although it may seem logical to run programs in the order in which they are submitted, this is not always the most practical approach. For instance, assume that five programs are submitted for processing within a short period of time. Suppose one program requires one minute of CPU time and the other four require one hour each. It may be reasonable to process the short program first. Or suppose one program will produce a vital report and the output of the others is less important. The more important program should probably be processed first. A system of priorities can be established based on considerations such as the required processing time and the need for the expected output.

Types of Processing Handled by Operating Systems

There are two basic types of operating systems: batch and online. In a batch operating system user programs ("jobs") are grouped into a batch to be processed one after the other in a continuous stream. For example, in the morning an operator may load all jobs to be processed during the day onto a tape. The batch operating system will direct processing without interruption until all jobs on the tape are completed, thus freeing the operator to perform other tasks.

An online operating system can respond to spontaneous requests for system resources, such as management inquiries entered from online terminals.

Operating systems currently in use can handle both batch and online applications simultaneously. These operating systems direct the processing of a job but also respond to **interrupts** from I/O devices such as online terminals (or workstations), printers, and secondary storage devices which communicate with the CPU through the operating system. When an I/O device sends a message to the CPU, normal processing is suspended (the CPU is interrupted) so that the CPU may direct the operation of the I/O device. It is the function of the operating system, therefore, to manage the resources of the CPU in its handling of batch and online processing and its control of peripheral devices.

Components of Operating Systems

As previously mentioned an operating system is an integrated collection of system programs. Each program performs specific duties. Because all operating system programs work as a "team," CPU idle time is avoided and utilization of computer facilities is increased. Operating system programs are kept online in a secondary storage device known as the **system residence device.** The secondary storage media most commonly used are magnetic tape drives (TOS—tape operating system) and magnetic disk drives (DOS—disk operating system). Magnetic-drum technology has the fastest processing time, but many existing operating systems use magnetic-disk technology.

Two types of programs make up the operating system: **control programs** and **processing programs.** Control programs oversee system operations and perform tasks such as input/output, scheduling, handling interrupts, and communicating with the computer operator or programmer. They make certain that computer resources are used efficiently. Processing programs are executed under the supervision of control programs and are used by the programmer to aid in the development of application programs.

CONTROL PROGRAMS. The **supervisor program** (also called the **monitor** or **executive**), the major component of the operating system, coordinates the activities of all other parts of the operating system. When the computer is first put into use the supervisor is the first program to be transferred into primary storage from the system residence device. Only the most frequently used components of the supervisor are initially loaded into primary storage. These components are referred to as **resident routines,** because they remain in primary storage as long as the computer is running. Certain other supervisor routines known as **transient routines** remain in secondary storage with the remainder of the operating system. Supervisor routines call for these nonresident system programs as needed and load them into primary storage. The supervisor schedules I/O operations and allocates channels to various I/O devices. It also sends messages to the computer operator indicating the status of particular jobs, error conditions, and so forth. Figure 10–1 illustrates how supervisor routines control the accessing of the system residence device programs.

HIGHLIGHT

What It Means to Be Open

Open systems—the concept is on the minds of most information system professionals who deal with operating systems. What are open systems? An "open" operating system is one that will run on different brands of hardware. For example, an open operating system would run equally well on Digital Equipment Corporation (DEC) computers, AT&T computers, and IBM computers. Why are open systems important? In the past when a buyer bought hardware she also had to buy the operating system from the same company, because the only operating system that would run on Company A's hardware was Company A's system. Buyers felt they often were locked into a product. Open systems would give the buyers more options.

Recently a group of vendors formed the Open Software Foundation (OSF). The member vendors are DEC, Hewlett-Packard, IBM, Nixdorf, Groupe Bull, and Apollo Computer, Inc. The purpose of the foundation is to set the industry standards on software so that operating systems and applications can be used on different brands of hardware. The group says working together will greatly decrease the amount of time it could take a single vendor to develop open systems. Will a group of competitors be able to work together to accomplish their goals? Information systems personnel are wondering that, too.

FIGURE 10–1

Operating System in Primary Storage and System Residence Device

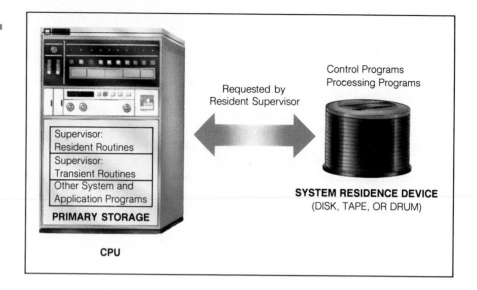

Requested by Resident Supervisor

Control Programs
Processing Programs

Supervisor:
Resident Routines

Supervisor:
Transient Routines

Other System and
Application Programs

PRIMARY STORAGE

CPU

SYSTEM RESIDENCE DEVICE
(DISK, TAPE, OR DRUM)

The operating system requires job-control information in order to instruct it as to how a particular job is to be carried out. (A *job* is a task to be processed by the CPU.) A **job-control language (JCL)** serves as the communication link between the programmer and the operating system. Job control languages are typically used in conjunction with the batch oriented portion of operating systems.

The term JCL was introduced by IBM for use on their systems. JCL is a very complex language with a large number of commands. Although other manufacturers have different names for their job-control languages, the term JCL has become so widely accepted that programmers generally use it to refer to any type of job-control language, regardless of the system.

In a batch operating system, job-control statements must be placed at the beginning of the job. These statements identify the beginning of the job, the user, and the specific program to be executed, describe the work to be done, and indicate the I/O devices required. The **job-control program** translates the job-control statements written by a programmer into machine-language instructions that can be executed by the computer.

In most computer systems, the data to be processed is kept on storage media such as magnetic tape or disk. On these systems, job-control statements and programs often are entered from a source other than that on which the data files are stored. For example, the JCL and program may be entered as a series of statements from magnetic tape, as shown in Figure 10–2a. Among other things, these JCL statements must specify which data files and I/O devices are required by the program.

On other systems, programs and data are read into storage from the same device used to submit the JCL (see Figure 10–2b). No additional I/O devices are required, but this is not an efficient method for processing large programs or data files. It is most often used when programs are being tested, before they are stored on a secondary-storage medium. Figure 10–3 shows a sample JCL used to translate a COBOL program into machine-readable form (that is, the 1s and 0s that the computer is capable of executing), which reads program data, processes the data, and then sends the results to a line printer.

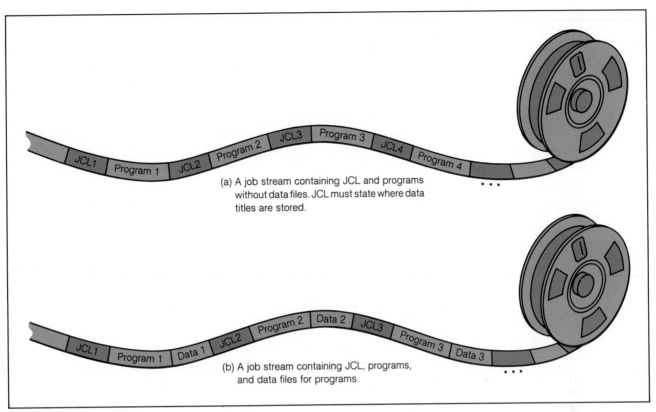

(a) A job stream containing JCL and programs without data files. JCL must state where data titles are stored.

(b) A job stream containing JCL, programs, and data files for programs.

FIGURE 10—2

Continuous Job Streams for a Batch Processing System

The first statement uniquely identifies the job and indicates what system message will be displayed concerning the translation. The second statement identifies the particular step of the overall job and invokes the COBOL language translator program. Although this JCL contains only one step, multiple steps can be contained in a single job, as demonstrated in Figure 10–2. The third statement identifies the beginning of the COBOL source program, and the fourth statement identifies the beginning of the program data. The source program would be placed between statements three and four and the data between statements four and five. Statement five defines the master file to be used, which in this case is a disk file. The final statement simply identifies the line printer as the output device.

A job is often thought of as a single program entered by a user into the computer. In fact, most data-processing jobs require the execution of many

FIGURE 10—3

Sample JCL

```
//PAY JOB ACCT, '***PAYROLL***', MSGLEVEL=(1,1)
//STEP1 EXEC COBVCG
//COB. SYSIN DD *

//GO. SYSIN DD *

//GO.FILE1 DD DSN=MASTER.FILE , DISP = SHR
//GO.OUTPUT DD SYSOUT=A
```

related programs. Thus, several job-control statements would be needed to indicate which operations should be performed and the devices needed to perform them.

The control programs of the operating system must be able to control and coordinate the CPU while receiving input from channels, executing instructions of programs in storage, and regulating output. I/O devices must be assigned to specific programs and data must be moved between them and specific memory locations. The **input/output management system** oversees and coordinates these processes.

PROCESSING PROGRAMS. The operating system contains several processing programs that facilitate efficient processing operations by simplifying program preparation and execution for users. The major processing programs contained in the operating system are the language translators, linkage editor, library programs, and utility programs. Language translators, linkage editors, and library programs will be discussed in greater detail in Chapter 12.

Operating systems include a set of **utility programs** that perform specialized functions. One such program transfers data from file to file, or from one I/O device to another. For example, a utility program can be used to transfer data from tape to tape, tape to disk, card to tape, or tape to printer. Other utility programs known as **sort/merge programs** are used to sort records into a particular sequence to facilitate the updating of files. Once sorted, several files can be merged to form a single, updated file. Job-control statements are used to specify the sort/merge program to be accessed; these programs or routines are then called into primary storage when needed. See Concept Summary 10–2 for a summary of the types and purposes of operating system programs.

CONCEPT SUMMARY 10–2

Types of Operating System Programs	
Control Programs	**Purpose**
Supervisor program	Coordinates activities of all other parts of the operating system
Job-control program	Translates job-control statements into machine language
I/O management system	Coordinates the CPU while receiving input, executing instructions, and regulating output
Processing Programs	**Purpose**
Utility programs	Perform specialized functions such as transferring data from one file to another
Sort/merge programs	Perform tasks such as sorting files into a particular order and merging several files into a single file

COMPUTERS AND INFORMATION PROCESSING

ADDITIONAL SOFTWARE. As mentioned at the beginning of the chapter, system programs are available from a variety of sources. Each data-processing department must decide which system programs should be included in its operating system. The original operating system is usually obtained from the manufacturer of the CPU. However, in some cases alternative operating systems can be purchased from software vendors.

Once the essential operating system has been purchased, optional programs may be obtained. These programs can either improve an existing operating system or provide additional capabilities to the existing operating system. For example, the operating system for a bank's computer might be supplemented with a program to interface with MICR equipment (discussed in Chapter 4). Applications requiring the use of light pens with display terminals also demand special system programs.

▨ MULTIPROGRAMMING

When the CPU is very active, the system as a whole is more efficient. However, the CPU frequently must remain idle because I/O devices are not fast enough. The CPU can operate on only one instruction at a time; furthermore, it cannot operate on data that is not in primary storage. If an input device is slow in providing data or instructions, the CPU must wait until I/O operations have been completed before executing a program.

In the earliest computer systems with simple operating systems, most programs were executed using **serial processing:** one at a time, one after the other. Serial processing was highly inefficient because the high-speed CPU was idle for long periods of time as slow input devices loaded data or output devices printed or stored the results.

Multiprogramming, or **multitasking,** increases CPU active time by effectively allocating computer resources and offsetting low I/O speeds. Under multiprogramming, several programs reside in the primary storage unit at the same time. Although the CPU still can execute only one instruction at a time, it can execute instructions from one program, then another, then another, and back to the first again. Instructions from one program are executed until an interrupt for either input or output is generated. While the I/O operation is handled by a channel, the CPU can shift its attention to another program in memory until that program requires input or output. This rotation occurs so quickly that the execution of the programs appears to be simultaneous. More precisely, the CPU executes the different programs **concurrently** which, in this context, is used to mean "within the same time interval." Figure 10–4 illustrates this process.

Although multiprogramming increases the system's flexibility and efficiency, it also creates some problems. First, the programs in primary storage must be kept separate. This is accomplished through the use of **regions** or **partitions.** Keeping programs in the correct region or partition is known as **memory management** or **memory protection.** A similar situation exists with I/O devices—two programs cannot access the same tape or disk drive at the same time. These problems are handled by operating system control programs.

A second problem that arises with multiprogramming is the need to schedule programs to determine which will receive service first. This requires that each program be assigned a priority. The highest-priority programs

FIGURE 10—4

Comparison of Serial Processing and Concurrent Processing

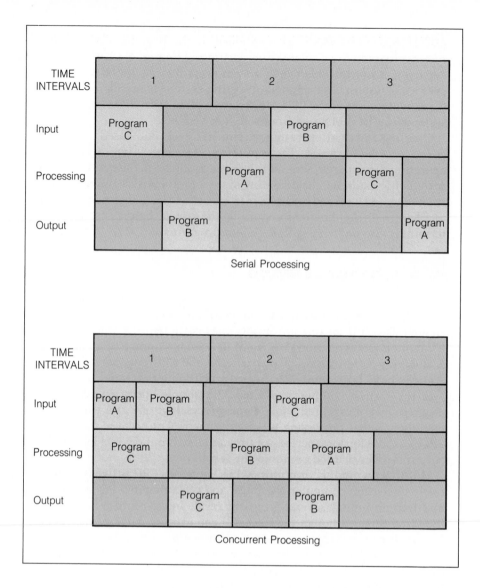

Serial Processing

Concurrent Processing

are loaded into **foreground partitions** and are called **foreground programs.** Programs of lowest priority are loaded into **background partitions** and are called **background programs** (see Figure 10–5). Background programs are typically executed in batch mode. When a foreground program is interrupted for input or output, control is transferred to another foreground program of equal or lower priority or to a background program.

For large systems with several foreground and background programs, scheduling is not a simple task. Two programs of the same priority may request CPU resources at the same time. The method of deciding which program gets control first may be arbitrary; for example, the program that has been in primary storage longer may receive control first. Fortunately, the operating system is capable of handling such problems as they occur and in most instances makes the process of multiprogramming invisible to the user.

FIGURE 10—5

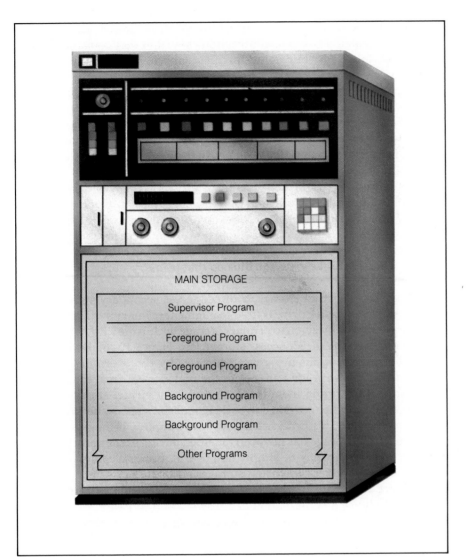

MAIN STORAGE

Supervisor Program

Foreground Program

Foreground Program

Background Program

Background Program

Other Programs

▬ VIRTUAL STORAGE

Multiprogramming increases system efficiency because the CPU can execute programs concurrently instead of waiting for I/O operations to occur. A limitation of multiprogramming, however, is that each partition must be large enough to hold an entire program; the program remains in memory until its execution is completed. Therefore, all the instructions of a program are kept in primary storage throughout its execution. As processing requirements increase, the physical limitations of memory become a critical constraint and the productive use of memory becomes increasingly important.

For many years, the space limitations of primary storage have been a barrier to applications. Programmers have spent much time trying to find ways to trim the size of programs so that they could fit into the available primary storage space. In some cases, attempts have been made to segment programs (break them into separate modules) so that they could be executed in separate job steps; but doing this manually is both tedious and time consuming. While hardware costs have decreased and storage capacities have increased, this storage problem still exists in high-volume processing systems that require large programs.

To alleviate the problem, an extension of multiprogramming called **virtual storage** (sometimes called **virtual memory**) has been developed. Virtual storage is based on the principle that only the immediately needed portion of a program must be in primary storage at any given time; the rest of the program and data can be kept in secondary storage. Since only part of a program is in primary storage at one time, more programs can reside in primary storage simultaneously, allowing more programs to be executed within a given time interval. Using virtual memory gives the system the ability to treat secondary storage as if it were merely an extension of primary storage. This technique gives the illusion that primary storage is unlimited, or "virtual."

To implement virtual storage, a direct-access secondary storage device such as a magnetic-disk drive is used to augment primary storage. The term **real storage** is usually given to primary storage within the CPU, while virtual storage refers to the direct-access storage (see Figure 10–6). Both real and virtual storage locations are given addresses by the operating system. If data or instructions needed are not in the real storage area, the portion of the program containing them is transferred from virtual storage into real storage, while another portion currently in real storage may be written back to virtual storage. This process is known as **swapping.** If the portion of the program in real storage has not been modified during execution, the portion from virtual storage may be simply laid over it, because copies of all parts of the program are kept in virtual storage.

There are two main methods of implementing virtual-storage systems, both of which use a combination of hardware and software to accomplish the task. The first method is called **segmentation.** Each program is broken

FIGURE 10–6

Schematic Drawing of Virtual Storage and Swapping

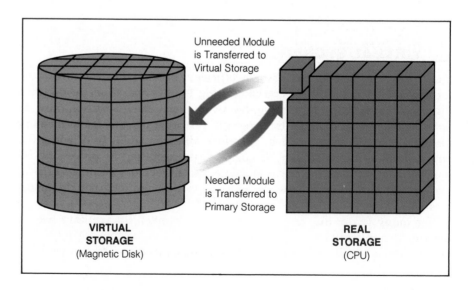

Unneeded Module is Transferred to Virtual Storage

Needed Module is Transferred to Primary Storage

VIRTUAL STORAGE
(Magnetic Disk)

REAL STORAGE
(CPU)

COMPUTERS AND INFORMATION PROCESSING

into variable-sized blocks called **segments,** which are logical parts of the program. For example, one segment may contain data used by the program; another segment may contain a **subroutine** of the program; and so on. The operating system software allocates storage space according to the size of these logical segments.

A second method of implementing virtual storage is called **paging.** Here, primary storage is divided into physical areas of fixed size called **page frames.** All page frames for all programs are the same size, and this size depends on the characteristics of the particular computer. In contrast to segmentation, paging does not consider the logical portions of the programs. Instead, the programs are broken into equal-sized blocks called **pages.** One page can fit in one page frame of primary storage (see Figure 10–7).

In both paging and segmentation, the operating system handles the swapping of pages or segments whenever a portion of the program that is not in real storage is needed during processing.

Virtual storage offers tremendous flexibility to programmers and system analysts designing new applications; they can devote their time to solving the problem at hand rather than fitting programs into storage. Moreover, as already explained, the use of primary storage is optimized, because only needed portions of programs are in primary storage at any given time.

One of the major limitations of virtual storage is the requirement for extensive online secondary storage. Also, the virtual-storage operating system is highly sophisticated and requires significant amounts of internal storage. If virtual storage is not used wisely, much time can be spent locating and changing program pages or segments; in some programs, little actual processing occurs compared with the amount of swapping. (This is known as **thrashing.**)

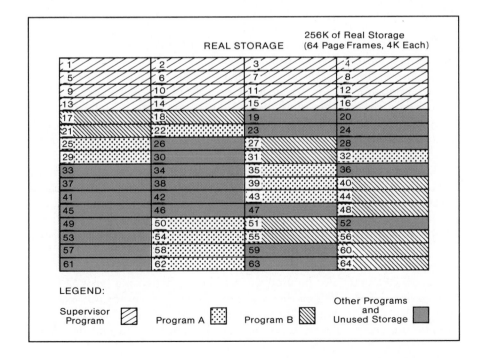

FIGURE 10–7

Paging

HIGHLIGHT

SAA, Systems Application Architecture

Although IBM is one of the leading manufacturers of computer hardware systems, it too must adapt to the changing needs of users. In the past IBM sold stand-alone systems; for example, a mainframe worked alone and was not connected to other mainframes or micros. Now users want to be able to transfer files and applications between systems. This is a problem because many of IBM's systems are not compatible. A microcomputer application program often does not work on the mainframe. In order to rectify the situation, IBM is developing Systems Application Architecture (SAA), a new framework for providing connectivity between networks.

SAA is a series of interfaces that will provide connectivity between certain IBM mainframes, minicomputers, and microcomputers. These interfaces follow standards in the areas of user access, communications support, applications, and programming. For example, in programming the software will all use such languages as C, FORTRAN, and COBOL. When SAA is complete, users should be able to view the same screen on either

their micros or on a mainframe. They should be able to perform functions on any size computer in one manner—there should be no need to learn a new system.

SAA is not supported by all IS professionals. Some feel IBM is unclear about how it will accomplish SAA. The skeptics feel SAA may not be able to create compatibility; if compatibility is possible, they feel, development will be slow and true compatibility will be a long way off. SAA may have a major effect on future computer systems, or it may fall by the wayside.

■ MULTIPROCESSING

Multiprocessing involves the use of two or more CPUs linked together for coordinated operation. Stored-program instructions are executed simultaneously, but by different CPUs. The CPUs may execute different instructions from the same program, or they may execute totally different programs. (In contrast, under multiprogramming, the computer appears to be processing different jobs simultaneously but is actually processing them concurrently, or within a given time interval.)

Multiprocessing systems are designed to achieve a particular objective. One common objective is to relieve a large CPU of tasks such as scheduling, editing data, and maintaining files so that it can continue high-priority or complex processing without interruption. To achieve this goal, a small CPU is linked to the large CPU. All work coming into the system from remote terminals or other peripheral devices is first channeled through the small CPU, which coordinates the activities of the large one. Generally, the small CPU handles all I/O interrupts and so on, while the large CPU handles the "number crunching" (large mathematical calculations). A schematic diagram of this type of multiprocessing system is shown in Figure 10–8. The small CPU in Figure 10–8 is commonly referred to as a **front-end processor.** It is an interface between the large CPU and peripheral devices such as online terminals.

A small CPU may also be used as an interface between a large CPU and a large data base stored on direct-access storage devices. In this case, the small CPU, often termed a **back-end processor,** is solely responsible for maintaining the data base. Accessing data and updating specific data fields are typical functions that a small CPU performs in this type of multiprocessing system.

Many large multiprocessing systems have two or more large CPUs. These large CPUs are no different from those used in single-CPU (stand-alone) configurations. Each may have its own separate memory, or a single memory may be shared by all of them. The activities of each CPU can be controlled in whole or in part by a common supervisor program. This type of

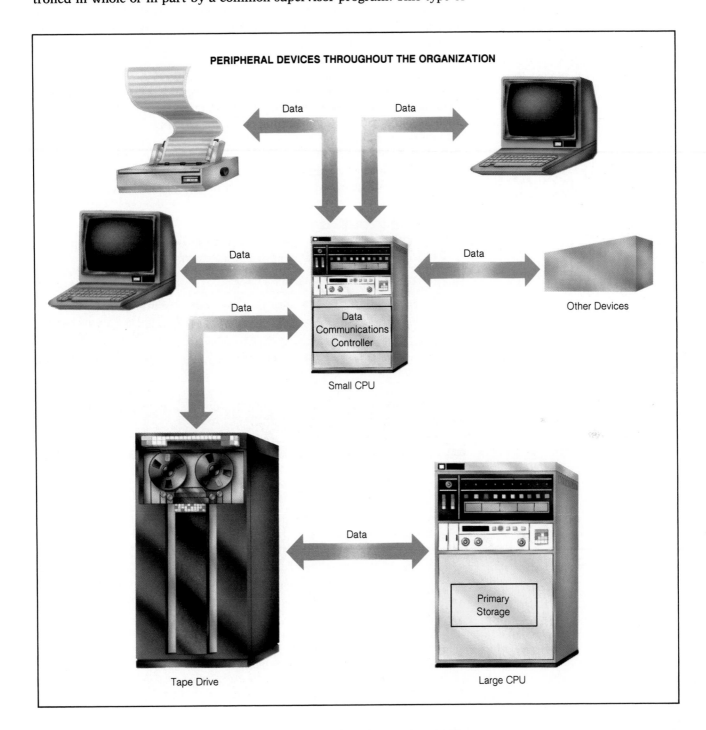

PERIPHERAL DEVICES THROUGHOUT THE ORGANIZATION

Data   Data

Data

Data Communications Controller

Small CPU

Data

Other Devices

Data

Tape Drive

Data

Primary Storage

Large CPU

system is used by organizations with extremely large and complex data-processing needs. Each large CPU may be dedicated to a specific task such as I/O processing or arithmetic processing. One CPU can be set up to handle online processing while another handles only batch processing. Alternately, two CPUs may be used together on the same task to provide rapid responses in the most demanding applications. Many multiprocessing systems are designed so that one or more of the CPUs can provide backup if another malfunctions. A configuration that uses multiple large CPUs is depicted in Figure 10–9. This system also uses a small CPU to control communications with peripheral devices and perform "housekeeping chores" (input editing, validation, and the like).

Coordinating the efforts of several CPUs requires highly sophisticated software and careful planning. The scheduling of workloads for the CPUs involves making the most efficient use of computer resources. Implementing such a system is a time-consuming endeavor that may require the services of outside consultants as well as those provided by the equipment manufacturers. The payoff from this effort is a system with capabilities extending far beyond those of a single-CPU system. See Concept Summary 10–3 for a review of multiprogramming, virtual storage, and multiprocessing.

CONCEPT SUMMARY 10—3

Developments that Improved Computer Efficiency

Multiprogramming	Virtual Storage	Multiprocessing
■ Involves storing several programs in primary storage at one time	■ Involves use of pages or segments of a program	■ Involves use of two or more CPUs linked together
■ Processes programs concurrently (that is, within a given time interval) by shifting back and forth among programs	■ Only needed portions of program reside in primary storage, giving illusion that primary storage is unlimited	■ Stored-program instructions are executed simultaneously

FIGURE 10-9

**Multiprocessing System Using
Multiple Large CPUs**

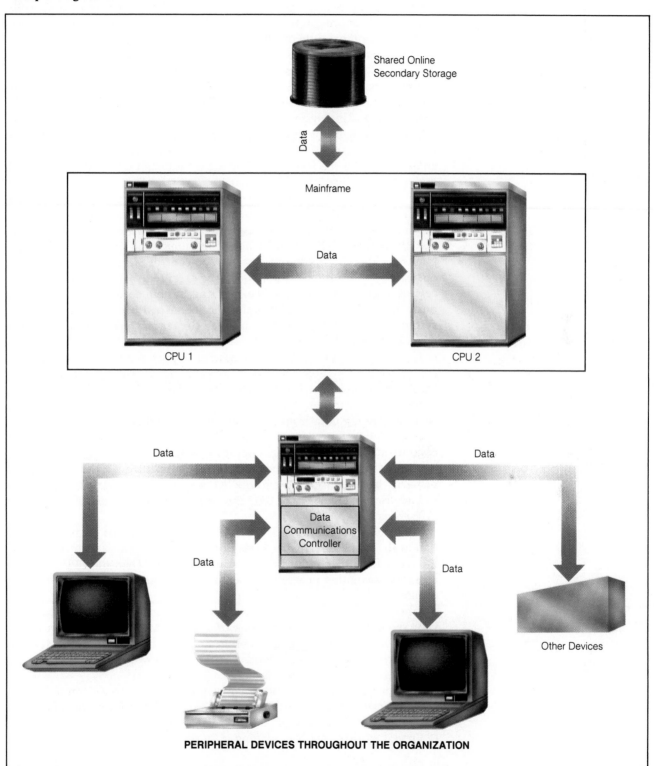

Shared Online
Secondary Storage

Data

Mainframe

Data

CPU 1

CPU 2

Data

Data

Data
Communications
Controller

Data

Data

Other Devices

PERIPHERAL DEVICES THROUGHOUT THE ORGANIZATION

■ SUMMARY POINTS

■ A program is a series of step-by-step instructions that a computer can use to solve a problem.

■ System programs are generally provided by the computer manufacturer or a specialized programming firm. Application programs can be developed within the organization or purchased from a software firm.

■ An operating system is a collection of programs designed to permit a computer system to manage its own operations. It allocates computer resources among multiple users, keeps track of all information required for accounting purposes, and establishes job priorities.

■ Batch operating systems allow uninterrupted processing of a batch of jobs without operator intervention. Online operating systems can respond to spontaneous requests for system resources, such as management inquiries entered from online terminals. Operating systems that handle both batch and online applications are standard.

■ An operating system consists of control programs and processing programs stored on the system residence device. The supervisor program, the major component of the operating system, controls the other subsystems.

■ A job-control language (JCL) is the communication link between the programmer and the operating system. Job-control statements instruct the operating system in how the job is to be executed. When using batch processing, each instruction that the operating system needs to execute the job must be stated at the beginning of the job. When using online operating systems, the user is prompted to enter the correct operating instruction when it is needed.

■ The input/output management system is part of the operating system control programs. It receives input from channels, regulates output, assigns I/O devices to specific programs, and coordinates all I/O activities.

■ Utility programs perform specialized functions like sorting and merging and transferring data from one I/O device to another.

■ Operating systems can be configured in a modular fashion by the addition of components to the original operating system.

■ The CPU may be idle for a significant amount of time because of the speed disparity between the CPU and the I/O devices. Multiprogramming is used to increase the efficiency of CPU utilization through the use of concurrent processing.

■ With multiprogramming several programs reside in the primary storage unit at the same time. Instructions from one program are executed until an interrupt for either input or output is generated. Then the CPU shifts its attention to another program in memory until that program requires input or output.

■ When multiprogramming is used, the programs in primary storage are kept separate by use of partitions or regions. Memory protection and a method of assigning priorities to programs are required. High-priority programs are loaded into foreground partitions and low-primary programs are loaded into background partitions.

■ Multiprogramming is limited by primary storage space limitations; a complete program may not fit into a partition. These problems are alleviated by the use of virtual storage.

■ Virtual storage involves loading only the part of a program needed in primary storage, while keeping the remainder of the program in secondary storage. This technique gives the illusion that primary storage is unlimited.

■ Segmentation is a method of implementing virtual storage whereby each program is broken into segments of variable size. Each segment is a logical subunit of the complete program. Paging, another method of implementing virtual storage, uses equal-sized blocks called pages without considering logical parts of the program.

■ Multiprocessing involves the use of two or more CPUs linked together for coordinated operation. Separate programs or separate parts of the same program can be processed simultaneously by different CPUs.

■ Small computers can be linked to mainframes as either front-end processors or back-end processors. The former act as interfaces between the CPU and the I/O devices; the latter act as interfaces between large CPUs and data bases stored on direct-access storage devices.

■ Large CPUs can be linked together to handle extremely large and complex data-processing needs. Each CPU may be assigned to a specific task, or it may be used with other CPUs on the same task to provide rapid response.

■ REVIEW QUESTIONS

1. Distinguish between application programs and system programs. Give examples of each and explain why they belong in that particular category.

2. What are the major functions performed by an operating system? Is an operating system that can handle batch processing more complex and sophisticated than one that allows online processing? Explain.

3. Into what two categories can operating system programs be divided? List some programs under each category.

4. What is the function of the supervisor program?

5. What are some of the functions performed by the job-control language?

6. What is the purpose of the system residence device?

7. What is a utility program?

8. Distinguish between multiprogramming and multiprocessing. What are some of the problems that must be solved in a multiprogramming environment?

9. What is the purpose of placing programs in either foreground or background partitions of memory?

10. Why were virtual-storage systems developed? Compare and contrast the two techniques—segmentation and paging—used to implement virtual-storage capabilities.

11. What is a major limitation of virtual storage?

Microsoft Corporation

Microsoft®

EARLY DEVELOPMENTS

The microcomputer industry began in the mid-1970s and since then has experienced rapid growth. Most visible have been the successes of various hardware suppliers—Apple Computer, Tandy Corporation, and IBM, to name a few. It was the marked achievements of these suppliers that stimulated the development of a number of related businesses—most notably companies that designed and manufactured software to run on the new machines.

Founded in 1974, Microsoft Corporation has quickly become the largest developer of software for microcomputers in the United States, establishing itself as a pioneer. Since 1977, sales have increased dramatically and staffing has jumped from 5 persons to more than 2500. Corporate headquarters in Redmond, Washington occupy a 53-acre site that more closely resembles a college campus. Microsoft has given new meaning to the concept of rapid expansion.

Beginning with Microsoft's initial product, the first BASIC language for microcomputers (still an industry standard), the company established a reputation for developing innovative, state-of-the-art products. One of the most notable features of Microsoft's design standards is that each new generation of software is compatible with the software of the previous generation.

Microsoft began as a partnership between William H. Gates and Paul G. Allen. It was reorganized as a privately held corporation in 1981 with Gates as executive vice president and chairman of the board and Allen as executive vice president. Jon Shirley joined the company as president in August 1983. Today, Microsoft is the leading independent software supplier of easy-to-learn and well-supported productivity tools, languages, and operating systems. Microsoft estab-lished foreign subsidiaries around the world that have contributed to making it the undisputed leader in international software, with more than 40 percent of total revenues generated outside the United States.

PRODUCT LINE

Microsoft has the most comprehensive range of microcomputer software products of any company in the world, maintaining a full line of language compilers, interpreters, operating systems, business tools, and even entertainment packages.

In 1980, Microsoft licensed the UNIX operating system from Bell Labs and began to develop its own enhanced version for microcomputers, which is called XENIX. UNIX is a powerful, multi-user operating system designed for microcomputers, and Microsoft successfully adapted it, with a number of improvements, to run on the 16-bit microprocessor. With the release of the XENIX operating system, Microsoft began providing maintenance, support, and even application assistance to original equipment manufacturers and end users. As a result, Microsoft rapidly became the main supplier of a popular, standardized, high-level 16-bit operating system that was powerful and also accessible to almost every microprocessor on the market. The XENIX operating system was developed to run on multi-user computers with 16-bit microprocessors and on DEC's PDP-11 series. To date, forty companies in eight different countries have licensed XENIX.

In 1988, Microsoft introduced an Intel 80386 based version of XENIX. An agreement between AT&T and Microsoft will permit the development of a new version of UNIX for the 80386 that will combine the best features of XENIX and AT&T System V technology. This marks the first time that AT&T has licensed its trademark UNIX.

Also in 1980, Microsoft developed and introduced the Microsoft SoftCard, a plug-in board that allows Apple II owners access to both Microsoft BASIC and the CP/M operating system for the Zilog Z-80 microprocessor, and thereby tens of thousands of software packages. The first year on the market, Microsoft sold 25,000 units; since then SoftCard has been installed in more than 100,000 Apple systems.

Approached by IBM and working closely with them, Microsoft developed a new 16-bit operating system. When IBM introduced its personal computer in August 1981, Microsoft MS-DOS was the only operating system for which IBM provided additional software. Within a year, IBM had announced full support of twelve Microsoft products, and by June 1982, thirty other companies had released software designed to run on Microsoft MS-DOS. Microsoft also adapted a number of 8-bit languages to the 16-bit microprocessor. Those languages include Microsoft BASIC interpreter and compiler, as well as Business BASIC, Pascal, COBOL, C, and FORTRAN compilers.

Microsoft has developed a number of second-generation software packages and tools, such as Multiplan electronic worksheet, a sophisticated electronic planning and modeling tool designed to be the friendliest and most powerful on the market. By the end of 1982, Multiplan was offered by thirty-six different microcomputer manufacturers and was available in seven languages.

In 1983, Microsoft introduced a low-cost, hand-held input device called the Microsoft Mouse. Mouse is small and lightweight and is used to quickly insert, delete, and reposition the cursor or blocks of text within a document without having to use the keyboard. Microsoft Mouse has been developed for use with the IBM Personal Computer and other systems that run on the MS-DOS operating system.

With the release of the Microsoft Mouse, Microsoft also introduced a highly sophisticated word-processing software package, Microsoft Word. Features like style sheets, footnotes, glossaries, columnar formatting, and multiple windows have helped make Word an industry leader. Typical of Microsoft's careful planning, Word was designed to take advantage of anticipated developments in computer printers by allowing users to specify not only paper and type sizes but also special character sizes, ink colors, and up to sixty-four different type fonts. Word has become a best seller among users of the Apple's Macintosh computer and Laserwriter printer.

Marketing best-selling software is a way of life at Microsoft. Excel is a complete spreadsheet with integrated business graphics and data base for both the Macintosh and IBM PC computers. Microsoft Windows is a graphical operating environment designed to support the MS-DOS operating system. Additional products such as WORKS integrate the capabilities of form applications: word processing, data-base management, spreadsheets, and communications.

In the area of entertainment, the most significant software package released by Microsoft is Flight Simulator, which has become one of the biggest selling programs for the IBM Personal Computer. With Flight Simulator, the players "pilot" an aircraft (similar to a Cessna Skylane) through takeoff and landings at more than twenty airports. They may alter the environment to simulate various weather conditions, as well as daytime or nighttime flight.

Possibly the most significant announcement for the future of Microsoft was made in April 1987. Two products designed for the new generation of IBM PS/2 personal computers were introduced. Microsoft OS/2 with the Presentation Manager is a new operating system environment that allows software to take advantage of the more powerful generation of newer processing chips. Microsoft OS/2 LAN Manager is an advanced local area network operating environment that permits users to interconnect various hardware and operating systems in a standard interface.

Microsoft, while continuing to develop other consumer applications and tools, is committed to the philosophy of constantly improving software and developing upwardly compatible versions of all established products for the newer generations of personal computers.

DISCUSSION POINTS

1. What key issues does Microsoft consider critical to software developers in the future, and why are these issues important?

2. Why is the development of standards for user interface an important consideration for a software developer?

CHAPTER

11

Software Development

OUTLINE

Introduction
Defining and Documenting the Problem
Designing and Documenting a Solution
The Four Basic Logic Patterns
Structured Programming Techniques

Top-Down Design
Pseudocode
Flowcharts
Action Diagrams
Using Structured Design Techniques in Industry
Writing and Documenting the Program
Structured Coding
Types of Statements

Debugging and Testing the Program
Summary Points
Review Questions

Trying Times: Lawsuits Threaten Developers

Michael Tucker
Computerworld

A litigation craze has hit the software business. Suddenly, software developers are finding themselves at risk in copyright disputes. For some of the smaller developers that can least afford legal fees, this new age offers both perils and promise.

Until recently, copyright laws were rarely invoked in the software industry. However, in the last year and a half, major lawsuits have been launched by some of the biggest computer firms in the business. Lotus Development Corp. led off the assault in 1987 with suits directed against makers of clone products that closely mimicked its 1-2-3 spreadsheet. In more recent months, Apple Computer, Inc. began a suit aimed at protecting the interface of its Macintosh.

How will these suits affect software developers? "The Lotus suit doesn't seem to be having much effect at all," says Richard M. Lucash, a partner with the Boston-based law firm of Lucash, Gesmer and Updegrove, which specializes in computer law. "With very few exceptions, there just weren't that many people out there making exact duplications of other people's software products. I know of maybe one product, a spreadsheet clone, that hasn't been released as a result of the suit."

Far more serious, though, has been the Apple suit. "That's where we have clients calling up and asking what chance Apple has of winning and how long it's going to take either way," Lucash says.

Lucash explains that the Apple suit is unique because it brings the copyright dispute to the interface level. "It means, for the first time, you can walk into a lawsuit without having a direct clone of somebody else's product."

Small developers that have invested their resources developing for Microsoft Corp.'s Windows or Hewlett-Packard Co.'s New Wave stand to suffer the most from the litigation, he says. Suddenly, they must put their products on hold until the issue is resolved. Some may even go out of business before that time.

Lucash, however, does not think the dispute will go on long. "I don't think this is going to go to trial. I think you're going to see a settlement whereby Apple will be able to extract a few more dollars from Microsoft. . . . You know, Bill Gates has always been known as a hard bargainer. Well, in a sense, he's getting a taste of his own medicine now."

But what accounts for the upsurge of legal activity in the software industry? Lucash claims it is the result of modifications of the copyright law made between 1985 and 1986. "For the first time," he says, "the law at least mentioned computer technology. It's taken three years for the courts to work out the basic issues of the new copyright law. And now we're seeing the consummation of that."

He also thinks the new laws will benefit smaller developers, even though they are the ones being hurt in the short run. In time, he says, small developers will be able to use the law to protect themselves from larger, better funded rivals that might otherwise pirate their work.

Other explanations are not so positive. One Cambridge, Mass.-based developer of 1-2-3 add-ins, who asked not to be named for fear of a lawsuit, explains the litigation boom simply and bitterly. He says, "The lawyers, they saw there was money in software and figured it was time to go get it."

Until recently, copyright laws did not cover computer software. Now the laws have been changed, and a number of lawsuits have been filed on infringements on computer software. What effect will these lawsuits have on the software development industry? Will software be produced more slowly and its cost rise? Right now it's a wait and see game.

INTRODUCTION

Augusta Ada, Countess of Lovelace, made the following statement concerning the analytical engine which she helped Charles Babbage to develop, "The Analytical Engine has no pretensions whatever to originate anything. It can do whatever we know how to order it to perform. It can follow analysis; but it has no power of anticipating any analytical relations or truths. Its province is to assist us in making available what we are already acquainted with."

This statement briefly explains the basic problem in programming: the programmer must know how to instruct the computer, in an ordered way, in the exact steps it must take to solve a programming problem. People often solve problems intuitively, without identifying each step they perform. Computers lack this human capability. Therefore, using a computer to help solve a problem requires planning. In the early days of the computer, the most significant changes came in the area of improvements to the hardware. Changes in the methodology of software development did not keep pace with these hardware advances. Only in recent years have the methods used to develop software become the object of intensive research. It has been determined that to efficiently develop a well-designed solution to a programming problem, four steps, collectively referred to as the **software development process,** should be followed:

1. Define and document the problem.
2. Design and document a solution.
3. Write and document the program.
4. Debug and test the program and revise the documentation if necessary.

Each of these steps will be discussed in detail in this chapter. See Concept Summary 11–1 for a review of the steps in the software development process.

DEFINING AND DOCUMENTING THE PROBLEM

It is virtually impossible to get somewhere if you do not know where you are going. Likewise, in programming, a clear and concise statement of the problem must be given before anything else is done. Despite this fact, many programming disasters have occurred because this step was glossed over. Often this situation occurs because the person who writes the program is not the same person who will be using it. Communication between these two people (or groups) can be inadequate, leading to misunderstandings concerning the desired results of the program and ultimately to programs that do not meet the user's needs. Therefore, before the project proceeds, the problem must be clearly defined and documented in writing and agreed upon by all parties involved. Because such analysis skills often differ from the skills required of a programmer, many corporations use system analysts to define and design a solution to the programming problem. The tasks of actually writing, debugging, and testing the program are then performed by members of the corporation's programming staff.

The documentation of the problem definition should include a description of:

■ *The desired output.* All output and the manner in which it is to be formatted should be described here. Formatting refers to the way in which the output is to be displayed or printed to make it easy for the user to read and use. For example, placing output in table form with appropriate headings is one way of formatting it.

CONCEPT SUMMARY 11–1

The Steps in the Software Development Process

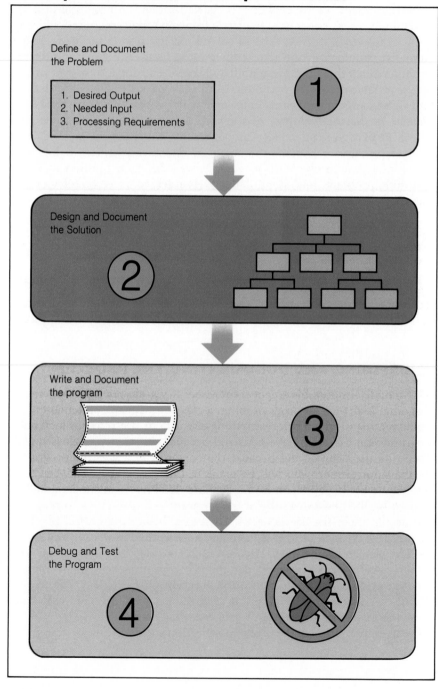

Define and Document
the Problem

1. Desired Output
2. Needed Input
3. Processing Requirements

1

Design and Document
the Solution

2

Write and Document
the program

3

Debug and Test
the Program

4

COMPUTERS AND INFORMATION PROCESSING

Groupware Can Make Groups Work

"Send it to committee." These words often strike fear in the hearts of people who want decisions and actions. Committees are notorious for taking a lot of time to make even simple decisions. A new type of software, called groupware, is trying to change this image. Instead of groups taking longer than an individual to decide on issues, the software developers say groupware will provide users with the benefits of a committee, such as different perspectives, but will also enable the users to reach decisions more quickly.

How will groupware work? Groupware is actually a combination of software products that enhance the productivity of groups in a number of ways. For example, how much time do committee members spend discussing when they can next meet? Some groupware products are used to schedule meeting times by accessing the calendars of all the members. Another product sends members a reminder for the meetings and the agenda. In addition, groupware is used to exchange information among members—for example, by group conferencing.

It is interesting to note that experts feel electronic mail is not a groupware product. Electronic mail users often get a lot of junk mail that they must sort through. This wastes time and lowers efficiency. One software developer, however, has a product that actually sorts mail for E-mail users. Are mail sorters considered groupware? That depends upon whom you ask. Groupware is still a new concept, and software developers are still defining its components. If they are successful, however, we may no longer hear groans when the word "committee" is mentioned.

■ *The input.* What data is needed to obtain the desired output? From where will this data be obtained? How will this data be formatted? The programmer or system analyst should make it as easy as possible for the user to enter the data that a program needs.

■ *The processing requirements.* Given the stated output specifications and the required input, the processing requirements can be determined.

The documentation for these three items, the input, output, and processing steps, is referred to as the **program specifications.**

As an example of this process, let's define and document a specific programming problem. The accounting department's payroll section is not functioning properly. Checks are issued late, and many are incorrect. Most of the reports to management, local and state governments, and union officials are woefully inadequate. The payroll section's personnel often work overtime to process the previous week's payroll checks.

The problem is fairly obvious—company expansion and new reporting requirements have strained the accounting department beyond its capacity. A new computerized payroll system has been suggested. Management has agreed with this assessment and has contacted the computer services department for help in solving the problem. The accounting department and computer services department, working together, have defined the problem as shown below.

Problem Definition: Write a program to process the company's payroll. This program will generate not only individual paychecks but appropriate summary reports.

Desired Output: First of all, the payroll program must issue the paychecks. It also must send a statement of weekly and monthly payroll expenses to management and an updated list of changes in employee salaries and positions to the personnel department. The local, state, and federal governments require a monthly report of income taxes withheld, and the union receives payment of employee dues deducted by the payroll section. Not only the checks but all of these reports must be printed by the program. The content and format (layout) of the reports should be determined at this time.

Needed Input: The next step in defining the problem is to determine the input needed to generate the output listed above. This input includes each employee's time card, which contains the employee number and the hours worked each day of the week. Another input, dealing with new employees and changes in pay scales, is sent by the personnel department. Supervisors provide a special form regarding employee promotions. The tax section sends updates of tax tables used to calculate local, state, and federal withholdings. The union provides information about the withholding of union dues. The format and content of the forms used for input must also be determined as part of the process of identifying the needed input.

Processing Requirements: Given the needed output and input, the processing required of the new computerized payroll system is illustrated in Figure 11–1. First, each employee's gross pay must be calculated from the employee's time card and pay scale. Second, each deduction regarding taxes and union dues must be determined from the tax rates provided by the tax department and the information regarding union dues provided by the union, and these deductions must be subtracted from the gross pay to arrive at the net, or take-home, pay. Third, each employee's paycheck must be printed. Totals must be kept of all employees' gross pay and net pay values as well as of taxes and union dues withheld. These totals are used to generate reports to management, government, and union officials. In addition, changes in any employee's work status must be reported to the personnel department.

FIGURE 11—1

Problem Definition Step for Payroll Example

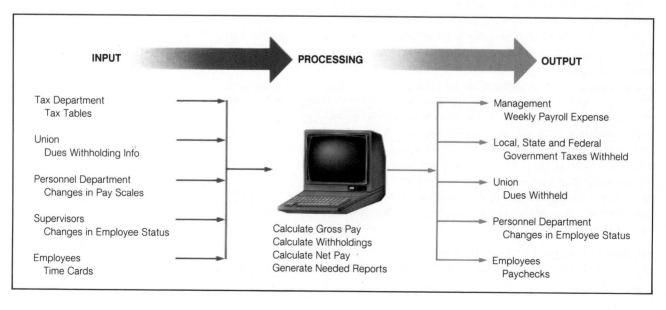

The programmer or system analyst must not only thoroughly understand the problem, but also must write the statement of the problem in a clear, concise style. By documenting the problem, it becomes apparent whether or not it is clearly understood. This written documentation should be shown to the potential user(s) of the program to determine if the analyst's understanding of the problem is the same as that of the user(s). Making certain of this early in the programming process will save time and increase the probability that everyone involved will be satisfied with the end product.

■ DESIGNING AND DOCUMENTING A SOLUTION

Once the necessary program input, output, and processing requirements have been determined, it is time to design a solution. It is not necessary to know what programming language will be used in order to develop the logic of a tentative solution. (In fact, knowing the processing requirements first helps the programmer to select the language best suited to those requirements.)

The Four Basic Logic Patterns

After the processing requirements are known, the actual logic of the solution can be determined. In order to do this, it is necessary to know the basic logic patterns that the computer is able to execute. The power of the computer comes in large part through the programmer's ability to specify the sequence in which statements in a program are to be executed. However, the computer can execute only four basic logic patterns: the simple sequence, the selection pattern, the loop, and the branch. Programming languages may have more complicated statements, but they all are based on various combinations of these four patterns.

SIMPLE SEQUENCE. In a **simple sequence** the computer executes one statement after another in the order in which they are listed in the program. It is the easiest pattern to understand. Figure 11–2 demonstrates the simple sequence pattern as it relates to the payroll example.

SELECTION. The **selection** pattern requires that the computer make a choice. The choice it makes, however, is based not on personal preference but on pure logic. Each selection is made on the basis of the results of a comparison. The computer can determine if a given value is greater than, equal to, or less than another value; these are the only comparisons the computer is capable of making. Complex comparisons are made by combining two or more simple comparisons. This process of requiring the computer to make a selection or choice is often referred to as conditional programming logic. Figure 11–3 illustrates the selection pattern by demonstrating how the logic of the payroll example would consider overtime pay.

LOOP. The **loop** or iterative pattern enables the programmer to instruct the computer to alter the normal next-sequential-instruction process and loop back to a previous statement in the program, so that a given sequence of

FIGURE 11—2

Simple Sequence Logic Pattern

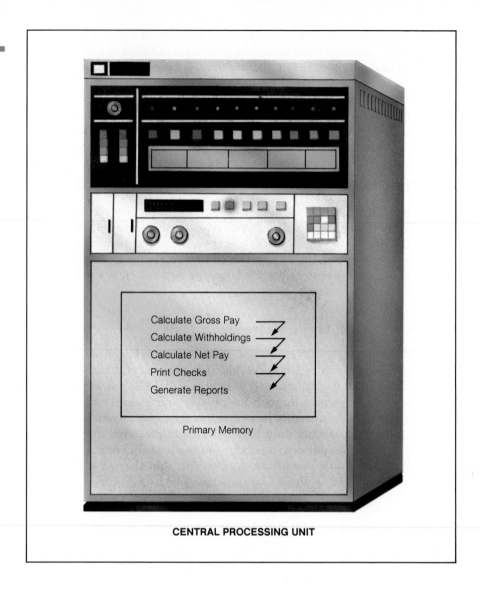

Calculate Gross Pay

Calculate Withholdings

Calculate Net Pay

Print Checks

Generate Reports

Primary Memory

CENTRAL PROCESSING UNIT

statements can be performed as many times as needed. This is especially useful if the same sequence of statements is to be executed, say, for each employee in a payroll program; the programmer need not duplicate the sequence of statements for each set of employee data processed. The looping pattern is illustrated in Figure 11–4.

BRANCH. The last and most controversial pattern is the **branch** (also called the GOTO), which is often used in combination with selection or looping (see Figure 11–5). This pattern allows the programmer to skip statements in a program, leaving them unexecuted.

Branching is controversial for several reasons. If a program uses branches too often, the logic of the program becomes very difficult to follow. Such programs are difficult and time consuming for programmers to maintain and modify. Therefore, the use of the branch statement is strongly dis-

FIGURE 11—3

Selection Logic Pattern

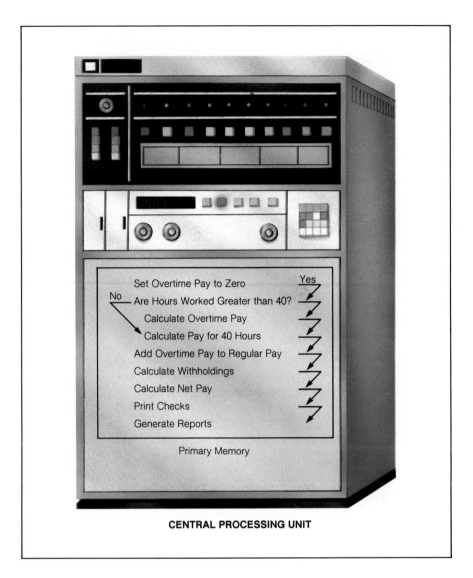

Set Overtime Pay to Zero

No — Are Hours Worked Greater than 40?   Yes

Calculate Overtime Pay

Calculate Pay for 40 Hours

Add Overtime Pay to Regular Pay

Calculate Withholdings

Calculate Net Pay

Print Checks

Generate Reports

Primary Memory

CENTRAL PROCESSING UNIT

couraged in most situations. When using most of the newer programming languages such as Pascal, Ada, and C, referred to as structured programming languages, there is very little need to use branch statements. Loops and selection patterns are used instead. These languages and their advantages will be discussed in Chapter 12.

Structured Programming Techniques

Data processing has come a long way since the days of the UNIVAC I, when the leading scientists of the period projected that the world would need only ten such machines for the rest of time. Today the world has millions of computers with processing capabilities billions of times greater than ten UNIVAC Is, and the demand for computing power continues to increase. In the first generation of computers, hardware was expensive, accounting for 80 percent of the total cost, whereas software accounted for approximately

FIGURE 11—4

Loop Logic Pattern

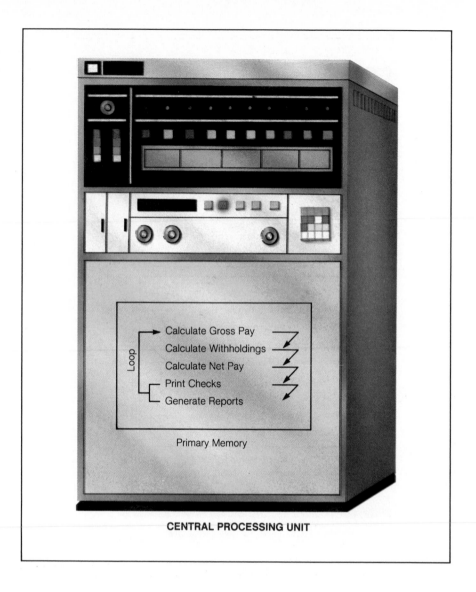

CENTRAL PROCESSING UNIT

20 percent. Today those figures are reversed, and it appears this trend will continue for some time. Figure 11–6 graphically depicts this situation.

As the sophistication of hardware increased rapidly, software technology did not keep pace. In the early days of software development, programming was very much an art. There were no standards or concrete rules. Many programmers approached their work haphazardly. Their main objective was to develop a program that executed properly, but they were not concerned about how this was accomplished. This situation created the following problems:

■ Programmer productivity was low. Developing a usable program of any significant size was a long, tedious process.
■ The programs often were not reliable. **Reliability** is the ability of a program to always obtain correct results. These early programs often produced incorrect results.

FIGURE 11—5

Branch Logic Pattern

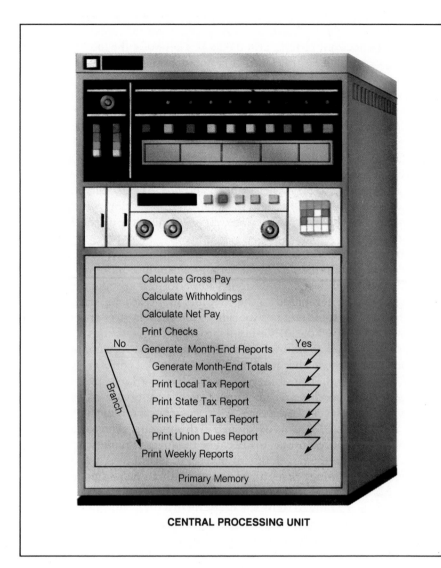

CENTRAL PROCESSING UNIT

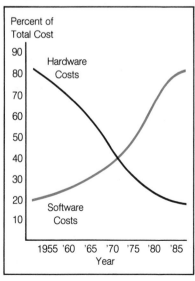

■ The programs could not always correctly handle invalid input. A well-written program should be able to handle any type of input. For example, if the user types in a letter of the alphabet when a number should have been entered, the program should be able to handle the situation appropriately by, for example, printing an error message.

■ The programs were not easy to maintain (that is, keep in working order). The original programmers did not concern themselves with making the logic of the program easy for others to understand. Therefore, if a different programmer had to modify an existing program at a later date (a situation that happens continually in industry), it was a difficult task.

As programmers became aware of these difficulties, their attention was turned to developing methods of improving programming techniques. One of the earliest developments was the discovery by two mathematicians, Guiseppe Jacopini and Corrado Bohm, that any programming problem could be solved using a combination of three basic logic patterns: the simple sequence, the selection pattern, and the loop. Therefore, the fourth pattern, the branch, was unnecessary. Until this point, branches were used often, leading to programs with convoluted, difficult-to-follow logic.

Another event in the development of structured programming occurred in 1968 when E. W. Dijkstra published a letter in the Communications of the ACM (Association for Computer Machinists) titled "Go To Statements Considered Harmful." Dijkstra stated in this now-famous letter that using the GOTO statement (which uses the branch logic pattern) made the logic of a program virtually impossible to follow because execution skipped haphazardly from one part of the program to another. At this stage computer scientists began to realize that it was important to develop programming languages that allowed programs to be written without the use of the GOTO statement.

At about this time, computer scientists also determined that program structure could be obtained by breaking a program into more manageable subprograms or **modules,** each designed to perform a specific task. These subprograms can be compared to the chapters in a textbook; each chapter deals with a specific topic and has specific goals. The chapters are combined to present a unified whole. Dividing a program into modules makes the program's logic easier to follow just as dividing a book into chapters (and subsections within those chapters) makes the facts and concepts presented easier to comprehend. The ability to easily divide a large program into fairly independent modules is an important characteristic of structured programming languages. Languages with this characteristic will be discussed in Chapter 12. Programs developed in this manner tend to have fewer errors than unstructured programs because the logic is readily apparent.

These events led to the development of a set of techniques, referred to as **structured programming.** Structured programming encourages programmers to think about the problem first and thoroughly design a solution before actually beginning to write the program in a programming language. Using structured programming encourages the development of well-written modular programs that have easy-to-follow logic and tend to be more error-free than other programs. There are many characteristics that distinguish structured programming. These characteristics can be divided into two broad categories: those that affect the manner in which the program solution is designed (structured design techniques) and those that affect the style in which the actual program is written (structured coding). Structured coding will be discussed in the section on writing programs (step 3 of the software development process). Structured design techniques will be presented next.

Top-Down Design

Using a computer to solve a problem is considerably different than most people think. The programmer needs to know only a little about the computer and how it works, but he or she must know a programming language. The most difficult aspect of programming is learning to organize solutions in a clear, concise way. One method of organizing a solution is to define the major steps or functions first, then expand the functions into more detailed steps later. This method, which proceeds from the general to the specific, is called **top-down design.** Top-down design employs the **modular approach,** which consists of breaking a problem into smaller and smaller subproblems. Sometimes this is referred to as the "divide-and-conquer" method, because it is easier to deal with a large job by completing it a small step at a time. When the actual program is written, these small steps can be written as separate modules, each of which performs a specific task. These modules are then joined together to form the entire program.

STRUCTURE CHARTS. **Structure charts** are used to document the results of the top-down design process by graphically illustrating the various modules and their relationship to one another. The most general level of organization is the main control module; this overall definition of the solution is the most critical to the success of the program. Modules at the next level contain broad descriptions of the steps in the solution process. These steps are further detailed in lower-level modules. The lowest-level modules contain the specific individual tasks the program must perform.

Figure 11–7 contains a structure chart that was developed to solve the payroll processing problem. Note that this structure chart has a total of four levels. The topmost level, Level 0, contains a statement of the general problem. Level 1 contains three basic processing steps the program must perform: read the needed data, process that data, and print the results. Level 2 contains further refinements of the steps in Level 1. In Level 3, only three steps from Level 2 are further refined.

Using top-down design has several advantages. It helps to prevent the programmer from becoming overwhelmed by the size of the job at hand. Also, the programmer is more likely to discover early in the programming process whether a specific solution will work. When the program is actually coded (written in a programming language), each box in the structure chart can be written as a separate module performing a specific task.

HIPO PACKAGES. The term **HIPO (Hierarchy plus Input-Process-Output)** is applied to a kind of visual aid commonly used to supplement structure charts. Whereas structure charts emphasize only structure and function, HIPO packages highlight the inputs, processing, and outputs of program modules.

A typical HIPO package consists of three types of diagrams that describe a program or system of programs from the general level to the detail level. At the most general level is the **visual table of contents,** which is almost identical to the structure chart but includes some additional information. Each block in the visual table of contents is given an identification number that is used as a reference in other HIPO diagrams. Figure 11–8 shows a visual table of contents for the payroll processing application.

Each module in the visual table of contents is described in greater detail in an **overview diagram,** which includes the module's inputs, processing, and outputs. The reference number assigned to the overview diagram shows where the module fits into the overall structure of the system as depicted in the visual table of contents. If the module passes control to a lower-level module in the hierarchy for some specific processing operation, that operation is also given a reference number. An overview diagram for the payroll

FIGURE 11—7

Structure Chart for Payroll Processing Problem

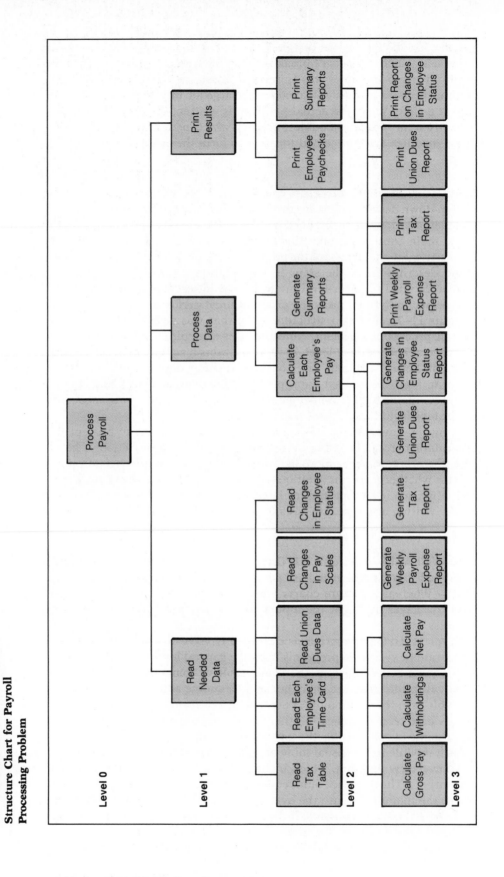

Level 0

Level 1

Level 2

Level 3

Process Payroll

Read Needed Data

Read Tax Table

Read Each Employee's Time Card

Read Union Dues Data

Read Changes in Pay Scales

Read Changes in Employee Status

Process Data

Calculate Each Employee's Pay

Calculate Gross Pay

Calculate Withholdings

Calculate Net Pay

Generate Summary Reports

Generate Weekly Payroll Expense Report

Generate Tax Report

Generate Union Dues Report

Generate Changes in Employee Status Report

Print Results

Print Employee Paychecks

Print Summary Reports

Print Weekly Payroll Expense Report

Print Tax Report

Print Union Dues Report

Print Report on Changes in Employee Status

FIGURE 11-8

Visual Table of Contents for Payroll Processing Example

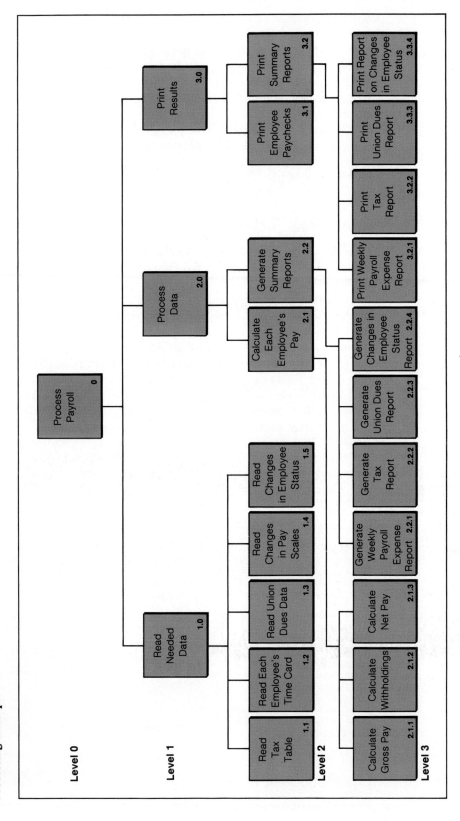

processing module (2.1), "Calculate Each Employee's Pay," is shown in Figure 11–9.

Finally, the specific functions performed and data items used in each module are described in a **detail diagram.** The amount of detail used in these diagrams depends on the complexity of the problem involved. Enough detail should be included to enable a programmer to understand the functions and write the code to perform them.

HIPO diagrams are an excellent means of documenting systems and programs. The varying levels of detail incorporated in the diagrams allow them to be used by managers, analysts, and programmers to meet needs ranging from program maintenance to the overhaul of entire systems.

Pseudocode

Once a structure chart has been developed for a program, the actual logic of the solution can be documented; one method often used is pseudocode. **Pseudocode** is a narrative, or English-like description, representing the logic of a program or program module. The programmer arranges these descriptions in the order in which corresponding program statements will appear. Using pseudocode allows the programmer to focus on the steps required to perform a particular process, rather than on the syntax (or grammatical rules) of a particular programming language. Each pseudocode statement can be transcribed into one or more program statements.

Pseudocode is easy to learn and use. Although it has no rigid rules, several key words often appear. They include PRINT, IF/THEN/ELSE, END, and READ. Some statements are indented to set off repeated steps or conditions to be met. The statements cannot be translated for execution by the computer, therefore *pseudo-* is an appropriate prefix for this type of programming code. Figure 11–10 shows how the three basic logic patterns used in

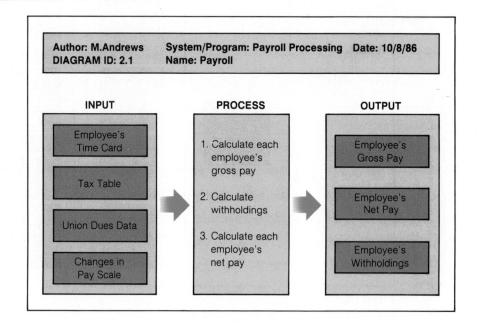

1. Simple Sequence Pattern

```
Read name
Read hours worked
Read hourly rate
Multiply hours worked by hourly rate
  to obtain gross pay
```

2. Selection Pattern

```
If hours worked is greater than 40
  Then subtract 40 from hours worked to
    obtain overtime hours
```

3. Loop Pattern

```
Begin loop; perform until no more records
  Read name
  Read hours worked
  Read hourly rate
  Multiply hours worked by hourly rate
    to obtain gross pay
End loop
```

FIGURE 11–10

Pseudocode Illustrating Three Logic Patterns

structured programming could be written in pseudocode. The pseudocode for the payroll program is shown in Figure 11–11.

Flowcharts

One way of graphically representing the logic of a solution to a programming problem is by using a **flowchart.** A flowchart shows the actual flow of the logic of a program, whereas a structure chart simply contains statements of the levels of refinement used to reach a solution. Each symbol in a flowchart has a specific meaning, as shown in Figure 11–12. Flowchart symbols are arranged from top to bottom and left to right. Flowlines connect the symbols and visually represent the implied flow of the program's logic. Arrowheads indicate the direction of flow. A disadvantage of flowcharts is

```
Begin
Begin loop; perform until no more employee records
  Read employee's name, hours worked, and hourly wage
  Calculate gross pay
  Calculate withholdings
  Calculate net pay
  Print check
End loop
Generate summary reports
End
```

FIGURE 11–11

Pseudocode for Payroll Processing Example

FIGURE 11–12

Flowchart Symbols

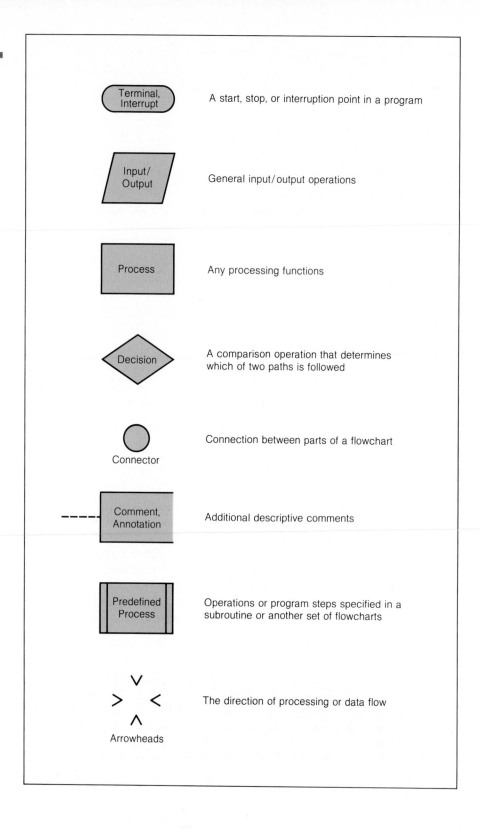

COMPUTERS AND INFORMATION PROCESSING

that they can take up many pages and grow more confusing as programs become more complex. Flowcharting is becoming outdated as more and more programming environments use pseudocode to represent a program's logic. Figure 11–13 shows examples of how the four basic logic structures could be flowcharted.

Action Diagrams

Action diagrams are an alternative form of documenting a designed solution to a problem. Action diagrams lend themselves to a top-down design because they can be used to document each level of the design. They can be used at a high level where structure charts or HIPO diagrams might be used as well as at a detailed level where pseudocode might typically be used. By using action diagrams, there can be a natural progression from a high level to a low level of detail because of the consistent method of documenting each level of the solution. This eliminates the need to mix alternate methods of documenting such as mixing structure or HIPO charts with pseudocode or flowcharts.

Action diagrams also use notation that supports structured programming techniques including modularization, functional decomposition, structured control constructs, and hierarchical organization. Action diagrams use brackets ([) as their basic building blocks. Figure 11–14 illustrates how the four basic logic patterns would be documented using action diagrams while Figure 11–15 shows an action diagram for the payroll processing example. Note that a bracket with a double bar at the top is used to denote a loop pattern and an arrow extending out through a bracket is used to indicate a GOTO.

Using Structured Design Techniques in Industry

The program to generate a company's payroll would be long and complex, having many modules. In large corporations, programs such as this are developed by programmers working in teams. These programmers would use the structured design methods such as top-down design that we discussed earlier. They also would generally employ other methods to develop the software in an organized manner. Two commonly used methods, the chief programmer team and the structured walkthrough, are discussed below.

CHIEF PROGRAMMER TEAM. An important first step in coordinating a programming effort involves the formation of a **Chief Programmer Team (CPT)**, which is a group of programmers under the supervision of a chief programmer. The number of team members varies with the complexity of the project. The purpose of this approach is to use each team member's time and abilities as efficiently as possible.

The chief programmer primarily is responsible for the overall coordination, development, and success of the programming project. He or she meets with the user(s) to determine the exact software specifications. Usually a backup programmer is assigned as an assistant to the chief programmer to

FIGURE 11—13

Flowchart Examples for Each of the Four Basic Logic Patterns

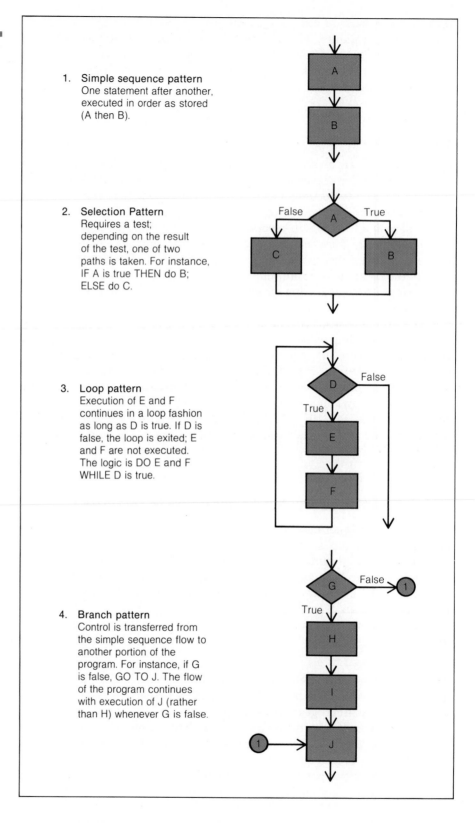

1. Simple sequence pattern
    One statement after another, executed in order as stored (A then B).

2. Selection Pattern
    Requires a test; depending on the result of the test, one of two paths is taken. For instance, IF A is true THEN do B; ELSE do C.

3. Loop pattern
    Execution of E and F continues in a loop fashion as long as D is true. If D is false, the loop is exited; E and F are not executed. The logic is DO E and F WHILE D is true.

4. Branch pattern
    Control is transferred from the simple sequence flow to another portion of the program. For instance, if G is false, GO TO J. The flow of the program continues with execution of J (rather than H) whenever G is false.

FIGURE 11—14

**Action Diagram for Four Basic
Logic Patterns**

```
┌─ A
│                          Simple Sequence Pattern
└─ B

┌─ IF A
│    B
├─ ELSE                    Selection Pattern
│
└─ C

┌──── DO WHILE D IS TRUE
│
│       E                  Loop Pattern
│
└──── F

┌───── IF G IS FALSE
│  ◄- - - - GO TO J
├───── ELSE               Branch Pattern
│         H
│         I
└─
   J
```

help design, test, and evaluate the software. Separate modules of the software are written and tested by programmers on the team. These modules are then integrated into a complete system.

The CPT also includes a librarian to help maintain complete, up-to-date documentation on the project and to relieve the team programmers of many

FIGURE 11—15

**Action Diagram for the Payroll
Processing Example**

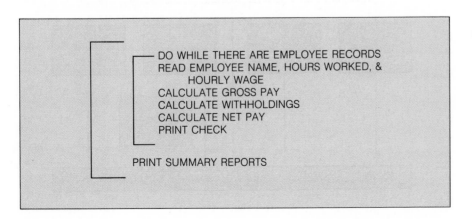

```
┌─┐
│ ┌──── DO WHILE THERE ARE EMPLOYEE RECORDS
│ │     READ EMPLOYEE NAME, HOURS WORKED, &
│ │         HOURLY WAGE
│ │     CALCULATE GROSS PAY
│ │     CALCULATE WITHHOLDINGS
│ │     CALCULATE NET PAY
│ │     PRINT CHECK
│ └───
│
└── PRINT SUMMARY REPORTS
```

clerical tasks. A librarian enhances communication among team members because he or she makes all program description, coding, and test results readily available to everyone involved in the effort. Figure 11–16 shows the organization of the chief programmer team.

The CPT approach facilitates top-down design and ongoing documentation of programs because each team member's tasks are clearly defined and coordinated as a team effort. This approach also helps with the testing of programs.

STRUCTURED REVIEW AND EVALUATION. An important goal of a programming effort is to produce an error-free program in the shortest possible time. Meeting this goal requires the early detection of errors in order to prevent costly modifications later. One approach used to try to detect program errors at an early stage is an **informal design review.** The system design documentation is studied by selected management, analysts, and programmers, usually before the actual coding of program modules. After a brief review period, each person responds with suggestions for additions, deletions, and modifications to the system design.

A **formal design review** is sometimes used after the detailed parts of the system have been sufficiently documented. The documentation at this point may consist of structure charts, HIPO charts, flowcharts, pseudocode, or any combination of these methods. Sometimes called a **structured walkthrough,** the formal design review involves distributing the documentation to a review team of two to four members, which studies the documentation

FIGURE 11–16

Organization of Chief Programmer Team

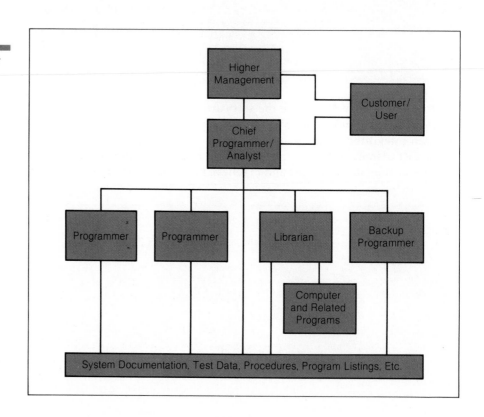

and then meets with the program designers to discuss the overall completeness, accuracy, and quality of the design. The reviewers and program designers often trace through the programs checking for errors. In large ongoing projects, formal design reviews are often held at various points in the software development process. Because other programmers have a fresh outlook on the program, they can often identify problem areas that the original programmer is not able to recognize.

WRITING AND DOCUMENTING THE PROGRAM

After the programming problem has been defined and a solution designed, the program is written in a specific programming language; this process is referred to as **coding.** Sometimes the proposed solution will limit the choice of languages that can be used in coding the program. Other constraints outside the scope of the problem and its solution may also affect the choice of a programming language. A programmer may have no choice in the selection of a language for a particular application; for instance, a business may require the use of COBOL because of its readability and because it is used in the company's existing software.

Once the programming language is chosen, the programmer should proceed to code the program according to the **syntax** (the grammatical rules) of the particular language and the rules of structured programming.

Structured Coding

When structured programming techniques are used to create a program, certain rules are followed during coding. Four major rules govern the use of branching statements, the size of program modules, the definition of a proper program, and thorough documentation.

As previously discussed, one characteristic of structured programming is the lack of branching (GOTO) statements. The programmer writes the program within the confines of three logic patterns: the simple sequence, selection, and the loop. This discipline limits the use of the branch to jump from one program statement to another in a random fashion.

When branching statements are avoided, the programmer can code each module as an independent segment. Each module should be relatively small (generally no more than 50 or 60 lines) to facilitate the translation of modules into program statements. When module size is limited in this manner, the coding for each module fits on a single page of computer printout paper, which simplifies program testing and debugging.

Yet another rule of structured coding dictates that modules should have only one entrance point and one exit point. A program segment that has only one entrance point and one exit point is called a **proper program** (see Figure 11–17). Following this rule makes the basic logic flow easy to follow and simplifies the modification of a program at a later date.

A final rule to follow in writing structured programs is to include documentation, or comment statements, liberally throughout the program. The comments should explain the data items being used in the main module and document each of the lower-level modules. Documentation aids in testing and debugging programs, which should occur at intervals throughout

FIGURE 11—17

Illustration of a Proper Program

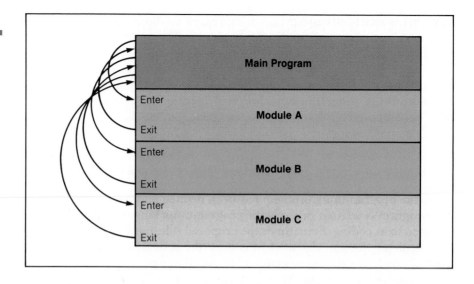

the coding phase. Documentation is also helpful when the program needs to be modified at a later date. See Concept Summary 11–2 for a review of structured programming techniques.

CONCEPT SUMMARY 11—2

Structured Programming Techniques	
Structured Design Techniques	
Top-Down Design	Reaches a problem solution by dividing a problem into more and more specific modules
Chief Programmer Team	Uses a team approach to develop software wherein a group of programmers work under the supervision of a chief programmer
Structured Review and Evaluation	A formal review of the design of a program to locate errors and problem areas as efficiently as possible
Structured Coding	
Avoidance of branching (GOTO) statements	Branching statements are discouraged so that program logic is easy to follow
Short program modules	The ideal length of a module is generally considered to be 50 to 60 lines
Proper program modules are used	Each program module has a single entrance point and a single exit point
Programs are well documented	The program is thoroughly documented to aid in testing, debugging, and later modification

Types of Statements

Certain types of programming statements are common to most high-level programming languages; they are comments, declarations, input/output statements, computations, comparisons, and loops.

COMMENTS. The type of statement known as the remark or comment has no effect on program execution; the computer simply ignores these statements. Comments are inserted at key points in the program as documentation—notes to anyone reading the program to explain the purpose of program statements. For example, if a series of statements sorts a list of names into alphabetical order, the programmer may want to include a remark to the effect: "This segment sorts names in ascending alphabetical order."

DECLARATIONS. The programmer uses declarations to define items used in the program. Examples include definitions of files, records, modules, functions, and variables.

INPUT/OUTPUT STATEMENTS. Input statements bring data into primary storage for use by the program. Output statements transfer data from primary storage to output media such as hard-copy printouts or displays on terminal screens. These statements differ considerably in form (though not so much in function) from one programming language to another.

COMPUTATIONS. Computational instructions perform arithmetic operations such as addition, subtraction, multiplication, division, and exponentiation.

COMPARISONS. This type of statement allows two items to be compared to determine if one is less than, equal to, or greater than the other. The action taken next depends on the result of this comparison.

LOOPS. The final type of statement is the loop, which allows a specified section of a program to be repeated as long as stated conditions remain constant.

▓ DEBUGGING AND TESTING THE PROGRAM

Using structured programming techniques encourages the development of programs with easy-to-follow logic, thus making them much less error-prone than unstructured programs. Nonetheless, programs of any significant length virtually always contain some errors, and correcting them can account for a large portion of the time spent in developing and maintaining software. Therefore, numerous techniques have been developed to make this process easier and more reliable.

The language translator can detect grammatical or syntax errors such as misspellings and incorrect punctuation. Such errors often occur because

H I G H L I G H T

NEW PRODUCT ANNOUNCEMENT

Title:	To be announced
Purpose:	Undecided
Available:	Soon
Price:	Yes

Of course this ad looks ridiculous, but unfortunately it is not as far from the real world of software development as it should be. Software development companies are now announcing new software products long before the products have been developed and tested. They claim users need to know what products will be available soon so they can effectively plan

Vaporware

their systems. Users agree they like to know what will soon be on the market, but announcements often create problems; that is, either the product is never completed, or it is completed at a much later date, or when it is produced it does not perform the functions stated in the announcement. Users now refer to promised software products as "vaporware." You can't get a clear answer on what it is or when it will be ready.

Many users are disgusted with vaporware. Some say they no

longer use product announcements for planning. Yet if premature announcements are causing problems, why do software companies make them? It is a marketing method of trying to prevent users from buying a competitor's product. In other words, the ads say don't buy their software, ours is even better and it will be available real soon. Wonder if software developers remember the story about the boy who cried wolf too many times?

the programmer does not fully know the programming language being used. Errors in programs are called **bugs,** and the process of locating, isolating, and eliminating bugs is called **debugging.** The amount of time that must be spent in debugging depends on the quality of the program. However, a newly completed program rarely executes successfully the first time it is run. In fact, one-third to one-half of a programmer's time is spent in debugging.

After all of the syntax errors are located and corrected, the program can be **tested.** This involves executing the program with input data that is either a representative sample of actual data or a facsimile of it. Often, sample data that can be manipulated easily by the programmer is used so that the computer-determined output can be compared with the programmer-determined correct results.

A complex program is frequently tested in separate modules so that errors can be isolated to specific sections, helping to narrow the search for the cause of an error. The programmer must correct all mistakes; running and rerunning a specific module may be necessary before the cause of an error can be found. The programmer then rewrites the part in error and resubmits it for another test. Care must be taken that correction of one error does not lead to several others.

Each section of the program must be tested (even sections that will be used infrequently). The programmer often finds **desk checking** helpful. With this method, the programmer pretends to be the computer and, reading each instruction and simulating how the computer would process a data item, attempts to catch any flaws in the program logic.

After a programmer has worked for a long time to correct the logic of a program, he or she may tend to overlook errors. For this reason, programmers sometimes trade their partially debugged programs among themselves. The programmer tracing through a "fresh" program may uncover mistakes in logic that were hidden to the original programmer.

In many cases, program errors prove especially difficult to locate. Two commonly used diagnostic procedures usually available to the programmer in such cases are dump programs and trace programs.

A dump lists the contents of registers and primary storage locations. The dump is often useful in locating an error because the values that were in the registers and primary storage at the time the error occurred can be checked for correctness. If an incorrect value is found, it can be used to help locate the error.

A trace, produced by a trace program, is apt to be easier to use than a dump. The trace lists the steps followed during program execution in the order in which they occurred. The programmer can specify that all or portions of a program be traced. The trace is often used in combination with the desk-checking procedure described above to see if the correct flow of execution has occurred. The values of selected variables (memory locations in primary storage) can also be displayed in the trace; this can be helpful in determining whether the necessary calculations have been performed correctly.

Although program testing, if conducted properly, will uncover most of the errors in a program, it is no guarantee that a program is completely correct. There may be errors that were overlooked in the testing process because of the extremely large number of execution paths a program can take. Therefore, the area of program **verification** is receiving increasing attention in the software development field. Verification involves the process of mathematically proving the correctness of a program through the use of predicate calculus. Although this area of study is still not refined to the level of commercial use, it is likely that it will be widely used in the near future.

It is important to remember that each time a program is modified, the documentation must also be modified to reflect any changes that were made to the program. This updating of documentation when changes are made is critical in industry because programs are continually being altered and expanded. If the documentation no longer matches the program, program maintenance can become very difficult.

▧ SUMMARY POINTS

■ A sequence of steps, collectively referred to as the software development process, is used to efficiently develop a programming problem solution. The steps are: (1) Define and document the problem. (2) Design and document a solution. (3) Write and document the program. (4) Debug and test the program and revise the documentation as necessary.

■ When a programming problem is defined, it is necessary to state the desired output, the needed input, and the processing requirements. These three items collectively are referred to as the program specifications.

■ After the problem is defined, a solution can be designed. When designing a solution, the programmer must realize that the computer is capable of executing only four basic logic patterns: a simple sequence (in which statements are executed in the order in which they occur), a selection pattern (in which a comparison is made), a loop (which allows for the repetition of a sequence of statements), and a branch (which allows for program execution to skip over statements). The branch pattern is controversial because its overuse can lead to programs with difficult-to-follow logic.

■ Numerous problems were encountered in the early days of software development. Some of these problems were that programmer productivity was low, programs often were not reliable and did not correctly handle invalid input, and programs were not easy to maintain. Consequently, structured programming techniques were developed. Structured programming can be divided into two categories: structured design techniques and structured coding.

■ When using structured design, top-down design is used to break a problem into smaller and smaller subproblems. Structure charts are used to graphically illustrate the result of the top-down design process. Each box in the structure chart can be written as a separate module when the program is coded.

■ HIPO packages are visual aids that supplement structure charts. Typically, an HIPO package consists of three types of diagrams: a visual table of contents, an overview diagram, and a detail diagram.

■ Pseudocode consists of an English-like description of the logic of a program.

■ Flowcharts graphically represent the logic of a programming problem solution. Each symbol has a specific meaning; flowlines and arrows indicate the direction of flow.

■ In business and industry, a number of programmers are typically assigned to work together on large programming projects. Several structured design techniques are often used in developing these large projects. Two of these are chief programmer teams and structured review and evaluation.

■ The chief programmer team (CPT) is a small group of programmers under the supervision of a chief programmer. Usually the chief programmer is assisted by a highly qualified backup programmer. A librarian is responsible for maintaining up-to-date documentation on the project. Other programmers are included on the team according to the needs of the particular project.

■ Software designs must be reviewed before they are implemented. In an informal design review, the design documentation is reviewed before coding takes place. Later, a formal design review may be held to discuss the overall completeness, accuracy, and quality of the design.

■ The process of writing the program in a programming language is referred to as coding. In structured coding, a number of rules are followed, including avoiding branch (GOTO) statements, dividing the program into independent modules each working together to form the entire program, writing each module so that it is a proper program (that is, containing only one entrance point and one exit point), and fully documenting the program.

■ Some of the general types of statements in a program are: comments, declarations, input/output statements, computations, comparison, and loops.

■ Although using structured programming techniques encourages the development of programs that are less error-prone than unstructured programs, programs of any length nearly always contain some bugs, or errors. Debugging is the process of locating and correcting these errors.

■ Testing programs involves running them with a variety of data to determine if they always obtain correct results. It is difficult to locate all program errors through testing. Therefore, program verification, which involves mathematically proving the correctness of a program, is an area of increasing interest in the software development field. Although program verification is not yet practical on a large scale, it is likely to prove useful in the near future.

■ REVIEW QUESTIONS

1. What are the four steps in the software development process? Identify which steps could be performed by a system analyst and which by a programmer.

2. Why should the system analyst consult with the potential program user(s) when developing software?

3. What is included in the program specifications?

4. Is it important for a system analyst to have a specific programming language in mind when performing the first two steps of the software development process? Why or why not?

5. What are the four basic logic patterns that the computer is capable of executing? Which of these patterns is avoided in structured programming? Why?

6. List four early problems in software development that led to the development of structured programming techniques.

7. What is meant by the term top-down design and how are structure charts used in this design methodology?

8. Explain each of the three types of diagrams that are usually included in an HIPO package.

9. Draw a flowchart that depicts the steps necessary to convert a Fahrenheit temperature to a Celsius temperature and print both temperatures. Then write the pseudocode for this problem.

10. What would be the advantage to using action diagrams rather than a combination of structure charts and pseudocode to document a design?

11. Explain the chief programmer team concept. What is the role of the librarian in this approach to software development?

12. List four rules that are followed in structured coding.

13. List and describe the different types of statements used in most high-level programming languages.

14. Explain the difference between program testing and program verification.

Eli Lilly

COMPANY HISTORY

On May 10, 1876, Colonel Eli Lilly, a Civil War veteran, established a small laboratory in downtown Indianapolis, Indiana, to manufacture medications. With total assets of $1,400 in fluid extracts and cash, Lilly began producing pills and other medicines. In 1881, the firm, which had since incorporated as Eli Lilly and Company, moved to the location just south of downtown Indianapolis that today continues to house its principal offices and research headquarters.

Two of the best-known medical discoveries to which Lilly made substantial contributions are insulin and Salk polio vaccine. More recently, the company has developed a number of important antibiotics, cancer treatment agents, and human insulin, the first human health product from recombinant DNA technology. Besides manufacturing pharmaceutical products, Lilly has diversified through its subsidiaries into agricultural products, medical instrument systems, and diagnostic products.

Products are manufactured and distributed through the company's own facilities in the United States, Puerto Rico, and 28 other countries. In 18 countries, the company owns or has an interest in manufacturing facilities. Its products are sold in approximately 130 countries.

LILLY TODAY

With interests in business and research scattered across the globe, Eli Lilly and Company has developed an extensive data-processing operation to support every department of the corporation. Two Corporate Data Centers comprise seven large IBM computers and seven DEC VAX computers, which receive and process data transmitted to the center via on-line teleprocessing, remote job entry (RJE), and time-sharing terminals located in user departments in the United States and in locations abroad. The Corporate Data Centers support more than 6,000 teleprocessing devices. In a typical business day, more than 20,000 programs are executed and about 1 million on-line transactions are processed. More than 3,000 personal computer work stations for professionals have been acquired, and about 1,000 secretarial workers now use office terminals. There are more than 8,000 users accessing data via computers.

The corporate information systems development and support groups employ approximately 600 people and are responsible for the analysis, design, development, and maintenance of all information systems worldwide. The systems area is decentralized into the various Strategic Business Units (SBUs) of the company, including medical, scientific, financial, marketing, pharmaceutical marketing, manufacturing, Elanco (agricultural products), engineering, medical instrument systems, and several European facilities.

Each of these groups reports to the client area and works with line management and staff groups to develop application systems designed to reduce operating expenses, improve productivity, or provide information for more effective management decisions. Some of the groups have remained centralized, including systems training, the information resource center, and data administration, all of which support both the clients and the decentralized systems groups.

Application development for selected administrative groups (industrial relations, legal, corporate affairs) is served centrally. The computer operations group is also centralized. Part of this group is production systems support, which maintains and enhances existing systems.

FAST—FRAMEWORK FOR SYSTEMS DEVELOPMENT TRAINING. When a customer department requests a new application, a project is initiated to begin a multiphase process called FAST (Framework for Application Systems Development Training). FAST is a framework for developing and maintaining systems worldwide. All systems analysts, management, and key clients are trained in this process. The key word in FAST is *framework*, which means that each systems group can build upon it as needed. It has the flexibility to apply to all technologies, large or small projects, built or purchased systems, development or production support, all builders of systems (systems personnel, client, or contractors), and centralized or decentralized systems groups worldwide.

Eli Lilly and Company now speaks one systems-development-methodology language. That language is FAST. It consists of five major phases: (1) analysis and definition, (2) design, (3) construction and testing, (4) implementation, and (5) ongoing support. Within each of the five phases are subphases which comprise our FAST Wheel (see art). FAST has been accepted while other approaches have not been. Here are the key reasons why:

1. The entire methodology is packaged in one small reference card and one reference guide.
2. All analysts, members of management, and clients have been or are being trained in the process.
3. For every ten analysts, there is one FAST framework consultant who has been especially trained to help others implement and understand the process.
4. The deliverables, documentation, controls, testing, and maintenance are built into each system as the analyst develops the system, not at the end of the project when the time may not allow for the completion of these segments.

In describing the FAST process, let's walk through the FAST reference card with its five phases. To help accomplish this, the FAST reference card is designed as a checklist within each of the five phases. Within each phase there are five components:

1. Phase and subphase objectives
2. Key results/deliverables for that phase
3. Key leadership activities
4. Controls germane to the phase
5. Tests germane to the phase.

Each of these five components is color-coded on the reference card for easier comprehension.

Phase 1: Analysis and Definition

The objective for the first phase, Analysis and Definition, requires the client and the systems area to define, describe, and obtain an agreement on the "business" functions of the proposed systems project. Written systems-requirement statements are developed for/with the client. These are carefully prepared to serve several purposes:

■ User and management sign-off helps ensure that the system will meet the business need.
■ The requirements will be measured and tested to ensure that the solutions solve the business problems.
■ Initial estimates serve as a basis for this phase and for the project.

Phase 2: Design

After the requirements have been tested and approved by systems and user managements, the second phase, Design, begins. The objective of the Design phase is to use the previously developed requirement to define, describe, and obtain agreement on the design of the new system. The Design phase consists of the logical/external design subphase and the physical/internal design subphase. In the logical/external design subphase, the users are given a detailed explanation of how the system will work from a user perspective.

At the beginning of the Design phase and throughout the remainder of the life of the project, change management begins. Change management oversees the adding, deleting, or changing of a systems requirement at the request of the client. A change request is submitted by the client and reviewed by the project team. The time-and-dollar impact is discussed with the client to determine whether to:

1. Make the change immediately,
2. Make the change after implementation, or
3. Cancel the request.

Data Flow Diagrams and Entity Relationship Diagrams explain the flow and the transactions for each part of the system. Users participate in report design, screen formats, test data, and inquiries. Controls appear in the system at input, process, and output execution. There are two parts to every control—detect and intervene. For each function in the design, analysts ask:

What can go wrong?
Do you care?
If you care, then
  Detect and prevent, or
  Detect and correct, or
  Detect and recover.

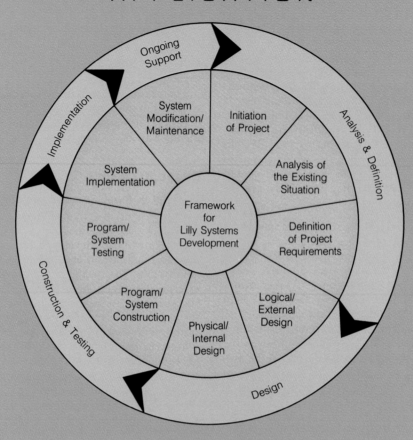

The next subphase, physical/internal design, produces the detailed system blueprints for the construction and testing of the system. The user language of the logical/external subphase is translated into technical terms. The system structure is divided into subsystems and programs. Specification describes the functions performed by each program. Data is now normalized and all data elements are defined in the data dictionary. Data files used for communication between programs are specified.

The ten key questions asked throughout the project are:

Function:	What function will this system accomplish? (Try to use a single sentence.)
Content:	What data does this system need? What data will it generate?
Frequency:	How often will the system be used?
Urgency:	How long after you have the need to know can you wait for information from the system? How long can the system wait for new data to be entered?
Distribution:	Who gets the output? Where are they located? Why do they get the output?
Volume:	How much data (pages, screens, etc.) are you producing?
Location:	Where are you putting the hardware?
Accuracy:	Are there any concerns for accuracy? What errors can you tolerate?
Constraints:	Are there any special constraints (security, environment, access, etc.)?
Security:	Are there specific security issues (access, distribution, etc.)?

During the Design phase, plans for the construction and testing phases are written and physical/internal systems-design documents are tested and published. Reviews are scheduled with users, management, and quality assurance to ensure that the design meets the systems requirements.

Phase 3: Construction and Testing

During the Construction and Testing phase, additional members, including contract programmers, often join the project team. The objective of the Construction and Testing phase is to translate the physical/internal design into the actual system. Final testing and integration of the system occurs at this time.

With the information from the design phase and firm staffing plans, the project leader is able to project a fairly reliable completion date. Each team member begins detailed design and construction of assigned programs. When coding is completed, the program is submitted for compilation. Any clerical errors should be detected during the compilation process. This step is repeated until an error-free compilation is achieved.

The analyst then conducts a programming walkthrough, explaining the purpose of the program to a previously uninvolved third party. This person, usually another analyst, can provide fresh insights into areas where the purpose of the program is unclear (and thus requires additional comments). The person can also desk-check the program to identify logic errors that the analyst has overlooked.

At this point, before the actual program testing begins, the program is usually recompiled according to a compiler program that optimizes the machine language code (builds instruction sequences that will be most efficient for repetitive processing purposes). It may also give diagnostic messages indicating possible logic problems.

The program is now ready to be executed using real, or "live," test data supplied by the end user that represents what may be processed in real-life situations. If the data is processed correctly, the program is ready for use. However, correct processing seldom occurs on the first run. To identify the causes of error, the analyst may submit trial runs with abnormal terminations that produce core dumps at the end of execution. Occasionally, an error is so subtle that the programmer cannot determine its cause by analyzing a dump. In this case, a trace program can be used to indicate the execution flow through the entire sequence of instructions. The analyst can then determine if the flow has mistakenly entered a wrong section of the program.

The system-test phase includes heavy user participation and is actually the beginning of user training. Each subsystem is thoroughly tested with user-supplied input data. Finally, the entire system is tested, usually running parallel with the old system.

Experienced analysts, not a part of the project team, conduct the detailed program and system testing to ensure that all functions are tested and errors corrected. It is very important that all the controls of the previous phases are tested during the Construction and Testing phase.

Phase 4: Implementation

The next phase is the Implementation phase, in which the system is placed in a stable production environment once the system-integration and acceptance tests are completed. Training of clients and production support personnel is completed. Data files are converted and all documentation is finalized. The actual system turnover process occurs in this phase. This is completed by the development team working in conjunction with the production support team who will be assuming the ongoing support for the system once the system has been approved and put in "production." The turnover review includes a check to see that (1) the system conforms to established standards, (2) system-development-documentation requirements have been satisfied, and (3) the system is ready to be assigned to "production" status. If the total application is found to be acceptable by both the client and production support, the system is implemented.

Phase 5: Ongoing Support

The last but not least important phase is the Ongoing Support phase. The objectives of this phase are to define, prioritize, and implement approved requested modifications to existing systems in accordance with organization policy. Modifications may be minor "fixits" or sizable enhancements. Enhancements in effect require the production-support analyst to follow the entire FAST process. During fix-its or enhancements all changes must cause the following:

1. Existing controls in the system retained
2. Modified system controls identified, tested, and implemented
3. All previous phase test results germane to the modification identified and executed
4. All documentation updated.

As fix-its or enhancements are requested, the requests for change are documented, reviewed, prioritized, and implemented.

APPLICATION

The complexity of activities in developing a new application or enhancing an existing one from the systems requirements through implementation of the system is justified by the financial and business needs of such an undertaking. Failure to properly perform any of the steps in the process can result in, at best, considerable difficulty and, at worst, a complete failure of the application. For this reason, Eli Lilly and Company has adopted a structured, yet flexible, framework described here that relates to all systems development and support projects throughout the corporation.

DISCUSSION POINTS

1. Why does Lilly involve users so heavily in designing a new application?
2. What procedures are used to test the applications prior to their implementation?

CHAPTER

12

Programming
Languages

O U T L I N E

Introduction
Standardization of Languages
Categorizing Languages
Translating Languages
Low-Level Languages
  Machine Language
  Assembly Language
High-Level Languages

FORTRAN
BASIC
Pascal
COBOL
Logo
APL
Ada
RPG
C
Modula-2

FORTH
LISP
Very-High Level Languages
Natural Languages
Programming Languages—
  A Comparison
Summary Points
Review Questions

C Edging Out Pascal as Developers' Language of Choice

Suzanne F. Williams
PC Week

Although the choice between programming in C and in Pascal is still a matter of personal preference, industry observers agree that C is largely taking over as the language of choice.

The movement toward C on the PC began in the mid-1980s, and it seemed to have happened overnight. According to James Gimpel, president of Gimpel Software, the Collegeville, Pa., developer of the C-terp C interpreter, there's a simple rule to tell when an application project got under way: "If it's written in Pascal, it got started in the '70s; if it's written in C, it got started in the '80s."

Pascal was designed as a language to teach programming methodologies. It is widely taught in universities, creating a vast pool of Pascal programmers.

Because Pascal is tightly structured and well-defined, it protects programmers from themselves, according to Greg Lobdell, product manager of the languages group at Microsoft Corp., of Redmond, Wash.

One safety feature inherent in the language is the strict control Pascal puts on types of data and how they are used within a program—so-called strong data typing.

Strong data typing or type checking ensures that input information matches the expected input. "If the function expects an integer, and [the programmer] gives it a string, it will let [the programmer] know," explained Rob Dickerson, vice president of product management at Borland International Inc., the Scotts Valley, Calif., developer of the Turbo line of language products, which include Turbo C and Turbo Pascal.

However, Pascal's safety features may leave programmers restrained in what they can and cannot do. Programmers may be backed into a corner.

C does not have this safety-net characteristic. "C assumes you know what you're doing," said Scott Hutchinson, systems programmer at VANCE (Value Added Networks for Computer Environments) Systems Inc. in Chantilly, Va. Mr. Hutchinson is using Borland's Turbo C to develop AST 1000, a network-analysis and testing system.

Jim Brodie, a consultant at Jim Brodie and Associates in Phoenix, Ariz., said he switched from Pascal to C. "I liked Pascal when I was using it, but it got stretched into environments it wasn't meant for. Pascal didn't have the features that are important for commercial programming. There was no separate compilation, which is necessary for serious development. I also needed loopholes, I needed to escape strong data typing," said Mr. Brodie.

One of the reasons programmers are choosing to program in C rather than in Pascal is to produce applications that will be sold as commercial products. Industry observers and programmers noted that commercial applications need to be compact and fast. C has the upper hand in both respects.

"C makes smaller executable [programs]," said Mr. Hutchinson. "Two hundred eighty kilobytes to 300K bytes of C code would be considerably larger in Pascal," he said.

Portability is another reason why programmers are choosing C over Pascal, observers say. Portability means that an application written to work on one type of machine under a certain operating system can be made to work on another machine and operating system with little or no rewriting of code.

PageMaker, a desktop-publishing system developed by Aldus Corp. of Seattle, was originally written in Pascal for the Macintosh. It is being rewritten in C so it will operate on both the Mac and on the PC in the Microsoft Windows environment, according to Jeremy Jaeck, Aldus's vice president of engineering.

Two compilers are being used to rewrite PageMaker: Think's LightspeedC, a C compiler developed by Symantec Corp., of Bedford, Mass., is being used on the Macintosh side; Microsoft's C is being used on the PC side.

C was chosen because Windows is written in C. Think's LightspeedC and Microsoft's C were chosen because their implementations of C were the same.

However, the movement toward C does not mean that Pascal is being banished completely. Two of Pascal's pluses—its safety and the vast pool of Pascal programmers available—made it the language of choice at Southern California Edison, a public utility located in San Diego County, Calif. Since Pascal is easy to program in, applications written in Pascal can also be supported by less-experienced programmers, according to Richard Messeder, computer-applications engineer at South California Edison.

A Pascal fan who uses the language to develop commercial applications in defiance of the trend toward C is Ben Myers, owner of Spirit of Performance Inc., a Harvard, Mass., software developer.

Mr. Myers sees himself as somewhat of a heretic. "I don't like C. While 85 percent of serious development work is done in C, C is error-prone, and the errors are sometimes not caught during the compile time, but during run time."

Mr. Myers chose to write the statistical and reporting portion of Personal Measure, a PC performance-measuring application, in Pascal and the terminate-and-stay-resident (TSR) part in assembler. "Pascal does a good job of defining data structures, whereas C is not quite adept."

The TSR portion was written in assembler language because it produces more compact and faster code than either C or Pascal. When writing TSR-type programs, the size of the program and speed are critical, according to industry observers.

There is no steadfast rule that decrees what language is best for writing what type of application. C is popular today, but that does not mean that other languages are fading fast.

"A wide variety of needs will prevent the complete ascendancy of any one language over another," said Jeffrey M. Gross, president of The Boston Information Group, a computer consulting firm located in Cambridge, Mass.

The decision as to what type of language to use for writing a program depends upon two variables—the characteristics of the language and the experience of available programmers. The user must match the requirements of the program, such as portability, with a language. If, however, users do not have programmers familiar with the selected language, they must either provide training for the programmers or use a different language. For example, fewer programmers are familiar with the languages C and Ada than with the highly used COBOL.

▦ INTRODUCTION

Languages are systems of communication. Programming languages are communication systems that people can use to communicate with computers. The earliest computers were programmed by arranging various wires and switches within the computer components. Up to 6,000 switches could be set on the ENIAC to execute one program. However, when a new program was to be run, all the switches had to be reset. This was clearly inefficient. The EDSAC, the first stored-program computer, allowed instructions to be entered into primary storage without rewiring or resetting switches. Codes that corresponded to the required on/off electrical states were needed to enter these instructions. These codes were called **machine language**. Later, **assembly language** (which uses simple codes to represent machine-language instructions) was developed to offset the tedium of writing machine-language programs. A disadvantage of both machine and assembly languages is that

CHAPTER

they are dependent on the type of computer system being used; the programmer must be familiar with the hardware for which the program is being written.

The development of FORTRAN in the mid-1950s signaled the beginning of a trend toward high-level languages that were oriented more toward the programmer than the computer. Since that time, a wide variety of high-level languages have been developed. At the present time there are more than two hundred distinct computer programming languages.

This chapter discusses some of the programming languages most commonly used today. As with languages such as English and German, each of these programming languages has a history of development and specific characteristics. The unique features, characteristics, advantages, and disadvantages of each language are explained in this chapter and typical applications are shown.

▓ STANDARDIZATION OF LANGUAGES

One of the advantages of using high-level languages is the potential for these programs to be **portable**; that is, to be able to be executed on a wide variety of systems with minimal changes. The problem with this idea is that the language must be standardized; that is, rules must be developed so that all of the language translator programs for a particular language will be able to translate the same program. Therefore, it is necessary that standards be established for programming languages. A number of agencies authorize these standards. The most influential is the American National Standards Institute (ANSI), which has developed or adopted widely used standards for many languages including FORTRAN, Pascal, BASIC, and COBOL (all of which will be discussed in this chapter). One difficulty is that many manufacturers do not entirely adhere to these standards. They often add extra features (referred to as "enhancements") to their language translator programs to make them more useful. This means that a program that will run on one computer system will not necessarily run on another system without modification.

▓ CATEGORIZING LANGUAGES

Computer scientists have long tried to categorize programming languages. This categorization helps the programmer in determining which language might be most useful in a particular situation. Some different ways in which it is possible to categorize languages are listed below:

▪ **Low-level or high-level.** This refers to the degree to which the language is oriented toward the hardware as compared to the programmer. Low-level languages are oriented toward the computer, whereas high-level languages are oriented more toward the programmer. Therefore, low-level languages are easier for the computer to execute, but high-level languages are easier for people to use and understand.

▪ **Structured or unstructured.** The characteristics of structured programming languages were discussed in Chapter 11. Briefly, these languages allow programmers to easily divide programs into modules, each performing a specific task. Also, structured programming languages provide a wide variety of control structures such as loops (to perform repetitive tasks) and selection statements (to make comparisons). These features result in programs with easy-to-follow logic that are easy to modify and maintain. Many languages that were developed before the widespread acceptance of structured programming have since been modified to include structured techniques (COBOL is an example).

■ **Procedure-oriented or problem-oriented.** Procedure-oriented languages place programming emphasis on describing the computational and logical procedures required to solve a problem. Commonly used procedure-oriented languages include COBOL, FORTRAN, and Pascal. A problem-oriented language is one in which the problem and solution are described without the necessary procedures being specified, therefore requiring little programming skill.

■ **General purpose or special purpose.** General-purpose languages are those languages that can be used to solve a wide variety of programming problems. BASIC and Pascal are examples of general-purpose languages. Some examples of categories of special-purpose languages might be educational languages, business languages, and scientific languages. For example, FORTRAN, a language used mostly for mathematical and scientific applications, is an example of a scientific language.

CONCEPT SUMMARY 12-1

Special-Purpose Languages		
Category	**Characteristics**	**Examples**
Education	Should teach good programming concepts and be fairly easy to learn; should be able to be used to write a variety of programs to give the beginner a range of experiences	Pascal Logo BASIC
Scientific	Able to perform complex mathematical operations with a high degree of accuracy	FORTRAN FORTH
Business	Able to handle large data files efficiently and to perform the types of data processing necessary in business	COBOL

Although it would be nice to be able to neatly categorize each language, many languages fall somewhere in between one extreme or the other in any specific category. For example, C, a programming language that we will discuss in more detail later, is often considered to be neither a low-level nor a high-level language, but somewhere in between. Nonetheless, these categories can prove useful in making generalized statements about languages and their appropriate uses. Therefore, where appropriate we will attempt to categorize the languages discussed in this chapter.

▆ TRANSLATING LANGUAGES

Translating a computer programming language is conceptually very similar to translating one spoken language into another. In order for an English-speaking person to understand Russian, for example, someone must translate the Russian language into English. This process of translating one language to another is also required by computers. Since machine language is the only language a computer can understand, all other languages must be translated into machine language.

H I G H L I G H T

That Really Bugs Me!

As in other professions, programmers have their own language. One of their often used phrases is to "debug" a program or find "the bugs" in a program, that is, to find the errors in a program. Few people realize that the phrase originated because a real live bug once caused problems in a computer system.

In the summer of 1945, something went wrong with the Mark II, a large electromechanical machine used by the Department of Defense. Though the machine was not working properly, the operating personnel could find no obvious problems. A continued search revealed a large moth beaten to death by one of the electromechanical relays. The moth was pulled out with tweezers and taped to a log book. "From then on," said Rear Admiral Grace Hopper, one of the people working with the machine, "when the officer came in to ask if we were accomplishing anything, we told him we were 'debugging' the computer."

And where is that infamous bug today? The insect is exhibited in the Naval Museum at the Naval Surface Weapons Center, in Dahlgren, Virginia.

Assembly and high-level languages are much more widely used by programmers than machine language. Since these languages cannot be executed directly by computers, they are converted into machine executable form by language-translator programs. The language-translator program translates the source program (that is, the sequence of instructions written by the programmer) into machine language. The translator program for assembly language programs is called an **assembler program.** A high-level language translator can be either a **compiler program** or an **interpreter program.** Assemblers, compilers, and interpreters are designed for specific machines and languages. For example, a compiler that translates a source program written in FORTRAN into a machine-language program can only translate FORTRAN programs.

This translated program (called the **object program**) is then "linked" with other object programs which reside in a **system library** to form what is referred to as the load module. It is the load module that is then executed by the CPU. The process of linking the application object program with the object programs in the system library is handled by the **linkage editor.** The object programs in the system library are combined to form the library and managed by the object module **librarian program.**

An interpreter, unlike assemblers and compilers, evaluates and translates a program one statement at a time. The interpreter reads each program statement checking for syntax errors and, if errors are found, generates an appropriate error message. If there are no errors, the interpreter translates the statement into machine language and executes it before proceeding to the next statement. This is in contrast to an assembler or a compiler, which first checks the entire program for syntax errors and then translates the entire program into an object program that is executed. An interpreter program is typically smaller than an assembler or compiler program. An interpreter, however, can be inefficient. Program statements that are used more than once during a program's execution must be evaluated, translated, and executed each time the statement is used.

■ LOW-LEVEL LANGUAGES

Machine Language

Remember from Chapter 3 that all data in digital computers is stored as either on or off electrical states which we represent through the use of 1s and 0s. Machine language must take the form of 1s and 0s to be understood by the computer. But coding a program in this binary form is very tedious; therefore machine language is often coded in either octal (base 8) or hexadecimal (base 16) codes.

The programmer using machine language must specify everything to the computer. Every step the computer must take to execute a program must be coded; therefore, the programmer must know exactly how the computer works. The actual numerical addresses of the storage locations containing instructions and data must be specified.

In order to accomplish the necessary specificity, each machine-language instruction has two parts. The **op code** (short for operation code) tells the computer what function to perform, such as adding two values. The **operand** tells the computer what data to use when performing that function. The operand takes the form of the specific storage address where the data is located. Figure 12–1 shows some examples of machine-language instructions.

The greatest advantages of machine language are that the computer can execute it efficiently and that generally it uses less storage space than high-level languages. It also allows the programmer to fully utilize the computer's potential because the programmer is interacting directly with the computer hardware.

On the other hand, this type of programming is extremely tedious, time consuming, and error prone. The instructions are difficult to remember and to use. In addition, programs written in machine language will execute only on the specific type of system for which they were written. Therefore, machine language is used only in rare instances today.

Assembly Language

Assembly languages were developed to alleviate many of the disadvantages of machine-language programming. When programming in an assembly language, the programmer uses **mnemonics** (symbolic names) to specify machine operations; thus, coding in 0s and 1s is no longer required. Mnemonics are alphabetic abbreviations for the machine-language op codes. Table 12–1 shows some common arithmetic operations coded in assembly language and in machine language. Assembly-language instructions differ depending on the type and model of computer being programmed. Thus, assembly-language programs, like machine-language programs, can be written only for the type of computer that will execute them.

48	00	23C0	
4C	00	23C2	
40	00	2310	
D2	01	2310	2310
48	00	2310	
4E	00	2028	
F3	17	3002	2028
9G	F0	3003	

FIGURE 12–1

Machine-Language Instructions Expressed in the Hexadecimal (Base 16) Number System

TABLE 12–1

Examples of Assembly-Language Mnemonic Code

Operation	Typical Assembly-Language Op Code	Typical Binary (Machine Language) Op Code
Add memory to register	A	01011010
Add (decimal) memory to register	AP	11111010
Multiply register by memory	M	01011100
Multiply (decimal) register by memory	MP	11111100
Subtract memory from register	S	01011011
Subtract (decimal) memory from register	SP	11111011
Move (numeric) from register to memory	MVN	11010001
Compare memory to register	C	01011001
Compare (decimal) memory to register	CP	11111001
Zero register and add (decimal) memory to register	ZAP	11111000

There are three basic parts to an assembly-language instruction: an op code and an operand, as in machine language, and a label. Table 12–2 shows a section of an assembly-language program with the parts of the instructions labeled. The **label** is a programmer-supplied name that represents the location in which a particular instruction will be stored. When the programmer wishes to refer to that instruction, he or she can simply specify the label, without regard to the actual address of the storage location.

The op code, as in machine language, tells the computer what operation to perform, but it is in mnemonic form. The operand, also in mnemonic form, represents the address of the item that is to be manipulated. Each instruction may contain one or two operands. The remainder of the line can be used for remarks that explain to humans the operation being performed (the remarks are optional and are simply ignored by the computer).

There are several advantages to using assembly language. The main advantage is that it can be used to develop programs that use storage space and processing time efficiently. As with machine language, the programmer is able to fully utilize the computer's processing capabilities. Second, the assembler program (the program that translates the assembly program into machine language) performs certain error-checking functions and generates error messages, if appropriate, that are useful to the programmer when debugging the program.

The main disadvantage of assembly language is that it is more cumbersome to use than high-level languages. Generally, one assembly-language instruction is translated into one machine-language instruction; this one-for-one relationship leads to long program preparation time. However, this feature makes it easier for the computer to translate the program into machine language than to translate a high-level language into machine language. Another disadvantage of assembly language is the high level of skill required to use it effectively. As with machine language, the programmer

TABLE 12—2

The Parts of an Assembly-Language Instruction

Label	Op Code	Operands A and B	Remarks
OVERTIME	AP	OVERTIME, FORTY	BEGIN OVERTIME COMPUTATION
	MP	OVERTIME, WKRATE	
	AP	GROSS, WKRATE	
	SP	WKHRS, FORTY	COMPUTE OVERTIME PAY
	MP	WKHRS, ONEHLF	
	MP	GROSS, WKHRS	
	MVN	GROSS +5(1), GROSS +6	
	ZAP	GROSS(7), GROSS (6)	
	AP	GROSS, OVERTIME	
TAXRATE	CP	GROSS, =P'25000'	BEGIN TAX COMPUTATION

must know the computer to be used and must be able to work with binary or hexadecimal numbers. Finally, assembly language, like machine language, is machine-dependent; a program written for one computer generally cannot be executed on another.

Assembly language is often used for writing operating system programs. Because operating systems are designed for particular computers, they are machine-dependent. The potential efficiency of assembly language also makes it well suited for operating-system programming.

CONCEPT SUMMARY 12—2

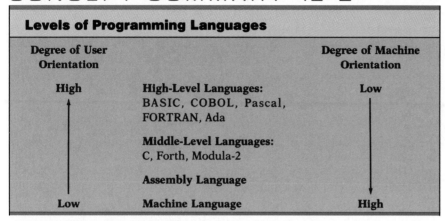

Levels of Programming Languages

Degree of User Orientation		Degree of Machine Orientation
High	**High-Level Languages:** BASIC, COBOL, Pascal, FORTRAN, Ada	Low
↑	**Middle-Level Languages:** C, Forth, Modula-2	↓
	Assembly Language	
Low	**Machine Language**	High

HIGH-LEVEL LANGUAGES

In this section we will discuss a cross-section of high-level languages. High-level languages are much easier to understand than low-level languages because they use meaningful words such as READ and PRINT in their instructions. One high-level statement may generate several machine-language statements. Therefore, high-level language programs are more difficult to translate into machine language than are assembly-language programs. Traditionally, high-level languages have not made as efficient use of computer resources as machine and assembly languages. However, with the ever-increasing sophistication of translator programs, this is no longer necessarily true.

FORTRAN

FORTRAN (FORmula TRANslator) is the oldest high-level programming language. It originated in the mid-1950s, when most programs were written in either assembly language or machine language. Efforts were made to develop a programming language that resembled English but could be translated into machine language by the computer. This effort, backed by IBM, produced FORTRAN—the first commercially available high-level language.

Early FORTRAN compilers contained many errors and were not always efficient in their use of computer resources. Moreover, several manufacturers offered variations of FORTRAN that could be used only on their particular computers. Although many improvements were made, early implementations of FORTRAN continued to suffer from this lack of standardization. In response to this problem, the American National Standards Institute laid the groundwork for a standardized FORTRAN. In 1966, two standard versions of FORTRAN were recognized, ANSI FORTRAN and Basic FORTRAN. A more recent version, FORTRAN 77, provides more enhancements to the language. A new FORTRAN standard (FORTRAN 8X) is also under consideration by the American National Standards Institute. In spite of the attempts to standardize FORTRAN, however, most computer manufacturers have continued to offer their own extensions of the language. Therefore, compatibility of FORTRAN programs remains a problem today.

In 1957, when the language was first released, computers were used primarily by engineers, scientists, and mathematicians. Consequently, FORTRAN was developed to suit their needs and its purpose has remained unchanged. FORTRAN is a procedure-oriented language with extraordinary mathematical capabilities. It is especially applicable when numerous complex arithmetic calculations are necessary. In general, FORTRAN is not a good business language. Its capabilities are not well suited to programs involving file maintenance, data editing, or document production. However, use of FORTRAN is increasing for certain types of business applications, such as feasibility studies, forecasting, and production scheduling. Another disadvantage of FORTRAN is that it does not resemble English as closely as many high-level languages; therefore, the programs must be well documented so that they are understandable. Figure 12–2 contains a simple FORTRAN program that calculates a payroll.

BASIC

BASIC, an acronym for Beginner's All-purpose Symbolic Instruction Code, was developed in the mid-1960s at Dartmouth College by Professors John Kemeny and Thomas Kurtz. It was originally developed for use on time-sharing systems to help students learn to program. Inspired by FORTRAN, BASIC is a simplified version of that first high-level language.

The growth in the use of time-sharing systems has been accompanied by an increase in the use of BASIC. Although BASIC was originally intended to be used by colleges and universities for instructional purposes, many companies have adopted it for their data-processing needs. In addition, the increased popularity of microcomputers in homes is furthering the use of BASIC, since it is the language most often implemented on these computers.

Among BASIC's most attractive features are its simplicity and flexibility. Because it is easy to learn, it can be used by people with little or no programming experience; a novice programmer can write fairly complex programs in BASIC in a matter of a few hours. It is a general-purpose language that can be used to write programs to solve a wide variety of problems. A BASIC program is shown in Figure 12–3.

The simplicity of BASIC has led many manufacturers to offer different versions of the language. Although there is an established standard (American National Standards Institute BASIC), few manufacturers adhere to this standard and virtually all of them have added their own quirks to the language. Therefore, BASIC programs written for one system often need substantial modification before being used on another.

The main criticism of BASIC focuses on the fact that traditionally it has not been a structured programming language. This means that many pop-

FIGURE 12—2

Payroll Program in FORTRAN

```
FORTRAN IV G LEVEL 21      MAIN              DATE = 81214

        WRITE (6,1)
1       FORMAT('1','EMPLOYEENAME',5X,'NETPAY'/'')
2       READ (5,3) NA,NB,NC,ND,NHOURS,WAGE,IEND
3       FORMAT (4A4, 12, 2X, F4.2, 54X, 12)
        IF (IEND.EQ.99) STOP
        IF (NHOURS.GT.40) GO TO 10
        GROSS = FLOAT(NHOURS)*WAGE
        GO TO 15
10      REG = 40.*WAGE
        OVERTM=FLOAT(NHOURS-40)*(1.5*WAGE)
        GROSS=REG+OVERTM
15      IF (GROSS.GT.250.) GO TO 20
        RATE = .14
        GO TO 25
20      RATE = .20
25      TAX=RATE*GROSS
        PAY = GROSS - TAX
        WRITE (6,50) NA,NB,NC,ND,PAY
50      FORMAT (' ', ,4A4, 3X, F6.2)
        GO TO 2
        END
```

Output

```
     EMPLOYEE NAME          NET PAY

     LYNN MANGINO           224.00
     THOMAS RITTER          212.42
     MARIE OLSON            209.00
     LORI DUNLEVY           172.00
     WILLIAM WILSON         308.00
```

ular versions of BASIC do not encourage dividing the program into modules nor do they contain adequate control statements. In many implementations of BASIC it is often necessary to use unconditional branches (commonly referred to as GOTO statements) that can cause program logic to be convoluted and difficult to follow.

Some newer versions of BASIC do encourage the development of structured programs. One of these is True BASIC, which was developed by the original developers of BASIC, Kemeny and Kurtz, and was put on the market in 1984. True BASIC retains many of the strengths of the first version produced twenty years ago; it is an economical language, using English-like commands. Yet it provides extensions and options that allow programmers to develop properly structured programs and sophisticated graphics and perform text processing. In addition, ANSI is in the process of adopting new standards for a structured BASIC. It will be interesting to see how widely implemented these new standards will be.

FIGURE 12–3

Payroll Program in BASIC

```
10 REM ***              PAYROLL PROGRAM            ***
20 REM ***    THIS PROGRAM CALCULATES A WEEKLY     ***
30 REM ***    PAYROLL.                             ***
40 REM
50 PRINT "EMPLOYEE NAME",,"NET PAY"
60 PRINT
70 READ NME$,HRS,WAGE
80 WHILE NME$ <> "END OF DATA"
90     IF HRS <=40 THEN GROSS = HRS * WAGE ELSE GOSUB 1000
100    IF GROSS > 250 THEN LET TAX = .2 ELSE LET TAX = .14
110    LET TAX2 = TAX * GROSS
120    LET PAY = GROSS - TAX2
130    PRINT NME$,,PAY
140    READ NME$,HRS,WAGE
150 WEND
999 END
1000 REM
1010 REM ***********************************************
1020 REM ***              SUBROUTINE OVERTIME        ***
1030 REM ***********************************************
1040 REM
1050 LET REG = 40 * WAGE
1060 LET OVRTIME = (HRS - 40) * (1.5 * WAGE)
1070 LET GROSS = REG + OVRTIME
1080 RETURN
1090 REM ***********************************************
2000 DATA "LYNN MANGINO",35,8.00
2010 DATA "THOMAS RITTER",48,4.75
2020 DATA "MARIE OLSON",45,5.50
2030 DATA "LORI DUNLEVY",40,5.00
2040 DATA "ERIC WILSON",50,7.00
2050 DATA "END OF DATA",0,0
```

Output

EMPLOYEE NAME	NET PAY
LYNN MANGINO	224
THOMAS RITTER	212.42
MARIE OLSON	209
LORI DUNLEVY	172
ERIC WILSON	308

Pascal

Pascal was the first major programming language to implement the ideas and methodology of structured programming. Niklaus Wirth, a Swiss computer scientist, developed Pascal between 1968 and 1970; in 1971 the first compiler became available. Wirth named the language after the French mathematician and philosopher Blaise Pascal, who invented the first mechanical adding machine. In 1982, ANSI adopted a standard for Pascal.

Like BASIC, Pascal was first developed to teach programming concepts to students, but it rapidly expanded beyond its initial purpose and has found increasing acceptance in business and scientific applications.

Pascal increasingly is becoming the first programming language taught to students at the college level; at present, it is the introductory programming course for computer science students at 80 percent of all universities.

It is relatively easy to learn, like BASIC; in addition, it is a powerful language capable of performing a wide variety of tasks including sophisticated mathematical operations. The main reason for the widespread use of Pascal as a teaching tool is that it is a structured language. Each Pascal program is made up of modules called procedures that can be nested within one another. Pascal contains a wide variety of useful control structures such as the IF/THEN/ELSE decision statement and the WHILE/DO loop. These features encourage students to develop good programming habits. Figure 12–4 contains a short program written in Pascal.

At first Pascal's availability was limited, but more computer manufacturers are now offering Pascal compilers for their machines. Some compilers developed for microcomputers, such as the popular TURBO Pascal implementation, are surprisingly inexpensive and versatile. Many of these compilers have good graphics capabilities. Programmers can create intricate, detailed objects using properly equipped display terminals. This feature is attractive to scientists and increasingly to business personnel as well. A disadvantage of Pascal is that many people believe it has poor input/output capabilities. Therefore, it is not particularly well suited to applications involving manipulation of large data files.

FIGURE 12–4

**Payroll Program in Pascal
(Continued Next Page)**

```
program payroll (emplfile, output);

(* This program calculates a weekly payroll. *)

type
    array20 = array[1..20] of char;

var
    emplfile : text;
    name : array20;
    wage, hours, grosspay, tax, netpay : real;

(******************************************************)

procedure readname (var name : array20);

var
    i : integer;
    count : integer;

begin   (* readname *)

    i := 1;
    while not eoln (emplfile) and (i <= 20) do
    begin   (* while *)
        read (emplfile, name[i]);
        i := i + 1
    end;   (* while *)
    readln (emplfile);

    for count := i to 20 do
        name[count] := ' '

end;   (* readname *)

(******************************************************)
```

```
            begin   (* payroll *)

                reset (emplfile);
                writeln;
                writeln ('EMPLOYEE NAME':13, 'NET PpcAY':27);

                while not eof (emplfile) do
                begin   (* while *)
                    readname (name);
                    readln (emplfile, wage, hours);

                    (* Calculate gross pay *)
                    if hours <= 40
                        then grosspay := hours * wage
                        else grosspay := hours * wage + (hours - 40) * wage * 0.5;

                    (* Calculate net pay *)
                    if grosspay > 250
                        then tax := 0.2 * grosspay
                        else tax := 0.14 * grosspay; temp1.p
                    netpay := grosspay - tax;
                    writeln (name:20, netpay:20:2)

                end   (* while *)

            end.   (* payroll *)
```

Output

```
  O |   EMPLOYEE NAME                  NET PAY        | O
    |   LYNN MANGINO                   224.00         |
    |   THOMAS RITTER                  212.42         |
  O |   MARIE OLSON                    209.00         | O
    |   LORI SANCHEZ                   172.00         |
    |   WILLIAM LUOMA                  308.00         |
  O |                                                 | O
```

FIGURE 12—4

Payroll Progam in Pascal
(Continued)

COBOL

COBOL (COmmon Business-Oriented Language) is the most frequently used business programming language. Before 1960 no language was well suited to solving business problems. Recognizing this inadequacy, the Department of Defense met with representatives of computer users, manufacturers, and government installations to examine the feasibility of developing a common business programming language. That was the beginning of the CODASYL (Conference Of DAta SYstems Languages) Committee. By 1960 the committee had established the specifications for COBOL and the first commercial versions of the language were offered later that year. The government furthered its cause in the mid-1960s by refusing to buy or lease any computer that could not process a program written in COBOL.

One of the objectives of the CODASYL group was to design a machine-independent language—that is, a language that could be used on any computer with any COBOL compiler, regardless of who manufactured it. Thus, when several manufacturers began offering their own modifications and extensions of COBOL, the need for standardization became apparent. In 1968 ANSI published guidelines for a standardized COBOL that became known as ANSI COBOL. In 1974 ANSI expanded the language definition in a revised version of the standard. These standards have been widely accepted in industry. After many years of difficult analysis and compromise, a new set of ANSI standards for COBOL was published in 1985. These new standards made many changes to the language including adding structured programming facilities. It will be several years before it is known how widely accepted and implemented this new COBOL standard will be.

A key objective of the designers of COBOL was to make the language similar to English. Their intent was that a program written in COBOL should be understandable even to casual readers, and hence self-documenting. You can judge how successful they were by looking at Figure 12–5, which shows a payroll application program written in COBOL.

COBOL programs have a formal, uniform structure. Many types of statements must appear in the same form and the same position in every COBOL program. The basic unit of a COBOL program is the sentence. Sentences are combined to form paragraphs; paragraphs are joined into sections; and sections are contained within divisions. COBOL programs must have four divisions: IDENTIFICATION, ENVIRONMENT, DATA, and PROCEDURE. The divisions appear in the program in this order and are identified by headings, as shown in Figure 12–5.

COBOL offers many advantages for business users. Because of its English-like nature, programs require very little additional documentation; well-written COBOL programs tend to be self-explanatory. This feature makes programs easier to maintain and modify. This is very important because large business programs are always being altered, expanded, and so forth. Since the logic of the program is easy to follow, testing and debugging procedures are simplified. In addition, programmers other than the original ones can read the program and quickly discern what the program does and how it does it. COBOL also has strong file-handling capabilities; it supports sequential, indexed, and direct-access files (see Chapter 6). This feature is very important to large corporations that must deal with enormous quantities of data stored in files.

Because COBOL is standardized, a firm can switch computer systems with little or no rewriting of existing programs. Its standardization also has implications for programmers: once programmers learn COBOL through college training or previous experience, they can transfer their learning with little adjustment to various computer systems and organizations.

However, the effort to make COBOL as English-like and self-explanatory as possible has created two disadvantages. First, COBOL programs tend to be wordy and rather long. Using COBOL usually requires more statements to solve a problem than using a more compact language such as Pascal. Second, a large, sophisticated translator program is needed to turn a COBOL source program into machine language. Such a program occupies a large portion of main memory.

Regardless of COBOL's disadvantages, it is likely to remain a popular language for many years. Polls indicate that more than 80 percent of business application programs are written in COBOL. Converting these hundreds of thousands of COBOL programs to other languages and retraining thousands of programmers and users would be neither inexpensive nor easy.

Logo

Logo is a procedure-oriented, interactive programming language developed initially by Seymour Papert and the MIT Logo group in the late 1960s. Like BASIC and Pascal, it was originally designed as a teaching tool. Logo's main

FIGURE 12—5

Payroll Program in COBOL
(Continued Facing Page)

```
IDENTIFICATION DIVISION.
PROGRAM-ID. PAYROLL.
INPUT-OUTPUT SECTION.
FILE-CONTROL.
    SELECT CARD-FILE ASSIGN TO UR-S-SYSIN.
    SELECT PRINT-FILE ASSIGN TO UR-S-OUTPUT.

DATA DIVISION.
FILE SECTION.
FD  CARD-FILE
    LABEL RECORDS ARE OMITTED
    RECORD CONTAINS 80 CHARACTERS
    DATA RECORD IS PAY-RECORD.
01  PAY-RECORD.
    03   EMPLOYEE-NAME      PIC A(16).
    03   HOURS-WORKED       PIC 99.
    03   WAGE-PER-HOUR      PIC 99V99.
    03   FILLER             PIC X(58).

FD  PRINT-FILE
    LABEL RECORDS ARE OMITTED
    RECORD CONTAINS 132 CHARACTERS
    DATA RECORD IS PRINT-RECORD.
01  PRINT-RECORD           PIC X(132).

WORKING-STORAGE SECTION.
77  GROSS-PAY              PIC 9(3)V99.
77  REGULAR-PAY            PIC 9(3)V99.
77  OVERTIME-PAY           PIC 9(3)V99.
77  NET-PAY                PIC 9(3)V99.
77  TAX                    PIC 9(3)V99.
77  OVERTIME-HOURS         PIC 99.
77  OVERTIME-RATE          PIC 9(3)V999.
77  EOF-FLAG               PIC X(3)        VALUE 'NO'.
01  HEADING-LINE.
    03   FILLER            PIC X           VALUE SPACES.
    03   FILLER            PIC X(21)       VALUE
         'EMPLOYEE NAME'.
    03   FILLER            PIC X(7)        VALUE
         'NET PAY'.

01  OUTPUT-RECORD.
    03   FILLER            PIC X           VALUE SPACES.
    03   NAME              PIC A(16).
    03   FILLER            PIC X(5)        VALUE SPACES.
    03   AMOUNT            PIC $$$$.99.
    03   FILLER            PIC X(103)      VALUE SPACES.

PROCEDURE DIVISION.
MAIN-LOGIC.
    OPEN INPUT CARD-FILE
         OUTPUT PRINT-FILE.
    PERFORM HEADING-ROUTINE.
    READ CARD-FILE
         AT END MOVE 'YES' TO EOF-FLAG.
    PERFORM WORK-LOOP UNTIL EOF-FLAG = 'YES'.
    CLOSE CARD-FILE
          PRINT-FILE.
    STOP RUN.
```

attraction is that it allows children and adults of all ages to begin to program and communicate with the computer in a very short period of time. Logo allows the user to draw images, animate them, and color them using very simple instructions.

```
HEADING-ROUTINE.
      WRITE PRINT-RECORD FROM HEADING-LINE
            BEFORE ADVANCING 2 LINES.
WORK-LOOP.
      IF HOURS-WORKED IS GREATER THAN 40
            THEN
                  PERFORM OVERTIME-ROUTINE
            ELSE
                  MULTIPLY HOURS-WORKED BY WAGE-PER-HOUR
                        GIVING GROSS-PAY.
      PERFORM TAX-COMPUTATION.
      PERFORM OUTPUT-ROUTINE.
      READ CARD-FILE AT END MOVE 'YES' TO EOF-FLAG.

OVERTIME-ROUTINE.
      MULTIPLY WAGE-PER-HOUR BY 40 GIVING REGULAR-PAY.
      SUBTRACT 40 FROM HOURS-WORKED GIVING OVERTIME-HOURS.
      MULTIPLY REGULAR-PAY BY 1.5 GIVING OVERTIME-RATE.
      MULTIPLY OVERTIME-HOURS BY OVERTIME-RATE
            GIVING OVERTIME-PAY.
      ADD REGULAR-PAY, OVERTIME-PAY GIVING GROSS-PAY.

TAX-COMPUTATION.
      IF GROSS-PAY IS GREATER THAN 250
            THEN
                  MULTIPLY GROSS-PAY BY 0.20 GIVING TAX
            ELSE
                  MULTIPLY GROSS-PAY BY 0.14 GIVING TAX.
      SUBTRACT TAX FROM GROSS PAY GIVING NET-PAY.

OUTPUT-ROUTINE.
      MOVE EMPLOYEE-NAME TO NAME.
      MOVE NET-PAY TO AMOUNT.
      WRITE PRINT-RECORD FROM OUTPUT-RECORD
            BEFORE ADVANCING 1 LINES.
```

Output

EMPLOYEE NAME	NET PAY
LYNN MANGINO	$224.00
THOMAS RITTER	$212.42
MARIE OLSON	$209.00
LORI DUNLEVY	$172.00
WILLIAM LUOMA	$308.00

Logo accomplishes this interactive programming of graphics through a triangular object called a turtle, which leaves a graphic trail in its path. The user can easily command the turtle to draw straight lines, squares, or other objects as his or her skill level increases. Figure 12–6 contains a Logo program that illustrates statements that can be used to draw a triangular figure.

Logo was developed as an education-oriented language; its strengths lie in its ability to help the inexperienced user learn logic and programming. Because it is a structured language, it encourages the beginning programmer to develop good programming habits. Logo helps the user to determine and develop the procedures required to solve a given problem using the computer. It also helps the user learn to communicate with the computer and to develop an understanding of what programming is all about, including how to debug programs.

The word and list processing capabilities of Logo add more power to an already powerful programming language that is used in teaching geometry, language, physics, art, music, and architecture, to name only a few subject areas.

APL

APL (A Programming Language), conceived in 1962 by Kenneth Iverson, became available to the public through IBM in 1968. Over the years it has been expanded and has gained many enthusiastic supporters. Many businesses now use APL to write application programs.

The full power of APL is best realized when it is used for interactive processing via a terminal. A programmer can use APL in two modes. In the execution mode, the terminal can be used much like a desk calculator. An

FIGURE 12–6

Logo Program to Draw a Triangular Figure

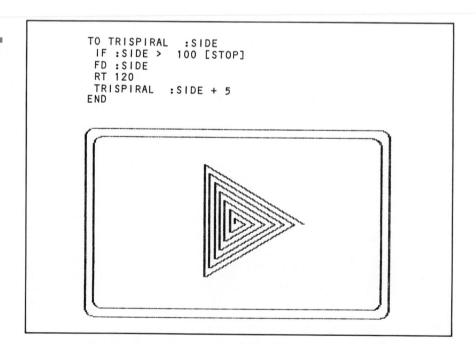

```
TO TRISPIRAL   :SIDE
  IF :SIDE >   100 [STOP]
  FD :SIDE
  RT 120
  TRISPIRAL   :SIDE + 5
END
```

COMPUTERS AND INFORMATION PROCESSING

instruction is keyed in on one line and the response is returned immediately on the following line. In the definition mode, a series of instructions is entered into memory and the entire program is executed on command from the programmer. The APL programmer enters statements to create a source program, system commands to communicate with the operating system, and editing commands to modify the source program. However, APL bears little resemblance to any other high-level language we will discuss.

Both character-string data and numeric data can be manipulated when APL is used. It is especially well suited for handling tables of related numbers, which are referred to as arrays. To simplify the programmer's task, a number of operations (up to fifty or more) are provided for array manipulation, logical comparisons, mathematical functions, branching operations, and so forth. The operators are represented by symbols on a special APL keyboard (see Figure 12–7). Some examples of APL coding are shown in Table 12–3. Figure 12–8 contains an interactive APL session.

APL operators can be combined to perform some very complex operations with a minimum of coding. APL's lack of formal restrictions on input and output and its free-format style make it a very powerful language. It is especially suited to handling tables of related numbers. It contains functions such as random-number generation, index generation, and matrix formation, making it very popular among statisticians. However, since it can be used for applications such as document production, graphics analysis, data retrieval, and financial analysis, APL also fills many business needs. APL is available through time-sharing networks for organizations that need only a limited amount of data processing.

APL has several disadvantages; one is that it is very difficult to read. A special keyboard is required to enter APL statements because of the number of unique symbols used; fortunately, the larger offering of new, low-cost terminals capable of handling several type fonts has greatly reduced this problem. Many people do not believe that APL is suitable for handling large data files. Another limitation of APL is the large amount of primary storage required by its translator program. Finally, APL is not available on as many different computer systems as are COBOL and Pascal.

Ada

Ada is a relatively new, state-of-the-art programming language developed by the Department of Defense. Ada is named after Augusta Ada Byron, Countess of Lovelace and daughter of the poet Lord Byron. Augusta Ada

FIGURE 12–7

APL Keyboard

TABLE 12-3

APL Coding

APL Coding	English Translation
A + B	A plus B
A ← 25	A = 25
ALB	Finds the smaller of A and B
V1 ← 2 5 11 17	Creates a vector of 4 components and assigns this vector to V1
r/V1	Finds the maximum value in the vector V1

HIGHLIGHT

Ada

When the U.S. Department of Defense adopted the advanced programming language Ada as its standard, the language was just being developed. There were no compilers and other software tools to support the language.

Now Ada is maturing, and supporters and users say it is much more productive than either FORTRAN or COBOL. The Department of Defense claims the language can increase programmer productivity by 18 percent. If indeed the Department is correct, businesses may also start using the language. Yet in order for businesses to benefit from Ada they must be able to develop Ada software. Since Ada is such a complex language, software companies are reluctant to develop software in the language until they are sure there is a market. In-house programmers may be reluctant to use Ada because most of them are unfamiliar with the language and they would need to acquire additional training. Yet as with any new technology or software, the first to develop and use it effectively can gain a significant edge over the competition.

Byron worked with Charles Babbage, programming his difference engine (see Chapter 2), and for this reason is often referred to as the first programmer. Ada is derived from Pascal and like Pascal is a structured language with many useful control statements.

The need for a language such as Ada was determined by a Department of Defense study conducted in 1974, which found that more than $7 billion was spent on software in 1973. Through further study it was found that no current high-level language could meet the needs of the Department of Defense and a new language would have to be developed. In 1980 the Department of Defense approved the initial Ada standard, and in 1983 ANSI approved it. Because of the considerable influence the Department of Defense has had and continues to have in this area, some people believe that Ada will someday replace COBOL as the most widely used programming language in business.

Ada is not a beginner's language; a skilled programmer may take six months to become proficient in the language. However, it has the sophistication and reliability (that is, the ability to always obtain correct results) that is necessary for programming in areas of defense, weather forecasting, oil exploration, and so forth.

Ada has the advantage of supporting the use of concurrent processing, which, as discussed in Chapter 10, is the capability of a single CPU to execute more than one program (or subpart of a program) at the same time. Concurrent processing allows computer resources to be used very efficiently.

RPG

RPG (Report Program Generator) is a problem-oriented language originally designed in the late 1960s to produce business reports. The programmer using RPG describes the type of report desired without having to specify much of the logic involved. A generator program is then used to build (generate) a program to produce the report. Little programming skill is required to use RPG.

Because RPG was originally developed to support punched-card equipment, it is used primarily with small computer systems. Many firms that formerly used electromechanical punched-card processing equipment have upgraded their data-processing operations to small computer systems. These

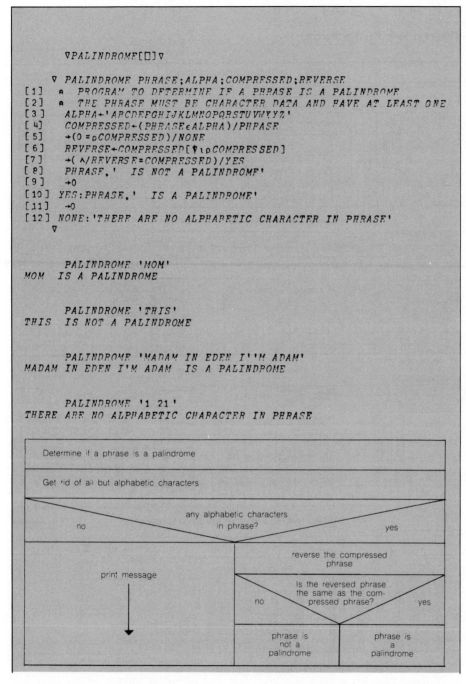

FIGURE 12—8

Sample APL Interactive Session

```
      ∇PALINDROME[□]∇

   ∇ PALINDROME PHRASE;ALPHA;COMPRESSED;REVERSE
[1]   ⍝  PROGRAM TO DETERMINE IF A PHRASE IS A PALINDROME
[2]   ⍝  THE PHRASE MUST BE CHARACTER DATA AND HAVE AT LEAST ONE
[3]   ALPHA←'ABCDEFGHIJKLMNOPQRSTUVWXYZ'
[4]   COMPRESSED←(PHRASE∈ALPHA)/PHRASE
[5]   →(0=⍴COMPRESSED)/NONE
[6]   REVERSE←COMPRESSED[⍒⍳⍴COMPRESSED]
[7]   →(∧/REVERSE=COMPRESSED)/YES
[8]   PHRASE,'  IS NOT A PALINDROME'
[9]   →0
[10] YES:PHRASE,'  IS A PALINDROME'
[11]  →0
[12] NONE:'THERE ARE NO ALPHABETIC CHARACTER IN PHRASE'
   ∇


      PALINDROME 'MOM'
MOM  IS A PALINDROME


      PALINDROME 'THIS'
THIS  IS NOT A PALINDROME


      PALINDROME 'MADAM IN EDEN I''M ADAM'
MADAM IN EDEN I'M ADAM  IS A PALINDROME


      PALINDROME '1 21'
THERE ARE NO ALPHABETIC CHARACTER IN PHRASE
```

firms usually have relatively simple, straightforward data-processing needs. In such cases, a small computer system supporting RPG can provide significantly improved data-processing operations. Management reports can be produced in a fraction of the time required by electromechanical methods.

When using RPG, the programmer does not code statements; instead, he or she completes specification forms such as those shown in Figure 12–9.

FIGURE 12–9

RPG Program Specification Forms

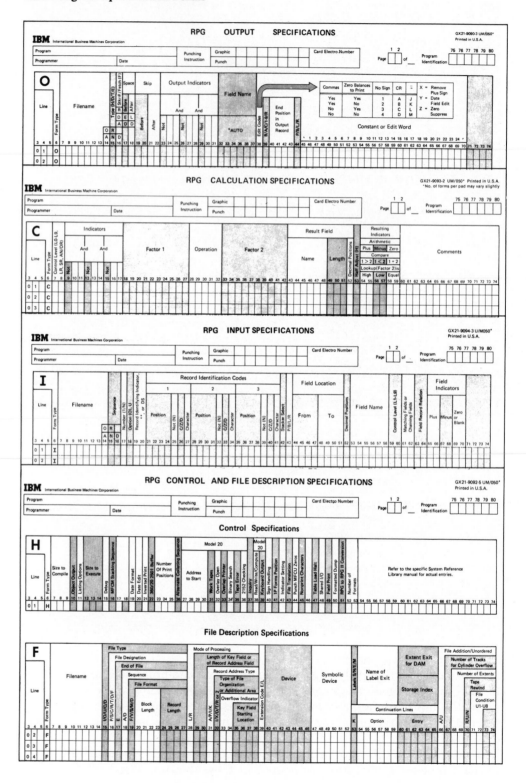

COMPUTERS AND INFORMATION PROCESSING

All files, records, and fields to be manipulated must be defined by entries in specific columns on the specification forms. The operations to be performed and the content and format of output files are described similarly. The RPG program builds an object program from the source program, and the object program is executed by the computer (see Figure 12–10).

Like other programming languages, RPG is constantly being improved. IBM introduced a new version named RPGII in the early 1970s for use on its IBM System/3 computers. This new version has been widely accepted and is now supported by many computer manufacturers; in fact, it has essentially replaced the original RPG. A third version introduced in 1979, RPGIII, features the ability to process data stored in a data base.

RPG is easy to learn and use because the basic pattern of execution is fixed. Because it does not require large amounts of primary storage, it is one of the primary languages of small computers and minicomputers. RPG provides an efficient means for generating reports requiring simple logic and calculations; it is commonly used to process files for accounts receivable, accounts payable, general ledgers, and inventory.

Unfortunately, the computational capabilities of RPG are limited. Some RPG compilers can generate machine-language instructions for up to thirty different operations. However, compared with COBOL, FORTRAN, and Pascal, RPG's looping, branching, and comparison-making capabilities are restricted. It is not a standardized language; therefore RPG programs may require a significant degree of modification if they are to be executed on a computer other than the one for which they were initially written. This is especially true if a firm changes computer manufacturers. However, if a firm stays with a particular manufacturer's equipment, its RPG programs can generally be run on a similar but more powerful computer with only slight modifications.

C

Developed in 1972, **C** is rapidly becoming popular for both system and application programming. It has some capabilities similar to those of assembly languages, such as the capability to manipulate individual bits and bytes in storage locations. Yet it also offers many high-level language features, such as a wide variety of useful control structures. Therefore, sometimes it is referred to as a *middle-level language.*

C is popular for several reasons. First, it is independent of machine architecture, so that C programs are portable. That is, the same program can be run on different computers. Second, C can be implemented on a wide variety of systems, from eight-bit microcomputers to supercomputers such as the Cray-1. Third, it includes many structured programming features found in languages like Pascal. Figure 12–11 contains a payroll program written in C.

C was designed by Dennis Ritchie at Bell Laboratories. One of the first uses was in the rewriting of Bell Laboratories' UNIX operating system. UNIX and its utilities include more than 300,000 lines of C source code, a very ambitious programming project. Today, many of the largest microcomputer manufacturers and software developers use C for system programs, utility programs, and graphics applications. Digital Research, for example, is using C for all its newer products, including CP/M-68K for the

FIGURE 12-10

Payroll Program in RPG
(Continued Facing Page)

```
00010H        0003          132
00020F*                  PAYROLL EXAMPLE
00030FCDIN    IP F  80  80           READ01
00040FPRINTR  O  F 132 132     OF   PRINTER
00050I* DEFINES INPUT
00060ICDIN    ZZ  01 80   CD
000701                                1     6 DATE
000801        ZZ  02
000901                                1    10DEPT  L1
001008                                2     5 EMPNO
001101                                6     92HRS
001201                               10    133RATE
001301                               14    140EXEMP
00510C*TO FIND GROSS PAY, NET PAY
00511C    40            SETOF                    30
00512C    N40 02        SETON                    3040
00520C    02     HRS    COMP  40.00              100909
00530C    02 09  RATE   MULT  HRS     GROSS  52H
00540C    02 10  HRS    SUB   40.00   OTHRS  42
00550C    02 10  RATE   MULT  40.00   REG    52
00560C    02 10  RATE   MULT  1.5     OTRT   43
00570C    02 10  OTHRS  MULT  OTRT    OVER   52
00580C    02 10  REG    ADD   OVER    GROSS  52
00590C    02     EXEMP  MULT  14.40   EXAMT  52H        EXEMPT AMT
00600C    02     GROSS  SUB   EXAMT   BASE   52
00610C    02     BASE   MULT  .12     INCTX  52HN       INCOME TAX DED
00620C    02     GROSS  SUB   INCTX   NET    52
00630C    02     GROSS  ADD   DGROSS  DGROSS 62
00640C    02     HRS    ADD   DHRS    DHRS   52
00650C    02     GROSS  ADD   GGROSS  GGROSS 72
00660C    02     HRS    ADD   GHRS    GHRS   62
001400* DEFINES HEADINGS AND OUTPUT
001500OPRINTR   H 0201   01
001600      OR          OF
001700                               10'DATE'
001800               DATE            19'  /  / '
002100                               67'PAYROLL'
002200                              120'PAGE'
002300               PAGE           125'  0'
002400         H 02    L1
002500      OR          OF
002600                               10'DEPT'
002700                               24'EMP NO'
002800                               37'HOURS'
002900                               49'RATE'
003000                               63'GROSS'
003100                               81'EXEMPTIONS'
003200                              100'INCOME TAX'
003300                              115'NET PAY'
003400         D 02    02
003500               L1 DEPT
003510               30 DEPT          8
003600                  EMPNO        23
003700                  HRS          37' . '
003800                  RATE         49' . '
003900                  GROSS        63' 0. '
004000                  EXEMP        76
004100                  INCTX        97' 0. '
004200                  NET         114' 0. '
004300         T 33    L1
004400                               27'DEPARTMENT
004500                  DGROSS  B    63'  , $0.  '
004600                  DHRS    B    37' 0.  '
004700         T 30    LR
004800                               29'GRAND TOTALS
004900                  GGROSS  B    63'  , $0.  '
005000                  GHRS    B    39' 0.  '
```

```
//GO.PRINTR DD SYSOUT=A
//GO.CDIN   DD =
052775
10029400031753
10087410029002
10141420044401
10160400026754
10387445049954
10401510037502
10403400029003
20037300024502
20098400029701
20201400044501
20221440041503
20485478541705
/*EOF
```

Output

				PAYROLL			
DEPT	EMP NO	HOURS	RATE	GROSS	EXEMPTIONS	INCOME TAX	NET PAY
1	0029	40.00	3.175	127.00	3	10.06	116.94
	0087	41.00	2.900	120.35	2	10.99	109.36
	0141	42.00	4.440	190.92	1	21.18	169.74
	0160	40.00	2.675	107.00	4	5.93	101.07
	0387	44.50	4.995	233.51	4	21.11	212.40
	0401	51.00	3.750	211.87	2	21.97	189.90
	0403	40.00	2.900	116.00	3	8.74	107.26
DEPARTMENT TOTALS		298.50		$1,106.65			
DEPT	EMP NO	HOURS	RATE	GROSS	EXEMPTIONS	INCOME TAX	NET PAY
2	0037	40.00	2.450	98.00	2	8.30	89.70
	0098	40.00	2.970	118.80	1	12.53	106.27
	0201	40.00	4.450	178.00	1	19.63	158.37
	0221	44.00	4.150	190.90	3	17.72	173.18
	0485	47.85	4.170	215.90	5	17.27	198.63
DEPARTMENT TOTALS		211.85		$801.60			
GRAND TOTALS		510.35		$1,908.25			

68000 microprocessor and the new Personal BASIC. Both Microsoft and VisiCorp have used C in products ranging from Multiplan and Xenix to Visiword and Visi On.

C is a general-purpose language that features economy of expression, modern data structures, and a rich set of operators. Although it is considered a system programming language, it is also useful for numerical, text-processing, and data-base programs. It is a "small" language, using many built-in functions. Therefore, the compilers are simple and compact. Unlike Pascal, which assumes that the programmer is often wrong and thus limits the chances for the programmer to write incorrect statements, C assumes that the programmer is always right and allows the programmer a freer programming style. Therefore, truly spectacular errors are easier to make in C. C is a compiled language and also contains rather cryptic error mes-

```
main()
{
/*****************************************************
      This program calculates a weekly payroll.
 *****************************************************/

    double atof();
    float wage, hours, grosspay, tax, netpay;
    char *chwage, *chhours, *name;

    flag = 0;
    printf ("EMPLOYEE NAME                    NETPAY \n");
    emplfile = fopen("payroll","r");
    while (1) {
/*****************************************************
                procedure read data
 *****************************************************/
        readname(name);
        if (flag)
                break;
        readname(chhours);
        readname(chwage);


/*****************************************************
            Calculate gross pay
 *****************************************************/
        wage = atof(chwage);                    /* convert the string  */
        hours = atof(chhours);                  /* to a float value    */
        if (hours <= 40)
                grosspay = hours * wage;
        else
                grosspay = hours * wage + (hours - 40.0) * wage * 0.5;


/*****************************************************
            Calculate net pay
 *****************************************************/
        if (grosspay > 250)
            tax = 0.2 * grosspay;
        else
            tax = 0.14 * grosspay;
        netpay = grosspay - tax;
```

FIGURE 12—11

**Payroll Program in C
(Continued Facing Page)**

sages that can confuse a novice programmer. For these reasons, C is clearly intended for the professional programmer.

Modula-2

Modula-2 is a descendant of Pascal. Designed by the creator of Pascal, Niklaus Wirth, Modula-2 contains all aspects of Pascal as well as features drawn from Modula, a language developed from experiments with concurrent processing. Like Ada, Modula-2 allows for the use of concurrent processing, thereby encouraging the efficient use of the CPU. Because Modula-2 is similar to Pascal, it is easy for programmers who already know Pascal to learn it.

As Pascal became widely implemented during the 1970s, it became evident that certain improvements to the language were possible. Wirth proposed to create a single, high-level language that also had low-level capabilities to interact more closely with its given hardware. In this respect,

```
/******************************************************
                Print the results
******************************************************/
        printf("%-24s  %7.2f\n",name,netpay);
        }  /* while loop closing bracket */
        fclose(emplfile);
} /* main closing bracket */

/******************************************************
                Subroutine readname
******************************************************/
readname(ts)
char *ts;
{
        int cc;
        char *cs;

        cs = ts;
        while ((cc = getc(emplfile)) != EOF)    /*look for EOF */
                {
                if (cc == 13)                   /* return if CR is seen */
                        break;
                if (cc != 10)                   /* do not process LF */
                        *cs++ = cc;             /* build the string */
                }
        if (cc == EOF) flag = 1;                /* if EOF we are done */
        *cs = '\0';                             /* make sure we terminate
                                                   a string value */
}
```

Output

```
 O |                                                              | O
   |   EMPLOYEE NAME                    NETPAY                     |
   |   LYNN MANGIN                      224.00                     |
   |   THOMAS RITTER                    212.42                     |
 O |   MARIE OLSON                      209.00                     | O
   |   LORI SANCHEZ                     172.00                     |
   |   WILLIAM LUOMA                    308.00                     |
 O |                                                              | O
```

Modula-2 is similar to C and FORTH (FORTH is discussed in the next section).

The most outstanding feature of Modula-2 is its use of the module, a concept drawn from its parent Modula. Each of these modules performs a specific task. It is a structured language that is easy to modularize and has a wide variety of useful control structures. Because Modula-2 is a new programming language, it remains to be seen how widely implemented it will be.

FORTH

Working at Kitt Peak National Observatory, Charles Moore developed **FORTH** in response to what he saw as a need for an adequate programming language to use in tracking satellites and studying the universe. Like C and Modula-2, FORTH is often categorized as a middle-level language. By using the many library commands to define new special-purpose commands, FORTH can be modeled to meet the programmer's particular needs.

A FORTH program consists of the definitions of many words (commonly called procedures or subroutines in other languages). A program is a list of words, with simple words defining more complex ones. The notation looks strange; the mathematical expression 8 + 4 * 5 would appear as 4 5 * 8 + in FORTH. The reason for this is that FORTH operates on the principle of a stack—a pile of objects from which you add or remove only the topmost element, just as you would from a stack of dishes. Other programming languages use stacks internally, but FORTH makes the stacks available to the programmer. Let's see how the idea of stacks works on the expression 4 5 * 8 + . If FORTH sees a number, it pushes that number onto the top of the stack. If it sees an operator such as * or +, it removes the top two numbers off the stack and applies the operation, then puts the result back onto the top of the stack. Therefore, 4 and 5 would be multiplied, leaving 20 on top of the stack. Then FORTH removes the 20 and the 8 from the stack and sees the symbol + . It adds 20 and 8, the next two numbers on the stack. The result is 28.

FORTH has become the standard language for astronomical observatories around the world. It also is used to guide automated movie cameras, run portable heart monitors, and simulate radar for the air force. In addition, it is being used increasingly for the less glamorous tasks involved in data base management and word processing.

The simplicity of FORTH makes it fast and efficient. Adding new features to FORTH is also possible. Because FORTH systems are interpreted, the programmer can write one word (procedure) at a time and test it thoroughly before writing the next word. However, this strange-looking language is hard to read, and sometimes strange names are given to the words. In the name of speed, FORTH lacks many of the safety features built into other languages, so it is difficult to debug.

LISP

LISP (or LISt Processing) is the language commonly associated with artificial intelligence (AI). Using concepts of lambda-calculus (a branch of mathematics) and a new idea in computing called list processing, John McCarthy developed the language in 1960 at Massachusetts Institute of Technology. LISP aids in the manipulation of nonnumeric data that change considerably in length and structure during execution of a program. Essentially, LISP involves performing built-in or user-defined functions on lists.

In LISP, a list is a group of elements in a particular order. The following example contains seven elements, A, LIST, IS, A, GROUP, OF, ELEMENTS.

(A LIST IS A GROUP OF ELEMENTS)

Using parentheses can separate elements of a list, as follows:

(A LIST IS A GROUP OF ELEMENTS (IN A PARTICULAR ORDER))

The elements of this list are A, LIST, IS, A, GROUP, OF, ELEMENTS, and IN A PARTICULAR ORDER.

To beginning programmers in LISP, the tangle of parentheses can be confusing. However, the lists can contain collections of functions, such as finding the square or cube of a number; sentences; mathematical formulas; logic theorems; or even complete computer programs. This capability makes LISP a powerful tool in applications such as the generation of mathematical proofs, algebraic manipulation, and simulations of human problem-solving techniques.

Another AI language, PROLOG, is also recognized by the academic community as a useful language in AI. Part of the reason for interest in PROLOG is that the Japanese have chosen it to be the standard language for their fifth-generation project, a project that could make Japan the world leader in advanced computer applications and expert systems.

■ VERY-HIGH-LEVEL LANGUAGES

Very-high-level, or fourth-generation, languages are programming languages that still require a specific or exact syntax but are much easier to learn and use. For example, someone who is not a professional computer programmer can use a very-high-level language to develop application software. Very-high-level languages allow the user to specify "what" needs to be accomplished without having to specify "how" it should be accomplished. The fourth-generation language itself is designed such that the user can designate what task is to be completed. Once the task has been specified, the fourth-generation language then goes about determining how the task will be accomplished by generating the instructions necessary to complete the task.

Very-high-level languages typically contain three tools that can be used in the development of an application program. These include query languages, report generators, and application generators. In addition, some very-high-level languages also include a data-base manager. The fourth-generation language FOCUS would be an example. The query language portion of the language requires the user to construct English-like statements to extract and manipulate data in the data base. Although easily understood, these English-like statements must still maintain an exact syntax.

The report generator portion of a very-high-level language allows a user to designate the format of reports that are created from data contained in the language's data base. Application generators give the user a simplified method of developing an application program. This program can then be used to enter and manipulate data within the data base. The application generator can be used to create "user friendly" applications by allowing the user a way of designing input screens. The application generator may also be used to designate verification rules to be performed on the data being entered. Calculations that are required may also be specified when using an application generator. Although they are easy to use, very-high-level languages are still limited in their capabilities. They are often not capable of developing complex programs such as those that may be created using COBOL, FORTRAN, or C.

■ NATURAL LANGUAGES

Computer scientists have always realized that computers can't achieve their full potential if only a few people know how to use them. Programmers have helped to make software "user friendly" by using menus and other devices to make the machines interact in humanlike ways. One way in which people's interaction with these machines could be greatly improved would be if data bases could be queried in plain English.

Natural languages are programming languages that attempt to allow the user to state queries in English sentences. The question is then translated into a form that the computer can understand. A sentence such as "HOW MANY WOMEN HOLD A POSITION AT LEVEL 10 OR ABOVE?" may be entered by a member of the personnel department to gain information for reporting purposes. In some cases, if the natural language processor does not fully understand the inquiry, it may request further information from the user in order to process the given inquiry.

Natural languages have been designed primarily for the novice computer user for use as online, data base, query languages. Natural-language processors normally are designed to be used with a vocabulary of words and definitions that allows the processor to translate the English sentences to machine-executable form. Currently, natural-language sentences are typed at the keyboard; however, in the future the combination of voice recognition technology and natural languages could result in a very powerful tool for computer users. The ability to interface natural-language systems with graphics software also provides a valuable tool for managers in decision making. Although limited to mainframe computers in the past, natural-language systems are being developed for minicomputer and microcomputer systems as well.

■ PROGRAMMING LANGUAGES—A COMPARISON

Implementing an information system involves making an important decision concerning the type of programming language to use. Some questions must be asked:

■ What languages does the selected (or available) computer system support?

■ Does the company require that the system be written in a particular language? For example, in some businesses, all application programs must be written in COBOL.

■ Will the application require mostly complex computations, file processing, or report generation?

■ Are equipment changes planned for the future? If so, is it important that the chosen language be implemented on a wide variety of computer systems?

■ How frequently will programs need modification?

■ What languages do the programmers who will program and maintain the system know?

The size of the computer system is an obvious constraint on language choice. The size of the primary storage of microcomputers limits the use of languages such as APL and ADA. But languages such as Pascal, C, and BASIC are widely available on microcomputers. Although the computational capabilities of RPG are limited, it can still supply sufficient information for the management of small firms.

COMPUTERS AND INFORMATION PROCESSING

For large systems, the type of processing is the key consideration in choosing a language. Business applications typically involve large amounts of data on which relatively few calculations are performed. Substantial file processing (requiring many I/O operations) is required; thus, many business applications are **input/output-bound.** In such cases, COBOL is the language generally chosen, although Ada is growing in popularity.

Scientific programming applications usually require many complex calculations on relatively small amounts of data. Therefore, they tend to be **process-bound.** The computational capabilities of FORTRAN make it ideal for such applications although Pascal also is often used because it is structured better than FORTRAN.

Because of the diversity of programming languages, many firms choose to use several. For example, a firm can write scientific programs in FORTRAN and file-updating programs in COBOL. It is also possible to write part of a program in one language and another part in a different language; this involves compiling the various portions of the program in separate steps and linking together the resultant object programs. For example, a program written in COBOL may call up an assembly-language program to perform extensive sorting of alphanumeric data, because assembly language can perform sorting tasks more efficiently than COBOL and thus save processing time.

Nevertheless, there has been a definite trend away from programming in assembly language. Because of the one-to-one relationship between assembly-language instructions and machine-language instructions, programming in assembly language is very time consuming. Assembly-language programs may be efficient, but writing them is laborious. In contrast, high-level languages shift the programming emphasis away from detailed computer functions toward procedures for solving problems. If it is necessary to use low-level language commands such as those involving bit and byte manipulation, one of the so-called "middle-level" languages such as C or Modula-2 should be considered. These languages incorporate the advantages of both high-level and low-level languages.

■ SUMMARY POINTS

■ Machine language and assembly language, which are low-level languages, require extensive knowledge of the computer system being used.

■ Machine language, consisting of 1s and 0s, is the only language that the computer is capable of executing directly. It is different for each type of computer.

■ Assembly-language statements use symbolic names (called mnemonics) to represent machine operations, making assembly-language programming less tedious and time-consuming than machine-language programming. Before assembly-language programs are executed, they must be translated into machine language. Because there is generally a one-to-one correspondence between assembly- and machine-language statements, this translation is easier to make than when a high-level language is used.

■ Programming languages can be divided into various categories, such as high level or low level, structured or unstructured, procedure-oriented or problem-oriented, and general or special purpose. Dividing programming languages into categories helps programmers in making generalizations about languages and in choosing the right language to meet a specific need.

■ Assembly-language programs are translated into machine language by an assembler. There are two types of translator programs for high-level language programs—compilers and interpreters. Compilers translate the entire source program into machine code, thereby creating an object program, which is then executed. Interpreters translate the source program one statement at a time. In general, interpreters are smaller than compilers and therefore take up less space in primary storage. However, interpreters can be less efficient than compilers because statements that are used more than once in a program must be retranslated each time.

■ High-level language statements contain English-like words such as READ and PRINT; these statements must be translated into machine language before execution. High-level languages are oriented toward the user, whereas low-level languages are oriented toward the computer hardware. A single high-level language statement may translate into many machine-language statements.

■ FORTRAN is the oldest high-level language and is commonly used for scientific applications because of its ability to perform mathematical calculations with a great deal of accuracy.

■ BASIC is an easy-to-learn language that is widely implemented on microcomputers and is often taught to beginning programmers.

■ Pascal is a structured language that was developed as an instructional language. It is relatively easy to learn and is useful in both business and scientific applications.

■ COBOL is the most popular business programming language. It was designed to be English-like and self-documenting. The main disadvantage of COBOL is that a large and sophisticated compiler is required to translate programs. A main advantage of COBOL is its ability to handle large data files efficiently.

■ Logo is an interactive, education-oriented language that uses an object called a turtle to help beginners become familiar with the computer and computer graphics.

■ APL is a powerful interactive language that can be used in execution mode or definition mode. Both character-string data and numeric data can be manipulated easily. Because APL includes a large number of unique symbols as operators, it requires a special keyboard. The APL compiler needs a large amount of primary storage; this restricts its use to medium-sized and large computers.

■ Ada is a relatively new, structured high-level language that was developed for use by the Department of Defense. It allows for the use of concurrent processing and is a sophisticated language that obtains the level of accuracy necessary for programming in areas such as defense, weather forecasting, and oil exploration.

■ RPG is a problem-oriented language designed to produce business reports. Because the RPG generator can build a program to provide specified output, little programming skill is required to use this language.

■ C is a structured high-level language that also includes low-level language instructions; therefore it is sometimes referred to as a middle-level language. It is a general-purpose language that features economy of expression, modern data structures, and a wide variety of operators. C is used for both system and application programming.

■ Modula-2, a descendant of Pascal, is based on the idea of structured subprograms, or modules, which are nested within one another. Like C, Modula-2 is a high-level language that includes low-level language instructions. Modula-2 also allows for concurrent processing, thereby helping the programmer make efficient use of the CPU.

■ FORTH is another high-level language that contains low-level language instructions, thereby allowing the programmer to interact closely with the computer's hardware. FORTH is used in astronomical observatories around the world.

■ LISP is the language commonly used in artificial intelligence programming and research. It involves performing built-in or user-defined functions on lists.

■ Very-high-level languages require adherence to a programming syntax but are much easier to use than high-level languages.

■ Natural languages are designed to allow the novice computer user to access the computer's capabilities more easily. For example, easy to write and understand English sentences allow the user to access information in a data base.

■ Factors to consider when selecting an appropriate programming language include: What languages can the computer support? Does the company require that application programs be written in a particular language? Are computations simple? Does the application require a great deal of handling of large data files? Are equipment changes planned in the future? How often will programs be modified? What languages do the programmers who will work on the project know?

REVIEW QUESTIONS

1. Distinguish between machine languages and assembly languages. What are the advantages and disadvantages of each?

2. How does a compiled programming language differ from an interpreted programming language? What would be an advantage of using an interpreted language rather than a compiled language?

3. Why were high-level languages developed? Name an advantage and a disadvantage high-level languages have over low-level languages.

4. Why is it desirable to attempt to standardize high-level languages? How does language standardization aid portability?

5. List four ways in which languages can be categorized. How is this categorization process helpful to programmers?

6. List three categories of special-purpose languages and name a language that fits into each category.

7. Give at least two reasons why Pascal has become a widely taught language for introductory programming students.

8. What are some common characteristics of scientific-oriented programming languages? How do these characteristics differ from business-oriented programming languages?

9. Describe some of the key advantages associated with the COBOL programming language.

10. List and discuss some of the factors that should be considered when a programming language is to be chosen for a particular application program.

11. How does a very-high-level language differ from a high-level language? How does a very-high-level language differ from a natural language?

12. What is the purpose of natural languages? For what type of user are they best suited?

13. How does a procedure-oriented language differ from a problem-oriented language? List some common procedure-oriented languages and a problem-oriented language.

United States Navy

NAVY CONTRIBUTES TO ADP HISTORY

The Naval Data Automation Command (NAVDAC) was established in 1977 to administer and coordinate the Navy Information Resources Management (IRM) and Information Systems (IS) programs. This mission includes: developing policy and procedures; approving IS development; setting up contracts for computers, communications equipment, software and services; managing IS technology transfer; managing computer security; and administering the Navy's IRM budget.

NAVDAC is the latest evolution of the Navy's office for managing it's critical computer resources. NAVDAC and its predecessor organizations have always been at the forefront of progress in computer technology. An excellent example of this is the Navy's significant role in the success of COBOL.

In 1967, there was a draft American National Standards Institute (ANSI) standard for COBOL, but the various vendor implementations of the draft standard were in no way consistent with one another. Portability of COBOL programs could not be achieved because each vendor interpreted the complex standard differently. The COBOL specification (and other programming language specifications, as it turned out) could not be written so as to promote a consistent interpretation.

The Navy, under Admiral Grace M. Hopper, opted to develop validation programs which each vendor was obliged to run successfully prior to selling their COBOL compiler to the Navy. The validation programs arbitrarily implemented a single interpretation (the Navy's interpretation, by and large) of the ANSI draft standard, thereby forcing vendors who wanted to sell to the Navy to comply. The concept worked so well that eventually the Navy was asked to validate all COBOL compilers coming into the federal government. Since all vendors wanted to sell to the federal government, all vendors compiled and the entire industry ultimately benefited from the consistency and portability of COBOL that resulted from this initiative.

Now, for the sake of increasing productivity, the Navy is migrating from COBOL to new language technologies. One example of this process is highlighted in the following account.

CHANGING TECHNOLOGIES, CHANGING LANGUAGES

Twenty years after its creation, COBOL was well ingrained as the standard programming language used for Navy's business applications (inventory, personnel, etc.). COBOL, along with FORTRAN, PASCAL and BASIC were, in fact, dictated in Navy standards as the only authorized languages for use in these systems unless IS developers could obtain a waiver to use some other lesser known or proprietary language to meet a special need.

The choice of COBOL as a standard language was based not only on its ability to automate the functions required, but on other life-cycle management issues and economics. COBOL was available to run on virtually all computer brands, and, in most cases, moving a system from one computer brand to another was about as easy as recompiling the program; trained COBOL programmers were always available in the marketplace; the English-like style made the program a useful part of documentation and helpful in keeping maintenance costs lower than more arcane languages.

As information systems and their technology became more complicated, the life-cycle management issues and economics related to COBOL became less significant and, at times, even an obstacle to meeting automation demands. An example of this occurred on a large Navy system which supported budget, scheduling, and inventory management for alterations of ships. The system was supporting all of these functions using the data stored in a well known data-base management system. There were both batch and on-line processes serving over one hundred users.

Around 1980, changes and improvements to this complicated ship alteration IS were being demanded faster than they could be met. The Navy was using twenty staff members to support system changes but was no longer able to keep up with end-user needs. This was happening because the procedures for analyzing, coding, testing, debugging, and implementing changes in a complex data-base environment were time consuming and highly subject to error. In addition, maintaining a staff experienced not only in COBOL but in the data-base language, job control language, and screen language was a problem. System users demanded more and more capabilities and were not willing to wait.

Finally, pressure was great enough to seek a solution through new technology. "4th generation languages," or 4GLs, were emerging from the technology advances at that time. These products promised more that a 700 percent increase in productivity in implementing user requirements. After some research, the Navy, under the sponsorship of NAVDAC, selected a product which had a programming language capable of replacing a full page of COBOL code with five or six statements; in addition, the product had a data-base management system which allowed a programmer to obtain data by merely identifying the data base and stating the data element names. The complex task of navigating through the data base was not required.

The 4th generation language used more computer resources, but technology had made those resources inexpensive, and the major problems and expenses in system development had become the time and costs associated with programming.

Within three months, the Navy had the 4GL running as a flexible adjunct to the ship alteration IS with its old proven COBOL code. As time permitted, the old code was phased out and the system began to run as a state-of-the-art example of a complex IS which is very responsive to its end users.

Based on the results of this effort, the Navy loosened its policy on COBOL as a standard language. Throughout the Navy, there are now examples of state-of-the-art systems in which the data base is centrally managed and end-users employ 4GLs to do adds, deletes, changes, and inquiries.

The Navy's actions in managing and implementing computer languages exemplify a critical factor for success in the computer field—the ability to adjust as technology changes.

DISCUSSION POINTS

1. Discuss the Navy's support for programming language standardization.
2. Why has the Navy chosen 4th generation languages for future development?

Application Software

OUTLINE

Introduction
**Advantages and Disadvantages of
    Commercial Application
    Software**
**General Categories of Application
    Software Packages**
Productivity Tools
  Word Processors
  Graphics Packages
  Spreadsheets
  File Managers
  Other Productivity Tools

Functional Tools
  Desktop Publishing Packages
  Accounting Packages
  Manufacturing Packages
  CASE Packages
  Sales and Marketing Packages
  Turnkey Systems
End-User Development Tools
  Simulation Software
Expert Systems
  Statistical Packages
  Data-base Management Systems

**Choosing an Application Software
    Package**
Summary Points
Review Questions

Financial Software: Brokers Power Up

R. D. R. Hoffmann
InformationWeek

Wall Street's meltdown of 1987 drew so much attention to the "dark side of the force" that few pundits noticed something interesting percolating in stock market technology. Brokers were asking for—and information managers were delivering—new ways to enhance brokers' productivity by bringing powerful systems to the desks of those selling stock to the public.

MIS executives at Prudential Bache, Kidder Peabody, and Shearson Lehman Hutton are stressing networked PCs and intelligent workstations on the hardware side, while developing their own software. Interestingly, these efforts at in-house development of distributed data systems and software on Wall Street have put MIS back in the software development driver's seat for retail brokerage systems, at least for the moment.

John Settel, product development and implementation director for Prudential Bache Securities, recently made the comment that the new Pru-Bache system, developed in concert with ADP's Brokerage Services Division and Convergent Technologies Inc., will give its brokers a two-year head start on the rest of The Street.

The Pru-Bache distributed data system runs on Convergent's N-Gen intelligent terminals. Under development since 1984, it went live in one Pru-Bache branch office on March 6th and will be fully operational, Settel says, by the end of the year.

That Pru-Bache is off and running with the new system is uncontested. That it is two years ahead of everyone else on the street is a point of contention. "Everyone's working hard in an extremely competitive environment, and I don't think we're two years behind anyone," says Jack Owens, executive vice president of EDP services for Shearson Lehman Hutton in New York. Shearson has been working with ADP for over a year on designing an advanced retail brokerage system, Owens notes. "The financial services industry historically has been running hard to keep up with ever-increasing volumes of business and trying to optimize the price/performance of technology," Owens observes. "Today, people are searching for the right technology."

Terry Quinn, a research analyst for Drexel Burnham Lambert in New York, say "Pru-Bache obviously has the lead at the moment," in retail brokerage systems. Quinn points out that "Merrill Lynch and Shearson are working with ADP on their own systems. I understand they're waiting to see what IBM does. By waiting, they may well close the gap very quickly."

Analyst Cato Carpenter, who follows the financial services software industry for the Baltimore-based Alex Brown brokerage firm, offers some reasons why MIS has taken the wheel. "There aren't software packages available for most applications, particularly in the newer technologies: micros, LANs, and departmental systems."

Carpenter observes that among the three categories he identifies as sources of financial services software (systems software firms, PC, and network software vendors, and specialty software developers) the only strong activity has been in the latter—and that primarily for the back office. Applications software to track and control international trading and mutual funds record-keeping systems are two areas in which specialty software developers have built sales with the major brokerage houses.

Quinn notes that brokers are focusing on "long-term strategies," that won't change "with every tic of the market." He believes, for example, that "none of the major firms changed their decisions on the roll-out of new systems" as a result of the October crash. Observers agree that what's on Wall Street's MIS drawing boards now is definitely "the wave of the future."

Many companies now recognize that in order to stay competitive they must always keep abreast of new computer developments, whether the developments are in hardware or software. For example, in the area of financial software, Prudential Bache Securities hopes its new Pru-Bache system will give the company at least a two-year edge over its competitors. Other companies are working vigorously to develop their own brokerage system because many times the first company to effectively use a technology becomes the leader in the field.

■ INTRODUCTION

In Chapter 11 we examined the software development process. This process can be used by a company to develop an application software package for in-house use or by a company to develop application software packages to sell. In recent years, the use of commercially written application software packages has increased dramatically. There are commercial packages available for everything from running a doctor's office to performing sophisticated statistical analysis on research data. This chapter focuses on application software for large computer systems. We will discuss some of the advantages and disadvantages of using commercially developed application software. Included in the chapter are discussions of different kinds of application packages—productivity tools, functional tools, and end-user development tools. The chapter concludes with some guidelines for choosing an application software package.

■ ADVANTAGES AND DISADVANTAGES OF COMMERCIAL APPLICATION SOFTWARE

Many factors have contributed to the increase in commercially developed software packages. You may recall from Chapter 2 that a court decision forcing IBM to "unbundle" its software had a major impact on the growth of the software industry. During that period companies also began to realize that developing programs in-house required a staff of highly talented and skilled programmers. Many found the cost of in-house software development prohibitive, so they began using commercially developed packages. Other factors contributing to the increased use of commercial packages include, first, the speed at which commercial packages can be implemented. Usually less time is needed to implement a commercial application package than to develop software in-house. Second, the quality and sophistication of commercial packages means that often a commercial package will contain more features than could realistically be included in a package developed in-house. Third, the reliability of the packages can be assumed. Because the package is already on the market, presumably it will work properly (or at least well enough to be usable). The reputation of the commercial developer is on the line; therefore, the developer is eager to market a package that will work properly. Because of the strong competition in the field, commercial software developers also have an incentive to provide good quality support for the user. Software support involves a variety of services including on-site training of users and "hot line" telephone support, which allows the users to talk to a staff of trained support representatives. These support representatives are typically employees of the company that has developed the application software package, who have been trained to answer user questions and solve user problems.

While there are benefits to using commercially developed software, there are also disadvantages. A commercially developed package may not meet the user's exact needs and therefore may require extensive modification. In industry, a general rule of thumb is that about 85 percent of an application package can be used exactly as it is written. The other 15 percent of the package must be modified according to user needs. The commercially developed packages can be modified, or customized, by the developer for a user, or, in some cases, commercial software developers sell the source code

HIGHLIGHT

Piracy

Software developers have been fighting piracy—the unauthorized copying of software—for many years. They feel that companies that rent software to users are actually enabling the software to be copied, so they are trying to introduce legislation that would make it illegal to rent software. Businesses that rent software say buyers have a right to try out software before they purchase it. The businesses say that providing software for rent actually eliminates the amount of software illegally copied.

Different software-rental bills have already been introduced in Congress three times; they have not passed because they were either too broad or too narrow. For example, a bill cannot eliminate a user's right to make a backup copy of software.

Another reason the software-rental bills have not passed is because it is difficult to estimate the amount of money companies lose each year from piracy. Recent court cases on piracy, however, show the amount is significant. For example, Inslaw, a small software company, provided the U.S. Department of Justice with a copy of its case-tracking product, called PROMIS. The company later found that the Department made twenty illegal copies of the product. The company sued the Department for $6.8 million. The judge ruled in favor of Inslaw, and although the Department of Justice is appealing the case, many software companies feel the precedent has been set—software pirates beware!

to the user so it can be modified to meet their needs. In addition, the customer usually depends on the vendor from whom the package was purchased to provide support. In the early days of commercial application packages, there were considerable problems in this area. Software developers did not have the personnel or the facilities to provide the needed support. Vendors would make impossible promises concerning the capabilities of their software, leaving many users highly dissatisfied. However, word quickly spread concerning unreliable software developers and vendors. Today most developers and vendors are extremely concerned about their reputations and produce and market high-quality products. Therefore, for many companies, buying and using commercial application software has become a way of life. For most companies, developing and maintaining application software has become costly; this cost can be reduced by purchasing commercial application software.

GENERAL CATEGORIES OF APPLICATION SOFTWARE PACKAGES

The computer industry has grown at a rate unmatched by any other industry. Because of this rapid growth, some areas of the industry are not clearly defined or are the subject of disagreement among industry professionals. Commercial application software development is one area in which some confusion exists. There is a lack of consensus among professionals about how to label or categorize software packages. In this chapter we will divide application software into three broad categories: productivity tools, functional tools, and end-user development tools. Although these categories overlap to some extent, they do provide a useful method of making generalized statements about the different types of application software currently available.

■ PRODUCTIVITY TOOLS

Productivity tools are software packages that can increase user productivity. Common examples of productivity tools are word processors, graphics packages, spreadsheets, and file managers. These tools can be used for a wide variety of tasks. Productivity tools are simply aids in achieving a goal; the exact goal may vary depending on the particular situation.

Word Processors

Software packages that allow the user to manipulate documents consisting of text, such as reports and tables, are referred to as **word processors.** Anyone who has ever used a word processor knows how helpful they are when creating and editing reports, tables, and so on. No longer are typing mistakes and organizational problems a major difficulty. Portions of the text can be easily deleted, inserted, or moved. Other features often included in word processors are the ability to justify the left and right margins and center headings. Footnotes can be inserted at the bottom of pages and pages can be numbered automatically. Most word processors allow the user to specify options such as italics, underlining, or boldface type. An example of a word processor containing all of the features mentioned above is WordStar.

Often word processors will include extensions such as **spelling checkers,** which compare each word in a specified document with the contents of an online dictionary. If a particular word does not appear in the dictionary, it is flagged so that the user can check it for correct spelling. Most spelling checkers allow the user to add words to the dictionary so that it can be customized to meet the user's needs and vocabulary.

Another popular extension to word processors is a mail-merge capability, which allows users to merge a mailing list with a form letter. This extension can allow users to create a form letter that can then be customized for each recipient from information contained in the mailing list. In some cases, the mailing list can be maintained in a file manager or data base (file managers and data bases will be discussed later in this chapter).

Graphics Packages

Graphics packages allow the user to create bar graphs, line graphs, pie charts, and so forth. Figure 13–1 shows examples of the different types of graphs that might be created with this type of application software. Normally, the user need only specify the type of graph desired and the size of each field within the graph. Different parts of the graph can be appropriately labeled. When using color monitors, the user can determine the colors of various parts of the graph, creating an attractive, professional-looking product in minimal time. Graphics packages are very useful for managers who must prepare reports summarizing complex information.

There are many specialized graphics packages available. Some allow geologists to create color-coded graphics of the earth's surface; these graphics

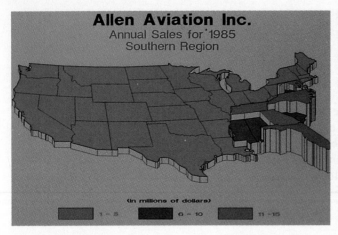

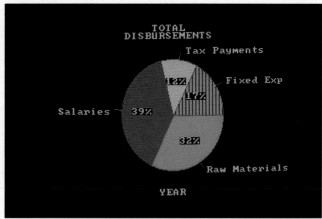

FIGURE 13—1

Examples of graphs developed with
graphics packages.

are based on aerial photographs. Presentation graphics packages are especially designed for managers and educators to use when preparing presentations of slidelike shows for groups. The packages allow figures and graphs to be pulled easily from other sources. Composite screens can be created and a wide range of display and dissolve techniques are generally available. Special cameras can create slides from images on terminal screens. In addition, special projectors designed to be attached to computer terminals can be used to project the images onto a screen.

Spreadsheets

A spreadsheet, or electronic ledger sheet, is primarily used in business by accountants for performing financial calculations and recording transactions. An **electronic spreadsheet** is simply a computerized version of a traditional spreadsheet. Electronic spreadsheets, however, are being used for more than just doing financial calculations and recording transactions. An electronic spreadsheet consists of a table of rows and columns used to store and manipulate any kind of numerical data. The point in a spreadsheet where a particular row and column meet is called a **cell.** Each cell is a unique location within the spreadsheet. Cells can contain labels, values, and formulas.

The use of formulas is what makes spreadsheets powerful. A formula can be applied to the contents of specified cells to obtain a result. For example, a user could calculate the amount of monthly payments on a loan, depending on the interest rate being charged. It would also be a simple matter to determine how much monthly payments would be if the length of payment time varied, say for thirty-six, forty-eight or sixty months. The ability to alter variables within the spreadsheet makes such calculations a simple matter. Figure 13–2 shows the variety of functions often available with spreadsheets that are part of integrated packages.

File Managers

File managers are designed to duplicate the traditional manual methods of filing. Before the use of computers for filing, sections or departments in a

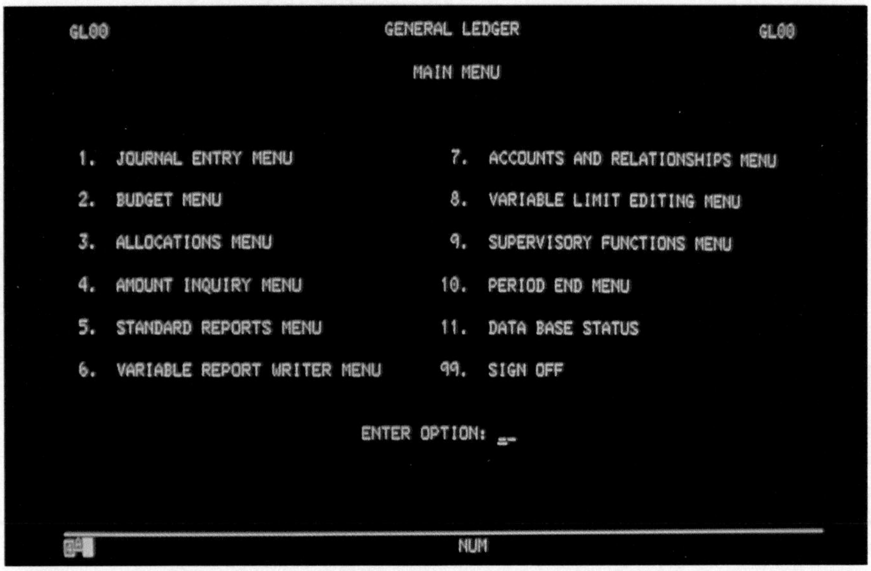

FIGURE 13—2

```
GL00                    GENERAL LEDGER                    GL00
                          MAIN MENU


   1.  JOURNAL ENTRY MENU          7.  ACCOUNTS AND RELATIONSHIPS MENU

   2.  BUDGET MENU                 8.  VARIABLE LIMIT EDITING MENU

   3.  ALLOCATIONS MENU            9.  SUPERVISORY FUNCTIONS MENU

   4.  AMOUNT INQUIRY MENU        10.  PERIOD END MENU

   5.  STANDARD REPORTS MENU      11.  DATA BASE STATUS

   6.  VARIABLE REPORT WRITER MENU 99.  SIGN OFF


                     ENTER OPTION: _



                              NUM
```

Integrated accounting packages, such as this one from Software International Corporation, allow the user to select from a menu of available functions.

business generally kept records that pertained only to their particular area of interest. The payroll department, for example, might keep an employee's name, number, address, salary, and number of deductions to facilitate the writing of paychecks. The personnel department might keep each employee's name, employee number, salary, job title, address, employment history, and spouse's name. Each department would keep its own information independently for its own use.

Computers and computerized record keeping made it possible for the procedures and methods of recording, filing, and updating data to be converted from paper file folders and file cabinets to computer software and storage devices. These computerized files can be updated easily and also can be accessed by more than one person at a time. Project Management is an example of a file manager produced by the SAS Institute, Inc.

Other Productivity Tools

Microcomputer software vendors have developed a number of software packages to aid a computer user's productivity. Desktop organizers such as sidekick combine a number of functions into one software package. These functions are made available to the user with a single keystroke. Functions such as a notepad, calculator, calendar, and telephone dialer for modems can help to improve a computer user's productivity. Text outlines like ThinkTank are designed to allow users to quickly produce outlines. Integrated software packages such as Framework increase a user's productivity by combining a word processor, spreadsheet, file manager, and graphics package into one with a common user interface. Keyboard macro packages such as superkey can also be used by someone to increase their productivity. Keyboard macro packages allow the user to define a series of keystrokes that can be played back as if they were being typed by the user. These macros can be played back by pressing one or two keys to activate them.

■ FUNCTIONAL TOOLS

Functional tools are software packages that perform a specific function. For example, an inventory program used by a grocery store has only one purpose: to keep track of the inventory. An enormous variety of functional tools are currently available, and the number increases daily.

Businesses are the most common users of these commercial application packages. Uses for the packages include accounting, manufacturing, sales, and marketing. We will discuss some popular types of packages here.

Desktop Publishing Packages

Desktop publishing software packages allow users to create near-typeset quality documents by using a laser printer in conjunction with their computer system. Desktop publishing can be used for documents such as company newsletters that may not require the quality of a typeset document. This can result in a significant savings to organizations that would normally send documents out to be typeset. Desktop publishing software allows both text and graphics to be placed on the same page without any cutting and pasting. A typical microcomputer-based desktop publishing system with a laser printer and hard disk drive would cost between $5,000 and $12,000. This can be a very insignificant cost to a business that would spend considerably more to have documents professionally typeset and printed. Desktop publishing software packages such as Aldus Corporation's PageMaker allow a user to view exactly what the printed page will look like on the computer monitor. This is known as a "what-you-see-is-what-you-get" (WYSIWYG) page description desktop publishing software package. With recent decreases in the cost of microcomputer hardware and laser printers, desktop publishing has become a viable alternative for small companies that might require a limited amount of near-typeset quality printing. Microcomputer systems purchased for desktop publishing can also be used by small companies to run other software packages to assist in the management of the business.

Accounting Packages

Most functional packages are built-in modules. For example, in accounting, a particular package might have payroll, billing, accounts receivable, and accounts payable modules. When a company purchases a particular package, only those modules needed are obtained. Others can be added on later, if desired. Therefore, the package is tailored to individual needs. Because these modules are then integrated into an entire package, they can interact with one another, passing data between them. These packages can be customized to generate well-designed reports that meet the needs of a specific company. Balance sheets and income statements can be produced, as well as other reports. Figure 13–3 shows a screen for an accounts payable package. Such packages can generate a wide variety of output (see Figure 13–4).

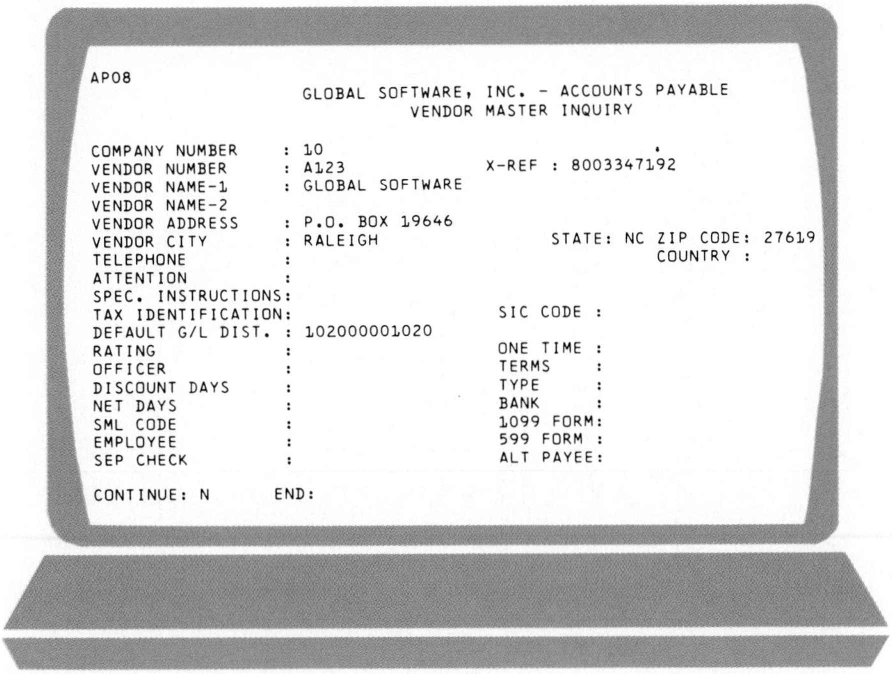

FIGURE 13–3

This screen demonstrates Global Software, Inc.'s Accounts Payable Ledger Inquiry.

```
AP08                    GLOBAL SOFTWARE, INC. - ACCOUNTS PAYABLE
                                   VENDOR MASTER INQUIRY

    COMPANY NUMBER    : 10
    VENDOR NUMBER     : A123           X-REF : 8003347192
    VENDOR NAME-1     : GLOBAL SOFTWARE
    VENDOR NAME-2     :
    VENDOR ADDRESS    : P.O. BOX 19646
    VENDOR CITY       : RALEIGH              STATE: NC ZIP CODE: 27619
    TELEPHONE         :                           COUNTRY :
    ATTENTION         :
    SPEC. INSTRUCTIONS:
    TAX IDENTIFICATION:            SIC CODE :
    DEFAULT G/L DIST. : 102000001020
    RATING            :            ONE TIME :
    OFFICER           :            TERMS    :
    DISCOUNT DAYS     :            TYPE     :
    NET DAYS          :            BANK     :
    SML CODE          :            1099 FORM:
    EMPLOYEE          :            599 FORM :
    SEP CHECK         :            ALT PAYEE:

    CONTINUE: N       END:
```

Manufacturing Packages

Manufacturing application packages, like other functional packages, tend to be composed of a number of integrated modules. The modules used depend on the needs of the particular company. In manufacturing, application packages are used to determine material requirements so that inventory needs can be projected to maintain a steady inventory of items on hand. This is important because keeping excess inventory on hand is expensive and ties up capital that could be used elsewhere. If a company maintains multiple warehouses, application packages can track down needed material, making operations run more smoothly overall and making efficient use of stock on hand.

Manufacturing resource planning (MRP) packages have been developed to meet these needs. MRP combines a variety of functions in the areas of business planning and production planning and scheduling. Such a system can maximize resources by helping to route materials efficiently; in addition, overhead is kept at a minimum because only needed inventory is kept on hand. Another important aspect of manufacturing is the scheduling of equipment and people. Often, equipment must be carefully scheduled so that it can be used in the most efficient way possible. A large amount of manufacturing time is used in setting up equipment. For example, if a lathe must be set up in a special way to turn the arms for a certain type of chair, all of the arms that will be needed over an established period of time should be cut at once.

MRP software has become popular and indeed essential because, if implemented correctly, it can save a company large amounts of money; the average return on the investment varies from 50 to 200 percent. In addition,

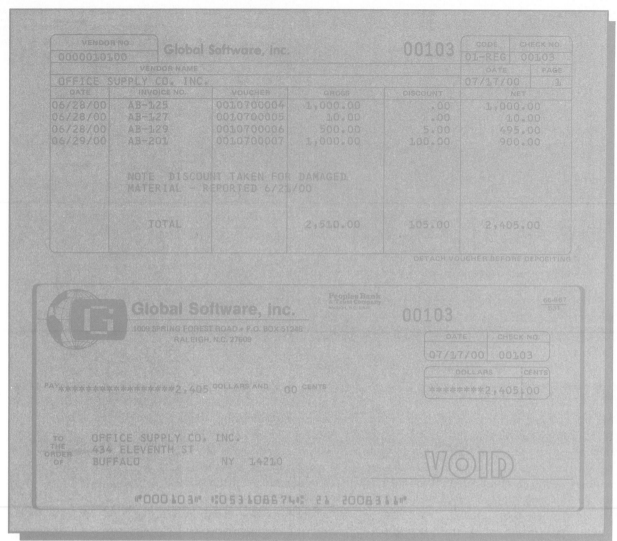

FIGURE 13—4

Global Software, Inc.'s Accounts Payable System can perform a variety of tasks such as generating correctly formatted checks.

the average MRP user reduces inventory by 17 percent, increases manufacturing productivity by 10 percent, and realizes cost reductions of approximately 7 percent.

In addition to **MRP** packages, computer-aided design (CAD), computer-aided engineering (CAE), and computer-aided manufacturing (CAM) packages have become an essential part of the overall manufacturing process. Computer-aided design allows a user to create a design for a single part or an assembly of parts by using two- or three-dimensional computer graphics. The CAD package allows an engineer or draftsman to rotate, enlarge, or quickly modify a portion of the design. These capabilities allow the user to be significantly more productive than if the design had to be created and modified using pencil and paper. Computer-aided engineering packages allow the design created by the CAD package to be tested and analyzed prior to the actual manufacture of the part or assembly. A CAE package, for example, can be used to conduct stress tests on parts that may ultimately fit into a car's suspension. Once the part or assembly has been designed and tested, a computer-aided manufacturing package can be used to actually create the end product.

CASE Packages

Computer-aided systems engineering (CASE) software packages are becoming popular with companies that develop application software. CASE software packages automate the step-by-step process of developing software by capturing the information required for each step of the process from the user. Once the information has been entered by the user, the CASE package then completes the requirements for the steps in an automated fashion. For example, some CASE packages are capable of allowing the user to design an input/output screen and then generate the program required to accept the input or display the output on the screen. CASE packages are very appealing because, in many cases, they can reduce the amount of time required to produce a particular application software package.

Sales and Marketing Packages

Sales analysis software is used to analyze data on sales transactions over a given period of time. The software generates reports stating sales made by each salesperson, quantity of sales of a particular item or in a particular region, profits, and so forth.

Another area in which sales departments commonly use application software is ordering. Excellent software packages are available to maintain order records. New orders are entered, the status of existing orders can be updated, and filled orders can be deleted. This type of package can be integrated with inventory and billing operations. For example, when an order is filled, the data concerning how much the customer owes can then be passed on to the software that performs the billing. When an order is shipped, the inventory package can be instructed to update the inventory.

Turnkey Systems

Functional tools can be aimed at either horizontal markets or vertical markets. A tool for the horizontal market would be an accounting package that was designed for general use and could therefore be used by any type of user that needed to perform general accounting tasks. Such a package would not be customized for a particular business. On the other hand, a set of application software packages to run a doctor's office is an example of a functional tool aimed at the vertical market. Such a group of packages has a very specific market, doctors' offices, and a specific purpose, helping to perform those tasks that can be computerized. Therefore, the package is designed to meet user's needs in ways that a more general package cannot.

Developing functional tools for the vertical market is a rapidly expanding field. Some software companies not only set up a complete system of integrated packages designed to meet the user's needs but also supply the necessary software. These packages, in which everything is provided for the user, including hardware, software, training, and support, are referred to as **turnkey systems.** These types of systems are very popular with small businesses that do not have the in-house expertise to locate and implement the appropriate hardware and software.

For example, a company that implements turnkey systems for dentists' offices might first determine the exact needs of a particular office and then set up a minicomputer system that will be capable of efficiently running the needed application packages such as scheduling, billing, storing patient records, and generating needed reports. This provides a single integrated system that is designed to meet a variety of needs in a specific situation.

Ortho-Track is one company that has designed a specific system for use in orthodontists' offices. Not only does Ortho-Track provide the hardware and software for the business, it also provides on-site training when the system is first implemented and a telephone hotline to handle later questions or problems. The software used by this system, like that for other systems, is modularized. Therefore, the office personnel can choose only those modules that are suited to their needs. The user can also customize the way in which output is displayed on the screen. The Ortho-Track system is typical of many of the systems aimed at the vertical market. The number of companies providing this type of specialized service is growing daily.

■ END-USER DEVELOPMENT TOOLS

End-user development tools (also referred to as **fourth-generation software development tools**) are software packages that allow a user to develop a software application to meet the specific needs of a particular situation. There are several reasons why end-users may choose to develop their own package rather than to buy a commercial package. Sometimes the user's needs are highly specialized; therefore the market for such a package is small and an appropriate one may not be available. In addition, by developing its own package, a company can tailor the software to the exact needs of the particular situation. There is a wide variety of end-user development tools on the market, including simulation software, statistical packages, decision support systems, and data-base management systems.

Creating a software package using these tools requires little skill. Often development tools allow users to solve problems that ordinarily would require the attention of data processing departments. This frees users from dependency upon data processing departments and is an important advantage in many companies where the data processing department may have a backlog of projects.

Fourth-generation programming languages, or query languages as they are often called, are used with these end-user development tools. The end-user can quickly learn to use these languages because they are similar to English. These languages allow managers to manipulate corporate data in a fast, friendly, flexible way. The user must learn the necessary commands and syntax, but because the statements are similar to English, they require little time or skill to learn.

Simulation Software

People establish theories based on what they observe and measure in reality. Models are then built to test the theory to see if it is correct. If the model works properly, it can be used for **simulation,** which is the use of a model to project what could possibly happen in a particular situation. A simple example of this process would be the development of a formula for converting Fahrenheit temperatures to Celsius. The reality is that any given temperature can be stated in terms of both the Fahrenheit and the Celsius scales. Therefore, a theory could be proposed that because these two scales are based on an absolute value (temperature), it should be possible to come up with a formula to convert a temperature stated in one scale to the other. Once a theory has been created, a model can be developed. One way of developing a model is to take a range of Fahrenheit and Celsius temperatures and determine the relationship. From this a model could be stated:

$$\text{Celsius} = \frac{5}{9} \times (\text{Fahrenheit} - 32)$$

If this model consistently yields correct results when used in simulation, it can be assumed to be reasonably accurate; if not, the model will have to be altered accordingly. After it has been shown that using the model in simulation consistently yields accurate results, it is no longer necessary to check the results against reality. Therefore, results are considered accurate simply by using the model. Concept Summary 13–1 explains the relationship between reality and simulation.

CONCEPT SUMMARY 13—1

Illustration of Relationship between Reality and Simulation	
Reality	The temperature of a given entity can be determined using either the Fahrenheit or Celsius scales
Theory	A specific, consistent correlation exists between these two scales; therefore, it should be possible to convert a temperature stated in one scale to its corresponding temperature in the other scale
Model	The proposed formula: Celsius = 5/9 × (Fahrenheit − 32)
Simulation	Convert a temperature in one scale to its equivalent in the other scale; after extensive testing, if these conversions are continually consistent with reality, the simulation can be assumed to be accurate

Simulation is particularly useful in making business decisions. For example, if a manager needs to know how cost-effective building a new plant would be, a simulation package can help in making such a decision. Usually such software makes use of a wide variety of information stored in the company's data base to arrive at a conclusion.

An example of a general-purpose simulation software package is GPSS (General Purpose Simulation System), developed by IBM. This package allows the user to establish variables and then alter the relationships between the variables. The software package will determine how these alterations will affect output.

DECISION SUPPORT SYSTEMS. Decision support systems (DSS) help managers to make and implement decisions. These software packages are capable of obtaining data from a wide variety of sources such as different departments within a company; they allow the user to analyze this data on an interactive basis. These systems also generally include a number of productivity tools that were previously discussed, such as graphics packages and spreadsheets. What makes the decision support system unique is the way in which these tools are integrated into a highly sophisticated package. Such systems are widely used by financial institutions, oil companies, automobile manufacturers, and other similar industries. The theory behind decision support systems will be discussed in detail in Chapter 15; our emphasis here is on the software used to implement these systems. Decision support systems use fourth-generation languages to query data bases to obtain necessary information; in addition they can be used to simulate specified conditions to determine the output of a particular situation. An example of such a system is the SAS System, developed by SAS, Inc. It is an integrated decision support system that includes 125 procedures including spreadsheets, statistical analysis, and decision support. Sophisticated graphics and report-generating features allow the output to be attractively displayed or printed. Figure 13–5 demonstrates the SAS System, which can also be used as a statistical package. (Statistical packages will be discussed later in this chapter.)

There are a number of application software packages available that allow the manager to interactively probe a computerized model for results concerning various decision alternatives. These packages include MARKET-PLAN and BRANDAID, which help in preparing marketing plans; CALL-

FIGURE 13—5

The results generated by the SAS decision support system can be displayed in a variety of ways, including easy-to-understand graphs.

PLAN and DETAILER, which aid in the allocation of a sales force; and MEDIAC, which helps to prepare advertising media schedules.

Another package is the Interactive Financial Planning System (IFPS). IFPS is an interactive planning package that centers around a model based on a manager's perception of the real-world system. Marketed by EXECUCOM Systems Corporation, IFPS can be considered a generalized planning or modeling system. As a generalized system, IFPS can be used for such applications as balance sheet and income statement preparation, operating budgets, forecasting, strategic planning, risk analysis, and capital budgeting. Because IFPS does not incorporate a specific model, it offers management a great deal of flexibility. See Figure 13–6 as an illustration of the decision support aspect of IFPS.

▨ EXPERT SYSTEMS

Expert systems are built using what is known of the human thought processes to mimic the decision-making processes of human experts in narrowly defined fields. Software designers try to program the computer to follow the same path of thinking as top experts in the specified field. Expert systems are different from decision support systems in that they only cover very small fields of knowledge; decision support systems attempt to allow managers to make decisions based on a wide range of data and factors (see Figure 13–7).

The heart of the system is a knowledge base that contains facts and rules used by experts. The user asks questions of the system through the use of fourth-generation programming languages. When responding to these questions, the expert system draws on its knowledge base.

Although the quality of these systems is growing rapidly, as yet they are unable to make the type of sophisticated inferences that a human expert

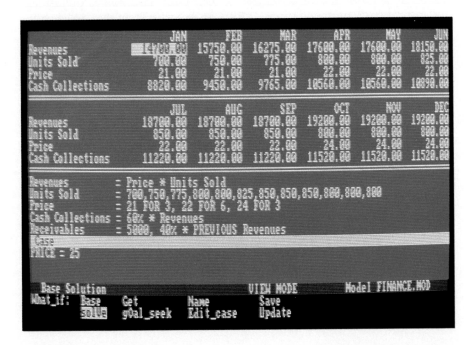

FIGURE 13–6

The What-If? feature of IFPS enables the user to calculate the effect of changes on selected values to the remaining values with a single menu selection.

FIGURE 13—7

IRA Master from Fogle Computing Corp. is an expert system used for investment purposes.

```
                    IRA MASTER MENU


   ENTER TRAN ID ■


   IMAS   LOGON/LOGOFF/CH DATE    IPOS   POST TRANSACTIONS
   IEDP   EDIT PARTICIPANT REC     IPNA   ADD REPEATING TRANS
   IEDI   EDIT INVESTMENT REC      IPNI   REPEATING INQUIRY
   IEDT   EDIT TRANSACTION REC     IPNR   REPEATING RELEASE
   IEDA   ADD INVESTMENT           IPRT   POST REPEATING
   INQP   PARTICIPANT INQUIRY      IPRE   PROFILE EDIT
   INQI   INVESTMENT INQUIRY       IPRO   PROFILE INQUIRY
   INQT   TRANSACTION INQUIRY      I002   DAILY SUMMARY REPORT
   IFND   FIND SS# BY NAME         INAC   ADD NEW PARTICIPANT
   ICSS   CHANGE SOCIAL SEC #      IPNE   EDIT REPEATING TRANS
```

can make. Nonetheless, expert systems offer a number of advantages over human experts. For example, knowledge is not lost as it may be when a human expert dies or moves to another job.

One expert system is MYCIN, which is used to diagnose infectious diseases and recommend appropriate drugs. Another interesting expert system is XCON, developed by J. McDermott, at Carnegie-Mellon University, which is used to determine the best configuration of Digital Equipment Corporation (DEC) minicomputer system components for a particular user. PROSPECTOR is an expert system that helps geologists in locating mineral deposits. Taxadvisor, developed by R. Michaelsen at the University of Illinois, helps users with estate planning. It determines ways in which the client can minimize income and death taxes and also makes investment and insurance recommendations. ILPRS, an expert system that assists businesses in long-range planning, and IPPMS, an expert system that assists businesses in managing projects, are expert systems developed by DEC. More expert systems in every conceivable field are being designed all the time. Typically, there are three approaches to the use of expert systems:

1. You can write your own expert system using programming languages such as LISP or PROLOG.
2. You can use an expert system shell such as VP-EXPERT, Level 5, Goldworks, or Exsys to develop an expert system. Expert system shells can be used to develop a customized expert system.
3. You can purchase an expert system from a software vendor. The Taxadvisor would be an example of an expert system sold by a software vendor.

Statistical Packages

An interesting application of prewritten software packages is in the area of statistics. Before the advent of these packages, scientists and statisticians spent many hours analyzing data, using calculators and complex mathematical formulas. Today, elaborate statistical procedures can be performed accurately and quickly with the aid of **statistical packages.** The user must write a simple program that then generates the needed statistics, but because the program is written in a fourth-generation language, these packages are easy for people with no programming experience to use. Three commonly used statistical packages are SAS (Statistical Analysis System), SPSS (Statistical Package for the Social Sciences), and Minitab. These packages can provide a wide variety of arithmetic and trigonometric functions. In addition, statistical functions calculating means, ranges, variances, and standard deviations, as well as more complicated statistics, are easily performed.

To use a statistical package, the user must write a program in a fourth-generation programming language designed specifically for that package. Figure 13–8 shows a sample SAS program and its output. In addition to performing a wide variety of statistical operations, SAS also allows the user to determine how the output will be printed. Statistical packages are often included as part of a decision support system, thereby allowing managers to analyze data as desired.

Data-base Management Systems

Data-base management systems (DBMS) consist of a series of programs that are used to design and maintain data bases. A data-base management system is more complex than a file manager because programs can be developed to access the data base in a variety of ways.

For example, if the accounting department accessed employee records contained in a data base, the records could be displayed in a way that was most convenient for their needs. Also, only the information needed by the accounting department would be displayed. On the other hand, a different program could be written to access the same employee records for the personnel department. This program would display only the information needed by personnel.

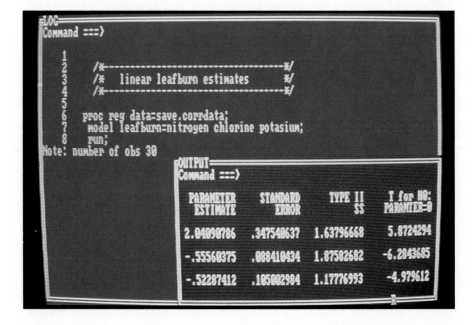

FIGURE 13–8

SAS/STAT® software performs simple and complex statistical analysis.

HIGHLIGHT

Expert Systems

One of the standard questions asked when a new computer technology is applied to business is "Will it put people out of work?" This same question is now being asked about companies who are using expert systems. Expert systems are presently being used by banks to help judge loan applications. Federal Express uses an expert system to assess credit card transactions. The airlines are another business now using expert systems; they use them for such operations as assigning gates for incoming flights. For example, United Airlines uses an expert system to assign gates at O'Hare Airport in Chicago.

So far, users of expert systems say they have not eliminated staff, although they have redefined positions. In other words, the positions are reassessed so that the expert system performs simple functions and the worker is able to concentrate on more challenging tasks. In the future, expert systems will continue to be applied to simple decision-making tasks, and this may cut down on the number of lower level jobs. But as many professionals point out, the system will never be able to replace the complicated thinking of real life experts!

Data-base management systems are divided into three categories depending on the way in which data contained in them is stored. The categories, which were explained in Chapter 7, are hierarchical, network, and relational. The oldest data-base structure is the hierarchical structure. An example of a hierarchical data base is IMS, which was developed by IBM and has been widely used for some time. A commonly used network data base is DBMS-20.

When using hierarchical or network systems, programs called **schemas** are written that determine the manner in which the records stored in the data base will be related to one another. These schemas are written in a **data definition language (DDL).** Once the DDL is written, a program written in a **data manipulation language (DML)** accesses the data base defined by the DDL. In these programs, data manipulation language statements are embedded in another language, such as COBOL. Therefore, writing a program to access a hierarchial or network data base requires a significant amount of programming skill.

On the other hand, when using a relational data base, the user simply accesses the data base directly through the use of a fourth-generation language. The American National Standards Institute (ANSI) has approved SQL (Structured Query Language) as the standard fourth-generation language to query relational data bases. Three relational data bases currently available are DB2, developed by IBM; ORACLE, developed by Oracle Corporation; and INGRES, developed by Relational Technology. All of these data bases can be queried by using the fourth-generation language SQL. Data bases provide an enormous amount of flexibility in allowing users to access data in a wide variety of ways.

CONCEPT SUMMARY 13—2

Categories of Application Software Packages

Category	Explanation	Examples
Productivity tools	Used to increase user productivity	Text processor Graphics package Spreadsheet File Manager
Functional tools	Perform a specific purpose	Payroll Billing Accounts receivable Inventory control Manufacturing resource planning
End-user development tools	Allow the end-user to develop software tailored to a specific situation, often through the use of a fourth-generation programming language	Decision support system (DSS) Data-base management system (DBMS)

COMPUTERS AND INFORMATION PROCESSING

■ CHOOSING AN APPLICATION SOFTWARE PACKAGE

The user who needs to decide whether to buy a commercial application package or to develop the needed software system in-house is facing a difficult decision. Some of the questions that should be asked are:

■ Does the data processing department have the needed system analysts and/or programmers with the needed skills to develop the package in-house?
■ Is there commercial application software that can meet the stated needs (or at least be easily modified to meet these needs)?
■ Will the appropriate commercial software run on the available computer system?
■ Is there adequate documentation?
■ Will the vendor or manufacturer provide the needed support?
■ Is there time available to write the software in-house, or is obtaining a package that can be quickly implemented a critical factor?

If after carefully considering the above factors it has been decided to purchase a commercial application package, it then must be determined which package will best meet the user's needs. If possible, the user should arrange to try the package on a trial basis to determine how well it will work day in, day out. Another source of information on the quality of application software is user surveys. Several publications conduct such surveys on a regular basis. For example, *DATAMATION* conducts a yearly survey of data processing managers called the Applications Software Survey, asking them to evaluate packages they are using. The results of this survey can be a very helpful guide in choosing software. According to *DATAMATION*, there are four areas of primary concern in evaluating these packages: performance, operations, I/O functionality, and vendor support. Performance is concerned with such factors as the efficiency of hardware utilization and the ease of use. I/O functionality covers data entry provisions and how quickly and easily output format changes can be made. The applications software packages covered in the survey fall into business categories such as general accounting, payroll and personnel, and business management and forecasting.

When choosing application software packages, customers often turn to resources within their specific field. Another method of evaluating application packages is simply word-of-mouth. Company management within a specific industry often have frequent contact with management in similar companies and can ask these people what types of packages they are using and how they would evaluate the performance of the software.

Probably the best method of choosing a package is to use a number of them on a trial basis to determine how each will actually perform on the job. Because the application package will probably be used for some time to come, the time spent in making an informed choice is well spent.

■ SUMMARY POINTS

■ The use of commercially written application software packages has increased dramatically in recent years. Such packages have a number of advantages over software written in-house, including generally lower cost, faster implementation, better quality, and reliability. There are some disadvantages, however, including the fact that a commercial package may not meet the user's needs as precisely as one developed in-house. Also, the user is dependent upon the vendor or the developer for support.

■ Application software can be divided into three broad categories: productivity tools, functional tools, and end-user development tools.

■ Productivity tools are packages that can be used in a wide variety of ways to increase the productivity of the user. Examples are word processors, graphics packages, spreadsheets, and file managers.

■ Functional tools perform a specific function or purpose. Functional packages are generally built from modules so that they can be customized to meet the user's needs. Accounting packages produce payrolls, balance sheets, and income statements. Desktop publishing packages are used to produce near-typeset quality printed documents. Manufacturing resource planning (MRP) packages are commonly used in manufacturing to handle inventory and schedule employees and equipment efficiently. In sales and marketing, software packages keep track of order status and generate sales reports.

■ Turnkey systems are popular with small businesses. Companies specializing in these systems supply the user with a complete package, including hardware, software, training of staff, and on-going support. Because the software is usually modularized, it can be customized easily to meet the user's needs.

■ End-user development tools allow the end-user to use fourth-generation programming languages to develop an application package to exact specifications. Fourth-generation programming languages are more English-like than high-level languages such as COBOL and require only a short period of time to learn.

■ Simulation software uses a model to project what will happen in a particular situation. Decision support systems help managers to make and implement decisions. They obtain data from a wide variety of sources, most commonly data bases. In addition, they incorporate a wide variety of packages such as graphics and spreadsheets. IFPS is a decision support system that allows the user to manipulate variables to determine how various results will be affected.

■ Expert systems attempt to mimic the decision-making processes of experts in narrowly-defined fields. These systems use a knowledge base to answer questions posed by the user.

■ Statistical packages quickly and accurately perform statistical analysis of data. SAS, SPSS, and Minitab are three examples of statistical packages.

■ Data-base management systems consist of a series of programs that are used to design and maintain data bases. When using hierarchical or network data bases, a data definition language (DDL) must be used to write a program that determines how the data base is organized. Then programs are written in data manipulation languages (DML) that allow the user to access the data base. The end-user can then access the data base through the use of a fourth-generation language. Relational data bases do not require the use of data definition languages or data manipulation languages. These data bases can be accessed directly by using fourth-generation languages.

■ When choosing an application package, many factors must be taken into account. Some of them are: (1) Can the package be written by the company's data processing department? Are the needed analysts and programmers available? (2) Is there a commercial package available that can meet the stated need and will this package run on the available computer system?

(3) Is there adequate documentation for the commercial software and will the vendor or manufacturer supply the needed support? (4) Is there time to develop the package in-house?

■ If a company decides to buy a commercial package, a particular package must be chosen. User surveys conducted by magazines and journals are one helpful method of determining if current users are satisfied with their software. Another method is to ask other companies in the same field how happy they are with the software they are using. But using the software on a trial basis is the best test of how well it will perform in a particular setting.

■ REVIEW QUESTIONS

1. What are some advantages of using commercially written application software? What are some disadvantages?

2. Into what three categories can application software be placed?

3. Explain what is meant by the term *productivity tool* and give three examples.

4. What is the difference between functional tools aimed at the vertical market and those aimed at the horizontal market?

5. List some functional tools commonly used in business.

6. Give a definition of simulation software.

7. What is an expert system? Why might such a system be preferable to a human expert? Why not?

8. What is the purpose of statistical packages? Name two commonly used statistical packages.

9. What is a data definition language?

10. Name some factors that should be considered when choosing an application software package.

Chase Manhattan

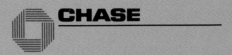

The Chase Manhattan Corporation started out in 1799 as a New York City water company, the brainchild of Aaron Burr. Through Burr's lobbying in the New York State Legislature, the company was permitted to use capital not required in the water business in other money transactions or operations. Thus on Sept. 1, 1799, the Bank of the Manhattan Company broke the monopoly of Alexander Hamilton's federal institution, The Bank of the United States.

In 1955 the Chase Manhattan Bank was formed by a merger between Chase National, the nation's third largest bank, and the Bank of The Manhattan Company, the fifteenth largest.

From its earliest days, the Bank of The Manhattan Company supported the nation's economic development. The bank made its first ship construction loan in 1805. It frequently financed East India trade in the early 1800s. It provided major funding for the construction of the Erie Canal.

In the years following World War II, Chase solidified its position as the bank to corporate America, and the bank's retail branch capabilities continued to grow. In the 1950s Chase developed one of the first corporate computer facilities. Then, in 1961, Chase installed a fully automated check processing and demand deposit accounting computer system, the first of its kind in New York City.

Today Chase is a global wholesale and consumer financial institution doing business in more than 100 countries. Quality—in people, products and technology—make Chase a recognized leader and innovator worldwide, providing corporations and individuals with superior products and service.

INVESTMENT BANKING BECOMES ELECTRONIC

Like many money-center institutions, Chase Manhattan is reaching beyond its breadth as a commercial bank and entering the investment banking and securities arena. And just as Chase created electronic products that supported traditional commercial banking activities, it's now looking to make the transactions of its new businesses electronic also.

The banks that will thrive in the global financial marketplace will be those which can provide lending, investment banking, and securities capabilities to their customers. Toward that end, Chase formed the Financial and Securities Products Division to be responsible for building and selling electronic investment banking and securities products. Formerly the banking component of Interactive Data Corporation, which was recently divested, the unit employs systems builders, product managers and marketing personnel. While many large banks have built similar investment banking securities products, Chase is one of the few currently selling these products for use directly to its customers as part of an overall service products market offering.

In the investment banking area, the Financial and Securities Products Division now sells two asset/liability management (ALM) tools or products used to manage interest rate risk exposure. ALM began as an issue for financial institutions and it has become an issue for corporations as well. Chase developed a Banking Risk Management System (BRMS) which provided the ability to evaluate an almost unlimited number of interest rate scenarios, pricing/volume strategies, interest rate swaps, options, and financial futures. In addition, Chase developed a system called Duration which calculates the effect of interest rate fluctuations on the market value of an instrument, on a portfolio of instruments, on an institution's equity and on net interest income. Duration helps identify the profit/loss implications of buying and selling financial instruments as well as optimizes the timing of such actions through understanding the cost/benefit of various hedging strategies.

Both Duration and BRMS were originally developed on Chase's mainframe computers for internal use. Recently, both systems have been redesigned to operate on personal computers (microBRMS and Chase Duration) and being marketed successfully to financial institutions of all sizes—from the smallest savings associations through the largest commercial banks, finance companies, building societies, and investment banks.

The Chase Electronics Swaps System (CHESS), another risk-management product, was developed by the division for the Chase Manhattan Capital Markets Corp. The possibility of broadening that system to encompass other interest rate hedgings such as futures and options is also being explored.

The division was also responsible for developing a corporate finance analysis tool called the Chase Financial Reporting System, or ChaseFRS, a product that has been adopted as a standard corporate finance credit analysis vehicle throughout the Global Bank. The system analyzes the forecasts and the financial needs and conditions of industrial corporations.

CHASE SYSTEMS ARCHITECTURE

At many major banks, the byword today is integration. For large global organizations such as banks, system integration is a necessity, requiring a technological infrastructure that provides for the rapid exchange of information across all products and markets. At Chase Manhattan Bank the integration is taking place against a long-term commitment to decentralization.

Chase employs over 5,000 information systems people in approximately 100 separate data-processing centers around the world and many times that number of products and systems of all sizes and makes. Since the mid-1970s, responsibility for these people and computers have been distributed among the various business units. This brought systems and business people closer together, making it possible for technology to become an integral part of many of the bank's lines of business and for individual business units to make the technology trade-offs they deemed worthwhile. The challenge today is finding the balance between the need for integration and the traditional independence of the business units.

In attempting to achieve that balance Chase has adopted a systems architecture model composed of four major components: Communications, Applications, Data, and Operating Environment. The objectives of adopting this architecture are:

■ Simple Access to Information and Processing Resources
■ Multi Vendor Systems Interoperability

■ Increased Cost Efficiency
■ Protection of Chase's Existing Systems Investment
■ User Sovereignty in Choosing Implementations
■ Data Integrity
■ Improvement of Development Productivity
■ Use of Universal Applications Tools

The benefits from this systems architecture approach will be realized over time as it is implemented in the operating units. Those benefits include the following:

■ Reduced development and maintenance costs for networking software and hardware.
■ Productivity, quality, and throughput improvements resulting from integrated information capabilities.

■ Improved use of scarce development resources resulting from the ability to concentrate on development of the application versus development of the tools.
■ More flexibility to change because of less customization.
■ Shorter development lead times.

The development and implementation of this systems architecture will be carried on over the next few years. It will be evolutionary rather than revolutionary and will serve as a guide for how systems being developed are to be integrated into an overall Chase systems network.

DISCUSSION POINTS

1. How is computer software integrated into Chase's marketing strategy for financial services?
2. Describe the philosophy behind the Chase model for systems architecture.

CHAPTER

14

System Analysis and Design

OUTLINE

Introduction
System Analysis
  Reasons for Conducting System
    Analysis
  Data Gathering
  Data Analysis
  System Analysis Report
System Design
  Reviewing Goals and Objectives
  Developing a System Model
  Evaluating Organizational
    Constraints

  Developing Alternative Designs
  Performing Feasibility Analysis
  Performing Cost/Benefit Analysis
  Preparing the Design Report
System Programming
  Programming
  Testing
  Documentation
  Special Considerations
System Implementation
  Personnel Training
  Conversion

System Audit and Review
  Evaluating System Performance
  Making Modifications and
    Improvements
  Responding to Change
Prototyping
Summary Points
Review Questions

Expert System Cuts Diagnosis Time

Michael Alexander
Computerworld

When a child in elementary school is having difficulty learning to read, it may not be because he has a bad attitude or disability. It may be because he is hungry. But some teachers may not recognize the problem for what it is and instead refer the child to a special education program.

"The teachers are overwhelmed, and special education is one of the few places to get help for getting these kids out of the classroom," explained Jacqueline Haynes, a researcher at Intelligent Automation in Rockville, Md.

Haynes is also the developer of an expert system called Computer-Assisted Planning for Educational Resources, or CAPER, designed to help elementary school teachers and administrators more accurately diagnose pupils and plan instructional programs for them.

"CAPER was developed to help children who are educationally at risk, including those who are having trouble adjusting to mainstream American schools; who are culturally different from many of their classmates; and who are not proficient English speakers," Haynes said.

Schools are devoting considerable resources and personnel to administrative and referral meetings to determine whether a particular child should be placed in a special education setting. Administrators often discover that if the teacher is unable to work with children with limited English proficiency or socioeconomic problems, he is apt to recommend that the children be placed in special education just to get rid of them.

Helping Educators

"Too often, many of these kids are referred for special education and identified as handicapped because teachers and school administrators do not have the knowledge or time to analyze complex individual situations and determine the best instructional plan for each student," Haynes said. "We saw the opportunity to build an expert system that would deliver reliable information and sound recommendations to elementary school personnel."

The expert system, which was developed using the Knowledge Engineering System from Software Architecture and Engineering, reduced the number of administrative and referral meetings in one school by more than 50% and received rave reviews from school administrators and faculty members, Haynes said.

CAPER is a family of 14 expert systems, each with two components. The first component, the problem analyzer, defines the pupil's problem in the classroom setting.

"The problem may be that the student does not speak English, is impoverished, does not read well, is not motivated, does not do homework or is withdrawn," Haynes explained. "It can be hard to figure out what the problem is [without CAPER], particularly because standard tests are not valid for students that do not speak English. In fact, the tests are not valid for the student who is not a native speaker."

The Strategic Selector

The second component, called the strategic selector, offers suggestions for resolving the problem as well as guidelines for steps to take in the referral process. Sometimes the solution may be as simple as recommending a change in seating assignments so that students are seated with more compatible classmates or recommending a reading program that includes oral discussion.

"The system may make the teacher aware that if the child is very inattentive in class that hunger could be the problem," Haynes said, "or alerts the teacher that the child may be acting this way because it is normal in this child's culture. A lot of emotional problems are due to cultural differences, and the system sensitizes the teacher to this fact."

No Cure-All

The system does not handle every sort of problem; it is designed to resolve problems related to reading, classroom behavior and language and cultural differences. Problem-solving components for math, study skills or motor skills, for example, will be added later if additional funding can be found to develop the system further.

Haynes and her colleagues began developing CAPER in October 1985 after receiving a grant for funding from the U.S. Department of Education. Work on the project began when Haynes was a research associate with the Institute for the Study of Exceptional Children and Youth at the University of Maryland's Department of Special Education.

During the first year, the CAPER team validated and tested modules of the expert system with teachers, administrators and other education experts. The completed system was installed at test sites in elementary schools in the Washington, D.C., area in January. The system, which can be configured for the characteristics and educational objectives of different schools, is also currently undergoing testing at school systems in Pennsylvania.

CAPER runs on an IBM Personal Computer XT or faster class of personal computer with 640K bytes of random-access memory and a hard disk drive. One advantage of using Knowledge Engineering System as the shell for developing this and other expert systems is that it can be ported to a wide variety of platforms ranging from PCs to mainframes.

Expert systems must be customized to a specific problem in order to effectively weigh the variables of the problem. Expert systems have been developed not only for business but for other areas, such as medicine and education, as well. Often the design of a good expert system requires the collaboration of a system expert and content expert—in this case, an educator.

INTRODUCTION

In computer-based information systems, the hardware and software technologies discussed in earlier chapters are applied as tools for the collection, storage, and retrieval of information that is either helpful to management or required for routine business practices. Information that is helpful to management might include sales analyses, while information that is required for normal business practices might include payroll processing or income tax reporting. It is necessary to understand the hardware and software technologies in order to develop an effective management information system.

This chapter focuses on how hardware and software technologies are used in the development of computer-based information systems and explains the various phases involved in designing and implementing such systems. Topics covered include system analysis, design, programming, implementation, and audit and review.

SYSTEM ANALYSIS

The first step of **system analysis** is to formulate a statement of overall business objectives—the goals of the system. Identifying these objectives is essential to the identification of information the system will require. The next step is for the analyst to acquire a general understanding of the scope of the analysis.

CHAPTER

14

By viewing the system from the top down, the analyst determines on what level the analysis should be conducted. Figure 14–1, for example, illustrates the potential levels at which analysis could be conducted for a company's marketing information system. Other information systems such as an accounting information system or a personnel information system may also exist within a company's organizational information system. The level at which the analysis should be conducted should be agreed upon with management and reviewed in the form of a proposal to conduct a system analysis. The proposal should provide management with the following:

■ A clear and concise statement of the problem or reason for the system analysis.
■ A statement clearly defining the level of the system analysis and its objectives.
■ An identification of the information that must be collected and the potential sources of this information.
■ A preliminary schedule for conducting the analysis.

The proposal ensures that management knows what resources will be required during the system analysis. It also helps the system user to make sure the analyst has identified the problems correctly and understands what the analysis should accomplish. Because system analysis is costly and time consuming, the scope of the analysis should be clarified in this way before the analyst continues.

Once the proposal has been accepted, the analysis can proceed. Data relevant to decision makers' information needs is gathered and analyzed. When the analysis is completed, the analyst communicates the findings to management in the **system analysis report.** On the basis of this report, management decides whether or not to continue with the next step in system development—system design.

Reasons for Conducting System Analysis

System analysis is performed for various reasons, which determine its scope or magnitude. An analysis may be required because of a need to solve a problem, as a response to new information requirements, as a method of incorporating new technology into a system, or as a means of making broad system improvements. The gathering and analyzing of data occur at different levels of intensity, depending upon the scope of the analysis. The reasons for conducting system analysis are discussed in the following sections.

SOLVING A PROBLEM. Sometimes information systems that do not function properly require adjustment. Perhaps a particular manager is not getting a report at the time it is needed, or an insufficient number of copies of a certain report are being printed, or the information a report provides is incorrect, or the information system is not effective in helping the company's management run the business.

In attempting to solve problems like these, the analyst may find that the effort expands into broad system improvements. One problem may lead to another, which may then lead to another, and so forth. Because this snowball effect frequently occurs, it is important for the analyst to determine the

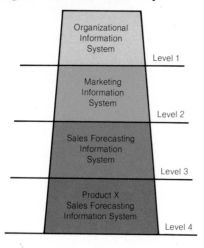

FIGURE 14–1

Top-Down View of an Organization's Information System

scope of the system analysis at the outset of the project, as described earlier. Analysts must use discretion and discipline in solving the problem at hand.

RESPONDING TO NEW REQUIREMENTS. Information systems should be designed to be flexible so changes can be made easily. Unfortunately, it is often difficult to anticipate future information needs; new requirements more often than not cause changes that require a new system analysis. For example, oil companies have experienced a series of changes in government regulations in recent years. Passage of the windfall profits tax followed by the earlier-than-expected deregulation of domestic oil prices created instant headaches for the companies and instant projects for system analysts. Information systems, especially for the accounting departments, had to be updated very rapidly in order to comply with new laws.

There are other areas in which government regulations have affected business information systems. Personnel is one of those areas; regulations governing hiring and firing practices are constantly changing. Another area affected by government regulations is privacy. New laws designed to protect the rights of citizens mandate that more and more information must be kept confidential.

New requirements also originate from nongovernment sources. A company may add a new product line, necessitating a whole new series of reports. A new labor agreement may require additional benefits and deductions or a different way of calculating base pay.

IMPLEMENTING NEW TECHNOLOGY. The introduction of new data-processing technology can cause major changes in information systems. Many companies started with punched-card, batch-processing environments. When magnetic tape became available, larger files could be processed and more information could be stored. The introduction of magnetic-disk technology opened up direct-access processing, causing major changes to information systems in the late 1960s. New input devices such as visual display terminals began to replace paper forms and punched cards for data entry.

In banking alone, the introduction of MICR (magnetic-ink character recognition) technology eliminated thousands of bookkeeping jobs because it allowed electronic posting of entries to accounts instead of manual posting. In grocery stores and other retail stores, bar-code readers and optical-character readers are being combined with point-of-sale devices to dramatically change internal accounting and checkout procedures. There are dozens of other ways in which new technology has led to changes in information systems. We could list many other examples, but the important thing to remember is that changes in technology often lead to changes in information systems.

MAKING BROAD SYSTEM IMPROVEMENTS. There may be times when an organization wants to update its entire information system. An increase in size or sales volume may make such a change necessary. Competition from a rival may provide an incentive to improve efficiency.

One example of a broad system improvement is the introduction and use of online ticketing by major airlines. As soon as the first company converted to this new method, other airlines had to follow suit to remain competitive. The new method forced changes in the airlines' entire accounting and reservations systems.

During the boom years of the 1950s and 1960s numerous companies discovered that their information systems were out of date because of mergers and acquisitions. Many companies found that it was advantageous to update their entire information systems rather than to just keep patching them.

A broad system improvement normally requires an extensive system analysis because it has a very broad scope.

Data Gathering

After the proposal to conduct system analysis has been accepted, the analyst sets out to gather data. The type and amount of data gathered depends upon the scope and goal of the system analysis. Data can be supplied by internal and external sources.

INTERNAL SOURCES. Some common sources of internal information are interviews, observations, system flowcharts, questionnaires, and formal reports. A brief description of each source follows.

Interviews. Personal interviews can be a very important source of data. Preliminary interviews provide data about current operations and procedures as well as the users' perception of what the system should do. The analyst must be diplomatic yet probing. Often during an interview the analyst discovers informal information in the form of reports, personal notes, and phone numbers that indicates how the current information system really works. Without interviews, these "extras" might never appear.

Observation. When an analyst is gathering data on an existing information system, observation can be used both to confirm data already obtained and to gather data on aspects of the system for which none exists. By observing an existing information system's data flow, a system analyst can gather data about the system on a first-hand basis.

System Flowcharts. After gathering the documents that provide the system input, the analyst turns to the system flowchart to identify the processing steps used in the system. Devices and files used in the system, the resulting output, and the departments that use the output are identified. (A more detailed discussion of system flowcharts will appear later in this chapter.)

Questionnaires. Questionnaires are used to collect details about system operations. By keying questions to specific steps in a system flowchart, the analyst can obtain detailed data on the volume of input and output. Information such as the frequency of processing, the time required for various processing steps, and the personnel used can also be identified.

Questionnaires are useful only if they are properly constructed. Further, the analyst must be careful to take note of who filled out a particular questionnaire; a manager might respond differently from an employee. The analyst must also be sure to follow up if a questionnaire is not returned (see Figure 14–2).

FIGURE 14—2

Sample Questionnaire

TITLE   *Report Analysis—Batch Payroll Report*
NUMBER   *378-Batch-Pay*
PURPOSE   *To determine demand for and timing of Batch Payroll Report*

1. Do you currently receive, or would you like to receive, the Payroll Report?
   ☐Yes   If yes, please answer the remaining questions.
   ☐No   If no, please go to the end of the questionnaire.

2. How often would you like to receive the Payroll Report?
   ☐Weekly   ☐Quarterly   ☐Annually
   ☐Monthly   ☐Semiannually

3. What would you be using the report for?
   ☐Department budgeting of payroll expenses
   ☐General information only
   ☐Other _____

4. How do you rank this report in relation to other reports you receive?
   ☐Above average   ☐Average   ☐Below average

5. Do you require more payroll information than is contained on the report?
   ☐Yes   ☐No
   If yes, please list the additional information you require:

6. Please indicate any other information that would be useful in revising or updating
   the Payroll Report.

   _____

   _____

                              Thank you for your cooperation.

Signed _____ Title _____

Department _____ Date _____

Formal Reports. Formal reports, the major output of many systems, should be studied carefully by the analyst (see Figure 14–3). The processing steps taken to convert data to information usually become apparent when these reports are examined. The number of copies of each report made and the people who receive them helps to identify the flow of information within an organization. Where and how a report is stored may indicate the degree of sensitivity and the importance of the information it contains. The advent of inexpensive paper copiers makes the task of determining all users of a particular report extremely difficult. The ease with which copies are made can be a disadvantage.

EXTERNAL SOURCES. Systems analysts should examine external sources of information during the data-gathering stage. Standard external sources

FIGURE 14-3

Example of a Formal Report

GB ELECTRIC AND GAS COMPANY			
PAYROLL REPORT			
NOVEMBER, 1989			

12/21/89   PAGE   2

DEPT. NO.	ID	EMPLOYEE	HOURS	GROSS PAY	TAX	NET PAY
---------	--	----------	------	-----------	----	--------
1	12345	BUXBAUM, ROBERT	75.0	$ 750.00	$ 60.00	$ 690.00
	23488	COSTELLO, JOSEPH S	82.1	$ 623.63	$ 49.89	$ 573.74

12/21/89   PAGE   3

DEPT. NO.	ID	EMPLOYEE	HOURS	GROSS PAY	TAX	NET PAY
---------	--	----------	------	-----------	----	--------
2	24567	ANDERSON, DAVID	80.4	$ 760.86	$ 60.87	$ 699.99
	31578	BREWER, BETTY	43.2	$ 791.85	$ 63.35	$ 728.50

12/21/89   PAGE   4

DEPT. NO.	ID	EMPLOYEE	HOURS	GROSS PAY	TAX	NET PAY
---------	--	----------	------	-----------	----	--------
3	15422	CALDWELL, SUSAN	75.9	$ 348.38	$ 13.94	$ 334.44
	16882	CLANCY, BETTY	55.7	$ 426.10	$ 25.57	$ 400.53

12/21/89   PAGE   5

DEPT. NO.	ID	EMPLOYEE	HOURS	GROSS PAY	TAX	NET PAY
---------	--	----------	------	-----------	----	--------
4	23451	ALEXANDER, CHARLES	90.2	$ 952.10	$ 95.21	$ 856.89
	32155	BROWN, WALLACE	77.5	$ 792.05	$ 63.36	$ 728.69
	51202	DUNIGAN, HENRY	66.5	$ 964.25	$ 96.43	$ 867.82
	70123	JACKSON, KENNETH	75.9	$ 977.59	$ 97.76	$ 879.83

```
                          TOTAL EMPLOYEES        4
                          OVERTIME EMPLOYEES     1
                          TOTAL TAX         $     352.76
                          TOTAL NET PAY     $   3,333.23
```

12/21/89   PAGE   6

DEPT. NO.	ID	EMPLOYEE	HOURS	GROSS PAY	TAX	NET PAY
---------	--	----------	------	-----------	----	--------
5	20988	FOX, WILLIAM	90.0	$1,941.80	$ 233.02	$1,708.78
	31254	HALLECK, FRANCES	120.0	$4,277.20	$ 513.26	$3,763.94
	32611	HEPNER, ELMER	110.4	$ 753.60	$ 60.29	$ 693.31
	52319	HORNE, ALBERT	92.0	$ 980.00	$ 98.00	$ 882.00
	67822	SAWYER, DAVID	80.0	$ 444.00	$ 26.64	$ 417.36
	78200	SIPE, CHARLES	75.0	$1,181.25	$ 141.75	$1,039.50
	89212	SMITH, JERRY	60.0	$ 539.40	$ 32.36	$ 507.04

```
                          TOTAL EMPLOYEES        7
                          OVERTIME EMPLOYEES     4
                          TOTAL TAX         $   1,105.32
                          TOTAL NET PAY     $   9,011.93


            REPORT TOTALS
                          TOTAL EMPLOYEES       39
                          OVERTIME EMPLOYEES    14
                          TOTAL TAX         $   4,069.91
                          TOTAL NET PAY     $  35,730.01
```

COMPUTERS AND INFORMATION PROCESSING

are books, periodicals, brochures, and product specifications from manufacturers. Customers and suppliers are sometimes good sources. For example, asking customers what information they would like to see on an invoice might aid in the analysis of an accounts receivable system. Analysts should also attempt to contact other companies that have developed or implemented similar information systems.

CONCEPT SUMMARY 14—1

Types of Data Gathering	
Internal Sources	**External Sources**
Interviews	Books
Observation	Periodicals
System flowcharts	Brochures
Questionnaires	Manufacturers' product specifications
Formal reports	Customers and suppliers

Data Analysis

After data has been collected, it must be organized so that it can be seen in proper perspective. While the focus during data collection is on *what* is being done, the focus during data analysis is on *why* certain operations and procedures are being used. The analyst looks for ways to improve these operations.

INFORMATION NEEDS. An analysis should be conducted to determine both management's information needs and the data that will be required to meet those needs. This will have a significant impact later when input/output requirements are being determined.

Determining information needs requires that the analyst use a top-down approach. In a file-processing environment, it is relatively easy to create and manipulate files. But many companies are rapidly moving into database environments. Creating and maintaining an effective data base requires that data items be maintained independently. This means that the data must be analyzed and organized from a corporate-wide perspective. A file can no longer be created for use by a single department; data must be accessible to many other departments as well. The goal is to properly relate each data item to all other data items, ignoring departmental boundaries.

Some techniques used to analyze data and determine information needs are grid charts, system flowcharts, and decision logic tables. While these techniques are some of the most frequently used, there are many others. Analysts should use the tools and techniques that are best suited for analyzing gathered data. In the following paragraphs grid charts, system flowcharts, and decision logic tables are explained.

Grid Charts. The **tabular** or **grid chart** is used to summarize the relationships among the components of a system. Relationships among components such as inputs, outputs, and files are often depicted on grid charts. Figure 14–4 is a grid chart indicating which department used what documents of an order-processing, billing, and inventory-control system. For example, the billing department uses shipping and invoice documents, while accounts receivable uses invoices, credit authorization, and monthly reports.

System Flowcharts. In Chapter 11, program flowcharts were concerned with operations on data. In contrast, **system flowcharts** emphasize the flow of data through the entire data-processing system, without describing details of internal computer operations. A system flowchart represents the inter-relationships among various elements of the information system.

The general input/output symbol used in program flowcharting is not specific enough for system flowcharting. A variety of specialized input/output symbols are needed to identify the wide variety of media used in input/output activities. The symbols are miniature outlines of the actual media (see Figure 14–5).

Similarly, specialized process symbols are used instead of the general process symbol ( ) to represent specific processing operations. For example, a trapezoid is used to indicate a manual operation such as key-to-tape data entry (see Figure 14–6).

The difference in emphasis in the two forms of flowcharting is due to the differences in the purposes they serve. A program flowchart aids the programmer by providing details necessary to the coding of the program. In contrast, system flowcharts are designed to represent the general information flow; often one process symbol is used to represent many operations.

Figure 14–7 is a sample system flowchart that shows the updating of an inventory master file. The **online storage** symbol ( ) indicates that the file is kept on an online external storage medium such as disk or tape. The file is used to keep track of the raw materials and finished products of the

FIGURE 14—4

Grid Chart

Document \ Department	Order Writing	Shipping	Billing	Inventory	Marketing	Accounts Receivable
Sales Order	X				X	
Shipping Order	X	X	X	X		
Invoice			X		X	X
Credit Authorization					X	X
Monthly Report					X	X

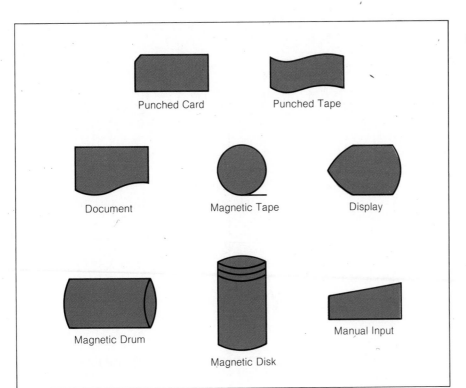

FIGURE 14–5

**Specialized Input/Output Symbols
for System Flowcharting**

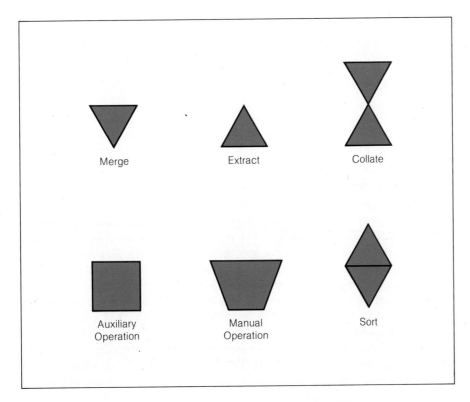

FIGURE 14–6

**Specialized Process Symbols for
System Flowcharting**

FIGURE 14—7

Sample System Flowchart

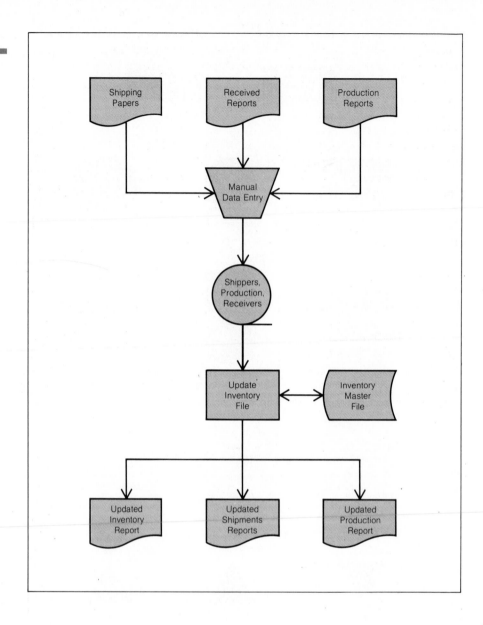

organization. Whether or not this information is current depends on how often the master file is updated. If it is updated as soon as a product is shipped or a raw material supply depleted, then the information it provides is up-to-date. Usually, however, the updating is done on a periodic basis. All changes that occur during a specific time period are batched and then processed together to update the inventory master file. Reports from the shipping, receiving, and production departments are collected. The data from this set of documents are entered into the computer via a CRT. The data entered on the CRT and the inventory master file then serve as input for the updating process.

The flowchart in Figure 14—7 outlines the steps in this process. In addition to updating the inventory master file, the system generates three reports, which give management information about inventory, order shipments, and production. Notice that in the system flowchart one process symbol encompasses the entire updating process. A program flowchart must be created to detail the specific operations to be performed within this process.

Decision Logic Tables. A **decision logic table (DLT)** is a tabular representation of the actions to be taken under various sets of conditions. The decision table expresses the logic for arriving at a particular decision under a given set of circumstances. The structure within the table is based on the proposition "if this condition is met, then do this."

The basic elements of a decision logic table are shown in Figure 14–8. The upper half lists conditions to be met and the lower half shows actions to be taken. That is, the **condition stub** describes the various conditions; the **action stub** describes the possible actions. **Condition entries** are made in the top right section. **Action entries** are made in the bottom right section.

A decision table is not needed when conditions can be communicated and understood easily. However, where multiple conditions exist, a decision table serves as a valuable tool in analyzing the decision logic involved. Figure 14–9 shows a decision table for selecting applicants for an assembly-line job.

The rules for selecting applicants are based on the age, education, and experience of the candidates. The applicants must be at least eighteen years old to be considered for the position. They must have at least a high school education or a year's experience to be interviewed for further evaluation. If they meet both requirements, they are hired directly. The Ys in the table mean yes, the Ns mean no, and the Xs indicate what actions are to be taken. The decision table is read as follows:

■ Rule 1: If the applicant's age is less than eighteen years, then reject him or her.

■ Rule 2: If the applicant is at least eighteen years old but has no high school education and less than one year's experience, then reject him or her.

■ Rule 3: If the applicant is at least eighteen years old, has no high school education, but has experience of more than one year, then call him or her for an interview. Once a candidate has been selected for an interview, another decision table may be needed to evaluate the interviewee.

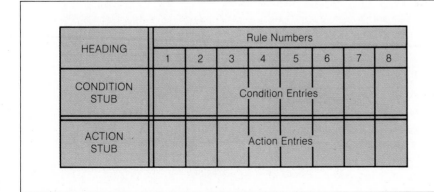

FIGURE 14—8

Decision Logic Table

FIGURE 14—9

Decision Logic Table for Selecting Applicants

SELECTING APPLICANTS		Rules				
		1	2	3	4	5
CONDITIONS	Age < 18 Years?	Y	N	N	N	N
	High School Education?		N	N	Y	Y
	Experience > 1 Year?		N	Y	N	Y
ACTIONS	Reject	X	X			
	Interview				X	X
	Hire					X

■ Rule 4: If the applicant is at least eighteen years old, has a high school education, but has less than one year's experience, then call him or her for an interview. Again, another decision table might be used to evaluate the interviewee.

■ Rule 5: If the applicant is at least eighteen years old, has a high school education, and has more than one year's experience, then hire him or her.

A more detailed decision logic table is shown in Figure 14–10. The first step in constructing such a table is to determine which conditions must be considered. In this case, the conditions are: (1) Is the customer's credit rating AAA? (2) Is the quantity ordered above or equal to the minimum quantity for a discount? (3) Is there enough stock on hand to fill the order? The conditions are listed in the condition stub section of the decision table.

The next step is to determine what actions can take place. These are: Either (1) bill at a discount price or (2) bill at a regular price; and either

FIGURE 14—10

Decision Logic Table for Order Processing

ORDER PROCESSING	Rules							
	1	2	3	4	5	6	7	8
Credit Rating of AAA	Y	Y	Y	Y	N	N	N	N
Quantity Order >= Minimum Discount Quantity	Y	N	N	Y	Y	N	Y	N
Quantity Ordered <= Stock on Hand	N	Y	N	Y	N	Y	Y	N
Bill at Discount Price	X			X				
Bill at Regular Price		X	X		X	X	X	X
Ship Total Quantity Ordered		X		X		X	X	
Ship Partial and Back-Order Remaining Amount	X		X		X			X

(3) ship the total quantity ordered or (4) ship a partial order and back-order the rest. These possibilities go in the action stub section.

Once the conditions and possible courses of action have been identified, the conditions can be related to corresponding action entries to indicate the appropriate decision. Thus, Rule 4 could be interpreted as follows: "If the customer has a credit rating of AAA and the quantity ordered is equal to or above the minimum discount quantity and there is enough stock on hand, then the customer is to be billed at the discount price and the total order is to be shipped."

Decision tables summarize the logic required to make a decision in a form that is easy to understand. They are used to record facts collected during the investigation of the old system and can also be used to summarize aspects of the new system. In the latter case, they guide programmers in writing programs for the new system.

System Analysis Report

After collecting and analyzing the data, the system analyst must communicate the findings to management. The system analysis report should include the following items:

- A restatement of the scope and objectives of the system analysis.
- An explanation of the present system, the procedures used, and any problems identified.
- A statement of all constraints on the present system and any assumptions made by the analyst during this phase.
- A preliminary report of alternatives that currently seem feasible.
- An estimate of the resources and capital required to either modify the present system or design a new one. This estimate should include costs of a feasibility study.

The system analyst proceeds to the detailed system design only if management approves this report.

■ SYSTEM DESIGN

If, after reviewing the system analysis report, management decides to continue the project, the system design stage begins. Designing an information system demands a great deal of creativity and planning. It is also very costly and time consuming. In system analysis, the analyst has focused on what the current system does and on what it should be doing according to the requirements discovered in the analysis. In the design phase, the analysis changes focus and concentrates on how a system can be developed to meet information requirements.

Several steps are useful during the design phase of system development:

- Reviewing goals and objectives.
- Developing a system model.
- Evaluating organizational constraints.
- Developing alternative designs.
- Performing feasibility analysis.
- Performing cost/benefit analysis.
- Preparing a system design report and recommendation.

Reviewing Goals and Objectives

The objectives of the new or revised system were identified during system analysis and stated in the system analysis report. Before the analyst can proceed with system design, these objectives must be reviewed, for any system design offered must conform to them.

In order to maintain a broad approach and flexibility in the system design phase, the analyst may restate users' information requirements to reflect the needs of the majority of users. For example, the finance department may want a report of customers who have been delinquent in payments. Since this department may be only one subsystem in a larger accounts-receivable system, the analyst may restate this requirement more generally. It might more appropriately be stated as follows: (1) maintain an accurate and timely record of the amounts owed by customers, (2) provide control procedures that ensure detection of abnormal accounts and report them on an exception basis, and (3) provide, on a timely basis, information regarding accounts receivable to different levels of management to help achieve overall company goals.

A well-designed system can meet the current goals and objectives of the organization and adapt to changes within the organization. In discussions with managers, the analyst may be able to determine organizational trends that help to pinpoint which subsystems require more flexibility. For instance, if the analyst is developing a system for an electric company, strong consideration should be given to providing flexibility in the reporting subsystem in order to respond to changing regulatory reporting requirements.

Developing a System Model

The analyst next attempts to represent symbolically the system's major components to verify understanding of the various components and their interactions. The analyst may use flowcharts to help in the development of a system model or may simply be creative in the use of diagrammatic representations.

In reviewing the model, the analyst refers to system theory to discover any possible omissions of important subsystems. Are the major interactions among subsystems shown? Are the inputs, processes, and outputs appropriately identified? Does the model provide for appropriate feedback to each of the subsystems? Are too many functions included within one subsystem?

Once a satisfactory system model has been developed, the analyst has an appropriate tool for evaluating alternative designs (discussed later in this section). Each alternative can be evaluated on the basis of how well it matches the requirements of the model. Figure 14–11 is an example of a conceptual model of an accounts-receivable system.

Evaluating Organizational Constraints

No organization has unlimited resources; most have limitations on financial budgets, personnel, and computer facilities and time constraints for system development. The system analyst must recognize the constraints on system design imposed by this limited availability of resources.

FIGURE 14—11

Model of an Accounts-Receivable System

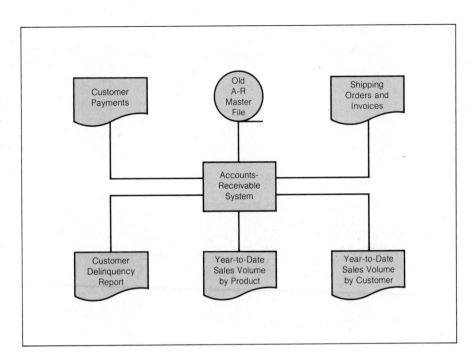

Few organizations request the optimal design for their information requirements. Businesses are profit-seeking organizations. Only in an extremely rare case does an organization request an all-out system development with no cost constraints. (Competition or technological developments, for example, may make such an uncharacteristic decision mandatory.)

The structure of the organization also affects subsequent designs developed by the analyst. A highly centralized management may reject a proposal for distributed processing. Similarly, an organization with geographically dispersed, highly autonomous decision centers may find designs that require routing reports throughout the central office unsatisfactory.

Human factors are also an organizational constraint that must be evaluated during the system design phase. Special consideration must be given to the users of the system. A proposed system design should be **user friendly.** In other words, the system must be designed not only to meet the needs of the user, but also to meet those needs through an easy-to-use, understandable design.

A **menu-driven** system design, for example, guides the user through the computerized system helping him or her attain the needed information. A menu-driven system displays menus (lists of available choices or actions) to the user (see Figure 14–12). With the menu-driven system, the user can be guided through the process of using the system.

Technological advances such as a mouse, touch-sensitive screens, or a voice recognition system may also help make a system design more compatible for its human users. The human factors of system design are extremely important.

Before proceeding with system design, the analyst must be fully aware of the various organizational constraints and critically evaluate their impact on the system design.

FIGURE 14—12

Sample Menu

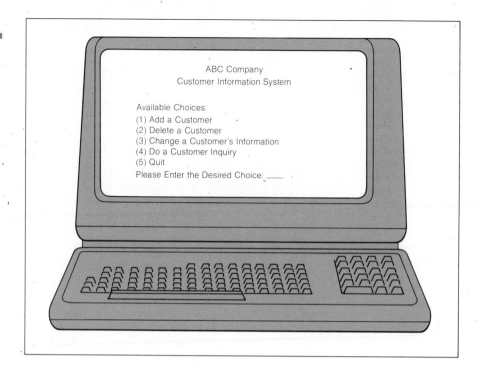

```
                    ABC Company
               Customer Information System

        Available Choices:
        (1) Add a Customer
        (2) Delete a Customer
        (3) Change a Customer's Information
        (4) Do a Customer Inquiry
        (5) Quit
        Please Enter the Desired Choice: ____
```

Developing Alternative Designs

Systems can be either simple or complex. Simple systems require simple controls to keep processes working properly. Complex systems, on the other hand, require complex controls. A business is a complex system; it requires vast numbers of interactions among its many interrelated subsystems. It naturally follows that information systems developed for business use must be complex, since they model the actual business.

There is more than one way to design a complex information system, and system analysts are generally required to develop more than one design alternative. This requirement is useful because it forces the analyst to be creative. By designing several possible systems, the analyst may discover valuable parts in each that can be integrated into an entirely new system. The alternative systems may also be designed in ascending order of complexity and cost; since management often desires alternatives from which to choose, designing alternative systems in this fashion is quite appropriate.

The analyst must work with a number of elements in designing alternative systems. Computerized information systems have many components. Inputs, outputs, hardware, software, files, data bases, clerical procedures, and users interact in hundreds of different ways. Processing requirements may also differ in each alternative. For example, one may require batch processing and sequential organization of files; another may provide random-access processing using direct-access storage and online terminals. The data collection, processing, storage, retrieval, and update procedures vary, depending on the alternative selected.

Each alternative developed by the analyst must be technically feasible. In some instances, analysts try to design at least one noncomputerized alternative. Although this may be difficult, it often reveals unique methods of information processing that the analyst has not considered when developing the computerized systems.

In designing each alternative, the analyst should include tentative input forms, the structures and formats of output reports, the program specifications needed to guide programmers in code preparation, the files or data base required, the clerical procedures to be used, and the process-control measures that should be instituted.

With the increasing use of online systems, the input forms are often input screens. These screens must be designed in as much detail as their hardcopy counterparts. The analyst, in consultation with those who will be inputting the data, must design each screen to maximize efficiency in data input. The screen format must be easy for users to view and understand (see Figure 14–13).

Output reports must be designed so that users can quickly and easily view the information they require. The analyst often prepares mock-up reports that approximate how the actual computer-generated report will look (see Figure 14–14). Most contain sample data. It is easier for users to relate their needs to such sample reports than to discuss them in abstract form with the analyst in an interview. Mock-up reports also allow the analyst to verify once again what is required of the system.

Once the input forms or screens and output reports have been designed, a detailed set of programming specifications for each alternative must be prepared. The analyst must determine what kind of processing is to occur in each of the system designs. The analyst often works in conjunction with the programming staff to determine these requirements and to develop cost estimates for program coding.

File and data-base specification is particularly important. The analyst must be aware of the physical layout of data in a file. The storage media

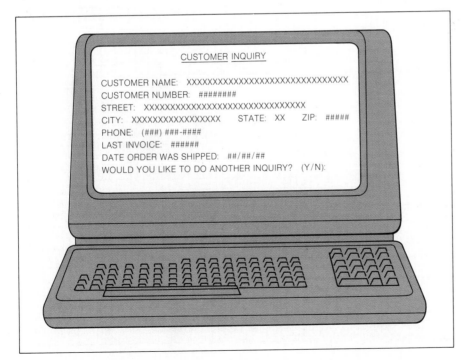

FIGURE 14–13

Screen Format

FIGURE 14–14

Output Report Format

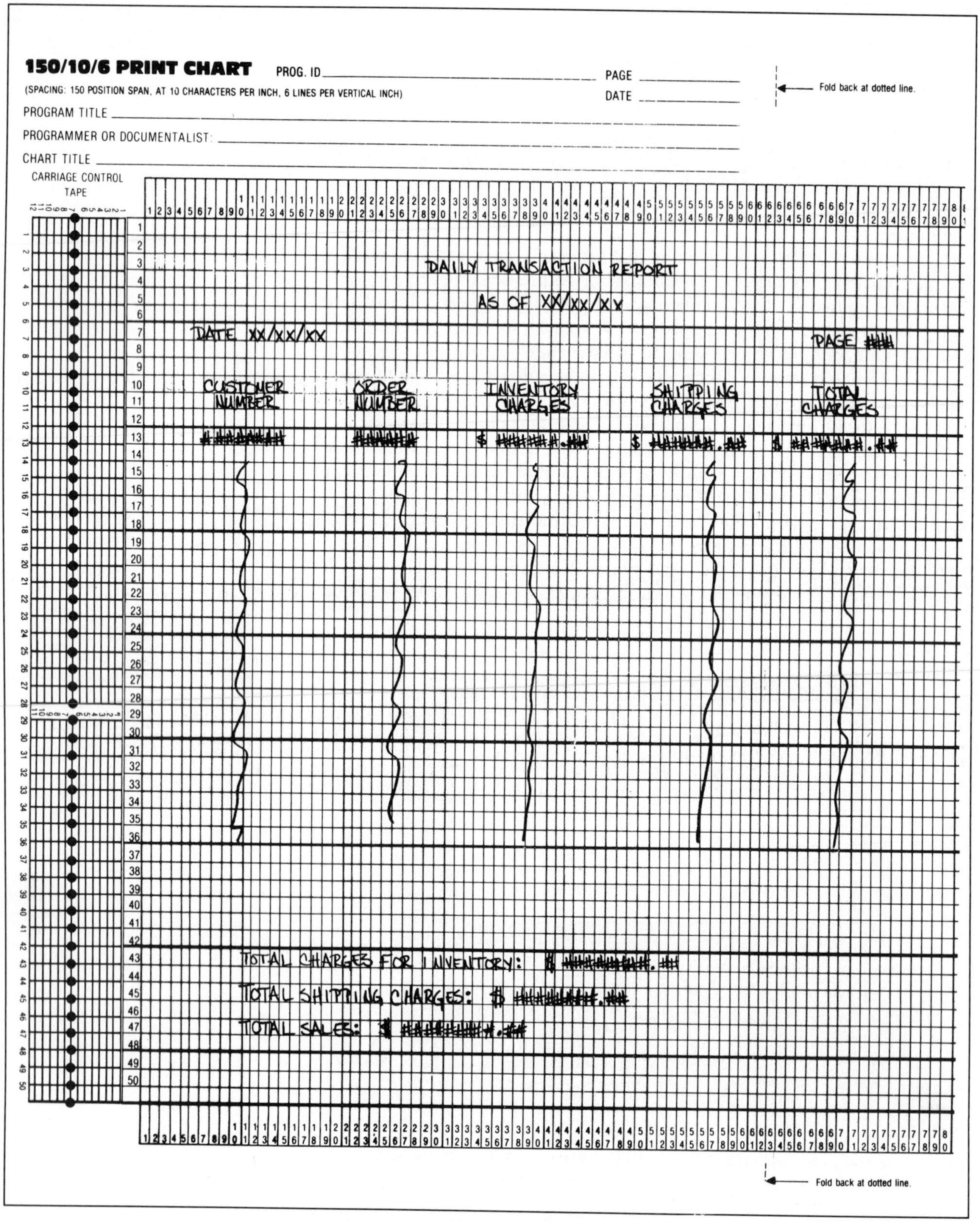

150/10/6 PRINT CHART PROG. ID _____ PAGE _____

(SPACING: 150 POSITION SPAN, AT 10 CHARACTERS PER INCH, 6 LINES PER VERTICAL INCH) DATE _____

PROGRAM TITLE _____

PROGRAMMER OR DOCUMENTALIST: _____

CHART TITLE _____

DAILY TRANSACTION REPORT

AS OF XX/xx/xx

DATE xx/xx/xx   PAGE ###

CUSTOMER   ORDER   INVENTORY   SHIPPING   TOTAL
NUMBER   NUMBER   CHARGES   CHARGES   CHARGES

#########   ####### $ ######.## $ #####.## $ ######.##

TOTAL CHARGES FOR INVENTORY: $ ########.##

TOTAL SHIPPING CHARGES: $ #######.##

TOTAL SALES: $ ########.##

and keys used to access data in the files need to be determined (see Chapter 7 for details on file design). The analyst should also determine the potential size of each file, the number of accesses and updates that may take place during a particular time period, and the length of time for which users may wish to retain each file. Since each of these specifications requires the use of computer facilities, the estimates help the analyst determine the potential cost of each design alternative.

The analyst must carefully examine each clerical procedure required in a particular system alternative. In a sense, the analyst must imagine himself or herself actually performing the steps required. From the receipt of data through the processing steps to the final output, the analyst must determine the most efficient methods for users to perform their required tasks.

Process-control measures were easier in the days of batch processing. With online systems, however, changes made to files and data bases are instantaneous. If the changes are made on the basis of incorrect data, incorrect values will be stored, accessed, and reported. The analyst must institute controls from initial data capture and entry through processing and storage to final reporting. Methods to restore data bases when errors in data entry occur should be developed. Security procedures should be instituted to prevent unauthorized access to stored data. Since the advent of privacy legislation (discussed in Chapter 17), the development of control procedures has become increasingly important.

Performing Feasibility Analysis

While developing each alternative system, the analyst must keep asking the question, "Is this feasible?" A design may require certain procedures that the organization is not staffed to handle; the design, therefore, must be discarded, or the appropriate staff acquired. The analyst may discover an alternative with great potential for reducing processing costs, but may find that the company does not own the hardware required to implement it. The analyst may choose to present this alternative to management rather than disregard it. The analyst must use personal judgment and experience to eliminate unfeasible alternatives.

In some cases, the question of a system's feasibility may also center around organizational constraints. Even though the proposed system may be technically feasible, questions such as, "Is the system practical?" and "Is the system cost effective or necessary as a competitive response?" also need to be considered. As was noted earlier in the chapter, organizational constraints may also affect whether a system is feasible or not.

The users' educational backgrounds and organizational positions must be taken into consideration. The lack of familiarity of some employees with computer-based information systems may prohibit the use of a complex system. Highly educated managers may resist a simple information system because they feel uneasy working with it. Companies in rural locations may be unable to properly staff data-processing departments.

Analysts must also determine whether there are legal constraints that affect the design of the system. For example, several presidents have proposed to Congress that a massive, integrated data base be created containing data about citizens receiving benefits from the government. The objective is to reduce fraud, inefficiency, and multiple payments. It is possible, however, that such a data base might violate privacy laws (see Chapter 17).

Although the system is feasible from a technical standpoint, the controls that would have to be incorporated to conform with legal constraints have hindered its development.

When performing a feasibility analysis, time is frequently a limiting factor. A time constraint may appear before system development begins, during the development process, or during implementation. The required completion date may preclude the selection of a complex alternative, necessitate changing the selected design to one less complex, or require that the system be developed in stages different from those suggested by the analyst.

The economic feasibility of a project is paramount. Many systems have fallen by the wayside because of budgetary constraints. The system's economic feasibility is determined by cost/benefit analysis, which is discussed in the next section. In performing this analysis, the analyst must be extremely careful. Costs that at first appear to exceed the budget may in fact give rise to greater benefits. The expression "you have to spend money to make money" is often applicable here. It is up to the analyst to foresee such possibilities.

Performing Cost/Benefit Analysis

Cost/benefit analysis is a procedure commonly used in business decision making. A firm has limited financial resources. They must be allocated to projects that appear to offer the greatest return on the costs of initial development. In order for cost/benefit analysis to be performed, both costs and benefits must be quantified. Costs are easier to determine than benefits. Some benefits are tangible (or realizable as cash savings). Others are intangible (not necessarily obvious reductions in costs). Naturally, intangible benefits are especially difficult to determine. How does one estimate the benefit from an improved information system that provides better customer service?

An analyst might approach the cost/benefit analysis of an accounts-receivable system in the following fashion. A company is unable to respond to 20 percent of customer orders because of inefficiencies in its current information system. A proposed new system will reduce lost sales by increasing the customer service level so that only 5 percent of orders remain unprocessed. By observing the current sales level and predicting how much sales will increase if the new system is implemented, the analyst can approximate the cash benefits of the alternative.

The costs of an alternative include direct costs like the initial investment required for materials and equipment; setup costs required to create computer files from old manual systems, install data-processing equipment, and hire personnel; and educational costs to train the users of the new system. Ongoing expenses resulting from employees' salaries, computer operations, insurance, taxes, and rent must also be identified.

It is not always necessary for positive economic benefits to exist for an alternative to be considered feasible. For example, environmental impact statements are required by law from some companies. Design alternatives for a system that must produce these reports need to provide accurate and timely information in spite of the cost/benefit relationship involved. Careful planning, however, will minimize the resources required to develop such a system.

The analyst can also use statistics in determining costs and benefits of large system designs. Sampling and modeling enable the analyst to provide cost/benefit figures not readily apparent from available information. By modeling the complex interactions of accounts-receivable, inventory, and service levels, the analyst may be able to determine how savings in one area affects costs in another. Other techniques, ranging from judgment to common sense to experience, are useful to the analyst attempting to choose the best alternative.

The design alternative that management selects often depends on the results of the cost/benefit analysis. The analyst must ensure that a comprehensive cost/benefit study has been performed on all alternatives.

Preparing the Design Report

Once the analyst has completed all of the steps described earlier, a report is prepared to communicate findings to management. The **system design report** should explain in general terms how the various designs will satisfy the information requirements determined in the analysis phase. The report should also review the information requirements uncovered in the system analysis, explain in both flowchart and narrative form the proposed designs, detail the corporate resources required to implement each alternative, and make a recommendation.

Since many organizational personnel may not have participated actively in the analysis stage of system development, the analyst restates information requirements in the design report to tell these decision makers the constraints considered in creating alternative designs. The restatement also shows that the analyst understands what information the new system should provide.

Each of the proposed alternatives should be explained in easy-to-understand narrative form. Technical jargon should be avoided. The purpose of the design report is to communicate; using words unfamiliar to the reader will hinder this communication process. Flowcharts for each alternative should be provided as well.

From the detailed design work performed on each alternative, the analyst should glean the important costs, benefits, and resources required for its implementation. This, more than any other portion of the report, will be analyzed carefully by those empowered to make a design selection. Their decisions will be based on the projected benefits of each design versus the corporate resources required to implement it.

Finally, the analyst should make a design recommendation. Due to familiarity with both the current system and each of the alternative designs, the analyst is in the best position to make a recommendation for implementing a successful alternative design. If the analyst has been thorough in analyzing resource costs and potential benefits, as well as objective in viewing corporate goals, this recommendation is apt to be adopted by management.

After evaluating the system design report, management can do one of three things: (a) approve the recommendation; (b) approve the recommendation with changes (this may include selecting another alternative); or (c) select none of the alternatives. The "do nothing" alternative is always feasible but will not solve any of the problems that led to the system analysis

HIGHLIGHT

A Case for CASE

In order to develop a new application program, the designer must work through the necessary design steps of analysis, design, programming, implementation, and evaluation. New software tools called CASE can make this process more efficient. CASE stands for Computer-Aided Software Engineering. CASE is not a system, but a combination of tools; the components of CASE depend upon the type of business and the design needs of the business.

Lower level CASE tools, also called back-end tools, are programs that automate tasks such as programming. A CASE tool can take programmers' instructions and write the code. For a language like COBOL, which requires great amounts of code, the CASE tool can save a significant amount of time. For example, Koppers and Co. of Pittsburgh, Pennsylvania, is a major supplier of construction materials. Koppers installed new hardware, and therefore had to rewrite nearly all their COBOL code. By using the CASE tool from Netron, Inc. the code was written in half the time it would have taken programmers to do the job.

Higher level (front-end) CASE tools can check design diagrams to make sure they flow logically and contain all the necessary functions. Other CASE products can actually diagram flowcharts from the specifications of a designer.

The CASE market continues to grow. Some experts say the market may reach $800 million in the next few years. It looks like design and programming in the 1990s will rely heavily on CASE tools.

in the first place. If the design of the system is approved, the analyst proceeds with implementation.

SYSTEM PROGRAMMING

Programming

A computerized information system depends on computer programs for converting data into information. Programs may be produced in-house or purchased in the form of commercially prepared software packages. If the programs are written in-house, the system analyst should help decide which language must be chosen. To make the system easier to maintain and change, programs should be developed in independent modules (see Chapter 11).

The analyst, in conjunction with the programming department, may wish to evaluate commercial software packages designed to perform tasks similar to those required of the selected design as an alternative to in-house programming. These software evaluations should be made on the basis of system compatibility and adaptability.

Testing

Before a system becomes operational, it must be tested and debugged. Testing should take place at all levels of operation. Programs are tested by dividing them into logical modules. Each module should be tested to ensure that input is accounted for, files are updated, and reports are correctly printed. Once all program testing is complete, system testing takes place. System testing involves checking all application programs that support the system. All clerical procedures used in data collection, data processing, and data storage and retrieval are included in system testing.

Documentation

Creating documentation involves taking an overview of the entire system including subsystems and their functions. Generally, documentation falls into one of three classifications: system documentation, program documentation, and procedure documentation. System documentation usually includes system flowcharts, forms and files input to the system's subsystems, and reports and files output from the subsystems. Program documentation includes program flowcharts, explanations of the program's logic patterns, and explanations of the data elements on computer files. Procedure documentation instructs users on how to perform particular functions in each subsystem. These instructions are designed to help users obtain the information they need quickly and easily.

Special Considerations

In designing solutions to business problems, analysts and programmers must be aware of other considerations besides developing the programs required to help solve a particular problem. Since system analysis and design concentrate on inputs, processing, and outputs, the following issues must be considered: (a) The form of input to the program determines how the program should ask for data. (b) Processing steps should verify the accuracy of data and identify potential errors. (c) The program may be required to produce output that is not in hard-copy form.

Today's computer systems give users a variety of ways to communicate with programs. The programmer must know in advance which input devices will be used to put data into the program. Different input devices require different input considerations. The input devices and forms of data input must be precisely defined before solution design begins, or considerable time may be required to rework programs designed to accept input in an inappropriate format.

Businesses are naturally concerned with the accuracy of data used to provide the information managers use to make decisions. Programmers must do their part to help keep data error free; merely designing a program with logically correct processing statements providing the required output may not be enough. Most programmers are required to include extensive edit checks on the data before storing it in data files. **Edit checks** are processing statements designed to identify potential errors in the input data.

Several broad types of edit checks can be incorporated into the solution design. In some situations, combinations of these edit checks are required. The determination of how many and what kinds of edit checks should be performed on input data is usually made by all personnel involved in the design solution. Users, management, system analyst, and programmers should all be involved in ensuring the integrity of the data input into the system.

In modern systems, not all data is entered directly into a program by users nor is all output fed directly to hard-copy reports. Many systems require the use of interdependent programs in which the output from one program is used as input to another. Programmers need to ensure that output from one program is in a form acceptable as input to another.

■ SYSTEM IMPLEMENTATION

In the implementation stage of the system methodology, the analyst is able to see the transformation of ideas, flowcharts, and narratives into actual processes, flows, and information. This transition is not performed easily, however. Personnel must be trained to use the new system procedures, and a conversion must be made from the old system to the new one.

Personnel Training

Two groups of people interface with a system. The first group includes the people who develop, operate, and maintain the system. The second group includes the people who use the information generated by the system to support their decision making. Both groups must be aware of their responsibilities regarding the system's operation and of what they can and cannot expect from it. One of the primary responsibilities of the system analyst is to see that education and training are provided to both groups.

The user group includes general management, staff personnel, line managers, and other operating personnel. It may also include the organization's customers and suppliers. These users must be educated as to what functions they are to perform and what, in turn, the system will do for them. Procedure documentation (mentioned above) provides information to the users of the system on what functions they should perform.

The personnel who operate the system must be trained to prepare input data, load and unload files on secondary storage devices, handle problems that occur during processing, and so on.

Education and training can be provided in large group seminars or in smaller tutorial sessions. The latter approach, though fairly costly, is more personal and more appropriate for complex tasks. Another approach, used almost universally, is on-the-job training. As the name implies, the employee learns while actually performing the tasks required.

Personnel training and education are expensive, but they are essential to successful system implementation.

Conversion

The switch from an old system to a new one is referred to as a conversion. Conversion involves not only changes in the mode of processing data but also changes in equipment and clerical procedures.

Several approaches can be used to accomplish the conversion process. The most important ones are explained below:

■ *Parallel conversion.* When **parallel conversion** is used, the new system is operated side by side with the old one for some period of time. An advantage of this approach is that no data is lost if the new system fails. Also, it gives the user an opportunity to compare and reconcile the outputs from both systems. However, this method can be costly.

■ *Pilot conversion.* **Pilot conversion** involves converting only a small portion of the organization to the new system. For example, a new system may be implemented on one production line. This approach minimizes the risk to the organization as a whole in case unforeseen problems occur, and enables the organization to identify problems and correct them before implementing

The Design Team

Designing application software is a long and complex process. Designers decide what the program should do and how it should be done. The programmers then transform the design into computer code. Software development groups are adding two new members to the development team—a trainer and a documentation specialist.

The trainer is the person responsible for training new users on the system. For example, when the system is sold, the trainer may hold on-site seminars to show users how to operate the application. The documentation specialist is the person who writes the text in the user guides. Even if the new user has been trained, all the procedures in the system cannot be covered in a seminar. The user will consult the user guides. The trainer and the documentation specialist are important to design teams because they view the

emerging system through the eyes of a user. They can point out parts of a system that are unclear or inconsistencies that might confuse the user.

For example, a trainer and documentation specialist would not assume that the user is familiar with common computer terms. They would determine the level of expertise of the user and define any terms that might be unfamiliar. Another example is the need to eliminate inconsistencies between titles of screens or windows in a screen. If the designer requires the use of the same screen a number of times, but refers to the screen by two different names, the user might get confused. Again, a documentation specialist or trainer would catch and help resolve the problem.

In the product services department of the Online Computer Library Center (OCLC) in Dublin, Ohio, manager Janet Mushruch says trainers and documentation specialists are included on their design teams because they head off problems early in the development phase. Robert Stahl, a consultant with Interface Design Group in Oakland, California, agrees with Mushruch saying that management must support the concept of trainers and documentation specialists on the design team in order for the process to work.

All good systems begin with good design. For many companies, that means having a design team that includes a trainer and a documentation specialist.

---

the system throughout the organization. A disadvantage of this method is that the total conversion process usually takes a long time.

■ *Phased conversion.* With **phased conversion,** the old system is gradually replaced by the new one over a period of time. The difference between this method and pilot conversion is that in phased conversion the new system is segmented and only one segment is implemented at a time. Thus, the organization can adapt to the new system gradually over an extended period while the old system is gradually being phased out. One drawback is that an interface between the new system and the old system must be developed for use during the conversion process.

■ *Crash conversion.* **Crash** (or **direct**) **conversion** takes place all at once. This approach can be used to advantage if the old system is not operational or if the new system is completely different in structure and design. Since the old system is discontinued immediately upon implementation of the new one, the organization has nothing to fall back on if problems arise. Because of the high risk involved, this approach requires extreme care in planning and extensive testing of all system components.

SYSTEM ANALYSIS AND DESIGN   **395**

SYSTEM AUDIT AND REVIEW

Evaluating System Performance

After the conversion process is complete, the analyst must obtain feedback on the system's performance. This can be done by conducting an audit to evaluate the system's performance in terms of the initial objectives established for it. The evaluation should address the following questions:

1. Does the system perform as planned and deliver the anticipated benefits? How do the operating results compare with the initial objectives? If the benefits are below expectation, what can be done to improve the cost/benefit tradeoff?

2. Was the system completed on schedule and with the resources estimated?

3. Is all output from the system used?

4. Have old system procedures been eliminated and new ones implemented?

5. What controls have been established for input, processing, and output of data? Are these controls adequate?

6. Have users been educated about the new system? Is the system accepted by users? Do they have confidence in the reports generated?

7. Is the processing turnaround time satisfactory, or are delays frequent?

All persons involved in developing the system should be aware that a thorough audit will be performed. The anticipated audit acts as a strong incentive; it helps to ensure that a good system is designed and delivered on schedule. As a result of the audit or of user requests, some modification or improvements of the new system may be required.

Making Modifications and Improvements

A common belief among system users is that after a system has been installed, nothing more needs to be done. On the contrary, all systems must be continually maintained. System maintenance detects and corrects errors, meets new information needs of management, and responds to changes in the environment.

One of the important tasks of the analyst during the system audit is to ensure that all system controls are working correctly. All procedures and programs related to the old system should have been eliminated. Many of the problems that the system analyst deals with during system maintenance and follow-up are problems that were identified during the system audit. A well-planned approach to system maintenance and follow-up is essential to the continued effectiveness of an information system.

Responding to Change

A well-designed information system is flexible and adaptable. Minor changes should be easily accommodated without large amounts of reprogramming. This is one of the reasons why structured programming was emphasized in Chapter 12; if each program module is independent, a minor change in one module will not snowball into other changes.

No matter how flexible or adaptable a system is, however, major changes become necessary over time. When the system has to be redesigned, the entire system cycle—analysis, design, programming, implementation, and audit and review—must be performed again. Keeping information systems responsive to information needs is a never-ending process.

■ PROTOTYPING

In the traditional method of system analysis and design, the system design phase involves developing a system model. The system model that is developed is based on data that has been gathered and analyzed by the system analyst. The model that is developed is typically diagrammed on paper so that the end user of the system can review it. Prototyping, however, differs from the traditional approach to system analysis by developing a working model, or *prototype*, of the system the analyst is proposing to the end user. The prototype is developed prior to the final design and is used as a tool to solicit feedback from the end user. The creation of a working prototype and the solicitation of the end user's feedback allows for the design of the system to be an evolutionary process. As the prototype is modified and adjusted, the design of the system is continually being refined to meet the user's specific needs. In the traditional approach to system analysis and design, the user would have to wait until the new system was implemented to have any hands-on experience with the system. As a result, any modifications or refinements to the system would have to be made at the end of the project. With prototyping, the user can gain hands-on experience with the system during the design phase rather than after the implementation phase. By incorporating this level of user input into the system being developed the final system should have a much higher probability of being accepted by the user as well as meeting his or her needs much more closely.

It has been found that when prototyping is used during the design phase the overall time required to produce a system is reduced thereby reducing the cost of the system. In addition, building a system that incorporates all of the features required by the end user is much more difficult without prototyping. Models that are diagrammed on paper are much more difficult to conceptualize than a working model. Prototyping also greatly aids the design of the user interface of a system. Once the prototype design is complete, it can also be used by the programmers assigned to develop the actual system. This too should reduce the amount of time and cost required to complete the development of the system.

Prototyping therefore serves as an alternative to a portion of the traditional approach to the system design phase of system analysis and design. Rather than developing and diagramming a system model and possible alternatives, the system analyst would develop a working model that the user could interact with. This interaction would lead to feedback which would then result in revisions and enhancements to the prototype and the design. By soliciting the user's feedback at this stage of the process overall time requirements and costs should be reduced. The following is a list of positive and negative aspects of prototyping.

Positive Aspects

■ Increased user involvement in the design of the system.
■ Potentially reduces development time and costs.
■ Increased user involvement should lead to increased user satisfaction.

Negative Aspects

■ Not all proposed systems will lend themselves to prototyping.

■ When prototyping is used the analyst must be careful not to neglect other phases of the system analysis and design.

■ The prototype may not be used in the final working version of the system.

CONCEPT SUMMARY 14—2

The Purposes and Steps of System Development Stages

Stage	Purpose	Steps
Analysis	To formulate overall objectives To determine focus of analysis	Gather data from internal and external sources Analyze data Prepare system analysis report
Design	To determine how a system can meet information requirements	Review goals and objectives Develop system model Evaluate organizational constraints Develop alternative designs Perform feasibility analysis Perform cost/benefit analysis Prepare system design report
Programming	To write programs that perform information tasks according to system requirements	Test system programs Document all parts of system
Implementation	To bring the new system into use	Train personnel Switch from old system to new
Audit and review	To obtain feedback on system's performance	Compare actual performance with objectives Direct and correct errors Make changes as necessary

▨ SUMMARY POINTS

■ System analysis is conducted for any of four reasons: to solve a problem, to respond to a new requirement, to implement new technology, or to make broad system improvements.

■ Problem solving is an attempt to correct or adjust a currently malfunctioning information system. The analyst must balance the desire to solve just the problem at hand with an attempt to get at the most fundamental causes of the problem. The latter could snowball into a major project.

■ A new requirement is caused by either internal or external change. A typical example is a new law or a change in government regulations.

■ New technology can force system analysis by making formerly infeasible alternatives feasible.

■ The most comprehensive system analysis is conducted for a broad system

COMPUTERS AND INFORMATION PROCESSING

improvement, which can be necessitated by rapid sales or rapid internal growth or by a desire to redesign the present system.

■ Data is gathered during system analysis from internal and external sources. Interviews are an excellent way of collecting data and often lead to unexpected discoveries. A system analyst's observation of an existing information system can also reveal its inner workings. System flowcharts help the analyst get a better understanding of how the components in a system interrelate. Questionnaires can be helpful, but they are sometimes difficult to design, administer, and interpret. Formal reports tell the analyst much about the present workings of the system.

■ An analyst should also collect data from external sources such as customers, suppliers, software vendors, hardware manufacturers, books, and periodicals.

■ Data should be analyzed in any manner that helps the analyst understand the system. Grid charts, system flowcharts, and decision logic tables are three of the tools analysts use to accomplish this task.

■ The final result of the system analysis stage is the system analysis report, a report to management reviewing the results of the analysis and the feasibility of proceeding with system design and implementation.

■ If the system analysis report is approved, the analyst begins the design stage. Goals and objectives of the new or revised system are reviewed. A system model is developed and organizational constraints are evaluated.

■ Alternative designs should always be generated in the design phase. There is always more than one way to design a system, and management likes to have alternatives from which to select.

■ When developing the various alternatives, the analyst must include tentative input forms or screens, output report formats, program specifications, file or data-base designs, clerical procedures, and process-control measures for each alternative.

■ Each alternative should undergo a feasibility analysis. This involves looking at constraints such as those imposed by hardware, software, human resources, legal matters, time, and economics.

■ A cost/benefit analysis should be conducted to determine which alternative is most viable economically. While tangible costs and benefits are easy to determine, intangible benefits are difficult to quantify.

■ The final step in system design is preparing a design report to present to management. This report should explain the various alternatives and the costs, benefits, and resources associated with each. The report includes the analyst's recommendation.

■ The next stage of the system methodology is system programming. Programming is one of the most time-consuming parts of the system methodology and begins almost immediately after management has approved a design.

■ Testing is performed when each program module is completed. When all program testing is done, system testing commences.

■ Documentation is a necessary part of system and program development. System documentation provides an overview of the entire system and its subsystems and includes system flowcharts and narratives describing the input forms and computer files as well as the output reports and computer files.

■ During implementation, converting to the new system can be done in several ways. In parallel conversion, the old and the new system operate together for a period of time. In pilot conversion, the new system is first implemented in only a part of the organization to determine its adequacies and inadequacies; the latter are corrected before full-scale implementation. In phased conversion, the old system is gradually replaced with the new system one portion at a time. In crash conversion, the new system is implemented all at once.

■ Once a new system is operational, it must be audited to ascertain that the initial objectives of the system are being met and to find any problems occurring in the new system. System maintenance is the continued surveillance of system operations to determine what modifications are needed to meet the changing needs of management and to respond to changes in the environment.

■ Prototyping involves the creation of a working model of a system that can be used to solicit user feedback during the design phase of system analysis and design.

■ Prototyping creates a situation where the model goes through an evolutionary process that ultimately results in the design of the system.

■ Using prototyping should result in a system that more closely meets the needs of the user.

■ REVIEW QUESTIONS

1. What is the purpose of the proposal to conduct system analysis? How will the definition of the scope of the analysis affect the overall system analysis?

2. Identify and briefly describe the possible reasons for conducting a system analysis.

3. Which five internal sources of data do analysts frequently use? Which one appears to be most effective?

4. Briefly describe what a decision logic table is and how it can be used by a system analyst and a programmer.

5. What type of information should be contained in the system analysis report?

6. How does the focus of system design differ from that of system analysis?

7. Why is it difficult to design a perfect information system?

8. What information should be contained in the system design report? To whom is the report to be presented, and how should it be presented?

9. What are some of the methods used to train personnel in new system procedures? What groups of individuals must undergo training?

10. Explain why the documentation of both systems and programs is important to the long-term success of a system.

11. List and briefly explain the types of conversion available for a system implementation. Given a situation in which a new computer-based information system is replacing a manual system, which method of conversion might be best?

12. Why is a system audit important? What is the difference between system audit and system maintenance?

13. How does prototyping differ from the traditional approach to system design?

14. What are some of the advantages to prototyping?

General Dynamics

GENERAL DYNAMICS

HISTORY OF GENERAL DYNAMICS

General Dynamics is one of the free world's largest defense firms. It is engaged in the design, development, and manufacture of highly sophisticated defense systems and in the production and delivery of general aviation aircraft, construction materials, and natural resources. The company uses its broad technological capabilities in the assembly of military aircraft, space vehicles, electronic products, land vehicles, and nuclear-powered submarines.

Nine divisions and six major operating subsidiaries make up General Dynamics. Some of them were independent companies in existence for many years before joining General Dynamics.

An example is the founding division of General Dynamics, Electric Boat, headquartered in Groton, Connecticut. Electric Boat, which today makes nuclear-powered attack and ballistic missile-firing submarines, traces its history to the formation in 1880 of a predecessor company, Electro Dynamic. (Electro Dynamic exists today as Electric Boat's facilities in Avenel, New Jersey) Electro Dynamic's birth coincided with the introduction of electricity into everyday life; the light bulb was patented in the same year. Electro Dynamic made electric motors, batteries, and other electrical equipment.

Electric Boat received its name in 1899 when the Electric Launch Company merged with the Holland Company. Electric Launch built electrically powered pleasure boats, while the Holland Company built the U.S. Navy's first operational submarine. In the years since, Electric Boat has concentrated on submarine design and construction, although its Elco division turned out more than half of the PT boats built during World War II. Electric Boat built 85 submarines during World War I and 78 during World War II. The

division brought submarines into a new age by making the first nuclear-powered submarine, the USS Nautilus, which was launched in 1954.

After World War II, Electric Boat expanded into other lines of business, prompting the company to change its name to General Dynamics in 1952 and designate Electric Boat as a division of the company.

Just two years later, General Dynamics merged with Convair, an aviation giant formed in 1923. During World War II, Convair, known before the war as Consolidated Aircraft Co. and during the war as Consolidated Vultee, produced the Allies' most widely used heavy bomber, the B-24 Liberator, and a family of amphibious aircraft that included the PBY Catalina.

After joining General Dynamics, Convair continued to produce military aircraft such as the B-36 Peacemaker and B-58 Hustler bombers and the F-102 and F-106 delta-wing interceptors. Today, Convair manufactures cruise missiles and airliner fuselages.

Four more divisions have evolved out of Convair: Pomona (1961), which produces antiaircraft and antiship weapons such as the Sparrow and Standard missiles and the Phalanx gun system; Electronics (1961), which makes military avionics and communications systems; Space Systems (1985), which makes the Atlas I and II launch vehicles for military and commercial customers; and Fort Worth (1961), which turns out the F-16 Falcon fighter for the United States and many of its allies.

The F-16 is one of General Dynamics' major product lines. Worldwide deliveries of the Fighting Falcon are expected to exceed 4,000 aircraft.

The next major firms to join General Dynamics after its merger with Convair were Material Service Corporation and Marblehead Lime in 1960. Material Service produces construction materials in the Midwest. Marblehead mines lime and produces brick. Freeman United Coal Mining Co. became part of GD in 1972.

General Dynamics expanded into the tank business in 1982 by buying the U.S. Army's only tank builder, Chrysler Defense, Inc. Renamed Land Systems Division, it has made over 48,000 tanks since 1941. Its current product, the M1A1 Abrams, the world's most advanced ground weapon system, is descended from a long line of tanks that include the M4 Sherman. The Sherman was the Western Allies' most widely used tank during World War II.

General aviation became General Dynamics' next activity when it bought Cessna Aircraft Company in

1985. Cessna has made over 177,000 aircraft since its formation in 1927, including the U.S. Air Force's first jet trainer, the T-37. Today, Cessna makes light utility aircraft and business jets. It has produced the world's largest fleet of business jets.

In 1985, the company also established Valley Systems Division in Rancho Cucamonga, California Valley Systems, formed out of Pomona Division, makes Stinger portable antiaircraft weapons and the Rolling Airframe Missile, which defends against antiship missiles.

Other units of General Dynamics include Data Systems Division, which provides in-house computer services; General Dynamics Services Co., which supplies product support services, operations and maintenance, and construction management; and American Overseas Marine Corporation, which mans and services Maritime Prepositioning Ships that are stocked and ready to serve as supply points for U.S. forces overseas during crises.

With more than 12,000 of its 105,000 employees working as scientists and engineers, General Dynamics has a strong technological research and development capability. The company is part of the team selected to develop the Navy's Advanced Tactical Aircraft and is a member of another team bidding for the Air Force's Advanced Tactical Fighter. It is one of three firms working on the preliminary design of the National Aero-Space Plane, which will take off like a conventional aircraft and achieve orbit at greater than five times the speed of sound. GD has been picked to build the Air Force's Medium Launch Vehicle, an expendable rocket to boost payloads into orbit, and has started its own commercial launch vehicle program by funding the construction of eighteen Atlas Is to boost commercial spacecraft. The company is also involved in the design of the Navy's newest attack submarine type, the Seawolf.

GENERAL COMPUTER USE

The Data Systems Division (DSD) provides corporate-wide guidance for, direction to, and management of the company's information resources and the information services required by the company's operating divisions.

Chartered in 1973 as Data Systems Services, General Dynamics intended that data-processing functions which were being performed by individual operating units be organized and consolidated to achieve more efficient and effective use of resources.

Over the next three years, seventeen separate data-processing functions were organized into three regional Data Centers which were geographically located in close proximity to General Dynamics' major operating divisions.

In 1981, Data Systems Services was elevated to divisional status in recognition of the importance of its services to the overall business of General Dynamics.

With division headquarters located in St. Louis, Missouri, DSD currently provides information services to General Dynamics from four regional Data Centers. Data Center management works closely with General Dynamics' product divisions, who are viewed as "customers", through the product divisions' Information Resource Management (IRM) functions. Each product divisions' IRM function acts as a focal point to coordinate computing requirements for the various departments within the product division. In this respect, user demand and DSD supply can be negotiated to continue efficient and effective use of resources and provide for optimum benefit to the corporation.

Information services provided by DSD include a full range of computer processing and systems development activities. Processing represents equipment and services relating to the processing of data. Development represents services relating to the design, development, and implementation of computer-based systems. These services are provided for all facets of company operations and include business systems, computer-aided design and manufacturing (CAD/CAM) systems, scientific and engineering systems, and deliverable software, which is software actually embedded in various product division products.

Business processing services are mainly run on IBM mainframe computers located within a central computing complex at each Data Center. CAD/CAM processing utilizes a variety of processors, including large-scale mainframe computers as well as engineering workstations. Scientific and engineering systems processing is performed on a wide range of mainframes and minicomputers, with a Cray XMP supercomputer as the top of the line.

Development services are provided for all of the areas outlined above; however, concentration is heaviest in the business systems and deliverable software areas.

APPLICATION

SYSTEMS DEVELOPMENT

Business systems development consists of planning, consulting, designing or enhancing, developing or purchasing, testing, implementing, and managing systems and data bases utilized for management information, operational processes, and financial control purposes. Examples of such systems include payroll and personnel systems, material control and warehousing systems, and automated data collection systems.

Business systems are developed according to standards established to provide an effective approach to developing quality business computer systems in a consistent, cost effective manner. The standards are comprised of six phases, each of which is composed of a group of related tasks and activities. Application of the standards will vary somewhat from project to project, allowing the project manager to tailor the standards to the size and complexity of the development effort. In general, larger projects will utilize most tasks and activities while smaller efforts will be more selective.

Phase I is the Proposal Phase. When DSD services are requested, the system sponsor (customer) is responsible for describing the business objectives. This includes the business opportunity or problem, as well as the requirements. Based upon customer input, DSD will establish the project scope, analyze alternatives (make/buy analysis), develop preliminary cost and schedule estimates, and prepare a proposal document.

Phase II is the Requirements Phase. The system sponsor and DSD work together to define detailed system requirements by developing, evaluating, and refining one or more iterations of a prototype system. The prototype is a working model of the system developed quickly to help the user refine system requirements and to identify missing requirements. When all requirements have been defined, the final iteration of the prototype becomes the basis for a document which clearly and concisely states the system requirements. This document includes functions to be performed, input/output purposes and formats, performance considerations, interfaces with other systems, system controls and security, hardware/software requirements, and system acceptance criteria.

Phase III is the System Design Phase. During this phase, requirements are transformed into a system design. Detailed specifications are developed to ensure that customer requirements are met when the system is installed. Design specifications include data structure, program specifications, input/output formats, test plans, implementation plans, and support materials (manuals). This phase contains two critical reviews which decide whether the project will proceed into development, test, and implementation. A Technical Design Review is held to verify that the system design is technically feasible and acceptable. A System Design Phase Review is held to provide a management summary of the project progress to date and to determine the feasibility of the work plan for remaining tasks and activities. Included in this review are updated cost and schedule estimates.

Phase IV is the Program Development Phase. This phase consists of program logic design, test data generation, program coding, unit testing, and integration testing. This phase is complete when the programs have been developed and thoroughly tested from the unit level to and including integration testing at the system level in preparation for customer acceptance testing.

Phase V is Acceptance Testing and Installation. During this phase, the entire system (programs, procedures, hardware, and system software) is tested by the system sponsor and appropriate product division personnel to verify that the system will satisfy the established acceptance criteria. User training is also conducted during this phase. At the conclusion of this phase, the system and all necessary support material have been tested/verified and turned over for use by the product division.

Phase VI is a Post Implementation Tuning Phase. The purpose of this phase is to retain project team expertise during the initial period of system operation. DSD and product division personnel support the "burn-in" period and finalize any documentation requiring updating. The system sponsor and DSD work together to identify and resolve any problems with the system after installation. All aspects of the system, ranging from computer usage to user training needs, are reviewed to identify areas where improvements can be made.

Deliverable software systems (i.e., those embedded in products) are generally developed according to applicable military specifications or contract line item specifications. Typical phases of development for these systems include preliminary analysis, requirements analysis, preliminary design, detailed design, coding and unit testing, software component integration and testing, software system integration and testing, acceptance testing, installation, and turnover.

DISCUSSION POINTS

1. Describe the interaction between computer professionals and customers during systems development at General Dynamics.

2. Discuss the role of documentation in this approach.

CHAPTER

15

Management Information Systems and Decision Support Systems

OUTLINE

Introduction
**Definition of a Management
    Information System (MIS)**
Levels of Management
  Top-Level Management
  Middle-Level Management
  Lower-Level Management
  Problems and Differences

Types of Reports
  Scheduled Listings
  Exception Reports
  Predictive Reports
  Demand Reports
Management and MIS
Design Methodology
  Top-Down Design
  Design Alternatives

Decision Support Systems
  The Purpose and Scope of a DSS
  A Model: The Heart of a DSS
  The Future of DSS
Summary Points
Review Questions

DSS/EIS Aids in Corporate Downsizing

Software Magazine

As Robert G. Wallace stepped down as president of Phillips 66 on Oct. 31, he left the executive suite in Bartlesville, Okla., with earned credits as a fighter and a visionary.

His legacy includes an executive information system which has played a vital role in the regeneration of the company's fortunes.

Those fortunes were at a low ebb in early '85. Phillips Petroleum was struggling for survival in a crippled oil market against two successive hostile takeover attempts. Rather than yield to the corporate marauders, Phillips chose to stand and fight.

Toning the corporate structure was a central, strategic aim. Wallace followed through at the Phillips 66 "downstream" subsidiary (Phillips Petroleum's refining/marketing/transportation arm) with a program that combined company reorganization, austerity, and enhanced management productivity.

In June 1985 Wallace trimmed Phillips 66 from 14 divisions to nine and made significant changes in leadership. He merged four separate MIS and operations analysis/control units, into one unit under the direction of E. L. (Gene) Batchelder. His title is manager of operations analysis and control, and management information systems.

Austerity thinned the executive ranks by 40% and severely reduced strategic support staff. Wallace believed a solution existed that would compensate for the leaner, decision-making structure.

In August 1985 Wallace commissioned Batchelder to develop a customized information system to meet the needs of the CEO and the nine divisional vice presidents. He gave Batchelder a year to plan and implement the project.

"I'm a financial man, not an MIS specialist," Batchelder disclosed. If not a total awareness, he had premonitions that the mission would lead to uncharted waters and that the outcome, at best, was uncertain.

He appointed two top staffers—B. J. Culpepper and Glenn Jones—to spearhead the project. Their abilities would prove decisive. "When we started," Batchelder recounted, "we didn't know we were building an EIS."

The plan evolved as information needs were analyzed, delivery requirements defined and systems options explored. Batchelder said, "we had to design for the response requirements of a market that presented greater volatility and competitive pressures than we ever faced."

For example, if motor fuel pricing was set a penny too low, it could mean a difference of as much as $40 million in annual profits. A similar mispricing of polyethylene could reduce an-

nual profits by as much as $15 million.

Addressing short-term events and reporting historical trends and forecasts required accelerated delivery. Managers needed to be able to monitor and assess information changes, and communicate action to all parties in the loop, with speed and efficiency consistent with the realities of competition.

User friendliness was just as important as system performance. System operations, including applications development, had to be easy to quell the apprehensions of executives who were unfamiliar with computing.

The approved design specified a micro-mainframe system running off the company's IBM 3081 IS mainframe, which provided central data storage, analysis, and graphics.

Focus, a 4GL/DBMS from Information Builders of New York, was used for PC-mainframe access, data integration, and EIS information analysis. Graphics were delivered by software designed by Phillips in collaboration with IBM. For E-Mail, calendar, and scheduling functions, the system ran the existing Profs software from IBM.

A scripting language from Software Corp. of America, Stamford, Conn., called 'Gateway PC' was used to write various menus. These simplified access to outside databases such as Dow-Jones News Retrieval.

In July 1986 Wallace's EIS workstation was operational. In November on schedule and within the budget, individually customized systems for the nine divisional vice presidents were

A R T I C L E

online. By December 1986, 50 reports were available to the executive users.

In January 1988 the EIS provided over 1,000 displays for 45 executives and 35 secretaries and staff managers, now supported by a 3090 host.

Division managers reported saving as much as 40 minutes a day in reading time, and productivity increased in every division.

Although many companies are decreasing the size of their information systems departments, these companies still recognize the need for quality information at all levels of management, including the executives. In order to provide this vital information with less personnel, companies are developing and implementing user-friendly systems that

can be operated by upper management. These systems, such as executive information systems, decision support systems, and expert systems help management sort through information and make timely decisions.

■ INTRODUCTION

For many years, computers have been used to perform routine and repetitive operations formerly done manually. When functions such as payroll preparation and order writing are computerized, many hours of human labor are saved. Each organization has specific needs that must be met by its computer system. The types of information that can be provided by a system are as diverse as the organization and the information. Since no two organizations are exactly alike, their computer systems are also different. Large hospitals, corporations, universities, or research laboratories usually need mainframe computers to handle their information needs while a microcomputer and peripherals might easily handle the data processing requirements for a small retail store or restaurant. Once the information is processed, it may or may not be helpful to management. This chapter explains how a management information system (MIS) ensures that the information that has been processed is useful to a company by focusing on the information needs of the organization.

■ DEFINITION OF A MANAGEMENT INFORMATION SYSTEM (MIS)

Information is data that has been processed and is useful in decision making. It helps decision makers by increasing knowledge and reducing uncertainty. Modern businesses cannot be run without information; it is the lifeblood of an organization. An information system can supply many types of information. Originally, information systems provided standard reports such as accounting statements, sales summaries, payroll reports, and personnel reports. More recently, information systems have been designed to provide information to support decision making. This application is called a **management information system (MIS).**

In Chapter 1, you learned how data processing takes raw facts called data and organizes them into information. Data processing is concerned with

HIGHLIGHT

Chief Information Officer

Businesses are recognizing the ever increasing importance of information. They are treating information as a company resource, much like goods and money. Now a number of companies have even created a new position, the Chief Information Officer (CIO), to oversee all functions pertaining to the management of corporate information. The CIO, who is equal to the CEO (Chief Executive Officer), is often in charge of the Information Systems Department and the Telecommunications Department.

What type of people are being made CIOs? Often the CIO did not move up through the ranks in an Information System Department. Although he or she may have a basic understanding of computers and data processing, the CIO is generally not a technical person. The CIO is business oriented and can see the potential of information for business applications. His or her view of needed information is not limited by the hardware and software presently being used. The CIO has a firm understanding of the company's business and where the company stands in relation to its competitors.

the immediate task of data organization. The emphasis in data processing is on the short-term or daily operations of an organization; it provides detailed kinds of information. An MIS is a formal information network using computers to provide management information for decision making. The emphasis in an MIS is on intermediate and long-range planning; therefore, less detailed and more summarized information is necessary. The goal of an MIS is to get the correct information to the appropriate manager at the right time and in a useful form. This is not always an easy task. See Concept Summary 15–1 for a review of the characteristics of data processing and management information systems.

CONCEPT SUMMARY 15—1

Data Processing vs. Management Information Systems

Characteristics of DP	Characteristics of MIS
Changes data into information	Provides correct and timely information to appropriate manager
Emphasis on short-term daily operations	Emphasis on intermediate and long-range operations
Provides detailed information	Provides summarized information

■ LEVELS OF MANAGEMENT

In order for an MIS to be successful, it is important to determine the kinds of information each manager needs. To do this, one must understand the various levels of management that exist and the kinds of decisions that are made at each level of an organization. Three levels of management generally exist within an organization, and managers at each of these levels make different types of decisions that require different types of information. Figure 15–1 depicts the three management levels.

Top-Level Management

Top-level managers are concerned with strategic decision making. Activities at this level are future-oriented and involve a great deal of uncertainty. Examples include establishing goals and determining strategies to achieve the goals. These strategies may involve introducing new product lines, determining new markets, acquiring physical facilities, setting financial policies, generating capital, and so forth.

Middle-Level Management

Middle-level managers are concerned with tactical decision making. The emphasis in middle level is on activities required to implement the strategies determined at the top level; thus, most middle-management decision making is tactical. Activities include planning working capital, scheduling production, formulating budgets, making short-term forecasts, and administering personnel. Much of the decision making at this level pertains to control and short-run planning.

FIGURE 15—1

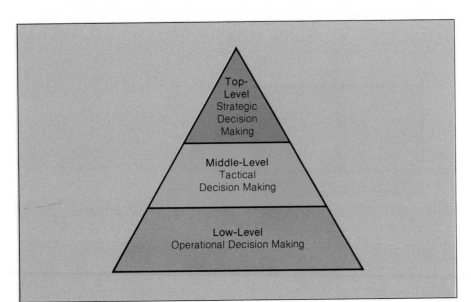

Lower-Level Management

Members of the lowest level in the management hierarchy (first-line supervisors and foremen) make operating decisions to ensure that specific jobs are done. Activities at this level include maintaining inventory records, preparing sales invoices, determining raw material requirements, shipping orders, and assigning jobs to workers. Most of these operations are structured and the decisions are deterministic—they follow specific rules and patterns established at higher levels of management. The major function of lower-level management is controlling company results—keeping the results in line with plans and taking corrective actions if necessary.

Problems and Differences

Managers at all levels must be provided with decision-oriented information. The fact that the nature of decisions differs at the three levels creates a major difficulty for those attempting to develop an MIS: the information must be tailored to provide appropriate information to all levels (see Figure 15–2).

Decisions made at the lower level are generally routine and well defined. The needs of first-level supervisors can be met by normal administrative data-processing activities such as preparation of financial statements and routine record keeping. Although this level of decision making is fairly basic, it provides the data-processing foundation for the entire organization. If the information system is faulty at this level, the organization faces an immediate crisis.

Tactical decision making is characterized by an intermediate time horizon, a high use of internal information, and significant dependence on rapid processing and retrieval of data. Many middle-level decisions are badly structured. The major focus of tactical decisions is how to make efficient use of organizational resources.

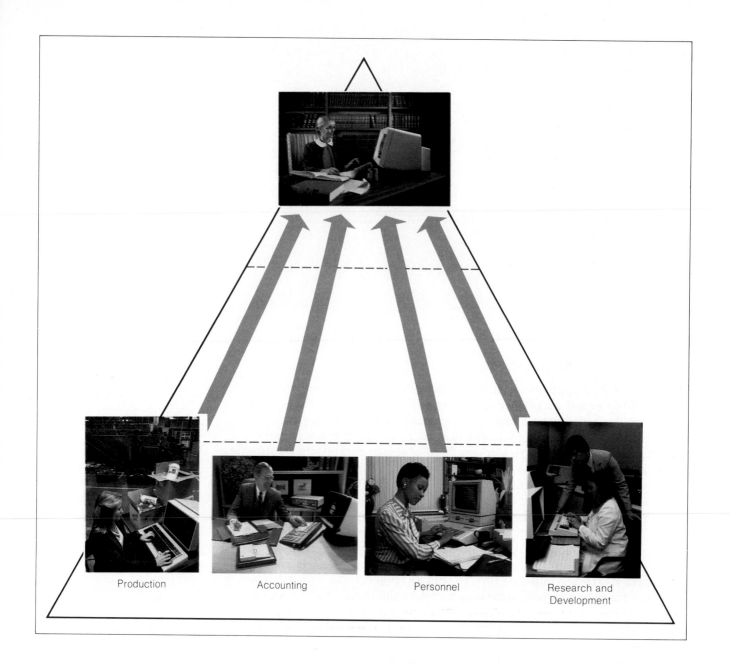

FIGURE 15—2

Functional Information Flow
Information at the lowest level contains the most detail. As information flows upward, details are weeded out; only important facts are presented to top management.

The main problems in MIS design arise when planners attempt to define and meet information requirements of top-level management. Delineating these information needs clearly is extremely difficult, if not impossible. Most problems are nonrepetitive, have great impact on the organization, and involve a great deal of uncertainty. Most information systems serve the needs of the two lower levels but are not adequately designed to cope with the variety of problems encountered by top management.

Since the information needs at the three levels differ, data has to be structured differently at each level. For routine operating decisions such as payroll preparation and inventory stocking, separate employee and inventory files are adequate. To serve the middle and top levels, the data should be organized to provide inquiry capabilities across functional lines and to handle routine information reports. Concept Summary 15–2 summarizes the differences among the decision-making levels.

CONCEPT SUMMARY 15–2

Differences among Decision-Making Levels			
	Levels of Decision Making		
Characteristics	Operational	Tactical	Strategic
Time horizon	Daily	Weekly/monthly	Yearly
Degree of structure	High	Moderate	Low
Use of external information	Low	Moderate	Very high
Use of internal information	Very high	High	Moderate
Degree of judgment	Low	Moderate	Very high
Information online	Very high	High	Moderate
Level of complexity	Low	Moderate	Very high
Information in real time	High	High	High

■ TYPES OF REPORTS

Management information systems typically generate several types of reports containing information that may be used in decision making. Reports generated include scheduled listings, exception reports, predictive reports, and demand reports.

Scheduled Listings

Scheduled listings are produced at regular intervals and provide routine information to a wide variety of users. Since they are designed to provide information to many users, they tend to contain an overabundance of data. Much of the data may not be relevant to a particular user. Such listings constitute most of the output of current computer-based information systems.

Exception Reports

Exception reports are action-oriented management reports. The performance of business systems is monitored, and any deviation from expected results triggers the generation of a report. These reports can also be produced during processing, when items are collected and forwarded to the computer in a group. Exception reports are useful because they ignore all normal events and focus management's attention on abnormal situations that require special handling.

Predictive Reports

Predictive reports are used for planning. Future results are projected on the basis of decision models that can be either simple or highly complex. The usefulness of these reports depends on how well they can predict future events. Management can manipulate the variables included in a model to get responses to "what if" kinds of queries. Predictive reports are especially suited to the tactical and strategic decision making performed in the middle and upper levels of management.

Demand Reports

As the name implies, demand reports are produced only on request. Since these reports are not required on a continuing basis, they are often requested and displayed on a computer terminal. The MIS must have an extensive and appropriately structured data base to provide responses to unanticipated queries. No single data base can meet all the needs of the user, but a data base in a well-designed MIS should include data that may be needed to respond to possible user queries. Because it requires a sophisticated data base, demand reporting can be expensive, but it allows decision makers to obtain relevant and specific information at the moment it is needed.

■ MANAGEMENT AND MIS

Although an MIS can help management make decisions, it cannot guarantee that the decisions will be successful. One problem that frequently arises is determining what information is needed by management. To many, decision making is an individual art. Experience, intuition, and chance affect the decision-making process. These inputs are all but impossible to quantify. In designing a system, the analyst relies on the user to determine information requirements. Frequently lacking precise ideas of what they need, managers request everything the computer can provide. The result is an overload of information. Instead of helping the manager, this information overload creates another problem: how to distinguish what is relevant from what is irrelevant.

After the MIS has been installed, management does not always consider the change beneficial. In some cases, however, the people who must use the system were not involved in the analysis and design; therefore their expectations are unrealistic. Managers frequently expect that decision making will be totally automatic after implementation of an MIS. They fail to recognize that unstructured tasks are difficult to program. Even though routine decisions (such as ordering materials when inventory stock goes below a certain point) can be programmed easily, decisions that depend on more than quantitative data require human evaluation, because the computer system has no intuitive capability.

Other problems may arise. As the computer takes over routine decisions, managers may resist further changes. They may fear that their responsibility for decision making will be reduced or that the computer will make their positions obsolete. They may fail to realize that the availability of good information can enhance their managerial performance.

The success of an MIS depends largely on the attitude and involvement of management. An MIS is most apt to be successful when it is implemented in an organization already operating on a sound basis, rather than in an organization seeking a miracle.

DESIGN METHODOLOGY

As the pace of technological innovation accelerates, data-processing departments must try to keep current with the changes. Software development is far behind existing technology, because software development is extremely labor-intensive. As a result, data-processing departments today face a productivity problem; they must obtain greater software development for each dollar invested. The basic ways of increasing productivity are: (a) to automate the software development process; (b) to require employees to work harder, or longer, or both; or (c) to change the way things are done. Structured design attempts to achieve greater productivity by focusing on the third method.

Top-Down Design

Top-down design is a structured approach to designing an MIS. The approach attempts to simplify a system by breaking it down into logical functions, or modules. These, in turn, are further divided. The system is first defined in terms of the functions it must perform. Each of these functions is then translated into a module. The correct system design may require several of these modules to perform all the required tasks.

In top-down design, the most general level of organization is the main module; this overall view of the organization is most critical to the success of the system design. Modules at this level contain only broad descriptions of functions in the system. These functions are further broken down into lower-level modules that contain more detail about the specific steps to be performed. Depending on the complexity of the system, several levels of modules may be required, with the lowest-level modules containing the greatest amount of detail.

The modules of the system design are related to each other in a hierarchical manner. These relationships can be depicted graphically in a structure chart. Figure 15–3 shows a portion of such a chart for the application process at a university. Using top-down design, the application process is broken down into its main modules: reviewing the applications, notifying applicants, and considering applicants for financial aid. Each of these functions can be broken down into more specific tasks. For example, the review process consists of checking the application form, obtaining transcripts to verify the grade-point average, obtaining official SAT or ACT scores, and reading the essays submitted by the applicant. These tasks may be broken down even further, if necessary.

Design Alternatives

The development of an MIS is an integrated approach to organizing a company's activities. The company's MIS must be structured in a way that will allow it to realize the full benefits of integration. When considering alternative organizational structures, the analyst faces virtually unlimited possibilities. This section describes four basic design structures: centralized,

HIGHLIGHT

Information Center

As PCs become more popular, other departments besides Information Services (IS) are now purchasing and using their own hardware and software. In response to the situation, some IS departments have developed Information Centers (ICs). The purpose of the IC is to provide users with assistance in using personal computers for particular business applications. The assistance can be in the form of helping users select hardware or adapt software. IC groups can also provide training for users.

In some cases the IC is a good solution to growing user demands for information. If users can run their applications on PCs, then the mainframe is free to run bigger jobs. This could decrease the backlog of programs that need to be run on the mainframe. Yet an IC can also present problems. Some IS professionals feel the security and integrity of data is jeopardized because so many users can access and change data. There is a much greater potential for either deliberate sabotage or careless error.

So what is the final word on ICs? So far IS professionals cannot agree whether the service is beneficial or hazardous. But one thing is certain, users like controlling their own data—and they intend to continue doing so—with or without the support of an IC provided by Information Services.

FIGURE 15–3

Structure Chart for the Application Process at a University

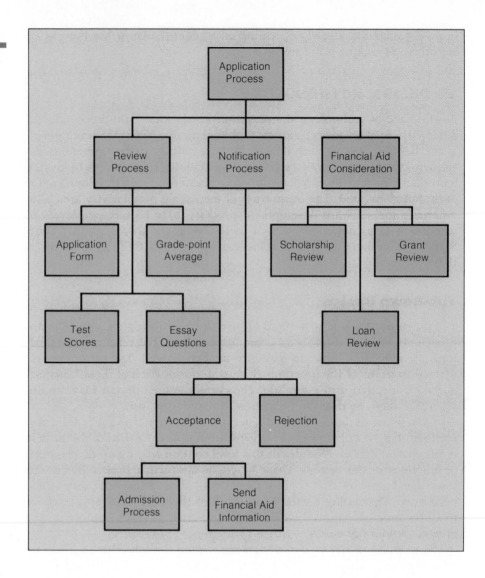

hierarchical, distributed, and decentralized. These structures should be viewed as checkpoints along a continuous range of design alternatives rather than as separate, mutually exclusive options. For example, a system design may incorporate characteristics from both the distributed system and the decentralized system.

The **centralized design** is the most traditional approach. It involves the centralization of computer power. A separate electronic data-processing (EDP) department is set up to provide data-processing facilities for the organization. This department's personnel, like other staff personnel, support the operating units of the organization. All program development, as well as all equipment acquisition, is controlled by the EDP group. Standard regulations and procedures are employed. Distant units use the centralized equipment by a remote access communication network. A common data base exists, permitting authorized users to access information (see Figure 15–4a).

When **hierarchical design** is used, the organization consists of multiple levels with varying degrees of responsibility and decision-making authority. In hierarchical design, each management level is given the computer power necessary to support its task objectives. At the lowest level, limited support is required, because the work is considered technical in nature. Middle-level support is more extensive, because managerial decisions at this level require more complicated analysis (hence, more information processing). Finally, top-level executives require little detailed information since they work with general issues requiring information that can be obtained only with greater processing and storage capabilities. An example of this design approach is shown in Figure 15–4b.

The **distributed design** approach identifies the existence of independent operating units but recognizes the benefits of central coordination and control. The organization is broken into the smallest activity centers requiring computer support. These centers may be based on organizational structure, geographical location, functions, operations, or a combination of these factors. Hardware (and often people) are placed within these activity centers to support their tasks. Total organizationwide control is often evidenced by the existence of standardized classes of hardware, common data bases, and coordinated system development. The distributed computer sites may or may not share data elements, workloads, and resources, depending on whether they are in communication with each other. An example of the distributed design approach is given in Figure 15–4c.

In a **decentralized design,** authority and responsibility for computer support are placed in relatively autonomous organizational operating units. These units usually parallel the management decision-making structure. Normally, no central control point exists; the authority for computer operations goes directly to the managers in charge of the operating units. Since there is no central control, each unit is free to acquire hardware, develop software, and make personnel decisions independently. Responsiveness to user needs is normally high because close working relationships are reinforced by the proximity of the system to its users. Communication among units is limited or nonexistent, thereby ruling out the possibility of common or shared applications. This design approach can only be used where an existing organizational structure supports decentralized management. Furthermore, it is not highly compatible with the MIS concept. An example of the decentralized design approach is shown in Figure 15–4d.

▬ DECISION SUPPORT SYSTEMS

Closely related to the MIS is the decision support system. Whereas an MIS supplies managers with information to support structured decisions, a **decision support system (DSS)** provides managers with information to support relatively unstructured decisions. For example, an MIS may provide information about sales trends, changes in productivity from one quarter to the next, or fluctuation in inventory levels. Information such as this tells the manager what has already happened. A DSS, on the other hand, may provide financial planning models or optimal production schedules that information managers can use to determine what *might* happen.

Essentially, a DSS and an MIS do the same thing—they process data to get information that is useful to managers. What, then, is the difference

FIGURE 15—4

Sample Design Structures

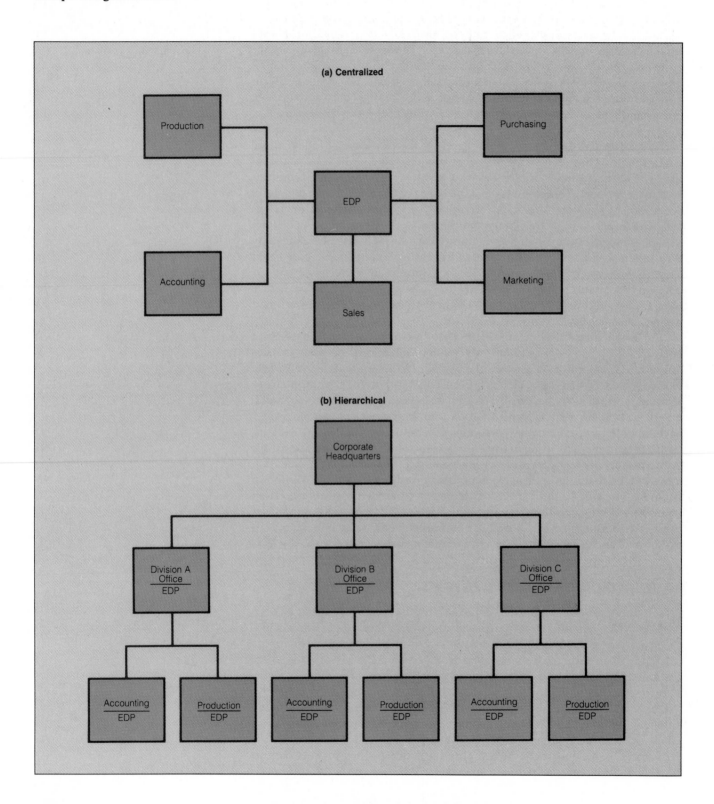

(a) Centralized

Production

Purchasing

EDP

Accounting

Marketing

Sales

(b) Hierarchical

Corporate Headquarters

Division A Office EDP

Division B Office EDP

Division C Office EDP

Accounting EDP

Production EDP

Accounting EDP

Production EDP

Accounting EDP

Production EDP

FIGURE 15—4

Continued

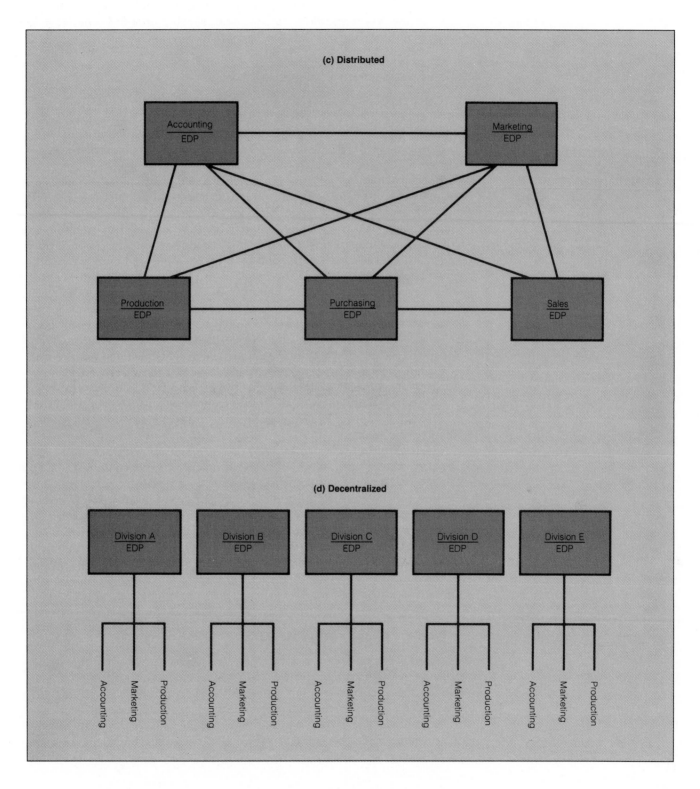

(c) Distributed

(d) Decentralized

between them? Some professionals in the information field believe the difference is that an MIS supports only structured or operational decisions, while a DSS supports unstructured or strategic decisions. The distinction is based on the type of decision supported. Others believe DSSs are merely subsystems of a larger MIS, capable of processing different types of data as a result of technological advances in hardware and software.

The Purpose and Scope of a DSS

Decision support systems separate structured (or operational) decision making from unstructured (or strategic) decision making. For example, a purchase order for a certain product may be generated automatically if an inventory stock level falls below a certain amount. Such a structured decision can be handled easily by a computer.

A decision support system, on the other hand, places more emphasis on semistructured or unstructured decisions. While the computer is used as an analytical aid to decision making, the DSS does not attempt to automate the manager's decision making or to impose solutions. For example, an investment manager must make recommendations to a client concerning the client's investments. The manager's decision is based on stock performance and requires a certain amount of judgment. The computer can be used to aid the decision but cannot make the actual recommendation to the client.

The primary use of computer technology within a DSS has been to speed the processing of the large amounts of data needed for the manager to consider the full effects of a possible decision. This permits managers to consider a greater number of alternatives—alternatives that otherwise might not have been considered, because of time constraints. But as previously stated, a DSS, and within it the use of computers, must be a normal and comfortable extension of the manager's overall method of problem solving and decision making.

Advocates of DSS, therefore, claim that its emphasis is toward improving the effectiveness and quality of decision making. The purpose of the DSS is not to replace management information systems but to enhance them. Because advances are being made in applying computer technology to the areas of tactical and strategic decision making, the rewards that can be realized are even greater than those that have occurred in the area of operational decision making. Computer applications in the areas of tactical and strategic decision making are a logical step forward in the application of computer technology to management science and a logical addition to and advancement in the area of management information systems.

A Model: The Heart of a DSS

As stated in the section on decision-oriented reports, predictive reports use decision models to project future results. Such models are suited to tactical and strategic decision making, which is the focus of a DSS.

A **model** is a mathematical representation of an actual system. The model contains independent variables that influence the value of a dependent variable. Think of the independent variables as the input and the dependent variable as the output.

In the real world, many relationships are based on the effect of an independent variable on a dependent variable. For example, the price of a sofa depends on the costs of the materials needed to make it. Sales of a new brand of toothpaste depend, in part, on the amount of money spent advertising it. The number of microwave ovens sold depends on, or is a function of, the price of the oven. This relationship between price and sales could be represented by the following mathematical model:

Microwave oven sales $=$ f(Price of the oven)

The relationship could be expressed as a mathematical equation. Then a manager could plug different prices into the equation and get some idea of how many microwave ovens would be sold at each price.

The fact that each manager must have a decision model based on his or her perception of the system is what has made the implementation of DSS so difficult. Managerial styles, as well as the environments in which people manage, are unique to each manager. In order for the DSS to be useful, it must be designed to aid a manager in his or her particular decision-making style.

Once the model for the DSS is developed, it must be incorporated into a decision support system that can be used by the manager. Some decision support systems are designed to be used to assist a manager in making specific types of decisions. For example, a DSS might be designed to assist an advertising manager in determining how much to spend for a particular advertising campaign. This type of DSS can be developed by a company for use by its managers or it could be purchased from a software vendor. An alternative to developing or purchasing a DSS to be used for a specific purpose would be to purchase packages that can be used to develop different types of decision support systems. These packages could possibly include both software and hardware and would be used by a company to develop a variety of decision support systems to be used for differing purposes. Electronic spreadsheets (discussed in Chapter 13) for example, have been used on microcomputer systems to create decision support systems that can be used for financial planning. Expert systems (also discussed in Chapter 13) can also be used to develop decision support systems. The decision support systems used by a particular company's management will depend upon the type of decision that needs to be made as well as the computer hardware and software expertise that exists within the company.

The Future of DSS

One of the key factors, if not the key factor, in the acceptance of decision support systems within business is management. How the management of a company views modeling and decision support systems is the critical factor that determines whether or not they are successfully implemented and used. Although decision modeling is used in a large number of firms, if its full potential is to be realized, obstacles such as management resistance, a lack of management sophistication, and interdepartmental communication problems must be overcome.

Many people feel that the acceptance and use of decision modeling and decision support systems in business is being slowed by the resistance of top management, which often has a skeptical attitude toward scientific management techniques and an unwillingness to accept and have confidence in these techniques. In addition, management is also sensitive to a situation in which the promise of what can be done with computers is far different from that which is finally accomplished. Before management will fully accept the use of computers and decision support systems, promises of what can be accomplished must be realistic. Until these promises are realized, management's willingness to accept new decision-making aids will be hindered.

Until recently, decision support systems have been discussed in a functional context. Each functional area of an organization may have its own DSS. The current trend, however, is the use of **simultaneous decision support systems,** or **corporate planning models.** The primary goal of simultaneous decision support systems is to combine into one system the various functional areas of an organization that affect the performance and output of other functional areas. The marketing areas of a firm, for instance, must coordinate advertising and sales efforts with production to ensure that the demand generated for a product can be met.

Organizations realize that consistent, overall strategic planning is required if the organization is to survive in a dynamic environment. For this reason, firms are attempting to develop simultaneous decision support systems that can coordinate the functional areas of a corporation as well as aid the organization's strategic and tactical planners. Figure 15–5 illustrates a possible structure for a simultaneous decision support system.

The number of organizations using simultaneous decision support systems or corporate planning models is growing. There is little doubt that the future of decision support systems lies in this direction. Advances in the areas of decision model development and applying computer technology

FIGURE 15–5

Possible Framework for Simultaneous Decision Support Systems

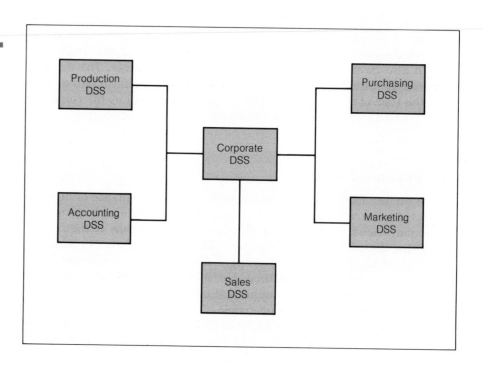

to managerial decision making are helping simultaneous decision support systems gain widespread acceptance and use.

■ SUMMARY POINTS

■ A management information system (MIS) is a formal information network that uses computer capabilities to provide management with the information necessary for decision making. The goal of an MIS is to get the correct information to the appropriate manager at the right time.

■ There are three levels of management: top-level management makes strategic and future-oriented decisions; middle-level management makes tactical decisions (implementing the strategies developed by top-level managers); and lower-level management makes the day-to-day decisions that keep the organization operating efficiently.

■ Managers at all levels must be provided with decision-oriented information. Since the information needs at the three management levels differ, data has to be structured differently at each level.

■ Decision-oriented reporting includes various types of reports required by management. Scheduled reports are produced at regular intervals and provide routine information. Exception reports are action-oriented and monitor performance—they indicate when a particular operation is not behaving as expected. Predictive reports use models to project possible outcomes of different decisions. Demand reports are usually one-time-only requests that cover unanticipated information needs.

■ Structured design is a method of breaking down a problem into logical segments, or modules. Each module performs a logical function. These modules, in turn, may be broken down further. Modules are related to one another in a hierarchical fashion, but each module is independent of the others.

■ The ways in which an MIS can be designed within the structure of an organization are virtually unlimited. Common approaches are centralized, hierarchical, distributed, and decentralized structures.

■ The centralized approach generally uses a single computer department to provide data processing for the entire organization.

■ The hierarchical approach gives each management level the computer power needed to support its task objectives.

■ The distributed approach places computer support in key activity centers, and information is shared among the various functions.

■ The decentralized approach places authority and responsibility for computer support in relatively autonomous organizational units.

■ Decision support systems emphasize effective decision making. Managers in strategic areas are provided with relevant information to help them make decisions. Support is provided for tasks that are not routine or structured. To be most useful, the decision support system should be compatible with the manager's decision-making processes.

■ The use of computers within decision support systems has primarily been to help speed the manager's analysis of decision alternatives.

■ A decision model acts as the heart of a decision support system. It is a mathematical representation of an actual system. The model should be developed by the manager who will use it so that it represents his or her perception of the actual system.

■ The future of DSS may lie in simultaneous decision support systems or corporate planning models, which are decision support systems designed to coordinate decision making within an entire organization.

■ REVIEW QUESTIONS

1. Describe the type of information that should be provided by decision-oriented reports. What level(s) of management benefit most from this type of information?

2. What levels of management exist in a typical organization? What are the information requirements at each level? What are some difficulties for the MIS attempting to supply needed information to each level?

3. Briefly explain how tactical decision making differs from strategic decision making, and how operational decision making differs from strategic decision making.

4. Identify the types of reports an MIS generates. Describe the uses of each type of report and show, by examples, where each could be utilized.

5. Contrast the distributed and centralized MIS design alternative. Which of them is likely to be more responsive to user needs?

6. Explain how "garbage in–garbage out" can affect the decision-making process in a negative way.

7. Explain the progression of the details presented in the top-down design approach of designing an MIS.

8. What is a decision support system? How does it differ from an MIS?

9. What is the purpose of a DSS? How should it interact with the manager who is using it?

10. What is a decision model? Is a model an exact replication of an actual system? Why or why not?

Pepsi-Cola Company

CAPSULE HISTORY

The roots of Pepsi-Cola Company trace to 1893, and to Caleb Bradham, a young New Bern, North Carolina pharmacist. Bradham formulated a drink combining carbonated water, sugar, vanilla, rare oils, and cola nuts, for sale in his drug store. Called "Brad's Drink" initially, it was renamed Pepsi-Cola in 1898, and trademarked in 1903.

Over the next several years Bradham expanded the business by selling licenses to bottle the product, and in 1907, syrup sales exceeded 100,000 gallons for the first time. By the following year, there were 250 independent Pepsi bottling franchises in twenty-four states.

The business prospered for ten more years, but with the end of World War I came the collapse of the sugar market—and Pepsi-Cola Company—and the start of an almost thirteen year struggle back to solvency. But, in the 1930s, prosperity returned, thanks to innovations like twelve ounces of Pepsi for the price of six ounces of other colas, and the first radio jingle ever to air nationally—"Pepsi-Cola hits the spot/Twelve full ounces, that's a lot . . ."

In 1948 the company moved its headquarters to New York City, and by the early 1950s, under the leadership of CEO Alfred Steele—whose wife was actress Joan Crawford—Pepsi was being advertised more as being part of a modern lifestyle than as a bargain.

Pepsi's worldwide expansion led to the formation of a separate international division in 1954, and in 1959 when then-Vice President Nixon provided Soviet Premier Krushchev with a sample, Pepsi became the hit of the Moscow World's Fair—auguring Pepsi's becoming the first American product ever licensed for manufacture in the Soviet Union, fifteen years later.

"Pepsi Generation" in 1963 became both the name for the young people born during the post-war baby boom and an advertising theme still in use today. It was in the '60s too, that Diet Pepsi and Mountain Dew were added to the company's product line, and PepsiCo, Inc. was formed with the merger of Pepsi-Cola and Frito-Lay.

During the 1970s the initiation of a program of strategic acquisitions—Pizza Hut in 1977, Taco Bell in 1978, and Kentucky Fried Chicken in 1986—resulted in PepsiCo's becoming the world's largest restaurant company.

On the advertising front, the Pepsi Challenge became the most successful comparative campaign in soft drink history, and in 1977, Pepsi-Cola became the number one-selling soft drink in food stores for the first time, as well as the number one-selling branded product of any kind in American supermarkets—a rank it continues to hold.

The company's tradition of innovation carried into the '80s, with Pepsi's newest product, Slice, the first soft drink with real fruit juice. In advertising, stars like Michael Jackson, Michael J. Fox, and Lionel Richie appeared in Pepsi commercials, while throughout the decade, the company continued its long-established pattern of growth at a pace well ahead of its industry.

PEPSI-COLA COMPANY

Pepsi-Cola Company, like most major corporations, relies on computers for virtually all of the fundamental data accumulation and processing necessary for the conduct of the business. Therefore, accounting and record-keeping constitute one of the key missions of the MIS function.

However, Pepsi information systems also play a key role in the overall decision-making and management of the business, the result of an MIS department philosophy of continually providing the improved systems and technology that help ease access to data and computing power for users throughout the company.

At the lowest operational level, Hewlett Packard and IBM mainframes are employed for transactional processing. General ledger functions—accounts receivable and payable—as well as other standard functions of the normal business cycle are processed and executed. Standardized reports of those transactions are

provided for management review and action by twenty-eight day period, monthly, quarterly, or in other desired formats.

These same data may also be integrated with data from other sources such as market research, syndicated data sources—Nielsen or Majers, for example—and configured specifically for research and analytical use. The information can then be accessed via specialized systems, IN*FACT on mainframe, or META-PHOR minicomputers.

Finally, these same data are again reconfigured, this time into summary formats for management decision support. Sales trends, profitability trends, regional, demographic, or seasonal performance, or any of dozens of other key performance indicators are routinely available or can easily be created on request.

The technical tools for presenting the data allow the individual manager to determine the most practical format for evaluation, and in effect, to configure reporting to his or her own needs. That capability, in conjunction with the ability to access the mainframe from a personal computer, significantly expands executive decision support capabilities.

PEPSI-COLA COMPANY: SPECIALIZED COMPUTER APPLICATIONS

The increased capacities and sophistication of general purpose computer systems, the advent of user-friendly, easy-to-use computer hardware and software, plus the growing awareness of computer capabilities on the part of nontechnical managers and executives are contributing to the changing role of the computer in large organizations.

At Pepsi, as elsewhere, those characteristics are helping to expand utilization of the computer in diverse areas of the business. Below, two typical applications are described.

Executive Information System

One of the more exciting and innovative uses of information technology at Pepsi-Cola is the Executive Information System, which provides information about key business indicators to senior level executives.

The system enables management to monitor overall performance, as well as category-specific performance, and to take appropriate managerial actions when indicated. Deviations from plan or other exception conditions, both positive and negative, are highlighted to enhance decision making.

EIS combines both the raw processing power and large data storage capabilities of the mainframe and the flexibility and ease of use of the personal computer. Data originate from a variety of sources—internal accounting systems, external tracking services, and on-line data bases, such as Dow Jones Newswire.

However, along with its other capabilities, EIS is also designed to prevent data overload, since the data provided to the executive are highly compressed, and customized into specific formats based on managerial needs.

As a result, one of the more attractive features of EIS is its ease of use. Instead of an elaborate training program, executives access the system through a highly "intuitive" user interface. With the interface, most activity is controlled through a hand held mouse instead of a keyboard. Companywide data are presented in previously formatted online reports. And when further levels of detail are desired, it's relatively simple to "bore down" into supporting data.

METAPHOR

METAPHOR is a relatively new technology for use in the development of effective marketing programs, sales planning, competitive analyses, and for enhancing research and analytical capabilities. Unlike EIS, which provides strategic information and is specifically targeted for the senior executive, METAPHOR is oriented toward tactical, short term issues.

So, for example, a market research analyst might utilize METAPHOR to produce research reports, which require both extensive processing and completion within strict deadlines. For that reason, METAPHOR provides a dedicated central processor for analytical purposes, separate from the mainframe.

Previously, automated research functions were provided entirely by a mainframe technology called IN*FACT. However, with METAPHOR, the frequently heavy processing and data storage required for research purposes can be accomplished outside the mainframe, reducing the demand on capacity.

As with EIS, much of the data available from METAPHOR is purchased from third party vendors, and augmented by data from internal accounting and transactional systems. However, because METAPHOR is concerned more with detail and specialty data than the summary-oriented EIS, it is considerably less user friendly.

Therefore, when a senior manager's information needs exceed the scope of EIS, the inquiry might pass over to a specialist, say, in market research. And since one of the strengths of the METAPHOR system is that it enables users to prepare complicated ad-hoc reports, it works as an information complement to EIS.

DISCUSSION POINTS

1. How does EIS support strategic decision making at Pepsi?
2. Why does Pepsi access external data bases?

CHAPTER

16

The Impact of Computers on People and Organizations

O U T L I N E

Introduction
Behavioral Aspects of Computer Use
  Computer Anxiety
  Computer Literacy
  Job Displacement and Retraining
  Changes in the Workplace

Office Automation
  Word Processing
  Communications
Computers in Business and Industry
  Computers in Business
  Computers in Industry

Summary Points
Review Questions

The Goal Is Working Smarter, Not Longer

Therese R. Welter
Industry Week

If you've ever done job-related work away from your office, you've telecommuted in the broadest sense of the word. But Jack Nilles, president of JALA Associates, Los Angeles, and the man who coined the word in 1973, is more specific. "Telecommuting is the partial or total substitution by telecommunications, possibly with the aid of the computer, for the commute to work," he says.

Either way, the old 9-to-5, time-oriented workday will become more flexible in the next decade as managers become more concerned with results than with controlling workers' time. In fact, "most large corporations already have a reasonable number of telecommuters—up to 5% or so," Mr. Nilles says. "But most corporations don't know." A 1987 study by Link Resources, New York, showed that 23.3 million Americans performed some or all of their job-related work at home. Projections for 1990 put that figure at 25 million to 40 million.

Perhaps the most obvious driver of this trend is the digitization of information, says Tom Miller, director of the telework group at Link Resources. "This makes work within the organization accessible from a remote location via the phone lines." Additionally, the last decade has been a harsh one for U. S. industry. In striving to remain successful in a world market, many companies have become leaner by decentralizing to cut the fat and serve markets more quickly.

The savings of telecommuting include: Less real-estate and facility maintenance, more efficient use of employees' time and individual productivity peaks, and the ability to attract specialized talent regardless of location.

SOCIAL PRESSURES. Three-fifths of all women over the age of 16 will be at work in the year 2000, says the *Workforce 2000* study done by the Hudson Institute. It cites the emerging problem of reconciling the conflicting needs of women, work, and families. Link Resources' analysis revealed that 70% of the work-at-home population are people of childbearing age. "The majority of these people are struggling with the challenge of balancing career and home lives," Mr. Miller says. "One solution is to look for extended flexitime in a corporate job."

No one is suggesting that people can simultaneously work and care for children, but telecommuting does offer a more flexible schedule for employees with the conflicting needs of child care and the traditional workday. JALA's Mr. Nilles even suggests that a company without a telecommuting option for employees in the 1990s may find itself at a disadvantage in attracting key talent.

NOT FOR EVERYONE. Even so, telecommuting will not be a universal practice. First and foremost, it must be voluntary. JALA's Mr. Nilles says that only about 5% to 15% of the U. S. workforce will use it. And most of those will be telecommuting part time in addition to reporting to the office. Yet the type of job one holds is not as important as the amount of face-to-face contact the job requires and the self-directedness of the worker. "Telecommuting is for the high-performance employee," says Carol D'Agostino, editor of Link Resources' telecommuting report. Any part of that employee's job that can be done, often with fewer distractions, away from the office—like computer programming, report writing, and planning—is appropriate.

Several unions have officially denounced the use of home-based workers because these people cannot easily be organized and protected from possible abuses. Pacific Bell, in fact, involves only salaried employees in telecommuting because of job-security issues with the union. Most experts in the early days of telecommuting thought the secretaries and data-entry people would be sent home to work, but, as Link Resources' Mr. Miller points out, "that really hasn't happened on a large scale. One reason is because it raises problems with the Fair Labor Standards Act. We often advise companies not to develop a program with FLSA-covered employees."

Perhaps the most common worry managers have about employing telecommuters is control: How do I know they're working if I can't see them doing it? In fact, studies done of telecommuters find them to be among the most professional, motivated, and productive employees in their companies. "Managers of telecommuters have to change from being cops to being *leaders*," says JALA's Mr. Nilles.

And this is the type of manager the corporation of the 1990s will require for the entire workforce anyway, not just those who telecommute, notes Joanne Pratt, author of a study on work-at-home commissioned by the National Center for Policy Analysis, Dallas. The successful manager of the future will need the ability to communicate effectively with employees and trust them, organize and schedule responsibilities more carefully, and manage for results.

Computers continue to have a major impact on when and how we work and play. As more companies develop telecommuting programs, the "average" employee may not spend 40 hours a week in the office, but may work a more productive 40 hours per week by telecommuting at least part of the time. Managers will be forced to evaluate employees on what really counts—the amount of work they perform, rather than just how much time the employees spend at the office.

INTRODUCTION

Computers, although incapable of conventional thought and feeling, greatly affect our personal lives and the world in which we live. Because of computer technology, the way in which we live has changed drastically in recent history. The computer revolution has had an impact on individuals and organizations alike. While most people agree that computers benefit our society, the computer revolution has had some negative effects on people and organizations.

This chapter discusses the impact the computer has had on both our individual lives and on organizations and their struggle to survive in an ever-changing environment. The behavioral aspects of the impact of computers is discussed, as is the nature of their impact on organizations in business, industry, and government. The chapter also reviews some of the effects the computer has had on the office environment by exploring office automation.

BEHAVIORAL ASPECTS OF COMPUTER USE

Computer Anxiety

The rapid pace at which computers have been integrated into our society has created a group of people who fear the effects computers have on their lives and society in general. People who have this fear are said to be suffering from **computer anxiety** or **computerphobia.** In many cases these individuals are intimidated by computers. Some people not familiar with computers

C H A P T E R

16

are afraid that if they make a mistake and press the wrong button, valuable information will be destroyed. Another common fear experienced by many people is the threat of job loss due to computerization. The overwhelming use of jargon associated with computers also leads to computer anxiety. Terms such as bits, bytes, Ks, ROM, CPU, disk drives, emulators, and networks can be confusing and intimidating to the computer novice.

Age, too, is a factor that contributes to computerphobia. People who grew up in an environment largely unaffected by computer technology tend to resist using the machines, while young people are much quicker to accept the new technology. The fear of the continuing advancement of computers into our lives—a fear of the unfamiliar—is often referred to as *high-tech anxiety*. High-tech anxiety is predominant among older people, who have had limited contact with the computer in general.

Another type of computer anxiety is thought to be gender related. Recent studies involving women in computer fields, however, have shown that women in computer-related jobs perform their duties with a skill and confidence equal to that of males. Genevieve Cerf, an instructor in electrical engineering at Columbia University, feels that women make better programmers than men. Many studies have found that women are more organized, more verbal, and more likely to consider the end user when writing computer programs. Studies by biologists and psychologists suggest that women are better than men at skills that depend on the left hemisphere of the brain—communication and logic skills. Logic skills, in particular, are essential to computer programming.

One benefit for women who obtain a computer science degree and enter the field is pay. According to a National Science Foundation study, women with computer science degrees earn nearly 100 percent of the salary that men holding a similar position earn. This fact may seem trivial; however, in some occupations women earn as little as 59 cents for every dollar earned by a man in a similar position. The equal pay issue draws much attention and may be one reason why women account for 26 percent of computer professionals.

Still another type of computer anxiety stems from a fear of depersonalization. To many people, the use of a computer for things such as record keeping and billing often leads to a feeling of being treated as a number rather than as a person. This factor of impersonalization has led many people to develop negative attitudes concerning computers.

Computer Literacy

There is currently no standard definition of **computer literacy.** Most people, however, feel that being comfortable using computers to solve problems of both an academic and a personal nature is important. This implies that students need some knowledge of basic computer use and the functions of various hardware components. Computer literacy courses have been designed to teach these subjects. As more and more children and adults take computer literacy courses, computer anxiety will also be reduced within the overall population.

One goal of high school computer literacy courses is to give students an understanding of how computers work. Students learn to identify the parts of a computer; they also learn to follow the path that electricity takes and see firsthand the practical need for and use of the binary number system. Computer literacy courses also examine the effect of computers on society. Knowing the history of computers, examples of current uses, and projected future trends is important to understanding how computers are changing our lives.

The importance of computer literacy was evidenced by the proposal introduced by the Federal Commission on Excellence in Education in May 1983 to implement new guidelines to stem the "rising tide of mediocrity" in our society. Among these guidelines was a suggestion that all students be required to take a half-year of computer science in high school. Despite all the controversial opinions generated by the report, that particular suggestion was questioned by very few people. Why? The most likely answer is that parents and other adults realize there is no way to stop the growing use of computers. Schools cannot be allowed the option of ignoring computers, because these machines alter jobs, entertainment, and home life so radically. It is becoming evident that people who learn about computers are advancing in their jobs, while people who avoid the use of computers may be forfeiting promotions and even job security. Although computer literacy is vital in the education of younger generations, members of the adult work force should also take steps to gain computer literacy.

Job Displacement and Retraining

Ever since the Industrial Revolution, automation has been a source of concern to people. Technology has automated processes leading to greater efficiency and lower costs but it has also eliminated many jobs. The growing use of computers has led to the growing fear of unemployment and depersonalization. Whether or not this fear is justified is yet to be seen. Evidence of the past three decades does not indicate that increased automation leads to increased unemployment. To be sure, workers have been displaced; but each new technology has created new employment opportunities that more than compensate for the jobs eliminated. For example, the invention of the automatic weaving machine eliminated many jobs in the garment industry; but this effect was offset by the creation of a whole new industry involved in the manufacture and marketing of the new equipment.

Several studies have been conducted to determine the effects of computer automation on jobs. While the results have not been conclusive, in general they indicate that a certain amount of job displacement can be expected because the computers take over many routine clerical jobs. The extent to which such displacement occurs depends on several factors, including the following:

■ The goals that are sought from the use of the computer. Is the objective to be able to handle an increasing workload with the same personnel, or is it to reduce costs by eliminating jobs?
■ The growth rate of the organization. If the organization is expanding, it can more easily absorb workers whose jobs are being eliminated, since many new jobs are created to cope with the increasing business.
■ The planning that has gone into the acquisition and use of the computer. With careful preparation, an organization can anticipate the personnel

changes a computer system will bring about and make plans either to reassign the affected people or to help them to find new jobs with other organizations. First-time use of a computer-based system will definitely create new jobs in the areas of computer operations, data entry, programming, and system analysis and design. Usually, though, the skills and education required for these jobs differ from those required for the eliminated jobs. Displaced employees can be trained, however, to handle jobs such as operating computer equipment and keying in data. Employees can also be sent to schools for more formal training.

The current task of retraining displaced and unemployed workers has been assumed by groups such as businesses (which provide internal retraining), colleges, vocational schools, private training centers, and the federal government (through aid to states). Some of the more popular programs for retraining include robotics maintenance, computer programming, numerical-control machinery programming and operation, word processing, computer maintenance, and electronics (see Figure 16–1).

Changes in the Workplace

Computers have made changes in the workplace common. Farmers, secretaries, and business managers alike have experienced the effects computers can have on their jobs. The office is one area that offers great potential for automation. Office automation is discussed in the following section, while the impact the computer has had on workers and workstations will be discussed here.

Worker interaction with computers has led to new concerns. Perhaps the concerns that have received the most publicity have been those regarding worker health. The biggest complaint of office workers in automated offices is that of eyestrain, followed closely by complaints of backstrain. The issue of whether the small amount of radiation given off by the CRT screen is

FIGURE 16–1

Retraining can help workers whose jobs are eliminated by the introduction of computers into the workplace.

COMPUTERS AND INFORMATION PROCESSING

Health Problems and VDTs

It looks like a small TV screen—a rather harmless piece of equipment—yet the possible health problems caused by using a VDT (visual display terminal) have been debated for years. Employees have stated that working on VDTs has caused headaches, eyestrain, and backaches. Supporters of VDT use have shown that it is often not the VDT but the work environment that causes these problems. The eyestrain (a possible cause of headaches) is often caused by a glare produced by overhead fluorescent lighting. The backaches are often caused by inappropriate chairs and desks. A keyboard placed on a regular desk is often too high for workers. Adjustable desks and chairs can ease the strain on an employee's neck, back, and shoulders.

Studies have also examined the relationship between VDTs and miscarriages; these studies were inconclusive. Recently, however, a study by the Kaiser Permanent Medical Group, Inc. showed that women who work at VDTs more than 20 hours per week had more than three times the number of miscarriages as non-VDT users. Although experts say they need to investigate the relationship further, they admit that VDTs may be the possible cause of the miscarriages.

In another area, a report from the VDT Clinic at the University of California at Berkeley showed that VDTs may cause more eye problems than was originally thought. Researchers have found that younger workers (20 to 30 year olds) who work at VDTs for about six hours a day require prescription eyeglasses sooner than non-VDT workers. Again, the relationship between VDTs and eye problems requires further study.

In the meantime, managers need to be sensitive to the possible health problems associated with VDTs. Positions should be designed so that working at a VDT is only part of an employee's responsibilities. Also, pregnant employees should have the option of working in a position that does not threaten the pregnancy.

hazardous has not been resolved satisfactorily. It is recognized, though, that with prolonged contact CRTs cause eyestrain, loss of visual acuity, changes in color perception, back and neck pain, stomachaches, and nausea.

To help alleviate some of the health concerns associated with the automated workplace, the science of ergonomics has emerged. **Ergonomics,** the method of researching and designing computer hardware and software to enhance employee productivity and comfort, promises a better, more productive workplace. Major areas of research include the different elements of the workstation and software.

To reduce such physical problems as eyestrain and backstrain, it is recommended that the time spent at a CRT be reduced to a maximum of two hours per day of continuous screen work, that periodic rest breaks be granted, and that pregnant women be permitted to transfer to a different working environment upon request. Recommendations have also been made regarding the design of the CRT and of the keyboard. Suggestions have been made regarding their slope, layout, adjustability, and the use of numeric keypads and function keys (see Figure 16–2).

Other problems with the workstation include poor lighting and noise generated by printers. Sound-dampening covers and internal sound dampening are recommended but still do not reduce the noise sufficiently. The best solution to date is to put the printers in a separate room or at least

FIGURE 16—2

Specially designed keyboards are part of a good working environment.

away from the workers' area. Along with these suggestions, recommendations have been made regarding the tables and chairs used for data-processing work.

The application of ergonomics to workstations has resulted in a 10 to 15 percent improvement in performance in some offices (see Figure 16–3).

OFFICE AUTOMATION

As computer technology enters the workplace, the office environment is experiencing changes. Businesses are realizing that automating office pro-

FIGURE 16—3

An ergonomically designed workstation can help improve worker health and productivity.

cedures is efficient, cost effective, and, in fact, necessary to deal with the exploding information revolution. **Office automation,** the comprehensive term applied to this transition, refers to all processes that integrate computer and communication technology with the traditional manual processes. Virtually every office function—typing, filing, and communications—can be automated.

This section will discuss the characteristics of the elements that comprise office automation: word processing, communications, and local area networks.

Word Processing

Word processing is often considered the first building block in automating the workplace. It is the most widely adopted office automation technology; an estimated 75 percent of U.S. companies employ some type of word processing. Word processing, the manipulation of written text to achieve a desired output, bypasses the difficulties and shortcomings associated with traditional writing and typing. Word processors offer many functions to increase efficiency in the text-manipulation process. You may recall from Chapter 13 that standard features include automatic centering, pagination (page numbering), alphabetizing, justification of type, and reformatting of paragraphs; word processors also usually have features enabling them to boldface, search and find, and move blocks of text.

Special function keys and codes are used to format the document being typed. The user may create, edit, rearrange, insert, and delete material—all electronically—until the text is exactly as desired. Then the text can be printed as well as stored on tape or disk for later use. Each copy of the text printed is an original; thus the output of a word-processing system is of a consistently high quality.

Word processing can be used for a variety of tasks. Some popular uses include editing lengthy documents (this eliminates the need to have a document completely retyped every time it is edited), producing original form letters, and completing lengthy forms where tab stops can be automatically generated to increase the typist's speed. Some other functions that can be performed on many word-processing systems are merging data with text, processing files, performing mathematical functions, generating the output of photocomposition devices, facilitating electronic filing, and distributing text after it has been created, which allows documents prepared in one location to be printed in others.

A typical word-processing system consists of a keyboard for data input, a CRT or LED display screen for viewing text material, a secondary storage unit (disk or tape), and a printer for generating output (see Figure 16–4). Word processing is available in a variety of configurations, including electronic typewriters, dedicated word processors, dedicated data processors, and small business computers.

The major advantages of word processing over traditional text preparation are increased productivity and reduction in preparation time. Word processing, like data processing, relieves workers of time-consuming and routine tasks, thereby increasing standards of productivity and quality. It is estimated that a secretary's productivity can be increased 25 to 200 percent by using word processing. Because a document does not have to be

FIGURE 16—4

Word-Processing System

retyped every time a change is made, the preparation time is reduced dramatically.

One disadvantage of word processing is the increase in the number of times a document is revised. Because it is so easy to change a document, personnel make changes more often than when documents are prepared manually. To a point this can be useful; however, there is a limit to the number of times a revision improves a document. Another disadvantage in the past has been the cost of purchasing and implementing a word-processing system. Decreasing equipment costs, however, are making word processing more affordable for companies of all sizes.

Only a fraction of computer capabilities were applied to word-processing techniques in the past. Currently, many systems offer such features as spelling checkers that handle personal names, built-in dictionaries of definitions to provide the user with the meaning of an unfamiliar word, and thesauruses that provide the user with alternative words to be used. Word processors may eventually automatically and correctly hyphenate words (they only guess now) and check for correctness of standardized abbreviations, commas around dates, and written-out numbers compared to numerals. In case the user's grammar is not up to par, some word processors may check and correct grammar and try to anticipate the next character to be typed. The user will be able to override the computer in case it does not select the correct character; however, this feature could save the user a considerable amount of time when lengthy words or phrases are duplicated throughout a document.

Color word processing should be available in the future. With this feature, each revision could be shown in a different color so that a distinction could be made as to the most recent revision. Also, different levels of management could have color codes so that informed decisions could be made as to what should be changed and what should not. Word processors have become much more portable; they are used on airplanes and in cars. A few offer voice-input capabilities, eliminating the initial typing requirement. Word processing is in its infancy, with many future capabilities not even thought of yet.

Communications

An important benefit of office automation is the communication capabilities it makes possible. Such capabilities allow the electronic exchange of information between employees. Communications may be accomplished through forms such as electronic mail, teleconferencing, and telecomputing.

ELECTRONIC MAIL. Electronic mail is the transmission of messages at high speeds over telecommunication facilities (see Figure 16–5). It is used primarily for internal, routine communications; however, with the development of new technology, it is beginning to replace the traditional postal service. The concept behind these computer-based mail systems involves the storage of messages in a special area until the recipient can access them. People using electronic systems can be in remote locations. Receivers are notified of waiting mail when they log on to their computer. They can then view the incoming mail items on a CRT screen or can have the items printed on their terminal. The mail can be revised, incorporated into other documents, passed along to new recipients, or filed like any other document in the system. Some electronic mail systems allow the sender to cancel the message if it has not yet been read by the recipient. The sender may also check to see if the messages he or she has sent have been read yet by the recipient by including a "receipt required" message with the document. Some systems also provide a delayed sending option, allowing the sender to create a message and have it sent at a set time in the future.

Computer systems and computer networks have electronic mail, or **e-mail,** systems that allow a user to send mail or memos to other users that

FIGURE 16–5

Electronic Mail System

H I G H L I G H T

Lending a Helping Hand

Computers have had a major impact not only in business. For the more than 36 million Americans with handicaps, computers provide avenues to independence. For example, microprocessors enable quadriplegics to maneuver their wheelchairs. Some wheelchairs even have four legs, which enables the user to go up and down stairs and step over obstacles. In another instance a deaf person can "call" a person by electronic mail. A sophisticated system developed by Sentrent Systems Technology, Inc. allows a handicapped person to control a computer with his eyes. The individual stares at a word or picture on the control panel. A light detects where the person is looking, and the image is then projected onto the screen.

Personal computers and voice synthesizers allow persons without speech to "speak". They key their conversation into the computer and the voice synthesizer says their words. Some of these systems are also battery powered, so they are portable.

These and other advances in technology have enabled handicapped people to gain employment. For example, Prab Command, Inc. in Kalamazoo, Michigan, has developed a robot workstation for their use with an arm that can perform functions such as filing papers. Another computer-controlled workstation, which is voice activated, can perform functions such as desktop publishing.

Computers are lending an electronic helping hand to handicapped people.

---

are also connected to the system or network. **Facsimile systems,** sometimes referred to as **telecopier** or **FAX systems,** are another form of electronic mail system that transmits across telephone lines. Facsimile systems produce a picture of a page by scanning it, as a television camera scans a scene or a copier scans a printed page. The image is then transmitted to a receiver, where it is printed.

Another type of electronic message system is the **voice message system (VMS),** or **voice mail.** In VMS, the sender records a message in the receiver's mail box. The spoken message is converted by the VMS into digital form and stored in the computer's memory. At the receiver's request, the message is reconverted into voice form. Unlike standard answering machines, with VMS recipients can fast-scan the messages. Voice mail also allows for longer messages than answering machines.

TELECONFERENCING. In an effort to reduce travel time and expenses associated with out-of-town travel, businesses are turning to teleconferencing. **Teleconferencing,** permitting two or more locations to communicate via electronic and image-producing facilities, offers businesses a viable alternative to long-distance, face-to-face communications.

Five forms of teleconferencing exist. The most basic form of conducting electronic meetings, **audio conferencing,** is simply a conference call linking three or more people. Ideal for impromptu conversations, audio conferencing requires no major equipment investments but is limited to voice only.

The next level, **augmented audio conferencing,** combines graphics with audio conferencing. In this situation, visual information accompanies the conversation in the form of facsimile, electronic blackboards, or freeze-frame slide shows. Augmented audio conferencing is frequently used for technical discussions that require supplemental graphics to explain concepts.

Computer conferencing is well suited for ongoing meetings among a number of people. Information is exchanged at the participants' convenience using computer terminals; participants need not attend at the same time. New material can be added or previously submitted ideas can be critiqued. This differs from electronic mail in that discrete messages are not transmitted; instead comments are input in reference to specific issues. Computer conferencing has been found to reduce decision-making time considerably.

Video seminars represent the next level of sophistication. They employ one-way, full-motion video with two-way audio. The most common application of video seminars is for formal presentations that involve a question-and-answer session such as a press conference. Individuals from the audience communicate with the presentation headquarters via a separate two-way phone link. The entire audience can hear the question and view the official response. Special facilities with television equipment are needed for this type of conferencing.

Finally, there is **videoconferencing**—the technology currently receiving the most attention. Videoconferencing, employing a two-way, full-motion video plus a two-way audio system, provides the most effective simulation of face-to-face communication (see Figure 16–6). It is the only form that meets the need for full interaction; the participants are able to see and hear each other's responses. Videoconferencing is best suited for planning groups, project teams, and other groups that want a full sense of participation. It is not suitable for all situations, however. It does not seem to be effective when a participant is trying to persuade an audience or to sell something.

The cost effectiveness of videoconferences depends upon the geographic dispersion of the company, the number of intracompany meetings, and the management structure of the company. If the company does not have major

FIGURE 16—6

Videoconferencing

offices throughout the country, videoconferencing may not be cost effective. Also, because different types of videoconferencing equipment are not compatible, it can only be used for conferences within the company, not with other companies.

TELECOMPUTING. Companies as well as individuals may subscribe to online information services—services that offer access to one or more data bases. This is often referred to as **telecomputing.** By accessing the online data bases, workers receive additional information and save considerable research time. There are many information services available that provide information on a wide variety of topics. Three of the more popular services are The Source, CompuServe, and Dow Jones News/Retrieval. Some of the services offered include news stories; potential news-making events; up-to-the-minute stock, bond, and commodity information; sports information; information on alcohol problems; and law libraries (see Figures 16–7 and 16–8).

Usually, a membership fee is charged from the user, and a password and account number are issued. The online service then usually charges the user for service time or connect time. The only equipment needed is a computer, a modem, and a communications software package to instruct the user's computer how to talk to the computer at the other end. Employees can receive up-to-the-minute information with a minimal amount of effort and time.

■ COMPUTERS IN BUSINESS AND INDUSTRY

As computers have entered American society, nowhere have they had more impact than in business and industry. Part of the reason is that using computers speeds operations, reduces mistakes in calculations, and gives com-

FIGURE 16–7

CompuServe offers users access to a number of online data bases.

COMPUTERS AND INFORMATION PROCESSING

FIGURE 16—8

panies efficient, cost-effective analyses that would be nearly impossible with manual operations. Another major reason for the great impact of computers is the domino effect. If Business A speeds up its operations through the use of computers, then Business B must also computerize to compete. The same applies to the use of automation in industry. Once one factory incorporates automation, it sets a standard to be imitated and repeated.

These factors have caused a phenomenal increase in the number and types of computer applications in business and industry. Some experts even claim that these computer applications are helping to trigger a new type of industrial revolution.

Computers in Business

Because businesses are so varied in purpose and structure, it is nearly impossible to examine all business uses of computers. However, it is possible to look at how computers are used in many businesses. Businesses have special uses of computers. For example, a retail store might be interested

CONCEPT SUMMARY 16—1

Forms of Electronic Communication	
Form	**Characteristic**
Electronic mail	Used primarily for internal communication
Teleconferencing	Used to reduce travel time and expenses
Telecomputing	Offers computer access to online data bases

in computerizing inventory, whereas a stock brokerage would be more interested in computerizing its customer files. In general, though, there are three areas in which computers are used in most businesses: accounting and finance, management, and marketing and sales.

ACCOUNTING AND FINANCE. In the past, financial transactions were tediously calculated, either by hand or by calculator, and recorded using pencil and paper. This method has rapidly become obsolete as computers have moved into virtually every area of accounting and finance. To illustrate this point, let us examine how computers are being used in the areas of general accounting, financial analysis, and information management.

General accounting software is a very popular type of business software. In fact, it was the first business software to be offered for personal computers. Some of the most common uses of general accounting software are for preparing checks, reports, and forms. Forms, because of their repetitive nature, are well suited to computer processing. General accounting packages that produce reports keep users informed of everything from inventory on hand to monthly credit account balances. Checks are a frequent form of output from general accounting software.

Today, the most common use of the computer in financial analysis is the electronic spreadsheet. Spreadsheets are used to design budgets, record sales, produce profit-and-loss statements, and aid in financial analysis. Refer to Chapter 13 for more information regarding spreadsheets.

Data management software for business computers gives them the capability of an electronic filing system. Data entered into selected categories can be retrieved by specifying, for example, files on employees receiving a certain salary or employees hired on a certain date. Systems like these make file retrieval faster and more flexible and decrease the amount of storage space required.

MANAGEMENT. Communication is an important part of business management, and computer graphics are becoming an essential part of business communication. In the average business, computers are used to produce graphs that keep management informed and up-to-date on company statistics, sales records, and the like.

It is well known in business that executives make 80 percent of their decisions based on 20 percent of the data—that 20 percent representing the core data necessary to run their businesses. Finding that data can be difficult for managers if they are presented with pages upon pages of data. Graphically displayed data makes the task much easier. It is widely agreed that such displays can help managers to make better decisions. Also, comparisons, relationships and trends, and essential points can be clarified more easily with graphics (see Figure 16–9). Finally, computer graphics are the most cost-effective means of presenting the manager with that 20 percent of core data.

MARKETING AND SALES. Businesses use computers in a variety of ways to facilitate sales, record sales, update inventories after sales, and make projections based on expected sales (see Figure 16–10). In addition to these

FIGURE 16—9

Graphically displayed data helps make decision making easier for managers.

standard functions, some computers are also being used in customer contact.

The Helena Rubenstein cosmetic firm was instrumental in the movement of computers onto the sales floor. The cosmetic computer assisted customers in their decisions about perfumes, makeup, and colorings. The firm's effort was very successful and inspired similar applications by other companies.

FIGURE 16—10

Salespeople use computers to keep track of sales data.

Computers in Industry

The financial and bookkeeping uses of computers apply to both business and industry. However, industry also uses computers in designing and manufacturing products. In this chapter, we will discuss four of those ways: CAD/CAM, CIM, nondestructive testing, and robotics.

CAD/CAM. One of the fastest growing areas of computer use in industry is **computer-aided design (CAD).** CAD allows the engineer to design, draft, and analyze a prospective product using computer graphics on a video terminal (see Figure 16–11). The designer, working with full-color graphics, can easily make changes, and thus can test many versions of a product before the first prototype is ever built. CAD can also analyze designs for poor tolerance between parts and for stress points. This can save companies a great deal of money by eliminating defective designs before the money is spent to build a product.

Computer-aided design is often coupled with **computer-aided manufacturing (CAM).** The combination is referred to as **CAD/CAM.** Using CAD/CAM, the engineer can analyze not only the product but also the manufacturing process.

Once the rough design of the product has been entered into the computer, the engineer can have the computer simulate any manufacturing step (see Figure 16–12). For example, if the product must be drilled, the engineer can use a computerized drill that can be guided, either by the engineer or the computer, to simulate the drilling process. This simulation can be very helpful in two ways. First, it indicates any major problems that may be encountered on the assembly line—before it is even set up. Second, the computer will record exactly how the tool moved and will store that information on magnetic tape. If that factory uses robotics and **numerically controlled machinery,** those tapes can be used to drive the actual machines

FIGURE 16–11

Computer-aided design is used by engineers to design products.

COMPUTERS AND INFORMATION PROCESSING

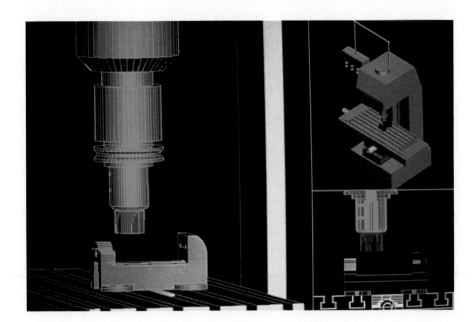

FIGURE 16—12

Computer-aided manufacturing is often coupled with computer-aided design in the manufacturing process.

in manufacturing the product. In this way, CAD/CAM can take the engineer from idea to final product.

COMPUTER INTEGRATED MANUFACTURING (CIM). For even greater savings and more efficient operation, manufacturers can tie CAD and CAM processes together with **computer-integrated manufacturing (CIM).** CIM is an attempt to link various departments of a company into a central data base. The CIM data base can help management run a more coordinated, efficient operation. The ideal CIM system would control the design and manufacture of a company's products without disruption. From raw materials to finished product, the operation would run smoothly. The CIM system would control scheduling and monitoring of operations.

In the United States no fully functional plants combine CAD/CAM and CIM. Some operations do employ the CIM concept in certain areas, though. Boeing, General Motors, and General Electric are experimenting with CIM. Boeing has saved $2.8 million annually by using CIM to link certain design and manufacturing operations.

To be successful, CIM requires a long-term commitment from management. General Electric found that CIM was most successful when implemented in a step-by-step plan. As the uses of CAD and CAM increase, CIM will become more common, too.

NONDESTRUCTIVE TESTING (NDT). Quality control has long been a problem for industry. Finding flaws or weaknesses in products is an important aspect of the successful operation of a company and is necessary for long-term growth. Until recently, most companies had to be content spotting flaws with a visual inspection or a physical stress test of their products. A visual inspection is effective only if the flaw is easily seen, and a stress test often destroys the object being tested.

Some manufacturers are relying on a new technology to test new and old products for flaws created during manufacturing or for weaknesses caused by wear and deterioration. The technology is called **nondestructive testing (NDT).** This process combines X rays, high-frequency sound waves, or laser beams with powerful microcomputers to inspect the interior of a product. Use of NDT locates the likely trouble while leaving the product intact. The process can detect the difference between dangerous flaws and harmless nicks.

Nondestructive testing is used to examine the interior of aircraft engines and to check welds in gas pipelines. Airplane mechanics may soon rely on NDT for early detection of metal deterioration. The growth in NDT is based on the increasing use of machines designed to operate near the limits of physical tolerance. Flaws that are not identified early could cause a disaster. Another reason for the growth of NDT is the increasing use of new, unpredictable materials. New construction materials may contain hard-to-discern flaws that could mean failure for a manufacturer.

Powerful new data-processing capabilities have made it possible for workers to determine the difference between serious and minor flaws. Being able to tell the difference between the two could save a company a great deal of money.

The use of computers in NDT to process data from radiology and ultrasound tests is growing in popularity. Radiology involves passing X rays or gamma rays through a product or structure. Flaws in the material appear as shadows on an X ray. Ultrasound testing uses high-frequency sound waves that are beamed into the test material. Flaws stop the sound beam, deflecting it to a source that collects and processes data about such things as the size and precise location of the defect.

ROBOTICS. Almost everyone is familiar with the terminology given workers: those who perform management-level jobs are referred to as white-collar workers; those performing unskilled tasks or factory jobs are called blue-collar workers. However, the influx of computers into the working world of the factories has created another category: the steel-collar worker. The steel-collar workers are nonhuman—robots.

Science fiction writer Isaac Asimov popularized the term *robotics*. **Robotics** is the science that deals with robots, their construction, capabilities, and applications.

Currently, American factories have tens of thousands of robots hard at work (see Figure 16–13). By 1990 this figure is expected to reach nearly 150,000. General Motors, General Electric, and Westinghouse are the three leading users of industrial robots. These steel-collar workers perform standard jobs, such as spot welding and spray painting, as well as more complex jobs like fitting light bulbs into the dashboards of cars. The automobile industry is the leading user of robots in the United States.

The steel-collar worker is not always as efficient as one may think. Robots perform well on the factory floor, but they have been known to go berserk. Swinging its powerful steel arm, a robot can deliver blows to anything within its reach. The problem—a crossed wire. Also, robots lack common sense and intelligence. For example, consider the case of a robot that drills holes in the doors of cars as they pass on the assembly line. If the car is not in the right position, the robot will drill holes in whatever is there.

FIGURE 16—13

Robots are used on the assembly line to manufacture cars.

Two generations of robots have appeared so far. The first generation possesses mechanical dexterity but no external sensory ability. These robots cannot see, hear, touch, or smell. Second-generation robots, however, possess more humanlike capabilities, including tactile sense or crude vision; they can "feel" how tightly they are gripping an object or "see" whether there are obstacles in their path.

Robots are appearing in places other than the factory, such as the area of sales. In Aurora, Colorado, an office supply store has robots for salespersons. For example, they will tell customers about the specials within the store while pointing to the wares displayed.

CONCEPT SUMMARY 16—2

Computers in Industry			
CAD	**CAM**	**CIM**	**NDT**
Computer-aided design	Computer-aided manufacturing	Computer-integrated manufacturing	Nondestructive testing
Using computers to design, draft and analyze prospective products	Using computers to simulate manufacturing steps	Using computers to link the departments of a company into a central data base	Using computers to identify hidden flaws in products

■ SUMMARY POINTS

■ Computer anxiety is the fear people experience about computers and the effects computers may have on individual's lives and society.

■ In order to prepare students for the future, computer literacy courses are being taught throughout elementary and secondary education systems.

■ Studies conducted by Genevieve Cerf at Columbia University have found that, overall, women may make better programmers than men.

■ Computer-related fields pay women and men equally for similar positions and work.

■ Job displacement and retraining are issues that must be dealt with as computer technology continues to automate more and more jobs and processes.

■ Ergonomics is the method of researching and designing computer hardware and software to enhance employee productivity and comfort. It has focused on recommendations for the workstation environment and for making software more user friendly.

■ Office automation refers to all processes that integrate computer and communications technology with traditional manual office processes.

■ The manipulation of written text to achieve a desired output is referred to as word processing; word processing is the most widely adopted office automation technology.

■ Communication capabilities derived from office automation allow the exchange of information electronically between employees.

■ Electronic mail is the transmission of messages at high speeds over telecommunications facilities and can be in the form of an e-mail system, a facsimile system, or a voice message system.

■ The method of two or more remote locations communicating via electronic and image producing facilities is called teleconferencing. Five forms of teleconferencing exist: (1) audio conferencing, (2) augmented audio conferencing, (3) computer conferencing, (4) video seminars, and (5) videoconferencing.

■ Accessing online information services, called telecomputing, can provide a vast amount of information for minimal time and money.

■ Computerization in business has taken place primarily in three functional areas: (1) accounting and finance, (2) management, and (3) marketing and sales.

■ General accounting software, electronic spreadsheets, and data management software have been heavily used in the area of finance.

■ Computer graphics have become a very important factor in business communication and decision making.

■ Computer-aided design (CAD) allows an engineer to design, draft, and analyze a potential product without leaving the computer terminal.

■ The combination of computer-aided design and computer-aided manufacturing (CAD/CAM) allows the engineer to analyze both the design and manufacturing process.

■ Computer-integrated manufacturing (CIM) is an attempt to link various departments of a company into a central data base. The CIM data base can help management run a more coordinated, efficient operation.

■ Nondestructive testing (NDT) combines X rays, high-frequency sound waves, or laser beams with powerful microcomputers to inspect the interior of a product. Use of NDT locates the flaws while leaving the product intact.

■ Robots are being used in factories, primarily in the manufacture of automobiles, for tasks such as spot welding, spray painting, and fitting fixtures.

▨ REVIEW QUESTIONS

1. What is computer anxiety? List some reasons why you feel computer anxiety is important to those who design, implement, and maintain computer applications.

2. What is ergonomics? What are some recommendations that have been made as a result of ergonomics?

3. What are some of the advantages of office automation?

4. Differentiate among the five forms of teleconferencing.

5. What is the difference between telecommuting and telecomputing?

6. Define a local area network and list some of its advantages.

7. Why have computer graphics become an important aspect of business management?

8. Explain how CAD/CAM is used in product development.

9. Define NDT and explain how it is used in product inspection.

10. In your opinion, what is the most identifiable effect computers have had on society?

11. Do you feel that we, as humans, will permit our society to be as automated as possible, or will there be some point in the future at which we will limit what computers can do? Briefly explain your answer.

EDS

EDS

COMPANY HISTORY

More than a quarter of a century ago, Electronic Data Systems Corporation (EDS) was founded in Dallas, Texas with only one employee. Today, EDS has more than 48,000 employees serving customers in 26 countries. The company's commitment to customer satisfaction and technological innovation has made EDS a world leader in information processing and communications services.

In 1962, EDS entered the commercial insurance industry and became the first information services company to provide industry-specific computer applications. Since that time, EDS' markets have expanded to include health care, finance, government, retailing, distribution, transportation, utilities and communications.

Many of the EDS customers within these markets rely on EDS for facilities management, a concept that was pioneered by EDS in the early 1960s. Under a facilities management agreement, EDS becomes the data processing department of its customer, providing the customer with computers, systems and people. In addition, an EDS communications facilities management agreement furnishes the customer with network capabilities and management of voice, video and data.

In 1970, EDS pioneered the Information Processing Center (IPC) concept. Located at 21 sites throughout the world, these centers expedite and process data for all of EDS' markets and now process 24 million transactions daily. Today, EDS owns and leases more than 350 mainframes worldwide and plans to exceed a processing capacity of 4 billion instructions per second by 1990.

EDS added the manufacturing arena to the list of markets it serves when it joined forces with General Motors (GM) in 1984 and became a wholly owned subsidiary, operating independently of GM. From office and plant automation, to computer-aided design, to systems integration, to communications with dealers and suppliers, to artificial intelligence and machine vision, EDS' services are far-reaching in virtually every area of GM.

EDS APPLICATIONS IN MANUFACTURING

EDS is the world's largest systems integrator, combining hardware, software, telecommunications and human resources into a cohesive information processing network. Because EDS is a vendor independent corporation, it is able to provide optimum systems integration solutions to its customers. In the manufacturing environment, these solutions enable all areas, from conceptual product design to final product delivery, to quickly access information from a common data base. EDS is using its successes in manufacturing systems at GM to open doors with other customers in the manufacturing industry.

In support of GM, EDS has assumed the worldwide systems integration responsibility for the management, operation, provision, and maintenance of all computer and information processing services, communications services and health care administration activities.

The largest GM systems integration and plant automation effort undertaken by EDS to date has been the GMT400 truck development program, which produces full-size Chevrolet and GMC pick-up trucks. In addition to the automation of three assembly and two stamping plants, EDS supported many of the computer systems integration projects within this program. These projects included systems architecture design, hardware evaluation and purchase, software design and development, user training and operations management. In total, the truck development program encompassed the development of 63 applications and resulted in a 40 percent increase in automation over all previous truck programs.

GMT400 also marked the first use of Manufacturing Automation Protocol (MAP) in a large-scale automated factory-floor production facility. MAP is a set of internationally accepted specifications for formatting and controlling information between computerized, automated devices in a manufacturing environment. MAP enables these intelligent devices to communicate with each other in a common language. On the GMT400 project, EDS was responsible for implementing MAP

into a single, plant-wide broadband communications network.

To further facilitate GM vehicle development and production, EDS designed and implemented a configuration of advanced computer-aided design (CAD), computer-aided manufacturing (CAM) and computer-aided engineering (CAE) systems for GM's engineering process. The integrated CAD/CAM/CAE applications are the computerized tools needed to communicate complex shapes and forms from the design environment to the engineering and manufacturing environments. CAD/CAM/CAE enables engineers to perform all parts modeling on a three-dimensional graphics system, thereby eliminating time-consuming clay modeling and manual drawing techniques. These tools give engineering and manufacturing departments nearly unlimited capabilities and flexibility in reducing product development time, improving quality and reducing costs.

EDS APPLICATIONS IN OTHER INDUSTRIES

In support of large-scale systems integration projects, EDS created EDS•NET, the world's largest private communications network. EDS•NET uses terrestrial, high-speed digital transmission lines, microwaves and private satellite earth stations to provide access to systems and transmission of information throughout the world. The network interfaces with a wide range of mainframes, minicomputers, microcomputers, teleprinters and interactive data terminals. EDS customers access EDS•NET through on-line terminals or direct telephone lines. Along with data transfer, EDS•NET capabilities include electronic mail, video conferencing and teleconferencing.

Linking more than 250,000 terminals, EDS•NET enables IPCs to communicate with their customers and other IPCs through one integrated system. EDS' largest

IPC, in Plano, Texas, can process more than 900 million instructions per second through central processing units. It can exchange information at its site and then transmit more than 1,300 million bits per second through telephone lines, microwave radio systems, fiber optics or satellite technology. The IPC has an on-line storage capacity of 5,000 billion bytes of information. With these technical capabilities, EDS has been able to undertake large, complex projects for its customers.

One example is the Army Standard Information Management System (ASIMS). EDS was awarded the ASIMS contract to improve the Army's automated data processing resources including hardware, software and communications at 47 installations in the continental United States, Hawaii, Alaska and Panama. ASIMS is the largest systems integration contracts ever awarded by the U.S. Army.

Another major undertaking for EDS was The Insurance Machine. This project set a precedent in research and development of mainframe software applications. EDS developed The Insurance Machine to automate virtually all of the key areas within a life insurance company and become that company's comprehensive data processing tool as well as support the processing of new products. Comprising 27 individual systems, including policy issue, billing, actuarial and client information, The Insurance Machine operates on specifications that interface with all the systems.

The Insurance Machine is based on logic separation, a process in which the programs that execute insurance transactions are not tied to the machine logic that runs the computer. In addition, each life insurance company can have its particular rules stored in its data base, and any product or procedural changes can be readily implemented. The Insurance Machine is user-friendly and has the flexibility to easily adapt to changing markets and strategies.

For more than 26 years, EDS has committed its resources to developing innovative products and services for its customers. Because of this commitment, the company is recognized today as the industry leader in information services, support and technology throughout the world.

DISCUSSION POINTS

1. Explain the concept of facilities management and the IPC.
2. Describe the impact of the close relationship between EDS and GM on both organizations.

Computer Security, Crime, Ethics, and the Law

OUTLINE

Introduction
Computer Crime and Security
   Computer Crime Defined
   Types of Computer Crime
   Crime Prevention and Detection
   Computer Security
Computer Ethics
Privacy
   Issues
   Legislation

Warranties, Copyright Law, Public-
   Domain Software, and
   Shareware
Warranties
Copyright Law
Public-Domain Software and
   Shareware

Summary Points
Review Questions

A Bold Raid on Computer Security

Phillip Elmer-DeWitt
Reported by Rhea Schoenthal and Dennis Wyss
Time

For months the computer intruder moved like an invisible man—until one day Clifford Stoll saw the footprints. The frizzy-haired Stoll, 37, a systems manager at California's Lawrence Berkeley Laboratory, knew something was amiss when one of the computers in his care revealed that an electronic trespasser was trying to use the lab's machines without providing a billing address. Suspecting the intruder might be a student prankster from the nearby University of California campus, Stoll launched a novel experiment. Instead of shutting out the interloper, he allowed him to roam at will through the system while carefully recording his every keystroke.

Thus began a game of cat and mouse that led Stoll and half a dozen investigative agencies far beyond the Berkeley campus. For ten months, they followed the hacker as he wended his way through the networks that link U.S. military and industrial computers all over the world. By the time the hacker was tracked to a ground-floor apartment in Hannover, West Germany, he had accomplished perhaps the most extensive breach of U.S. computer security to date. While no top secrets appear to have been uncovered, the incident shows how easy it can be to go fishing for sensitive information via phone lines and personal computers.

The case first came to light in the West German weekly *Quick*, which identified the suspect as a 24-year-old computer-science student with the pseudonym Mathias Speer. In a press conference last week, his pursuer,

Stoll, described how the young hacker used the Lawrence Lab computer as a gateway to Internet, a U.S. Government-owned network that connects some 20,000 computers handling scientific research and unclassified military work. While Speer used fairly standard techniques for cracking passwords, he showed uncommon persistence. He attacked some 450 different computers and gained access to more than 30. Victims ranged from the Navy Coastal Systems Command in Panama City, Fla., to the Buckner Army Base in Okinawa.

The intruder's appetite for military data is what eventually did him in. To trick him into staying connected long enough to effect a telephone trace, Stoll dangled an irresistible lure: a file of bogus Star Wars information titled SDI Network Project. The sting worked. The hacker stayed on the line for more than an hour, greedily loading the phony data into his home computer. (The information was booby-trapped as well, containing an address in Berkeley for more information on the fictitious project.) West German authorities, working with the FBI, traced the call to the Hannover apartment, questioned its occupant, and later confiscated his machine.

The intrusions came to an abrupt halt, but the mystery persists. Was Speer simply a clever hacker? Or was he a would-be mercenary or even an East bloc spy? Speer is apparently not telling, and the West Germans lack sufficient evidence to haul him into court. But back in Berkeley, an intriguing new lead has surfaced. Three months after Speer took the Star Wars bait, the lab received a request for more information on the bogus project. Postmarked Pittsburgh, it was signed by a reputed arms dealer with ties to Saudi Arabia. How could he have got the address? The only way, lab officials insist, was to have been in cahoots—or at least in contact—with the Hannover hacker.

In this information society, simply viewing confidential information, even if you do not destroy or change it, is a crime. Often possessors of information do not know that their data is being accessed, and if they discover their files are being viewed or tampered with, often they cannot catch the culprit. As computer technology becomes more sophisticated, the type of criminal involved in computer crimes is frequently a very skilled technician.

▦ INTRODUCTION

There is no doubt that computers have had a very significant impact on our lives and our society. By the same token, extensive use of computers has created new problems that must be dealt with. Just as the computer's success is attributed to people's imagination, many of the problematic situations that must be dealt with result from human nature. Computer crime and security, for example, are two issues that have created considerable concern among individuals who use computers for personal and business purposes. With computers being used as the main means of storage of personal information on credit, employment, taxes, and other aspects of a person's life, privacy is becoming a growing concern.

This chapter reviews some of the human issues associated with the use of computers. Computer crime and security as well as ethics and privacy are discussed. The chapter concludes with a discussion of warranties and copyright law.

▦ COMPUTER CRIME AND SECURITY

Computer crime is a greater problem than most people realize. Americans are losing billions of dollars to high-technology criminals whose crimes go undetected and unpunished; estimates of losses range from at least $2 billion to more than $40 billion a year. While no one really knows how much is being stolen, the total appears to be growing fast.

The earliest known instance of electronic embezzlement occurred in 1958, just a few years after IBM began marketing its first line of business computers. By the mid-1970s, scores of such crimes were being reported every year, and yearly losses were estimated to be as high as $300 million.

Many more problems appear to be ahead. Home computers and electronic funds transfer (EFT) systems pose a new threat to the billions of dollars in data banks accessible through telephone lines (see Figure 17–1). Already,

FIGURE 17–1

Electronic funds transfer made possible with a home computer and telephone lines poses a threat to billions of dollars in data banks.

criminals have made illegal switches of money over the phone, and more cases can be expected as EFT systems become widespread. Furthermore, the trend to distributed systems presents many opportunities for security and privacy violations.

Computer Crime Defined

What is meant by the term *computer crime?* The legal community has been focusing on answering this question through legislation and court opinions. Taking a broad but practical view, computer crime can be defined as a criminal act that poses a greater threat to a computer user than it would to a non-computer user, or a criminal act that is accomplished through the use of a computer.

Computer crime, therefore, consists of two kinds of activity: (a) the use of a computer to perpetrate acts of deceit, theft, or concealment that are intended to provide financial, business-related, property, or service advantages; and (b) threats to the computer itself, such as theft of hardware or software, sabotage, and demands for ransom. Because computer crimes seldom involve acts of physical violence, they are generally classified as white-collar crimes. While there is no single type that commits computer crimes, computer criminals are often young and ambitious with impressive educational credentials. They tend to be technically competent and come from all employee levels, including technicians, programmers, managers, and high-ranking executives.

Types of Computer Crime

Computer crimes can be classified into four broad categories: sabotage, theft of services, property crimes, and financial crimes. This section examines each of these categories and gives examples drawn from actual crimes.

SABOTAGE. Sabotage of computers results in destruction or damage of computer hardware. This type of computer crime often resembles traditional sabotage because the computer itself is not used to carry out the destruction. Sabotage may require some sophistication if computer-assisted security systems must be thwarted or if the system is manipulated to do harm to itself.

Computers are targets of sabotage and vandalism especially during times of political activism. Dissident political groups during the 1960s, for instance, conducted assaults on computer installations, often causing extensive damage. Other forms of physical violence have included flooding the computer room and shooting a computer with a revolver. One fired employee simply walked through the data storage area with an electromagnet, thereby erasing valuable company records.

Obviously, these acts of violence do not require any special expertise on the part of the criminal. Sabotage may, however, be conducted by dissatisfied former employees who put to use some of their knowledge of company operations to gain access to and destroy hardware and software.

A form of sabotage that has been used on microcomputers is a program that acts as a time bomb; when it goes off it can destroy the contents of either a hard disk or floppy disk. These programs are called **viruses.** They are called that because they can infect microcomputer systems by attaching themselves to programs that reside on floppy disks that are then carried to other microcomputers. Viruses can also attach themselves to programs that are copied to microcomputers from electronic bulletin boards. Once a virus is in a microcomputer system and has replicated itself a predetermined number of times, it attempts to erase the hard disk or diskette it resides on. This can be extremely damaging to the unsuspecting microcomputer user. These virus programs are very difficult to guard against; however, there are programs available that can detect viruses and counteract them. Another method of virus prevention would be to prevent diskettes from being written to whenever possible. This can be accomplished by using diskettes without a write protect notch or by placing a write protect tab over the write protect notch (see Chapter 6).

THEFT OF SERVICES. Computer services may be abused in a variety of ways. Some examples of theft of computer services have involved politicians using a city's computer to conduct campaign mailings and employees conducting unauthorized free-lance services on a company computer after working hours.

Time-sharing systems have been exposed to abuse due to inadequate or nonexistent security precautions. It is much easier to gain unauthorized access to a time-sharing system than to a closed system. Though most systems require the user to have a password to gain access, a system is only as good as the common sense and caution of its users. A time-sharing system that does not require regular changing of access codes is inviting the theft of valuable computer time. The amazing lack of care exercised by supposedly sophisticated users made national headlines when a group of high school computer buffs in Milwaukee were discovered accessing numerous information systems, including banks, hospitals, and the defense research center in Los Alamos, New Mexico. The students reportedly gained access by using each system's password. Some of the passwords had not been changed for years, while others were obtained from public sources.

Wiretapping is another technique used to gain unauthorized access to a time-sharing system. By tapping into a legitimate user's line, one can have free access to the system whenever the line is not being used by the authorized party.

One of the prime examples of computer services theft took place at the University of Alberta. In 1976, a student at the university began an independent study under the supervision of a professor. The purpose of the study was to investigate the security of the university's computer system, a time-sharing system with more than 5,000 users, some as far away as England. After discovering several gaps in the system's security, the student was able to develop a program that reduced the possibility of unauthorized use and tampering. The student brought this program to the attention of the computer center, which took no action on the student's recommendations. It was assumed that planned changes in the system would remove security shortcomings. However, the changes were not implemented for another nine months. During that period, the program, which was capable of displaying passwords, was leaked to several students on campus. "Code Green," as the program was nicknamed, was eventually run several thousand times.

The university attempted to crack down on the unauthorized users and revoked several students' access privileges. Two of the students involved could get the computer to display the complete listing of all user passwords, including those at the highest privilege levels. In essence, this gave them unlimited access to the computer's files and programs. These students retaliated against the university administration by occasionally rendering the system inoperable or periodically inserting an obscenity into the payroll file. With an unlimited supply of IDs, they were able to escape detection, compiling a library of the computer's programs and monitoring the implementation of the new security system. The desperate university computer personnel focused exclusively on this situation, keeping a detailed log of all terminal dialogues. This effort led them to a terminal in the geology department one evening, and the students were apprehended.

THEFT OF PROPERTY. The most obvious computer crime that comes to mind concerning crimes of property is the theft of computer equipment itself. Thefts have become more common with the increasing miniaturization of computer components and the advent of home computers. These crimes are easily absorbed into traditional concepts of crime and present no unique legal problems. More intriguing is the issue of what actually constitutes property in the context of computer crimes. Different courts have come to very different conclusions on this issue.

Computer crimes of property theft frequently involve merchandise from a company whose orders are processed by computers. These crimes are usually committed by internal personnel who have a thorough knowledge of the operation. By record manipulation, dummy accounts can be created, directing a product order to be shipped to an accomplice outside the organization. Similarly, one can cause checks to be paid out for receipt of nonexistent merchandise.

Theft of property need not be limited to actual merchandise but may also extend to software. People with access to a system's program library can easily obtain copies for personal use or, more frequently, for resale to a competitor. Technical security measures in a computer installation are of little use when dishonest personnel take advantage of their positions of responsibility.

This kind of theft is by no means limited to those within the company structure, however. A computer service having specialized programs but poor security may open itself up to unauthorized access by a competitor. All that is necessary is that the outsider gain access to proper codes. This is accomplished in a number of ways, including clandestine observation of a legitimate user logging on from a remote terminal or use of a remote minicomputer to test for possible access codes.

FINANCIAL CRIMES. Although not the most common type, financial computer crimes are perhaps the most serious in terms of monetary loss. With the projected increasing dependence on electronic fund transfers, implications for the future are serious.

A common method of committing this kind of crime involves checks. Mass-produced, negotiable instruments can be manipulated in a number of ways. An employee familiar with a firm's operations can direct that multiple checks be made out to the same person. Checks can also be rerouted to a false address. These crimes do not seem so incredible when one realizes the scope of *unintentional* mistakes that have been made with computerized checks. For example, the Social Security Administration once accidentally sent out 100,000 checks to the wrong addresses while the system's files were being consolidated.

Another form of a financial computer crime is known as the "round-off fraud." In this crime, the thief, perhaps a bank employee, collects the fractions of cents in customers' accounts that are created when the applicable interest rates are applied. These fractions are then stored in an account created by the thief. The theory is that fractions of cents collected from thousands of accounts on a regular basis will yield a substantial amount of money.

Still another crime involves juggling confidential information, both personal and corporate, within a computer. Once appropriate access is gained to records, the ability to alter them can be highly marketable. One group operating in California engaged in the business of creating favorable credit histories to clients seeking loans.

These cases exemplify the types of electronic crime being committed: manipulating input to the computer; changing computer programs; and stealing data, computer time, and computer programs. The possibilities for computer crime seem endless. It has been suggested that computers are used extensively by organized crime and that a computer-aided murder may already have taken place.

The unique threat of computer crime is that criminals often use computers to conceal not only their own identities but also the existence of the crimes. Law officers worry because solving computer crimes seems to depend on luck. Many such crimes are never discovered because company executives do not know enough about computers to detect them. Others go unreported to avoid scaring customers and stockholders. Many reported crimes do not result in convictions and jail terms because the complexities of data processing mystify most police officials, prosecutors, judges, and jurors. For a summary of the types of computer crimes, see Concept Summary 17–1.

CONCEPT SUMMARY 17–1

Types of Computer Crime

Type of Crime	Description of Crime
Sabotage	Destruction or damage of computer hardware
Theft of service	Unauthorized use of computer time
Theft of property	Stealing computer equipment
Financial crime	Using a computer to steal money from an individual or organization

Crime Prevention and Detection

The computer's ability to make statistical analyses is used in New York City to help authorities pinpoint buildings that are likely targets for arson. Several agencies contribute information to the computer about fires. Further data is available on fires that have occurred in the recent past. The computer constructs profiles of the most probable targets of arsonists. The city can keep a watch on the likely buildings and tell their owners how to lessen the risk of fires. The program is also intended to decrease the owners' incentive to burn the buildings to collect the insurance proceeds. Part of the data mix fed into the computer is the names of landlords who are behind in their taxes or who have been cited for safety or occupancy violations.

Another computerized crime predictor maintained by the FBI has drawn a good deal of criticism—some of it from members of Congress. No complaints are heard about the system as it pertains to tracking known criminals. But people are worried that the Justice Department may use the system to monitor people who are considered a threat to officials but who have never been convicted of a crime. Under the plan, the Secret Service can place in the FBI's National Crime Information Center computer the names of persons considered to be threats to the president, vice president, presidential candidates, visiting heads of state, or anyone else the Secret Service must protect. Among the most elaborate communication systems in the world, the National Crime Information Center is linked to 64,000 federal, state, and local justice agencies (see Figure 17–2).

The Secret Service receives about 9,000 reports a year about people who might constitute a danger to public figures. Of these, 300 to 400 are considered dangerous. By putting these names in the bureau's massive computer, the Secret Service is able to learn immediately if any of its suspects are arrested and can keep track of their movements. In addition, any local law enforcement agency can quickly determine if a person they are considering arresting or have arrested is a Secret Service suspect. Those concerned about civil liberties express fears that through this system anyone's name might find its way into the computer, possibly causing damage to an innocent person.

Not only have computers aided in crime prevention, they have also made some headlines in crime detection (see Figure 17–3). A far-ranging computer

FIGURE 17–2

The FBI's National Crime Information Center (NCIC) computer is linked to state and local law enforcement agencies.

FIGURE 17–3

Computer technology has become an important tool in police work.

system helped put an end to the string of child killings in Atlanta. Using two IBM computers and several data bases, the Atlanta police department was able to pinpoint Wayne Williams as the prime suspect in the twenty-eight killings and ultimately convict him for the murder of two.

Because ten different law enforcement agencies were involved in the Atlanta cases, officials agreed early in the investigation that a system was needed for handling and cross-checking the great volume of investigative data and tips that poured in. The computer system was designed so that key words could be fed into it to generate a printout of all other data that contained those words. For example, if someone reported seeing a blue van in the area where a body was discovered, operators could ask the computer to bring up all other references to "blue" and "van." Through such repeated uses of the computer, Williams was finally apprehended. When Williams went to trial, the computer system was used to check defense testimony against prior statements, and the results were factored into the cross-examination.

Computer Security

Computer security involves the technical and administrative safeguards required to protect a computer-based system (hardware, personnel, and data) against the major hazards to which most computer systems are exposed and to control access to information (see Figure 17–4).

Physical computer systems and data in storage are vulnerable to several hazards: fire, natural disaster, environmental problems, and sabotage.

PHYSICAL THREATS TO SECURITY.

Fire. Fire is a problem because most computer installations use combustible materials—magnetic tape, paper, and so on. If a fire starts, water cannot

FIGURE 17—4

Italcable, an intercontinental telecommunications service, utilizes a computer-assisted security system to meet its stringent security and building operation requirements.

be used to extinguish it, because water can damage magnetic storage media and hardware. Carbon-dioxide fire-extinguisher systems are hazardous because they would endanger employees, if any were trapped in the computer room. Halon, a nonpoisonous chemical gas, can be used in fire extinguishers, but such extinguishers are costly.

Natural Disasters. Many computer centers have been damaged or destroyed by floods, cyclones, hurricanes, and earthquakes. Floods pose a serious threat to the computer hardware and wiring. However, water in the absence of heat will not destroy magnetic tapes unless the tapes are allowed to retain moisture over an extended period of time. Protection against natural disasters should be a consideration when the location for the computer center is chosen; for example, the center should not be located in an area prone to flooding.

Environmental Problems. Usually, computers are installed in buildings that were not originally planned to accommodate them. This practice may lead to environmental problems. For example, water and steam pipes may run through a computer room; bursting pipes could result in extensive damage.

Pipes on floors above the computer room are also potentially hazardous; so all ceiling holes should be sealed. Data on magnetic media can be destroyed by magnetic fields created by electric motors in the vicinity of the computer room. Other environmental problems include power failures, brownouts (temporary surges or drops in power), and external radiation.

Sabotage. Sabotage represents the greatest physical risk to computer installations. Saboteurs can do great damage to computer centers with little risk of apprehension. For example, magnets can be used to scramble code on tapes, bombs can be planted, and communication lines can be cut. Providing adequate security against such acts of sabotage is extremely difficult and expensive.

DATA SECURITY MEASURES. In addition to safeguarding their computer systems from these physical difficulties, companies must protect stored data against illegitimate use by controlling access to it. There is no simple solution to these security problems. Organizations such as government agencies and businesses have instituted various security measures—most to restrict access to computerized records, others to provide for reconstruction of destroyed data. Some examples are given below:

■ Backup copies of data are stored outside the organization's location, and recovery procedures are established.

■ Authorized users are given special passwords. Users are only given access to areas or levels of the system warranted by their job responsibilities. Codes and passwords should be changed frequently.

■ The scope of access to the computer system is proportionate to the user's security clearance and job responsibility. Access to specific portions of the data base can be gained only by those whose jobs necessitate it.

■ Installations are guarded by internal security forces. For example, access to the data-processing department may be restricted to personnel with special badges and keys (see Figure 17–5).

■ The use of computer professionals to test security. They try to break into a computer system in order to point out weak spots in the system's security.

FIGURE 17—5

Devices such as data keys (left) and identification cards (right) help protect stored data by limiting access to the data.

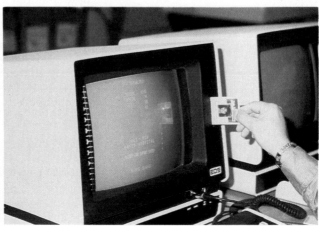

■ Data is **encrypted,** or translated into a secret code, by complex coding devices that scramble information before it is transmitted or stored. When data is transmitted to or from remote terminals, it is encrypted at one end and **decrypted,** or translated back into plain text, at the other. Files can also be protected by the data's being encrypted before it is stored and decrypted after it has been retrieved. Data is principally encrypted on its way out of the computer and decrypted on its way back in.

■ Computer installations use detectors that identify legitimate individual computer users by fingerprints or voice patterns. For example, computer makers have developed attachments that grant access only to operators who put proper thumbprints on glass plates. Adoption of these expensive devices is slow, however, because they deter the main objectives of using computers: economy and convenience.

■ The use of call-back modems which restrict usage to authorized terminals only. The user calls in to connect to the system, and then the system hangs up and calls back on a predetermined number allocated only to the location of the user's terminal.

ESTABLISHING COMPUTER SECURITY. While these security measures help protect data, they are not complete. They may not prevent internal sabotage, fraud, or embezzlement. For example, an employee with a special access code may steal classified information. Banks and insurance companies are especially susceptible. Often, these companies do not wish to report the incidents because of the bad publicity and the difficulty in solving such crimes.

How, then, can organizations establish computer security? First, computer users must recognize their role in security. If a high-level priority is assigned to security in the company, employees must be made aware of it and of the security measures that are being taken.

Second, many organizations recognize the need to have a well-trained security force—a department of security guards who specialize in maintaining data security, conducting system audits, and asking the right kinds of questions on a daily basis. Computerized records should be scrutinized regularly to see that everything is in order.

Third, a company should exercise a great deal of care in the selection and screening of the people who will have access to computers, terminals, and computer-stored data. Companies should choose programmers as carefully as they select attorneys or accountants.

CONCEPT SUMMARY 17-2

Computer Security	
Physical Threats to Security	**Security Measures**
Fire	Make backup copies
Natural disaster	Issue passwords to authorized users
Environmental problems	Encrypt data
Sabotage	Post security guards and identification detectors

Last, companies must discharge employees who stray beyond legal and ethical boundaries. Whenever these incidents occur, it is imperative that it be shown that they will not be tolerated and that, however hard the necessary course of action, those responsible for security and protection have the integrity to follow through.

COMPUTER ETHICS

Another issue facing both organizations and individuals in relation to computer use is computer ethics. Computer ethics are also largely dependent on human nature.

The term **computer ethics** refers to the standard of moral conduct in computer use. Although some specific laws have been enacted in problem areas such as privacy invasion and crime, ethics are a way in which the "spirit" of some laws can be carried to other computer-related activities. Some of the topics currently being addressed under the ethics issue include hacking, the security and privacy of data, employee loyalty, and the copying of computer software. Security and privacy of data are discussed in other sections of the chapter, while discussions of hacking, employee loyalty, and software copying follow.

HACKING. Hacking is a computer term used to describe the activity of computer enthusiasts who are challenged by the practice of breaking computer security measures. Hackers do this for a number of reasons including to gain access to confidential data or illegal computer time, or simply, for the challenge. Computer users should be aware that seemingly innocent activities such as hacking are actually criminal acts. Regardless of the reason, hacking is the same as intentionally committing a crime. Gaining unauthorized access to another computer can be as serious as breaking into someone's home.

The case discussed earlier in which a group of Milwaukee high school students gained access to the defense research center's computer in Los Alamos, New Mexico is a prime example of hacking. The youths, after being caught, stated that they did not see any classified information, but that they did accidentally erase some files. The same group of students accessed another computer in a New York cancer center. The computer, which was used to monitor 250 cancer patients, failed for a short time due to the activity of these youths. When questioned about why they behaved this way, the group said they did not know it was a crime, and it gave them something to do in the evenings!

EMPLOYEE LOYALTY. Employee loyalty is another ethical issue that has surfaced in the area of data processing. Because the field of data processing is a dynamic environment with a shortage of qualified personnel, there are many job opportunities. There is also a great deal of job changing among data-processing personnel. Because an employee has some obligations to his or her current employer, there have been a number of court cases that address the issue of employee loyalty to employers.

HIGHLIGHT

Who Goes There?

One Saturday morning a programmer at UAPA, Inc. had trouble running the payroll program. Instead of running as usual, the program erased 168,000 records. The company shut down the system for two days and in the meantime found that the company's former security officer, Donald G. Burleson, had planted other "bombs" in the system that were set to go off. A trial by jury found Burleson guilty of harmful access to a computer. He can face up to ten years in prison for this felony.

This case is important to users of computer systems. It shows that computer systems must be secured from present and past personnel. UAPA would have lost substantial computer time and money if the time bombs had not been found. Although the company says it checked the system after Burleson left and didn't see any apparent problems, systems need to be checked more thoroughly when computer personnel leave—especially when the ex-employee is a highly skilled technician.

On the positive side, this case is a victory for computer users. Initially lawyers were afraid to try the case because they thought it was too technical. Now that the precedent has been set that technical cases can be tried and the defendants can be convicted of felonies, more companies and lawyers may prosecute computer criminals.

Hackers—No Longer Harmless

What is a hacker? A computer whiz who enjoys the challenge of accessing "secure" data or a computer terrorist who creates havoc by changing or destroying data that belongs to someone else? The answer is both. Hackers are often computer experts who are very creative and persistent. They believe that for every system that is secure there is *some* way into the system. Many hackers are proud of their "hobby." They have created clubs where they share methods of accessing business and government systems. Some hackers have even written books, such as Steven Levy's *Hackers: Heroes of the Computer Revolution* and Herwart Holland's *Hacker's Bible.*

Some of the hackers have played harmless jokes on companies, such as displaying the word "Peace" simultaneously on all ter-

minals. Other hackers feel they are providing the users of computer systems a service—they are showing how vulnerable the systems are to unauthorized access and manipulation of data. Yet hackers have also cost businesses billions of dollars. Companies lose money because hackers use their computer time and telecommunication lines. One example is a bank in Germany where hackers charged $75,000 in telephone charges to the bank in only two days! Hackers are also invading military and government systems. A hacker recently accessed 30 military and military research systems. Although he chose not to

change or damage the data, he did print it.

Hackers seem to ignore the issue that they do not have the right to access, change, or destroy information that is not theirs. The few that have been caught (it took months to catch the hacker that invaded the government systems) show little remorse for their actions. Companies hesitate to prosecute hackers because they do not want the publicity that shows their computer systems are insecure. Yet as more government and business information is placed on computer systems, the threat posed by hackers increases. Hackers are no longer harmless pranksters. They now threaten both government security and business operations.

In one particular case, a data-processing consultant employed by Firm A was seeking a similar job with Firm B. Firm B was in competition for consulting contracts with Firm A. Prior to being offered a position with Firm B, the consultant was asked to attend an interview with a potential client on behalf of the firm. Unbeknownst to either the consultant or Firm B, Firm A was also seeking a contract from the client.

When Firm A became aware of the situation they sued the consultant, who at that time worked for Firm B. The suit alleged that the consultant breached his duty of loyalty to Firm A. The day the consultant attended the interview, he had called in sick to Firm A. The court criticized the consultant, finding that the illness excuse not only permitted him to aid himself but also aid the competitor on the employer's time. An appellate court disagreed. The court ruled that since neither Firm B nor the consultant knew Firm A was also competing for the contract, the employee had the right to seek alternate employment. The court believed that employees have the right to change jobs as long as they are not under contract for a definite term. The court felt that the right should be exercisable without the necessity of revealing the plans to the current employer.

Although the court opinions differed, it should be noted that the courts do recognize some degree of duty of loyalty to the employer on the part of the employee. For this reason, all employees in the area of data processing should be aware of their obligations and rights as employees and as potential employees. Actions taken in the process of changing positions should be conducted in an ethical fashion.

SOFTWARE COPYING. Another area of ethical concern is **software copying,** or **piracy.** Software piracy is the unauthorized copying of a computer program that has been written by someone else. Many software manufacturers write security measures into their programs so that they cannot be copied without authorization. However, some computer enthusiasts are challenged by trying to break this form of security as well. Whether done for personal use or to sell for profit, software piracy is a crime.

Computer ethics cannot be emphasized enough. It is the responsibility of each computer user to evaluate his or her own actions and determine the standard of morals to be followed. Only through ethical behavior will the ultimate security and privacy of computers and computer data be assured. Public-domain software and shareware are disussed later in the chapter. Both of these topics also deal with the copying of computer software.

▪ PRIVACY

The widespread use of computers, information systems, and telecommunications systems has created a major concern in recent years—the invasion of individual privacy. **Privacy** involves an individual's ability to determine what, how, and when personal information is communicated to others. With computers becoming the main means of storing personal information relating to credit, employment, taxes, and other aspects of a person's life, the issue of privacy assumes great importance.

Issues

Before computerized record keeping became widespread, most business and government decisions about such benefits as credit, educational grants, and Medicare were based on personal knowledge of the individuals involved and the limited data obtained from a decentralized system of public records. Privacy was protected to some extent by the inefficiency of the sources and methods of collecting data. The details of people's lives were maintained in widely dispersed, manually maintained files and in the memories of people who knew them. It was difficult to compile from these sources a detailed dossier on any individual.

Because computers have made data both easier to obtain and easier to store, more data is collected and stored (see Figure 17–6). Often an individual's data stored in one main file can be accessed easily by entering his or her social security number. The increased ease of obtaining data tempts organizations to collect more data than necessary. People have less control over who has access to personal data when it becomes part of a huge data base. They are unaware of whether their personal data files are complete and accurate. People may not even be aware that certain information is being kept.

FIGURE 17—6
(opposite page)

The stacks and rows of magnetic tapes show how easily just one corporation can accumulate and store huge amounts of data using computer systems. Multiply one corporation's data base by the many data bases kept by other organizations including the federal government, and you can see how John Q. Public could be completely unaware of what data is recorded about him. The ease with which organizations can record, store, and access data has led to concerns about data privacy and correct use of data.

The major concerns about the issue of privacy can be summarized as follows:

■ Too much personal data about individuals is collected and stored in computer files. This data is too easy to access and share.
■ Organizations are often making decisions solely on the basis of these files.
■ Much of the personal data collected about individuals may not be relevant to the purpose for which it is to be used.
■ The accuracy, completeness, and currency of the data may be unacceptably low.
■ The security of stored data is a problem.

Of course, the same computer systems that erode individual privacy are also allowing private and public institutions to operate more efficiently. For example, a firm must control its risks when issuing credit and, therefore, needs enough information about individuals to make responsible decisions. The solution to the privacy issue must be an appropriate balance between the legitimate needs of organizations for information about people and the rights of individuals to maintain their privacy.

The data bases that are responsible for the privacy concerns are most prevalent within the federal government (see Figure 17–7). Much of the data is acquired from census returns filed each decade and income tax returns filed annually. The Department of Transportation records owners of boats and aircraft. This department also notes any drivers' licenses that are withdrawn, suspended, or revoked by any state. Data about veterans, social security or welfare recipients, aliens, minority businesses, and dealers in alcohol, firearms, and explosives are stored away in huge data bases. Some people fear that using debit cards and computers for making purchases will create new opportunities for compiled assumptions about their habits and personal lives. The government could glean statistics concerning everything from where and how often a family dines out to what kinds of magazines and books they read.

Legislation

Since the early 1970s several laws have been enacted to protect privacy by controlling the collection, dissemination, and transmission of personal data. By far the most numerous have been passed by the federal government to protect against abuse of the government's own record-keeping agencies. But state legislatures are also beginning to recognize the widespread abuses that computer technology has created, and numerous states are taking action to stop the abuse.

FEDERAL LEGISLATION. One of the first federal laws to address the problem of abuse was passed in 1970, while a second was passed in 1973. The Freedom of Information Act of 1970 allows individuals access to data about themselves in files collected by federal agencies. The law was passed because of the potential for the government to conceal its proceedings from the public. The Crime Control Act of 1973 protects the privacy of data collected for state criminal systems that are developed with federal funds.

Perhaps the most sweeping federal legislation was the Privacy Act of 1974. Signed on January 1, 1975, this act is designed to protect the privacy of

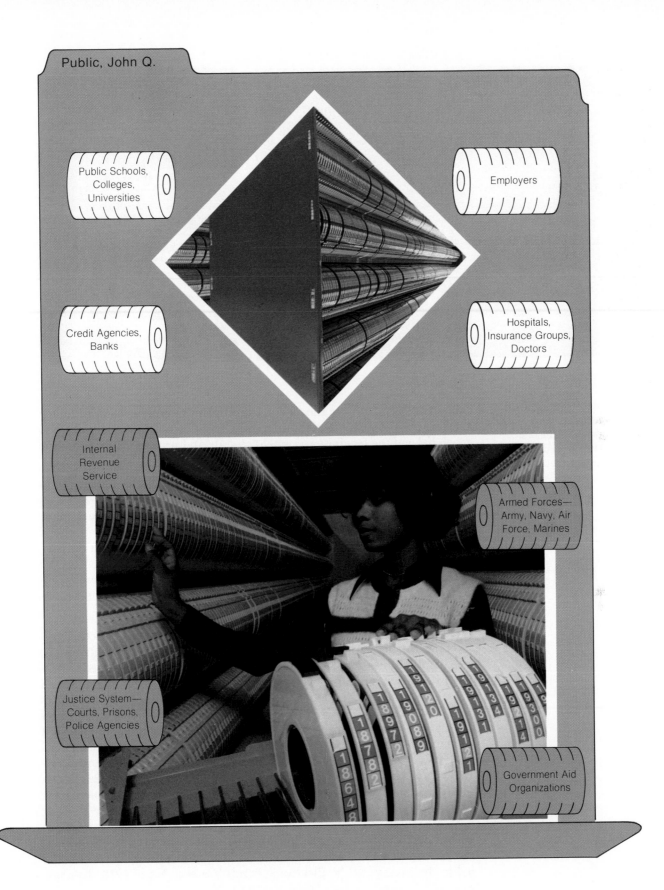

Public, John Q.

Public Schools, Colleges, Universities

Employers

Credit Agencies, Banks

Hospitals, Insurance Groups, Doctors

Internal Revenue Service

Armed Forces— Army, Navy, Air Force, Marines

Justice System— Courts, Prisons, Police Agencies

Government Aid Organizations

FIGURE 17—7

Huge data bases such as the one maintained by the IRS lead many people to fear abuse of their privacy.

individuals about whom the federal government maintains data. Although the act was a step in the right direction, it was criticized for its failure to reach beyond the federal government to state and private institutions. The act contains these provisions:

■ Individuals must be able to determine what information about themselves is being recorded and how it will be used.
■ Individuals must be provided with a way to correct inaccurate information that is collected about themselves.
■ Information collected for one purpose cannot be used for another purpose without the consent of the individual involved.
■ Organizations creating, manipulating, using, or divulging personal information must ensure that the information is reliable and must take precautions to prevent misuse of the information.

Several other laws have been passed by the federal government in an attempt to control data-base misuse and protect the privacy of individuals. The Family Educational Rights and Privacy Act of 1974 is designed to protect privacy by regulating access to computer-stored records of grades and behavior evaluations in both private and public schools. The act provides that no federal funds will be made available to an educational agency that has a policy of denying parents and students access to the student's relevant educational records. The Tax Reform Act of 1976 was passed to safeguard the confidentiality of personal tax information. The Right to Financial Privacy Act of 1978 provides further protection by limiting government access to the customer records of financial institutions, protecting to some degree the confidentiality of personal financial data.

As computer use has continued to grow during the 1980s, the federal government has continued to enact legislation directed toward protecting the privacy of individuals. The increased use of electronic funds transfer led to the passage of the Electronic Funds Transfer Act of 1980. This law

Do Computers and Medicine Really Mix?

Computers have been used and accepted in medicine for many years. They are used for both diagnosis (CAT scans) and treatment (pacemakers) of medical problems. Yet, medical devices controlled by computers have been known to malfunction. A computer may misdiagnose a medical problem or mistreat a disease. For example, two cancer patients died because they were given overdoses of radiation treatment.

The Food and Drug Administration (FDA) has decided it must regulate computer software because a "bug" in a program can be fatal for patients. The FDA will not regulate all programs—say, they won't monitor, hospital ac-

counting programs. They will regulate software that has no "competent human intervention" between a patient and a computer-controlled device. In other words, in the case of the deceased cancer patients, the computer determined the level for treatment and then treated the patients. There was no human intervention. If the level of radiation had to be checked by a medical professional before the patient was treated, the FDA would not need to regulate the software.

Will these regulations help the situation? That is difficult to say. It may depend on whether the FDA has the personnel and the money to test complex software. On the other hand, software developers are conscious of possible lawsuits and may begin monitoring their work themselves. Computers have been tremendously helpful in medicine and will continue to serve us well as long as we remember that they are only as good as the people who make them.

requires financial institutions to notify customers whenever a third party accesses a customer's account. The Comprehensive Crime Control Act of 1984 provides for protection from computer abuse in some areas that were overlooked in earlier legislation. In this act only a few limited categories of privacy abuse are defined. One provision of the law prohibits individuals without authorization from knowingly accessing a computer to obtain either information that is protected by the Right to Financial Privacy Act of 1978 or information contained in the file of a consumer reporting agency. Another provision prohibits individuals from knowingly accessing a government computer and using, modifying, destroying, or disclosing information stored in the computer or preventing the use of the computer. More recently, concern has focused on abuses of privacy during the actual transmission of data. This concern led to the drafting of the Electronic Communication Privacy Act of 1986 which prohibits the interception of data communications, for example, electronic mail. The act has undergone consideration by both houses of congress and is expected to become a law very soon.

STATE LEGISLATION. Many state laws regarding government record-keeping practices are patterned after the Privacy Act of 1974. Most states have enacted some controls on such practices in the public sector. Most of the laws have been passed since 1978. By the end of 1985, thirty-six state legislatures had passed laws regarding computer crime, and most states addressed the privacy issue in one form or another. Computer crime laws on the state level are generally quite similar to each other. Differences lie mainly in how each state defines a particular term or violation. Some state laws address the unlawful access to data bases in more detail than the federal Comprehensive Crime Control Act of 1984.

Relatively few information-privacy violation cases have been litigated, whether on the state or federal level. Since one problem of privacy violation is that data is transferred and disclosed without the knowledge or consent of the subjects, people are not likely to know how their personal data is used and probably will not realize they may have a claim to take to court. Furthermore, privacy litigation is something of a contradiction in terms: by taking claims to court, litigants may expose private aspects of their lives to a far greater extent than the initial intrusion did.

■ WARRANTIES, COPYRIGHT LAW, PUBLIC-DOMAIN SOFTWARE, AND SHAREWARE

This portion of the chapter discusses two of the legal issues associated with owning a computer system—the warranties for hardware and software and the copyright law as it applies to computer software. A discussion of express and implied warranties will be followed by a review of copyright law and its application to the writing of computer programs. The section concludes with a brief discussion on public-domain software and shareware.

Warranties

The **Uniform Commercial code (UCC)** is a set of provisions proposed by legal experts to promote uniformity among the state courts in their legal treatment of commercial transactions. By using Article Two of the UCC, the courts have a common basis for rendering decisions concerning the sale of computer hardware and software by vendors.

Common law, on the other hand, is based on customs and past judicial decisions in similar cases. If Article Two of the UCC does not apply to a transaction, then the common law of contracts will apply. The UCC is a far better system since it is more modern and basically abolishes the concept of *caveat emptor* (a Latin legal maxim meaning "let the buyer beware"). Under Article Two of the UCC, for example, the computer user is given implied warranty protection, whereas under common law, buyer protection is not presumed or implied and must be negotiated and agreed upon in the final contract. Most computer vendors are reluctant to agree to such negotiations.

Two main conditions must be satisfied for the UCC to apply to computer acquisitions. First, the contract must be one for goods, not services. As a general rule, the UCC is not applicable to contracts for services. Second, the contract should be for the *sale* of goods. Article Two of the UCC does not normally apply to leases or licenses.

EXPRESS WARRANTIES. Under Article Two of the UCC, **express warranties** are created when the seller makes any promise or statement of fact concerning the goods being sold which the purchaser uses as a basis for purchasing the goods. By doing so, the seller warrants, or guarantees, that the goods are those that will meet the purchaser's needs. An express warranty may be created by the supplier's use of a description, sample, or model in attempting to sell the goods, although the seller's contract terms will often attempt to limit or disclaim all such warranties. Express warranties are also found in the written contract, such as statements that defective equipment will be replaced or repaired for up to one year after delivery. **A breach of contract** occurs if the goods fail to conform to the express warranty, in which case the buyer is entitled to a reduction in the price of the goods as compensatory damages. One drawback of express warranties is that the purchaser must keep the defective equipment. Therefore, unless expressly stated in the contract, the computer hardware or software would not have to be replaced, only reduced in price.

IMPLIED WARRANTIES. Implied warranties were also created under Article Two of the Uniform Commercial Code. **Implied warranties** suggest that a contract for the sale of goods automatically contains certain warranties that exist by law. An implied warranty need not be verbally made nor included in the written warranties of a contract to be effective. Two major types of implied warranties include implied warranty of merchantability and implied warranty of fitness for a particular purpose.

The **implied warranty of merchantability** only exists if the seller is considered a merchant. Computer and software vendors are classified as merchants because they are in the business of selling computer-related products on a repetitive basis. In the case of a purchased computer system, an implied warranty of merchantability guarantees the user that the system will function properly for a reasonable period of time. As in the case of express warranties, however, the purchaser must keep the defective equipment.

To create an **implied warranty of fitness** for a particular purpose, the purchaser must communicate to the supplier the specific purpose for which the product will be used. The purchaser must then rely upon the supplier's judgment, skill, and expertise to select suitable computer hardware and software. If the computer hardware or software later fails to meet those needs, the supplier has breached this implied warranty and is liable for damages. The violation of this warranty permits the purchaser to recover only a certain amount of the sales price.

Copyright Law

Computer software, or computer programs, have been accepted for copyright registration since 1964. In order for a program to be protected under the copyright law, it must contain a notice of copyright that is visible to the user. This notice of copyright must consist of three things: (1) the © symbol, the word *copyright*, or the abbreviation *copr.*; (2) the year of the work's first publication; and (3) the name of the copyright owner (see Figure 17–8). If these three items are not given, however, the copyright is not necessarily forfeited—but the duplicator of the program may not be liable for damages. Unpublished programs are also eligible for protection under the copyright law, and registration is not required since copyright protection exists from the moment of creation. Registration is only required to obtain the right to sue for copyright infringement.

Current copyright law only protects against unauthorized copying and not against unauthorized use. It is not against copyright law, however, to

FIGURE 17—8

Copyright information is often displayed prominently as part of the opening screen.

make a copy of a program that is in a magazine, for example, or for archival purposes. There is some question whether copyright law applies to a program in machine-readable form—such as object code—if a copyright was obtained on the source program. In some cases, the program output can also be copyrighted.

Public-Domain Software and Shareware

Software that is increasingly used in the computer field is **public-domain software.** Public-domain software is software that is unprotected by copyright law and, therefore, falls into the "public domain" of unrestricted use. Public-domain software, frequently obtained from electronic bulletin boards, is free to all users. The only cost associated with a public-domain program is the cost of the phone service needed to reach the bulletin board on which the program appears or the cost of the disk to which the program is copied.

Public domain-programs were originally written by computer hobbyists and amateurs to fill the void of commercial software available for microcomputers. The programs, which appeared on bulletin boards or were passed among members of user groups, were often undocumented and full of "bugs." Today there are fewer bugs in the programs, and many come with sophisticated documentation. Besides bulletin boards and user groups, public-domain software now can be obtained from online services such as CompuServ and The Source. Most public-domain programs include the source code for user convenience.

Closely related to public-domain software is **shareware.** Authors of shareware retain the copyright to their work. They make their programs available to the public with the idea that, if a user likes the program, he or she will make a donation to the author. Generally the source code is not distributed with a shareware program. Users of shareware are encouraged to copy and distribute the programs freely. The basic philosophy behind shareware is that users are in the best position to judge the value of a program and that authors, if they know their fees depend upon it, will produce a quality product. For this reason, the quality of shareware programs tends to surpass that of public-domain programs.

▨ SUMMARY POINTS

■ Taking a broad view, computer crime can be defined as any criminal act that poses a greater threat to a computer user than it would to a non–computer user, or a criminal act that is accomplished through the use of a computer.

■ Computer crimes can be classified in four categories: sabotage, theft of services, theft of property, and financial crimes.

■ Uses of computers in the prevention and detection of crimes include pinpointing likely arson targets, monitoring people who are potential threats to public officials, and handling and cross-checking data and tips in murder investigations.

■ Physical threats to computer security exist in the forms of fire, natural disasters, environmental problems (such as power failures, brownouts, and external radiation), and sabotage.

■ Data security is an issue that must also be addressed by organizations that store sensitive data on computers. Illegitimate use of data must be controlled through access-security measures.

■ Computer ethics refers to the standard of moral conduct for computer use. Computer ethics are largely dependent on human nature.

■ Hacking is the practice of breaking computer security measures to gain unauthorized access to a computer system. Hacking is a criminal act.

■ Employee duty or loyalty is an ethical issue that can pose a serious problem to companies in competition for both business and employees.

■ Unauthorized software copying, or piracy, is a crime whether done for personal use or for profit.

■ The Freedom of Information Act of 1970 allows individuals access to data about themselves in files collected by federal agencies. The Crime Control Act of 1973 protects the privacy of data collected for state criminal systems.

■ The Privacy Act of 1974 is designed to protect the privacy of individuals about whom the federal government maintains data.

■ The Family Educational Rights and Privacy Act of 1974 is designed to protect privacy by regulating access to computer-stored records of grades and behavior evaluations in both private and public schools. The Tax Reform Act of 1976 was passed to safeguard the confidentiality of personal tax information, while the Right to Financial Privacy Act of 1978 limits government access to customer records in financial institutions.

■ The Fair Credit Reporting Act of 1970 attempts to regulate the information practices of private organizations and is intended to deter privacy violations by lending institutions that use computers to store and manipulate data.

■ As computer use has continued to grow during the 1980s, the federal government has continued to enact legislation directed toward protecting the privacy of individuals. The increased use of electronic funds transfer led to the passage of the Electronic Funds Transfer Act of 1980. The Comprehensive Crime Control Act of 1984 provides for protection from computer abuse in some areas that were overlooked in earlier legislation. The Electronic Communication Privacy Act of 1986 prohibits the interception of data communications, for example, electronic mail.

■ By the end of 1985, thirty-six states had passed legislation regarding computer crime; most of these laws addressed the privacy issue in one form or another. Computer-crime laws on the state level are generally quite similar to each other, the differences being in the way terms or violations are defined.

■ The Uniform Commercial Code (UCC) is a set of provisions established by legal experts to act as a uniform guide to state courts for resolving contract disputes.

■ For the UCC to be applicable, the contract must be one for goods rather than services, and the contract should be for the sale of goods, not for leases or licenses.

■ Under Article Two of the UCC, express warranties and implied warranties can be created on behalf of the purchaser.

■ Copyright law is one method of protecting computer programs from being illegally copied. Copyright registration is not required, but is necessary in order to seek damages for a copyright infringement.

■ Public-domain software is software that is unprotected by copyright law and thus falls into the "public domain" of unrestricted use.

■ Authors of shareware retain the copyright to their work. Programs are made available to the public with the idea that a user will make a donation to the author.

■ REVIEW QUESTIONS

1. What is computer crime? Do you feel computer crime is a serious problem in our society?

2. Describe some of the ways computers are being used in the detection and prevention of crimes.

3. Briefly explain some of the measures that can be taken by an organization to insure data security.

4. What is meant by the term *computer ethics?* Describe some instances, other than those discussed, in which computer ethics would be required.

5. Do you feel that computer ethics within an organization should be described through a formal company document that establishes what is ethical and what is not, or should computer ethics be a personal issue left to the discretion of each employee? Briefly explain your answer.

6. Why has the issue of privacy become so important? Do you feel that organizations that maintain information on individuals should be required to disclose this information to those people to verify its correctness? Why or why not?

7. What are the areas of privacy abuse addressed by the Comprehensive Crime Control Act of 1984?

8. Distinguish between express warranties and implied warranties. What are the two types of implied warranties?

9. Why is the copyright law important to a computer software vendor? Would a vendor be protected even if he or she neglected to register the copyright for the software?

10. Distinguish between public-domain software and shareware.

ALCOA

COMPANY HISTORY

Aluminum, which is the most plentiful metallic element in the earth's crust, occurs only as a chemical compound. For many years, the difficulty of reducing it to metallic aluminum made the metal too expensive for commercial use. In 1886, two young men—independently but simultaneously—unlocked the secret of a low-cost, electrolytic process for separating aluminum from its oxide. One of the men, Charles Martin Hall, a graduate of Oberlin College in Ohio, was able to bring his discovery to commercialization, and in 1888, six Pittsburgh industrialists financed the formation of the Pittsburgh Reduction Company, which later was renamed Aluminum Company of America (ALCOA).

Once aluminum was available at low cost, uses for the metal grew steadily. An early successful application was cooking utensils. The steel industry was also an early customer. Aluminum alloys became useful in the making of automobile parts after the turn of the century. As the uses for aluminum grew, so did ALCOA. World War II was a major turning point for the company. Wartime needs required vast amounts of additional aluminum, and ALCOA built many plants for the government. After the war, antitrust regulations required ALCOA to sell all but one of its wartime plants. Despite this setback, post-World War II growth was strong, and ALCOA prospered. Today, ALCOA and affiliated companies sell aluminum throughout the world. The past decade has brought major changes in the worldwide environment for aluminum producers, and ALCOA is becoming a broader-based company with a research thrust toward chemicals, ceramics, polymers, laminates, and advanced manufacturing systems.

DATA SECURITY

As ALCOA has become a more complex organization with an emphasis on research and development, data security has become an important aspect of the company's success. At ALCOA, the focus of data security is on support and acceptance by the user community. To ensure the support of the thousands of computer users at many remote locations, ALCOA has decentralized the responsibility for data security administration to several middle-level managers throughout the company.

ALCOA's security policy, security software, and positive user attitudes are all equally important to the effectiveness of the program. Of these, positive user attitudes are undoubtedly the most difficult to achieve. This is due partly to the logistics of creating security awareness among large numbers of users and partly to the inclination of people to adopt convenient data access practices rather than those intended to safeguard the corporation's data resources. Since people are more easily influenced by individuals whom they know well, local administrators are obviously in a better position to promote security than an unknown central administrator whose office may be three time zones away.

At ALCOA, the belief in positive user attitudes and local data security administrators is strong. According to national surveys, the odds that a computer criminal is a company insider are an astonishing 9 to 1. Central administrators are at a disadvantage in preventing crimes and abuses because they neither know nor are known by more than a few of the individuals who interface with the computer. ALCOA's local administrators, on the other hand, are likely to have job responsibilities that keep them in relatively close contact with the groups of computer users they control, either functionally or geographically. These administrators are more likely to know which users are high security risks. Traditionally, high security risks include employees who are disgruntled, are having money or drug problems, or are being transferred or terminated.

Local administrators can respond quickly to such situations by making direct on-line adjustments via security software. They are not deterred by the notion that security is someone else's problem, and they are not impeded by the phone calls and paperwork that are the bane of central administration. Also, potential

had to fill out more specialized change request forms, have them approved and signed by an authorized individual, and mail them to the home office. At the home office, the signatures were validated, and the forms were reviewed, processed, and returned by mail to the individual who authorized them. This procedure took one to two weeks. Today, ALCOA's local security administrator makes these changes on-line with immediate confirmation of accuracy.

The success of a decentralized program depends upon a central individual to give direction to the overall program and ensure that all local administrators are observing certain standard rules. This may be one of the reasons that relatively few corporations (less than 20 percent) have adopted the decentralized approach to data security and accessing mainframe computers that has successfully been implemented at ALCOA. Also important to the success of a decentralized program are good naming conventions for data security programs, user-friendly security packages that spare local administrators from having to master a great deal of technical jargon, the coordinating of necessary changes to various data sets when user IDs are added or deleted, and the reporting of unauthorized access attempts to the administrators responsible for both the user and the data.

All of these measures and many more have helped make decentralization successful. From corporate headquarters to the grass roots level, decentralization has won the approval of the Aluminum Company of America.

violators are less likely to misuse the computer or commit a crime if they know and respect their local data security administrator.

One of the benefits of the decentralized security system at ALCOA has been increased productivity, as well as improved security and a decrease in costs. Decentralization has increased productivity by eliminating the need for central support personnel to process requests and the staff of central administrators to review and approve the requests. The task of processing requests for user IDs and file accesses has been automated by a combination of purchased security software and programs written in house.

Decentralization has also increased user productivity by reducing the time users wait for computer change requests to be processed. Before decentralization, users

DISCUSSION POINTS

1. Discuss how decentralization has improved data security at ALCOA.
2. Why is positive user attitude the most difficult aspect of data security to achieve?

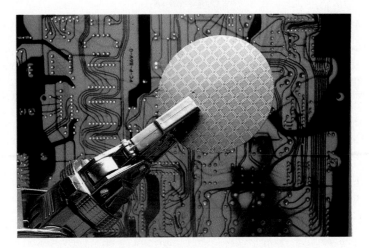

Computers in Our Lives: Today and Tomorrow

OUTLINE

Introduction
Trends in Hardware Technology
  Chip Technology
  Laser Technology
  Parallel Processing
Artificial Intelligence
  Voice Recognition
  Robotics

Computers in Medicine
  Computer-Assisted Diagnosis
  Computer-Assisted Treatment
Computers in Science
Computers for All of Us
  Microcomputers at Home
  Interactive Video
  The Card: Who's Watching Whom?
  Education: The Newly
     Disadvantaged?

Summary Points
Review Questions

Computer 'Virus' Plague Is Feared

Vin McLellan
New York Times

It could be a science-fiction nightmare come to life. In the past nine months, computer viruses—which could subvert, alter or destroy the computer programs of banks, corporations, the military and the government—have infected personal computer programs at corporations and universities in the United States, Israel and Europe.

Security experts say they fear that terrorists, hackers or practical jokers could invent viruses that would wreak havoc in the computer world—and in the business and military operations that have become so dependent on it.

Like its biological counterpart, a computer virus can be highly contagious. It can instantaneously clone a copy of itself and then bury those copies inside other programs. All infected programs then become contagious, and the virus passes to other computers with which the software comes into contact. Virus infections also can be transmitted between computers over telephone lines. A single strategically placed computer with an infected memory—say, a personal-computer-based electronic bulletin board—can infect thousands of small systems.

The most virulent outbreaks have occurred in personal computers. But security experts say the greatest risk would come from infected large computers, such as those governing the air traffic controllers' system or the Internal Revenue Service.

Fred Cohen, a University of Cincinnati professor, has been doing research on the threat of computer viruses since 1983. He said his research has shown that most mainframe computers can be subverted within an hour. And networks—even a huge international network with thousands of computers spread over continents—can be opened to an illicit intruder within days, he said. The possibility of computer networks becoming a primary medium for subversion and warfare "has become much more real," Cohen said.

Complicating the problem is the fact that the virus can evade the security barriers in even the most secure computers. "A virus is deadly because it can jump—actually slide right through—the barriers everyone uses to control access to valuable information," said Kenneth Weiss, technical director at Security Dynamics Technologies Inc., a computer-security company in Cambridge, Mass. "The solution is to put a wall with a good solid gate around the jungle; most computers still have the equivalent of a sleepy guard at the door."

Computer experts have been warning about the danger of such viruses for three or four years. But only in the past nine months have actual reports of viruses surfaced, including infections striking personal computer programs used by IBM employees on the East Coast, and others used by workers at Hewlett-Packard, Apple Computer and several small companies in the San Francisco area, security consultants said.

College administrators report widespread virus infection among students and faculty using personal computers at the University of Delaware and Lehigh University in Bethlehem, Pa.

"It's apparently going to be the game this year: to see who can come up with the best virus," said Dennis Steinaur, a senior security specialist at the National Bureau of Standards, which promotes computer security in the public and private sector. "We're all vulnerable."

Yet he said the bureau planned no immediate recommendations on the threat. "With limited resources," he said, "we like to put our priorities in areas where we can see a solution."

Viruses circulating in the United States were designed eventually to destroy data in IBM and compatible personal computers, the Apple Macintosh and Commodore Technology's Amiga, said company officials, and employees. In most of the reported cases, the virus codes were overtly malicious.

One of the most troubling reports has come from Israel, where a virus code was spread widely over a two-month period last fall and apparently was intended as a weapon of political protest. Yuval Rakavy, a student at Hebrew University who discovered, then dismantled the virus code, said the code contained a "time bomb" that on Friday,

May 13, 1988, would have caused infected programs to erase all stored files. May 13 will be the 40th anniversary of the last day Palestine existed as a political entity; Israel declared its independence May 14, 1948.

William Murray, a security consultant at Ernst & Whinney and former IBM spokesman on security issues, said efforts to contain viral infections were hampered by "all the things you have to do in the face of a viral attack," such as restricting the exchange and sharing of information. Those things, he said, "are almost as disruptive as the attack."

One reason viruses can thrive is that industry has widely adopted networks between computers to foster profitable cooperation and information sharing, despite the fact that these links generally have weakened security. Another productive change, the widespread adoption of personal computers, has depended in large part on free distribution of thousands of noncopyrighted "public domain" programs, ranging from those that help people balance their checkbooks to others that would connect with sophisticated mainframe computers.

Many companies, such as Hewlett-Packard, are trying to contain the spread of the virus by forbidding employees to bring public-domain software into the office.

Although most of the viruses that have surfaced so far appear to be malicious, more benign uses apparently are possible. Already, the idea of using a hidden virus code for constructive purposes appears to fascinate many programmers.

At a personal-computer software house outside of San Francisco, a research project developed a virus to count its generations and keep track of software duplication, said Philip McKinney, an executive at Thumbscan, an Oakbrook, Ill., security firm.

"A couple of the programmers working on the project got fascinated with the whole idea, and soon they and a few of their friends at other companies were using them to play practical jokes on each other," McKinney said. "Some of them got loose and they're all over the place in the (Silicon) Valley. They're generally not destructive, just irritating, messing up the screen and stuff like that."

"That's part of the problem: They're just so enticing," said Eric Hansen, vice president at Digital Dispatch Inc. in Minneapolis. To counter the threat of viruses, the company developed Data Physician, which identifies and removes viruses on IBM PC and Unix systems. Since 1985 it has sold 500 copies, more than half to U.S. military buyers.

"We would have dropped it long ago if we didn't get a couple calls from U.S. military sites every month, urging us to keep it available," Hansen said. Now, growing concern about viral infection means the product will stay on the market.

Although a few computer viruses have been harmless, the damage already done and the potential harm that can be caused by malicious viruses is compelling computer users to have their systems cleansed. Although unauthorized accessing, changing, or destroying someone else's data is illegal, these criminals are very hard to trace and prosecute. And often the victims never recover their data.

CHAPTER

18

▧ INTRODUCTION

Only forty-five years ago, vacuum tubes controlled the electrical circuits in computers. Today, scientists dream of "growing" electronic circuits from protein material. In the 1930s and 1940s, robots played important roles in science fiction. Today robots are no longer visions of the future. They are working in our factories and helping our young people learn in school. A February 1964 *U.S. News and World Report* article, "Is the Computer Running Wild?" announced that the first computers run by integrated circuits would make their debut that year. Today, Hewlett-Packard scientists have placed 450,000 transistors on a single, quarter-inch-square silicon chip. Computer technology has advanced so rapidly that computer scientists who grew up on vacuum tubes, transistors, and science fiction are performing research in biochips and gallium arsenide.

The gains in technology have benefited many areas: artificial intelligence, robotics, medicine and science, home use, and education. This chapter discusses some of the current directions and concerns in these fields as well as some trends in hardware technology.

▧ TRENDS IN HARDWARE TECHNOLOGY

In 1958, Jack S. Kilby of Texas Instruments introduced the first integrated circuit. It was a crude little piece of metal with several fine wires and other components sandwiched with solder. Later, Robert N. Noyce of Fairchild Semiconductor designed another type of integrated circuit that better protected the circuits on the chip. Soon a single chip less than one-eighth of an inch square contained sixty-four complete circuits. The number of circuits etched on a single chip continued to increase until, in September 1984, IBM announced a defect-free prototype of a one million bit (megabit) chip. Circuits have become so miniaturized that writers describe them in terms of angels dancing on the head of a pin and house-by-house maps of large cities etched on postage stamps (see Figure 18–1).

FIGURE 18—1

A Computer Chip
This chip with 450,000 transistors provides as much computing power as yesterday's room-sized computer, yet is only large enough to cover Lincoln's head on a penny.

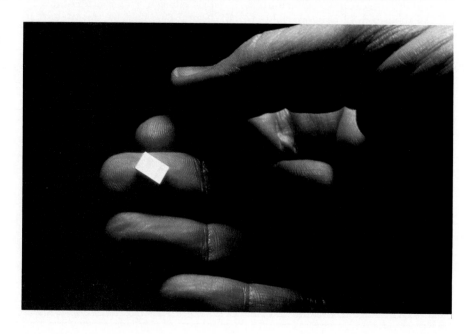

Still scientists explore the building of even higher speed, ultralarge-scale integrated circuits. Experts predict that by 1990 a single chip may contain as many as sixteen million transistors. Packing many components in such a small space reduces the distance that electricity travels and achieves extremely fast computer speeds.

When electronic components are crowded closer together to decrease these distances, however, two problems arise. The first problem is one that plagued the users of early computers: the generation of heat. The densely packed circuits in ultralarge-scale integrated circuits create enough heat and use enough power to burn out the chips. The second problem is an offshoot of the first. As circuits are crowded closer together, the chance increases that one circuit will receive unwanted signals from nearby circuits in what is often termed *cross talk*. (Cross talk resembles the problem you may experience when you make a long-distance telephone call and hear another conversation in the background.) The following sections discuss several ways in which scientists are solving these problems: the raw materials for making chips, laser technology, and parallel processing. Many people feel the development of technologies that solve these problems is signaling a movement into the fifth computer generation.

Chip Technology

As scientists address these problems, they try different materials to make chips. For example, silicon may have met its match in a material called gallium arsenide. Integrated circuits made with gallium arsenide achieve speeds five to seven times those of the fastest silicon computer chips. Gallium arsenide chips also require lower voltages to operate, generate less heat, and create less cross talk than silicon chips. Although expensive, the chips are being used in a variety of ways. Their speed makes them suitable for use in supercomputers. Because the chips resist radiation, they can be used effectively in missile guidance, electronic warfare, radar systems, and surveillance satellites.

Perhaps the most revolutionary idea in chip development is the **biochip.** Scientists believe that tiny computer circuits can be grown from the proteins and enzymes of living material such as *E. coli* bacteria. Like other life forms, they would require oxygen and the signals they would send would be most like those sent and received by our brains. Since biochips would be made from a living material, they could repair and reproduce themselves. They would be ten million times as powerful as today's most advanced computers.

Biochips could be used as "microscopic noses" that would sense odors indicating unusual or dangerous conditions. The chips could also be implanted in a person's brain and linked to a visual sensor like a miniature camera in order to help the blind see. Some biochips placed in the human bloodstream could monitor and correct chemical imbalances.

Laser Technology

Lasers aid computer technology in an important way: they carry signals through hair-thin fibers of the purest glass in a technology known as **fiber optics.** Optical fibers carry tiny staccato pulses of light that can turn on and off ninety million times per second. Fiber-optic cables are being used for linking computer terminals and mainframes in large industrial complexes (see Figure 18–2). They are also rapidly replacing conventional telephone lines. Fiber optics offers several advantages. Transmission of data by fiber optics is faster and more accurate than transmission by ordinary telephone lines. The actual cables are small: an optical cable one-half inch in diameter can carry as much data as a copper cable as thick as a person's arm. The fibers are immune to electromagnetic and noise interference and are difficult to tap. Finally, the raw material used to make the fibers is sand, a cheap and common resource.

Manufacturers of computer chips may also benefit from the use of laser beams. An ultraprecise laser beam could be used as a tiny blowtorch in correcting defective chips, sometimes 50 to 65 percent of the total production. Eventually, researchers hope to use lasers, computers, and robots in building circuits on chips and automatically making all the interconnections between the circuits.

Parallel Processing

Traditional processing occurs serially. A single channel carries all the data bit by bit, one by one, between primary storage and the control unit. The concepts of multiprogramming and virtual storage give the illusion to multiple users that a computer is performing many tasks at once. The computer is really processing several programs during the same period of time by rotating segments of the programs in quick succession.

The human brain, on the other hand, processes information in parallel sequence. It deals with large amounts of data and handles many different cognitive tasks effortlessly and *simultaneously*. Innovative forms of hardware architecture facilitate **parallel processing** by computer. Parallel processing imitates the brain's behavior by dividing a problem into several portions and processing the portions simultaneously. The architecture involves two or more CPUs or microprocessors.

FIGURE 18–2

A Fiber-Optic Cable

Parallel processing increases computer speed without further miniaturizing the circuitry and encountering the problems associated with densely packed electronic components. Applications using parallel processing occur on supercomputers and include speech understanding, interpretation of data from many sensing devices, simulations, navigation uses, and artificial intelligence.

■ ARTIFICIAL INTELLIGENCE

The term *number crunching* was born in the vacuum tube era of computing when mathematicians, scientists, and engineers used the machines for manipulating huge amounts of numerical data. Even today number crunching is what most computers do best. As programmers and developers of computer languages become more proficient at designing advanced software, however, number crunching will give way to more conceptual applications. Scientists will need faster, more powerful computers for these applications, which include voice recognition, robotics, and the ability to understand natural language.

The new computers and languages only begin to imitate human intelligence at higher levels of abstraction. Humanlike thinking, common sense, self-teaching, and decision-making skills performed by machines are termed **artificial intelligence (AI).** Since human intelligence is not clearly understood, current AI programs incorporate just a few aspects of it. The most common AI applications are **expert systems.** These systems imitate an expert in a field, drawing conclusions and making recommendations based on huge data bases of information and on *heuristics*, guidelines that help reduce options or uncertainty.

An example of an expert system is Dr. Lawrence Weed's medical diagnosis program, Problem-Knowledge Coupler (PKC). The patient and doctor enter history, symptoms, and test results on the computer keyboard and, after making cross-references, the computer responds with a list of diseases or conditions that the patient might have. This helps the doctor decide on a diagnosis and treatment.

Expert systems also help people in business and industry. Financial Advisor from Palladian Software is used for analyzing financial data for an organization. It takes into account inflation, taxes, and other economic factors. Ford Motor Company has signed an agreement with Carnegie Group of Pittsburgh for the development of programs that can approve credit applications and diagnose brake systems. Westinghouse Electric Corp. uses an expert system for selecting materials for pressurized water-reactive steam generators used in nuclear energy plants.

Many of these expert systems are not prepared from scratch. Rather, they are programmed into software, such as KEE (Knowledge Engineering Environment by Intellicorp), a "shell" or frame on which to build a tailor-made expert system for a particular user.

Many experts in AI contend that expert systems do not qualify as true AI. Intelligence involves coping with change and incorporating new information for improving performance, and expert systems do neither. The country's top researchers have taken different approaches to the way the wealth of human knowledge must be organized inside the computer. John McCarthy, director of Stanford's Artificial Intelligence Laboratory, is optimistic about the use of **nonmonotonic logic** in building computer knowledge.

Neurocomputing

Artificial intelligence, expert systems—scientists are still trying to make a computer "think" like a person. The latest step in computers imitating human thought is called neural networking. Neural networks are brain-like circuitry in the computer that does more than simply apply rules to logic. The computer can actually be taught to recognize patterns. It is shown a number of patterns. It is given a "problem" where it must decide if a particular pattern fits. The computer is then given feedback as to whether it was right or wrong and why.

Neural networks can also examine a small piece of information and then determine if there is any association between it and other information in its memory. For example, in the area of image analysis the computer may have images in memory. If the computer is then shown a small portion of a picture it can "remember" and retrieve the complete picture.

Scientists believe a "taught" computer with neural networks can be applied in such areas as risk analysis in business; instead of the user listing all the risks in a decision, the computer will "remember" factors and point them out to the user.

Some experts have reservations about neural networks. They feel it is too early to predict the value—if any—of neural networks. Still, neural network supporters say the computers may soon be able to solve problems humans have difficulty even understanding.

Monotonic logic allows conclusions to be drawn from assumptions, and if more assumptions are added, the new conclusions will not make the previous conclusions wrong. For example, "If X is a bird and birds can fly, then X can fly" is monotonic logic. But what if X is a dead bird or a penguin? As you can see, monotonic logic doesn't always hold true. Nonmonotonic logic adapts to this by saying "X can fly unless something prevents it." In other words, it allows for unusual situations.

Another approach is being taken by other researchers, primarily Marvin Minsky at Massachusetts Institute of Technology and Roger Schank at Yale University. It is based on the **script theory,** which says that in any particular situation, humans have an idea of how the thinking or dialogue would go. For instance, we each have a dentist's office script, a classroom script, and a restaurant script. Memories of past events are usually filed in our minds under keys associated with the structure of these scripts.

What these researchers want is to give the computer a way to use common sense and make inferences based on the situation at hand. They realize, though, that the inferences need some boundaries. It is defining and programming these boundaries that presents the challenge. If AI is to be developed further, experts need more accurate descriptions of human thought processes, improved programming for imitating those processes, large data bases, and improved hardware architecture.

Advances in AI will lead to natural English communication with computers. Intelligent computers could read books, newspapers, journals, and magazines and prepare summaries of the material. They could scan mail and sort all letters but those with the most illegible addresses. Used in education, AI could help students learn to read, remember, and think and also help researchers understand how people think. Among the current applications for advanced AI systems are voice recognition systems and robotics.

Voice Recognition

Although the simplest way to input data into a computer is to speak, voice recognition technology is still primitive. Today's systems may recognize many words, but they are usually limited to one speaker or one pitch range. "Speaker-independent" systems—those that accept a variety of voices—cost more than $10,000 and have a vocabulary limited to one or two dozen words. More versatile systems must be trained by the user to understand a particular vocabulary and recognize the user's voice pitch, accent, and inflection (see Figure 18–3). Each word must be enunciated and spoken discretely, that is, not run together with other words in a phrase. And heaven forbid that the user catch a cold!

Because of these limitations, voice recognition is best used with short-answer data. Tomorrow's systems will improve with advancements in AI and computer memory. Research in voice recognition now focuses on the ability to accept larger vocabularies, different voices, and continuous, or flowing, speech.

Some experts believe that keyboardless systems based on voice recognition and AI will become popular in the future. Users could hook the systems to their telephone lines to access just about any data base, leave messages on electronic bulletin boards, and conduct transactions—all without a single keystroke. Such systems would need to recognize natural language and overcome the problems associated with syntax and ambiguity. Users would not need to type specific codes or speak according to a standard question format but could simply request information in the same way they might ask another person. They could also direct computers to write application

FIGURE 18–3

Voice Recognition System
A voice-data entry system in GE's Maryland appliance plant lets workers talk directly to a computer as they monitor the quality of parts moving past on a conveyor.

programs from general descriptions of needs. Natural language would provide a simple yet precise way of stating these descriptions. (See Chapter 10 for a discussion of natural languages.)

Robotics

Robotics will change as AI develops, too. Scientists are working hard to develop robots that are more mobile and sophisticated. Existing robots are deficient in four areas: vision, touch, mobility, and methods of instruction.

Perhaps the most crucial problem to overcome is that of vision. Robots see in only two dimensions, length and width; unlike humans they do not judge depth. Some scientists are designing robots that use fiber-optic "eyes" as tiny cameras for relaying images to their computers. As AI becomes more sophisticated, engineers can program robots to "see" objects and rotate them until recognition is possible. Robots with this capability work as bin-pickers, sorting different parts from huge baskets of parts used in building machinery or other products. When special chips designed for processing and analyzing images are perfected, the robots can recognize objects much faster through parallel processing. With these advances, robots would be able to navigate throughout a person's home without bumping into objects. A robot could travel to the next room through a door, rather than being stopped by the wall. In addition, when confronted with an object in its path, the robot could decide whether to roll over it, move it out of the way, travel around it, or call for help.

A second difficulty, robot touch, has improved greatly with the development of sophisticated sensors. Some robots are equipped with several kinds of hands—after all, a robot does not really care what it looks like! Ichiro Kato has developed a robot hand dexterous enough to play a Schumann melody on the piano. Karen Hensley, a robot researcher, designed a hand that enables a robot to turn a doorknob. In a janitorial catalogue, she found a gripper that janitors use on the end of a long pole for changing light bulbs on high ceilings. Hensley's "hand" will be worn by Pluto, a robot developed by Hans Moravec, a professor at the Robotics Institute in Pittsburgh. Other robot hands can pick up a raw egg as easily as a heavy paperweight. Computer-driven robot arms can feed a bedridden patient and assist in nursing care.

Although most sensors are used to give robots skills in handling objects, scientists are experimenting with sensors that enable a robot to maintain balance while walking. Most of today's mobile robots travel on wheels, with the front two wheels providing the power to move and the back one or two wheels acting as balancers. Walking robots must maintain their own balance, and how do you program balance? Research in designing walking robots has been aided by a desk-high robot that bounces around on one leg, as if riding a pogo stick. The longer the robot can keep its balance, the more successful the engineers have been.

Finally, a robot is useless without an adequate way to receive instructions, learn new tasks, and even make rudimentary decisions. Most industrial robots are just one or two steps away from human-operated machines. The features that distinguish them are their typical crane, or arm, shape and their ability to operate by themselves once the instructions are completed.

Although current software can guide a robot to perform welding jobs, drill holes, trim vinyl dashboards, paint fenders, sort parts for manufacturing processes, and assemble minute electronic components, robots cannot use a bank of programs in learning a new job or making decisions. Software is only now enabling robots to distinguish shapes in three dimensions. In order to pass rigorous tests for home or hospital use, a mobile robot or robot arm must be able to distinguish between a glass of water and a cup of soup. It must recognize its master's voice and respond to natural language commands. It must recognize objects in its path and determine whether to proceed or stop. It must be able to sense how fast it is moving and how tightly it is clutching. And it must be able to synthesize existing programs so that the user can program it by simple English statements to do new tasks. All these abilities stem from research into human learning behavior and AI (see Figure 18–4). Researchers at the Veterans Administration Hospital in Palo Alto, California, are only beginning to realize the potential of such robots. At the hospital, a quadriplegic learns to work with a robot that will fetch objects, help him eat, and hold a book. Perhaps one day robots will help quadriplegics the way seeing-eye dogs help the blind.

CONCEPT SUMMARY 18–1

Improvements in Technology	
Idea	**Improvement**
Gallium arsenide chips	These chips are five to seven times faster than silicon chips, and help avoid the problem of cross talk
Biochips	Although chips in theory only, biochips would be much smaller and more powerful than today's chips and could be used to improve the condition of the human body
Parallel processing	This concept allows computers to use two or more CPUs to process data simultaneously rather than in sequence
Lasers	Lasers in fiber optics improve telecommunications, and lasers can be used in the manufacture of chips
Voice recognition	New voice-recognition systems would be able to accept larger vocabularies, different voices, and continuous or flowing speech
Robotics	Research in robots is geared toward improving robot vision, touch, mobility, and methods of receiving instruction

COMPUTERS IN MEDICINE

Medical personnel diagnose illnesses, provide treatments, and monitor patients. Computer technology is used in facilitating the timeliness and accuracy of these jobs, which in turn affects the quality of life.

FIGURE 18—4

Synthesizing Concepts of AI into a Robot

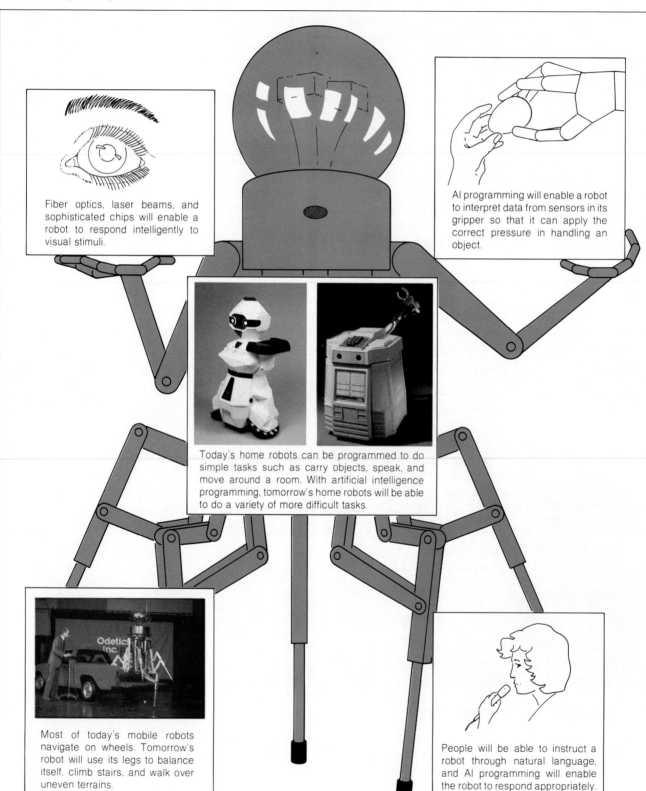

Fiber optics, laser beams, and sophisticated chips will enable a robot to respond intelligently to visual stimuli.

AI programming will enable a robot to interpret data from sensors in its gripper so that it can apply the correct pressure in handling an object.

Today's home robots can be programmed to do simple tasks such as carry objects, speak, and move around a room. With artificial intelligence programming, tomorrow's home robots will be able to do a variety of more difficult tasks.

Most of today's mobile robots navigate on wheels. Tomorrow's robot will use its legs to balance itself, climb stairs, and walk over uneven terrains.

People will be able to instruct a robot through natural language, and AI programming will enable the robot to respond appropriately.

Computer-Assisted Diagnosis

Computers are increasingly combined with testing equipment to provide diagnostic tools in hospitals and clinics (see Figure 18–5). Four common forms—multiphasic health testing, expert systems, computerized axial tomography, and nuclear magnetic resonance scanning—help with preventive health care and offer nonsurgical testing techniques. In **multiphasic health testing,** computer equipment aids in performing a series of tests, stores the results of the tests, and reports the results to doctors. Physical examinations are performed by trained technicians and paramedics using the computer equipment. Procedures include electrocardiograms, X-ray tests, blood tests, vision and hearing tests, blood pressure tests, and height and weight measurement. The computer system compares the results of the tests to predetermined standards of normal health. The patient's physician receives a report of the test results and meets with the patient. Multiphasic testing permits the doctor to spend more time on diagnosis and treatment, and can be valuable in preventive health care.

Expert systems also help physicians in making diagnoses. Among these systems are Mycin, developed at Stanford University for diagnosing blood diseases, and Chest Pain, developed by Dr. Evlin Kinney, a research cardiologist in Miami Beach, Florida, for analyzing chest pain. The latter program was built on an existing expert system shell, Expert Ease, from Human Edge Software in Palo Alto, California. Dr. Kinney cautions, however, that medical expert systems provide only one more factor for consideration in making a diagnosis. The physician may want to reason through his or her conclusions again if they differ from the diagnosis offered by the expert system.

Computerized axial tomography, commonly known as CAT scanning, is a diagnostic aid that joins two tools—X-rays and computerized evaluations of X-ray pictures. A CAT scan can do something that ordinary X-ray tests cannot: it can provide clear pictures of cross-sections of the body. Using

FIGURE 18—5

Computers in Diagnosis
Graphic representation of a patient's eye motion is depicted by the CENOG on the screen (left). An operator at a computer terminal monitors the patient in the testing chamber (right).

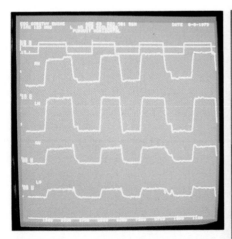
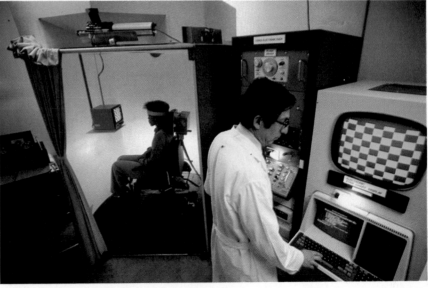

many cross-sections together provides a three-dimensional composite of an organ or bone (see Figure 18–6).

Medical Data Systems of Ann Arbor, Michigan, has taken the CAT scan one step further. The company markets a computer system that constructs a three-dimensional image of a human organ on a video monitor and also re-creates the actual movement of the organ in the simulated organ on the screen. Doctors are able to identify parts of the organ that are not functioning normally.

Nuclear magnetic resonance (NMR) scanning may soon replace the CAT scan in hospitals. Unlike X-ray tests or CAT scans, NMR can "see" through thick bones. Moreover, NMR works without radiation. Magnetic pulses react differently when they come into contact with different parts of the body. A computer is used for collecting the results and creating a detailed picture of the inside of the body. Often NMR scanning is more successful in detecting problems than CAT scanning. Since the procedure does not use radiation, it can be used for testing children and pregnant women. There are some drawbacks to NMR scanning, however. For example, it does not produce clear images of bones or spot breast cancer.

Both CAT scans and NMR scans allow doctors to conduct tests without invading the body through surgery. This prevents the infections, blood clots, and fatigue associated with surgery.

Computers also help ensure the success of reconstructive surgery. Computer-generated pictures can predict the results of reconstructive surgery. In the case of a patient with a deformed skull, CAT scan cross-sections are used to produce three-dimensional pictures of the skull. The computer studies the results of the CAT scan and presents a picture of the skull after reconstruction. Models based on the computer picture help the doctor plan the proper surgical techniques. They also help the patient visualize the outcome of the surgery.

The applications of computers in medicine are almost limitless. In the future computers could be used for testing the skills and efficiency of doc-

FIGURE 18–6

CAT Scan
A technician studies the image produced by a CAT scan that will help diagnose a medical problem.

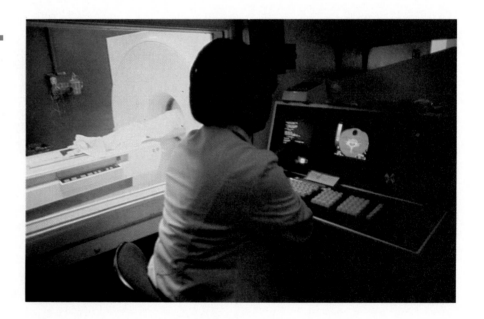

COMPUTERS AND INFORMATION PROCESSING

tors. Computers may also be combined with robots for performing delicate surgery, sometimes from another location across the country. In addition, computers will be used increasingly in hospitals and doctors' offices in the everyday record-keeping and accounting procedures of any business.

Computer-Assisted Treatment

New uses for computers in treatment are emerging daily, while other uses are being improved. For example, due to microprocessors, today's pacemakers are lighter in weight than earlier models. In addition, they can simulate the beating of a healthy heart: doctors can enter up to thirty separate functions, such as delay between pulses, pulse width, and energy output per pulse. In this way, a pacemaker can deal with each patient's particular heart problems.

Microprocessors also control the movements of artificial limbs. Electrical signals from muscles in an amputee's upper arms, for instance, can generate natural movements in an artificial arm and hand. These new artificial limbs are so sophisticated that they are powerful enough to open jars or crack walnuts, yet deft enough to pick up a tomato or a styrofoam cup full of coffee (see Figure 18–7).

An application using microprocessors that is still in the experimental stages involves the controlled release of medication or other treatments by devices implanted in the body. One device currently undergoing testing is called PIMS (Programmable Implantable Medicine System). PIMS is a three-inch computer that is programmed to release measured doses of a drug over time. When a drug is taken orally, once or twice a day, it is distributed throughout the whole body. Frequently, only a small amount of the drug reaches the correct organ. Also, the amount of the drug present in the bloodstream varies over time as each dose is administered. PIMS and other similar devices are designed to overcome these problems. One experimental

FIGURE 18–7

Jennifer Smith, a paraplegic, demonstrates the new hybrid walking system under development at Wright State University's National Center for Rehabilitation Engineering in Dayton, Ohio. The experimental system includes the WSU computer-controlled walking system, a lightweight reciprocating brace from Louisiana State University, and a walker or canes.

device being tested by diabetic patients dispenses a forty-day supply of insulin from a refillable reservoir using a miniature pump. The reservoir is refilled with a hypodermic needle. Radio telemetry and a desktop computer console allow doctors to monitor a diabetic's blood sugar level and reprogram the rate at which the pump dispenses medicine. The device has the potential of eliminating some of the life-threatening side effects of diabetes.

Another use of computers in the treatment of patients involves using computer-controlled lasers. During surgery, lasers are used to destroy tiny, hard-to-reach tumors once considered inoperable. X-ray films taken before surgery pinpoint the tumor's location. The surgeon uses a powerful microscope with a laser attached to it to locate the tumor. After correctly positioning a dot of light that indicates where the laser will strike when activated, the surgeon presses a foot pedal that fires the laser and destroys the tumor. Computer-controlled lasers are also being used in the treatment of kidney stones. A patient being treated for kidney stones is submerged in a tank of water and a computer-controlled laser is aimed at the stone, already located by use of X-rays and dye injections. When the laser strikes the kidney stone, it is dissolved into minute harmless particles. Conventional treatment of kidney stones involves major surgery. The laser technique does not require cutting into the body cavity, thereby eliminating the complications of surgery and reducing the recovery period for the patient.

COMPUTERS IN SCIENCE

Scientists perform calculations, simulate real situations, and observe equipment and conditions while doing their research. Because of the enormous volumes of data that must be stored and processed for some scientific tasks, scientists use large computers for handling the data and producing output in a form that is easy to read and interpret. Often the tasks that require large amounts of data involve monitoring the environment, chemical industries, nuclear power plants, and the weather. Immediate alert to problems in these areas is crucial. For example, the crisis that occurred at the Three Mile Island nuclear power plant when the temperature of the nuclear reactor exceeded safe limits and threatened to melt down the core may be avoided in the future with emergency management systems. The fatal gas leak at the Union Carbide plant in Bhopal, India, might have been prevented with computerized warning systems.

An emergency management system developed by Form & Substance in Westlake Village, California, was designed for the chemical industry. It contains information such as the properties of the chemicals manufactured at the particular plant site, evaporation rates of the chemicals, the influence of the surrounding land on wind patterns and flow, and backup plans of any number of possible accident situations. The computerized data bank is constantly updated with information supplied by chemical sensors around the plant. These sensors keep track of temperature, toxin levels, and wind velocity and direction (see Figure 18–8).

In the event of an emergency, the system will supply instructions and appropriate emergency telephone numbers for notifying authorities and warning nearby residents. Similar emergency management systems are required in nuclear power plants by the Federal Nuclear Regulatory Commission. Following the April 1986 core meltdown in a nuclear plant at

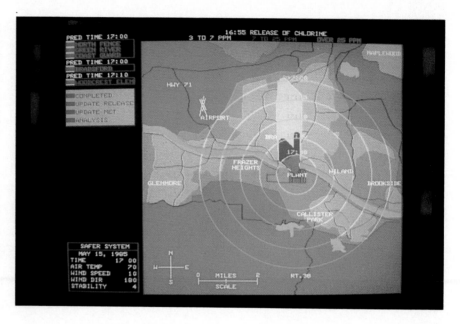

Chernobyl in the Soviet Union, U.S. officials and citizens will be even more concerned about safety and warning systems in North American nuclear plants. Although an emergency management system will not guarantee that a crisis can be averted, it will make emergency evacuation and response much more efficient.

The forecasting of weather is one of the most interesting applications of computers. Several variables, such as air pressure, wind velocity, humidity, and temperature are fed into huge computers for the processing of complex mathematical equations that describe the interaction of these variables. By combining the data with mathematical models, forecasters can predict the weather.

Although local forecasters use radar data directly, they also rely on national and international weather information. The world's weather information is collected by the National Weather Service in Maryland (see Figure 18–9) from a variety of locations: hundreds of data-collecting programs (DCPs) placed on buoys, ships, weather balloons, and airplanes; about seventy weather stations; and four satellites. Two of the satellites orbit the earth over the poles and send pictures revealing the movement and shape of clouds. The other two satellites are in stationary orbits above the equator.

The Weather Service's "brain" consists of fourteen computers housed at the meteorological center. These computers receive information from some of the DCPs whose data is beamed up to the two stationary satellites above the equator. The computers also receive information from other DCPs; the information travels from ground station to ground station. The fourteen computers use all of this incoming data to construct a mathematical description of the atmosphere. These weather reports—2,000 daily—are sent to local weather offices. Manual processing would take so much time that the results would not be available until the weather conditions had already occurred.

Another application of scientific monitoring involves volcano watching. The May 1980 prediction of the eruption of Mount St. Helens in the state

FIGURE 18–8

Emergency Management System
The SAFER system (left) is an emergency response system that alerts industrial companies to toxic releases that could pose potential harm to the employees and the neighboring area. The system displays actions to take in a variety of emergency situations. The display frame (right) illustrates the essential graphic information helpful in an emergency.

FIGURE 18—9

Weather Forecasting
This meteorologist is using the Centralized Storm Information System in forecasting severe weather across the United States.

of Washington was predicted by scientists with the help of data analyzed by computers. Devices such as tiltmeters, which show trends in the tilt of the crater floor, and seismometers, which measure harmonic tremors around the volcano, sent data to a laboratory in Vancouver, Washington, every ten minutes. In the laboratory, computers analyzed that data, helping scientists predict volcanic activity. Because instruments like these are located inside the volcano, volcanic eruptions can be predicted within thirty minutes; this allows time for scientists working near and on the volcano to be quickly evacuated by helicopter. One thing that cannot be predicted, however, is the fury of the eruption and the extent of the mudflow it creates. Mount St. Helens, one of the most heavily monitored volcanoes in the world, surprised the scientists monitoring it with the heavy mudflow that followed its eruption.

Computers can also control scientific instruments and devices. The use of computers in this area frees the scientists to spend valuable time conducting other experiments rather than overseeing the instruments. For example, computers reduce both the time and cost involved in the study of cells at the California Institute of Technology in Pasadena. Deoxyribonucleic acid (DNA) is a chemical that carries genetic information in human cells (see Figure 18–10). Strands of DNA once were synthesized (cloned) by a manual process that took weeks and sometimes months, and cost from $2,000 to $3,000. A computer can perform the same task in less than a day for only $2 to $3. Since the procedure involves much repetition, it was easy for technicians to make mistakes. By turning the tasks over to a computer, the mistakes were eliminated and the procedure became more economical.

■ COMPUTERS FOR ALL OF US

Much of our discussion has centered on computer technology that benefits research and industry. Eventually, the technology will trickle down into our everyday lives. In the meantime, what can we expect in the near future

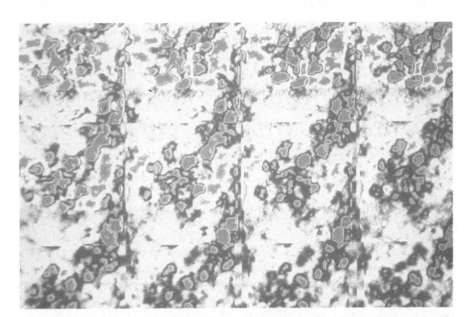

FIGURE 18—10

DNA Synthesis
This is a computer-generated reconstruction of DNA.

CONCEPT SUMMARY 18—2

Computers in Medicine and Science	
Diagnosis	Multiphasic health testing
	Expert systems
	Computerized axial tomography (CAT) scanning
	Nuclear magnetic resonance (NMR)
Monitoring	Emergency management systems (for chemical plants and nuclear plants)
	Weather
	Volcanic activity
Procedures	Pacemakers
	Artificial limbs
	PIMS (Programmable Implantable Medicine System)
	Laser surgery
	Synthetic DNA

in the areas of personal computing, laser technology, and education? The following sections discuss ways in which we might use the new technologies at home and examine some issues involved with our increased dependence upon computers and related technologies.

Microcomputers at Home

Despite the slump in sales of microcomputers for home use, many analysts predict sales will go up when new and faster computers are introduced. In addition, they believe that more people will get used to making transactions through home computers and trying out home-control and robotic devices linked to microcomputers. People will try out these applications for fun, preferring human interaction for most transactions and believing that home-control and robots cannot be cost-justified. As the technology becomes more prevalent, more families will become accustomed to these applications as routine. They will avoid the costs of driving and the irritation of traffic in running small errands, and they will find ways to decrease the responsibilities of chores in a two-income family. Homes of the future will not only be labor- and energy-saving for the homeowner, but also will help handicapped people in achieving independence.

The microcomputers that will be used at home in the future will have powerful graphics and computational capabilities. They will use less power than a 150-watt lightbulb. Screen displays will be larger and have a higher degree of resolution. The amount of primary storage will increase to handle many types of applications including artificial intelligence and intelligent tutors. And the prices will be affordable for most families.

Families will use their computers and telephones to conduct some banking and purchasing transactions and keep up with the status of their bank accounts, credit ratings, and store charges (see Figure 18–11). They will receive video versions of major newspapers, stock market reports, restaurant listings, computer graphic art, music, and movie reviews. They will be able to finish high school or take college courses for credit through their microcomputers. They will learn to program their computers for customized tasks by inputting commands in English (or whatever language they speak naturally). Finally, they will use microcomputers increasingly in controlling the home environment and security. The center of the home may even move from the kitchen and fireplace to a new center, the electronic hearth where all these activities will take place.

In addition, more people will own personal robots that actually are useful rather than merely entertaining. The robots will perform household chores such as laundry and house cleaning.

FIGURE 18–11

A Home Information System

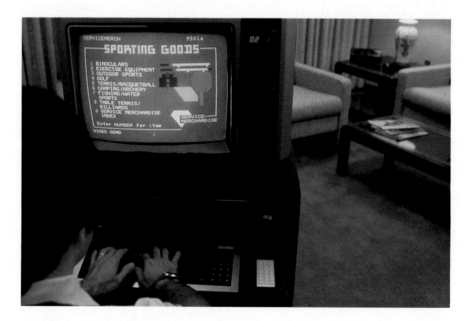

COMPUTERS AND INFORMATION PROCESSING

I'd Rather Stay Home

A computer in every home? Well, maybe not yet, but those people who do have home computers are using them for more than games! For example, some of these people are using their PCs to take college courses and earn degrees. New educational institutions, such as the Electronic University Networks in San Francisco, enable students to take courses via their personal computers. The students receive and return their assignments in electronic mailboxes. In some cases, the only time the student must actually leave home is to take a proctored final exam. This type of telecommuting provides the student with the same advantages as people who telecommute to work—that is, flexible hours, and not having to spend your whole life driving or trying to get one of the few parking spaces on campus!

Home computers have also provided the means for people to start their own businesses. For example, a young couple in New Jersey use their IBM PC to run their at-home business Reunion Time, which organizes high school and college reunions. Home-based word-processing companies can be found in nearly every city. Writers are using word processing and desktop publishing software to open businesses that write and design newsletters for companies and organizations. Accountants have found that spreadsheets can be used at home as well as in the office, and many of them now have their own consulting companies.

People are finding that a computer at home provides easy access to the outside world, for education, for work, or for pleasure. In the future computers may become as common in homes as televisions.

In Arizona, a computer-controlled house has been built as a showcase of automated systems. Called Ahwatukee (a Crow Indian word meaning "house of dreams"), this house is described as the state of the art in technology, ecology, and sociology. Visitors come by the thousands each month to view the house in a half-hour tour. Five microcomputers are linked to run the five systems in the house. Heating, cooling, and the opening and shutting of doors and windows is the primary function of the environmental control system. The security system protects against intruders with the use of television cameras, sensors, and a password-controlled front door. The sensors also watch for fire and will sound a warning if necessary. An electrical switching system uses sensors to note people moving through the house and adjust lights appropriately. Cost-efficient use of electricity is assured with the energy management system, and an information storage and retrieval system is provided for personal or home business needs.

Another such house, called Xanadu, Home of the Future, is located in Kissimmee, Florida. This "intelligent home of the future" features such attractions as a robotic chess set, an electronic art gallery, a children's electronic learning center, and an automatic clothes retrieval system that stores and cleans all clothing (see Figure 18–12).

Less elaborate systems are available for just about any home user. These systems govern appliance use and regulate energy consumption and ventilation. Among them are TomorrowHouse from Compu-Home Systems International in Denver, Colorado; Waldo from Artra Corporation in Arlington, Virginia; and HomeBrain from HyperTek in Whitehouse, New Jersey.

a.

b.

FIGURE 18—12

Xanadu, Home of the Future
a. The kitchen/greenhouse produces its own fresh fruits and vegetables, while meals are planned, prepared, and served by computer-controlled devices.
b. The children's room is a private entertainment and education center.
c. Xanadu's Exterior.

c.

Interactive Video

The combination of optical disks and computer programming has created a promising tool called **interactive video.** Some educators believe it will replace the computer, the instructional film, and perhaps even textbooks in many fields. Interactive video merges graphics and sound with computer-generated text by linking an optical disk (videodisk), a videodisk player, a microcomputer with a color monitor and disk drive, and computer software. Using this equipment, a person can watch news footage of historical events, learn about the most current advances in science, and listen to the music of great composers or the speeches of famous people. The interactive process begins when the user responds to computer-generated questions and forms inquiries to input into the system. The videodisk can be accessed at a chosen point, and motion sequences can be shown in slow motion or still frame for observing critical details.

Videodisk technology will change the way we share information. As a student, you may receive a homework package consisting of software on a floppy disk and graphics on a videodisk to play on your equipment at home. As an employee, you could use the technology for learning how to show new cars, trade shares on a stock exchange, or maintain and repair large earth-moving equipment. As a consumer, you will buy huge data bases of information on any topic ranging from medical subjects to career guidance or browse through videodisk catalogs of the latest merchandise. Interactive video has become so attractive that some people believe the videodisk player will become the most important peripheral device of this decade. The technology will become even more appealing when disks are developed that can be erased and reused. It will become one more technology to add to our electronic hearth.

The Card: Who's Watching Whom?

If our lives do not become centered around an electronic hearth, another technology has the potential for governing our lives. It is "smart cards," plastic cards or keys with embedded information. So far, smart cards are used only for specialized functions. Blue Cross-Blue Shield is issuing the LifeCard, a wallet-sized card on which medical history is stored by laser beam (see Figure 18–13). In Japan, Nipponcoinco vending machines accept laser cards as payment for food. The machine reduces the card's value, originally $40, each time the user buys food. Other cards will be used for recording car repairs, guiding a student's learning, and reporting economic news. The cards act almost like credit cards, and the owner controls their use.

Why not have just one card containing a dedicated computer that performs all personal and financial transactions? Such a card may be more of a reality than we think, says George Morrow, founder and chairman of the board of Morrow, Inc., maker of personal computers and other computer equipment (see Figure 18–14). Banks and creditors face mounting piles of

FIGURE 18—13

Smart Card
A wallet-sized laser card can be used for a variety of purposes.

FIGURE 18—14

Laser Card
This laser card can hold as much data as the disks in the background.

paper, bad checks, and unpaid bills. They have already begun to solve the first problem through automatic tellers and EFT, and people now accept the use of credit cards. The next step could be a card that would identify you, provide a personal audit, balance your checkbook, and pay your utility bills. You would use the card to buy food and clothing. You would never have to balance a checkbook, worry about money being lost in the mail, or face being mugged. Banks and stores would benefit because you could not buy goods without having sufficient funds to cover your purchases. Criminals and thieves could be easily tracked: in a cashless society, they could make no purchases without their cards. In addition, a remote computer could sense when a convicted criminal travels more than two blocks from home. People with a drinking and driving violation or more than four speeding tickets could no longer buy gasoline because a remote computer would program their cards, denying them that privilege. Even governments would benefit. Cash-only deals would be eliminated, guaranteeing the federal government its income tax and state and local governments their sales taxes.

Although many benefits could be realized from using these cards, there are negative implications, too. Governments would have control of everyone's money and could thereby ensure "correct" behavior. The cards could monitor the kinds of things we buy. Our tastes in reading material might be recorded and categorized as "acceptable," "suspicious," or "criminal." People in marketing research could access our records and determine purchasing and travel habits. Our cards could not be used to purchase candy and pie if we were overweight. We might have to use the cards to take breaks at work. Our lives could revolve around the cards.

Education: The Newly Disadvantaged?

Some futurists believe that one day almost every type of job will require employees to use computers. Education will certainly change through computer use and access to data bases. Most transactions will take place via computers and telecommunications. People with little computer experience will be profoundly affected. They will not be able to access a data base, read the material on the screen, or hold a job that requires a great deal of computer use. Therefore, some educators are pressing for extensive computer education in schools.

Computer education includes computer literacy and computer programming. Computer literacy courses teach technical knowledge about computers, the ability to use computers in solving problems, and awareness of how computers affect society. Programming classes often involve learning to program a computer in popular programming languages.

On the other hand, other researchers believe that computer education as a prerequisite for jobs is largely a myth. They say that only a small percentage of jobs will require actual knowledge of technical areas involving electronic circuits, computer programming, and hardware. Rather, they believe that reading and thinking skills and general knowledge will distinguish the haves from the have-nots (see Figure 18–15). If computers are to be used, they must become tools in learning these skills. Educators group software packages meant for teaching into an all-encompassing category: **computer-assisted instruction (CAI).** Through CAI, students encounter a patient "teacher" that allows them to learn at their own rates, receive

FIGURE 18–15

Some believe that in the future, almost every type of job will require the use of computers. Others believe that only a small percentage of jobs will require actual knowledge of electronic circuits, computer programming, and hardware and most computers will be used as tools for learning reading and thinking skills.

immediate feedback, and feel comfortable with both successes and mistakes. Included in CAI is a wide selection of software:

■ Drills for quizzing the student.
■ Tutorials for introducing students to new material and skills and quizzing them on their understanding of the material.
■ Simulations that imitate real-world situations, allowing students to learn through experience and induction without having to take actual risks.
■ Games for learning new concepts and practicing new skills.
■ Problem-solving software that encourages exploration and application of previous knowledge (see Figure 18–16).

Although a trend toward accountability in measuring how much a student learns may make the drills and tutorials attractive to teachers, educators realize the importance of computer use in developing thinking skills. Among the software packages that do more than drill and tutor are Rocky's Boots and Robot Odyssey I from The Learning Company, Menlo Park, California; Where in the World Is Carmen Sandiego? from Broderbund Software, San Rafael, California; and The Incredible Laboratory, The King's Rule, and The Puzzle Tank from Sunburst Communications, Pleasantville, New York. Adults as well as students use these packages.

FIGURE 18—16

Microcomputers in School
This student uses a computer as an
aid in a chemistry experiment.

Regardless of which computer skills are learned, people are realizing the
many ways in which computers can help them learn, conduct business, take
care of their health, and achieve competency at work. Although not everyone
may learn how to write a computer program or how a computer works,
most people can learn to use computers in meeting challenges of the future
and enriching their lives.

■ SUMMARY POINTS

■ Scientists are working on strategies to overcome two major problems
with miniaturizing integrated circuits: heat generation and cross talk.

■ Gallium arsenide can be used to make chips that are faster, require less
power, generate less heat, and are more resistant to radiation than silicon
chips.

■ Biochips are chips in name only; no prototypes have been developed. If
developed, these chips will be grown from the proteins and enzymes of
living material such as *E. coli* bacteria. They could repair and reproduce
themselves.

■ Research in fiber optics aids telecommunication development because
digital pulses can be sent through the glass fibers, which are immune to
electromagnetic and noise interference, and are difficult to tap.

■ Parallel processing facilitates development of applications using forms
of artificial intelligence because processing occurs simultaneously rather
than serially.

■ Today's artificial intelligence applications are called expert systems. These
systems imitate an expert in a field, drawing conclusions and making recommendations based on a huge data base. Some scientists believe expert
systems are not true artificial intelligence.

■ Principles of AI can improve voice recognition systems. Research focuses
on the ability to accept larger vocabularies, different voices, and continuous
or flowing speech.

- Artificial intelligence will increase robot powers of sight and touch, help robots walk, and give them the ability to make decisions.
- Computers are increasingly combined with testing equipment to provide diagnostic tools in hospitals and clinics. In multiphasic health testing (MPHT), computer equipment aids in performing a series of tests, stores the results of the tests, and reports the results to doctors. Doctors also use expert systems that help diagnose various conditions, including blood diseases and chest pain, for example.
- Two noninvasive diagnostic aids used in hospitals and clinics are computerized axial tomography (CAT or CT), commonly known as a CAT scan, and nuclear magnetic resonance (NMR) scanning.
- Microprocessors help in treatments, for example, in pacemakers, artificial limbs, and PIMS (Programmable Implantable Medicine System).
- Laser surgery for such conditions as kidney stones allows a surgeon to destroy the stones without cutting into a person.
- Scientists use computers for solving many problems including monitoring chemical plants, nuclear plants, the weather, and volcanoes. In addition, scientists can use computers for performing repetitive tasks such as creating synthetic DNA, thus freeing themselves for conducting valuable experiments.
- People will begin to use microcomputers for many tasks at home: monitoring energy consumption and security, accessing commercial data bases, performing business transactions; taking high school or college courses, and entertaining themselves.
- Because of the potential for interactive video (learning in an interactive way using a computer system), some experts believe the videodisk player will become the most important peripheral device for microcomputer systems in this decade.
- Electronic technology presents new challenges. One involves cards used for financial transactions, which could become monitoring devices of people's behavior.
- Some experts believe people who cannot use computers will be the newly disadvantaged. Others believe reading and thinking skills and general knowledge will determine the haves and have-nots of the future. Students can use computers for computer-assisted instruction (CAI) to learn such skills. CAI software includes drills, tutorials, simulations, games, and problem-solving software.

▦ REVIEW QUESTIONS

1. Why is gallium arsenide a better material for building faster chips?

2. What tasks would biochips perform if they existed?

3. How are laser beams used with fiber optics?

4. How do expert systems compare with scientists' criteria for artificial intelligence?

5. What are some of the difficulties that must be overcome in voice recognition?

6. What are some of the difficulties that must be overcome before robots are useful in homes?

7. Explain how multiphasic health testing can help a physician in making a diagnosis.

8. What is the difference between a CAT scan and NMR scanning?

9. Name and explain three ways microprocessors are being used in the treatment of patients.

10. Briefly describe how computers are used for monitoring volcanic activity.

11. How might computers be used in homes in the next decade or two?

12. What are some of the objections people have to carrying one card that can be used for a multitude of financial purposes?

13. Name five ways that computers can be used in building reading and thinking skills and general knowledge in education.

Marshall & Melhorn

MARSHALL &MELHORN

In 1896 Edwin J. Marshall and Harold W. Fraser announced their association for the practice of law in Toledo, Ohio. Mr. Marshall had recently completed postgraduate work in corporate law at Cornell University and was destined to become the leading authority on the subject in Ohio. Mr. Fraser was a renowned orator who would become recognized as a masterful trial lawyer involved in numerous landmark cases. Their goal was to provide service to their clients both in the boardroom and courtroom.

Today, Marshall & Melhorn carries forward this philosophy of total client service. Over forty lawyers make up the professional staff, with areas of speciality ranging from intellectual property to corporate finance and labor law to litigation. Marshall & Melhorn represents many of the largest corporations in the United States and is extremely active in the international field. The law firm has established a unique relationship with Jones Day, the second largest law firm in the world, to further support their concept of delivering the highest level of service to clients.

Within Marshall & Melhorn there is an operating unit, the Computer Law Group, which specializes in computer related matters. Their case load includes a broad range of activities from negotiating contracts to criminal proceedings, from copyright filings to corporate financing. In one particular case, they literally covered the country while representing parties in Hawaii, New York, Ohio, and Texas. The lawyers in this group are internationally recognized experts and have authored the leading textbooks in the field.

As part of their commitment to total client support, Marshall & Melhorn has implemented state-of-the-art computer technology to assure the cost-effective delivery of legal services. Every attorney, paralegal, administrator, and secretary has a desk-top personal computer. These systems have been networked together to permit the sharing and transfer of programs and files. In addition, the telephone system has been integrated to support remote-access computing and a totally electronic office. Productivity has improved significantly while support service has been greatly expanded. The financial accounting is run on a separate minicomputer so as to ensure integrity of the billing process.

The heart of the office system is two Novelle networks, each controlled by a 80386-based file server with approximately 45 stations. One network system is designated for office support (word processing, time sheets, etc.) and the other network is assigned for case support (legal research, docket control, etc.). However, there is a bridge between the two networks consisting of five data channels so that any station can communicate directly with either network. There is also a special bridge or channel between the networks and the minicomputer allowing authorized personnel to access the financial data directly from their stations.

The networks have been designed to be totally redundant and fail-safe so that if one network file server is nonoperational, the system will continue to perform for the users with minimal degradation. As a further backup, each station is a fully configured personal computer so that in the event both networks are down, every individual can continue operating in an independent mode. The firm has chosen the WordPerfect family of application software as their standard.

Many of the promises of networking are being realized at Marshall & Melhorn. A secretary completes

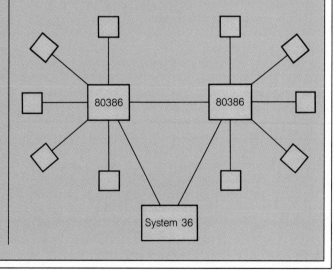

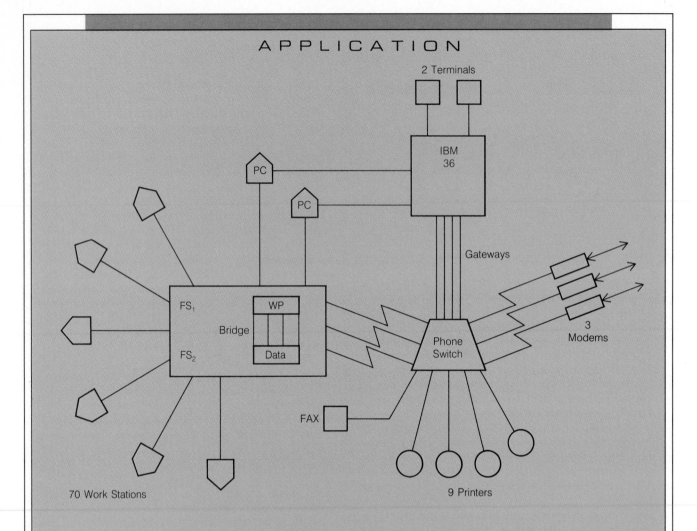

2 Terminals

IBM 36

PC

PC

FS₁

Bridge

WP

Data

FS₂

Gateways

Phone Switch

3 Modems

FAX

70 Work Stations

9 Printers

an initial draft of a contract and leaves for lunch. The attorney retrieves the document in his or her office and makes revisions. Prior to finalizing the contract, the attorney sends an electronic message and the document file to the senior billing attorney for peer review. This billing attorney then can take one of several actions depending upon the need for further modifications. Eventually the document returns to the secretary's station along with electronic instructions on how to proceed. Regardless of whether the document is to be printed or electronically transmitted, the secretary is in total control from her workstation.

Legal records management is extremely critical in a large case with numerous depositions and documents. By placing such records on the network, attorneys may search and retrieve necessary information in a manner never before cost justifiable. Utilizing one of the portable computers that the law firm has

acquired, a lawyer can execute such searches anywhere a telephone line is available, even from the courthouse.

Marshall & Melhorn has established itself as a force in the field of computer law and an innovator in the use of information systems. The benefits to their clients in improved service and productivity are apparent. In the future practice of law, the business advantage will be held by those firms capable of properly implementing computer technology.

DISCUSSION POINTS

1. Describe how backup is built into the design of the computer system at Marshall & Melhorn.
2. How has the computer affected interpersonal office communication?

BASIC Supplement

O U T L I N E

Section I: Introduction to BASIC
Introduction
What Is Programming?
The Programming Process
Interacting with the Computer
Summary Points
Review Questions
Section II: BASIC Fundamentals
Introduction
Components of the BASIC
    Language
Elementary BASIC Statements
Comprehensive Programming
    Problem
Summary Points
Review Questions
Debugging Exercises
Programming Problems
Section III: Input and Output
Introduction
The INPUT Statement
The READ and DATA Statements

A Comparison of Two Methods of
    Data Entry
Printing Results
Comprehensive Programming
    Problem
Summary Points
Review Questions
Debugging Exercises
Programming Problems
**Section IV: The Decision Statement
    and Functions**
Introduction
The GOTO Statement:
    Unconditional Transfer
The IF Statement: Conditional
    Transfer
Library Functions
User-Defined Functions
Comprehensive Programming
    Problem
Summary Points
Review Questions
Debugging Exercises
Programming Problems

Section V: Looping
Introduction
The FOR/NEXT Loop
The WHILE Loop
Comprehensive Programming
    Problem
Summary Points
Review Questions
Debugging Exercises
Programming Problems
Section VI: Modularizing Programs
Introduction
The Importance of Modularizing
    Programs
Writing Subroutines
Using the Structure Chart to
    Modularize a Program
Single-Entry, Single-Exit
    Subroutines
Comprehensive Programming
    Problem
Summary Points
Review Questions
Debugging Exercises
Programming Problems

■ PREFACE

BASIC has traditionally been accepted as an effective programming language for instructional purposes. In recent years, many businesses and computer manufacturers have recognized the potential for additional uses for this language. Today most small business computer systems and microcomputers allow for the use of BASIC programming. One major problem associated with the increasing use of BASIC has been the lack of controls in the implementation of the language. Although there is a national standard (ANSI) version of BASIC, normally it is not strictly followed by software designers. Therefore, there are differences in the versions of BASIC used by various computers. The main implementation of BASIC covered in this supplement is VAX BASIC, which runs on VAX computers. All programs have been run on this system. In addition, coverage of several microcomputer implementations of BASIC is given: Microsoft on the IBM Personal Computer, Microsoft on the Macintosh, Applesoft on the Apple IIe and Apple IIGS, and TRS-80 Model 4 BASIC.

Color coding has been used in programming examples throughout this supplement to help the reader. The legend for this coding is shown below:

BLUE	Computer Output
BROWN SHADING	Statements Referenced in Text
RED	User Response

■ INTRODUCTION

BASIC, an acronym for Beginner's All-purpose Symbolic Instruction Code, was developed in the mid-1960s at Dartmouth College by Professors John Kemeny and Thomas Kurtz. It is a high-level language that uses English-like words and statements such as LET, READ, and PRINT. It is easy to learn and is considered a general-purpose programming language because it is useful for a wide variety of tasks.

BASIC, like English and other languages used for communication, includes rules for spelling, grammar, and punctuation. In BASIC, however, these rules are very precise and allow no exceptions. They enable the programmer to tell the computer what to do in such a way that the computer is able to carry out the instructions. This supplement will teach you the rules for writing programs in BASIC.

■ WHAT IS PROGRAMMING?

Programming is the process of writing instructions (a program) for a computer to use to solve a problem. These instructions must be written in a programming language. A program can be anything from a simple list of instructions that adds a series of numbers together, to a large, complex structure with many subsections, which calculates the payroll for a major corporation.

When computers were first developed, programming was extremely complex and programmers were happy simply to get their programs to work. There was little concern over writing programs in a style that was easy for other people to understand. Gradually, however, programmers began to realize that working with such programs was very difficult, particularly when someone other than the original programmer had to alter an existing program.

Because of this problem, programmers began developing ways to make programs easier to understand and modify. These techniques, which have been developed over the last twenty years, are referred to as **structured programming.** Structured programming has two basic characteristics: (a) the program logic is easy to follow; and (b) the programs are divided into smaller **subprograms,** or **modules,** which in BASIC are referred to as subroutines. Thus, structured programming avoids large, complex programs in favor of more manageable subprograms, each designed to perform a specific task. Because the logic of structured programs is easier to follow than that of unstructured programs, they are more likely to be free of errors and are easier to modify at a later date.

This supplement will emphasize the concepts of structured programming. Because many versions of BASIC were developed before the concepts of structured programming were clearly understood, these versions do not easily lend themselves to this type of programming. We will try to present techniques for working around these difficulties whenever possible.

■ THE PROGRAMMING PROCESS

Software is a program or a series of programs that tells the computer hardware what to do. Because the computer must be able to read and interpret each instruction, the program must be precisely written. To know

S E C T I O N

Introduction to BASIC

O U T L I N E

Introduction
What Is Programming?
The Programming Process
  Defining and Documenting the
    Problem
  Designing and Documenting a
    Solution
  Writing and Documenting the
    Program
  Debugging and Testing the Program
Interacting with the Computer
  The VAX
  The IBM Personal Computer
  The Macintosh
  The Apple IIe and IIGS
  The TRS-80 Model 4
Summary Points
Review Questions

what instructions are required to solve a problem, the programmer follows five steps, commonly called the **programming process:**

1. Define and document the problem.
2. Design and document a solution.
3. Write and document the program.
4. Submit the program to the computer.
5. Test and debug the program and revise the documentation if necessary.

Defining and Documenting the Problem

The person who writes a program may not be the same person who will be using it, and communication between these two people (or groups) may be inadequate. Misunderstandings concerning the desired results of a program can lead to programs that do not meet the user's needs. Therefore, before the programmer begins work, the problem must be clearly defined and documented in writing. **Documentation** consists of any comments, diagrams, or other information that explains how a program is to be designed or describes the actual program. Documentation can be contained within the program *or* it can be separate from the program.

Let's practice defining and documenting a simple problem. Suppose you need a program to convert a given number of feet to miles. The output is the number of miles in the stated number of feet. The input is the number of feet to be converted. You will also need to know the conversion formula (that is, how many feet there are in one mile). You now have all the information needed to solve the problem. This information could be documented as follows:

Problem Definition
Write a program to convert a given number of feet to miles.

Needed Input
The number of feet to be converted.

Needed Output
The number of miles in a given number of feet.

Designing and Documenting a Solution

Once the programming problem is thoroughly understood and the necessary input and output have been determined, it is time to write the steps needed to obtain the correct output from the input. The sequence of steps needed to solve a problem is called an **algorithm.** In an algorithm, every step needed to solve a problem must be listed in the order in which it is to be performed. Developing an algorithm is an important step in all programming. Let's develop an algorithm for the problem of converting feet to miles. The steps could be stated like this:

1. Read the number of feet to be converted to miles.
2. Find the number of miles by dividing the number of feet by 5,280 (the number of feet in one mile).
3. Print the number of miles.

TOP-DOWN DESIGN. To use a computer to solve a problem, the programmer does not need a detailed understanding of how the computer works. However, he or she must know a programming language. The most difficult aspect of programming is learning to organize solutions in a clear, concise way. This is where **top-down design** becomes helpful. When using top-down design, the programmer proceeds from the general to the specific, attempting to solve the major problems first and worrying about details later. The problem is broken down into smaller and smaller subparts. Sometimes this is referred to as the "divide-and-conquer" method, because it is easier to deal with a large job by completing it a small step at a time. This approach prevents the programmer from becoming overwhelmed by the size of the job at hand.

Top-down design can be applied to solving the problem of converting feet into miles. The problem can be divided into three basic subtasks:

1. Get the number of feet to be converted into miles.
2. Divide the feet by the number of feet in one mile.
3. Display the resulting number of miles.

The diagram in Figure I–1 is called **a structure chart.** This chart graphically illustrates how the steps listed above are related to one another. Level 0 contains the general statement of the problem, while Level 1 contains the substeps. This is a very simple structure chart. However, structure charts for complex problems usually have many levels of substeps.

FLOWCHARTS. Once a solution has been developed, it must be documented. One method is by using a structure chart as was done in the feet-to-miles example. The structure chart graphically depicts how the individual subtasks are related to one another. Two other commonly used ways to document programming problem solutions are flowcharts and pseudocode.

Flowcharts graphically illustrate the steps necessary in solving a programming problem. A flowchart shows the actual flow of logic, whereas a structure chart simply shows how the problem can be divided into subtasks. The meanings of different flowchart symbols are stated in Figure I–2. At this point, do not worry if you do not understand them all.

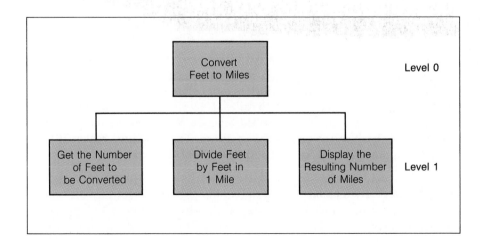

FIGURE I–1

Structure Chart for Conversion Problem

FIGURE 1—2

Commonly-Used Flowcharting Symbols

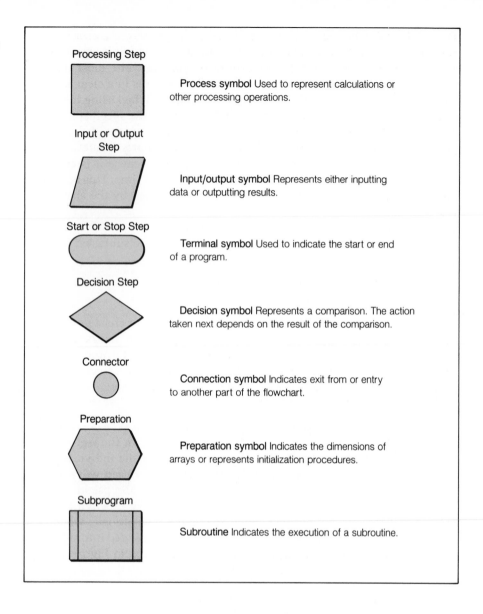

Processing Step

Process symbol Used to represent calculations or other processing operations.

Input or Output Step

Input/output symbol Represents either inputting data or outputting results.

Start or Stop Step

Terminal symbol Used to indicate the start or end of a program.

Decision Step

Decision symbol Represents a comparison. The action taken next depends on the result of the comparison.

Connector

Connection symbol Indicates exit from or entry to another part of the flowchart.

Preparation

Preparation symbol Indicates the dimensions of arrays or represents initialization procedures.

Subprogram

Subroutine Indicates the execution of a subroutine.

Figure 1—3 shows a flowchart depicting the steps needed to solve the problem of converting feet into miles. Notice how the symbols are shown in logical order, top down, connected by arrows. The first symbol indicates the start of the program. The second symbol shows an input step—the number of feet are entered. The third symbol shows the processing done by the program—conversion of feet to miles. Next, the number of miles in the stated number of feet are output so they can be read. Finally, another start/stop symbol signifies the end of the program. The flowchart makes it easy to see the input, processing, and output steps of the program.

PSEUDOCODE. Pseudocode is an English-like description of the solution to a programming problem. It is a type of algorithm in that all of the steps needed to solve the problem must be listed. However, algorithms can be written to solve all types of problems, whereas pseudocode is developed specifically to solve programming problems. Unlike a flowchart, which is a graphic representation of the solution, pseudocode is similar to the actual program. It lets the programmer concentrate on a program's logic rather than the **syntax,** or grammatical rules, of a programming language. All of the logical structures present in programs can be written in pseudocode. There are no rigid rules concerning the writing of pseudocode, but once you have developed a style, it is a good idea to follow it consistently.

The problem solution shown in the flowchart in Figure I–3 could be written in pseudocode like this:

```
Start
Input the number of feet
Convert the feet to miles
Display the number of miles in the stated number of feet
Stop
```

Writing and Documenting the Program

If the solution has been designed carefully, the third step—writing and documenting the program—should be relatively easy. All that is required is to translate the flowchart or pseudocode into BASIC statements. Figure I–4 shows this program written in BASIC. As you can see, many BASIC words, such as INPUT and PRINT, are easy to interpret. The symbol "/" in line 90 means to divide. The REM (short for REMark) statements in lines 10–70 are used to document the program. The computer skips over REM statements. Compare the coded BASIC statements in Figure I–4 to the flowchart in Figure I–3. Even if you've never seen a BASIC program before, you can probably determine which statement in the program corresponds to

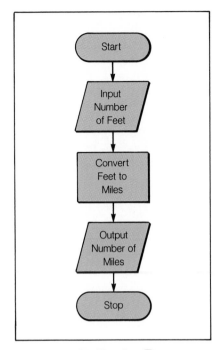

FIGURE I–3

Flowchart for Conversion Problem

FIGURE I–4

Program to Convert Feet to Miles

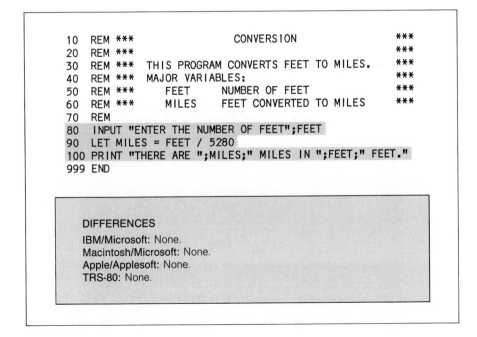

```
10   REM ***                  CONVERSION                    ***
20   REM ***                                                ***
30   REM ***   THIS PROGRAM CONVERTS FEET TO MILES.         ***
40   REM ***   MAJOR VARIABLES:                             ***
50   REM ***      FEET      NUMBER OF FEET                  ***
60   REM ***      MILES     FEET CONVERTED TO MILES         ***
70   REM
80   INPUT "ENTER THE NUMBER OF FEET";FEET
90   LET MILES = FEET / 5280
100  PRINT "THERE ARE ";MILES;" MILES IN ";FEET;" FEET."
999  END
```

```
DIFFERENCES

IBM/Microsoft: None.
Macintosh/Microsoft: None.
Apple/Applesoft: None.
TRS-80: None.
```

which symbols in the flowchart. Do not worry if you don't understand the entire program. It is given here to merely present an idea of how BASIC programs are written. The rest of this supplement will teach you how to write BASIC programs.

Debugging and Testing the Program

Structured programming techniques encourage the development of programs with easy-to-follow logic and fewer errors than unstructured programs. Nonetheless, programs of any significant length virtually always contain some errors, and correcting them can account for a large portion of the time spent in program development.

Debugging is the process of locating and correcting program errors. The most common errors made by a beginning programmer are simple typing mistakes, referred to as **syntax errors.** Carefully proofreading program statements as they are typed can prevent the majority of these errors.

Once the computer is able to run your program, you will need to test it with a variety of data to determine if the results are always correct. A program may obtain correct results when it is run with one set of data, but incorrect results when run with different data. This type of error is referred to as a **logic error.** It is caused by a flaw in the program's algorithm.

How the programmer is able to determine that a program contains an error depends upon the type of error that has been made. If a typing error is made, the computer usually will not be able to execute the program and an error message will be displayed. If the programmer makes a logic error, the program may stop executing prematurely or it may execute properly but obtain incorrect results. Once errors are corrected in a program, the programmer must also remember to revise any corresponding documentation.

Figure I–5 shows the output of the conversion program. The conversion example is relatively simple, but shows each of the steps required to develop a program. Although other problems may be more complex, the steps involved are the same. Successful programming can only come about through application of the five steps in the programming process.

▓ INTERACTING WITH THE COMPUTER

An important step in BASIC programming is learning to use the computer. Although this section cannot present the full operational details for each

FIGURE I–5

Output of Program to Convert Feet to Miles

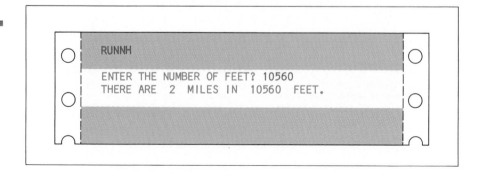

```
RUNNH

ENTER THE NUMBER OF FEET? 10560
THERE ARE  2  MILES IN  10560  FEET.
```

COMPUTERS AND INFORMATION PROCESSING

type of computer covered, we will discuss the principles of how to turn the computer on, access the BASIC system, retrieve a program from external storage, display the program, run the program, and save it for future use.

The instructions used in BASIC programming can be divided into two categories: BASIC statements and BASIC commands. Some of the instructions—for example, LET, READ, and INPUT—are BASIC statements and are used in BASIC programs. BASIC commands, on the other hand, are used by the programmer to communicate with the operating system of the computer in order to perform functions such as saving programs for future use and executing in programs. Some commands—for example, LIST, RUN, and NEW—are used on virtually all BASIC systems. Table I–1 lists some commonly used commands. Below is a list of commands with a brief explanation of the purpose of each.

NEW. The NEW command tells the computer to erase any program currently in main memory. It prepares the computer to have a new program entered. Always use the NEW command before entering a new program. Remember, however, if the old program in main memory is not saved before the NEW command is executed, it will be lost.

LIST. After typing in a program, you will want to check your work. Type LIST to display the program on the screen. If you have a very short program, LIST can display the whole program at one time. However, if the program has more lines than the screen can display, only the last part of the program will remain on the screen. Most screens allow twenty-four lines to be displayed at a time. You can display portions of programs by specifying the lines to be listed (LIST 150–300, for example). It is called *scrolling*, when the beginning of your program disappears off the top of the screen to make room for more lines at the bottom. Most computers also allow you to suppress the scrolling. By pressing one or two keys the user can "freeze" the screen. The exact method of controlling scrolling on each system is shown in Table I–2. The scrolling can then be resumed when the user is ready.

T A B L E I—1

Commonly Used BASIC Commands

Purpose	VAX BASIC	Apple/Applesoft	IBM/Microsoft	Macintosh/Microsoft*	TRS-80
Erase current program from main memory	NEW filename	NEW	NEW	NEW	NEW
List a program in main memory	LIST	LIST	LIST	LIST	LIST
Execute a program	RUN or RUNNH	RUN	RUN	RUN	RUN
Store program on disk	SAVE	SAVE filename	SAVE "filename"	SAVE "filename"	SAVE "filename"
Retrieve program from disk	OLD filename	LOAD filename	LOAD "filename"	LOAD "filename"	LOAD "filename"

*On the Macintosh, commands can be selected from menus.

TABLE 1—2

Scroll Control

	Scroll Stop	**Scroll Start**
VAX (VT-100 terminal)	Press NO SCROLL key.	Press NO SCROLL key
IBM PC	Hold Ctrl and Num Lock keys down at the same time.	Press any key
Macintosh	*	
Apple II	Hold Ctrl and S keys down at the same time.	Press any key
TRS-80	Hold the Shift and the @ keys down at the same time.	Press any key

*To stop scrolling output, click the Run menu at the top of the screen, and then click Suspend, which is found in the Run menu. To resume scrolling, click the Run menu again. Then click Continue, found in the Run menu.

RUN. The purpose of the RUN command is to begin execution of a program. Typing the word RUN will execute the program currently in memory.

SAVE. After you have typed in a program, you will want to avoid losing it when the computer is turned off. To prevent this, you have to copy the program from main memory to secondary storage. (Large systems may use disks or magnetic tape for secondary storage, whereas microcomputers most commonly use floppy or hard disks.) The SAVE command is used to copy the program. Generally, there are several options to this command. You will also need to supply a name under which the program is to be saved.

LOAD. This command copies the designated program from secondary storage into main memory. Before loading a program, any program previously in main memory is erased. On the VAX system, the OLD command is used instead of LOAD.

The following sections discuss specifics about using each of the systems covered in this supplement.

The VAX

All of the programs in this text were run on a VAX 8530, using the VMS operating system. The implementation of BASIC used was VAX BASIC, Version 3.2.

Logging On and Off. Accessing a large computer system is referred to as "logging on" the system. Before logging on, turn the terminal's power switch on. A message appears stating some general information, such as the type of VAX being accessed. The system first prompts you to enter your user name (often called an account name):

```
Username:
```

After entering your user name, press the return key. The system then prompts you for your password:

```
Password:
```

Notice that when you type in your password, it does not appear on the screen. This is so that anyone happening to be looking on will not see it. Passwords should only be made available to those who are responsible for the account. The system will now display the date, time, and other general information. The system prompt $ will appear, indicating that the system is ready to accept your commands. Type

```
$BASIC <Return>
```

to access the BASIC system. The BASIC system prompt will appear:

```
Ready
```

Before entering a program, use the NEW command to erase any programs currently in main memory:

```
NEW
New file name--PROG1.BAS
Ready
```

Notice that the system prompts you to enter a name for this new program. This is the name under which the program will be saved in secondary storage. You may wish to practice typing in the program in Figure I–4.

SAVING AND LOADING PROGRAMS. To save a program, use the SAVE command:

```
SAVE
```

The program is now copied onto secondary storage under the name given in the NEW command. It can be loaded back into main memory by using the OLD command:

```
OLD PROG1.BAS
```

RUNNING PROGRAMS. There are two versions of the RUN command in VAX BASIC: RUN and RUNNH. Both will execute the program currently in main memory. However, RUN also displays some system messages, whereas RUNNH eliminates these messages. If we executed the program in Figure I–4 using RUN, the output would be similar to the following:

```
RUN
FIG14    30-AUG-1988 12:11

ENTER THE NUMBER OF FEET? 10560
THERE ARE 2 MILES IN 10560 FEET.
Ready
```

Using the RUNNH command displays only the output:

```
RUNNH

ENTER THE NUMBER OF FEET? 10560
THERE ARE 2 MILES IN 10560 FEET.
Ready
```

All programs in this supplement are executed using RUNNH so that no headings are displayed.

The IBM Personal Computer

The IBM Personal Computer runs an enhanced version of Microsoft (MS) BASIC. We will discuss using BASIC on a PC with two floppy disk drives. If your computer has a hard disk, check with your instructor for directions on accessing BASIC.

STARTING THE COMPUTER. Place the disk operating system (DOS) diskette into Drive A (the left drive). Then turn on the computer. The power switch is located at the right rear of the machine. Remember to turn on the monitor and to turn up the brightness dial, too. As soon as the computer is turned on, it will attempt to load the DOS. Once the DOS has been loaded (or "booted"), the computer asks for the date and the time. If you do not wish to enter the date and/or time, simply press the Enter <↵> key after the prompts, which will be similar to the following:

```
Current data is Tue 1-01-1980
Enter new date (mm-dd-yy):
Current time is 0:00:49.32
Enter new time:
```

After you have responded to the time prompt and pressed <↵>, the computer responds with a display similar to the following:

```
The IBM Personal Computer DOS
Version 3.10 (C)Copyright International Business Machines Corp
1981, 1985
                (C)Copyright Microsoft Corp 1981, 1985
A>
```

The A> is the system prompt. To load BASIC, type the following:

```
BASIC <↵>
```

Then you will see the BASIC prompt:

```
Ok
```

Now you are ready to enter your program. Type in the program just as you would using any keyboard. If you make an error, use the cursor control keys to move up (↑), down (↓), left (←), or right (→). You may wish to type in the program shown in Figure I–4 for practice.

SAVING AND LOADING PROGRAMS. After typing in a program, you may want to save it on a disk. The system allows you to choose the name of the file in which the program will be saved. The following statement will save a program under the name TESTS:

```
SAVE "TESTS" <↵>
```

The length of the file name should be less than or equal to eight characters. Blank spaces are not allowed within the file name. For example, TEST 1 is not a valid file name. To load file TESTS from disk back into the computer's main memory, type:

```
LOAD "TESTS"  <↵>
```

RUNNING THE PROGRAM. To run a program that is currently in main memory, enter:

```
RUN <↵>
```

Program output will be displayed on the screen.

The Macintosh

The implementation of BASIC used on the Macintosh for this supplement is Microsoft 2.0.

STARTING THE COMPUTER. Turn on the Macintosh power switch, which is located on the lower left side of the back of the computer. Now place the Microsoft BASIC disk in the disk drive. When the screen comes on you will be in the "Finder," or monitor mode. On the lower half of the screen you will see several icons, or symbols, representing the forms of BASIC that are available for use. The two versions of BASIC available are the decimal version and the binary math version. For the types of programs written in this supplement, the decimal version is the more appropriate one.

To start BASIC, use the mouse to maneuver the cursor to the decimal BASIC icon. Then "double-click" the button on the mouse. Double-clicking consists of pressing the mouse button rapidly two times in a row. Figure I–6 shows the BASIC screen that will appear.

The Command window, which appears at the bottom of the screen, indicates that you are in BASIC. All BASIC commands can be entered in two ways: by using the Command window or by selecting the command from the menus. Only the Command window method will be explained here. Consult your manual for details on alternate methods of performing operations. To begin, type the following:

```
NEW <Return>
```

You can now begin typing in a BASIC program. You may wish to practice by typing in the program in Figure I–4. After you press <Return>, each statement will be displayed in the Output window, which is currently labeled "Untitled." To list your program, type:

```
LIST <Return>
```

If you wish to correct a line of your program, simply "double-click" on that line in the List window. The line will be displayed in the Command window so that you can alter it as needed. Move the cursor to the spot needing correction and insert new letters as needed. Incorrect letters can be deleted by using the Backspace key.

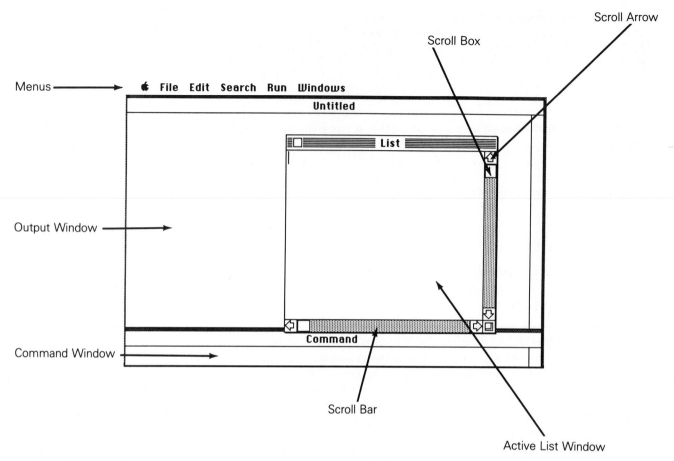

Menus

Scroll Box

Scroll Arrow

File Edit Search Run Windows

Untitled

List

Output Window

Command Window

Command

Scroll Bar

Active List Window

FIGURE I—6

Macintosh BASIC Screen (Decimal Version)

SAVING AND LOADING PROGRAMS. To save a program named TESTS, for example, type:

```
SAVE "TESTS" <Return>
```

The program will now be saved on disk in a file named TESTS. The program can be loaded back into main memory by the following command:

```
LOAD "TESTS"
```

After a program is loaded, you can use the LIST command to display it in the List window.

RUNNING A PROGRAM. To execute a program currently in main memory, simply enter:

```
RUN <Return>
```

Any output generated by the program will be displayed in the Output window.

The Apple IIe and IIGS

The Apple IIe automatically "comes up" in Applesoft BASIC. To enter Applesoft BASIC when using the IIGS, the BASIC.SYSTEM file must be opened. The steps for accessing BASIC with either of these system are listed below.

STARTING THE COMPUTER. To use BASIC on an Apple IIe, place an Apple DOS (disk operating system) disk in the disk drive. Turn the power on by flipping the switch located at the left rear of the computer. An external monitor is required, so you must remember to turn on power to this device also. The computer will now begin to load DOS. When it is through, the following prompt will appear:

```
]
```

This indicates that the computer is in Applesoft BASIC.

If you are using an Apple IIGS, first place the system disk in the disk drive. Turn on both the power and the monitor switches. The system will load the disk operating system (ProDOS). When the list of files on the system disk appears, select the BASIC.SYSTEM file. To do this, use the mouse to move the cursor so that it is on the BASIC.SYSTEM file and "double-click" the mouse button. You will now be in Applesoft BASIC as indicated by the prompt:

```
]
```

You can now type in BASIC statements just as you would using any keyboard. If you make mistakes, use the mouse to move the cursor to the location where corrections must be made.

SAVING AND LOADING PROGRAMS. When using the Apple IIe, programs can be saved on disk by using the SAVE command. The following statement will save the program currently in main memory in a file named TESTS:

```
]SAVE TESTS <Return>
```

To load this program from disk back into main memory, type:

```
]LOAD TESTS <Return>
```

The TRS-80 Model 4

The following description of the TRS-80 computer refers to the Model 4, with model 4 Disk BASIC.

STARTING THE COMPUTER. Place the system disk with Model 4 Disk BASIC into Drive 0 (zero), the bottom drive. Turn on the power switch, which is located under the right side of the keyboard. As soon as the computer is turned on, it will load the disk operating system (TRSDOS). You will see the TRSDOS start-up logo and a prompt to enter the date. If you wish to enter the date, use the MM/DD/YY format and press <ENTER>. For example, to enter the date December 16, 1989, type:

```
12/16/89 <ENTER>
```

If you don't wish to enter the date, simply press <ENTER>. After the computer displays the date, the system prompt appears:

```
TRSDOS Ready
```

This message indicates that you are at the operating system level. To enter BASIC, type:

```
BASIC <ENTER>
```

A paragraph with copyright information appears on the screen, followed by:

```
Ready
```

You can now begin using BASIC.

SAVING AND LOADING PROGRAMS. To save a program, you need to assign it a file name. For example, if you wanted to save a practice program under the name TESTS, you could use the following command:

```
SAVE "TESTS"
```

After the computer is through writing the program to disk, the BASIC prompt will reappear. If you want to use the program again, it must be loaded back into main memory by using the LOAD command:

```
LOAD "TESTS"
```

RUNNING PROGRAMS. A program that is currently in main memory can be executed by typing:

```
RUN
```

▨ SUMMARY POINTS

■ BASIC (Beginners All-purpose Symbolic Instruction Code) was developed in the mid-1960s by Professors John G. Kemeny and Thomas E. Kurtz.

■ Structured programming languages were developed to encourage the writing of easy-to-understand, more error-free programs. Such languages have two basic characteristics: the logic of the program is easy to follow, and the program is divided into subprograms, each performing a specific task.

■ The following are the five steps in the programming process: (1) define and document the problem; (2) design and document a solution; (3) write and document a program; (4) enter it into the computer; and (5) test and debug the program, and revise the documentation if necessary.

■ Programs are best designed by using a top-down approach, in which a large task is divided into smaller and smaller subtasks, moving from the general to the specific.

■ Program design can be documented by structure charts to show top-down design and by flowcharts to graphically display the program's logic.

■ BASIC has rules of grammar (syntax) to which programmers must adhere.

■ BASIC commands are used by the programmer to communicate with the operating system of the computer. Some commonly used ones are NEW, LIST, RUN, and SAVE.

▰ REVIEW QUESTION

1. What is BASIC?
2. What is the purpose of using top-down design?
3. What are some of the characteristics of structured programs?
4. What is an algorithm, and how is it used in the programming process?
5. Name the five steps of the programming process.
6. What is a syntax error?
7. Explain the function of the NEW command.
8. Explain the function of the SAVE command.

BASIC Fundamentals

O U T L I N E

Introduction
Components of the BASIC language
 Line Numbers
 Constants
 Variables
 Reserved Words
Elementary BASIC Statements
 The REM Statement
 The LET Statement
 The PRINT Statement
 The END Statement
Comprehensive Programming Problem
 Problem Definition
 Solution Design
 The Program
Summary Points
Review Questions
Debugging Exercises
Programming Problems

▦ INTRODUCTION

This section begins by discussing some components of the BASIC language: line numbers, constants, character strings, and variables. Four elementary BASIC statements are explained: REM, LET, PRINT, and END. REM (short for REMark) statements are used to explain the program to humans. The LET statement allows the program to assign values to variables. The PRINT statement allows program results to be displayed on the terminal screen. Processing is stopped with the END statement.

▦ COMPONENTS OF THE BASIC LANGUAGE

BASIC statements are composed of special programming command words (words that have specific meanings to the BASIC system) and parts of the language. A BASIC program is a sequence of statements that tells the computer how to solve a problem. Figure II–1 is an example. This program calculates the gross pay of an employee whose wage rate is $5.50 an hour and who has worked forty hours.

Line Numbers

Line numbers tell the computer the order in which statements are to be executed. However, as we shall see later, certain statements can be used to alter this order. Execution starts at the lowest line number and continues in ascending numerical order to the highest number. Line numbers must be integers between 1 and 32767, although the upper limit may be lower, depending on the system being used (refer to Table II–1 for the limit on your system). No commas or embedded spaces can be included in a line number. Below are some examples of valid line numbers:

```
  10
4000
9041
 530
```

Line numbers in BASIC are often referred to as labels, because they "label" a specific statement in a program. In Figure II–1, the number 80 is the label for the statement PRINT MESSAGE$; PAY.

In VAX BASIC and Macintosh/Microsoft BASIC, line numbers are optional. These computers could execute both of the following program segments without any problems:

```
10 LET NAM$ = "SAM"          LET NAM$ = "SAM"
20 LET MESS$ = "MY NAME IS " LET MESS$ = "MY NAME IS "
30 PRINT MESS$,NAM$          PRINT MESS$,NAM$
99 END                       END
```

However, because line numbers are required in the other implementations of BASIC discussed here and can be helpful when writing programs, they will be used in the programs in this supplement.

Line numbers do not have to be in increments of 1. In fact, it is best to use increments of 10 or 20, in order to allow for insertion of lines at a later time, if necessary. Statements need not be entered in ascending numerical order; the computer will rearrange them in this order for execution. This

FIGURE II–1

Program to Compute Gross Pay

```
10 REM *** THIS PROGRAM COMPUTES AN ***
20 REM *** EMPLOYEE'S GROSS PAY.    ***
30 REM
40 LET HOURS = 40
50 LET RTE = 5.5
60 LET PAY = HOURS * RTE
70 LET MESSAGE$ = "GROSS PAY = $"
80 PRINT MESSAGE$;PAY
99 END
```

```
RUNNH
GROSS PAY = $ 220
```

DIFFERENCES
IBM/Microsoft: None.
Macintosh/Microsoft: None.
Apple/Applesoft: None.
TRS-80: None.

feature of BASIC makes it easy to insert new lines between existing lines. For example, if you type:

```
10 LET NAM$ = "SAM"
20 PRINT MESS$,NAM$
99 END
```

and then realize you forgot a statement that should go between lines 10 and 20, you can simply add the needed statement like this:

```
15 LET MESS$ = "MY NAME IS "
```

TABLE II–1

Minimum and Maximum Line Numbers

Type of BASIC	Lowest Number	Highest Number
VAX BASIC*	1	32767
Apple/Applesoft	0	63999
IBM/Microsoft	0	65529
Macintosh/Microsoft*	0	65529
TRS-80	0	65529

*Line numbers are not required.

When the program is listed, it will appear like this:

```
10 LET NAM$ = "SAM"
15 LET MESS$ = "MY NAME IS "
20 PRINT MESS$,NAM$
99 END
```

Because we incremented the line numbers by 10, it was a simple matter to insert a new line. For this reason, programmers generally use increments of at least 10.

If you find that you have made an error on a line, simply retype the line number and the corrected BASIC statement. This procedure corrects the error because, if two lines are entered with the same line number, the computer saves and executes the most recently typed one. To demonstrate this fact, assume that line 160 should print SUM, but the following was typed instead:

```
160 PRINT SUN
```

To correct this, simply retype line 160:

```
160 PRINT SUM
```

The computer will discard the current line 160 and replace it with the new version of line 160.

Constants

Constants are values that do not change during program execution. There are two kinds: **numeric constants** and **character-string constants.**

NUMERIC CONSTANTS. BASIC allows numbers to be represented in two ways: as real numbers, which include a decimal point (also called floating-point numbers), or as integers (numbers with no decimal portion). The following rules must be observed when using numbers in BASIC:

1. No commas can be embedded in the number. The computer interprets the digits before and after a comma as two separate numbers. For example, the computer would interpret 3,751 as the number 3 and the number 751. The valid form of the number is 3751.
2. If a number is negative, it must be preceded by a minus sign, as in the number -21.
3. If no sign is included, the number is assumed to be positive: 56 is the same as $+56$.
4. Fractions must be written in decimal form. For example, 2.75 is the correct representation for 2¾.

Exponential notation, or scientific notation, is often used for very large or very small positive or negative numbers. Some examples are:

```
3.865312E+09     6.18E-05     4E+08
```

The number preceding the E is called the *mantissa*, and in most systems must lie between 1.000 and 9.999. The E represents base 10, and the signed number following the E is the power of 10 by which the mantissa is multiplied (in other words, the number of places the decimal point must be shifted to obtain the value). If the plus sign is omitted after the E, positive exponentiation is assumed. Some examples follow:

DECIMAL NUMBER	EXPONENTIAL NOTATION
53860	5.386E04
0.00531	5.31E-03
−658310	−6.5831E+05

CHARACTER-STRING CONSTANTS. The other type of constant is the **character string.** Character strings are composed of any combination of alphabetic, numeric, or special characters (such as the percent sign, %) which are enclosed in quotation marks. The maximum number of characters allowed in a character string depends on the system being used. On all the BASIC systems used in this supplement, the maximum character string length is 255 characters. The program in Figure II–1 contains a character string in line 70:

```
70 LET MESSAGE$ = "GROSS PAY = $"
```

This character string has a length of 13. Not only does each letter count as a character, but each space is also counted.

Variables

The computer has a great number of individual storage locations, each with a specific address, or numbered position. A storage location containing a value that can change during program execution is referred to as a **variable.** A variable can contain only one value at a time; if it receives a new value, the old one is destroyed.

In BASIC, the programmer identifies variables by assigning each a unique name. The programmer can then refer to a specific storage location by using its name. It is not necessary to know where the computer is storing a certain variable; you need simply to know the name of that variable. Variable names should describe the values that they identify because using meaningful names makes it easier to understand the program. Most computers permit variable names of various lengths; however, some systems (such as the Apple and the TRS-80) recognize only the first two characters of a variable name. For example, these systems would recognize the variables QUANTITY and QUEUE as being identical. When using these computers, the programmer must make sure that the first two characters of each variable name are unique. BASIC has two types of variables: numeric and string.

NUMERIC VARIABLES. A **numeric variable** represents a number that is either supplied to the computer by the programmer or internally calculated by the computer during execution of the program. A numeric variable name must begin with an alphabetic character, followed by letters and/or digits. The following examples show valid and invalid numeric variable names:

Valid	Invalid and Reason	
TAX	3TAX	(Must begin with a letter)
S1SUM	AGE 1	(No blanks allowed)
BIG50	BIG$	($ invalid for numeric variable)
SMALLEST	SM-NUM	(Hyphen not allowed)

The program in Figure II–1 contains three numeric variables: RTE, HOURS, and PAY.

STRING VARIABLES. A **string variable** can be used to represent a character string such as a name, address, book title, and so forth. String variable names are distinguished from numeric variable names by the use of the dollar sign ($) as the last character of the name. The following are examples of valid and invalid string variable names:

Valid	Invalid and Reason	
SSN$	PAY	(Last character must be $)
HEADING$	3HEAD$	(First character must be a letter)
DAY$	FLIGHT$T	(Last character must be $)
PET$	B#DAY$	(# not allowed)

Examples of the proper use of string variables can be seen in lines 70 and 80 of the sample program in Figure II–1:

```
70 LET MESSAGE$ = "GROSS PAY = $"
80 PRINT MESSAGE$;PAY
```

Reserved Words

Certain words have specific meanings to the BASIC system. These are **reserved words,** which cannot be used as variable names. Table II–2 lists some of the most common reserved words.

Some systems, such as the Apple and the TRS–80, scan all BASIC statements for reserved words. Any reserved words embedded in a variable name are seen by the computer as reserved words and cannot be used in a variable name. For example, RATE cannot be used as a variable name on such a system because it contains the reserved word AT.

■ ELEMENTARY BASIC STATEMENTS

We will now turn our attention to four elementary BASIC statements: REM, LET, PRINT, and END. These statements are useful in solving a variety of programming problems.

The REM Statement

The REM (remark) statement provides information for the programmer or anyone else reading the program. It provides no information for the com-

TABLE II—2

Reserved Words

ABS	END	GOSUB	LOG	REM	STOP
BASE	EXP	GOTO	NEXT	RESTORE	TAB
CALL	FN	IF	ON	RETURN	TAN
COS	FOR	INPUT	OPEN	RND	THEN
DATA	ELSE	INT	PRINT	SIN	TO
DEF	GET	LET	PUT	SGN	UNTIL
DIM	GO	LIST	READ	SQR	VAL
				STEP	WHILE

puter; the computer simply skips over REM statements. The REM statement documents the program; the programmer generally uses it to explain program segments, to describe variables, or to note any special instructions. Notice lines 10 and 20 of the program in Figure II–1:

```
10 REM *** THIS PROGRAM COMPUTES AN ***
20 REM *** EMPLOYEE'S GROSS PAY.    ***
```

These statements describe the purpose of the program. The computer does not execute these statements. The asterisks before and after each comment are not required, but many programmers use asterisks to separate comments from the rest of the program so that the REM statements can be easily identified when looking through long program listings. The REM statement of line 30 does not contain a comment; it is used to make the program more readable by separating the remarks from the body of the program. REM statements can be placed anywhere in the program. The general format of the REM statement is as follows:

line# REM comment

The LET Statement

The purpose of the LET, or assignment, statement is to store a value in the location allotted to a given variable. In a flowchart, an assignment statement is illustrated by a processing symbol (☐). An example of a LET statement is found in line 50 of the sample program (Figure II–1):

```
50 LET RTE = 5.5
```

When an assignment statement such as this is encountered, the computer stores the value of the expression on the right side of the equal sign in the location represented by the variable on the left side of the equal sign. After line 50 is executed, the variable RTE contains the value 5.5. Line 70 of the same program shows how a string variable receives the value of a character string:

```
70  LET MESSAGE$ = "GROSS PAY = $"
```

When line 70 is executed, the character string enclosed in quotation marks (but not the quotation marks themselves) is placed in the location called MESSAGE$.

The expression on the right side of the equal sign can be a constant, as in the preceding examples, or it can be a variable or an arithmetic expression. In line 60 of the sample program, the values in locations RTE and HOURS are multiplied, and the result is stored in location PAY.

```
60 LET PAY = HOURS * RTE
```

The values in RTE and HOURS remain unchanged. When a LET statement assigns a value to a variable on the left side of an equation, it actually is putting that value in a storage location in memory—a location labeled by that variable name. Therefore, only a variable can be on the left—nothing else would represent a storage location.

The general format of the LET statement is as follows:

line# LET variable = expression

On most computer systems, the word LET is optional. These statements are recognized as being equivalent on such computers:

```
10 LET X = 17
10 X = 17
```

The following table provides examples of assignment statements, along with descriptions of how they would be executed:

Statement	Computer Execution
100 LET HOURS = 30.5	The numeric value 30.5 is stored in the location called HOURS.
110 LET NUMBER = J	The value in location J is also stored in location NUMBER. J remains unchanged.
120 LET CNT = CNT + 1	The value 1 is added to the current value in CNT. This new value replaces the previous value of CNT.
130 LET SUM = A + B	The values in locations A and B are added together, and the result is stored in location SUM.

ARITHMETIC EXPRESSIONS. In BASIC, arithmetic expressions are composed of constants, numeric variables, and arithmetic operators. Here are the arithmetic operators that can be used:

BASIC Arithmetic Symbol	Operation	Arithmetic Example	BASIC Expression
+	Addition	10 + 2	10 + 2
−	Subtraction	10 − 2	10 − 2
*	Multiplication	10 × 2	10 * 2
/	Division	10 ÷ 2	10 / 2
^	Exponentiation	10^2	10 ^ 2

Some examples of valid arithmetic expressions in assignment statements are shown here:

```
10 LET VOLUME = LNGTH * WDTH * HGHT
20 AREA = (BASE * HGHT) / 2
30 LET SUM = A + 7
```

HIERARCHY OF OPERATIONS. When more than one operation is to be performed in an arithmetic expression, the computer follows a **hierarchy of operations.** The hierarchy of operations states the order in which arithmetic operations are to be performed. When parentheses are present in an expression, the operation within the parentheses is performed first. If parentheses are nested—that is, one set of parentheses is inside another—the operation in the innermost set of parentheses is performed first. Thus, in the following expression, the first operation to be performed is to add 2 to the value of Y:

$$30 * (80 - 5 / (2 + Y) * 6)$$

When there are no parentheses, operations are performed according to the following rules:

Priority	Operation	Symbol
First	Exponentiation	^
Second	Multiplication or division	*, /
Third	Addition or subtraction	+, −

Operations with high priority are performed before operations with lower priority. If more than one operation at the same level is performed, as in the following expression:

$$5 * 4 / 2$$

the computer evaluates them from left to right. In this example, the 5 is multiplied by 4, and then the result, 20, is divided by 2. The answer is 10. The following are some more examples of evaluating expressions:

Statement	Evaluation Process
1. Y = 1 + 2 * 5	First : 2 * 5 = 10 Second: 1 + 10 = 11 Result : Y = 11
2. Y = 2 * (5 + 1)	First : 5 + 1 = 6 Second: 2 * 6 = 12 Result : Y = 12
3. Y = (3 + (6 + 2) / 4) + 10 ^ 2	First : 6 + 2 = 8 Second: 8 / 4 = 2 Third : 3 + 2 = 5 Fourth : 10 ^ 2 = 100 Fifth : 5 + 100 = 105 Result : Y = 105

It should be noted that two operators cannot be placed next to one another. For example, the expression P ∗ − X is invalid on most systems. Parentheses should be used to separate the operators. Thus, P ∗ (− X) is valid.

The PRINT Statement

The PRINT statement can be used to display processing results on the terminal screen. It also permits formatting, or arranging, of output so that it is more readable. The PRINT statement can take several forms, depending on the output required. This is the general format of the PRINT statement:

$$\text{line\# PRINT} \begin{cases} \text{variables} \\ \text{literals} \\ \text{arithmetic expressions} \\ \text{any combination of the above} \end{cases}$$

PRINTING THE VALUES OF VARIABLES. We can tell the computer to print the value assigned to a storage location simply by using the reserved word PRINT with the name of the variable listed after it:

```
100 PRINT AMOUNT
```

If the value of more than one variable is to be printed, each variable name can be separated by a comma:

```
110 PRINT AMOUNT,DAY,YEAR
```

The commas are used to separate the variable names from one another; they also cause the output to be spaced across the print line. In Section III we will learn more about controlling the spacing of output.

Printing has no effect on the contents of a storage location. The PRINT statement only gets the value of a variable and displays it on the screen. Usually, each time the computer encounters a PRINT statement, it begins printing on a new line. Exceptions to this are discussed in Section III.

PRINTING LITERALS. A literal is an expression consisting of alphabetic, numeric, or special characters, or any combination of these. There are two types of literals: character string and numeric.

A character-string literal is any combination of letters, numbers, or special characters enclosed in quotation marks. Whatever is inside the quotation marks is printed exactly as is. For example,

```
10 PRINT "EXAMPLES$%#"
```

would display the following on the screen

```
EXAMPLES$%#
```

Note that the quotation marks are not printed.

Literals can be used to print headings for output. To print column headings, for example, put each heading in quotation marks and separate them with commas:

```
50 PRINT "ITEM","PRICE","QUANTITY"
```

When line 50 is executed, the following output appears:

```
ITEM          PRICE          QUANTITY
```

Numeric literals are numbers in the PRINT statement that are displayed in the output. They do not have to be enclosed in quotation marks. For example, the statement

```
40 PRINT 100
```

will display the following:

```
100
```

PRINTING THE VALUES OF EXPRESSIONS.

PRINTING THE VALUES OF EXPRESSIONS. The BASIC system can display not only the values of literals and variables, but also the values of arithmetic expressions. Consider the following program segment:

```
50 LET X = 15.0
60 LET Y = 26.0
70 PRINT (X + Y) / 2, X / Y
```

The BASIC system will evaluate each expression in line 70, according to the hierarchy of operations, and then print the result:

```
20.5          .576923
```

If the expression is an extremely large or extremely small number, the computer may print it in exponential notation.

PRINTING BLANK LINES. Inserting blank lines in program output makes the output more readable and can be achieved by using a PRINT statement alone:

```
100 PRINT
```

To skip more than one line, simply include more than one such statement:

```
110 PRINT
120 PRINT
```

The END Statement

The END statement instructs the computer to stop program execution. In a flowchart, it is indicated by the start/stop symbol ($\bigcirc$). The general format of the END statement is as follows:

line# END

The END statement is always the last line that is executed. To make the END statement readily identifiable, many programmers give it a line number of all 9s. All programs in this supplement will follow this practice. Line 99 of the sample program in Figure II–1 is an example of an END statement.

■ COMPREHENSIVE PROGRAMMING PROBLEM

Problem Definition

Smith's Warehouse needs a program to calculate its monthly ending inventory and the value of that inventory. Smith's has provided you with the following inventory data:

Beginning inventory = 430 units
Receipts = 86 units
Orders issued = 112 units
Cost per unit = $11.50

The program should produce a report that displays the beginning inventory, receipts, orders issued, ending inventory, and the value of the ending inventory.

Input and output for the program are easily seen: the input is simply the data given, and the output consists of three of the input values, plus two calculated values: the ending inventory and its value. Since the output is in the form of a report, an appropriate heading should also be displayed. The processing requires a formula to first calculate the ending inventory:

Ending Inventory = Beginning Inventory + Receipts − Orders issued

From this we can calculate the value of the ending inventory by using the following formula:

Value of ending inventory = Ending inventory × Cost per unit

With the input, processing, and output defined, we can design a solution.

Solution Design

We can now consider the general problem of producing the specified report and determine whether it can be divided into subproblems. Keeping in mind the flow of data processing, we can determine at least three smaller tasks to be performed:

1. Access the given data.
2. Perform the calculations.
3. Display the report.

The second step involves two formulas, so this step can be further divided:

2.A. Calculate the ending inventory.
2.B. Calculate the ending inventory value.

The report should contain a heading plus the requested values; therefore, the third step can be divided as follows:

3.A. Display a heading.
3.B. Display the requested values.

All of the tasks listed are shown in the structure chart in Figure II–2.

Next we need to consider what program steps will accomplish these tasks. A flowchart of a possible solution is shown in Figure II–3. In order to use the given data, we assign the starting values to variables. This is referred

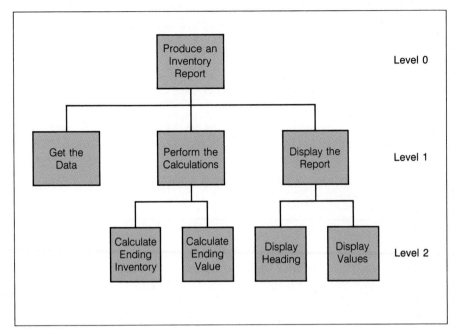

FIGURE II—2

Structure Chart for Inventory Problem

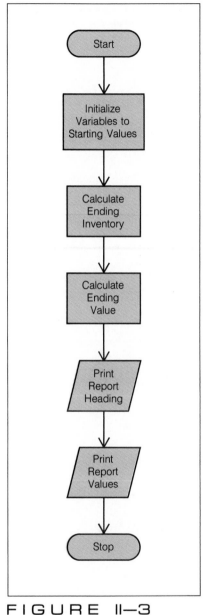

FIGURE II—3

Flowchart for Inventory Problem

to as *initializing* the variables. Next, the two calculations are performed. A heading is then printed, followed by the needed values.

The Program

Figure II–4 shows the final program and its output. The REM statements in lines 10 through 110 describe the program and document the contents of the variables. Lines 130, 190, and 230 give descriptions of the statements that follow them. Lines 140 through 170 assign the inventory values to variables. Line 200 calculates the ending inventory and assigns it to EINV. This result is then multiplied by the cost per unit in line 210, which yields the value of the ending inventory and assigns it to the variable VLUE.

Lines 240 and 250 improve the readability of the output by causing two blank lines to be printed before the following statement prints labels for each field of output followed by the field value. The program concludes with the END statement.

FIGURE II—4

Inventory Program

```
10  REM *** THIS PROGRAM COMPUTES THE MONTHLY ENDING    ***
20  REM *** INVENTORY AND VALUE FOR SMITH'S WAREHOUSE,  ***
30  REM *** AND DISPLAYS AN INVENTORY REPORT.           ***
40  REM ***                                             ***
50  REM *** MAJOR VARIABLES:                            ***
60  REM ***     BINV      BEGINNING INVENTORY           ***
70  REM ***     EINV      ENDING INVENTORY              ***
80  REM ***     ISSUED    NUMBER OF UNITS ISSUED        ***
90  REM ***     RECPT     NUMBER OF UNITS RECEIVED      ***
100 REM ***     CST       COST PER UNIT                 ***
110 REM ***     VLUE      ENDING INVENTORY VALUE        ***
120 REM
130 REM *** ASSIGN THE INPUT VALUES TO THE VARIABLES.   ***
140 LET BINV = 430
150 LET RECPT = 86
160 LET ISSUED = 112
170 LET CST = 11.5
180 REM
190 REM *** CALCULATE THE ENDING INVENTORY AND VALUE. ***
200 LET EINV = BINV + RECPT - ISSUED
210 LET VLUE = EINV * CST
220 REM
230 REM *** DISPLAY THE INVENTORY REPORT. ***
240 PRINT
250 PRINT
260 PRINT "INVENTORY STATUS"
270 PRINT
280 PRINT "BEGIN INV.",BINV
290 PRINT "RECEIPTS",RECPT
300 PRINT "ISSUED",ISSUED
310 PRINT "ENDING INV.",EINV
320 PRINT "VALUE        $",VLUE
999 END
```

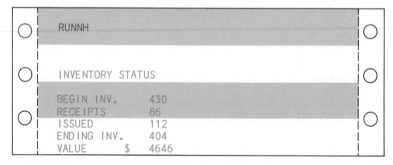

```
RUNNH


INVENTORY STATUS

BEGIN INV.      430
RECEIPTS        86
ISSUED          112
ENDING INV.     404
VALUE        $  4646
```

DIFFERENCES

IBM/Microsoft: None.
Macintosh/Microsoft: None.
Apple/Applesoft: None.
TRS-80: None.

SUMMARY POINTS

■ A BASIC program contains a series of instructions. Each one contains a line number and a BASIC statement.

■ The line numbers serve (a) as labels by which statements can be referenced, and (b) as devices to specify the order in which statements will be executed. Line numbers are optional in VAX BASIC and Macintosh/Microsoft BASIC.

■ Using line numbers in increments of 5 or 10 permits easy insertion of new statements.

■ BASIC statements are composed of reserved words, constants, variables, and operators.

■ Constants are values that do not change during program execution. A valid numeric constant is any integer or real number. Character strings are made up of letters, numbers, and special symbols and are enclosed in quotation marks.

■ Variables are storage locations containing values that can change during program execution. Variable names are programmer-supplied names that identify specific variables. Numeric variables store numbers, whereas string variables contain character strings. String variable names must have the $ symbol as their last character to distinguish them from numeric variables.

■ The purpose of the LET statement is to assign values to variables. The computer evaluates the expression on the right side of the equal sign and stores its value in the variable on the left side.

■ Arithmetic expressions are evaluated according to a hierarchy of operations: first, operations in parentheses; second, exponentiation; third, multiplication or division; and finally, addition or subtraction. Multiple operations at the same level are evaluated from left to right.

■ The PRINT statement displays the results of processing. It can be used to print the values of variables, literals, arithmetic expressions, or a combination of these values.

■ The END statement causes program execution to stop.

REVIEW QUESTIONS

1. What is the difference between numeric constants and character-string constants?

2. What are reserved words? Name three reserved words.

3. What is a variable? Name two types of variables and explain how they differ.

4. Which of these are invalid numeric constants?
   a. 0.73
   b. 1072 –
   c. – 275,210
   d. + 6029

5. Which of the following are illegal variable names, and why?
   a. 7$
   b. D
   c. %BIG
   d. END
   e. Z9
   f. NM$FRST

6. Evaluate the expression

```
10 LET A = 2.5 + (X * (Y ^ 2) / C) * (Y + X)
```

where X = 2, Y = 4, and C = 8.

7. What is the purpose of the PRINT statement? How can a blank line be output?

8. What is the output of the following program segment?

```
10 LET X = 952
20 LET Y = 56
30 PRINT 5.3 + X + (Y * 10)
```

■ DEBUGGING EXERCISES

Identify and correct any errors in the following programs or program segments.

```
1. 10 REM *** THIS PROGRAM CALCULATES      ***
   20 REM *** THE AVERAGE OF TWO NUMBERS.   ***
   30 REM
   40 LET 10 = A
   50 LET B = 20
   60 LET X = A + B / 2
   70 PRINT X
   99 END
```

```
2. 10 REM THIS PROGRAM PRINTS THE
   20 NAME AND AGE OF A PERSON.
   30 REM
   40 LET A = 21
   50 LET N$ = STACY
   60 PRINT N$,A
   99 END
```

■ PROGRAMMING PROBLEMS

1. Write a program that will compute the current balance in your checking account. At the beginning of the month, the balance was $46.19. During the month, you made purchases of:

Record	$ 8.83
Jeans	$15.60
Book	$14.89

You also deposited $30.00. Use a PRINT statement to display your balance.

2. Write a program that will display the name and telephone number of the following people:

Linda Jones	818-7081
Anna McGee	223-8764
Leroy Price	449-5062

The output should have the following format:

```
NAME                TELEPHONE #
XXXXXXXXXX          XXX-XXXX
```

3. Currently, tuition at Famous University is $1,200 per year and room and board fees are $3,600 per year. Next fall, tuition is expected to rise by 15 percent and room and board fees by 10 percent. Karl Perry wants to know what the fees will be and whether he will have enough money to cover them. Karl earns approximately $3,000 in the summer and $2,500 during the school year and gets no additional help for his college expenses. Write a program to help Karl. The format of the output should be similar to the following:

```
TUITION        ROOM/BOARD    TOTAL         EXCESS INCOME
XXX.XX         XXXX.XX       XXXX.XX       XXX.XX
```

4. You own an apartment building with eight identical apartments, each having two rooms that need carpeting. One room in each apartment has a length of 12 feet and a width of 9 feet, while the other has a length of 15 feet and a width of 12 feet. Carpeting costs $14.50 a square yard. Write a program that will calculate the amount of carpeting needed to cover the entire building, as well as the total cost of the carpeting. The output should include both figures. (The area of a room is equal to the length multiplied by the width.) Be sure to document your program.

5. The Rich Rug Company's top salesperson is Emmet Mitchell. He earns a base salary of $95.00 a week. In addition, he earns commissions of 6 percent on all Oriental rugs sold and 4 percent on all other items. The total salary is calculated as follows:

Total salary = Base salary + Commission

You are to write a program to calculate his salary. Then print his total weekly salary with an appropriate label. Use the following data:

| Oriental rugs sold | $3892.00 |
| Other sales | $ 989.00 |

S E C T I O N

Input and Output

O U T L I N E

Introduction
The INPUT Statement
The READ and DATA Statements
A Comparison of Two Methods of
    Data Entry
Printing Results
  Print Zones and Commas
  Using Semicolons
Comprehensive Programming Problem
  Problem Definition
  Solution Design
  The Program
Summary Points
Review Questions
Debugging Exercises
Programming Problems

INTRODUCTION

The first half of this section explains two ways of entering data to a program: the INPUT statement and the READ and DATA statements. The INPUT statement allows the user to enter data while the program is running. When the READ and DATA statements are used, the data is entered as part of the program itself. The second half of this section discusses ways of printing program results so that they are attractive and easy to read.

THE INPUT STATEMENT

In many programs, the data changes each time the program is executed. Suppose you need a program that calculates the gas mileage for your car. Each time you run this program, you will want to enter new values for the number of miles traveled and the amount of gas used. The program could use assignment statements to assign these values to variables, as shown in lines 30 and 40 of the program in Figure III–1. These statements would have to be changed every time you wanted to calculate your gas mileage. A more practical approach to this problem is to use the INPUT statement.

The INPUT statement is used for inquiry and response when a program calls for a question-and-answer, or interactive, situation. The INPUT statement allows the user to enter data at the keyboard while the program is running. Its general format is:

line# INPUT variable list

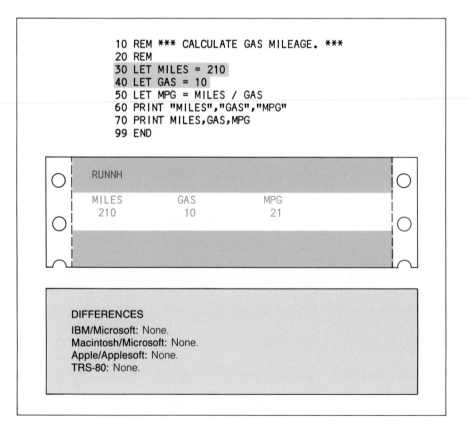

```
10 REM *** CALCULATE GAS MILEAGE. ***
20 REM
30 LET MILES = 210
40 LET GAS = 10
50 LET MPG = MILES / GAS
60 PRINT "MILES","GAS","MPG"
70 PRINT MILES,GAS,MPG
99 END
```

```
RUNNH

MILES          GAS           MPG
210            10            21
```

DIFFERENCES
IBM/Microsoft: None.
Macintosh/Microsoft: None.
Apple/Applesoft: None.
TRS-80: None.

F I G U R E   III—1

**Gas-Mileage Program Using
Assignment Statements**

A sample INPUT statement looks like this:

```
60 INPUT AGE,HGT
```

When this statement is run, a question mark will appear on the screen. The user should then enter two numbers and press the Return key. Below is an example of how the screen might appear when this statement is executed:

```
RUNNH

? 15,62.5 <Return>
```

The first value entered, 15, will be assigned to AGE and the second value, 62.5, will be assigned to HGT.

It is possible to place these variables in two separate INPUT statements:

```
60 INPUT AGE
70 INPUT HGT
```

When this program segment is run, the user will enter only one value (AGE) before pressing Return. Another question mark will appear for the second INPUT statement, and the user will enter a value for HGT before pressing Return. Below is an example of what might happen when these two statements are executed:

```
RUNNH

? 15 <Return>
? 62.5 <Return>
```

The variables listed in an INPUT statement can be string or numeric, but the user must be careful to always enter a number when a numeric variable is listed. In other words, the type of data should match the type of the variable to which it is to be assigned. If the user attempts to enter a character string to a numeric variable, an error message such as the following will appear:

```
Redo from start
```

The user can, however, assign a numeric value to a character string variable. The computer treats the numeric value as a string of characters and stores it in the corresponding string variable, but it cannot perform calculations with this value.

INPUT statements are placed where data values are needed in the program. This is determined by the logic of the program. In the previous short example, when the INPUT statement was executed only a question mark (?) appeared on the terminal screen when it was time for the user to enter data. The user was not told what type of data or how many data items to enter. To clarify matters, the programmer should always use a **prompt** to tell the user what data is to be entered. A prompt can consist of a PRINT statement, placed before the INPUT statement in the program, which tells the user the type and quantity of data to be entered. A PRINT statement could be placed before the INPUT statement asking for a person's age and height:

```
60 PRINT "ENTER YOUR AGE AND HEIGHT"
70 INPUT AGE, HGT
```

Now when this program is executed, the user will be prompted to enter his or her age and height:

```
RUNNH

ENTER YOUR AGE AND HEIGHT
? 15,62.5
```

Remember that the computer displays the prompt and the question mark. The user then enters the age and height before pressing Return. It is also possible to include the prompt in the INPUT statement:

```
60 INPUT "ENTER YOUR AGE AND HEIGHT";AGE,HGT
```

Notice that the prompt is enclosed in quotes and followed by a semicolon. The variables are placed after the semicolon. When this statement is executed, the screen looks like this:

```
RUNNH

ENTER YOUR AGE AND HEIGHT ? 15,62.5
```

Let us revise the program in Figure III–1 by replacing lines 30 and 40 with two INPUT statements so that the user can enter values for the miles traveled and gas used while the program is executing. Lines 30 and 40 could be rewritten as follows:

```
30 INPUT "ENTER THE MILES TRAVELED";MILES
40 INPUT "ENTER THE AMOUNT OF GAS USED";GAS
```

The entire program is shown in Figure III–2. Examine the output. When the program is run, two prompts will appear. The user enters a value in response to each prompt, assigning values to MILES and GAS. Once this is done, the program calculates and displays the mileage.

The INPUT statement offers a great deal of flexibility; each time this program is executed, new values can be entered. Thus, if you want to calculate the mileage for another time period, simply run the program again and enter the new values for MILES and GAS. You do not have to change any program statements.

▰ THE READ AND DATA STATEMENTS

The READ and DATA statements provide another way to enter data into a program. These statements differ from the INPUT statement in that the user does not enter data values during program execution; instead, the programmer assigns them within the program itself. Values contained in DATA statements are assigned to variables listed in READ statements. The general format of the READ and DATA statements is as follows:

line# READ variable list
line# DATA constant list

The variables and constants in the lists are separated by commas. READ statements, like INPUT statements, are located wherever the logic of the program indicates the need for data. DATA statements, however, are non-executable and may be located anywhere in the program. The computer collects the values from all of the DATA statements in a program and places them in a single list, referred to as the **data list.** This list is formed by taking

```
10 REM *** CALCULATE GAS MILEAGE. ***
20 REM
30 INPUT "ENTER THE MILES TRAVELED";MILES
40 INPUT "ENTER THE GAS USED";GAS
50 LET MPG = MILES / GAS
60 PRINT
70 PRINT "MILES","GAS","MPG"
80 PRINT MILES,GAS,MPG
99 END
```

```
RUNNH

ENTER THE MILES TRAVELED? 210
ENTER THE GAS USED? 10

MILES          GAS            MPG
210            10             21
```

DIFFERENCES
IBM/Microsoft: None.
Macintosh/Microsoft: None.
Apple/Applesoft: None.
TRS-80: None.

the values from the DATA statements in order, from the lowest to the highest line number and from left to right within a single line. When a READ statement is encountered, the computer goes to the data list and assigns the next value from that list to the corresponding variable in the READ statement. If the variable is numeric, the data value must also be numeric. If it is a string variable, the value should be a character string.

Figure III–3 shows the gas-mileage program rewritten using READ and DATA statements. Line 30 says the following to the computer: Take the value from the beginning of the data list, and put it in the storage location named MILES (throwing away any value already in MILES). Then take the next value from the data list, and assign it the variable GAS. Line 30 performs the same function as the INPUT statement in the program in Figure III–2, except that when INPUT statements are used the program user enters a value during execution. With READ and DATA statements, in contrast, the MILES and GAS values are already contained within the program in line 90. The output is unchanged. If you wanted to run this program again using different data, you could change line 90, the DATA statement.

Let us now consider another program using READ and DATA statements. The program in Figure III–4 prints a report of wages for two employees. The computer combines the values in lines 120 and 130 into a single data list. After line 30 is executed, the character string MARIA SMITH is in storage location NAM$, the number 25 is in location HOURS, and the number 4.5 is in location RTE. This leaves the character string JOHN DOE as the next available value in the data list. The next program line, line 40,

FIGURE III–3

Gas-Mileage Program Using READ and DATA Statements

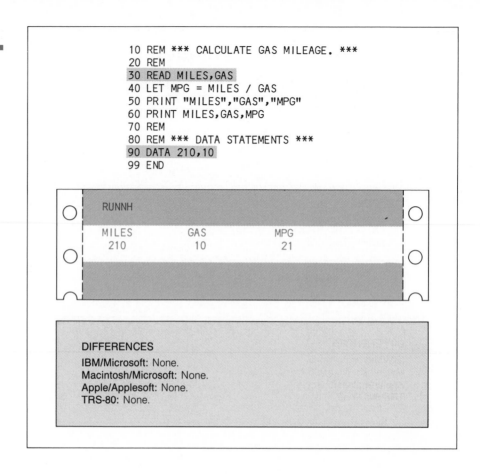

```
10 REM *** CALCULATE GAS MILEAGE. ***
20 REM
30 READ MILES,GAS
40 LET MPG = MILES / GAS
50 PRINT "MILES","GAS","MPG"
60 PRINT MILES,GAS,MPG
70 REM
80 REM *** DATA STATEMENTS ***
90 DATA 210,10
99 END
```

```
RUNNH

MILES           GAS             MPG
210             10              21
```

DIFFERENCES
IBM/Microsoft: None.
Macintosh/Microsoft: None.
Apple/Applesoft: None.
TRS-80: None.

does not use any data list values; it assigns the product of the values in HOURS and RTE to the storage location PAY. Line 50 provides a heading for the output, and line 60 prints the current value of each variable.

The same process occurs when the computer encounters line 70. The next available data list value, JOHN DOE, is placed in NAM$. The number 14 is stored in HOURS, and the value 4.25 in RTE. When these values are assigned, the values previously stored in the variables are destroyed. Therefore, the calculation in line 80 uses the most recently read values; the old ones are lost and cannot be retrieved. Once the data items have been assigned to storage locations, they remain there until new data items are recorded over them. Thus, all three variables of the READ statements represent more than one value during execution, but never more than one at a time.

If a READ statement is attempted after the data list has been exhausted, an error occurs and an OUT OF DATA error message is printed to indicate that the end of the data list has been reached. Execution of the program stops at that point. The number of READ statements and the number of DATA statements do not need to be equal. However, a DATA statement value should be available for each READ statement variable, in order to avoid an error.

The order of the variables and values is important. Make sure that the arrangement of values in the DATA statements corresponds to the data

FIGURE III—4

READ/DATA Payroll Example

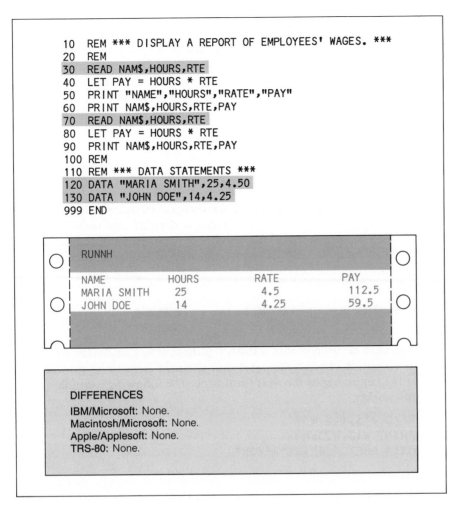

```
10   REM *** DISPLAY A REPORT OF EMPLOYEES' WAGES. ***
20   REM
30   READ NAM$,HOURS,RTE
40   LET PAY = HOURS * RTE
50   PRINT "NAME","HOURS","RATE","PAY"
60   PRINT NAM$,HOURS,RTE,PAY
70   READ NAM$,HOURS,RTE
80   LET PAY = HOURS * RTE
90   PRINT NAM$,HOURS,RTE,PAY
100  REM
110  REM *** DATA STATEMENTS ***
120  DATA "MARIA SMITH",25,4.50
130  DATA "JOHN DOE",14,4.25
999  END
```

```
RUNNH

NAME          HOURS         RATE          PAY
MARIA SMITH   25            4.5           112.5
JOHN DOE      14            4.25          59.5
```

DIFFERENCES
IBM/Microsoft: None.
Macintosh/Microsoft: None.
Apple/Applesoft: None.
TRS-80: None.

required in the READ statements—that is, that character strings are assigned to string variables, and numbers to numeric variables.

■ A COMPARISON OF TWO METHODS OF DATA ENTRY

The INPUT and the READ/DATA statements can both be used to enter data to BASIC programs. Which method is best? That depends on the particular application. Here are some general guidelines:

1. The INPUT statement is used when a question-and-answer (also called inquiry-response) situation is desired. It is also a good method to use when data values are likely to change frequently. INPUT statements might be helpful when entering data about hospital patients—a situation where people are checked in and out every day, and data about a particular patient changes frequently.

2. The READ/DATA statements are most useful when data values are the same for each execution of the program. The main disadvantage of using the READ and DATA statements is that the program itself must be altered when the data values change.

■ PRINTING RESULTS

Section II explained that the PRINT statement lets us display the results of processing. When more than one item is to be printed on a line, commas and semicolons can be used to control the spacing of the output. The TAB function and PRINT USING statement are also useful in formatting; however, they will not be discussed here. For information on them, refer to your BASIC manual.

Print Zones and Commas

The number of characters that can be printed on a line varies from system to system. Most screens can display a maximum of 80 characters on a single line. On many terminal screens, each line is divided into sections called print zones. The zone size and the number of zones per line depend on the system. When using VAX BASIC, each print zone is 14 characters wide, with five zones per line. The beginning columns of the five print zones are shown below:

ZONE 1	ZONE 2	ZONE 3	ZONE 4	ZONE 5
Col 1	Col 15	Col 29	Col 43	Col 57

Commas can be used within a PRINT statement to control the format of printed output. A comma indicates that the next item to be printed will start at the beginning of the next print zone. The following example shows how this works:

```
10 READ W1$,W2$,W3$
20 PRINT W1$,W2$,W3$
30 DATA "BE","SEEING","YOU"
```

The first item in the PRINT statement is printed at the beginning of the line, which is the start of the first print zone. After that, the comma between W1$ and W2$ causes the computer to space over to the next print zone; then the value in W2$ is printed. The second comma directs the computer to space over to the next zone (Zone 3) and print the value in W3$. The output is as follows (the labels for each zone are shown for reference):

ZONE 1	ZONE 2	ZONE 3
RUNNH		
BE	SEEING	YOU

If there are more items listed in a PRINT statement than there are print zones in a line, the print zones of the next line are also used, starting with the first zone. Notice the output of the following example:

```
10 READ SEX$,AGE,CLASS$,MAJ$,HRS,GPA
20 PRINT SEX$,AGE,CLASS$,MAJ$,HRS,GPA
30 DATA "M",19,"JR","CS",18,2.5
```

RUNNH

M	19	JR	CS	18
2.5				

Notice that the number 2.5 starts in column 2 instead of column 1. This is because the computer has left a space for the sign (in this case, an assumed plus sign). If this number had a sign, it would have been printed in the first column.

If the value to be printed exceeds the width of the print zone, the entire value is printed, regardless of how many zones it occupies. Placing a comma after the output causes printing to continue in the next print zone, as shown in the following example:

```
10 SPOT$ = "BAGHDAD"
20 PRINT "YOUR NEXT DESTINATION WILL BE",SPOT$
```

RUNNH

YOUR NEXT DESTINATION WILL BE   BAGHDAD

Table III–1 shows the formatting differences among the five computer systems discussed in this supplement. Columns 2 and 3 give the number of columns and rows available on each system and columns 4 and 5 give the number of print zones per line and the zone widths. Note that some systems enable the user to determine the screen and zone dimensions. Columns 6 and 7 indicate whether leading and trailing spaces are provided for numeric values.

A print zone can be skipped by using consecutive commas:

```
10 PRINT "ARTIST",,"ALBUM"
```

This causes the literal ARTIST to be printed in Zone 1, the second zone to be blank, and the literal ALBUM to be printed in Zone 3:

RUNNH

ARTIST   ALBUM

T A B L E   III—1

Computer Display Characteristics

Computer	Screen Width (Characters)	Screen Height (Lines)	Number of Print Zones	Zone Width	Space for Sign?	Space after Number?
VAX	80/132*	24/16*	5/9*	14	Yes	Yes
Apple	40/80**	24	3	16	No	No
IBM/Microsoft	80	24	5	14	Yes	Yes
Mac/Microsoft	***	***	***	***	Yes	Yes
TRS-80	64/32*	15	4/2*	16	Yes	Yes

*The slash indicates both options are available to the user.
**The Apple IIe must be equipped with an 80-column card in order to use the 80 column format.
***The number of characters that can be printed on one line of the screen varies, because reserved words are boldfaced and thus occupy more space than variable names and numbers. A line is not limited to the screen width; it can have up to 255 characters. To display a line exceeding the screen width, the Macintosh automatically scrolls to the left. The user sets the zone width, and in turn the number of print zones per line, by using the WIDTH statement.

If a comma appears after the last item in a PRINT statement, the output of the next PRINT statement encountered will begin at the next available print zone. Thus, the statements

```
10 READ NME$,AGE,SEX$,VOICE$
20 PRINT NME$,AGE,
30 PRINT SEX$,VOICE$
40 DATA "SHICOFF",32,"M","TENOR"
99 END
```

produce the following output:

```
RUNNH

SHICOFF          32              M               TENOR
```

Using Semicolons

Using a semicolon instead of a comma causes output to be placed closer together on the output line. This alternative gives the programmer greater flexibility in formatting output. In the following examples, notice the difference in spacing when semicolons are used instead of commas:

```
60 PRINT "JASON","JACKSON"
```

```
RUNNH

JASON           JACKSON
```

```
60 PRINT "JASON";"JACKSON"
```

```
RUNNH

JASONJACKSON
```

The semicolon between the items tells the computer to skip to the next column to print the next item—not to the next print zone, as with the comma. The above example shows what happens when semicolons are used with character strings. The letters run together. The best way to avoid this problem is to enclose a space within the quotes:

```
60 PRINT "JASON";" JACKSON"
```

```
RUNNH

JASON JACKSON
```

When numbers are printed, most computers (the Apple is the exception) print the number with a preceding space if the number has no sign, such as 104 or 48. If the number has a sign, such as −176 or +32, no preceding space is printed, because the sign is printed in that position. In either case, a space is left after the number to separate it from the next value that is printed. Therefore, on most computers, when numeric values are separated by a semicolon, the printed digits are not adjacent as in the case of the character strings. The following example demonstrates this point:

```
10 PRINT 100;-200;300
```

RUNNH

```
 100 -200  300
```

Notice that the output shows only one space before −200. This is because the computer left a space after printing the number 100. But there are two spaces before 300. Not only was a space left after −200, but a space was left for the sign (an assumed positive) of the number 300.

If the semicolon is the last character of the PRINT statement, carriage control is not advanced when the printing of the statement is completed; therefore, the output generated by the next PRINT statement continues on the same line. For example,

```
60 PRINT 495207;
70 PRINT "JASON";" JACKSON"
```

RUNNH

```
 495207 JASON JACKSON
```

Line 60 causes 495207 to be printed. The semicolon after this number keeps the output on the same line; then, when line 70 is encountered, JASON JACKSON is printed on the same line.

■ COMPREHENSIVE PROGRAMMING PROBLEM

Problem Definition

You are a loan officer for the local credit union. Your client, Ms. Rodgers, wants to borrow $70,000 to purchase a house in your neighborhood. She wants to know the amount of her monthly payments. The annual interest rate for her loan is 12 percent, and the term of the mortgage is twenty years. Since you must make this type of calculation often, you decide to write a program that will report all the pertinent mortgage information for you.

The input for the problem consists of the given mortgage amount, interest rate, and term. The desired output is a report that lists this information along with the calculated monthly payment. To calculate the monthly payment from the given data, you must first determine the monthly interest rate by using the following formula:

Monthly interest rate = Annual interest rate / 12

Don't forget to convert percentages to decimal numbers for the computer (12% = 0.12). To convert back to percentage rates, simply multiply by 100 (0.01 × 100 = 1%).

The monthly interest rate is used to calculate the mortgage multiplication factor:

$$\text{Mortgage multiplication factor} = \text{Monthly interest rate} /$$
$$[(1 + \text{Monthly interest rate})\,\hat{}$$
$$(\text{Years of term} \times 12) - 1] +$$
$$\text{Monthly interest rate}$$

The monthly payments can then be calculated based on the following formula:

$$\text{Monthly payment} = \text{Mortgage multiplication factor} \times \text{Mortgage amount}$$

Solution Design

The general problem we must solve is to produce a mortgage loan report. By examining the flow of data processing, we can determine that there are three smaller problems to solve:

1. Enter the given data.
2. Calculate the monthly payment.
3. Display the report.

Three formulas are involved in calculating the monthly payment, so the second step can be divided as follows:

2.A. Calculate the monthly interest rate.
2.B. Calculate the mortgage multiplication factor.
2.C. Calculate the monthly payment.

The display of the report can also be divided into smaller tasks:

3.A. Display the heading.
3.B. Display the report values.

The structure chart in Figure III–5 shows the subtasks needed to solve this problem.

FIGURE III–5

Structure Chart for Mortgage Payment Problem

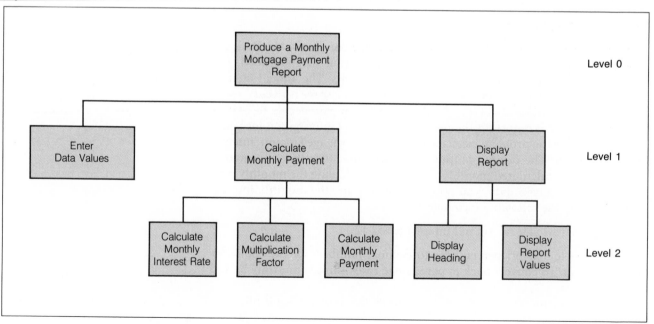

We will next decide what program steps are needed to perform these tasks and the order in which they should be performed. Figure III–6 shows the flowchart for a possible solution. We will make this an interactive program since it will be used with frequently changing values. First the input values must be entered. Next, the calculations are performed and the report is displayed.

The Program

In Figure III–7, lines 40 through 80 document the major variables used by the program. Lines 110 through 130 ask the user for the needed data values. Lines 160 through 180 perform the calculations. The commas in lines 230 and lines 260 through 280 cause the heading and report information to start in the second print zone.

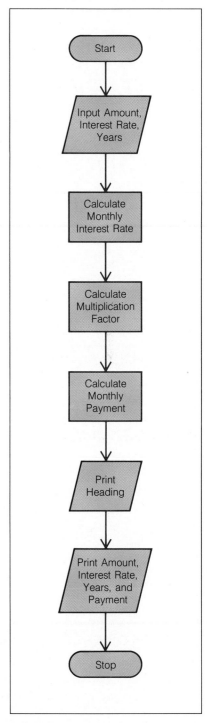

FIGURE III—6

Flowchart for Mortgage Payment Problem

FIGURE III—7

Mortgage Payment Program

```
10   REM *** THIS PROGRAM COMPUTES THE MONTHLY PAYMENTS  ***
20   REM *** FOR MORTGAGES AND DISPLAYS A REPORT.         ***
30   REM *** MAJOR VARIABLES:                             ***
40   REM ***     ANNLRTE    ANNUAL INTEREST RATE          ***
50   REM ***     MMFACTR    MORTGAGE MULTIPLICATION FACTOR ***
60   REM ***     AMOUNT     MORTGAGE AMOUNT               ***
70   REM ***     YEARS      LENGTH OF MORTGAGE            ***
80   REM ***     PAYMNT     MONTHLY PAYMENT               ***
90   REM
100  PRINT
110  INPUT "ENTER AMOUNT OF THE MORTGAGE";AMOUNT
120  INPUT "ENTER ANNUAL INTEREST RATE";ANNLRTE
130  INPUT "ENTER YEARS OF MORTGAGE";YEARS
140  REM
150  REM *** PERFORM THE CALCULATION. ***
160  LET MNTHRTE = (ANNLRTE / 100) / 12
170  LET MMFACTR = MNTHRTE / ((1 + MNTHRTE) ^ (YEARS * 12) - 1)
         + MNTHRTE
180  LET PAYMNT = MMFACTR * AMOUNT
190  REM
200  REM *** DISPLAY THE REPORT. ***
210  PRINT
220  PRINT
230  PRINT,"MORTGAGE REPORT"
240  PRINT
250  PRINT
260  PRINT,"MORTGAGE AMOUNT      $";AMOUNT
270  PRINT,"ANNUAL INT. RATE     ";ANNLRTE;"%"
280  PRINT,"MONTHLY PAYMENT      $";PAYMNT
999  END
```

```
RUNNH


ENTER AMOUNT OF THE MORTGAGE? 70000
ENTER ANNUAL INTEREST RATE? 12
ENTER YEARS OF MORTGAGE? 20


                MORTGAGE REPORT


         MORTGAGE AMOUNT      $ 70000
         ANNUAL INT. RATE       12 %
         MONTHLY PAYMENT      $ 770.76
```

DIFFERENCES

IBM/Microsoft: None.
Macintosh/Microsoft: None.
Apple/Applesoft: None.
TRS-80: None.

■ SUMMARY POINTS

■ The INPUT statement is used to allow data to be entered at the keyboard during program execution. Each value entered is assigned to the corresponding variable in the INPUT statement. The variables must be separated by commas.

■ Prompts should be used to instruct the user as to the type of data to be entered.

■ The READ and DATA statements can also be used to read values to variables. In this case, the input is placed in DATA statements within the program. READ statements are used to read these values and assign them to variables.

■ The INPUT statement is useful because it allows the user to enter data at the keyboard. It is particularly well suited for situations in which data changes often. The READ/DATA statements are most useful in cases where data values will not change often.

■ Processing results can be formatted by using commas in PRINT statements. Commas cause the following output to be displayed in the next available print zone. Using commas allows the programmer to place output in table form.

■ Using semicolons in PRINT statements causes the next output to be displayed in the next available column.

■ REVIEW QUESTIONS

1. What two ways were presented in this chapter to enter data to a program?

2. What does the computer do when it comes to an INPUT statement?

3. What is the purpose of using prompts?

4. Is the following a valid INPUT statement? Why or why not?

```
10 INPUT "ENTER THE NAME OF YOUR DOG";N
```

5. After the following READ/DATA statements are executed, what is the value of each variable?

```
10 READ A,B,C$
20 READ S$,X
30 DATA 256,49
40 DATA "TAMPA BAY"
50 DATA "FLORIDA",40421
```

6. What happens when a PRINT statement ends with a comma? What happens when a PRINT statement ends with a semicolon?

7. In which print zone will the word RETURNS appear if the following statement is executed?

```
70 PRINT "HAPPY","RETURNS"
```

8. What will be the output of the following program segment?

```
230 X$ = "MOUNTAIN"
240 Y$ = "MOLEHILL"
250 PRINT X$;Y$
```

DEBUGGING EXERCISES

Identify and correct any errors in the following programs or program segments.

```
1.  10 INPUT "ENTER CITY AND STATE";CITY$,ST
    20 INPUT "AND ZIP CODE",ZIP
    30 PRINT CITY$,ST,ZIP
2.  30 READ W1$,W2$,W3$
    40 READ X,Y,Z
    50 X = X - 10
    60 Y = Y + 5
    70 PRINT W1$;W2$;W3$
    80 DATA "WHAT'," IS","LIFE?",8,5,15
```

PROGRAMMING PROBLEMS

1. Plastic Cards, Inc. wants a program to compute the new balance for its credit card customers. The input is the customer's account number, the old balance on the account, the amount of the payment, the new charges, and the finance charge rate. The output should be displayed in a format similar to the following:

ACCT. NO.	OLD BALANCE	PAYMENT	CHARGES	NEW BALANCE
XXXXX	XXX.XX	XXX.XX	XX.XX	XXX.XX

Write the program.

2. Write a program that asks for the name of an object and its weight in pounds. The program should then calculate the weight in kilograms (1 pound = 0.453592 kilograms) and print the name of the object, its weight in pounds, and its weight in kilograms, each in a different print zone.

3. Mrs. Mathey wants to know how much it would cost her to fertilize her garden, which measures 15 by 20 feet, using economy fertilizer. The economy fertilizer costs $1.75 per pound, and one pound covers 20 square feet. She also wants to know how much it would cost if she used the deluxe fertilizer, which is $2.00 per pound (one pound of it also covers 20 square feet). The program you write should output the cost of using each and the difference between the two costs.

4. Martha's Dance School charges a flat hourly rate of $6.75. Martha would like a program to determine the total amount owed by each student and the dance school's total income. The output should be in table form. Use READ and DATA statements to place the following data in the program:

Name	Monday (hours)	Tuesday (hours)	Wednesday (hours)	Thursday (hours)	Friday (hours)
Karen	2	3	3	4	2
Alex	3	2	2	2	3

Help Martha with this programming problem.

5. The Acme Concrete Company has bought a new computer, and would like a program to compute the cost of a given amount of concrete and the cost of the labor to pour it. The input should be the length, width, and depth, in feet, of the concrete to be poured. Also, concrete costs $32 per cubic yard and labor costs $20 per cubic yard (a cubic yard has 27 cubic feet). The output should appear similar to the following:

CONCRETE COSTS

IN FEET:			CUBIC	CONCRETE AT	LABOR AT	TOTAL
LEN	WID	DEP	YARDS	$32/CU. YD.	$20/CU. YD.	COST
xx	xx	xx	xxx	$xx.xx	$xx.xx	$xxx.xx

Create the program.

SECTION IV

The Decision Statement and Functions

OUTLINE

Introduction
The GOTO Statement: Unconditional Transfer
The IF Statement: Conditional Transfer
The Single-Alternative IF Statement
The Double-Alternative IF Statement
Library Functions
Numeric Functions
String Functions
User-Defined Functions
Comprehensive Programming Problem
The Problem
Solution Design
The Program
Summary Points
Review Questions
Debugging Exercises
Programming Problems

INTRODUCTION

This section introduces the **control statement**, a powerful programming tool that will be used in all programs from this point on. Control statements allow the programmer to control the order in which program statements are executed. These control statements compare the values of variables. Two types of control statements will be discussed in this section: The **unconditional transfer statement** (or **unconditional branch**) and the **decision statement.** When an unconditional transfer statement is executed, control is always transferred to a specified line number. The GOTO statement is used to perform unconditional transfers. A decision statement makes a comparison. The IF statement is the type of decision statement that will be explained here.

At the end of this section, functions (that is, subprograms that determine a single value) will be discussed.

THE GOTO STATEMENT: UNCONDITIONAL TRANSFER

The GOTO statement can be used to transfer program control to a specified line number. The following statement transfers control to line 100:

```
20 GOTO 100
```

All lines between line 20 and line 100 will not be executed. The following program segment demonstrates how the GOTO statement works:

```
30 X = 75
40 Y = 40
50 GOTO 80
60 X = X + 5
70 Y = Y + 5
80 PRINT X,Y
99 END
```

```
RUNNH
 75              40
```

Notice that values were assigned to X and Y in lines 30 and 40. These values were not incremented by 5 because lines 60 and 70 were skipped.

The GOTO statement can cause a great deal of difficulty for programmers. It leads to programs with difficult-to-follow logic. Therefore, it is preferable to avoid its use whenever possible. Generally, most programs can be written by using loops or the IF statement instead.

THE IF STATEMENT: CONDITIONAL TRANSFER

The GOTO statement always transfers control. Often, however, it is necessary to transfer control only when a specified condition exists. The IF statement is used to test for such a condition. Therefore, it is called a **conditional transfer statement.** The path of program execution is dependent upon whether the condition is true. There are two variations of the IF statement: the single-alternative IF statement (IF/THEN) and the double-alternative IF statement (IF/THEN/ELSE). We will discuss the single-alternative IF statement first.

The Single-Alternative IF Statement

A single-alternative IF statement tests a condition: if the condition is true, the action stated after the THEN part of the statement is executed; if it is false, no action is taken and program execution simply continues on to the next statement. A flowchart of the single-alternative IF statement follows:

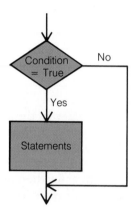

Here is an example of this type of statement:

```
20 IF NMBR > 10 THEN PRINT "THIS IS A LARGE SIZE."
```

In this example, the THEN clause, PRINT "THIS IS A LARGE SIZE.", is executed only if NMBR is greater than 10. Otherwise, no action is taken. Execution then continues on to the next program statement. The THEN clause can contain any number of statements. On the VAX, this can be accomplished by separating the statements with backslashes (\). We could rewrite the above statement so that the THEN portion consisted of two statements:

```
20 IF NMBR > 10 THEN PRINT "THIS IS A LARGE SIZE." \ LET LRGE = LRGE + 1
```

If NMBR is greater than 10, the specified message will be displayed and the value of LRGE will be incremented by 1. Note that the statement is on two different lines. However, it is contained in a single *physical line*. A physical line continues until the Return key is pressed. The statement has "wrapped around" on the screen. On most microcomputers, multiple statements appearing on one physical line are separated by a colon:

```
20 IF NMBR > 10 THEN PRINT "THIS IS A LARGE SIZE." : LET LRGE = LRGE + 1
```

It is possible to replace the THEN clause with a transfer line number (as in a GOTO statement), as shown here:

```
20 IF NMBR > 10 THEN 80
```

If NMBR is greater than 10, program control will transfer to line 80; otherwise, it will continue on to the next executable statement after line 20.

Notice the use of the greater than (>) symbol in the above IF statements. This is an example of a **relational symbol.** Relational symbols are used to compare two values. The result of any such comparison is always either true or false. Relational symbols can be used to compare either numbers or character strings. Below are the relational symbols that can be used in BASIC. All of the examples in the right column are true.

Symbol	Meaning	Example
<	Less than	1 < 10
<=	Less than or equal to	"Y" <= "Z"
>	Greater than	1043.4 > 1042
>=	Greater than or equal to	"SAMUEL" >= "SAM"
=	Equal to	10 + 4 = 14
<>	Not equal to	"Jones" <> "Done"

The program in Figure IV–1 calculates the pay for a salesperson. The person receives a base pay of $150 per week. Two bonuses are also available: a $25 bonus if the agent sold more than twenty products that week, and a $15 bonus if the agent was requested by at least eight customers.

The program prompts the user to enter the salesperson's name, the number of products sold, and the number of customer requests. The base pay is established in line 100. The condition for the first bonus is tested by an IF/THEN statement in line 130:

```
130 IF QUANT > 20 THEN PY = PY + 25
```

The value in QUANT is compared to 20. If it is greater, then $25 is added to the pay; otherwise, the THEN clause is ignored and nothing is added to the pay.

The condition for the second bonus is tested in line 160:

```
160 IF REQSTS > 7 THEN PY = PY + 15
```

The bonus is added only if the value in REQSTS is greater than 7. Execution then continues on to line 200, which starts to print the results.

The Double-Alternative IF Statement

The double-alternative variation of the IF statement also tests a condition. The following statement shows an example of the IF/THEN/ELSE statement:

```
20 IF NMBR > 10 THEN PRINT "LARGE" ELSE PRINT "SMALL"
```

If the condition is true, the action stated after the THEN part of the statement is executed, and the ELSE part is ignored; if it is false, the action after the ELSE part of the statement is executed, and the THEN portion is ignored. The flowchart for a double-alternative IF statement is as follows:

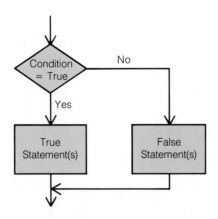

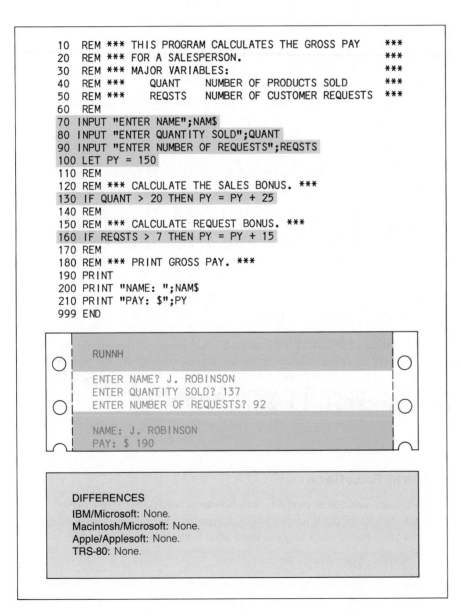

FIGURE IV—1

Program Using IF/THEN Statement

```
10   REM *** THIS PROGRAM CALCULATES THE GROSS PAY   ***
20   REM *** FOR A SALESPERSON.                       ***
30   REM *** MAJOR VARIABLES:                         ***
40   REM ***    QUANT     NUMBER OF PRODUCTS SOLD     ***
50   REM ***    REQSTS    NUMBER OF CUSTOMER REQUESTS ***
60   REM
70   INPUT "ENTER NAME";NAM$
80   INPUT "ENTER QUANTITY SOLD";QUANT
90   INPUT "ENTER NUMBER OF REQUESTS";REQSTS
100  LET PY = 150
110  REM
120  REM *** CALCULATE THE SALES BONUS. ***
130  IF QUANT > 20 THEN PY = PY + 25
140  REM
150  REM *** CALCULATE REQUEST BONUS. ***
160  IF REQSTS > 7 THEN PY = PY + 15
170  REM
180  REM *** PRINT GROSS PAY. ***
190  PRINT
200  PRINT "NAME: ";NAM$
210  PRINT "PAY: $";PY
999  END
```

```
RUNNH

ENTER NAME? J. ROBINSON
ENTER QUANTITY SOLD? 137
ENTER NUMBER OF REQUESTS? 92

NAME: J. ROBINSON
PAY: $ 190
```

DIFFERENCES

IBM/Microsoft: None.
Macintosh/Microsoft: None.
Apple/Applesoft: None.
TRS-80: None.

The Apple does not contain an IF/THEN/ELSE statement. If you are using an Apple, refer to the box titled: "For Apple users: Simulating the IF/THEN/ELSE Statement." As with the single-alternative IF statement, the statements following the THEN and ELSE can be replaced by transfer line numbers, as shown here:

```
20 IF NMBR > 10 THEN 60 ELSE 100
```

If NMBR is greater than 10, program control will transfer to line 60; otherwise, it will transfer to line 100.

Some more examples of the IF/THEN/ELSE statement follow:

```
10 IF X = Y THEN PRINT "EQUAL" ELSE PRINT "NOT EQUAL"
20 IF C = A * B THEN X = 1 ELSE X = 0
30 IF M < R THEN 100 ELSE 150
```

Figure IV–2 shows a program that uses an IF/THEN/ELSE statement to calculate the cost of T-shirts. There are two sizes of T-shirts: small or large. Small T-shirts are $8 and large ones $10. The user is prompted to enter the quantity and type of T-shirts requested. The amount owed is calculated in the IF/THEN/ELSE statement in line 160.

It is also possible to place IF statements inside of one another. This is referred to as nesting and allows the statement to check for multiple conditions. For example, we could rewrite the IF/THEN/ELSE statement in Figure IV–2, line 160, so that it checked for three sizes of T-shirts:

```
160 IF SIZE$ = "SMALL" THEN PAY = QUANTITY * 8 ELSE IF SIZE$ =
    "MEDIUM" THEN PAY = QUANTITY * 10 ELSE PAY = QUANTITY * 12
```

This statement first determines if SIZE$ is SMALL. If it isn't, the statement then determines if SIZE$ is MEDIUM. If SIZE$ isn't MEDIUM, it's assumed that it's LARGE. By nesting an IF/THEN/ELSE inside the ELSE portion of another IF/THEN/ELSE, this statement is able to check for three different conditions.

■ LIBRARY FUNCTIONS

A useful feature of BASIC is the **function,** a subprogram designed to perform a specific task and return a single value. BASIC has numerous **library functions,** functions that have been built into the BASIC language. The programmer can use these functions simply by using a function call which is a statement that includes the name of the function and one or more **arguments.** The argument is the value that the function manipulates to obtain its·result.

Numeric Functions

Many library functions perform arithmetic operations. For example, the function that finds the square root of a number, SQR, could be used in the following statement that assigns the value 5 to the variable SUM:

```
110 SUM = SQR(4) + 3
```

The value of SQR(4) is 2, which is then added to 3. Table IV–1 contains some commonly used arithmetic functions. SIN, COS, TAN, ATN, and LOG

▬ FOR APPLE USERS: SIMULATING THE IF/THEN/ELSE STATEMENT

For those systems, such as the Apple, which do not provide an IF/THEN/ELSE statement, the logic of the double-alternative IF statement can be achieved by using the IF/THEN and GOTO statements. The following flowchart is correct for both Solution A and Solution B program segments:

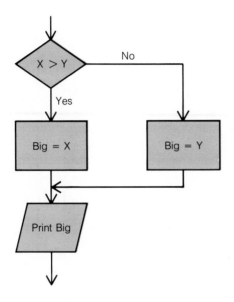

SOLUTION A

```
40 IF X > Y THEN BIG = X ELSE BIG = Y
50 PRINT BIG
```

SOLUTION B

```
40 IF X > Y THEN 70
50 BIG = Y
60 GOTO 80
70 BIG = X
80 PRINT BIG
```

In both segments the condition is the same, and both take the same actions for the true and false conditions. In Solution B the false action is contained in line 50, with a GOTO statement in line 60 to bypass the following THEN action. Notice that in Solution B, control is passed to line 80 after the ELSE action (via line 60) and after the THEN action (via normal execution flow). Whether the IF/THEN/ELSE statement or the IF/THEN statement is used, there should be a single common exit point for any double-alternative decision structure.

```
10  REM *** DETERMINES COST OF T-SHIRT ORDER.  ***
20  REM *** MAJOR VARIABLES:                   ***
30  REM ***     QUANTITY   QUANTITY OF T-SHIRTS ***
40  REM ***     SIZE$      SMALL OR LARGE       ***
50  REM ***     PAY        COST OF T-SHIRTS     ***
60  REM
70  PRINT "ROCK TOUR T-SHIRT ORDER"
80  PRINT "SIZES AVAILABLE:  SMALL OR LARGE"
90  PRINT "-------------------------------"
100 PRINT
110 INPUT "ENTER NUMBER OF T-SHIRTS";QUANTITY
120 INPUT "ENTER SIZE";SIZE$
130 PRINT
140 REM
150 REM *** CALCULATE COST ACCORDING TO SIZE. ***
160 IF SIZE$ = "SMALL" THEN PAY = QUANTITY * 8 ELSE PAY = QUANTITY * 10
170 REM
180 PRINT "TOTAL COST FOR ";QUANTITY;SIZE$;" T-SHIRTS = $";PAY
999 END
```

```
RUNNH

ROCK TOUR T-SHIRT ORDER
SIZES AVAILABLE:  SMALL OR LARGE
----------------------------------

ENTER NUMBER OF T-SHIRTS? 6
ENTER SIZE? SMALL

TOTAL COST FOR  6 SMALL T-SHIRTS = $ 48
```

DIFFERENCES

IBM/Microsoft: None.
Macintosh/Microsoft: None.
Apple/Applesoft: No IF/THEN/ELSE: refer to box titled
                 "Stimulating the IF/THEN/ELSE Statement."
TRS-80: None.

FIGURE IV–2

**Program Using IF/THEN/ELSE
Statements**

are trigonometric functions. The function EXP(X) raises the constant e (which is approximately equal to 2.718) to the specified power. The value returned by the SGN function is dependent on whether X is positive. The examples below illustrate how it works:

Statement	Value returned	
10 LET N1 = SGN(3)	N1 = +1	(positive argument)
20 LET N2 = SGN(0)	N2 = 0	(argument = 0)
30 LET N3 = SGN(-14)	N3 = -1	(negative argument)

Use the ABS function to obtain the absolute value of number:

T A B L E   I V—1

Common Numeric Functions

Function	Operation
ABS(X)	Absolute value of X
ATN(X)	Trigonometric arc tangent of X radians
COS(X)	Trigonometric cosine of X radians
EXP(X)	e^x
LOG(X)	Natural logarithm (if x = e, LOG(X) = Y)
RND*	Random number between 0 and 1
SGN(X)	Sign of X; +1 if X > 0, 0 if X = 0, −1 if X < 0
SIN(X)	Trigonometric sine of X radians
SQR(X)	Square root of X
TAN(X)	Trigonometric tangent of X radians

*On the TRS-80, an argument of 0 is needed, and on the Apple, a positive argument is needed.

Statement	Value returned

```
160 LET V = ABS(-148)    V = 148
```

The random number function (RND) returns a random number between 0 and 1. The RND function is useful in writing programs involving statistics, simulations, or computer games.

String Functions

BASIC also includes some string functions. Many business applications require sophisticated manipulations of strings. Some common string functions are shown in Table IV–2.

Two or more strings can be concatenated (joined together) as shown below:

```
270 T$ = "NIGHT" + "MARE"
```

The value NIGHTMARE is now assigned to T$.

The length of LEN function returns the number of characters in the string that is its argument. (Remember that blanks inside quotation marks are also part of the string.) The following statement assigns the value 9 to NMBR:

```
310 NMBR = LEN("YOUR NAME")
```

The LEFT$ function returns a string that consists of the leftmost portion of the string argument, from the first character to the character position specified by the expression. For instance, the following statement assigns the value BE SEEING to the variable X$:

```
30 X$ = LEFT$("BE SEEING YOU!",9)
```

The microcomputers discussed in this supplement handle the RIGHT$ function differently than the VAX does. On the VAX, the RIGHT$ function returns the rightmost part of the string, from the *character position* given

Common String Functions

Function	Operation	Example
string1 + string2	Concatenation; joins two strings	"KUNG" + "FU" is "KUNG FU"
LEFT$ (string, integer expression)	Returns the number of leftmost characters of a string specified by the expression	LEFT$("ABCD",2) is "AB"
LEN (string)	Returns the length of a string	IF N$ = "HI THERE", THEN LEN(N$) is 8
MID$(string, expression1, expression2)	Starting with the character at expression1, returns the number of characters specified by expression2	MID$("MARIE",2,3) is "ARI"
RIGHT$(string, expression)	*VAX:* Returns the rightmost characters of a string, starting with character specified by the expression	RIGHT$("ABCDE",2) is "BCDE"
	Micros: Returns the number of rightmost characters specified by the expression	RIGHT$("ABCDE",2) is "DE"
STR$(expression)	Converts a number to its string equivalent	STR$(123) is "123"
VAL(string)	Returns the numeric value of a number string	IF N$ = "352 63" THEN VAL(N$) is 35263

by the expression to the end of the string. Thus, the following statement assigns the value SEEING YOU! to X$:

```
30 X$ = RIGHT$("BE SEEING YOU!",4)
```

With the microcomputers, however, this function returns the *number of characters* specified by the expression from the right end of the string, which is in this case the value SEEING YOU!:

```
30 X$ = RIGHT$("BE SEEING YOU!",11)
```

The MID$ function is more complicated. Here is the general format:

MID$ (string,expression1[,expression2])

Sometimes expression #2 is omitted; in that case, the characters—from the starting point to the end of the string—are returned. The following statement assigns to X$ a string four characters long, starting at the fifth character: NDIP.

```
20 X$ = MID$("SERENDIPITY",5,4)
```

The VAL function converts a numeric string expression (such as "12.34") into its equivalent numeric value. The characters of the argument string can include the digits 0 through 9, the plus and minus signs, and the decimal point. Any leading blanks in the string are ignored. By using the VAL function, it is possible to change a number in a character string to a number that can be used in mathematical computations. In the program segment below, the user is supposed to enter a single digit from zero through nine.

The digit is read to the string variable N$ and is then converted to a numeric value and assigned to N1:

```
40 INPUT "ENTER A DIGIT FROM 0 THROUGH 9";N$
50 N1 = VAL(N$)
```

The STR$ function is the opposite of VAL. It causes a numeric value to be converted to the corresponding string value. Once it is a string, it cannot be used in mathematical operations. After this statement is executed, the value stored in N$ will be "101":

```
70 N$ = STR$(101)
```

USER-DEFINED FUNCTIONS

The DEF, or definition, statement can be used by the programmer to define a function not already included in the BASIC language. Once a function has been defined, the programmer can use it as many times as necessary in the program. The DEF statement can be placed anywhere in the program before the function is first called, but in the interests of clarity and organization, all DEF statements should appear near the beginning of the program. The general format of the DEF statement is as follows:

line# DEF function name(argument list) = expression

The function name consists of the letters FN followed by a valid variable name (for example, FNROUND, FNAREA, or FNX). The arguments are one or more variables that are replaced by values given when the function is called. (The Apple allows for only a single argument.) The expression contains the operations to be performed by the function. The entire DEF statement cannot exceed one line. A function call is used to execute the function. A call to a user-defined function has the following format:

function name(expression list)

The function name must match the name appearing in the DEF statement. In program execution, the one or more expressions are evaluated, and the results are used to replace the arguments of the DEF statement on a one-to-one basis. Figure IV–3 shows a program that uses a function to convert a Fahrenheit temperature to Celsius. The function is in line 80:

```
80 DEF FNTEMP(F) = (F - 32) * (5 / 9)
```

The function is called in line 100

```
100 CTEMP = FNTEMP (FTEMP)
```

When line 100 is executed, control passes to the function and the value entered for FTEMP is manipulated by the function to obtain the Celsius temperature. This value then is assigned to CTEMP.

COMPREHENSIVE PROGRAMMING PROBLEM

The Problem

The Acme Car Rental Company charges customers for the use of its rental cars based on the type of car, number of days, miles traveled, and type of

FIGURE IV—3

Program Containing a User-Defined Function

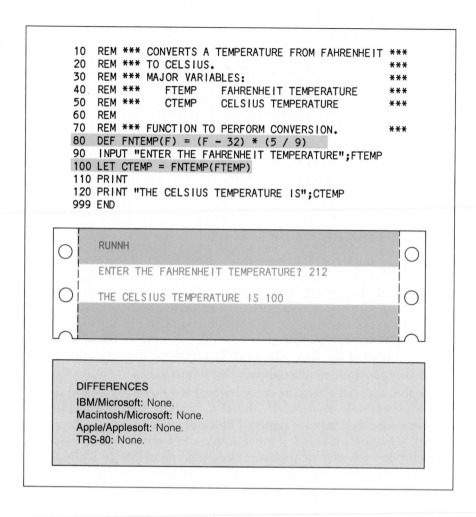

```
10  REM *** CONVERTS A TEMPERATURE FROM FAHRENHEIT ***
20  REM *** TO CELSIUS.                              ***
30  REM *** MAJOR VARIABLES:                         ***
40  REM ***     FTEMP     FAHRENHEIT TEMPERATURE     ***
50  REM ***     CTEMP     CELSIUS TEMPERATURE        ***
60  REM
70  REM *** FUNCTION TO PERFORM CONVERSION.          ***
80  DEF FNTEMP(F) = (F - 32) * (5 / 9)
90  INPUT "ENTER THE FAHRENHEIT TEMPERATURE";FTEMP
100 LET CTEMP = FNTEMP(FTEMP)
110 PRINT
120 PRINT "THE CELSIUS TEMPERATURE IS";CTEMP
999 END
```

```
RUNNH

ENTER THE FAHRENHEIT TEMPERATURE? 212

THE CELSIUS TEMPERATURE IS 100
```

DIFFERENCES
IBM/Microsoft: None.
Macintosh/Microsoft: None.
Apple/Applesoft: None.
TRS-80: None.

insurance chosen. They would like a program that will calculate a customer's bill for them. The company leases three types of cars:

Type	Daily Charge	Mileage Charge
1	$ 8.00	.06
2	$10.00	.08
3	$15.00	.12

The company offers two insurance plans:

Plan	Cost
1	20 percent of the daily and mileage charges
2	$4 per day of use

The program should prompt the user to enter the type of car rented, the number of days, the mileage, and the type of insurance plan. The total amount of the bill should then be displayed.

Solution Design

There are three basic tasks to be performed:

1. Determine the basic rental charge.
2. Determine the insurance charge.
3. Display the total bill.

Step 1 can be further divided as follows:

1.A. Determine the type of car, days rented, and miles driven.
1.B. Multiply daily rate × days rented.
1.C. Multiply mileage charge × miles driven.
1.D. Add rate charge to mileage charge.

Step 2 involves simply prompting the user to enter the type of insurance and assigning the cost. Step 3 can be broken into two parts:

3.A. Add rental charge to insurance charge.
3.B. Display the total bill.

The structure chart for this problem is shown in Figure IV–4. Now let us examine the flow of data processing to determine what types of statements we will need. In the first step, we must choose between three rates. Therefore, we can use a nested IF/THEN/ELSE statement to determine which rate is appropriate.

   Selecting the insurance rate is simpler. Because there are only two rates, a simple IF/THEN/ELSE statement can assign the desired rate. The insurance rate can then be added to the basic charge. The flowchart is shown in Figure IV–5.

FIGURE IV–4

Structure Chart for Rental Car Problem

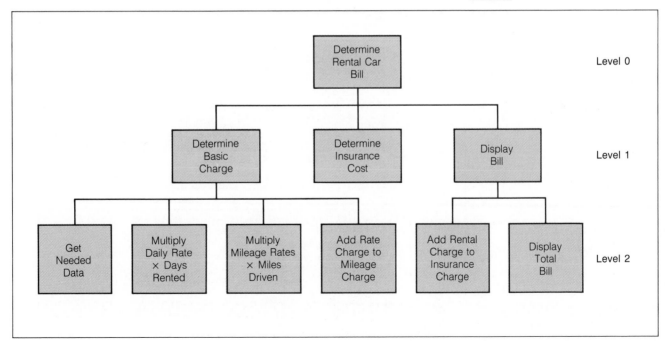

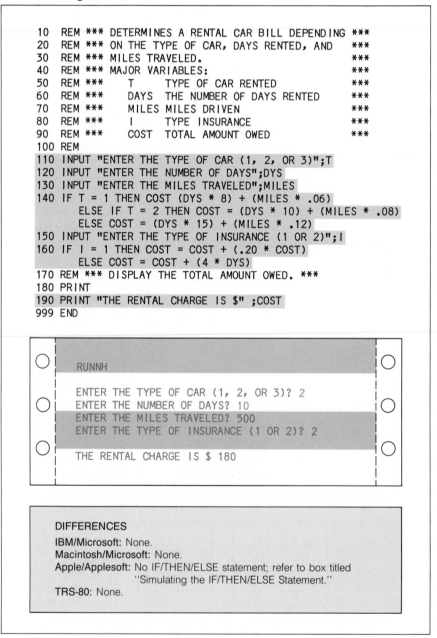

The Program

Examine the program in Figure IV–6. The needed data is obtained by lines 110 through 130 and line 150. The nested IF/THEN/ELSE statement in line 140 determines which of the three rates should be applied. Line 160 uses another IF/THEN/ELSE to add the appropriate insurance charge to the previously calculated amount. The resulting total is then displayed in line 190.

FIGURE IV–6

Rental Car Program

```
10   REM *** DETERMINES A RENTAL CAR BILL DEPENDING ***
20   REM *** ON THE TYPE OF CAR, DAYS RENTED, AND    ***
30   REM *** MILES TRAVELED.                         ***
40   REM *** MAJOR VARIABLES:                        ***
50   REM ***    T      TYPE OF CAR RENTED            ***
60   REM ***    DAYS   THE NUMBER OF DAYS RENTED     ***
70   REM ***    MILES  MILES DRIVEN                  ***
80   REM ***    I      TYPE INSURANCE                ***
90   REM ***    COST   TOTAL AMOUNT OWED             ***
100  REM
110  INPUT "ENTER THE TYPE OF CAR (1, 2, OR 3)";T
120  INPUT "ENTER THE NUMBER OF DAYS";DYS
130  INPUT "ENTER THE MILES TRAVELED";MILES
140  IF T = 1 THEN COST (DYS * 8) + (MILES * .06)
         ELSE IF T = 2 THEN COST = (DYS * 10) + (MILES * .08)
         ELSE COST = (DYS * 15) + (MILES * .12)
150  INPUT "ENTER THE TYPE OF INSURANCE (1 OR 2)";I
160  IF I = 1 THEN COST = COST + (.20 * COST)
         ELSE COST = COST + (4 * DYS)
170  REM *** DISPLAY THE TOTAL AMOUNT OWED. ***
180  PRINT
190  PRINT "THE RENTAL CHARGE IS $" ;COST
999  END
```

```
RUNNH

ENTER THE TYPE OF CAR (1, 2, OR 3)? 2
ENTER THE NUMBER OF DAYS? 10
ENTER THE MILES TRAVELED? 500
ENTER THE TYPE OF INSURANCE (1 OR 2)? 2

THE RENTAL CHARGE IS $ 180
```

DIFFERENCES

IBM/Microsoft: None.
Macintosh/Microsoft: None.
Apple/Applesoft: No IF/THEN/ELSE statement; refer to box titled
              "Simulating the IF/THEN/ELSE Statement."
TRS-80: None.

FIGURE IV–5

Flowchart for Rental Car Problem

■ The GOTO statement is an unconditional transfer of control that causes program control to pass to a specified line number. Its use should be avoided whenever possible.

■ The IF statement is a conditional transfer statement. It causes a transfer of control that depends on whether a specified condition is met.

■ The single alternative IF statement (IF/THEN statement) causes the action following the THEN to be taken only if the specified condition is true.

■ In the double alternative IF statement (IF/THEN/ELSE statement) one action is taken if the condition is true, another if it is false.

■ It is possible to "nest" IF statements inside one another. This allows for the checking of more than one condition.

■ The BASIC language includes many library functions that can be used by the programmer. These functions can manipulate both numeric and string values.

■ The programmer can define functions to meet specific needs by using the DEF statement.

REVIEW QUESTIONS

1. Why is the GOTO statement called an unconditional transfer?

2. Which of the following IF statements are valid?

```
a. 40 IF X$ = "FRANCO" THEN M = M + 1
b. 10 IF Y$ <> "YES" THEN GOTO 40
c. 20 IF Z THEN GOTO 1000
d. 60 IF N > 0 PRINT "+" ELSE PRINT "NOT +"
```

3. Is the ELSE clause of the IF/THEN/ELSE executed when the condition is true, or when it is false?

4. Explain the difference between a single-alternative IF statement and a double-alternative IF statement.

5. Give the statement(s) corresponding to the following flowchart:

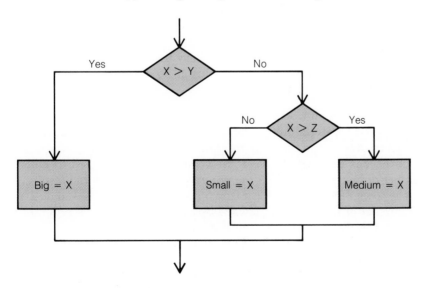

6. What is a function? Name two commonly used numeric functions.
7. What possible values can the SGN function return?
8. State the value of S$ after execution of each of the following:
   a. 10 S$ = LEFT$("TODAY",2)
   b. 20 S$ = "FIRST" + "SECOND"
   c. 30 S$ = MID$("TODAY",2,3)

▓ DEBUGGING EXERCISES

Identify and correct any errors in the following programs or program segments.

```
1. 10 REM *** THIS PROGRAM CALCULATES A GRADE  ***
   20 REM *** AS FOLLOWS:                       ***
   30 REM ***     GOOD     80 - 100             ***
   40 REM ***     AVERAGE 79 - 60               ***
   50 REM ***     POOR     BELOW 60             ***
   60 REM
   70 INPUT "ENTER THE SCORE";SCR
   80 IF SCR > 80 THEN G$ = "GOOD" ELSE IF SCR > 60
          THEN G$ = "AVERAGE" ELSE G$ = "POOR"
   90 PRINT G$
   99 END
2. 10 REM *** IF A$ IS NOT EQUAL TO "Y" THEN      ***
   20 REM *** PROGRAM EXECUTION SHOULD TERMINATE. ***
   30 REM
   40 INPUT "DO YOU WISH TO CONTINUE;A$
   50 IF A$ = "Y" THEN 99 ELSE INPUT "ENTER THE NAME";N$
   99 END
```

▓ PROGRAMMING PROBLEMS

1. Write a program that prompts the user to enter three values and displays the largest.

2. Write a program for converting military time (24 hour) to civilian time. For example, if the user enters the value 23.30, the output should be:

The civilian time is 11.30 PM.

3. Steve Cavanaugh works for Uptown Lumber Company on weekends and evenings. He receives $3.60 an hour for the first fifteen hours and $3.75 for the hours over fifteen. Write a program that Steve can use to display how much he has earned in a week. Steve should be prompted to enter the number of hours worked and the program should display the result.

4. The town of Micropolis has taken a poll of its ten families to determine the number of television sets owned by each family. Write a program that will prompt the user to enter this data and then calculate the average sets per family. Write a user-defined function to calculate the average. Display the results with appropriate labels.

5. The Wastenot Utility Company charges customers for electricity according to the following scale:

Kilowatt Hours (KWH)	Cost
0–300	$10.00
301–1000	$10.00 + .03 for each KWH above 300
1001 or above	$40.00 + .02 for each KWH above 1000

Write a program that accepts as input the customer's name and the old and new meter readings, and calculates the amount of the bill. The output should include the customer's name, the old and new readings, the number of KWH used, and the amount of the bill.

SECTION V

Looping

O U T L I N E

Introduction
The FOR/NEXT Loop
  Processing Steps for the FOR/NEXT
    Loop
  Rules for Using the FOR/NEXT Loop
  Nested FOR/NEXT Loops
  Advantages and Disadvantages of
    Using the FOR/NEXT Loop
The WHILE Loop
Comprehensive Programming Problem
  Problem Definition
  Solution Design
  The Program
Summary Points
Review Questions
Debugging Exercises
Programming Problems

■ INTRODUCTION

In Section IV, we learned how to use the IF statement to transfer program control. In this section, we will learn how to write another type of control statement: the **loop.** The loop is a control structure that allows a segment of a program to be repeated as many times as necessary. Because computers are well suited to performing repetitive tasks such as reading large quantities of data, loops are widely used in programming.

■ THE FOR/NEXT LOOP

The FOR and NEXT statements are used together to form a loop that is repeated a specified number of times. Figure V–1 contains a simple program that uses a FOR/NEXT loop to add ten numbers together. In this program, the value of SUM is initially set at zero. The FOR/NEXT loop is then entered. The variable I is referred to as a **loop control variable**; it is the variable that determines whether the loop will be executed. When the FOR statement is executed for the first time, the loop control variable is set to an initial value (which in this case is 1). This value is tested against the terminal value (which is 10). As long as the value of I is less than or equal to the terminal value, the loop will be executed. Here is a FOR statement with each of its parts labeled:

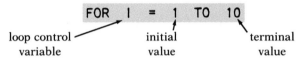

Each time this loop is executed, the value of I is incremented by one. When I is greater than 10, the loop will not be executed again.

In Figure V–1, the statements in lines 50 and 60 constitute the body of this loop; the body of a loop contains the actions that the loop performs. For each execution of the loop, the next number is read from the DATA statement and added to SUM. Notice that the loop body is indented. Indenting statements makes no difference to the computer but makes the program more readable for humans.

When the NEXT statement in line 70 is reached, the value of I is incremented by one and program control is transferred to the top of the loop. If the current value of I is less than or equal to the terminal value, the body of the loop is executed again; if I is greater than the terminal value, program control is transferred to the first statement following the NEXT statement. In this example, after the loop has executed ten times, control will be transferred to line 80 and the sum of the ten numbers will be printed.

In the loop in Figure V–1, the initial and terminal values are both numeric constants. These values can also be numeric expressions or variables. In the following example, the initial value is a numeric expression, and the terminal value is a numeric variable.

```
10 LET A = 10
20 FOR I = 2 + 4 TO A
30     PRINT I
40 NEXT I
```

This loop will execute five times. The output will appear as follows:

```
6
7
8
9
10
```

It is possible to alter the value by which the loop control variable is incremented. This is done by placing a step value at the end of the FOR statement. The FOR statement in the first program in Figure V–2 has a step value of 2. The FOR/NEXT loop in this program will execute ten times and the even numbers from 2 through 20 will be displayed. It is also possible to have a negative step value, as shown in the second program in Figure V–2. This program prints the even numbers from 20 through 2. If a FOR statement contains no step value, a step value of +1 is assumed. Therefore, the two FOR statements here are equivalent to each other.

```
10 FOR I = 10 TO 20          10 FOR I = 10 TO 20 STEP 1
```

We can now state the general format of the FOR/NEXT loop as follows:

line# FOR loop control variable = initial value TO terminal value [STEP step value]
.
.
.

line# NEXT loop control variable

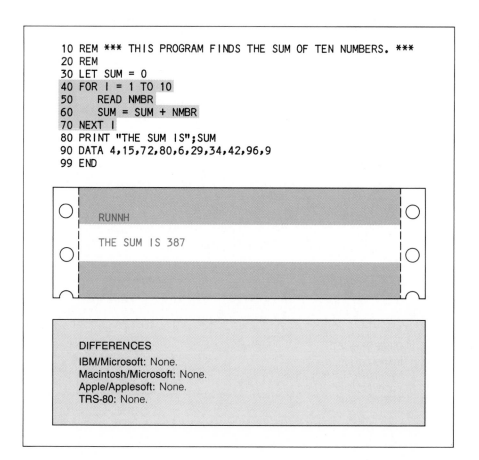

FIGURE V–1

Program to Add Ten Numbers

```
10 REM *** THIS PROGRAM FINDS THE SUM OF TEN NUMBERS. ***
20 REM
30 LET SUM = 0
40 FOR I = 1 TO 10
50    READ NMBR
60    SUM = SUM + NMBR
70 NEXT I
80 PRINT "THE SUM IS";SUM
90 DATA 4,15,72,80,6,29,34,42,96,9
99 END
```

```
RUNNH

THE SUM IS 387
```

DIFFERENCES
IBM/Microsoft: None.
Macintosh/Microsoft: None.
Apple/Applesoft: None.
TRS-80: None.

Notice that because the step value is optional, this part of the format statement is in brackets.

Processing Steps for the FOR/NEXT Loop

Let us review the steps followed by the computer when it encounters a FOR statement:

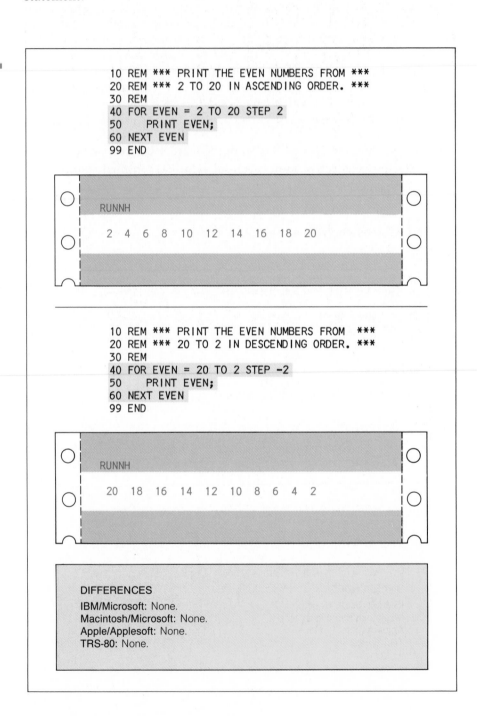

FIGURE V—2

FOR/NEXT Loops Using Positive and Negative Step Values

```
10 REM *** PRINT THE EVEN NUMBERS FROM ***
20 REM *** 2 TO 20 IN ASCENDING ORDER. ***
30 REM
40 FOR EVEN = 2 TO 20 STEP 2
50     PRINT EVEN;
60 NEXT EVEN
99 END
```

```
RUNNH
 2   4   6   8   10   12   14   16   18   20
```

```
10 REM *** PRINT THE EVEN NUMBERS FROM  ***
20 REM *** 20 TO 2 IN DESCENDING ORDER. ***
30 REM
40 FOR EVEN = 20 TO 2 STEP -2
50     PRINT EVEN;
60 NEXT EVEN
99 END
```

```
RUNNH
 20   18   16   14   12   10   8   6   4   2
```

DIFFERENCES

IBM/Microsoft: None.
Macintosh/Microsoft: None.
Apple/Applesoft: None.
TRS-80: None.

COMPUTERS AND INFORMATION PROCESSING

■ It sets the loop control variable to the initial value indicated.

■ It tests to see whether the value of the loop control variable exceeds the indicated terminal value. (This may occur the first time the FOR statement is executed—except on the Apple which always executes a FOR/NEXT loop at least once.)

■ If the value of the loop control variable does not exceed the terminal value, the statements in the loop are executed.

■ If the value of the loop control variable exceeds the terminal value, control is transferred to the statement following the NEXT statement.

When the NEXT statement at the end of the loop is encountered, the following actions are taken:

■ The loop control variable is incremented (or decremented) by the step value. If no step value is indicated in the FOR statement, the value is assumed to be +1.

■ The loop control variable is compared to the terminal value.

■ If the value of the loop control variable exceeds the terminal value, control transfers to the first statement after the NEXT; otherwise control transfers to the first statement after the FOR statement.

Rules for Using the FOR/NEXT Loop

To avoid errors in using the FOR and NEXT statements, be aware of the following rules:

■ The body of the loop is not executed if the initial value is greater than the terminal value when using a positive step, or if the initial value is less than the terminal value when using a negative step. For example, a loop containing either of the following statements would not be executed at all:

```
10 FOR X = 10 TO 5 STEP 2

20 FOR COUNT = 4 TO 6 STEP -1
```

■ The initial, terminal, and step values cannot be modified in the loop body.

■ It is possible to modify the loop control variable in the loop body, but this should *never* be done. Note how unpredictable the execution of the following loop would be. The value of I is dependent on the integer entered by the user.

```
10 FOR I = 1 TO 10
20    INPUT "ENTER AN INTEGER";X
30    I = X
40 NEXT I
```

■ If the step value is zero, an **infinite loop,** which is a loop that will never stop executing, is created. Here is an example:

```
10 FOR X = 10 TO 20 STEP 0
```

■ Each FOR statement must be associated with a corresponding NEXT statement.

Nested FOR/NEXT Loops

In Section IV we learned to nest IF statements to check for multiple conditions. It is also possible to nest FOR/NEXT loops. Below is an example:

```
10 FOR I = 1 TO 4
20    FOR J = 1 TO 2
30       PRINT I;J
40    NEXT J
50 NEXT I
```

Notice that the inner loop (loop J) is indented so that the reader can identify its boundaries. Each time the outer loop (loop I) is executed once, loop J is executed twice because J varies from 1 to 2. When the inner loop is through executing, control passes to the first statement after NEXT J, which in this case is the statement NEXT I. This statement causes I to be incremented by 1 and tested against the terminal value of 4. If I is still less than or equal to 4, the body of loop I is executed again. The J loop is again encountered, the value of J is reset to 1, and the inner loop is executed until J is greater than 2. Altogether, the outer loop is executed I (4) times and the inner loop is executed I × J times (4 × 2 = 8 times). The output of this program segment will be:

```
1   1
1   2
2   1
2   2
3   1
3   2
4   1
4   2
```

It is easy to make mistakes when nesting loops. Always make sure that the inner loop is entirely inside of the outer loop. Each loop must have its own loop control variable and its own NEXT statement.

Advantages and Disadvantages of Using the FOR/NEXT Loop

The FOR/NEXT loop is used often because it performs many tasks automatically. The loop control variable is incremented (or decremented, if a negative step value is used) automatically. Also, the condition that controls loop repetition is automatically checked each time the NEXT statement is executed. Therefore, the programmer does not need to write the statements that perform these tasks.

The FOR/NEXT loop is useful when writing programs that use counting loops. When a **counting loop** is used, the exact number of loop repetitions must be known before the loop is executed for the first time. The program in Figure V–3 contains a counting loop. In this program, the user is asked to enter the number of paychecks that need to be calculated for a payroll. This number, which is assigned to variable NMBR, is then used to control the number of times the FOR/NEXT loop will execute. In this way, each time the program is executed, the user can determine the number of paychecks that will be calculated.

FIGURE V–3

Program Using a FOR/NEXT Loop to Calculate a Payroll

```
10   REM *** CALCULATE PAYROLL FOR CITY ELECTRIC.              ***
20   REM
30   REM *** DETERMINE NUMBER OF PAYCHECKS TO BE CALCULATED. ***
40   INPUT "HOW MANY PAYCHECKS NEED TO BE CALCULATED";NMBR
50   REM
60   REM *** LOOP TO CALCULATE EACH PAYCHECK. ***
70   FOR I = 1 TO NMBR
80      PRINT
90      INPUT "ENTER NAME";NME$
100     INPUT "ENTER HOURS WORKED";HRS
110     INPUT "ENTER HOURLY RATE";RTE
120     LET WAGE = RTE * HRS
130     PRINT "NAME","WAGE"
140     PRINT NME$,WAGE
150  NEXT I
999  END
```

```
RUNNH

HOW MANY PAYCHECKS NEED TO BE CALCULATED? 3

ENTER NAME? J. JONES
ENTER HOURS WORKED? 40
ENTER HOURLY RATE? 4.0
NAME            WAGE
J. JONES        160


ENTER NAME? S. ROBINSON
ENTER HOURS WORKED? 30
ENTER HOURLY RATE? 5.0
NAME            WAGE
S. ROBINSON     150


ENTER NAME? C. KUMATA
ENTER HOURS WORKED? 40
ENTER HOURLY RATE? 6.0
NAME            WAGE
C. KUMATA       240
```

DIFFERENCES

IBM/Microsoft: None.
Macintosh/Microsoft: None.
Apple/Applesoft: None.
TRS-80: None.

■ THE WHILE LOOP

A second type of loop is the WHILE loop. Its general format follows:

line# WHILE expression

.

.

.

line# NEXT

Notice that the NEXT statement in this loop is not followed by a variable. Any statements between the WHILE and NEXT statements will be executed each time the loop is repeated. The WHILE loop will be executed as long as the expression in the WHILE statement is true. When the expression is no longer true, control is transferred to the first statement after the NEXT statement.

In contrast to the FOR/NEXT loop, the WHILE/NEXT loop involves no automatic initialization or incrementing of the loop control variable. Below is an example of a WHILE loop:

```
100 LET CNT = 40
110 WHILE CNT < 50
120     PRINT CNT
130     LET CNT = CNT + 1
140 NEXT
```

The statement in line 100 initializes CNT to 40. CNT will be the loop control variable and must be assigned a starting value before the loop is entered. Line 110 specifies that the loop will continue to execute as long as CNT is less than 50. Line 130 increments the value of CNT by one each time the loop is executed. When line 140 is reached, control branches back to the top of the loop and the condition "CNT < 50" is tested again. This loop will execute ten times before the condition becomes false. Consider the following version of this WHILE loop:

```
100 LET CNT = 40
110 WHILE CNT < 50
120     PRINT CNT
130 NEXT
```

When this loop is executed, the expression in line 110 will never become false. This is because CNT is never incremented. Therefore, this program segment creates an infinite loop.

Some implementations of BASIC (such as IBM, Macintosh, and TRS–80) create WHILE loops using the WHILE and WEND statements rather than the WHILE/NEXT statements. In these implementations, the end of the loop is indicated by using the WEND statement as follows:

```
100 LET CNT = 40
110 WHILE CNT < 50
120     PRINT CNT
130     LET CNT = CNT + 1
140 WEND
```

The WHILE loop is not implemented on the Apple. Refer to the box titled: "For Apple Users: Simulating the WHILE Loop" for instructions on working around this problem.

■ **FOR APPLE USERS: SIMULATING THE WHILE LOOP**

On systems such as the Apple which do not provide the WHILE loop, the same program logic can be obtained by using the IF and GOTO statements. Both of the following programs display a countdown from 5 to 1:

```
10 REM *** COUNTING WITH THE WHILE LOOP. ***
20 REM
30 LET CNT = 5
40 WHILE CNT > 0
50    PRINT CNT
60    LET CNT = CNT - 1
70 NEXT
99 END
```

```
10 REM *** COUNTING WITHOUT THE WHILE LOOP. ***
20 REM
30 LET CNT = 5
40 IF CNT <= 0 THEN 99
50    PRINT CNT
60    LET CNT = CNT - 1
70 GOTO 40
99 END
```

Any WHILE loop can be simulated using the IF and GOTO statements. Take care that the condition used in the IF statement is the correct one for the loop execution you desire. However, if your BASIC system provides for a WHILE loop, it is always preferable to use it and thereby avoid the use of the GOTO statement.

Refer back to Figure V–3 that calculated a payroll using a FOR/NEXT loop. A basic problem with this program is that the user must know how many paychecks are to be processed. This is often difficult to determine before the processing starts. Therefore, we will rewrite this program using a WHILE loop in place of the FOR/NEXT loop. The altered program is shown in Figure V–4. Note the condition controlling the loop repetition:

```
40 WHILE NME$ <> "DONE"
```

This loop will continue to execute until the user enters DONE for the value of NME\$. DONE is referred to as a **trailer value** (or **sentinel value**). A trailer value is a dummy value that marks the end of the input data. It signals the program that all of the data has been processed and loop repetition should stop. The trailer value can be either a numeric value or a character string, depending on the type of data being input. Notice that the first name is entered in line 30. This is so the variable NME\$ will have a value when the condition in line 40 is tested. Subsequent names are read at the bottom of the loop in line 110. Line 120 then transfers control to the top of the loop at line 40.

FIGURE V—4

Program Using a WHILE Loop to Calculate a Payroll

```
10   REM *** CALCULATE PAYROLL FOR CITY ELECTRIC. ***
20   REM
30   INPUT "ENTER NAME";NME$
40   WHILE NME$ <> "DONE"
50      PRINT
60      INPUT "ENTER HOURS WORKED";HRS
70      INPUT "ENTER HOURLY RATE";RTE
80      LET WAGE = RTE * HOURS
90      PRINT "NAME","WAGE"
100     PRINT NME$,WAGE
110     INPUT "ENTER NAME (ENTER 'DONE' TO STOP)";NME$
120  NEXT
999  END
```

```
RUNNH

ENTER NAME? J. JONES

ENTER HOURS WORKED? 40
ENTER HOURLY RATE? 4.0
NAME            WAGE
J. JONES         160
ENTER NAME (ENTER 'DONE' TO STOP)? S. ROBINSON

ENTER HOURS WORKED? 30
ENTER HOURLY RATE? 5.0
NAME            WAGE
S. ROBINSON      150
ENTER NAME (ENTER 'DONE' TO STOP)? DONE
```

DIFFERENCES

IBM/Microsoft: 120 WEND.
Macintosh/Microsoft: 120 WEND.
Apple/Applesoft: No WHILE loop; refer to box titled
                 "Simulating the WHILE Loop."
TRS-80: 120 WEND.

▨ COMPREHENSIVE PROGRAMMING PROBLEM

Problem Definition

The salespeople at Jack's OK Cars would like to have a program to calculate the cost of the cars they sell. They would like the program to calculate the cost of any number of cars. The salesperson should be prompted to enter the following information while the program is running:

Model of the car
Base price
The type of options and the cost of each option
Amount to be deducted for trade-in

A 6% sales tax should be added to the final cost. The output should be formatted similar to the following:

```
MODEL:ESCORT      $ 9000
TOTAL OPTIONS     $ 500
TRADE-IN          $ 1500
TAX               $ 480
                  ---------
TOTAL COST        $ 8480
```

Solution Design

This problem can be subdivided as follows:

1. Get the model of the car and the base price.
2. Get the type and cost of each option and add to base price.
3. Get price of trade-in and subtract from car's price.
4. Add 6% sales tax to price.
5. Display the total price.

Step 2 is the most complicated and contains two basic tasks:

2.A. Determine type and price of each option.
2.B. Add the price to total price of the options.

The structure chart for this problem is shown in Figure V–5.

Because we want the program to calculate the price for an unknown number of cars, we will need to use a WHILE loop. The loop can be controlled by a sentinel value. We can then prompt the user to enter the needed data. A loop will also be needed to get the information on the options. Because we don't know how many options there will be, this loop should also be controlled by a sentinel value. Figure V–6 contains the flowchart for this problem.

The Program

The completed program is contained in Figure V–7. The user is prompted to enter the model and base price of the first car before the loop is entered. Then the model is compared to the sentinel value of 'XXX'. If the value entered was not the sentinel value, the loop is executed and the user is prompted to enter the first option and its price. Another WHILE/NEXT loop allows the user to enter each option and add its price to OTTL (total price of all options). After the option loop is exited, the user is prompted to enter the trade-in value in line 250. The total price is calculated in line 270 by adding BPRICE and OTTL together and subtracting the value of TRADE. The final price is determined by adding the 6% tax. Lines 320 through 390 display the pricing information. In line 420, the user is prompted to enter information on the next car. Line 430 returns control to the top of the outer WHILE loop in line 160.

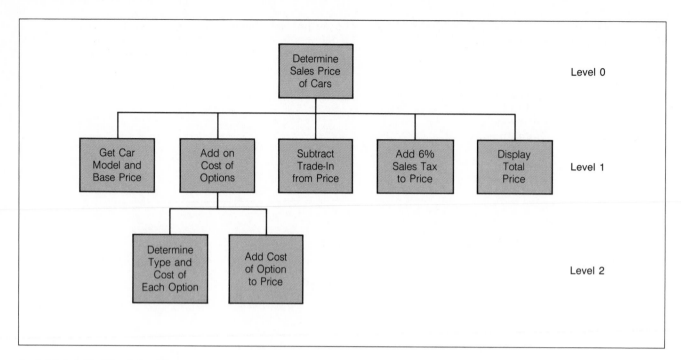

FIGURE V—5

Structure Chart for Car Price Problem

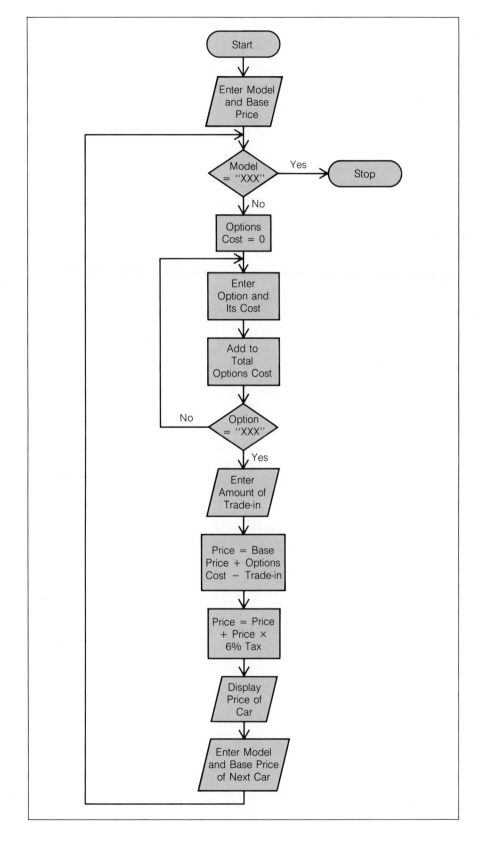

FIGURE V–6

Flowchart for Car Price Problem

FIGURE V—7

Car Price Program

```
10   REM *** DETERMINES THE TOTAL PRICE OF A CAR        ***
20   REM *** DEPENDING ON THE BASE PRICE, THE OPTIONS   ***
30   REM *** SELECTED, AND AMOUNT GIVEN ON A TRADE-IN.  ***
40   REM *** MAJOR VARIABLES:                           ***
50   REM ***    MDL$       CAR MODEL                    ***
60   REM ***    BPRICE     BASE PRICE                   ***
70   REM ***    OPTN$      OPTION                       ***
80   REM ***    OPRICE     PRICE OF EACH OPTION         ***
90   REM ***    OTTL       TOTAL PRICE OF ALL OPTIONS   ***
100  REM ***    TRADE      TRADE-IN ALLOWANCE           ***
110  REM ***    TAX        6% TAX                       ***
120  REM ***    TTL        TOTAL PRICE                  ***
130  REM
140  REM *** ENTER MODEL AND BASE PRICE. ***
150  INPUT "ENTER MODEL OF THE CAR";MDL$
160  WHILE MDL$ <> "XXX"
170     INPUT "ENTER THE BASE PRICE";BPRICE
180     LET OTTL = 0
190     INPUT "ENTER THE FIRST OPTION AND ITS PRICE";OPTN$,OPRICE
200     WHILE OPTN$ <> "XXX"
210        LET OTTL = OTTL + OPRICE
220        PRINT "ENTER THE NEXT OPTION AND ITS PRICE."
230        INPUT "ENTER 'XXX,0' TO STOP";OPTN$,OPRICE
240     NEXT
250     INPUT "ENTER AMOUNT TO BE DEDUCTED FOR TRADE-IN";TRADE
260     REM *** CALCULATE THE TOTAL PRICE WITHOUT THE TAX. ***
270     LET TTL = BPRICE + OTTL - TRADE
280     REM *** ADD THE TAX. ***
290     LET TAX = TTL * .06
300     LET TTL = TTL + TAX
310     REM *** DISPLAY PRICE INFORMATION. ***
320     PRINT
330     PRINT
340     PRINT "MODEL:";MDL$,"$";BPRICE
350     PRINT "TOTAL OPTIONS","$";OTTL
360     PRINT "TRADE-IN","$";TRADE
370     PRINT "TAX","$";TAX
380     PRINT,"--------"
390     PRINT "TOTAL COST","$";TTL
400     REM *** GET MODEL OF NEXT CAR. ***
410     PRINT
420     INPUT "ENTER MODEL OF CAR ('XXX' TO STOP)";MDL$
430  NEXT
999  END
```

FIGURE V–7

Car Price Program continued

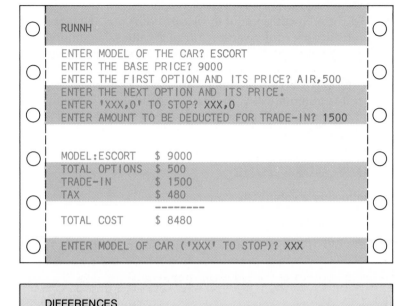

```
  O      RUNNH                                                   O

  O      ENTER MODEL OF THE CAR? ESCORT                         O
         ENTER THE BASE PRICE? 9000
         ENTER THE FIRST OPTION AND ITS PRICE? AIR,500
  O      ENTER THE NEXT OPTION AND ITS PRICE.                   O
         ENTER 'XXX,0' TO STOP? XXX,0
         ENTER AMOUNT TO BE DEDUCTED FOR TRADE-IN? 1500

  O      MODEL:ESCORT     $ 9000                                O
         TOTAL OPTIONS    $ 500
         TRADE-IN         $ 1500
         TAX              $ 480
  O                       ---------                             O

         TOTAL COST       $ 8480

  O      ENTER MODEL OF CAR ('XXX' TO STOP)? XXX                O
```

```
DIFFERENCES
IBM/Microsoft: 430 WEND.
Macintosh/Microsoft: 430 WEND.
Apple/Applesoft: No WHILE loop; refer to box titled
               "Simulating the WHILE Loop."
TRS-80: 430 WEND.
```

▰ SUMMARY POINTS

■ Loops allow a specified portion of a program to be repeated as many times as needed.

■ The FOR/NEXT loop executes the number of times specified in the FOR statement. The NEXT statement increments the loop control variable, tests it against the terminal value, and returns control to the statement immediately following the FOR statement if another loop execution is required. Otherwise, execution continues with the statement following the NEXT statement.

■ A step value may be placed in a FOR statement to determine the value by which the loop control variable should be incremented (or decremented) with each loop repetition.

■ The FOR/NEXT loop is useful when writing counting loops. With counting loops, the number of repetitions needed can be determined before the loop is first executed.

■ Advantages of the FOR/NEXT loop are that the loop control variable is initialized, incremented, and tested automatically. Therefore, the programmer need not worry about these tasks. The major disadvantage is that it cannot be used when the number of loop repetitions needed cannot be determined before loop execution begins.

■ The body of a loop contains the action that the loop performs and should be indented to make the program more readable.

■ The WHILE statement is useful in writing both counting loops and loops that are controlled by trailer values. A trailer value is a dummy value that indicates the end of the input data. When it is encountered, loop repetition is stopped.

■ Because the WHILE loop does not initialize, increment, or test the loop control variable automatically, these tasks must be performed by the programmer. This makes writing WHILE loops more complex than FOR/NEXT loops.

▇ REVIEW QUESTIONS

1. Is the following a valid FOR statement?

```
20 FOR C$ = 1 TO 10 STEP 2
```

2. When is a WHILE loop a more appropriate choice than a FOR/NEXT loop?

3. What is the output of the following statements?

```
30 LET L = 10
40 FOR L = 1 TO 6
50      PRINT L
60 NEXT L
```

4. What is meant by the term *counting loop*?

5. What happens when the step value of a FOR statement is zero?

6. How many times is the following inner loop executed? How many times is the outer loop executed?

```
10 LET Z = 10
20 LET W = 5
30 LET Q = 4
40 FOR L1 = (Q - Z) TO 1 STEP -1
50      FOR L2 = 1 TO W STEP 1
60          PRINT L1,L2
70      NEXT L2
80 NEXT L1
```

7. Explain how a sentinel value can be used to control loop execution.

8. Is the following a valid WHILE loop?

```
10 X = 14
20 Y = 7
30 WHILE Y < X
40      PRINT "X = ";X,"Y =";Y
50      INPUT Z
60      IF Z < Y THEN PRINT "Z = ";Z
70 NEXT
80 PRINT "ALL DONE"
99 END
```

DEBUGGING EXERCISES

Identify and correct any errors in the following programs or program segments.

1.
```
10 REM *** READ AND PRINT EIGHT CITIES. ***
20 REM
30 FOR I = 1 TO I
40    READ CTY$
50 NEXT I
60 PRINT CTY$
70 DATA "BOSIE","TAMA","MIDLAND","WHAT CHEER"
80 DATA "BIG TIMBER","PORTLAND","TOLEDO","SAN JOSE"
99 END
```

2.
```
10 REM *** READ AND PRINT A LIST OF EIGHT CITIES. ***
20 REM
30 READ CTY$
40 WHILE CTY$ <> DONE
50    PRINT CTY$
60    READ CTY$
70 NEXT
80 DATA "BIG TIMBER","PORTLAND","TOLEDO","SAN JOSE"
99 END
```

PROGRAMMING PROBLEMS

1. Write a WHILE loop to count by 5s until a given value is reached. For example, if the value read is 49, output should be similar to the following:

5   10   15   20   25   30   35   40   45

2. Write a program to print the following design. Use FOR/NEXT loops.

```
        *
        *
        *
        *
*********
        *
        *
        *
        *
```

3. The computer science department needs a program that will display, in a horizontal bar graph, the number of students in each of the class sections 300 through 309. Write a program that will create this graph with appropriate headings. Use the following data:

Section	Students
300	20
301	15
302	32
303	17
304	28
305	35
306	26
307	29
308	19
309	27

Use a FOR loop to print a line of asterisks indicating the number of students in each class. The first few lines of output should be similar to the following:

```
CLASS    SIZE
300      ********************
301      **************
302      *******************************
```

4. Write a program to display a multiplication table. The user should be allowed to enter the upper and lower limits of the table. Use the following format for the table:

```
X   1   2   3    4
1   1   2   3    4
2   2   4   6    8
3   3   6   9   12
4   4   8  12   16
```

5. The Olympics Judging Committee has asked you to write a program for the diving competition. The program must read a diver's name and seven scores in the range 0.0 through 10.0. The highest and lowest scores are thrown out; then the total and average of the remaining five scores are calculated. The diver's name, average, and total scores should be output. Use the following input:

Apollo Creed	7.5,	5.5,	6.5,	6.0,	5.7,	6.1,	8.0
Yani Petrok	3.1,	4.5,	3.8,	5.0,	4.9,	4.5,	3.9
Pedro Valecia	5.7,	6.1,	6.9,	5.9,	6.8,	4.9,	6.4
Igor Stephan	8.0,	8.2,	7.0,	9.1,	7.5,	8.3,	9.2
Thomas Kerry	6.5,	6.6,	6.5,	4.8,	5.7,	6.8,	6.0
Gino Balducci	9.1,	8.5,	9.9,	8.1,	8.8,	4.6,	7.8
Mietek Peters	7.7,	8.3,	6.5,	6.9,	7.5,	7.7,	8.0
Johann Mueller	2.1,	1.8,	3.0,	3.1,	2.8,	0.8,	2.5
Claude Berne	5.5,	6.8,	3.1,	9.7,	8.5,	2.3,	7.5

INTRODUCTION

We have previously discussed the two main characteristics of structured programs:

1. They incorporate easy-to-follow logic, which is achieved mainly by using decision and looping structures whenever possible, instead of using GOTO statements.
2. They are divided into subprograms, each of which is designed to perform a specific task.

Decision and looping structures were introduced in the two previous sections. This section will explain how programs are divided into subprograms which in BASIC are called **subroutines.** The GOSUB and ON/GOSUB statements are two methods of executing a subroutine in BASIC, and both will be covered here.

THE IMPORTANCE OF MODULARIZING PROGRAMS

The process of dividing a program into subroutines is called modularizing the program. This process is useful for two reasons:

1. The logic of a program that is divided into subroutines, each performing a distinct task, is easier to follow.
2. The same module can be executed any number of times.

For example, if the program needs to do the same task at two different points, the subroutine that performs this task may simply be executed twice. Without the subroutine, the programmer would have to write the same program segment twice.

WRITING SUBROUTINES

A subroutine is a sequence of statements, typically located after the main body of the program. Two statements in BASIC can be used to **call** a subroutine, that is, cause it to be executed. These two statements are the GOSUB and the ON/GOSUB statements.

The GOSUB Statement

The GOSUB statement transfers the flow of program control from the calling program to a subroutine. A subroutine can be called either from the main program or from another subroutine, the format of the GOSUB statement is:

line# GOSUB transfer line#

The transfer line number must be the first line number of the subroutine to be executed. This is very important, because the BASIC system will not detect an error if it is instructed to branch to an incorrect line. It will detect an error only if the transfer line number does not exist in the program. The GOSUB statement causes an unconditional branch to this specified line number. For example, the following statement will always cause a branch to the subroutine starting at line 1000:

```
120 GOSUB 1000
```

S E C T I O N

VI

Modularizing Programs

O U T L I N E

Introduction
The Importance of Modularizing
    Programs
Writing Subroutines
    The GOSUB Statement
    The RETURN Statement
    A Program Containing Multiple Calls
        to the Same Subroutine
    The ON/GOSUB Statement
Using the Structure Chart to
    Modularize a Program
Single-Entry, Single-Exit Subroutines
Comprehensive Programming Problem
    Defining the Problem
    Solution Design
    The Program
Summary Points
Review Questions
Debugging Exercises
Programming Problems

The RETURN Statement

After a subroutine is executed, the RETURN statement causes program control to return to the line following the one that contains the GOSUB statement. The format of the RETURN statement is as follows:

line# RETURN

Note that no transfer line number is needed in the RETURN statement. The BASIC system automatically returns control to the statement immediately following the GOSUB statement that called the subroutine. If the line returned to is a nonexecutable statement, such as a REM statement, the computer simply goes on to the next statement. Each subroutine must contain a RETURN statement. Otherwise, the program cannot branch back to the point from which the subroutine was called. The RETURN statement should always be the last line in the subroutine.

A Program Containing Multiple Calls to the Same Subroutine

Examine the program in Figure VI–1. This program displays a simple multiplication table. It contains a subroutine that displays a row of asterisks to divide the multiplication table into sections to make it more readable. The subroutine is called from three places in the main program: line 70, line 90, and line 190. Each time this subroutine is called, program control

FIGURE VI–1

Program Demonstrating Multiple Calls to a Subroutine

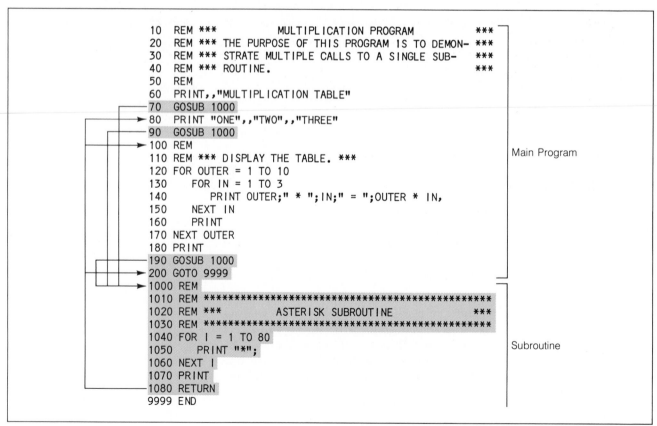

```
 10  REM ***          MULTIPLICATION PROGRAM          ***
 20  REM *** THE PURPOSE OF THIS PROGRAM IS TO DEMON- ***
 30  REM *** STRATE MULTIPLE CALLS TO A SINGLE SUB-   ***
 40  REM *** ROUTINE.                                 ***
 50  REM
 60  PRINT,,"MULTIPLICATION TABLE"
 70  GOSUB 1000
 80  PRINT "ONE",,"TWO",,"THREE"
 90  GOSUB 1000
100  REM
110  REM *** DISPLAY THE TABLE. ***
120  FOR OUTER = 1 TO 10
130      FOR IN = 1 TO 3
140          PRINT OUTER;" * ";IN;" = ";OUTER * IN,
150      NEXT IN
160      PRINT
170  NEXT OUTER
180  PRINT
190  GOSUB 1000
200  GOTO 9999
1000 REM
1010 REM ***********************************************
1020 REM ***          ASTERISK SUBROUTINE          ***
1030 REM ***********************************************
1040 FOR I = 1 TO 80
1050     PRINT "*";
1060 NEXT I
1070 PRINT
1080 RETURN
9999 END
```

Main Program

Subroutine

transfers to line 1000. Because lines 1000 through 1030 are nonexecutable statements, execution skips down to line 1040. Lines 1040 through 1060 contain a FOR/NEXT loop that is used to display a line of 80 asterisks. Then program control returns to the line following the statement that called the subroutine. In Figure VI–1, both the main program and the subroutine are labeled. Arrows are drawn to show the flow of execution of the program.

In this example, the subroutine is very short, so it would be relatively easy to repeat the necessary series of statements each time they are needed. If the subroutine were 10, 20, or more lines long, however, it would be tedious and wasteful to type it three times. Using the subroutine simplifies the program logic by organizing specific tasks into neat, orderly subsections.

Notice that the subroutine in Figure VI–1 begins at line 1000. To make programs more readable, programmers often start subroutines at readily identifiable line numbers, such as multiples of 1000. For example, the first subroutine might start at line 1000, the second at line 2000, and so forth.

FIGURE VI—1

Program Demonstrating Multiple Calls to a Subroutine continued

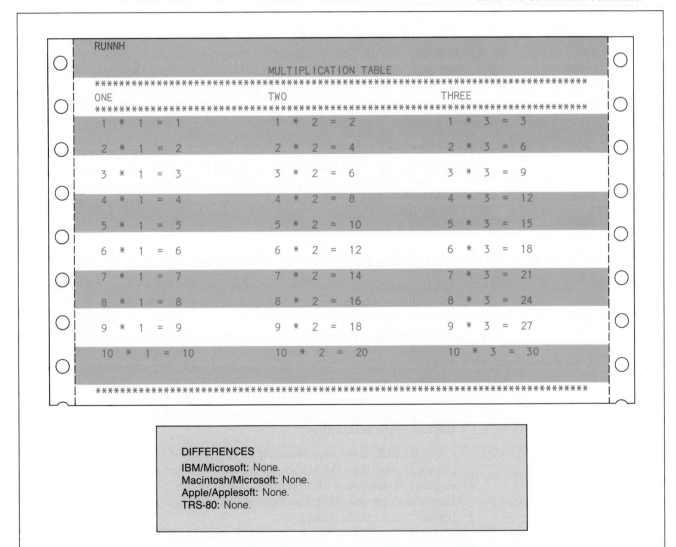

```
RUNNH
                              MULTIPLICATION TABLE
********************************************************************************
ONE                      TWO                      THREE
********************************************************************************
   1  *  1  =  1            1  *  2  =  2            1  *  3  =  3
   2  *  1  =  2            2  *  2  =  4            2  *  3  =  6
   3  *  1  =  3            3  *  2  =  6            3  *  3  =  9
   4  *  1  =  4            4  *  2  =  8            4  *  3  =  12
   5  *  1  =  5            5  *  2  =  10           5  *  3  =  15
   6  *  1  =  6            6  *  2  =  12           6  *  3  =  18
   7  *  1  =  7            7  *  2  =  14           7  *  3  =  21
   8  *  1  =  8            8  *  2  =  16           8  *  3  =  24
   9  *  1  =  9            9  *  2  =  18           9  *  3  =  27
  10  *  1  =  10          10  *  2  =  20          10  *  3  =  30

********************************************************************************
```

DIFFERENCES
IBM/Microsoft: None.
Macintosh/Microsoft: None.
Apple/Applesoft: None.
TRS-80: None.

In Figure VI–1, when program execution reaches the last line of the main program (line 200) it is ready to stop. We do not want to execute the subroutine again at this point, because it has already been called where it was needed in the program. Therefore, it is necessary to branch to the END statement, which has a line number of 9999. This branch statement will skip over any subroutines that have been placed between the end of the main program and the END statement.

The ON/GOSUB Statement

Because the GOSUB statement is an unconditional transfer statement, it always transfers program control to the subroutine starting at the indicated line number. Sometimes, however, it is necessary to branch to one of several subroutines depending on existing conditions. The ON/GOSUB statement is useful for this purpose.

The ON/GOSUB statement allows for the conditional transfer of program control to one of several subroutines. The format of the ON/GOSUB statement is:

line# ON expression GOSUB transfer line#1 [,transfer line#2]...

The ON/GOSUB uses an expression to determine the line number to which program control will transfer. The expression must be arithmetic. The transfer line numbers in the ON/GOSUB statement, however, are not within the calling program. Each transfer line number indicates the beginning of a subroutine. Consider the following ON/GOSUB statement:

```
100 ON NMBR GOSUB 2000,3000,5000
```

This statement will cause program control to transfer to one of three subroutines: the one starting at line 2000, or the one starting at 3000, or the one at 5000. The current value of NMBR determines which subroutine will be executed. If NMBR is equal to 1, control will branch to line 2000, if it is equal to 2, control will branch to line 3000, and if it is equal to 3, control will branch to line 5000.

The general execution of the ON/GOSUB can be stated as follows:

1. The expression is evaluated as an integer. On the VAX and the Apple II, this value is truncated if it is a real number; on the other systems it is rounded to the nearest integer.
2. Depending on the value of the expression, control passes to the subroutine starting at the corresponding line number. If the value of the expression is 1, control passes to the first line number listed, if it is 2, control passes to the second line number listed, and so on.
3. After the specified subroutine is executed, control is transferred back to the line following the ON/GOSUB statement by a RETURN statement at the end of the subroutine.

On the VAX, if the expression in an ON/GOSUB statement evaluates as a number larger than the number of transfer line numbers indicated, an error message is displayed and program execution terminates. When this situation occurs on the microcomputers, program control is simply passed to the next executable statement.

Figure VI–2 demonstrates a simple use of the ON/GOSUB statement. The user enters an integer value representing his or her year in college (1, 2, 3,

```
10    REM ***              GRADUATION PROGRAM           ***
20    REM ***                                           ***
30    REM *** THIS PROGRAM DISPLAYS THE CLASS A STUDENT ***
40    REM *** BELONGS TO (FRESHMAN, SOPHOMORE, JUNIOR,  ***
50    REM *** SENIOR) AND THE YEAR OF GRADUATION WHEN    ***
60    REM *** THE CORRESPONDING INTEGER (1, 2, 3, OR 4) ***
70    REM *** IS ENTERED.                                ***
80    REM *** MAJOR VARIABLES:                           ***
90    REM ***     STUDENT$        STUDENT'S NAME         ***
100   REM ***     YR             YEAR                    ***
110   REM
120   REM *** ENTER THE NECESSARY DATA. ***
130   INPUT "ENTER THE STUDENT'S NAME";STUDENT$
140   INPUT "ENTER THE STUDENT'S YEAR (1, 2, 3, OR 4)";YR
150   REM
160   REM *** BRANCH TO SUBROUTINE TO DISPLAY MESSAGE. ***
170   ON YR GOSUB 1000,2000,3000,4000
180   GOTO 9999
1000  REM
1010  REM ************************************************
1020  REM ***              SUBROUTINE FRESHMAN          ***
1030  REM ************************************************
1040  REM
1050  PRINT STUDENT$;" IS A FRESHMAN"
1060  PRINT "AND WILL GRADUATE IN 1993."
1070  RETURN
2000  REM
2010  REM ************************************************
2020  REM ***              SUBROUTINE SOPHOMORE         ***
2030  REM ************************************************
2040  REM
2050  PRINT STUDENT$;" IS A SOPHOMORE"
2060  PRINT "AND WILL GRADUATE IN 1992."
2070  RETURN
3000  REM
3010  REM ************************************************
3020  REM ***              SUBROUTINE JUNIOR            ***
3030  REM ************************************************
3040  REM
3050  PRINT STUDENT$;" IS A JUNIOR"
3060  PRINT "AND WILL GRADUATE IN 1991."
3070  RETURN
4000  REM
4010  REM ************************************************
4020  REM ***              SUBROUTINE SENIOR            ***
4030  REM ************************************************
4040  REM
4050  PRINT STUDENT$;" IS A SENIOR"
4060  PRINT "AND WILL GRADUATE IN 1990."
4070  RETURN
9999  END
```

or 4). This integer value is assigned to the variable YR, which is then used to determine which subroutine will be executed. Depending on the subroutine called, a message will be displayed stating the year that the student will graduate.

FIGURE VI–2

Program Using the ON/GOSUB Statement continued

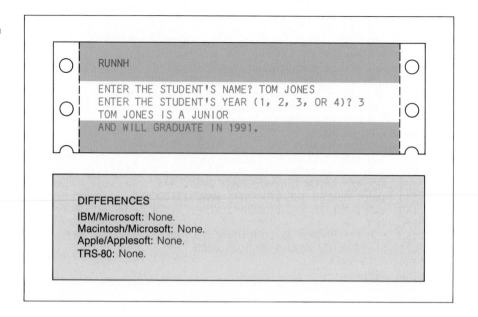

```
RUNNH

ENTER THE STUDENT'S NAME? TOM JONES
ENTER THE STUDENT'S YEAR (1, 2, 3, OR 4)? 3
TOM JONES IS A JUNIOR
AND WILL GRADUATE IN 1991.
```

DIFFERENCES
IBM/Microsoft: None.
Macintosh/Microsoft: None.
Apple/Applesoft: None.
TRS-80: None.

USING THE STRUCTURE CHART TO MODULARIZE A PROGRAM

So far in this supplement, we have been using structure charts to help analyze the steps necessary to solve programming problems. Structure charts enable us to visualize the specific tasks a program must perform to achieve the desired overall result. Because structure charts represent the subtasks involved in solving a problem, they are helpful in developing modularized programs. Once the tasks of a program are identified, often each of these can be implemented in the program as a separate subroutine.

We will illustrate this use of structure charts with a simple problem. We are going to write a program that will calculate the cost of a long distance phone call based on the following table (note that the user should enter the number of miles as an integer value):

Distance of Call	Cost per Minute
Within 90 miles	12¢ per minute for first 5 minutes, 10¢ per minute thereafter
Between 100 and 199 miles	15¢ per minute for the first 5 minutes, 13¢ per minute thereafter
Between 200 and 299 miles	18¢ per minute, regardless of length of call

No phone calls can be placed outside the 299-mile radius.

First we need to develop an algorithm for this problem. The steps needed to solve this problem can be listed in this way:

1. Enter the distance and the length of time of the call.
2. Calculate the cost of the call based on the distance.
3. Print the cost of the call.

A structure chart for this problem is shown at the top of Figure VI–3. Steps 1 and 3 are simple enough to implement: Step 1 can be written as a subroutine that allows the user to enter the distance and length of time of the call, and Step 3 can be written as a subroutine that displays the final cost with an appropriate label. Because these are such simple steps, they could be included within the main program itself. In this example, however, we

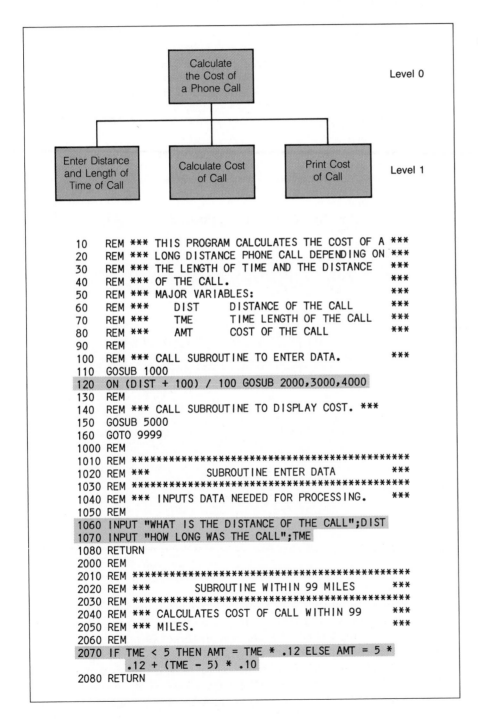

continued on next page

FIGURE VI–3

Program Using a Calculated Value in an ON/GOSUB Statement

FIGURE VI—3

**Program Using a Calculated Value
in an ON/GOSUB Statement**
continued

```
3000 REM
3010 REM *******************************************
3020 REM ***          SUBROUTINE 100 - 199 MILES        ***
3030 REM *******************************************
3040 REM *** CALCULATES COST OF CALL IN 100 - 199 ***
3050 REM *** MILE RANGE.                             ***
3060 REM
3070 IF TME < 5 THEN AMT = TME * .15 ELSE AMT = 5 *
         .15 + (TME - 5) * .13
3080 RETURN
4000 REM
4010 REM *******************************************
4020 REM ***          SUBROUTINE 200 - 299 MILES        ***
4030 REM *******************************************
4040 REM *** CALCULATES COST OF CALL IN 200 - 200 ***
4050 REM *** MILE RANGE.                             ***
4060 AMT = TME * .18
4070 RETURN
5000 REM
5010 REM *******************************************
5020 REM ***             SUBROUTINE PRINT COST           ***
5030 REM *******************************************
5040 REM *** PRINTS COST OF THE TELEPHONE CALL.    ***
5050 REM
5060 PRINT "THE COST OF THIS PHONE CALL IS ";AMT
5070 RETURN
9999 END
```

```
RUNNH

WHAT IS THE DISTANCE OF THE CALL? 100
HOW LONG WAS THE CALL? 5
THE COST OF THIS PHONE CALL IS  .75
```

DIFFERENCES

IBM/Microsoft: 120 ON (DIST +50)/100 GOSUB 2000, 3000, 4000.
Macintosh/Microsoft: 120 ON (DIST + 50)/100 GOSUB 2000, 3000, 4000.
Apple/Applesoft: No IF/THEN/ELSE statement.
TRS-80: 120 ON (DIST + 50)/100 GOSUB 2000, 3000, 4000.

are including them as subroutines to demonstrate how every task in the program can be modularized.

Step 2 is more complex. We want the program to use one of three rates in determining the cost, depending on the distance. This is a situation that is well suited to the ON/GOSUB statement; three subroutines can be used to perform these calculations as shown in Figure VI–3. The following ON/GOSUB statement will cause program control to be transferred to the needed subroutine if the computer system being used is one that truncates the value of the ON/GOSUB expression (such as the VAX or the Apple):

```
120 ON (DIST + 100) / 100 GOSUB 2000,3000,4000
```

Let's test this expression by assuming that the number of miles entered is 199. When 199 is substituted for DIST the statement looks like this:

```
120 ON (199 + 100) / 100 GOSUB 2000,3000,4000
```

The expression (199 + 100) / 100 is equal to 2.99. This number is truncated to 2, so the program will branch to the second subroutine, which starts at line 3000. This is the subroutine used to calculate phone bills in the 100- to 199-miles radius, which is exactly what we want.

Test this statement yourself, using different values for the distance. If your BASIC system rounds the expression rather than truncating it (the IBM, Macintosh, and TRS–80 all round the expression), the expression must be written differently, in this form:

```
120 ON (DIST + 50) / 100 GOSUB 2000,3000,4000
```

The expression evaluates as 2.49, which rounds to 2. This value will cause the program to correctly branch to the subroutine starting at line 3000.

It is often possible to use expressions similar to the preceding one in ON/GOSUB statements. They can simplify the programming process, but they must be thoroughly tested to make certain that they will always evaluate as expected.

Examine the program in Figure VI–3. Note that the main program contains only four executable statements, three of which are used to call subroutines; the fourth statement branches to the end of the program. This is an example of a **driver program,** that is, a program whose main purpose is to call subprograms. These subprograms then perform the actual processing.

■ SINGLE ENTRY, SINGLE EXIT SUBROUTINES

Each subroutine should have only one entry point and one exit point. This is an important principle of structured programming. A subroutine may be called any number of times in a given program, but it should always be entered at the first line of the subroutine. Branching to the middle of a subroutine makes program logic virtually impossible to follow and often leads to errors.

Figure VI–4 illustrates two program segments, both of which perform the same task. The top segment is incorrectly written, because the IF/THEN/ELSE statement in line 110 can allow control to be passed either to the first line of the subroutine (line 1000) or to the middle of the subroutine (line 1060). The bottom example shows how this segment can be correctly written. Note that an IF/THEN statement within the subroutine is used to control execution.

Likewise, a subroutine should contain only one RETURN statement, which should be the last statement of the subroutine. This rule is referred to as the single-exit-point principle. At the top of Figure VI–5 is a program segment that is incorrectly written because it contains two RETURN statements, one in line 1050 and another in line 1080. The bottom program segment accomplishes the same task by using an IF/THEN statement (line 1050) to branch to the RETURN statement at the end of the subroutine.

FIGURE VI—4

Demonstration of Single-Entry Subroutine Principle

```
100   INPUT "ENTER YOUR SCORE";PTS
110   IF PTS > 80 THEN GOSUB 1000 ELSE GOSUB 1060
120   GOTO 9999
1000 REM
1010 REM ***********************************************
1020 REM ***                SUBROUTINE                ***
1030 REM ***********************************************
1040 REM
1050 PRINT "YOU DID VERY WELL!"
1060 PRINT "YOU PASSED THE COURSE."
1070 RETURN
9999 END
```

Incorrectly Written Program Segment With Branch to the Middle of Subroutine

```
100   INPUT "ENTER YOUR SCORE";PTS
110   GOSUB 1000
120   GOTO 9999
1000 REM
1010 REM ***********************************************
1020 REM ***                SUBROUTINE                ***
1030 REM ***********************************************
1040 REM
1050 IF PTS > 0 THEN PRINT "YOU DID VERY WELL!"
1060 PRINT "YOU PASSED THE COURSE."
1070 RETURN
9999 END
```

Correctly Written Program Segment With a Single-Entry Point to Subroutine

DIFFERENCES

IBM/Microsoft: None.
Macintosh/Microsoft: None.
Apple/Applesoft: None.
TRS-80: None.

■ COMPREHENSIVE PROGRAMMING PROBLEM

Defining the Problem

Kelley's Best Burgers would like a program to calculate the cost of customer orders. Kelley's has only four items on its menu:

Hamburgers	$1.00
Cheeseburgers	$1.25
French fries	$0.80
Soft drinks	$0.75

The manager would like the program to display a list of the items available and allow the customer to choose the item to be purchased. The customer should then be prompted to enter the quantity of that item desired. The

FIGURE VI–5

Demonstration of Single-Exit Subroutine Principle

```
100   INPUT "ENTER YOUR SCORE";PTS
110   GOSUB 1000
120   GOTO 9999
1000 REM
1010 REM *********************************************
1020 REM ***              SUBROUTINE              ***
1030 REM *********************************************
1040 REM
1050 IF PTS < 80 THEN PRINT "YOU FAILED" \ RETURN
        ELSE PRINT "YOU PASSED"
1060 CREDITHR = CREDITHR + 4
1070 ST$ = "OK"
1080 RETURN
9999 END
```

Incorrectly Written Program Segment With Multiple RETURNs

```
100   INPUT "ENTER YOUR SCORE";PTS
110   GOSUB 1000
120   GOTO 9999
1000 REM
1010 REM *********************************************
1020 REM ***              SUBROUTINE              ***
1030 REM *********************************************
1040 REM
1050 IF PTS < 80 THEN PRINT "YOU FAILED" \ GOTO 1080
        ELSE PRINT "YOU PASSED"
1060 CREDITHR = CREDITHR + 4
1070 ST$ = "OK"
1080 RETURN
9999 END
```

Correctly Written Program Segment With a Single RETURN

DIFFERENCES

IBM/Microsoft: Line 1050: Use colons to separate statements.
Macintosh/Microsoft: Line 1050: Use colons to separate statements.
Apple/Applesoft: Line 1050: Multiple statements on a single line not allowed.
TRS-80: Line 1050: Use colons to separate statements.

---

program should allow the customer to enter as many items as desired. When the customer is through ordering, the total bill should be displayed.

Solution Design

This program needs to display a menu listing the choices available. Menus are used to allow the user to choose from a number of options. The menu should appear as follows:

```
CODE NUMBER    ITEM            COST OF ITEM

------------------------------------------------------------

1              HAMBURGER       $1.00
2              CHEESEBURGER    $1.25
3              FRENCH FRIES    $0.80
4              SOFT DRINK      $0.75

5                              END OF ORDER

ENTER CODE FOR FOOD ITEM (5 TO FINISH) ?
```

The customer can enter the integer value representing the desired item. If the order is complete, the customer should enter a 5. The total amount of the order can then be displayed. This problem can be divided as follows:

1. Display a menu listing the items and their prices.
2. Determine each item to be purchased and the quantity of that item.
3. Display total bill.

Because there are four items, step 2 can be further divided as follows:

2.A. Determine cost of hamburgers and add to total.
2.B. Determine cost of cheeseburgers and add to total.
2.C. Determine cost of french fries and add to total.
2.D. Determine cost of soft drinks and add to total.

A structure chart for this program is shown in Figure VI–6.

We will want to use a WHILE loop to allow the customer to select as many items as desired. A subroutine can be used to display the menu so that the customer can select the desired item. An ON/GOSUB statement can then be used to branch to one of five subroutines. Subroutines 2 through

FIGURE VI–6

Structure Chart for Restaurant Bill Problem

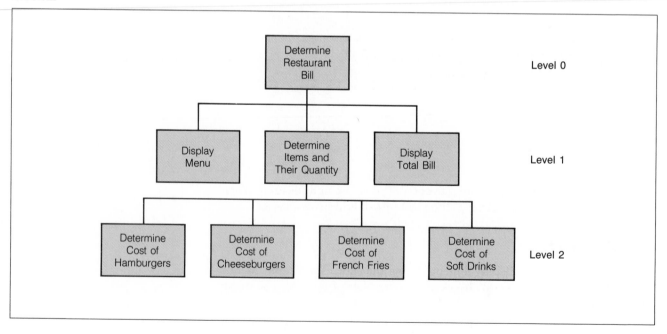

COMPUTERS AND INFORMATION PROCESSING

5 can calculate the amount owed for each type of food. The sixth subroutine can be executed when the customer enters a 5, indicating that the order is complete. This last subroutine should display the total amount of the bill. Figure VI–7 contains a flowchart for this problem.

continued on next page

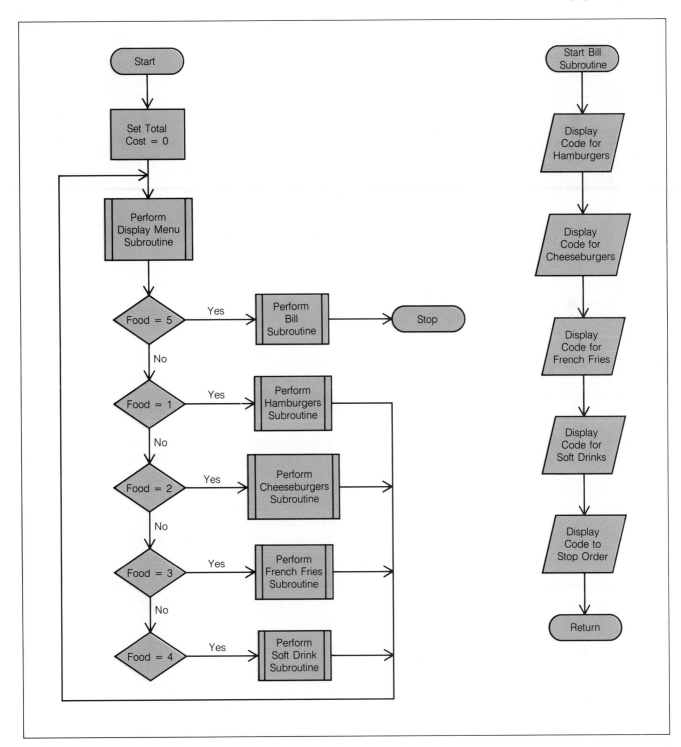

FIGURE VI–7

Flowchart for Restaurant Bill Problem

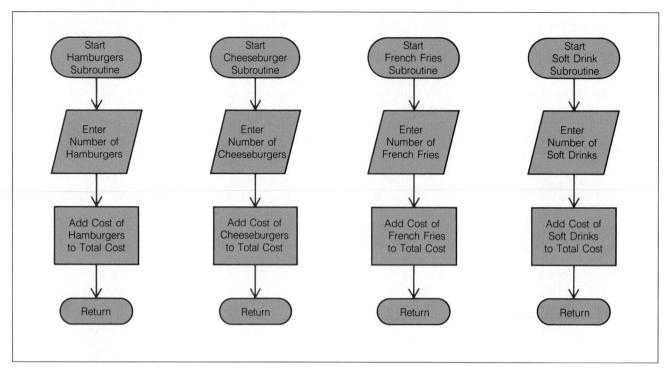

FIGURE VI-7

Flowchart for Restaurant Bill Problem continued

The Program

The completed program is shown in Figure VI–8. Notice that the main program contains only six executable statements. First, the total amount owed (TTCST) is set to zero. Then a WHILE loop is entered to allow the customer to enter as many items as desired. At the beginning of each execution of the loop, control is transferred to the subroutine at line 1000 which displays the menu. Line 220 contains an ON/GOSUB statement which determines which of five subroutines is executed, depending on the value entered for FOOD. For example, if the customer enters a 1, control is transferred to the subroutine starting at line 2000 and CST is assigned the price of a hamburger (1.00). The customer is prompted to enter the desired number of hamburgers and this value is multiplied by CST to get the total cost of the hamburgers. This amount is added to TTCST to give the current total bill.

This process continues until the customer enters a 5, indicating the end of the order. Control is then transferred to the subroutine at line 6000 where the amount owed is displayed.

FIGURE VI–8

Program for Calculating Restaurant Bill

continued on next page

```
10   REM ***                  PROGRAM MEAL COST                   ***
20   REM ***                                                      ***
30   REM *** THIS PROGRAM CALCULATES THE COST OF A PURCHASE       ***
40   REM *** AT A FAST FOOD RESTAURANT. THE USER IS PROMPTED      ***
50   REM *** TO ENTER AN INTEGER REPRESENTING THE ITEM TO BE      ***
60   REM *** BE PURCHASED.  THE USER THEN ENTERS HOW MANY OF      ***
70   REM *** THAT ITEM ARE DESIRED.  THE COST OF THAT ITEM IS     ***
80   REM *** THEN CALCULATED.  THE USER IS ALLOWED TO ORDER       ***
90   REM *** AS MANY ITEMS AS DESIRED.  WHEN THE ORDER IS         ***
100  REM *** COMPLETED, THE TOTAL BILL IS DISPLAYED.              ***
110  REM *** MAJOR VARIABLES:                                     ***
120  REM ***    FOOD     CODE INDICATING TYPE OF FOOD             ***
130  REM ***    CST      COST OF AN ITEM                          ***
140  REM ***    NMBR     QUANTITY OF AN ITEM                      ***
150  REM ***    TTCST    TOTAL COST OF ORDER                      ***
160  REM
170  REM *** INITIALIZE TOTAL COST TO ZERO. ***
180  LET TTCST = 0
190  REM *** LOOP TO MAKE SELECTIONS. ***
200  WHILE FOOD <> 5
210     GOSUB 1000
220     ON FOOD GOSUB 2000,3000,4000,5000,6000
230  NEXT
240  GOTO 9999
1000 REM ******************************************************
1010 REM ***              SUBROUTINE DISPLAY MENU             ***
1020 REM ******************************************************
1030 REM
1040 PRINT
1050 PRINT "CODE NUMBER","ITEM","COST OF ITEM"
1060 PRINT
1070 FOR I = 1 TO 60
1080    PRINT "-";
1090 NEXT I
1100 PRINT
1110 PRINT 1,"HAMBURGER","$1.00"
1120 PRINT 2,"CHEESEBURGER","$1.25"
1130 PRINT 3,"FRENCH FRIES","$0.80"
1140 PRINT 4,"SOFT DRINK","$0.75"
1150 PRINT
1160 PRINT 5,"END OF ORDER"
1170 PRINT
1180 INPUT "ENTER CODE FOR FOOD ITEM (5 TO FINISH) ";FOOD
1190 RETURN
2000 REM ******************************************************
2010 REM ***              SUBROUTINE HAMBURGERS               ***
2020 REM ******************************************************
2030 REM
2040 LET CST = 1.00
2050 INPUT "HOW MANY HAMBURGERS DO YOU WANT TO ORDER";NMBR
2060 TTCST = TTCST + (CST * NMBR)
2070 RETURN
3000 REM ******************************************************
3010 REM ***             SUBROUTINE CHEESEBURGERS             ***
3020 REM ******************************************************
3030 REM
3040 LET CST = 1.25
3050 INPUT "HOW MANY CHEESEBURGERS DO YOU WANT TO ORDER";NMBR
```

FIGURE VI–8

Program for Calculating Restaurant Bill continued

```
3060 TTCST = TTCST + (CST * NMBR)
3070 RETURN
4000 REM ****************************************************
4010 REM ***              SUBROUTINE FRENCH FRIES         ***
4020 REM ****************************************************
4030 REM
4040 LET CST = 0.80
4050 INPUT "HOW MANY FRENCH FRIES DO YOU WANT TO ORDER";NMBR
4060 TTCST = TTCST + (CST * NMBR)
4070 RETURN
5000 REM ****************************************************
5010 REM ***              SUBROUTINE DRINKS               ***
5020 REM ****************************************************
5030 REM
5040 LET CST = 0.75
5050 INPUT "HOW MANY SOFT DRINKS DO YOU WANT TO ORDER";NMBR
5060 TTCST = TTCST + (CST * NMBR)
5070 RETURN
6000 REM ****************************************************
6010 REM ***                SUBROUTINE BILL               ***
6020 REM ****************************************************
6030 PRINT
6040 PRINT "THE TOTAL AMOUNT DUE IS $";TTCST
6050 RETURN
9999 END
```

```
RUNNH

CODE NUMBER     ITEM          COST OF ITEM
--------------------------------------------------
   1            HAMBURGER      $1.00
   2            CHEESEBURGER   $1.25
   3            FRENCH FRIES   $0.80
   4            SOFT DRINK     $0.75

   5            END OF ORDER

ENTER CODE FOR FOOD ITEM (5 TO FINISH) ? 2
HOW MANY CHEESEBURGERS DO YOU WANT TO ORDER? 4

CODE NUMBER     ITEM          COST OF ITEM
--------------------------------------------------
   1            HAMBURGER      $1.00
   2            CHEESEBURGER   $1.25
   3            FRENCH FRIES   $0.80
   4            SOFT DRINK     $0.75

   5            END OF ORDER

ENTER CODE FOR FOOD ITEM (5 TO FINISH) ? 3
HOW MANY FRENCH FRIES DO YOU WANT TO ORDER? 3
```

```
CODE NUMBER    ITEM           COST OF ITEM

----------------------------------------------------------
 1             HAMBURGER      $1.00
 2             CHEESEBURGER   $1.25
 3             FRENCH FRIES   $0.80
 4             SOFT DRINK     $0.75

 5             END OF ORDER

ENTER CODE FOR FOOD ITEM (5 TO FINISH) ? 4
HOW MANY SOFT DRINKS DO YOU WANT TO ORDER? 3

CODE NUMBER    ITEM           COST OF ITEM

----------------------------------------------------------
 1             HAMBURGER      $1.00
 2             CHEESEBURGER   $1.25
 3             FRENCH FRIES   $0.80
 4             SOFT DRINK     $0.75

 5             END OF ORDER

ENTER CODE FOR FOOD ITEM (5 TO FINISH) ? 5

THE TOTAL AMOUNT DUE IS $ 9.65
```

DIFFERENCES
IBM/Microsoft: 240 WEND.
Macintosh/Microsoft: 240 WEND.
Apple/Applesoft: No WHILE loop.
TRS-80: 240 WEND.

FIGURE VI–8

Program for Calculating Restaurant Bill continued

SUMMARY POINTS

- Modularizing programs involves dividing them into subroutines, each of which performs a specific task.
- The use of subroutines makes program logic easier to follow. Also, a given subroutine can be called any number of times.
- Two BASIC statements can be used to call subroutines: the GOSUB and the ON/GOSUB.
- The GOSUB statement is an unconditional branch that causes the flow of execution to be passed to the line number contained in the GOSUB statement.
- The RETURN statement causes control to be transferred back to the statement after the one that called the subroutine.
- The ON/GOSUB statement allows for a conditional branch to one of several stated subroutines, depending on the evaluation of the expression in the ON/GOSUB statement.

■ An important rule in structured programming is that all subroutines should have a single entry point and a single exit point. Otherwise, the possibility of an error in the program is greatly increased. Also, entering or exiting from the middle of a subroutine makes the logic of the program convoluted and difficult to follow.

▦ REVIEW QUESTIONS

1. Name the advantages of modularizing programs.

2. Why is the GOSUB statement referred to as an unconditional transfer statement?

3. How can a structure chart help in modularizing a program?

4. Why is it important that a subroutine have only one entry point and one exit point?

5. Where will program control be transferred if the following statements are executed?

```
260 LET X = 4 + 23
270 LET N = X / 8 + 1
280 ON N GOSUB 1000,2000,3000,4000
```

6. Rewrite the following program segment using a single ON/GOSUB statement:

```
350 IF X = 1 THEN GOSUB 2000
360 IF X = 2 THEN GOSUB 3000
370 IF X = 3 THEN GOSUB 4000
```

7. Explain how the ON/GOSUB statement works. How is it different from the GOSUB statement?

8. What is a driver program?

▦ DEBUGGING EXERCISES

Identify the following programs and program segments that contain errors and correct them.

```
1. 10 REM *** BRANCH TO SUBROUTINE TO DISPLAY    ***
   20 REM *** GRADE DEPENDING ON VALUE OF SCORE. ***
   30 INPUT "ENTER STUDENT'S SCORE (1-5);PTS$
   40 ON PTS$ GOSUB 1000,2000,3000,4000,5000
2. 10 GOSUB 1000
   20 PRINT X
      .
      .
      .
   1000 REM ***           SUBROUTINE        ***
   1010 REM
   1020 LET X = 12 * 77
   9999 END
```

▨ PROGRAMMING PROBLEMS

1. Assume that a numeric variable named AMT can contain the value 2, 4, 6, or 8. Write a program segment that asks the user to enter a value to AMT. The program should then call one of three subroutines depending on the value of AMT:

AMT = 2, go to subroutine starting at line 1000

AMT = 4, go to subroutine starting at line 2000

AMT = 6, go to subroutine starting at line 3000

AMT = 8, go to subroutine starting at line 5000

2. Think of a song you know that contains a refrain. Write a program that will display the words to this song. Use a different subroutine for each of the verses and a subroutine for the refrain. Then after each verse is displayed, call the refrain subroutine to display the refrain.

3. Write a subroutine that will calculate the area and the volume of a cube. Call a subroutine to perform the calculations. The user should be prompted to enter the dimensions of the cube during program execution. The results should then be displayed.

4. World Travel wants a program that displays a menu with a list of cities to which it has special discount rates. After the user enters the name of a particular country, the program should display all cities in that country for which the special rates are available. Use the following data:

Country	Cities
France	Nice
	Cannes
	Nantes
	Chamonix
Italy	Milan
	Verona
	Venice
	Naples
U.S.A.	Chicago
	San Francisco
	New York
	Miami

5. Stan's Television Corporation needs a program to help with the billing of its customers. The user should be able to enter the due date for all bills to be processed. For each customer, enter a name, address, and the applicable charges selected from the following list:

Standard service	$7.00
Cable service	4.00
Home Cinema Channel	2.00
Continual Cartoon Channel	2.00

All customers receive the standard service. The program should print an itemized bill showing the total amount due and the amount owed for late payment, which is the total plus 5 percent. Use your own test data. Your output should resemble the following:

NAME: DUE DATE:
ADDRESS:

SERVICES:

    STANDARD SERVICE $ 7.00
    CABLE SERVICE   4.00
    CONTINUAL CARTOON CHANNEL   2.00

    TOTAL AMOUNT DUE: $13.00
    AFTER DUE DATE: $13.65

BASIC Glossary

Algorithm A sequence of steps arranged in a specific, logical order, which is followed to solve a problem.

Argument A value used by a function to obtain its result.

Call To cause a subroutine to be executed. When a subroutine is called, program execution is transferred to that subroutine.

Character-string constants Alphanumeric data that is enclosed in quotation marks. The quotation marks are not part of the character string, but serve only to delimit the string.

Conditional transfer statement A statement in which a condition is tested; the path of program execution is dependent on the result of this test.

Constant A value that does not change during program execution.

Control statement A statement that allows the programmer to alter the order in which statements are executed.

Counting loop A loop that is executed a specified number of times; the number of executions must be determined before the loop is entered for the first time.

Data list A single list containing the values in all of the data statements in a program; the values appear in the list in the order in which they occur in the program.

Debug To locate and correct program errors.

Decision statement A statement that makes a comparison; the action that is taken next depends on the result of this comparison.

Documentation Statements that explain a program to people; documentation is ignored by the computer.

Driver program A program whose main purpose is to call subroutines, which do the actual work of the program.

Flowchart A graphic representation of the solution to a programming problem.

Function A subprogram that is designed to perform a specific task and return a single value.

Hierarchy of operations The order in which arithmetic operations are performed.

Infinite loop A loop that will continue to execute until the computer system's resources are exhausted.

Library function A function built into the BASIC language.

Logic error A flaw in an algorithm developed to solve a programming problem.

Loop A control statement that allows a specified segment of a program to be repeated as many times as necessary.

Loop control variable A variable that determines whether a loop will be executed.

Module See Subprogram.

Numeric constant A numeric value that does not change during program execution.

Numeric variable A variable that contains numeric data.

Programming The processing of writing instructions for a computer to use to solve a problem.

Programming process The steps used to develop a solution to a programming problem.

Prompt A statement that explains to the user what data items are to be entered.

Pseudocode An English-like description of a program's logic.

Relational symbol A symbol that is used to specify a relationship between two values. The relational symbols in BASIC are $<$, $<=$, $>$, $>=$, $<>$, and $=$.

Reserved word A word that has a specific meaning to the BASIC compiler or interpreter. These words cannot be used as variable names.

Sentinel value See Trailer value.

Software A program or a series of programs.

String variable A variable that contains string data.

Structure chart A diagram that visually illustrates how a problem solution has been developed and indicates how the subtasks are related to one another.

Structured programming A method of programming in which programs have easy-to-follow logic and are divided into subprograms, each designed to perform a specific task.

Subprogram A distinct part of a larger program designed to perform a specific task. In structured programming, subprograms are used to make a program's logic easier to follow.

Subroutine A subprogram in a BASIC program containing a sequence of statements designed to perform a specific task; it usually follows the main program.

Syntax The grammatical rules of a language.

Syntax error A violation of the grammatical rules of a language.

Top-down design A method of solving a problem that proceeds from the general to the specific.

Trailer value A value used to control loop repetition; it indicates the end of the input data.

Unconditional branch See Unconditional transfer statement.

Unconditional transfer statement A statement that always transfers control to a specified line.

Variable A storage location which contains a value that can change during program execution.

West Student Pro Pack™ (IBM®/MS-DOS®) Supplement

O U T L I N E

Section A: Introduction to Word Processing and WordPerfect
Introduction
Definitions
Uses of Word Processors
Guide to WordPerfect
Getting Started with WordPerfect
Creating a New Document
Editing a Document
Section B: Advanced WordPerfect
Introduction
Formatting a Document
More Advanced Features
Section C: Introduction to Spreadsheets and VP-Planner Plus
Introduction
Definitions
Uses of Spreadsheets
Guide to VP-Planner Plus
Getting Started with VP-Planner Plus
Saving and Retrieving Files
Getting Help with VP-Planner Plus
Quitting a File and Quitting the Access System
Creating a Worksheet
Changing the Appearance of a Worksheet
Printing a Worksheet
Section D: Advanced VP-Planner Plus
Introduction
Copy and Move
The Difference between Global and Range Commands

Functions
Copying Formulas
Freezing Titles
Order of Precedence
Spreadsheet Analysis
Graphics
Section E: Introduction to Data Managers and dBASE III PLUS
Introduction
Definitions
Uses of Data Managers
Guide to dBASE III PLUS
Getting Started with dBASE III PLUS
Using the Assistant Menu
Selecting Menu Options
Getting Help with dBASE III PLUS
Quitting dBASE III PLUS
Defining the Structure of a Data-Base File
Entering Data into a Data-Base File
Updating a Data-Base File
Managing Files with the Tools Option
Relational and Logical Operators
Going to a Specific Record
dBASE III Summary Commands
Section F: Advanced dBASE III PLUS
Introduction
Sorting a Data-Base File
Indexing a File
Searching an Indexed Data-Base File
Creating a Report with dBASE III PLUS
Modifying a Report

Printing a Report
Summary of dBASE III PLUS Menus
Section G: Introduction to Expert Systems and VP-Expert
Introduction
Definitions
Uses of Expert Systems
Guide to VP-Expert
Getting Started with VP-Expert
Getting Help with VP-Expert
Creating a Knowledge Base from an Induction Table
Understanding the Parts of an Induction Table
Editing a Knowledge Base
Checking for Errors in the Knowledge Base
VP-Expert Clauses
Adding Variables to the Knowledge Base
Section H: Advanced VP-Expert
Introduction
Using Confidence Factors
Assigning Multiple Values to a Variable
Using the Logical Operator OR
Using the Why? and How? Commands
Formatting the Consultation
Printing a Hard Copy of Display Text
Using Mathematical Operations
Assigning Values to Variables with End User Input

S E C T I O N

A

Introduction to Word Processing and WordPerfect

O U T L I N E

Introduction
Definitions
Uses of Word Processors
Learning Check
Guide to WordPerfect
Getting Started with WordPerfect
Learning Check
Creating a New Document
   Entering Text
   Saving a Document
   Retrieving a Document
Learning Check
Editing a Document
   Moving the Cursor
   Removing Text
   Moving Blocks of Text
   The Speller and Thesaurus
   Printing
Learning Check
Summary Points
WordPerfect Exercises
WordPerfect Problems

■ INTRODUCTION

Of all the application software available, word processors meet the largest variety of users' needs. The number of programs that have been developed to serve this incredibly wide range of needs has made word processing the largest and most competitive market in application software. Word processors not only are a useful tool for more users than any other application program, they are the easiest application software program to learn. These two facts combine to make word processors huge sellers.

Word processors have not only improved, but enhanced the writing process. In the first generation of word processors, users were satisfied with simply being able to edit text before it appeared on paper. Word processors enable users to change, move, or erase words, sentences, and paragraphs without retyping the whole document. The final version is printed only after the writer is completely satisfied with it. Today, such standard features are old hat. Many word processors now enhance the writing process by checking spelling, offering a better word choice with a thesaurus, and automatically compiling an index or a table of contents.

This section introduces you to word processing—what it is and what its uses are. In addition, it provides instructions on how to get started using WordPerfect, one of the most popular word-processing packages on the market today.

■ DEFINITIONS

A **word processor** is a program or set of programs which enables a computer user to write, edit, format, and print text. As characters are typed on a keyboard, they appear on the computer screen. Mistakes can be corrected easily because the text has not yet been put on paper. Words, sentences, and even entire paragraphs can be moved by special commands. Nothing is printed on paper until the user is satisfied with the results.

Word processing refers to the act of composing and editing text. The words are composed and rearranged in the user's mind; the word processor and the hardware provide a convenient way to display, store, edit, and recall the creative work that has been done.

A **word-processing system** includes the hardware and software used for the purpose of word processing. There are two general types of word-processing systems: (a) **dedicated systems,** which are basically microcomputers equipped to handle only word processing; and (b) **multipurpose microcomputers,** which are equipped to handle a wide variety of processing tasks, including word processing.

In the early days of word processing, the serious user's only choice was a dedicated system. With the development of faster and more sophisticated microcomputers, however, came the development of microcomputer-compatible word processors such as WordPerfect. Today most, if not all, multipurpose microcomputers on the market have at least one word processor available for them.

Although a word processor is actually a program or programs, many people refer to the combination of both software and hardware as a word processor. Table A–1 provides a quick reference to other terms often used in connection with word processors.

Frequently Encountered Word Processing Terms

Term	Definition
Automatic pagination	A feature that enables a word processor to number the pages of the printed copy automatically.
Block	A group of characters, such as a sentence or paragraph.
Block movement	A feature that allows the user to define a block of text and then perform a specific operation on the entire block. Common block operations include block move, block copy, block save, and block delete.
Boldface	Heavy type, for example, this is **boldface.**
Character	A letter, number, or symbol.
Character enhancement	Underlining, boldfacing, subscripting, and superscripting.
Control character	A coded character that does not print but is part of the command sequence in a word processor.
Cursor	The marker on the display screen indicating where the next character can be displayed.
Default setting	A value used by the word processor when it is not instructed to use any other.
Deletion	A feature by which a character, word, sentence, or larger block of text can be removed from the existing text.
Document-oriented word processor	A word processor that operates on a text file as one long document.
Editing	The act of changing or reformatting text.
Format	The layout of a page; for example, the number of lines, margin settings, and so on.
Global	An instruction that will be carried out throughout an entire document, for example, global search and replace.
Header	A piece of text that is stored separately from the text and printed at the top of each page.
Incremental spacing	A method by which the printer inserts spaces between words and letters to produce justified margins; also called *microspacing*.
Insertion	A feature in which a character, word, sentence, or larger block of text is added to the existing text.
Justification	A feature for making lines of text even at the margins.
Line editor	The type of editor that allows the user to edit only one line at a time.

Table continued on next page

TABLE A—1

Continued

Term	Definition
Memory-only word processor	A word processor that cannot exchange text between internal memory and disk during the editing process.
Menu	A list of commands or prompts on the display screen.
Page-oriented word processor	A word processor that operates on a text file as a series of pages.
Print formatting	The function of a word processor which communicates with the printer to tell it how to print the text on paper.
Print preview	A feature that enables the user to view a general representation on the screen of how the document will look when printed.
Screen editor	The type of editor that enables the user to edit an entire screen at a time.
Screen formatting	A function of a word processor which controls how the text will appear on the screen.
Scrolling	Moving a line of text onto or off the screen.
Search and find	A routine that searches for, and places the cursor at, a specified string of characters.
Search and replace	A routine that searches for a specified character string and replaces it with the specified replacement string.
Status line	A message line above or below the text area on a display screen which gives format and system information.
Subscript	A character that prints below the usual text baseline.
Superscript	A character that prints above the usual text baseline.
Text buffer	An area set aside in memory to hold text temporarily.
Text editing	The function of a word processor that enables the user to enter and edit text.
Text file	A file that contains text, as opposed to a program.
Virtual representation	An approach to screen formatting which enables the user to see on the screen exactly how the printed output will look.
Word wrap	The feature in which a word is moved automatically to the beginning of the next line if it goes past the right margin.

■ USES OF WORD PROCESSORS

Word processors are used in many settings, including homes, businesses, and schools. In 1986, *PC Magazine* identified three categories of word processors: personal, professional, and corporate. By 1988, *PC Magazine* reported that the breadth of suitable uses for word processors had grown to such an extent that grouping word processors by distinct categories was no longer appropriate. As the quality of word processors has improved, the difference between personal, corporate and professional programs has become less distinct. Even though word processors can no longer be grouped by rigid categories, obviously some are better suited for certain applications than others. Looking at the *uses* of word processors, *PC Magazine* added two groups to the list: personal, professional, corporate, legal, and desktop publishing.

At home, word processors can be used to write school reports, personal letters, or minutes from a meeting. Most word processors for home use are easier to operate than those designated for business use because they usually have fewer features than business word processors. For example, print-formating capabilities, which control page breaks, page numbering, and character enhancements, are limited in a word-processing package for home use.

Schools are increasing their use of word processors. Students can write essays or reports on the computers in their classroom. Often, teachers can format tests and worksheets on a computer much faster than on a typewriter. Of course, school secretaries can use word processors to prepare school reports and letters.

In offices, word processors are used to produce reports, formal correspondence, brochures, and other important documents. They merge names and addresses into form letters to personalize the letters. They check the spelling of documents. Today, standard features of a business-oriented word-processing package include mail-merge, a spelling checker, a thesaurus, and an outlining facility.

Obviously, the legal profession is an area that handles a great deal of written material; for that reason some word-processing programs have taken into account the unique needs of lawyers. These packages include such features as a style checker for legal citations, the inclusion of legal terminology in the spelling checker, the ability to create a table of authorities, automatic line numbering, and red-lining—a function that makes it possible to compare additions and deletions in successive versions of a document.

More and more, word-processing programs are encroaching on the low end of desktop publishing. Desktop publishing enables professional-quality documents to be created and printed through the use of a microcomputer and a laser printer. Desktop publishing features found on some word processors include the ability to integrate graphics into text documents, manipulate the placement of text and graphics on a page, and mix type sizes and fonts within a document.

1. A _____ is a program or set of programs designed to enable a user to enter, manipulate, format, print, store, and retrieve text.

a. word processor
b. word processing
c. word-processing system
d. dedicated system

LEARNING CHECK

2. The two general types of word-processing systems are _____ and _____ .

3. A _____ is the hardware and software that enable a user to write, edit, format, and print text on a computer.

a. word processor

b. word processing

c. word-processing system

d. dedicated system

4. Word processing is the act of _____ and _____ text on a computer.

5. (True or False?) A dedicated system handles a wide range of processing tasks, including word processing.

ANSWERS

1. a.

2. dedicated systems; multipurpose microcomputers

3. c.

4. composing; editing

5. False

GUIDE TO WORDPERFECT

The remainder of Section A focuses on how to use the Limited-Use Version of WordPerfect 4.2. WordPerfect, a state-of-the-art word-processing program from WordPerfect Corporation, is extremely powerful, yet easy to use. Memos, letters, reports, and term papers can be created with WordPerfect.

Some of the directions for using WordPerfect vary, depending on whether the computer has two floppy disk drives or a hard disk drive. The directions in this section are written for computers with two floppy disk drives.

Each of the following sections introduces one or more features of WordPerfect. At the end of each section there is a hands-on activity called Your Turn. Do not try the hands-on activities before you have carefully read the section preceding them.

From now on, the key marked ↵ is referred to as the <Return> key (sometimes it is also called the <Enter> key). Throughout this chapter, when instructed to press the <Return> key, press the key marked <←>.

WordPerfect uses the ten function keys on the left side of the keyboard to activate most of its features. A template for your use is provided with this book. Place the template around these ten keys (see Figure A–1). The template lists, next to each key, the four functions which that key activates.

Each key has four functions, which are activated either by pressing the key alone or by pressing the <Alt>, <Shift>, or <Ctrl> key at the same time. The template's functions are color coded to indicate whether the key is pressed alone or with one of the other keys:

Black Press the indicated function key only

Blue Hold down the <Alt> key and press the indicated function key

Green Hold down the <Shift> key and press the indicated function key

Red Hold down the <Ctrl> key and press the indicated function key

A few other keys are important in using WordPerfect. The <Num Lock> key is used to control the ten-key number pad on the right side of the keyboard. If the <Num Lock> key is pressed once, the pad is used for writing numbers to the screen. If not pressed, or pressed twice, it allows the keypad to be used for controlling the cursor. The ← key, hereafter referred to as the <Backspace> key, allows mistakes to be erased by backing the cursor

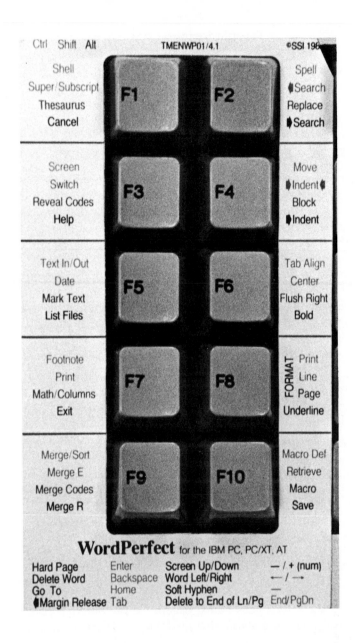

over them. The Cancel function, which is activated by pressing the <F1> key, allows a feature to be cancelled after it has been called up.

The following symbols and typefaces appear throughout the chapter. This is what they mean:

Type **B:**   The information in boldface indicates a command that should be typed to the screen.

Type Job Opening   Magenta colored characters indicate text that is to be entered into a document.

Press <Return>   The angle brackets (<>) are used to signify a specific key on the keyboard. Press the key whose name is enclosed by the angle brackets.

WP Tip:	This phrase introduces important information needed to run WordPerfect successfully.
EXIT WP? (Y/N)	All capital letters indicate phrases that appear on the computer screen. They also indicate the names of WordPerfect functions or commands.

▦ GETTING STARTED WITH WORDPERFECT

To **boot** the computer and start WordPerfect, you need a DOS disk, the WordPerfect Program Disk that comes with this book, and a formatted disk that will serve as your data disk. All the documents or files you create will be saved on your data disk.

To boot the computer involves loading an operating system into the computer's main memory. If a two-disk-drive system is used, the data disk is always inserted in drive B. Unless instructed otherwise, the computer automatically saves files on whatever disk is in drive A. Because your data disk is always in drive B, you need to instruct the computer to store the documents you create on the data disk in drive B, which you will learn to do in the section on "Saving a Document."

Follow these steps to boot the computer and start WordPerfect:

1. Insert the DOS disk into drive A. Close the disk drive door. Turn on the computer.
2. When asked to type the date, enter the current date (for example, 9-28-89) and press <Return>. When asked to enter the correct time, either enter the time using a twenty-four-hour format (14:26:24) and press <Return>, or simply press <Return> to bypass the time-set feature.
3. When the system prompt A> appears on the screen, remove the DOS disk from drive A. Insert the WordPerfect Program disk into drive A and close the disk drive door.
4. Insert your data disk into drive B. Close the disk drive door.
5. Type **wp** and press <Return>.

After typing **wp** and pressing <Return>, information about the Training Version of WordPerfect 4.2 appears on the screen. At the bottom of the screen is the prompt, PRESS ANY KEY TO CONTINUE. After the user presses a key, the screen goes blank, except for the blinking cursor in the upper left corner and the **status line** in the lower right corner (see Figure A–2).

▦ Your Turn

Turn on and boot your computer, and start WordPerfect. Your screen should match Figure A–2. Next, follow these directions to exit from WordPerfect:

- ▪ Press <F7> for EXIT
- ▪ Type **N**
- ▪ Type **Y**

Turn off your computer and monitor. In the next Your Turn exercise you will boot the computer and start WordPerfect again.

1. WordPerfect uses _____*C*_____ to activate most of its features.

a. letter keys   c. function keys

b. menus   d. the ten-key number pad

2. Each function key has _____*D*_____ function(s).

a. one   c. three

b. two   d. four

3. If the function that you want to use is printed on the function-key template in black, what key do you press with the listed function key? _____*D*_____

a. <Ctrl>   c. <Alt>

b. <Shift>   d. Press the function key alone

4. If the function that you want to use is printed on the function-key template in red, what key do you press with the listed function key? _____*A*_____

a. <Ctrl>   c. <Alt>

b. <Shift>   d. Press the function key alone

5. What key do you press in order to restore deleted text? _____*D*_____

a. <F3>   c. <F2>

b. <Delete>   d. <F1>

ANSWERS

1. c.   4. a.

2. d.   5. d.

3. d.

FIGURE A–2

The WordPerfect Status Line and Editing Window

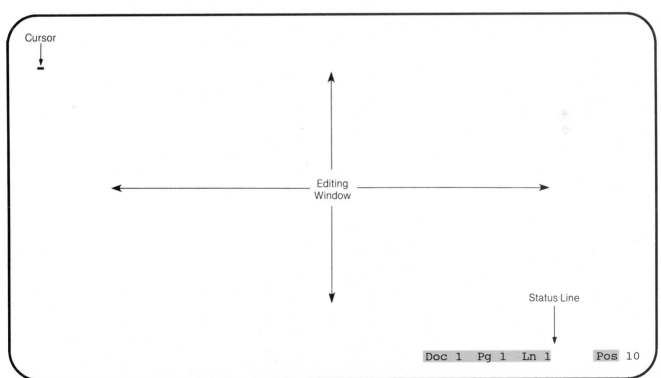

CREATING A NEW DOCUMENT

The files created with WordPerfect are similar to files in a file cabinet—each file is a unit of storage. Files can be used to store memos, letters, and term papers. For example, when a memo or letter is completed, that file is saved to a disk. Once saved, that file can be reentered in order to revise, edit, or print its contents.

Entering Text

Each time WordPerfect is started, a blank screen appears with a blinking cursor in the upper left corner. The status line is in the lower right corner (refer to figure A–2). The status line displays the number of the document and the cursor's location. The number following Pg is the page number. The number following Ln is the number of the horizontal line where the cursor is located. The number following Pos is the position number, or the number of spaces from the left margin, of the cursor's location.

The remainder of the screen is often referred to as the **editing window.** The editing window displays your words as they are typed. All editing of a document takes place in the editing window, which can contain twenty-four lines of text. When you type a document that is longer than twenty-four lines, the lines at the beginning of the document **scroll** off the top of the screen to make room for any additional lines.

When entering text, you need to use both upper- and lowercase letters. If the letters are all capitals when you begin typing, press the <Caps Lock> key. Letters should appear in both upper- and lowercase. Pressing the <Caps Lock> key once again produces all capital letters. In order to enter the symbols found on the top half of some of the keys, you have to press the <Shift> key rather than the <Caps Lock> key.

The <Return> key does not need to be pressed when the end of a line is reached. WordPerfect has a feature called **word wrap,** which automatically moves a word to the beginning of the next line if it crosses the right margin. The <Return> key is used to begin new paragraphs and to add blank lines to the text.

Features such as margins, tabs, and spacing are set automatically according to **default** settings. The default setting is the setting that a program automatically assumes when no other setting is designated by the user. These settings can be changed easily, but for now you should just use the default settings.

■ Your Turn

In this exercise, you are going to start WordPerfect on the computer and enter a letter.

1. Insert the DOS disk into drive A. Close the disk drive door. Turn on the computer and the monitor. The date prompt appears on the screen. Enter the current date. The time prompt appears on the screen. Press <Return>.
2. The system prompt A> appears on the screen. Remove the DOS disk from drive A. Insert the WordPerfect Program disk into drive A and close the disk drive door. Insert your data disk into drive B. Close the disk drive door.

- Type **wp**
- Press <Return>

Information about the Training Version of WordPerfect 4.2 appears on the screen. At the bottom of the screen is the prompt, PRESS ANY KEY TO CONTINUE.

- Press any key

The editing window should be on the screen and the blinking cursor should be in the upper left corner.

3. You are now going to enter a letter that should be typed exactly as it appears here. Do not worry about any errors you make; they can be corrected easily later. Do not press <Return> unless instructed to do so. Let word wrap move the cursor to the next line. Follow the directions closely.

Before typing the letter, you are going to activate the FLUSH RIGHT and DATE functions. Remember that functions are activated through the combined use of the ten function keys and the <Ctrl>, <Shift>, and <Alt> keys. Use the color-coded function-key template to find the proper combination. In this case, FLUSH RIGHT appears in blue beside the <F6> key and DATE appears in green beside the <F5> key.

- Press the <Alt> and <F6> keys for FLUSH RIGHT.

The cursor jumps to the right side of the screen.

- Press the <Shift> and <F5> keys for DATE

At the bottom of the screen, a line with three numbered choices for the Date function appears.

- Type **1**

The date is inserted automatically, flush with the right margin. (Note: If you bypassed setting the date when starting up DOS, the date will be incorrect).

- Press <Return> four times
- Type Kim Landon
- Press <Return>
- Type 4332 University Road
- Press <Return>
- Type Toledo, Ohio 43403
- Press <Return> twice
- Type Dear Ms. Landon,
- Press <Return> twice

Now type the body of the letter as follows:

As your advisor, I want to help you in any way possible with your job hunt. Since graduation is only six short months away, I'm sure finding a job is a top priority for you right now. I just received some information form the placement service office that I would like to pass along to you. I think this information will help you in your job-search efforts.

■ Press <Return> twice

The placement service is sponsoring a series of seminars designed to help upcoming graduates locate potential employers, write cover letters and resumes, and improve interviewing skills. There is no cost for attending this seminar, but if you plan to attend, you must register with the placement office no later than Monday, February 20. These seminars will be divided up according to majors. The seminar for Accounting majors is scheduled for Saturday, February 25. I have enclosed a tentative schedule of events.

■ Press <Return> twice

I hope you plan to attend this seminar. I think it will be well worth your time.

■ Press <Return> twice

Sincerly,

■ Press <Return> four times

Professor Hubert Melville

■ Press <Return> twice

See enclosure

4. When you have finished, your screen should look like Figure A–3. Leave the letter on the screen. You are going to save it in the next hands-on exercise.

FIGURE A–3

Entering Text

```
received some information form the placement service office that
I would like to pass along to you.  I think this information will
help you in your job-search efforts.

The placement service is sponsoring a series of seminars designed
to help upcoming graduates locate potential employers, write
cover letters and resumes, and improve interviewing skills.
There is no cost for attending this seminar, but if you plan to
attend, you must register with the placement office no later than
Monday, February 20.  These seminars will be divided up according
to majors.  The seminar for Accounting majors is scheduled for
Saturday, February 25.  I have enclosed a tentative schedule of
events.

I hope you plan to attend this seminar.  I think it will be well
worth your time.

Sincerly,


Professor Hubert Melville

See enclosure
B:\JOBSEM.1                            Doc 1   Pg 1   Ln 37      Pos 23
```

Saving a Document

To save a document, activate the EXIT function by pressing the function key marked <F7>. When the prompt SAVE DOCUMENT?(Y/N) Y appears in the lower left corner of the screen, press <Return> to save the document. You do not have to type **Y** because the program's default setting is Y. If you do not wish to save the document before leaving it, type **N**, which will replace the Y.

The prompt DOCUMENT TO BE SAVED appears next. Type **B:** and a name for the document. It is helpful to give your files names that will remind you of their contents. Do not insert a space between the colon and the first letter of the document name. Typing **B:** causes your work to be saved on the disk in drive B, which is your data disk. You do not want to save your work on the program disk in drive A.

WP Tip: When naming a file, remember the following rules:

1. The name can be from 1 to 8 characters long, with no spaces.
2. The characters in a file name can be the letters of the alphabet, the numbers 0 through 9, or the special characters $#@!()-{}_.
3. An optional extension can be used following the file name. The extension can have from 1 to 3 characters with no spaces, and is separated from the file name by a period(.).
4. Try to give the file a name that reminds you of what it contains.

After naming a file, the prompt EXIT WP? (Y/N) N appears. If you want to continue using WordPerfect, press <Return> to accept the default setting of N for No. If you want to exit the program, type **Y.** When the system prompt appears and the red lights on the disk drives are off, you can take the disks out of the disk drives and turn off the computer and monitor.

■ Your Turn

In this exercise, you are going to save the letter just entered.

1. The letter should still be on the screen.

■ Press <F7> for EXIT

The prompt SAVE DOCUMENT appears at the bottom of the screen.

■ Press <Return> to accept the default setting **Y** for Yes

The prompt DOCUMENT TO BE SAVED appears at the bottom of the screen.

2. You are going to name the document JOBSEM.1 for job seminar.

■ Type **B:JOBSEM.1**
■ Press <Return>

The prompt EXIT WP appears.

■ Type **Y**

The system prompt appears in the lower left corner of the screen.

Retrieving a Document

To edit a document that already exists, activate the RETRIEVE command by pressing the <Shift> and <F10> keys. The prompt DOCUMENT TO BE RETRIEVED appears. Type the name of the document that is to be edited, and press <Return>. If there is a file that corresponds to the name entered, the document appears on the screen, ready to be edited.

If you do not remember the name of the document you want to retrieve, activate the LIST FILES command by pressing <F5>. The prompt DIR A:*.* appears in the lower left corner of the screen and the instruction TYPE = TO CHANGE DEFAULT DIRECTORY appears in the lower right corner. You will always want to retrieve the listing of files in Directory B, which contains your data disk. To access Directory B, press the equal sign key. The prompt NEW DIRECTORY = A:\ appears. Type **B:** and press <Return>. The prompt Dir B:*.* appears. Press <Return>. A list of all the files on the disk in drive B appears. Highlight the name of the file to be retrieved by typing the name of the file. Press <Return>.

A list of options appears at the bottom of the screen. Next to the RETRIEVE option is the number one. To retrieve the highlighted file, type **1.** The desired document appears on the screen.

■ Your Turn

In this exercise, you are going to retrieve the JOBSEM.1 file.

1. Start WordPerfect.

2. A blank editing window should be on the screen.

- ■ Press <Shift> <F10> for RETRIEVE
- ■ Type **B:JOBSEM.1**
- ■ Press <Return>

The letter appears on the screen.

3. Now you are going to retrieve the letter again, using the directory. First you have to exit from the file.

- ■ Press <F7> for EXIT

The SAVE DOCUMENT prompt appears. You do not have to save the letter again since it has already been saved once and you have not yet made any changes to it.

- ■ Type **N**
- ■ Press <Return>

The prompt EXIT WP? (Y/N) N appears.

- ■ Press <Return>

A blank editing window appears.

- ■ Press <F5> for LIST FILES
- ■ Press =
- ■ Type **B:**
- ■ Press <Return> twice

The directory for disk B appears on the screen. The JOBSEM.1 file is listed.

■ Type **JOBSEM.1**

The highlighting is on the JOBSEM.1 file in the directory. The file name appears in the lower left corner as you type it.

■ Press <Return>

A list of options appears at the bottom of the screen.

■ Type **1** for RETRIEVE

The letter appears in the editing window.

4. Exit WordPerfect.

LEARNING CHECK

1. Each time WordPerfect is started up, ___ _C_ ___ appears.

a. a menu
b. a blank screen

c. a blank screen with a blinking cursor in the upper left corner
d. a list of formatting options

2. What key do you press to save a file? _F 7_

3. How long can a WordPerfect file name be?

4. What is the feature called which automatically moves words that run over the right margin to the next line? _WORD WARP_

5. Which function keys activate the LIST FILES and RETRIEVE functions? _F5 7 Sft F10_

ANSWERS

1. c.
2. The EXIT function key, <F7>
3. Eight characters, with three additional characters following a period if desired.

4. word wrap
5. <F5>; <F10> and <Shift>

EDITING A DOCUMENT

Now that a document has been saved on a disk, it can be edited. The **text editing** function of a word processor enables the user to enter and edit text. The most fundamental aspect of this function is the word processor's ability to accept and store the text that is typed in at the keyboard. Without this ability, all the other functions and procedures would be useless.

Text editing also includes the ability of the word processor to **insert** and **delete** characters, words, lines, paragraphs, and larger blocks of text. The insert and delete modes are two of the most often-used text editing features of any word processor. The text editing features of most word processors, including WordPerfect, also allow blocks of text to be moved and copied. These features make it easier to rearrange and retype documents.

The exercises in this section demonstrate the commands used to edit a document. You will practice using these commands on the JOBSEM.1 document you created.

Moving the Cursor

Before starting to work on a file, you need to be able to control the position of the cursor. The cursor is controlled by the arrow keys in the numeric keypad on the right side of the keyboard. The down arrow < ↓ > moves the cursor one line down. The up arrow $<\uparrow>$ moves the cursor one line up. The left arrow $<\leftarrow>$, which should not be confused with the <Backspace> key, moves the cursor one position to the left. The right arrow $<\rightarrow>$ key moves the cursor one position to the right. Remember, the keypad can be used to move the cursor only when the <Num Lock> key is off. If the numbers 2, 4, 6, 8 appear on the screen when you are trying to move the cursor, then the <Num Lock> key is on. Press it once to turn it off, and use the <Backspace> key to delete the numbers.

The cursor can also be moved a specified number of lines by using the <Esc> key. Press <Esc> and the prompt N = 8 appears in the lower left corner of the screen. Enter the number of lines you want the cursor to move and press either the $<\downarrow>$ or $<\uparrow>$ key. The cursor moves down the number of lines specified if the $<\downarrow>$ key was pressed, and up the specified number of lines if the $<\uparrow>$ key was pressed.

The cursor can also be moved word by word or page by page through the document. Table A–2 summarizes the cursor commands.

■ Your Turn

In this exercise, you are going to practice moving the cursor.

1. Start WordPerfect. A blank editing window should be on the screen.

TABLE A–2

Commands for Moving the Cursor

Keys	Description
$<\leftarrow>$	Moves the cursor one character to the left
$<\rightarrow>$	Moves the cursor one character to the right
<Ctrl>$<\rightarrow>$	Moves the cursor one word to the right
<Ctrl>$<\leftarrow>$	Moves the cursor one word to the left
<Home>$<\rightarrow>$	Moves the cursor to the right edge of the screen
<Home>$<\leftarrow>$	Moves the cursor to the left edge of the screen
<Home><Home>$<\rightarrow>$	Moves the cursor to the far right of the line
<Home><Home>$<\leftarrow>$	Moves the cursor to the far left of the line
$<\uparrow>$	Moves the cursor up one line
$<\downarrow>$	Moves the cursor down one line
<Home>$<\uparrow>$	Moves the cursor to the top of the screen
<Home>$<\downarrow>$	Moves the cursor to the bottom of the screen
<Ctrl><Home>$<\uparrow>$	Moves the cursor to the top of the current page
<Ctrl><Home>$<\downarrow>$	Moves the cursor to the bottom of the current page
<Pg Up>	Moves the cursor to the top of the previous page
<Pg Dn>	Moves the cursor to the top of the next page
<Home><Home>$<\uparrow>$	Moves the cursor to the beginning of the document
<Home><Home>$<\downarrow>$	Moves the cursor to the end of the document
<Ctrl><Home>#	Moves the cursor to the page number entered
<Esc>#$<\uparrow>$	Moves the cursor up the number of lines entered
<Esc>#$<\downarrow>$	Moves the cursor down the number of lines entered

COMPUTERS AND INFORMATION PROCESSING

2. Retrieve the JOBSEM.1 file. Look at the status line. The cursor should be on Page 1, Line 1, Position 10.

■ Press < ↓ > key 10 times.

The cursor should be under the *A* in the first word of the first sentence. Look at the status line. It now reads Line 11 rather than Line 1.

■ Press <Home><Home><→>

The cursor is now on Line 11, Position 75, at the very end of the first line of the letter.

■ Press <Home>< ↓ >

The cursor will move to the bottom of the screen.

■ Press <Home><Home>< ↓ >

The word Repositioning flashes briefly on the screen as the cursor repositions itself at the end of the document.

■ Press <Esc>

The prompt N = 8 appears in the lower left corner of the screen.

■ Type **10**
■ Press < ↑ >

The cursor moves up ten lines. Continue to practice all the ways to move the cursor. Watch the Line and Position numbers in the status line as you move the cursor.

Removing Text

There are several ways to remove text from a WordPerfect document. The most efficient method depends upon the text to be removed and the user's typing style.

Pressing <Backspace> moves the cursor one space to the left, removing the character from that position. If you hold the <Backspace> key down, it continues to remove characters until you release it.

Pressing <Del> removes the character immediately above the cursor. The <Del> key can also be used in conjunction with the BLOCK command (<Alt><F4>). Position the cursor at the beginning of the block of text that is to be deleted. Press <Alt><F4> to activate the block command. The words BLOCK ON begin flashing in the lower left corner of the screen. Use the arrow keys to highlight the block of text to be deleted. Press <Del>. The prompt DELETE BLOCK? (Y/N) N appears in the lower left corner of the screen. To delete the block of text that is highlighted, press **Y.** To cancel the Block command, press <Return> and then press <F1> for CANCEL. The highlighting disappears from the text.

The <Ins> key can be used for removing and replacing text. If <Ins> is pressed once, the word TYPEOVER appears in the lower left corner of the screen and the **overtype** mode is on. When WordPerfect is in overtype mode, text can be changed by typing over the characters above the cursor. For example, if the cursor is under the *d* in "The *d*og ran up the street" and TYPEOVER appears on the screen, typing *cat* produces the sentence "The cat ran up the street." Typing *elephant,* however, results in the sentence "The elephantup the street." For one word to replace another, the two must have the same number of letters. Usually it is not efficient to work with the overtype feature on, because important information could easily be written over. Pressing <Ins> again puts WordPerfect back into Insert mode.

Text can also be deleted by pressing either <Ctrl><End> or <Ctrl> <PgDn>. Pressing <Ctrl> <End> deletes text from the cursor's position to the end of the line. Pressing <Ctrl><PgDn> deletes text from the cursor's position to the end of the page.

If text is deleted by accident, pressing <F1> for the CANCEL command enables you to undo the deletion. This function has limitations, however. It can restore only the most recently removed text.

■ Your Turn

In this exercise you are going to practice the various ways to delete text. The JOBSEM.1 document should be on the screen. If necessary, move the cursor to position it at Page 1, Line 1, Position 10.

1. Because the JOBSEM.1 document is a modified block form letter, the date needs to be moved back to the left margin.

■ Press the <→> key to position the cursor under the first letter in the date
■ Press <Backspace> once

The prompt DELETE [ALN/FLSR]? (Y/N) N appears in the lower left corner of the screen. The prompt is asking if you want to delete the Flush Right function.

■ Press **Y**

The date moves over to the left margin.

2. Move the cursor to Line 14 Position 37, under the *o* in *form.*

■ Press <Del> twice to delete *or*

Make sure TYPEOVER does not appear in the lower left corner of the screen.

■ Type ro

The word should now be *from.*

3. Keep the cursor in Line 14 and move it until it is under the *p* in *placement.* You are going to change the lowercase *p,s,* and *o* in *placement service office* to uppercase letters.

■ Press <Ins>

TYPEOVER appears in the lower left corner of the screen.

■ Type P

Move the cursor until it is under the *s* in *service.*

■ Type S

Move the cursor until it is under the *o* in *office.*

- Type O
- Press <Ins> to turn the Typeover mode off

4. The word TYPEOVER should no longer be on the screen. Move the cursor to the beginning of the sentence in Line 15 that starts: "I think this information . . ." You are going to delete the entire sentence using the BLOCK command. The cursor should be under the *I*.

- Press <Alt><F4> for BLOCK

The words BLOCK ON start flashing in the lower left corner of the screen.

- Press < ↓ > once
- If necessary, press <→> until the highlighting includes the period after *efforts*

The entire sentence is now highlighted.

- Press <Del>

The prompt **DELETE BLOCK** appears.

- Type **Y**

The entire sentence is deleted.

5. Move the cursor to Line 17. Using the <Ins> key, change the lowercase *p* and *s* in *placement service* to uppercase letters.

6. Move the cursor to Line 22. Using the BLOCK command and the <Del> key, delete this entire sentence: "These seminars will be divided up according to majors." Replace it with the following sentence: Each seminar will focus on a different major.

7. Change the lowercase *p* and *o* in *placement office* in Line 21 to capital letters using the <Ins> key. Do not forget to turn the overtype mode off after the corrections have been made.

8. Move the cursor to the *t* in the word *it* in the following sentence which starts on Line 27: "I think *it* will be well worth your time." Use the <Backspace> key to change this sentence to: "It will be well worth your time."

9. Move the cursor to the *l* in the word *Sincerly* in Line 30.

- Type e

You are now going to save the corrections you just made.

- Press <F10> for SAVE

The prompt **DOCUMENT TO BE SAVED: B:\WP\JOBSEM.1** appears at the bottom of the screen.

- Press <Return>

The prompt **REPLACE B:\WP\JOBSEM.1? (Y/N) N** appears at the bottom of the screen. This prompt is asking if you want to replace the original JOBSEM.1 file with the file you just created by making corrections. Because there is no need to save the first letter, you are going to replace the file.

- Type **Y**

The new JOBSEM.1 file with corrections should stay on the screen. You are going to continue to make more changes in the next hands-on exercise.

Moving Blocks of Text

Manipulating a document a character at a time is extremely slow when working with large blocks of text. To help speed operations, WordPerfect includes a **block movement** feature. This feature defines a block of text— either a sentence, paragraph, or page—and then either copies it or moves it elsewhere in the document.

To be able to move a block of text, it first must be highlighted. Position the cursor under the first letter of the text to be moved. Activate the MOVE function by pressing <Ctrl><F4>. A menu appears at the bottom of the screen that offers three move options: 1 SENTENCE; 2 PARAGRAPH; 3 PAGE. Select the appropriate number. Depending on the number selected, either a sentence, paragraph, or page is highlighted.

Next, the prompt 1 CUT; 2 COPY; 3 DELETE appears at the bottom of the screen. If the text is to be moved to another part of the document, type **1** for CUT. Move the cursor to the position where the cut text should be inserted. Activate the MOVE function again by pressing <Ctrl><F4>. When the menu reappears, press **5** for TEXT to place the text at its new position.

The MOVE function can also be used to copy a block of text that is to be repeated a number of times throughout a document. Move the cursor to the beginning of the block of text to be copied. Activate the MOVE function (<Ctrl><F4>). Select either **1**, **2**, or **3**, depending on whether a sentence, paragraph or page needs to be copied. When the 1 CUT; 2 COPY prompt appears, type **2** for COPY. The text is copied into memory, but also is left in its original position. The block of text can be reproduced as many times as needed. Simply place the cursor at the position where the copied text is to appear and activate the MOVE function (<Ctrl><F4>). Select **5** to place the copied text at the cursor's position. To reproduce the text again, move the cursor to the next location where the copied text is to appear, activate the MOVE function, and press **5** for text. This process can be repeated as many times as necessary to place copied text. The text stays in memory until a new block of text is copied.

■ Your Turn

Use the JOBSEM.1 document, which should be on your screen, to practice using the BLOCK function.

1. Move the cursor to the *A* in the opening sentence, "As your advisor, I want to help you in any way possible with your job hunt."

■ Press <Ctrl><F4> for MOVE

The menu appears at the bottom of the screen.

■ Type **1** for SENTENCE

The entire first sentence is highlighted and the prompt 1 CUT; 2 COPY; 3 DELETE appears at the bottom of the screen (see Figure A–4). You are going to cut this sentence and move it to a new location.

■ Type **1**

The sentence is cut from the letter.

COMPUTERS AND INFORMATION PROCESSING

```
February 6, 1989


Kim Landon
4332 University Road
Toledo, Ohio  43403

Dear Ms. Landon,

As your advisor, I want to help you in any way possible with your
job hunt.  Since graduation is only six short months away, I'm
sure finding a job is a top priority for you right now.  I just
received some information from the Placement Service Office that
I would like to pass along to you.

The Placement Service is sponsoring a series of seminars designed
to help upcoming graduates locate potential employers, write
cover letters and resumes, and improve interviewing skills.
There is no cost for attending this seminar, but if you plan to
attend, you must register with the Placement Office no later than
Monday, February 20.  Each seminar will focus on a different
major.  The seminar for Accounting majors is scheduled for
Saturday, February 25.  I have enclosed a tentative schedule of
1 Cut; 2 Copy; 3 Delete: 0
```

2. Move the cursor to the word *I* in the sentence that begins "I just received some information . . .,"

- ■ Press <Ctrl><F4> for MOVE
- ■ Type **5** for TEXT

The sentence that was cut is now inserted as the second sentence of the letter.

3. Move the cursor to the first letter of the sentence in the second paragraph that begins: "There is no cost for attending this seminar . . ." You are going to move this sentence so that it is the last sentence of the paragraph.

- ■ Press <Ctrl><F4> for MOVE
- ■ Type **1** for SENTENCE
- ■ Type **1** for CUT

Move the cursor to the space immediately following the period at the end of the last sentence in the paragraph. Press the <Space Bar> so that there are two spaces after the period.

- ■ Press <Ctrl><F4> for MOVE
- ■ Type **5** for TEXT

The sentence that was cut now appears as the last sentence of the paragraph.

4. Save the corrections you have made. Again, you can replace the old JOBSEM.1 with the newly revised file JOBSEM.1.

FIGURE A—4

Moving a Block of Text

The Speller and Thesaurus

WordPerfect comes with two very useful functions called the Speller and the Thesaurus. The Speller checks the spelling in a document and if it finds a misspelled word, it suggests the correct spelling. The Speller can analyze a word phonetically (as though it were sounding it out). If a word is close to the correct spelling, the Speller can suggest the right spelling. The Thesaurus checks a selected word from a document and displays a list of synonyms and other words related to the selected word. When you are not particularly satisfied with a word you have used in a document, the Thesaurus helps you find a better word with which to replace it.

In the commercial version of WordPerfect 4.2 there are over 115,000 words in the Speller dictionary alone. Because of the space limitations on WordPerfect's training disk, the entire Speller and Thesaurus cannot be included. There is, however, a file included on the training disk that enables you to learn how the Speller and Thesaurus work.

■ Your Turn

You are going to learn how to use WordPerfect's Speller and Thesaurus. On the WordPerfect Program disk is a file called README. Working with this file gives you the opportunity to learn all the functions of the Speller and Thesaurus. The JOBSEM.1 document should be on your screen. You need to clear your screen. Press <F7> for EXIT. You do not have to save the document again and you do not want to exit WordPerfect. The editing window should be blank.

1. First, you have to copy the README file from the program disk in drive A to your data disk in drive B.

■ Press <F5> for LIST FILES

In the bottom right corner of the screen the line DIR B: *.* appears. You want to see the directory for drive A because the README file is on the disk in drive A.

■ Press = (the equal sign)

In the bottom right corner of the screen the line NEW DIRECTORY = B: appears.

■ Type **A:**
■ Press <Return>

In the bottom right corner of the screen the line now reads DIR A:*.*.

■ Press <Return>

The directory for the disk in drive A appears. One of the files on the disk in drive A is called README. Using the arrow keys, move the highlighting to the line that says README. One of the options in the menu at the bottom of the screen is COPY. You are now going to copy the README file from the disk in drive A to your data disk in drive B.

■ Press **8** for COPY

The prompt COPY THIS FILE TO appears at the bottom of the screen.

- Type **B:README**
- Press <Return>

After a few moments the file is copied and the menu returns to the bottom of the screen. Now you want to retrieve the file you just copied.

- Press **7** for CHANGE DIRECTORY
- Type **B:**
- Press <Return>

In the bottom right corner of the screen the line DIR B:*.* appears.

- Press <Return>

The directory for the disk in drive B appears. Move the highlighting to the README file.

- Press **1** for RETRIEVE

2. The README file appears. Read the two paragraphs that are on the screen. First you are going to practice using the thesaurus. Using the arrow keys, move the cursor to the word *Fools*.

- Press <Alt><F1> for THESAURUS

Your screen should look like Figure A–5. A list of words related to the word *fool* is presented. Read over the entire list. Notice that the list of words in the first column all have a corresponding letter. Pressing the letter that is next to the word is the means by which that word is selected. At the bottom of the screen is a menu. The words with dots next to them (*idiot, genius, sage*) are called headwords. You can look up headwords in the thesaurus to

FIGURE A—5

Looking Up a Word in the Thesaurus

```
   left-hand corner of the screen.)

            Fools rush in where angels fear to tread.


  ┌fool=(n)════════════════╤═══════════════════════════════
  │  1 A   blockhead        │        cheat
  │    B   dolt             │        defraud
  │    C   dunce            │
  │    D  ·idiot            │   5    jest
  │    E   oaf              │        joke
  │                         │
  │  2 F   buffoon          │   6    feign
  │    G   clown            │        pretend
  │    H   harlequin        │
  │    I   jester           │ fool─(ant)──────────────
  │                         │   7   ·genius
  │ fool─(v)────────────────│       ·sage
  │  3 J   deceive          │ ────────────────────────
  │    K   dupe             │
  │    L   mislead          │
  │    M   trick            │
  │                         │
  │  4 N   bilk             │
  1 Replace Word; 2 View Doc; 3 Look Up Word; 4 Clear Column: 0
```

get a listing of even more words. Since *idiot* is a headword, you are going to look it up in the thesaurus.

■ Press **3** for LOOK UP WORD

The word you want to look up is *idiot*. The letter corresponding to the word *idiot* is D. This is the letter you use to indicate that *idiot* is the word you want to look up.

■ Press **D**
■ Press <Return>

There is now a new column 2 that contains a list of words related to the word *idiot*. Notice that the letters moved over to column 2. At this moment only words from column 2 can be selected because that is the column of words in front of which the letters appear. This new list of words contain another headword you can look up, *simpleton*.

■ Press **3** for LOOK UP WORD
■ Press **G**
■ Press <Return>

Now, a new column 3 appears with words related to *simpleton*. There are no new headwords that you can look up. Say you wanted to replace the word *fools* with *buffoons*. At this moment you cannot select *buffoon* because the letters by which you select a word are now in column 3. The arrow keys move the column of letters.

■ Press <←> twice

The letters should now be in column 1.

■ Press **1** for REPLACE WORD
■ Press **F**

The thesaurus disappears and the word *Fools* is replaced by *Buffoon* in the sentence.

■ Press **s** to make the word plural

3. Now you are going to look up the word *rush* in the thesaurus. Move the cursor to the word *rush*.

■ Press <Alt><F1> for THESAURUS

Now you are going to look up the headword *race*.

■ Press **3** for LOOK UP WORD
■ Press **D**
■ Press <Return>

Two new columns of words appear. In addition to synonyms, the thesaurus also lists antonyms. You decide to replace *rush* with an antonym, *mosey*. First you have to move the column of letters so you can select *mosey*.

■ Press <→> once
■ Press **1** for REPLACE WORD
■ Press **E**

Rush has now been replaced with *mosey*. Move the cursor to *angels*.

- Press <Alt><F1> for THESAURUS
- Press **3** for LOOK UP WORD
- Press **E**

You decide you like the word *spirit*.

- Press <←> to move the column of letters
- Press **1** for REPLACE WORD
- Press **E**
- Type **s** to make the word plural.

Move the cursor to the word *fear*.

- Press <Alt><F1> for THESAURUS

You decide you like the word *dread*.

- Press **1** for REPLACE WORD
- Press **I**

Move the cursor to *tread*.

- Press <Alt><F1> for THESAURUS

You decide you like the word *tread* better than any of the new words listed, so you are not going to replace *tread*.

- Press **0** for CLEAR COLUMN

Your screen should look like Figure A–6.

FIGURE A–6

Replacing Words Using the Thesaurus

```
    left-hand corner of the screen.)

            Buffoons mosey in where spirits dread to tread.




    ================================================================================

    Instructions: While holding down the Ctrl key, push F2.  Next,
    push 2 to check a page, and then follow the prompts and status
    line as you like.

        We hold theese truths to be self-evedent, that all men are
        are created equal, that they are endoud by their Creator
        with certain unalienable Rights, that among these are Life,
        Liberty and the prusuit of Happiness.  That to secure these
        rights, Goverments are instituted among Men, deriving their
        just powers from the consent of the governed.


    B:\README                              Doc 1  Pg 1  Ln 16     Pos 61
```

4. You are now ready to practice using the Speller. Read the second set of instructions near the bottom of the screen. Move the cursor to the word *We* in the sentence that begins *"We hold theese truths . . ."*

■ Press <Ctrl><F2> for SPELLER

A menu appears at the bottom of the screen. The Speller can check a document a word at a time, page at a time, or it can check the spelling of the entire document. To check the spelling of one word or page, the cursor must be placed anywhere within the word or page before activating the SPELL function. When the menu appears at the bottom of the screen, pressing **1** for WORD checks a single word, pressing **2** for PAGE checks the spelling in an entire page, and pressing **3** for DOCUMENT checks the spelling of the entire document.

■ Press **2** for PAGE

Your screen should look like Figure A–7. The highlighting is on *F2* because *F2* is not contained in WordPerfect's Speller dictionary. Notice the menu at the bottom of the screen.

■ Press **3** for IGNORE WORDS CONTAINING NUMBERS

The next word the speller finds is *theese*. A replacement list appears on the screen. The replacement list includes words that are similar to the misspelled word; its purpose is to help you find the correct spelling of the highlighted word. If the highlighted word can be replaced by one of the words in the replacement list, simply press the letter corresponding to the correct word. The Speller replaces the highlighted word with the word selected from the replacement list, and continues checking the spelling.

■ Press **A** to replace *theese* with *these*
■ Press **A** to replace *evedent* with *evident*

FIGURE A–7

Using the Speller

```
================================================================================

Instructions: While holding down the Ctrl key, push F2.  Next,
push 2 to check a page, and then follow the prompts and status
line as you like.

     We hold theese truths to be self-evedent, that all men are
     are created equal, that they are endoud by their Creator

================================================================================




Not Found!  Select Word or Menu Option (0=Continue): 0
1 2 Skip; 3 Ignore words containing numbers; 4 Edit
```

COMPUTERS AND INFORMATION PROCESSING

Next the Speller finds a double word. The word *are* has been entered twice.

- Press **3** for DELETE 2ND
- Press **A** to replace *endoud* with *endowed*
- Press **A** to replace *prusuit* with *pursuit*
- Press **A** to replace *Goverments* with *governments*

Notice that when the last replacement was made, WordPerfect automatically capitalized the *g* in *Governments*. The Speller can find no more misspelled words. The message WORD COUNT: 82 PRESS ANY KEY TO CONTINUE appears at the bottom of the screen.

- Press any key

You are now ready to leave the README file.

- Press <F7> for EXIT
- Press **Y**
- Press <Return>
- Press **Y**
- Press **N**

You should have a blank editing window on your screen.

Printing

There are several ways to print with WordPerfect. One way is to retrieve the document to be printed. Make sure that the computer is hooked up to the printer, and that the printer has plenty of paper and is online. With the document on the computer screen, press <Shift><F7> for PRINT. A menu appears at the bottom of the screen. Press **1** to print the entire text or press **2** to print just a page of the text. Quickly, then, the document is printed.

A document also can be printed without retrieving it. With a blank editing window on the screen, press <Shift><F7> for PRINT. When the menu appears, press **4** for PRINTER CONTROL. The Printer Control menu appears (see Figure A–8). Press **P** for PRINT A DOCUMENT. Type the name of the document. Both the disk drive and file name have to be included. For example, to print the JOBSEM.1 document using this method, you would type **B:JOBSEM.1** and press <Return>.

The prompt STARTING PAGE appears. If desired, only certain pages from a document can be printed. For example, pages 4 through 6 from a ten-page document could be printed. Enter the page number of the first page to be printed. If the entire document is to be printed, enter **1.** Press <Return>.

Next the prompt ENDING PAGE appears. If the entire document is to be printed, press <Return>. If only a portion of the document is to be printed, enter the page number of the last page that is to be printed and press <Return>.

When you are finished using the Printer Control menu, press <F1> for CANCEL. A blank text editing window appears on the screen.

When printing a document using the training version of WordPerfect 4.2, the code *WPC* may be printed intermittently throughout the document. If *WPC* appears in the documents you print using the training version of WordPerfect 4.2, it is not because you have made an error. It is part of the program to print this code occasionally.

```
    Printer Control                  C - Cancel Print Job(s)
                                     D - Display All Print Jobs
    1 - Select Print Options         G - "Go" (Resume Printing)
    2 - Display Printers and Fonts   P - Print a Document
    3 - Select Printers              R - Rush Print Job
                                     S - Stop Printing
    Selection: 0


    Current Job

    Job Number: n/a                  Page Number:  n/a
    Job Status: n/a                  Current Copy: n/a
    Message:     The print queue is empty

    Job List

    Job   Document          Destination          Forms and Print Options




    Additional jobs not shown: 0
```

FIGURE A—8

WordPerfect's Printer Control Menu

FIGURE A—9

Printing a Document

```
February 6, 1989



Kim Landon
4332 University Road
Toledo, Ohio  43403

Dear Ms. Landon,

Since graduation is only six short months away, I'm sure finding
a job is a top priority for you right now.  As your advisor, I
want to help you in any way possible with your job hunt.  I just
received some information from the Placement Service Office that
I would like to pass along to you.

The Placement Service is sponsoring a series of seminars designed
to help upcoming graduates locate potential employers, write
cover letters and resumes, and improve interviewing skills.
Each seminar will focus on a different major.  The seminar for
Accounting majors is scheduled for Saturday, February 25.  I have
enclosed a tentative schedule of events.  There is no cost for
attending this seminar, but if you plan to attend, you must
register with the Placement Office no later than Monday, February
1 Full Text; 2 Page; 3 Options; 4 Printer Control; 5 Type-thru; 6 Preview: 0
```

■ Your Turn

You are going to print the JOBSEM.1 document.

1. The blank editing window should still be on your screen.

- ■ Press <Shift><F10> for RETRIEVE
- ■ Type **JOBSEM.1**
- ■ Press <Return>

2. The JOBSEM.1 document should appear on the screen.

- ■ Press <Shift><F7>

3. A menu appears at the bottom of the screen (see Figure A–9).

- ■ Type **1** for FULL TEXT to print the entire document

The message PLEASE WAIT flashes briefly in the lower left corner of the screen and the document is printed. When your document is printed, it should look like Figure A–10. Remember, the code *WPC* may be inserted in your document by the WordPerfect program.

FIGURE A—10

The JOBSEM.1 Document

```
          February 6, 1989
          *WPC


          Kim Landon
          4332 University Road
          Toledo, Ohio  43403*WPC

          Dear Ms. Landon,

          Since graduation  is only six short months away, I'm sure finding
          a job is a top priority for you  right now.  As  your advisor, I
          want to  help you in any way possible with your job hunt.  I just
          received some information from the Placement  Service Office that
          I would like to pass along to you.  *WPC

          The Placement Service is sponsoring a series of seminars designed
          to help  upcoming  graduates  locate  potential  employers, write
          cover  letters  and  resumes,  and  improve  interviewing skills.
          Each seminar will focus on a  different major.   The  seminar for
          Accounting majors is scheduled for Saturday, February 25.  I have
          enclosed a tentative schedule of events.   There  is no  cost for
          attending  this  seminar, but  if  you  plan to attend, you must
          register with the Placement Office no later than Monday, February
          20.  *WPC

          I hope  you plan  to attend  this seminar.  It will be well worth
          your time.

          Sincerely,*WPC



          Professor Hubert Melville
          *WPC
          See enclosure
```

1. The _____ function of a word processor enables the user to enter and edit text.

2. What function needs to be activated to move blocks of text in a document?

3. If the <Ins> key is pressed once, _____ appears in the lower left corner of the screen.

4. If text is deleted by accident, the _____ function allows the text to be recovered.

5. (True or False?) The WordPerfect Speller can not only search for misspelled words, it can also suggest correct spellings.

ANSWERS

1. text editing
2. MOVE; <Ctrl><F4>
3. TYPEOVER

4. CANCEL; <F1>
5. True

SUMMARY POINTS

■ Word processing is the act of composing and manipulating text with the aid of a computer.

■ A word processor is a program or set of programs which enables users to write, edit, format, and print data.

■ A word-processing system includes both the hardware and software that enable users to operate a word processor. There are two general types of word-processing systems: (a) dedicated systems, which can handle only word processing; and (b) multipurpose systems, which are equipped to handle various processing tasks including word processing.

■ Word processors can be used in many different places, such as businesses, schools, and homes. Uses for word processors include writing business documents, school reports, and personal letters.

■ The two primary functions of a word processor are text editing (which involves entering and manipulating text) and print formatting (which involves communicating to the printer how to format the printed copy).

■ Common writing and editing features of word processors include cursor positioning, word wrap, scrolling, insertion, replacement, deletion, spelling correction, block movement, searching, undo, and save.

WORDPERFECT EXERCISES

1. Start Up WordPerfect
Assuming that the computer is shut off, describe all the necessary steps to start WordPerfect. Start WordPerfect. How are most of WordPerfect's functions activated? What is the significance of the color coding on the function-key template?

2. Creating a New Document
  a. What actions do you have to take to begin working on a new document in WordPerfect? Take the steps necessary to begin entering text into a document.
  b. How do you tell where you are in a document? Locate the status line on your screen.

3. Entering a Document
  a. Type the following paragraphs exactly as they appear here:

COMPUTERS AND INFORMATION PROCESSING

The development of the microcomputer-driven lasser printer has ushered in a new era of neat, quickly, produced business letters. Incedentally, and perhaps even more significantly, inexpernisve in-house typesetting was made possible as welll. since many of the relatively inexpensive laser printers available today can produce a number of different typefaces, at near typeset quality, the microcomputer/laser printer mariage has started an entire new industry—desktop publishing.

Large businesses are effecting huge reductions in costs through the use of the new technology, while smaller businesses are finding entirely new avenues to pursue profit. Not only are the costs of text production dropping dramatically due to desktop publishing, but prodcution time is cut dramatically as well. Often it is possible to not commit documents to paper at all until the final product is printed. A growing number of newspapers around the country have picked up this procedure, and other businesses are taking note of the positive results.

4. Using the Editing Commands
   a. Correct the following typing mistakes:

■ Delete an *s* from *lasser* in the first sentence.
■ In the second sentence, change *Incedentally* to *Incidentally* and remove the extra *l* from *well*.
■ In the third sentence, capitalize the *s* in *since*. Correct the misspelled word *mariage*.
■ Using <Pg Dn>, move the cursor to the end of the text; replace the words *picked up* with the word *adopted*.
■ Correct any other errors that you may find.

   b. Delete the following sentence using the BLOCK function and <Del>: "Not only are the costs of text production dropping dramatically due to desktop publishing, but production time is cut dramatically as well." Make sure you also delete the two spaces following this sentence.
   c. Move the cursor back to the beginning of the first paragraph. Copy the first sentence of the first paragraph. Reproduce this sentence at the end of the second paragraph, using the MOVE function.

5. Saving and Retrieving a Document
   a. What steps are taken to save the work you have completed and quit WordPerfect? Save the document and exit WordPerfect.
   b. You decide to restore the sentence removed in 4b above. To do so, you need to reboot WordPerfect and retrieve the file containing the document. Describe the steps required to do this. Retype the sentence at the appropriate place and save the document again.

6. Review
List all of the WordPerfect functions that you used in this section.

■ WORDPERFECT PROBLEMS

To complete the following problems, use the SUBSCRIP file included on the Student File Disk. Start WordPerfect. Place the Student File Disk in drive B. When you have a blank editing window on your screen, press <F5> to list the files. Change the directory to drive B. A list of all the files on the Student File Disk, which is in drive B, should be on your screen.

1. Make a copy of the SUBSCRIP file using the LIST FILES command and selecting the appropriate choice from the menu beneath the directory. Name the copy SUBSCRIP.2. Describe the steps necessary to copy the file.

2. After copying the SUBSCRIP file, press the <Space Bar> to clear the screen. Press <F5> to LIST FILES again. Press <Return>. You can now access the SUBSCRIP.2 file. Use the SUBSCRIP.2 file to answer the remaining questions. Retrieve the SUBSCRIP.2 file.

3. The document is an order to a publishing firm. Assume that you are Helen Turoff, the writer. You want to use the same format used in the SUBSCRIP.2 file to order another magazine. Because you made a copy of the SUBSCRIP file, you can make changes to it using the SUBSCRIP.2 file, employing the original format. Enter the current date as the fourth line in the return address in the upper right corner. Press <Return>.

4. Using the BLOCK function and the <Del> key, delete the supplier address and replace it with the following new address:

Midwest Publishing
112 Lassalle Street
Chicago IL 60610

5. Change the name of the magazine to *News Weekly.*

6. Add the phrase, *Starting next month,* to the beginning of the first sentence. Change the *P* in *Please* from uppercase to lowercase.

7. Add the following name to the list of persons receiving the subscription:

Mr. Mark Steiner
M.I.S. Department

8. Using the Block function and the <Del> key, delete the following sentence: "I am accepting your special offer—$15 for the first subscription, $8 for each additional copy."

9. Proofread your letter carefully. Make any necessary corrections.

10. Save and print your work.

INTRODUCTION

Many simple documents such as memos, letters, and short papers can be created with the WordPerfect functions learned in Section A. Resumes, term papers, and other types of documents, however, require the use of WordPerfect's more advanced features. These features can make the creation of a complicated-looking document a relatively easy task. This chapter explains how to use formatting features to enhance the appearance of a document, and how to add footnotes or endnotes to a document.

FORMATTING A DOCUMENT

The **formatting** function of a word processor involves a variety of features that communicate with the printer to tell it how to print the text on paper. Some of the more common formatting features include setting margins and tab stops; selecting single- or double-spaced text; and performing **character enhancements,** such as underlining and boldfacing. Figure B–1 illustrates a typical page format.

As mentioned in Section A, WordPerfect's default settings provide a standard page format; the user does not have to enter any information to set up a standard document. These default settings can be changed, however, to accommodate the formatting needs of complex documents. Most of WordPerfect's formatting functions fall into one of three categories: print format, line format, and page format. Each of these categories is controlled by the function key <F8>. Notice that the word FORMAT is printed vertically on the WordPerfect template next to the <F8> function key. The exercises in the following sections will guide you through the process of formatting a document so that it can be custom designed.

Print Format

The PRINT FORMAT function is activated by pressing <Ctrl> <F8>. Do not confuse this with the PRINT function triggered by <Shift> <F7>. The PRINT function actually prints the document. The PRINT FORMAT function enables the user to select print enhancements, such as right **justification,** that determine how the document will look when it is printed. When the PRINT FORMAT function is activated, the Print Format Menu appears (see Figure B–2). When an option from the Print Format Menu is selected, a code is placed in the document at the cursor's position. The printing is affected from the cursor's position forward. This means that several different print formats can be selected for the same document.

There are nine options on the Print Format menu. Table B–1 explains the purpose of each option.

At the bottom of the Page Format Menu is the prompt SELECTION. To select a prompt option, enter its selection number. The cursor moves to that option. Type the appropriate number and press <Return>. When all the selections have been made, press the EXIT function (<F7>) to return to the document.

Line Format

The FORMAT function, which enables the user to set margins, tabs, spacing, and hyphenation, is activated by pressing <Shift> <F8>. The Line Format

Advanced WordPerfect

OUTLINE

Introduction
Formatting a Document
  Print Format
  Line Format
  Indenting Paragraphs
Learning Check
  Character Enhancements
  Viewing Command Codes
More Advanced Features
  Page Format
  Footnotes and Endnotes
  Search
Learning Check
Summary Points
WordPerfect Exercises
WordPerfect Problems

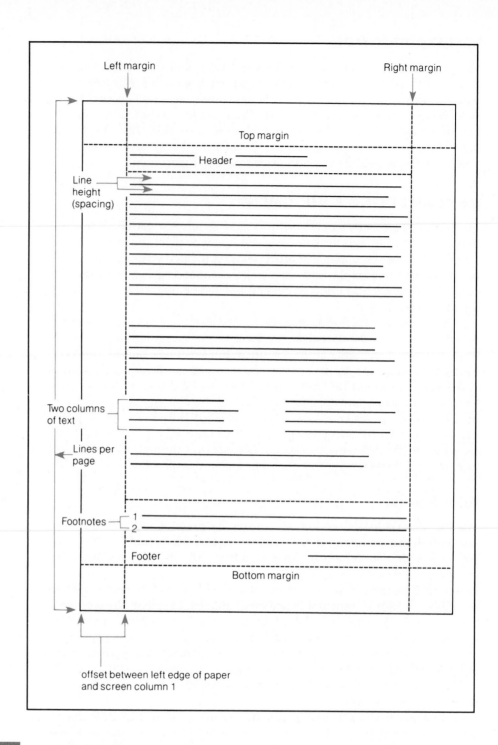

FIGURE B–1

A Typical Page Format

Menu (see Figure B–3) has six options. Table B–2 explains the purpose of each option.

To set the right and left margins, press **3** for margins when the Line Format Menu appears. The prompt [MARGIN SET] 10 74 TO LEFT = appears in the lower left corner of the screen. A standard size piece of paper is 8½ inches wide. If the document is to be printed at 10 characters per inch,

```
          Print Format

              1 - Pitch                    10
                  Font                     1

              2 - Lines per Inch           6

          Right Justification              On
              3 - Turn off
              4 - Turn on

          Underline Style                  5
              5 - Non-continuous Single
              6 - Non-continuous Double
              7 - Continuous Single
              8 - Continuous Double

              9 - Sheet Feeder Bin Number  1

              A - Insert Printer Command

              B - Line Numbering           Off

          Selection: 0
```

FIGURE B—2

The Print Format Menu

there will be 85 columns across the page, assuming that the first column is
0. If the document is to be printed at 12 characters per inch, there will be
102 columns across the page. The margin setting designates the column
number of the left and right margin. For example, if a document is printed
at 10 characters per inch, setting the margins at 10 and 74 would provide
1-inch margins. If the pitch is set at 12 characters per inch, setting the
margins at 18 and 83 would provide 1½-inch margins.

To set the left margin, enter the column number of the left margin at the
prompt and press <Return>. The prompt RIGHT = appears. Enter the
column number of the right margin and press <Return>. The editing window returns to the screen.

To select tab stops, press **1** or **2** when the Line Format Menu appears.
Two lines representing the width of the document appear. Along the lines
are *L*s which indicate the current tab settings. *L* stands for left tab alignment.

There are several ways to set or delete tabs. First, the column number
can be entered by typing the number of the column where the tab is to be
set and pressing <Return>. Another method is to place the cursor on the
line at the bottom of the screen where the tab is to be set and type **l** or **t**.

FIGURE B—3

The Line Format Menu

```
      1 2 Tabs; 3 Margins; 4 Spacing; 5 Hyphenation; 6 Align Char: 0
```

TABLE B—1

Options from the Print Format Menu

Selection Number	Option	Description
1	Pitch	The Pitch sets the number of characters per inch. Ten characters per inch, which is the default setting, and 12 characters per inch are the pitches most commonly used.
1	Font	The Font sets the print style. To use this option, you must know which fonts your printer is capable of printing.
2	Lines per Inch	Lines per Inch sets the number of vertical lines printed in an inch. Word-Perfect prints either six or eight lines per inch. The default setting is six.
Right Justification:		
3	Off	The Right Justification option can either be turned on or off.
4	On	If it is set to ON the right margin is justified, which means that the lines of text are even at the right margin. If it is set to OFF the lines at the right margin are ragged or uneven. The default setting is ON.
Underline Style:		
5	Non-continuous-Single	Non-continuous underlining, which does not underline the spaces between words; one-line underlining. The default setting is for non-continuous, single underlining.
6	Non-continuous-Double	Non-continuous underlining, which does not underline the spaces between words; two-line underlining.
7	Continuous-Single	Continuous underlining that also appears between spaces; one-line underlining.
8	Continuous-Double	Continuous underlining; underlines between spaces; two-line underlining.
9	Sheet Feeder Bin Number	Applies only to printers with sheet feeders. Selects the bin from which the paper will come when the document is printed.

TABLE B—2

Options from the Line Format Menu

Selection Number	Option	Description
1 2	Tabs	Enables the user to set tab stops. The default setting is one tab stop at every five spaces.
3	Margins	Enables the user to set the left and right margins. The default setting is right margin = 10; left margin = 74.
4	Spacing	Enables the user to set the line spacing. A setting of 1.5 = one-and-a-half lines of spacing; 1 = single spacing, 2 = double spacing, 3 = triple spacing, and so on. The default setting is 1 for single spacing.
5	Hyphenation	Enables the user to set the hyphenation feature either on or off. If the feature is off, none of the words entered are hyphenated. If the feature is on, the user can select where words should be hyphenated. The default setting is off.
6	Alignment	Enables the user to select the symbol around which characters are aligned when the TAB ALIGN function is used. The default setting is a decimal point.

Finally, multiple tab stops can be set by typing the column number where the first tab is to be set, followed by a comma and the interval at which the tabs are to occur. For example, if tabs are to be set every 15 spaces starting at the left margin, **0,15** should be entered.

To delete all set tabs, position the cursor on or before the first tab setting. Activate the DELETE TO EOL (end of line) function by pressing <Ctrl><End>. All the tabs from the cursor forward are deleted. To delete individual tabs, move the cursor to the *L* representing the tab stop to be deleted and press <Del>.

When you have finished setting the tabs, press <F7> for EXIT to exit the Tab Menu. To return to the text without saving any of the tabs that were set, press <F1> for CANCEL. Tabs can be set as many times as necessary in a document. Only the text entered after tabs have been set will be affected.

To select the line spacing, press **4** when the Line Format Menu appears. The prompt [SPACING SET] 1 appears in the lower left corner of the screen. Enter the desired spacing and press <Return>. The editing window returns to the screen.

Indenting Paragraphs

In addition to using tab stops, WordPerfect has two INDENT functions that enable the user to easily indent an entire paragraph from the left margin only or from both the left and right margins. The INDENT function that indents a paragraph from both the right and left margin is activated by pressing <Shift> <F4>. The tab stops also are used for indent stops, so the cursor moves to the next tab stop when the INDENT function is activated. Every line is then indented an equal distance from the left and right margins. Pressing the <Return> key cancels the INDENT function and the lines that follow return to the normal margin.

To indent a paragraph from the left margin only, press <F4>. The paragraph indents one tab stop each time <F4> for INDENT is pressed. Pressing <Return> cancels the function and the lines that follow return to the normal margin.

A hanging paragraph, in which the first line begins at the left margin while the remaining lines are indented, can also be created using the INDENT function. To create a hanging paragraph, press <F4> for INDENT. Then press <Shift><Tab> to move the first line of the paragraph one tab stop to the left. Type the paragraph. The first line of the paragraph starts at the left margin, while the remaining text is indented. To end a hanging paragraph, press <Return>.

■ Your Turn

For this exercise, you are going to practice using the PRINT FORMAT, LINE FORMAT, and INDENT functions by creating an outline. Figure B–4 depicts the final document.

1. Start WordPerfect on the computer. There should be a blank editing window on the screen.

2. First, turn the right justification off.

■ Press <Ctrl> <F8> for PRINT FORMAT
■ Type: **3** for RIGHT JUSTIFICATION OFF

```
The Placement Service Office is pleased you are attending one of our job
placement seminars.  This is the third year we have sponsored these
seminars and they have proven to be quite successful.  The seminar for
Accounting majors is Saturday, February 25 from 8:00 a.m. to 5:00 p.m.  The
following introduces you to the people leading the seminar and outlines the
day's schedule.

         Dr. Kate Clifford, Head of Placement Service.  Dr. Clifford has
         been the head of the Placement Service Office at Ohio State for
         over fifteen years.  Before coming to Ohio State, she worked
         for the executive recruiting firm, Cyphers,and Porter, Inc.

         Mr. Keith Goldman, Audit Manager, Thales Electronic, Inc.  As
         Audit Manager, Mr. Goldman is responsible for hiring close to
         twenty auditors a year.  Mr. Goldman's published articles
         include, "Marketing Your Accounting Degree," and "The Hiring
         Trend in Accounting."

   I.    8:00-8:30   Registration

   II.   8:30-10:00   Locating Employers

         A.  What Are the Job Opportunities for Accounting Majors and Who is
             Doing the Hiring?
         B.  Informational Interviews:  What They Are and How to Get One
         C.  Word of Mouth:  How Talking to Everybody Can Get You a Job

   III.  10:00-12:00   Cover Letters and Resumes

         A.  The Content of a Resume:  What Should and Should Not Be Included
         B.  The Form of a Resume:  What a Resume Should and Should Not Look
             Like
         C.  How to Write a Cover Letter

   IV.   12:00-1:00   Break for Lunch

   V.    1:00-2:00   Interviewing Skills

         A.  First Impressions:  How to Make a Positive Impression in the
             First Five Minutes of an Interview
         B.  Being Prepared for Any Interview Question
         C.  Knowing What Questions You Should Ask

   VI.   2:00-5:00   Utilizing the Placement Service Office

         A.  Using the Career Library
         B.  Interviews Through the Placement Office
```

FIGURE B—4

**Using Formatting Functions to
Create an Outline**

The word OFF now appears next to RIGHT JUSTIFICATION on the Print
Format Menu.

3. Exit from the Print Format Menu.

■ Press <F7> for EXIT

4. Next, change the margin settings.

■ Press <Shift> <F8> for LINE FORMAT

The Line Format menu appears.

■ Type: **3** for MARGINS

The prompt [MARGIN SET] 10 74 TO LEFT = appears. Set the margins at 5 and 79.

- Type: **5**
- Press <Return>
- Type: **79**
- Press <Return>

The editing window appears.

5. Now, reset the tab stops.

- Press <Shift> <F8> for LINE FORMAT

Type either **1** or **2** to access the Tab Menu.

- Type: **1** for TABS

The Tab Menu appears (see Figure B–5).

- Press <Ctrl><End> to delete all the tab stops

The left margin is set in column 5. You want the first tab stop to be six spaces in from the left margin and the second tab stop to be four spaces from the first tab stop.

- Type: **11**
- Press <Return>
- Type: **15**
- Press <Return>

The letter *L* appears on the line at column 11 and column 15.

- Press <F7> for EXIT

The editing window appears. Type the following:

The Placement Service Office is pleased you are attending one of our job placement seminars. This is the third year we have sponsored these seminars and they have proven to be quite successful. The seminar for Accounting majors is Saturday, February 25 from 8:00 a.m. to 5:00 p.m. The following introduces you to the people leading the seminar and outlines the day's schedule.

- Press <Return> twice

The following two paragraphs are to be indented from both the left and right margins.

- Press <Shift> <F4> for INDENT

FIGURE B–5

The Tab Menu

```
L....L....L....L....L....L....L....L....L....L....L....L....L....L....L...
567890123456789012345678901234567890123456789012345678901234567890123456789012
    10        20        30        40        50        60        70        80
Delete EOL (clear tabs); Enter number (set tab); Del (clear tab);
Left; Center; Right; Decimal; .= Dot leader; Press EXIT when done.
```

- Type the following:

Dr. Kate Clifford, Head of Placement Service. Dr. Clifford has been the head of the Placement Service Office at Ohio State for over fifteen years. Before coming to Ohio State, she worked for the executive recruiting firm, Cyphers and Porter, Inc.

- Press <Return> twice

Pressing <Return> cancels the INDENT function, so it is necessary to reactivate the INDENT function before entering the second paragraph.

- Press <Shift> <F4> for INDENT
- Type the following:

Mr. Keith Goldman, Audit Manager, Thales Electronic, Inc. As Audit Manager, Mr. Goldman is responsible for hiring close to twenty auditors a year. Mr. Goldman's published articles include, "Marketing Your Accounting Degree," and "The Hiring Trend in Accounting."

- Press <Return> twice

6. Now, enter the outline.

- Type: I.
- Press the <Tab> key
- Type: 8:00–8:30 Registration
- Press <Return> twice
- Type: II.
- Press the <Tab> key
- Type: 8:30–10:00 Locating Employers
- Press <Return> twice

Next, use the INDENT function that indents lines from the left margin only.

- Press <F4> for INDENT
- Type: A.
- Press <F4> for INDENT
- Type the following:

What Are the Job Opportunities for Accounting Majors and Who is Doing the Hiring?

Notice that when the line wraps around, it lines up under the indentation.

- Press <Return>
- Press <F4> for INDENT
- Type: B.
- Press <F4> for INDENT
- Type the following:

Informational Interviews: What They Are and How to Get One

- Press <Return>
- Press <F4> for INDENT
- Type: C.
- Press <F4> for INDENT

■ Type the following:

Word of Mouth: How Talking to Everybody Can Get You a Job

■ Press <Return> twice

7. You should now be familiar with how the INDENT function works. Type the rest of the outline as follows:

III.   10:00–12:00 Cover Letters and Resumes

     A. The Content of a Resume: What Should and Should Not Be Included
     B. The Form of a Resume: What a Resume Should and Should Not Look Like
     C. How to Write a Cover Letter

IV.   12:00–1:00 Break for Lunch

V.   1:00–2:00 Interviewing Skills

     A. First Impressions: How to Make a Positive Impression in the First Five Minutes of an Interview
     B. Being Prepared for Any Interview Question
     C. Knowing What Questions You Should Ask

VI.   2:00–5:00 Utilizing the Placement Service Office

     A. Using the Career Library
     B. Interviews Through the Placement Office

8. Proofread the document carefully. Correct any errors that you find. Save the document; name it **PLASER.LET** for Placement Service letter.

9. Use the PRINT function (<Shift> <F7>) to print the document, which should look like Figure B–4. The *WPC* code may appear in your document. Exit from the document.

1. For the most part, WordPerfect formatting changes are controlled by _____ .

2. To change margins, activate the _____ function.

3. How do you turn off the right justification?

4. What is a hanging paragraph indention?

5. Examples of character enhancements are _____ and _____ .

LEARNING CHECK

ANSWERS

1. <F8>
2. LINE FORMAT
3. Activate the PRINT FORMAT function and press **3** when the menu appears.

4. Every line of a paragraph being indented except the first one.
5. underlining; boldfacing

Character Enhancements

A character enhancement is any special printing effect. Character enhancements such as underlining and boldfacing are quite useful when creating reports, resumes, and other documents. Whether you can use all of the print enhancements included in WordPerfect depends on your printer. Your instructor can tell you which print enhancements your printer is capable of producing.

To activate the BOLD function, press <F6>. Any text entered after activating the BOLD function appears in boldface when printed. To end the BOLD function, press <F6> again.

To boldface text that has already been entered, use the BLOCK function to define the text to be bolded. While the words BLOCK ON are still flashing in the lower left corner of the screen, activate the BOLD function by pressing <F6>. The text that was marked with the BLOCK function will be in boldface when printed. Activating the BOLD function turns the BLOCK function off. The words BLOCK ON stop flashing in the lower left corner of the screen.

To activate the UNDERLINE function, press <F8>. Any text entered after activating the UNDERLINE function is underlined when printed. To end the UNDERLINE function, press <F8> again.

To underline text that has already been entered, use the BLOCK function to define the text to be underlined. While the words BLOCK ON are still flashing in the lower left corner of the screen, activate the UNDERLINE function by pressing <F8>. The text that was marked with the BLOCK function will be underlined when printed. Activating the UNDERLINE function turns the BLOCK function off. The words BLOCK ON stop flashing in the lower left corner of the screen.

Text can be centered by pressing <Shift> <F6> for the CENTER function. Any text entered after pressing <Shift> <F6> is automatically centered. Pressing <Return> cancels the CENTER function and the text that follows returns to the margin settings.

Viewing Command Codes

WordPerfect is a what-you-see-is-what-you-get word processor. That is, what you see on the screen resembles as closely as possible how the text will look when printed on a piece of paper. However, activating most of WordPerfect's functions causes command codes to be inserted into the text. Because codes are not printed, they do not appear on the screen unless the user wants to view them. Revealing the command codes enables a user to easily delete commands.

Pressing <Alt> <F3> activates the REVEAL CODES function. When the REVEAL CODES function is activated, the screen is divided in two by the Tab Ruler. The same text is displayed above and below the Tab Ruler, but the text below the Tab Ruler also displays all the codes. Seven lines of text can be displayed in both windows: the line where the cursor is currently positioned and three lines above and below it. The cursor on the bottom window is displayed as a blinking line. The cursor can be moved using the arrow keys. Either the <Backspace> key or the <Del> key can be used to delete command codes. Pressing any other key cancels the REVEAL CODES function and the editing window returns to normal.

■ Your Turn

For this exercise you are going to create a resume. Figure B–6 illustrates the final corrected document. Start with a blank editing window on your screen.

```
KIM LANDON
                                    322 Spring Road
                                    Columbus, Ohio  44322
                                    (612) 555-1214

                          Objective

To develop skills in managerial accounting with a major
corporation and to become a controller.

                          Education

B.S. Accounting, Ohio State University, 1989
Minor:  Economics with emphasis in corporate finance
Significant courses include:

Accounting                     Business
Financial Accounting           Topics in Corporate Management
Cost Accounting                Industrial Economics
Advanced Accounting            Management Information Systems
Advanced Federal Tax Law       Business Communications

                         Experience

Summers    Intern, Price Waterhouse, Columbus, Ohio, 1988
           Worked on various audit assignments, including stock
           inventory at Mills International.

College    Assistant, University Financial Aid Office, 1988
           Reviewed applications for financial aid; verified their
           conformity with tax returns and other supportive
           documents.

           Orientation Leader, University Admissions Office, 1987
           Met with prospective students and their parents;
           conducted tours of campus; wrote reports for each
           orientation meeting.

                    Computer Experience

Proficient in running VP-Planner Plus and WordPerfect on an IBM
PC.

                         Activities

Alpha Beta Psi, 1986-1988
Student Senator, Served on budget committee, 1987-1988

                         References

Credentials and References available upon request.
```

FIGURE B—6

Resume Using Several Print Enhancements

1. Before you start typing the resume, some formatting changes need to be made. First, the right margin should not be justified.

- Press <Ctrl> <F8> for PRINT FORMAT

The Print Format Menu appears.

- Type: **3** for RIGHT JUSTIFICATION; TURN OFF

The word OFF now appears next to the words RIGHT JUSTIFICATION.

- Press <F7> for EXIT

The blank editing window returns to the screen.

2. Next you need to set the tab stops.

- Press <Shift> <F8> for LINE FORMAT
- Press **1** or **2** for TABS
- Press <Ctrl><End> to clear all the current tabs
- Type: **20**
- Press <Return>
- Type: **45**
- Press <Return>

You now have tabs set at positions 20 and 45.

- Press <F7> for EXIT

3. Now you are ready to start typing the resume. The name Kim Landon is in capital letters and boldface.

- Press <F6> for BOLD
- Type: **KIM LANDON**
- Press <F6> to quit BOLD
- Press <Return>
- Press the <Tab> key twice
- Type: 322 Spring Road
- Press <Return>
- Press the <Tab> key twice
- ▪   Columbus, Ohio 44322
- Press <Return>
- Press the <Tab> key twice
- Type: (612) 555-1214
- Press <Return> twice

4. All the titles for the major divisions in the resume need to be boldfaced and centered.

- Press <Shift> <F6> for CENTER
- Press <F6> for BOLD
- Type: **Objective**
- Press <F6> to quit BOLD
- Press <Return> twice
- Type the following:

To develop skills in managerial accounting with a major corporation and to become a controller.

- Press <Return> twice
- Press <Shift> <F6> for CENTER
- Press <F6> for BOLD
- Type: **Education**
- Press <F6> to quit BOLD
- Press <Return> twice

- Type the following:

B.S. Accounting, Ohio State University, 1989

- Press <Return>
- Type the following:

Minor: Economics with emphasis in corporate finance

- Press <Return>
- Type the following:

Significant courses include:

- Press <Return> twice

5. The next subtitles are to be underlined.

- Press <F8> for UNDERLINE
- Type: <u>Accounting</u>
- Press the <Tab> key
- Type: <u>Business</u>
- Press <F8> to quit UNDERLINE
- Press <Return>
- Type: Financial Accounting
- Press the <Tab> key
- Type: Topics in Corporate Management
- Press <Return>
- Type: Cost Accounting
- Press the <Tab> key
- Type: Industrial Economics
- Press <Return>
- Type: Advanced Accounting
- Press the <Tab> key
- Type: Management Information Systems
- Press <Return>
- Type: Advanced Federal Tax Law
- Press the <Tab> key
- Type: Business Communications
- Press <Return> twice
- Press <Shift> <F6> for CENTER
- Press <F6> for BOLD
- Type: **Experience**
- Press <F6> to quit BOLD
- Press <Return> twice

The next two subheadings also will be underlined.

- Press <F8> for UNDERLINE
- Type: <u>Summers</u>
- Press <F8> to quit UNDERLINE

Indent the next paragraph.

- ■ Press <F4> for INDENT
- ■ Type: Intern, Price Waterhouse, Columbus, Ohio, 1988
- ■ Press <Return>
- ■ Press <F4> for INDENT
- ■ Type the following:

Worked on various audit assignments, including stock inventory at Mills International

- ■ Press <Return> twice
- ■ Press <F8> for UNDERLINE
- ■ Type: <u>College</u>
- ■ Press <F8> to quit UNDERLINE
- ■ Press <F4> for INDENT
- ■ Type: Assistant, University Financial Aid Office, 1988
- ■ Press <Return>
- ■ Press <F4> for INDENT
- ■ Type the following:

Reviewed applications for financial aid; verified their conformity with tax returns and other supportive documents.

- ■ Press <Return> twice
- ■ Press <F4> for INDENT
- ■ Type: Orientation Leader, University Admissions Office, 1987
- ■ Press <Return>
- ■ Press <F4> for INDENT
- ■ Type the following:

Met with prospective students and their parents; conducted tours of campus; wrote reports for each orientation meeting.

- ■ Press <Return> twice
- ■ Type the remainder of resume using the CENTER and BOLD functions as necessary:

Computer Experience

Proficient in running VP-Planner Plus and WordPerfect on an IBM PC.

Activities

Alpha Beta Psi, 1986–1988
Student Senator, Served on budget committee, 1987–1988

References

Credentials and References available upon request.

6. Next, save the document.

- ■ Press <F10> for SAVE
- ■ Type: **Kim.Res** (For Kim's resume)
- ■ Press <Return>

7. You have decided you want to underline the name at the top. To do this, mark the name as a block of text and activate the underline function. Move the cursor under the *K* in *Kim* (Page 1, Line 1, Position 10).

- Press <Alt> <F4> for BLOCK
- Press <→> 10 times so that the entire name is highlighted
- Press <F8> for UNDERLINE

The name will now be underlined when printed.

8. Now you have decided to delete the underlining from the subtitles *Summers* and *College*. Move the cursor so that it is under the *S* in *Summers*.

- Press <Alt> <F3> for REVEAL CODES

The screen is divided in two (see Figure B–7). Below the Tab Ruler line is the text with all of the command codes revealed. Notice the word *Summers* has a [U] symbol in front of it and a [u] symbol after it. These are the command codes for underlining. To delete the underlining, delete the command code. The blinking cursor should be to the right of the [U] symbol. If it is not, use the arrow keys to move it so that it is between the [U] symbol and the *S* in *Summers*.

- Press <Backspace>

Now you need to delete the underlining from *College*.

- Press < ↓ > four times
- Press <→> once

The blinking cursor should be between the [U] symbol and the *C* in *College*.

- Press <Backspace>
- Press <Return>

The editing window returns to normal.

9. Proofread the resume carefully. The formatting should match Figure B–6. Correct any errors that you find. When you are satisfied with the resume, print it.

Before exiting from this document, however, make sure you save it again because changes were made to the resume after it was saved the first time.

FIGURE B—7

Revealing Command Codes

```
                          Experience

Summers     Intern, Price Waterhouse, Columbus, Ohio, 1988
            Worked on various audit assignments, including stock
            inventory at Mills International.

B:\KIM.RES                              Doc 1  Pg 1  Ln 25      Pos 10
[        ▲                    ▲                        ]
[HRt]
[C][B]Experience[b][c][HRt]
[HRt]
_[U]Summers[u][->Indent]Intern, Price Waterhouse, Columbus, Ohio, 1988[HRt]
[->Indent]Worked on various audit assignments, including stock[SRt]
inventory at Mills International.[HRt]
[HRt]
```

■ MORE ADVANCED FEATURES

WordPerfect includes sophisticated features that are not mandatory for all documents. If mastered, however, they can be convenient time-savers. These features, which are covered in the remainder of this chapter, can help you create professional-looking documents with little effort.

Page Format

The PAGE FORMAT function is activated by pressing <Alt> <F8>. After activating the PAGE FORMAT function, the Page Format Menu appears (see Figure B–8). This menu has ten options.

Options on the Page Format Menu that help users create professional-looking documents include **headers** and **footers.** A header is a piece of text that is printed at the top of a page, such as a title that appears on each page (see Figure B–9). A footer is a piece of text that is printed at the bottom of a page, such as a page number. Headers and footers can take up as many lines as needed. They can be printed on odd-numbered pages only, even-numbered pages only, or on both odd and even pages.

The Page Format Menu also offers the option of eliminating "widows" and "orphans" from documents. In publishing, a widow is a single line that has been separated from a paragraph and appears by itself at the top of a page. An orphan is a single line separated from a paragraph that appears at the bottom of a page. All the options in the Page Format Menu are explained in Table B–3.

FIGURE B–8

The Page Format Menu

```
Page Format

    1 - Page Number Position

    2 - New Page Number

    3 - Center Page Top to Bottom

    4 - Page Length

    5 - Top Margin

    6 - Headers or Footers

    7 - Page Number Column Positions

    8 - Suppress for Current page only

    9 - Conditional End of Page

    A - Widow/Orphan

Selection: 0
```

COMPUTERS AND INFORMATION PROCESSING

find out what he or she wants to know, as the newest
college graduate just coming into the job market.[1]

This in not the impression most people looking for jobs have of

those who have the power to hire or not hire them.

Bolles explains why interviewers may be so uncomfortable

with the process:

> The odds are very great that the executive who does the
> interviewing was hired because of what they could
> contribute to the company, and not because they were
> such a great interviewer. In fact, their gifts in this
> arena may be rather miserable.[2]

David Roman agrees with Bolles. Roman states:

> As interviewers, ... managers may be out of their
> element. They're in the business of running a ...
> department, not of interviewing job applicants.[3]

Since the person running the interview is probably just as

uncomfortable as you are, there are several things you as a

person being interviewed can do to take advantage of the

situation and turn the interview into a pleasant and rewarding

experience.

⎯Footnotes

---

[1] Bolles, Richard. <u>What Color Is Your Parachute?</u>, Berkeley:
10 Speed Press, 1983, p. 181.

[2] Ibid.

[3] Roman, David. "Why MIS/DP Job Interviews Go Wrong," in
<u>Computer Decisions</u>, November 19, 1985, p. 66.

FIGURE B—9

Headers and Footnotes

TABLE B-3

Options from the Page Format Menu

Selection Number	Option	Description
1	Page Number Position	Enables the user to select where the page numbers appear on pages. The default setting is for no page numbers to appear.
2	New Page Number	Enables the user to renumber pages; the user can choose either roman- or arabic-style numbers.
3	Center Page Top to Bottom	Centers a page from top to bottom when it is printed.
4	Page Length	Enables the user to change the page length and the number of lines that are to be printed on the page.
5	Top Margin	Enables the user to set the top margin. The top margin is set in half lines. The default setting is 12, which provides a one-inch margin.
6	Headers or Footers	Enables the same text to be printed at the top or bottom of each page.
7	Page Number Column Positions	Enables the user to define the column positions for the Page Number Position option. The default settings are: 10 for page numbers appearing on the left side of the page; 42 for page numbers appearing at the center of the page; 74 for page numbers appearing on the right side of the page.
8	Suppress for Current Page Only	Enables the user to turn off any combination of page formats for the current page only.
9	Conditional End of Page	Enables the user to keep a block of text together at all times.
A	Widow/Orphan	Enables the user to keep at least two lines of a paragraph together at the top or bottom of a page.

Footnotes and Endnotes

One of the most tedious tasks involved in writing documents such as term papers is typing the footnotes. WordPerfect simplifies this task tremendously.

With WordPerfect, both footnotes and endnotes can be included in the same document. Footnotes and endnotes provide information about cited works. The only difference is that footnotes appear at the bottom of the page and endnotes are compiled at the end of the document. Footnotes and endnotes created with WordPerfect are automatically numbered. All the user has to do is type the text of the note.

To create a footnote or endnote, the cursor must be placed at the space where the note number is to appear. Activate the FOOTNOTE function by pressing <Ctrl> <F7>. The Footnote Menu appears. Type **1** for CREATE to create a footnote; type **5** for CREATE ENDNOTE to create an endnote. A special editing screen appears. The number of the note is in the upper left corner of the screen. Enter the note contents, and then press <F7> for EXIT. The document returns to the editing window.

To edit a note that has already been entered, activate the FOOTNOTE function (<Ctrl> <F7>). When the Footnote Menu appears, type **2** for EDIT to edit a footnote or type **6** for EDIT ENDNOTE. Next, the number of the footnote or endnote has to be entered. The note is retrieved and changes can then be made to it. Once the changes are made, press <F7> for EXIT. The document returns to the screen.

To delete a footnote or endnote, move the cursor to the note number in the document. Press <Backspace> or <Del> to delete the note number. The prompt DELETE [NOTE]? (Y/N) appears. Type **Y** and the note is deleted.

Search

If you have ever written a lengthy document and discovered that a key term has been used incorrectly throughout the text you know how difficult and time consuming it is to correct the mistake. This problem has been eliminated by incorporating a **search and find** routine in WordPerfect and most other word processors. The user tells the program the specific character string to search for, and it finds and positions the cursor at the first occurrence of the string.

WordPerfect can search for text in a forward or reverse direction. The SEARCH function, activated by pressing <F2>, searches forward from the cursor's position for the specified text. The SEARCH function activated by pressing the <Shift> <F2> keys searches for the specified text backward from the cursor's position. Once the SEARCH function is activated, the SRCH prompt appears at the bottom of the screen with an arrow that indicates the direction of the search. Enter the character string to be searched for and press either <F2> or <Shift> <F2> again. The cursor stops after the first match is found.

■ Your Turn

In this exercise, you are going to type a paper that includes footnotes. A blank editing window should be on the screen.

1. Before you start typing the paper, some formatting changes have to be made. First, you want each page of the paper to have a header.

■ Press <Alt> <F8> for **PAGE FORMAT**

The Page Format Menu appears.

■ Type: **6** for **HEADERS OR FOOTERS**

The Header/Footer Specification screen appears (see Figure B–10).

FIGURE B—10

The Header/Footer Specification Screen

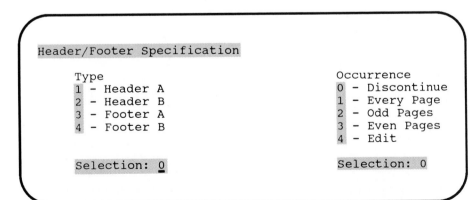

```
Header/Footer Specification

    Type                        Occurrence
    1 - Header A                0 - Discontinue
    2 - Header B                1 - Every Page
    3 - Footer A                2 - Odd Pages
    4 - Footer B                3 - Even Pages
                                4 - Edit

    Selection: 0                Selection: 0
```

■ Type: **1** for HEADER A

The cursor moves to the OCCURRENCE column. You want the header to occur on every page.

■ Type: **1** for EVERY PAGE

A special screen appears in which the header is entered. Type the following header:

Job Placement Seminar (**Press** <Return>)
February 25

■ Press <F7> for EXIT

The Page Format Menu returns to the screen.

2. Next, choose the page number position; they should appear at the top right corner of every page.

■ Type: **1** for PAGE NUMBER POSITION
■ Type: **3** for TOP RIGHT OF EVERY PAGE

The Page Format Menu returns to the screen.

3. Finally, you want to eliminate any widows or orphans.

■ Press **A** for WIDOWS/ORPHANS
■ Type: **Y** in response to the Widow/Orphan Protect prompt
■ Press <F7> for EXIT

The blank editing window reappears.

4. The right margin in this paper will not be justified.

■ Press <Ctrl> <F8> for PRINT FORMAT
■ Type: **3** for RIGHT JUSTIFICATION; TURN OFF
■ Press <F7> for EXIT

5. This term paper uses both double- and single-spacing. The body of the paper is double-spaced and the quotations are single-spaced. As you type the paper, you will switch back and forth between double- and single-spacing. Because the default setting is single-spacing, switch to double-spacing to begin typing the body of the paper.

■ Press <Shift> <F8> for LINE FORMAT
■ Type: **4** for SPACING
■ Type: **2**
■ Press <Return>

The editing window returns to the screen.

6. Now you are ready to begin typing the paper. First, type the title.

■ Press <Shift><F6> for CENTER
■ Press <F8> for UNDERLINE
■ Type: <u>Interviews: Wretched or Rewarding?</u>
■ Press <F8> to quit UNDERLINE
■ Press <Return>

■ Type the following:

For many people, interviews have a peculiar Dr. Jekyll and Mr. Hyde quality to them. While these people are job hunting, they anxiously await the phone call or letter issuing the coveted invitation for an interview. After all their hard work of scouting out the job market, finding openings in their field, and writing resumes and cover letters, an interview seems like a well-deserved reward. But, once attained, the golden interview turns into a nerve-shattering monster. Sleepless nights are spent worrying over such questions as, what will I wear, what will I say, what if they ask a question I can't answer? All of a sudden, the job hunter feels like the hunted as visions of the mighty interviewer, whose sole purpose is to expose all the inadequacies of the interviewee, become inescapable.

Interviews do not have to turn into such horrible monsters. Exposing some of the myths about interviews helps to alleviate the fear we all attach to the interviewing process.

Often, the interviewee has a totally inaccurate image of the interviewer. Many prospective employees assume the interviewer is highly skilled in conducting interviews. This is not necessarily the case, as Richard Boles points out in the following quotation:

7. Now you are ready to type the first quotation. The cursor should still be in the space following the colon. Press the <Return> key once to create space between the text and the quotation. The quotation should be single spaced, so you need to activate the LINE FORMAT function.

■ Press <Shift> <F8> for LINE FORMAT
■ Type: **4** for SPACING
■ Type: **1**
■ Press <Return>

The quotation needs to be indented five spaces from each margin.

■ Press <Shift> <F4> for INDENT
■ Type the quotation as follows:

. . . the interviewer may be as uncomfortable with this process as you are, and as ill-equipped to know how to find out what he or she wants to know, as the newest college graduate just coming into the job market.

8. Now you need to insert the first footnote.

■ Press <Ctrl> <F7> for FOOTNOTE

The Note Menu appears at the bottom of the screen.

■ Type: **1** for CREATE

The special screen for entering the footnote text appears. Notice the 1 for footnote 1 has already been inserted.

■ Type the footnote as follows, underlining the title of the book:

Boles, Richard, <u>What Color Is Your Parachute?</u> Berkeley: 10 Speed Press, 1983, p. 181.

9. After entering the footnote text, activate the EXIT function. The 1 for footnote 1 is automatically placed in the text (see Figure B–11). The series

```
inadequacies of the interviewee, become inescapable.

      Interviews do not have to turn into such horrible monsters.

Exposing some of the myths about interviews helps to alleviate

the fear we all attach to the interviewing process.

      Often, the interviewee has a totally inaccurate image of the

interviewer.  Many prospective employees assume the interviewer

is highly skilled in conducting interviews.  This is not

necessarily the case as Richard Boles points out in the following

quotation:

      . . . the interviewer may be as uncomfortable with this
      process as you are, and as ill-equipped to know how to
      find out what he or she wants to know, as the newest
----------------------------------------------------------------
      college graduate just coming into the job market.1
                                    Doc 1  Pg 2  Ln 1        Pos 65
```

FIGURE B—11

Adding Footnotes to a Document

of dashes that go across the screen indicates a page break. Notice that there is one line from the quotation by itself at the top of the second page. This is a widow. Change the spacing back to double space.

■ Press <Return> to create space between the quotation and the next line of text in the document

10. After pressing <Return>, notice that WordPerfect automatically moves the next-to-last line from the quotation onto the second page to eliminate the widow.

■ Type the following:

This is not the impression most people looking for jobs have of those who have the power to hire or not hire them.

Boles explains why interviewers may be so uncomfortable with the process:

■ Press <Return> to create a space before the next quotation

Change the spacing to single and activate the INDENT function that indents the paragraph from both margins. Enter the quotation as follows:

The odds are very great that the executive who does the interviewing was hired because of what they could contribute to the company, and not because they were such a great interviewer. In fact, their gifts in this arena may be rather miserable.

Activate the FOOTNOTE function.

■ Type the following footnote:

Ibid.

Activate the EXIT function to return to the document. Return to double spacing.

■ Press <Return> to create space between the quotation and the next line of text
■ Type the following:

David Roman agrees with Boles. Roman states:

■ Press <Return>

Change the spacing to single, and activate the INDENT function to indent the quotation from both margins.

■ Type the following:

As interviewers, . . . managers . . . may be out of their element. They're in the business of running a . . . department, not of interviewing job applicants.

Activate the FOOTNOTE function and type in the following footnote:

Roman, David, "Why MIS/DP Job Interviews Go Wrong," in Computer Decisions, November 19, 1985, p. 66.

Exit back to the document. Change the spacing to double.

■ Press <Return> to create space between the quotation and the next line of text
■ Finish typing the text:

Since the person running the interview is probably just as uncomfortable as you are, there are several things you as an interviewee can do to take advantage of the situation and turn the interview into a pleasant and rewarding experience.

11. You now discover that you misspelled a name throughout the text. The author's name is *Bolles*, not *Boles*.

■ Move the cursor to the beginning of the document (Page 1, Line 1, Position 10)

Use the REPLACE function to locate and correct all occurrences of *Boles*.

■ Press <Alt> <F2> for REPLACE

The prompt WITH CONFIRM? (Y/N) N appears. The prompt is asking if you want to confirm every correction.

■ Type: **Y**

The prompt -> SRCH appears in the lower-left corner of the screen.

■ Type: Boles
■ Press <Alt> <F2> for REPLACE

The prompt REPLACE WITH appears in the lower-left corner of the screen.

■ Type: Bolles
■ Press <Alt> <F2> for REPLACE

The cursor stops on the first occurrence of *Boles*. The prompt CONFIRM? (Y/N) N appears in the lower-left corner of the screen.

■ Type: **Y**

The cursor stops on the second occurrence of *Boles* and the confirm prompt appears at the bottom of the screen.

■ Type: **Y**

The cursor stops on the third occurrence of *Boles* and the confirm prompt appears at the bottom of the screen.

■ Type: **Y**

All corrections have now been made in the text; but footnote 1 still contains a misspelling of the author's name, so you need to edit a footnote.

■ Press <Ctrl> <F7> for FOOTNOTE
■ Type: **2** for EDIT

The prompt FTN #? 3 appears in the lower left corner of the screen.

■ Type: **1**
■ Press <Return>

The first footnote appears on the screen. Change the spelling of *Boles* to *Bolles*. Exit from the note screen after the correction has been made.

12. Now you decide that the word *interviewee* is too informal for this paper.

■ Return the cursor to the beginning of the document (Page 1, Line 1, Position 10)
■ Press <F2> for SEARCH

The prompt -> SRCH appears on the screen, with *Boles* entered as the search string because that was the last text searched for.

■ Type: interviewee
■ Press <F2> for SEARCH

The cursor stops at the first occurrence of *interviewee*.

■ Use the <Backspace> key to delete *interviewee*
■ Enter: applicant to take its place
■ Press <F2> for SEARCH again

The prompt appears with *interviewee* entered as the search string.

■ Press <F2> for SEARCH one more time

The cursor stops at the next occurrence of *interviewee*.

■ Use the <Backspace> key to delete *interviewee*
■ Enter: person being interviewed to take its place

Activate the SEARCH function again. When the program finds the third occurrence of *interviewee*, replace it with prospective employee. Notice that you will also have to change the preceding *an* to *a*.

13. Next you need to proofread the entire document carefully.

■ Return the cursor to the beginning of the document one more time. Correct any errors you find.
■ Save the document as INTER.PAP (for interview paper)

14. Print the entire document. Exit WordPerfect.

1. What are the functions required for bolding existing text?

2. What function enables the user to delete command codes from an existing document?

3. What function is activated to create a footnote?

4. What function is activated to create a header?

5. In a word processor program, the _____ routine can locate a specified character string.

CHECK

ANSWERS

1. BLOCK (\<Alt> \<F4>); BOLD (\<F6>)	4. PAGE FORMAT (\<Alt> \<F7>)
2. REVEAL CODES (\<Alt> \<F3>)	5. Search and Find
3. FOOTNOTE (\<Ctrl> \<F7>)	

■ SUMMARY POINTS

■ Word processors, such as WordPerfect, include formatting features that determine how the text is printed on paper.

■ Common formatting features include setting tab and margin stops, single- or double-spacing the text, and performing character enhancements.

■ Common character enhancements include underlining and boldfacing.

■ Headers and footers are pieces of text that are printed on every page in a document. A header is printed at the top of a page, and a footer is printed at the bottom of a page.

■ Search and find routines locate a specific string of characters.

■ WORDPERFECT EXERCISES

1. Changing a Document's Formatting

a. What are the steps required to change the formatting for a Word-Perfect document? Start up WordPerfect to begin a new document.

b. Describe the process for setting margins. Set the margins for your document at 15 and 70.

c. How do you change the spacing in a document? Change to double-spacing for this exercise.

d. Tell how to center and underline the title of the document. Format and type in the title of this exercise, Microcomputers in Business.

e. Type the following:

   Microcomputers have had a major impact on small businesses. Studies have found that nearly two million small companies in the United States use micros. Many small businesses that could not afford large computers are now able to perform all their processing on micros. This enables small businesses to maintain accurate and timely information and to improve their quality control. Micros have also helped small businesses control the size of their staffs by increasing the productivity of the present staff. Some small business owners claim if they did not use a micro, they would have to hire at least two or three more employees for functions such as accounting and bookkeeping.

Microcomputers are changing the concept of an average work day. Some companies are now allowing employees to take micros home and work from their residence. The time frames of these home workers varies. Some companies allow their employees to regularly work at home two or three days a week. Other employers allow staff to work at home for limited periods of time because of special circumstances, such as recovering from an illness or attending to an ill family member. Many employers state that staff productivity increases—in some cases as much as 40 percent—when employees are allowed to work at home.

2. Changing Command Codes in an Existing Document

a. What function is used to view the commands made in a document? Describe the procedure for changing those commands. Use this function to change the spacing to single in the preceding document by deleting the Double-space command in the command screen.

b. Delete the Underline command for the title.

3. Footnotes

a. What is the procedure for inserting footnotes in a WordPerfect document? Insert the following footnote after the first paragraph:

Dock, Thomas and James Wetherbe. Computer Information Systems for Business, St. Paul: West Publishing Company, 1987, p. 389.

b. Return to the document. Now use the FOOTNOTE function again to edit the footnote. Change the date of publication from 1987 to 1988.

4. Review all of the functions that you have used in this chapter.

▨ WORDPERFECT PROBLEMS

To complete the following problems, use the APPLY file included on the Student File Disk. To start WordPerfect, boot the system with the DOS disk. At the A> prompt, insert the WordPerfect system disk in drive A and the Student File Disk in drive B. Type **wp** and press <Return>.

1. Copy the APPLY file onto the disk in drive B by pressing <F5> for LIST FILES, changing the directory to B, highlighting the apply file in the directory and pressing **8** for COPY. Name the new file APPLY2.

2. Use the APPLY2 file to answer the remaining questions. To be able to retrieve the APPLY2 file, you must exit from the drive B directory, and then use the LIST FILES command again. Retrieve the APPLY2 file.

3. Read the APPLY2 file. APPLY2 is a solicited application letter used to answer an advertisement for an accounting job. Assume that you have just graduated from college with a major in marketing rather than accounting. You are looking for a job in the marketing field. Delete the sender's address using the BLOCK function and the <Del> key. Replace it with your own address. Use the FLUSH RT command when inserting your address. Include the current data as the last line.

4. Delete the company's address, and replace it with the address of a company that you know.

5. Delete the phrase _Daily Mirror_ on April 9 from the first sentence of the letter. Insert the following to take its place: Tribune No. 350. (Make sure that the word _Tribune_ is underlined.)

6. Using the REPLACE function, replace all occurrences of the word _accounting_ with the word _marketing_.

7. In the second paragraph, delete *Ohio State University*. Type the name of your college.

8. Delete the following sentence: "As an intern at Price Waterhouse, I worked on the audit of Mills International."

9. Insert the following in place of the sentence just deleted:

As a project assignment, I conducted a market survey on fast food businesses in Northwest Ohio. This survey was used for the implementation of a new fast food chain in the area.

10. Move the cursor to the name of the applicant. Replace the name *Kim Landon* with your own name.

11. Proofread the letter carefully. Correct any errors you find. Print the letter.

12. Now that you have seen a hard copy of the letter you decide to make some changes to the format design. Make the following changes:

   a. Change the top margin from 1 inch to 1½ inches.

   b. Set the right and left margins so that they are both 1½ inches wide.

   c. Make the right margin ragged rather than justified.

13. Proofread and print the letter again.

Introduction to Spreadsheets and VP-Planner Plus

O U T L I N E

Introduction
Definitions
Uses of Spreadsheets
Learning Check
Guide to VP-Planner Plus
Identifying Parts of the Worksheet
Learning Check
Getting Started with VP-Planner Plus
Moving Around the Worksheet
Menus and Menu Options
Saving and Retrieving Files
Saving a New File
Saving an Amended File
Getting Help with VP-Planner Plus
Quitting a File and Quitting the
Access System
Creating a Worksheet
Entering Labels
Entering Values
Ranges
Entering Formulas
Formatting Cells
Erasing a Cell
Learning Check
Changing the Appearance of a
Worksheet
Aligning Labels
Adjusting Column Widths
Inserting and Deleting Rows and
Columns
Printing a Worksheet
Learning Check
Summary Points
VP-Planner Plus Exercises
VP-Planner Plus Problems

INTRODUCTION

A manual **spreadsheet** is used to record business transactions and perform calculations. A **spreadsheet program** uses a computer's memory capability to solve mathematically-oriented problems. With a spreadsheet program, columns of numbers can be set up to keep track of money or objects.

Typically, a pencil, a piece of paper, and a calculator are the tools used to solve mathematical problems. A spreadsheet program makes the process much faster and easier. This capability is useful with complicated formulas or lengthy, tedious calculations. Imagine that after finishing your tax returns, you realized you had forgotten to include income you received from a temporary job. Every calculation following that part of the form would be incorrect. With a spreadsheet program, you would simply insert the forgotten number and direct the program to recalculate all the totals. With the ability to calculate, store, print, merge, and sort numeric information, a spreadsheet is an extremely useful tool.

This section looks at some of the features that make spreadsheet programs so popular. It also provides instructions on how to get started using VP-Planner Plus.

DEFINITIONS

Ledger sheets are used primarily by accountants and business managers for financial calculations and the recording of transactions. A spreadsheet actually is a ledger sheet like the one shown in Figure C–1. To keep numbers in line, ledger sheets have columns in which the numbers are written.

An **electronic spreadsheet** keeps numbers in line with a grid consisting of columns and rows that appear on the display screen. The spreadsheet is used to manipulate numeric data that is stored in the computer's memory. Some software packages, like VP-Planner Plus, refer to an electronic spreadsheet as a **worksheet.** For the remainder of this chapter, the word *worksheet* refers to the grid of rows and columns used by VP-Planner Plus to store and manipulate numeric data. Table C–1 provides a quick reference to other terms frequently encountered when using an electronic spreadsheet.

In a spreadsheet, numbers, or **values,** are entered into **cells** formed by the columns and rows. Each cell relates to a certain storage location in the computer's memory. **Labels** also can be entered to tell the user what the numbers mean (see Figure C–2).

Formulas, as well as values, can be entered into cells. A formula is a mathematical expression that can contain constant numbers and numbers from other cells. If one number in a cell is changed, the program automatically recalculates any formula that uses the changed number. This is probably one of the most significant advantages of an electronic spreadsheet over a traditional spreadsheet.

USES OF SPREADSHEETS

Managers in decision-making positions frequently use spreadsheets. These people are responsible for making sure their companies run smoothly. An important part of running any business is managing money. A spreadsheet program can help people manage not only money, but goods and employees.

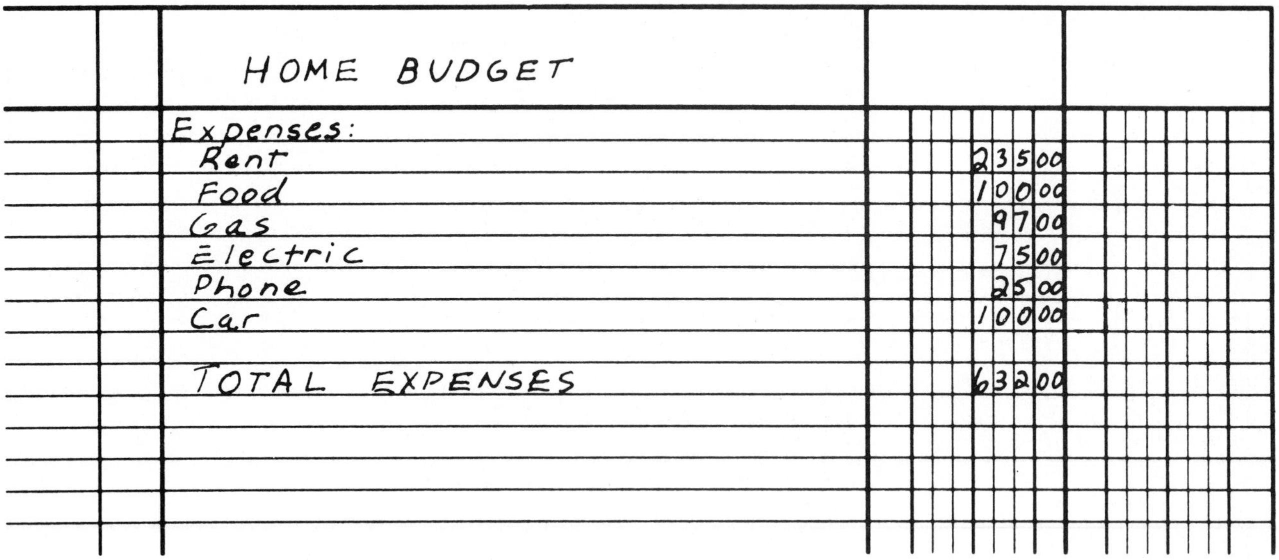

HOME BUDGET

Expenses:	
Rent	235 00
Food	100 00
Gas	97 00
Electric	75 00
Phone	25 00
Car	100 00
TOTAL EXPENSES	632 00

FIGURE C—1

Ledger Sheet

Business data, such as sales figures, expenses, payroll amounts, prices, and other numbers, are stored in the spreadsheet. A manager can enter formulas to calculate profits and losses. Other formulas compute the percentage of profits paid in taxes or any other useful calculation.

A number in a spreadsheet can be changed to show how that change affects the other numbers. For example, an increase in the cost of a material used in manufacturing can be entered into a spreadsheet to show how the increase affects the profits gained from selling the item. By using an electronic spreadsheet, a manager can spend more time thinking about how to run the business. The answers to "what if" questions are quickly calculated. This ability has made such spreadsheets a popular business tool.

TABLE C—1

Terms Associated with Electronic Spreadsheets

Term	Definition
Cell	A storage location within a spreadsheet used to store a single piece of information relevant to the spreadsheet.
Coordinates	The column letter and row number that define the location of a specific cell.
Formula	A mathematical expression used in a spreadsheet.
Label	Information used for describing some aspect of a spreadsheet. A label can be made up of alphabetic or numeric information, but no arithmetic can be performed on a label.
Value	A single piece of numeric information used in the calculations of a spreadsheet.
Window	The portion of a worksheet which can be seen on the computer display screen.

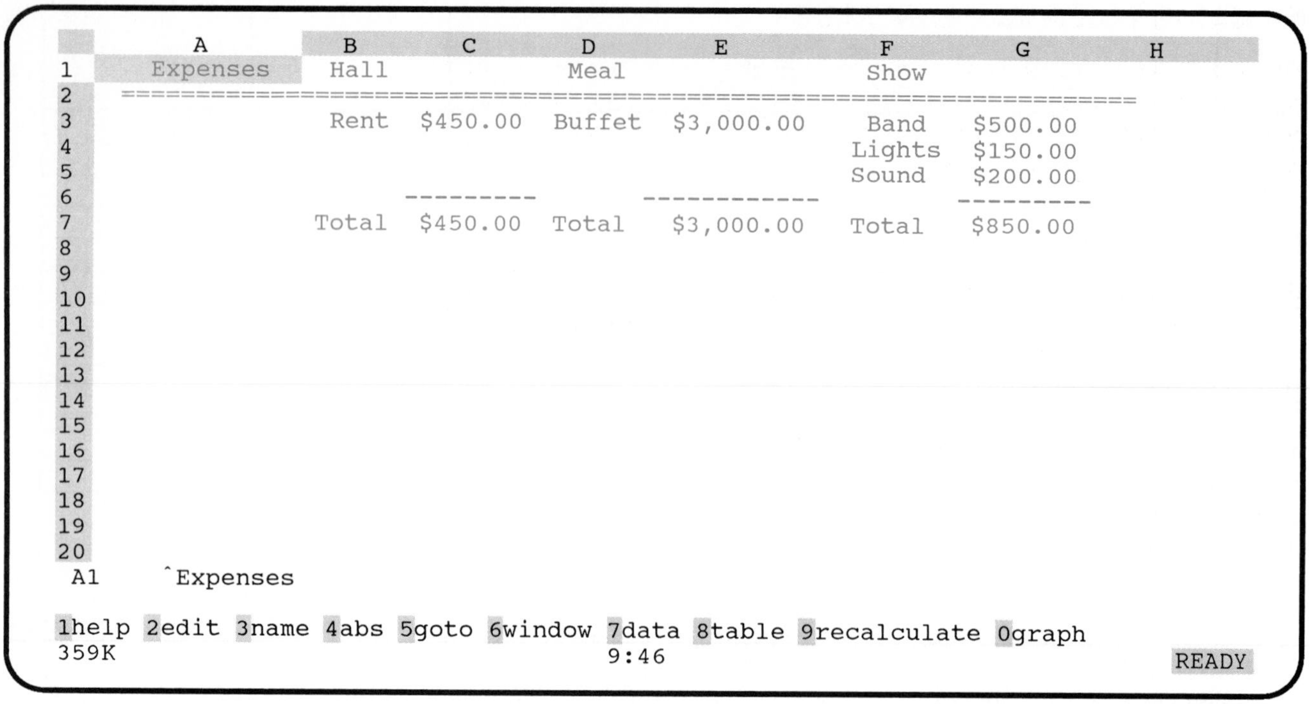

```
         A         B         C         D         E         F         G         H
 1  Expenses   Hall                Meal                Show
 2  ==========================================================================
 3             Rent   $450.00   Buffet  $3,000.00   Band    $500.00
 4                                                  Lights  $150.00
 5                                                  Sound   $200.00
 6                    ---------         ---------           ---------
 7             Total  $450.00   Total   $3,000.00   Total   $850.00
 8
 9
10
11
12
13
14
15
16
17
18
19
20
 A1        ^Expenses

 1help 2edit 3name 4abs 5goto 6window 7data 8table 9recalculate 0graph
 359K                              9:46                              READY
```

FIGURE C–2

Values and Labels

Columns A, B, D and F contain labels. Columns C, E, and G contain values.

Owners of home computers can also benefit from using spreadsheets. Spreadsheets simplify any task that requires calculating numbers. One common use of a spreadsheet program is to keep track of household expenses. The program can figure the percentage of each paycheck that goes to rent, electricity, and food. You can then see which expenses increase and which decrease each month. You can also find out how much should be saved each month for a family vacation or a new appliance.

A spreadsheet program can keep track of a team's weekly bowling scores. It can record and calculate charitable contributions. It can keep track of your grades at school and determine the marks you need to get the grades you want.

Complex spreadsheets are used in science and engineering. Scientists can use spreadsheets to calculate the outcomes of their experiments under different conditions.

LEARNING CHECK

1. An electronic spreadsheet is made up of _____ and _____ used to store and manipulate numeric information.

2. The numbers, or numeric information, used in the calculations of a spreadsheet are called _____.

3. Mathematical expressions that can contain numbers from other cells and constant numbers are called _____.

4. One reason why spreadsheets are so popular in business is because they can quickly calculate the answers to "_____" questions.

5. The location of a cell within a spreadsheet is called a _____.

ANSWERS

1. columns; rows
2. values
3. formulas
4. what if
5. coordinate

▨ GUIDE TO VP-PLANNER PLUS

The remainder of this section introduces VP-Planner Plus, a software package that combines a spreadsheet with data-base, graphics, and report generation functions. Section C and Section D cover the spreadsheet and graphics capabilities of VP-Planner Plus.

Identifying Parts of the Worksheet

When a new VP-Planner Plus worksheet is loaded into the computer, a screen like the one shown in Figure C–3 appears. Numbers listed down the left side of the grid represent the rows. The letters listed across the top of the grid represent the columns.

Each cell in the spreadsheet has a cell address or **coordinate.** The coordinate of a cell consists of a letter for its column and a number for its row. For example, the coordinate, or cell address, C4 represents the cell where column C and row 4 intersect. The **cell pointer** is a highlighted bar that indicates which cell or cells are active or can accept information. The cell indicated by the cell pointer is called the **active cell.** In Figure C–3, the cell pointer is in cell A1; so A1 is the active cell.

The bottom three lines of the screen constitute the **control panel.** The first line of the control panel is the status line, which provides information such as the cell address, the type of entry, and the cell contents.

The second line of the control panel, the input line, is a work line that displays data as it is typed in at the keyboard. Data entered in the input line can be edited and changed before the <Return> key is pressed. Once

FIGURE C–3

A Blank VP-Planner Plus Worksheet

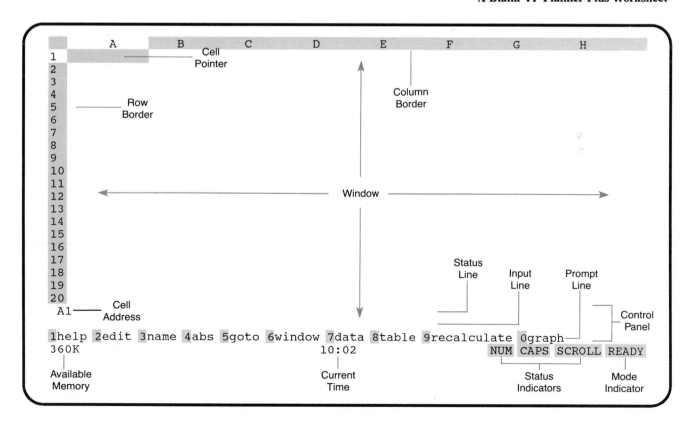

the <Return> key is pressed, however, the data moves from the entry line to the status line and enters the worksheet.

The third line in the control panel, the prompt line, displays the function keys that are available when VP-Planner Plus is in the ready mode, or it shows user menu options.

Three other pieces of information are found at the bottom of the screen. The available memory, the amount of RAM memory remaining for the current worksheet, is displayed in the left corner. The current time is displayed in the center. In order for this time to be correct, the time of day has to be entered at the DOS command when the computer is first started. The current mode of operation is displayed in the right corner. VP-Planner Plus is always in the READY mode when first started. This is the mode that enables you to move the cell pointer around the worksheet. Typing any other valid character or command activates one of the other modes. Table C–2 describes some of VP-Planner's mode indicators.

In the lower right corner of the worksheet next to the mode indicators are the status indicators. Table C–3 describes some of VP-Planner's status indicators.

T A B L E C–2

VP-Planner Plus Mode Indicators

Indicator	Description
EDIT	An entry is being edited.
HELP	A Help screen relating to the current worksheet operation is displayed.
LABEL	A label is being entered.
MENU	A menu is displayed and a menu option is being selected.
POINT	A cell or a range of cells is being specified.
READY	VP-Planner Plus is waiting for a command or cell entry.
VALUE	A number or formula is being entered.

T A B L E C–3

VP-Planner Plus Status Indicators

Indicator	Description
CAPS	The Caps Lock key is on. Letters will be typed in upper case.
ERROR	An error condition has been created; press <Esc> or <Return> to fix the error.
NUM	The Num Lock key is on. Keypad produces numbers rather than cursor movement.
SCROLL	The Scroll Lock key is on. Cursor keys move the worksheet under the cursor, rather than the cursor over the worksheet.
WAIT	User must wait for the program to perform an operation that is not instantaneous.

1. The bottom three lines of a VP-Planner Plus worksheet are called the _____.

2. The _____ is the first line of the control panel and includes information such as the cell address and cell contents.

3. The _____ displays data as it is typed in at the keyboard.

4. In VP-Planner Plus, the _____ indicates the current mode of operation.

5. In VP-Planner Plus, the _____ indicates to the user such things as whether or not the Caps Lock or Num Lock key is on.

ANSWERS

1. control panel
2. status line
3. input line

4. mode indicator
5. status indicator

▉ GETTING STARTED WITH VP-PLANNER PLUS

Some of the procedures for using VP-Planner Plus depend on whether you are using a system with two floppy disk drives or one with a hard disk drive. The directions in this section are for a system with two floppy disk drives.

Each of the following sections introduces one or more features of VP-Planner Plus. At the end of each section, there is a hands-on activity marked Your Turn. Be sure to read the preceding section carefully before trying the hands-on activity.

The key on the IBM PC keyboard marked ← is the <Return> key, also called the <Enter> key. Whenever you are instructed to press the <Return> key, press the key marked ←.

Throughout this chapter, the following symbols and typefaces appear. This is what they mean:

Type: **/WEY**	Any information in boldface should be typed. All entries that begin with the slash symbol (/) indicate a series of commands to be selected from the menus.
Press the <Return> key	The angle brackets (<>) are used to signify a specific key on the keyboard. Press the key enclosed by the angle brackets.
ENTER RANGE OF LABELS	All capital letters indicate phrases that appear on the computer screen.
Type: MONTHLY BUDGET	Magenta-colored characters indicate text that is to be entered into the worksheet.
VP-Planner Tip:	This phrase introduces important information needed to run VP-Planner Plus successfully.

To start VP-Planner Plus, you need a DOS disk, a VP-Planner Plus program disk, and a formatted disk that is your data disk. Follow these steps whenever you need to start VP-Planner Plus:

1. Insert the DOS disk in drive A. Turn on the computer.
2. When asked to type the date, enter today's date using the same format that appears next to "Current Date" on the screen. When asked to type the time, enter the current time using the same format that appears next to

"Current Time" on the screen. If you do not enter the time, the clock displayed on the worksheet will be incorrect.

3. When the system prompt (A>) appears, remove the DOS disk from drive A. Insert the VP-Planner Plus system disk in drive A.

4. Insert the formatted data disk, the disk on which the VP-Planner Plus files that you create will be stored, into drive B.

5. Type **VPP** and press <Return>.

A worksheet with the copyright message is displayed on the screen. Press <Return>. The copyright information disappears and a blank worksheet is on the screen.

■ Your Turn

Start VP-Planner Plus. After you have followed all the steps, a blank worksheet should be on the screen.

Moving Around the Worksheet

The VP-Planner Plus worksheet contains 64 columns, which are labeled A through BL, and 256 rows, which are numbered 1 through 256. The part of the worksheet that appears on the screen at one time is the **window.** For example, in Figure C–3 cells A1 through H20 appear in the window.

There are several ways to move around the VP-Planner Plus worksheet and to see parts of the worksheet outside of the window. The first is by using the pointer-movement keys (also called cursor control keys) located on the numeric keypad at the right of the keyboard. Table C–4 lists the pointer-movement keys and describes where the cell pointer moves when

T A B L E C–4

Pointer-Movement Keys

Keys	Description
<Home>	Pressing the <Home> key always returns the cell pointer to cell A1.
<PgUp>	Pressing <Page Up> moves the cell pointer up twenty cells.
<PgDn>	Pressing <Page Down> moves the cell pointer down twenty cells.
<↑>	Pressing <↑>, the up arrow key, moves the cell pointer one cell up.
<→>	Pressing <→>, the right arrow key, moves the cell pointer one cell to the right.
<↓>	Press <↓>, the down arrow key, moves the cell pointer one cell down.
<←>	Pressing <←>, the left arrow key, moves the cursor one space to the left.
<Tab>	Pressing <Tab> moves the cursor one screenful of columns to the right.
<Shift><Tab>	Pressing these keys together moves the cursor one screenful of columns to the left.

each key is pressed. (The <Ctrl> key is located at the left side of the keyboard.)

VP-Planner Tip: Because the worksheet is so large, it is possible to lose track of your position on it. If this happens, simply press <Home>—returning the cell pointer to cell A1—to reorient yourself on the worksheet.

The other way to move the cell pointer around the worksheet is with the <F5> key, one of the ten function keys at the left of the keyboard. Pressing <F5> moves the cell pointer to any cell on the worksheet. For example, if the cell pointer is in cell A1 and you want to go to cell R30, simply press <F5>. The prompt ENTER DESTINATION CELL appears. Type R30, and press <Return>. The cell pointer immediately moves to cell R30. The <F5> key quickly moves the cell pointer large distances in the spreadsheet.

■ Your Turn

Start with a blank VP-Planner Plus worksheet on the screen.

1. Practice moving the cell pointer by doing the following:

■ Press the < ↓ > key three times

The cell address in the status line should be A4.

■ Press the <→> key ten times

The cell address should be K4.

■ Press <PgDn>

Watch the row border. The cell pointer remains in the same place and the row numbers change. The cell address should be K24.

■ Press <Tab>

The cell address should be L24.

■ Press <Home>

The cell pointer should be back to A1.

■ Press <F5>
■ Type **L24**
■ Press <Return>

The cell pointer immediately moves to cell L24. Check the cell address to make sure that is the location of the cell pointer.

■ Press <PgUp>

The cell address should be L4.

■ Press <Home>
■ Press <F5>
■ Type **Z199**
■ Press <Return>
■ Press <Home>

2. Continue practicing moving the cell pointer with the pointer movement keys and with <F5>. When you have finished practicing, press <Home> to return to A1.

Menus and Menu Options

For the command menu to be activated, VP-Planner Plus must be in the READY mode. Typing the slash </> key activates the MENU mode. Two menus appear. The menu on the left side of the screen in a single-lined box is the main command menu. When it first appears, it is also the first-level menu. The first-level menu is the menu from which an option can be selected. The second-level menu is displayed in a double-lined box to the right of the first-level menu (see Figure C–4). The main command menu lists eleven options. When the main command menu first appears, the menu pointer is always on the Worksheet option. The menu pointer is the highlight that indicates which option is currently selected.

There are two ways to select an option. The first is by highlighting the option with the menu pointer. To highlight an option, move the menu pointer to the option using the < ↑ > or < ↓ > keys. When the option is highlighted, press <Return>. The second way to select an option is by pressing the first letter of the option name. Selecting an option using this second method is faster, as it eliminates having to move the menu pointer and press the <Return> key.

Each entry in the first-level command menu has its own corresponding second-level menu. In Figure C–4, the second-level menu corresponds to the Worksheet option from the first-level command menu.

FIGURE C–4

The VP-Planner Plus Command Menu

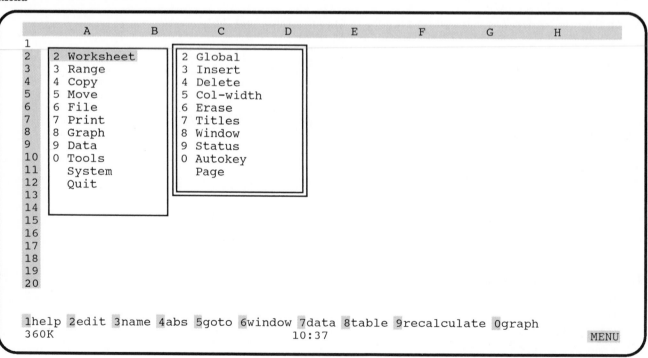

COMPUTERS AND INFORMATION PROCESSING

If a menu is activated by mistake, or if you begin to use an option and decide you do not want that option, pressing the <Esc> key lets you back out of any selection one menu at a time until you return to the READY mode. Each time <Esc> is pressed, the current menu is replaced with the one previous to it.

■ Your Turn

1. Start with a blank VP-Planner Plus worksheet on the screen.

■ Press the slash key (/).

The VP-Planner Plus main command menu and a second-level menu appear. Note that the mode indicator says MENU and the cell pointer is on WORK-SHEET, the first option in the first-level menu. The second-level menu corresponds to the WORKSHEET option.

■ Press the < ↓ > key

The cell pointer is on RANGE in the first-level main command menu, and a second-level menu corresponding to the RANGE option appears.

■ Press the < ↓ > key

The cell pointer is on COPY in the first-level main command menu, and a second-level menu corresponding to the COPY option appears.

2. Move through the main command menu one command at a time, using the < ↓ > key. Stop when the cell pointer is on QUIT.

■ Press the < ↓ > key twice

The cell pointer moves back to the first command, WORKSHEET.

3. With the cell pointer on the WORKSHEET command, press the <Return> key. The second-level menu corresponding to the WORKSHEET option has now become a first-level menu and a new second-level menu corresponding to the GLOBAL option appears (see Figure C–5).

■ Press the < ↓ > key

The cell pointer moves to the second command, INSERT, and a new second-level menu corresponding to the INSERT command appears. Move through the entire first-level menu using the < ↓ > key. When the PAGE command is highlighted, use the < ↑ > key to move backward through the menu until the cell pointer is on GLOBAL.

■ Press the <Esc> key

Pressing the <Esc> key moves VP-Planner Plus back one command level. The main command menu is now the first-level menu.

4. Now let's change modes.

■ Press the <Esc> key again

The menus have disappeared and the mode indicator has changed from the MENU mode to the READY mode.

■ Press the slash key (/)

The main command menu appears.

■ Type **P**

The **PRINTER** command is immediately activated.

■ Press <Esc>
■ Type **R** to activate the RANGE command
■ Type **N** to activate the NAME command
■ Press <Esc> two times to move backwards through the menus until the main command menu is the first-level menu.

5. Practice moving through the first- and second-level menus both by using the < ↑ > and < ↓ > keys and pressing <Return> and by using the first letter of the command name. When you have finished practicing, return the worksheet to the READY mode by using the <Esc> key.

■ SAVING AND RETRIEVING FILES

Worksheets are permanently saved in files on your data disk. Once saved, the file can be retrieved at any time to be used and changed as necessary.

VP-Planner Plus saves files to a **directory** located on a disk. When instructed to save a file, VP-Planner Plus checks the location of the current directory. The current directory can be on either the disk in drive A or the disk in drive B. The **default setting** is the disk in drive A, but your data disk is in drive B, so you want the current directory to be in drive B.

To find where the current directory is located, type the slash character (/) to view the main command menu. Type **F** for File, and then **D** for Di-

FIGURE C—5

First- and Second-Level Menus

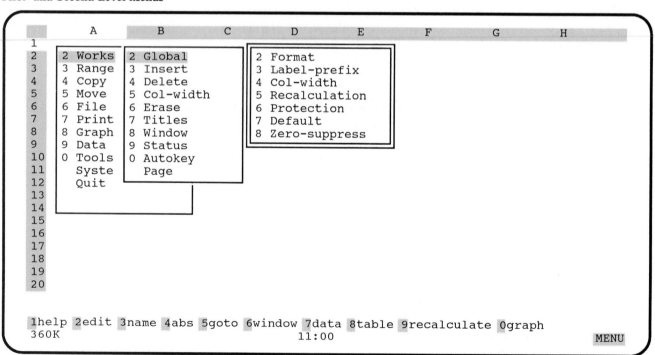

rectory. The entry line reads ENTER PATH: followed by either A:\ or B:\. If it says B:, the location of the current directory does not need to be changed. It is already in drive B, where your data disk is. If that is the case, simply press <Return>.

If, however, it says A:, the current directory has to be changed to drive B. To change the directory to drive B, type **B:** and press <Return>. Whenever you first start VP-Planner Plus on your computer, you should always check to make sure the current directory is located in drive B.

■ Your Turn

Start with a blank VP-Planner Plus worksheet on the screen. Since it is more efficient to select options from the menus by typing the first letter of the option name, the remaining Your Turn exercises will instruct you, for example, to *Type: /FD*, meaning to press the slash key to activate the main command menu, press the F key to select the File option from the main command menu, and press the D key to select the Directory option from the File menu.

1. Whenever you start working with VP-Planner Plus, you must check to make sure the current directory is in drive B. Find out where the current directory is located by doing the following:

■ Type: **/FD**

2. If the entry line reads ENTER PATH: B:\, press <Return>. If the entry line reads ENTER PATH: A:\, change the location of the current directory to drive B by doing the following:

■ Type **B:**
■ Press <Return>

The worksheet returns to the READY mode. Leave the blank worksheet on your screen.

Saving a New File

Once the current directory designation is drive B, a worksheet can be saved. To save a worksheet in a file, type a slash (/) to view the main command menu. Next, select the File command and the Save command.

The prompt ENTER FILE NAME: B:\ then appears in the entry line. A file name can be up to eight characters long, and it can be a combination of letters and numbers. Try to give the file a name that indicates the information contained on that worksheet. Type the name of the file and press <Return>. The mode indicator switches to WAIT for a few seconds and then changes to READY. When VP-Planner Plus returns to the READY mode, the worksheet has been saved.

When VP-Planner Plus saves the worksheet, a file extension ".WKS" (for "worksheet") is automatically added to the name given the worksheet. The extension is separated from the file name by a period. For example, if you named a file BUDGET, VP-Planner Plus would save the file as BUDGET.WKS.

To retrieve an existing file, type the slash (/) when the worksheet is in the READY mode. Type **F** for File and **R** for Retrieve. The prompt ENTER FILE

NAME:B:\ appears in the entry line. A window listing all the existing files also appears in the upper left corner of the screen. To select a file to retrieve, highlight its name using the <↑> or <↓> keys if necessary and press <Return>.

■ Your Turn

You should still have a blank VP-Planner Plus worksheet on your screen.

1. VP-Planner Plus should be in the **READY** mode, with the cell pointer at A1.

- ■ Type: VP-Planner Plus
- ■ Press <Return>

2. Something is now entered into the worksheet. To save this worksheet, do the following:

- ■ Type: **/FS**

The prompt ENTER FILE NAME:B:\ appears in the entry line.

- ■ Type: **Practice**
- ■ Press <Return>

Next, you are going to quit the worksheet.

- ■ Type: **/QY**

The system prompt returns to the screen.

3. Now you want to start VP-Planner Plus again and retrieve the file you just created.

- ■ Type: **VPP**
- ■ Press <Return>

A worksheet with the copyright message is displayed on the screen.

- ■ Press <Return>

The copyright information disappears and a blank worksheet is on the screen.

- ■ Type: **/FD**

If the entry line reads ENTER PATH: B:\, press <Return>. If the entry line reads ENTER PATH: A:\, change the location of the current directory to drive B by doing the following:

- ■ Type **B:**
- ■ Press <Return>

The worksheet returns to the READY mode.

4. Retrieve the file just saved by doing the following:

- ■ Type: **/FR**

In the box that appears in the upper left corner of the screen should be the file name PRACTICE.WKS. The highlighting should be on PRACTICE.WKS.

- ■ Press <Return>

The worksheet with "VP-Planner Plus" typed into cell A1 should appear on the screen.

Saving an Amended File

Once a worksheet has been created, it can be retrieved and changes made to it. Data can be added or deleted, values and labels can be changed, and so on. When a previously saved file has been retrieved and amended, there are two methods by which to save it.

The first method is to save the amended file as a new file, in which case the original file remains in VP-Planner's memory and can be retrieved again if necessary. The second method is to replace the original file with the amended file, so that only the amended file is saved and the original file is erased from memory.

To save an amended file, first select the File option from the main command menu. Next, select Save. The prompt ENTER FILE NAME: B:\ appears in the entry line. The response to this prompt determines whether the amended file replaces the original file or is saved as a new file.

To save the amended file as a new file, type in a different file name and press <Return>. If your wish, though, is to replace the original file, press <Return>, indicating that the file name of the original file is to be used as the file name of the amended file. After pressing <Return>, a menu appears that enables you to either cancel the Save command, keeping the original file intact, or, by selecting Replace, you can erase the original file and replace it with the amended file.

■ Your Turn

Start with the PRACTICE worksheet on the screen.

1. The words "VP-Planner Plus" should be in cell A1.

- ■ Go to cell **A2**
- ■ Type: Practice File
- ■ Press <Return>

The PRACTICE file has now been amended, since new data has been entered into A2.

2. To save the amended file, do the following:

- ■ Type: **/FS**

The prompt ENTER FILE NAME: B:\PRACTICE.WKS appears in the entry line. If you wanted to save the amended file as a separate file from the original PRACTICE file, you would enter a new file name. Instead, replace the original PRACTICE file with the amended PRACTICE file, which now has data in A2, by doing the following:

- ■ Press <Return>

The first-level menu that appears has three options: CANCEL, REPLACE, and BACKUP.

- ■ Type: **R**

The mode indicator returns to READY, and the new PRACTICE worksheet remains on the screen.

▨ GETTING HELP WITH VP-PLANNER PLUS

VP-Planner Plus includes a Help function that provides information about how to use the program. Pressing <F1> accesses the Help function. The help provided by the VP-Planner Plus Help function is contextual. That is, whenever you press <F1>, the information provided is specifically related to the current activity on the worksheet. For example, if you were using the Worksheet Global Default command when you pressed <F1>, information specifically related to that command would appear on the screen. Other Help screens that might provide you with further relevant information are also noted.

To access the Help function, press <F1>. As soon as <F1> is pressed, the worksheet disappears and a detailed explanation of the current activity on the worksheet appears. After you have read the information provided by that particular Help screen, you can access other Help screens by pressing <PgDn>, <PgUp>, or <F5> and the screen number. There are 150 different Help screens. When you are ready to leave the Help function, press <Esc>. The worksheet returns to the screen.

▨ Your Turn

Start with the PRACTICE file on the screen.

1. In this exercise you are going to practice using the Help function.

■ Type: **/WGF**

You have selected the Worksheet Global Format command. Now you want to get help with this command.

■ Press <F1>

2. The worksheet disappears and Help screen 48 on Setting Numeric Format appears (see Figure C–6). Read the screen. It provides information on each of the Format options. Note at the bottom of the screen it says:

NEXT SCREEN:
(49) NUMERIC FORMAT CONTINUED

More information on formatting is contained in the next screen.

■ Press <PgDn>

The next screen, screen 49 appears. Read the information on this screen.

■ Press <PgUp>

Screen 48 appears again. Pressing <PgUp> accesses the previous Help screen and pressing <PgDn> accesses the next Help screen.

3. Note at the bottom of the screen it says <F1> INDEX. Pressing <F1> accesses an index to all the Help screens.

■ Press <F1>

The screen numbers and titles for Help screens 1 through 58 are listed.

```
                    (48)   Setting Numeric Format

  These are the Worksheet Global (/WG) and Range (/R) options for numeric format:

    <F2> Fixed        Fixed number of decimal places (0 - 15).

    <F3> Scientific   Exponential notation (e.g., 3.1417E+09).

    <F4> Currency     Show dollar sign, commas, decimal point, and given number of
                      decimal places (e.g.,$10,000.00).

    <F5> , (comma)    Same as Currency, but without dollar sign (e.g., 10,000.00).

    <F6> General      No non-significant zeros after the decimal point.  Long
                      numbers shown in scientific notation.

    <F7> +/-          For horizontal bar graph: shows +'s for positive values, -'s
                      for negative values (e.g., 3 = +++).

    <F8> Percent      Percentage (value/100) shown with percent sign (%).

                                    Next Screen:
                                    (49) Numeric Format continued
  -----------------------------------------------------------------------------
        <F1> index   <PgDn> next   <PgUp> previous   <F5> goto   <ESC> exit
```

FIGURE C—6

Using Help Screens

■ Press <PgDn>

The screen numbers and titles for Help screens 58 through 120 are listed.

■ Press <PgDn>

The screen numbers and titles for Help Screens 121 through 150 are listed.

■ Press <PgUp>

4. Now you are going to access more information on file commands.

■ Press <F5>

The prompt GO TO SCREEN: appears at the bottom of the screen.

■ Type: **61**
■ Press <Return>

A help screen providing information on file commands appears.

■ Press <F1>

Now access the Help screen for editing cell entries.

■ Press <F5>
■ Type: **29**
■ Press <Return>

Look over the Help screen.

■ Press <F1>

5. Take a minute to look over some more Help screens. When you have finished, press <Esc> until the PRACTICE worksheet returns to the screen.

VP-Planner Tip: When using VP-Planner Plus you are bound to make a mistake at some point. First try using the Help function which provides useful information on the current worksheet activity. If you still don't know what to do, press the <Esc> key to terminate your last command. Repeatedly pressing the <Esc> key eventually takes you back to the READY mode. Once back to the READY mode, you can start all over.

■ QUITTING A FILE AND QUITTING THE ACCESS SYSTEM

When you no longer want to work on a particular worksheet, you need to leave the VP-Planner Plus program. Be sure to save the file before leaving VP-Planner Plus. Once the file is saved, type a slash (/) to view the main command menu. Next type **Q** for Quit. The prompt YOU HAVE ASKED TO QUIT THE WORKSHEET. ARE YOU SURE? (Y/N) appears in the entry line. Typing **N** cancels the Quit command and returns the worksheet to the READY mode.

If you select the Quit command before saving the worksheet, the prompt MODIFICATIONS TO THIS WORKSHEET ARE ABOUT TO BE LOST appears. If this happens and you want to save the worksheet, type **N** to cancel the Quit command and type /**FS** to save the worksheet. You can then issue the Quit command again.

If you want to quit the VP-Planner Plus program, type /**Q.** When the prompt YOU HAVE ASKED TO QUIT THE WORKSHEET. ARE YOU SURE? (Y/N) appears, take the VP-Planner Plus system disk out of drive A. Place the DOS disk into drive A. Type **Y** for yes. The system prompt appears on the screen. Once the system prompt appears, take the disks out of drives A and B and turn off the computer and monitor.

■ Your Turn

Start with the PRACTICE file on the screen and the worksheet in the READY mode.

■ Type: /**Q**

The prompt YOU HAVE ASKED TO QUIT THE WORKSHEET. ARE YOU SURE? (Y/N) appears. Take the VP-Planner Plus system disk out of drive A. Place the DOS disk into drive A.

■ Type: **Y**

The system prompt appears on the screen. You can now remove the disks from drives A and B and turn off the computer and monitor.

■ CREATING A WORKSHEET

In the first part of this section, you learned how to move around the worksheet and how to use first- and second-level menus. You used two commands, Save and Retrieve, and you entered data into the worksheet (when you typed "VP-Planner Plus" into cell A1). The remainder of the section introduces more commands by having you create a raw materials purchases budget for a company that manufactures chairs.

Entering Labels

As explained at the beginning of the chapter, one of three categories of data can be entered in a cell: a label, a value, or a formula. Labels usually are letters or words used as titles or captions to help identify the items in a column or a row.

Labels can be entered only when the worksheet is in the READY mode. If an attempt is made to enter a label while in any other mode, VP-Planner Plus beeps and nothing happens. Before you enter a label, check to make sure the worksheet is in the READY mode.

Entering a label in a cell involves three steps:

1. First, the cell pointer has to be moved to the cell where the label is to be entered. Either the <F5> key or the pointer-movement keys can be used to move the cell pointer.
2. Next, the label is typed. As soon as you start typing the label, the mode indicator changes to LABEL and the label appears in the entry line.
3. The final step is to store the label in the cell. There are two ways to store the label. The first is by pressing the <Return> key. The second is by pressing the Up < ↑ >, Down < ↓ >, Left <←>, or Right <→> pointer-movement keys. As soon as one of these keys is pressed, the label is stored in the cell.

Three things happen once the label is stored: The label moves to the status line, it appears in the appropriate cell on the worksheet, and the mode indicator returns to READY.

Using the pointer-movement keys, rather than the <Return> key, to store a label can be a time-saver because the pointer-movement keys perform two functions with one keystroke. If <Return> is pressed to store the label, the label is stored but the cell pointer remains in the same cell. Before you can make the next entry, the cell pointer has to be moved to a new cell. If the < ↑ >, < ↓ >, <←>, or <→> key is used to store a label, the cell pointer also moves automatically one cell in the direction the arrow is pointing. For example, if labels must be entered in cells A1, A2, A3, and A4, time is saved by pressing < ↓ >, after each label is typed because the cell pointer moves to the next cell where a label is to be entered.

A typing error can be corrected before the <Return> key or one of the cell pointer keys is pressed by using the <Backspace> key, which is located to the left of the <Num Lock> key. The <Backspace> key should not be confused with the Left pointer-movement key, which also has a left arrow on it (←). Each time <Backspace> is pressed, one character is erased. After erasing the mistake, retype and store the label.

There are two ways to edit data already stored in a cell. One way is to go to the cell where the label is located, retype the entire label, and store it. The new label replaces the old one. Once a label has been replaced, it is erased from memory and cannot be retrieved. The second way is to use the Edit key, <F2>, which allows the information in the entry line to be edited. To use the Edit key, go to the cell to be edited, press <F2> and make the correction.

The default setting for the width of a cell in VP-Planner Plus is nine characters. That is, unless otherwise specified, a cell can hold only nine characters. When entering labels, however, VP-Planner Plus uses an automatic spill-over feature: if a label longer than nine characters is entered, it spills over automatically into the next cell.

■ Your Turn

Start with a blank VP-Planner Plus worksheet on the screen.

1. Make sure the worksheet is in the READY mode and the current cell address is A1.

- ■ Type: RAW MATERIALS PURCHASES BUDGET
- ■ Press <Return>

Notice that the title RAW MATERIALS PURCHASES BUDGET spills over into cells B1 and C1 because it is longer than nine characters. Also notice the cell pointer remains in cell A1.

2. Go to cell A4 by using either the <F5> key or the pointer-movement key <↓>. When you are instructed to go to a specific cell, always check the cell address to make sure the cell pointer is in the correct cell.

- ■ Type: TOTAL BUDGET
- ■ Press <↓>

Notice that the cell pointer automatically moves one cell down, to cell A5. By now you should be familiar with the three steps involved in entering a label: going to a specific cell location, typing the label, and pressing either the <Return> key or the Up <↑>, Down <↓>, Left <←>, or Right <→> arrow key. For the remainder of the chapter, whenever you are instructed to "Enter A Label in A1", for example, this means go to cell A1, type A Label, and either press <Return>, <↓>, <↑>, <←>, or <→>.

- ■ Enter Materials in A7
- ■ Enter Lumber in A9
- ■ Enter Nails in A10
- ■ Enter Screws in A11
- ■ Enter Wood Stain in A12
- ■ Enter Paint in A13
- ■ Enter Glue in A14
- ■ Enter Varnish in A15
- ■ Enter Foam Padding in A16
- ■ Enter Fabric in A17
- ■ Enter TOTAL in A19
- ■ Enter Budgeted in C7
- ■ Enter Actual in D7
- ■ Enter Difference in E7
- ■ Enter Per of Total in G6
- ■ Enter Budget in G7

3. Now practice using <F2>, the Edit key:

- Go to G6
- Press <F2>

The mode indicator reads EDIT, and the label moves from the status line to the entry line.

- Press <←> nine times or until the cursor is one space to the right of the *r* in *Per*
- Press the <Backspace> key three times to erase *Per*
- Type: *%*
- Press <Return>

4. When all the labels are entered, the screen should look like Figure C–7. Save the worksheet under the file name BUDGET1.

Entering Values

Values are either numbers or formulas. Like all spreadsheet programs, VP-Planner Plus processes labels and values differently. A value, unlike a label, can be used in an arithmetic calculation. A label can spill over into several cells, but a value must be confined to one cell. Because VP-Planner Plus distinguishes labels from values, care must be taken in making entries.

The first character of an entry distinguishes it as either a label or a value. Because most labels are words, VP-Planner Plus assumes that an entry is a label if its first character is a letter. If the first character is a number, VP-Planner Plus assumes the entry is a value. For the most part, the following rules apply:

FIGURE C–7

Entering Labels in the BUDGET1 Worksheet

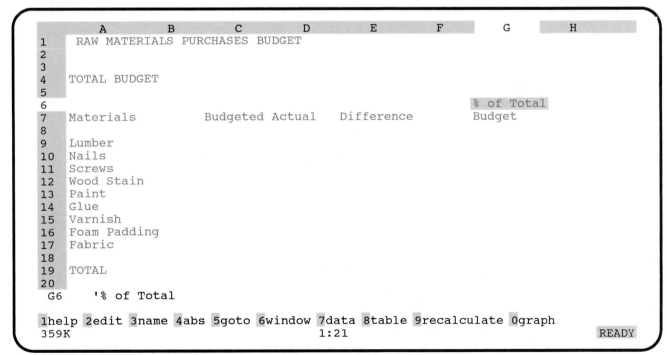

```
              A         B         C         D         E         F         G         H
  1    RAW MATERIALS PURCHASES BUDGET
  2
  3
  4    TOTAL BUDGET
  5
  6                                                                        % of Total
  7    Materials            Budgeted Actual    Difference                  Budget
  8
  9    Lumber
 10    Nails
 11    Screws
 12    Wood Stain
 13    Paint
 14    Glue
 15    Varnish
 16    Foam Padding
 17    Fabric
 18
 19    TOTAL
 20
   G6        '% of Total


 1help 2edit 3name 4abs 5goto 6window 7data 8table 9recalculate 0graph
 359K                                    1:21                              READY
```

■ The entry is interpreted as a value if the first character is one of the following: 0123456789+ −(.@#$.

■ If the first character is any character other than those listed above, the entry is interpreted as a label.

Values are entered into a cell in the same way as labels. The worksheet must be in the READY mode. The cell pointer is moved to the appropriate cell, the number is typed into the cell, and the number is stored in the cell by pressing <Return>, <↑>, <↓>, <←>, or <→>.

Values also are edited the same way as labels. A value can be edited with the <Backspace> key before it has been stored in the cell. After a value has been stored, it can be changed either by typing a new entry or by using the <F2> key.

■ Your Turn

Start with the BUDGET1 file on your screen. For this hands-on exercise, you are going to enter numbers into cells on the worksheet.

■ Enter 110000 in C4

Notice that   mode indicator changes to VALUE as soon as a number is typed.

■ Enter 24000 in C9
■ Enter 2000 in C10
■ Enter 2500 in C11
■ Enter 7250 in C12
■ Enter 12300 in C13
■ Enter 5200 in C14
■ Enter 9400 in C15
■ Enter 18300 in C16
■ Enter 29050 in C17
■ Enter 24000 in D9
■ Enter 2300 in D10
■ Enter 2350 in D11
■ Enter 7200 in D12
■ Enter 12800 in D13
■ Enter 4800 in D14
■ Enter 9250 in D15
■ Enter 18300 in D16
■ Enter 29000 in D17

When all the values have been entered, your worksheet should look like Figure C–8.

Ranges

A **range** is a rectangular block of one or more cells in the worksheet which VP-Planner Plus treats as one unit. A range can be composed of a single

```
         A          B            C          D            E         F         G          H
  1    RAW  MATERIALS  PURCHASES  BUDGET
  2
  3
  4    TOTAL  BUDGET           110000
  5
  6                                                            % of  Total
  7    Materials              Budgeted  Actual   Difference    Budget
  8
  9    Lumber                   24000    24000
 10    Nails                     2000     2300
 11    Screws                    2500     2350
 12    Wood  Stain               7250     7200
 13    Paint                    12300    12800
 14    Glue                      5200     4800
 15    Varnish                   9400     9250
 16    Foam  Padding            18300    18300
 17    Fabric                   29050    29000
 18
 19    TOTAL
 20
      D17      29000


     1help 2edit 3name 4abs 5goto 6window 7data 8table 9recalculate 0graph
     359K                                        0:35                          READY
```

FIGURE C—8

**Entering Values in the BUDGET1
Worksheet**

cell, one row, one column, or a block of rows and columns that form a
rectangle (see Figure C–9). Ranges are among the valuable assets of electronic spreadsheets. Instead of performing a particular function on one cell
at a time, the user can define a range of cells and have a function performed
on the entire range. For example, ranges can be used to copy, move, or erase
entire sections of a worksheet.

■ Your Turn

1. Start with the BUDGET1 worksheet on the screen.

- ■ Go to cell A5
- ■ Type: \ = (the backslash key followed by the equal sign)
- ■ Press <Return>

Notice that, even though the equal sign was only pressed once, the double
lines fill the entire cell. That is because the backslash was pressed before
the equal sign. In VP-Planner Plus, the backslash functions as a repeating
label prefix. Whatever is typed after the backslash repeats itself until it fills
the entire cell.

2. Next, we need to define a range.

- ■ Type: /C

The message SOURCE CELL RANGE: A5..A5 appears in the entry line, and
the mode indicator says POINT. A5 is the current location of the cell pointer,
and it is also a one-cell range. You are now going to copy this one-cell range.
Because A5 is the only cell to be copied, press the <Return> key. The prompt
DESTINATION CELL RANGE: A5 appears. You now need to indicate the

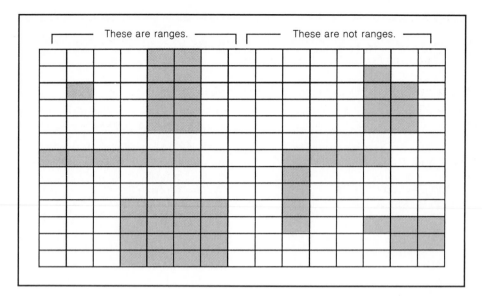

These are ranges. ———— These are not ranges. ————

FIGURE C—9

Ranges

range of cells into which you want the double lines copied. There are two ways to indicate a range. The first way is to type the cell addresses that comprise the range, separated by a period:

- Type: **B5.H5**
- Press <Return>

3. The second way to indicate a range is to extend the highlighting to include all the cell addresses that constitute the range:

- Go to A8
- Type: \ –
- Press <Return>
- Type: /C

The prompt SOURCE CELL RANGE: A8..A8 appears in the entry line. Again, this one-cell range is what you want to copy, so press <Return>. The prompt DESTINATION CELL RANGE: A8 appears. This time you are going to indicate the range by expanding the highlighting. The range must first be "anchored" before the highlighting can be expanded. Typing a period after the cell address where the highlighting is to begin anchors the highlighting—that is, it indicates the address of the first cell in the range.

- Type . (period) to anchor the first cell of the range in cell A8

Notice that the prompt now reads, DESTINATION CELL RANGE: A8..A8. Once the period was pressed, VP-Planner Plus automatically added ..A8. You can tell if a range is anchored by looking at this notation by the prompt. If there is just a cell address, such as A8, the range is not anchored. If there is a notation of a range, such as A8..A8, the range is anchored.

- Press <→> seven times

Notice that the highlighting now extends through the range of cells A8–H8, and that the notation by the prompt in the entry line reads A8..H8

■ Press <Return>

Pressing <Return> confirms the range indicated by the highlighting. The single line is copied into that range of cells.

VP-Planner Tip: If the range is anchored in the wrong cell, press <Esc> to release the range, move the cell pointer to the correct cell, and type a period(.) to re-anchor the range.

Entering Formulas

Formulas are mathematical expressions. When writing formulas with VP-Planner Plus, you can use addition, subtraction, multiplication, division, and exponentiation, as well as advanced financial and statistical analysis. Formulas can contain references to particular cells (using their cell addresses) and can indicate mathematical operations to be performed on the values within those cells.

Formulas are entered on a worksheet the same way as labels and numbers are entered—by typing them into cells. A formula typically is created by entering either a value or a cell address, then a mathematical operator, and then another value or cell address, and so on. The mathematical operators most frequently used in formulas are:

+ add
− subtract
* multiply
/ divide

Formulas often contain cell addresses. For example, a formula might be A5 + A6 + A7. Because formulas are values and VP-Planner Plus assumes an entry beginning with a letter is a label, formulas often begin with a plus sign (+) to indicate that what follows is a formula, not a label. If the previous example were entered into a worksheet, it would be entered as +A5 + A6 + A7.

There are two ways to enter formulas into cells: (a) by typing the formula, and (b) by pointing to the cells included in the formula. The following exercise uses both methods.

■ Your Turn

Start with the BUDGET1 worksheet on your screen. For this hands-on exercise, you are going to enter formulas into cells on the worksheet.

1. First, you are going to enter formulas by typing them.

　■ Go to C19
　■ Type: **24000 + 2000 + 2500 + 7250 + 12300 + 5200 + 9400 + 18300 + 29050**

Notice that the mode indicator changes to VALUE and the formula you typed appears in the entry line.

　■ Press <Return>

The mode indicator changes to READY, the formula moves to the status line, and the sum appears in cell C19.

2. The next formula is entered by using cell addresses rather than numbers.

- Go to D19
- Type: **+D9+D10+D11+D12+D13+D14+D15+D16+D17**

Remember that the plus sign (+) must be the first character typed to indicate to VP-Planner Plus that this is a value, not a label.

- Press <Return>

Again, the sum appears in the cell where the formula was entered, even though you used cell addresses rather than numbers in the formula.

3. When a formula is long like this one, typing in all the numbers or cell addresses is time-consuming and making a typing error would be easy. A more efficient way to enter formulas is by pointing to the cells included in the formula. Reenter the two formulas just entered, using this new method:

- Go to C19
- Type: **+**
- Using the < ↑ > key, move to C17

Notice that the mode indicator says POINT and that +C17 is in the entry line.

- Type: **+**

The cell pointer moves back to C19.

- Using the < ↑ > key, move to C16
- Type: **+**

Again, the cell pointer moves back to C19.

- Move to C15
- Type: **+**
- Move to C14
- Type: **+**
- Move to C13
- Type: **+**
- Move to C12
- Type: **+**
- Move to C11
- Type: **+**
- Move to C10
- Type: **+**
- Move to C9
- Press <Return>

4. The formula, using cell addresses, is in the status line. The sum is in cell C19. Using the same pointing method, reenter the formula for cell D19.

5. The column titled Difference shows the difference between what was budgeted and what was actually spent. Enter formulas in cells E9 through E17 to show this difference:

- Go to E9
- Type: **+**
- Move to C9
- Type: **−**

- Move to D9
- Press <Return>

The formula appears in the status line, the mode indicator says READY, and the difference appears in cell E9.

- Go to E10
- Type: **+**
- Move to C10
- Type: **−**
- Move to D10
- Press <Return>

Because $300 more than what was budgeted was actually spent, the number appears as a negative.

- Go to E11
- Type: **+**
- Move to C11
- Type: **−**
- Move to D11
- Press <Return>

Continue to enter formulas into cells E12 through E17 which calculate the difference between what was budgeted and what was actually spent.

6. Save the amended worksheet.

Formatting Cells

Values in a VP-Planner Plus worksheet can be formatted. That is, they can be made to appear with dollar signs, with commas, or rounded off to a certain number of decimal places. Either one cell or a range of cells can be formatted.

To format a cell, first select the Range option from the main command menu. Then select Format. The options for the Format command appear in the second-level menu. Table C–5 lists these options and the functions they perform.

If Fixed, Scientific, Currency, Comma (,), or Percent is selected as a format, VP-Planner Plus prompts you to enter the number of decimal places you would like displayed. Up to 15 decimal places can be displayed. Values are rounded to the number of decimal places specified.

■ Your Turn

Start with the BUDGET1 worksheet on the screen.

1. To begin formatting,

- Go to C9
- Type: **/RFC**

The prompt ENTER DESIRED DECIMAL POSITION appears in the entry line. The default setting is 2. You do not want a decimal position.

- Type: **0**
- Press <Return>

TABLE C-5

Format Command Options

Option	Description
Fixed	Values are rounded to a fixed number of places. Example: 8.67
Scientific	Exponential notation. Example 2.56E + 05
Currency	Dollars and cents. Example: $30.45 Negative numbers are placed in parentheses. Example (5,469)
,	Commas are added to long numbers. Example: 32,450
General	No fixed number of decimal places is set. Example: 8.671
Percent	Value is multiplied by 100 and a % sign added. Example: 58%
Date	Date format. Example: DD-MMM-YY (28-Sep-53)
Text	Displays the formula in the cell.
Reset	Returns cell or cells to the global default format, which, if not changed, is General
Hide	Hides the cell entries.

2. The prompt in the entry line reads SELECT RANGE OF CELLS TO BE ALTERED: C9..C9.

- Press the < ↓ > key ten times or until the range reaches C19.
- Press <→> twice

The range from C9 to E19 is now selected, as indicated by the highlighting on the worksheet and the prompt in the entry line.

- Press <Return>

All the values in cells C9 to E19 now appear in the currency format. Notice that the negative numbers now appear within parentheses rather than having a minus sign in front of them. The status line reads C9: (C0) 24000. The C0 within parentheses indicates how the cell has been formatted. It stands for Currency rounded to 0 decimal places.

3. The column titled % of Total Budget is used for figuring out what percentage of the budgeted total was actually spent on each of the raw materials. The formula used to figure this percentage is the amount spent divided by the budgeted total. For example, the formula to be entered into G9 is 24000/110000 or D9/C4. Enter the appropriate formulas into cells G9 through G17. Remember, if you use cell addresses in your formulas, you must use the + prefix.

4. Next, format cells G9–G17 using the Percent format option:

- Go to G9
- Type: **/RFP**

The prompt in the entry line reads ENTER DESIRED DECIMAL POSITION: 2.

- Type: **0**
- Press <Return>
- Press < ↓ > eight times or until the cell range G9 to G17 is selected.
- Press <Return>

The percentages appear in column G. In the status line, (P0) stands for the Percentage format carried out to 0 decimal places.

5. Save the amended BUDGET1 worksheet.

Erasing a Cell

Erasing a cell or a range of cells on a VP-Planner Plus worksheet is easy. First select Range from the main command menu, then select Erase. The prompt, SELECT RANGE OF CELLS TO BE BLANKED appears in the entry line. Using the $<\rightarrow>$, $<\leftarrow>$, $<\uparrow>$ and $<\downarrow>$ keys, select the range to be erased and press <Return>.

If a value that has been used in a formula is erased, the formula using that value will automatically recalculate without the value.

■ Your Turn

1. Start with the BUDGET1 worksheet on your screen.

- ■ Go to A17
- ■ Type: **/RE**

The prompt, SELECT RANGE OF CELLS TO BE BLANKED: A17..A17 appears in the entry line. Only one cell, A17, is to be erased, so press <Return>.

- ■ Enter Upholstery in A17

2. Save the amended worksheet BUDGET1.

LEARNING CHECK

1. The Edit key is _____.

a. F1
b. F2
c. F5
d. F10

2. If the first character of an entry is a number, VP-Planner Plus assumes the entry is a _____.

3. A _____ is a rectangular block of cells in a worksheet which VP-Planner Plus treats as one unit.

4. If the first entry in a formula is a cell address, the formula must be preceded with a _____.

5. Changing the way a value appears in a cell, for example adding a dollar sign, percent sign, or comma, is called _____ a cell.

ANSWERS

1. b.
2. value
3. range
4. plus sign (+)
5. formatting

■ CHANGING THE APPEARANCE OF A WORKSHEET

Having a worksheet that is easy to read is important. VP-Planner Plus includes such options as being able to align labels, adjust column widths, and insert and delete rows and columns, in order to create a neat and easily understandable worksheet. These options are discussed in the following sections.

Aligning Labels

A label prefix determines the alignment of a label—that is, whether it aligns on the left side of the cell, is centered within the cell, or is aligned on the right side of the cell. A label prefix is the first character typed when entering a label. Table C–6 lists the label prefixes and explains their functions.

VP-Planner's default prefix is the apostrophe. That is, if no prefix is indicated, VP-Planner Plus aligns the labels on the left side of the cell.

Label prefixes also enable a heading that begins with a number to be used as a label. For example, if you wanted to use 1987, 1988, and 1989 as labels, VP-Planner plus would read them as values unless you used a label prefix. Just as the plus sign is typed in as the first character of a formula beginning with a cell address, so a label prefix must be the first character of a label beginning with a number. In this example, you would type the following into the cells: ˆ1987, ˆ1988, ˆ1989. (The label prefix character does not appear in the cell as part of the label.)

There are two methods for setting up label prefixes. The first is to type in the prefix as part of the title. The second, which is explained in the following exercise, is to align a range of labels.

▨ Your Turn

1. Start with the BUDGET1 worksheet on your screen.

- ▪ Go to A7
- ▪ Type: **/RL**

The options LEFT, RIGHT, CENTER, and FLUSH-RIGHT appear in the first-level menu. The difference between right and flush-right is right-justified labels include a space between the end of the label and the edge of the cell. Flush-right labels do not include that space. Currently the labels are aligned at the left side of the cell. You are going to change the labels so that they are right-justified.

- ▪ Type: **R**

T A B L E   C—6

Label Prefixes

Label Prefix	Purpose
' (apostrophe)	To align labels on the left side of the cell
ˆ (caret)	To center labels within the cell
" (double quotation mark)	To align labels on the right side of the cell. A space is included between the end of the label and the edge of the cell.
' (left single quote)	To align labels on the right side of the cell. There is no space between the end of the label and the edge of the cell.
\ (backslash)	To repeat a single character or a set of characters for the length of the cell

The prompt SELECT RANGE OF CELLS TO BE ALTERED: A7..A7 appears in the entry line.

- Press <→> seven times, or until the range of cells from A7 through H7 is selected.
- Press <Return>

Move the cell pointer through row 7. Notice that each label is preceded by the double quotation label prefix.

- Go to A7
- Type: **/RLC**
- Enter the range of labels A7 through H7
- Press <Return>

Move the cell pointer through row 7. Now the ^ label prefix is in front of each label, indicating that you have now centered these labels.

2. Save the amended worksheet BUDGET1.

Adjusting Column Widths

The default column width in VP-Planner Plus is nine characters. The column width can be adjusted, however, from 0 to 240 characters. The width of individual columns can be set, or the width of all the columns in the worksheet can be set.

■ Your Turn

1. Start with the BUDGET1 worksheet on your screen. You have decided you want all the values to appear as currency carried out to two decimal places rather than zero decimal places.

- Go to C4

In the previous hands-on exercise, when cells were changed to the currency format, cell C4 was not formatted. Now you are going to format this cell.

- Type: **/RFC**
- Press <Return> to accept the default decimal position of 2
- Press <Return> again to accept a range of one cell, C4

Notice that asterisks now fill C4. Changing the format to currency carried out to two decimal places added enough characters to 110000 that it is now too long to fit in the column at its present width. Look at the status line. Even though asterisks appear on the worksheet, VP-Planner Plus still has the value 110000 stored in cell C4.

2. Keep the cell pointer at C4. You are now going to change the width of the column so that the actual value, rather than asterisks, appears on the worksheet in cell C4.

- Type: **/WCS**

ENTER DESIRED COLUMN WIDTH (1..240): 9 now appears in the entry line, because 9 is the current width of the column.

- Press <→> once

Notice that the 9 in the entry line changed to a 10. The current column width is now 10. Asterisks still appear in the cell.

■ Press <→> twice

$110,000.00 now appears on the worksheet in C4. A column width of 12 is enough space for this value.

■ Press <Return>

The control panel now reads C4: (C2) 110000. This indicates that cell C4 is formatted as currency carried out to two decimal places and the value in C4 is 110000. Now you are going to change the format of the rest of the values in column C to currency carried out to two decimal places.

■ Go to C9
■ Format the range of cells C9 to C19 as currency carried out to two decimal places

Because the width of the entire column is 12, the correct value (rather than asterisks) appears in cell C19. When you are changing the width of a column, the cell pointer can be on any cell in the column.

3. Move the cell pointer to any cell in column D and change the width of column D to 12. Then format the range of cells D9 to D19 as currency carried out to two decimal places.

Column F is too wide. Move the cell pointer to column F and change the width to 3. When the prompt ENTER COLUMN WIDTH (1..240) appears in the entry line, type **3** and press <Return>.

4. Save the amended worksheet BUDGET1.

Inserting and Deleting Rows and Columns

Sometimes the appearance of a worksheet can be enhanced by adding a row or column. Perhaps a row or column has to be added to accomodate additional data, or data that is no longer relevant has to be deleted from a worksheet. Adding or deleting rows and columns on a VP-Planner Plus worksheet is a simple task that involves pointing to the location where the row or column is to be added or deleted.

To add a row or column, first position the cell pointer. The cell pointer must be positioned to the right of where a column is to appear and under where a row is to appear. Select the Worksheet option from the main command menu. Next select Insert. The option of selecting either Column or Row appears next. After you select Row or Column, the prompt SELECT RANGE OF COLUMNS (ROWS) TO INSERT appears in the entry line. If only one column or row is to be inserted, simply press <Return>. If more than one column or row is to be inserted, the range of the insertion can be indicated either by using the pointer-movement keys or typing in the range. Once the <Return> key is pressed, the row or column is added and the worksheet returns to the READY mode.

Deleting a row or column is similar to adding a row or column. Select Worksheet from the main command menu and select Delete. Next you choose to delete either a row or a column and indicate the range of columns or rows to be deleted. Pressing the <Return> key deletes the designated rows or columns and the worksheet returns to the READY mode.

Be very careful when deleting rows and columns. Once a row or column is deleted, it is erased from memory and cannot be retrieved. Accidentally deleting a row when you intended to delete a column could be disastrous.

■ Your Turn

Start with the BUDGET1 worksheet on the screen.

1. You are going to delete row 2 from the worksheet.

- ■ Go to A2
- ■ Type: **/WDR**
- ■ Press <Return>, because you want to delete row 2 only.

2. Now you are going to add a row between TOTAL BUDGET and the double lines:

- ■ Go to A4
- ■ Type: **/WIR**
- ■ Press <Return>, because you want to add one row only.

Your worksheet should look like Figure C–10 when completed.

3. Save the amended BUDGET1 file.

■ PRINTING A WORKSHEET

There are times when it is useful to have a hard copy of a worksheet. Printing a VP-Planner Plus worksheet is described in this section.

Before printing a worksheet, make sure to save the file so that the hard copy will include the latest changes or additions. Select the Print option

FIGURE C–10

Changing the Appearance of the BUDGET1 Worksheet

	A	B	C	D	E	F	G	H
1	RAW MATERIALS PURCHASES BUDGET							
2								
3	TOTAL BUDGET		$110,000.00					
4								
5	==							
6						% of Total		
7	Materials		Budgeted	Actual	Difference	Budget		
8	--							
9	Lumber		$24,000.00	$24,000.00	$0	22%		
10	Nails		$2,000.00	$2,300.00	($300)	2%		
11	Screws		$2,500.00	$2,350.00	$150	2%		
12	Wood Stain		$7,250.00	$7,200.00	$50	7%		
13	Paint		$12,300.00	$12,800.00	($500)	12%		
14	Glue		$5,200.00	$4,800.00	$400	4%		
15	Varnish		$9,400.00	$9,250.00	$150	8%		
16	Foam Padding		$18,300.00	$18,300.00	$0	17%		
17	Upholstery		$29,050.00	$29,000.00	$50	26%		
18								
19	TOTAL		$110,000.00	$110,000.00				
20								

A4

1help 2edit 3name 4abs 5goto 6window 7data 8table 9recalculate 0graph
357K   5:00   READY

from the main command menu. The options PRINTER and FILE appear next. A VP-Planner Plus worksheet can be sent directly to a printer, or it can be stored in a print file for later processing. Select Printer. Ten Printer options appear in the first-level menu. These options offer choices regarding the appearance and format of the printout. Table C–7 lists the Printer options and describes their functions.

The only printer option that must be selected to print a worksheet is Range. After you select Range, the prompt SELECT RANGE OF CELLS FOR PRINTING appears in the entry line. To specify the range to be printed, move the cell pointer to the first cell to be printed. The address of that cell appears after the prompt in the entry line. Type a period (.) to anchor the range, and then move the cell pointer to the last cell to be printed. Press <Return>. The Printer options return to the entry line.

Make sure the printer is connected to your computer and is online. Select Go from the Printer options, and the worksheet is printed. The Printer options remain in the entry line after the worksheet has been printed. When you no longer want to print, select Quit and the worksheet returns to the READY mode.

■ Your Turn

1. You are going to print the entire BUDGET1 worksheet.

- ■ Type: **/PPR**

Move the cell pointer to A1.

- ■ Type a period (.) to anchor the range
- ■ Press <→> 7 times to select the columns A through H
- ■ Press <↓> 18 times to select the rows 1 through 19

The entire worksheet should now be highlighted.

TABLE C–7

Printer Options

Option	Description
Range	Specifies the range of the worksheet to be printed. The range must be specified even if all the data on the worksheet is being printed.
Line	Advances the paper one line.
Page	Advances the paper one page.
Options	Allows a number of choices to be made regarding the appearance of the worksheet. These choices include specifying a header or footer to be printed on each page, setting margins, specifying border columns and rows, and specifying the number of lines per page.
Clear	Resets all of the print settings.
Align	Resets the alignment of the paper to the top of the page.
Go	Starts the printing process.
Quit	Returns to the READY mode.
Status	Displays the current Print command settings.
Eject	Advances the paper to the top of the next sheet.

■ Press <Return>

The worksheet is no longer highlighted and the menus return to the worksheet.

2. Make sure your computer is connected to the printer and is online.

■ Type: **G**

The BUDGET1 worksheet is printed. It should look like Figure C–11.

■ Type: **Q**

LEARNING
CHECK

1. The label prefix _____ aligns labels on the right side of the cell.

a. ' (apostrophe)
b. " (double quotation mark)
c. ^ (caret)
d. \ (backslash)

2. The label prefix _____ repeats a single character or set of characters for the length of the cell.

a. ' (apostrophe)
b. " (double quotation mark)
c. ^ (caret)
d. \ (backslash)

3. (True or False?) A heading beginning with a number can only be used as a label if a label prefix precedes it.

4. The default column width in VP-Planner Plus is _____ characters.

a. 6
b. 9
c. 8
d. 10

5. (True or False?) When a row has been deleted accidentally on a VP-Planner Plus worksheet, it can be retrieved.

ANSWERS

1. b.
2. d.
3. True

4. b.
5. False

FIGURE C–11

The BUDGET1 Worksheet

```
RAW MATERIALS PURCHASES BUDGET

TOTAL BUDGET        $110,000.00


=================================================================
                                                      % of Total
Materials          Budgeted     Actual    Difference  Budget
-----------------------------------------------------------------
Lumber            $24,000.00  $24,000.00        $0       22%
Nails              $2,000.00   $2,300.00     ($300)       2%
Screws             $2,500.00   $2,350.00      $150        2%
Wood Stain         $7,250.00   $7,200.00       $50        7%
Paint             $12,300.00  $12,800.00     ($500)      12%
Glue               $5,200.00   $4,800.00      $400        4%
Varnish            $9,400.00   $9,250.00      $150        8%
Foam Padding      $18,300.00  $18,300.00        $0       17%
Upholstery        $29,050.00  $29,000.00       $50       26%

TOTAL            $110,000.00 $110,000.00
```

▣ SUMMARY POINTS

■ A spreadsheet program simulates the operations of a calculator and stores the results in the computer's memory.

■ An electronic spreadsheet is displayed as a table of columns and rows.

■ The three categories of items which can be entered into an electronic spreadsheet are labels, values, and formulas.

■ Labels are used to identify the contents of a spreadsheet. A value is a single piece of numeric information used in the calculations of a spreadsheet.

■ A formula is a mathematical expression that is assigned to a cell in the spreadsheet.

The two major areas of a worksheet are the control panel and the window. The control panel displays important information about the worksheet. The window is the portion of the worksheet which is currently displayed.

▣ VP-PLANNER PLUS EXERCISES

To complete the following exercises you need a DOS disk, a VP-Planner Plus system disk, and a formatted disk that will be your data disk.

1. Starting VP-Planner Plus

a. Start the computer with a DOS disk. At the A> prompt, insert the VP-Planner Plus system disk in drive A.

■ Type: **VPP**
■ Press <Return>
■ Type /

What is the name of the menu that appears on the left? How do you select an option from a menu?

2. Moving through the Worksheet and Entering Data

Now that a worksheet is displayed, you are going to practice moving through the worksheet. First, insert your data disk in drive B.

a. The cell pointer is positioned on cell A1. Enter the words last name into that cell. Describe the different steps you use to do this. Which key do you press to go to B1?

b. In B1, type first name and press < ↓ >. Where is the cell pointer positioned after this action? Which key do you press to go to A2?

c. Use the GOTO key to go to cell L130.

■ Enter the number 145.6.

d. Use the <Home> key to return to cell A1.

3. Building a New Worksheet

Now you are going to enter a new worksheet. First, type a slash (/) to activate the main menu. Then type **WE** to clear the screen and start a new worksheet. This step deletes the information you previously entered. Assume that you want to prepare the following report on the total quantity of items ordered by customers during the past week. In the report X stands for a figure to be computed.

Summary of Products Ordered During Week 30

PRODUCT NAME	CODE	MON	TUE	WED	THR	FRI	TOT
Skirts	1	80	90	50	70	110	X
Shorts	2	120	130	110	140	150	X
Blouses	3	30	30	20	60	70	X
Shirts	4	180	170	150	180	180	X
Socks	5	110	105	120	140	150	X
Jeans	6	165	170	140	150	170	X
Total		X	X	X	X	X	X

a. Make sure the cell pointer is positioned at cell A1 and start typing the title of the report: Summary of Products Ordered During Week 30. In which cell(s) is the text displayed? What do you call this?

b. Start typing the labels. Move the cell pointer to cell A3. Type PROD-UCT NAME and press <→>. Where is the cell pointer positioned now? Type the next label, CODE, and press <→> again. Type all the labels in row 3.

c. Move the cell pointer back to cell A3. What happens to the cell entry? Type /WCS to set the width of column A to 15 characters. Describe all the steps taken to change the column width.

d. Move the cell pointer to cell A5. You are now ready to enter the data for each line.

■ Type the first product name and press <→> to move the pointer to the right. Use the label-prefix ^ to center the name.
■ Type the code and press <→> again to move the cell pointer to the right.
■ Type the quantities ordered during the week for product 1 in the appropriate cells.
■ Repeat these steps to enter name, code number, and daily quantities for the remaining products.

e. You are now ready to compute the totals and complete the report.

■ Start with the totals per day. For this purpose, move the cell pointer to cell C12. Total orders for the first day are equal to +C5+C6+C7+C8+C9+C10. Enter this formula using the pointing method.
■ Enter the appropriate formulas in cells D12, E12, F12, and G12 using the pointing method.
■ Move the cell pointer to H5. This cell should contain the total for skirts ordered during week 30, that is, the sum of cells C5 through G5. Enter the appropriate formula in cell H5.
■ Enter the appropriate formulas in cells H6, H7, H8, H9, H10, and H12. What is the grand total of products ordered during the week?

f. To improve the appearance of the report, you want to draw a horizontal line between the last line of data and the totals. Move the cell pointer to cell C11.

■ Type \ −

What appears in that cell? Copy this cell entry to the remaining cells through H11.

    g. The report is now ready. Save the worksheet under the name SALES30.

    h. Print the report.

    i. When you have finished, return to DOS using the appropriate steps.

▨ VP-PLANNER PLUS PROBLEMS

You are an administrative assistant in the sales department. The manager asks you to prepare a variance report in order to analyze each division's activity and the performance of the sales force during the past year. To complete the problem, you need to use the VP-Planner Plus system disk and the SALES file included on your Student File Disk.

1. Following the appropriate steps, start VP-Planner Plus and insert the Student File Disk with the permanent files into drive B.

2. Retrieve the file SALES and save it under the new name NEW. From now on, use the file NEW. The original data will always be in the file SALES if you need to start over or if you want to work through the questions again.

3. Retrieve the file NEW. You now have access to the data provided to you by the manager. Move the cell pointer through the worksheet to familiarize yourself with the information. Notice that this worksheet contains the forecast and actual sales for the previous calendar year.

4. You want to compute all the totals per division and per quarter, and the grand total for the year. First compute the annual forecasted sales for each division:

    a. Go to cell F7. Using the pointing method, enter the formula that finds the total of the Northwest division's yearly forecasted sales.

    b. Using the pointing method, enter the formulas in cells F8, F9, and F10 which find the total yearly forecasted sales for the East Coast, Midwest, and Central divisions respectively.

Next, compute the total forecasted sales per quarter and for the total year:

    c. Go to B12. Using the pointing method, enter the formula that finds the total of all the divisions' forecasted sales in the first quarter.

    d. Using the pointing method, enter the formulas in cells C12, D12, and E12 which find the total for all the divisions' forecasted sales in the second, third, and fourth quarter, respectively.

    e. Go to F12. Compute the total forecasted sales for all the divisions for the entire year.

Repeat steps a through e for realized sales, starting at cell F15.

5. Now you want to compute the variances per quarter and per division. Variances are deviations of the actual results from what was expected. For one quarter, the variance is equal to realized sales minus forecasted sales. For example, the formula to compute the variance for the Northwest division in the first quarter is +B15–B7.

    a. Go to B23. Enter the formula that computes the variance for the Northwest division in the first quarter.

b. In cells C23, D23, and E23, enter the formulas that compute the variances for the Northwest division in the second, third and fourth quarters, respectively.

c. Follow the same procedure to find the variance for the East Coast, Midwest, and Central divisions.

d. In cells B28, C28, D28, and E28, compute the total variances per quarter.

e. In cells F23, F24, F25, and F26 compute the total variances per division.

f. In cell F28, compute the total variance for the entire company for the entire year.

6. Now that you have finished building the worksheet, you would like to improve its appearance.

a. Insert a row below the subtitles (Forecasted sales, Realized sales, and Variance report).

b. Insert a column before the "Total Y1" column.

c. Increase the first column width to 15 in order to be able to read "East Coast" completely.

d. Type Thousands $ under the main title.

e. Above each total line, draw a horizontal line using the repeating label prefix (\ −). Start at column B.

f. Below each total line, draw a double line using the repeating label prefix (\ =).

7. Save and print the report.

8. Look over the report. What are your first conclusions concerning the activity of the firm? Which division has performed best? Do you think that there is a problem with their forecasts?

S E C T I O N

D

Advanced VP-Planner Plus

O U T L I N E

Introduction
Copy and Move
The Difference between Global and
    Range Commands
Functions
Copying Formulas
Freezing Titles
Order of Precedence
Spreadsheet Analysis
Learning Check
Graphics
    Bar Graphs and Pie Charts
    Creating a Bar Graph and a Pie
        Chart
    Printing a Graph
Learning Check
Summary Points
Summary of Frequently Used VP-
    Planner Plus Menus
VP-Planner Plus Exercises
VP-Planner Plus Problems

■ INTRODUCTION

In Section C, the fundamentals for creating a basic worksheet were covered. VP-Planner Plus has many advanced features that simplify the task of creating more complex worksheets. These features, such as copy and move and @functions, will be covered now. In addition, this section describes how to create graphs using VP-Planner Plus.

Another important concept that will be covered is **spreadsheet analysis.** Spreadsheet analysis (or "what-if" analysis) is the mental process of evaluating information contained within an electronic spreadsheet. It often involves comparing various results generated by the spreadsheet. Analysis sometimes employs modeling. A **model,** in terms of a spreadsheet, is a numeric representation of a real-world situation. For example, a home budget is a numeric representation of the expenses involved in maintaining a household and therefore can be considered a model. The hands-on exercises in the following sections provide an introduction to spreadsheet analysis.

■ COPY AND MOVE

Some of the data entered into complex worksheets is repetitive. For example, the same labels or the same formulas may be repeated. VP-Planner Plus has a copy and move feature that enables the user to copy any cell or cells in the worksheet and move them to any other part of the worksheet, instead of needing to type the same data two or more times.

The Copy command is one of the options from VP-Planner's main command menu. After the user selects Copy, the prompt SOURCE CELL RANGE appears in the entry line. The range to be copied is then selected, either by using the pointer-movement keys or by typing the range of cells. After this range has been selected, the prompt DESTINATION CELL RANGE appears in the entry line. Move the pointer to the first cell of the range where the data is to be copied and press <Return>. All the data moves automatically to the new range. You need not specify a range equal in size to the range that was copied.

■ Your Turn

In this exercise, you are going to create a new worksheet.

1. Start with a blank worksheet on the screen.

    ■ Enter the following labels in the cells indicated:

Cell	Label
A1	INCOME
A3	Rent
A5	Apt. #1
A6	Apt. #2
A7	Apt. #3
A9	EXPENSES
A11	Repairs
B3	^1986
C3	^1987
D3	^1988
E3	^1989
F3	^1990
G3	^1991

(Remember to use the ^ label prefix because these dates are labels, not values.)

2. Now you are going to copy cells B3 through G3 and move them to cells B11 through G11. You will also copy cells A5 through A7 and move them to cells A13 through A15.

- Go to B3
- Type: **/C**

When the SOURCE CELL RANGE prompt appears, move the cell pointer using the <—→> key to G3. Press <Return>. When the prompt DESTINATION CELL RANGE appears, move the cell pointer to B11 using the < ↓ > key. Press <Return>. The labels are copied automatically to cells B11 through G11.

- Go to A5
- Type: **/C**
- Select the range A5 through A7
- Go to A13
- Press <Return>

The labels are copied automatically to cells A13 through A15.

3. Save this worksheet as EXAMPLE on your data disk.

VP-Planner Tip: Before copying a range, make sure there is no data in the range where the data will be written. If there is data in that range, the Copy command will write over it, and that data will be irretrievably lost.

■ THE DIFFERENCE BETWEEN GLOBAL AND RANGE COMMANDS

Many VP-Planner Plus commands can be applied either to a specific range of cells or to the entire worksheet. For example, if every value in a particular worksheet is currency, the entire worksheet can be formatted one time and all the values in that worksheet will appear as currency.

To use the Global command, first select Worksheet from the main command menu. Next select Global, and a menu of all the Global options appears. Table D–1 lists these options and describes their functions.

■ Your Turn

Start with the EXAMPLE file on the screen.

1. Enter the following values in the cells indicated.

Cells	Values	Cells	Values
B5	2280	B13	250
B6	4080	B14	190
B7	3880	B15	312
C5	2460	C13	235
C6	4260	C14	285
C7	4060	C15	345
D5	2700	D13	310
D6	4500	D14	308
D7	4300	D15	296
E5	3000	E13	433
E6	4800	E14	507
E7	4600	E15	472

TABLE D–1

Global Options

Option	Description
Format	Sets a global format. For example, the entire worksheet could be formatted as currency.
Label-prefix	Sets a global label alignment prefix. For example, all the labels in the worksheet could be centered.
Column-width	Sets a global column width. For example, every column in the worksheet could be 12 characters wide.
Recalculation	Determines when, in what order, and how many times formulas in the worksheet are recalculated.
Protection	Prevents changes from being made to cells.
Default	Enables the user to select his or her own default settings for the type of printer being used and its connection; the directory VP-Planner automatically uses when searching for files; international display formats; the method of using the help facility; and the type of clock display on the screen.
Zero-suppress	Determines whether values of zero are displayed on the screen.

2. All the values in this particular worksheet are currency, so you are going to format the entire worksheet as currency:

■ Type: **/WGFC**

When the prompt ENTER DEFAULT DECIMAL POSITION appears, press <Return> to accept the default setting of 2.

Asterisks appear in many of the cells because the columns are not wide enough to display some of the values.

3. You are going to change the column width of the entire worksheet:

■ Type: **/WGC**

When the prompt ENTER DESIRED COLUMN WIDTH appears, type **12** and press <Return>. The worksheet is now globally formatted for currency and for a column width of 12. A value entered in any cell on the worksheet appears on the screen as currency, and every column on the worksheet has a width of 12 characters. When completed, your worksheet should look like Figure D–1.

4. Save the amended EXAMPLE file.

▆ FUNCTIONS

In Section C, you learned how to enter formulas either by typing them or by using the pointing method. Using VP-Planner's @functions is a quicker and more accurate way to enter certain formulas. **Functions** reduce the number of keystrokes needed to enter a formula as well as reducing the likelihood of an error occurring. The @functions are built-in formulas that perform specialized calculations.

	A	B	C	D	E	F
1	INCOME					
2						
3	Rent	1986	1987	1988	1989	1990
4						
5	Apt #1	$2,280.00	$2,460.00	$2,700.00	$3,000.00	
6	Apt #2	$4,080.00	$4,260.00	$4,500.00	$4,800.00	
7	Apt #3	$3,880.00	$4,060.00	$4,300.00	$4,600.00	
8						
9	EXPENSES					
10						
11	Repairs	1986	1987	1988	1989	1990
12						
13	Apt #1	$250.00	$235.00	$310.00	$433.00	
14	Apt #2	$190.00	$285.00	$308.00	$507.00	
15	Apt #3	$312.00	$345.00	$296.00	$472.00	
16						
17						
18						
19						
20						

E15   472

1help 2edit 3name 4abs 5goto 6window 7data 8table 9recalculate 0graph
358K   17:24   READY

FIGURE D—1

The EXAMPLE File with a Global Currency Format and Global Column-Width Settings

In VP-Planner Plus, these functions are called "at functions" because each one begins with the "at" character (@). An @function is comprised of three parts: the at symbol (@), the name of the function, and an argument or arguments enclosed by parentheses. The argument, which indicates what data the function applies to, can be a single value or a range of cells.

VP-Planner Plus includes both simple @functions, such as one that adds a range of cells, and more complex @functions, such as those that calculate loans, annuities, and cash flows over a period of time. VP-Planner Plus includes twelve categories of functions:

- Database Statistical Functions
- Date Functions
- Financial Functions
- Information Functions
- Logical Functions
- Lookup Functions
- Mathematical Functions
- Special Functions
- Statistical Functions
- String Functions
- Time Functions
- Trigonometric Functions

Table D—2 lists some of the more commonly used @functions.

Your Turn

Start with the EXAMPLE file on the screen.

TABLE D-2

@Functions

Function	Description
@AVG	Calculates the average of a list of values
@MAX	Determines the maximum value in a list
@MIN	Determines the minimum value in a list
@SUM	Determines the sum of a list of values
@RAND	Determines a random number between 0 and 1
@ROUND	Rounds a value to a specified number of places
@SQRT	Determines the positive square root of a value

1. You are going to use an @function to find the total income from rent in 1986 and the total expenses spent on repairs in 1986. First, some changes need to be made to the worksheet. You have to add two rows for the totals.

- Go to A9
- Type: **/WIR**

When the prompt, SELECT RANGE OF ROWS TO INSERT appears, enter the range A9 to A10. Press <Return>.

- Enter Total in cell A9
- Enter Total in cell A19
- Go to B9
- Enter **@SUM(B5.B7)**
- Press <Return>

The total of cells B5, B6, and B7 immediately appears in cell B9.

- Go to B19
- Enter **@SUM(B15.B17)**
- Press <Return>

Your worksheet should look like Figure D–2. Notice that the formula using the @SUM function is in the status line.

2. Save the amended EXAMPLE file.

▆ COPYING FORMULAS

Previously you learned how to use the Copy command by copying and moving labels in the EXAMPLE file. The Copy command also can be used to copy formulas, but it works differently in this case, as explained in this section.

When a cell containing a formula is copied, VP-Planner Plus does not copy the value displayed in the cell on the worksheet. Rather, VP-Planner Plus copies the formula displayed in the status line. When the formula is copied, VP-Planner Plus automatically inserts the appropriate argument or arguments. For example, suppose a worksheet contains a list of values in columns B, C, and D, and a sum for each column needs to be calculated. First, the @SUM function would be used to calculate the total for column B. Then,

	A	B	C	D	E	F
1	INCOME					
2						
3	Rent	1986	1987	1988	1989	1990
4						
5	Apt #1	$2,280.00	$2,460.00	$2,700.00	$3,000.00	
6	Apt #2	$4,080.00	$4,260.00	$4,500.00	$4,800.00	
7	Apt #3	$3,880.00	$4,060.00	$4,300.00	$4,600.00	
8						
9	TOTAL	$10,240.00				
10						
11	EXPENSES					
12						
13	Repairs	1986	1987	1988	1989	1990
14						
15	Apt #1	$250.00	$235.00	$310.00	$433.00	
16	Apt #2	$190.00	$285.00	$308.00	$507.00	
17	Apt #3	$312.00	$345.00	$296.00	$472.00	
18						
19	TOTAL	$752.00				
20						

B19   @SUM(B15..B17)

1help 2edit 3name 4abs 5goto 6window 7data 8table 9recalculate 0graph
358K   17:33   READY

FIGURE D—2

Using @Functions

that formula is copied into columns C and D to calculate the totals for those columns. VP-Planner Plus automatically inserts the appropriate range of cells in the arguments for each formula.

■ Your Turn

Start with the EXAMPLE file on the screen.

1. You are going to copy the formula in B9 into C9, D9, and E9. You also will copy the formula in B19 into C19, D19, and E19.

- ■ Go to B9
- ■ Type: **/C**

When the prompt SOURCE CELL RANGE appears, press <Return> to copy just the formula in B9. When the prompt DESTINATION CELL RANGE appears, move the cell pointer to C9. Type a period to anchor the range and move the cell pointer to E9. Press <Return>.

The totals for columns C, D, and E immediately appear. Go to C9 and look at the formula in the status line. It should say @SUM(C5..C7). VP-Planner Plus automatically changed the argument from (B5..B7) to (C5..C7) when the formula was copied into cell C9.

2. Next you are going to copy the formula to sum expenses.

- ■ Go to B19
- ■ Type: **/C**
- ■ Press <Return>
- ■ Move the cell pointer to C19
- ■ Type . (period)

- Move the cell pointer to E19
- Press <Return>

The totals appear in cells C19, D19, and E19. Your worksheet should look like Figure D–3.

3. Save the amended EXAMPLE file.

▅ FREEZING TITLES

Up to this point, all the worksheets you have used have fit within the window. More complex and larger worksheets, however, may not fit in that space. As the user moves around a large worksheet, columns and rows of information scroll off the computer screen. Usually this is not a problem, unless titles identifying the rows and columns also scroll off the screen. A screen full of numbers with no identifying labels can be confusing. VP-Planner Plus solves that problem by including a feature that "freezes" titles. If a row or column of titles is frozen, those titles do not scroll off the computer screen as the user moves around a large worksheet.

To freeze titles, the user must position the cell pointer one row below the rows to be frozen and one column to the right of the columns to be frozen. After positioning the cell pointer, select the Worksheet option from the main command menu; then select Titles. There are four Titles options from which to select. Table D–3 lists these options and describes their functions.

The cell pointer keys cannot be used to move into a row or column that has been frozen. To go to a cell within a row or column that is frozen, use the Goto key, <F5>.

A second copy of the title row or column is displayed on the screen. There are two ways to remove this second copy. If the Clear option is selected

FIGURE D–3

Copy @Functions

	A	B	C	D	E	F
1	INCOME					
2						
3	Rent	1986	1987	1988	1989	1990
4						
5	Apt #1	$2,280.00	$2,460.00	$2,700.00	$3,000.00	
6	Apt #2	$4,080.00	$4,260.00	$4,500.00	$4,800.00	
7	Apt #3	$3,880.00	$4,060.00	$4,300.00	$4,600.00	
8						
9	TOTAL	$10,240.00	$10,780.00	$11,500.00	$12,400.00	
10						
11	EXPENSES					
12						
13	Repairs	1986	1987	1988	1989	1990
14						
15	Apt #1	$250.00	$235.00	$310.00	$433.00	
16	Apt #2	$190.00	$285.00	$308.00	$507.00	
17	Apt #3	$312.00	$345.00	$296.00	$472.00	
18						
19	TOTAL	$752.00	$865.00	$914.00	$1,412.00	
20						

B19   @SUM(B15..B17)

1help 2edit 3name 4abs 5goto 6window 7data 8table 9recalculate 0graph
358K   17:38   READY

COMPUTERS AND INFORMATION PROCESSING

TABLE D-3

Titles Options

Option	Description
Both	Both the rows above the cell pointer and columns to the left of the cell pointer will not scroll off the screen.
Horizontal	The rows above the cell pointer will not scroll off the screen.
Vertical	The columns on the screen to the left of the cell pointer will not scroll off the screen.
Clear	All the existing titles are unfrozen.

from the Titles menu, all the existing titles are unfrozen and the second copy is removed. Another way to remove the second copy is to press the <PgDn> key and then the <PgUp> key for rows or the tab <Tab> key and then the <Backtab> key for columns. (The <Backtab> key is the <Shift> key used in combination with the <Tab> key.)

■ Your Turn

Start with the EXAMPLE file on your screen.

1. You are going to freeze column A.

- ■ Go to B1
- ■ Type: **/WTV**

Column A is now frozen and will not scroll off the screen.

2. Suppose you wanted to start projecting some costs for 1991. To do that, you need to move to column G:

- ■ Press <F5>
- ■ Type: **G1**
- ■ Press <Return>

Your screen should look like Figure D–4. Notice that column A remains on the screen. Without those titles, the worksheet would not make much sense.

- ■ Press <F5>
- ■ Type: **A1**
- ■ Press <Return>

Notice that there are now two column As. That is because VP-Planner Plus copied the frozen column.

3. Remove the frozen column by pressing <Tab> and then <Backtab>.

4. Save the EXAMPLE file. Exit from the VP-Planner Plus program.

■ ORDER OF PRECEDENCE

When more complex formulas are used on a worksheet, VP-Planner Plus performs calculations in a specific order of **precedence**. The order of precedence, or the order of operations, is the order in which calculations are

```
              A              G              H              I              J              K
1     INCOME
2
3     Rent           1991
4
5     Apt #1
6     Apt #2
7     Apt #3
8
9     TOTAL
10
11    EXPENSES
12
13    Repairs        1991
14
15    Apt #1
16    Apt #2
17    Apt #3
18
19    TOTAL
20
 G1

1help 2edit 3name 4abs 5goto 6window 7data 8table 9recalculate 0graph
358K                              17:48                                    READY
```

FIGURE D—4

Freezing Titles

performed in a formula that contains several operators. Table D–4 shows operators that can be used in formulas, together with the order in which the operations are performed. If a formula contains operations that have the same precedence, they are performed sequentially from left to right.

There is a way to override the order of precedence listed in Table D–4. Operations contained within parentheses are calculated before operations outside the parentheses. The operations within the parentheses are performed according to the order of precedence. For example, the formula C12*(B12+C12) would be calculated in the following order:

1. The contents of cell B12 are added to the contents in cell C12.
2. The result of the calculation in step 1 is multiplied by the contents of cell C12.

TABLE D—4

Order of Precedence

Order	Operator	Operation
First	^	Exponentiation
Second	*/	Multiplication, Division
Third	+ −	Addition, Subtraction

COMPUTERS AND INFORMATION PROCESSING

Your Turn

For this hands-on exercise you will design a model that will help the owner of an apartment building project the income that each unit in the building will generate per month.

1. Load the VP-Planner Plus program. Make sure the location of the current directory is drive **B.** A blank worksheet should be on the screen. First, you will globally change the column width and enter all the labels:

■ Type: **/WGC**

When prompted to **ENTER DESIRED COLUMN WIDTH,** enter **10.** Now, enter the following labels in the cells indicated: (Remember, any number used as a label must be preceded by the ^ symbol.)

Cells	Label	Cells	Label
A1	^803 NORTH WOOSTER, BOWLING GREEN, OHIO		
B3	Yearly	D5	^1989
D3	Projected	E5	^1990
E3	Projected	F5	^1991
F3	Projected	A7	Apt #1
B4	Increase	A8	Apt #2
D4	Income	A9	Apt #3
E4	Income	A10	Apt #4
F4	Income	A11	Apt #5
A5	Unit	A12	Apt #6
B5	Rate	A13	Apt #7
C5	^1988	A15	Average
		A17	Total

2. Next, format cells B7 through B13 to percentages carried out to one decimal place:

■ Go to B7
■ Type: **/RFP**

When the prompt, **ENTER DESIRED DECIMAL POSITION** appears, type **1** and press <Return>. Format the range B7 through B13.

3. The rest of the worksheet values should be formatted as currency, carried out to 0 decimal places:

■ Go to C7
■ Type: **/RFC**

When the prompt, **ENTER DESIRED DECIMAL POSITION** appears, type **0** and press <Return>. Format the range C7 through F17.

4. Enter the following values in the appropriate cells.

Cells	Values
B7	.065
B8	.08
B9	.065
B10	.05
B11	.08
B12	.05

B13	.10
C7	250
C8	530
C9	275
C10	350
C11	540
C12	325
C13	750

5. To find the average rent for the apartments in this building, use the @AVG function:

- Go to C15
- Enter **@AVG(C7.C13)**

Copy this formula into cells D15 through F15:

- Go to C15
- Type: **/C**

Press <Return> when the prompt SOURCE CELL RANGE appears. When the prompt DESTINATION CELL RANGE appears, select the range D15 through F15. Notice the letters ERR, for error, appear in cells D15, E15, and F15. This is because the formulas entered into those cells include the contents of cells that are currently empty. For now, ignore the ERR message.

6. To find the total rent per month for each year, use the @SUM function.

- Go to C17
- Enter **@SUM(C7.C13)**

Copy this formula into cells D17 through F17:

- Go to C17
- Type: **/C**

Press <Return> when the prompt SOURCE CELL RANGE appears. When the prompt DESTINATION CELL RANGE appears, select the range D17 through F17. Notice that $0 appears in cells D17 through F17. That is because currently the cells in columns D, E, and F are empty.

7. Now you need to enter a formula that finds the new monthly rent, given the yearly increase percentage rate for each apartment.

- Go to D7
- Enter **(C7*B7)+C7**

Because of the order of precedence, the operation within the parentheses is calculated first. This operation (C7*B7) finds the rent increase each month, given the yearly increase rate. That amount then is added to the current rent, which is the value in C7. The result is the rental cost for the apartment in 1989. This formula can now be copied into cells D8 through D13:

- Go to D7
- Type: **/C**
- Press <Return> to copy from D7
- Select the range D8 through D13 to copy to

Notice that once formulas were entered into column D, ERR in cell D15 was replaced by a value.

8. Now formulas need to be entered into cells E7 and F7.

- Go to E7
- Enter **(D7∗B7)+D7**
- Go to F7
- Enter **(E7∗B7)+E7**
- Copy the formula in cell E7 into cells E8 through E13
- Copy the formula in cell F7 into cells F8 through F13

When completed, your worksheet should look like Figure D–5.

9. Save this worksheet under the file name RENT.

▰ SPREADSHEET ANALYSIS

Once a worksheet has been created, it is easy to experiment with various options. After changes are made, VP-Planner Plus automatically recalculates the worksheet to reflect those changes. Numerous alternatives to a single plan can be projected and evaluated, making the spreadsheet an invaluable tool in decision making.

▰ Your Turn

Start with the RENT file on the screen. You are going to experiment with "what if" analysis by making changes to the Yearly Increase Rate and to the rent for each unit.

The owner of this apartment building is thinking of hiring a building manager in 1989. The owner cannot afford to pay a building manager's salary, however, unless the total income per month from the apartments is

FIGURE D–5

The RENT Worksheet

	A	B	C	D	E	F	G
1	803 NORTH WOOSTER, BOWLING GREEN, OHIO						
2							
3		Yearly		Projected	Projected	Projected	
4		Increase		Income	Income	Income	
5	Unit	Rate	1988	1989	1990	1991	
6							
7	Apt #1	6.5%	$250	$266	$284	$302	
8	Apt #2	8.0%	$530	$572	$618	$668	
9	Apt #3	6.5%	$275	$293	$312	$332	
10	Apt #4	5.0%	$350	$368	$386	$405	
11	Apt #5	8.0%	$540	$583	$630	$680	
12	Apt #6	5.0%	$325	$341	$358	$376	
13	Apt #7	10.0%	$750	$825	$908	$998	
14							
15	Average		$431	$464	$499	$537	
16							
17	Total		$3,020	$3,248	$3,495	$3,762	
18							
19							
20							

F7   (C0)   (E7*B7)+E7

1help 2edit 3name 4abs 5goto 6window 7data 8table 9recalculate 0graph
357K   10:08   READY

$3,800. The owner wants to know if raising the Yearly Increase Rate for each unit by 1 percent would generate enough income to hire a building manager in 1989. Change the values in cells B7 through B13 to reflect a 1 percent greater increase in the Yearly Increase Rate. Could the owner afford to hire a building manager in 1989? In what year could the owner afford to hire a building manager?

The other option for increasing income is to raise the rent. Increase each apartment's rent in column **C** by $30.00. In what year can the owner afford to hire a building manager?

Continue to experiment with "what if" analysis. When you have finished, do not save the amended file. You want to save the file as it was before you began experimenting with "what if" analysis. The following commands enable you to save the RENT file in its original form:

■ Type: **/QY**

If you quit without using the / FILE SAVE command, the file will remain as it was originally entered.

LEARNING CHECK

1. In _____, different results generated by the spreadsheet often are compared.

2. A(n) _____ is a numeric representation of a real-world situation.

3. VP-Planner Plus commands that apply to the entire worksheet are called _____ commands.

4. A built-in formula already stored in a spreadsheet program is called a(n) _____.

5. The order in which calculations are performed in a formula with several operators is called the _____.

ANSWERS

1. spreadsheet analysis
2. model
3. global

4. function
5. order of precedence

GRAPHICS

The purpose of business graphics is to develop charts and **analytical graphs** for financial analysis. Numeric statistics can be transformed into multi-colored charts and graphs for analyzing markets, forecasting sales, comparing stock trends, and planning business and home finances. Frequently used in presentations and reports, business graphics can often present information more effectively than a column of numbers. Two of the more commonly used graphs are bar graphs and pie charts.

Bar Graphs and Pie Charts

A bar graph can be used to make a quantitative comparison of several subjects' performances. Numeric values are represented as vertical bars, each of which depicts the value of a single cell in the worksheet. The X axis, a horizontal line, has labels identifying what each bar represents. The Y axis, a vertical line, has scaled numeric divisions corresponding to the worksheet values being represented.

Two types of bar graphs are often used as analytical graphs. A simple bar graph depicts the changes in one set of values, whereas a multiple bar graph depicts the relationships among changes in several sets of values. For example, a simple bar graph might chart how many blue jeans a clothing store sold in 1986, 1987, and 1988 (see Figure D–6). A multiple bar graph might compare the numbers of blue jeans sold to the numbers of corduroy slacks and chino pants sold in 1986, 1987, and 1988. Each year would have three bars above it: one bar for blue jeans, one for corduroy slacks, and one for chino pants (see Figure D–7).

In Figure D–6, the vertical line, or Y axis, contains the numeric data ranges from 0 to 45000. The first bar in this graph reaches the 30000 mark on the Y axis, meaning 30,000 blue jeans were sold in 1986.

A pie chart represents a whole subject divided into parts. It looks like a circle divided into wedges, like slices of a pie, and shows the relationships among the sizes of the wedges and the whole pie. The pie stands for the total, and each wedge stands for one data item. In Figure D–8, the entire pie represents the total number of pants sold in 1988. Each wedge represents one style of pants. This pie chart indicates that in 1988, 44 percent of all the pants sold were blue jeans, 31.9 percent were corduroys, and 24.2 percent were chinos.

With VP-Planner Plus, data contained in a worksheet can be transformed easily into a graph. In addition, if a number is changed on the worksheet, that change is immediately reflected in the graph. Five different types of

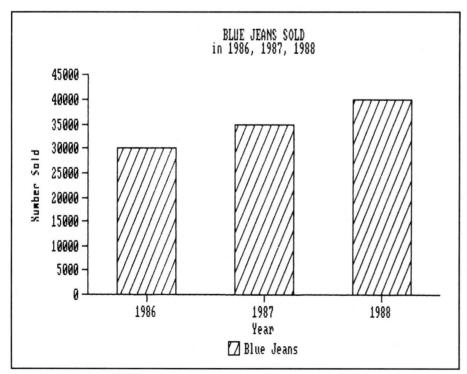

A Simple Bar Graph

FIGURE D-7

A Multiple Bar Graph

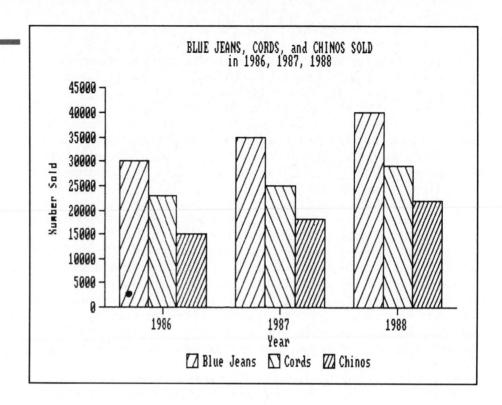

graphs can be drawn with VP-Planner Plus: line graphs, bar graphs, stacked-bar graphs, pie charts, and XY graphs. Bar graphs and pie charts are covered in this chapter.

FIGURE D-8

A Pie Chart

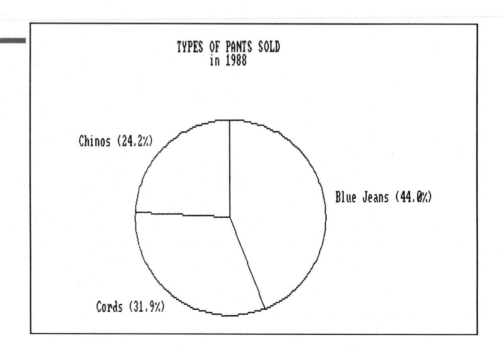

COMPUTERS AND INFORMATION PROCESSING

Creating a Bar Graph and a Pie Chart

In order to use VP-Planner's graphics feature, your computer must be equipped with a graphics adapter. VP-Planner Plus supports the IBM Color Graphics Adapter (**CGA**) in its high resolution monochrome mode, the IBM Enhanced Graphics Adapter (**EGA**) in its high resolution 16-color mode, the Hercules Monochrome Graphics Adapter (**MGA**), and compatible graphics adapters.

The default setting for graphics is **CGA.** If you have an IBM Enhanced Graphics Adapter or a Hercules Monochrome Graphics Adapter, you have to change the hardware configuration. The following command enables you to change the hardware configuration: **/WGDHV.** Once this command is typed, the CGA, Hercules, EGA, and other options are available. Using $<\uparrow>$ and $<\downarrow>$ highlights the appropriate graphics adapter for your computer. Press <Return> after making your choice. (The IBM Monochrome Adapter displays text only, and does not support graphics. If the computer you are using is equipped with an IBM Monochrome Adapter, you cannot display or print graphs with VP-Planner Plus.)

Commands from the VP-Planner Plus Graph menu are used to create a graph. The first step is to retrieve the file containing the data to be used for the graph. Next, the graph type has to be selected. To select the type of graph, choose the Graph option from the main command menu. The Graph options appear in the entry line. Table D–5 lists these options and describes their functions.

After you have selected Type from the Graph menu, the options LINE, BAR, XY, STACKED-BAR, and PIE are in the first-level menu. Select the type of graph to be drawn.

Once the type of graph has been selected, the Graph menu becomes the first-level menu. The next step in creating a graph is to specify which data ranges are to be used for this graph, and what labels are to be used to

TABLE D—5

Graph Options

Option	Description
Type	Enables the user to select which of the five types of graphs is to be drawn.
Reset	Cancels all or some of the previous range specifications.
View	Enables the user to view the current graph.
Print	Enables the current graph to be printed.
Save	Saves the current graph in a file for later printing.
Options	Enables the user to add legends or titles to the graph or to alter its appearance.
Name	Enables the user to save the current graph settings under a graph name.
Quit	Returns the worksheet to the Ready mode.
Look	Enables the user to view a graph that has been saved as a .PIC file.
X, A–F (Ranges)	Enables the user to select the ranges of the worksheet from which the graph is to be drawn and labeled.

describe that data. The options used to accomplish this step are the range commands (X, A, B, C, D, E, F,) from the Graph menu.

The X option is used to select the range of labels. On a bar graph, each label on the X axis corresponds to a bar or multiple bars. On a pie chart, each label corresponds to one slice of the pie. The A–F options are used to specify ranges of data. Up to six ranges can be specified for a bar graph, but only one range can be specified for a pie chart. After the data ranges and labels have been specified, the graph can be viewed by using the View option from the Graph menu.

▩ Your Turn

You are going to create a simple bar graph and a multiple bar graph using the RENT file. Start with the RENT file on the screen.

1. The first bar graph you will create compares the rent paid for each apartment in 1988.

   ■ Type: **/GTB**

The Graph menu should be the first-level menu. You need to identify the labels to be used for the bar graph. Because the graph will compare the rents for the apartments, the apartment numbers are the appropriate labels.

   ■ Type: **X**

The prompt ENTER DATA RANGE appears.

   ■ Go to A7
   ■ Type a period (.) to anchor the range
   ■ Using the < ↓ > key, move to A13
   ■ Press <Return>

2. Now you need to specify the range of data to be used in the graph. You want to compare the rent for each unit in 1988, so the data to be used is in cells C7 through C13. The Graph menu should be the first-level menu.

   ■ Type: **A**

The prompt ENTER DATA RANGE appears.

   ■ Go to C7
   ■ Type a period (.) to anchor the range
   ■ Using the < ↓ > key, move to C13
   ■ Press <Return>

3. You can now view the graph. Select View from the graph menu. What happens after you select View depends on the hardware being used and on how the system is configured. The system must be equipped with both a graphics monitor and a graphics card. If it is not, when View is selected, the computer beeps and nothing happens.

If the computer you are using has a graphics card and either a monochrome or color screen, the bar graph is displayed after selecting View. When you have finished viewing the graph, press <Esc>.

4. Now you are going to create a multiple bar graph that includes three more data ranges. Say you want to compare the rent paid on each unit in

1988 with the projected rent to be paid on each unit in 1989, 1990, and 1991. Option B from the Graph menu can hold the data from the data range D7 through D13, option C can hold the data from E7 through E13, and option D can hold the data from the range F7 through F13.

- Type: **B**
- Enter the data range D7 through D13
- Type: **C**
- Enter the data range E7 through E13
- Type: **D**
- Enter the data range F7 through F13
- Type: **V**

Now there are four bars for each apartment unit. Each of these four bars represents the monthly rent for that unit in 1988, 1989, 1990, and 1991, respectively. When you are finished viewing the graph, press <Esc>.

5. The graph would become more meaningful if it had a title and labels. A two-line title can be printed at the top of the graph. You are now going to provide a title for the graph.

- Type: **O**

Your screen should look like Figure D–9. These are the graph options commands; they enable you to add enhancements to your graph.

- Type: **T**

The highlighting moves to the TITLES option. The highlighting should be on FIRST.

- Press <Return>

FIGURE D—9

Graph Options Commands

```
2 DATA-LABELS      5 SCALE                    6 FORMAT                    7 GRID
  2 A none           2 X-axis  2 Automatic      2 Graph                     2 Horiz
  3 B none           3 Y-axis  3 Manual         3 A B   2 Lines             3 Vert
  4 C none                     4 Lower          4 B B   3 Symbols           4 Both
  5 D none                     5 Upper          5 C B   4 Both              5 ClearX
  6 E none                     6 Format         6 D B   5 Neither
  7 F none                     7 Indicator      7 E B                     8 COLOR
  8 Quit                       8 Quit           8 F B                     9 B&W     X
3 TITLES                                        9 Quit                    0 Quit
  2 First            4 Skip
  3 Second                                                       Type:  Bar
  4 X-axis
  5 Y-axis                                                       Data Ranges:
4 LEGEND                                                          X A7..A13
  2 A                                                             A C7..C13
  3 B                                                             B D7..D13
  4 C                                                             C E7..E13
  5 D                                                             D F7..F13
  6 E                                                             E none
  7 F                                                             F none


                                                                           MENU
```

The prompt ENTER TITLE appears.

- Enter RENT INCREASE ON EACH UNIT
- Press <Return>
- Type: **TS**

The prompt ENTER TITLE appears again.

- Enter FOR 1988, 1989, 1990, AND 1991
- Press <Return>
- Type: **TX**

The prompt ENTER TITLE appears. You are now going to enter a title for the X and Y axes.

- Enter Apartment
- Press <Return>
- Type: **TY**
- Enter Rent Per Month
- Press <Return>

6. Now you want to add a legend. Each one of the bars stands for a year and is filled in with a different fill-pattern. To identify what each fill-pattern stands for, you have to designate a legend. The graphics options should still be on your screen.

- Type: **LA**

The prompt ENTER LEGEND appears.

- Enter 1988
- Press <Return>
- Type: **LB**
- Enter 1989
- Press <Return>
- Type: **LC**
- Enter 1990
- Press <Return>
- Type: **LD**
- Enter 1991
- Press <Return>

You are now ready to leave the graph options.

- Type: **Q**

7. Now you want to save the bar graph.

- Type: **S**

The prompt ENTER FILE NAME appears.

- Type **Rentbar**
- Press <Return>

When VP-Planner Plus saves the graph, the extension PIC is added automatically to whatever name the graph is given.

■ Type: **Q**

The worksheet returns to the READY mode.

■ Your Turn

In this hands-on exercise, you will use the RENT file to create a pie chart to compare apartment unit rents in 1988.

1. Start with the RENT file on the screen.

■ Type: **/GTP**

The Graph menu should be the first-level menu.

■ Type: **X**

Since each piece of the pie is to represent one apartment, you want to leave the X range setting intact. It should already be set at the range A7 through A13.

■ Press <Return>
■ Type: **A**

2. The range C7 through C13 should still be selected. Because the pie chart is to compare rents in 1988, you want to leave the A range setting intact.

■ Press <Return>

Unlike a bar graph, a pie chart is limited to comparisons based on one criterion. Therefore, the only settings to be made from the Graph menu are X, to set the X range, and A, to set the first (and only) data range.

None of the other data used in the bar graph is to be used in the pie chart, so you need to reset options B, C, and D.

■ Type: **RBCDQ**

The Graph menu should now be the first-level menu.

3. Next, you need to provide a title for the pie chart.

■ Type: **OTF**

The prompt ENTER TITLE appears. The title from the bar graph may be entered after the prompt. If it is, ignore it. You are just going to type over it.

■ Enter MONTHLY INCOME 803 NORTH WOOSTER
■ Press <Return>
■ Type: **TS**

The prompt ENTER TITLE appears. If the second line from the bar graph appears after the prompt, ignore it.

■ Enter FOR THE YEAR 1988
■ Press <Return>
■ Type: **Q**

4. You now want to view the pie chart.

- Type: **V**

The pie chart illustrates what percentage the rent on each unit contributes to the total monthly income for the building. When you are finished viewing the pie chart, press <Esc>.

5. Now you need to save the pie chart.

- Type: **S**

When the prompt ENTER FILE NAME appears, enter **Rentpie.**

- Type: **Q**

The worksheet returns to the Ready mode.

Printing a Graph

Before trying to print a graph, you need to make sure the printer being used is capable of printing graphics. Also, make sure the printer is properly hooked up to the computer, is online, and has plenty of paper.

There are two ways to print a graph. A graph can be printed as soon as it is created by typing **P** for PRINT from the Graph menu. As soon as **P** is pressed, the current graph will immediately begin printing. If, however, you want to print a graph that was created previously and saved as a .PIC file, you must first access that graph with the LOOK option from the Graph menu. Type **L** for LOOK. A window listing all the graph files that have been saved appears in the upper left corner of the screen. Using < ↑ > or < ↓ >, highlight the graph file you want to print and press <Return>. The graph appears on the screen. Press the two keys <Shift><PrtSc> at the same time. The graph immediately begins to print.

Your Turn

You are going to print the bar graph and pie chart you created in the last Your Turn exercises.

1. The RENT worksheet should be on your screen.

- Type: **/GL**
- If necessary, press < ↓ > or < ↑ > until RENTBAR.PIC is highlighted
- Press <Return>

The RENTBAR bar graph appears on the screen.

- Press <Shift><PrtSc>

The graph begins to print. When the graph has finished printing, press <Esc> to return to the worksheet. Your bar graph should look like Figure D–10.

2. Now print the pie chart.

- Type: **L**
- Move the highlighting to RENTPIE.PIC
- Press <Return>
- Press <Shift><PrtSc>

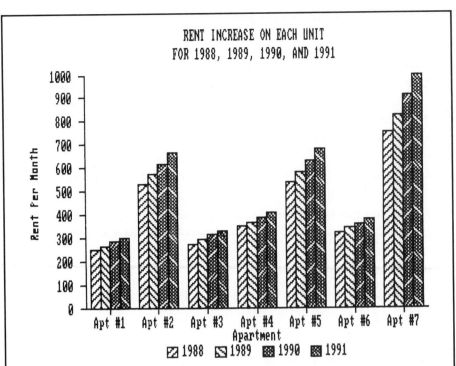

Your pie chart should look like Figure D–11. Press <Esc> when the graph
has finished printing.

- Type: **Q**
- Type: **/Q**

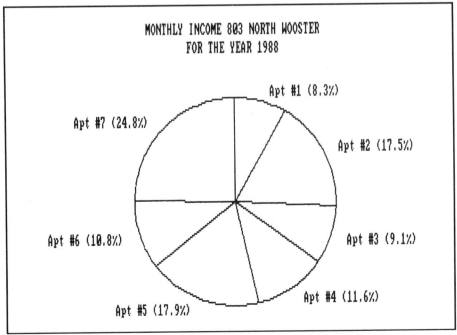

Turn off your computer and monitor.

LEARNING CHECK

1. Business graphics used for financial analysis are called _____.

2. A _____ bar graph illustrates the changes in one set of values and a _____ bar graph illustrates the relationship among changes in several sets of values.

3. (True or False?) A pie chart makes comparisons based on only one criterion.

4. (True or False?) Each bar in a bar graph depicts an entire range of cells from a worksheet.

5. In a bar graph, the labels identifying what the bars represent appear along the _____ and the scaled numeric divisions appear along the _____.

ANSWERS

1. analytic graphs
2. simple; multiple
3. True

4. False
5. X axis; Y axis

SUMMARY POINTS

■ Spreadsheet analysis is the mental process of evaluating information contained within a spreadsheet. It often involves comparing various results generated by a spreadsheet.

■ A model is a numeric representation of a real-world situation.

■ Functions, which are built-in formulas included in a spreadsheet program, save time by reducing the number of keystrokes needed to enter a formula. Functions also reduce the likelihood of error.

■ Formulas involving several operators are calculated according to the order of precedence. Parentheses can be used to override the order of precedence.

SUMMARY OF FREQUENTLY USED VP-PLANNER PLUS MENUS

A. MAIN COMMAND MENU

Command	Keys	Description
Worksheet	/W	Set of commands that affect the entire worksheet. Format, Erase the entire worksheet. Insert and Delete rows and columns. Set titles, windows, page break characters.
Range	/R	Set of commands that affect particular cells. Format, Label, Erase, Name, Justify, Protect, Unprotect a range of cells.
Copy	/C	Copy cell entries to other locations in the worksheet.

Move	/M	Move cell entries to other locations in the worksheet.
File	/F	Retrieve, Save, Combine, Import files. Set the current directory drive.
Print	/P	Output a range to a printer or a print file.
Graph	/G	Create graphs.
Data	/D	Create, Modify, Sort a data base. Search for records.
Tools	/T	Invoke word processing and graphics features to enhance worksheets and printed reports.
System	/S	Invoke the DOS command interpreter.
Quit	/Q	End VP-Planner Plus session and return to DOS.

B. WORKSHEET COMMAND MENU

Command	Keys	Description
Global	/WG	Select entire worksheet settings.
Insert	/WI	Insert a blank column to the left of the specified range or a row above the specified range.
Delete	/WD	Delete specified rows or columns.
Column-width	/WC	Set individual column widths.
Erase	/WE	Erase the entire worksheet. Worksheet should be saved before using this command.
Titles	/WT	Set titles horizontal, vertical, or both. Clear titles.
Window	/WW	Set split screen and synchronized scrolling.
Status	/WS	Display worksheet settings.
Autokey	/WA	Record keystrokes and store them in a macro.
Page	/WP	Insert a page break above the cell pointer.

C. RANGE COMMAND MENU

Command	Keys	Description
Format	/RF	Format a cell or range of cells.
Label	/RL	Align a label or range of labels.
Erase	/RE	Erase a cell or range of cells.
Name	/RN	Create, delete, or modify range names.
Justify	/RJ	Adjust width of a column of labels.
Protect	/RP	Disallow changes to a range if protection is enabled.
Unprotect	/RU	Allow changes to a range.
Input	/RI	Enter data into the unprotected cells in a range.
Column	/RC	Set column width for one or more adjacent columns.
Value	/RV	Copy range, converting formulas to values.
Transpose	/RT	Copy range, switching columns and rows.

D. FILE COMMAND MENU

Command	Keys	Description
Retrieve	/FR	Erase the current worksheet and display the selected worksheet.
Save	/FS	Store the entire worksheet in a worksheet file.
Combine	/FC	Incorporate all or part of a worksheet file into the worksheet.

Xtract	/FX	Store a cell range in a worksheet file.
Erase	/FE	Erase a worksheet, print, or graph file.
List	/FL	Display names of VP-Planner Plus files in the current directory.
Import	/FI	Read text or numbers from a print file into the worksheet.
Directory	/FD	Display and/or set the current directory.
Utility	/FU	Rename a file.

E. PRINT COMMAND MENU TO PRINTER

Command	Keys	Description
Range	/PPR	Specify a range to print.
Line	/PPL	Advance one line.
Page	/PPP	Advance one page.
Options	/PPO	Header, Footer, Margins, Borders, Setup, Page-length, Others.
Clear	/PPC	Reset some or all print settings.
Align	/PPA	Reset to top of page.
Go	/PPG	Print the specified range.
Quit	/PPQ	Return to Ready mode.
Status	/PPS	Display print settings for the current worksheet.
Eject	/PPE	Eject paper to top of the next physical page.

F. GRAPH COMMAND MENU

Command	Keys	Description
Type	/GT	Set graph type.
Reset	/GR	Cancel graph settings.
View	/GV	View the current graph.
Print	/GP	Print the current graph.
Save	/GS	Save the current graph in a file for later printing.
Options	/GO	Legend, Format, Titles, Grid, Scale, Color, B & W, Data, Labels.
Name	/GN	Use, Create, Delete, or Reset named graphs.
Quit	/GQ	Return to Ready mode.
Look	/GL	View a graph saved as .PIC file.
X	/GX	Set X range.
A	/GA	Set first data range.
B	/GB	Set second data range.
C	/GC	Set third data range.
D	/GD	Set fourth data range.
E	/GE	Set fifth data range.
F	/GF	Set sixth data range.

G. DATA COMMAND MENU

Command	Keys	Description
Fill	/DF	Fill a range with numbers.
Table	/DT	Create a table of values.

COMPUTERS AND INFORMATION PROCESSING

Sort	/DS	Sort data records.
Query	/DQ	Find all data records satisfying the given criteria.
Distribution	/DD	Calculate frequency distribution of a range.
External	/DE	Transfer data between current worksheet and a data-base file.
Input	/DI	Input data into a worksheet table from a data entry form.

VP-PLANNER PLUS EXERCISES

Managing a business successfully involves endless decision making. Electronic spreadsheets have been a tremendous aid to this complicated decision-making process. One way an electronic spreadsheet is used in business is for profit planning. In order to project the profit of a company, decisions must be made regarding labor expense, overhead expense, cost of materials, number of goods manufactured, and so on. By examining the past year's figures in all these areas and predicting how the figures will change in the coming year, management can project the following year's profit.

In this exercise you are going to create an income statement for a company called Arville and Associates.

1. At the DOS A> prompt, insert the VP-Planner Plus program disk in drive A and your data disk in drive B. Start VP-Planner Plus and load a new worksheet.

2. Enter the following labels in the cells indicated:

Cells	Labels
C1	ARVILLE AND ASSOCIATES INCOME STATEMENT
A3	Sales
A5	Cost of goods sold:
A6	Direct materials
A7	Direct labor
A8	Factory overhead
A11	Gross Profit
A13	Commercial expenses:
A14	Marketing expenses
A15	Administrative expenses
A17	Operating Income

3. Format the range of cells E3 through E35 to currency with zero decimal places.

4. Change the column-width of column F to 5. Change the column-width of column G to 12.

5. Format the range of cells G3 through G35 to currency with zero decimal places.

6. Enter the following values in the cells indicated:

Cells	Values
E6	3900000
E7	3000000
E8	2550000
E14	1300000
E15	1050000
G3	15000000

7. Go to cell E9.

■ Type: \ −

Go to cell G9.

■ Type: \ −

Go to cell E16

■ Type: \ −

Go to cell G18

■ Type: \ =

8. Go to cell G8. Enter a formula that finds the total of the cost of goods sold (materials plus labor plus overhead).

9. Go to cell G11. Enter a formula that calculates the gross profit (sales minus total cost of goods sold).

10. Go to cell G15. Enter a formula that calculates total expenses (marketing expenses plus administrative expenses).

11. Go to cell G17. Enter a formula that calculates the operating income (gross profit minus total expenses).

12. Now you are ready to project the gross profit and operating income for next year. Management has predicted the following for next year:

Sales to increase by 20%
Cost of direct materials to increase by 8%
Cost of direct labor to increase by 12%
Cost of factory overhead to increase by 3%
Marketing expenses to increase by 7%
Administrative expenses to increase by 5%

Go to cell A19.

■ Type: FORECAST

13. Copy the content of cells A3 through A17 to cells A21 through A35.

14. Go to cell G21. Using the predictions provided by management, enter a formula that calculates the forecasted sales.

15. In cells E24, E25, and E26, enter formulas that calculate the cost of materials, labor, and overhead based upon managements' predictions.

16. In cells E32 and E33, enter formulas that calculate marketing and administrative expenses based upon managements' predictions.

17. In cell G26, enter a formula that calculates the total forecasted cost of goods sold.

18. In cell G29, enter a formula that calculates the forecasted gross profit.

19. In cell G33, enter a formula that calculates the total forecasted commercial expenses.

20. In cell G35, enter a formula that calculates the forecasted operating income.

21. Save and print the worksheet.

▬ VP-PLANNER PLUS PROBLEMS

To complete the following problems, use the INCOME file included on the Student File Disk.

1. If you are not yet in VP-Planner Plus, use the necessary steps to start the worksheet program. Insert the Student File Disk in drive B.

■ Type: **/FR**

When the window with the file names of the files on the disk in drive B appears, highlight INCOME.WK1 and press <Return>. You should see the worksheet with the title INCOME STATEMENT on the screen.

■ Type: **/FS**

The prompt ENTER FILE NAME appears.

■ Type: **INCOME1**

When you do this, the file INCOME is copied to INCOME1. From now on, you are going to use the file INCOME1 and keep the file INCOME intact in case you want to start over again or you make a mistake. Use the **/FR** command again to retrieve the file INCOME1.

2. The file INCOME1 contains the summary of income statements for the LL&T CO. for the past seven years. You will have to update it and make a comparative analysis of the data.

a. Use the arrow keys to move around the worksheet and discover the structure of the model. Look closely at column D. This column contains simple entries in cells D6, D7, D10, D13, and D16; and formulas for totals and subtotals in cells D9, D12, D15, and D18. This structure is the same for all years.

b. Go to cell D3 and enter the following: (Thousand dollars) (Remember that this is a label and not a value.)

c. Now assume that you have just received the following data for 1988:

NET SALES	1 650.41
COST OF GOODS SOLD	1 251.30
GENERAL EXPENSES	214.68
INTEREST EXPENSE	15.65
STATE TAXES	73.26
COMMON SHARES	27 500
DIVIDENDS PAID	29 900

You are going to update the worksheet in column B.

■ Go to cell B4 and type 1988 with the label prefix that centers the label.

■ Enter the numbers in the appropriate columns.

■ Copy the formulas from cells D9, D12, D15, and D18 to the equivalent cells in column B. As you can see, the totals are updated as you enter the formulas.

3. Now you would like to compute the differences between years for the following items: NET SALES, COST OF GOODS SOLD, GROSS PROFIT, GEN. ADM. EXPENSES, and NET INCOME.

a. First, freeze column A so that you will always be able to see those titles. To do this, move the cell pointer to column B. Type: **/WTV**. Now column A will remain on the screen as you move one screen to the right.

b. Now, start with the differences between 1988 and 1987.

■ Move the cell pointer to cell E4 and type D88/87. Remember that this is a label and not a value.

■ Move the cell pointer to cell E6 to calculate the first difference in NET SALES. The formula should be: (+B6−D6)/D6. Type the formula into that cell.

■ Copy it to the cells corresponding to the other items for which a difference is requested.

c. Change the format of the cells in that range to the percent format.

■ Move the cursor to cell E6.

■ Type: **/RFP**

■ When asked for the decimal places, type **2** and press <Return>.

■ When asked for the range, use the pointing method to define the following range: E6..E18. You should see all the differences displayed on the worksheet in the PERCENT format.

d. Now compute the differences for the remaining years.

■ Enter the column titles as above (for example, D87/86 in cell G4 for the differences between 1987 and 1986).

■ Because the formulas already have been computed once, simply use the COPY command to copy them to the appropriate cells for the remaining columns.

■ If necessary, change the format of the cells to PERCENT as in 3C, to display the differences using the PERCENT format.

■ Clear the frozen titles.

■ Move the cell pointer to cell A20. Enter \ = (using the repeating label prefix) and copy this cell entry to the range B20..R20, to draw a horizontal double line.

4. Compute the income per share and dividends per share for each year. Start with 1988.

> INCOME PER SHARE = NET INCOME/COMMON SHARES
> DIVIDEND PER SHARE = DIVIDENDS PAID/COMMON SHARES

a. Freeze both column A and row 4.

b. Define the formulas with their cell addresses and enter them in the appropriate cells (B23 and B27).

c. Copy the formulas to the remaining columns.

d. You would like to show a $ sign before INCOME/SHARE, DIVIDENDS PAID, and DIVIDEND/SHARE. Type **/RFC.** When asked for the number of decimal positions, type **2** and press <Return>. When asked for a range, use the pointing method to define the range B23 through P27.

e. Clear the frozen titles.

5. Save the INCOME1 file.

6. Print the INCOME1 file.

7. Now assume that you want to draw a bar graph showing the evolution of NET SALES over the past seven years. To draw this graph, you need the years for the horizontal axis and the net sales for the vertical axis. The data should be in a continuous set of cells. Therefore, you first have to copy them.

a. Copy the net sales for the eight years to the cells S6 to S13. For example, the cell B6 entry (net sales for 1988) should be copied to cell S6, and the cell D6 should be copied to cell S7.

b. Move the cell pointer to cell R6 and type 1988. Type 1987 in cell R7. Repeat this until you have typed the appropriate year for each net sales amount.

c. Select the GRAPH command from the main command menu. The Graph menu should be the first-level menu.

d. Type: **TB.** Notice that after the graph type is selected, the Graph menu is once again the first-level menu.

e. Type: **X.** When asked for the range, enter **R6..R13** and press <Return>.

f. Type: **A.** When asked for the range, use the pointing method to define the range S6..S13 and press <Return>.

g. Type: **V** to view the graph. Press <Esc> after you have viewed the graph.

h. Give a title to the graph by doing the following:

- Type: **OTF**
- Enter the following title: Evolution of sales from 1981 to 1988
- Press <Return>
- Type: **TX**
- Enter Year
- Press <Return>
- Type: **TY**
- Enter Sales
- Press <Return>
- Type: **Q** to quit

i. Save the graph. Name the graph SALES.

8. Print the bar graph SALES.

SECTION E

Introduction to Data Managers and dBASE III PLUS

OUTLINE

Introduction
Definitions
Uses of Data Managers
Learning Check
Guide to dBASE III PLUS
Getting Started with dBASE III PLUS
Using the Assistant Menu
Selecting Menu Options
Getting Help with dBASE III PLUS
Quitting dBASE III PLUS
Learning Check
Defining the Structure of a Data-Base
    File
    Naming a Data-Base File
    Defining Fields
    Displaying the Structure of a Data-
        Base File
    Editing the Structure of a Data-Base
        File
Entering Data into a Data-Base File
Updating a Data-Base File
    Editing a Record
    Browsing Through Records
    Adding a Record
    Deleting a Record
    Displaying and Printing a Data-Base
        File
Learning Check
Managing Files with the Tools Option
    Setting the Disk Drive
    Copying a File
    Renaming a File
    Listing the File Directory
    Erasing a File
Relational and Logical Operators
Going to a Specific Record

■ INTRODUCTION

Schools, hospitals, restaurants, and all types of businesses store data. The ability to retrieve, sort, and analyze data quickly and efficiently can make the difference between a company's success and failure. The types of data collected include employee records, bills, supply lists, budgets, and insurance information. Before microcomputers became standard business equipment, the most common way to organize data was to store records in folders in file cabinets. File cabinets use a lot of space, however, and sometimes several departments may keep the same data. This duplication of data is a waste of time, effort, and space, and can lead to confusion or errors if one copy is updated and the others remain unchanged.

Data managers are software packages that computerize record-keeping tasks. The term **data-base management system (DBMS)** also is often used when referring to the systematic organization and handling of a large collection of data stored in a computer system. In this book the computerization of record-keeping tasks is referred to as data management, and the programs that make this task possible are called data managers. This section explains what a data manager is and how it works. It also introduces dBASE III PLUS, a sophisticated and powerful data-management tool.

■ DEFINITIONS

A data manager software package is used to organize files. Data managers use secondary storage devices, such as floppy disks, to store the type of data that is kept in folders and envelopes in a manual filing system.

It is easy to understand how data is stored in a filing cabinet. Folders with related data are kept in the drawers of the cabinet. Each folder has a label that identifies the contents. All the folders in each drawer may be related to a certain topic. To find one data item, the appropriate drawer has to be selected, and then the specific folder containing the needed information has to be found.

With a data manager, data is recorded electronically on floppy disks, hard disks, or magnetic tapes. Instead of people looking through drawers and folders for a certain item, the computer searches the disk or tape for it.

Each data item, such as a student's name, insurance-policy number, or amount of a bill, is called a **field.** A group of related fields forms a **record.** Your school may keep records about each student. A student's record contains fields such as the person's name, home address, parents' names, class standing, courses taken, and grade-point average.

A **file** is a group of related records. For example, all the student records in a school could make up one file. The school might have other files for teacher records, financial records, and school board records. Figure E–1 illustrates how a data-base software package might be organized for a business.

Data managers are useful because they perform many tasks faster and more easily than a manual filing system. Most data managers can perform the following:

■ Add or delete data within a file
■ Search a file for specific data
■ Update or change data in a file

- Sort data into a particular order
- Print all or part of the data in a file

Because different files may contain the same information, **data redundancy** can occur and cause problems for a business. Data redundancy is the repetition of data in different files. Because of the difficulty of keeping one piece of information—such as an employee's address—current in several files, large companies have developed data-base packages. A **data base** consolidates various independent files into one integrated unit while allowing users access to the information they need. Each data item is stored once, so it is easy to maintain. Users can search for, update, add, or delete data on all the records at one time.

Data-base packages store data that can later be accessed for many uses. A university data base might be accessed by the admissions, registrar's, financial aid, and dean's offices. A college dean might request the names of students who will graduate with academic honors, whereas the financial aid director might need a list of all students participating in a work-study program.

Since microcomputers were introduced, data managers also have become popular with small businesses and home users.

dBASE III Summary Commands
  Count
  Sum
  Average
Learning Check
Summary Points
dBASE III PLUS Exercises
dBASE III PLUS Problems

FIGURE E-1

The Organization of a Simple Data-Base File

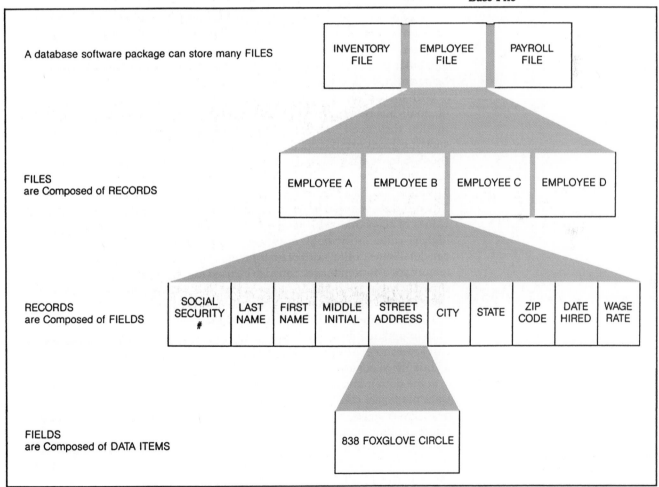

A database software package can store many FILES

FILES are Composed of RECORDS

RECORDS are Composed of FIELDS

FIELDS are Composed of DATA ITEMS

■ USES OF DATA MANAGERS

Data managers are popular software packages for home use. They can be used to create and organize a computerized address book, holiday card list, or recipe file. A data manager can be used for just about any type of record keeping. Collectors of coins, stamps, baseball cards, or any other items can keep an up-to-date file of their collections.

By computerizing recording and filing tasks in the home, you can keep records in a compact form. Instead of having numerous notebooks and folders that must be maintained manually, you enter new data into the computer. You can store files on several floppy disks.

Besides storing files in a compact form, data managers can find specific data stored in a file much faster than a person looking through folders and notebooks. For example, data managers can be used to prepare reports for the filing of taxes. You could keep a record of financial transactions throughout the year and place a file labeled "Tax Deductible" in the data record to indicate whether a transaction was tax related. At tax time, the data manager could be used to pick out the tax-related transactions and print a report. Other home uses of data managers include keeping personal records, creating mailing lists, keeping appointment calendars, and indexing books in a personal library.

Data bases lie at the heart of most businesses' use of computers. Data bases are used to maintain employee records, control inventory, and list suppliers and customers. Data bases can generate payroll checks, invoices and balance sheets. Most of the critical elements of running a business can be performed on a data base.

With the increasing sophistication of low-end data managers, even owners of small businesses can now have the kind of timely and accurate information they need to manage their business well. For example, a small sporting goods retail store could computerize its inventory to improve sales through more efficient and timely record keeping. By recording daily sales, managers can see when the stock levels are low, and know when to reorder. The store can have an ample supply of items at all times.

Some data managers perform mathematical tasks. They can total the values of the same field in each record or find records with the lowest or highest value in the field. A data manager with mathematical capabilities can determine dollar sales of an item for a certain period. The mathematical features of a data manager can also be used for inventory control. Employees would not need to count the items in the store. The data manager can display subtotal and total inventory for tax reporting at the end of the year.

A major benefit of computerized record keeping is the savings in time both in updated data and in searching for information. Data managers free employees to concentrate on tasks that can only be done by humans, such as talking to customers or planning new displays.

Some data managers are designed for use in special or unique situations. Data managers can be designed to meet the unique need of a specific business. Pharmacies, for example, use data bases to store drug and patient information to help pharmacists avoid giving patients medicines that may be harmful. With a data base, a pharmacist could determine if a particular drug would react adversely with another drug the patient was taking, or if the patient was allergic to a drug.

Creating mailing lists is another popular specialized application. A data manager can store data about people, such as their names, addresses, interests, hobbies, and purchases. People's interests and hobbies can be determined from studying the products they order or magazines they receive. For example, the data manager can sort and print a list of people who order a sewing or craft item or who receive craft catalogs. The data manager can then print mailing labels for these people.

Data managers can be used with word processors to produce personalized form letters for individuals or organizations found on the mailing lists. They can supply the names and addresses to be inserted in the letter.

LEARNING CHECK

1. A _____ C _____ is a meaningful item of data, such as an employee address.

a. data base   c. field
b. record   d. file

2. A _____ B _____ is a collection of related data fields that constitute a single unit, such as all the relevant data about one employee.

a. data base   c. field
b. record   d. file

3. A grouping of independent data files into an integrated whole is a _____ A _____.

a. data base   c. field
b. record   d. file

4. A _____ d _____ is a group of related data records.

a. data base   c. field
b. record   d. file

5. By storing each data item only once, eliminating duplication of information in many different files, a data base reduces problems caused by _____ S _____.

ANSWERS

1. c.
2. b.
3. a.

4. d.
5. data redundancy

▰ GUIDE TO dBASE III PLUS

The remainder of this section focuses on how to use an educational version of dBASE III PLUS, a data manager developed by Ashton-Tate. dBASE III PLUS is a data-management program that enables users to perform many functions of data-base management easily.

Some of the directions for using dBASE III PLUS vary depending on whether the computer has two floppy disk drives or a hard disk drive. The directions in this section are written for computers with two floppy disk drives.

Before using dBASE III PLUS, you must know the amount of available memory on the computer you are using. The minimum computer memory required to run dBASE III PLUS is 256K. However, if you are using a computer with 256K of memory, you must use a DOS Version 2.X to start the system. If the computer you are using has 384K or more of memory, then any version of DOS can be used to start the system.

Each of the following sections introduces one or more features of dBASE III PLUS. At the end of each section there is a hands-on activity called Your Turn. Do not try the hands-on activities until you have carefully read the sections preceding them.

The key on the IBM PC keyboard marked ↵ is the <Enter> or <Return> key. In the previous sections this key was called the <Return> key. However, the dBASE III PLUS program refers to this key as the <Enter> key. Therefore, throughout this section, the key marked ↵ is called the <Enter> key. When you are instructed to press the <Enter> key, press the key marked ↵.

The following symbols and typefaces appear throughout this section:

Enter: Number	Magenta-colored characters indicate data that should be entered into a file.
Press *S*	Italicized text indicates a letter that should be pressed. Usually the key activates a dBASE III PLUS menu. The letter does not appear on the monitor when it is pressed.
Add new record? [Y/N] (prompt) **File is already open** (message) Select **List** (menu option) Type: **Address** (text)	Boldface text indicates words or phrases that appear on the computer screen. The text could be a prompt, message, name of a menu option, or text that the user is typing.
Press <PgDn>	Angle brackets are used to signify a specific key on the keyboard. Press the key whose name or symbol is enclosed by the angle brackets.
Press <Enter>	dBASE III PLUS refers to the key labeled ↵ on the IBM PC keyboard as the ENTER key. Whenever instructed to press <Enter>, press the key marked ↵.
Press <Ctrl>-<N>	<Ctrl> is always used in conjunction with another key. In this example, <Ctrl> is held down while the letter N is pressed. Both keys are released together. The caret symbol (^) is

	used to denote the <Ctrl> key on the dBASE III PLUS menus. If you see the ^ symbol on the computer screen, it means press <Ctrl>.
The ADDRESS file	The names of files appear in all capital letters.

There are two ways to enter commands in dBASE III PLUS. One way is by using the Assistant Menu. The second way is by typing commands at the dot prompt. For beginning users of dBASE III PLUS, entering commands using the Assistant Menu is an easier method for learning how to use the program. Therefore, this section approaches learning the dBASE III PLUS program by using the Assistant Menu. Typing commands at the dot prompt is not covered.

▦ GETTING STARTED WITH dBASE III PLUS

To **boot** a computer (load an operating system into a computer's main memory) and start dBASE III PLUS, you need a DOS disk, the dBASE III PLUS Sampler Disk #1, dBASE III PLUS Sampler Disk #2, and a formatted data disk. Remember, if your computer has a memory of only 256K, then you must use a DOS Version 2.X. If you use a DOS Version 3.1 or above to boot a computer with 256K, you will receive an insufficient memory error message when you try to complete the advanced exercises in this section. All the files you create must be saved on your data disk. The files you create have to be saved on your data disk because there is not enough room to save them on the dBASE III PLUS Sampler Disk. Follow these steps to boot the computer and start dBASE III PLUS:

1. Insert the appropriate DOS disk into drive A. Close the disk drive door. Turn on the computer and monitor.

2. When asked to type in a date, enter today's date using the same format that appears next to CURRENT DATE on the screen and press <Enter>. When asked to type the time, enter the current time using the same format that appears next to CURRENT TIME on the screen and press <Enter>. The computer is set to conform to a twenty-four time format. That is, if it is 9:30 A.M. enter **09:30:00.** If it is 9:30 P.M. enter **21:30:00.**

3. When the system prompt (A>) appears on the screen, remove the DOS disk from drive A. Insert the dBASE III PLUS System Disk #1 into drive A and close the disk drive door.

4. Type **dbase** and press the <Enter> key. A message screen stating the dBASE III PLUS Software License Agreement appears. After a few moments, the following message appears at the bottom of the screen:

Insert Sampler Disk 2 in drive A and a Data Disk in drive B and press ENTER or press Ctrl-C to abort.

5. Remove the dBASE III PLUS Sampler Disk 1 from drive A. Insert the dBASE III PLUS Sampler Disk 2 into drive A and your formatted data disk into drive B. Close the disk drive doors. Press <Enter>. When the Assistant Menu appears, you are ready to start using dBASE III PLUS.

■ Your Turn

In this exercise start dBASE III PLUS on the computer.

1. Before you begin, make sure you have a DOS disk, Sampler Disk #1, Sampler Disk #2, and your Student File Disk that comes with this book.

- ■ Insert the DOS disk into drive A
- ■ Turn on the computer and monitor.

2. After a few moments a prompt appears instructing you to enter the date.

- ■ Enter the current date using the mm-dd-yy format
- ■ Press <Enter>

Another prompt appears instructing you to enter the time.

- ■ Enter the current time using the twenty-four hour format
- ■ Press <Enter>

3. The **A>** system prompt appears on the screen.

- ■ Remove the DOS disk from drive A
- ■ Insert the Sampler Disk #1 into drive A
- ■ Type: **dBase**
- ■ Press <Enter>

The message screen containing the dBASE III PLUS Software License Agreement appears. At the bottom of the screen is a prompt instructing you to insert the Sampler Disk #2 into drive A.

- ■ Remove the Sampler Disk #1 from drive A
- ■ Insert the Sampler Disk #2 into drive A
- ■ Insert your Student File Disk into drive B
- ■ Close the disk drive doors
- ■ Press <Enter>

The Assistant Menu appears on the screen. Your screen should look like Figure E–2. Leave the Assistant Menu on the screen while you read the following section.

■ USING THE ASSISTANT MENU

A **menu** is a list of choices or options shown on the display screen from which the user selects a command or option. The Assistant Menu acts as a home base for the dBASE III PLUS program. All the commands needed to create and maintain a data-base file are in the Assistant Menu. Before creating data-base files, you must understand the components of the Assistant Menu (see Figure E–2).

At the top of the Assistant Menu is a Menu Bar that lists eight options:

- ■ Set Up
- ■ Create
- ■ Update
- ■ Position
- ■ Retrieve
- ■ Organize
- ■ Modify
- ■ Tools

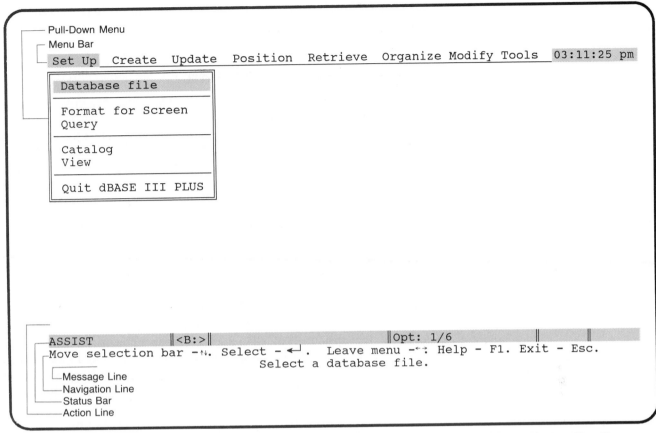

Pull-Down Menu
Menu Bar

Set Up Create Update Position Retrieve Organize Modify Tools 03:11:25 pm

Database file

Format for Screen
Query

Catalog
View

Quit dBASE III PLUS

ASSIST   ‖<B:>‖   ‖Opt: 1/6   ‖   ‖   ‖
Move selection bar - ↖. Select - ↵. Leave menu - ↩ Help - F1. Exit - Esc.
                    Select a database file.
Message Line
Navigation Line
Status Bar
Action Line

FIGURE E–2

The Assistant Menu

To the right of the Menu Bar is a space that keeps track of the current time. If you did not enter the correct time when the dBASE III PLUS program was first loaded, the time that appears on the screen will be incorrect.

When the Assistant Menu first appears after loading the dBASE III PLUS program, the Set Up Menu is open. The options from the Set Up Menu are listed in a pull-down menu. Each of the options on the Menu Bar has a corresponding pull-down menu.

There are four lines at the bottom of the screen. The first is called the Action Line; it is located immediately above the highlighted bar. In Figure E–2 the Action Line is empty, but in the next hands-on exercise you will see an entry in it. The highlighted bar is called the Status Bar. It keeps track of what you are doing. For example, in Figure E–2 the first box in the Status Bar shows that you are using the Assistant Menu, and the second box indicates which disk drive the computer is currently accessing. The remaining boxes in the Status Bar will be explained in the following hands-on exercise.

Underneath the Status Bar is the navigation line. The navigation line explains how to move between the menus and menu options. Finally, the message line at the bottom of the screen describes the option currently selected. In Figure E–2, the message **Select a database file** describes the option currently highlighted, which is the **Database file** option from the Set Up Menu.

As you use the Assistant Menu, get in the habit of reading the Status Bar and the action, navigation, and message lines. They provide useful information that will help you to work with data-base files.

▉ SELECTING MENU OPTIONS

There are two ways to open a menu on the Menu Bar. The first method is to use the right and left arrow keys located on the numeric keypad at the right of the keyboard. Pressing <→> moves the highlighting on the Menu Bar to the right. Pressing <←> moves the highlighting to the left. As a new menu is opened, its pull-down menu appears. If the highlighting is on the Set Up Menu, which is the first menu on the Menu Bar, pressing <←> moves the highlighting to the Tools Menu, the last one on the bar. Conversely, if the highlighting is on the Tools Menu, pressing <→> moves the highlighting to the first menu, the Set Up Menu.

The second way to open a menu is to press the letter corresponding to the first letter of the name of the menu. For example, if you want to open the Retrieve Menu, press *R*. If you want to open the Update Menu, press *U*, and so on.

Pressing < ↑ > and < ↓ > moves the highlighting up and down through a pull-down menu. When the option you want is highlighted, press <Enter> to select the option. Typically, another menu appears after you press <Enter>. The method for moving through that menu and all subsequent menus is the same: Press < ↑ > or < ↓ > until the desired option is highlighted, and press <Enter>. You cannot select an option from within a pull-down menu by entering the first letter of the option's name. That method only works if you are selecting an option from the Menu Bar. To make a selection from a pull-down menu, highlight the option and press <Enter>.

If you choose an option from a menu and then decide you do not want it, press <Esc> to cancel the selection. Each time <Esc> is pressed, you are taken back one step. Continue to press <Esc> until you are back to the desired menu. If <Esc> is pressed from one of the menus on the Menu Bar, the entire screen goes blank except for the Status Bar and a dot at the bottom of the screen. It is called a dot prompt. If you were entering commands by typing them at the dot prompt rather than selecting them from the Assistant Menu you would want this dot prompt on your screen. However, in this section you will only be entering commands using the Assistant Menu. If the dot prompt appears on the screen, type **Assist** and press <Enter>. The Assistant Menu will reappear.

▉ Your Turn

In this exercise practice moving around the Assistant Menu and selecting menu options.

1. The Assistant Menu should be on your screen from the previous exercise. First, practice moving along the Menu Bar. Currently the Set Up Menu is open.

■ Press <→>

Notice that the Create Menu is now open.

■ Press <→>

Now the Update Menu is open.

■ Press <→> five times

The Tools Menu is now open.

■ Press <→>

Notice that the highlighting moved back to the beginning of the Menu Bar, and the Set Up Menu is open.

■ Press <←>

The Tools Menu is now open.

■ Press <←> two times

Now the Organize Menu is open.

■ Press <→> four times

The highlighting wrapped around to the beginning of the Menu Bar again, and the Create Menu is now open. Try making selections from the Menu Bar by pressing the first letter of the option.

■ Press O

The Organize Menu is open.

■ Press T

The Tools Menu is open.

■ Press P

The Position Menu is open.

■ Press C

The Create Menu is open.

2. Next, practice moving up and down in the pull-down menus.

■ Press < ↓ > two times

The highlighting moved down to the **View** option on the Create Menu.

■ Press < ↓ > four times

Notice that the highlighting moved from the **Label** option, the last on the list, to the **Database file** option, the first on the list.

■ Press < ↑ >

The highlighting moved back to **Label,** the last option on the list.

■ Press <→>

The Update Menu is open.

■ Press < ↓ >

Notice that nothing happened. None of the options on the Update Menu are available to you now. That is because you have not yet accessed any files that could be updated.

3. Practice making menu selections.

■ Press <←> two times

The Set Up Menu should be open with the **Database file** highlighted. Select the **Database file** option.

■ Press <Enter>

A submenu listing all of the possible disk drives that can be used appears.

■ If necessary, use < ↓ > to highlight **B:**
■ Press <Enter>

A list of all the dBASE III PLUS files stored on the Student File Disk in drive B is displayed.

■ Highlight the file name **CUSTOMER.DBF**
■ Press <Enter>

The prompt **Is the file indexed? [Y/N]** appears. You will learn about indexed files in Section F.

■ Press *N*

The Set Up Menu remains open. Look at the Status Bar; some of its entries have changed. The first box still has **ASSIST** in it because you are using the Assistant Menu. The second box has <**B:**> in it because you are accessing disk drive B. The third box always displays the name of the file that currently is being used. **CUSTOMER** now appears in this box. It was accessed when the CUSTOMER.DBF file was highlighted from the list of files on the disk in drive B and <Enter> was pressed. **Rec: 1/12** appears in the fourth box. This box provides information on the status of the records in the current file. The first number tells you which record the program is currently accessing, and the second number reports the total number of records in the current data-base file. Therefore, **Rec: 1/12** means that the computer is currently accessing record 1, and there are a total of twelve records in the CUSTOMER file. The next box, which is currently empty, indicates the status of <Ins> and <Del>. <Ins> and <Del>, the Insert and Delete keys, are used when editing a data-base file. The last box in the Status Bar indicates the status of <Caps Lock>. If the capitals lock key is on, **Caps** appears in this box.

■ Press <Caps Lock>

Caps should now appear in the box. Anything you type while **Caps** appears in the Status Bar will be in all capital letters.

■ Press <Caps Lock>

The last box in the Status Bar should be empty again. <Caps Lock> is a toggle switch, which means that if you press it once it is on, if you press it a second time it is off, and pressing it a third time turns it on again.

4. Next, practice pressing <Esc> to cancel a selection.

■ Press *R*
■ Press < ↓ >

Display is highlighted.

■ Press <Enter>

A new menu appears and the entry **Command: DISPLAY** is in the Action Line. The Action Line always displays the command that was selected from the Assistant Menu. Because the dBASE III PLUS command DISPLAY was selected, **Command: DISPLAY** appears in the Action Line.

■ Press < ↓ >

Specify a scope is highlighted.

■ Press <Enter>

A third menu appears. Next, escape from all of the menus.

■ Press <Esc>

The third menu disappears.

■ Press <Esc>

The second menu disappears. You have moved all the way back to the options on the Menu Bar.

■ Press <Esc>

The Assistant Menu disappears from the screen and (Demo) followed by the dot prompt appears at the bottom of the screen. Notice that **ASSIST** no longer appears in the Status Bar. This is because the Assistant Menu was canceled the last time <Esc> was pressed. It is easy, however, to retrieve the Assistant Menu.

■ Type: **Assist**
■ Press <Enter>

The Assistant Menu returns to the screen.

5. Next, look at the CUSTOMER file.

■ Press *U*
■ Press < ↓ >

Edit is highlighted.

■ Press <Enter>

Record 1 from the CUSTOMER file appears on the screen, which should look like Figure E–3. The CUSTOMER file keeps track of customers' names, addresses, and business-related numbers. At the top of the screen is an editing and cursor-movement menu. The purpose of this menu is to remind you what keys to press to edit and move the cursor through the record. Underneath the menu is a record from the CUSTOMER file. You can tell, from the entry **Rec: 1/12** on the Status Bar, that this file contains twelve records and the current record is 1. Each record contains six fields: Name, Address, City, State, ZIP, and CNumber.

6. Look at the menu at the top of the screen. The first box in the menu indicates how to move the cursor from character to character and word to word. The second box indicates how to move the cursor from field to field and record to record. The last two boxes have information on editing a record. Practice moving around a record and moving from record to record.

■ Press <→>

```
┌──────────────────────────────────────────────────────────────────────────────┐
│  CURSOR    <-- -->      UP   DOWN  │   DELETE     │ Insert Mode:  Ins          │
│    Char:    ←   →   Field:  ↑    ↓  │ Char:   Del  │ Exit/Save:   ^End          │
│    Word:  Home End  Page: PgUp PgDn │ Field:   ^Y  │ Abort:        Esc          │
│                     Help:   F1      │ Record:  ^U  │ Memo:       ^Home          │
└──────────────────────────────────────────────────────────────────────────────┘
   NAME        Eileen Shonk
   ADDRESS     920 Conneaut Ave.
   CITY        Bowling Green
   STATE       Ohio
   ZIP         43402
   CNUMBER     4498




   EDIT              ║<B:>║CUSTOMER              ║Rec: 1/12        ║        ║
```

FIGURE E–3

Record 1 from the CUSTOMER File

The cursor moves to the next character, the *i* in *Eileen*.

■ Press < ↓ >

The cursor moves down to the next field, the Address field.

■ Press < ↓ >

The cursor moves down to the City field.

■ Press <End>

The cursor moves to the second word in the City field.

■ Press <End> again

The cursor moves to the end of the City field.

■ Press <Home>

The cursor moves one word to the left.

■ Press <Home> again

The cursor moves another word to the left.

■ Press <PgDn>

Record 2 appears. The entry in the Status Bar now reads **Rec: 2/12.**

■ Press <PgDn> again

Record 3 appears.

■ Press < ↓ > six times

The cursor moved through record 3 and now record 4 appears.

■ Press <PgUp>

Record 3 appears again. Pressing <PgUp> brought the previous record to the screen. Notice that the cursor is in the first field in record 3.

■ Press <↑>

Record 2 appears on the screen. There are two ways to move from record to record. First, pressing <PgUP> brings the previous record to the screen, and pressing <PgDn> brings the next record to the screen. The second way is to move the cursor to the first or last field in the record and press <↑> or <↓>. Pressing <↑> when the cursor is in the first field in the record brings the previous record to the screen. Pressing <↓> when the cursor is in the last field in the record brings the next record to the screen.

■ Press <Ctrl>-<End>

The Assistant Menu returns to the screen. Leave the Assistant Menu on the screen. You will be using it in the next hands-on exercise.

▓ GETTING HELP WITH dBASE III PLUS

dBASE III PLUS has a very useful Help feature. When using dBASE III PLUS you can obtain information about the menu option currently selected by pressing <F1>. If you get lost or stuck while trying to perform an operation, try to solve the problem by pressing <F1> and reading the Help screen that appears. The Help feature provides information only on the menu option that is highlighted.

▓ Your Turn

In this exercise you are going to practice using the Help function.

1. The Assistant Menu should still be on your screen.

■ Press C
■ Press <F1>

A Help screen appears that describes the Create option, which is used with the dot prompt. Notice the prompt at the bottom of the screen in the navigation line: **Press any key to continue work in ASSIST.**

■ Press any key

2. The Assistant Menu returns to the screen.

■ Press R
■ Press <↓> four times
■ Press <F1>

A Help screen describing the SUM command appears. Read the screen.

■ Press any key to return to the Assistant Menu

▓ QUITTING dBASE III PLUS

The command to exit from dBASE III PLUS is found in the Set Up Menu. The last option on the Set Up Menu, **Quit dBASE III PLUS,** allows the user to exit from dBASE III PLUS and return the DOS system prompt to the screen. The only way you can exit from dBASE III PLUS is by selecting this option. If you exit using any other method, you risk losing information stored in your data files. When the system prompt appears and both red lights on the disk drives are off, you can remove your disks from drives A and B and turn off the computer and monitor.

■ Your Turn

In this exercise you are going to exit from dBASE III PLUS.

1. The Assistant Menu should be on your screen.

■ Press *S*
■ Press < ↑ >

2. The option **Quit dBASE III PLUS** should be highlighted.

■ Press <Enter>

The message **END RUN dBASE III PLUS** and system prompt return to the screen. When the lights on both of the disk drives are off, take your disks out of drives A and B and turn off the computer and monitor.

**LEARNING
CHECK**

1. A _____/A_____ is a list of choices or options shown on the computer screen from which an option or command can be selected.

2. (True or False?) The only way to open a menu from the menu bar is to move the highlighting to that option by pressing the arrow keys.

3. (True or False?) The only way to select an option from a pull-down menu is to move the highlighting to that option and press <Enter>.

4. If the Assistant Menu disappears from the screen after pressing <Esc>, type _____ and press <Enter> to bring it back.

5. When a menu from the menu bar is open, a _____ appears below it.

ANSWERS

1. menu
2. False
3. True

4. Assist
5. pull-down menu

■ DEFINING THE STRUCTURE OF A DATA-BASE FILE

The first step in creating a data-base file is to define its structure. That is, you have to decide what fields will be included in each record, the names of the fields, maximum number of characters each field is likely to contain, and whether the data to be stored in a field is alphanumeric, numeric, or logical. Although the structure of a data-base file can be edited and changed after it has been created, prior planning can be a time-saver. Before entering the structure on the computer, take some time to think about and organize the data to be stored in the data-base file you are creating.

Naming a Data-Base File

Before the structure of a data-base file can be defined, the file has to be given a name. To name a data-base file, the Create option on the Menu Bar in the Assistant Menu must be selected. The Create option is the second choice on the Menu Bar; to choose it, either move the highlighting using the arrow keys to Create and press <Enter>, or type the letter *C*. When Create has been selected, the Create Submenu appears.

The first option in the Create Submenu is Database file, and it is highlighted. Select this option by pressing the <Enter> key. The Drive Selection Submenu appears. Select drive B. The prompt **Enter the name of the file** appears in the middle of the screen. You can now enter a name for the data-base file.

File names can be up to eight characters long. The first character must be a letter, but the name can contain numbers and underscore characters. The file name cannot contain any blank spaces. The file name MY DATA would not be acceptable because of the space. The following file name would be acceptable because an underscore instead of a space is used: MY_DATA.

If you make a mistake while typing in the file name, use the <Backspace> key to delete the error and retype the entry. Once the <Enter> key has been pressed, the only way to change the file name is to cancel the operation by pressing the <Esc> key. If the <Esc> key is pressed, the prompt **Are you sure you want to abandon operation? (Y/N)** appears. Pressing **Y** for yes cancels the operation for naming a file, and you can start the file-naming procedure again. Pressing **N** for no enables you to continue creating the data-base file and keep the file name that was entered.

dBASE III PLUS automatically adds a file extension to file names. A file extension is a period and three letters that follow the file name. File extensions help identify different types of files. When creating a data-base file, dBASE III PLUS automatically adds the file extension .dbf (for data-base file) after the file name. An example of another type of file that can be created with dBASE III PLUS is label form file, which is used for creating mailing labels. dBASE III PLUS adds the file extension .lbl (for label) after a label form file. By looking at the file extensions, a user can easily tell the difference between a data-base file and a file that contains a form for mailing labels.

■ Your Turn

In this exercise, you are going to boot your computer, load the dBASE III PLUS program and name a data-base file. When instructed to select an option from a menu, move the highlighting to that option using the arrow keys and press <Enter>.

1. The computer should be turned off. Have your Sampler Disk #1, Sampler Disk #2, and data disk ready.

- ■ Insert the DOS disk in drive **A**
- ■ Turn on the computer

The prompt **Enter current date** appears on the screen.

- ■ Enter today's date
- ■ Press <Enter>

The prompt **Enter current time** appears on the screen.

- Enter the current time
- Press <Enter>

2. The system prompt A> appears on the screen.

- Remove the DOS disk from drive A
- Insert the Sampler Disk #1 into drive A
- Type: **dBase**

The first dBASE III PLUS message screen appears.

- Press <Enter>

3. At the bottom of the screen is a prompt instructing you to insert the Sampler Disk #2 into drive A.

- Remove the Sampler Disk #1 from drive A
- Insert the Sampler Disk #2 into drive A
- Insert your data disk into drive B
- Close the disk drive doors
- Press <Enter>

4. The Assistant Menu appears on the screen.

- Select **Create**

The Create Submenu appears.

- Select **Database file**

The Drive Selection Submenu appears.

- Select **B:**

The prompt **Enter the name of the file:** appears (see Figure E–4).

- Type: **photos**
- Press <Enter>

The dBASE III PLUS field definition form appears on the screen (see Figure E–5). Leave this form on your screen while reading the next section. You will enter data into this form in the next Your Turn exercise.

Defining Fields

Defining a field consists of establishing the field's name, type, and width. A field name identifies its contents. Common field names are LASTNAME, FIRSTNAME, CITY, STATE. Notice there are no spaces in LASTNAME or FIRSTNAME. Like file names, field names cannot contain any spaces. Underscores, in addition to letters and numbers, are permitted. Therefore, LAST_NAME or FIRST_NAME would be acceptable field names. A field name may include up to ten characters; the first character must be a letter.

The field type identifies the kind of data stored in the field. A field can be defined as one of the following types:

- Character
- Date
- Logical

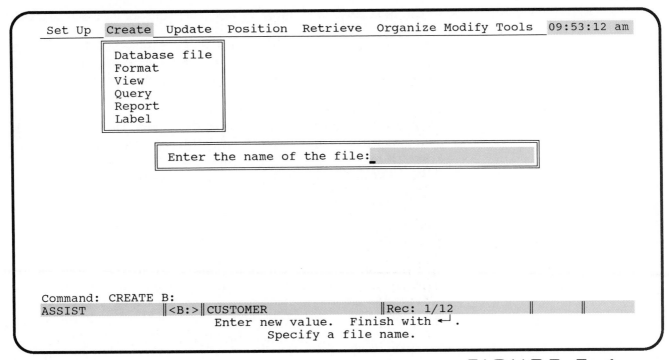

FIGURE E-4

Creating a Data-Base File

■ Memo
■ Numeric

Character fields are used to store data comprised of any of the letters, numbers, or special characters found on the keyboard. Date fields are used to store dates. Unless instructed to do otherwise, dBASE III PLUS stores

FIGURE E-5

The Field Definition Form

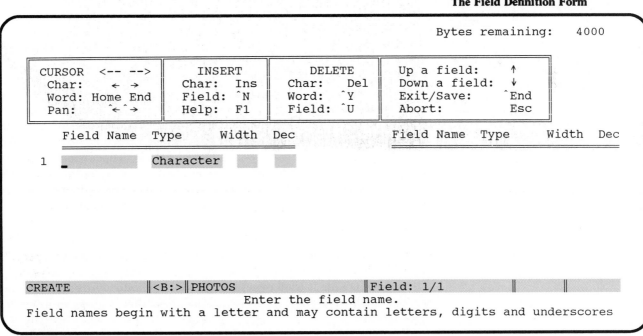

and displays dates in the mm/dd/yy format (*m* stands for the month, *d* stands for day, and *y* for year).

Logical fields are used to store data based on the response to a true/false question. An example of a logical field might be PAID. If a customer had paid for an item, either a T, for true (or Y, for yes) would be the data entered into the PAID field. If the customer had not paid, F, for false (or N, for no) would be entered into the field.

Memo fields are used to store large blocks of text. They hold the same kind of data as that of character fields (letters, numbers, and special characters). However, memo fields can store 5,000 characters or more, while character fields can only store up to 254 characters. Memo fields, for example, might contain notes on the individual records.

Numeric fields are used to store numbers that are used in mathematical formulas. A numeric field can be either integer or decimal. An integer number is one that would never have a decimal place. The number of books checked out of a library is an example of an integer number.

Not all fields that store numbers are numeric. A field is defined as numeric only if the numbers stored in it are used in a computation. Fields that store ZIP codes, Social Security, telephone, or employee numbers would be character rather than numeric fields because those numbers would not be used in a formula. Fields that store the quantity of an item ordered or the cost of an item would be numeric because those numbers could be used in a formula. Multiplying the number stored in the QUANTITY field by the number stored in the COST field would result in the total amount owed, for example.

The field width is the maximum number of characters required to store information in the field. For example, in a STATE field the width would be two because the maximum number of characters the field would have to hold is two (OH for Ohio, CA for California, etc.). Because the field width that is defined for each field takes up memory space, it is a good idea to know as closely as possible how many storage characters are necessary for all fields. That is, if a data-base file contains a LASTNAME field, it is a waste of memory to define the field width as 30 if most of the last names stored in the file are going to be 20 characters or less.

Each type of field has a limit as to how many characters it can store. Character fields have a maximum field width of 254. Date fields always have a field width of eight. The only possible width for a logical field is one, because the entry will always be one letter (T, F, Y, or N). dBASE III PLUS automatically inserts a field width of eight whenever a date field is defined and a field width of one whenever a logical field is defined since these are the only possible widths for these two fields. When defining the width of a numeric field decimal points and negative signs must be considered because they count as digits. The maximum width of a numeric field is 19.

▇ Your Turn

Start with the field definition form on your screen. The file name PHOTOS should be in the Status Bar.

The PHOTOS file is used by a photography studio to store data on photo sessions. Following is a description of each field that is going to be in the PHOTOS file.

COMPUTERS AND INFORMATION PROCESSING

Field Name	Description
FIRSTNAME	This field stores the first name of the customer.
LASTNAME	This field stores the last name of the customer.
PHONE	This field stores the telephone number of the customer.
CATEGORY	This field stores what type of photo session has been ordered. There are four possible categories: I (Individual) for a photo session with just one person, C (couple) for a photo session with two individuals, G (Group) for a photo session with three people or more, and W (Wedding) for photographing a wedding.
DATE	This field stores the date that the photo session is to take place.
COST	This field stores the cost of the photo session.
PAID	This field stores whether or not the customer has paid for the photo session.
NOTES	This field stores additional notes on the particular photo session.

You are now ready to start defining the fields. The blank table for defining field structure should still be on your screen. The cursor is in field 1 under the words *Field Name*.

1. The name of the first field is FIRSTNAME. It is a character field and its field width is 15.

■ Type: **FIRSTNAME**

Do not worry about capitalization. dBASE III PLUS automatically capitalizes all the field names as you enter them regardless of whether you type upper- or lowercase letters.

■ Press <Enter>

The cursor moves to the Type column. The word CHARACTER already appears in the Type column. The FIRSTNAME field is a character field, so this is the field type you want.

■ Press <Enter>

The cursor moves to the Width column. The field width for this field is 15.

■ Type: **15**
■ Press <Enter>

The first field is now defined. Notice the cursor skipped over the Dec column. *Dec* stands for decimal and the cursor moves to that column only if a numeric field has been defined.

2. The cursor is now in the Field Name column for field 2.

■ Type: **LASTNAME**
■ Press <Enter>

The LASTNAME field is also a Character field.

■ Press <Enter>

The field width for the LASTNAME field is 20.

- Type: **20**
- Press <Enter>

The cursor has moved to the Field Name column for field 3.

- Type: **PHONE**
- Press <Enter>

Even though the PHONE field is going to store numbers (telephone number), it is still a Character field since these numbers are not going to be used in a formula.

- Press <Enter>

The field width for the PHONE field is 13. The field width is so long because the parentheses around the area code and the hyphen in the phone number have to be considered when calculating the field width. When the phone numbers are entered into the file they will be entered as follows: (999)999-9999.

- Type: **13**
- Press <Enter>

The cursor has moved to the Field Name column for field 4.

- Type: **CATEGORY**
- Press <Enter>

The CATEGORY field is a Character field.

- Press <Enter>

The field width for the CATEGORY field is 1.

- Type: **1**
- Press <Enter>

The cursor has moved to the Field Name column for field 5.

- Type: **DATE**
- Press <Enter>

The field type for the DATE field is Date. Notice the following statement in the navigation line at the bottom of the screen: PRESS SPACE TO CHANGE THE FIELD TYPE. One way to change the field type is to press the <Space Bar> until the appropriate field type appears in the Type column.

- Press the <Space Bar>

Numeric appears in the Type column.

- Press the <Space Bar> again

Date now appears in the Type column.

- Press <Enter>

Notice that the number 8 was automatically placed in the Width column and the cursor has now moved to the Field Name column for field 6. dBASE III PLUS automatically inserts a field width of eight whenever Date is selected as the field type.

- Type: **COST**
- Press <Enter>

The COST field is a Numeric field. Another way of selecting the field type, other than pressing the <Space Bar> until the appropriate field type appears in the Type column, is to type the first letter of the field type (**C** for Character; **D** for Date; **L** for Logic; **M** for Memo; **N** for Numeric).

- Type: **N**

NUMERIC now appears in the Type column and the cursor automatically moved to the Width column without your having to press the <Enter> key. The field width for the COST field is 10.

- Type: **10**
- Press <Enter>

Since the COST field is a Numeric field, the cursor moved into the Decimal column. You have to define how many decimal places are to be stored for the numbers being entered into this field. You would like the numbers to have two decimal places.

- Type: **2**
- Press <Enter>

The cursor has moved to the Field Name column for field 7.

- Type: **PAID**
- Press <Enter>

The PAID field is a Logical field.

- Type: **L**

Notice that a field width of one was automatically entered and the cursor moved to the Field Name column for field 8. Since Logical fields can only have a width of one, dBASE III PLUS automatically enters the 1 for you.

- Type: **NOTES**
- Press <Enter>

The NOTES field is a Memo field.

- Type: **M**

dBASE III PLUS automatically entered the field width of 10 for you because the NOTES Memo field will be stored in a different file and only 10 characters of it will actually be stored in the PHOTOS file.

3. You have finished defining all the fields for the PHOTOS file. Look over your entries carefully. Your screen should look like Figure E–6. If you find you have made a mistake in one of the fields, use the up arrow key < ↑ > or down arrow key < ↓ > to move to the field where the mistake was made. Once the cursor is located in the correct field, use the left arrow key <←> or right arrow key <→> to move to the column where the error was made. Pressing the arrow keys moves the cursor from character to character. If you wish to move the cursor from column to column, press the <Enter> key. Once the cursor is in the field and column where the error appears, type in the correct entry and press <Enter>.

4. When you are sure all your entries are correct, you are ready to save the structure for the PHOTOS data-base file. Pressing <Ctrl>-<End> saves the structure for the data-base file.

■ Press <Ctrl>-<End>

The prompt PRESS ENTER TO CONFIRM. ANY OTHER KEY TO RE-SUME appears in the Navigation line at the bottom of the screen. Pressing <Enter> saves the structure for the data-base file. Pressing any other key cancels the save command and enables you to make further changes to the structure.

■ Press <Enter>

The prompt INPUT DATA RECORDS NOW? (Y/N) appears in the Navigation line. If you were immediately ready to enter data into the records, you would type **Y** for yes. You will not be entering data into the records until a hands-on exercise later in the chapter, so for now, you will select no.

■ Type: **N**

The Assistant Menu returns to the screen.

Displaying the Structure of a Data-Base File

After the structure for a data-base file has been defined, the user can view the structure. By displaying the structure on the screen, a user can find out what fields are included in the file, its field names, widths, and field types.

Before the structure of a data-base file can be displayed, however, the file has to be active. The file whose name appears in the Status Bar is the one currently in use—the active file. If you want to display the structure of a file other than the one whose name is in the Status Bar, or if there is no file

FIGURE E-6

Defining the Fields for the PHOTOS File

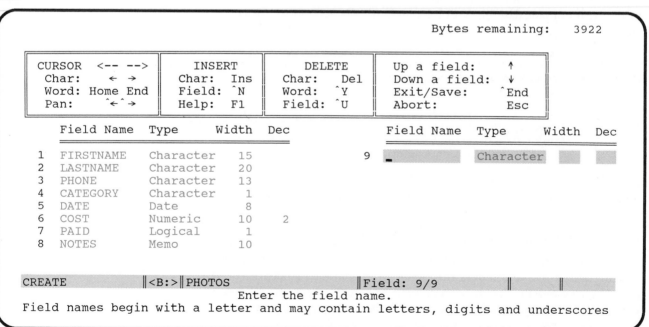

COMPUTERS AND INFORMATION PROCESSING

name listed in the Status Bar, you must first access the data-base file. To access the data-base file, select the Setup option from the Menu Bar in the Assistant Menu. Next, select the Database file option from the Set Up Submenu, the disk drive where the files are stored, and the name of the file whose structure you want to display. The prompt **Is the file indexed? [Y/N]** appears on the screen. Indexed files are covered in Section F. For now you will type **N** in response to this prompt. After responding to the prompt, the file name appears in the Status Bar.

To display the structure of a data-base file whose name is in the Status Bar, select the Tools option from the Menu Bar in the Assistant Menu. Next, select the List structure option from the Tools Submenu. The prompt **Direct the output to the printer? [Y/N]** appears on the screen. If you wish to have a hard copy of the structure for future reference, type **Y.** If you do not need a hard copy of the structure, type **N.** The structure of the data-base file then appears on the screen. To exit from the display, press any key. The Assist Menu returns to the screen.

■ Your Turn

In this exercise you are going to display the structure of the PHOTOS data-base file. Look at the Status Bar. Notice that the file name PHOTOS appears. Because the PHOTOS file is currently active, you do not have to access it.

1. The Assistant Menu should be on your screen.

- ■ Select **Tools** from the Menu Bar
- ■ Select **List structure** from the Tools Submenu

2. The prompt **Direct the output to the printer? [Y/N]** appears on the screen. You do not need a hard copy of the structure.

- ■ Type: **N**

3. The structure for the PHOTOS data-base file appears. Your screen should look like Figure E–7. Notice that the first line displays the disk drive where the file is stored and its file name. The second line lists the number of records that are stored in the data-base file. Because no records have been added to the PHOTOS data-base file, a zero appears in this line. The next thing listed is the date of the last change made to the file. Finally, the field numbers, names, types, widths, and the decimal places for each field in the data-base file are listed.

4. Look the structure over carefully.

- ■ Press any key

The Assistant Menu returns to the screen.

Editing the Structure of a Data-Base File

It is easy to make changes to the structure of a data-base file. Fields can be added, deleted, or redefined; field names, widths, or types can be changed.

The data-base file to be edited must be active. That is, its name has to appear in the Status Bar. If you want to edit the structure of a file other than the one whose name is in the Status Bar, or if there is no file name

```
┌──────────────────────────────────────────────────────────────────┐
│  Set Up  Create  Update  Position  Retrieve  Organize Modify Tools  10:25:50 am │
│  ────                                                                            │
│                                                                                  │
│                                                                                  │
│  Structure for database: B:photos.dbf                                           │
│  Number of data records:        0                                                │
│  Date of last update   : 08/29/88                                                │
│  Field   Field Name  Type        Width    Dec                                    │
│      1   FIRSTNAME   Character      15                                            │
│      2   LASTNAME    Character      20                                            │
│      3   PHONE       Character      13                                            │
│      4   CATEGORY    Character       1                                            │
│      5   DATE        Date            8                                            │
│      6   COST        Numeric        10        2                                   │
│      7   PAID        Logical         1                                            │
│      8   NOTES       Memo           10                                            │
│  ** Total **                        79                                            │
│  ─────────────────────────────────────────────────────────────────────────────  │
│  ASSIST           ║<B:>║ PHOTOS                    ║Rec: None      ║      ║        │
│                   Press any key to continue work in ASSIST._                      │
└──────────────────────────────────────────────────────────────────┘
```

FIGURE E-7

The Structure of the PHOTOS File

listed in the Status Bar, access the data-base file by selecting the Setup option from the Menu Bar in the Assistant Menu. Next, select the Database file option from the Set Up Submenu, select the disk drive where the files are stored, and the name of the file whose structure you want to display. The prompt **Is the file indexed? [Y/N]** appears on the screen. Until you learn about indexed files, you will type **N** in response to this prompt. After responding to the prompt, the file name appears in the Status Bar.

Once the data-base file to be edited is active, select the Modify option from the Menu Bar in the Assistant Menu. Next, select Database file from the Modify Submenu. The structure for the data-base file, along with a menu that identifies how to move the cursor around the structure and insert and delete, appears on the screen. The words *Modify structure* appear in the Status Bar.

To edit the structure of the data-base file, move the cursor to the field that is to be changed. Pressing the up arrow key moves the cursor up a field; pressing the down arrow key moves the cursor down a field. Pressing the left and right arrow keys moves the cursor one character to the left or right, respectively. Pressing <End> moves the cursor through the structure category by category. That is, the cursor jumps from the field name, to the type, width, decimal (if there is an entry in that column), and then down to the field name of the following field, and so on.

To insert a character, position the cursor where the character is to be inserted, press <Ins>, and enter the character or characters. To delete a character, position the cursor under the character to be deleted and press <Del>.

To insert a new field, position the cursor where the field is to be inserted and press <Ctrl>-<N>. A new field is inserted, and all the fields following the new field move down one position. The field's name, type, width, and, if necessary, decimal places must then be entered. To delete a field, position the cursor on the field to be deleted and press <Ctrl>-<U>. The field is deleted and all the fields following the deleted field move up one position. If only a word, rather than an entire field, is to be deleted, place the cursor on that word and press <Ctrl>-<Y>. The word is deleted and a new entry can be made.

After all of the changes have been made, pressing <Ctrl>-<End> saves and exits from the Modify Structure Command. The prompt **Press ENTER to confirm. Any other key to resume** appears on the screen. If you are sure all the editing changes have been made, press <Enter>. The changes are saved and the Assistant Menu returns to the screen. If you want to cancel the option to save the data-base structure, press any key other than <Enter>. You can then continue to make changes to the data-base structure.

■ Your Turn

In this exercise, you are going to make changes to the PHOTOS data-base structure.

1. The Assistant Menu should be on your screen and the PHOTOS file should be active. Check the Status Bar to make sure that the PHOTOS file is active. If it is not, use the Set Up option to access the PHOTOS data-base file. The word PHOTOS should appear in the Status Bar.

- ■ Select **Modify** from the Menu Bar on the Assistant Menu
- ■ Select **Database file** from the Modify Submenu

2. Your screen should look like Figure E–8. At the top of the screen is a menu that lists the keys used to move the cursor, insert and delete. Underneath the menu is the structure for the PHOTOS data-base file.

FIGURE E—8

Modifying the Structure of a Data-Base File

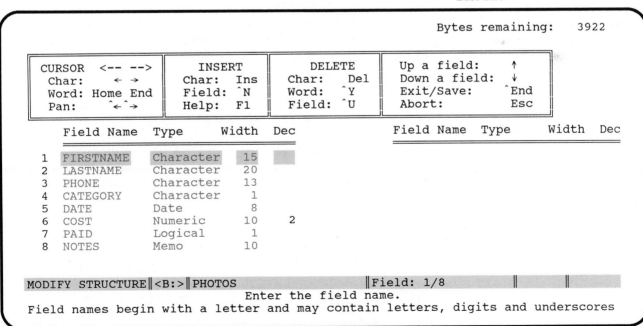

```
                                              Bytes remaining:    3922

 ┌─────────────────┬─────────────────┬─────────────────┬──────────────────────┐
 │ CURSOR  <-- -->  │    INSERT       │    DELETE       │ Up a field:      ↑   │
 │ Char:     ← →    │ Char:   Ins     │ Char:   Del     │ Down a field:    ↓   │
 │ Word: Home End   │ Field:  ^N      │ Word:   ^Y      │ Exit/Save:     ^End  │
 │ Pan:     ^←^→    │ Help:   F1      │ Field:  ^U      │ Abort:          Esc  │
 └─────────────────┴─────────────────┴─────────────────┴──────────────────────┘

       Field Name   Type     Width  Dec        Field Name   Type      Width  Dec

  1  FIRSTNAME   Character    15
  2  LASTNAME    Character    20
  3  PHONE       Character    13
  4  CATEGORY    Character     1
  5  DATE        Date          8
  6  COST        Numeric      10     2
  7  PAID        Logical       1
  8  NOTES       Memo         10

 MODIFY STRUCTURE ‖<B:>‖ PHOTOS                    ‖Field: 1/8    ‖       ‖
                            Enter the field name.
     Field names begin with a letter and may contain letters, digits and underscores
```

You have decided you would like the field names FIRSTNAME and LAST-NAME to look like two words rather than one. To do this, you are going to insert an underscore between the letters *T* and *N* in each field name. The cursor is now under the *F* in *FIRSTNAME*.

■ Press the right arrow key five times so that it is under the *N* in *FIRSTNAME*
■ Press the <Ins> key

Notice the word INS now appears in the right corner of the Status Bar.

■ Type: ＿ (the underscore character)

You now need to move down to the next field.

■ Press the down arrow key once

The cursor moves to field 2. It is under the *L* in *LASTNAME*.

■ Press the right arrow key four times to move the cursor to the *N* in *LASTNAME*

Notice the <Ins> key is still on because the word <INS> appears in the Status Bar. You do not have to press <INS> again to insert the underscore in *LASTNAME*

■ Press ＿ (the underscore character)

You have now finished inserting characters

■ Press <Ins>

The word <INS> is now gone from the Status Bar and the <Ins> key is off.

3. You now want to add a field to the PHOTOS data-base file. You need a field named LOCATION that stores the location of where the sitting is to take place. The LOCATION field is to be a character field, and its width is 40. You want to add the LOCATION field before the COST field, after the DATE field.

■ Press the down arrow key three times

The cursor should be in field 5, the DATE field.

■ Press <Ctrl>-<N>

There is now space to add a new field 5. Notice that the last four fields in the data-base file all moved down one spot. For example, the DATE field is now field 6. The cursor should be in the Field Name column for field 5.

■ Type: **LOCATION**
■ Press <Enter>

The LOCATION field is a character field.

■ Press <Enter>
■ Type **40**
■ Press <Enter>

The new field has now been added.

4. You now want to switch the order in which the fields appear. You want the DATE field to come right after the PHONE field. To do this, you are going to delete the DATE field from where it now appears and reinsert it in its new location. Use the arrow keys to move the cursor to the DATE field.

- Press <Ctrl>-<U>

The DATE field is deleted and all the fields that came after it moved up one spot.

- Press the up arrow key twice

The cursor should now be in field 4, the CATEGORY field.

- Press <Ctrl>-<N>

There is now room to add a new field 4.

- Type: **DATE**
- Press <Enter>
- Press. **D** to enter the Date field type

The DATE field is now inserted in its new location. You are now ready to save the edited PHOTOS data-base file.

- Press <Ctrl>-<End>

The prompt PRESS ENTER TO CONFIRM. ANY OTHER KEY TO RE-SUME appears at the bottom of the screen.

- Press <Enter>

The Assistant Menu returns to the screen.

■ ENTERING DATA INTO A DATA-BASE FILE

Once the structure for the data-base file has been completed, records can be entered into the file. Records can be added immediately following the creation of the data-base file structure. When creating the data-base file structure for the first time, the prompt **Input data now? [Y/N]** appears as soon as you press <Ctrl>-<End> to save the data-base structure. Pressing **Y,** for yes, enables you to begin entering records.

Records do not have to be entered as soon as the data-base file structure is completed. If you choose to enter records at a later point, make sure the data-base file to which the records are to be added is the active file. The active file is the file whose file name appears in the Status Bar. If the file to receive the records is not the active file, access that file by selecting Set Up from the Menu Bar on the Assistant Menu, and selecting Database file from the Set Up Submenu. Next, select the disk drive where the file is stored and, finally, select the appropriate file name.

Once the file is active, access the data-entry form by selecting Update from the Menu Bar in the Assistant Menu, and then selecting Append from the Update Submenu. The data-entry form appears on the screen along with a menu. The data is entered on the data-entry form in the space provided for each field. After typing the data for one field, press <Enter> and the cursor moves to the next field. If the data fills the field completely you do not have to press <Enter>; the cursor automatically moves to the next field. After data for the last field in the record has been added, a blank data-entry form for the next record appears. dBASE III PLUS saves the data that is entered record by record. That is, once the blank entry form for the next record appears, the previous record is saved.

If you make a typing mistake while entering data into a field and have not pressed <Enter>, use the backspace key to delete your mistake and type the entry again. If you notice a mistake that has already been entered into a field, use the up or down arrow keys to move the cursor to that field. Use either <Backspace> or <Del> to delete the error and enter the correction.

If you want to move back to check the entries in a previous record, press <PgUp>. Pressing <PgUp> moves to the previous record. To move to the next record in the file, press <PgDn>.

As you enter each record into the data-base file, dBASE III PLUS assigns it a record number. The record number for the current record is displayed in the Status Bar. dBASE III PLUS displays two record numbers separated by a slash. The first is the number of the current record; that is, the record that appears on the screen. The second is the total number of records in the data-base file.

Remember, when creating the structure for a data-base file, capitalization does not matter because dBASE III PLUS automatically capitalizes all the field names. Capitalization does, however, make a difference when entering records into the data-base file. dBASE III PLUS stores the data in the records exactly as you enter them, including whatever capitalization is used.

When all the records have been entered, end the data-entry process by using one of two methods. The first is by pressing <Enter> when the blank data-entry form for the next record appears. For example, say there are twenty records in a data-base file and you have just entered all the data for record 20. A blank data-entry form for record 21 appears on the screen. Pressing <Enter> when the blank form for record 21 appears terminates the data-entry process. Only 20 records will be saved (records 1 through 20); the empty record 21 will not be saved.

Another way to end the data-entry process is by pressing <Ctrl>-<End>. It does not matter what record appears on the screen if you press <Ctrl>-<End> to end the data-entry process. For example, say there are 20 records in a data-base file and you have entered all of them. Before ending the entry process you want to return to record 10 to check and make sure you entered the data in that record correctly. You would press <PgUp> to return to record 10. Once you had checked that record, you could leave it on the screen and press <Ctrl>-<End>. All the records in the file would be saved without having to return to record 20.

If a blank data-entry form is on the screen when you press <Ctrl>-<End>, that record will be saved in the data-base file. For example, say you entered the 20 records and pressed <Enter> after data for the last field in record 20 was entered. A blank data-entry form for record 21 appears on the screen. If <Ctrl>-<End> is pressed while this blank form is on the screen, dBASE III PLUS saves all 21 records; record 21 is saved although it contains no data. If this happens, the blank record can be removed. Later in this section you will learn how to delete an unwanted data-base record.

▨ Your Turn

In this exercise, you are going to enter eight records into the PHOTOS file. Check to make sure the PHOTOS file is the active file. If the file name PHOTOS does not appear on the Status Bar, access the file by selecting SET UP from the Menu Bar on the Assistant Menu, selecting DATABASE FILE from the Set Up Submenu, selecting the disk drive where the PHOTOS file is stored and finally selecting the PHOTOS file.

1. Once the PHOTOS file is the active file, you are ready to access the data-entry form

- ▪ Select **UPDATE** from the Menu Bar on the Assistant Menu
- ▪ Select **APPEND** from the Update Submenu

A blank data-entry form appears. Your screen should look like Figure E–9.

2. The cursor is in the space next to FIRST_NAME.

- ▪ Type: Donald
- ▪ Press <Enter>

Notice that the cursor moves to the next field.

- ▪ Type: Gross
- ▪ Press <Enter>
- ▪ Type: (404)555-3478

Notice that the computer beeped and the cursor automatically moved to the DATE field. The beep is a reminder to you not to press the <Enter> key because the data entered filled the field, causing the cursor to automatically move to the next field.

FIGURE E–9

A Data-Entry Form

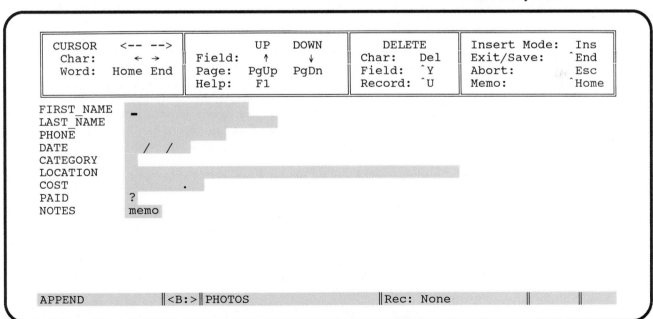

- ■ **Type:** 011590

The cursor automatically moves to the CATEGORY field. Notice in the DATE field that the slash marks separating the month from the date and the date from the year are already entered into the data-entry form so that you do not have to type them.

- ■ **Type:** I

The cursor automatically moves to the LOCATION field.

- ■ **Type:** Studio
- ■ **Press** <Enter>
- ■ **Type:** 45
- ■ **Press** <Enter>

Notice the decimal point and the two zeros are automatically entered without your having to type them. The cursor is now in the PAID field.

- ■ **Type:** T

The cursor automatically moves to the NOTES field, which is a memo field. To enter data into a memo field, you have to access the blank memo screen.

- ■ **Press** <Ctrl>-<PgDn>

The cursor is in the blank screen and you are ready to type the note.

- ■ **Type the following:**

Donald is an actor and wants 8 × 10 B&W glossies to accompany his resume. He wants five good poses—four close-ups of face only and one full-body shot.

You are now ready to save the note and return to the records in the database file.

- ■ **Press** <Ctrl>-<PgUp>

The record for Donald Gross returns to the screen. Look over the data you just entered. If you need to make any corrections, move the cursor to the field you want to edit using the up and down arrow keys. Delete the mistake either by using the <Backspace> key or the <Del> key. To insert a character into a word, press the <Ins> key. When you are sure all the entries are correct, you are ready to enter data into record 2.

- ■ **Press** <PgDn>

3. The blank form for record 2 appears.

- ■ **Type:** Karen
- ■ **Press** <Enter>
- ■ **Type:** Janiszewski
- ■ **Press** <Enter>
- ■ **Type** (404)555-9032
- ■ **Type:** 011890
- ■ **Type:** G

- **Type:** 13399 Peachtree Way, Atlanta
- **Press <Enter>**
- **Type:** 55
- **Press <Enter>**
- **Type:** T
- **Press <Ctrl>-<PgDn>**
- **Type the following:**

This family portrait is going to be taken inside the home. Bring light trees and lights to the appointment.

- **Press <Ctrl>-<PgUp>**

Look over your entries for record 2. If they are correct, press <PgDn>. If there are any errors, correct them and then press <PgDn>.

4. The blank data-entry form for record 3 appears. You should now be familiar with the data-entry process. Enter the following data into the remaining six records. Some of the records do not include notes in the memo field. If there are no notes for a record, simply press <PgDn> after entering the data in the PAID field.

FIRST_NAME:	Beatrice
LAST_NAME:	Weiss
PHONE:	(404)555-2600
DATE:	012090
CATEGORY:	W
LOCATION:	Temple B'nai Israel, Atlanta
COST:	400
PAID:	T
FIRST_NAME:	Samantha
LAST_NAME:	Mancuso
PHONE:	(404)555-3623
DATE:	012190
CATEGORY:	I
LOCATION:	Studio
COST:	45
PAID:	F
NOTES:	Samantha is bringing her two dogs to be included in the portrait.
FIRST_NAME:	Peter
LAST_NAME:	Schwartz
PHONE:	(404)555-4052
DATE:	012690
CATEGORY:	C
LOCATION:	115 Taylor, Atlanta
COST:	55
PAID:	F
NOTES:	This portrait is being taken inside the home. Bring light trees and lights to the appointment.
FIRST_NAME:	Shawn
LAST_NAME:	Montague
PHONE:	(404)555-5609
DATE:	012990

CATEGORY:	I
LOCATION:	Carter Park, Atlanta
COST:	55
PAID:	T
FIRST__NAME:	Gary
LAST__NAME:	Wasserman
PHONE:	(404)555-7382
DATE:	012990
CATEGORY:	G
LOCATION:	Studio
COST:	45
PAID:	F
FIRST__NAME:	Max
LAST__NAME:	O'Dell
PHONE:	(404)555-7382
DATE:	012990
CATEGORY:	C
LOCATION:	Studio
COST:	45
PAID:	T

Once the record for Max O'Dell is entered, press the <PgUp> key to browse through all the records to make sure the entries are correct. Correct any errors you find.

5. When you are sure all the records are correct, you are ready to save the data-base file.

■ Press <Ctrl>-<End>

The Assistant Menu returns to the screen.

▬ UPDATING A DATA-BASE FILE

Very rarely is a data-base file ever finalized. Typically changes such as adding or deleting records and updating the data stored in the records are continually made to a data-base file. Editing a data-base file is a very easy operation using the Assistant Menu.

Editing a Record

To edit records in an active data-base file, first select the Update Option from the Menu Bar in the Assistant Menu. Next select Edit from the Update Submenu. The current record, whose number is displayed in the Status Bar, appears on the screen. The word **EDIT** appears in the Status Bar.

If the record that is displayed is not the record needing to be edited, press <PgUp> or <PgDn> to browse through the records until the one you want to edit is displayed. Pressing the up and down arrow keys moves you through the records as long as you do not go past the first or last field. For example, if the cursor is in the first field of the record and you press < ↑ >, the previous record appears on the screen. If the cursor is in the last field of the record and you press < ↓ >, the next record appears on the screen.

Once the appropriate record is displayed, use the up and down arrow keys to move to the field to be edited. Use the left and right arrow keys to move through the characters in a particular field. Use <Backspace> or <Del> to delete characters. If you want to insert characters, press <Ins>. If you try to enter characters without pressing <Ins> first, the characters you enter will type over the characters that were already there. Typing over characters is, of course, another method for editing data.

After making editing changes to one record, you can edit other records by pressing <PgUp> or <PgDn>. As many data records can be edited as necessary.

When editing is complete, there are two ways to exit from the editing process. If you want to save all the changes that were made, press <Ctrl>-<End>. If you want to leave the editing process but you do not want to save the changes made to the current record, press <Esc>.

■ Your Turn

In this exercise you are going to edit several of the records in the PHOTOS data-base file. Make sure the PHOTOS data-base file is active.

1. When the PHOTOS file is active, start the process of editing records.

■ Select **Update** from the Menu Bar in the Assistant Menu
■ Select **Edit** from the Update Submenu

Record 1 appears on the screen. Notice the word **EDIT** in the Status Bar. Also notice the words **REC: 1/8** in the Status Bar. This is telling you that record 1 is currently displayed and that there are a total of eight records in the PHOTOS data-base file.

2. The PHOTOS file needs to be edited because the following four things have happened:

Karen Janiszewski had to change the date of her sitting. She also decided she wants the portrait taken outside rather than indoors.
Samantha Mancuso has a new telephone number.
Peter Schwartz wants to have a group sitting rather than a couple sitting.
Max O'Dell decided to have his pictures taken at home rather than in the studio.

You are going to edit the records to reflect these changes. Record 1 should still be on your screen.

■ Press <PgDn>

Record two, which is the record for Karen Janiszewski, appears on the screen. Karen has changed her appointment from January 18 to January 25.

■ Press the down arrow key until the cursor is in the date field
■ Press the right arrow key until the cursor is under the numeral 1 in the number 18

Make sure the <Ins> key is not on. The word INS should not appear in the Status Bar. If it does appear, press the <Ins> key once.

■ Type: 25

The data in the DATE field should now read 01/25/90. You now have to edit the NOTES field.

- Press the down arrow key until the cursor is in the NOTES field
- Press <Ctrl>-<PgDn>
- Move the cursor until it is one space after the period following the word *appointment*
- Press the <Backspace> key until the entire note is deleted
- Type the following:

This portrait is being taken in front of the home. No special lighting equipment needed.

- Press <Ctrl>-<PgUp>

The record for Karen Janiszewski returns to the screen.

- Press <PgDn>

The edited record is now saved.

- Press <PgDn> until Samantha Mancuso's record appears

Samantha's new phone number is 555-5025.

- Press the down arrow key until the cursor is in the phone field
- Press the right arrow key until the cursor is under the first numeral 3 in her phone number
- Type: 5025
- Press <PgDn>

Peter Schwartz's record should appear. Peter wants to change from a couple to a group sitting.

- Move the cursor to the CATEGORY field
- Type: G
- Press <PgDn> until Max O'Dell's record appears

Max wants his pictures taken at his home rather than in the studio. This change involves three fields in the record. The LOCATION field now has to list Max's address. Also, the fee to have a sitting at a location away from the studio is ten dollars more, so the COST field must also be changed. Finally a memo has to be added to the NOTES field.

- Move the cursor to the LOCATION field
- Type: 50 Court Street, Atlanta
- Move the cursor so that it is under the 4 in 45.00 in the COST field
- Type: 5
- Move the cursor to the NOTES field
- Press <Ctrl>-<PgDn>
- Type the following:

This portrait is being taken in the back yard of the home. No special lighting equipment is needed.

- Press <Ctrl>-<Up>

3. The records have now been edited. You are ready to exit from the editing procedure.

■ Press <Ctrl>-<End>

Browsing Through Records

Records can also be listed for editing by using the Browse option from the Update Submenu. To list records using the Browse option, select Update and Browse; records from the current data-base file are displayed. Instead of displaying one record at a time, however, the Browse option displays a set of records. Up to 17 records can be displayed vertically down the screen, and up to 80 characters can be displayed horizontally across the page. If a data record contains more than 80 characters, only the first 80 are displayed.

■ Your Turn

In this exercise you are going to use the Browse option to display records from the PHOTOS file.

1. Make sure the PHOTOS data-base file is active.

■ Select **Update** from the Menu Bar in the Assistant Menu
■ Select **Browse** from the Update Submenu

Record 8 should be displayed on your screen.

2. Notice that only five of the nine fields in the PHOTOS file are displayed. Whenever you use the Browse option, only those fields that will fit across the screen horizontally are displayed. To see all the fields in a data-base file, use the Edit option. Only the first five fields of the PHOTOS file will fit across the screen horizontally. Also notice the Editing Menu at the top of the screen. Records can be edited from the Browse option.

■ Press < ↑ >

Record 7 appears.

■ Press < ↑ > six times

All the records in the file should now appear.

■ Press <→>

The cursor moves to the *o* in *Donald.*

■ Press <→> fourteen times

The cursor moves to the next field. You can move through a record using <←> and <→>.

■ Press < ↓ > until record 8 is highlighted
■ Press < ↓ > one more time

The message **Add new records? (Y/N)** appears. New records can be added using the Browse option.

■ Type: **N**
■ Press <Ctrl>-<End>

Adding a Record

To add a record to an active data-base file, select the Update option from the Menu Bar in the Assistant Menu. Next, select Append from the Update Submenu. A blank data-entry form appears on the screen. The word Append is in the Status Bar. The letters EOF are in the area of the Status Bar that indicates what record is currently active. EOF stands for End of File. When records are added to an existing data-base file using the Append command, they appear at the end of the existing file.

The data-entry form is filled out using the same method as that for entering data into the data-base file for the first time. As many records as necessary can be added. Pressing <PgDn> or <Enter> after entering data into the last field in the file accesses another blank data-entry form. After all the records have been added, press <Ctrl>-<End> or <Enter> when the next blank data-entry form appears; either ends the process of adding records to the file.

■ Your Turn

In this exercise, you are going to add two new records to the PHOTOS file. Make sure the PHOTOS file is active before you begin.

1. The following two people have made appointments to have their pictures taken:

FIRST_NAME:	Sonia
LAST_NAME:	Hoffberg
PHONE:	(404)555-0526
DATE:	020190
CATEGORY:	I
LOCATION:	Riverside Park, Atlanta
COST:	55.00
PAID:	F

FIRST_NAME:	Lawrence
LAST_NAME:	Beech
PHONE:	(404)555-6200
DATE:	020690
CATEGORY:	W
LOCATION:	St. Michael's Episcopal Church, Atlanta
COST:	550.00
PAID:	T
NOTES:	The wedding is being video-taped in addition to being photographed. Bring all video equipment.

You need to add their records to the data-base file.

- Select **UPDATE** from the Menu Bar in the Assistant Menu
- Select **APPEND** from the Update Submenu

A blank data-entry form appears on the screen. In the Status Bar, the words **REC: EOF/8** should appear. This means that you are at the end of the file and there are a total of eight records in the PHOTOS data-base file.

2. You are now ready to add the two new records. The cursor should be in the FIRST_NAME field. Enter the data for Sonia Hoffberg as it appears above. After entering F in the PAID field press <PgDn>. A blank data-entry form for record 9 appears. Enter the data for Lawrence Beech. When all the data is entered, press <Ctrl>-<End> to save the records and end the process of adding records to a data-base file. The Assistant Menu returns to the screen.

Deleting a Record

Deleting records using dBASE III PLUS is a two-step process. First, mark the records for deletion, and then remove the marked records from the data-base file. By marking the records first, you have the option of retrieving the material before it is permanently removed from the data-base file. Once they are removed from the data-base file they are irretrievable, so be careful with deleting records. You do not want to lose data that you may need later.

To mark records for deletion, select Update from the Menu Bar on the Assistant Menu. Access the record that is to be deleted so that it appears on the screen. Pressing <Ctrl>-<U> marks the record for deletion. The word Del appears in the right corner of the Status Bar, indicating that the record has been marked for deletion.

<Ctrl>-<U> is a **toggle.** That is, if you press it once, it is active and the record is marked; if pressed again, it is no longer active and the record is no longer marked. Pressing <Ctrl>-<U> a third time marks the record again.

When all the records to be deleted are marked, press <Ctrl>-<End> to exit from the Edit Function. At this point, the records are only marked; they have not been removed from the data-base file. If you decide to retain the records, remove the deletion marks by selecting Update from the Menu Bar and Recall from the Update Submenu. Then select the marked records to be recalled.

To delete marked records from the data-base file, select Update from the Menu Bar on the Assistant Menu. Next, select Pack from the Update Submenu. When Pack has been selected, the records are permanently removed from the data-base file.

■ Your Turn

In this exercise you are going to delete two records from the PHOTOS data-base file: The PHOTOS data-base file should be active.

1. The sitting for Donald Gross has been completed, so his record can be deleted. Peter Schwartz cancelled his appointment, so his record also needs to be deleted.

- ■ Select **Update** from the Menu Bar on the Assistant Menu
- ■ Select **Edit** from the Update Submenu

One of the records from the PHOTOS data-base file appears on your screen.

2. The first record you want to delete, the record for Donald Gross, is record 1.

- ■ Press <PgUp> or <PgDn> until record 1 appears on your screen
- ■ Press <Ctrl>-<U>

Your screen should look like Figure E–10. Notice the word **Del** appears in the Status Bar.

```
┌────────────────────┬──────────────────────┬───────────────────┬─────────────────────────┐
│ CURSOR    <-- -->  │         UP    DOWN   │     DELETE        │ Insert Mode:   Ins      │
│ Char:      ← →     │ Field:    ↑     ↓    │ Char:     Del     │ Exit/Save:    ^End      │
│ Word:   Home End   │ Page:   PgUp  PgDn   │ Field:    ^Y      │ Abort:         Esc      │
│                    │ Help:    F1          │ Record:   ^U      │ Memo:         ^Home     │
├────────────────────┴──────────────────────┴───────────────────┴─────────────────────────┤

   FIRST_NAME   Donald
   LAST_NAME    Gross
   PHONE        (404)555-3478
   DATE         01/15/90
   CATEGORY     I
   LOCATION     Studio
   COST             45.00
   PAID         T
   NOTES        memo



   EDIT              ‖<B:>‖PHOTOS              ‖Rec: 1/10        ‖     Del‖
```

FIGURE E—10

Deleting a Record

■ Press <Ctrl>-<U> again

Because <Ctrl>-<U> is a toggle, the word **Del** is no longer in the Status Bar and record 1 is no longer marked for deletion.

■ Press <Ctrl>-<U> a third time

Again, record 1 is marked for deletion. Leave it marked. Look at the Status Bar. It should say **Rec: 1/10,** which means there are 10 records in the database file.

■ Press <PgDn> until record 5, the record for Peter Schwartz, is on the screen.

■ Press <Ctrl>-<U>

Record 1 and record 5 are now marked for deletion.

■ Press <Ctrl>-<End>

3. You are now ready to permanently remove records 1 and 5 from the PHOTOS data-base file. The Update Submenu should appear on your screen. Notice that, according to the Status Bar, there are now a total of 10 records in the PHOTOS data-base file.

■ Select **Pack**

The message **8 records copied** appears at the bottom of the screen.

■ Press any key to return to the Assistant Menu

Now look at the Status Bar. Notice that there are now a total of 8 records in the PHOTOS data-base file. Check to make sure the record was deleted.

■ Select **Edit** from the Update Submenu

Record 1 should be on the screen. Record 1 is now the record for Karen Janiszewski rather than Donald Gross.

- Press <PgDn> until record 5 appears on the screen

Record 5 is now the record for Gary Wasserman rather than for Peter Schwartz.

- Press <Ctrl>-<End> to return to the Assistant Menu

Displaying and Printing a Data-Base File

To display records, the data-base file whose records you wish to display must be the active file. Select the Retrieve option from the Menu Bar on the Assistant Menu. Next, select the List option from the Retrieve Submenu. A submenu for the List option appears. The option **Execute the command** is highlighted. Selecting this option causes all the fields from all records to be listed on the computer screen. Usually all the fields in a record will not fit on one line across the screen. dBASE III PLUS displays the fields that do not fit on the following line. Listing the records in this fashion, however, is confusing and difficult to read. Usually you will want to select the specific fields from the records that you want to list.

To select specific fields from a record to be listed, choose the **Construct a field list** option from the List Submenu. When this option is selected, a list of all the fields in the data-base structure is displayed on the screen. The first field name in the list is highlighted. You can move the highlighting by pressing the up or down arrow keys. The field name, type, width, and decimal points, if there are any, of the highlighted field appear in another box on the screen. To select a field to be included in the list, press <Enter> when the field is highlighted. The name of the field just selected appears in the Action Line. You can then highlight another field and press <Enter>. The name of the second field appears in the Action Line. The order in which the fields are selected determines the order in which they will appear in the list. You can select as many fields as you want.

Once all the fields have been selected, press the right arrow key <→> to exit from the selection process. Next, select **Execute the command** from the List Submenu. The prompt **Direct the output to the printer? [Y/N]** appears on the screen. If the list is to be printed, the computer must be connected to a printer and the printer must be online. Press **Y** for yes to print the list. If the list is to be displayed only on the screen, press **N** for no. The data stored in all the records for the fields that were selected is then listed on the screen and, if **Y** was pressed, printed. If a data-base file contains more records than will fit on the screen, the first records in the file scroll off the top of the screen. Press any key and the Assistant Menu returns to the screen.

If you press **Y** to print the list, you may notice that the last line of the list does not print. Some printers have a buffer area that stores individual characters in a line before printing that line. This print buffer is like a holding zone. Because of the particular way the dBASE III PLUS program works, a printer with a print buffer will not print the very last line. To print the last line, you must enter the dot prompt mode. Do not move the paper in the printer once the first part of the list is printed. When the first part of the list has finished printing, press any key to return to the Assistant Menu, then press <Esc>. The Assistant Menu disappears and the dot prompt with the word **DEMO** in front of it appears at the bottom of the screen.

Type the word **Eject** and press <Enter>. This dot prompt command ejects the last line from the print buffer and prints it at the end of the list where it belongs. To return to the Assistant Menu, type **Assist** and press <Enter>.

■ Your Turn

In this exercise you are going to display and print the records in the PHOTOS data-base file. Check to make sure the PHOTOS file is the active file. In order to print the files, your computer must be hooked up to a printer and the printer must be loaded with paper and online. If your computer is not hooked up to a printer, you can display the records as instructed in this exercise.

1. Once the PHOTOS file is the active file, you are ready to start the process of displaying the records.

- ■ Select **Retrieve** from the Menu Bar in the Assistant Menu
- ■ Select **List** from the Retrieve Submenu
- ■ Select **Execute the command** from the List Submenu

The prompt **Direct the output to the printer? [Y/N]** appears on the screen.

- ■ Press **N**

Your screen should look like Figure E–11.

Look at your screen closely. All the fields from all the records are listed. Since the fields did not all fit on one line, the data for each record is listed on two lines. The LOCATION field is split in two: The first two characters in the field are on the first line and the remainder is on the second line.

FIGURE E—11

Listing Records

```
┌─────────────────────────────────────────────────────────────────────────────┐
│  Set Up  Create  Update  Position  Retrieve  Organize Modify Tools  07:08:10 pm│
│                                                                               │
│  Record#  FIRST_NAME      LAST_NAME           PHONE          DATE     CATEGORY LO│
│  CATION                                    COST PAID NOTES                     │
│      1  Karen           Janiszewski        (404)555-9032 01/25/90 G        13 │
│  399 Peachtree Way, Atlanta               55.00 .T.  Memo                      │
│      2  Beatrice        Weiss              (404)555-2600 01/20/90 W        Te │
│  mple B'nai Isreal, Atlanta              400.00 .T.  Memo                      │
│      3  Samantha        Mancuso            (404)555-5025 01/21/90 I        St │
│  udio                                      45.00 .F.  Memo                     │
│      4  Shawn           Montague           (404)555-5609 01/29/90 I        Ca │
│  rter Park, Atlanta                        55.00 .F.  Memo                     │
│      5  Gary            Wasserman          (404)555-7382 01/29/90 G        St │
│  udio                                      45.00 .T.  Memo                     │
│      6  Max             O'Dell             (404)555-6743 02/01/90 C        50 │
│   Court Street                             55.00 .T.  Memo                     │
│      7  Sonia           Hoffberg           (404)555-0526 02/01/90 I        Ri │
│  verside Park, Atlanta                     55.00 .F.  Memo                     │
│      8  Lawrence        Beech              (404)555-6200 02/06/90 W        St │
│  . Michael's Episcopal Church, Atlanta    550.00 .T.  Memo                     │
│  ─────────────────────────────────────────────────────────────────────────── │
│  ASSIST           ‖<C:>‖PHOTOS          ‖Rec: EOF/8       ‖         ‖          │
│           Press any key to continue work in ASSIST._                           │
└─────────────────────────────────────────────────────────────────────────────┘
```

2. As they appear now, the records are very confusing to read. To make the records easier to read, you are going to display only a few fields at a time from each record.

■ Press any key to end the display process

The Retrieve Submenu appears. The List Option is already highlighted.

■ Press <Enter>
■ Select **Construct a field list** from the List Submenu

A list of all the fields in the PHOTOS data-base file appears in the upper-left corner of the screen. A box containing a description of the structure for the first field, FIRST_NAME, appears in the center of the screen (see Figure E–12).

3. You can move through the list of field names by pressing the up < ↑ > or down < ↓ > arrow keys.

■ Press < ↓ > twice

The highlighting is now on the PHONE field. Notice that the structure for the PHONE field is now displayed in the box in the center of the screen.

■ Press < ↓ > four times

The highlighting is now on the COST field, and its structure is displayed in the center box.

■ Press < ↑ > twice

The highlighting is on the CATEGORY field, and its structure is displayed in the center box.

FIGURE E–12

Constructing a Field List

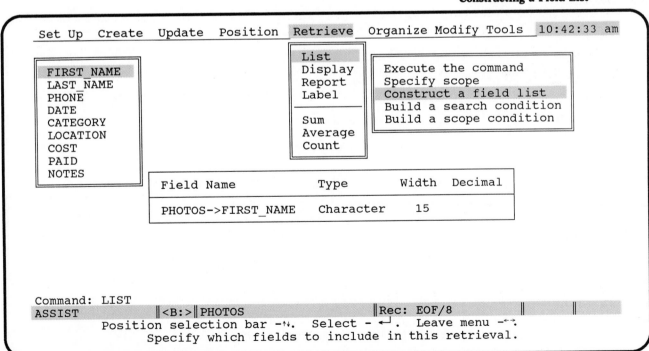

4. Now you are ready to select the specific fields to be displayed in the list. First, you want to display the LAST_NAME, CATEGORY, and LOCATION fields.

■ Press < ↑ > until the field name LAST_NAME is highlighted
■ Press <Enter>

Look at the Action Line. Notice that it says **Command: LIST LAST_NAME.** The name of the field just selected appears in the Action Line.

■ Press < ↓ > until the LOCATION field is highlighted
■ Press <Enter>
■ Press < ↑ > until the CATEGORY field is highlighted
■ Press <Enter>

You have finished selecting the fields to be displayed. Your screen should look like Figure E–13. Notice that all the field names selected appear in the Action Line at the bottom of the screen.

5. You are ready to leave the selection process.

■ Press <→>

The list of fields from the PHOTOS data-base file leaves the screen. The List Submenu is still on the screen.

■ Press < ↑ > until **Execute the command** is highlighted
■ Press <Enter>

The prompt **Direct the output to the printer? [Y/N]** appears on the screen.

■ Press **Y**

FIGURE E–13

Selecting Fields from a Data-Base File

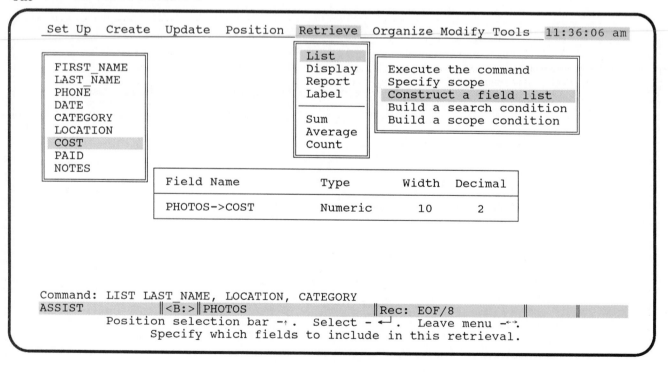

```
   Set Up   Create   Update   Position   Retrieve   Organize Modify Tools   11:36:06 am
  ┌──────────────────┐       ┌──────────┐ ┌───────────────────────────────┐
  │ FIRST_NAME       │       │ List     │ │ Execute the command           │
  │ LAST_NAME        │       │ Display  │ │ Specify scope                 │
  │ PHONE            │       │ Report   │ │ Construct a field list        │
  │ DATE             │       │ Label    │ │ Build a search condition      │
  │ CATEGORY         │       │          │ │ Build a scope condition       │
  │ LOCATION         │       │ Sum      │ └───────────────────────────────┘
  │ COST             │       │ Average  │
  │ PAID             │       │ Count    │
  │ NOTES            │       └──────────┘
  └──────────────────┘  ┌─────────────────────────────────────────────┐
                        │ Field Name          Type      Width  Decimal │
                        ├─────────────────────────────────────────────┤
                        │ PHOTOS->COST        Numeric      10      2    │
                        └─────────────────────────────────────────────┘



  Command: LIST LAST_NAME, LOCATION, CATEGORY
  ASSIST           ‖<B:>‖PHOTOS                    ‖Rec: EOF/8      ‖       ‖
           Position selection bar -↑.  Select - ↵.  Leave menu -↩.
               Specify which fields to include in this retrieval.
```

The data-base file prints then, and your screen should look like Figure E–14. Before moving the paper in the printer, take a close look at what was printed. If the last record printed is record 7, your printer is holding record 8 in the print buffer. The following steps enable you to print record 8.

■ Press any key
■ Press <Esc>

The Assistant Menu disappears, and the dot prompt with **(DEMO)** in front of it appears at the bottom of the screen.

■ Type: **Eject**
■ Press <Enter>

The last line of the list is printed. A second dot prompt appears at the bottom of the screen.

■ Type: **Assist**
■ Press <Enter>

The Assistant Menu returns to the screen.

The LAST_NAME, LOCATION, and CATEGORY fields for all the records are displayed. This time, reading the display is very easy. Notice that the fields are printed in the order they were selected (LOCATION precedes CATEGORY) rather than in the order in which they appear in the data-entry form (CATEGORY preceding LOCATION).

■ Press any key to exit from the display

6. The Retrieve Submenu appears on the screen.

■ Select **List**
■ Select **Construct a field list**

FIGURE E–14

Listing Selected Files

```
 Set Up   Create   Update   Position   Retrieve  Organize Modify Tools   07:14:57 pm




  Record#   LAST_NAME             LOCATION                                    CATEGORY
        1   Janiszewski           13399 Peachtree Way, Atlanta                G
        2   Weiss                 Temple B'nai Isreal, Atlanta                W
        3   Mancuso               Studio                                      I
        4   Montague              Carter Park, Atlanta                        I
        5   Wasserman             Studio                                      G
        6   O'Dell                50 Court Street                             C
        7   Hoffberg              Riverside Park, Atlanta                     I
        8   Beech                 St. Michael's Episcopal Church, Atlanta     W
  ASSIST            ‖<C:>‖PHOTOS                 ‖Rec: EOF/8      ‖        ‖
                    Press any key to continue work in ASSIST._
```

This time display the DATE, FIRST_NAME, LAST_NAME, and PHONE fields, in that order.

- Press < ↓ > until DATE is highlighted
- Press <Enter>
- Press < ↑ > until FIRST_NAME is highlighted
- Press <Enter>
- The LAST_NAME field should be highlighted
- Press <Enter>
- The PHONE field should be highlighted
- Press <Enter>

Look at the Action Line. It should say **Command: LIST DATE, FIRST_ NAME, LAST_NAME, PHONE.**

- Press <→>
- Select **Execute the command** from the List Submenu
- Press **Y**

Again, the data-base file is printed. Your hard copy should look like Figure E–15.

- Press any key to exit from the display.

LEARNING CHECK

1. (True or False?) In dBASE III PLUS, the file name for the data-base file can be up to eight characters long and must begin with a letter.

2. _____ fields are used to test for true/false conditions.

a. Character
b. Numeric

c. Logical
d. Date

3. _____ fields store any character that can be entered from the keyboard.

a. Character
b. Numeric

c. Logical
d. Date

4. The option that enables a user to edit the structure of a data-base file is found in the _____ Submenu.

a. Set-Up
b. Update

c. Create
d. Modify

5. (True or False?) Once a dBASE III PLUS record has been marked for deletion, it is removed from the file.

ANSWERS

1. True
2. c.
3. a.

4. d.
5. False

▄▄ MANAGING FILES WITH THE TOOLS OPTION

After working with dBASE III PLUS, you will begin to accumulate a lot of files on your data disk. Appropriate management of the files is extremely important. The Tools option on the Menu Bar in the Assistant Menu includes several commands that enable users to maintain files that have been created and stored. The following sections explain these options from the Tools Submenu.

COMPUTERS AND INFORMATION PROCESSING

```
Record#   DATE       FIRST_NAME    LAST_NAME       PHONE
     1    01/25/90   Karen         Janiszewski     (404)555-9032
     2    01/20/90   Beatrice      Weiss           (404)555-2600
     3    01/21/90   Samantha      Mancuso         (404)555-5025
     4    01/29/90   Shawn         Montague        (404)555-5609
     5    01/21/90   Gary          Wasserman       (404)555-7382
     6    01/29/90   Max           O'Dell          (404)555-7382
     7    02/01/90   Sonia         Hoffberg        (404)555-0526
     8    02/06/90   Lawrence      Beech           (404)555-6200
```

FIGURE E—15

Printing Records in a Data-Base File

Setting the Disk Drive

The first option on the Tools Submenu is Set drive. If the disk drive the computer is currently accessing needs to be changed, select this option from the Tools Submenu. Another submenu appears with the letters of the disk drives available for selection. For example, if you are using a computer with two floppy disk drives, the letters A: and B: appear. Highlight the drive to be accessed and press <Enter>.

Copying a File

There are two methods for copying files. One is used to copy a file that is open (a file whose name is displayed in the Status Bar). The other method is used to copy files that are not open. Making at least one copy, called a backup, of any file that you create is extremely important. If anything should happen to your original file (for example, if it is accidentally erased) and you do not have a backup copy, all of your valuable work is lost forever.

The command to copy a file that is already open is found in the Organize Submenu. First, make sure the file whose name appears in the Status Bar is the file you want to copy, and then select the Organize option from the Menu Bar in the Assistant Menu. Next, select Copy. A menu with disk drive options appars. Select the disk drive where the new file is to be stored. The prompt **Enter the name of the file** appears. You must enter a file name that is different from the original file name. The new file name can be up to eight characters long. Ending the file name with the letters *BK* is a convenient way to easily identify the files on your disk that are backup copies. Enter the file name and press <Enter>. Another submenu appears. Select Execute the command. When the number of records that were copied appears in the Action Line at the bottom of the screen, you can press any key to return to the Assistant Menu.

To copy a file that is not open, select the Tools option from the Menu Bar in the Assistant Menu. Next, select Copy file. A menu with disk drive options appears. Select the disk drive where the file to be copied is stored. Another menu appears that lists all the files that are stored on the disk drive just selected. Select the file to be copied. Again, a menu with disk drive options appears. This time, select the disk drive where the new file is to be stored. The remainder of the procedure for copying an unopened file is similar to that for copying an opened file. The prompt **Enter the name of the file** appears. The file name can be up to eight characters long; ending it with the letters *BK* (for backup) will easily identify the file as a backup copy.

Press <Enter> after the file name has been entered. When the number of records that were copied appears in the Action Line at the bottom of the screen, press any key to return to the Assistant Menu.

If you try to copy a file that is open using the Copy file command from the Tools Submenu, the message **File is already open** appears. If you get this error message, press <Enter> to get back to the Assistant Menu, and copy the file using the Copy command from the Organize Submenu.

▤ Your Turn

The PHOTOS file should still be active. If the file name PHOTOS does not appear in the Status Bar, select it by using the Set Up option on the Menu Bar in the Assistant Menu. In this hands-on exercise make a copy of the PHOTOS file.

1. Because the PHOTOS file is open, use the Copy command from the Organize option on the Menu Bar of the Assistant Menu.

- ▤ Select **Organize**
- ▤ Select **Copy**
- ▤ Select **B:**

2. The prompt **Enter the name of the file** appears.

- ▤ Type: **PHOTOSBK**
- ▤ Press <Enter>
- ▤ Select **Execute the command**

3. When the file is copied the message **8 records copied** should appear in the Action Line at the bottom of your screen. A copy was made both of the PHOTOS.DBF and the PHOTOS.DBT file, the memo file associated with PHOTOS.

- ▤ Press any key to return to the Assistant Menu

Renaming a File

If it is necessary to change the name of a file, it can be easily accomplished with the Rename option on the Menu Bar of the Assistant Menu. After selecting Rename, a submenu with a list of the disk drives appears. Select the disk drive where the file to be renamed is stored. A list of all the files stored on that disk appears. Select the file to be renamed. The prompt, **Enter the name of the file** appears. Enter the new file name including the extension. When renaming files, you must include the extension in the new file name. Press <Enter>. The message **Press any key to continue work in ASSIST** appears once the file has been renamed.

▤ Your Turn

In this exercise you are going to rename the PHOTOSBK file.

1. The Assistant Menu is on your screen and the PHOTOS file is active.

- ▤ Select **Tools**

- Select **Rename**
- Select **B:**

2. A list of all the files stored on your disk in drive B appears.

- Select **PHOTOSBK.DBF**

3. The prompt **Enter the name of the file** appears.

- Type **PHOTOBK1.DBF**
- Press <Enter>

4. When the message **Press any key to continue work in ASSIST** appears, the file has been renamed.

Listing the File Directory

It is often very useful to be able to list the names of the files that are stored on a disk. After creating several files you might forget some of their names or need to know how much storage space you have on your disk. You can access this information by listing the file directory.

The Directory command is found on the Tools Submenu. To list the file directory, select Directory and then choose the disk drive on which the files are stored. Another submenu appears that lists extensions used in dBASE III PLUS. You can list all the files that are stored or only those with a particular extension. For example, if you want the names of all data-base files you can list only those that have a DBF extension rather than all the files that are stored. After selecting which files you want to list in the directory, the names of the designated files appear on the screen. When all the files are listed, press any key to return to the Assistant Menu.

Your Turn

In this exercise, you are going to practice listing the file directory.

1. The Assistant Menu should be on your screen and the Tools Submenu should still be open.

- Select **Directory**
- Select **B:**

2. The submenu listing dBASE III PLUS extensions appears. Your screen should look like Figure E–16. The only file extension that you have been instructed to use is .dbf for Database File.

- Select **.dbf Database Files**

The two data-base files PHOTOS.DBF and PHOTOBK1.DBF should be listed on your screen. Also, the bytes of memory used by the two files and bytes of memory remaining on your disk are listed. Bytes are used for measuring computer memory. A byte is what the computer treats as one unit of information. Periodically checking the available memory is useful to see how much room you have left on your disk. If you think you may be running out of disk space, find out by listing the directory of the disk.

- Press any key to return to the Assistant Menu

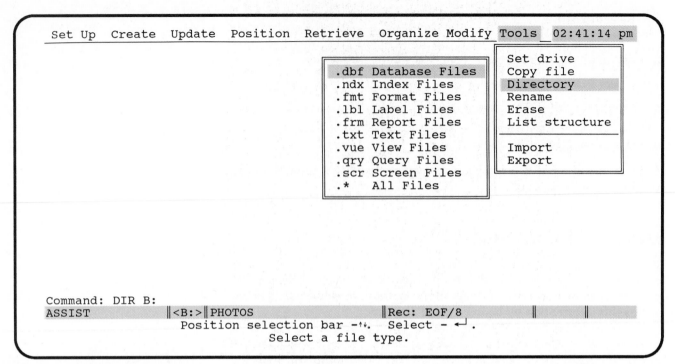

```
  Set Up  Create  Update  Position  Retrieve  Organize Modify  Tools   02:41:14 pm
                                                              ┌─────────────────────┐
                                      ┌─────────────────────┐ │ Set drive           │
                                      │ .dbf Database Files │ │ Copy file           │
                                      │ .ndx Index Files    │ │ Directory           │
                                      │ .fmt Format Files   │ │ Rename              │
                                      │ .lbl Label Files    │ │ Erase               │
                                      │ .frm Report Files   │ │ List structure      │
                                      │ .txt Text Files     │ │                     │
                                      │ .vue View Files     │ │ Import              │
                                      │ .qry Query Files    │ │ Export              │
                                      │ .scr Screen Files   │ └─────────────────────┘
                                      │ .*   All Files      │
                                      └─────────────────────┘




  Command: DIR B:
  ASSIST              ║<B:>║PHOTOS              ║Rec: EOF/8      ║       ║
               Position selection bar -↕.  Select - ↵ .
                      Select a file type.
```

FIGURE E–16

Listing the File Directory

Erasing a File

The command to erase a file is also found on the Tools Submenu. To erase a file, select the Tools option from the Menu Bar in the Assistant Menu. Next, select Erase from the Tools Submenu. A list of disk drives appears; select the drive where the file to be erased is stored. A list of all the database files stored on the disk in the drive that you selected appears next. Select the file you want to erase. Be absolutely certain this is the file to be erased before pressing <Enter>. When the <Enter> key is pressed, the file is deleted from the disk. If a file is mistakenly selected for deletion and the <Enter> key is pressed, the file is lost unless there is a backup copy.

After pressing <Enter> the message **File has been deleted** appears in the Action Line. To return to the Assistant Menu, press any key.

■ Your Turn

In this hands-on exercise, you are going to make a second copy of the PHOTOS.DBF file and then erase the copy.

1. The Assistant Menu should be on your screen and the PHOTOS file should be active. If the file name PHOTOS does not appear in the status line, open the file by using the Set Up option.

- ■ Select **Organize**
- ■ Select **Copy**
- ■ Select **B:**
- ■ Type: **PHOTOBK2.DBF**
- ■ Press <Enter>
- ■ Select **Execute the command**

2. The message **8 records copied** appears in the Action Line, indicating that there is now a second copy of PHOTOS.DBF. Next, delete the copy just made.

- Select **Tools** from the Menu Bar on the Assistant Menu
- Select **Erase** from the Tools Submenu
- Select **B:**
- Select **PHOTOBK2.DBF**

Before pressing <Enter>, be certain that you have the right file name highlighted.

- Press <Enter>

The message **File has been deleted** appears in the Action Line.

- Press any key to return to the Assistant Menu

3. Now you want to erase PHOTOBK2.DBT, the second copy of the memo file that is associated with the PHOTOS file.

- Select **Erase** from the Tools Submenu
- Select **B:**
- Select **PHOTOBK2.DBT**

Again, make sure the right file is highlighted before pressing <Enter>.

- Press <Enter>

Press any key to return to the Assistant Menu.

■ RELATIONAL AND LOGICAL OPERATORS

At times it is useful to be able to display specific records. For example, you might want to display only those records that meet certain conditions. Using the PHOTOS file as an example, suppose you want to know which sessions cost more than $50. Relational operators enable the user to display only those records that meet certain conditions, such as "cost more than $50." Table E–1 defines the relational operators available in dBASE III PLUS.

To display only those records that meet certain requirements, first select the Retrieve option from the main Menu Bar. Next, select Display. From the Display Submenu, select **Build a search condition.** A list of all the fields from the current file appears. Select the search field, that is, the field upon which the search is to be based. For example, if you want to find all the

T A B L E E–1

Relational Operators

Relational Operator	Relation
=	Equal to
<	Less than
>	Greater than
<=	Less than or equal to
>=	Greater than or equal to
<> or #	Not equal to

sessions in the PHOTOS file that cost more than $50, the COST field is the search field on which the search is based.

Once a search field has been selected, a menu listing all the relational operators appears. Select a relational operator. If the search field is character/text, the prompt **Enter a character string** appears. If the search field is numeric, the prompt **Enter a numeric value** appears. After either a character string or numeric value has been entered, a logical operator can be selected.

Logical operators allow more than one condition to be set up for displaying records. For example, say you want to display only the records of sessions from the PHOTOS file that cost more than $50 and have not yet been paid for. To conduct this kind of search, it is necessary to select a logical operator. Table E–2 lists and explains the logical operators.

If a logical operator is selected, a list of the fields from the current file appears again and another search condition can be set up. When all the desired conditions have been set up, select **No more conditions**. Next select **Execute the command**. All the records that meet the designated conditions will be displayed.

■ Your Turn

The PHOTOS file should be active. In this exercise you are going to practice using relational and logical operators.

1. First, display all the sessions that cost more than $50.

- ■ Select **Retrieve**
- ■ Select **Display**
- ■ Select **Build a search condition**

A list of the fields in the PHOTOS file appears at the left of the screen. A description of the highlighted field appears in the center of the screen. Because you are interested in locating records of all sessions that cost more than $50, select the cost field.

- ■ Select **COST**

A menu of the relational operators appears (see Figure E–17).

- ■ Select > **Greater Than**

The prompt **Enter a numeric value** appears.

- ■ Type: **50.00**
- ■ Press <Enter>

Another menu appears that enables you to add more conditions, if you wish. For this situation, however, you do not want to add more conditions.

TABLE E—2

Logical Operators

Logical Operator	Comparison
.AND.	Both expressions must be true.
.OR.	Either one expression or the other must be true (or both).

- Select **No more conditions**
- Select **Execute the command**

A list of the five sessions costing more than $50 appears on the screen. Look over the list carefully.

- Press any key

2. Now you want to know how many sessions are scheduled for in the studio.

- Select **Retrieve**
- Select **Display**
- Select **Build a search condition**
- Select **LOCATION**
- Select **= Equal To**

The prompt **Enter a character string (without quotes)** appears.

- Type: **Studio**

The character string must be entered exactly as it appears in the record. For example, if you type *studio* instead of *Studio*, dBASE III PLUS cannot find the records.

- Press <Enter>
- Select **No more conditions**
- Select **Execute the command**

The three sessions scheduled in the studio are displayed on the screen.

- Press any key

FIGURE E–17

Relational Operators

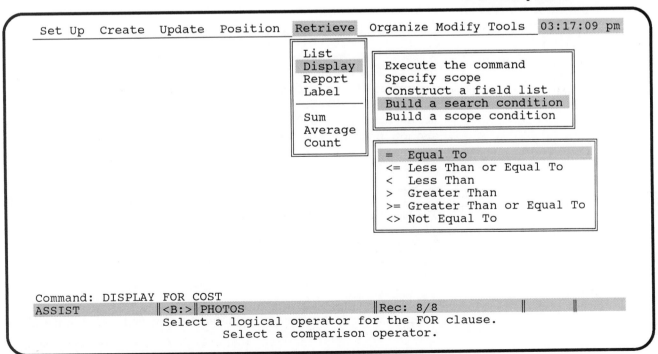

3. Now suppose you want to combine two commands to display the sessions that cost over $50 that have been paid for. The logical operator .AND. must be selected.

- Select **Retrieve**
- Select **Display**
- Select **Build a search condition**
- Select **COST**
- Select **> Greater Than**
- Type: **50.00**
- Press <Enter>

Next, select a logical operator.

- Select **Combine with .AND.**

Now you are ready to build the second search condition, which is all the sessions that have been paid for.

- Select **PAID**

Notice that the relational operators do not appear. That is because PAID is a logical field and there are only two options, true or false. Either the session has been paid for or it has not been paid for. dBASE III PLUS is automatically going to list all the conditions where PAID is equal to true; that is, all the records in which the session has been paid for.

- Select **No more conditions**
- Select **Execute the command**

dBASE III PLUS displays the four sessions that cost more than $50 that have been paid for.

- Press any key

GOING TO A SPECIFIC RECORD

A specific data record can be displayed by using the Goto Record option from the Position Menu. The options from the Goto Record Submenu are TOP, BOTTOM, and RECORD. If TOP is selected, record 1 becomes the active record. If BOTTOM is selected, the last record in the file becomes the active record. If RECORD is selected, the prompt **Enter a numeric value** appears. Enter the number of the record that you want placed in active status and press <Enter>.

Your Turn

The PHOTOS file should be active.

1. Practice using the Goto Record option.

- Select **Position**
- Select **Goto Record**
- Select **TOP**

Notice that the Status Bar now says **Rec: 1/8.** The first record in the file is now the active record.

- Select **Retrieve**
- Select **Display**
- Select **Execute the command**

Record 1 is displayed.

- Press any key

2. Now you want to display the last record in the file.

- Select **Position**
- Select **Goto Record**
- Select **BOTTOM**

Notice that the Status Bar now says **Rec: 8/8.** The last record in the file is now the active record.

- Select **Retrieve**
- Select **Display**
- Select **Execute the command**

Record 8 is displayed.

- Press any key

3. Now you want to go to a specific record.

- Select **Position**
- Select **Goto Record**
- Select **RECORD**
- Type: **5**
- Press <Enter>

Notice the Status Bar now says **Rec: 5/8.** The fifth record in the file is now the active record.

- Select **Retrieve**
- Select **Display**
- Select **Execute the command**

Record 5 is displayed.

- Press any key

▆ dBASE III PLUS SUMMARY COMMANDS

Thus far this section has introduced dBASE III PLUS commands that enable users to create, edit, and display data files. When a file has been created, it can provide valuable information about a variety of subjects through the use of summary commands. In fact, the summarizing of data is one of dBASE's most significant functions. The summary commands Sum, Average, and Count are found in the Retrieve Menu.

Count

The Count option can be used in several ways to tally the records in a file. An unconditional Count command counts all the data records in a file. To use the unconditional Count command, select Count from the Retrieve Menu, then **Execute the command.** A message such as *28 records* appears on the screen; this indicates the total number of records currently stored in the file.

A conditional Count command only counts records that meet a specified condition. To build a condition for the Count command, first select Count from the Retrieve Menu, and then **Build a search condition.** Building a condition upon which to base the Count command is exactly the same as building a condition upon which to display only records that meet a specific condition.

More than one condition can be specified in the Count command by selecting the option Combine with .AND., or the option Combine with .OR. These logical operators perform the same functions when used with the Count option that they do when used with the Display option.

■ Your Turn

The PHOTOS file should be active.

1. Practice using the Count option. Because you want to count the records in the file, it is necessary to make sure the first record in the file is the current record. That is, you need to make sure that the record pointer is on record one.

- ■ Select **Position**
- ■ Select **Goto Record**
- ■ Select **TOP**

The Status Bar should read **Rec: 1/8.**

- ■ Select **Retrieve**
- ■ Select **Count**
- ■ Select **Execute the command**

The message **8 records** appears at the bottom of the screen because the PHOTOS file currently has 8 data records stored in it.

- ■ Press any key

2. Now you want to find out how many weddings you have scheduled.

- ■ Select **Retrieve**
- ■ Select **Count**
- ■ Select **Build a search condition**

A list of the fields in the PHOTOS file appears.

- ■ Select **CATEGORY**
- ■ Select **= Equal To**
- ■ Type: **W**
- ■ Select **No more conditions**
- ■ Select **Execute the command**

The message **2 records** appears at the bottom of the screen. Thus, two weddings have been scheduled.

- ■ Press any key

3. Now you want to know how many sessions have been scheduled after January 25 that are not in the studio.

- Select **Retrieve**
- Select **Count**
- Select **Build a search condition**
- Select **DATE**
- Select **> Greater Than**
- Type: **01/25/90**
- Select **Combine with .AND.**
- Select **LOCATION**
- Select **<> Not Equal To**
- Type: **Studio**
- Press **<Enter>**
- Select **No more conditions**
- Select **Execute the command**

The message **3 records** appears at the bottom of the screen; three sessions have been scheduled after January 25 that are not in the studio.

- Press any key

Sum

The contents of numeric fields can be added using the Sum option from the Retrieve Menu. The unconditional Sum command calculates the sum of all the values in the specified data field. To use the unconditional Sum command, select Sum from the Retrieve Menu. Next, select **Execute the command.** If there is only one numeric field in the file, dBASE III PLUS automatically totals all the entries made in that field. If there is more than one numeric field, you must designate the field for which you want to calculate a total. The Sum command also can include relational and logical operators.

■ Your Turn

The PHOTOS file should be active.

1. You are going to find out the total cost of the sessions scheduled by using the SUM command.

- Select **Retrieve**
- Select **Sum**
- Select **Execute the command**

The message **8 records summed COST 1250.00** appears. This message indicates that 8 records were added together in the COST field and the total cost for all the photo sessions is $1250.00.

- Press any key

2. Now you are going to find out how much income is from weddings.

- Select **Retrieve**
- Select **Sum**
- Select **Build a search condition**

- Select **CATEGORY**
- Select **= Equal To**
- Type: **W**
- Select **No more conditions**
- Select **Execute the command**

The message **2 records summed COST 950.00** appears. The income from weddings scheduled is $950.00

- Press any key

3. Now you want to find out how much income is from studio shots during the month of January.

- Select **Retrieve**
- Select **Sum**
- Select **Build a search condition**
- Select **DATE**
- Select **> Greater Than**
- Type: **12/31/89**
- Select **Combine with .AND.**
- Select **DATE**
- Select **< Less Than**
- Type: **02/01/90**
- Select **Combine with .AND.**
- Select **LOCATION**
- Select **= Equal To**
- Type: **Studio**
- Press **<Enter>**
- Select **No more conditions**
- Select **Execute the command**

A message appears indicating $90.00 income is to be generated from studio shots during the month of January.

- Press any key

Average

The Average option from the Retrieve Menu calculates an average value for the contents of a numeric field. The unconditional Average command computes the average using the specified field from all the records. The conditional Average command computes the average using the numeric fields that meet the specified conditions. The Average command also can include logical operators.

Your Turn

The PHOTOS file should be active.

1. Find the average cost of all the photography sessions.

- Select **Retrieve**
- Select **Average**
- Select **Execute the command**

The message **8 records averaged COST 156.25** appears. The average cost of all the appointments is $156.25.

■ Press any key

2. You are now finished working with the PHOTOS file and can exit from dBASE III PLUS.

■ Select **Set Up**
■ Select **Quit dBASE III PLUS**

LEARNING
CHECK

1. The command to copy a file is found in the _____ Submenu.

a. Create   c. Organize
b. Tools   d. Update

2. The command to erase a file is found in the _____ Submenu.

a. Create   c. Organize
b. Tools   d. Update

3. _____ operators enable the user to access only those records that meet certain conditions.

4. _____ operators enable the user to set up more than one condition for accessing records.

5. Which of the following is not a dBASE III PLUS summary command?

a. Count   c. Sum
b. Not   d. Average

ANSWERS

1. c.   4. Logical
2. b.   5. b.
3. Relational

▒ SUMMARY POINTS

■ A data manager (data management package) can be used for the same purposes as a manual filing system: to record and file information.

■ Data managers can be used in the home for such tasks as creating a computerized holiday card list or recipe index file, helping balance a checkbook, and keeping a personal appointment calendar.

■ In business, data managers have many uses, such as keeping employee and inventory control records and lists of customers and suppliers.

■ Data managers enable businesses to maintain records quickly and efficiently.

■ Some specialized uses of data managers include preparing mass mailings and creating form letters, in conjunction with word processors.

■ The first step in creating a data-base file is to define its structure. That is, the field name, width, and type must be defined for each field in a record. The field name identifies the contents of that field. The field width indicates the maximum length of an entry into that field. There are five field types: Character, Date, Logical, Memo, and Numeric.

■ The structure of a data-base file can be edited by adding or deleting fields or redefining field names, widths, or types.

- Records can be listed for editing with either the Edit option, or the Browse option from the Update Submenu. Records can be added to a data-base file with the Append option from the Update Submenu. Records are deleted from a data-base file by selecting the Edit option from the Update Submenu, accessing the record to be deleted, and pressing <Ctrl>-<U>. The record is not permanently removed from the data-base file until the Pack option is selected from the Update Submenu.
- Specific fields from a record can be displayed and printed with the Construct a field list option from the List Submenu.
- dBASE III PLUS files can be managed with the Tools option. The Tools option enables a user to set the disk drive, copy a file, rename a file, list the file directory, and erase a file.
- Relational and logical operators enable the user to display only those records that meet certain requirements.
- The dBASE III PLUS summary commands Sum, Average, and Count, are used to summarize data stored in a data-base file in a variety of useful ways.

■ dBASE III PLUS EXERCISES

1. Start dBASE III PLUS. Describe the steps required.

2. Assume you have been hired by Kenneth Fretwell, D.D.S., to establish a data-base management system for his office. Use dBASE III PLUS to create a data-base file named PATIENTS.

3. Your PATIENTS file has eight fields. For each field, enter the following information into the field description form.

Field Name	Type	Width	Dec
First_Name	Character	10	
Last_Name	Character	10	
Address	Character	15	
City	Character	10	
St	Character	2	
ZIP	Character	5	
Age	Character	2	
Balance	Numeric	6	2

4. Enter the following data in the PATIENTS file:

First_Name	Last_Name	Address	City	St	ZIP	Age	Balance
David	Busch	552 Wallace	Columbus	OH	78654	27	58.60
Patricia	Busch	552 Wallace	Columbus	OH	78654	28	0
Tom	Allen	67 Curtis	Columbus	OH	78653	78	8.90
Eileen	Spires	890 Pine	Columbus	OH	78651	56	120.00
Dave	Jenkins	10 W. Wooster	Columbus	OH	79123	13	93.50
Pamela	Weaver	16 Clough	Columbus	OH	78654	10	0
Bradley	Busch	552 Wallace	Columbus	OH	78654	07	25.00
William	Bentley	77 Palmer	Dayton	OH	89213	45	0

After the eighth record has been added, press <Enter> to end the process of adding data records.

5. Proofread all the records you entered. Make any corrections necessary and save the changes.

6. Add the following records to the PATIENTS file:

First_Name	Last_Name	Address	City	St	ZIP	Age	Balance
Wilma	Lukes	909 Clough	Columbus	OH	78653	89	280.09
Douglas	Swartz	9 Main	Dayton	OH	89213	32	46.90
Linda	Plazer	12 Vine	Columbus	OH	78651	25	176.00
Ann	Bressler	25 Baldwin	Columbus	OH	78653	25	0

7. Tom Allen and William Bentley changed dentists. Delete their records from the file.

8. The Busch family moved. Their new address is 41 Normandie in Columbus. Update their records (assume their ZIP code is the same).

9. Dr. Fretwell is going to start a No Cavities Club for children under the age of 16. List all of Dr. Fretwell's patients who are eligible for membership in the club.

10. What is the total balance due from all of the patients? Which patients owe more than $35? Which patients have a zero balance?

11. Print a hard copy of the PATIENTS file.

▆ dBASE III PLUS PROBLEMS

To complete the following exercise you need a DOS disk, the dBASE III PLUS System Disk #1, System Disk #2, and the Student File Disk.

1. Start dBASE III PLUS and insert the Student File Disk in drive B.

2. You are going to use a data-base file that has already been created. Assume that you are working in the payroll department of a company. The company uses a file called PAYROLL to keep information regarding employees' names, addresses, job names, and hourly salaries. Access the PAYROLL file. Before you begin the exercise, make a copy of the files. That way, if you make a mistake, you will always have the original file. Name the copy PAYROLL1.

3. Access the PAYROLL1 data-base file. How do you display a file's structure? Display the structure of the PAYROLL1 file. How many fields are there in the file? How many numeric fields? What is the width of the field Jobname? The field Status defines the personnel status (F for full-time and P for part-time). What is its type? How many data records are in the file?

4. Now you want to see the records of the employees. Display all the records. What option do you select to ensure that all the records will be displayed? What is the name of the employee corresponding to record 5? What is his job title? What is the name of the last employee?

5. Now you want to list only the last name, first name, and job title of all employees. Describe the steps necessary to obtain this information.

6. Now list the same information for full-time employees only. How many full-time employees are employed by the company?

7. List the last name, first name, employee number, and job title for all part-time employees who are writers.

8. What is the average hourly wage of all the employees? Which employees earn more than $9 an hour?

9. The payroll department manager wants you to create a new data-base file that will store information about the employees who worked during March. The file should contain the following information:

Field Name	Field Type	Width	Dec	Description
EMPLNUM	Character	3		Employee number
MONTH	Character	2		Month of work
ENDPER	Date	8		Ending period
NORMHRS	Numeric	5	2	Total hours of work

Create a new data-base file and name it MONTH3.

10. Enter the structure of the new file using the information in step 9. What prompt does dBASE III PLUS display when all of the fields have been entered? Answer **N** and use the List structure option from the Tools Menu to review the file structure.

11. The following field should be added to the file:

Field Name	Field Type	Width	Dec	Description
EXTRAHRS	Numeric	6	2	Extra hours

Use the Database file option from the Modify Menu to add this new field. Change the Normhrs field width to 6. When you are satisfied with the structure, use the appropriate command to save your modifications.

12. What is the command to add records to a file?

Using this command, enter the following data into the file.

EMPLNUM	MONTH	ENDPERIOD	NORMHRS	EXTRAHRS
1	3	033190	160.00	30.00
2	3	033190	160.00	40.00
3	3	033190	160.00	0.00
4	3	033190	140.00	0.00
6	3	033190	160.00	0.00
7	3	033190	160.00	20.00
8	3	033190	160.00	20.00
9	3	033190	160.00	0.00
10	3	033190	160.00	0.00
11	3	033190	100.00	0.00
13	3	033190	160.00	0.00
15	3	033190	80.00	0.00
16	3	033190	90.00	0.00

Save the data. Exit from dBASE III PLUS

INTRODUCTION

Section E presented all the commands needed to create a data-base file with dBASE III PLUS. Once a file has been created, it can be manipulated in many useful ways. The purpose of Section F is to introduce users to more advanced dBASE III PLUS commands that make it possible to efficiently arrange data stored in a data-base file so that it can be used to create a report.

SORTING A DATA-BASE FILE

As discussed in Section E, a data-base file is made up of records that a user enters into the data-entry form. As each record is entered, dBASE III PLUS automatically assigns a chronological record number to it. The data records are stored in the file in the order in which they are entered, but this may not be the order that provides the most useful information. For example, records in a payroll file are not entered in alphabetical order. They are added when employees are hired and deleted when workers leave a company. To be useful, however, a data-base program must be able to arrange a payroll file in alphabetical order. In dBASE III PLUS, the Sort option found in the Organize Menu enables users to rearrange the data records according to the contents of a specified field, which is called the key field. In the example of a payroll file being sorted alphabetically by last name, the field containing the last names would be the key field.

Sorting physically rearranges the records in the active data-base file; to maintain the original data-base file, dBASE III PLUS copies the sorted data-base file into what is called the target file. The user must designate a new file name for the target file. When the sorting procedure is complete, the data records in the target file are arranged by the key field as specified.

Your Turn

You are going to sort a data-base file using the Sort option from the Organize Menu. First, however, you need to create a file called ACCOUNTS that contains data-base information for a company called ProSoft. ProSoft has created two software packages that it sells to businesses. One package is a program for computing payroll. The other package is used for project management. The data base contains the following information:

Field	Description
ACCOUNT	This is the account number. The letters PA, PM, or PP precede each account number. If the company purchased the payroll program, PA precedes the account number. If the company purchased the project management program, PM precedes the account number. If the company purchased both programs, PP precedes the account number.
LAST_NAME FIRST_NAME	This is the name of the person who authorized the purchase of the software.
COMPANY ADDRESS CITY STATE ZIP	This is the name and address of the company that purchased the software.

S E C T I O N

F

Advanced dBASE III PLUS

O U T L I N E

Introduction
Sorting a Data-Base File
Conditional Sorts
Indexing a File
Indexing on Multiple Fields
Searching an Indexed Data-Base File
Learning Check
Creating a Report with dBASE III PLUS
Designing the Report
Modifying a Report
Printing a Report
Learning Check
Summary of dBASE III PLUS Menus
Summary Points
dBASE III PLUS Exercises
dBASE III PLUS Problems

SOLD_BY	This is the last name of the salesperson who made the sale of the software to the company.
SERVICE	Included in the price of the software are quarterly service calls. This is the date of the next service call to this company.
BALANCE	This is the balance due on this company's account.

1. Start dBASE III PLUS. Using the Create option, create a data-base file named ACCOUNTS.

■ Enter the following information in the field definition form

Field	Field name	Type	Width	Dec
1	ACCOUNT	Character	6	
2	LAST_NAME	Character	15	
3	FIRST_NAME	Character	10	
4	COMPANY	Character	25	
5	ADDRESS	Character	25	
6	CITY	Character	10	
7	STATE	Character	2	
8	ZIP	Character	5	
9	SOLD_BY	Character	15	
10	SERVICE	Date	8	
11	BALANCE	Numeric	8	2

■ Press <Ctrl>-<End>

If the entries are correct, press <Enter>. If they are not correct, make the necessary corrections and press <Ctrl>-<End> and <Enter>.

2. When the field information has been entered you may input data into the records. The prompt **Input data records now? (Y/N)** should be on the screen.

■ Type: **Y**

■ Enter the following into the data records

ACCOUNT	PA1001
LAST_NAME	Faulks
FIRST_NAME	Tim
COMPANY	Michaels & Associates
ADDRESS	78 Main St. Suite 101
CITY	Columbus
STATE	OH
ZIP	43219
SOLD_BY	Mitchell
SERVICE	08/05/90
BALANCE	2086.00

ACCOUNT	PA1005
LAST_NAME	Bulas
FIRST_NAME	Irene
COMPANY	B & H Plastics
ADDRESS	908 W. Industrial Pkwy
CITY	Cygnet
STATE	OH
ZIP	43409
SOLD_BY	Louys

| SERVICE | 08/14/90 |
| BALANCE | 1203.87 |

ACCOUNT	PM2001
LAST_NAME	Klein
FIRST_NAME	Tom
COMPANY	Fischer Label
ADDRESS	12 Yong St.
CITY	Columbus
STATE	OH
ZIP	43219
SOLD_BY	Santiago
SERVICE	08/15/90
BALANCE	969.50

ACCOUNT	PM2010
LAST_NAME	Wilcox
FIRST_NAME	Bill
COMPANY	Master Printing
ADDRESS	6 Williams Rd. #301
CITY	Fremont
STATE	OH
ZIP	43098
SOLD_BY	Santiago
SERVICE	08/20/90
BALANCE	3000.00

ACCOUNT	PP3025
LAST_NAME	Ornelas
FIRST_NAME	Tina
COMPANY	S & P Productions
ADDRESS	123 First St. Suite 35
CITY	Canton
STATE	OH
ZIP	43012
SOLD_BY	Louys
SERVICE	08/28/90
BALANCE	2005.30

ACCOUNT	PM2100
LAST_NAME	Lord
FIRST_NAME	Pamela
COMPANY	Holmes Manufacturing
ADDRESS	98 Pike St.
CITY	Oregon
STATE	OH
ZIP	42876
SOLD_BY	Mitchell
SERVICE	09/05/90
BALANCE	1576.90

ACCOUNT	PP3100
LAST_NAME	Busch
FIRST_NAME	Brad
COMPANY	Dryer Supplies, Inc.
ADDRESS	32 Bradner Pkwy
CITY	Columbus
STATE	OH
ZIP	43219

SOLD_BY	Louys
SERVICE	09/06/90
BALANCE	5245.70
ACCOUNT	PA1345
LAST_NAME	Weaver
FIRST_NAME	Chris
COMPANY	Baldwin and Sons
ADDRESS	909 Clough #1C
CITY	Portage
STATE	OH
ZIP	43213
SOLD_BY	Mitchell
SERVICE	09/15/90
BALANCE	680.70
ACCOUNT	PM2045
LAST_NAME	Engel
FIRST_NAME	Chuck
COMPANY	Poe Research, Inc.
ADDRESS	1432 Indian Rd.
CITY	Hamler
STATE	OH
ZIP	43406
SOLD_BY	Santiago
SERVICE	09/28/90
BALANCE	1218.00
ACCOUNT	PA1554
LAST_NAME	Wilks
FIRST_NAME	Cleo
COMPANY	McCloud Development
ADDRESS	76 Gorrel Suite 56
CITY	Lima
STATE	OH
ZIP	43420
SOLD_BY	Mitchell
SERVICE	10/03/90
BALANCE	1096.20
ACCOUNT	PP3701
LAST_NAME	Bressler
FIRST_NAME	Ann
COMPANY	Midway Construction
ADDRESS	45 S. Luke St.
CITY	Palma
STATE	OH
ZIP	43316
SOLD_BY	Louys
SERVICE	08/31/90
BALANCE	4872.75
ACCOUNT	PP3801
LAST_NAME	Hocks
FIRST_NAME	Arthur
COMPANY	H & H Products
ADDRESS	90 Kellog Rd.
CITY	Portage
STATE	OH

ZIP	43213
SOLD_BY	Mitchell
SERVICE	09/23/90
BALANCE	4462.90
ACCOUNT	PA1742
LAST_NAME	DeSalvo
FIRST_NAME	Liz
COMPANY	Tarkett, Inc.
ADDRESS	9 W. Second Suite 201
CITY	Columbus
STATE	OH
ZIP	43207
SOLD_BY	Louys
SERVICE	10/18/90
BALANCE	168.00
ACCOUNT	PM2908
LAST_NAME	Friedman
FIRST_NAME	Mark
COMPANY	Shawnee Distributors
ADDRESS	3426 Little St.
CITY	Palma
STATE	OH
ZIP	43316
SOLD_BY	Santiago
SERVICE	10/17/90
BALANCE	336.80
ACCOUNT	PP3907
LAST_NAME	Crope
FIRST_NAME	Trish
COMPANY	Stockman & Associates
ADDRESS	67 Brackner Suite 22
CITY	Cygnet
STATE	OH
ZIP	43409
SOLD_BY	Louys
SERVICE	09/30/90
BALANCE	1750.90

3. When the records have been entered, use the Sort option from the Organize Menu to sort all the records alphabetically by last name.

■ Select **Organize**
■ Select **Sort**
■ Select **LAST_NAME**

Next, name the target file on which the sorted data-base will be stored. To do this you must press the right arrow key.

■ Press <→>

A list of disk drive options appears. Select the drive where the floppy disk onto which the sorted data-base file is to be stored is located.

■ Select **B:**

The prompt **Enter the name of the file** appears. Enter a name for the target file.

- Type: **Alphaname**
- Press \<Enter\>

ALPHANAME is the name of the file that now stores the records listed in alphabetical order by the customer's last name. After pressing \<Enter\>, the message **100% Sorted 15 Records sorted** appears on the screen.

- Press any key

4. To see the new sorted file, select the Database file option from the Set Up Menu to change the active file to ALPHANAME. Currently, ACCOUNTS is the active file.

- Select **Set Up**
- Select **Database file**
- Select **B:**
- Select **ALPHANAM.DBF**
- Type: **N**

To check if the records have been sorted alphabetically by name, use the Display option from the Retrieve menu.

- Select **Retrieve**
- Select **Display**
- Select **Specify Scope**
- Select **ALL**
- Select **Construct a field list**
- Select **LAST_NAME**
- Press \<→\>
- Select **Execute the command**

The names should appear on the screen listed in alphabetical order.

- Press any key

5. Now you are going to sort all the records by the balance owed on the account in descending order. The sorted file will be called BALANCE.

- Select **Set Up**
- Select **Database file**
- Select **B:**
- Select **ACCOUNTS.DBF**
- Type: **N**
- Select **Organize**
- Select **Sort**
- Select **BALANCE**
- Press \<→\>
- Select **B:**
- Type: **Balance**
- Press \<Enter\>

The records are now sorted by the balance owed.

- Press any key

6. Look at the records sorted by the balance.

- Select **Set Up**

COMPUTERS AND INFORMATION PROCESSING

- ■ Select **Database file**
- ■ Select **B:**
- ■ Select **BALANCE.DBF**
- ■ Type: **N**
- ■ Select **Retrieve**
- ■ Select **Display**
- ■ Select **Specify Scope**
- ■ Select **ALL**
- ■ Select **Construct a field list**
- ■ Select **LAST__NAME**
- ■ Select **BALANCE**
- ■ Press **<→>**
- ■ Select **Execute the command**

The last names of the customers and the balance owed on their accounts should appear on the screen listed in order by the balance owed.

- ■ Press any key

Conditional Sorts

A condition can be added to the dBASE III PLUS Sort option dictating that only those records that satisfy the condition are included in the sort. dBASE III PLUS tests each record for the condition and includes the record in the sort only if the condition is met.

To sort only a selected set of records, you must first create a query file that specifies the conditions for selecting records. To create a query file, select Query from the Create Menu. Next, select the disk drive where the new query file is to be stored, and then enter a file name for the file. A query table, by which you can designate the conditions for the sort, appears.

■ Your Turn

Use the ACCOUNTS file to perform a conditional sort. You want to know which customers have an account balance of $1500.00 or more.

1. First, make the ACCOUNTS file the active file.

- ■ Select **Set Up**
- ■ Select **Database file**
- ■ Select **B:**
- ■ Select **ACCOUNTS.DBF**
- ■ Type: **N**

Now that the ACCOUNTS file is the active file, you are ready to create the query file.

- ■ Select **Create**
- ■ Select **Query**
- ■ Select **B:**

The prompt, **Enter the name of the file** appears.

- ■ Type: **Balance2**
- ■ Press **<Enter>**

Your screen should look like Figure F–1, which is the query table.

2. You are now ready to designate the condition for the sort. Remember, you only want balances that are equal to or greater than 1500.

- Select **Field name**
- Select **BALANCE**
- Select **Operator**
- Select **>= More than or equal**
- Select **Constant/Expression**
- Type: **1500**
- Press <Enter>

Your screen should look like Figure F–2. You have created the condition and are ready to exit from the query table.

- Select **Exit**
- Select **Save**

3. Next, sort the ACCOUNTS file by the conditions established in the query file. First, set up the BALANCE2 query file.

- Select **Set Up**
- Select **Query**
- Select **B:**
- Select **BALANCE2.QRY**

Now that you have set up the BALANCE2 query file, only those records that meet the query conditions will be sorted.

- Select **Organize**
- Select **Sort**

FIGURE F–1

A Query Table

```
┌──────────────────────────────────────────────────────────────────────────────┐
│  Set Filter           Nest           Display            Exit  10:55:15 am      │
│   ┌──────────────────────────────────────────────────┐                         │
│   │ Field Name                                        │                         │
│   │ Operator                                          │                         │
│   │ Constant/Expression                               │                         │
│   │ Connect                                           │                         │
│   │                                                   │                         │
│   │ Line Number          1                            │                         │
│   └──────────────────────────────────────────────────┘                         │
│                                                                                 │
│   ┌───────┬───────┬──────────────┬────────────────────────┬───────────┐        │
│   │ Line  │ Field │ Operator     │ Constant/Expression    │ Connect   │        │
│   ├───────┼───────┼──────────────┼────────────────────────┼───────────┤        │
│   │  1    │       │              │                        │           │        │
│   │  2    │       │              │                        │           │        │
│   │  3    │       │              │                        │           │        │
│   │  4    │       │              │                        │           │        │
│   │  5    │       │              │                        │           │        │
│   │  6    │       │              │                        │           │        │
│   │  7    │       │              │                        │           │        │
│   └───────┴───────┴──────────────┴────────────────────────┴───────────┘        │
│                                                                                 │
│  CREATE QUERY      ‖<B:>‖B:BALANCE2.QRY            ‖Opt: 1/2        ‖       ‖    │
│       Position selection bar –↑↓.  Select – ↵.  Leave menu –←→.                 │
│            Select a field name for the filter condition.                        │
└──────────────────────────────────────────────────────────────────────────────┘
```

```
┌──────────────────────────────────────────────────────────────────────────┐
│  Set Filter            Nest          Display           Exit  11:10:26 am   │
│  ┌─────────────────────────────────────────────────────┐                   │
│  │ Field Name            BALANCE                         │                   │
│  │ Operator              More than or equal              │                   │
│  │ Constant/Expression   1500                            │                   │
│  │ Connect                                               │                   │
│  │                                                       │                   │
│  │ Line Number           1                               │                   │
│  └─────────────────────────────────────────────────────┘                   │
│                                                                            │
│  ┌───────┬──────────┬──────────────────┬────────────────────┬───────────┐ │
│  │ Line  │ Field    │ Operator         │ Constant/Expression│ Connect   │ │
│  ├───────┼──────────┼──────────────────┼────────────────────┼───────────┤ │
│  │  1    │ BALANCE  │ More than or equal│ 1500              │           │ │
│  │  2    │          │                  │                    │           │ │
│  │  3    │          │                  │                    │           │ │
│  │  4    │          │                  │                    │           │ │
│  │  5    │          │                  │                    │           │ │
│  │  6    │          │                  │                    │           │ │
│  │  7    │          │                  │                    │           │ │
│  └───────┴──────────┴──────────────────┴────────────────────┴───────────┘ │
│                                                                            │
│  CREATE QUERY     ‖<B:>‖B:BALANCE2.QRY          ‖Opt: 4/5      ‖    ‖      │
│        Position selection bar -↕.   Select - ↵.   Leave menu -↩.          │
│           Select a logical connector for the filter condition.            │
└──────────────────────────────────────────────────────────────────────────┘
```

FIGURE F-2

Creating a Sort Condition

■ Select **BALANCE**
■ Press <→>
■ Select **B:**

The prompt **Enter the name of the file** appears. You need to provide a file name for the data-base file which will hold only those records that met the condition of the sort. You are going to use the file name **BALANCE2** just to remind yourself that this data-base file is a result of the BALANCE2 query.

■ Type **BALANCE2**
■ Press <Enter>

The message **100% Sorted 8 Records sorted** appears at the bottom of the screen.

■ Press any key

4. To see the customer names and corresponding balances that are over $1500, make BALANCE2 the active file.

■ Select **Set Up**
■ Select **Database file**
■ Select **B:**
■ Select **BALANCE2.DBF**
■ Type: **N**
■ Select **Retrieve**
■ Select **Display**
■ Select **Specify scope**
■ Select **ALL**
■ Select **Construct a field list**

- Select **LAST_NAME**
- Select **BALANCE**
- Press <→>
- Select **Execute the command**

Eight records are displayed, each one showing the customer's last name and balance. The balances range from $1576.90 to $5245.70.

- Press any key

■ INDEXING A FILE

In some respects the Index option is similar to the Sort option. Both can arrange records in ascending order alphabetically, chronologically, or numerically, and place the newly sorted file into a separate target file. There are, however, some significant differences between the two options.

Indexed files, unlike sorted files, automatically update changes made to the data base. For example, if a record is added or deleted, or if the information stored in a record is edited, the changes are made automatically in all open Index files. Thus, as the data base grows larger or is modified, the records do not have to be reordered constantly.

With the Index option, as with the Sort option, the field being indexed must be a numeric, character, or date field. When a file is indexed, it must be the active file before it can be viewed.

■ Your Turn

Use the Index option to create three indexed files for fields ACCOUNT, ZIP, and SOLD_BY. The account numbers are used to identify what software was purchased. The index on the ZIP field will list the customers according to ZIP code. The list could be used for a mass mailing. The index on the SOLD_BY fields will list customers according to the salesperson.

1. First, make ACCOUNTS the active file.

- Select **Set Up**
- Select **Database file**
- Select **B:**
- Select **ACCOUNTS.DBF**
- Type: **N**

2. Now that ACCOUNTS is the active file, set up the Index files.

- Select **Organize**
- Select **Index**
- Type: **Account**
- Press <Enter>
- Select **B:**
- Type: **Acct_Number**
- Press <Enter>

The message **100% indexed 15 Records indexed** appears.

- Press any key

Next, index on the ZIP field to a file named MAILING. That is, you are going to create a file called MAILING in which the records are arranged in ascending order by ZIP code. Producing a mass mailing would be much easier with the records arranged by ZIP code.

- Select **Organize**
- Select **Index**
- Type: **ZIP**
- Press <Enter>
- Select **B:**
- Type: **Mailing**
- Press <Enter>

The message **100% indexed 15 Records indexed** appears.

- Press any key

Now you want to index on the SOLD_BY field to a file named SALES. That is, you are going to create a file called SALES in which the records are arranged, according to the salesperson. All of Mitchell's customers will be grouped together, all of Louys' customers will be grouped together and all of Santiago's customers will be grouped together.

- Select **Organize**
- Select **Index**
- Type: **Sold_By**
- Press <Enter>
- Select **B:**
- Type: **Sales**
- Press <Enter>

The message **100% indexed 15 Records indexed** appears.

- Press any key

3. Now you want to view one of the indexed files.

- Select **Set Up**
- Select **Database file**
- Select **B:**
- Select **ACCOUNTS.DBF**
- Type: **Y**

Because you indicated the file is indexed, a list of the indexed files appears. An indexed file is opened by selecting it from this list. The first file selected is the master index. Up to seven indexed files can be open at a time on a computer that has 384K or more of memory. On a computer with 256K, only two index files can be open at a time. You are going to open two of the indexed files.

- Select **ACCT NUM.NDX**
- Select **MAILING.NDX**

Your screen should look like Figure F–3.

- Press <←> to close the menu

4. You still want to view one of the indexed files.

```
  Set Up  Create  Update  Position  Retrieve  Organize Modify Tools   11:58:05 am
 ┌─────────────────────────┐
 │ Database file           │  ┌──────────────────────────┐
 │                         │  │ ACCT_NUM.NDX Master      │
 │ Format for Screen       │  │ MAILING.NDX   02         │
 │ Query                   │  │ SALES.NDX                │
 │                         │  └──────────────────────────┘
 │ Catalog                 │
 │ View                    │
 │                         │
 │ Quit dBASE III PLUS     │
 └─────────────────────────┘



 Command: USE B:ACCOUNTS INDEX ACCT_NUM, MAILING
 ASSIST             ║<B:>║ACCOUNTS                    ║Rec: 2/15      ║       ║
          Position selection bar -↑↓.  Select - ←┘.  Leave menu -←↩.
   Select up to seven index files.  The first file selected is the master index.
```

FIGURE F–3

Opening an Indexed File

- Select **Retrieve**
- Select **Display**
- Select **Specify scope**
- Select **ALL**
- Select **Construct a field list**
- Select **LAST__NAME**
- Select **ACCOUNT**
- Press <→>
- Select **Execute the command**

Your screen should look like Figure F–4. Notice that the ACCT__NUMBER index is displayed. You can tell it is the ACCT__NUMBER index because the records are listed with the PA account numbers in ascending order, followed by the PM account numbers in ascending order, followed by the PP account numbers in ascending order.

5. Next, look at the record numbers. Remember that the Sort option renumbered the records consecutively in ascending order. When a file is indexed, however, records maintain their original record numbers. The record numbers in Figure F–4 are 1, 2, 8, 10, 13, 3 and so on.

6. Now you are going to add a record to the file. The ACCT__NUMBER index and the MAILING index are open. Therefore, the added record will be incorporated into these two indexes automatically. Since the SALES index is not open, the added record will not be incorporated into it.

- Press any key
- Select **Update**
- Select **Append**

COMPUTERS AND INFORMATION PROCESSING

```
 Set Up   Create   Update   Position   Retrieve   Organize Modify Tools   12:07:57 pm



    Record#   LAST_NAME        ACCOUNT
          1   Faulks           PA1001
          2   Bulas            PA1005
          8   Weaver           PA1345
         10   Wilks            PA1554
         13   DeSalvo          PA1742
          3   Klein            PM2001
          4   Wilcox           PM2010
          9   Engel            PM2045
          6   Lord             PM2100
         14   Friedman         PM2908
          5   Ornelas          PP3025
          7   Busch            PP3100
         11   Bressler         PP3701
         12   Hocks            PP3801
         15   Crope            PP3907
 ASSIST                 ‖<B:>‖ACCOUNTS                      ‖Rec: 1/15        ‖           ‖
                   Press any key to continue work in ASSIST._
```

FIGURE F—4

Displaying an Indexed File

A data entry form for record 16 appears.

■ Use the following information to fill in the form

ACCOUNT	PA0050
LAST__NAME	Diaz
FIRST__NAME	Kate
COMPANY	Bartlett Press
ADDRESS	75 Hilltop Ave.
CITY	Detroit
STATE	MI
ZIP	48233
SOLD__BY	Louys
SERVICE	09/27/90
BALANCE	90.00

■ Press <Enter> after the data is entered

7. Check to make sure the two indexes are updated.

■ Select **Retrieve**
■ Select **Display**
■ Select **Specify scope**
■ Select **ALL**
■ Select **Construct a field list**
■ Select **ACCOUNT**
■ Select **LAST__NAME**
■ Select **COMPANY**
■ Press <→>
■ Select **Execute the command**

Record 16, for Kate Diaz, is the first record listed. It's listed first because the ACCT—NUMBER index is the active index and the Diaz account number is the lowest number.

8. Now check to make sure that record 16 also is in the MAILING index. To do this, change the active index using the Set Up option.

- Press any key
- Select **Set Up**
- Select **Database file**
- Select **B:**
- Select **ACCOUNTS.DBF**
- Type: **Y**
- Select **MAILING.NDX**
- Press <←>
- Select **Retrieve**
- Select **Display**
- Select **Specify scope**
- Select **ALL**
- Select **Construct a field list**
- Select **LAST—NAME**
- Select **ADDRESS**
- Select **CITY**
- Select **STATE**
- Select **ZIP**
- Press <→>
- Select **Execute the command**

Record 16 is the last record listed because it is the record with the highest ZIP code number. Notice that the records are now listed in ascending order according to ZIP code. They are listed this way because the active index is now the MAILING index.

- Press any key

Indexing on Multiple Fields

There are times when indexing on more than one field is useful. To index on more than one field, join the fields with plus signs when the prompt **Enter an index key expression** appears. This command can only be used on fields of the same type. For example, you cannot have a character/text field combined with a numeric field in the index key expression. All the fields must be either character/text or numeric.

The order in which the fields are listed in this command is significant. dBASE III PLUS first arranges all the records by the first field listed, then by the second field listed, and so on. When using this command, make sure the fields are listed in the order that produces the desired results.

■ Your Turn

Use the Index option on multiple fields to list the customers in account number order by salesperson.

1. First, make the SALES file the master index.

- Select **Set Up**
- Select **Database file**
- Select **B:**
- Select **ACCOUNTS.DBF**
- Type: **Y**
- Select **SALES.NDX**
- Press **<←>**
- Select **Retrieve**
- Select **Display**
- Select **Specify scope**
- Select **ALL**
- Select **Construct a field list**
- Select **ACCOUNT**
- Select **LAST_NAME**
- Select **COMPANY**
- Select **SOLD_BY**
- Press **<→>**
- Select **Execute the command**

Notice that Kate Diaz is not on the list. She is not on the list because the SALES index was closed when her record was added. Look at how the accounts are listed. They are grouped according to salesperson, but the accounts themselves are in no particular order. This index will be more useful if the customers are listed not only by salesperson, but also by account number. Indexing on multiple fields enables you to do this.

- Press any key

2. You are now going to index both the ACCOUNT and SOLD_BY fields.

- Select **Organize**
- Select **Index**

The prompt **Enter an index key expression** appears. You are going to enter two fields connected with a plus sign.

- Type: **Sold_By + Account**
- Press **<Enter>**
- Select **B:**
- Type: **Sales2**
- Press **<Enter>**

3. Take a look at the SALES2 index.

- Select **Retrieve**
- Select **Display**
- Select **Specify scope**
- Select **ALL**
- Select **Construct a field list**
- Select **ACCOUNT**
- Select **SOLD_BY**
- Select **COMPANY**
- Press **<→>**
- Select **Execute the command**

Your screen should look like Figure F–5. The records are still grouped by

```
 Set Up   Create   Update   Position   Retrieve   Organize Modify Tools   02:57:19 pm


 Record#    ACCOUNT  SOLD_BY         COMPANY
      16    PA0050   Louys           Bartlett Press
       2    PA1005   Louys           B & H Plastics
      13    PA1742   Louys           Tarkett, Inc.
       5    PP3025   Louys           S & P Productions
       7    PP3100   Louys           Dryer Supplies
      11    PP3701   Louys           Midway Construction
      15    PP3907   Louys           Stockman & Associates
       1    PA1001   Mitchell        Michaels & Associates
       8    PA1345   Mitchell        Baldwin and Sons
      10    PA1554   Mitchell        McCloud Development
       6    PM2100   Mitchell        Holmes Manufacturing
      12    PP3801   Mitchell        H & H Products
       3    PM2001   Santiago        Fischer Label
       4    PM2010   Santiago        Master Printing
       9    PM2045   Santiago        Poe Research, Inc.
      14    PM2908   Santiago        Shawnee Distributors
 ASSIST              ||<B:>||ACCOUNTS              ||Rec: 16/16        ||        ||
             Press any key to continue work in ASSIST._
```

FIGURE F—5

Indexing on Multiple Fields

salesperson—all of Louys' accounts together, all of Mitchell's accounts together, and all of Santiago's accounts together—but now the customers also are listed in ascending order according to account number.

■ Press any key

SEARCHING AN INDEXED DATA-BASE FILE

When data-base files become large, it can be a tedious chore to look for a particular record. dBASE III PLUS eliminates that problem with the Seek option from the Position Menu. The Seek option searches an indexed file for a particular alphanumeric string. dBASE III PLUS searches the indexed file for the first record containing the string specified. If the string for which you are searching is character/text, that string has to be enclosed in quotation marks when dBASE III PLUS prompts you to enter the string for which you are searching. When a record with the string is found, dBASE places a record pointer on it. That record can then be displayed. The Seek option works only on indexed files.

■ Your Turn

Create an index in which all the customers are listed alphabetically. Then use that index to search for specific customers. The ACCOUNTS file should be active.

1. First create a new index file that lists the customers in alphabetical order.

■ Select **Organize**
■ Select **Index**

COMPUTERS AND INFORMATION PROCESSING

- Type: **Last_Name**
- Press <Enter>
- Select **B:**
- Type: **Alphaname**
- Press <Enter>
- Press any key

Now open the ALPHANAME index.

- Select **Set Up**
- Select **Database file**
- Select **B:**
- Select **ACCOUNTS.DBF**
- Type: **Y**
- Select **ALPHANAM.NDX**

Press <←>

2. Next, use the Seek option with the ALPHANAME index.

- Select **Position**
- Select **Seek**

The prompt **Enter an expression** appears. Because the expression to be entered is character/text, it has to be enclosed in quotation marks.

- Type: **"Desalvo"**
- Press <Enter>

The message **No find** appears. There is a client whose last name is DeSalvo, and her name is in the data-base file, but dBASE III PLUS did not find the record because it distinguishes capital and lowercase letters. For dBASE III PLUS to find the record, the name must be typed exactly as it appears in the record.

- Press any key
- Select **Position**
- Select **Seek**
- Type: **"DeSalvo"**
- Press <**Enter**>

This time the record is found but does not appear on the screen. You know the record was found because the **No find** prompt did not appear.

- Press any key

Next, display the record.

- Select **Retrieve**
- Select **Display**
- Select **Construct a field list**
- Select **FIRST_NAME**
- Select **LAST_NAME**
- Select **COMPANY**
- Press <→>
- Select **Execute the command**

The record for Liz DeSalvo appears.

- Press any key

3. Now you are going to look for the record of a client whose last name is Weaver.

- Select **Position**
- Select **Seek**
- Type: **"Weaver"**
- Press <Enter>
- Press any key
- Select **Retrieve**
- Select **Display**
- Select **Construct a field list**
- Select **FIRST_NAME**
- Select **LAST_NAME**
- Select **COMPANY**
- Select **SOLD_BY**
- Press <→>
- Select **Execute the command**

The record for Chris Weaver appears.

- Press any key

LEARNING CHECK

1. When using the Sort option, the field by which the data-base file is being sorted is called the _____ field.

a. target   c. sort
b. key   d. query

2. Since sorting a data-base file physically rearranges the records in the data-base file being sorted, dBASE III PLUS copies the sorted records into the _____ file.

a. target   c. sort
b. key   d. query

3. To sort only those records in a data-base file that satisfy a certain condition, a _____ file must be created.

a. target   c. sort
b. key   d. query

4. (True or False?) When indexing on multiple fields, all the fields have to be of the same type.

5. (True or False?) If you are searching for a character string using the Seek option, the string has to be enclosed in quotation marks when responding to the prompt telling you to enter the string for which you are searching.

ANSWERS

1. b.   4. True
2. a.   5. True
3. d.

■ CREATING A REPORT WITH dBASE III PLUS

Data stored in a data-base file can provide users with helpful information. Until the information can take the form of a report on paper, however, its usefulness is limited. The following section explains how to create a hard copy report using dBASE III PLUS files.

A dBASE III PLUS report is created with the Report option from the Create Menu. After selecting Report from the Create Menu, dBASE III PLUS guides you through the creation of the report by displaying a series of screens and prompts.

■ Your Turn

Start dBASE III PLUS if necessary. The next several hands-on exercises take you through the creation of a report using the ACCOUNTS file. The AC-COUNTS file should be the active file.

1. Once the ACCOUNTS file is active, you are ready to start the process of creating a report.

- ■ Select **Create**
- ■ Select **Report**
- ■ Select **B:**

The prompt **Enter the name of the file** appears. Provide the report file with a name.

- ■ Type: **Accounts**
- ■ Press <Enter>

The names of the data-base file and the report are the same: ACCOUNTS. This does not cause a problem because dBASE III PLUS automatically adds the extension .FRM to the report. The two files, ACCOUNTS.DBF and AC-COUNTS.FRM, are stored as two separate files. Using the same name for the data-base file and report can help to clarify the contents of the files. Your screen should look like Figure F–6. Leave the report screen on your monitor while you read the next section.

Designing the Report

The dBASE III PLUS report screen has a menu with five options: Options, Groups, Columns, Locate, and Exit. The Options Menu enables users to design the format of a report, that is, how the report will look on paper. The first option in the Options Menu is Page title. You can enter up to four lines of text that will be printed at the top of each report page. The rest of the options from the Options Menu already have default settings. You can change such things as the width of the page, left and right margins, how many lines will print on the page, and so on. However, for most standard reports, the default settings will be acceptable.

The Groups Menu enables users to group together certain portions of the data-base file when it is printed. For example, if the data-base file is alphabetized by last name, a report can be printed with all the last names beginning with A grouped together, all the last names beginning with B grouped together, and so on.

The Columns Menu enables users to designate which fields will be included in a report. In addition, a heading for each column can be entered from the Columns Menu. The Locate Menu enables users to move to certain columns in a report. The Exit Menu enables users to save a report.

```
┌─────────────────────────────────────────────────────────────────────────┐
│  Options          Groups         Columns        Locate      Exit  03:20:34 pm │
│  ┌──────────────────────────────────────┐                                  │
│  │ Page title                           │                                  │
│  │ Page width (positions)     80        │                                  │
│  │ Left margin                 8        │                                  │
│  │ Right margin                0        │                                  │
│  │ Lines per page             58        │                                  │
│  │ Double space report        No        │                                  │
│  │ Page eject before printing Yes       │                                  │
│  │ Page eject after printing  No        │                                  │
│  │ Plain page                 No        │                                  │
│  └──────────────────────────────────────┘                                  │
│                                                                            │
│  ┌────────────────┬──────────────────────┬───────────────────┬───────────────────┐ │
│  │ CURSOR  <-- -->│ Delete char:    Del  │ Insert column: ^N │ Insert:    Ins   │ │
│  │  Char:   ← →   │ Delete word:    ^T   │ Report format: F1 │ Zoom in:  ^PgDn  │ │
│  │  Word: Home End│ Delete column:  ^U   │ Abandon:      Esc │ Zoom out: ^PgUp  │ │
│  └────────────────┴──────────────────────┴───────────────────┴───────────────────┘ │
│  CREATE REPORT    ‖<B:>‖B:ACCOUNTS.FRM          ‖Opt: 1/9      ‖        ‖       │
│         Position selection bar -↕.  Select - ⏎.  Leave menu -↔.              │
│     Enter up to four lines of text to be displayed at the top of each report page. │
└─────────────────────────────────────────────────────────────────────────┘
```

FIGURE F—6

Creating a Report

■ **Your Turn**

The ACCOUNTS file should be active and the report screen should be on your monitor.

1. First, enter a page title for the report.

■ Select **Options**
■ Select **Page title**
■ Type: PROSOFT, INC.
■ Press <Enter>
■ Type: CLIENT ADDRESSES
■ Press <Enter> three times

2. Next, indicate the columns to be included in the report.

■ Select **Columns**
■ Select **Contents**

At this point, you must designate the field to be included in the report. To see a list of the available fields, press <F10>.

■ Press <F10>

The fields from the ACCOUNTS file appear at the left of the screen. You decide that the report will contain the company name, address, city, and state for all the clients in the file.

■ Select **COMPANY**

The word *COMPANY* moves into the Columns menu next to the Contents option.

COMPUTERS AND INFORMATION PROCESSING

■ Press <Enter>

Notice that **25** now appears next to width. That is because the FIRST_ NAME field has a width of 25. Now you are going to enter a column heading to describe the contents of this column. The header can be up to four lines long and 60 characters wide. The field headers are printed at the top of each page above the corresponding columns.

■ Select **Heading**
■ Type: COMPANY
■ Press <Enter> four times

The first column has now been defined. To define the second column, you must press the <PgDn> key.

■ Press <PgDn>

The Columns menu is once again empty.

■ Select **Contents**
■ Press <F10>
■ Select **ADDRESS**
■ Press <Enter>
■ Select **Heading**
■ Type: ADDRESS
■ Press <Enter> four times
■ Press <PgDn>
■ Select **Contents**
■ Press <F10>
■ Select **CITY**
■ Press <Enter>
■ Select **Heading**
■ Type: CITY
■ Press <Enter> four times
■ Press <PgDn>
■ Select **Contents**
■ Press <F10>
■ Select **STATE**
■ Press <Enter>
■ Select **Heading**
■ Type: STATE
■ Press <Enter> four times
■ Press <PgDn>
■ Select **Exit**
■ Select **Save**

The Assistant Menu returns to the screen.

MODIFYING A REPORT

When the report form has been designated and saved, it can be recalled for editing or modification if necessary. To edit a report, select Report from the Modify Menu. Next, select the disk drive where the report is located, and finally select the name of the report you want to edit. The report screen appears. The menu at the bottom of the screen lists the keys used for editing.

▰ PRINTING A REPORT

When a report is entered into a data-base file, hard copy of the report can be printed. To print a report, select Report from the Retrieve menu. Next, select the disk drive where the report is located. Select the report to be printed and the option **Execute the command.** The prompt **Direct the output to the printer? [Y/N]** appears. Type **Y** for yes and the report will be printed. When printing a report, dBASE III PLUS does not hold the last line of the report in a print buffer. The entire report is printed.

▰ Your Turn

Print a copy of the ACCOUNTS report. Make sure that your computer is hooked up to a printer and that the printer has plenty of paper and is online.

1. Check to make sure the ACCOUNTS file is the active file.

   - ▪ Select **Retrieve**
   - ▪ Select **Report**
   - ▪ Select **B:**
   - ▪ Select **ACCOUNTS.FRM**
   - ▪ Select **Execute the command**
   - ▪ Type: **Y**

2. The report is both displayed on the screen and printed. Your printed report should look like Figure F–7.

   - ▪ Press any key

FIGURE F–7

ProSoft Client Report

```
Page No.      1
09/01/88
                          PROSOFT, INC.
                          CLIENT ADDRESSES

COMPANY                   ADDRESS                     CITY        STATE


Midway Construction       45 S. Luke St.              Palma       OH
B & H Plastics            908 W. Industrial Pkwy      Cygnet      OH
Dryer Supplies            32 Bradner Pkwy             Columbus    OH
Stockman & Associates     67 Brackner   Suite 22      Cygnet      OH
Tarkett, Inc.             9 W. Second   Suite 201     Columbus    OH
Bartlett Press            75 Hilltop Ave.             Detroit     MI
Poe Research, Inc.        1432 Indian Rd.             Hamler      OH
Michaels & Associates     78 Main St. Suite 101       Columbus    OH
Shawnee Distributors      3426 Little St.             Palma       OH
H & H Products            90 Kellog Rd.               Portage     OH
Fischer Label             12 Yong St.                 Columbus    OH
Holmes Manufacturing      98 Pike St.                 Oregon      OH
S & P Productions         123 First St. Suite 35      Canton      OH
Baldwin and Sons          909 Clough   #1C            Portage     OH
Master Printing           6 Williams Rd. #301         Fremont     OH
McCloud Development        76 Gorrel   Suite 56        Lima        OH
```

1. When designing a report, the _____ Menu on the report screen enables you to determine how the report will look on paper.

a. Options
b. Columns

c. Groups
d. Locate

2. When designing a report, the _____ Menu on the report screen enables you to group together certain portions of the data-base file when it is printed.

a. Options
b. Columns

c. Groups
d. Locate

3. When designing a report, the _____ Menu on the report screen enables you to designate which fields will be included in a report.

a. Options
b. Columns

c. Groups
d. Locate

4. (True or False?) You cannot name a report the same name as an existing data-base file.

5. (True or False?) Once a report form has been created and saved, it cannot be modified.

ANSWERS

1. a.
2. c.
3. b.

4. False
5. False

LEARNING
CHECK

▰ SUMMARY OF dBASE III PLUS MENUS

Set Up Menu

Option	Description
Database file	Selects which data-base file is to be used.
Format for screen	Selects a custom screen that has been previously designed.
Query	Selects a query file that has been previously created.
Quit dBASE III PLUS	Exits from the dBASE III PLUS program.

Create Menu

Option	Description
Database file	Creates a new data-base file.
Format	Creates a custom screen form for data entry and custom report generation.
View	Creates a view file used for relating different data-base files.
Query	Creates a query file used for accessing records that meet specified conditions.
Report	Creates a report form file.
Label	Creates a label format file.

Update Menu

Option	Description
Append	Allows records to be added to the end of a data-base file
Edit	Allows records from a data-base file to be edited, one record at a time.
Display	Displays the contents of records in a data-base file.
Browse	Allows records from a data-base file to be edited, several records at a time.
Replace	Allows the contents of a field to be edited in all of the records in a data-base file at the same time.
Delete	Marks a record for deletion.
Recall	Erases the deletion mark from a record.
Pack	Permanently removes all deleted records from the file.

Position Menu

Option	Description
Seek	Searches for an index key that matches a specific expression.
Locate	Searches for a record that meets a specific condition.
Skip	Moves the file pointer by skipping records.
Goto record	Moves the file pointer to a designated record.

Retrieve Menu

Option	Description
List	Lists the contents of the records in the data-base file to the screen or printer.
Display	Displays the contents of the records in the data-base file.
Report	Displays the contents of the records in a data-base file using an existing report format.
Label	Displays the contents of the records in a data-base file using an existing label format.
Sum	Calculates the sum of values in a specified numeric field.
Average	Calculates the average value for the contents of a numeric field.
Count	Counts the number of records in the active data-base file.

Organize Menu

Option	Description
Index	Creates an index file in which all records are ordered according to the field specified.
Sort	Rearranges data records in order according to the field specified.
Copy	Copies records from one data-base file to another.

Modify Menu

Option	Description
Database file	Allows changes to be made to the structure of the active data-base file.
Format	Allows changes to be made to the structure of a custom screen design.
View	Allows changes to be made to the structure of a view file.
Query	Allows changes to be made to the structure of a query file.
Report	Allows changes to be made to the structure of a report form file.
Label	Allows changes to be made to the structure of a label format file.

Tools Menu

Option	Description
Set drive	Changes the default disk drive.
Copy file	Copies the contents of a data-base file to a new file.
Directory	Displays the contents of a disk directory.
Rename	Renames a data-base file.
Erase	Erases a data-base file.
List structure	Displays the structure of the current data-base file.

SUMMARY POINTS

■ Two ways to rearrange the order of records within a dBASE III PLUS file are by using the Sort option and the Index option from the Organize Menu.

■ The Seek option from the Position Menu searches indexed files for relevant data.

■ The Report option from the Create Menu enables the user to create a hard copy report using dBASE III PLUS files.

dBASE III PLUS EXERCISES

In this exercise you are going to create a data-base file for the personnel department of the Central Data Corporation. An employee of Central Data has a choice of four different insurance plans. This data-base file keeps track of the insurance plan selected by each employee.

1. If you are not in dBASE III PLUS, use the procedures to start it. Make sure your work disk is in drive B.

2. Use the Create option to start a new file, and name it ENROLL. The file should have the following structure:

Field Name	Type	Width
LAST_NAME	Character	10
FIRST_NAME	Character	10
ADDRESS	Character	16
CITY	Character	15
STATE	Character	2
DEPARTMENT	Character	15
PROGRAM	Character	4

The DEPARTMENT field indicates for which department the employee works within Central Data, and the PROGRAM field indicates the insurance program the employee selected. There are four options for the insurance programs:

HO-I	Health insurance only for an individual
HO-F	Health insurance only for a family
HD-I	Health and dental insurance for an individual
HD-F	Health and dental insurance for a family

Enter the structure information.

3. At the prompt INPUT DATA RECORDS NOW? (Y/N), type **Y** and enter the following information:

LAST_NAME	Mansfield
FIRST_NAME	Carolyn
ADDRESS	190 Main Street
CITY	Bowling Green
STATE	OH
DEPARTMENT	Data Processing
PROGRAM	HD-F

LAST_NAME	Magpoc
FIRST_NAME	William
ADDRESS	1200 Victory Rd.
CITY	Toledo
STATE	OH
DEPARTMENT	Marketing
PROGRAM	HO-I

LAST_NAME	Rath
FIRST_NAME	Alexis
ADDRESS	221 Maple Ave.
CITY	Perrysburg
STATE	OH
DEPARTMENT	Research
PROGRAM	HD-I

LAST_NAME	Byrtum
FIRST_NAME	Laura
ADDRESS	849 Napoleon Rd
CITY	Bowling Green

STATE   OH
DEPARTMENT   Personnel
PROGRAM   HO-F

LAST_NAME   Burkett
FIRST_NAME   Lynn
ADDRESS   12 Central
CITY   Toledo
STATE   OH
DEPARTMENT   Training
PROGRAM   HD-F

LAST_NAME   Catayee
FIRST_NAME   Monique
ADDRESS   110 Main Street
CITY   Maumee
STATE   OH
DEPARTMENT   Training
PROGRAM   HD-I

LAST_NAME   Marin
FIRST_NAME   Bernard
ADDRESS   12 King Rd.
CITY   Huron
STATE   OH
DEPARTMENT   Research
PROGRAM   HD-I

LAST_NAME   Byler
FIRST_NAME   Diane
ADDRESS   333 Anderson
CITY   Bowling Green
STATE   OH
DEPARTMENT   Personnel
PROGRAM   HO-F

LAST_NAME   Heil
FIRST_NAME   Pascal
ADDRESS   302 West St.
CITY   Bowling Green
STATE   OH
DEPARTMENT   Research
PROGRAM   HO-I

LAST_NAME   Jaccoud
FIRST_NAME   Lynn
ADDRESS   120 S. Main St.
CITY   Sandusky
STATE   OH
DEPARTMENT   Data Processing
PROGRAM   HO-F

LAST_NAME   Wegman
FIRST_NAME   Nelly
ADDRESS   430 Clough
CITY   Maumee
STATE   OH
DEPARTMENT   Data Processing
PROGRAM   HO-F

LAST_NAME	Pinkston
FIRST_NAME	Mark
ADDRESS	65 High St.
CITY	Toledo
STATE	OH
DEPARTMENT	Marketing
PROGRAM	HD-I
LAST_NAME	Burroughs
FIRST_NAME	Beverly
ADDRESS	26 S. Summit
CITY	Huron
STATE	OH
DEPARTMENT	Research
PROGRAM	HO-F
LAST_NAME	King
FIRST_NAME	Seth
ADDRESS	201 E. Wooster
CITY	Bloomdale
STATE	OH
DEPARTMENT	Personnel
PROGRAM	HO-F
LAST_NAME	Paulin
FIRST_NAME	Jack
ADDRESS	102 High
CITY	Sylvania
STATE	OH
DEPARTMENT	Training
PROGRAM	HO-I
LAST_NAME	Proctor
FIRST_NAME	Chris
ADDRESS	34 Eighth St.
CITY	Lancaster
STATE	OH
DEPARTMENT	Personnel
PROGRAM	HO-I
LAST_NAME	Priess
FIRST_NAME	Ronald
ADDRESS	120 Prout St.
CITY	Bowling Green
STATE	OH
DEPARTMENT	Research
PROGRAM	HO-F
LAST_NAME	Atkins
FIRST_NAME	Lee
ADDRESS	12560 Euclid
CITY	Perrysburg
STATE	OH
DEPARTMENT	Data Processing
PROGRAM	HD-F
LAST_NAME	Asik
FIRST_NAME	Jennifer
ADDRESS	22 Mercer
CITY	Weston

STATE	OH
DEPARTMENT	Marketing
PROGRAM	HO-I
LAST_NAME	Dowell
FIRST_NAME	Gail
ADDRESS	112 Ridge
CITY	Toledo
STATE	OH
DEPARTMENT	Training
PROGRAM	HD-I

4. Use the Browse option to review the data; make sure that everything is accurate. If you find errors, correct them.

5. How do you index a file? Index the ENROLL file on the DEPARTMENT field. Name the indexed file DEPT.

6. How do you access an indexed file? Access the DEPT file.

7. Use the Display option to display the records in the DEPT file. Use the Specify scope option and select ALL to display all the records. Use the Construct a field list option and select the LAST_NAME, FIRST_NAME, and DEPARTMENT as the fields you want to display. Is there any difference in the order of the records? What is it?

8. Now you want to index on both the DEPARTMENT field and the PROGRAM field. Name the indexed file PROG. Access the PROG file. Use the Display option to display all the records in the PROG file. Display the LAST_NAME, FIRST_NAME, DEPARTMENT, and PROGRAM fields.

9. Create an indexed file on the PROGRAM field. Name the file REPORT1. Access the display of the REPORT1 file to make sure the records are grouped by insurance programs.

10. With the REPORT1 file as the master index, create a report and name it REPORT1. Enter the following for a page title:

Employees' Health Care Plan

Use the LAST_NAME, FIRST_NAME, and PROGRAM fields as the contents for three columns. Enter appropriate column headings. Group the report on the PROGRAM field. Save the Report form.

11. Print the REPORT1.FRM report.

12. Access the ENROLL data-base file. Use the List option to list the last name, department, and program for all employees who selected health insurance only for an individual. How many employees selected this option? How many employees selected health and dental coverage for a family? Finally, how many employees selected health and dental coverage for an individual? Print a hard copy of each listing.

■ dBASE III PLUS PROBLEMS

To complete the following problems, you need the DOS disk, dBASE III PLUS System Disk #1, System Disk #2, and the Student File Disk.

Businesses often use data bases to store information on their clients. An example of such a data-base file can be found on the Student File Disk. The name of the file is CAST. It is a data-base file for a casting agency in New

York City. There are fourteen fields in the CAST file. A description of the fields is offered below:

Field Name	Description
NUMBER	The client's number used for record-keeping purposes by the agency.
NAME	The client's name.
PHONE	The client's telephone number.
BIRTHDAY	The client's date of birth.
SEX	The client's gender, either M for male or F for female.
HEIGHT	The client's height entered as feet:inches—for example 5:07 for five feet seven inches.
WEIGHT	The client's weight.
EYE	The client's eye color
HAIR	The client's hair color
THEATRE	The client's theatre experience, entered as Y if the client has experience and N if the client has no theatre experience.
DANCE	The client's dance experience, entered as Y if the client is a dancer and N if the client cannot dance.
MOVIE	The client's movie experience, entered as Y if the client has experience in film and N if the client has no film experience.
COMMERCIAL	Client's experience making commercials, entered as Y if client has made a commercial and N if client has not made a commercial.
SING	Client's ability to sing, entered as Y if client can sing and N if client cannot sing.

1. Start the computer and load dBASE III PLUS and insert the Student File Disk into drive B. Access the CAST data-base file and make a copy of it. Name the copy CAST1. Access the CAST1 data-base file.

2. Display the structure of the CAST1 data-base file. How many data records are there in the file? Use the Display option to view the name, height, and weight fields of all records in the data-base file. What is the name, height, and weight of the client in the last record?

3. Add the following records to the CAST1 file:

NUMBER:	2567
NAME:	Lieberwitz, Ann
PHONE:	780-8962
BIRTHDAY:	02/21/50
SEX:	F
HEIGHT:	5:06
WEIGHT:	135
EYE:	brown
HAIR:	brown
THEATRE:	Y
DANCE:	N
MOVIE:	Y
COMMERCIAL:	Y
SING:	N
NUMBER:	2670
NAME:	Sanino, Maria
PHONE:	780-8662

BIRTHDAY:	11/26/59
SEX:	F
HEIGHT:	5:07
WEIGHT:	125
EYE:	brown
HAIR:	brown
THEATRE:	N
DANCE:	N
MOVIE:	Y
COMMERCIAL:	Y
SING:	N

4. Edit records in the file as follows:

■ Blair Lindsay has a new telephone number. His number is now 780-9211.

■ Richard Garcia made a movie. In his record, change the entry in the MOVIE field to Y.

■ Judith Ritchie made a commercial. In her record, change the entry in the COMMERCIAL field to Y.

5. A request has come in for anyone with previous film-making experience. Print a report that lists the names, telephone numbers, and birthdates of all qualified clients.

6. A request has come in for anyone with dance experience. Print a report that lists the names, heights, eye color, and hair color of all qualified clients.

7. A request has come in to the agency for females with black hair who have previous experience making commercials. Print a hard copy of a report that lists the names, phone numbers, and birthdates of all the qualified women.

8. A request has come in to the agency for males who are six feet or taller and who can both sing and dance. Print a hard copy of a report that lists names, eye color, hair color, and height of all the eligible men.

O U T L I N E

Introduction
Definitions
Uses of Expert Systems
Learning Check
Guide to VP-Expert
Getting Started with VP-Expert
Getting Help with VP-Expert
Creating a Knowledge Base from an Induction Table
Understanding the Parts of an Induction Table
  The ACTIONS Block
  Rules
  Statements
Learning Check
Editing a Knowledge Base
Checking for Errors in the Knowledge Base
VP-Expert Clauses
  The DISPLAY Clause
Adding Variables to the Knowledge Base
Learning Check
Summary Points
VP-Expert Exercises
VP-Expert Problems

INTRODUCTION

Expert systems technology is a subfield of research in the area of **artificial intelligence.** Artificial intelligence is concerned with developing techniques whereby computers can be used to solve problems that appear to require imagination, intuition, or intelligence. Artificial intelligence is a very broad concept encompassing a number of applications, one of which is expert systems technology.

Expert systems technology is the development of computer software that simulates human problem-solving abilities. An expert system uses human knowledge that has been collected and stored in a computer to solve problems that ordinarily can be solved only by a human expert. Expert systems imitate the reasoning process experts go through to solve a specific problem.

The purpose of this chapter is to introduce you to the concept of expert systems. It includes an explanation of expert systems, how they work, and how they are used. In addition, it provides instructions on how to get started using Paperback Software's VP-Expert, a rule-based expert system development tool.

DEFINITIONS

One outcome of research in artificial intelligence is, to repeat, the development of expert systems technology. In 1957, Allen Newell of the RAND Corporation and Herbert Simon from Carnegie-Mellon University began work on a machine that could reason. They wanted to create a machine capable of incorporating problem-solving techniques applicable to a broad range of problems. They called their machine the General Problem Solver.

In order to identify the problem-solving techniques they wanted their machine to emulate, Newell and Simon gathered together human subjects and gave them problems to solve. They asked their subjects to do all their thinking aloud. By closely analyzing how humans solve problems, they began to identify specific problem-solving techniques. This method of learning how people reason by asking human experts to reason aloud while they are solving a problem is still used today by developers of expert systems.

The object of an expert system is to transfer the expertise of a human expert from that person to a computer and then from the computer to other humans who may not be experts in the field. When an end user accesses information from an expert system, it is called a **consultation.**

The first step in developing such a system is to gather as much information about the specific **domain** as possible. The domain is the field or area of activity. Examples of various domains are medicine, law, tax analysis, geology, and engineering. The **domain knowledge,** or the knowledge pertaining to a specific domain, could be gathered from books, manuals, human experts, data bases, special research reports, or a combination of all these sources.

The domain knowledge partly makes up the **knowledge base.** The knowledge base contains everything necessary for understanding, formulating, and solving the problem. In addition to the domain knowledge, the knowledge base contains a **rule base** that is the actual expertise of the system. The rules in the rule base are generally stated as IF/THEN propositions. The following is an example of a rule:

COMPUTERS AND INFORMATION PROCESSING

```
IF        temperature > 98.6   AND
          temperature < = 102
THEN      fever = moderate
```

Such a rule could be used to help diagnose an illness. Basically this rule says if the body temperature is greater than 98.6 degrees but less than 102, then the person has a moderate fever.

The unique feature of an expert system is its ability to reason. The computer is programmed so that it can make inferences from data stored in the knowledge base. The "brain" of an expert system is the **inference engine,** the component where the reasoning is performed. The inference engine includes procedures regarding problem solving.

Obviously, developing and programming an expert system from scratch is the work of professionals. The designers or **developers** of expert systems typically are artificial intelligence specialists. Usually, the developers are not the people who will perform consultations on the systems. The people who will use the system, the **end users,** generally have little or no knowledge of artificial intelligence. Expert systems have to be designed with the end user in mind. Therefore, the **user interface** is an important consideration in designing expert systems. The user interface in an expert system has to enable an end user to easily perform a consultation regardless of previous computer experience.

Today, expert systems are available to people who do not have access to developers capable of programming a system from scratch. Programs called expert system shells or expert system development tools can be purchased as an application software package. These programs, such as VP-Expert, provide the inference engine, the user interface, and the commands of an expert system. In fact, the only thing that has to be provided is the domain knowledge. Providing the domain knowledge is no small order. But expert system development tools have increased the availability of expert systems to the general public.

Parts of the business sector have high hopes for expert systems. Some developers predict that expert systems will soon become an essential part of office decision making. Expert systems are seen as a possible solution to the productivity problem in American manufacturing. Tasks such as ordering supplies, designing products, and monitoring quality control now account for more than 70 percent of the cost of manufacturing a product. Expert systems could take over many of these tasks.

USES OF EXPERT SYSTEMS

Expert systems are used in the fields of law, medicine, engineering, business, geology, financial analysis, and tax analysis, among others. Expert systems have the potential of functioning better than any single human expert in making judgments within these expertise areas. These systems perform such functions as recommending strategies, diagnosing illnesses, analyzing structures, and training personnel. In general, expert systems can advise, consult, diagnose, recommend, teach, and train.

Some specific examples of expert systems that have been developed will help to demonstrate how they are used. The ACE system, developed by Bell Laboratories, identifies trouble spots in telephone networks and recommends appropriate repair and preventative maintenance. The DART system, developed by Stanford University, assists in diagnosing faults in computer hardware systems using information about the design of the device being diagnosed. The MYCIN system, also developed at Stanford, identifies bacterial diseases of the blood and prescribes antibiotic therapies. The CATS-1 system diagnoses malfunctions and prescribes repairs for General Electric's diesel electric locomotive engines. STEAMER is a system used to train inexperienced workers to operate complex ship engines. PROSPECTOR is a mineral-exploration expert system that has been used to discover mineral deposits in Washington valued at $100 million.

IBM has one hundred expert systems that, among other things, test computer disk drives. Yearly savings from the disk-drive expert systems are estimated to be eight million dollars. The Internal Revenue Service will soon be using an expert system to detect suspicious deductions and errors on tax returns. American Express uses an expert system to authorize questionable charges. Previously, charges that were not authorized by a computer program were passed on to human authorizers. These authorizers had a four-inch-thick rule book, several computer screens filled with account information, and seventy seconds to make a decision. Now, an expert system analyzes questionable transactions.

In addition to highly specialized expert systems like the ones mentioned above, more and more expert systems are being developed that have broader purposes. One school system developed a trouble-shooting expert system for its teachers. Many of the teachers had little computer experience and were having problems using the computers. As a result, far too many repair calls were being made, incurring a great expense in terms of both lost computer time and repair bills. Many, if not most, of the problems could be solved by the teachers themselves. The expert system, by asking a series of simple questions, helped teachers identify and fix their problems. This expert system ended up saving the school system an enormous amount of money in needless computer repairs.

The Center for Law and Computer Science at Northeastern University in Boston uses VP-Expert to teach students how to use expert systems. Students have designed systems that will, for example, determine tax deductions and federal assistance eligibility. The Bank of Montreal in New York is using VP-Expert to develop a system to approve credit checks and assist in loan processing.

Some expert systems have even been designed for home use. One example of an expert system to be used in the home is a system by Paperback Software, the developers of VP-Expert. This system helps the user choose from over 600 top-rated American wines the appropriate wine to serve for any meal or occasion.

1. When an end user accesses information from an expert system he or she performs a(n) _Consultation_

2. The actual expertise of an expert system is called a(n) _____.

a. domain   c. knowledge base
b. rule base   d. inference engine

3. The __d__ is the "brain" of the expert system.

a. domain   c. knowledge base
b. rule base   d. inference engine

4. In an expert system, the _____C_____ contains all the data needed for understanding, formulating, and solving the problem.

a. domain
b. rule base

c. knowledge base
d. inference engine

5. An end user consults an expert system to gain information about a particular field or _____A_____.

a. domain
b. rule base

c. knowledge base
d. inference engine

ANSWERS

1. consultation
2. b.
3. d.

4. c.
5. a.

▄▄ GUIDE TO VP-EXPERT

The remainder of this chapter focuses on how to use the educational version of VP-Expert 2.0. VP-Expert is a rule-based expert system development tool by Paperback Software that allows quick and easy expert system development.

Some of the directions for using VP-Expert vary depending on whether the computer has two floppy disk drives or a hard disk drive. The directions in this section are written for computers with two floppy disk drives. VP-Expert will run on IBM PCs and compatibles with 384K or more RAM.

Each of the following sections introduces one or more features of VP-Expert. At the end of each section there is a hands-on activity called Your Turn. Do not try any of the hands-on activities until you have carefully read the section preceding it.

From now on the key marked ↵ is referred to as the <Return> key (sometimes it is also called the <Enter> key). Throughout this chapter, when instructed to press the <Return> key, press the key marked ↵.

The following symbols and typefaces appear throughout the chapter. This is what they mean:

What is the name of the example file? (prompt) **Error in line 15** (message) Select **Induce** (menu option) Type: **vpx** (text)	Boldface text indicates words or phrases that appear on the computer screen. The text could be a prompt, message, name of a menu option, or text that the user is typing.
Type: IF color = red	Magenta-colored characters indicate text that is to be entered.
Press <Return>	The angle brackets (<>) are used to signify a specific key on the keyboard. Press the key whose name is enclosed by the angle brackets.
ACTIONS	All capital letters indicate key words. Key words are commands to VP-Expert.

There are three ways to make a menu selection using VP-Expert. One way is to press the first letter of the option name. For example, if you wanted to select the **Induce** option from VP-Expert's Main Menu, you would press the letter **I.** The second method is to move the highlighted bar, using <→> or <←>, to the option you wish to select and press <Return>. Finally, you can press the function key that corresponds to the selection you wish to make. For example, the number **2** appears in front of the **Induce** option on VP-Expert's Main Menu. You could select the **Induce** option by pressing the <F2> function key. When the directions in this and the following chapter instruct you to "Select" an option, use the method you prefer to make the appropriate selection.

▆ GETTING STARTED WITH VP-EXPERT

Before you can use VP-Expert on a computer system with two floppy disk drives, you need to copy a file from the VP-Expert Sample Files Disk that comes with this book to your data disk. Use a blank, formatted disk for your data disk. Complete the following directions to copy the file onto your data disk.

1. Insert the DOS disk into drive A. Close the disk drive door. Turn on the computer.
2. When asked to type the date, enter the current date (for example 9-28-89) and press <Return>. When asked to enter the correct time, either enter the time using a twenty-four-hour format (14:26:24) and press <Return>, or simply press <Return> to bypass the time-set feature.
3. When the system prompt A> appears on the screen, take the DOS disk out of drive A. Place the VP-Expert Sample Files disk that comes with this book into drive A. Place your blank, formatted disk that will be your data disk into drive B.

  ▪ Type: **Copy A:VPXI.EXE B:**
  ▪ Press <Return>

The message "1 File(s) copied" along with the A> prompt should appear. When this message appears, you know the file has been copied and you can take the disks out of the disk drives and turn the computer and monitor off.

To **boot** the computer and start VP-Expert, you need a DOS disk (2.xx or 3.xx), the VP-Expert Program Disk that comes with this book, and a formatted disk that will serve as your data disk.

Booting the computer involves loading an operating system into the computer's main memory. If a two-disk-drive system is used, the program disk is inserted in drive A and the data disk is inserted in drive B. Follow these steps to boot the computer and start VP-Expert:

1. Insert the DOS disk into drive A. Close the disk drive door. Turn on the computer.
2. When asked to type the date, enter the current date (for example 9-28-1989) and press <Return>. When asked to enter the correct time, either enter the time using a twenty-four-hour format (14:26:24) and press <Return>, or simply press <Return> to bypass the time-set feature.
3. When the system prompt A> appears on the screen, remove the DOS disk from drive A. Insert the VP-Expert Program Disk into drive A and close the disk drive door.

4. Insert your data disk into drive **B.** Close the disk drive door.

5. Type **vpx** and press <Return>.

After typing **vpx** and pressing <Return>, the VP-Expert opening screen appears (see Figure G–1).

Whenever you first begin working with the VP-Expert program, you must switch the working directory from drive A to drive B. If you do not switch directories, the program will try to save files onto the disk in drive A. There is not enough room on the VP-Expert Program Disk in drive A to store any files, so you must remember to switch directories. Follow these steps to change the working directory:

1. One of the options on the VP-Expert Main Menu is **Path.** There are three methods by which you can select the Path option: press **P** for **Path,** press <→> to move the highlighted bar to **Path** and then press <Return>, or press the <F7> function key.

■ Select **Path**

2. The message **What is the new path?** appears.

■ Type **B:**
■ Press <Return>

The VP-Expert Main Menu returns to the screen.

■ Your Turn

Turn on and boot your computer. Start VP-Expert. Change the working directory to drive B. Your screen should match Figure G–1.

FIGURE G–1

VP-Expert's Main Menu

```
              V P - E X P E R T
                 Version 2.01
              Copyright (c) 1988
                 Brian Sawyer
              All Rights Reserved

    Editor Portion Copyright (c) 1984, 1985, 1987, Idea Ware Inc.

                    Educational Version
            Published by Paperback Software International




    1Help      2Induce    3Edit     4Consult   5Tree      6FileName 7Path      8Quit
    1Help 2Go 3Whatif 4Variable 5Rule 7Set 8Quit
```

▨ GETTING HELP WITH VP-EXPERT

VP-Expert has a very useful Help System that provides help as to how to use the program. The Help System is itself a knowledge base. The Help System can be activated at any point by pressing the <F1> function key. VP-Expert also has the ability to "observe" a user as he or she develops a knowledge base. If the user repeatedly has difficulty with the same area of development, VP-Expert automatically offers "advice" based on its observation of the mistakes being made.

▨ Your Turn

In this hands-on exercise you are going to practice using the VP-Expert Help System.

1. VP-Expert's Main Menu should still be on your screen. Notice that the first option on the menu is **Help.** Remember, there are three methods by which you can select the Help option: press **H** for **Help,** press <←> to move the highlighted bar to **Help** and then press <Return>, or press the <F1> function key.

   ■ Select **Help**

The message **Insert 'Sample Files' Disk in Drive B and Press ENTER or Press Esc to Quit** appears. Take your data disk out of drive B and place the VP-Expert Sample Files disk that comes with this book into drive B and press <Return>.

   The Help Screen for VP-Expert's Main Menu appears. The Help Screen explains each of the selections from the Main Menu. Read this screen.

2. Notice the menu at the bottom of the screen. The first option on the menu indicates you can scroll up a line at a time by pressing the up arrow key or scroll down a line at a time by pressing the down arrow key. The second option indicates you can scroll up a page at a time by pressing <PgUp> or scroll down a page at a time by pressing <PgDn>. The third and fourth options indicate that pressing <Home> takes you to the top of the current file and pressing <End> takes you to the bottom of the current file. The fifth option indicates pressing <Esc> accesses more help topics. The final option indicates that pressing **P** enables you to print.

   ■ Press <Esc>

3. A list of VP-Expert's Help topics appears on the screen. You can move through the list either by pressing <↑>, <↓>, <Home>, or <End>.

   ■ Press <End>

The highlighted bar moves to the bottom of the list.

   ■ Press <Home>

The highlighted bar moves to the top of the list.

   ■ Press <↓> until **CONFIDENCE FACTORS** is highlighted.
   ■ Press <Return>

A Help Screen describing confidence factors appears. Read the screen. Notice at the end of the screen it says, **See also TRUTHTHRESH.**

- Press <Esc>
- Press <PgDn> until you see **TRUTHTHRESH**
- Highlight **TRUTHTHRESH**
- Press <Return>

Read the Help Screen that appears and then press <Esc>

4. Continue looking up topics on the Help System. When you have finished, press <Esc> to exit from the Help System and return to VP-Expert's Main Menu. Take the Sample Files Disk out of drive B and place your data disk into drive B.

■ CREATING A KNOWLEDGE BASE FROM AN INDUCTION TABLE

Perhaps the easiest way to create a knowledge base is to use VP-Expert's ability to automatically generate a knowledge base from an induction table. An induction table is a table that represents examples in the form of rows and columns. The following is an example of an induction table:

Age	Weight (lbs.)	Calcium (mg.)
1	13	360
1	20	540
3	29	800
6	44	800
10	62	800
14	100	1200
16	130	1200

Look at this induction table closely. The purpose of the table is to recommend daily dietary allowances of calcium. The recommendation is based on the age and weight of the child. The table is comprised of rows and columns. The top row provides column headings. These headings define the variables. The column furthest to the right contains the goal variable, that is, the variable determined by the two preceding variables.

As was mentioned earlier, VP-Expert is a rule-based expert system. If this table were to be used as part of a knowledge base, it would have to be translated into rules. This table would be translated as follows:

IF *Age* is 1 and *Weight* is 13 THEN *Calcium* is 360 mg.

IF *Age* is 1 and *Weight* is 20 THEN *Calcium* is 540 mg.

IF *Age* is 3 and *Weight* is 29 THEN *Calcium* is 800 mg.

IF *Age* is 6 and *Weight* is 44 THEN *Calcium* is 800 mg.

IF *Age* is 10 and *Weight* is 62 THEN *Calcium* is 800 mg.

IF *Age* is 14 and *Weight* is 100 THEN *Calcium* is 1200 mg.

IF *Age* is 16 and *Weight* is 130 THEN *Calcium* is 1200 mg.

VP-Expert's Induce command automatically creates a knowledge base from an induction table. That is, it automatically interprets a table into a set of rules such as the ones above. The knowledge base created using the Induce command is limited in its complexity, but for some applications, the Induce command is the most efficient way to start a knowledge base.

An induction table can be created using several different methods. It can be created in the text editor that comes with VP-Expert, in a dBASE database file, or in a VP-Planner Plus spreadsheet file. In the next Your Turn exercise you will create an induction table using VP-Expert's text editor.

Creating an induction table using the text editor that comes with VP-Expert is not difficult. VP-Expert's Editor is similar to a word processor. Creating an induction table is simply a matter of entering text in columns. Table G–1 lists the editing commands used in the VP-Expert Editor.

■ Your Turn

In this hands-on exercise you are going to create an induction table using VP-Expert's text editor. Before you begin, check to make sure your data disk is in drive B. Also, be sure that the VPXI.EXE file has been copied from the VP-Expert Sample File Disk onto this data disk.

1. First, you are going to change the working directory to drive B.

■ Select **Path**
■ Type **B:**
■ Press <Return>

TABLE G—1

VP-Expert Editing Commands

Key	Function
<↓>, <↑>	Moves the cursor down or up a line.
<←>, <→>	Moves the cursor left or right one character.
<Ctrl><←>	Moves the cursor left one word.
<Ctrl><→>	Moves the cursor right one word.
<PgUp>	Moves the cursor to the preceding screen.
<PgDn>	Moves the cursor to the following screen.
<Ctrl><PgUp>	Moves the cursor to the beginning of the file.
<Ctrl><PgDn>	Moves the cursor to the end of the file.
<Home>	Moves the cursor to the beginning of the line.
<End>	Moves the cursor to the end of the line.
<Ins>	Turns the insert mode on or off. The default setting is on.
<Tab>	Moves the cursor to the next tab stop.
<Shift><Tab>	Moves the cursor back one tab stop.
<Ctrl><Return>	Pressing these two keys together adds a blank line of space.
<Del>	Deletes the character at the cursor position.
<Ctrl><Y>	Deletes the entire line in which the cursor is located.
<Alt><F6>	Saves the file and exits from the Editor.
<Alt><F8>	Abandons the file without saving or updating it.
<Alt><F5>	Updates the file without exiting from the Editor.

VP-Expert's Main Menu should return to your screen.

- Select **Induce**

The VP-Expert Induce Menu appears.

- Select **Create**

The prompt **What is the name of the examples file?** appears. You need to provide a file name for the induction table file.

- Type: **Media**
- Press <Return>

The VP-Expert Editor appears. Your screen should look like Figure G–2.

2. VP-Expert's text editor works much like a word processor. The blank space is the editing window into which you will enter text. The flashing box in the upper left corner is the cursor. The name of the file is in the upper right corner. Notice that VP-Expert automatically added the extension **tbl** to the file name **Media.** The triangles at the bottom of the screen indicate tab stops, which are set for every five spaces.

You are going to type in an induction table to help someone decide the best advertising media to be used based on the following criteria:

Audience to be reached: a small, selective audience (for example, people who fall within a certain age group), or a broad, mass audience

Budget: Small—under $10,000; Medium—$10,000–$50,000; Large—over $50,000

- Type: Audience
- Press <Tab> twice

Creating an Induction Table

```
                                    Editing: New File b:\media.tbl
 -













 +   ▲     ▲     ▲     ▲     ▲     ▲     ▲     ▲     ▲    ▲     ▲     ▲     ▲     ▲
 Insert On     Document Off                           Boldface Off Underline Off
    1Help     2Reform 3TabSet 4Margin  5Center6        7Bold  8Ulin   9Dcumn10Print
```

- **Type:** Budget
- **Press <Tab> once**
- **Type:** Media
- **Press <Return>**

A left triangle appears at the end of the line, and the cursor moves to the next line. The left triangle indicates that the <Return> key was pressed.

3. You have now entered the column headings. Complete the induction table by typing the following under each column heading. When typing in two-word entries, such as *Mass_Market*, be sure to include the underscore between the two words. (The underscore or underline is found on top of the hyphen on the right side of the first row of keys on the keyboard.) When finished, your screen should look like Figure G–3.

Audience	Budget	Media
Mass_Market	Large	Television
Selective	Small	Direct_Mail
Selective	Medium	Radio
Selective	Large	Magazine
Mass_Market	Medium	Outdoor_Billboards
Mass_Market	Small	Newspaper

When you have finished, look over your induction table carefully and make sure it looks like Figure G–3. The entries must be correct and lined up in the proper columns. Make sure there are no spelling mistakes and that you included the underscore in *Mass_Market*, *Direct_Mail* and *Outdoor_Billboards*. Make any necessary corrections. When you are satisfied with your induction table, press <Alt><F6> to save it.

FIGURE G–3

The MEDIA Induction Table

```
                                        Editing: New File b:\media.tbl

   Audience       Budget       Media◄
   Mass_Market    Large        Television◄
   Selective      Small        Direct_Mail◄
   Selective      Medium       Radio◄
   Selective      Large        Magazine◄
   Mass_Market    Medium       Outdoor_Billboards◄
   Mass_Market    Small        Newspaper◄
```

```
+   ▲     ▲     ▲     ▲     ▲    ▲    ▲    ▲    ▲    ▲    ▲    ▲    ▲    ▲   +
Insert On      Document Off                     Boldface Off Underline Off
   1Help    2Reform 3TabSet 4Margin 5Center6       7Bold 8Ulin  9Dcumn10Print
```

- The prompt **Save as "b:\media.tbl" (Y or N)?** appears.
- Type: **Y**

4. The Induce Menu appears. You now want to create a knowledge base from your MEDIA induction table.

- Select **Text**

The message **Insert 'Sample Files' Disk in Drive B and Press ENTER or Press Esc to Quit appears.** Your data disk onto which you copied the VPXI.EXE file should be in drive B. DO NOT REMOVE IT TO REPLACE IT WITH THE SAMPLE FILES DISK. Leave your data disk in drive B and press <Return>.

The prompt **What is the name of the example file?** appears. The MEDIA file should be listed and highlighted on the screen.

- Press <Return> to select the MEDIA file

Next, the prompt **What is the name of the rule file to create?** appears. The MEDIA file with the new file extension KBS (for *knowledge base*) appears on the screen and is highlighted. You are going to name the knowledge base that you are creating from your induction table **MEDIA.KBS.**

- Press <Return> to select **MEDIA.KBS**

5. The Induce Menu returns to the screen.

- Select **Quit**

The VP-Expert Main Menu returns to the screen. Now you are going to run a consultation using the MEDIA.KBS knowledge base.

- Select **Consult**

The prompt **What is the name of the knowledge base you want to use?** appears. The MEDIA file name appears on the screen and is highlighted.

- Press <Return>

Three boxes should appear on your screen. The top box is called the **consultation window.** This is where the actual consultation will take place. The window in the lower left corner is called the **rules window.** The rules window will display the processing performed by the inference engine during the consultation. The window in the lower right corner is called the **results window.** The results window displays conclusions reached during the consultation.

- Press G for **Go**

Your screen should look like Figure G–4. The system is asking the end user if the advertising is for the mass market or for a selective audience. There are three steps required to select an option. First, use the left and right arrow keys to highlight the desired response. Next, press <Return> to select the highlighted response and, finally, press <End> to move on to the next question.

- Press <→> to select **Selective**
- Press <Return>
- Press <End>

```
What is the value of Audience?
 Mass_Market              Selective




┌─────────────────────────────────────────────┐  ┌──────────────────────────┐
│ Finding Media                                 │  │                          │
│ Testing 0                                     │  │                          │
│ RULE 0 IF                                     │  │                          │
│ Audience = Mass_Market AND                    │  │                          │
│ Budget = Large                                │  │                          │
│ THEN                                          │  │                          │
│ Media = Television CNF 100                    │  │                          │
│ Finding Audience                              │  │                          │
└─────────────────────────────────────────────┘  └──────────────────────────┘

↑↓→←Enter to select    END to complete    /Q to Quit    ? for Unknown
```

FIGURE G—4

Running a Consultation

The next question, regarding the size of the budget, appears.

- Press <→> twice to select **Medium**
- Press <Return>
- Press <End>

The result of the consultation, **Media = Radio,** appears in the results window. Notice that the rules processed by the inference engine appear in the rules window. Also notice that **CNF 100** appears in both the rules window and the results window. This indicates the confidence factor, and in this case the confidence factor is 100%. Try another consultation.

- Press <Return> to start the consultation again
- Press <Return> to select **Mass_Market**
- Press <End>
- Press <→> to select **Small**
- Press <Return>
- Press <End>

This time the system advised using the newspaper as the advertising media. Continue experimenting with making consultations. When you have finished, press <F8> to quit. The VP-Expert Main Menu should return to your screen. If you want to quit at this point, select **Quit** from the VP-Expert Main Menu. When the A> system prompt appears on the screen, remove your disks from the disk drives and turn off the computer and the monitor.

▓▓ UNDERSTANDING THE PARTS OF A KNOWLEDGE BASE

A knowledge base created with VP-Expert consists of three parts: the AC-TIONS block, rules, and statements. In addition, a fourth element, called clauses, is found in the ACTIONS block, as well as in rules. Each of these knowledge base elements are explained in the following sections.

The ACTIONS Block

The ACTIONS block defines the problems of the consultation. That is, it tells the inference engine what it needs to find out. This information is conveyed to the inference engine in FIND clauses. FIND clauses instruct VP-Expert to find the value or values for one or more variables. The FIND clause actually sets up the "goal" that is to be achieved by the consultation. For this reason, the variable listed in the FIND clause is called the **goal variable.** The ACTIONS block also determines the order in which the variables are to be found.

The ACTIONS block is comprised of three elements:

- the key word "ACTIONS"
- clauses
- a semicolon

The ACTIONS block must begin with the key word "ACTIONS." After the key word "ACTIONS" comes one or more clauses, one of which must be a FIND clause. Finally, the ACTIONS block must end with a semicolon.

Rules

Rules are always stated as IF/THEN propositions. The actual knowledge of an expert system is contained within the rules. Rules enable the system to make decisions; they are comprised of four elements:

- the rule name
- the rule premise
- the rule conclusion
- a semicolon

Each rule must begin with the key word "RULE," followed by a label or rule name. Each rule in a knowledge base has to have a different name. The name can be made up of letters, numbers, and the symbols _$%^|. Often, it is easiest to use numbers (0,1,2,3, and so on) as rule names.

Following the rule name is the rule premise. The rule premise, which is always introduced with the key word "IF," states one or more conditions that compare the contents of a variable to a value. The following six comparisons can be made:

=	is equal to
<	is less than
<=	is less than or equal to
>	is greater than
>=	is greater than or equal to
<>	is not equal to

An example of a rule premise is, IF gpa >= 3.3.

A rule premise can contain up to ten conditions. Conditions are added to the rule premise by using the logical operators AND and OR. The following conditions could be added to the previous example of a rule premise:

```
IF gpa >= 3.3 AND
income < 12000 OR
family > 4
```

When the AND condition is used, both statements must be true; when the OR statement is used, one or both conditions must be true. Therefore, in order for this rule premise to "pass"—that is, to be considered as true—the value for the "gpa" variable must be greater than or equal to 3.3 *and* either the value for the "income" variable must be less than 12000, *or* the value for the "family" variable must be greater than 4, or both.

Every rule premise must be followed by a rule conclusion. Rule conclusions begin with the key word THEN and must contain at least one equation, the purpose of which is to assign a value to a variable when the IF premise is true. For example, in the following rule:

```
RULE 1
    IF gpa >= 3.3 AND
    income < 12000 OR
    family > 4
    THEN scholarship = eligible
```

The value "eligible" is to be assigned to the variable "scholarship" when the premise "IF gpa >= 3.3 AND income < 12000 OR family > 4 is evaluated as true.

Statements

Statements provide further directions to the expert system. The purpose of most VP-Expert statements is to assign specific characteristics to variables. Three examples of statements are ASK statements, CHOICES statements, and PLURAL statements. The purpose of these three types of statements is explained in this section. A list of all of VP-Expert's statements appears at the end of Section H.

The ASK statement assigns a value to all the variables the user must define. The following ASK statement

ASK gpa: "What is your grade point average?";

assigns to the variable "gpa" whatever value the user enters in response to this question.

CHOICES statements accompany ASK statements. When the question from an ASK statement is displayed during a consultation, values from the corresponding CHOICES statement are displayed as a menu. Look at the following example:

ASK gpa: "What is your grade point average?";
CHOICES gpa: under_3.3, 3.3_to_3.6, over_3.6;

Notice that both the ASK statement and the CHOICES statement include the same variable "gpa." A CHOICES statement must include a variable that is named in an ASK statement. In this example, when the consultation is run, the question "What is your grade point average?" will be displayed with the three options listed: under 3.3, 3.3, to 3.6, over 3.6. The end user selects an option by moving the highlighted bar over his or her choice and pressing the <Return> key. When the end user selects an option, that value is assigned to the appropriate variable. In this example, if the end user selected 3.3 to 3.6, the value for the variable gpa would become 3.3 to 3.6.

The PLURAL statement enables more than one value to be assigned to a variable. Look at the following example:

ASK Quarter: "What quarter will you be attending school?";
CHOICES Quarter: Fall, Winter, Spring, Summer;
PLURAL: Quarter;

During the consultation the question "What quarter will you be attending school?" would appear on the screen with the options Fall, Winter, Spring, and Summer listed below it. In this example, the end user could select more than one option because the PLURAL statement enables the variable "Quarter" to be assigned more than one value.

▤ Your Turn

In this exercise, you are going to look at the knowledge base that VP-Expert created from your MEDIA induction table.

1. If necessary, start the VP-Expert program. Remember to change the working directory to drive B. The VP-Expert Main Menu should be on your screen.

■ Select **FileName**

The prompt **What is the name of the knowledge base you want to use?** appears. The filename **MEDIA** appears and is highlighted.

■ Press <Return>

The VP-Expert Main Menu returns to the screen.

■ Select **Edit**

The MEDIA knowledge base appears. Your screen should look like Figure G–5.

2. You are now going to look over the MEDIA knowledge base carefully to familiarize yourself with the three parts of a knowledge base. Notice the first word in the knowledge base is the key word **ACTIONS.** This introduces the ACTIONS block which, you will remember, leads the consultation, telling the inference engine what to do. Here, the ACTIONS block is directing the consultation to **FIND Media,** that is find a value for the Media variable. Remember that the FIND clause establishes the goal of the consultation. In this example **Media** is the goal variable. The semicolon following the word **Media** indicates the end of the ACTIONS block.

The rules follow the ACTIONS block. Remember, the rules are the IF/THEN propositions that enable the system to make decisions. Each rule statement has a name, which is in this case a number. The first rule, **RULE 0,** states, if the value for Audience is equal to Mass—Market and the value for Budget is equal to Large, then the value for Media is equal to Television.

Use < ↓ > to scroll down through the entire knowledge base and read all five rules. Notice that each rule is introduced with a rule name, **RULE 0,**

```
                                        Editing: Old File media.kbs


     ACTIONS ◄
             FIND Media; ◄
     ◄
     ◄
     RULE 0 ◄
     IF      Audience=Mass_Market AND ◄
             Budget=Large ◄
     THEN    Media=Television; ◄
     ◄
     RULE 1 ◄
     IF      Audience=Selective AND ◄
             Budget=Small ◄
     THEN    Media=Direct_Mail; ◄
     ◄
     RULE 2 ◄
     IF      Audience=Selective AND ◄
             Budget=Medium ◄
     THEN    Media=Radio; ◄

     +    ▲    ▲    ▲     ▲    ▲    ▲     ▲    ▲    ▲     ▲    ▲    ▲     ▲    ▲
     Insert On    Document Off                      Boldface Off Underline Off
       1 Help    2 Reform 3 TabSet 4 Margin 5 Center 6         7 Bold 8 Ulin  9 Dcumn 10 Print
```

FIGURE G—5

Displaying the MEDIA Knowledge Base

RULE 1, RULE 2, and so on, and that each rule ends with a semicolon. The semicolon has to be present to indicate to the system that the end of that particular rule has been reached.

3. After RULE 5 there is an ASK statement, followed by a CHOICE statement. Remember, statements provide further directions to the system. The statements say:

ASK Audience: "What is the value of Audience?";
CHOICES Audience: Mass_Market, Selective;

Remember when you ran the **MEDIA** consultation, the first question to appear in the consultation window was "What is the value of Audience?" This ASK statement directed the system to display that question in the consultation window. The CHOICES statement directed the system to list the options Mass Market and Selective. Whenever you made a selection of either Mass Market or Selective, that value was assigned to the variable "Audience."

If necessary, press < ↓ > to read the second ASK and CHOICES statements. The second ASK statement directs the system to display the question, "What is the value of Budget?" so that a value for the variable "Budget" can be established. The choices are Large, Small, and Medium. Based on the option selected by the end user, the system assigns a value to the Media variable.

4. Using the up and down arrow keys, read over the MEDIA knowledge base carefully. Make sure you understand the three parts of the knowledge base: the ACTIONS block, rules, and statements. When you are finished, press <Alt> <F8> and **Y** to quit without making any changes to the knowledge base. The VP-Expert Main Menu returns to the screen.

1. In VP-Expert, an induction table has to be translated into _RULES_ before it can be used as part of a knowledge base.

2. The problem to be solved by the consultation is defined in the _b_.

a. CHOICES statement   c. PLURAL statement
b. ACTIONS block   d. rule premise

3. (True or False?) Each rule in a knowledge base must have a rule name.

4. An ASK statement and its corresponding CHOICES statement both include the same _variable_.

5. (True or False?) The ACTIONS block and each rule in a knowledge base must end with a semicolon.

ANSWERS

1. rules
2. b.
3. True

4. variable
5. True

EDITING A KNOWLEDGE BASE

When using an induction table to create a knowledge base, the knowledge base that is created has an arbitrary format that is not particularly user friendly. For example, in the current MEDIA consultation, the end-user is asked **What is the value of Audience?** and **What is the value of Budget?** In addition, the result of the consultation appeared in the results window, but at the end of the consultation it was not readily apparent exactly what or where the result was. Someone not familiar with the knowledge base would have no idea of the meaning of such a question as "What is the value of Audience?" nor would they know where to look to find the result of the consultation.

A knowledge base created with the Induce command can easily be edited to make it more user friendly. Before editing a knowledge base, however, you must be familiar with VP-Expert's formatting rules. Table G–2 describes these rules.

Your Turn

In this hands-on exercise you are going to refine the MEDIA knowledge base to make it more user friendly.

1. The VP-Expert Main Menu should be on your screen.

■ Select **Edit**

If necessary, highlight **Media** as the name of the knowledge base you want to use and press <Return>. The MEDIA knowledge base should be on your screen.

2. First you are going to edit the ASK statements so that they are easier to understand.

■ Press < ↓ > until it is in the line that begins **"ASK Audience . . ."**

Currently, the question that is displayed is "What is the value of Audience?" You want to change this question to "Is the advertising to appeal to a mass market or a selective audience?"

TABLE G—2

Rules for Formatting a VP-Expert Knowledge Base

- The ACTIONS block must begin with the word ACTIONS.
- Rule statements must begin with the key word RULE. The key word RULE must be followed by a label that cannot be longer than 20 characters.
- Rule labels, variable names, and values cannot contain spaces. The underline character can be used to indicate a space. VP-Expert will replace the underline character with a space in display text during a consultation.
- Rule labels and variable names may contain numbers, letters, and the special characters __$%ˆ and |. Variable names must begin with a letter.
- In statements that create onscreen messages, such as ASK and DISPLAY, the text that is to appear onscreen must be in double quotes.
- The ACTIONS block must end with a semicolon. Every rule and every statement must end with a semicolon. The only other place a semicolon can appear in a knowledge base is inside the double quotes surrounding display text.
- VP-Expert key words cannot be used as variable names. A complete list of VP-Expert key words is given at the end of Section H.
- Comment lines, which are notes that are to be ignored by the inference engine, can be included by beginning each comment line with an exclamation mark (!). Syntax errors will occur if the exclamation point is left out.

■ Press <→> until the cursor is on the *W* in *What*
■ Press <Ctrl> <T>

The word *What* is deleted.

■ Press <Ctrl> <T> twice

The word *is* is deleted. Continue pressing <Ctrl> <T> until the entire sentence is deleted. The opening double quotation mark should still be on the screen. If it is not, enter a double quotation mark.

■ Type: Is the advertising to appeal to a mass market or
■ Press <Ctrl> <Return>

You have to press <Ctrl> <Return> together, rather than just <Return>, to create a new line for the additional text to be entered.

■ Type: a selective audience?'';

Your screen should look like Figure G—6.

Check to make sure the question that is to be displayed on the screen is contained within double quotations marks and that there is a semicolon after the last quotation mark.

3. Using the arrow keys, move the cursor so that it is on the *W* in *What* in the sentence "What is the value of Budget?"

■ Press <Ctrl> <T> until the whole sentence is deleted

The opening double quotation mark should still be on the screen. If it is not, enter a double quotation mark.

■ Type: Is your advertising budget small (under $10,000),

```
◄
RULE 3 ◄
IF      Audience=Selective AND◄
        Budget=Large ◄
THEN    Media=Magazine; ◄
◄
RULE 4 ◄
IF      Audience=Mass_Market AND◄
        Budget=Medium◄
THEN    Media=Outdoor_Billboards; ◄
◄
RULE 5◄
IF      Audience=Mass_Market AND◄
        Budget=Small◄
THEN    Media=Newspaper; ◄
◄
ASK Audience: "Is the advertising to appeal to a mass market or ◄
a selective audience?'; ◄
```

```
+   ▲   ▲   ▲   ▲   ▲   ▲   ▲   ▲   ▲   ▲   ▲   ▲   ▲   ▲   ▲   ▲
Insert On    Document Off                    Boldface Off Underline Off
  1Help    2Reform 3TabSet4Margin 5Center6        7Bold 8Ulin  9Dcumn10Print
```

FIGURE G—6

Editing the MEDIA Knowledge
Base

■ Press <Ctrl> <Return>

■ **Type:** medium (between $10,000 and $50,000) or large (over $50,000)?'';

Again, check to make sure the question to be displayed on the screen is between quotation marks and that there is a semicolon after the last quotation mark.

■ Press <Alt> <F6> to save the revised knowledge base

The prompt **Save as "b:\media.kbs" (Y or N)?** appears

■ Press **Y**

The VP-Expert Main Menu returns to the screen.

CHECKING FOR ERRORS IN THE KNOWLEDGE BASE

If anything is entered incorrectly in the knowledge base, an error message will appear when you try to run a consultation. Following is an example of a typical error message:

Missing ';'
(Press any key to go on)
Error in line 15

This message indicates that line 15 in the knowledge base is missing a mandatory semicolon. When you press any key to continue, the knowledge base will appear on your screen with the cursor in the line indicated in the error message. In this example, the cursor would appear in line 15. A summary of common VP-Expert error messages is found at the end of Section H. Refer to this summary to help you correct your mistakes.

VP-Expert can only make an educated guess at the line number where the error occurs. Look over the line where the cursor appears, carefully. If you cannot find the error in that line, check previous lines for errors. Table G–3 will help you find some common knowledge base mistakes. Once the knowledge base is entered correctly, the three consultation windows appear and the message **File loaded** is displayed.

■ Your Turn

You are going to check your edited MEDIA knowledge base to make sure there are no errors in it.

1. The VP-Expert Main Menu should be on your screen.

■ Select **Consult**

If you made the editing changes correctly, the three consulting windows appear and **media.kbs loaded** is in the upper left corner. If you get an error message, read the error message carefully, press any key, and see if you can correct your error. Refer to the Summary of Common VP-Expert Error Messages at the end of Section H for help.

2. Once your knowledge base is loaded, run a consultation to see the changes you made to the file.

■ Select **Go**

Now the question in the consultation window reads, **Is the advertising to appeal to a mass market or a selective audience?**

■ Press <Return> to select **Mass_Market**
■ Press <End>

Your edited second question appears.

■ Press <Return> to select **Large**
■ Press <End>

TABLE G—3

Checklist for Finding Errors within a Knowledge Base

● The ACTIONS block ends with a semicolon.
● Each rule ends with a semicolon.
● Each statement ends with a semicolon.
● A semicolon does not appear anywhere in the knowledge base other than at the end of an ACTIONS block, at the end of a rule, at the end of a statement, or within the double quotation marks surrounding text that is to be displayed during a consultation, that is, text in an ASK statement, DISPLAY clause, etc.
● All VP-Expert key words must be spelled correctly.
● Rule labels, variable names, and values can only contain letters, numbers, and the characters __$%^ and |. There can be no spaces in rule labels, variable names, or values.
● VP-Expert key words cannot be used as variable names.

The result of the consultation, **Television,** still is not very easy to find. In the next section, you'll learn how to insert a DISPLAY clause to display the result of the consultation in a more user-friendly fashion.

■ Select **Quit**

The VP-Expert Main Menu returns to the screen.

■ VP-EXPERT CLAUSES

In the discussion on the elements that comprise a knowledge base, it was mentioned that the fourth element, clauses, appears in the ACTIONS block and in the rules of the knowledge base. Clauses provide further instructions to the knowledge base.

The DISPLAY Clause

The DISPLAY clause can be used both in the ACTIONS block and in rules. The DISPLAY key word introduces text that is to appear on the screen during a consultation. DISPLAY clauses that occur in the ACTIONS block will always appear in the order that they occur in the block. When used in rules, DISPLAY clauses appear only if the rule with which they are associated is evaluated as true. In the following example,

RULE 1
IF gpa > = 3.3 AND
income < 12000 OR
family > 4
THEN scholarship = eligible
DISPLAY "The candidate is eligible for a scholarship.";

If Rule 1 evaluates as true, then the sentence that appears in quotes after the key word DISPLAY will appear on the screen during the consultation. The text to be displayed must always appear between double quotation marks in the knowledge base.

■ Your Turn

In this exercise you are going to add two DISPLAY clauses to the ACTIONS block.

1. The VP-Expert Main Menu should be on your screen.

■ Select **Edit**

If necessary, select **Media** in response to the prompt **What is the name of the knowledge base you want to use?** The MEDIA knowledge base appears.

2. First you want to add a DISPLAY clause that will help to introduce the consultation.

■ Press <→> until the cursor is on the triangle that follows the *S* in *ACTIONS*
■ Press <Ctrl> <Return>

There should now be a line of space between the key word **ACTIONS** and the **FIND** clause.

- Press <Tab>
- Type: DISPLAY "What is the best advertising media for your product?
- Press <Ctrl> <Return>
- Type: To find out, press any key to begin the consultation.~"

Make sure you enter the ~ symbol after the period and before the quotations mark. When used in a DISPLAY clause this symbol causes the program to pause until a key has been pressed.

3. Now you are going to add a DISPLAY clause that will indicate to the end user the result of the consultation.

- Press < ↓ > until the cursor is at the beginning of a line of space following the **FIND** clause.
- Press <Tab>
- Type: DISPLAY "An appropriate advertising media for your product is {Media}.";

Make sure the variable **Media** is contained within the curly brackets. When the consultation is run, the value for **Media** will appear in place of {*Media*}.

4. Notice that you included a semicolon at the end of the DISPLAY clause. This semicolon marks the new end of the ACTIONS block. Therefore, you have to delete the original semicolon that appeared after the **FIND** clause.

- Move the cursor to the semicolon following the word *Media* in the **FIND** clause
- Press <Del>

5. You have now added the two DISPLAY clauses. Your screen should look like Figure G–7.
Check to make sure you entered the DISPLAY clauses correctly.

- Press <Alt> <F6> to save the edited knowledge base

The prompt **Save as "b:\media.kbs" (Y or N)?** appears.

- Type: **Y**

The VP-Expert Main Menu appears.

6. Now you want to run another consultation to see what changes the DISPLAY clauses made.

- Select **Consult**
- Select **Go**

Your DISPLAY clause, "What is the best advertising media for your product? To find out, press any key to begin the consultation." should appear on the screen.

- Press any key.

The first consultation question appears.

- Select **Mass_Market**
- Press <Return>
- Press <End>

```
ACTIONS◄
DISPLAY "What is the best advertising media for your product?◄
To find out, press any key to begin consultation.~"◄
        FIND Media◄
    DISPLAY "An appropriate advertising media for your product is {Media}.";◄
◄
RULE 0◄
IF      Audience=Mass_Market AND◄
        Budget=Large◄
THEN    Media=Television;◄
◄
RULE 1◄
IF      Audience=Selective AND◄
        Budget=Small◄
THEN    Media=Direct_Mail;◄
◄
RULE 2◄
IF      Audience=Selective AND◄

+    ▲    ▲    ▲    ▲    ▲    ▲    ▲    ▲    ▲    ▲    ▲    ▲    ▲    ▲
Insert On    Document Off                    Boldface Off Underline Off
  1Help    2Reform 3TabSet4Margin 5Center6        7Bold  8Ulin  9Dcumn10Print
```

FIGURE G—7

The DISPLAY Clause

The second consultation question appears.

- ▪ Select **Small**
- ▪ Press <Return>
- ▪ Press <End>

The second DISPLAY clause appears with the value "Newspaper" inserted in place of {Media}. If you wish, run a few more consultations to see the effect the DISPLAY clauses have. When you are finished, exit from the consultation and return to VP-Expert's Main Menu.

▆ ADDING VARIABLES TO THE KNOWLEDGE BASE

The more variables a knowledge base contains, the greater is the breadth of information the knowledge base can impart. When variables are added to a knowledge base, the original knowledge base has to be edited, ASK and CHOICES statements must be added, and the number of rules increases.

Block commands help to make the process of adding variables to the knowledge base easier. Table G–4 lists the block commands that can be used with VP-Expert's text editor.

▪ Your Turn

In this exercise you are going to add a variable to the MEDIA knowledge base. Adding the variable is going to double the number of rules.

1. The VP-Expert Main Menu should be on your screen.

- ▪ Select **Edit**

TABLE G—4

VP-Expert Block Commands

<Ctrl> <F3>	Pressing <Ctrl> <F3> marks the beginning of the block.
<Ctrl> <F4>	Pressing <Ctrl> <F4> marks the end of the block.
<Ctrl> <F7>	Pressing <Ctrl> <F7> copies a marked block.
<Ctrl> <F5>	Cancels a marked block.

If necessary, select **Media** as the name of the file you wish to edit. The MEDIA knowledge base appears on your screen.

2. You want to add a variable to the MEDIA knowledge base that allows the end user to identify the stage of the advertising campaign. That is, is this a new product just being introduced, or is it a product that has been on the market for awhile?

- Move the cursor to the very end of the knowledge base
- Type: ASK Stage: "At what stage is the product in its life cycle?";
- Press <Return>
- Type: CHOICES Stage: Introduction, Market_Maturity;

3. Next, you need to edit the rules and add new rules. Move the cursor to Rule 0. Currently, Rule 0 states:

RULE 0
IF   **Audience = Mass_Market AND**
         Budget = Large
THEN   **Media = Television**

You need to add a condition for the Stage variable. Move the cursor so that it is on the triangle following the word *Large* in Rule 0.

- Press the <Spacebar> once
- Type: AND
- Press <Ctrl> <Return>

The cursor should move into a blank line of space created by pressing <Ctrl> <Return>.

- Press <→> until the cursor is beneath the *B* in *Budget*
- Type: Stage = Introduction

Your screen should look like Figure G—8

4. Now you want to copy Rule 0 by blocking it.

- Move the cursor to the beginning of the blank line of space between Rule 0 and Rule 1
- Press <Ctrl> <Return> two times to create space
- Move the cursor to the *R* in *RULE 0*
- Press <Ctrl> <F3> to begin marking the block
- Move the cursor to the end of Rule 0

All of Rule 0 should be highlighted.

```
ACTIONS◄
DISPLAY "What is the best advertising media for your product?◄
To find out, press any key to begin consultation.~"
        FIND Media◄
    DISPLAY "An appropriate advertising media for your product is {Media}.";◄
◄
RULE 0◄
IF      Audience=Mass_Market AND◄
        Budget=Large AND◄
        Stage=Introduction◄
THEN    Media=Television;◄
◄
RULE 1◄
IF      Audience=Selective AND◄
        Budget=Small◄
THEN    Media=Direct_Mail;◄
◄
RULE 2 ◄
```

```
+    ▲   ▲   ▲    ▲    ▲    ▲    ▲    ▲    ▲     ▲     ▲    ▲     ▲    ▲
Insert On     Document Off                         Boldface Off Underline Off
  1Help   2Reform 3TabSet4Margin 5Center6       7Bold   8Ulin   9Dcumn10Print
```

FIGURE G—8

Adding Variables to the MEDIA Knowledge Base

■ Press <Ctrl> <F4> to end marking the block

■ Move the cursor to the beginning of the two lines beneath the marked block

■ Press <Ctrl> <F7> to copy the block

A copy of Rule 0 should appear underneath the original Rule 0

■ Press <Ctrl> <F5> to cancel the block

5. Now you want to edit this rule you just copied. First you must give it a new rule name.

■ Move the cursor to the triangle following *RULE 0* of the *copied* block

■ Type: A

Now you want to replace the value **Introduction** with the value **Market__ Maturity.**

■ Move the cursor to the *I* in *Introduction* in Rule 0A

■ Press <Ctrl> <T> to delete the word

■ Type: Market__Maturity

■ Move the cursor to the *T* in *Television* in Rule 0A

■ Press <Ctrl> <T>

■ Type: National__Newspaper;

Don't forget to type the semicolon to end the new RULE 0A.

6. You should now be familiar with the editing process. Remember, if you are inserting an entire line, you must press <Ctrl> <Return> to insert a blank line of space for the new line. Edit Rule 1 so it looks like the following (the changes you have to make appear in italicized text):

RULE 1

IF   Audience = Selective AND
                Budget = Small *AND*
                Stage = Market__Maturity

THEN   Media = Direct__Mail;

Create a few lines of blank space after Rule 1 and copy Rule 1. Edit the *copy* of Rule 1 to look like the following:

RULE 1*A*

IF   Audience = Selective AND
                Budget = Small AND
                Stage = *Introduction*

THEN   Media = *Circulars;*

Don't forget the semicolon after **Circulars.**

7. Edit the remainder of the MEDIA knowledge base as follows. Use the Copy function to help you in your editing:

RULE 2

IF   Audience = Selective AND
                Budget = Medium *AND*
                Stage = Market__Maturity

THEN   Media = Radio;

RULE 2*A*

IF   Audience = Selective AND
                Budget = Medium AND
                Stage = *Introduction*

THEN   Media = *Promotional__Novelties;*

RULE 3

IF   Audience = Selective AND
                Budget = Large *AND*
                Stage = Introduction

THEN   Media = *Monthly__Magazine;*

RULE 3*A*

IF   Audience = Selective AND
                Budget = Large AND
                Stage = *Market__Maturity*

THEN   Media = *Catalogs;*

RULE 4*A*

IF   Audience = Mass__Market AND
                Budget = Medium *AND*
                Stage = Market__Maturity

THEN   Media = *Weekly__Magazine;*

RULE 4*A*

IF   Audience = Mass__Market AND
                Budget = Medium AND
                Stage = *Market__Maturity*

THEN   Media = *Weekly__Magazine;*

RULE 5

IF	Audience = Mass_Market AND
	Budget = Small *AND*
	Stage = Introduction
THEN	Media = *Local_Newspaper;*

RULE 5A

IF	Audience = Mass_Market AND
	Budget = Small AND
	Stage = *Market_Maturity*
THEN	Media = *Bus&Train_Cards;*

Look over the MEDIA knowledge base carefully. Make sure you included a semicolon after each rule. Check for spelling mistakes. When you are satisfied the MEDIA knowledge base has been edited correctly, press <Alt> <F6> to save it.

8. Run a new consultation to see the changes made by adding the new variables. If you get an error message, read it carefully and correct the error. Run a few consultations with the edited knowledge base. You will notice it takes longer to run the consultation because there is more information the knowledge base has to sort through. When you have finished running consultations, leave the knowledge base and select **Quit** from VP-Expert's Main Menu to exit from the program.

1. (True or False?) In knowledge base statements that create onscreen messages, such as ASK statements and DISPLAY statements, the text that is to appear onscreen must be within double quotation marks.

2. (True or False?) If there is an error in the knowledge base, VP-Expert always identifies the exact line number in which the error is located.

3. (True or False?) VP-Expert key words can be used as variable names.

4. (True or False?) When DISPLAY clauses are used in rules, the text is displayed onscreen only if the rule evaluates as true during the consultation.

5. When copying a block using VP-Expert's text editor, pressing _____ marks the beginning of the block.

a. <Ctrl> <F5>
b. <Ctrl> <F7>
c. <Ctrl> <F3>
d. <Ctrl> <F4>

ANSWERS

1. True
2. False
3. False
4. True
5. c.

▧ SUMMARY POINTS

■ Expert systems technology, the development of computer software that simulates human problem-solving abilities, is an area of research in the field of artificial intelligence.

■ A consultation takes place when an end user accesses information from an expert system.

- The knowledge base of an expert system is comprised of the domain knowledge and the rule base.
- The "brain" of an expert system is the inference engine. The inference engine is the component where reasoning is performed.
- Some of the areas in which expert systems are used include law, medicine, engineering, business, geology, financial analysis, and tax analysis.
- An induction table is a table that represents examples in the form of rows and columns. VP-Expert's Induce command converts an induction table into a workable knowledge base.
- There are four elements to a knowledge base: the ACTIONS block, rules, statements, and clauses. The ACTIONS block is comprised of the key word ACTIONS, clauses, and a semicolon. Rules are comprised of the rule name, the rule premise, the rule conclusion, and a semicolon. Statements and clauses are always introduced with a VP-Expert key word.

VP-EXPERT EXERCISES

To complete the following exercises you will need a DOS disk, the VP-Expert 2.0 program disk, and your data disk.

1. Start the VP-Expert program by doing the following:

- Insert the DOS disk into drive A. Close the disk drive door. Turn on the computer.
- Enter the date at the date prompt. Press <Return> at the time prompt.
- Remove the DOS disk from drive A. Insert the VP-Expert Program Disk into drive A and close the disk drive door.
- Insert your data disk into drive B. Close the disk drive door.
- Type **vpx** and press <Return>.
- Select **Path** and change the working directory to drive B.

The VP-Expert Main Menu should be on your screen.

2. You are going to create an expert system to help someone decide what kind of a car to purchase. The end user will be able to specify whether he or she is interested in a small, sporty, or compact car. In addition, the end user will specify a price range he or she can afford: under $6,000, between $6,000 and $10,000, or over $10,000. You will create the knowledge base from an induction table.

- Select **Induce**
- Select **Create**
- Type: **CAR**
- Press <Return>

A blank editing window appears for you to enter the induction table. Key in the induction table as follows:

Style	Cost	Car
Small	Under_6000	Chevrolet_Sprint
Small	6000–10000	Ford_Escort
Small	Over_10000	Toyota_Corolla
Sporty	Under_6000	None
Sporty	6000–10000	Pontiac_Fiero

Sporty	Over__10000	Mazda__RX-7
Compact	Under__6000	Dodge__Aries
Compact	6000–10000	Toyota__Camry
Compact	Over__10000	Volkswagen__Quantum

Look over your induction table carefully, checking for spelling mistakes. Make sure you included all the necessary underscores between words. When you are ready to save the induction table, press <Alt> <F6>. At the prompt **Save as "b:\car.tbl" (Y or N)?** type **Y**.

3. The Induce Menu should appear on your screen.

■ Select **Text**

The message **Insert 'Sample Files' Disk in Drive B and Press ENTER or Press Esc to Quit** appears. Your data disk onto which you copied the VPXI.EXE file should be in drive B. DO NOT REMOVE IT TO REPLACE IT WITH THE SAMPLE FILES DISK. Leave your data disk in drive B and press <Return>.

The prompt **What is the name of the examples file?** appears.

■ Select **Car**

The prompt **What is the name of the rules file to create?** appears.

■ Select **CAR.KBS**

4. You are now ready to run a consultation. The Induce Menu should be on your screen.

■ Select **Quit**

You may need to make the CAR knowledge base the active knowledge base. The VP-Expert Main Menu should be on your screen. To make the CAR file the active file, do the following:

■ Select **FileName**

The prompt **What is the name of the knowledge base you want to use?** appears.

■ Select **CAR**

The VP-Expert Main Menu returns to the screen.

■ Select **Consult**

The prompt **What is the name of the knowledge base you want to use?** appears.

■ Type: **Car**
■ Press <Return>

If there are any errors in the knowledge base, read the error message carefully and correct the mistake.

■ Select **Go** to begin the consultation

Run a couple of consultations. When you have finished, select **Quit**.

5. Now you want to edit the knowledge base so that it is more user friendly.

■ Select **Edit**

The CAR knowledge base appears. Move the cursor to the end of the knowledge base. Edit the two ASK statements to the following:

ASK Style: "What style of car do you prefer?";
ASK Cost: "Within which price range would you like the car to fall?";

Next, edit the ACTIONS block so that it looks like this:

>**ACTIONS**
>**DISPLAY "Interested in buying a new car?**
>**Press any key to help you pick one out.~"**
>**FIND Car**
>**DISPLAY "You might consider test driving a {Car}.";**

Save your edited CAR knowledge base and run another consultation to make sure all your changes are correct. When you are sure your knowledge base is working correctly, exit from VP-Expert.

■ VP-EXPERT PROBLEMS

To complete the following exercises you will need a DOS disk, the VP-Expert 2.0 program disk, and the Student File Disk that comes with this book.

1. Start the VP-Expert program by doing the following:

■ Insert the DOS disk into drive A. Close the disk drive door. Turn on the computer.
■ Enter the date at the date prompt. Press <Return> at the time prompt.
■ Remove the DOS disk from drive A. Insert the VP-Expert Program Disk into drive A and close the disk drive door.
■ Insert your data disk into drive B. Close the disk drive door.
■ Type **vpx** and press <Return>.
■ Select **Path** and change the working directory to drive B.

The VP-Expert Main Menu should be on your screen.

2. On the Student File Disk is a knowledge base named CAREER. It's purpose is to help people select a career in which they might be interested. Run a consultation using the CAREER knowledge base to become familiar with it.

3. Edit the ACTIONS block to the following. All the DISPLAY clauses must appear exactly as they do here, including where one line ends and the next line begins. For example, in the first DISPLAY clause, press <Ctrl><Return> after typing "... *to enter as a*" in order to insert a blank line and to move the cursor to the next line so you can type, "*career, press any key ...*" and so on.

>**ACTIONS**
>**DISPLAY "If you're beginning to consider what field to enter as a career, press any key to receive some suggestions.~"**
>**FIND job**
>**DISPLAY "You may want to further explore the job occupation of {job} as a possible career option.";**

4. Edit the ASK statements as follows:

> **ASK environment: "Is your preference to work in an office, work outdoors, or work at a job that includes a lot of travel?";**
> **ASK salary: "What is the range of salary you expect to receive?";**

5. You want to add a variable to the CAREER knowledge base. You want to give the end user the option of selecting law or medicine as an area of interest. This requires extensive editing of the CAREER knowledge base. First add the following ASK and CHOICES statement to the end of the CAREER knowledge base:

ASK field: "In which one of the following fields are you interested?";
CHOICES field: law, medicine;

6. Edit the rules in the CAREER knowledge base to look like the following. Use VP-Expert's block commands:

RULE 0
IF   **environment = office AND**
        salary = 10000–15000 AND
        field = law
THEN **job = legal_secretary;**

RULE 1
IF   **environment = office AND**
        salary = 15000–20000 AND
        field = law
THEN **job = court_reporter;**

RULE 2
IF   **environment = office AND**
        salary = 20000–25000 AND
        field = law
THEN **job = paralegal;**

RULE 2A
IF   **environment = office AND**
        salary = 10000–15000 AND
        field = medicine
THEN **job = medical_secretary;**

RULE 2B
IF   **environment = office AND**
        salary = 15000–20000 AND
        field = medicine
THEN **job = medical_assistant;**

RULE 2C
IF   **environment = office AND**
        salary = 20000–25000 AND
        field = medicine
THEN **job = physical_therapist;**

RULE 3

IF   environment = outdoors AND
salary = 10000–15000 AND
field = law

THEN   job = security_guard;

RULE 4

IF   environment = outdoors AND
salary = 15000–20000 AND
field = law

THEN   job = park_ranger;

RULE 5

IF   environment = outdoors AND
salary = 20000–25000 AND
field = law

THEN   job = conservationist;

RULE 5A

IF   environment = outdoors AND
salary = 10000–15000 AND
field = medicine

THEN   job = emergency_medical_technician;

RULE 5B

IF   environment = outdoors AND
salary = 15000–20000 AND
field = medicine

THEN   job = zoologist;

RULE 5C

IF   environment = outdoors AND
salary = 20000–25000 AND
field = medicine

THEN   job = veterinarian;

RULE 6

IF   environment = travel AND
salary = 10000–15000 AND
field = law

THEN   job = reporter;

RULE 7

IF   environment = travel AND
salary = 15000–20000 AND
field = law

THEN   job = labor_relations_specialist;

RULE 8

IF   environment = travel AND
salary = 20000–25000 AND
field = law

THEN   job = attorney;

RULE 8A

IF	environment = travel AND
	salary = 10000–15000 AND
	field = medicine
THEN	job = home_health_care;

RULE 8B

IF	environment = travel AND
	salary = 15000–20000 AND
	field = medicine
THEN	job = speech_pathologist;

RULE 8C

IF	environment = travel AND
	salary = 20000–25000 AND
	field = medicine
THEN	job = hospital_administration;

7. When you have finished keying in the changes to the knowledge base, proofread your knowledge base carefully. Check for spelling mistakes. Check to make sure there is a semicolon at the end of each rule. Check to make sure all the necessary underscores between words are keyed in. After proofreading the knowledge base, run a consultation. If there are any errors in the knowledge base, correct them. When your consultation runs without any problems, exit from VP-Expert.

SECTION H

Advanced VP-Expert

OUTLINE

Introduction
Using Confidence Factors
Assigning Multiple Values to a
　　Variable
Using the Logical Operator OR
Using the Why? and How? Commands
　　Adding a BECAUSE Statement to a
　　　Knowledge Base
Learning Check
Formatting the Consultation
　　Using the CLS Clause
　　Using the EXECUTE Statement
　　Using the RUNTIME Statement
Printing a Hard Copy of Display Text
　　Using the PRINTON and PRINTOFF
　　　Clauses
　　Using the EJECT Clause
Using Mathematical Operations
Assigning Values to Variables with
　　End User Input
Learning Check
Summary Points
Summary of VP-Expert Key Words
Summary of VP-Expert Statements
Summary of VP-Expert Clauses
Summary of Common VP-Expect
　　Error Messages
Summary of VP-Expert Function Key
　　Commands
VP-Expert Exercises
VP-Expert Problems

■ INTRODUCTION

In the previous section, you learned the basics of creating an expert system by using an induction table. In this section you will be introduced to VP-Expert's more advanced capabilities, such as computing the confidence factor and using mathematical calculations in a knowledge base. In addition, you will be introduced to more formatting commands that enable you to create a professional looking, user friendly consultation.

■ USING CONFIDENCE FACTORS

In VP-Expert, confidence factors are numbers that indicate the level of certainly of a value. These numbers can be input into the knowledge base itself. That is, the developer can assign a confidence factor to the conclusion drawn by a rule. For example, in the following rule

```
RULE 1
IF        climate = humid AND
          moisture = high
THEN      crop = rice CNF 80;
```

The number 80 indicates that this conclusion was drawn with 80% certainty. The letters *CNF* are used to identify the confidence factor in the rule.

Confidence factors can also be entered by the end user during a consultation. That is, the end user can input his or her level of certainty in an answer being provided during a consultation. To enter a confidence factor during a consultation, highlight the option to be selected, press <Home>, enter a number between 0 and 100 as a confidence factor, press <Return>, and press <End>.

If the end user enters a confidence factor of less than 50, that selection is negated. VP-Expert includes a truth threshold which requires the confidence factor to be above a certain number in order for the rule to evaluate as true. The default setting for the truth threshold is 50. If no confidence factor is entered by the end user, VP-Expert assumes the confidence factor is 100%.

■ Your Turn

In the hands-on exercises in this section you will be creating a knowledge base to help businesses decide on an appropriate area of the country to relocate, based upon criteria such as climate, health care, and available transportation. In this exercise you are going to begin the knowledge base by entering an induction table.

1. Turn on the computer and start the VP-Expert program. Make sure your data disk onto which the VPXI.EXE file has been copied is in drive B. The VP-Expert Main Menu should be on your screen.

　■ Select **Path**
　■ Type **B:**
　■ Press <Return>
　■ Select **Induce**
　■ Select **Create**

The prompt **What is the name of the examples file?** appears.

- Type: **Locate**
- Press <Return>

2. You are now ready to type the induction table. To begin, you are going to enter data concerning climate, housing, and health care. When a consultation is run, the end user will be able to identify if a warm or cool climate is preferred; if housing costs in the area can run between $50,000–$70,000 or between $70,000–$90,000; and, if the number of hospitals and physicians in the area is a primary concern. Based on the user input, the expert system suggests an area for relocation.

Carefully enter the following:

Climate	Housing	Health	Location
Warm	$50000–70000	Yes	Albuquerque__NM
Warm	$50000–70000	No	Winter__Haven__FL
Warm	$70000–90000	Yes	Portland__OR
Warm	$70000–90000	No	Austin__TX
Cool	$50000–70000	Yes	St__Louis__MO
Cool	$50000–70000	No	Pittsfield__MA
Cool	$70000–90000	Yes	Minneapolis__MN
Cool	$70000–90000	No	Billings__MT

When you have finished, your screen should look like Figure H–1.

Look over your induction table carefully. Check for spelling mistakes. Make sure there is an underscore between words wherever necessary. When you are certain the induction table is entered correctly, press <Alt> <F6> to save it. The prompt **Save as "b:\locate.tbl" (Y or N)?** appears.

FIGURE H—1

Entering the Location Induction Table

```
                                          Editing:  New File b:\locate.tbl


        Climate     Housing        Health      Location◄
        Warm        $50000-70000   Yes         Albuquerque_NM◄
        Warm        $50000-70000   No          Winter_Haven_FL◄
        Warm        $70000-90000   Yes         Portland_OR◄
        Warm        $70000-90000   No          Austin_TX◄
        Cool        $50000-70000   Yes         St_Louis_MO◄
        Cool        $50000-70000   No          Pittsfield_MA◄
        Cool        $70000-90000   Yes         Minneapolis_MN◄
        Cool        $70000-90000   No          Billings_MT◄




        +      ▲     ▲     ▲     ▲     ▲     ▲    ▲    ▲    ▲     ▲    ▲    ▲      ▲    ▲
        Insert On     Document Off                        Boldface Off Underline Off
          1 Help    2 Reform 3 TabSet 4 Margin 5 Center 6      7 Bold  8 Ulin   9 Dcumn 10 Print
```

■ Press **Y**

3. Next you want to create the knowledge base from the induction table you just created and then run a consultation to make sure there are no errors.

■ Select **Text**

The message **Insert 'Sample Files' Disk in Drive B and Press ENTER or Press Esc to Quit** appears. Your data disk onto which you copied the VPXI.EXE file should be in drive B. DO NOT REMOVE IT TO REPLACE IT WITH THE SAMPLE FILES DISK. Leave your data disk in drive B and press <Return>.

The prompt **What is the name of the examples file?** appears.

■ Select **LOCATE**

The prompt **What is the name of the rule file to create?** appears.

■ Select **LOCATE.KBS**
■ Select **Quit**

When the VP-Expert Main Menu appears, you are ready to run a consultation.

■ Select **FileName**
■ Select **LOCATE**
■ Select **Consult**

If you get an error message, correct your error. Run a few consultations to make sure the system is working properly.

4. Next, you want to edit the knowledge base.

■ Select **Quit** to exit from the consultation
■ Select **Edit**

The LOCATE knowledge base appears on the screen. Edit the ACTIONS block so it appears exactly as it does here. Press <Ctrl> <Return> at the end of each line to move the cursor to the next line of space.

> **ACTIONS**
> **DISPLAY "This relocation planner will help you to select an appropriate location for your company based upon your specific requirements. Press any key to begin the consultation.~"**
> **FIND Location**
> **DISPLAY "You should consider {Location} as a location for your company.";**

5. Edit the ASK and CHOICES statements at the end of the knowledge base so they appear exactly as they do here. Press <Ctrl> <Return> at the end of each line to move the cursor to the next line of space.

ASK Climate: "Would you like your company to be located in a warm climate or a cool climate?";
CHOICES Climate: Warm, Cool;
ASK Housing: "Would you prefer that the cost of housing in the area be between $50,000 and $70,000 or between $70,000 and $90,000?";
CHOICES Housing: $50000–70000, $70000–90000;
ASK Health: "Is the number of health care facilities and physicians in the

area a prime consideration in your location selection?'';
CHOICES Health: Yes, No;

When you have finished editing the knowledge base, save it and run another consultation to make sure there are no errors.

6. Now you want to enter confidence factors. In order to do this, you are going to edit the knowledge base in two ways. You are going to enter a confidence factor next to each city, and you are going to include instructions to the end user on how to enter confidence factors. Exit from the consultation and access the LOCATE knowledge base in order to edit it. Edit the ACTIONS block to look like the following (boldface type indicates the changes). Remember to press <Ctrl> <Return> at the end of each line.

> **ACTIONS**
> **DISPLAY "This relocation planner will help you to select an appropriate location for your company based upon your specific requirements. Press any key to begin the consultation.~"**
> ***DISPLAY "If you wish, for each question asked during the consultation you can enter your degree of certainty in your answer. For example, entering 80 would indicate you are 80% confident in your response to the question. To enter your confidence level, move the highlighting to your selection, press the HOME key, type a number between 0 and 100, press RETURN and press END. If you do not enter a number, the system assumes you are 100% confident in your response. Press any key to continue with this consultation.~"***
> **FIND Location**
> **DISPLAY "You should consider {Location} as a location for your company.";**

7. Next you want to add confidence factors into the knowledge base itself. In each of the rule's THEN statements add *CNF 90;* at the end of the statement. For example, the THEN statement in RULE 0 should be edited to look like the following (italicized text indicates the changes):

THEN   Location = Albuquerque__NM *CNF 90;*

In other words, you are entering a confidence factor of 90 by each of the cities in the knowledge base. Be sure to leave a space between the state and **"CNF" and between "CNF" and "90;".**

8. Finally, you want to edit the knowledge base so that the final confidence factor is displayed. The final confidence factor takes into consideration the confidence factor the user enters together with the confidence factor already in the knowledge base next to each city. In order for the final confidence factor to be displayed, edit the third DISPLAY statement in the knowledge base as follows (italicized text indicates the change):

DISPLAY "You should consider {*#* Location} as a location for your company.";

When a consultation is run, the confidence factor will display in place of the number symbol. Save the edited knowledge base and run a few consultations to make sure the program is working properly. Be sure to enter confidence factors as you run the consultations. Notice how the confidence factors entered by the end user affect the final confidence factor that is displayed at the end of the consultation. After running a few consultations, exit from the consultation and return to VP-Expert's Main Menu.

■ ASSIGNING MULTIPLE VALUES TO A VARIABLE

In the knowledge bases you have created so far, all the variables have been assigned only one value. During a consultation, a user can select more than one option by moving the highlighting to his or her first choice, pressing <Return>, moving the highlighting to the second choice, pressing <Return>, and finally pressing <End>. That is, the user can make as many selections as desired by highlighting the choice and pressing <Return>. The selection process is not ended until the <End> key is pressed.

If a variable is going to be assigned more than one value, that variable has to be designated as a plural variable in the knowledge base. A PLURAL statement in the knowledge base enables a variable to be assigned more than one value. In the following example,

ASK Season: "During what season will you be planting?";
CHOICES Season: Fall, Winter, Spring, Summer;
PLURAL: Season;

the PLURAL statement makes it possible for the end user to select more than one season.

■ USING THE LOGICAL OPERATOR OR

In addition to the keyword AND, the keyword OR is used to combine conditions in a rule. If a rule contains the logical operator OR, either one or the other of the conditions must be true in order for the rule to evaluate as true. Look over the following example:

RULE 1
IF   soil_temp >= 45 AND
        season = spring OR
        season = fall OR
        rainfall = 2
THEN   planting = okay;

To translate this rule, if the soil temperature is greater than or equal to 45 degrees *and* either the season is spring *or* the season is fall *or* rainfall is equal to 2 inches, then planting is equal to okay. That is, in order for this rule to evaluate as true, both the soil temperature has to be equal to or greater than 45 and *one* of the following three statements (season = spring; season = fall; rainfall = 2) have to be true.

Sometimes it helps to understand rules that use both the AND and OR logical operators to imagine a set of parentheses surrounding the expressions separated by OR. To use the rule above as an example:

RULE 1
IF   soil_temp >= 45 AND
        (season = spring OR
        season = fall OR
        rainfall = 2)
THEN   planting = okay;

This helps you to visualize the necessary requirements for the rule to pass as true—that is, the first condition must be true and at least one of the following conditions must be true. Do not use parentheses when creating your knowledge base, however, as this will result in a syntax error.

■ Your Turn

In this exercise you are going to introduce another variable, transportation, into the LOCATE knowledge base. The transportation variable is going to be defined as plural so the end user can select more than one option. The VP-Expert Main Menu should be on your screen.

1. The first step is to edit the existing LOCATE knowledge base.

■ Select **Edit**

The LOCATE knowledge base should appear on your screen. It is a good idea to copy the LOCATE knowledge base and work with the copy in case you make some mistakes and want to start over with this Your Turn exercise. Do the following to make a copy of the LOCATE knowledge base:

■ Press <Alt> <F6> to save the LOCATE knowledge base

The prompt **Save as "locate.kbs" (Y or N)** appears.

■ Press **N** for no

The prompt **Please enter the file where you want to save your text** appears.

■ Type: **b:\Locate2**
■ Press <Return>

Now you want to access your backup copy of the LOCATE knowledge base.

■ Select **Filename**
■ Select **Locate2**
■ Select **Edit**

The LOCATE2 knowledge base should appear on your screen. Check the upper right corner to make sure the file name says **locate2**. You are now ready to edit the knowledge base.

2. Move the cursor to the end of the knowledge base. Add the following statements at the very end of the knowledge base (remember to press <Ctrl> <Return> at the end of each line):

ASK Transportation: "Which of the following modes of transportation need to be readily accessible? Up to three options can be selected.";
CHOICES Transportation: Public, Air, Amtrack;
PLURAL: Transportation;

3. Next, each of the rules have to be edited to account for the new variable. In editing the rules, you are going to use the logical operator OR. Edit Rule 0 to look like the following (italicized text indicates the changes):

RULE 0
IF   **Climate = Warm AND**
                Housing = $50000–70000 AND
                Health = Yes *AND*
                Transportation = Public OR
                Transportation = Air OR

Transportation = Amtrack

THEN   Location = Albuquerque__NM CNF 90;

4. Next you are going to block from Rule 0 the new lines pertaining to the transportation variable and copy them into all the remaining rules in the knowledge base. To begin, place the cursor on the *A* in *AND* in the line **Health = Yes AND** in Rule 0

- Press <Ctrl> <F3> to start the block
- Move the cursor to the triangle following the *k* in *Amtrack*
- Press <Ctrl> <F4> to end the block

Your screen should look like Figure H–2.

Move the cursor so that it is on the triangle following the line **Health = No** in Rule 1

- Press the Spacebar once
- Press <Ctrl> <F7> to copy the block

The transportation block now appears in Rule 1. Move the cursor so that it is on the triangle following the line **Health = Yes** in Rule 2.

- Pres the Spacebar once
- Press <Ctrl> <F7> to copy the block

The transportation block now appears in Rule 2. Continue copying this block into Rules 3 through 7. When this new segment of text is properly inserted into all the rules, press <Ctrl> <F5> to cancel the block.

5. Not all of the cities have Amtrack service, so further editing is needed. Move the cursor to Rule 3. Austin, Texas, does not have Amtrack service. First, you are going to insert a new rule that provides for a city that does have Amtrack service. Block Rule 3 and copy it so that it comes immediately before Rule 4. Edit the new Rule 3 so that it looks like the following:

RULE 3A

IF   **Climate = Warm AND**
         Housing = $70000–90000 AND
         Health = No AND
         Transportation = Public OR
         Transportation = Air OR
         Transportation = Amtrack
THEN   Location = *Charlottesville__VA CNF 90;*

After editing the new Rule 3A, go back to Rule 3 and make the following changes:

- Delete the entire line that reads **Transportation = Amtrack**
- Delete the word *OR* from the line that reads **Transportation = Air OR**

6. Billings, Montana, does not have Amtrack service. Move the cursor to RULE 7. Insert a new rule that provides for a city that does have Amtrack service by blocking Rule 7 and copying it so that it follows the original Rule 7. Edit the new Rule 7 so that it looks like the following:

RULE 7A

IF   **Climate = Cool AND**
         Housing = $70000–90000 AND
         Health = No AND

```
◄
RULE 0◄
IF      Climate=Warm AND◄
        Housing=$50000-70000 AND◄
        Health=Yes AND◄
        Transportation=Public OR◄
        Transportation=Air OR◄
        Transportation=Amtrack◄
THEN    Location=Albuquerque_NM CNF 90;◄
◄
RULE 1◄
IF      Climate=Warm AND◄
        Housing=$50000-70000 AND◄
        Health=No◄
THEN    Location=Winter_Haven_FL CNF 90;◄
◄
RULE 2◄
IF      Climate=Warm AND◄

+    ▲    ▲    ▲    ▲    ▲    ▲    ▲    ▲    ▲    ▲    ▲    ▲    ▲    ▲    ▲
Insert On      Document Off                        Boldface Off Underline Off
  1Help    2Reform 3TabSet 4Margin 5Center 6      7Bold  8Ulin   9Dcumn 10Print
```

FIGURE H—2

Copying a Block in the LOCATE2 Knowledge Base

> **Transportation = Public OR**
> **Transportation = Air OR**
> **Transportation = Amtrack**
> **THEN   Location =** *Provo__UT CNF 90;*

After editing the new Rule 7A, go back to Rule 7 and make the following changes:

- Delete the entire line that reads **Transportation = Amtrack**
- Delete the word *OR* from the line that reads **Transportation = Air OR**

7. The changes you just made to the LOCATE knowledge base made it possible for more than one city to meet the end user's specifications; therefore, you have to insert another variable in the PLURAL statement. Move the cursor to the very end of the knowledge base. Edit the PLURAL statement as follows:

PLURAL: Transportation, *Location;*

8. Save your edited knowledge base and try to run a consultation. If you get an error message, try to figure out your mistake and fix it. Use the Summary of Common VP-Expert Error Messages at the end of this chapter to help you. Once you have corrected all errors, run a few consultations. Be sure to try out all the options. That is, enter confidence factors and select more than one mode of transportation. Remember, the way to select more than one option is to move the highlighting to your first selection, press <Return>, move the highlighting to the next selection, press <Return> and so on. When all the options have been selected, press <End>. If more than one city meets the criterion of a consultation, they both will be listed in the final DISPLAY clause. After running several consultations, select **Quit.** The VP-Expert Main Menu returns to your screen.

■ USING THE WHY? AND HOW? COMMANDS

At any point in a consultation being performed with VP-Expert, the end user can select the Why? or How? command to find out why a certain question is being asked or how a particular value was determined. To use the Why? and How? commands during a consultation, when a prompt appears asking the end user to make a selection, press the slash key </>. The Go Menu then appears at the bottom of the screen. Select **Why?** to find out why that particular question is being asked. One of two things will happen. Either the rule that caused that question to be asked is displayed, or text is displayed that explains why the question is being asked. In order for text to be displayed, BECAUSE text has to be included in the knowledge base. If there is no BECAUSE text in the knowledge base, then the rule that caused the question to be asked is displayed.

Adding a BECAUSE Statement to a Knowledge Base

In order for explanatory text to appear in response to the Why? command, BECAUSE text has to be added to the rules. BECAUSE text must come at the end of the rule, and it must end with a semicolon. The text that is to appear during the consultation has to be enclosed in quotation marks. The following example illustrates how BECAUSE text is incorporated into a rule:

RULE 1
IF soil_temp >= 45 AND
   season = spring OR
   season = fall OR
   rainfall = 2
THEN planting = okay

BECAUSE "The soil temperature, season, and amount of rainfall are needed to determine whether or not planting is appropriate.";

■ Your Turn

In this exercise you are going to first use the Why? command without BECAUSE text in the LOCATE knowledge base. Then, you will add BECAUSE text to each of the rules in the LOCATE2 knowledge base.

1. The VP-Expert Main Menu should be on your screen.

 ■ Select **Consult**
 ■ Select **Go**

Begin the consultation, pressing any key as necessary. The first prompt, **Would you like your company to be located in a warm climate or a cool climate?** appears.

 ■ Press the slash key </> to access the Go Menu

 ■ Select **Why?**

Your screen should look like Figure H–3.
Since there is no BECAUSE text in the LOCATE2 knowledge base, the rule that caused the prompt to appear is displayed in a box in the center of the

```
answer.  For example, entering 80 would indicate you are 80%
confident in your response to the question.  To enter your
confidence level, move the highlighting to your selection,
press the HOME key, type a number between 0 and 100, press RETURN
and press END.  If you do not enter a number, the system
assumes you are 100% confident in your response.  Press any key
to continue with this consultation.
Would you like your company to be located in a warm
                        ┌───────────────[ WHY ]───────────────┐
  Housing = $50000-70000 AND
  Health = Yes AND
  Transportation = Public OR
  Transportation = Air OR
  Transportation = Amtrack
  THEN
  Location = Albuquerque_NM CNF 90

  (Press Any Key To Continue)

 Finding Climate


  1Help      2How?      3Why?      4Slow      5Fast      6Quit
  Ask why a question was asked
```

FIGURE H—3

Using the Why? Command

screen. Notice, however, the rule is too long for all of it to fit in the box. To read the entire rule, the end user can use the **Slow** option from the Go Menu. This causes the rule to scroll slowly enough for the end user to read it.

■ Press any key to continue
■ Press the slash key </>
■ Select **Slow**
■ Press the slash key </>
■ Select **Why?**

This time the rule executes slowly enough for you to read it. If you wish to restore the original speed, press the slash key and select **Fast.**

2. Next, you are going to use the How? command. The prompt **Would you like your company to be located in a warm climate or a cool climate?** should still be active.

■ Select **Warm**

The housing prompt appears.

■ Select **$70000–90000**

The health care facilities prompt appears.

■ Select **No**

You now want to use the How? command.

■ Press the slash key </>

The highlighting is already on **How?**

■ Press <Return>

You have to select **How?** by pressing <Return>. If you try to select it by typing **H** for **How,** you will get the Help Menu. Your screen should look like Figure H–4.

The purpose of the How? command is to tell the end user how a value was assigned to a variable. The prompt that appears is asking the end user to indicate which variable he or she wants to know about.

■ Press <→> to highlight **Housing**
■ Press <Return>

The prompt that appears states:

Housing was set because:
You said so.
(Press any key to continue)

That is, the end user selected the value for the housing variable. If the value had been assigned in a rule, the rule would have appeared. In the LOCATE2 knowledge base, all the values are determined by the end user, so this same prompt would appear no matter which variable was selected. The How? command is only available during a consultation. That is, you can never execute the How? command after an option for the final prompt has been made, because at that point, VP-Expert finds a value for the goal variable and the consultation is ended. For example, you cannot use the How? command in a consultation using the LOCATE2 knowledge base after selecting options to the modes of transportation prompt.

■ Press any key and complete the consultation

3. Now you want to add BECAUSE text to the LOCATE2 knowledge base. Quit the consultation and select **Edit.** The LOCATE2 knowledge base ap-

FIGURE H–4

Using the How? Command

```
between $50,000 and $70,000 or between $70,000 and $90,000?
 $50000-70000              $70000-90000◄

Is the number of health care facilities and physicians in the
area a prime consideration in your location selection?
 Yes                      No◄

Which of the following modes of transportation need
─────────────────────────[ HOW ]─────────────
Name of variable you are asking about?
 Climate                  Housing
 Health                   Transportation
 Location



 (Select with ↑,↓,→,← PgUp, or PgDn, then press ENTER)

Finding Transportation


1Help      2How?      3Why?      4Slow      5Fast      6Quit
Ask how a conclusion was reached
```

COMPUTERS AND INFORMATION PROCESSING

pears on your screen. Edit Rule 0 to look like the following (italicized text indicates the changes). Remember to press <Ctrl> <Return> at the end of each line when entering the BECAUSE text:

RULE 0

IF	**Climate = Warm AND**
	Housing = $50000–70000 AND
	Health = Yes AND
	Transportation = Public OR
	Transportation = Air OR
	Transportation = Amtrack
THEN	**Location = Albuquerque_NM CNF 90**

BECAUSE "Your preference in climate, cost of housing, number of health care facilities, and types of transportation are needed to help determine a location site.";

Do not forget to delete the semicolon after the THEN clause and insert the new semicolon after the BECAUSE text.

4. Block the BECAUSE text and copy it into its proper location in all of the rules. Again, do not forget to delete the semicolon at the end of the THEN clauses. When the BECAUSE text has been copied into all of the rules, save the edited LOCATE2 knowledge base. Run a consultation. If an error message appears, fix your mistake. During the consultation, be sure to select the Why? command to see the results. When you have finished, quit the consultation. The VP-Expert Main Menu appears on your screen.

LEARNING
CHECK

1. (True or False?) Confidence factors can be input into a knowledge base either by the developer or by the end user.

2. (True or False?) During a consultation using VP-Expert, a variable can be assigned only one value.

3. (True or False?) The following rule will evaluate as true if the temperature is 30, the wind is 10 miles an hour and the snowfall is 4 inches an hour.

RULE 1

IF	temp <= 32 AND
	wind > 15_mph OR
	snowfall > 3_inches_per_hour
THEN	condition = blizzard

4. (True or False?) If BECAUSE text does not appear in a knowledge base, the Why? command is inoperable.

5. To find out how a particular value was determined during a consultation, select _____ from the Go Menu.

ANSWERS

1. True	4. False
2. False	5. How?
3. True	

▬ FORMATTING THE CONSULTATION

You may have noticed by now that the consultation screen seems slightly crowded. In addition, the constant display of the inference engine in the rules window can be distracting. To an end user who has no interest in the workings of the inference engine, it can be confusing. The CLS clause and the EXECUTE and RUNTIME statements are VP-Expert commands that help make a consultation a little more user friendly.

Using the CLS Clause

The purpose of the CLS clause is to clear the consultation window so that DISPLAY text does not build up on the screen. CLS is inserted in the knowledge base at the point where the screen is to be cleared. The following example illustrates how the CLS clause can be used:

ACTIONS
     DISPLAY "The purpose of this consultation is to help you determine the appropriateness of planting various crops. Press any key to continue.~"

     CLS

     DISPLAY "A series of questions will follow. To make a selection, highlight your choice using the arrow keys, press <Return>, and then press <End>. To continue with this consultation, press any key.~"

     CLS

     DISPLAY "....

The CLS clauses in this example clear the screen of each DISPLAY text before the next DISPLAY text appears.

Using the EXECUTE Statement

The purpose of the EXECUTE statement is to enable the consultation to begin immediately after the end user selects **Consult** from VP-Expert's Main Menu. It eliminates having to select **Go** from the Consult Menu. The following example illustrates how the EXECUTE statement can be used:

EXECUTE;
ACTIONS
     DISPLAY "The purpose of this consultation is to help you determine the appropriateness of planting various crops. Press any key to continue.~"

In this example, the DISPLAY text "The purpose of this consultation . . ." will appear immediately after the end user selects **Consult** from the VP-Expert Main Menu.

Using the RUNTIME Statement

The purpose of the RUNTIME statement is to eliminate the rules window and the results window from the screen during a consultation. The following example illustrates how the RUNTIME statement can be used:

RUNTIME;
EXECUTE;
ACTIONS
     DISPLAY "The purpose of this consultation is to help you determine the appropriateness of planting various crops. Press any key to continue.~"

COMPUTERS AND INFORMATION PROCESSING

In this example, when a consultation is run, the only thing that will appear on the screen is the DISPLAY text. A RUNTIME statement can appear anywhere within the knowledge base.

■ Your Turn

In this exercise you are going to edit the LOCATE2 knowledge base by inserting two CLS clauses, a RUNTIME statement, and an EXECUTE statement.

1. The VP-Expert Main Menu should be on your screen.

■ Select **Edit**

The LOCATE2 knowledge base should appear on your screen. Edit the beginning of the knowledge base so that it looks like the following (italicized text indicates the changes):

RUNTIME;
EXECUTE;
ACTIONS
     DISPLAY "This relocation planner will help you to select
an appropriate location for your company based upon your specific
requirements. Press any key to begin the consultation.~"
CLS
     DISPLAY "If you wish, for each question asked during the
consultation you can enter your degree of certainty in your answer.
For example, entering 80 would indicate you are 80% confident in your
response to the question. To enter your confidence level, move the
highlighting to your selection, press the HOME key, type a number
between 0 and 100, press RETURN and press END. If you do not enter a
number, the system assumes you are 100% confident in your response.
Press any key to continue with this consultation.~"
CLS
FIND LOCATION

Save the edited LOCATE2 knowledge base

2. You now want to run a consultation to see the effect of the changes.

■ Select **Consult**

If an error message appears, fix your mistake. Once your additions have been made correctly, your screen should look like Figure H–5.
There are several things you should notice. First the consultation began immediately. You did not have to select **Go** from the Consult Menu. Second, the results window and rules window are no longer displayed.

■ Press any key

The first DISPLAY text disappears and the second DISPLAY text appears.

■ Press any key

The climate prompt is displayed. Complete the consultation. When you finish, the final DISPLAY text with the goal variable is displayed so fast, you can hardly read it. The VP-Expert Main Menu should be on your screen. One more change needs to be made to the knowledge base.

```
This relocation planner will help you to select an
appropriate location for your company based upon your specific
requirements.  Press any key to begin the consultation.
```

FIGURE H—5

**Running a User-Friendly
Consultation**

■ Select **Edit**

The LOCATE2 knowledge base should appear. Move the cursor to the third
DISPLAY clause. Edit it so it looks like the following (italicized text indicates
the changes):

**DISPLAY "You should consider {#Location} as a location for your
company. *Press any key to continue.*~";**

Save the edited knowledge base and run another consultation. This time
the result of the consultation remains on the screen until you press any key.
Notice how much faster the consultation runs. This is because the inference
engine is no longer being displayed. Pressing any key at this point takes
you back to VP-Expert's Main Menu. To run another consultation, the end
user would simply select **Consult** again. Press any key to return to
VP-Expert's Main Menu.

PRINTING A HARD COPY OF DISPLAY TEXT

In some cases it would be useful to the end user for a hard copy of certain
text that is displayed during a consultation to be printed. The PRINTON
and PRINTOFF clauses together with the EJECT clause enable the developer
of the knowledge base to indicate text that should be printed during the
run of a consultation.

Using the PRINTON and PRINTOFF Clauses

The PRINTON and PRINTOFF clauses are used in conjunction with DIS-
PLAY clauses. Their purpose is to enable the DISPLAY text to be not only
displayed on the screen, but sent to the printer as well. The following example illustrates how the PRINTON and PRINTOFF clauses can be used.

COMPUTERS AND INFORMATION PROCESSING

ACTIONS
   DISPLAY "The purpose of this consultation is to help you determine the appropriateness of planting various crops. Press any key to continue.~"

   CLS

   DISPLAY "A series of questions will follow. To make a selection, highlight your choice using the arrow keys, press <Return>, and then press <End>. To continue with this consultation, press any key.~"

   CLS
   FIND Crop
   PRINTON
   DISPLAY "You should consider {crop} as an appropriate crop to plant."
   PRINTOFF;

In this example, during the consultation the text in the first two DISPLAY clauses will not print because they are not included within the PRINTON and PRINTOFF clauses. However, the text to the third DISPLAY clause will be both displayed on the screen and printed. In order for the PRINTON and PRINTOFF clauses to work, the computer has to be hooked up to a printer and the printer has to be loaded with paper and be online during the consultation.

Using the EJECT Clause

The EJECT clause is used with a DISPLAY clause. The purpose of the EJECT clause is to tell the printer to eject the remainder of the current page and go to the top of the next page. The EJECT clause is only necessary if the PRINTON and PRINTOFF clauses are being used. The following example illustrates how the EJECT clause can be used.

   PRINTON
   DISPLAY "You should consider {crop} as an appropriate crop to plant.";
   PRINTOFF
   EJECT

In this example, the EJECT clause causes the printer to eject the page upon which "You should consider . . ." was printed and move the printer head to the top of the next page. The clause is useful only with continuous-feed paper.

■ Your Turn

In this exercise you are going to insert PRINTON, PRINTOFF, and EJECT clauses into the LOCATE2 knowledge base. Before you start this exercise, make sure the computer you are using is connected to a printer and that the printer is loaded with paper and is online.

1. The VP-Expert Main Menu should be on your screen.

   ■ Select **Edit**

The LOCATE2 knowledge base appears. Edit the ACTIONS block so it looks like the following (italicized text indicates the changes):

> **FIND LOCATION**
> *PRINTON*
> **DISPLAY "You should consider {#Location} as a location for your company. Press any key to continue.~"**
> *PRINTOFF*
> *EJECT;*
> **RULE 0**

Since the PRINTOFF and EJECT clauses are being added at the end of the ACTIONS block, the semicolon has to be deleted from the end of the DISPLAY text, which was the original end of the ACTIONS block, and inserted following EJECT, which is the new end of the ACTIONS block. Save the edited LOCATE2 knowledge base.

2. Run a consultation. The text in the final DISPLAY clause should both appear on the screen and print out on the printer. Press any key. The VP-Expert Main Menu returns to the screen.

▨ USING MATHEMATICAL OPERATIONS

There are two ways in which mathematical operations can be used in a knowledge base. First, they can be used to indicate a value in a rule condition. For example, in the following rule

RULE1
IF   total_rainfall <= (.1 * average_rainfall)
THEN   conditions = drought

if the value for the total_rainfall variable is less than or equal to the value of the average_rainfall variable multiplied by .1, then the value for the conditions variable equals drought.

The second way mathematical operations can be used is to assign a value to a variable. For example, if the following rule passes

RULE1
IF   crop = corn
THEN   herbicide = (acres * 5)

then five times the value of the acres variable is assigned to the herbicide variable.

VP-Expert uses the following symbols to represent mathematical operations:

+   Addition
−   Subtraction
*   Multiplication
/   Division

The math operations must be enclosed in parentheses. Notice in the above two examples, (.1 * average_rainfall) and (acres * 5) are enclosed by parentheses.

▨ ASSIGNING VALUES TO VARIABLES WITH END USER INPUT

In all the examples used so far, values for variables were assigned by having the end user select an option or options provided in a menu. Instead of selecting an option from a menu, it is possible for the end user to key in the answer to a prompt. If the end user is to key in a response to a prompt, the ASK statement that generates that prompt does not have a corresponding CHOICES statement. When the end user keys in his or her response and presses <Return>, the entry made by the end user is assigned as the value for the variable in the ASK statement.

■ Your Turn

In this exercise you are going to create a new knowledge base called TAXES that can be used in conjunction with the LOCATE2 knowledge base. The purpose of the TAXES knowledge base is to compute the local taxes for any of the locations included in the LOCATE2 knowledge base. In creating the TAXES knowledge base you will use a mathematical operator, and you will have the end user input a response to a prompt.

1. The VP-Expert Main Menu should be on your screen. This time, you are going to enter the knowledge base directly rather than using an induction table.

- Select **Filename**
- Type: **Taxes**
- Select **Edit**

A blank text editing window appears. Key in the TAXES knowledge base as follows. Remember to press <Ctrl> <Return> at the end of each line:

```
RUNTIME;
EXECUTE;
ACTIONS
     DISPLAY "This consultation is to be used in conjunction with the
relocation planner. Its purpose is to compute the local taxes for the
location identified by the relocation planner. Press any key to begin the
consultation.~"
CLS
     FIND Taxes
     DISPLAY "The taxes taken out of this salary would amount to {Taxes}.
Press any key to continue.~";
RULE 0
     IF        Location=Albuquerque_NM OR
               Location=Winter_Haven_FL OR
               Location=Austin_TX AND
               Salary>0
     THEN      Taxes=(Salary * .01);
RULE 1
     IF        Location=St_Louis_MO OR
               Location=Billings_MT AND
               Salary>0
     THEN      Taxes=(Salary * .03);
RULE 2
     IF        Location=Charlottesville_VA OR
               Location=Pittsfield_MA AND
               Salary>0
     THEN      Taxes=(Salary * .04);
```

RULE 3

    IF   Location = Portland_OR OR
              Location = Minneapolis_MN OR
              Location = Provo_UT AND
              Salary>0
    THEN   Taxes = (Salary * .05);
ASK Location: "For which one of the following locations would you like to
compute the local taxes?";
CHOICES Location: Albuquerque_NM, Winter_Haven_FL, Portland_OR, Austin_TX,
Charlottesville_VA, St_Louis_MO, Pittsfield_MA, Minneapolis_MN, Provo_UT, Billings_MT;
ASK Salary: "Enter the salary upon which the tax computation should be
based. Do not use a dollar sign or commas. For example, type 25000 for a
$25,000 salary. Type the salary, press RETURN.";

Read over your knowledge base carefully. When you think it is entered correctly, save the TAXES knowledge base.

2. Run a consultation. If there are any errors, find your mistakes and fix them. Run several consultations to make sure the program works properly. When you are sure the program works, exit from VP-Expert.

LEARNING CHECK

1. Using _____ in a knowledge base clears the consultation window.

a. an EXECUTE statement   c. a CLS statement
b. a PRINTON clause   d. a RUNTIME statement

2. Using _____ in a knowledge base enables the consultation to begin immediately after the end user selects **Consult** from VP-Expert's Main Menu

a. an EXECUTE statement   c. a CLS statement
b. a PRINTON clause   d. a RUNTIME statement

3. Using _____ in a knowledge base removes the rules window and the results window from the screen during a consultation.

a. an EXECUTE statement   c. a CLS statement
b. a PRINTON clause   d. a RUNTIME statement

4. To print DISPLAY text during a consultation, the DISPLAY clause to be printed must be preceded by _____.

a. an EXECUTE statement   c. a CLS statement
b. a PRINTON clause   d. a RUNTIME statement

5. (True or False?) Any mathematical operation used in a knowledge base must be enclosed by parentheses.

ANSWERS

1. c.   4. b.
2. a.   5. True
3. d.

■ SUMMARY POINTS

■ A confidence factor is a number that indicates the level of certainty of a value.

■ During a consultation, a variable can be assigned more than one value if an appropriate PLURAL statement is included in the knowledge base.

■ If a rule contains the logical operator OR, either one or the other of the conditions connected by the OR operator must be true in order for the rule to pass.

■ The Why? command enables the end user to find out why a particular question is being asked. The How? command enables the end user to find out how a particular value was determined.

■ The CLS clause clears the consultation window during a consultation. The EXECUTE statement enables the consultation to begin as soon as **Consult** is selected from the VP-Expert Main Menu; use of the Consult Menu is eliminated. The RUNTIME statement deletes the rules window and the results window from the screen during a consultation.

■ The PRINTON and PRINTOFF clauses enable designated DISPLAY text to be printed as well as displayed on the screen.

■ The mathematical operations of addition (+), subtraction (−), multiplication (∗), and division (/) can be included in a knowledge base.

▨ SUMMARY OF VP-EXPERT KEY WORDS

@ABS	CLOSE	POP
@ACOS	CLS	PRINTOFF
@ASIN	COLOR	PRINTON
@ATAN	COLUMN	PUT
@COS	DISPLAY	PWKS
@EXP	EJECT	RECEIVE
@LOG	ELSE	RECORD_NUM
@SIN	END	RESET
@SQT	ENDOFF	ROW
@TAN	EXECUTE	RULE
ACTIONS	FIND	RUNTIME
ALL	FORMAT	SAVEFACTS
AND	GET	SHIP
APPEND	IF	SHOWTEXT
ASK	INDEX	SORT
AUTOQUERY	LOADFACTS	THEN
BCALL	MENU	TRUTHTHRESH
BECAUSE	MENU_SIZE	UNKNOWN
BKCOLOR	MRESET	WHILEKNOWN
CALL	NAMED	WKS
CCALL	OR	WORKON
CHAIN	PDISPLAY	
CHOICES	PLURAL	

▨ SUMMARY OF VP-EXPERT STATEMENTS

ACTIONS	CHOICES	PLURAL
ASK	ENDOFF	RULE
AUTOQUERY	EXECUTE	RUNTIME
BKCOLOR		

■ SUMMARY OF VP-EXPERT CLAUSES

APPEND	FORMAT	PWKS
BCALL	GET	RECEIVE
CALL	INDEX	RESET
CCALL	LOADFACTS	SAVEFACTS
CHAIN	MENU	SHIP
CLOSE	RESET	SHOWTEXT
CLS	PDISPLAY	SORT
COLOR	POP	TRUTHTHRESH
DISPLAY	PRINTOFF	WHILEKNOWN
EJECT	PRINTON	WKS
END	PUT	WORKON
FIND		

■ SUMMARY OF COMMON VP-EXPERT ERROR MESSAGES

Error in math expression	A number or parentheses may be missing; the formula might be illogical.
Illegal confidence factor	Confidence factors must be within the range of 0 to 100.
Illegal statement	There is an invalid statement in the knowledge base. Check to make sure all key words are spelled correctly; check statement syntax.
Math expression too long	A math expression cannot be longer than 256 characters.
Missing comma	Variables in ASK, CHOICES, and PLURAL statements must be separated by commas.
Out of memory error	The memory limit has been exceeded.
Premature end of file	Check to make sure that the last character in the knowledge base is a semicolon (;).
Syntax error	There is a syntax error in a clause or a statement.
Text string too long	ASK, BECAUSE, and DISPLAY text is limited to 1,000 characters.
Too many columns	Induction tables cannot contain more than 11 columns.
Too many examples	Induction tables cannot contain more than 150 rows.
Word too long	Rule names and most variables and values cannot exceed 20 characters.

■ SUMMARY OF VP-EXPERT FUNCTION KEY COMMANDS

On-Screen Formatting: The Function Keys Used Alone

Keys	Function	Description
<F1>	Help	Pressing <F1> provides on-screen Help
<F2>	Reformat	Pressing <F2> enables a paragraph to be reformatted. Paragraphs are readjusted to margin settings after editing has altered line lengths.

<F3>	Tab Set	Pressing <F3> places a tab set or deletes an existing tab set at the cursor's current location.
<F4>	Margins/ Justify	Pressing <F4> displays a screen that enables you to change the left and right margins as well as to turn justification on or off.
<F5>	Center	Pressing <F5> centers the line where the cursor is currently located.
<F7>	Bold	Pressing <F7> turns boldfacing on and off.
<F8>	Underline	Pressing <F8> turns underlining on and off.
<F9>	Document	Pressing <F9> turns the Document Mode on and off. The default setting is off. When the Document Mode is off, wordwrap, justify, centering, and reformatting are inoperable.
<F10>	Print	Pressing <F10> activates the Print Menu, from which you can print a file.

File Saving, Listing, and Reformatting:
The Function Keys Used with the ALT Key

Keys	Function	Description
<Alt><F2>	Global Reformat	Pressing <Alt><F2> reformats the entire document from the cursor's current location forward. Document Mode must be on to use this command.
<Alt><F4>	Insert File	Pressing <Alt><F4> enables you to insert an existing file at the cursor's current location.
<Alt><F5>	Update File	Pressing <Alt><F5> enables you to save your document without exiting from the text editor.
<Alt><F6>	Save File	Pressing <Alt><F6> enables you to save your file and exit from the text editor.
<Alt><F7>	Disk Directory	Pressing <Alt><F7> enables you to list the files on the disk in the current directory or in a designated directory.
<Alt><F8>	Abandon Edit	Pressing <Alt><F8> enables you to exit from the text editor without saving changes made since the last save.

Manipulating Blocks of Text: The Function Keys Used with the CTRL Key

Keys	Function	Description
<Ctrl><F3>	Start Block	Pressing <Ctrl><F3> marks the cursor's current location as the beginning of a block of text.
<Ctrl><F4>	End Block	Pressing <Ctrl><F4> marks the cursor's current location as the end of a block of text.
<Ctrl><F5>	Cancel Block	Pressing <Ctrl><F5> cancels a block of text that has been marked.
<Ctrl><F6>	Move Block	Pressing <Ctrl><F6> moves a block of text that has been marked to the cursor's current location. The block of text is deleted from its original position.

<Ctrl><F7>	Copy Block	Pressing <Ctrl><F7> copies a block of text that has been marked to the cursor's current location. The block of text remains in its original position.
<Ctrl><F8>	Delete Block	Pressing <Ctrl><F8> deletes a block of text that has been marked.
<Ctrl><F9>	Change Attributes	Pressing <Ctrl><F9> accesses a list of attributes such as normal, underline, boldface, or combined (underline and boldface). Typing the first letter of one of these attributes causes the block of text that has been marked to take on that attribute.
<Ctrl><F10>	Recall Block	Pressing <Ctrl><F10> recalls the most recently deleted word, line, or block to the cursor's current location.

Search and Replace: The Function Keys Used with the SHIFT Key

Keys	Function	Description
<Shift><F3>	Search Forward	Pressing <Shift><F3> moves the cursor forward to the first instance of a designated text string.
<Shift><F5>	Replace Forward	Pressing <Shift><F5> replaces the next instance of a designated text string with a new text string.
<Shift><F7>	Global Replace	Pressing <Shift><F7> replaces every instance of a designated text string with a new string.
<Shift><F9>	Repeat Search	Pressing <Shift><F9> repeats the most recent Search, Search and Replace, or Global Replace command.

▬ VP-EXPERT EXERCISES

To complete the following exercises you will need a DOS disk, the VP-Expert 2.0 program disk, and your data disk onto which the VPXI. EXE file has been copied.

1. Start the VP-Expert program. Change the working directory to drive B. The VP-Expert Main Menu should be on your screen.

2. You are going to create a knowledge base that will help a student determine if he or she has met a college's general English Composition, Foreign Language, and Social Sciences requirements for graduation. The requirements are as follows:

English Composition	English 110 English 112
Foreign Language (FL stands for the particular language: French, Spanish, etc.)	FL 101 or FL 111 FL 201
Social Studies	A variety of classes can be taken, but the student must take a total of six classes.

Create the knowledge base directly from the text editor. Name the knowledge base REQUIRE. Key in the knowledge base as follows:

ACTIONS
    DISPLAY "This consultation will help you determine what courses you have left to take to complete your English Composition, Foreign Language, and Social Sciences requirements for graduation.
Press any key to continue.~"
    FIND Require
    DISPLAY "You have the following requirements left to fulfill (the first number indicates the number of Social Science courses you have left to take):
{Require}";

RULE 0
    IF   Eng = Both__110__&__112
    THEN   Require = English__Comp__None;

RULE 1
    IF   Eng = ENG112__only
    THEN   Require = ENG110;

RULE 2
    IF   Eng = ENG110__only
    THEN   Require = ENG112;

RULE 3
    IF   FL = Both__101__&__201 OR
              FL = Both__111__&__201 OR
              FL = All__3__classes
    THEN   Require = Foreign__Lang__None;

RULE 4
    IF   FL = FL101__only OR
              FL = FL111__only
    THEN   Require = FL201;

RULE 5
    IF   FL = FL201__only
    THEN   Require = FL101__or__FL111;

RULE 6
    IF   SS = 6
    THEN   Require = zero;

RULE 7
    IF   SS < 6
    THEN   Require = (6 − SS);

ASK Eng: "Which of the following English Composition classes have you taken (select one option)?";
CHOICES ENG: ENG110__only, ENG112__only, Both__110__&__112;
ASK FL: "Which of the following Foreign Language classes have you taken (select one option)?";
CHOICES FL: FL101__only, FL111__only, FL__201__only, Both__101__&__201, Both__111__&__201, All__3__classes;
ASK SS: "How many Social Sciences classes you have taken? Enter a number between 0 and 6 and press RETURN.";

Look over your work carefully. When you are sure your REQUIRE knowledge base is entered correctly, save it.

3. Before you run a consultation, there are some editing changes you need to make. Access the REQUIRE knowledge base so that you can edit it. The REQUIRE variable has to be designated as a PLURAL variable. Add the appropriate PLURAL statement.

4. You want to eliminate the rules window and results window from the screen during the consultation. Add the appropriate statement to the RE-QUIRE knowledge base that accomplishes this.

5. You want the DISPLAY clause to be cleared from the screen during a consultation. Add the appropriate clause to the REQUIRE knowledge base that accomplishes this.

6. You want the consultation to start immediately after the end user selects **Consult** from the VP-Expert Main Menu. Add the appropriate statement to the REQUIRE knowledge base that accomplishes this.

7. Save the edited REQUIRE knowledge base and run a consultation. If you receive an error message, locate you mistake and fix it. Once the knowledge base is working correctly, run several consultations making various selections.

8. You want to edit the REQUIRE knowledge base further. Quit from the consultation and access the REQUIRE knowledge base. You want the final DISPLAY text to remain on the screen until the end user presses a key, and you want this final DISPLAY text to be printed. Make the needed changes to the REQUIRE knowledge base. Save the edited REQUIRE knowledge base and run some consultations to make sure the knowledge base is working properly. Be sure to run the consultations on a terminal that is connected to a printer to make sure the DISPLAY text prints as it should.

9. You need to add another value for the Eng and FL variables. As the REQUIRE knowledge base stands now, the student can enter 0 if he or she has not taken a Social Science class, but if the student has not taken an English Composition or Foreign Language class, there is no appropriate option to select. You want to edit the knowledge base so that the option None appears with both the English Composition and Foreign Language prompts. You must edit the rules so that if the student selects None at either of these prompts, the appropriate answer is listed with the goal variable during the final display. That is, if the student selects None at the English Composition prompt, then the student has to take both ENG110 and ENG112. If the student selects None at the Foreign Language prompt, then the student has to take either FL101 or FL111 and FL201. Remember, you have to keep the names of the values to twenty characters or less. It is a good idea to make a backup copy of the REQUIRE knowledge base and make the necessary editing changes to the backup. That way if you make a mistake and want to start over, you will still have your original REQUIRE knowledge base. Make the necessary changes. Save the edited knowledge base. Run several consultations to make sure it is working properly.

▬ VP-EXPERT PROBLEMS

To complete the following exercises you will need a DOS disk, the VP-Expert 2.0 program disk, and the Student File Disk that comes with this book.

1. Start the VP-Expert program. The VP-Expert Main Menu should be on your screen.

COMPUTERS AND INFORMATION PROCESSING

2. On the Student File Disk is a knowledge base named INVEST. It's purpose is to suggest some investment alternatives to first-time investors with $500 to $1000 to invest. Run through a couple of consultations using the INVEST knowledge base to become familiar with it.

3. Edit the INVEST knowledge base as follows in order to make it more user friendly:

■ Add the appropriate clause to the knowledge base to clear the screen of the opening DISPLAY text.

■ Add the appropriate statement to the knowledge base that enables the end user to begin the consultation immediately after selecting **Consult** from the VP-Expert Main Menu.

■ Add the appropriate statement to remove the results window and the rules window from the screen during the consultation.

■ Edit the final display text that identifies the goal variable in order to have it remain on the screen until the end user presses any key.

After making these changes, save the revised INVEST knowledge base and run a few consultations to make sure it is working properly.

4. Next you want to add confidence factors to the INVEST knowledge base. Edit the INVEST knowledge base so that the following confidence factors are assigned to each goal variable:

Goal Variable	Confidence Factor
Mutual Funds	90
Life Insurance	85
NOW Account	95
Certificate of Deposit	90
REITs	80
Common Stock	80

In addition, add a second DISPLAY clause in the ACTIONS block that instructs the end user as to how he or she can enter confidence factors during the consultation. Include a clause that will clear this DISPLAY text as well from the screen before the consultation begins. Edit the DISPLAY text, identifying the goal variable so that the final confidence factor will be displayed on the screen with the goal variable. Save the edited INVEST knowledge base. Run a few consultations to make sure the program is working properly. Be sure to enter confidence factors as you run your consultations.

5. Next you want to add BECAUSE statements to the knowledge base. Edit the INVEST knowledge base so that the following will be displayed when the end user selects the Why? command during a consultation:

The time frame of the investment and the risk level of the investment help to determine where the money should be invested.

Edit the DISPLAY text that instructs the end user how to enter confidence factors, to include instructions on how to use the Why? command. Save the revised INVEST knowledge base. Run a few consultations using the Why? command to make sure the program is working properly.

6. You now want to create a new knowledge base to be used along with the INVEST knowledge base. It is for the end user who does not have any money to invest, but would like to begin setting aside some money so that eventually he or she will be able to make an investment. This new knowledge base is to compute how much money will have to be set aside each month, based upon amount of money the end user eventually wants to have to invest and how soon the end user wants to have the investment money. Name the new knowledge base INVEST2.

The INVEST2 knowledge base has to enable the end user to input the values for two variables:

Amount—the total amount of money the end user wants to have to invest
Time—the number of months the end user is willing to save

For example, if the end user wanted to have $1000 within one year, he or she enters 1000 for the amount of money they want to have to invest and 12 for how soon they want the investment money to be available (the number of months). The program should then compute and display the amount of money that needs to be set aside each month in order for the end user to have $1000 in 12 months.

Mathematical operations have to be included in the knowledge base. Keep the computation simple. That is, take the value the user assigns to the amount variable and divide it by the value the user assigns to the time variable. (In the above example, 1000 would be divided by 12.) Have the goal variable be displayed in a message that informs the end user how much money they will have to save each month in order to reach their goal. Include in this message a statement informing the end user that this calculation does not take into account any interest they may earn on the monthly savings. Obviously, if interest is included, they will reach their goal sooner.

West Student Pro Pack (IBM/MS-DOS) Supplement Index

A

action line, A-135
ACTIONS block, A-233, A-235, A-238
active cell, in spreadsheets, A-63
analytical graphs, A-110
artificial intelligence, see expert systems
assistant menu, A-134–A-135
"at" functions, A-101–A-102, A-104
automatic pagination, A-3
average option, A-184

B

BECAUSE statement, A-262
block movement, A-3 A-20–A-21
BOLD function, A-42
boldface A-3, A-41–A-42
boot procedure, A-8, A-133, A-262
both titles freezing option, A-105
business graphics, A-110

C

CAPS indicator, A-64
CATS application software, A-222
cell
    copying of, A-102
    erasing of, A-87
cell pointer, in spreadsheet, A-63
cells
    formatting of, A-85
    in spreadsheets, A-60–A-61
character enhancement, A-3, A-33
    on WordPerfect, A-41–A-42
character fields, A-144
CLS clause, A-266
column menu, A-207
columns
    deleting of, A-90
    width of, A-89
commands
    copy, A-102, A-104
    summary, A-181

confidence factors, A-255
consultation
    formatting of, A-265
    in expert systems, A-220, A-231–A-232
    user friendly, A-268
consultation window
control panel, in spreadsheet, A-63
coordinate
    in spreadsheet, A-61, A-63
copy and move function, A-98
Copy command, A-98
count option, A-181–A-182
currency format, A-86
cursor, A-3, A-15–A-16

D

DART application software, A-222
data managers, A-128–A-219
    definition of, A-128
    uses of, A-130
data redundancy, A-129
data base files, A-142–A-143
data base management system (DBMS),
        A-128
date fields, A-144
date format, A-86
dBASE III PLUS, A-128–A-219
    action line, A-135
    assistant menu, A-134, A-135
    average option, A-184
    booting of, A-133
    columns menu, A-207
    count option, A-181–A-182
    creating a report on, A-206–A-208
    data-base files, A-143
    designing a report on, A-207
    fields, A-144
    file
        adding records on, A-164
        copying of, A-173–A-174
        deleting records on, A-165–A-166
        displaying, A-167, A-180
        editing of, A-155–A-156

entering data on, A-155–A-156
    erasing of, A-176
    printing of, A-167, A-173
    renaming of, A-174
    sorting of, A-189
    structure of
        display of, A-150
        edit of, A-151–A-153
    viewing of, A-163
file management
    with tools submenu, A-172
goto record option, A-180
Help feature, A-141
index option, A-198
indexing of, A-198, A-200–A-202, A-204
logical operators, A-178
memory needed, A-131
menus, A-207, A-211–A-213
modifying a report on, A-209
navigation line, A-135
query files, A-195
query table, A-196
quitting of, A-141
relational operators, A-177, A-179
selecting menu options on, A-136–A-138
sort option on, A-189, A-195, A-197
status bar, A-135
sum option, A-183
dedicated systems, A-2
default setting, A-3, A-10, A-70
deleting text, A-17–A-18
directory command, A-175
DISPLAY clause, A-241–A-243, A-269
domain in expert systems, A-220

E

EDIT indicator, A-64
editing A-3, A-15–A-16
editing window, A-9–A-10
editor, line, A-3
editor, screen, A-4
education application software, A-222
electronic spreadsheet, A-60–A-61

end users, of expert systems, A-221
endnotes, A-50
ERROR indicator, A-65
EXECUTE statement, A-266
exit menu, A-207
expert system shells, A-221
expert systems, A-220–A-280
   statements in, A-234
   uses of, A-221–A-222
expert system development tools, A-221
expert systems induction table,
      A-227–A-229
expert systems knowledge base, A-236
expert systems rules, A-246–A-247
expert system development tools, A-221
expert systems technology
   definition of, A-220
   developers of, A-221

F

field
   defining of, A-144
   definition of, A-128
   indexing of, A-198, A-202
   width of, A-146
file
   copying of, A-173–A-174
   definition of, A-128
   deleting records on, A-165–A-166
   displaying of, A-163, A-167, A-180
   editing on, A-160–A-161
   entering data on, A-155–A-156
   erasing of, A-176
   indexing of, A-198
      displaying, A-201
      opening, A-200
      searching for, A-204
   printing of, A-167
   renaming of, A-174
   sorting of, A-189, A-195, A-197
   updating of, A-160
file directory, A-175–A-176
file query, A-195
file structure
   display of, A-150
   edit of, A-151–A-153
fixed format, A-86
footers, A-48–A-49, A-51
footnotes, A-50, A-54
format, A-3, A-33–A-36
format command options, A-86
FORMAT function, A-33
formatting
   of cells, A-85
   screen, A-4
formatting function, A-33
formulas
   copying of, A-102
   in cells, A-60–A-61
   in VP-Planner Plus, A-83
functions, A-100–A-101

G

general format, A-86
General Problem Solver, A-220
global commands, A-99
global instruction, A-3
global options, A-100
goto record option, A-180
graph option, A-113–A-114
graph option commands, A-115
graphs, A-110–A-114
groups menu, A-207

H

header, A-3, A-48–A-49, A-51
Help function, A-74–A-75, A-141
HELP indicator, A-64
help system, A-226–A-227
Hercules Monochrome Graphics Adapter
      (MGA), A-113
hide format, A-86
horizontal title freezing option, A-105
How? command, A-262, A-264

I

IBM Color Graphics Adapter, A-113
IBM Enhanced Graphics Adapter (EGA),
      A-113
IF/THEN clause, A-246
IF/THEN propositions, A-220–A-221, A-233
incremental spacing, A-3
indents, A-37
Induce option, A-224, A-228–A-229
induction table, A-227, A-229–A-230
inference engine, A-221, A-265–A-266
insertion, A-3
Internal Revenue Service, and expert
      systems, A-222

J

justification, A-3

K

key field, A-189
keywords
   AND, OR, A-258
   summary of, A-273
knowledge base, A-236
   adding statements to, A-262
   adding variables to, A-243, A-245
   copying in, A-261
   editing of, A-237–A-239
   finding errors in, A-239–A-240
   formatting on, A-238
   in expert systems, A-220

mathematical operations on, A-270
parts of, A-232

L

LABEL indicator, A-64
label prefixes, A-88
labels
   aligning of, A-88
   entering of, A-77, A-79
   in spreadsheets, A-61–A-62
line editor, A-3
line format, A-33
line format menu options, A-36
locate menu, A-207
location induction table, A-256–A-257
logical fields, A-144–A-145
logical operators, A-178

M

medical software, A-222
memo fields, A-145–A-146
menu
   definition of, A-134
   Page Format A-33, A-48, A-50
   Print format, A-33
   tab, A-39
MENU indicator, A-64
menu options, A-68, A-136–A-138
menus, A-68
microcomputers, A-2
mineral-exploration software, A-222
mode indicators, A-64
model, spreadsheet, A-98
MOVE function, A-20
MYCIN application software, A-222

N

naming a file, A-13
navigation line, A-135
Newell, Allen, A-220
NUM indicator, A-64
numeric fields, A-145–A-146

O

operators, A-178–A-179
options menu, A-207
order of precedence, in spreadsheets,
      A-105–A-106
orphans, in format, A-45
overtype mode, A-17

P

PAGE FORMAT function, A-48
page format menu, A-50

paragraph indents, A-37
percent format, A-86
PLURAL statement, A-258
POINT indicator, A-64
position menu, A-204
print
    formatting of, A-4
    on WordPerfect, A-27
    preview, A-4
print enhancements, A-42
PRINT FORMAT function, A-33
print format menu, A-33, A-35–A-36
printer control menu, A-28
printer options, A-92
printing
    of graphs, A-118
    of VP-Planner Plus worksheet, A-91–A-92
    on dBASE III PLUS, A-173
    on VP-Expert, A-268
    on WordPerfect, A-27
PRINTOFF clause, A-268
PRINTON clause, A-268
PROSPECTOR application software, A-222

R

range, A-80–A-81
range commands, A-99
READY indicator
    in VP-Planner Plus, A-64
record, definition of, A-128
relational operators, A-177, A-179
report
    creating of, A-206–A-208
    designing of, A-207
    modifying of, A-209
    printing of, A-210
reset format, A-86
results window, A-231
RETRIEVE function, A-14
retrieving files, A-70
REVEAL CODES function, A-42
routines, search, A-4
rule base, in expert systems, A-220,
        A-233–A-234
rules window, A-231, A-266
RUNTIME statement, A-266

S

SAVE function, A-13
saving amended files, A-73
saving files, A-70–A-71
scientific format, A-86
screen editor, A-4
screen formatting, A-4
SCROLL indicator, A-64
scrolling, A-4, A-104
search and find routine, A-4, A-51
search and replace, A-4

seek option, A-204
Simon, Herbert, A-220
sort option, A-189, A-195, A-197
sorting
    alphabetically, A-189
    conditional, A-195
Speller
    on WordPerfect, A-22, A-26–A-27
spreadsheet, A-60–A-127
    active cell, A-63
    analysis, A-98, A-109
    cell pointer, A-63
    cells, A-61
    control panel, A-63
    coordinate, A-61, A-63
    definition of, A-60
    formulas, A-61
    labels, A-61, A-62
    program, A-60
    uses of, A-60, A-61
    values, A-61, A-62
    windows, A-61
statements, of expert systems, A-234
status bar, A-135
status indicators, A-64
status line, A-4, A-9
STEAMER application software, A-222
storage, A-175
subscript, A-4
sum option, A-183
summary command, A-181
superscript, A-4
systems analysis, of expert systems, A-222

T

tab menu, A-39
table, A-196
text
    block movement of, A-20
    deletion of, A-17–A-18
    editing of, A-15–A-16
    search in, A-51
text buffer, A-4
text format, A-86
Thesaurus, A-22–A-25
title freezing
    in VP-Planner plus, A-104–A-106
toggle, A-165
tools submenu, A-175

U

UNDERLINE function, A-42
user interface, A-221

V

VALUE indicator, A-64

values
    entering of, A-79–A-81
    formatting of, A-85
    in spreadsheets, A-60–A-62
variables, assigning values to, A-270
vertical title freezing option, A-105
virtual representation, A-4
VP-Expert, A-221–A-280
    printing of, A-268
    ACTIONS block, A-233, A-235
    BECAUSE statement, A-262
    block commands, A-244
    clauses, A-241, A-242, A-243, A-273
    commands, A-262, A-266
    confidence factors, A-255
    consultations, A-258, A-265
    editing commands, A-228
    error messages, A-273
    function key commands, A-273
    guide to, A-223
    How? command, A-264
    keywords, A-258, A-272
    knowledge base
        adding variables to, A-243
        copying in, A-261
        editing of, A-237, A-238, A-239
        finding errors in, A-239–A-240
        formatting on, A-238
    knowledge base, A-232
    location induction table, A-256–A-257
    logical operators, A-258
    PLURAL statement, A-258
    printing of, A-268
    statements, A-272
    Why? command, A-262–263
VP-Planner Plus, A-63–127
    "at" functions, A-101–A-102, A-104
    analytical graphs
        bar graphs, A-110–A-114
        pie charts, A-111–A-114
    business graphics, A-110
    cell, erasing of, A-87
    cell formatting, A-85
    column widths, A-89
    commands, A-99
    default setting, A-70
    deleting columns, A-90
    description of, A-63
    director, A-70
    format command options, A-86
    formulas, A-83
    global options, A-100
    graphs, printing of, A-118
    Help function, A-74
        screens, A-75
    inserting columns in, A-90
    labels, A-77, A-79, A-88
    menu options, A-68
    mode indicators, A-64
    pointer-movement keys, A-66
    printer options, A-92
    quitting, A-76

ranges, A-80–A-81
retrieving files, A-70
saving files, A-70–A-71, A-73
spreadsheet, A-60
status indicators, A-64
title freezing, A-104
values, A-79, A-80–A-81, A-85

W

WAIT indicator, A-64
window
  in spreadsheets, A-61
  in VP-Planner Plus, A-66
WordPerfect
  boldfacing text, A-41, A-42
word processing, A-2–A-59
  character enhancements, A-33
  dedicated systems, A-2
  definition of, A-2

formatting, A-33
in legal profession, A-5
in schools, A-5
terminology of, A-3, A-4
word processor
  definition of, A-2
  document-oriented, A-3
  memory-only, A-4
  page-oriented, A-4
word processors, A-5
word wrap, A-4, A-10
WordPerfect, A-2, A-6–A-59
  boldfacing in, A-41–A-42
  color codes, A-6
  command codes, A-42, A-47
  endnotes, A-50
  entering text, A-10, A-12
  EXIT, A-13
  footers, A-48, A-51
  footnotes, A-50, A-54
  FORMAT function, A-33

headers, A-48, A-51
line format, A-35
PAGE FORMAT function, A-48
paragraph indents, A-37
print format, A-35
PRINT FORMAT function, A-33
printer, A-27, A-28
RETRIEVE, A-14
REVEAL CODES function, A-42
routines, A-51
SAVE, A-13
symbols for, A-7, A-8
tabs, A-39
to start, A-8
underlining text, A-41, A-42
worksheet cell, A-87
  creating of, A-76
  definition of, A-60
  formulas in, A-83
  printing of, A-91–A-92

Glossary

Abacus An early device used for mathematical calculations; it consists of a rectangular frame with beads strung on wires.

Access To get or retrieve data from a computer system.

Access mechanism The device that positions the read/write head of a direct-access storage device over a particular track.

Accounting machine A mechanically operated forerunner of the computer; could read data from punched cards, perform calculations, rearrange data, and print results in varied formats.

Acoustic-coupler modem A device used in telecommunications that is attached to a computer by a cable and that connects to a standard telephone handset.

Action entries One of four sections of a decision logic table; specifies what actions should be taken.

Action stub One of four sections of a decision logic table; describes possible actions applicable to the decision being made.

Activity The proportion of records processed during an update run.

Ada A high-level programming language developed for use by the Department of Defense. Named for Augusta Ada Byron, Countess of Lovelace and daughter of the poet Lord Byron, Ada is a sophisticated structured language that supports concurrent processing.

Address A unique identifier assigned to each memory location within primary storage.

American Standard Code for Information Interchange (ASCII) A seven-bit standard code used for information interchange among data-processing systems, communication systems, and associated equipment.

Amount field The field where a clerk manually inserts the amount of the check; used in the processing of bank checks.

Analog computer A computer that measures the change in continuous electrical or physical conditions rather than counting data; contrast with digital computer.

Analog transmission Transmission of data over communication channels in a continuous wave form.

Analytical engine A machine (designed by Charles Babbage) capable of addition, subtraction, multiplication, division, and storage of intermediate results in a memory unit. Too advanced for its time, the analytical engine was forgotten for nearly a hundred years.

APL (A Programming Language) A terminal-oriented high-level programming language that is especially suitable for interactive problem solving.

Application program A sequence of instructions written to solve a specific user problem.

Application programmer The person who converts a design for a system into instructions for the computer; they are responsible for testing, debugging, documenting, and implementing programs.

Arithmetic Logic Unit (ALU) The section of the processor or CPU that handles arithmetic computation and logical operations.

Artificial intelligence (AI) Field of research currently developing techniques whereby computers can be used to solve problems that appear to require imagination, intuition, or intelligence.

ASCII-8 An eight-bit version of ASCII developed for computers that require eight-bit rather than seven-bit codes.

Assembler program The translator program for an assembly language program; produces a machine-language program (object program) which can then be executed.

Assembly language A low-level programming language that uses convenient abbreviations called mnemonics rather than the groupings of 0s and 1s used in machine language. Because instructions in assembly language generally have a one-to-one correspondence with machine-language instructions, assembly language is easier to translate into machine language than are high-level language statements.

Attribute A characteristic field within a record in a computer file.

Audio conferencing A conference call that links three or more people.

Audit trail A means of verifying the accuracy of information; a description of the path that leads to the original data upon which the information is based.

Augmented audio conferencing A form of teleconferencing

that combines graphics and audio conferencing.

Automatic teller machine (ATM) Remote terminal that allows bank customers to make transactions with the bank's central computer; user can check account balances, transfer funds, make deposits, and so forth.

Auxiliary storage *See* Secondary storage.

Back-end processor A small CPU serving as an interface between a large CPU and a large data base stored on a direct-access storage device.

Background partition In a multiprogramming system, a partition handling a lower-priority program that is executed only when high-priority programs are not using the system.

Background program In a multiprogramming system, a program that can be executed whenever the facilities of the system are not needed by a high-priority program.

Backup copies Second copies of original magnetic storage tapes made to prevent data loss.

Bandwidth Also known as grade; the range of width of the frequencies available for transmission of a given channel.

Bar-code reader A device used to read a bar code by means of reflected light, such as a scanner that reads the Universal Product Code on supermarket products.

BASIC (Beginners' All-purpose Symbolic Instruction Code) A high-level programming language commonly used for interactive problem solving by users; it is widely implemented on microcomputers and is often taught to beginning programmers.

Binary number system Number system used in computer operations that uses the digits 0 and 1 and has a base of 2; corresponds to the two possible states in machine circuitry, "on" and "off."

Binary representation Use of a two-state, or binary, system to represent data, as in setting and resetting the electrical state of semiconductor memory to either 0 or 1.

Binary system *See* Binary number system.

Biochip In theory, a chip whose circuits will be built from the proteins and enzymes of living matter such as *E. coli* bacteria.

Bit Short for BInary digiT; the smallest unit of data that the computer can handle and that can be represented in the digits (0 and 1) of binary notation.

Bit cells The name for storage locations in semiconductors.

Bletchley Park A computer built by two Englishmen, Dilwyn Knox and Alan Turing, that was used successfully during World War II to decipher German codes.

Block *See* Blocked record.

Blocked record Records grouped together on magnetic tape or magnetic disk to reduce the number of interrecord gaps and more fully utilize the storage medium.

Boot To load instructions into the computer's memory.

Branch A statement used to alter the normal flow of program execution.

Breach of contract The instance when goods fail to meet the terms of either an express warranty or implied warranty.

Broad-band channel A communication channel that can transmit data at rates of up to 120,000 bits per second; for example, microwaves.

Bubble memory A memory medium in which data is represented by magnetized spots (magnetic domains) resting on a thin film of semiconductor material.

Buffer Storage used to compensate for a difference in the rate of flow of data, or time of occurrence of events; used when transmitting data from one device to another.

Bug A program error.

Bus configuration A configuration often used with local-area networks in which multiple stations connected to a communication cable can communicate directly with any other station on the line.

Byte A fixed number of adjacent bits operated on as a unit.

C A high-level structured programming language that includes low-level language instructions, C is popular because it is portable and is implemented on a wide variety of computer systems.

Cache memory Also known as a high-speed buffer; a working buffer or temporary area used to help speed the execution of a program.

CAD/CAM The combination of computer-aided design and computer-aided manufacturing with which an engineer can analyze not only a product but also the manufacturing process.

Cell The unique location in an electronic spreadsheet where a row and a column intersect.

Central processing unit (CPU) Acts as the "brain" of the computer; composed of three sections—arithmetic/logic unit (ALU), control unit, and primary storage unit.

Centralized design An information structure in which a separate data-processing department is used to provide data-processing facilities for the entire organization.

Chain printer An output device that has the character set engraved in type and assembled in a chain that revolves horizontally past all print position; prints when a print hammer (one for each column of the paper) presses the paper against an inked ribbon that presses against the characters on the print chain.

Channel A limited-capacity computer that takes over the tasks of input and output in order to free the CPU to handle internal processing operations.

Character A single letter, digit, or special sign (like $, #, or *). Characters are represented by bytes in computer storage.

Charge-coupled device (CCD) A storage device made of silicon that is nearly 100 times faster than magnetic bubble storage.

Check bit *See* Parity bit.

Chief Programmer Team (CPT) A method of organization used in developing software systems in industry in which a chief programmer supervises the development and testing of software; programmer productivity and software reliability are increased.

Clock speed The number of electronic pulses a microprocessor can produce each second.

Clustered key-to-tape device The tying together of several keyboards to one or two magnetic-tape units.

COBOL (COmmon Business-Oriented Language) A high-level programming language generally used for business applications; it is well suited to manipulating large data files.

Coding The processing of writing a programming problem solution in a programming language.

Common law Law that is based on customs and past judicial decisions in similar cases.

Communication channel A medium for carrying data from one location to another.

Compact disk (CD) A nonerasable 4¾ inch disk used as a storage medium for microcomputers; it can store about 1,000 times more bytes than a single-sided floppy disk.

Compatibility The ability to use equipment or software produced by one manufacturer on a computer produced by another manufacturer.

Compiler program The translator program for a high-level language such as FORTRAN or COBOL; translates the entire source program into machine language, creating an object program tha tis then executed.

Composite color monitor A computer monitor offering composite color and resolution slightly better than a TV.

Computer-aided design (CAD) Process of designing, drafting, and analyzing a prospective product using computer graphics on a video terminal.

Computer-aided engineering (CAE) A system, used in the design of electronic products, that allows engineers to interact with the computer during simulation runs as errors are identified.

Computer-aided manufacturing (CAM) Use of a computer to simulate or monitor the steps of a manufacturing process.

Computer-assisted instruction (CAI) Use of a computer to instruct or drill a student on an individual or small-group basis.

Computer anxiety A fear individuals have of the effects computers have on their lives and society in general.

Computer conferencing A form of teleconferencing that uses computer terminals for the transmission of messages; participants need not be using the terminal in order to receive the message—it will be waiting the next time they use the terminal.

Computer crime A criminal act that poses a greater threat to a computer user than to a non-computer user, or a criminal act that is accomplished through the use of a computer.

Computer ethics A term used to refer to the standard of moral conduct in computer use; a way in which the "spirit" of some laws are applied to computer-related activities.

Computer-integrated manufacturing (CIM) An arrangement that links various departments within an organization to a central data base for the purpose of improving the efficiency of the manufacturing process.

Computer literacy General knowledge about computers; includes some technical knowledge about hardware and software, the ability to use computers to solve problems, and awareness of how computers affect society.

Computer operator The person responsible for setting up equipment; mounting and removing tapes, disks, and diskettes; and monitoring the operation of the computer.

Computer phobia Fear of computers and their effects on society.

Computer security Instituting the technical and administrative safeguards necessary to protect a computer-based system against the hazards to which computer systems are exposed and to control access to information.

Computerized axial tomography (CT or CAT) scanning Form of noninvasive physical testing that combines x-ray techniques and computers to aid diagnosis.

Concentrator A device that systematically allocates the use of communication channels among several terminals.

Concurrent Taking place within the same time interval. In multiprogramming, concurrency occurs when processing alternates between different programs.

Condition entries One of four sections of a decision logic table; answers question in the condition stub.

Condition stub One of four sections of a decision logic table; describes all options to be considered in making a decision.

Continuous form A data-entry form, such as cash register tape, utilized by OCR devices.

Control program A routine, usually part of an operating system, that aids in controlling the operations and management of a computer system.

Control unit The section of the CPU that directs the sequence of operations by electrical signals and governs the actions of the various units that make up the computer.

Copy A feature of electronic spreadsheets that allows the user to duplicate a cell or group of cells on another part of the spreadsheet.

Corporate planning model *See* Simulation decision support system.

Crash conversion A method of system implementation in which the old system is abandoned and the new one implemented at once.

Cut form Data-entry form such as a phone or utility bill; used by OCR devices.

Cylinder The tracks on all disk surfaces that may be read without repositioning the read/write arm.

Daisy-wheel printer An output device resembling an office typewriter; it employs a flat disk with petal-like projections, each having a character at its tip; printing occurs one character at a time.

Data Facts; the raw material of information.

Data base Collection of data that is commonly defined and consistently organized to fit the information needs of a wide variety of users in an organization.

Data-base administrator (DBA) The person who controls all the data resources of an organization.

Data-base analyst The person responsible for the analysis, design, and implementation of the data base.

Data-base management system (DBMS) A set of programs that serves as the interface between the data base and the programmer, operating system, and users; also programs used to design and maintain data bases.

Data buffering Reading data into a separate storage unit normally contained in the control unit of the input/output system.

Data communication The electronic transmission of data from one site to another, usually over communication channels such as telephone or microwave.

Data definition language (DDL) The language in which the schema, which states how records within a data base are related, is written. This language differs depending on the type of data-base management system being used.

Data-entry operator The person who transcribes data into a form suitable for computer processing.

Data manipulation language (DML) The language used to access a hierarchical or a relational data base to provide a way for users to access the data base. The data manipulation language is different for each type of data-base management system.

Data set *See* Modem.

Data structure A particular relationship between the data elements in a computer file.

Datacom handler Another name for multiplexer and concentrator.

Debugging The process of locating, isolating, and correcting errors in a program.

Decentralized design An information structure in which the authority and responsibility for computer support are placed in relatively autonomous organization operating units.

Decimal number system A number system based on the powers of ten.

Decision logic table (DLT) A table that organizes relevant facts in a clear and concise manner to aid a decision-making process.

Decision support system (DSS) An integrated system that draws on data from a wide variety of sources such as data bases to provide a supportive tool for managerial decision-making. Generally, managers use fourth-generation programming languages to access decision support systems.

Decrypted Data that is translated back into regular text

after being encrypted for security reasons.

Demodulation The process of retrieving data from a modulated carrier wave.

Desk checking A method used in both system and application program debugging in which the sequence of operations is mentally traced to verify the correctness of program logic.

Detail diagram Used in HIPO packages to describe the specific functions performed and data items used in a given module.

Digital computer Type of computer commonly used in business applications; operates on distinct data (for example, digits) by performing arithmetic and logic processes on specific data units.

Digital transmission The transmission of data as distinct on and off pulses.

Direct-access storage device (DASD) Auxiliary storage device that allows data to be stored and accessed either randomly or sequentially.

Direct-connect modem A device used in telecommunications that is attached to a computer by a cable and that connects directly to a telephone line by plugging into a standard phone jack.

Direct conversion *See* Crash conversion.

Directory Contains record keys and their corresponding addresses; used to obtain the address of a record with a direct-access file design.

Disk address The method used to identify a data record on a magnetic disk; consists of the disk surface number, track number, and record number.

Disk drive The mechanical device used to rotate a disk pack during data transmission.

Disk pack A stack of magnetic disks.

Diskette *See* Floppy disk.

Distributed computing A system in which processing is done at a site other than that of the central computer.

Distributed data processing (DDP) *See* Distributed computing.

Distributed design An information structure in which independent operating units have some data-processing facilities but there is still central control and coordination of computer resources.

Dot-matrix printer A type of impact printer that creates characters through the use of dot-matrix patterns.

Drum printer An impact printer that consists of a metal cylinder with rows of characters engraved on its surface; one line of print is produced with each drum rotation.

Dump A hard-copy printout of the contents of computer memory; valuable in debugging programs.

E-mail *See* Electronic mail.

Edit checks Processing statements designed to identify potential errors in the input data.

EDVAC (Electronic Discrete Variable Automatic Computer) A stored-program computer developed at the University of Pennsylvania.

Electronic data processing (EDP) Data processing performed largely by electronic equipment, such as computers, rather than by manual means.

Electronic funds transfer (EFT) A cashless method of managing money; accounts involved in a transaction are adjusted by electronic communications between computers.

Electronic mail Transmission of messages at high speeds over telecommunication facilities.

Electronic spreadsheet An electronic ledger sheet used to store and manipulate any type of numeric data.

Electrostatic printer A nonimpact printer in which electromagnetic impulses and heat are used to affix characters to paper.

Electrothermal printer A nonimpact printer that uses a special heat-sensitive paper; characters are formed when heated rods in a matrix touch the paper.

Encrypted A term describing data that is translated into a secret code for security reasons.

End-user development tools Tools that allow the end-user to develop an application package, usually through the use of a fourth-generation programming language. Examples of end-user development tools are simulation software, statistical packages, and data-base management systems.

ENIAC (Electronic Numerical Integrator and Calculator) The first general-purpose electronic digital computer; it was developed by John W. Mauchly and J. Presper Eckert at the University of Pennsylvania.

Erasable programmable read-only memory (EPROM) A form of read-only memory that can be erased and reprogrammed, but only by being submitted to a special process such as exposure to ultraviolet light.

Ergonomics The method of researching and designing computer hardware and software to enhance employee productivity and comfort.

Even parity A method of coding in which an even number of 1 bits represent of each character; used to enhance the detection of errors.

Executive *See* Supervisor program.

Expert system Form of artificial intelligence software designed to imitate the same decision-making and evaluation processes of experts in a specific field.

Express warranty Created when the seller makes any promise or statement of fact concerning the goods being sold, which the purchaser uses as a basis for purchasing the goods.

Extended Binary Coded Decimal Interchange Code (EBCDIC) An eight-bit code for character representation.

External storage *See* Secondary storage.

Facsimile system Produces a picture of a page by scanning it.

FAX system *See* Facsimile system.

Feedback A check within a system to see whether prede-termined goals are being met; the return of information about the effectiveness of the system.

Fiber optics A data transmission concept using laser pulses and cables made of tiny threads of glass that can transmit huge amounts of data at the speed of light.

Field A meaningful collection of characters, such as a social security number or a person's name.

File A grouping of related records, such as student records; sometimes referred to as a data set.

File manager An application package designed to duplicate the traditional manual methods of filing records.

First-generation computer Computer that used vacuum tubes; developed in the 1950s; much faster than earlier mechanical devices, but very slow in comparison to today's computers.

Flexible disk *See* Floppy disk.

Floppy disk A low-cost direct-access form of data storage made of plastic and coated with a magnetizable substance upon which data are stored; disks come in varying sizes.

Floppy diskette *See* Flexible disk.

Flowchart Of two kinds: the program flowchart, which is a graphic representation of the types and sequences of operations in a program; and the system flowchart, which shows the flow of data through an entire system.

Foreground partition Also called foreground area; in a multiprogramming system, a partition containing high-priority application programs.

Foreground program In a multiprogramming system, a program that has high priority.

Formal design review Also called a structured walkthrough; an evaluation of the design of a software system by a group of managers, analysts, and programmers to determine completeness, accuracy, and quality of the design.

FORTH A high-level programming language that includes low-level language instructions, FORTH is the standard language used in astronomical observatories around the world.

FORTRAN (FORmula TRANslator) The oldest high-level programming language, it is used primarily in performing mathematical or scientific operations.

Four-bit binary coded decimal (BCD) A four-bit computer code that uses four-bit groupings to represent digits in decimal numbers.

Fourth-generation computer Computer that uses chips made by large-scale integration and offers significant price and performance improvements over earlier computers.

Fourth-generation software development tools See End-user development tools.

Front-end processor A small CPU serving as an interface between a large CPU and peripheral devices.

Fully distributed configuration A network design in which every set of nodes in the network can communicate directly with every other set of nodes through a single communication link.

Functional tools A category of application software packages that perform specific tasks or functions, such as inventory control.

Garbage in-garbage out (GIGO) A phrase illustrating the fact that the meaningfulness of computer output relies on the accuracy or relevancy of the data fed into the processor.

Grade *See* Bandwidth.

Graphic display device A visual-display device that projects output in the form of graphs and line drawings and accepts input from a keyboard or light pen.

Graphics package An application software package designed to allow the user to display images on the display screen or a printer.

Graphics tablet A flat board-like object that, when drawn on, transfers the image to a computer screen.

Grid chart (tabular chart) A chart used in system analysis and design to summarize the relationships between functions of an organization.

Hacking A term used to describe the activity of computer enthusiasts who are challenged by the practice of breaking computer security measures designed to prevent unauthorized access to a particular computer system.

Hard copy Printed output.

Hardware Physical components that make up a computer system.

Hard-wired Memory instructions that cannot be changed or deleted by other stored-program instructions.

Hashing *See* Randomizing.

Hexadecimal number system A base 16 number system commonly used when printing the contents of primary storage to aid programmers in detecting errors.

Hierarchical configuration A network design for multiple CPUs in which an organization's needs are divided into multiple levels that receive different levels of computer support.

Hierarchical design An information structure in which each level within an organization has necessary computer power; responsibility for control and coordination goes to the top level.

Hierarchical structure Also called tree structure; the data structure in which one primary element may have numerous secondary elements linked to it at lower levels.

High-speed buffer *See* Cache memory.

Impact printer A printer that forms characters by physically striking a ribbon against a paper.

Implied warranty A warranty that provides for the automatic inclusion of certain warranties in a contract for the sale of goods.

Implied warranty of fitness A situation in which the purchaser relies on a seller's expertise to recommend a good that will meet his or her needs; if the good later fails to meet the purchaser's needs the seller has breached the warranty.

Implied warranty of merchantability Guarantees the purchaser that the good purchased will function properly for a reasonable period of time.

Information Data that has been organized and processed so that it is meaningful.

In-house An organization's use of its own personnel or resources to develop programs or other problem-solving systems.

Ink-jet printer A nonimpact printer that uses a stream of charged ink to form dot-matrix characters.

Input Data submitted to the computer for processing.

Input/output bound A situation in which the CPU is slowed down because of I/O operations, which are extremely slow in comparison to CPU internal processing speeds.

Input/output control unit A device located between one or more I/O devices that performs code conversion.

Input/output management system A subsystem of the operating system that controls and coordinates the CPU while receiving input from channels, executing instructions of programs in storage, and regulating output.

Instruction set The fundamental logical and arithmetic procedures that the computer can perform, such as addition, subtraction, and comparison.

Integrated circuit An electronic circuit etched on a small silicon chip less than ⅛-inch square, permitting much faster processing than with transistors and at a greatly reduced price.

Interactive video A multimedia learning concept that merges computer text, sound, and graphics by using a videodisk, videodisk player, microcomputer with monitor and disk drive, and computer software.

Interblock gap (IBG) A space on magnetic tape that facilitates processing; separates records grouped together on the tape.

Internal memory *See* Primary storage.

Internal modem A modem that plugs into the internal circuitry of a computer; no external cables or connections are needed.

Internal storage *See* Primary storage.

Interpreter A high-level language translator that evaluates and translates a program one statement at a time; used extensively on microcomputer systems because it takes up less primary storage than a compiler.

Interrecord gap (IRG) A space that separates records stored on magnetic tape; allows the tape drive to regain speed during processing.

Interrupt A condition or event that temporarily suspends normal processing operations.

Inverted structure A structure that indexes a simple file by specific record attributes.

Job-control language (JCL) A language that serves as the communication link between the programmer and the operating system.

Job-control program A control program that translates the job-control statements written by a programmer into machine-language instructions that can be executed by the computer.

Josephson junction A primary storage unit that will be housed in liquid helium to reduce the resistance to the flow of electricity that currently exists in semiconductor memory.

K (kilobyte) A symbol used to denote 1,024 (2^{10}) storage units (1,024 bytes) when referring to a computer's primary storage capacity; often rounded to 1,000 bytes.

Key The unique identifier or field of a record; used to sort records for processing or to locate specific records within a file.

Keypunch A keyboard device that punches holes in a card to represent data.

Keypunch operator Person who uses a keypunch machine to transfer data from source documents to punched cards.

Label A name written beside a programming instruction that acts as an identifier for that instruction; also, in spreadsheets, information used to describe some aspect of the spreadsheet.

Large-scale Integration (LSI) Method by which circuits containing thousands of electronic components are densely packed on a single silicon chip.

Laser printer A type of nonimpact printer that combines laser beams and electrophotographic technology to form images on paper.

Laser storage system A secondary storage device using laser technology to encode data onto a metallic surface; usually used for mass storage.

Librarian The person responsible for classifying, cataloging, and maintaining the files and programs stored on cards, tapes, disks and diskettes, and all other storage media in a computer library.

Librarian program Software that manages the storage and use of library programs by maintaining a directory of programs in the system library and appropriate procedures for additions and deletions.

Light pen A pen-shaped object with a photoelectric cell at its end; used to draw lines on a visual display screen.

Linear structure A data structure in which the records in a computer file are arranged sequentially in a specified order.

Link A transmission channel that connects nodes.

Linkage editor A subprogram of the operating system that links the object program from the system residence device to primary storage.

LISP (LISt Processing) A high-level programming language commonly used in artificial intelligence research and in the processing of lists of elements.

Local system Peripherals connected directly to the CPU.

Logical file The combination of data needed to meet a user's needs.

Logo An education-oriented, procedure-oriented, interactive programming language designed to allow anyone to begin programming and communicating with computers quickly.

Loop A structure that allows a specified sequence of instructions to be executed repeatedly as long as stated conditions remain constant.

Machine language The only set of instructions that a computer can execute directly; a code that designates the proper electrical states in the computer as combinations of zeros and ones.

Magnetic core Iron-alloy, doughnut-shaped ring about the size of a pinhead of which memory can be composed; individual cores can store one binary digit (its state is determined by the direction of an electrical current); the cores are strung on a grid of fine wires that carry the current.

Magnetic disk A direct-access storage medium consisting of a metal platter coated on both sides with a magnetic recording material upon which data are stored in the form of magnetized spots.

Magnetic domain A magnetized spot representing data in bubble memory.

Magnetic drum Cylinder with a magnetic outer surface on which data can be stored by magnetizing specific positions on the surface.

Magnetic-ink character reader A device used to perform magnetic-ink character recognition (MICR).

Magnetic-ink character recognition (MICR) A process that involves reading characters composed of magnetized particles; often used to sort checks for subsequent processing.

Magnetic tape A sequential storage medium consisting of a narrow strip of plastic upon which spots of iron-oxide are magnetized to represent data.

Mainframe A type of large, full-scale computer capable of supporting many peripheral devices.

Main memory *See* Primary storage.

Main storage *See* Primary storage.

Maintenance programmer The person who maintains large programs by making needed changes and improvements.

Management information system (MIS) A formal network that uses computers to provide information used to support structured managerial decision making; its goal is to get the correct information to the appropriate manager at the right time.

Management Information System (MIS) manager The person responsible for planning and tying together all the information resources of a firm.

Mark I First automatic calculator.

Mark sensing *See* Optical-mark recognition.

Master file A file that contains all existing records organized according to the key field; updated by records in a transaction file.

Materials requirement planning (MRP) A manufacturing system that ties together different manufacturing needs such as raw materials planning and inventory control into interacting systems. The interacting systems allow a manufacturer to plan and control operations efficiently.

Megahertz (MHz) One million times per second; the unit of measurement for clock speed.

Memory management In a multiprogramming environment, the process of keeping the programs in primary storage separate.

Memory protection *See* Memory management.

Menu driven An application program is said to be menu-driven when it provides the user with "menus" displaying available choices or selections to help guide the user through the process of using the software package.

Message switching The task of a communications processor of receiving messages and routing them to appropriate destinations.

Microcomputer A small, low-priced computer used in homes, schools, and businesses; also called a personal computer.

Microprocessor A programmable processing unit (placed on a silicon chip) containing arithmetic, logic, and control circuitry; used in microcomputers, calculators, and microwave ovens and in many other applications.

Microprogram A sequence of instructions wired into read-only memory; used to tailor a system to meet the user's specific processing requirements.

Minicomputer A type of computer with the components of a full-sized system but with smaller primary storage capacity.

Mnemonics A symbolic name (memory aid); used in symbolic languages (for example, assembly language) and high-level programming languages.

Model A mathematical representation of an actual system, containing independent variables that influence the value of a dependent variable.

Modem Also called a data set; a device that modulates and demodulates signals transmitted over communication facilities.

Modula-2 A high-level structured programming language that is a descendant of Pascal; it is based on the concept of modules that are nested within one another. Modula-2 supports concurrent processing and also incorporates low-level language commands.

Modular approach A method of simplifying a programming project by breaking it into segments or subunits referred to as modules.

Modulation A technology used in modems to make data processing signals compatible with communication facilities.

Module Part of a whole; a program segment or subsystem; a set of logically related program statements that perform one specified task in a program.

Monitor *See* Supervisor program.

Monochrome monitor A computer monitor that displays amber, green, or white characters on a black background.

Multiphasic health testing (MPHT) Computer-assisted testing plan that compiles data on patients and their test results, which are compared with norms or means to aid the physician in making a diagnosis.

Multiplexer A device that permits more than one I/O device to transmit data over the same communication channel.

Multiplexor channel A limited-capacity computer that can handle more than one I/O device at a time; normally used to control slow-speed devices such as card readers, printers, or terminals.

Multiprocessing A multiple CPU configuration in which jobs are processed simultaneously.

Napier's Bones A portable multiplication tool (described by John Napier) consisting of ivory rods that slide up and down against each other; forerunner of the slide rule.

Narrow bandwidth channel A communication channel that can transmit data only at a rate between 45 and 90 bits per second; for example, telegraph lines.

Natural language Designed primarily for novice computer users; uses English-like statements usually for the purpose of accessing data in a data base.

Network The linking together of several CPUs.

Network structure The data structure in which a primary data element may have many secondary elements linked to it and any given secondary element may be linked to numerous primary elements.

Next-sequential-instruction feature The ability of a computer to execute program steps in the order in which they are stored in memory unless branching takes place.

Node The endpoint of a network; consists of CPUs, printers, CRTs, or any other physical devices.

Nondestructive read/destructive write The feature of computer memory that permits data to be read and retained in its original state, allowing it to be referenced repeatedly during processing.

Nondestructive testing (NDT) Testing done electronically to avoid breaking, cutting, or tearing apart a product to find a problem.

Nonimpact printer The use of heat, laser technology, or photographic techniques to print output.

Nonmonotonic logic A type of logic that adapts to exceptions to ordinary monotonic logical statements and allows conclusions to be drawn from assumptions.

Nuclear magnetic resonance (NMR) A computerized, non-invasive diagnostic tool that involves sending magnetic pulses through the body to identify medical problems.

Numeric bits The four rightmost bit positions of six-bit BCD used to encode numeric data.

Numerically controlled machinery Manufacturing machinery that is driven by a magnetic punched tape created by a tape punch that is driven by computer software.

Object program A sequence of machine-executable instructions derived from source-program statements by a language-translator program.

Octal number system Number system in which each position represents a power of eight.

Odd parity A method of coding in which an odd number of 1 bits is used to represent each character; facilitates error checking.

Office automation Integration of computer and communication technology with traditional office procedures to increase productivity and efficiency.

Online storage In direct communication with the computer.

On-us field The section of a check that contains the customer's checking-account number.

Op code The part of a machine or assembly language instruction that tells the computer what function to perform.

Operand The part of an instruction that tells where to find the data or equipment on which to operate.

Operating system A collection of programs designed to permit a computer system to manage itself and to avoid idle CPU time while increasing utilization of computer resources.

Operation code (op code) The part of an instruction that indicates what operation is to be performed.

Optical character A special type of character that can be read by an optical-character reader.

Optical-character recognition (OCR) A method of electronic scanning that reads numbers, letters, and other characters and then converts the optical images into appropriate electrical signals.

Optical disk A secondary storage device that stores data as the presence or absence of a pit burned into the surface of the disk by a laser beam.

Optical-mark page reader A device that senses marks on an OMR document as the document passes under a light source.

Optical-mark recognition (OMR) Mark sensing; a method of electronic scanning that reads marks on a page and converts the optical images into appropriate electrical signals.

Output Information that comes from the computer, as a result of processing, into a form that can be used by people.

Overview diagram Used in an HIPO package to describe in greater detail a module shown in the visual table of contents.

Packaged software A set of standardized computer programs, procedures, and related documentation necessary for solving specific problems.

Page Material that fits in one page frame of primary storage.

Page frame In a virtual storage environment, one of the fixed-sized physical areas into which primary storage is divided.

Paging A method of implementing virtual storage: data and programs are broken into fixed-sized blocks, or pages, and loaded into real storage when needed during processing.

Parallel conversion A system implementation approach in which the new system is operated side by side with the old one until all differences are reconciled.

Parallel processing A type of processing in which instructions and data are handled simultaneously.

Parity bit A bit added to detect incorrect transmission of data; it conducts internal checks to determine whether the correct number of bits is present.

Partition In multiprogramming, the primary storage area reserved for one program; it may be fixed or variable in size; see also Region.

Pascal A high-level structured programming language that was originally developed for instructional purposes and that is now commonly used in a wide variety of applications.

Pascaline A device invented by Blaise Pascal used to add and subtract; a series of rotating gears performed the calculations.

Peripheral device Device that attaches to the central processing unit, such as a secondary storage device or an input or output device.

Phased conversion A method of system implementation in which the old system is gradually replaced by the new one.

Physical file The way data is stored by the computer.

Pilot conversion The implementation of a new system into an organization on a piecemeal basis.

Plotter An output device that prepares graphic, hard copy of information; it can produce lines, curves, and complex shapes.

Point-of-sale (POS) system A computerized system that records information required for such things as inventory control and accounting at the point where a good is sold; see also source-data automation.

Point-of-sale (POS) terminal An input device that records information at the point where a good is sold.

Poll The process used by a concentrator to determine if an input/output device is ready to send a message to the CPU.

Portable The characteristic of a program that can be run on many different computers with minimal changes.

Portable computer A computer light enough to be carried; does not require an external power source.

Primary key A unique field for a record; used to sort records for processing or to locate a particular record within a file.

Primary storage/memory Also known as internal storage/ memory and main storage/memory; the section of the CPU that holds instructions, data, and intermediate and final results during processing.

Primary storage The section of the CPU that holds instructions, data, and intermediate results during processing.

Print-wheel printer An impact printer with 120 wheels each containing 48 characters. To produce characters on paper, the wheels rotate into position, forming an entire line of characters, then a hammer presses paper against the wheels.

Printer-keyboard An output device similar to an office typewriter; prints one character at a time and is controlled by a program stored in the CPU of the computer.

Privacy An individual's right regarding the collection, processing, storage, dissemination, and use of data about his or her personal attributes and activities.

Process To transform data into useful information by classifying, sorting, calculating, summarizing, or storing.

Process-bound A condition that occurs when a program monopolizes the processing facilities of the computer, making it impossible for other programs to be executed.

Processing program A routine, usually part of the operating system, that is used to simplify program preparation and execution.

Processor The term used collectively to refer to the ALU and control unit.

Productivity tools Application software packages that can increase the productivity of the user. Examples are text processors and graphics packages.

Program specifications The documentation for a programming problem definition; it includes the desired output, needed input, and the processing requirements.

Programmable communications processor A device that relieves the CPU of the task of monitoring data transmission.

Programmable read-only memory (PROM) Read-only memory that can be programmed by the manufacturer or by the user for special functions to meet the unique needs of the user.

Programming language A communication system people can use to communicate with computers.

Proper program A structured program in which each individual segment or module has only one entrance and one exit.

Pseudocode An informal design language used to represent the logic of a programming problem solution.

Public domain software Programs unprotected by copyright law for free, unrestricted public use.

Punched card A heavy paper storage medium on which data is represented by holes punched according to a coding scheme much like that used on Hollerith's cards.

Random-access memory (RAM) A form of primary storage

into which instructions and data can be read, written, and erased; directly accessed by the computer; temporary memory that is erased when the computer is turned off.

Random-access memory (RAM) disk A portion of RAM memory that is temporarily treated as a secondary storage device.

Randomizing A mathematical process applied to the record key that produces the storage address of the record.

Reading The process of accessing the same instructions or data over and over.

Read-only memory (ROM) The part of computer hardware containing items (circuitry patterns) that cannot be deleted or changed by stored-program instructions because they are wired into the computer.

Read/write head An electromagnet used as a component of a tape or disk drive; in reading data, it detects magnetized areas and translates them into electrical pulses; in writing data, it magnetizes appropriate areas and erases data stored there previously.

Read/write notch The oblong or rectangular opening in the jacket of a floppy disk through which the read/write head accesses the disk.

Real storage *See* Primary storage: contrast with virtual storage.

Record A collection of data items, or fields, that relates to a single unit, such as a student.

Region In multiprogramming, with a variable number of tasks, a term often used to mean the internal space allocated for a particular program; a variable-sized partition.

Register An internal computer component used for temporary storage of an instruction or data; capable of accepting, holding, and transferring that instruction or data very rapidly.

Relational structure The data structure that places the data elements in a table with rows representing records and columns containing fields.

Reliability The ability of a program to consistently obtain correct results.

Remote system A system in which terminals are connected to the central computer by a communication channel.

Remote terminal A terminal that is placed at a location distant from the central computer.

Remote-terminal operator A person involved with the preparation of input data at a location at some distance from the computer itself.

Resident routine A frequently used component of the supervisor that is initially loaded into primary storage.

Retrieve To access previously stored data.

RGB (red-green-blue) monitors A computer monitor that displays in three colors with high resolution.

Ring configuration A network design in which a number of computers are connected by a single transmission line in a ring formation.

Robotics The science that deals with robots, their construction, capabilities, and applications.

RPG (Report Program Generator) A problem-oriented high-level language that requires little skill on the part of the programmer to use. RPG was originally designed to produce business reports and requires the programmer to fill out specification forms; the generator program then builds the needed program.

Secondary key Fields that are used to gain access to records on a file; may not be unique identifiers.

Secondary memory *See* Secondary storage.

Secondary storage Also known as external or auxiliary storage; supplements primary storage and is external to the computer; data is accessed at slower speeds.

Second-generation computer A computer that used transistors; it was smaller, faster, and had larger storage capacity than the first-generation computers.

Segment A variable-sized block or portion of a program used in a virtual storage system.

Segmentation A method of implementing virtual storage; involves dividing a program into variable-sized blocks, called segments, depending on the program logic.

Selection A logic pattern that requires the computer to make a comparison; the result of the comparison determines which execution path will be taken next.

Selector channel A channel that can accept input from only one device at a time; generally used with high-speed I/O devices such as a magnetic tape or magnetic-disk unit.

Semiconductor memory Memory composed of circuitry on silicon chips; smaller than magnetic cores and allows for faster processing; more expensive than core memory and requires a constant power source.

Sequential file design Records are organized in a file in a specific order based on the value of the key field.

Sequential processing The process of creating a new master file each time transactions are processed; requires batch file access.

Serial processing A method of processing in which programs are executed one at a time; usually found in simple operating systems such as those used on the earliest computer systems.

Shareware Programs that are distributed to the public; the author retains the copyright to the programs with the expectation that users will make donations to the author based upon the value of the program to the users.

Silicon chip Solid-logic circuitry on a small piece of silicon used to form the primary storage of third- and fourth-generation computers.

Simple sequence A logic pattern in which one statement is executed after another, in the order in which they occur in the program.

Simple structure A data structure in which the records in a computer file are arranged sequentially.

Simulation software Application software that uses a model to project the outcome of a particular real-world situation.

Simultaneous decision support system A decision support system that attempts to incorporate into one system the decision making of various functional areas of an organization so that consistent, overall decisions can be made by management.

Six-bit Binary Coded Decimal (BCD) A data representation scheme that is used to represent the decimal digits 0 through 9, the letters A through Z, and twenty-eight special characters.

Soft copy A temporary, or nonpermanent, record of machine output; for example, a CRT display.

Software Program or programs used to direct the computer in solving problems and overseeing operations.

Software development process A sequence of four steps used to develop the solution to a programming problem in a structured manner. The steps are: (1) Define and document the problem. (2) Design and document a solution. (3) Write and document the program. (4) Debug and test the program and revise the documentation, if necessary.

Sort/merge program A type of operating system utility program; used to sort records to facilitate updating and subsequent combining of files to form a single, updated file.

Source-data automation The use of special equipment to collect data at its source.

Spelling checker Application software that checks words in a document against a dictionary file. Any words in the document that are not in the file are flagged. Spelling checkers are often included in text processing packages.

Stand-alone key-to-tape device A self-contained unit that takes the place of a keypunch device.

Star configuration A network design in which all transactions must go through a central computer before being routed to the appropriate network computer.

Statistical package A software package that performs statistical analysis of data. Examples are SAS, SPSS, and Minitab.

Stepped Reckoner Machine designed by von Liebniz that could add, subtract, multiply, divide, and calculate square roots.

Stored program Instructions stored in the computer's memory in electronic form; can be executed repeatedly during processing.

Stored-program concept The idea that program instructions can be stored in primary storage (computer memory) in electrical form so that no human intervention is required during processing; allows the computer to process the instructions at its own speed.

Structure chart A graphic representation of the results of the top-down design process, displaying the modules of the solution and their relationships to one another; of two types, system and process.

Structured programming A collection of techniques that encourages the development of well-designed, less error-prone programs with easy-to-follow logic. Structured programming techniques can be divided into two categories:

(1) structured design techniques, such as top-down design, that are used in designing a problem solution, and (2) structure coding techniques, which state the rules that are followed when a program is actually coded.

Structured walkthrough *See* Formal design review.

Subroutine A sequence of statements not within the main line of the program; saves the programmer time by not having to write the same instructions over again in different parts of the program.

Supercomputer The largest, fastest, most expensive type of computer in existence, capable of performing millions of calculations per second and processing enormous amounts of data; also called maxicomputer or monster computer.

Supermicrocomputer A microcomputer built around a 32-bit microprocessor that is powerful enough to compete with low-end minicomputers.

Supervisor program Also known as a monitor or executive; the major component of the operating system; coordinates the activities of all other parts of the operating system.

Swapping In a virtual-storage environment, the process of transferring a program section from virtual storage to real storage, and vice versa.

Symbolic language The use of mnemonic symbols to represent instructions; must be translated into machine language before being executed by the computer.

Synergism The interaction that the combined efforts of all parts of an information system have to achieve a greater effect than the sum of the individual efforts.

Syntax The grammatical rules of a language.

System A group of related elements that work toward a common goal.

System analysis report A report given to top management after the system analysis phase has been completed to report the findings of the system study; includes a statement of objectives, constraints, and possible alternatives.

System analyst The person who is responsible for system analysis, design, and implementation of computer-based information systems and who is the communication link or interface between users and technical persons.

System design report The phase of the system life cycle in which information system design alternatives are developed and presented to management. These alternatives should contain information on system inputs, processing, and outputs.

System flowchart The group of symbols that represents the general information flow; focuses on inputs and outputs rather than on internal computer operations.

System library A collection of files in which various parts of an operating system are stored.

System program Programs that coordinate the operation of computer circuitry and assist in the development of application programs. System programs are designed to facilitate the efficient use of the computer's resources.

System programmer The person responsible for creating and maintaining system software.

System residence device An auxiliary storage device (disk, tape, or drum) on which operating-system programs are stored and from which they are loaded into primary storage.

Tabular chart *See* Grid chart.

Tape cassette A sequential-access storage medium used in small computer systems for high-density digital recording.

Tape drive A device that moves magnetic tape past a read/write head.

Telecommunication The combined use of communication facilities, such as telephone systems and data-processing equipment.

Telecommuting Method of working at home by communicating via electronic-machine telecommunication facilities.

Telecomputing A term referring to the use of online information services that offer access to one or more data bases; for example, CompuServe, The Source, and Dow Jones News/Retrieval.

Teleconferencing The method of two or more remote locations communicating via electronic and image-producing facilities.

Telecopier system *See* Facsimile system.

Teletypewriter system Transmits messages as strings of characters.

Terminals An input/output device through which data can be input or output from a system.

Testing The process of executing a program with input data that is either a representative sample of actual data or a facsimile of it to determine if it will always obtain correct results.

Third-generation computer A computer characterized by the use of integrated circuits, reduced size, lower costs, and increased speed and reliability.

Thrashing Programs in which little actual processing occurs in comparison to the amount of swapping.

Time-sharing system An arrangement in which two or more users can access the same central computer resources and receive what seem to be simultaneous results.

Time slicing A technique used in a time-sharing system that allocates a small portion of processing time to each user.

Top-down design A method of defining a solution in terms of major functions to be performed, and further breaking down the major functions into subfunctions; the further the breakdown, the greater the detail.

Touch-tone device A terminal used with ordinary telephone lines to transmit data.

Track A horizontal row following the length of a magnetic tape on which data can be recorded; one of a series of concentric circles on the surface of a magnetic disk.

Transaction file A file containing changes to be made to the master file.

Transient routine A supervisor routine that remains in primary storage with the remainder of the operating system.

Transistor A type of circuitry characteristic of second-generation computers; smaller, faster, and more reliable than vacuum tubes but inferior to third-generation, large-scale integration.

Transit field The section of a check, preprinted with magnetic ink, that includes the bank number.

Transparent system An operating system that is user-friendly—that requires little involvement by the user.

Transportable computer A computer that is larger than a portable, but is still small enough to be carried; requires an external power source.

Tree structure *See* Hierarchical structure.

Turnkey system An integrated system including hardware, software, training, and support developed for particular businesses.

Uniform Commercial Code (UCC) A set of provisions proposed by legal experts to promote consistency among state courts in the legal treatment of commercial transactions between sellers and purchasers.

UNIVAC I (UNIVersal Automatic Computer) One of the first commercial electronic computers; became available in 1951.

Universal Product Code (UPC) A machine-readable code consisting of thirty dark bars and twenty-nine spaces that identifies a product and its manufacturer; commonly used on most grocery items.

User friendly An easy-to-use, understandable software design that makes it easy for noncomputer personnel to use an application software package.

Utility program A program within an operating system that performs a specialized function.

Vacuum tube A device (resembling the light bulb) from which almost all air has been removed and through which electricity can pass; often found in old radios and televisions; used in first-generation computers to control internal operations.

Variable A meaningful name assigned by the programmer to storage locations of which the values can change.

Verification Mathematically proving that a program or a program module is correctly designed.

Very-Large-Scale Integration (VLSI) A type of circuitry replacing large-scale integration in fourth-generation computers; smaller, faster, and less costly than large-scale integration.

Videoconferencing A technology that employs a two-way, full-motion video plus a two-way audio system for the purpose of conducting conferences between two remote locations through communication facilities.

Video seminar A form of teleconferencing that employs a one-way, full-motion video with two-way radio.

Virtual memory *See* Virtual storage.

Virtual storage An extension of multiprogramming in which portions of programs not being used are kept in secondary storage until needed, giving the impression that primary storage is unlimited; contrast with real storage.

Virus A form of sabotage; a program that acts as a time bomb that can destroy the contents of a hard or floppy disk.

Visual display terminal A terminal capable of receiving output on a cathode-ray tube (CRT) and, with special provisions, capable of transmitting data through a keyboard.

Visual table of contents Used in HIPO packages; includes blocks with identification numbers that are used as a reference in other HIPO diagrams.

Voice mail *See* Voice message system.

Voice message system (VMS) The sender activates a special "message" key on the telephone, dials the receiver's number, and records the message. A button lights on the receiver's phone, and when it is convenient, the receiver can activate the phone and listen to the message.

Voice-grade channel A communication channel that has a wider frequency range and can transmit data at rates between 300 and 9,600 bits per second; for example, a telephone line.

Volatility The frequency of changes made to a file during a certain period of time.

Wand reader A device used in reading source-data represented in optical bar-code form.

Wire-matrix printer *See* Dot-matrix printer.

Word processing The use of computer equipment in preparing text; involves writing, editing, and printing.

Word processor *See* Text processor.

Word size The number of bits that can be manipulated at one time.

Writing The process of storing new instructions or data in computer memory.

Xerographic printer A type of nonimpact printer that uses printing methods similar to those used in common xerographic copying machines.

Zone bit A bit used in different combinations with numeric bits to represent numbers, letters, and special characters.

Index

A

abacus, 29–30
access mechanism, 138
accounting computers, 35, 68, 442
ACM, see Association for Computing
      Machinery
acoustic-coupler modem, 223
action diagrams, 293
action entries, 381
action stub, 381
Ada programming language, 327–328
add-ons, 211
address, on disk, 141
AFIPS, see American Federation of
      Information Processing Societies
AI, see artificial intelligence
Aiken, Howard, 33
airplane design, computerized, 7
algorithm
   definition of, 512
   pseudocode, 514
Allen, Paul, 272
ALU, see arithmetic/logic unit
American Federation of Information
      Processing Societies, 50
American National Standards Institute,
      241, 312, 317–320, 362
American Standard Code for Information
      Interchange, 96
amount field, 110
analog computers, 14
analog transmission, 222
Anixter, Ben, 28
ANSI, see American National Standards
      Institute
ANSI COBOL, 323
ANSI FORTRAN, 318
APL coding, 328
APL interactive session, 329
APL programming language, 326–327
apparel manufacturers
   and computers, 58
application architecture, 266
application computer programs, 254

application generators, 337
application programs, 255
application programmers, 46
application software, 346–368
   arithmetic/logic unit in, 80
   commercial, 347–348
   comparisons of, 363
   computer-aided systems engineering in,
      355
   function of, 81
   design of, 395
arithmetic expressions, 532
arithmetic operations, 15
Army Standard Information Management
      System, 452
artificial intelligence, 40–42, 336–337
   and neural networking, 486
   and parallel processing, 484–485
   and robotics, 488–489
   and RISC, 28
   and script theory, 486
   definition of, 485
ASCII, see American Standard Code for
      Information Interchange, 96
ASIMS, see Army Standard Information
      Management System
Asimov, Isaac, 446
ASM, see Association of Systems
      Management
assembler program, 314
assembly language, 315–317
   advantages of, 316
   definition of, 311
assembly language programs, 339
Association for Computing Machinery, 50,
      286
Association of Systems Management, 51
Atanasoff, John V., 34
ATM, see automatic teller machine
attributes, of data, 170
audit trail, 60
audio conferencing, 438
auto design, computerized, 2
automobiles, and computer maps, 61
automatic teller machine, 234

automation, and competition, 7
auxiliary storage, see secondary storage

B

Babbage, Charles, 31, 328
back-end processor, 266
background programs, 262–263
backup copies, 136
banking, computers in, 5
bar codes, 113
Barron, Clarence W., 25
BASIC
   and personal computers, 520
   and the Apple, 563
   and the Apple IIe, 522
   and the IBM PC, 520
   and the Macintosh, 521–522
   and the TRS, 522
   arithmetic expressions, 532
   constants
      character strings, 529
      numeric, 528
   DATA statement, 544–546
   END statement, 535
   flowchart, 533
   functions, 562
   hierarchy of operations, 533
   INPUT statement, 542–546
   LET statement, 531–532
   line numbers, 536
   LOAD command, 518
   loading in, 519
   numeric functions, 565
   origin of, 272, 511
   PRINT statement, 534
   printing of, 534–535, 548–550
   programs, 596
   READ statement, 544–546
   reserved words, 530
   RUN command, 518
   SAVE command, 518
   statements, 517, 530
      END, 353

GOSUB, 591
ONGOSUB, 594–595, 597–599
PRINT, 534
RETURN, 592
string functions, 565–566
variables, 529–530
Basic FORTRAN, 318
batch file access, 158
batch processing systems, 256
in banking, 166
Bates, Barbara, 220
BCD, see binary coded decimal
Berger, Paul, 58
billing operations, 161
binary coded decimal, 95–96
binary conversion, 95
binary digit, see bit
binary equivalent values, 94
binary representation, 90–91
biochip, 483
bismuth, in superconductors, 148
bit
cells, 86
definition of, 9, 85
parity, 98
transfer in microcomputers, 189
zone, 96
blocked records, 133
booting, 196
Boyd, Woody, 106
Bradham, Caleb, 423
branch logic pattern, 294
branch programming pattern, 282, 285
Brand, Stewart, 2
Brandt, Richard, 154
briefcase computer, 190
broad-band communication channels, 228
bubble memory, 86–87, 129
data representation in, 90
budgets, computerized, 69
Buderi, Robert, 2
buffer, 224
bus configuration, 238
businesses
competition in, 428
and information systems, 58
and telecommuting, 429
computers in, 5, 36, 40
software for, 202
byte, 96
definition of, 10

C

cache memory, 90
CAD, see computer-aided design
CAE, see computer-aided engineering
calculator, 33
CAM, see computer-aided manufacturing
Canion, Rod, 216

Canin, Jeff, 78
CAPER, see Computer-Assisted Planning
for Educational Resources
cartridge tape, 144
definition of, 143
CASE, see computer-aided systems
engineering
CAT scan, see computerized axial
tomography
cathode-ray tubes, 122
CCD, see charge-coupled device
CCITT, see Consultative Committee on
International Telephone &
Telegraph
C computer language, 310–313, 331,
333–334
CD ROM, see compack disc read-only
memory
cell, in electronic spreadsheet, 350
centralized management system design,
414
central processing unit
definition of, 12, 80
operations, 83
outlook for, 195
stand-alone, 267
Cerf, Genevieve, 430
CGA, see color graphics adapters
chain printer, 119
channel communication, 225
channel transmission modes, 230
channels, 224–225
character, 9
charge-coupled devices, 144
check bit, see parity bit
chief programmer team, 293, 296
CIM, see computer-integrated
manufacturing
circuit, integrated, 482
clock speed, in microprocessors, 194
clustered key-to-tape device, 108
coaxial cable, 226
COBOL, 313, 323–324, 339, 362, 392
beginning of, 38, 322
code checking, 98
coding, 297
color graphics adapters, 200
comment programming statement, 299
commercial application software, 347
commercial data bases, see information
services
communication channel, 225, 227
communications network, 451
compact disk
advantages and disadvantages, 147
interactive, 147
read-only memory, 128
compact disks
advantages of, 146
competition
in the automobile industry, 72, 346

of businesses, 428
compiler program, 314
compilers, Pascal, 321
composit color monitors, 200
Comprehensive Crime Control Act, 471
computation programming statement, 299
computer
binary system, 91
bugs, 300
functions of, 17
information systems, 58
peripherals, 39
uses of, 2
message transmission, 222
computer access control, 220
computer analysts
and cost/benefit analysis, 390
in design, 386–387
computer animation, 2
computer anxiety, 429–430
computer applications
in banking, 367–368
on open systems, 257
computer authentication, 220
computer careers, 45–49
data-base specialists, 48–49
data-processing operations personnel,
45–46
information system managers, 49
system development personnel, 46–48
computer chip, trends, 482–483
computer classifications, 17
computer coding, 90, 95
computer conferencing, 439
computer crime, 221, 235, 348
definition of, 456
detection of, 460
military, 454
prevention of, 459
types of, 459
computer data
representation, 90
computer development, 337
computer documentation, 393
definition of, 512
flowcharts, 513
symbols of, 514
computer dump, 93
computer encryption, 220
computer ethics, 465
computer files, 152
computer games, 273
introduction of, 40
computer hardware, 78–103
computer laboratories, 2
computer language
translating, 313–314
computer law, 276, 507–508
computer librarian, 295–296
definition of, 45
computer literacy, 430–431

computer logic
  errors in, 516
  nonmonotonic, 485–486
  patterns of, 281
computer memory
  bubble, 86–87
  cache, 90
  erasable programmable read-only, 89
  programmable read-only, 88
  registers, 90
computer modems, 223
computer modules, 511
computer network, 237–238
  in business, 248
computer operating systems, 196, 253
computer operator
  definition of, 45
  training of, 394
computer privacy, 220
computer processing storage, address, 84
computer programmers
  definition of, 46
  demand for, 47
  division of, 286
  reliability of, 284
  steps in, 277
  women as, 67, 430
computer programming
  background partitions, 262
  background programs, 262
  counting loop, 578
  debugging, 393
  foreground programs, 262
  infinite loop, 577
  loop control variable, 574
  partitions, 261
  pseudocode, 514
  regions, 261
  structure chart, 513
  syntax, 515
computer programs, 254
  definition of, 4
computer program statements,
  conditional transfer, 558
  control, 558
  decision statement, 558
  double-alternative, 560
  unconditional transfer, 558
computer security, 47, 454–478
  and computer viruses, 480
  and encryption of data, 464
  and voice recognition, 487
  breach of, 454
  establishment of, 464
  threats to, 461
computer scanners, 199
  benefits of, 70
computer software
  accounting, 351
  application, 363
  decision support systems, 358–359

definition of, 511
executive, 406–407
expert systems, 359–360
file managers, 350
financial, 346
functional tools, 352
graphics, 349–350
in business, 366–368
in manufacturing resource planning,
    353–354
mail-merge, 349
productivity tools, 351
sales analysis, 355
simulation, 356–357
statistical, 360–361
turnkey systems, 355–356
computer storage, 127
computer support services, 43
computer system
  cash conversion, 395
  definition of, 62
  design of, 384, 386–387
  evaluation of, 396
  parallel conversion, 394
  parts of, 80
  phased conversion, 395
  pilot conversion, 394
  local, 237
  testing of, 392
  time-sharing, 237–238
  top-down design, 413
  user friendly, 385
computer theft, 220
computer training, 206
computer transmission links, 239
computer trends, 482
computer viruses, 220, 480
  containment of, 481
  definition of, 457
computer voices, 226
computer warranties, 472–473
computer-aided design, 71, 354, 444–445,
    450–451
computer-aided engineering systems, 354,
    392, 451
  definition of, 71
computer-aided manufacturing, 5–6, 354,
    444–445, 451
computer-assisted manufacturing, 122
computer-assisted planning for educational
    resources, 370
computer-assisted treatment, 492
computer-controlled machines, 5, 7
computer-integrated manufacturing, 445
computerized axial tomography, 491
computerized cash registers, 55
computerized file processing, 156
computer phobia, see computer anxiety
computers
  accuracy of, 15
  and office automation, 7

and fire, 461
and health-related problems, 433
and the American Federation of
    Information Processing
    Societies, 50
and the Association for Computing
    Machinery, 50
and the Association of Systems
    Mangement, 51
and the Data Processing Management
    Association, 51
and the Institute of Certification of
    Computer Professionals, 51
and the Society for Information
    Management, 52
benefits of, 58
competition in, 182
corporate, 406
cost of, 22, 253, 390–391
damage to, 462
decentralizations of, 478
demand for, 283
educational, 370
  and BASIC, 318
evolution of, 28–56
"father" of, 32
faults, 97
first generation of, 36–37
fourth generation of, 40
functions of, 15
future of, 2, 40
generations of, 34
impact of, 429–452
in airline reservations, 150
in apparel manufacturing, 58
in banking, 5
in business, 4–5, 346
in education, 146, 500–501
in football, 12
in industry, 447
in manufacturing, 5
in management, 5
in medicine, 80, 146, 471, 489
  computerized axial tomography, 491
  diagnosis, 485
  in rehabilitation, 492
  multiphasic health testing, 491
in pharmaceuticals, 178–179
in publishing, 25–26
in science research, 493–494
in travel reservation systems, 147
  APL in, 326
language of, 322
  RPG in, 328
mainframe, 101
menu-driven, 385
micro, 190–191
miniaturization of, 40–41
next generation of, 28
portable, 191
purchase of, 22

second generation of, 36
size of, 29
speed of, 16–17, 146
standardization of, 39
storage in, 16
third generation of, 38–39
types of, 2, 14
theft in, 459
voice recognition, 107
voice-controlled, 2
concentrators, 229–231
concurrent processing, 268, 328
condition entries, 381
conditional programming logic, 281
conditional transfer statement, 558
continuous form, 114
Consultative Committee on International
Telephone & Telegraph, 241
control programs, 257
control statement, 558
control unit, 80–81
Conversational Desktop, 2
copyright law, 276, 473
core storage, 90
corporate planning models, 420
cost/benefit analysis, 390
counting loop, 578
CPU, see central processing unit
CPT, see chief programmer team
crash conversion, 395
Cray X-MP Supercomputer System, 18
crime control, computers, in, 157
crime prevention, 460–461
cross-talk, 483
CRT, see cathode-ray tubes
customer files, 158
customer identification, 116
customer lock-in, 58
customer master file, 161
customer record, processing, 160
cut forms, 114

D

daisy print wheel, 118–119
DASD, see direct-access storage devices
data
binary representation of, 91
definition of, 9
completeness of, 60
in information systems, 66
rate of growth, 58
relevancy of, 60
data analysis, 377–378
data base, 169–179
assessment of, 176
definition of, 11, 169
design in, 170
data-base administration, 170
data base management systems, 175, 362

data base, of FBI, 157
data base programs, 154
data buffering, 224
data communication channels, 221, 229
data conversion, 95, 223–224
data a definition language, 362
data design, 155
data entry methods, 66, 108–109, 116
data flow, 11, 224
data list, 544
data manipulation language, 362
data modulation, 223
data output, 106–125, 116
data privacy, 468, 470
data processing, 8, 29
data record storage, 178
data security measures, 463
data storage, 90, 128–150, 143, 178
trends of, 144
data structures, 170
data timeliness, 60
data transmission
analog, 222
bandwidth, 227
broad-band channels, 228
channel modes, 228
coaxial cables, 226
communication channels, 227
digital, 222
fiber optics, 226
in business, 249
microwave channels, 226
types of channels, 229
verification, 60
voice-grade channels, 228
datacom handlers, see multiplexers and
concentrators
Data Processing Management Association,
51
data-base administrator, 49
data-base analyst, 48
data entry operator, 46
DBA, see data-base administrator
DBMS, see data base management systems
DCP, see data-collecting program
DDL, see data definition language
DDP, see distributed data processing
deaf people, and computers, 438
debugging
definition of, 300, 516
origin of, 314
programs, 299
decentralized management system design,
415
decimal conversion, 95
decimal equivalent values, 94
decimal number system, 91
decision logic table, 381–382
decision statement, 558
decision support system, 415
advantages of, 418
future of, 419

decision support systems, 358–359,
406–428
declaration programming statement, 299
demand reports, 412
demodulation, 223
desk checking method, 300
desktop publishing, software, 352
detail diagram, 290
DeWitt, Philip Elmer, 2
digital transmission, 222
Dijkstra, E. W., 286
direct-access capability, 168
direct-access file design, 163, 169
assessment of, 165–166
direct-access media, 136
direct-access storage devices, 163
direct-connect modem, 223
direct conversion, see crash conversion
directory file, 163
disk
address, 139, 141
drive, 138
pack, 136–137
storage units, 139
surface, 137
diskette, see floppy disk, 141
disks, optical, 145
distributed computing, 236–237
distributed data processing, 225, 233
distributed management system design,
415
Dixon, David, 79
DLT, see decision logic table
DML, see data manipulation language
double-alternative IF statement
documentation specialist, 395
dot-matrix character set, 119
dot-matrix printer, 117
Dow, Charles, H., 25
Dow Jones Average, 25
DPMA, see Data Processing Management
Association
drug research, 79
drugstores, computers in, 178–179
drum printer, 120
DSS, see decision support system
dump, computer, 93, 301

E

e-mail, see electronic main
earthquake prediction, 7
EBCDIC, see Extended Binary Coded
Decimal Interchange Code
Eckert, J. Presper, 33
EDI, see electronic data interchange
edit checks, 393
EDP, see electronic data processing
education, 7, 370

and need for computer literacy, 431
computers in, 7–8
HyberCard, 146
in Pascal, 320
EDVAC, see Electronic Discrete Variable
Automatic Computer
EFT, see electronic funds transfer
EGA, see enhanced graphics adapters
electroluminescence display, 200
electronic banking, 233–234, 366–368
and Electronic Funds Transfer Act, 470
electronic bulletin boards, 244–245
electronic communication
forms of, 441
electronic data interchange, 239
electronic data processing, 414
definition of, 8
Electronic Discrete Variable Automatic
Computer, 34
electronic funds transfer, 233, 455
crime in, 458
Electronic Funds Transfer Act, 470
electronic homes, 499
electronic ledger sheet, 350
electronic maps, 61
electronic mail, 5, 126, 192, 233, 437
sorting of, 279
electronic newspapers, 2
Electronic Numerical Integrator and
Calculator, 33–34
electronic predictions, 36
electronic speech recognition, 28
electronic spreadsheets, 202, 350, 442
electrostatic printer, 121
electrothermal printer, 212
Elmer-DeWitt, Philip, 28, 128
employees
and computer security, 465
and telecommuting, 429
rights of, 466
employee files, 156–157, 162
based on zip codes, 164
design of, 167
employee security
and computers, 431–432
encryption technology, 220, 464
end-user development tools, 356
engineering, computer-aided, 71
enhanced graphics adapters, 200
ENIAC, see Electronic Numerical
Integrator and Calculator
environmental problems, and computers, 7
EPROM, see erasable programmable read-
only memory
erasable programmable read-only memory,
89
ergonomics, 433–434
Esber, Edward, 154
Estridge, Philip, 186
even parity, 98
exception reports, 411
executive information systems, 406

example of, 424–425
executive program, see supervisor program
expert system, 359–360, 362, 370, 371, 485
Extended Binary Coded Decimal
Interchange Code, 96, 131
external storage, see secondary storage

F

facsimile systems, 438
Family Educational Rights and Privacy
Act, 470
FAST, see Framework for Application
Systems Development Training,
304
"father" backup copies, 159
FAX, see telecopier, systems
fault tolerance system, 97
Federal Bureau of Investigation, 8
feedback
definition of, 62
in information processing, 14
fiber optics, 226, 483–484
field, 10, 110, 166, 168
fifth-generation languages, 337
file, 152
definition of, 11
inverted, 171–172
organization of, 154–169
physical and logical, 170
file access, 158
file arrangements, 155
file design, 158, 163, 169
file managers, 350
file processing, 156
firmware, 87
first-generation computers, 34–35
fixed hard disk, 202
flexible disk, see floppy disk
flight simulator, 273
floppy disk, 201, 210
definition of, 108, 141
parts of, 142
flowchart symbols, 292
flowcharts, 291
FOCUS programming language, 337
Food and Drug Administration, 471
football
computers in, 12
foreground partitions, 262
foreground programs, 262–263
forensic dentistry
computers in, 157
formal design review, 296
FORTH programming language, 335–336
FORTRAN, 312–313, 318, 339
origin of, 317
FORTRAN X, 318
four-bit binary coded decimal, 95
fourth generation computers, 40, 337

fourth generation software development
tools, 356
Framework for Application Systems
Development Training, 304–305
front-end processing, 268
front-end processor, 231, 267
definition of, 266
full-duplex transmission channel, 228, 230
fully distributed configuration, 239

G

gallium arsenide, 483
garbage in-garbage out
definition of, 59
Gates, William, 272
general purpose computer language, 313
Gibson, C. Scott, 182
GIGO, see garbage in-garbage out
Gimpel, James, 310
Goldman, Murrary, 28
GOTO, see branch programming pattern
GOTO statements, 286, 319
"grandfather" backup copies, 159
graphic display device, 122
graphics software, 349
graphics tablets, 199

H

hacking, 465–466
half-duplex transmission channel, 228, 230
Hall, Charles Martin, 477
Hammonds, Keith, 182
Handler, Gary, 252
hard copy, 12
hard disks, 108, 201
on microcomputer, 210
hardware, 78–103
backup system, 97
definition of, 4
in information systems, 65
microcomputer, 209
trends, 482–484
hard wiring, 88
hard-wired instruction, 87
Harris, Jim, 216
hashing, see randomizing
Heller, Andrew, 28
hexadecimal conversion, 95
hexadecimal equivalent values, 94
hexadecimal number system, 93
hierarchical configuration, 239
hierarchical data structure, 172
hierarchical structure, 173
computer language of, 362
hierarchy of operations, 533
hierarchy plus input-process-output,
287–289
diagram of, 290

high-level computer language, 312, 317
high-speed buffer, see cache memory, 90
high-tech anxiety, 340
HIPO, see Hierarchy plus Input-Process-Output
Hoff, Ted, 40, 184
Hollerith, Herman, 32, 101, 108
hologram, 2
Home Shopping Club, computers in, 106
hybrid, 55
hypermedia, 146

I

IAM, see index access method
IBG, see interblock gaps
ICCP, see Institute of Certification of Computer Professionals
icons, in microcomputers, 197
impact printers, 117
  definition of, 116
index access method, 178
index table, 166
indexed-sequential file design, 166
  assessment of, 168
indexed-sequential files, 167, 169
  inquiries to, 168
indexed-sequential record layout, 167
infinite loop, 577
informal design review, 296
information services, 241–244
  Information Centers, 47, 413
information output, 116
  information processing, 3–25
    definition of, 8
    overview of, 14
information retrieval, 7
information services, 413
  military, 402
information systems, 58–75
  corporate, 423
  in insurance business, 74
  in management, 407
  model of, 418–419
  synergism in, 67
information system manager, 49
in-house time-sharing system, 238
ink-jet printer, 121
input
  definition of, 11, 62, 107
  types of, 82
input devices
  of microcomputers, 198
input/output bound, 225, 339
  definition of, 224
input/output control unit, 223, 225
input/output programming statement, 299
Institute of Certification of Computer Professionals, 51
instruction set,

in microcomputers, 196
insurance, and
  computers, 74, 450, 452
integrated circuit
  definition of, 38
  miniaturization of, 40
integrated software
  definition of, 203
interactive multimedia, see compact disk interactive
interactive programming pattern, see loop programming pattern
interactive video, 500
interblock gaps, 133
internal modem, 223
internal storage/memory, see primary storage
International Business Machines Corporation, 32
International Organization for Standardization, 241
interpreter program, see compiler program
interrecord gaps, 133
interrupts, 257
inventory control
  computerized, 69
    in grocery stores, 70
    in materials requirement planning, 70
inverted data structure, 171
  definition of, 170
IRGs, see interrecord gaps
IS, see information systems
ISO, see International Organization for Standardization
Iverson, Kenneth, 326

J

Jacquard, Joseph-Marie, 31
JCL, see job-control language
job search, computers in, 243
job-control language, 258–259
Jobs, Steven, 185
Jones, Edward D., 23
Josephson, Brian, 147
Josephson junction, 147

K

Kay, Alan, 2
Kemeny, John, 318, 511
keypunch operator, 46
key value, 158
keys, 168
Kilby, Jack S., 38, 482
Kilgore, Barney, 25
Knox, Dilwyn, 33
Kurtz, Thomas, 318, 511

L

LCD, see liquid crystal display
LAN, see Local Area Network
large-scale integration, 40, 56
laser card, 501–502
lasers
  in computers, 483–484
  in medicine, 493
laser printers, 44, 121
laser storage system, 144
laser technology, 144
Levine, Jonathan, 182
Lewinski, Richard, 33
librarian program, 314
light pen, 199
Lilly, Eli, 304
Lindbergh, Charles, 150
linear integrated circuits, 55
line-at-a-time printers, 118
linkage editor, 314
liquid crystal display, 200
LISP programming language, 336–337
LIST command, 517
LOAD command, 518
load module, 314
Local Area Network, 47, 245
  for businesses, 233
  data communication in, 231
local system, 237
logging on, 518
logical comparisons, 13
logical file, 170
Logo computer language, 324–326
loop logic pattern, 294
loop programming pattern, 281
loop programming statement, 299
low-level computer language, 312, 314
LSI, see large-scale integration
Lumena software, 6
Lybrand, Terry, 78

M

machine language, 314
  advantages of, 315
  definition of, 35, 311
machine vision, 29
magnetic bubble memory, 144
magnetic cores, 37
magnetic disk
  advantages and disadvantages of, 142
  beginning of, 38
  characteristics of, 142
  definition of, 136
magnetic domains, 86
magnetic drums, 35, 129
magnetic tape, 108
  advantages of, 134–135
  and interrecord gaps, 133

characteristics of, 136
definition of, 129
disadvantages of, 135
in processing customer records, 160
magnetic-ink character reader, 110
magnetic-ink character recognition,
    110–111, 373
magnetic-ink character set, 111
magnetic-ink characters, 109
magnetized media, 108
main storage/memory, see primary storage
main system board, 188
mainframe, 81
mainframe computers, 19, 101
    manufacturers of, 20
maintenance programmer, 47
management
    computers in, 5
    decision-making levels, 411
    functional information flow to, 410
management information system, 49,
    406–428
    compared to data processing, 408
    definition of, 407
    levels of, 408–410
    problems of, 412
    reports in, 411–412
management system design, 416–417
manufacturing
    and materials requirement planning, 70
    competition in, 7, 58
    computers in, 5
manufacturing application packages, 353
manufacturing automation protocol, 450
manufacturing resource planning, 353
maps, computerized, 61
marketing, and information systems, 69
mark-sensing, see optical-mark recognition
Massachusetts Institute of Technology, 2
mass storage, 143
master file, 159
materials requirement planning, 70
Mauchly, John, 33
McCarthy, John, 336
MCGA, see multicolor graphics array
McKelvey, John, 79
Media Laboratory, 2
megahertz, 194
memory
    cache, 90
    chips, 86
    erasable programmable read-only, 89
    primary, 295
    programmable read-only, 88
    registers, 90
    words, 92
memory management, 261
memory segmentation, 82
menu-driven computer system, 385
message switching, 231
MHz, see megahertz, 194

MICR, see magnetic-ink character
    recognition
microcomputer, relational programs for,
    154
microcomputer add-ons, 211
microcomputer development, 185
microcomputer monitors, 199
microcomputer peripherals, 198
microcomputer ports, 189
microcomputer printers, 210
microcomputers, 20, 182–217
    advantages of, 498
    in the insurance business, 75
    popularity of, 21, 40
    commercial, 185
    competition in, 186, 187
    cost of, 183
    development of, 216
    future of, 192
    guide to purchase, 205–206, 211–212
    in kit form, 185
    portables, 190
    sale of, 204, 497
    uses of, 192
microprocessors, 148
    compared to mainframes, 182
    development of, 20
    definition of, 184
    evolution of, 28
    speed of, 195
    uses of, 187
microprograms, 88
microwave communication channels, 226
middle-level computer language, 331, 335
military intelligence, computers in, 7
mini supercomputers, 18
minicomputers, 19–20
    compared to micro networks, 233
    relational data bases, 155
    software for, 154
Minsky, Marvin, 2, 486
miscarriages, and visual display terminals,
    433
MIS, see management information system
mneumonic symbols
    in programming, 315
    in symbolic languages, 36
modems, 229
Modula-programming language, 334
modular approach, to software design, 287
modulation, 223
    definition of, 286
molecular modeling, on computers, 78
monitor program, see supervisor program
monitor resolution, 209
monochrome monitors, 199
Moore, Charles, 335
Morosky, Robert, 58
motherboard, see main system board
mouse, computer, 424
    development of, 273

MRP, see materials requirement planning
multicolor graphics array, 200
multiple CPU networks, 238
multiplexors, 229, 232
multiplexor channel, 225
multiprocessing, 267–268
    definition of, 266
    diagram of, 269
multiprogramming, 261, 268
    virtual storage in, 263
multitasking, see multiprogramming
Murto, Bill, 216

N

National Bureau of Standards, and
    computer viruses, 480
National Cancer Institute, 79
National Crime Information Center, 157,
    460
National Semiconductor, Corporation, 55
natural programming languages, 337, 338
NCIC, see National Crime Information
    Center
NDT, see nondestructive testing
Negroponte, Nicholas, 2
nested loop, 578
network data structure, 173–174
network configurations, 239–240
network systems, 362
neurocomputing, 486
newspapers, electronic, 2
next-sequential-instruction, 82
Nilles, Jack, 428
NMR, see nuclear magnetic reasonance
node
    definition of, 238
nondestructive read, 88
nondestructive read/destructive write, 84
nondestructive testing, 445–446
nonimpact printers, 116
nonmonotonic logic, 485–486
nonproprietary networks, 245–246
notebook computer, 200
Noyce, Robert N., 482
nuclear magnetic resonance, 491
numerically controlled machinery, 444
numeric bits, 96

O

object program, 314
OCR characters, 115
OCR, see optical-character recognition
octal (base) number system, 92
octal number system, see hexadecimal
    number system, 93
odd parity, 98
office automation
    and computers, 7

definition of, 435
OMR, see optical-maker recognition
on line file access, 158
online operating systems, 256
online storage, 201
    and data analysis, 378, 380
"on-us" field, 110
op code, see operation code
Opel, John, 186
Open Software Foundation, 257
open systems, 266
    definition of, 257
operand, 314
    function of, 81
    mneumonic, 316
operating systems, 44
    control programs, 257
    development of, 255
    functions of, 255
    job-control language, 258
    multiprogramming, 261
    nonproprietary, 252
    processing programs, 257, 260
    proprietary, 252
    serial processing, 261
optical characters, 114
optical disk storage, 144
optical disks, and hypermedia, 146
optical readers, 113
optical-character recognition, 114
optical-mark recognition, 110, 112
output, definition of, 12, 62, 107
overview diagram, in HIPO, 287

P

packaged software, 20
page frames, 265
pages, in virtual storge, 265
paging
    definition of, 265
Papert, Seymour, 2, 324
parallel conversion, 394
parallel processing, 182, 484–485
    definition of, 40
parity bit, 98
Pascall, Blaise, 30, 313, 321
patterns, of computer logic, 281
payroll, computerized, 68–69
Pelton, Charles, 128
peripheral devices, 4
peripherals
    compatibility of, 197
    for microcomputers, 189
    manufacture of, 44
    of microcomputers, 198
    standardization of, 39
personal computer, see microcomputer
personal identity number, 235
personnel record keeping, 70

Peters, Dave, 78
pharmaceutical research,
    and computers, 78–79, 304
phased conversion, 395
physical file, 170
Piaget, Jean, 2
pilot conversion, 394
PIN, see personal identity number
Pique, Mike, 79
plotter, 122
point-of-sale systems, 113
point-of-sale terminal, 115, 117
political elections,
    computer predictions in, 36
Port, Otis, 182
portable microcomputers, 190, 192, 216
portability,
    of computer programs, 311, 312
ports, 190
Powell, Casey, 182
predictive reports, 412
primary key field, 166
primary memory, see primary storage
primary storage
    function of, 81
    Josephson junction, 147
print-wheel, 119
print-wheel printer, 118
printer
    chain, 119
    daisy-wheel, 118
    dot-matrix, 117
    drum, 120
    electrostatic, 121
    impact, 116
    ink-jet, 121
    laser, 121
    line-at-a-time, 118
    microcomputer, 210
    nonimpact, 116, 121
    plotters, 122
    xerographic, 121
privacy
    and computers, 157, 467
    and the Family Educational Rights and
        Privacy Act, 470
    and the Right to Financial Privacy Act,
        470
    legislation for, 468, 470
probability theory,
    in insurance, 74
problem-oriented computer language, 313
procedure documentation, 393
processing
    definition of, 12
    functions of, 13
    parallel, 182
processor chips, 101
productivity tools, 349
professional associations, 50, 52, 54
program documentation, 393

programmable communications processor,
    231
programmable read-only memory, 80
    definition of, 88
programming
    label, 316
    languages, 310–344
        comparison of, 338
        levels of, 317
    new
        and branch patterns, 283
    statements
        structured, 511
    top-down design, 513
    types of, 299
PROLOG programming language, 337
PROM, see programmable read-only
        memory
proper program
    diagram of, 298
    in structured coding, 297
proprietary networks, 245
prototyping, 397–398
pseudocode, 293, 514
    definition of, 290
    diagram of, 291
punched cards, 129

Q

quality control, 445
query languages, see fourth-generation
        programming languages

R

RAM disk, 146
RAM, see random-access memory
random-access memory, 81, 89, 195–196
randomizing, 163
read-only memory, 80, 147
    definition of, 87
    erasable, 89
    in microcomputers, 195
    programmable, 88
read/write head, 131
read/write notch, 142
real storage, 264
reduced instruction set computer, 28, 196
Reingold, Edwin M., 28
registers, 90
relational data base programs, 154
relational data bases, 155
    and structure query language, 169, 362
relational data structure
    definition of, 173
    example of, 174, 175
relevancy of data, 60
remote terminal operator
    definition of, 46

remote terminals, 39, 115
removable hard disk, 202
reserved words, 530
resident routines, 257
RGB monitors, 200
Right to Financial Privacy Act, 470
ring configuration, 239
RISC, see reduced instruction set computer
Ritchie, Dennis, 331
Roach, John, 186
Roberts, Ed, 184
robots, 7, 446–447, 490
    and artificial intelligence, 488–489
ROM, see read-only memory
Rosen, Ben, 216
RPG programming language, 328–333
Ryan, Alan J., 106

S

SABRE, beginning of, 150
sales analysis software, 355
sales order processing, 69
scanners,
    computer, 199
scheduled listings, 411
Schmandt, Chris, 2
scientific computer language, 313, 335
Scouting Information Systems, 12
script theory, 486
scrolling, 517–518
Sculley, John, 185
second generation computers, 37
    storage in, 85
secondary key field, 166
secondary storage, 85
    for microcomputers, 210
secondary storage media, 130
segmentation, 264–265
selection logic pattern, 294
selection programming patterns, 281
selector channel, 225
SEMATECH, 56
semiconductor data storage innovations, 144
semiconductor memory, 81, 86, 129, 147
semiconductor RAM, 144–145
semiconductor storage, 90
semiconductors, 28
    in microcomputers, 185
    retail sale of, 58
    storage in, 86
sentinel value, see trailer value
sequential file, 159
sequential file design, 162
    definition of, 158
sequential processing, 159–160, 166
sequential-access media, 129
serial ports, 190
serial processing, 261–262

Shirley, Jon, 272
silicon chips
    function of, 86
    introduction of, 40
    vs. gallium arsenide, 483
Silicon Valley, 28
    beginning of, 55–56
simple data structure, 171
    definition of, 170
simple sequence computer pattern, 281, 294
simplex transmission channel, 228, 230
SIM, see Society for Information Management
simulation software, 356
simultaneous decision support systems, 420
single-alternative IF statement, 559
size-bit binary coded decimal, 96
smart card, 501–502
social security numbers, 164
Society for Information Management, 52, 59
Society for Worldwide Interbank Financial Telecommunications, 235
soft copy, 12
software
    and copyright law, 473
    bugs, 301
    compatibility of, 198
    competition in, 154–155
    copyrights, 474
    cost of, 284–285
    definition of, 4
    design
        phases of, 305, 306, 307
        top-down, 286
        top-down design, 287
    development process, 276–307, 395
    industry, 44
        beginning of, 39
    in information systems, 65
    litigation, 276
    Lumena, 6
    microcomputer, 272
        evaluation of, 206–208
    packaged, 20
    piracy, 348
    program specifications, 279
    purpose computer language, 313
    public domain, 474
    regulation of, 471
    sale of, 45
    theft, 220, 467
    tools, 392
    utilities, 203
    word processing, 202
sort/merge programs, 260
source-data automation
    definition of, 109
spelling checkers, 349

spelling programs, 436
Sporck, Charles, 55
Sprague, Peter, 55
SQL, see structured query language
stand-alone key-to-tape device, 108
star configuration, 239
statistical software, 360–361
Steele, Alfred, 423
storage, 16–17, 129
    blocks, 133
    concept, 34, 83–84
    devices, 127
    locations
        variables in, 85
    media, 129, 201
    on compact discs, 128
    program
        definition of, 84
    retrieval operations, 15
structure chart, 287–288
structured coding, 297
structured computer language, 312
structured design techniques, 293
structured programming, 296, 298
structured programs, 319
structured query language, 169, 362
structured walk-through, 296
supercomputers, 17, 40, 78
    as microcomputer clusters, 182
    mini, 18
superconductors, 147
supermicrocomputers, 183, 193
supermini computers, 20
supervisor program, 257
swapping, 264
symbolic languages, 36
synergism in information systems, 67
syntax, 515–516
Synthetic Performer, 2
system analysts
    and data design, 170
    and program development, 393
    definition of, 48
system analysis, 370–404
system computer, 62–63
    data gathering in,
        internal sources, 374–375
        types of, 377
    definition of, 371
    military, 401–402
    purpose of, 373
    report, 383
system computer programs, 254
system design
    alternatives to, 413
    for defense, 401–402
    prototyping, 397–398
    steps in, 383
system design report, 391
system development, 403
    stages of, 398

system documentation, 393
system flowcharting, 378–380
system implementation, 394
system library, 314
system programmers, 47
system residence device, 257
system software, 251–273
system theory, 63

T

tabular chart, 378
Tandy, Charles, 186
tape storage, 16
tape cartridge, 135
    microcomputer, 210
tape cassette, 134–135
tape drive, 131
telecommunications, 220–249
    in insurance, 75, 241
telecommuting, 7, 235, 499
    origin of, 428
telecomputing, 440–441
teleconferencing, 2, 7, 438
telecopier systems, 438
terminals
    for data communication, 221
    point-of-sale, 115
    remote, 115
third generation computers, 38
    storage in, 85
Thomas, R. David, 125
thrashing, 265
timeliness, of data, 60
time slicing, 237
time sharing systems, 237–238
top-down design, 286–287, 413, 513
total system package, 102
touch-tone devices, 116
trace
    definition of, 301
track, 136
trailer value, 581
Tramiel, Jack, 185–186
transaction file, 159
transaction records, 160
transient routines, 257
transistors, 55
    definition of, 37
transit field, 110
transparent operating system, 197

transportable microcomputers, 190
tree data structure, see heirarchical data
        structure
True BASIC, 319
TSP, see total system package
Tucker, Michael, 276
TURBO Pascal, 321
Turning, Alan, 33
turnkey systems, 356
    definition of, 355
turtle, in Logo, 326

U

UCC, see Uniform Commercial Code
Unconditional transfer statement, 558
Uniform Commercial Code, 472
Uninterrupted power source, 97
UNIVACI, 34
Universal Product Code, 113
    computerized, 70
unstructured computer language, 312
UPC, see Universal Product Code
UPS, see uninterrupted power source
used computers, sale of, 84
user friendly system, 385
users group, 204
utility programs, 44, 203, 260

V

vacuum tubes, 34, 36
    problems of, 34
Vadasz, Leslie, 182
variables, 529
VAX system, 518
VDT, see visual display terminal
verifying data, 60
very-large-scale integration, 56
    definition of, 40
very-large-scale integration logic, 102
VGA, see Video graphics array
videoconferencing, 439
video graphics array, 200
video seminars, 439
virtual storage, 264, 268
viruses, computer, 457
visual display terminals, 116
    and health-related problems, 433
    definition of, 112

VLSI, see very-large-scale integration
voice grade communication channels, 228
voice response system, 106–107
volatility, of a computer application, 162
von Leibniz, Gottfried, 31
von Neumann, John, 34
vaporware, 300
verification, of software, 301
very-high-level computer languages, 337
virtual storage, 268
visual table of contents, 287, 289
VMS, see voice message system
voice mail, see voice message system
voice message system, 487
voice-data entry system, 487

W

wand reader, 114
warranties, computer, 472–743
Watson, Thomas J., 32
Willman, Barry, 78
Wimmer, Erich, 78
Wirth, Niklaus, 320, 334
Witten, Matthew, 80
women
    as programmers, 67
    in the work force, 428
word processing software, 202, 349
word size, in microprocessors, 194
WORM, see write once read many
Wozniak, Stephen, 185
write once read many, 147
writing, computer definition of, 84
word processing, 5
    definition of, 435
    disadvantages of, 436
    in color, 436

X

xerographic printers, 121

Z

Zachmann, William, 182
Zeltzer, David, 2
zone bits, 96

Articles

Chapter 1: Copyright 1987 Time Inc. All rights reserved. Reprinted by permission from TIME.
Chapter 2: Copyright 1988 Time Inc. All rights reserved. Reprinted by permission from TIME.
Chapter 3: Reprinted with permission of *DECISIONS Magazine,* copyright by Baetech Publishing Company, L.P.
Chapter 4: Reprinted with permission of the *St. Paul Pioneer Press Dispatch.*
Chapter 5: Copyright 1988 by CW Publishing, Inc., Framingham, MA, 01701. Reprinted from *Computerworld.*
Chapter 6: Copyright 1988 Time Inc. All rights reserved. Reprinted by permission from TIME.
Chapter 7: Reprinted from February 8, 1988 issue of *Business Week* by special permission, copyright © 1988 by McGraw-Hill, Inc.
Chapter 8: Reprinted from September 26, 1988 issue of *Business Week* by special permission, copyright © 1988 by McGraw-Hill, Inc.
Chapter 9: Copyright 1988 *InformationWEEK.*
Chapter 10: Reprinted from March 13, 1988 issue of *Business Week* by special permission, copyright © 1988 by McGraw-Hill, Inc.
Chapter 11: Copyright 1988 by CW Publishing, Inc., Framingham, MA, 01701. Reprinted from *Computerworld.*
Chapter 12: Reprinted by permission from August 22, 1988 issue of *PCWEEK,* copyright 1988.
Chapter 13: Copyright 1988 *InformationWEEK.*
Chapter 14: Copyright 1988 by CW Publishing, Inc., Framingham, MA 01701. Reprinted from *Computerworld.*
Chapter 15: Reprinted from *Software Magazine,* November 1988. Copyright 1988, Sentry Publishing Company, Inc., Westborough, MA, 01581.
Chapter 16: Reprinted with permission from *Industry Week,* April 18, 1988. Copyright, Penton Publishing, Inc., Cleveland, Ohio.
Chapter 17: Copyright 1988 Time Inc. All Rights reserved. Reprinted by permission from TIME.
Chapter 18: Copyright © 1988 by The New York Times Company. Reprinted by permission.

Chapter Opening Photos

1 Gregory Heisle, The Image Bank: **27** Lou Jones, The Image Bank; **57** Roger Ressmeyer-Starlight © 1989; **77** Jay Freis, The Image Bank; **105** © Hank Morgan, Science Source/Photo Researchers, Inc.; **127** © Michael Salas, The Image Bank; **153** © 1988 Roger Ressmeyer, all rights reserved; **181** Ken Cooper, The Image Bank; **219** © Paul Shambroom, Science Source/Photo Researchers, Inc.; **251** Gregory Heisler, The Image Bank; **275** © Zao-Longfield, The Image Bank; **309** Benn Mitchell, The Image Bank; **345** © Paul Shambroom, Science Source/Photo Researchers, Inc.; **369** © 1986 Walter Bibikow, The Image Bank; **405** © Gary Gladstone, The Image Bank; **427** Lou Jones, The Image Bank; **453** © Gary Gladstone, The Image Bank; **479** A. M. Rosario, The Image Bank.

Text Photos

5 Courtesy of International Business Machines Corporation; **6 (top)** Courtesy of Bethlehem Steel Corporation; **6 (bottom)** © 1985 Time Arts Inc. Artist: James Dowlen; **8** Photo courtesy of FBI; **9** Courtesy of Blyth Software; **16** The Huntington National Bank; **18** Courtesy of Cray Research, Inc.; **19** Courtesy of International Business Machines Corporation; **20** Courtesy of International Business Machines Corporation; **21** Courtesy of International Business Machines Corporation; **30 (top)** Courtesy of International Business Machines Corporation; **30 (bottom left)** Courtesy of International Business Machines Corporation; **31 (top)** Crown Copyright, Science Museum, London; **31 (bottom left)** Courtesy of International Business Machines Corporation; **32 (left)** Courtesy of International Business Machines Corporation; **32 (right)** Courtesy of International Business Machines Corporation; **33** Courtesy of Sperry Corporation; **35 (top)** The Institute for Advanced Study, Princeton, New Jersey; **35 (bottom)** Courtesy of Sperry Corporation; **36** Photograph courtesy of the National Museum of American History; **37 (top)** Courtesy of International Business Machines Corporation; **37 (bottom)** Courtesy of International Business Machines Corporation; **38** Courtesy of International Business Machines Corporation; **39** Photo courtesy of Digital Equipment Corporation; **41 (top)** Courtesy Motorola, Inc.; **41 (bottom)** Courtesy of International Business Machines Corporation; **43** Courtesy of International Business Machines Corporation; **44** Photo courtesy of Hewlett-Packard Company; **56** Courtesy of National Semiconductor Corporation; **65 (bottom left)** Photo courtesy of Hewlett-Packard Company; **65 (top right)** Chicago Tribune; **65 (bottom right)** Photo courtesy of Hewlett-Packard Company; **65 (top left)** Steve Uzzell, III, Courtesy of Planning Research Corporation; **66** Courtesy of International Business Machines Corporation; **68** Courtesy of Honeywell Inc.; **71 (top)** Photo courtesy of Hewlett-Packard Company; **71 (bottom)** Photo courtesy of Rockwell International; **73** Courtesy of PRUPAC; **86** Courtesy of International Business Machines Corporation; **87** Courtesy of AT&T Bell Laboratories; **88** Courtesy of AT&T Bell Laboratories; **89** Courtesy of Motorola, Inc.; **102** Courtesy of IBM; **109** Courtesy of International Business Machines Corporation; **114** Steve Uzzell, III, Courtesy of Planning Research Corporation; **115 (top)** Photo courtesy of NCR Corporation; **117 (top)** Courtesy of Albertson's, Inc.; **117 (bottom)** Photo courtesy of Northern Telecom, Inc.; **118 (top)** Courtesy of International Business Machines Company; **119 (top right)** Courtesy of Dataproducts Corporation; **121** Xerox Corporation; **122** Permission granted by Nicolet Computer Graphics; **123** Courtesy of International Business Machines Company; **126** Courtesy of Wendy's International Inc.; **132 (top)** The Huntington National Bank; **135 (top)** Courtesy Verbatim Corporation; **135 (bottom)** Photo courtesy 3M; **137 (bottom)** Photograph courtesy of BASF Systems Corporation; **139 (top)** Reprinted courtesy of DIALOG R Information Services, Inc.; **140 (left)** Photo courtesy 3M; **140 (right)** Photo courtesy 3M; **145 (top)** Photo courtesy 3M; **145 (bottom)** Courtesy of International Business Machines Corporation; **147** Courtesy of International Business Machines Corporation; **150** Courtesy of American Airlines; **151** Courtesy of American Airlines; **183** Courtesy of International Business Machines Corporation; **184** Courtesy of AT&T Bell Laboratories; **185** Courtesy of Apple Computers, Inc.; **186** Courtesy of International Business Machines Corporation; **188 (top)** Courtesy of International Business Machines Corporation; **188 (bottom)** Courtesy of International Business Machines Corporation; **189 (top)** Courtesy of Blyth Software; **189 (bottom)** Courtesy of Blyth Software; **190** Courtesy of International Business Machines Corporation; **197** Courtesy of Blyth Software; **199** Courtesy of Apple Computers, Inc.; **200 (top)** Photo courtesy of Hewlett-Packard Company; **200 (bottom)** Courtesy of International Business Machines Corporation; **201** Courtesy of Maxtor Corporation; **207** Courtesy of Blyth Software; **209** Courtesy of NEC Information Systems, Inc.; **217** Courtesy of Compaq Computer Corporation; **223 (left)** Photo courtesy of Hewlett-Packard Company; **223 (middle)** Photo courtesy of Anderson Jacobson, Inc.; **223 (right)** Photo courtesy of Hayes Microcomputer Products; **227 (top)** Courtesy of BRIntec Corporation; **227 (bottom)** Courtesy of Gould, Inc.; **234** Photo courtesy of Hewlett-Packard Company; **242** Courtesy of CompuServe; **248** Courtesy of Texas Instruments; **249** Courtesy of Texas Instruments; **342** Courtesy of United States Navy; **351** Photo courtesy of Software International Corporation; **358** Courtesy of SAS Institute, Inc., Cary, N.C.; **359** Courtesy of Execucom Systems Corporation; **361** Courtesy of SAS Institute Inc., Cary, N.C.; **367** Courtesy of Chase Manhattan; **432** The DOW Chemical Company; **434 (top)** Photo courtesy of TRW, Inc.; **434 (bottom)** This photo supplied courtesy of Lear Siegler, Inc./Data Products Division; **436** Courtesy of Mead; **437** Photo courtesy of Wang Laboratories, Inc.; **439** Boeing Computer Services; **440** CompuServe Incorporated; **441** Photo courtesy of Source Telecomputing Corporation; **443 (top)** Courtesy Execucom Systems Corporation; **443 (bottom)** Courtesy of International Business Machines Corporation; **444** Courtesy of International Business Machines Corporation; **445** Photo courtesy of Automation Technology Products "CIMPLEX"; **447** Photo courtesy of Hewlett-Packard Company; **451** Courtesy of EDS; **455** Printed with the permission of Pronto, USA; **460** Courtesy of Honeywell, Inc.; **461** Courtesy: Los Angeles Police Department; **462** Courtesy of Honeywell, Inc.; **463 (left)** Photo courtesy of Datakey, Inc., Burnsville, MN; **463 (right)** Courtesy of Yale-New Haven Hospital; **470 (left)** Photos courtesy of Internal Revenue Service; **470 (right)** Courtesy Sperry Corporation; **474** Courtesy of the Software Link, Inc.; **478** Courtesy of ALCOA; **482** Courtesy of Calma Company, a wholly-owned subsidiary of General Electric Company; **487** Courtesy of General Electric Company; **491** Courtesy of Dr. Robert S. Ledley, Medical Computing & Biophysics Division, Georgetown University Medical Center, Washington, D.C.; **492** Courtesy of Parkland Memorial Hospital; **493** Courtesy of Wright State University; **495** Courtesy of SAFER Emergency Systems, Inc.; **496** Courtesy of National Severe Storms Forecast Center; **497** Ada L. Olins and Donald E. Olins, University of Tennessee and the Oak Ridge National Laboratory; **498** Courtesy of AT&T Bell Laboratories; **500 (top left)** Xanadu-Home of The Future; **501 (top)** Courtesy of Drexler Technology Corporation; **501 (bottom)** Courtesy of Drexler Technology Corporation; **503** Courtesy of International Business Machines Corporation; **504** Courtesy of Apple Computer, Inc.

TO: User's of the Limited-Use version of WordPerfect 4.2
FROM: Wordperfect Corporation
RE: The limitations of Limited-Use Wordperfect 4.2
DATE: June 30, 1987
        ****

The Limited-Use introductory version of WordPerfect 4.2 (L-WP)
is intended to allow one to <u>learn</u> the features of WordPerfect
4.2; however, the L-WP is not intended 'to allow one to print
usable academic or professional documents**.

Certain limitations which should not deter <u>learning</u> WordPerfect
through the L-WP have been encrypted into the L-WP to guard
against productive use, and are as follows:

I.   One may work with as large a document on screen as desired,
        but one may only save to disk a data file no larger than
        50,000k (approximately 25-30 regular pages).

        1.   A data file created with the L-WP cannot be imported
             into regular WordPerfect, nor can a file created in
             regular WordPerfect be imported into L-WP.

II.   Data files of any size may be printed through parallel
        printer port "1" without defining a printer, but font
        changes and extended ASCII characters are not allowed.
        Also, "*WPC" will be printed after each paragraph.

III.   One will be able to learn all the functions of WordPerfect
        4.2's speller and thesaurus by calling up the "readme.wp"
        and following the step-by-step directions; however, one
        cannot use the L-WP speller and thesaurus with any of one's
        own documents because there are only a limited number of
        words in the L-WP speller and thesaurus. (The regular
        speller has 115,000 words, and the regular thesaurus has
        approximately 150,000 words.)

IV.   The help file of L-WP allows the user to retrieve the
        function-key template, but similar to the speller and the
        thesaurus described above, the space will not allow the
        full help files on the L-WP disk.

L-WP is designed to be used for introductory, word processing
courses and thus far has been well received in these types of
environments. Notwithstanding the broad abilities provided in
the L-WP, presumably the L-WP will not satisfactorily substitute
for regular WordPerfect 4.2, and therefore the full feature
version may be obtained directly from WordPerfect Corporation
via the enclosed order form at a 75% educational discount.

        **"*WPC" will be automatically printed after each paragraph
of text to discourage academic or professional use of the L-WP.

EXCLUSIONS OF WARRANTIES AND LIMITATION OF LIABILITY

THE COPY OF THE dBASE III PLUS PROGRAM MADE AVAILABLE FOR USE WITH THIS
TEXTBOOK IS A LIMITED FUNCTIONALITY VERSION OF dBASE III PLUS, AND IS
INTENDED SOLELY FOR EDUCATIONAL, TRAINING AND DEMONSTRATION PURPOSES.
ACCORDINGLY, THIS COPY OF dBASE III PLUS IS PROVIDED "AS IS," WITHOUT
WARRANTY OF ANY KIND FROM ASHTON-TATE OR WEST PUBLISHING COMPANY.
ASHTON-TATE AND WEST PUBLISHING HEREBY DISCLAIM ALL WARRANTIES OF ANY
KIND WITH RESPECT TO THIS LIMITED FUNCTIONALITY COPY OF dBASE III PLUS,
INCLUDING WITHOUT LIMITATION THE IMPLIED WARRANTIES OF MERCHANTABILITY
AND FITNESS FOR A PARTICULAR PURPOSE. NEITHER ASHTON-TATE NOR WEST
PUBLISHING SHALL BE LIABLE UNDER ANY CIRCUMSTANCES FOR CONSEQUENTIAL,
INCIDENTAL, SPECIAL OR EXEMPLARY DAMAGES ARISING OUT OF THE USE OF THIS
LIMITED FUNCTIONALITY COPY OF dBASE III PLUS, EVEN IF ASHTON-TATE OR
WEST PUBLISHING HAS BEEN APPRISED OF THE LIKELIHOOD OF SUCH DAMAGES
OCCURRING. IN NO EVENT WILL ASHTON-TATE'S OR WEST PUBLISHING'S
LIABILITY (WHETHER BASED ON AN ACTION OR CLAIM IN CONTRACT, TORT OR
OTHERWISE) ARISING OUT OF THE USE OF THIS LIMITED FUNCTIONALITY COPY OF
dBASE III PLUS EXCEED THE AMOUNT PAID FOR THIS TEXTBOOK.

LIMITED USE SOFTWARE LICENSE AGREEMENT

DEFINITIONS

The term "Software" as used in this agreement means the Limited Use
version of dBASE III Plus which is made available for use in conjunction
with this Textbook solely for educational, training and/or demonstration
purposes. The term "Software Copies" means the actual copies of all or
any portion of the Software, including back-ups, updates, merged or
partial copies permitted hereunder.

PERMITTED USES

You may:

-- Load into RAM and use the Software on a single terminal or a single
   workstation of a computer (or its replacement).

-- Install the Software onto a permanent storage device (a hard disk
   drive).

-- Make and maintain up to three back up copies provided they are used
   only for back-up purposes, and you keep possession of the back-ups.
   In addition, all the information appearing on the original disk
   labels (including copyright notice) must be copied onto the back-up
   labels.

This license gives you certain limited rights to use the Software and
Software Copies for educational, training and/or demonstration purposes.
You do not become the owner of and Ashton-Tate retains title to, all the
Software and Software Copies. In addition, you agree to use reasonable
efforts to protect the Software from unauthorized use, reproduction,
distribution or publication.

All rights not specifically granted in this license are reserved by Ashton-Tate.

USES NOT PERMITTED

You may not:

-- Make copies of the Software, except as permitted above.

-- Rent, lease, sublicense, time-share, lend or transfer the Software, Software Copies or your rights under this license except that transfers may be made with Ashton-Tate's prior written authorization.

-- Alter, decompile, disassemble, or reverse engineer the Software.

-- Remove or obscure the Ashton-Tate copyright and trademark notices.

-- Use the Software or Software Copies outside the United States or Canada.

DURATION

This agreement is effective from the day you first use the Software. You license continues for fifty years or until you return to Ashton-Tate the original disks and any back-up copies, whichever comes first.

If you breach this agreement, Ashton-Tate can terminate this license upon notifying you in writing. You will be required to return all Software Copies. Ashton-Tate can also enforce our other legal rights.

GENERAL

This agreement represents the entire understanding and agreement regarding the Software and Software Copies and supersedes any prior purchase order, communication, advertising or representation.

This license may only be modified in a written amendment signed by an authorized Ashton-Tate officer. If any provision of this agreement shall be unlawful, void, or for any reason unenforceable, it shall be deemed severable from, and shall in no way affect the validity or enforceability of the remaining provisions of this agreement. This agreement will be governed by California law.

VP-PLANNER PLUS SOFTWARE LICENSE AGREEMENT

The Software in this package is offered only on the condition that you agree to the following terms and conditions:

1. You agree that this Software remains the property of Paperback Software International (PSI), but that PSI grants you a nonexclusive license to use this Software subject to this Agreement. This Software and this Manual are copyrighted.

2. You agree that this Software and this Manual are licensed to you for your use, and that this license is not a sale of this original Software or any copy.

3. You agree that you may make backup or archival copies of this Software to protect your investment from loss and/or to run this Software from a fixed disk or other disk media.

4. You agree that neither this Software disk nor any of the copies made may be given, distributed, transferred, loaned, leased, or sold to any other person, company or entity to whom or which this Software is transferred consents to the terms of this Agreement.

5. You agree that you may not make any copies of this Software and/or this Manual other than those which are specifically authorized above or without the separate express written approval of PSI.

6. You agree that you may not disassemble, change, or modify this Software or any copy, and/or this Manual or any copy, in whole or in part, for any purpose, without express written approval of PSI.

7. You agree that this Software will only be used on one computer by one person at one time.

8. You agree that PSI designed this software for use with the computer system(s) listed in this Manual, and that with proper application this Software will perform substantially as described in this Manual. You also agree that PSI does not warrant that the functions contained in this Software will meet your particular requirements or that the operation of this Software will be uninterrupted or error free. The diskette(s) delivered to you on which this Software is recorded are free from defects in materials and faulty workmanship under normal use. The representations above do not cover items damaged, modified, or misused after delivery to you.

    If a diskette should prove defective or if this Software does not perform as described in this Manual, you shall immediately return any defective diskette or non-conforming Software to West Publishing Company and, as your sole remedy, West Publishing Company shall either replace the diskette or Software or refund the purchase price at West Publishing Company's election.

THE FOREGOING WARRANTIES ARE LIMITED IN DURATION TO THE PERIOD OF 90 DAYS FROM THE DATE OF ORIGINAL DELIVERY TO YOU. THE FOREGOING WARRANTIES ARE IN LIEU OF ALL OTHER WARRANTIES, EXPRESS OR IMPLIED, INCLUDING, BUT NOT LIMITED TO, THE IMPLIED WARRANTIES OF MERCHANTABILITY AND FITNESS FOR A PARTICULAR PURPOSE ON THE DISKETTES AND THE SOFTWARE. WEST PUBLISHING COMPANY SHALL IN NO EVENT BE LIABLE FOR ANY INDIRECT, INCIDENTAL, OR CONSEQUENTIAL DAMAGES, WHETHER RESULTING FROM DEFECTS IN THE DISKETTE(S) OR FROM ANY DEFECT IN THE SOFTWARE ITSELF OR DOCUMENTATION THEREOF. IN NO EVENT SHALL THE LIABILITY OF WEST PUBLISHING COMPANY FOR DAMAGES ARISING OUT OF OR IN CONNECTION WITH USE OR PERFORMANCE OF THE SOFTWARE OR DISKETTE(S) EXCEED THE LICENSE FEE ACTUALLY PAID BY YOU.

Any implied warranties which are found to exist are hereby limited in duration to the 90-day life of the express warranties on the diskettes given above. Some states do not allow the exclusion or limitations may not apply to you. Warranties give you specific legal rights and you may also have other rights which vary from state to state.

9. You agree that if you violate any of the terms and conditions in this Agreement, PSI may terminate this Agreement and the license granted and shall be entitled to all rights and remedies available in law or equity, including, without limitation, specific performance. Upon termination of this Agreement, you agree to return your copy of this Software to PSI at your expense and to erase any and all copies of this Software which you have made.

10. This Agreement is construed in accordance with, and governed by the laws of the State of California and the United States of America. Should any part of this Agreement be declared invalid or unenforceable, the validity and enforceability of the remainder of this Agreement shall not be affected thereby. This Agreement can only be modified by a written agreement signed by you and PSI.

Special Student Upgrade Offer
VP-Planner Plus™
Professional Version
*$89.*⁹⁵

*A*s an owner of the Educational Version,

you are entitled to obtain the Professional Version of
VP-Planner Plus
at a special educational upgrade price of $89.⁹⁵

*T*o order your upgrade,

fill out and send this order form with your payment
to the address below. Please allow 3-4 weeks for delivery.

Price includes shipping and handling within U.S.A.
Add $10.⁰⁰ shipping and handling for Canadian orders. Offer good in U.S.A. and Canada only.

___$89.95___ One copy of VP-Planner Plus Professional Version
_____ CA residents ONLY add 7% sales tax ($6.75)
_____ Canadian orders ONLY add $10.00 shipping/handling
_____ TOTAL

❏ Check Enclosed
❏ MasterCard
❏ VISA

Ship to: (please print)

_____
(Name)

_____
(Card Number)

_____
(Address)

_____
(Expiration Date)

_____
(City, State, Zip)

_____
(Signature as it appears on card)

_____
(Phone)

Detach this coupon (copies not accepted)
and mail with your payment to:

_____
(Name of Institution)

_____
(Course Title)

Paperback Software International • Educational Upgrade Offer • 2830 Ninth Street • Berkeley, CA 94710

VP-EXPERT SOFTWARE LICENSE AGREEMENT

The Software in this package is offered only on the condition that you agree to the following terms and conditions:

1. You agree that this Software remains the property of Paperback Software International (PSI), but that PSI grants you a nonexclusive license to use this Software subject to this Agreement. This Software and this Manual are copyrighted.

2. You agree that this Software and this Manual are licensed to you for your use, and that this license is not a sale of this original Software or any copy.

3. You agree that you may make backup or archival copies of this Software to protect your investment from loss and/or to run this Software from a fixed disk or other disk media.

4. You agree that neither this Software disk nor any of the copies made may be given, distributed, transferred, loaned, leased, or sold to any other person, company or entity to whom or which this Software is transferred consents to the terms of this Agreement.

5. You agree that you may not make any copies of this Software and/or this Manual other than those which are specifically authorized above or without the separate express written approval of PSI.

6. You agree that you may not disassemble, change, or modify this Software or any copy, and/or this Manual or any copy, in whole or in part, for any purpose, without express written approval of PSI.

7. You agree that this Software will only be used on one computer by one person at one time.

8. You agree that PSI designed this software for use with the computer system(s) listed in this Manual, and that with proper application this Software will perform substantially as described in this Manual. You also agree that PSI does not warrant that the functions contained in this Software will meet your particular requirements or that the operation of this Software will be uninterrupted or error free. The diskette(s) delivered to you on which this Software is recorded are free from defects in materials and faulty workmanship under normal use. The representations above do not cover items damaged, modified, or misused after delivery to you.

    If a diskette should prove defective or if this Software does not perform as described in this Manual, you shall immediately return any defective diskette or non-conforming Software to West Publishing Company and, as your sole remedy, West Publishing Company shall either replace the diskette or Software or refund the purchase price at West Publishing Company's election.

THE FOREGOING WARRANTIES ARE LIMITED IN DURATION TO THE PERIOD OF 90 DAYS FROM THE DATE OF ORIGINAL DELIVERY TO YOU. THE FOREGOING WARRANTIES ARE IN LIEU OF ALL OTHER WARRANTIES, EXPRESS OR IMPLIED, INCLUDING, BUT NOT LIMITED TO, THE IMPLIED WARRANTIES OF MERCHANTABILITY AND FITNESS FOR A PARTICULAR PURPOSE ON THE DISKETTES AND THE SOFTWARE. WEST PUBLISHING COMPANY SHALL IN NO EVENT BE LIABLE FOR ANY INDIRECT, INCIDENTAL, OR CONSEQUENTIAL DAMAGES, WHETHER RESULTING FROM DEFECTS IN THE DISKETTE(S) OR FROM ANY DEFECT IN THE SOFTWARE ITSELF OR DOCUMENTATION THEREOF. IN NO EVENT SHALL THE LIABILITY OF WEST PUBLISHING COMPANY FOR DAMAGES ARISING OUT OF OR IN CONNECTION WITH USE OR PERFORMANCE OF THE SOFTWARE OR DISKETTE(S) EXCEED THE LICENSE FEE ACTUALLY PAID BY YOU.

Any implied warranties which are found to exist are hereby limited in duration to the 90-day life of the express warranties on the diskettes given above. Some states do not allow the exclusion or limitations may not apply to you. Warranties give you specific legal rights and you may also have other rights which vary from state to state.

9. You agree that if you violate any of the terms and conditions in this Agreement, PSI may terminate this Agreement and the license granted and shall be entitled to all rights and remedies available in law or equity, including, without limitation, specific performance. Upon termination of this Agreement, you agree to return your copy of this Software to PSI at your expense and to erase any and all copies of this Software which you have made.

10. This Agreement is construed in accordance with, and governed by the laws of the State of California and the United States of America. Should any part of this Agreement be declared invalid or unenforceable, the validity and enforceability of the remainder of this Agreement shall not be affected thereby. This Agreement can only be modified by a written agreement signed by you and PSI.

Special Student Upgrade Offer
VP-Expert™
Professional Version
$89.⁹⁵

*J*ust look at the added features you'll get when you decide
to take advantage of this special offer
to upgrade the version of VP-Expert included in this book
to the full professional version of
VP-Expert:

✓ You'll register yourself as owner of the professional version of
VP-Expert™.

✓ Many powerful new features including hypertext, dynamic
graphics, mouse support, forward chaining and Smartforms.

✓ Rule bases larger than 16K bytes (up to available memory).

✓ Unlimited chaining to other rule bases.

✓ Full read and write access to VP-Planner®, VP-Planner Plus™,
Lotus 1-2-3®, or Lotus Symphony® spreadsheet files.

✓ Full read and write access to VP-Info®, dBASE II®, dBASE III®
database files.

✓ Your own set of VP-Expert diskettes for use at school or home.

THE PROFESSIONAL VERSION of VP-Planner Plus is fully compatible with the academic version of VP-Planner Plus included in this book.

To order your upgrade, fill out the order form on the back of this page, tear out this entire page and mail it to the address shown on the form. Only one upgrade is available for each copy of this book. YOU MUST INCLUDE THIS ORIGINAL ORDER FORM to receive your upgrade. Copies will not be accepted.

VP-Planner Plus and VP-Expert are trademarks and Paperback Software is a registered trademark of Paperback Software International. Other brand and product names are trademarks or registered trademarks of their respective holders. West Publishing.

Paperback Software International • Educational Upgrade Offer • 2830 Ninth Street • Berkeley, CA 94710

Limited Use Software License Agreement
for the WordPerfect 4.2 Textbook Version

1. **WHAT THIS IS.** This page contains the WordPerfect Corporation Limited Use Software License Agreement (the "Agreement") which will govern your use of the WordPerfect Textbook Education Version of WordPerfect Professional Release 4.2.

2. **GRANT OF LICENSE.** WordPerfect hereby grants you, and you accept, a limited license to use the enclosed disk(s) ("Software"). You may use the Software only on a single computer terminal or on its temporary or permanent replacement. If you wish to use the Software on more than one computer terminal you must license an additional copy of the Software. You may not transfer or sublicense, either temporarily or permanently, your right to use the software under this Agreement without the prior written consent of WordPerfect.

3. **TERM.** This Agreement is effective from the day you open the sealed package containing the diskettes and continues until you return the original diskettes to WordPerfect, in which case you must also certify in writing that you have destroyed any archival copies you may have recorded on any memory system or magnetic medium.

4. **WORDPERFECT'S RIGHTS.** You acknowledge that the software is the sole and exclusive property of WordPerfect. By accepting this Agreement, you do not become the owner of the Software, but you do have the right to use the Software in accordance with this Agreement. You agree to use your best efforts and take all reasonable steps to protect Software from use, reproduction, or distribution, except as authorized by this Agreement. You agree not to disassemble, decompile, or otherwise reverse engineer the Software.

5. **YOUR ORIGINAL DISKETTE/ARCHIVAL COPIES.** The magnetic diskettes enclosed contain an original WordPerfect label. Use the original diskettes to make up to three (3) "back-up" or archival copies for the purpose of running the Software program. You should not use the original diskettes in your terminal except to create the archival copies. After recording the archival copies, place the original diskettes in a safe place. Other than these archival copies, you agree that no other copies of the Software will be made.

6. **LIMITED WARRANTY.** WordPerfect warrants for a period of ninety (90) days from the date of purchase that, under normal use, the material of the magnetic disk(s) will not prove defective, that the Software program will prove to operate substantially in accordance with what is described in the manuals and in WordPerfect's advertising for the Software, and that the Software program is properly recorded on the diskettes.

If during the ninety day period, the Software should fail to meet the above warranty, you may return it to the Publisher or to WordPerfect for replacement without charge, or for a refund at Publisher's or WordPerfect's option.

EXCEPT FOR THE LIMITED WARRANTY DESCRIBED ABOVE, THERE ARE NO WARRANTIES, EITHER EXPRESS OR IMPLIED PROVIDED WITH THIS SOFTWARE. THESE INCLUDE, BUT ARE NOT LIMITED TO, IMPLIED WARRANTIES OF MERCHANTABILITY OR FITNESS FOR A PARTICULAR PURPOSE, AND ALL SUCH WARRANTIES ARE EXPRESSLY DISCLAIMED.

7. **LIABILITY.** You agree that WordPerfect's liability for any damages to Institution or to any other party shall not exceed ten times the license fee paid for the Software.

WORDPERFECT WILL NOT BE RESPONSIBLE FOR ANY DIRECT, INCIDENTAL, OR CONSEQUENTIAL DAMAGES RESULTING FROM USE OR REPRODUCTION OF THE SOFTWARE OR ARISING OUT OF ANY BREACH OF THE WARRANTY, EVEN IF WORDPERFECT HAS BEEN ADVISED OF THE POSSIBILITY OF SUCH DAMAGE.

SOME STATES DO NOT ALLOW THE LIMITATION OR EXCLUSION OF LIABILITY FOR INCIDENTAL OR CONSEQUENTIAL DAMAGES, SO THE ABOVE LIMITATION OR EXCLUSION MAY NOT APPLY TO YOU. YOU MAY ALSO HAVE OTHER RIGHTS THAT VARY FROM STATE TO STATE.

8. **TERMINATION OF AGREEMENT.** If any of the terms and conditions of this agreement are broken, WordPerfect has the right to terminate the Agreement and demand that you return the Software to WordPerfect. At that time you must also certify in writing that you have not retained any copies of the Software.

9. **GOVERNING LAW.** This agreement is to be governed by, and interpreted in accordance with, the laws of the State of California and the United States. Any terms or conditions of the Agreement found to be unenforceable, illegal, or contrary to public policy in any jurisdiction will be deleted, but will not affect the remaining terms and conditions of the Agreement.

10. **ENTIRE AGREEMENT.** This Agreement constitutes the entire agreement between Institution and WordPerfect.

School Software Direct Order Form

❑ Ship to student ❑ Ship to reseller (replacement stock)

Qualifying teachers, as well as college, university, and other post-secondary students, can now purchase WordPerfect Corporation (WPCORP) software directly from WPCORP at a reduced price. To qualify, a participant must be a full time teacher/administrator or currently enrolled as a full-time post-secondary student, and must agree in writing not to resell or transfer any package purchased under this program.

If you satisfy these qualifying conditions and would like to purchase software directly from WPCORP under the School Software Program, complete the following six steps and sign at the bottom of the form.

Step 1. From the list below, select the appropriate software and disk size for your computer (please note that you are limited to *one* package of each program) and mark an "x" in the corresponding boxes).

Product	Price*	Disk Size
❑ WordPerfect -- IBM PC & Compatibles	$125.00	❑ 3 1/2" ❑ 5 1/4"
❑ WordPerfect -- Apple IIe/IIc	59.00	❑ 3 1/2" & 5 1/4"
❑ WordPerfect -- Apple IIGS	59.00	❑ 3 1/2"
❑ WordPerfect -- Amiga	99.00	❑ 3 1/2"
❑ WordPerfect -- Atari ST	99.00	❑ 3 1/2"
❑ WordPerfect -- Macintosh	99.00	❑ 3 1/2"
❑ PlanPerfect -- IBM PC & Compatibles	99.00	❑ 3 1/2" ❑ 5 1/4"
❑ WordPerfect Library -- IBM PC & Compatibles	59.00	❑ 3 1/2" & 5 1/4"
❑ WordPerfect Executive -- IBM PC & Compatibles	79.00	❑ 3 1/2" & 5 1/4"
❑ Junior WordPerfect -- IBM PC & Compatibles	35.00	❑ 5 1/4"
❑ WordPerfect. Foreign Versions -- IBM PC & Compatibles	175.00	❑ 3 1/2" ❑ 5 1/4"
Language _____		
❑ WordPerfect Speller. Foreign Versions -- IBM PC & Compatibles	40.00	❑ 3 1/2" ❑ 5 1/4"
Language _____		
No changes or additions can be made to this list.		

Step 2. Make a photocopy of your current Student ID or Faculty card *and* a photocopy of some well known form of identification displaying your social security number, such as your Driver License or Social Security Card. (WPCORP) will hold this information strictly confidential and use it only to guard against duplicate purchases.) Your school ID must show current enrollment. (If it does not show a date, you must send verification of current enrollment.) If you have serious reservations about providing a social security number, call the Education Division at (801) 227-7131 to establish clearance to purchase any of the above software products at these special prices.

Step 3. Enter your social security number: __ __ __--__ __--__ __ __ __.

Step 4. Enclose payment for the total cost of the package(s) ordered with personal check, money order, Visa, or MasterCard.

Account # _____ Expiration Date _____ ❑ VISA ❑ MasterCard
(Make check or money order payable to WordPerfect Corporation.)

Step 5. List your shipping address

Ship To _____

_____

_____

Phone _____

West Publishing Company

Step 6. Enclose this signed and completed form, the photocopies of your identification cards, and your signed check or money order (or Visa or MasterCard account number and expiration date) in an envelope and mail to School Software Program, WordPerfect Corporation, 288 West Center Street, Orem, UT 84057.

The information provided herein is correct and accurate, and I will abide by the restricting conditions outlined by WPCORP in this document. I understand that at its sole discretion, WPCORP may refuse any order for any reason.

Signature _____ Date _____

*Utah residents add 6.25 % sales tax. Prices are quoted in U.S. dollars and apply to U.S. delivery for U.S. customers *only*.

WordPerfect Corporation • 288 West Center Street • Orem, Utah 84057 • (801) 225-5000

IMPORTANT:PLEASE READ BEFORE OPENING DISKETTE PACKAGE.
THIS TEXT IS NOT RETURNABLE IF SEAL IS BROKEN.

DATA DISK LIMITED USE LICENSE

By accepting this license, you have the right to use the Data Disk and the accompanying documentation, but you do not become the owner of these materials.

1. PERMITTED USES

You are granted a non-exclusive limited license to use the Data Disk under the terms and conditions stated in this License. You may:

a. Use the Data Disk on a single computer.

b. Make a single copy of the Data Disk in machine readable form solely for backup purposes in support of your use of the Data Disk on a single machine. You must reproduce and include the copyright notice on any copy you make.

c. Transfer this copy of the Data Disk and the License to another user if the other user agrees to accept the terms and conditions of this License. Transfer of this license may only be within education. If you transfer this copy of the Data Disk you must also destroy the backup copy you made. Transfer of this copy of the Data Disk and the License automatically terminates this License as to you.

2. PROHIBITED USES

You may not use, copy, modify, distribute or transfer the Data Disk or any copy, in whole or in part, except as expressly permitted in this License.

3. TERMS

This License is effective when you open the diskette package and remains in effect until terminated. You may terminate this License at any time by ceasing all use of the Data Disk and destroying this copy and any copy you have made. It will also terminate automatically if you fail to comply with the terms of this License. Upon termination, you agree to cease all use of the Data Disk and destroy all copies.

4. DISCLAIMER OF WARRANTY

Except as stated herein, the Data Disk is licensed "as is" without warranty of any kind, express or implied, including warranties of merchantability or fitness for a particular purpose. You assume the entire risk as to the quality and performance of the Data Disk. You are responsible for the selection of the Data Disk to achieve your intended results and for the installation, use, and results obtained from it. West Publishing and West Services do not warrant the performance of nor results that may be obtained with the Data Disk. West Services does warrant that the diskette(s) upon which the Data Disk is provided will be free from defects in materials and workmanship under normal use for a period of thirty days from the date of delivery to you as evidenced by a receipt. Some states do not allow the exclusion of implied warranties so the above exclusion may not apply to you. This warranty gives you specific legal rights. You may also have other rights which vary from state to state.

5. LIMITATION OF LIABILITY

Your exclusive remedy for breach by West Services of its limited warranty shall be replacement of any defective diskette upon its return to West at the above address, together with a copy of the receipt, within the warranty period. If West Services is unable to provide you with a replacement diskette which is free of defects in material and workmanship, you may terminate this License by returning the Data Disk and the license fee paid hereunder will be refunded to you. In no event will West be liable for any lost profits or other damages including direct, indirect, incidental, special, consequential or any other type of damages arising out of the use or inability to use the Data Disk even if West Services has been advised of the possibility of such damages.

6. GOVERNING LAW

This Agreement will be governed by the laws of the State of Minnesota.

You acknowledge that you have read this license and agree to its terms and conditions. You also agree that this license is the entire and exclusive agreement between you and West and supersedes any prior understanding or agreement, oral or written, relating to the subject matter of this agreement.

West Publishing Company